THE FORTY FOUR PRESIDENTS OF THE UNITED STATES OF AMERICA

BY

PAT O'BRIEN

ISBN: 978-1-907107-48-1

A CIP catalogue for this book is available from the National Library.

This book was published in cooperation with Choice Publishing & Book Services Ltd, Drogheda,
Co Louth, Ireland
Tel: 041 9841551 Email: info@choicepublishing.ie
www.choicepublishing.ie

Acknowledgement

I would like to pay tribute to the following people whose contribution to this book is deeply appreciated

John Mahon PHD whose understanding of Trinity Library gave me access to rare and historical books in its comprehensive catalogue on which I based my book.

Michelle Hanlon for her computer literacy and patient editorial work and research which helped to design the format of the book.

Anne Galvin - Drumcondra Secretarial Services for her dedicated and skilful contribution and advice over the many years she worked alongside the author to produce the finished product.

Nikki O'Brien a professional artist for her artistic work producing the cover graphics.

Amanda Duggan Assistant Secretary responsible for a sizeable portion of the secretarial work.

Avis Reynolds BA BSc whose constructive criticism on the book as it developed was much appreciated.

Avis My wife, Last but not least my long suffering wife Avis whose home was taken over by an untidy pile of books, magazines and manuscripts for years. Her loving patience and tolerance was unbelievable. Thank you.

The author of "The Forty Four Presidents of the United States of America" Pat O'Brien, is a retired official of the Irish Electricity Supply Board where he worked for thirty-six years.

In 1956 he studied Commerce, Accountancy and Social-Political theory in Trinity College, Dublin. Pat's main hobby has been song writing in which he achieved moderate success by reaching the finals of three National Eurovision Song Contests.

In 1993 Pat decided to change direction and set about researching and writing about all 44 Presidents of the United States. In 2010 he completed the project which took approximately sixteen years and half a million words.

If you enjoy a good story, a fascinating script, thousands of famous players in a wonderful supporting cast from the greats of history then just read on.

Preface

This book "The forty four Presidents of the United States of America" derives its inspiration from published material in the public domain.

Listed are over 180 books, 20 newspaper articles and 3 TV documentaries the use of which I acknowledge with grateful thanks to all concerned in these publications.

Apart from my own amateur comments they have been my library for the anecdotes, statistics, facts, fables, quotes, opinions, rumours, and commentaries by historians, politicians, newspapermen, journalists, writers and Statesmen world wide.

The result I hope is an entertaining reservoir of stories that capture the heart and soul of the times we pass through in the 18th, 19th, 20th and 21st centuries.

This wonderful spectrum of political and social history includes the assassination of four U.S. Presidents - Lincoln, McKinley, Garfield and Kennedy.

We will also follow the dramatic scenes when Ronald Reagan was almost assassinated. We follow him from the shooting to the hospital and the fight to save his life in the operating theatre.

You will hear about the tragedy of the Indian or Native American race whose conflict with the white man remains unresolved to this day in 2010.

We will march with the rookie soldiers into the battlefields of the Civil War or stand with the "Hooverites" on the breadlines of the 1932 Depression.

We will sit inside the cockpit of the "Enola Gay" and afterwards witness the horror of the nuclear bomb dropped on the people of Nagasaki and Hiroshima that ended the Second World War.

The awful events of the Titanic will be played out before our eyes during the Presidency of the 27th President William Howard Taft. The sheer helplessness of the radio operator in the radio room of the stricken liner as he clung to his machine crying out to the world for help will almost break your heart.

The glory of the moonwalkers will be experienced again by the readers as Nixon the 36th President talks to them from an aircraft carrier in the Pacific. We will read their words on how it affects their lives. Reluctantly we will watch the execution of Saddam Hussein on the gallows in Iraq. Finally we will walk the unbelievable journey of Barack Obama, the first coloured American President all the way from Hawaii to the White House.

I have made every effort in my research to get the facts right. However if I have failed at times I can only trust in the generosity and indulgence of those readers more informed than your writer.

Perhaps some stories may upset you. Perhaps others may touch you profoundly but as we travel together down these years I know you will share with me a deep sense of reverence for the awesome title President of the United States of America.

So, now let us start with our first quotation from Article 11 Section 1 of the Constitution of the United States as follows:-

1. "The executive power shall be vested in a President of the United States of America. He shall hold his office during the term of four years and together with the Vice President, chosen for the same term be elected as follows"

(Details can be found in the Constitution of the United States.)
2. The Inauguration ceremonies for each President have been officially set for January 20th following the election of the President. This is the final day when his predecessor vacates office as set out by Amendment xx Section 1 of the Constitution.

The oath of office reads as follows,

3. "I do solemnly swear that I will faithfully execute the Office of President of the United States and will to the best of my ability preserve, protect and defend the Constitution of the United States."

4. The Presidents term of office is limited to no more than two four year terms as set out in the 22nd Amendment of the Constitution.

5. Finally, after the new President takes the oath of office, the outgoing President steps off the rostrum and walks straight into history no longer head of the most powerful democracy on earth.

The time has now come for us to start this odyssey. The date is July 2, 1776.

You find General George Washington seated on his horse at the head of his army ready to give his historical address to the troops.

Our journey starts now, so let's begin.

Table of Contents

1: George Washington
Leader of the American Revolution and the historic birth of a nation. The 234 year journey of the Presidency now begins in the hands of a Deity. (p1)

2: John Adams
The parting of two friends Jefferson and Adams was a personal tragedy for both of them. However the real story we concentrate on is the formidable First Lady Abigail Adams. (p13)

3: Thomas Jefferson
Inventor, Philosopher, Intellectual. Jefferson organized an expedition into the West led by Captains Merryweather and Clark exploring Indian territories and mapping the future trails for the covered wagons of the pioneers into the West. (p 29)

4: James Madison
"The great little Madison Father of the Constitution" has all the constitutional answers for Congress, while Dolly Madison, his glamorous wife and First Lady, host their lavish banquets at home. (p 43)

5: James Monroe
Creator of "The Monroe Doctrine" closes the door on all future attempts to colonize in America. His Presidency was the known as "the era of good feeling". (p 57)

6: John Quincy Adams
The son of John Adams, he was a rough, tough debating bruiser who enjoyed the infighting of politics. He was a loud passionate anti-slavery voice which he addressed fearlessly to the secessionists. (p 65)

7:Andrew Jackson
Sworn enemy of the Indian Nation known by them as "sharp knife" and "the devil". Known to others as an "atrocious saint". He was also a great General. (p 75)

8: Martin Van Buren
He was Americas first "spin doctor" through his political contacts and the expertise of his political machine called "The Albany Regency". His clients were almost unbeatable in elections. (p 85)

9: William H Harrison
Indian wars were rampant on his watch. They included "The fall of the Sioux nation", "Custer's last stand" and "The life and times of Geronimo". William Harrison only lived for one month of his Presidency. (p 95)

10: John Tyler
A difficult character, at war with everyone. He gave a devastating speech to his cabinet to put them in their place making enemies of them all. His death was ignored for fifty years by his fellow politicians, such was his unpopularity. (p 107)

11: James Knox Polk
An impassioned supporter of "Manifest Destiny". This was the right of Americans to move westward to own their own land, usually confiscated from the Indians. (p 115)

12: Zachary Taylor
He spent forty years on horseback in the army. He broke his wife's heart when he became President against her wishes. His daughter Sarah eloped to marry a famous soldier Jefferson Davis, future leader of the Confederates. Sarah died a few years after she eloped, and Jefferson Davis returned to Zachary Taylor. (p 125)

13: Millard Fillmore
Physically very handsome, he was born in a log cabin in the wilderness but became a lawyer. After the Presidency he toured Europe and was feted by all who met him.
(p 133)

14: Franklin Pierce
He is said to be an ancestor of George W Bush. Had a sad life. He was a heavy drinker with anti-Lincoln views. A freak accident saw his little son Benny killed before his eyes in a horrific train accident. Pierce later died without friends or family, alone in the White House. (p 147)

15: James Buchannan
A brilliant lawyer, politician, statesman, and ambassador before he was President yet as President he was weak, scared, and dysfunctional as the Civil War approached. He hated being President. (p 157)

16: Abraham Lincoln
He lasted only one month into his second term, but at the moment of victory came his awful assassination. He was as sure about the evil of slavery as other Presidents were unsure. He led his army against slavery in the Civil War in which over 600,000 were killed. Lincoln never got to enjoy the fruits of his victory. (p 169)

17: Andrew Johnson
Reconstruction was badly needed in the South. Devastation was everywhere, like Berlin after World War II. Johnson gave an amnesty to all Confederates while Congress was on holidays. Later he was impeached unsuccessfully for his vetoes.
 (p 195)

18: Ulysses Grant
Victorious General of the Civil War. He was not as good in politics as he was in the army. He duly retired and made a very successful world tour. His liking for cigars may have caused him the cancer from which he died. He wrote a brilliant book described as a classic, the royalties of which became his pension. He finished the book on his death bed. It was entitled "Let Us Have Peace".
(p 215)

19: Rutherford Birchard Hayes
He lived a very patrician lifestyle. Very rich with a beautiful estate called "Spiegal Grove." Moved gently among the academics in Washington University before the Presidency. His victory by a narrow margin called for a recount. He won the recount but Tilden, his opponent took the defeat so badly he retired from politics, some say with a broken heart. (p 235)

20: James Garfield
Garfield was shot on July 2, 1881 and died on September 20 1881, eight days later. His Presidency had lasted 200 days from March 4 1881 to September 20 1881. The reason he was shot was because his assassin was refused a job by the Administration. The trial of his murderer was a shambles because Charles Guiteau, who shot him, seemed seriously deranged. If the trial took place today I'm certain it would have collapsed. (p 251)

21: Chester Alan Arthur
Arthur was scoffed at as a choice of President. He was a "Dandy" who loved socialising, but was in the pocket of the chief New York spin doctor Boss Conkling. He turned his back on Boss Conkling forever and ran a benign Presidency to everyone's relief. A statue has been erected to him in Madison Square Park. (p 269)

22 & 24: Grover Cleveland
A fierce, confrontational man. Had two terms as President from 1885-1889 and from 1893-1897.
He was as fiery as Theodore Roosevelt. In his second term a terrible botched up arrest happened.
Indian police, sent to arrest Sitting Bull, shot and butchered him in a fight. Sitting Bulls friend
Crazy Horse, hero of the battle called "Little Big Horn", was bayoneted. (p 277), (p 297)

25: William Mc Kinley
He was the third President to be assassinated. During his Presidency the Indians were in rebellion.
Mc Kinley's assassination was carried out by an anarchist, Leon F Czolgosz, as a protest against the
moral decay of the society he saw around. (p 303)

26: Theodore Roosevelt
Theodore arrived on the scene like a knight in shining armour. His mission was to reform society
as Governor of New York. His Presidency was one major news story after another and he proved
to be a treasure trove for the headline writers. He was the cousin of Franklin D Roosevelt, the 32nd
President. (p 325)

27: William Howard Taft
A strange enigma of a man, who should never have been a politician, for his consuming passion
was always the Law. The Titanic tragedy, which I've covered in detail, happened on his watch and
filled the newspapers for weeks. Taft finally arrived where he truly belonged as Chief Justice of the
Supreme Court for nine years. (p 349)

28: Woodrow Wilson
Woodrow Wilson will forever be associated with the First World War. His efforts to secure a fair
armistice were sabotaged by the French Prime Minister, Clemenceau. He was also opposed by
politicians back home against his idea of the League of Nations. A loner, forging his own lonely
furrow in a futile pursuit of his dream. Stress eventually killed him. (p 363)

29: Warren Gamaliel Harding
Another man who should never have become President. The reason being his heart never left the
world of the Newspaper Man. He died later of a massive heart attack in far off Canada whilst still
pining for his beloved newspaper life in "The Marion Star" newspaper. The storyline proves that
Harding's Presidency was hijacked off him by crooks. (p 383)

30: Calvin Coolidge
Was not known as "Silent Cal" for nothing. Famous for his one liners in conversation. One lady
told him at a party "I have a bet to get at least three words from you." "You Lose," was his reply.
He was lucky to be President in the richest time in America called "The Roaring 20s". Yet the Wall
Street Crash was only around the corner. Strangely he was a certainty for a second term yet chose
to resign. Why we, will never know. (p 401)

31: Herbert Hoover
Known as "The Engineer". Had he retired an engineer he could have remained a hero for his
humanitarian work in the First World War. America's money markets went out of control and
Hoover retired in ignominy. (p 419)

32: Franklin D Roosevelt(FDR)
Roosevelt was a cousin of the famous Theodore Roosevelt (26th President). But disaster struck
him when he developed Polio and was crippled for the rest of his life. That didn't prevent him
becoming a towering figure in the depression of 1932. He sorted out the money markets and went
on to partner Churchill and Eisenhower in winning the Second World War. (p 435)

33: Harry S Truman

He has gone down in history as the man who dropped the Atom Bomb on Japan. Very independent, he had opinions of his own which saw him sack most of FDR's Cabinet. The Berlin Airlift happened on his watch. Both he and his wife Bess were very popular on Capitol Hill. Finished his Presidency with a party and a singsong around the piano in the White House. (p 455)

34: Dwight Eisenhower

He was one of the most charismatic Generals in American history and a proud product of WestPoint. Roosevelt made him Supreme Commander of the Allied forces fighting the Nazi's throughout Europe and North Africa. Some of his speeches in the Presidency will go down in history - and were praised by the Russians in the cold war. He never went to war again. (p 479)

35: John F Kennedy

He was the first of a new well-educated, sophisticated breed of politician and a millionaire from the time of his youth. He was the fourth President to be assassinated and will always be remembered as a tragic figure never to achieve his full political potential. His brother Bobby was also assassinated ending the Kennedy dynasty in politics. (p 507)

36: Lyndon Johnson (LBJ)

Successor to Kennedy he was the most accomplished parliamentarian ever in Congress. One of his most heartbreaking defeats was his failure to launch his "great society", a vision he had for social and political reform throughout America. Korea destroyed his will to fight for a second term. (p 531)

37: Richard Nixon

Mention Richard Nixon and people will think of Watergate. The first President to resign in nearly 200 years. Watergate was a self-inflicted wound which got worse as time went on. He was rehabilitated back into politics as an international expert before he died. (p 551)

38: Gerald R Ford

He must be the only man who ever stood and watched the downfall of a King while he stood in the wings as heir to the Kings dynasty. As President , Ford's first act caused an outrage - he pardoned Nixon. (p 577)

39: Jimmy Carter

He was a Southerner who amazed Washington when he entered the race for the Presidency. They said "Jimmy who"? He used his knowledge of the South to achieve political success. Amazingly he is still having success to this day as an international peacemaker thirty years later. (p 601)

40: Ronald Reagan

The most colourful of Presidents whose film star career gave him a real quality Hollywood polish. It was his relationship with Gorbachev, the Russian Premier that brought down the Berlin wall. Unfortunately his family life was not as successful as his political one. Sadly he died of Alzheimer's disease for which there is no cure today. (p 620)

41: George Bush (Snr)

He is remembered for "Desert Storm" which was his declaration of war on Saddam Hussein. Bush was part of the "old money" dynasty in America with a political family going back two or three generations. He personally told Richard Nixon, it was time for him to quit! Bush was followed into office later by his son George W Bush. (p 648)

42: William Jefferson Clinton

The story of the Bill Clintons Presidency is really the story of a love affair between himself and his wife Hillary. One of his greatest roles is remembered in Ireland where he had "a hands on" input into the "Good Friday Agreement", which brought an end to violence in Northern Ireland. Hillary is now Secretary Of State in the Obama Presidency. Their marriage now flourishes into a joyful future after the Monica Lewinsky. (p 668)

43: George W Bush
George Bush will tell you himself how he was headed for "skid row" preferring Jack Daniels and Johnnie Walker "whiskeys" to Abraham Lincoln. This didn't prevent him from reforming and becoming a jet pilot, a university graduate and a fluent Spanish speaker. He met and married a beautiful woman and had two lovely daughters. What blew his Presidency apart was the bombing of the Twin Towers in New York on September 11 2001, after that it became a war Presidency. (p 692)

44: Barack Obama
The first coloured President to enter the White House. His sense of history was there in everything he did from Hawaii to college, from college to university and beyond. He deserves to have providence on his side. Barracks arrival on Capitol Hill is indeed the end of Civil War politics after one hundred and fifty years in America. He has so much to accomplish if only the American people believe in his dream. (p 730)

1st President   George Washington

"Father of his Country"
Born 1732
Died 1799
67 Years of age
2 Terms
1789 – 1797
Age 57

Party: Federalist
Profession: Planter & soldier
County: Virginia
Ancestry: English
Estate: $530,000, land poor
Hobbies: Fishing, Riding, Races, Billiards, Theatre

Physical Description: Height 6 foot 2 inches; weight 175 lbs; brown sandy hair, powdered, under powdered wig, blue eyes; high brow, scar on left cheek, black mole under right ear, pock-marks on nose and cheeks, strongly pointed chin; false teeth, powerful physique, broad sloping shoulders.

Extracts from his inaugural address Thursday April 30, 1789
"When I was first honoured with a call into the service of my country – then on the eve of an arduous struggle for its liberties - the light in which I contemplated my duty required that I should renounce every pecuniary compensation. From this resolution I have in no instance departed……………"

GEORGE WASHINGTON

A gentle breeze rustled the leaves overhead as George Washington gazed over his army, a vast sea of young, eager, trusting faces ready for battle. This beautiful day should have been no different from all the other sunlit days in Virginia up to now. Looking into the distance to the green rolling hills beyond he realized this one was different. Today America would march into history in pursuit of a dream. Today they would set out to win for America their God given right to rule over their own land. The rolling meadows, the golden valleys, the rushing rivers, the singing streams, the hamlets and villages, towns and cities of this majestic country they all loved. His well-groomed chestnut pawed impatiently at the grass beneath him disturbing his soaring thoughts. Facing his troops he addressed them with a loud clear distinctive voice on the morning of July 2, 1776. His speech carried to the outer ranks of his far flung soldiers. "The time is now near at hand which must probably determine whether Americans are to be freemen or slaves, whether they are to have any property they can call their own. The fate of unborn millions will now depend, under God, on the courage and conduct of the army. Our cruel and unrelenting enemy leaves us only the choice of brave resistance or the most abject submission. We have therefore to resolve to conquer or to die." - (General Orders July 2, 1776 from the writings of George Washington Volume 5 -1932.)

And so began the most momentous event in world history - The American Revolution. The leader General George Washington, a planter by profession, was about to embark upon an adventure that would one day march him into the hearts of the American people as the 1st President of the United States of America.
Victory over Great Britain was to change the whole future for this so far unexplored Continent whose boundaries spread thousands of miles westward to the Pacific Ocean, northwards to Canada and southwards to the Gulf of Mexico.

The United States emerged from the war with impressive gains. Not only did the outcome achieve independence from Great Britain, it actually doubled the size of the country adding a vast area later known as Michigan, Wisconsin, Ohio, Indiana, Illinois, Kentucky, Tennessee, Alabama and Mississippi. But most important of all for the first time in its history, America took its place among the foremost nations of the world under their new leader and first President George Washington.

And who, you may ask was George Washington? What was his background? How did he have the military skills to lead the revolutionaries to victory after eight years fighting? Why did he become involved?

Washington was a planter enjoying all the privileges of planter life in Virginia. To take such a course of rebellion was to invite trouble and unforeseen consequences to a secure a comfortable social lifestyle.

It was his experience working for the British Empire and its officials in the army, and his dealings with them in the market place when selling his crops that changed him forever.

He gradually came to the conclusion that colonists like himself regardless of talent or background would always be regarded as second class citizens by the establishment. The native born Englishman would always be favoured over the provincials. Consequently Virginia was left to cope alone against a blazing frontier. Many Virginians suffered and died as a result of decisions made in far off London where powerful faceless men determined America's destiny.

Another developing problem was the slave trade. The number of slaves had risen from 19,000 to 190,000 and had got out of hand. Slave insurrection was a distinct possibility and a threat to his own planter class. The developing situation was also a threat to future stability in a changing market making the transition from tobacco to agriculture imperative. However, England would not tamper with the lucrative slave trade.

Virginia was also starved of money to defend itself against marauding Indians on its borders because no constructive policy was coming from London. Finally lands west of the mountains were declared British and not open to American exploitation. America was like a trussed up Turkey under the control of powerful forces in England. So entered Washington into America's historic destiny.

Despite his love of the planter's life, Washington had a secret love affair with army life which really started when he was appointed Adjutant to the Virginian Militia by Governor Robert Dunwiddie.

Being an ambitious young man of twenty he pushed for a commission with the British Army and Dunwiddie duly appointed him Lieutenant Colonel, in charge of one hundred and fifty badly equipped troops in the war against the French.

However it never became a Royal Commission as British Army officers were preferred to those who held Colonial Commissions. Washington resigned. He later was invited to become Aide-de-Camp to Major General Edward Braddock. During forest warfare General Braddock was mortally wounded and Washington was appointed Commander-in-Chief of the colonies troops with the rank of Colonel. For the next three years he acquired invaluable experience defending the frontiers of Virginia against the French. He then resigned and returned to planter life once again. It was this background that made him an ideal choice of Commander-in-Chief of the first U.S. Army in the revolution.

The story of George Washington really begins seventy-five years before he was born. In 1657 two brothers, John and Lawrence Washington emigrated from England aboard "The Seahorse of London" and set up home in Virginia. In three generations, by hard work and enterprise in the farming industry and land buying, they brought a measure of wealth to the family raising them to the status of planters with 10,000 acres and fifty slaves.

George was born on February 22, 1732 in the family home Mount Vernon near Popes Creek. They say that he was related to the aristocracy in Britain going back to King Edward III through his paternal grandmother Mildred Warner Washington.

His father died in 1743 when George was only nine years old and his stepbrother Lawrence became his guardian. Lawrence himself was married to Lady Anne Fairfax, a sister of Lord Fairfax who owned property far larger than the Washington's in the wilder reaches of Virginia.

As he grew older George Washington learned all the skills of surveying a very popular career in those days when frontiers were expanding further and further westwards. It was a talent that ultimately made him a very rich man.

He spent his youth on the lands of Fairfax which embraced an area of five million acres in the wild upper reaches of Virginia. It was here Washington at sixteen had his first adventure when he was taken on an expedition which lasted a month to locate the Fairfax holdings west of the Shenandoah Valley. Travelling by horseback and canoe George recorded as follows: "We slept in the open in pitched tents covered by threadbare blankets full of fleas and lice. We cooked in open fires and our spit was two forked sticks. Dishes we had none. Pioneers came out of the forests to see us and roads were the worst ever trod by man or beast." George set out on the expedition as a boy but came home a frontiersman. He received a doubloon a day for his troubles which he saved to buy land for himself later.

The world Washington lived in was a tough one. People died young from smallpox, malaria, typhoid and gout of the stomach. Slavery was the norm in a society that had no conscience about it or any resentment of British rule. All that came later.

You may be wondering at this point what family life was like in frontier America. Furniture was simple and serviceable. Homemade beds were the norm with straw stuffed into ticks. Tables and chairs were also homemade. Cooking was carried out on wide stone fireplaces with a built in brick oven which was kept lighting all day. Breakfast consisted of rye pudding or Indian porridge, bean or pea soup, flavoured with pork or salt fish. Dinner consisted of the same, plus turnips and other vegetables. Supper served up gingerbread cake.

Female education was considered a vain and idle thing because it was widely accepted that women should "mind their own business", and that their business was cooking, washing, sweeping and bearing children. As you can see women were way down the list in society's pecking order. Families were large and nine children were considered a medium sized family. Unfortunately maternal and infant mortality rates were sky high. The evidence for this was laid out in the graveyards which were filled with gravestones to young wives who went to their deaths prematurely worn out by childbirth. Some of them were buried alongside five or six of their children. Their cold and draughty houses, bad diet and congenital weakness caused by too frequent parenthood were a grim commentary on a harsh and demanding environment that only the strongest managed to survive.

Physically, Washington was a tall powerful man six foot two inches in height, fourteen stone, muscular and fit. A man of enormous integrity and honesty; tough and firm in debate with a quick temper which he was always struggling to control. Yet underlying all this he was a shy man especially with strangers. He had many pastimes and hobbies especially dancing, cards, billiards, raffles, barbeques, fox hunting and mule breeding.

It is not generally known that Washington was a bit of a romantic at heart writing his thoughts in stilted poetry to those women he tried to woo. This was not always successful for him with a Betsy Fauntleroy who rejected his proposal of marriage not once but twice. His bachelor days finally came to an end however when he married an attractive widow Martha Dandridge Custis aged twenty-seven who had two surviving children from her first marriage John and Martha. They were married on her estate prophetically called The White House at 1.10 p.m. on January 6, 1759 but returned to live out the remaining forty-three years of their days at Mount Vernon.

Martha Custis was described according to her parents as short, plump and plain but gracious and kind. Her wealth was considerable for she owned one hundred slaves, 6,000 acres and her liquid assets were valued at £12,000. It was a very happy marriage but sadly it produced no children. The marriage significantly increased Washington's bank balance for Martha was indeed a very wealthy woman. Washington was now a very rich man too because he had also inherited Mount Vernon and it's estates from his brother Laurence when he was only twenty years old.

Yet although he loved plantation life George had another dream. He wanted to go to sea. Perhaps he was impressed by the tales he heard from the transatlantic merchants who cruised up and down the Rappahannock River nearby or tales from his brother Laurence who had served under Admiral Vernon in the Caribbean. The house Mount Vernon was called after the Admiral. However he was discouraged by his mother and uncle Joseph Ball who dismissed such a career as "nothing better than a Tinker's apprentice".

Actually his only trip by sea was to Barbados with his brother Laurence. Unfortunately that trip resulted in him developing smallpox; a disease which left him facially scarred for life however it did give him immunity to smallpox which served him well during an outbreak among his troops during operations.

Planter Profession

Of course there were many more wealthy planters around at that time such as the Randolphs, the Byrds and the Harrisons who lived on tidal creeks and rivers exporting tobacco to England and importing in return luxuries such as port, porcelain and mahogany furniture which allowed them to live in the lifestyle of the English gentry thus enjoying a very privileged existence. They sent their sons to the best schools learning manners and law and finally attending the ultimate college of "William and Mary". Yet for Washington life was different and for some strange reason college was not the route chosen by him. He received no formal education though he did have private tutors who taught him mathematics and the one hundred rules of social graces. Washington preferred to live the rough and ready life of the planter cum frontiersman preferring the art of canoeing, horse-riding, hunting and fishing to reading the classics in a stuffy classroom.

There are two further stories worth telling about Washington. A loan of $3,750 was owed by a Captain John Posey to Washington. Being unable to repay the debt Posey cleared it by turning over his lands, a ferry and a fishery to Washington in lieu of cash. Washington operated the ferry and sold fish from his own boats right up to the revolution.

The second story concerns an attempt to kidnap or kill him. The conspiracy was lead by the Tory Governor of New York, William Tryon and many others including his own bodyguard. The bodyguard Thomas Hickey was publicly hanged in a field near the Bowery Lane watched by 20,000 people. Washington described the act as a disgraceful one for a soldier and his execution was a lesson to all serving in the Army against the crime of sedition. Washington took the role of a soldier very seriously and once issued an order from his headquarters severely reprimanding those who swore in the course of their duties. He described it as a "vice so mean and low to be uncharacteristic of the life of a soldier." But the army Washington took over early in 1775 was anything but the finished product he aspired to as Commander-in-Chief of the first U.S. Army.

Building his new Army 1776.

The troops he took over for the monumental task ahead was nothing but a ramshackle collection of farmers, cowhands and shop keepers with a sprinkling of hard bitten frontiersmen mixed in. They were undisciplined, under-trained, under-fed, under-clothed, under-equipped and badly paid. Some even remained unpaid at the end of the campaign. After many battles in Congress, Washington managed to establish conscription for three years instead of six months and pushed through the reforms he needed to fund his army.

Looking at them he would often complain in despair - "They don't salute officers. They gamble, drink, curse and swim openly in rivers with women and children on the banks nearby." He noted officers fraternized with the men giving them haircuts and repairing their shoes. Yet somehow he saw the raw material there for good soldiers. "All they need is animation and a cause," he said. "No one expects the same standards of veterans and raw recruits. What they need are good officers to train them."

Lamenting the state of affairs in his rag taggle army Washington wrote to his brother about it. His criticism of the army he had inherited could not be expressed openly. He said "Many of my difficulties and distresses were of so peculiar a cast that in order to conceal them from my friends I was thereby subjecting my conduct to interpretations unfavourable to my character".

The Job

Perhaps if Washington had known the size of the job he was taking on as Commander-in-Chief of the first U.S. Army he would have been horrified. Nevertheless on July 3 he halted his horse under a tree on the common at Cambridge, drew his sword and formally took charge of his army giving the speech with which we opened this story. There would be many triumphs, heartbreaks and defeats ahead for a rookie General and a collection of misfits who later were to prove themselves more than a match for the best the British Empire could throw at them.

Washington drew first blood at the battle of Bunker Hill. Still the appalling indiscipline, insubordination, sickness and desertions troubled him. Even more of a worry was the lack of gunpowder. Furthermore the troops he faced in New York were made up of hard-bitten German mercenaries fighting not for glory but for money. I won't bore my readers with the details of the war as I'm certain this information is available from more informed sources than your writer. There were to be many illustrious battles to come such as the Battle of Lovy Island, the Battle of White Plains, the Battle of Trenton, the Battle of Princeton and the Battle of Brandywine, to mention just a few. Historians will remember others such as Germantown, Saratoga and Valley Forge among the glorious battles that go down in the folklore of American history. There were also failures waiting for him when he marched South. Savannah, Georgia, Charlestown (now Charleston) and South Carolina fell to the new British General, Cornwallis.

It wasn't only the tough rip roaring recruits of Washington's army who achieved victory for America. There was another army out there who may not have won any medals but they certainly made their own contribution to the war. Families paid higher taxes; women made bullets, sewed shirts and made uniforms for the soldiers. They even gathered intelligence and worked as spies. An amazing 20,000 women went with the army cooking, washing and nursing the wounded soldiers while keeping the camps clean.

They also paid a terrible price back home for not a family was untouched by the war. They too had to suffer the sacrifice of losing a loved one for months at a time, many of whom never came home. Even the civilians fell victim of the war from diseases they picked up from nearby armies or were brought home by returning soldiers on leave. Last but not least while leading a vast army of veterans is tough, directing and managing such an unwieldy machine that "clanked and clattered" during it's early stages was a nightmare for Washington yet he persevered and finally against all the odds he got it right. But he paid a price for his success. His casualties were not insignificant. 25,000 of the Continental Army died as well as countless others in the militias. Yes, throughout the thirteen States many young men paid a price for the new Republic with their own blood sacrifices. Many died unknown but not forgotten.

Just before Washington's last battle at Yorktown tragedy struck him. His stepson, Martha's twenty-six year old son Jacky got ill with camp fever. Despite rushing to his side Jacky's condition worsened and he died within days of Washington's visit. Washington returned to Mount Vernon where he stayed with Martha for five days so grief stricken he was unable to concentrate on his duties. But life went on and he duly set out again to continue the campaign.

The end came on a pleasant sunny evening in the fall of 1781 at Yorktown when the English Generals appeared on the surrender field that up to then had been a killing ground. Cornwallis was not there. Betraying no emotion Washington accepted the arms laid down by the remaining 7,241 British soldiers under the golden autumn sunset of October 19, 1781. Typical of the man, Washington gave his officers and men all the credit for the victory in his address to Congress one week later. A sign of the times was the fact that news of the surrender did not reach Europe for five weeks.

A sad postscript to all the excitement of the victory is about poor John Adams who had had a brush with death when he collapsed some weeks earlier. He was too weak and feeble to spring with joy or shout exultantly as was his style. He just wrote to a friend "The infant Hercules triumphantly strangled Cornwallis."

Back in Britain its Parliament had already surrendered refusing to support the war any more. What a wonderful moment of triumph for Washington. So wonderful, some people, with the backing of army sources wanted to make him King over a new American Monarchy. This idea was totally at odds with Washington's pride in the army he loved and he called his officers together to end a well meaning but potentially serious mistake.

Peace was officially declared on April 19, 1783 when the last British boats headed for the ships waiting for them in New York Bay for their long journey back to England. Britain had left America forever.

The final accolade for Washington was leading his victorious army down Broadway into the heart of New York to the cheers of thousands. His farewell private dinner for his senior Generals ended with informal embraces and emotional tears that ended army friendships forever. Then he stepped out into the night and was gone, returning back home to his beloved Mount Vernon. The Peace of Paris finally sealed the victory and for the first time America joined the family of nations in her own right thanks to Washington's army.

America was now almost twice the size it was before the war because Britain had ceded thirteen colonies in the surrender. These vast areas would later become Michigan, Wisconsin, Ohio, Indiana, Kentucky, Tennessee, Alabama and Mississippi. It gave America control of the Ohio River and access to the heart of the Continent by means of the Mississippi River.

America would later be doubled again when Napoleon sold 827,000 square miles to the U.S. in what is known as The Louisiana Purchase. That is a fascinating story we will tell you about later under the Presidency of Thomas Jefferson, the 3rd President of the United States.

After the war Washington resigned his Commission and returned to life on his beloved plantation Mount Vernon.

Despite his reluctance to bask in the glory of his achievements, despite his desire to sink into obscurity on his plantation, fate had other ideas. He was the automatic choice as first President of the United States and destiny claimed him for that role on April 30, 1789.
The inauguration ceremony, the first of its kind was one of great pomp and celebration as would befit an occasion never before witnessed in American history. By way of light relief a small anecdote is worth recounting. Washington among the richest men of his time had to borrow $600 for his inauguration. It seems he was "land poor" meaning his lands were valuable but unsaleable because the crops were so poor.

Meanwhile, Washington duly arrived by boat for his inauguration. Thirteen pilots in sailors' uniforms rowed the barge. The boat with two flags astern moved up the Hudson River to Murray's Wharf at the foot of Wall Street to the sound of a twenty cannon salute from his old adversary the British Navy in New York Bay. This being the United States' first Presidential election the occasion was duly recorded by the U.S. Chronicle of May 21, 1789.

The newspaper report went roughly like this. "The parade from Wall street was led by a troop of horse artillery and veterans of the army in uniform. Next came the principal officers of State, followed by the Governor of New York, the clergy and the ordinary citizens."

Washington took the oath of office out of doors on the balcony of the Senate Chamber. After his inauguration speech he was escorted to the first Presidential mansion at number one Cherry Street, New York, where he lived for ten months. When the house in Cherry Street was found to be too small for the guest lists George Washington had to move to bigger premises on Broadway. But settling into their new home was again disrupted when they had to move to a third house in the newly created capital of Philadelphia in 1790. This was far more private than New York.

Soon Martha opened up her house for a New Year's Day party that was to continue, except for the war years, right up to 1933 when President Hoover stopped it. It seems future parties got far too big to handle for it was beginning to attract thousands. When George Washington died permission was requested of the First Lady to transfer his body to a newly constructed marble tomb in the Capital. Martha died and by the time the idea came up again thirty years later her survivors had already constructed a family tomb at Mount Vernon. That is where he was finally laid to rest.
But let us not digress. Let us return again to Washington's inauguration.

The evening celebrations opened and closed with the firing of thirteen rockets and thirteen cannons, and the inaugural ball was held a week later on May 7, 1789 in the assembly rooms on the east side of Broadway. All the leading politicians and dignitaries of the day including the French and Spanish Ministers and the majority of Congress and the Senate were there. Today in 2009 the President and his First Lady are expected to dance the night away at six or seven specially chosen hotels.

Special medallions were struck for that occasion. Strangely the First Lady Martha Washington was not there; preferring not to arrive until the event was all over at the end of May 1789. They both returned to Mount Vernon the following year where they lived happily during his Presidency and his retirement eight years later.

Washington's first official engagement was a 3,000 mile tour of the North and South with the help of a private secretary, six servants, nine horses, a luggage wagon and his Aide-de-Camp Major William Jackson.

On his return Washington set about his tasks as President by surrounding himself with the best brains available to him. Three of these Jefferson, Adams and Madison became future Presidents. Together they were the driving force behind the awesome task of moulding a far flung Continent into one cohesive harmony of multi-racial nation States under one flag and one Government. Those times in the New America were a cauldron of political ideas and philosophies. It was a pressure cooker of political thought bursting to be free after centuries of suppression and stagnation. America was on the move at last with the safe hands of George Washington on the steering wheel of history.

Through the eight years of his Presidency Washington always had a detached disdain for the political infighting he saw around him. Down the years this was the one facet of his personality that endeared him most to the American people leaving him more popular on his retirement than he was on his inauguration.

In fact during the Civil War eighty years later in 1861 Washington's estate Mount Vernon was declared neutral by both sides Unionists and Confederates, and so well was he respected by all sides in politics he received the honorary degree of L.L.D. from five separate universities.

George Washington's Presidency eventually came to an end on March 3, 1797, eight years after his inauguration. He declined a third term which was his for the asking and left behind him an America firmly in the forefront of international politics.

If you think the story of George Washington ends here you may be surprised to hear his retirement was every bit as colourful as all that went before. The energy and commitment he applied to his previous career soon found an outlet in an unbelievable frenzy of activity to conclude the story of a remarkable man. His lifestyle in retirement was breathtaking for a man of sixty-four.

Retirement

It consisted of an early rise in the dark before dawn, two hours correspondence, then a fifteen mile round trip on horseback to oversee the days labour on his estate returning in mid afternoon for a large meal lasting two hours. He entertained visitors constantly showing them around his estate and his day finally ended at 9 p.m. with his family.

Washington could never get close to men as a General because of the authority of his position. But civil life did not change him much and his main friendships were kept within the family circle with George Fairfax, Bryan Fairfax and his brother-in-law Burwell Bassett.

He nevertheless had a good sense of humour and being a good listener conversed easily with the simple and the powerful. For such a serious man Washington was truly a great socialiser. He loved the races, theatre, cockfights, cards and billiards, an evening in the Tavern including parties and dances but hunting was always his first love. Yes, he certainly knew how to enjoy himself.

His plantation though, run by one hundred slaves was not profitable so he switched successfully to farming. An astute businessman he raised livestock, bought and sold horses, bought a schooner and launched a fishing business that exported one million shad and herring.

Andrew Barnaby, an English traveller in 1759 described Washington's house Mount Vernon as a sparsely furnished eight roomed one storey and a half house so unspectacular he took no notice of it.

Built to impress however in breathtaking surroundings on a high hill overlooking the Potomac River surrounded by water, cliffs and woods it was more a comfortable house than a mansion. But Washington true to form set out to correct that image by buying for his estate every tract of land around the original site till it sprawled over 7,300 acres stretching for ten miles along the Potomac River. He tripled Mount Vernon's floor space to four thousand feet by adding another floor on top and facing it to the West towards the frontier he had conquered. Yet it was devoid of ostentatious pomp and captured the modesty of its owner.

Today in 2009 it is a place of pilgrimage for millions of tourists.

They arrive on the Mansion Tours everyday between April and October. The property has passed down the line from Washington to his nephew Bushrod Washington and onto John Augustine Washington. Then by charter to Virginia it was bought for $200,000 by Mount Vernon Ladies Association in 1858. It is now run by the Ladies Association "not for profit but for the benefit of all who come here".

Though he was a simple man, Washington, during the three short years of his retirement loved the Patrician lifestyle on his army gratuity of $64,647. To achieve this he imported from London an incredible variety of goods from the best suppliers in Europe. Items like crystal, silver, pewter, china, furniture, liquor, wine, beer, guns, ammunition, swords, knives, engraved whips, exotic food like cheese, candy, olives, dates, honey, tea and coffee, farm tools and kitchen equipment and a new carriage for Martha; genteel and light. He also purchased musical instruments for his grandchildren. The cost came to twice the annual income of a skilled artisan. His library one tenth the size of Harvard College library in 1790 held books on theology, law, philosophy, anatomy, medicine dictionaries, encyclopaedias and classics by contemporary authors. But it is obvious Washington did not depend on his army gratuity to purchase these items.

Being part of the 18th century American aristocracy Washington was already a very wealthy and influential man long before the first shot in the War of Independence rang out in July 1776.

Much of his assets were inherited from his parents, his brother Lawrence and his wife Martha Dandridge Custis. The rest came from shrewd business deals and land speculation at which he was a past master. In fact his skills at buying land had been honed since he was a youth. Land became an obsession with him, almost a pastime.
It may not be generally known but Washington owned vast expanses of property from a land buying company called "The Ohio Company" set up by his brother Lawrence. He also owned "The Mississippi Company" that had title to a wide area of land between the Wabash and the Mississippi. Finally he was given land by a donation of 200,000 acres to be shared among his men by General Dunwiddie. Privates received 400 acres and Commanders 50,000 acres. His holdings covered acreages in Maryland, Pennsylvania, North Carolina, nine Virginian Counties and West Virginia.

As a businessman they say he was a hard shrewd taskmaster. He compelled his managers and labourers to work as hard as he did himself. They worked by order from daybreak to dark. If a slave was idle Washington directed he get a good whipping and it is on record he sanctioned the flogging of female slaves. This may shock modern readers but in the plantation life of the late 18th century this was considered quite the norm. Martha also played her part in running the house. Washington complimented her to his mother. "She runs Mount Vernon like a well resorted Tavern," he said.

A tough negotiator in business deals even his former Aide-de-Camp in the French Indian wars ruefully remarked "I never desire to deal with him for six cents in future." Yet we must remember this was the man who fought not only on the battlefields of America but in the corridors of power for his soldiers – for uniforms, equipment, rations, training funds, conscription, finance, wages and a host of problems that once made him sigh in despair – "I should retire now to the back country and live in a wigwam."
But life in retirement was soon to come to an end. Alas, like Kennedy and Lincoln in another century the Gods had other plans for him.

Early on the morning of December 14, 1799 he awoke with an inflamed throat. His condition rapidly worsened. It was a normal ailment by today's standards that could easily be cured by a course of antibiotics. Unfortunately the only medical treatment available to him in those days was frequent blood-letting which did more harm than good. He deteriorated rapidly and knowing the end was near he bravely described death as "a debt we all had to pay." He died that night December 14, 1799 at 11.30 p.m. of complications caused by inflammatory quinsy. He was sixty-seven years of age. His retirement had only lasted three years. Nevertheless George Washington left behind a United States proudly facing into a glorious future.

To speak of the wealth he left behind may not do the great man justice. Suffice it to say his Will records leaving over half a million dollars in land and livestock spread throughout Virginia, Kentucky, Pennsylvania, Washington, New York and the Northern territories. He left his five swords to each of his five nephews with the admonition they were to remain unsheathed and only used in self defence.

Washington the man however, left behind him something else, the love and respect of a grateful nation.

At his funeral his friend General Henry Lee said "He was first in war, first in peace and first in the hearts of his people."

His successor as President, his number two John Adams was even more moving in his tribute. He said "His example is now complete and it will teach example and virtue to magistrates, citizens and men not only in the present age but in future generations as long as history shall be read."
I guess we cannot even try to improve on that.
George Washington was buried on his magnificent estate Mount Vernon in the family vault he specially built for that purpose. His beloved wife Martha was entombed alongside him three years later when she died in 1802.

2nd President   John Adams

"Duke of Braintree"
Born 1735
Died 1826
91 Years of age
1 Term
1797 – 1801
Age 62

Party: Federalist
Profession: Lawyer
County: Massachusetts
Estate: $30,000
Ancestry: English
Hobbies: Unknown

Physical description: Height 5 foot 7 inches; corpulent; bald; expanded eyebrows.
He had lost all his teeth.

Extract from his inaugural address on Saturday March 4, 1797

"And may that Being who is supreme over all, the Patron of Order, the foundation of justice, and the protector in all ages of the world of virtuous liberty, continue his blessings upon this nation and its Government, and give it all possible success and duration consistent with the ends of his providence."

JOHN ADAMS

When George Washington refused a third term as President of the United States a whole new breed of politician came on the scene at the end of the 18th century.

Washington was a frontiersman and a soldier revered for his achievements on the battlefield with no pretensions to academic qualifications. He was a people's President.

The two candidates who fought out the final stages of the second Presidential election to succeed him, John Adams and Thomas Jefferson, were giants of the academic world.

Winning the war against Britain was a colossal achievement by Washington against all the odds but having launched the new America on the world stage new laws, legislation and political structures were needed to guide the new country on its journey into the future.

It was people like Adams Jefferson, Franklin and Madison men of truly honest, unselfish and patriotic vision who came together to accomplish that mission and they succeeded brilliantly.

At the age of sixty-two John Adams was duly elected on March 4, 1797 to take up the mantle of the great George Washington.

Adams was born on October 3, 1735 the first son of John Adam's, a farmer in Braintree, now Quincy, Massachusetts. His mother Suzanna Boylston before marriage came from a Boston family of noted physicians. The Adams family it is said dated back to the Pilgrim Fathers and the land on which they farmed had been cleared by his great-grandfather one hundred years previously in 1640.

Adam's father combined three jobs, Minister of religion, leather worker and farmer. Both of John Adams's parents enjoyed a great passion for learning and education. However their son John did not share their zeal. Like all young lads his only passion was fishing, hunting, swimming, hiking and reading. Soon having a son as Minister was an ambition they had to abandon.

But their prayers were answered in another way and John duly went to college and boarding school then university from where he graduated in law. After three years teaching he started a law practice in Braintree.

The call of Boston was too much for him and at twenty-seven years of age he moved there to practise law. Soon he was so successful, he found himself moving in very exalted circles as a lawyer to the rich and famous and a welcome guest in Boston society.

He took on all sorts of cases and became a specialist in Government law unexcelled in colonial America of that time.

One of his most notorious cases was known as the Boston Massacre. Although Adams supported agitation against the British he did not condone mob violence. When a crowd incited British soldiers to fire on them Adams was asked to defend the soldiers against a charge of murder. He successfully defended them and all but two were acquitted.

Such was his reputation as a patriot he was successfully elected to the Massachusetts Legislature despite the case.

Adams a profound writer on political philosophy produced many works of renown in this field the most famous of which was A Defence of the Constitution of Governments of the United States of America which ran to three volumes.

Adams's incisive legal mind and his hunger for change caused him painful frustration at times because of the pedestrian rate of change in a democracy. His pent-up creative energy made him shake his head in despair.

"America is a great unwieldy body," he complained, "like a large fleet sailing under convoy. The fleetest sailor must wait for the dullest and slowest."

It was his writings in Common Sense a popular pamphlet published by Adams - which reached an amazing 100,000 sales - that stirred the country to a frenzy of patriotism when passions seemed to be at their lowest ebb. Urging his public urgently onwards he wrote "Why is it that we hesitate? For God's sake let us come to a final separation. The birthday of a new world is at hand." It was a call to war and independence. The voice of the revolution.

You can appreciate therefore how proud he was to be called upon to join the committee consisting of himself, Franklyn his close friend, Jefferson Livingstone and Sherman to draw up "The Declaration of Independence" which was finally passed by Congress on July 4, 1776. His later comments reflect his sense of a joyful celebration at this historic event.

In a letter to Abigail his wife, he revealed how deeply aware he was of the historic nature of The Declaration of Independence when he wrote "It will be celebrated by succeeding generations as the great anniversary festival. It ought to be commemorated as the day of deliverance with pomp and parade, with guns, bells, bonfires and illuminations from one end of the Continent to the other."

His involvement was complete when he was made chairman of the Board of War and Ordinance for the rebellion charged with the job of supplying troops, raising money for their pay and naming officers of the army. As an instrument in the conduct of war this took over his life right up to 1777.

It is intriguing that the man who helped to declare war on Britain was later appointed to Paris to negotiate an honourable end to the conflict. The Treaty of Paris was finally agreed on September 3, 1788 and a boundary between the U.S. and Canada was established. Having done his job he asked to be recalled from Paris and in 1788 after ten years diplomatic service in France he came home. But America was still a mere teenager in politics.

As you can see times were turbulent and in a constant state of social evolution. A new Constitution of the United States was created and a new Party system came into being. The rate of change was breathtaking. A proud tribute to the unselfish patriotism and intellectual fertility in this vast unfolding dream of the new America. And Adams was at the centre of it all.

Yet despite his record of apparent success and his clarity of thought on the most profound political subjects Adams was a strange mixture of fierce determination complicated by conflicting self-doubts and personal dissatisfaction with his life. "How difficult the task to quench out the fires of personal ambition," he wrote, "how often are the laurels worn by those who have not earned them," he said bitterly. This restless frame of mind could have robbed history of a great man if it had not been for the reassurance and support he received from his wife Abigail.

It was this chemistry which balanced all his trials and tribulations, his successes and failures. She was the lifelong umbilical cord on which his life depended. Theirs was truly a love affair of two careers - Adams's political life and Abigail's marriage. Neither of these two elements could ever be separated. Without Abigail we might never be writing about John Adams, 2nd President of the United States.

But why did such an accomplished man feel such a need for reassurance. Perhaps because physically he was very unimpressive and he knew it. He was small, only 5 foot 6 inches tall. He was also plump and had lost all his teeth from a gum disease years previously. Sometimes called "his rotundity" and the "Duke of Braintree" by his enemies he once said "I have been too abused by painters ever to sit for them again."

Unfortunately his personality had no compensating features. He was reputed to be the most ungracious person in public life. He took himself far too seriously, was vain, tactless, arrogant and aloofly distant with others, being impatient and patronising at the flaws in his opponents. He was even known to have criticised Washington himself, "not to harm," he hastened, "but to humanise a deity." Yet he balanced his criticism by telling a group of Cadets, who came to visit him at home in his frail old age, to model themselves on Washington. "I have never sacrificed my judgment to Kings, Ministers or people and I never will," he boasted.

So is it surprising he made so many enemies? Deep down, he was aware of this personality problem. Yet this indiscriminate honesty in his opinion was a trait which did no justice to a very warm personality and was only understood by those who knew him personally.

To understand John Adams and his Presidency it is impossible to separate his life as a politician from his life with Abigail his wife for fifty-four years of marriage. It was Abigail who gave meaning to everything he achieved. Their letters to one another are now a national treasure. In their pages no other Presidency has been captured so intimately. They opened up a window on life in the White House during the four years they lived there. The letters they wrote revealed a warm and tender love affair better than any modern documentary could have achieved today.

In them we find sadness, loneliness, happiness, celebration and so many human faults never shared with the world by any future President. Some extracts may help to paint the picture of this love affair with all its joys, heartaches and tears.

First of all who was Abigail Adams and what did she look like? When were they married? Had they any children?

Their love story began on October 25, 1764. She was a twenty year old daughter of a Congregational Minister and he was the son of a farmer. His age was twenty-nine. They were both married on that day in October 1764 by her father at her home in Weymouth, Massachusetts. The marriage produced five children, three boys and two girls. John Quincy destined to be the 5th President of United States. Charles, Thomas, Amelia and Susanna. Abigail was destined to be the serene supporting wife with unshaken confidence in her husband's abilities.

She has been described as "having an oval face ending in a sharp chin, a long arched nose and brilliant piercing widespread eyes. As commanding a face a woman can have and still remain feminine" was one sneering description of her.

Abigail became known as the most popular and intellectually blessed First Lady ever to grace the White House. Yet she started out in life with all the disadvantages of any daughter in the

American society of the mid 18th century. Because she was a female she was not allowed to be formally educated in America of the 18th century something she resented all her life. This was in stark contrast to the sons of planters who were groomed by the fathers very early on in their lives. In early Virginia "The breeching of the boy" was a custom that emphasised this. At six years of age the boy was dressed in a man's clothes and for the first time entered a man's world thus bonding more towards the father than the mother. He was taught to ride, attend races and cockfights, learned the art of supervision of a plantation and even had his own slave. They were schooled as gentlemen and learnt a code of honour distinguishing them from their social inferiors. It was the age of the planter aristocrat.

So Abigail at every opportunity sought to redress this loss and imbalance in her life. She read vociferously in philosophy, history and politics and despite her handicap she sought to write constantly on any subject to enhance her expertise and knowledge. Besides, letter writing was a wonderful way to bridge the width of the vast Atlantic Ocean that often separated her from her husband during his long lonely trips abroad.

In fact conscious of her literary shortcomings she once pleaded with her husband "I wish you would burn all my letters." John Adams replied to the relief of future generations of historians "the conclusion of your letter makes my head throb more than a cannonade would. You bid me burn your letters but I must forget you first."

Abigail's letters to Adams were full of imagery of people, places and events big and small. Writing about home she mingled the momentous with the intimate. Descriptions of butlers, Generals and politicians went side by side with prattle from her children, requests for a green umbrella or the conditions of the Adams household in Boston after the British evacuation. They were a fascinating account of family life in the house of one of the Founding Fathers. A true history of human feelings in the Adams household.

Once she wrote a nostalgic description of Boston on a summer's day. "I have this day taken a long ramble with my son and the weather is as delightful as you can imagine. There is not in the month of May a softer air, a warmer sun or a more delicious appearance of things about Boston."

The hurt of their separation can be felt in this extract.

June 6, 1777 – "I should greatly rejoice to see you. I know of no earthly blessing which would make me happier. No separation was ever more painful than the last. May the joy of meeting again be equal to the pain of separation?"

Adams' thoughts were just as revealing. Here is one dated June 23, 1777 – "I have just retired to my chamber but an impulse seizes me to write you a few lines before I close my eyes. I often come and sit myself down alone to think of my absent friend."

And lest she be jealous in her heart at his female company he wrote on February 26, 1779 - "We expect to honour Mr Targot the famous financier. If there should be some ladies at the feast it will not be at my invitation and therefore you need not be uneasy." The journey from Paris to America by sailing ship took six weeks so letters were infrequent and late.

Abigail writes on July 17, 1779 - "I have delayed writing till the vessel is ready to sail that my letters may not lay three weeks or months after they are written as is commonly the case."

On July 31, 1776 Abigail complained about his letters, "I wish you would even write me letters half as long as I write you."

April 5, 1776 - "I want to hear much oftener from you than I do. March 8, 1776 was the last date."
His absence from home on foreign trips brought out the loneliness and heartache she endured for his career.

Braintree - May 27, 1776 – "What can be the reason I have not heard from you since the April 20 and now it is May 27. My anxious foreboding heart fears every evil. I have sent and sent again to the Post Office. I fear you are sick."

Abigail did not spare her son Quincy - destined to be the 5th President - from her scolding pen. She wrote on November 27, 1785 – "Never was there a young man deserved more severe punishment than yourself. I am so out of patience with you that I am quite at a loss in what way to avenge myself. Month after month has elapsed. Ship after ship has arrived from New York and six months have passed since you left us and I as yet received but one letter."

What a roasting. The human side of Quincy Adams, her offending son emerged in one exasperated letter about his mother, "I wish she would not be so concerned about me I had rather be killed by a ball than live in such continual fears as she does. I wish she had a little of your fortitude," he wrote to his dad.

John Adams' letters sometimes got him into trouble. He wrote, "There is in the Congress a collection of the greatest men on this Continent but because they are all great men they talk too much." He scoffed "The Philadelphians eat and drink too much." He also referred to the fidgets, the whims, the caprice and the vanity of some. This letter was published to his embarrassment later. In a letter from Paris he expressed fears that Americans might be seduced by the siren songs of idleness and luxury that Europe spread before him on his travels.

Throughout his political life Adams shared all his difficulties with his wife and valued her opinions which were many and varied on all sorts of subjects.

She did not hesitate to voice the most controversial advice to him. "Do not put unlimited powers into the hands of husbands," she warned. And another passion of hers, the rights of women, prompted the comment "We are determined to ferment rebellion and will not hold ourselves bound by any laws in which we have no representation." She would have made a powerful suffragette in the England of a century later.

Her pen pictures of great men of her time are revealing. George Washington deeply impressed her. "I was struck with Washington. You had prepared me to entertain a favourable opinion of him," she wrote to her husband. "Dignity with ease and complacency. The gentleman and the soldier look agreeably blended."

But her reference to General Lee was rather tongue-in-cheek: July 16, 1775 "General Lee looks like a careless hardy veteran. The elegance of his pen far exceeds that of his person."

Yet ever the practical wife and mother she did her own cooking by the open hearth at Braintree and spun and wove clothes for both of them – her day starting at 5 a.m.
Abigail's role was fundamental to the Adams household and Presidency. Despite his long

absences abroad she ran her home crowded with children with little help, local epidemics, and soaring taxes and she ran his farm for him like any modern manager. Her grandson Charles wrote of Abigail his grandmother admiringly, "She's a farmer cultivating the land, discussing the weather and the crops, making up invoices, a politician speculating on the probability of war and a mother. In all she appears equally." Adams himself was not really a farmer. He had two servants and two farm hands. He planted wheat and grain, a meadow for fodder and an apple orchard for both family and animals. There were three cows, two calves, twenty sheep, one rooster, two horses and a one eyed mare. Yet Adams the lawyer when he was on the farm dug ditches, shovelled manure, spread fertilizer and worked under a hot sun stacking hay and mowing meadows. Outside this he had no interest in farming and looked on his Braintree farm as a pastime supplementing his income and insurance for his old age.

His work on the farm also revitalised him for his hectic law practice. Adams was one of the first commuters, residing on his farm and working in Boston, travelling between the two on horseback, a ride of thirty or forty minutes hail, rain or snow. Naturally he soon tired of this lifestyle, his day running from nine in the morning till nine at night. And so he decided to move the whole family to Boston leaving the farm in the care of his workers and Abigail's management. It was truly a union of friendship, esteem, respect and love. Abigail was as absorbed in her domestic life as deeply as he was in his career.

The year 1765 stood out for him for political reasons while it stood out for Abigail because it was marked by the birth of their first child. He was a distant father who only seemed to notice the children's disruptions to his life. This cantankerous trait naturally caused discord between them but the marriage seemed to flourish on her accommodating role to his career.

His time was so taken up by his pursuit of knowledge in law and the whole legal system. He could be seen attending Court as a spectator despite the hours he spent there as a Judge. He prospered in his practice earning £900 per annum which helped him to purchase an imposing residence in Boston. He also earned interest on loans which improved his income still further out of which he built the largest law library in Massachusetts. As you will have noticed John Adams was a workaholic travelling vast distance on horseback to Court cases from Maine to Cape Cod. The inconvenience of this coupled with poor food, bad accommodation, fatigue and separation from his family got him down. He described it bitterly as "his vagabond lifestyle". His cases were varied some exciting, others boring, many covering mob violence, homicide, rape, assaults and battery, defamation and counterfeiting. After ten years it became tedious and the ambitious Adams looked more and more to politics to distract him from the treadmill he walked.

Yet he feared with his customary self-doubt he would become corrupted by power and destroyed by it. He also feared for his health. The inevitable happened one day and he suffered a minor stroke which perhaps today would have been diagnosed as thyroid trouble. He recovered after four months rest and returned to politics climbing to Vice President and later President of the United States.

During this time his political ambition seemed to fuel him with an all consuming passion to the exclusion of everything else in his life. To follow his political dream his absences from ome became nomadic and was a tremendous strain on a marriage which could only have survived by a love affair that was truly remarkable.

The following anecdote should explain what I mean. In the summer of 1779 Franklin was appointed Minister to France and Adams already in Paris as a Diplomat was recalled to

America. At that time Adams and Abigail had been apart for eighteen months which is a long time in any marriage. He duly set sail for home on the powerful sailing ship "La Sensible".

After six weeks travel on the high seas from France to America Adams arrived at Braintree where his family awaited him. However it was not long before he was asked to return to Paris, this time to negotiate the Peace Treaty to end hostilities between the U.S. and Britain. Once again Abigail had to endure what she considered "A very painful price for his career." "Why?" she demanded, "must she be called upon so often to struggle with the pain of separation from her spouse?"

His answer that "The sacrifice was a public virtue to build a better world for her and the children" seemed to convince her but she knew also that her husband was a man driven by vanity and ambition and the hunger for recognition and immortality. Abigail also realized they both were confronted by irreconcilable urges. "Honour and fame moved him," she said, "but domestic happiness was paramount for her."

And so after only seventy-one days at home he set sail again for France on the same ship "La Sensible" on an autumn day in 1779 leaving a tearful Abigail on the shore thinking herself a widow and the children thinking of him as a stranger.

Abigail was disturbed that John Adams her husband seems to have been the exception in his willingness to make such sacrifices for the cause. Washington himself was deeply upset for political reasons that other major players were pursuing their own private ambitions leaving Congress denuded of talent.

William Jefferson did not escape such censor from Washington. He seemed more concerned about the completion of his mansion Monticello than he did about the final Peace Treaty. Adams was of the opinion that only a handful of truly dedicated and competent people were left in Congress. "Where is Jefferson?" some Virginian soldiers had asked at his constant unexplained absences in Congress.

Public opinion helped change his mind and soon Jefferson returned to a full-time commitment to Congress and the Treaty.

The foregoing picture of the Statesmen of that time is mentioned to underline just how dedicated and unselfish was Adams in comparison, but most of all how praiseworthy and remarkable was his wife Abigail who had no political lust for power to sustain her. Hers was a true love affair with Adams, his family and her marriage.

The number of sea voyages taken on by Adams in pursuit of politics was truly amazing because one of the most frightening things about life in the 18th century was the hazard of travel by sea in sailing ships not designed for passenger traffic.

On one of these journeys Adams was foolish enough to bring his young son John Quincy and recorded a storm at sea in one of these sailing ships that could have had mortal consequences.

Adam writes "It was with the utmost difficulty that my little son and I held ourselves in our beds with both hands, bracing ourselves against the boards, planks and timbers with our feet. There was a horrendous terrifying crash as a bolt of lightening hit the main mast very near the powder room. Twenty seamen were injured. One man, a hole burned in the top of his head would die raving mad. The wind blowing against the current of the Gulf Stream produced a tumbling sea, vast mountains of which crashed against each other and not infrequently breaking on the ship threatening to bury us all at once in the deep. The shrouds and every other rope in the ship exposed to the wind became a chord of very harsh music. Their vibrations produced a constant and hideous howl."

Of his son Adams wrote "His behaviour throughout the storm gave me satisfaction I cannot express..... There were moments I had severe regret for bringing him." Of Adams himself, Tucker the salty old sea Captain said admiringly "Damn and bugger my eyes I found him after a while as sociable as any marblehead man."

The bravery of the Adams family was tested again sometime later. Abigail was terrified by the sea but on hearing Adams was suffering another serious illness in Paris from fever she made up her mind to go to him. She left the house in the care of a former slave of her fathers with detailed instructions as follows. "You are to be allowed a pint of milk per day, a seven week old pig, 3 lbs of hogs lard and what salt beef is left in the house. Take care of the furniture by airing, rubbing and cleaning it. No books in the library are to be lent out." She gave further instructions to give various sums of money to particular people she named. Then, sailed to England en route to France on June 20, 1784 aboard the sailing ship "Inactive".

Unfortunately the ship, a cargo vessel left a lot to be desired. It was filthy with a cargo of potash and whale oil. She had a small cabin next to the main one where the men slept.

Inevitably they hit a storm which sent plates and bottles crashing to the deck and Abigail had to be tied in a chair. But when the storm abated and the sun came out Abigail true to form set about cleaning up. She took charge of the scrapers, brushes and vinegar and in her own words "It was soon a different ship than the one I first boarded." The rest of the journey was uneventful until a storm blew up in the English Channel requiring everyone to be taken off and lowered over the side into a pilot boat. This boat with all its passengers was hit by a huge wave as they neared the shore which lifted it high up on the beach. They had arrived in England four weeks after setting sail despite the storms on July 20, 1784.

As if this was not challenging the Gods to do their worst Abigail then drove by carriage seventy-two miles to London and beyond to the English Channel risking the dangers posed by highway men, robbery, violence and maybe worse. At home women travelled alone in safety and hazards like these were totally alien to her.

On her journey she witnessed the capture of a twenty year old lad caught in the act of robbery. When she learned he was sure to swing it filled her with dread and compassion towards him. "Long may my country be free of such villainies," she wrote.

Her journey ended in Paris without further excitement. There were now four Adams – sister and brother, father and mother renting a house in the rural village of Auteuil just outside Paris. Abigail ever the holder of the purse complained to her sister Mary in her letters home about the cost of running the house with the expected eight servants on a budget of $9,000 – Adams' Congress salary. The money available to her was limited on a salary that for Paris she complained "was like a sprat in a whale's belly."

That did not stop her embarking on a small shopping spree when she got there to rent furniture, buy new table linen, some china glassware, and acquire a songbird in a cage. She also set about having the garden fountain repaired.

Yet all around her although she spent frugally the extravagance of other Embassies was the measure of the person's office. The British Ambassador had fifty servants. The Spanish Ambassador had seventy-five. It was the fashion and to be out of fashion was criminal.

Yet impressed as she was with Paris the state of sanitation left a stench which appalled her. The buildings she observed were handsome but most of them were covered with soot. The number of prostitutes amazed her while arranged marriages of the rich and the titled depressed her. It was simply unbelievable that there were places designated throughout the entire city to hold abandoned babies. In a weary moment she described France of the late 18th century as a country grown old in debauchery and lewdness. And yet the Bois de Boulogne she noted "was filled with people on Sunday's, playing music and making jollity and mirth."

However there was one redeeming feature about Paris that brightened her nights and helped her to forget its gaudy side – Theatre life.

Back in Braintree she could only read plays. Now she could see them performed and by the greatest actors. She also enjoyed visits to the Opera and wrote enthusiastically of these wonderful nights when even the buildings came in for excited descriptions to her sister Betsy back home.

"Those wonderful two hundred candled chandeliers that shone magnificently on everything. Fancy my dear Betsy this building filled with two thousand well dressed men," she wrote totally unaware of the sense of loss it must have instilled in her absent sister 3,000 miles away.
Even the stagecraft of the dancers enthralled her for she was a woman who had lived all her life in rural Braintree far removed from such glamour and excellence.

Is it any wonder then that Paris would have a life shattering impact on a lady of Abigail's simplicity?
But the long planned chance to share each others company was at last upon them. What a pleasure it was to walk together in the local parks free from wars and no more separations were the thoughts uppermost in their hearts and the dominant dream between them for the future.

But there is no such thing as happy ever after in this life. In January, word came from home that their little daughter Lucy, aged two had died of whooping cough leaving them devastated. Now they had two of their five children left alive, Nabby and John living with them there in Paris.

John Quincy Adams spent much of his time now with Jefferson and became amazingly accomplished in his studies and was mature beyond his years living as he did under the influence of his father John Adams himself, Jefferson and Franklin. Russia and Europe were his much travelled playground. He excelled in Greek and the classics, Aristotle and Euclid.

His grooming was the ideal training for the future Presidency.

But one day Abigail made a nostalgic observation. Remarking about the snow that was falling in Paris she wrote home "It looks so American," she sighed, "What a sad misfortune it is to have the body in one place and the soul in another." Yes home sickness was fast setting in. As she recalled her home in America more now than ever, she really appreciated her husband's perseverance in his job so far from America. Her regard for him was never greater.

But Abigail's longing for home was not to be satisfied just yet for her husband John Adams had been called to the British court and arrangements were soon in hand for another journey, another country and another people. They left Auteuil for London on the afternoon of May 20, 1785.

On the journey Adams read Jefferson's new book, his now famous Notes on the State of Virginia and he was moved by Jefferson's denunciation in it of the depravity of slavery. This topic of slavery was never far from the hearts of both of these great architects of the new America.

It was like a persistent painful irremovable thorn.

The Adams family duly arrived in London and met King George III. The ritual of the Court was so overwhelming it left John Adams speechless. This was the same King he had described in the Declaration of Independence as the tyrant unfit to be ruler of a free people.

To the King Adams was the despised traitor fit for a hangman's noose.

After meeting the King Adams was led through servants, flunkeys and porters to his waiting carriage in a protocol that was very impressive. However one group who were not impressed by him was the press. "An Ambassador from America, good heavens what a sound," they sneered. To Abigail "the whole thing was an elaborate stage play full of derision and animosity." Deep down she knew she was not going to like the English.

"Who knows what they would have said about the great George Washington had he come to London," she mused.

These were heady days for the Adams family sharing events that would go down in history. Meeting the Queen was another ritual about which Abigail wrote home. A large drawing room full of two hundred guests including Diplomats and their wives, in a large circle, some of whom had stood for hours awaiting the arrival of the dignitaries. Abigail's unflattering gaze noticed how the ladies of the court looked rather plain, ill shaped and ugly and yet she found the Royal Family quite affable. The French press however never let up in its vilification of John Adams which left Abigail with a dislike for the press that would last a lifetime.

Perhaps they could be excused for as Adams wrote to Richard Henry Lee "The British seem to believe that the States are in confusion and Congress has lost authority. There are no laws over there - poverty, distress, ruin and wretchedness are everywhere." Even British Statesmen refused to comprehend the new situation in America. But with no TV, radio programmes or Internet in those days who can blame them. Soon the day of their return to America was here and that fearful return journey had to be faced again. After her goodbyes and last letters to her sister and to John Quincy now at Harvard, John and Abigail set off on Sunday March 30, 1788 from Portsmouth on the sailing ship Lucretia bound for Boston. Abigail hoped never to see England or Europe again.

As they sailed for home the political upheaval of the coming French Revolution was not far away. Adams knew they had lived through the fading days of a changing Europe.

To Adams' surprise far from being forgotten, thousands of people stood on the pier to welcome them home to Boston harbour. It was a noisy generous celebration. Church bells and cheering crowds applauded them for the rest of the day. At last they were glad to slip quietly away to a welcome armchair by the fireside in their house in Quincy.

But lets fast forward now to the upcoming Presidential election. The outcome was doubtful for despite Adams' wide political experience, his self-opinionated blunt vain personality didn't help. Eventually he was elected Vice President to the illustrious George Washington despite the treachery of Hamilton working secretly against him.

More than forty carriages flanked by cavalry escorted him out of Boston that day for his journey to New York. He arrived at Manhattan Island after a week on the road and at 4 p.m. on April 20, 1789 he was met by cavalry and taken to John Jay's palatial home on Broadway.

Moving forward again eight years to the election of a second President, the final ultimate reward came to John Adams for his faithful hard-working patriotic work at the highest level of post revolutionary America. Now having lived side by side with George Washington himself as a Founding Father to the American dream he was about to take over the ship of State. On March 4, 1797 at sixty-two years of age he was inaugurated the second U.S. President to succeed Washington in the then capital city of Philadelphia.

But the storyline has a cloud on the horizon for unfortunately it was a prize that would turn to ashes before four more years had elapsed. John Adams retained the same Cabinet that surrounded Washington but little did he know it was a decision that proved disastrous for him.

One of the inherited problems of the Presidency he had to deal with was a diplomatic conflict with France. There was talk of war. To further complicate matters France had almost declared war on America by belligerently seizing U.S. ships at sea. Unfortunately Jefferson, his old friend and Vice President belonged to an opposing Party within the Cabinet and a rift developed between them. Adams preferred diplomacy to war and just like the political bruiser he was he stuck to his policy which proved right in the long term but at a terrible cost later. The history of this situation that engulfed Adams in his early years as President is best left to the historians. Let's just say Jefferson did not give him the same loyalty as President that he Adams had given to Washington. That is the way I read it from published material I have used.

The story of his troubles, triumphs and failures in the Presidency is a sad one. I am sure there are many opinions for and against Adams given his turbulent personality. Adams created a new Navy and Washington himself was recalled as Commander-in-Chief of the defence forces. It seems that within the Cabinet unrest was fermenting beneath the surface the flames of which were fanned by Alexander Hamilton, a West Indian who had ambitions of his own and personally disliked Adams. His agenda some say was to undermine Adams from within the Cabinet. There were now two factions at war with each other which left Adams no choice but to work unilaterally for the good of the country outside the Cabinet. He outmanoeuvred the hawks led by Hamilton who wanted war with the French.

During this time Adams wrote to Abigail "I am old, old very old and never shall be very well. Certainly in this office for the drudgery of it is too much for my years and strength."

The victory of Nelson over the French on the Nile was a fortuitous piece of luck for Adams which helped him sue for a peace settlement with the French. This was a dramatic political victory over the Hawks in his Cabinet but the price he paid for it was ignominious defeat in his attempt to achieve a second term as President by three votes and a new enemy – his old friend Jefferson. Ten years as a Diplomat in Europe, eight years as Vice President to Washington, four years as President and his contribution to the Declaration of Independence and the new Constitution which still survives to this day, stood for nothing.

Strangely Winston Churchill suffered a similar fate at the hands of the electorate at the pinnacle of his greatest triumph as war hero in 1945. Such are the cruel contradictions of Democracy.

And so at four o'clock on the morning of March 4, 1801 inauguration day for Jefferson, John Adams made his heartbreaking exit from politics travelling home by public stagecoach. The night was cold and crystal clear and the time was eight hours before Jefferson took the oath of office. Adams passed lonely darkened houses along silent empty streets in a trough of despair, all his glory a thing of the past.

In later days he was criticised for his early departure without a goodbye as "the petulance of an old man." Yet perhaps his absence could be explained differently. Perhaps he was never really invited to stay. It is also thought provoking that his old friend Jefferson who had helped in the education of Adams' son Quincy never even mentioned Adams in his inauguration speech.

Only three future Presidents would repeat this scene. His son Quincy, Andrew Jackson and Richard Nixon.

Back home on his arrival in Quincy the heavens opened and a wild nor'easter struck with a ferocity not seen for years. Black skies, violent winds, floods and incessant rain kept him indoors for five days. The Gods it seemed were in sympathy with John Adams on the shabby end of a wonderful political career. His old friend Jefferson now President would not write again for eleven years.

Meanwhile Abigail continued to share John Adams life for seventeen years into his retirement. It had been a happy, always exciting, sometimes lonely yet wonderfully fulfilling love affair that is now recorded for history.

Sadly mortality is inevitable even for someone like Abigail Adams.

Towards October 1818, Abigail took seriously ill with typhoid fever. She was ordered to bed to lie still and not to speak. What could be more horrific for a woman of so many opinions and such energy? At seventy-four years of age, typhoid was very serious in those days. She was dosed with quinine and seemed to improve.

But on Monday morning October 26, 1818 she told John Adams "I am dying and if it is the will of heaven I am ready."

"I cannot bear to see her in this state," Adams murmured in despair. His distress was so intense he trembled visibly and had to sit down.

On the Wednesday at 1 p.m. October 28, 1818 Abigail Adams passed away semi-conscious to the end. She was buried three days later on November 1, 1818. One of the greatest partnerships in history was sadly, very sadly over. All of Quincy town went into mourning. As John Adams himself would remember – "In the storm as well as the smooth sea of life her virtues were ever the object of my trust and veneration."

The story of John Adams ends here with Abigail's departure. His life in retirement continued but it was really the epilogue to a magnificent love affair.

Every good story deserves a happy ending and the life of John Adams was no exception. He enjoyed the quiet solitude of life on his farm for another eight years. Although he never again took an active part in politics he lived to enjoy the political triumphs of his son Quincy who became the 6th President of the United States succeeding Munroe. Twelve months after Quincy's inauguration John Adams died. What a compensation you will agree for the bitter events of the last few years of his political life. I am sure Adams was proud of the fact that the wheel of fortune had indeed turned a full circle for him.

To complete my story, by an amazing coincidence of history, not only did he pass away at ninety-one years on the same day as his dear friend Jefferson – they had become reconciled some years previously – but the date itself was strangely significant. They both died on July 4, 1826 on the 50th anniversary of the Declaration of Independence. Yes stranger than fiction perhaps but then again destiny can be an unpredictable bedfellow.

On the day of their burial a genuine outpouring of love and loss was felt right across the nation for both Jefferson and Adams. Adams was laid to rest alongside Abigail in the family vault prepared for the Adam's family inside The First Unitarian Church in their hometown Quincy.
As John Ferling recorded in his fascinating book Setting the World Ablaze "Throngs numbering thousands held mock funerals in dusty villages and the largest cities to mourn these greats."
Quoting John Ferling again we read "Looking back two hundred years we will remember Washington, Adams and Jefferson as the grand triumvirate of the revolutionary era with Washington in the upper sky. It is now safe to say Adams and Jefferson have long since taken their place in the constellation."

With opinions like that written about him Adams need never again feel overlooked and unrewarded by the people.

3rd President   Thomas Jefferson

"Philosopher of Democracy"
Born 1743
Died 1826
83 Years of age
2 Terms
1801 – 1809
Age 58

Party: Democratic – Republican
Profession: Lawyer, Writer
County: Virginia
Estate: In debt $40,000
Ancestry: Welsh
Hobbies: Riding, Hiking and Reading

Physical description: Height 6 foot 2.5 inches; sandy, reddish hair; prominent cheekbones and chin; large hands and feet, Hazel eyes.

Extract from his inaugural address on Wednesday March 4, 1801
"Let us then fellow citizens unite with one heart and one mind. Let us restore to social intercourse and harmony and affection without which liberty and even life itself are but dreary things. And may that infinite power which rules the destinies of the universe lead our councils to what is best and give them a favourable issue for your peace and prosperity."

THOMAS JEFFERSON

As John Adam's horse drawn carriage made its lonely journey back home to Quincy he left behind his old friend Jefferson standing on a rostrum listening to the cheering crowds and the thunder of fireworks greeting his inauguration as the 3rd President of the United States of America.

What a terrible contrast are these twin pictures of triumph and failure.

If ever we needed an example of the cruelty of politics need we look any further?

But life goes on and political life reminds one of an ever flowing river carrying all before it into the future. Like time and tide it waits for no man.

So just how do you start and finish a painting of the life of a colossus. It is impossible to capture the talents of a genius like Thomas Jefferson, 3rd President of the United States of America. You certainly will not succeed with simple brushstrokes, that is for sure.

Looking backwards through the pages of history he seems to have been more suited to a professorship in the hallowed halls of a university as a thinker, philosopher, political theorist, architect, linguist, inventor and intellectual – dilatant than to the rough and tumble world of a politician. He once said "Lions and tigers were mere lambs compared with politicians." Jefferson did not seem to belong in politics and was full of surprises. He grew tobacco but never smoked it. He ate little meat and drank even less alcohol. He was a fine horseman yet unlike his fellow planters he never hunted. His interests were all consuming in any subject that stimulated debate. Yet he was a very quiet conservative man who loved life to the full in the Virginian fraternity of planter society. A big gangling red head with hazel eyes and well over six foot tall he had attractive warmth in his personality with a good sense of humour. He sailed through his teenage years a happy young man though he sometimes accused himself of being a romantic failure due no doubt to his rejection by a girl called Rebecca Burwell. Actually this relationship was doomed from the beginning because he preferred travel to romancing. When he returned from one of his journeys he found her married on this return. It seems she was not prepared to wait around even for the great Thomas Jefferson.

Thomas Jefferson was born at Shadwell, the family estate on April 13, 1743. His father Peter although an uneducated mapmaker was a prosperous planter who was also involved in Virginian politics as a member of the House of Burgesses.

His mother who is rarely mentioned in his life came from a distinguished line of Virginian aristocrats, the famous planter family called The Randolphs.

His father died when he was only fourteen and left him everything including his 2,750 acre plantation, making him a very wealthy young man indeed. Naturally Jefferson lived a very privileged lifestyle enjoying a classical education. Little is known of these early years but when not pursuing his insatiable thirst for knowledge in architecture, engineering, music, landscaping, fine wines and inventing things he found time for hobbies like hiking and reading. He also excelled in languages, literature and poetry. His first school was a one room plantation school house where he was tutored privately.

Later he attended boarding school from nine to fourteen years of age and went on to graduate from the foremost college of that time "William and Mary". It was here he met Dr. William

Small, a professor of mathematics. Later Jefferson said "his influence fixed the destiny of my life."

In 1767, aged twenty-four he was called to the Bar and two years later he entered politics. This was for him a strange decision for he abhorred public speaking. Adams said of him "During the whole time I sat with him in Congress I never heard him utter three sentences." However watching politicians at work around him Jefferson was not impressed by what he saw.

Jefferson also came to dislike the law and lost interest in its practice. Perhaps this was because he seemed to have a towering contempt for his colleagues in practice. He described them as "A disagreeable crowd, mostly parasitic ephemeral insects, who subsisted off the malice avarice and the mendacity of others." "The Lawyers trade," he once remarked, "is to question everything – yield nothing and talk by the hour." The only reason he persisted in its practice was the financial uncertainty of tobacco planting.

Around the time he started in politics three significant events took place. (1) His old home Shadwell was burnt down. (2) Work started on building his new home Monticello. (3) Most important of all Jefferson got married to the love of his life Martha Wayles Skelton – called "Patsy" the twenty-three year old daughter of a rich Welsh immigrant planter. She was a widow with a three year old son John. As Jefferson put it "When I fell in love with Martha I was touched by heaven." She was described by relatives as being tall and slender with auburn hair and hazel eyes. A bright graceful woman of many talents. She was a skilled equestrian, played the Harpsichord had a beautiful singing voice besides being an eloquent conversationalist who put him at his ease. Yet their marriage brought with it the seeds of personal tragedy. The couple waited until Monticello was finished to marry on New Year's Day 1772. They then rode away on their honeymoon into the worst blizzard of the century through snow drifts three foot deep to arrive by carriage half-frozen but happy at Monticello.

The marriage which lasted for ten years was the cornerstone of Jefferson's life. It produced five children but tragically they all died young. Martha died aged eighteen, Mary died at twenty-six, Jane died aged eighteen months and Lucy died aged six months. A further child also name Lucy died at three years of age. Her own child John died aged three years, seven months just before she married Jefferson.

Martha herself was not a very strong woman and was cared for by Jefferson for most of the marriage.

September 6, 1782 was the blackest day of his life. Martha died. Jefferson was struck with such devastating grief he withdrew from politics for a very long time. Torn apart by grief he was inconsolable. As his daughter Martha observed "He imprisoned himself in his own room for three weeks pacing the floor night and day only stopping to lie down when nature left him exhausted."

Eventually Jefferson relinquished his hold on grief. His self inflicted isolation from politics ended when he was invited to the Confederation Congress. All his old hunger returned and soon he was enjoying himself drafting reports and sitting on committees. It was a time of inspiration for him in which he produced Notes on the Establishment of a Money Unit, the very basics of the modern American decimal currency which has survived the test of time for the past two hundred years.

He also became part of a nomadic squad of Statesmen who went wherever they were needed throughout the country problem solving. He was now part of the new Republican Party taking shape at that time; made up of farmers, workers and producers and having a much broader appeal than the old Federalist Party drawn from the privileged planter class.

On June 10, 1776 he was elected chairman of a committee to prepare the draft of the Declaration of Independence. Other members of that committee were John Adams, Benjamin Franklin, Roger Sherman and Robert R Livingston. Being an expert in the draughtsmanship of political documents the committee gave him permission to write it. It was accepted on June 28, 1776 after much political debate and opposition from those who did not want to offend friends in England. The wording was changed here and there to avoid offence. References to slavery were struck out to appease South Carolina, Georgia, and some Northerners engaged in the slave trade. The result was a masterpiece. Listed were all the crimes of the crown as they affected America.

Some extracts are as follows; "He has plundered our seas, burnt our towns and destroyed the lives of our people….. He has endeavoured to bring on the inhabitants of our frontiers, the merciless Indian savages whose whole rule of warfare is an undisguised destruction of all ages, sexes and conditions of existence……. He is transporting large armies of foreign mercenaries to complete the work of death desolation and tyranny."

The Declaration was signed on July 4, 1776 and on parchment on August 2, 1776.

Actually there were some other much stronger passages that were reworded. One deleted phrase ran as follows, "The good people of these States reject and renounce all allegiance and subjection to the King of Great Britain and all others who may hereafter claim by through or under them. We utterly dissolve all political connection which may heretofore have subsisted between us and the people of Great Britain and finally we do assert and declare the colonies to be free and Independent States."

Jefferson's love affair with politics was only matched by his undying attraction for another great passion of his – Monticello, his new home. His whole life was like an ongoing lover's quarrel that always found him returning to his first love Monticello and the planter's way of life whenever politics dissatisfied him.

His main preoccupation and expense was developing Monticello, the house on the hill above Shadwell he had dreamed about as a boy. Washington pursued the same goal but only in his retirement years. Jefferson's pursuit of his goal was a lifelong obsession. His love of architecture and all its problems fascinated him. For example building on a hill was not commonplace due to a plantation's need to be on a river to facilitate trade. An elevated site meant leveling the mountaintop, cutting roads through rugged forests, hauling building material great distances, access to water for domestic use and the hazard of wind damage.

Despite all these obstacles Jefferson persevered and surmounted them all eventually. Now from his mountaintop home he could look down on the swirling storms in the valley below or gaze at the green hills around bathed in the evening sunset. As a French visitor observed "From this lofty height a person might contemplate the universe."

No matter how hard one tries with Jefferson it is impossible to avoid straying down other fascinating avenues far removed from his Presidency.

One story concerns the remarkable coincidence of his presence in Paris as a Diplomat during the French Revolution.

During Jefferson's time there he became a great friend of Lafayette, one of the leaders who in later years paid a high profile visit to America where he was feted at Virginia University. The visit of Lafayette ended of course with a trip to Monticello as Jefferson's guest.

In Paris, Jefferson mixed freely with Statesmen of every nationality. It was this experience in diplomacy, society, art, science, revolution and even love that changed him forever.

He soaked up the bohemian atmosphere of Paris spending hours in secondhand bookshops gathering a library of rare books and manuscripts he would later bequeath to Congress. He also became a favourite figure in the salons and houses of the leading intellectuals of French society. Strangely, although he had much in common with fellow Diplomat Benjamin Franklin who created America's postal system and measured the Gulf Stream, founded the University of Pennsylvania and invented bi-focals somehow they were totally incompatible. Perhaps they were too much alike. The behaviour of great men can always be unpredictable.

Was it not an amazing coincidence that someone with the stature of Jefferson should be living in Paris at the height of the French Revolution? The raw material for his eloquent pen was laid out before him like a tapestry and he did not disappoint us.

Writing to John Jay from Paris on July 19, 1789 he painted a graphic picture of events as they unfolded in the streets around him.

He wrote "The winter was 20 degrees below freezing and jobs closed down throwing thousands of people out of work. Scarce money had to be used by the Government for buying wood to light fires on the crossroads around which vast crowds gathered to avoid perishing with the cold. Bread allowances were issued to those who could not pay for it. People with means had to contribute to street food kitchens for the poor. This continued into high summer in July. Riots broke out on rumours alone." Another extract from his writings describes events in Paris at that time. "The people were silent and sullen as the King passed through the streets to Parliament and 20,000 or 30,000 police were placed between Paris and Versailles." Describing the King's journey in procession with guards riding before and after it he noted that on all sides the crowds were armed with muskets, pistols, swords, pikes, pruning forks, hooks and scythes. Some were shouting from windows and doors "Vive La Nation, Vive Le Roi." For a so called weak King it was an extraordinary act of bravery. Jefferson even went to Versailles itself to witness the crowd scenes there.

But how can one go to Paris without finding love and Jefferson was no different. Like any other mortal man it seems he fell in love with a ravishing beauty named Maria Cosway, the wife of an artist and she seemed to return his admiration. His head eventually overruled his heart however when Washington called him home to become Secretary of State in October 1798. Sailing away from France he was never to return again. The French experience left him light years ahead of his time as a political philosopher and intellectual visionary.

Jefferson was a profound thinker whose observations on civilization prompted him to commit the following thoughts to paper.

"To preserve the freedom of the human mind every spirit should be ready to devote itself to martyrdom." He believed that genius flourished as liberally among the poor as the rich. He also felt passionately that the growth of cities would only complicate society requiring even more regulation. Finally on Government he said "It s a necessary evil for by its nature it restricts the freedom of the individual."

Washington seemed to understand Jefferson's restless soul because Jefferson's conflict with Alexander Hamilton constantly pushed him to the brink of retirement but Washington, his Commander–in–Chief always succeeded in steering him back to politics.
In the meantime his restless energies continued to develop Monticello, he invented the plough which was to revolutionize agriculture and entertain lavishly his many new found European friends.

Although retirement to Monticello was his ultimate ambition in life the finger of fate one day called Jefferson to fulfill his true destiny.

He was persuaded to run for the Presidency and was beaten by John Adams by the narrowest of margins to become Vice President. His destiny arrived four years later when on Wednesday March 4, 1801 he became the 3rd President of the United States.

Incidentally, Hamilton the man who almost drove him out of politics made an enemy of one too many when on July 12, 1804 he was killed in a duel with Aaron Burr. They were indeed colourful times.

As first Republican President of the United States he set about the job with all the enthusiasm and dedication one would expect of Jefferson.

Democracy is something we take for granted today but in Jefferson's time it was a brand new concept looked on with suspicion by the new America. When Jefferson became President he was looked on with anxiety especially because of his French connections.

But remodeling American society on French lines would not happen. Jefferson was no Robespierre. The foundation of what became know as Jeffersonian Democracy was in safe hands and during his term of eight years America grew and prospered. The prize had been achieved – unlike the French experience – without firing a shot, and without sacrificing freedom or limiting human liberty Jefferson was true to his inaugural promises, "To leave men free to regulate their own pursuits."

Two outstanding features of his office was the reduction of the National Debt from $83 million to $57 million and the "Louisiana Purchase". The story behind the "Louisiana Purchase" is truly remarkable. It seems Napoleon needed the money for a new campaign in Europe and since he wished to conduct his war without being encumbered defending Louisiana against the British he offered it for sale to Jefferson – 827,000 square miles at three cents an acre for $15 million. The offer was accepted with delight by Jefferson. As Henry Adams the historian said later "Never did the United States Government get so much for so little."

Through all of his time in office Jefferson never lost the touch of the common man. As President his informal approach to the job was not only unorthodox but openly defied convention. Pomp and ceremony went out the window. After his inauguration it is said he returned on foot to his boarding house and ate dinner at the common table. During dinner in the White House he was quite unconcerned wearing shabby carpet slippers or a frayed coat. He wore the same outfit meeting Diplomats in their full beribboned regalia. There was no such thing as rank or status for the guests who were left free to choose their own places at the table.

"Equal rights for all," was his motto. He called it "The law of Pell-Mell". At stag parties he even served food himself. Round tables were also used to encourage conversation. In this way he came to know every Congressman personally. It is not surprising this paid handsome dividend which resulted in a landslide re-election for him.

The Louisiana Purchase we told you about earlier was the beginning of an adventure which I feel should be told in a little more detail to give you the reader a deeper understanding of what the Louisiana Purchase involved. The adventure took place under the strict instruction and wide ranging duties set out by Jefferson himself and was called The Merryweather Clark Expedition. It is described in five volumes covering the three years it took to complete the exploration of The American West to the Rocky Mountains and back.

It was Jefferson's meticulous instincts and visionary eye on the America of the future that inspired him to have these vast newly acquired lands surveyed and mapped for future generations.

To carry out this task he appointed his secretary, Captain Merryweather Lewis and an ex-soldier Captain William Clark with instructions to explore westwards to the Pacific Ocean. Merryweather Lewis had wide army experience and Captain Clark was an expert in negotiating with Indians.

They were to start at the mouth of the Missouri River and follow it to its source in the Rocky Mountains. While doing so they were to note "The longitude and latitude at remarkable points of the river, at rapids, at islands and recognizable points for future travellers."

More detailed instructions were then laid out by a President who had made a profound study of nature at work in his book on his native Virginia. He had left nothing to chance for Merryweather and Clark. The books title was Notes on the State of Virginia.

I list here just some of the information they were to bring back with them and remember there were no landline phones or internet, laptop computers or mobile phones to consult with the White House as they went West. They literally disappeared into the unknown wilderness of internal America which was full of potential dangers from hostile Indians, traders, animals and the weather for three years. Here is a rough list of their orders from Jefferson.
1. Study the Indians and the limits of their possessions.
2. Their relationship with other tribes.
3. Their language and traditions.
4. Their ordinary occupations in agriculture, fishing, hunting, war and the arts.
5. Their food, clothing and accommodation, disease and remedies.
6. Their moral and physical circumstance to compare with Indians back home.
7. Their laws, customs and commerce.
8. The soil, vegetables, animals, minerals, climate variations, plants, birds and reptiles.

They even had instructions on what to survey on the Pacific West Coast and if necessary to find their way back by ship around the Cape of Good Hope using an open credit on the exchequer of the U.S. in any port of the world to complete their journey back home.

The expedition started on Monday May 14, 1804 at 5 a.m.

It returned to St. Louis on September 23, 1806 at 12 a.m. – two and a half years later approximately. A total of forty-five people including Captain Lewis and Captain Clark were in the expedition. There were nine men from Kentucky, fourteen U.S. soldiers, two Canadian watermen, one Indian hunter who acted as interpreter, one Negro servant of Captain Clark, and sixteen boat hands. Stores included seven bales filled with food and clothing. Working utensils, locks, flints and powder balls, fourteen bales and one box of Indian presents consisting of richly laced coats, medals, flags, knives and tomahawks for the Chiefs, ornaments of different kinds, coloured beads, looking glasses, mirrors, handkerchiefs and paints. There would be three boats, one fifty-five foot long with one large square sail and twenty-two oars, a cabin, lockers and a deck ten foot wide. Two open boats of six oars and seven oars and two horses for the bank of the river.

They passed the winter encamped in preparation for the journey at Wood River, east of the Mississippi. And so on Monday May 14, 1804 at five o'clock in the morning, the party set off on a journey into history the significance of which just never occurred to any of them. As they travelled further and further West into the unknown they managed to ship back to Jefferson boxes of samples, plants, minerals, bones and animal skins wherever they could. I presume traders they met did so for a fee.

They had only gone a short distance when they had their first set back. Their two horses were stolen by Sioux Indians. After tracking them through the woods, their hunter Labiche had to admit defeat as he knew by their tracks their horses were travelling too fast. Two other horses had to be bought from the Sioux later. Wolves or dogs stole their meat hung out on a scaffold so already their learning curve was kicking in. The combination of wolves and buffalo in great numbers signalled the start of buffalo country.

The most valuable role they had was to make friends with the Indian tribes in the lands they travelled. The account of the expedition was a masterpiece of reporting and is a valuable historical document to this day. A copy is kept under strict security in five volumes in Trinity College Library, Dublin.

Their skills in diplomacy were superb and they were accepted with friendships wherever they went. Indian folklore and stories abound in it. One account was a pen picture of the Yanktous, a tribe of the Sioux nation who were famous for their dignity and bravery and their code of honour never to retreat in battle. This may have been a foolhardy philosophy that although bringing the tribe a place in the top councils of the Sioux nation it eventually led to their demise. They were fond of decoration and the use of paint, porcupine quills and feathers. They traditionally wore a necklace of white bear claws three inches long closely strung together around their necks and were armed with bows and arrows.

Descriptions of the prairies were equally detailed. These descriptions were filled with a panoramic view of the terrain covered with elk, buffalo, river rapids, lush forests of oak and ash and walnut trees. Plains teeming with abundance unlike the grassland and prairies back home were abounding in hazelnuts, summer grapes, plums and gooseberries of superior quality.

Here is a small extract from daily diaries written briefly about the type of weather and the behaviour of bird and animal life they encountered.

Year 1804
Jan 1:   Snow now one inch deep
Jan 4:   Missouri River covered in ice.
Jan 21:   Ice running out of Missouri - nine inches thick
Feb 14:   Mississippi not broken up

May 25: Strawberries on Prairie ripe and abundant
June 1:   Wood duck in abundance
Sept 21: The elk is now rutting. Buffalo nearly ceased. Swallow has disappeared
Oct 14: Cottonwoods all yellow and leaves beginning to fall
Dec 14: Captain Clark set out with a hunting party on the ice with sleighs

Year 1805
May 8: The bald eagles in great numbers have their young
May 17: The geese have their young. The elk begin to produce their young
May 18: Saw the wild rose in bloom
May 31: The antelope now brings forth its young
June 5: Great numbers of sparrows, larks, curlews and other small birds common to prairies are now laying their eggs and sitting. Their nests are in great abundance
June 27: Hail the size of pigeons' eggs fall. Have to shelter under canoes. Some men were badly bruised. On striking the ground they would rebound into the air ten or twelve feet. Captain Clark measured one seven inches in diameter
June 28: Young blackbirds are abundant and beginning to fly

Year 1806
Mar 28: This evening we saw many swans passing to the North as if on a long flight

One of the outcomes of their journey according to the information they solicited from the Indians they met was a report they wrote on the behaviour of traders towards their customers the Indians.
It read as follows: "The stimulation or bribing of Indians to war against each other or against other traders or even against U.S. citizens must stop. They constituted a constant danger of fermenting trouble which in the long run endangered the Indians themselves."
The report strongly recommended taking control of the traders en bloc because of their negative influence on the Indians. Perhaps control of the Indians by withholding goods was also necessary. "If we do not do this the Government's job over the Indians is lost," they wrote. The report continued "Perhaps regulated commercial posts was the answer as whiskey was the main means of inducement used by the traders, or maybe control under strict regulations was the answer. Finally, over hunting on Indian lands with superior techniques, and guns by intruders are depleting stocks and causing great concern to the Indians. 9/10ths of the Indian wars are caused by this behaviour."

Incidentally Sacajawea, the wife of their French interpreter was a major help to them on their final journey by canoe to the Pacific Ocean.

The scene on reaching the Pacific was described by Captain Clark as follows:
"On reaching the sea we climbed a mountain with the Indian guide and found before us a beautiful scene. The ocean breaks with fury on the Cape Disappointment as far as the eye could see northwards. To the boisterous scene, the Columbus with its tributary waters widening into bays as it approaches the ocean. Immediately beneath our feet are stretched rich prairies enlivened by three beautiful streams which conduct the eye to the small lakes at the foot of the hills. We then followed our guide down the steep mountain covered with a very thick growth of timber, chiefly pine and fir. We returned with the guide to the Killamuck villages and gathered much information from them on their lives. Those Killamucks were part of a much larger nation of the Killamuck."

The explorers were soon retracing their footsteps home through prairies, rivers and

woodlands; meeting and talking to many Indian tribes on the way.
Final entries in their log books read as follows;

September 18, 1806 "We overtook the hunters who had been sent ahead. They had not been able to kill anything. Our total stock left was one biscuit for each person but because pawpaws were in abundance we did not worry."

Year 1806 "On September 19 "We worked the oars all day not bothering to hunt and camped at the entrance of the Osage River. At this point our eyeballs were burning from the sun."
Sept 20, 1806 "We reached the little French village called La Charette which we saluted by a discharge of four guns and three hearty cheers. A Scotsman who was going to trade with the Osage Indians was surprised to see us. He had long since abandoned any hope of seeing the expedition again."
Sept 23, 1806 "It had been raining most of the morning when we reached the safety of St. Louis at twelve o'clock."

The expedition of Merryweather and Clark was a spectacular achievement. Not one person was lost despite the hostile nature of the country, the inhabitants, the animals and reptiles, the thunder storms, snow, ice , scorching heat and raging winds they had endured. It had been three years living together in pursuit of a dream. They were all a credit to the expedition, this small army led by two remarkable men Captain Merryweather and Captain Clark.

The expedition was a glorious success and acclaimed by everyone on their return home. Their maps and discoveries of passes through the Rockies to the Pacific were used by thousands of pioneers in covered wagons for years to come.

Summary
Finally, I have added a rough summary of their journey extracted from three volumes of a book written by Elliott Coues based on the manuscripts and field notes of Merryweather and Clark. I trust you will find them helpful. The period of the journey was from 5 a.m. on the morning of Monday May 14, 1804 to 12 a.m. on September 28, 1806 – two and a half years approximately. I regret any errors in the extraction of the above information. They can be checked out in Trinity College Dublin with the permission of their librarian.

Summary of Merryweather – Lewis Report filed in Trinity College, Dublin
History of the expedition under the command of Lewis and Clark to the sources of the Missouri River across the Rocky Mountains and down the Columbian River to the Pacific Ocean performed during the years 1804 –05 –06 by order of the Government of the United States.Book based on original manuscripts, journals and field notebooks of the explorers.
Author Elliott Coues in four volumes.
Publisher Henry Stevens and Son New York, Francis P Harper 1892.
25C – 31, 25 – 2 – 32, 25 & 32, 25 & 34

Volume 1 - Journey out
Up country to the Platte River
The Platt to the Vermillion River
Vermillion to Teton River
Teton to Mandans (stay with Mandans Indians)
Fort Mandan to Yellowstone
Yellowstone to Musselshell
Musselshell to Marias River (See vol. 2.)

Volume 2 – Journey Continues
From Marias River to the Great Falls
Great Falls to the Three Forks
(The Jefferson, Madison and Gallatin Rivers)
Up the Jefferson to its main forks
From Beaverhead (on Jefferson) to Rocky Mountains, the source of Missouri
Across the Great Divide to Columbian Waters
Stay with the Shoshones of Lemhi River
Bitter Root Mountains down the Kooskooskee River
Down the Snake and Columbia Rivers
Down the Columbia to the Tidewater
Columbia Tidewater to the Pacific Ocean
Establishing Fort Clatsop
Stayed with Indian tribes of Clatsop in Vicinity.

Volume 3 and 4 – Journey Home
Homeward bound on Columbia Tidewater
Columbia from Sandy River to Dalles
From Dalles to Walls Walla River
Overland East of Columbia
Kooskooskee to Commearp Creek
Camp Chopunnish Bitter Root Mountains
Expedition Divides
Captain Lewis – Exploration of Big Blackfoot and Marias Rivers
Reunion of Expedition
Captain Clark explores The Yellowstone
Captain Clark descends the Yellowstone
Reunion of Expedition
Down Missouri to White River
Return to Safety of St. Louis.

Well that concludes the background story of Jefferson's Louisiana Purchase. Now we must move on.
One day the inevitable happened. Having completed eight years in the Presidency and four years as Vice President the time had come for that retirement Jefferson always yearned for.

Knowing the man now, can you see Jefferson in carpet slippers and frayed smoking jacket sitting on the porch of Monticello passing in the years in peaceful inactivity?

I guess it was not in the character of the man. He always had a dream of founding Virginia's first university. That is why in the last seven years of his retirement he devoted all his time to this task. Looking back he always looked on this as his own crowning glory – the ambition nearest and dearest to his heart.

Free from political duties he threw himself into the work and gathered together the most distinguished faculty available to him. He designed the buildings and the curriculum. Brought in exclusive library books and even designed the school bell which was lovingly dovetailed into this his most cherished treasure. The university was opened in the winter of 1825.

But how can we finish this story of Jefferson without expecting the unexpected always a feature of the great man's life. True to form it came about just as he put his feet up to relax.

He went broke!

But how did this come about you may ask. After all he had no family to lavish his money on. Well, like most intellectuals money was always secondary to him. His generosity to friends left debts that were never repaid. He spent most of his money on the arts, his books, his travels and of course his beloved Monticello. But what is little known was the debt he inherited from his father-in-law John Wayles who left him 11,000 acres and 135 slaves. Unfortunately he also left him liabilities. Jefferson sold half the estate to clear these debts but was paid in the depleted currency of the revolution and for the rest of his life he was liquidating debts to John Wayles creditors.

So Jefferson was forced to make a heartrending decision – to sell Monticello. Such was his popularity however, a group of private citizens immediately set up a fund to ward off such a tragedy and Monticello was saved for him and the nation. Gratefully he thanked all those involved describing the gesture as "An act of pure unsolicited offering of love."

Sadly his health prevented him from attending the 50th Anniversary of The Declaration of Independence in 1826 but he did not let the occasion go without a comment from his illustrious pen. He wrote, "Let the annual return of this day forever refresh our recollections of these rights and an undiminished devotion to them."

By the miraculous coincidence of history, which could only happen to Jefferson, he passed away on Independence Day July 4, 1826 just after his 83rd birthday. It was the same day his lifelong friend John Adams also passed away. The Almighty could not have planned it better.

His instructions for his tombstone were written by Jefferson himself. The words of his epitaph reads as follows, "Here was buried Thomas Jefferson, author of the Declaration of American Independence of the Statute of Virginia for religious freedom, and father of the University of Virginia." His wishes were duly carried out and appear on his tombstone to this day.

4th President   James Madison

"The Great Little Madison"
Born 1751
Died 1836
85 Years of age
2 Terms
1809 – 1817
Age 58

Party: Republican
Profession: Lawyer
County: Virginia
Ancestry: English
Estate: Unknown
Hobbies: Chess, Nature walks and horse riding

Physical Description: Height 5 foot 4 inches (smallest President in stature): weight about 100 lbs; blond hair; blue eyes; weak speaking voice.

Extracts from inaugural address on Saturday March 4, 1809
"It is my good fortune moreover to have the path in which I am to tread lightly by examples of illustrious services successfully rendered in the most trying difficulties by those who have marched before me. It has been the true glory of the United States to cultivate peace by observing justice."

JAMES MADISON

Irving Grant set out to write the life story of James Madison in 1937, one hundred years after Madison's death in 1836, hoping to finish it in two volumes inside two years. Twenty-three years later he was still writing and was on his sixth volume when he completed it in 1961.

This is not as surprising as it seems for the first three Presidents – Washington, Adams and Jefferson had political and personal lives so exciting and unbelievable it was not possible to tell the world about them in less than eighty volumes.

The life of "The great little Madison" is no exception. Yet strangely it is not for his eight years in the Presidency that he is recognized, colourful as they were, but in the leading role he played at the Continental Congress in Philadelphia in May 1787. It was here he earned the respect and admiration of all the other delegates who had come to the Continental Congress to draw up the Constitution of the United States. This was twenty-two years before he became President. Yet for the rest of his life he was known as The Father of the Constitution with the title "The great little Madison".

One of the most regrettable aspects of Madison is the way history seems to have failed to give him his proper place in the forefront of the world's most influential political thinkers. He was truly one of the greats.

Having someone of Madison's legal and political ability could not have been timelier for a nation just emerging from revolutionary turmoil. It was his vision; expertise and eloquence that helped build the framework upon which the new nation would grow into, the economic and political colossus we know today as the United States of America.

But let us start at the beginning of the Madison Era.

James Madison was born on March 16, 1751 at the family home Montpelier in Orange County. His father and mother James and Eleanor Conway Madison were considered refined, comfortable and cultured of the slave-owning planter class but at a modest level. It is said his father James had roots going back to 1640 and involved himself in community work as well as working to develop his large estate. Madison's mother was also of the same class being the daughter of a tobacco planter.

Young James grew up on his father's estate and because of his studious nature some people claimed he never had a childhood. Perhaps this was because he was educated at home by private tutors in Greek, Latin, French, Spanish and Mathematics. He continued his education at Princeton College finally graduating with a BA degree at twenty. He then added a further year studying Hebrew and Ethics. Unfortunately he became so engrossed in studying his health suffered and in a bout of depression convinced himself he had a very short life ahead of him. He was not to know he would live to be eighty-five years of age after a very challenging, turbulent and demanding political career.

It was four more years before he discovered politics at the age of twenty-five when he was selected as a delegate to the Williamsburg Convention. It was here he met Jefferson and formed a friendship with him that not only lasted for fifty years but was to influence his ideas for the rest of his life. Around this time he restarted his studies to acquire a law degree. He eventually graduated but was never called to the Bar. His reason for seeking a new qualification was, as he put it, "to depend as little as possible on the labour of slaves." But he need not have worried for his political life extended for another thirty-nine years right up to the day he retired as President of the United States in 1817.

The thirty years of his political life before his inauguration was spent in the company of the Greats of American Politics, Founding Fathers such as Washington, Adams, Jefferson, Franklin and Hamilton among others. His curriculum vitae covered many areas - the Virginian House of Representatives, The Continental Congress, The Constitutional Convention, Secretary of State in Jefferson's Cabinet and finally The Presidency itself.

One of Madison's greatest obsessions was his love of books especially those on authoritive works dealing with political philosophy, jurisprudence and international law. When Jefferson was working in Paris he supplied Madison with a great stockpile of books that Madison listed for him in comprehensive detail. Jefferson admired and appreciated Madison "for the rich resources of his luminous mind" and although only eight years his senior he was devoted to Madison like a father to a son.

One would imagine a man of Madison's stature would be physically imposing but in reality he was quite tiny for he was only five foot four, weighing 100 lbs with a weak constitution. He also had a quiet and nervous disposition. He had brown hair, blue eyes and dressed meticulously. Away from the spotlight he was an advisor to the great George Washington himself. He loved chess, nature walks and was a natural horseman. The truth is he dominated politics by his sheer intellectual brilliance. One of the fundamental driving forces that influenced him can be summed up in two of his quotes. (1)"All Confederations fly apart without supreme Central Authority," and (2) "The advice nearest my heart and deepest in my convictions is that the Union of States be cherished." He went on "Let the open enemy to it be regarded as a Pandora's Box with her box open." Near the end of his life when the seeds of the coming Civil War started to produce their bitter fruits the word "Nullification" haunted his old age. In it was all the fear of failure to his past achievements. He shook his head and sighed "It has the effect of putting powder under the Constitution and Union and a match in the hand of every Party to blow them up at leisure." There were ominous signs at that time in the Southern States of this desire to opt out of the Union. Madison prophetically wrote "It would break the Union into parts that only a miracle could unite." In this it can be seen Madison was a man whose thoughts straddled the past, the present and the future and his precious Constitution was the umbilical cord of future generations. It is easy now to appreciate what a gigantic task faced the legislators in those critical days during May 1788 in Philadelphia in writing the Constitution of the United States.

It was to be a superstructure of laws, rules and penalties to please representatives of millions of people all with their own hopes and fears to ensure justice for everyone in every possible situation for years to come and where necessary to compromise in harmony. Today we can see what an awe inspiring necessity it was for these great visionaries. But Madison had come to the Convention well prepared with months of research and detailed analysis of every eventuality the Convention would investigate. Madison's expertise was so impressive delegates left their seats to gather round him as he almost whispered his explanations and arguments to the hall.

From then on he was known as "The Father of the Constitution" and it was said, "When the great Madison took the mike everyone listened." Even years into the future people still sought him out to interpret and explain passages of the Constitution.

Madison felt the Government was there to protect the people. The Constitution was there to protect the rich against the poor and the poor against the rich should either come to dominate. The questions he was asked were many. Should new inexperienced Western States be treated as equals? The South needed reassurance that they had nothing to fear from a

Northern majority. Should Congress have the unlimited right to raise armies thus risking the fear of a military dictatorship? A two year budget was suggested as the answer. Post roads for the mail were agreed but nobody foresaw modern rail or air travel. Every power necessary to keep control by Central Government was advised and not left to future generations. The issue of paper money was criticised but the war could not have taken place without it. Finally to keep States in their places it was decided every law Congress might pass was the Supreme Law of the land. There was to be no nullification. No State could opt out of this. This was the central plank of everything.

Also debated were questions like – What rights these new States had in Congress? Would they be greater or lesser in Congress? Would their laws be special to themselves only? Could Congress discriminate between old and new States? How many Representatives would a State have? Would it be based on population? Should only rich property owners be elected for Congress? How could the slave question effect representation? What contribution to the common treasury was payable and on what basis? The slave question came more and more into every problem that arose and the seeds of Civil War politics was not far from the surface in this new America Madison was grappling with. Should the Southern States have more votes in Congress because of their slave population? This was solved by only counting 3/5ths of the slaves in the sums. Would plantation States be undermined by rich industrial Northern States? Would the restriction or abolition of slavery in future effect the South's voting power in Congress? How would the commercial East be affected by the new farming States in the West?

When studied in retrospect it seems underlying the whole debate was the problem of slavery which it never resolved satisfactorily. The question of the importation of slaves came up. What States now had such a right? Would abolition of slavery come about by law or evolutionary change? Right at that time Georgia and South Carolina were openly importing slaves from abroad. Vested interests were having a great run for their money. Finally, and also disastrously, the problem of slavery was left to fester as a "general fudge". The will simply was not there to tackle it.

Madison in a letter to a Philadelphia journalist Robert Walsh actually denied the power of Congress to attaché an anti-slavery condition to new States and questioned the constitutionality of anti-slavery laws preventing or excluding slavery from national territories.

It was indeed a terrible dilemma for a man so committed to the peaceful development of a new America. His opinion was clear "An unconstitutional law is no law," he said. Meanwhile there seemed nothing that the writers of the Constitution could or would do about the slave question.

Unfortunately that resolve would have to come in different times under different circumstances and under a different President who would lose his life and the lives of half a million soldiers in pursuit of a solution to it and it would not happen until 1861, seventy-three years later.

The Constitution was finally ratified by 88 to 79 votes on June 26, 1788.

Years later, two years after his retirement from the Presidency, Madison wrote to Robert J. Evans on June 15, 1819. "Whites and blacks living together would not be tolerated by the whites. The incorporation of the two is with most whites insuperable." We now can see how gifted with foresight was this man of vision as we look back at events from the vantage point of history nearly two hundred years later. His remarks forecasting a split between black and white citizens were made forty-six years before the 13th Amendment to the Constitution abolishing slavery forever on January 13, 1865. Alas, being slaveholders themselves how compromised were both Madison and Jefferson throughout the drafting of the Constitution?

After the Constitutional Convention in Philadelphia, Madison was involved in many historical events. He became leader of the now Democratic Republican Party. He was also the proposer of the nine Amendments of ten to the Constitution that would guarantee freedom of the press and freedom of religion among others. This became known as the Bill of Rights. Another significant decision by Congress was to nominate a Southern State as the capital so Washington DC became that capital. Finally for eight years he served as Secretary of State in Jefferson's Cabinet. All of this expertise and political experience made him a hot favourite to become the 4th President in the 1809 Presidential election which he was to win by a landslide beating Charles Pinckney by 122 electoral votes to 47. But let us slow things down a little for there were other amazing events to take place in his life before that happened.

No matter how we look at his life, his long list of political achievements pales into insignificance beside one terrible catastrophe that was to indirectly change his life forever.

It happened like this. Just after the signing of the Constitution in 1788 a terrible disease struck Philadelphia. It was a malignant fever which raged with frightening violence in every village and homestead in Philadelphia. Little did Madison know how this awful chain of events would shape the rest of his life? The fever struck down an unknown Quaker lawyer name John Todd who did not survive the attack. One year later the dedicated bachelor James Madison married Todd's widow Dolly Payne Todd on September 15, 1794 and Madison's priorities changed forever.

It was a truly tragic sequence of events that lead to Madison's new status as a married man. Dolly, besides losing her husband John, also lost one of her children. Another child John Todd Junior survived and Madison became a stepfather overnight. There was one happy outcome for Dolly when she inherited John Todd's house and other property leaving Dolly Madison a very wealthy woman. What a change took place in Madison's lifestyle almost overnight. The youngster John Junior would cause him a lot of heartache in his old age but let us not get ahead of the story. Dolly Madison was to become one of the characters of American history and the most colourful First Lady ever to grace the White House.

Living only one block from Congress, Dolly was known to quite a few Congressmen such as Aaron Burr and Isaac Coles her cousin among others. She was also related to George Washington through her sister Lucy who was married to Washington's nephew.

Was it really so surprising then that a woman as dazzling as Dolly would come to the notice of a bachelor like Madison? Aaron Burr seems to have played cupid passing on the news of Madison's interest. A meeting at "Montpelier" Madison's mansion was arranged and after some minor hiccups it eventually took place. Madison always a bookworm and a bit of a recluse had no chance. He was bowled over completely by Dolly. She was twenty-six and very beautiful and he was seventeen years her senior at forty-three. Despite Madison's claim to greatness somehow it is impossible to write about him without including the anecdotes of Dolly Payne Madison his First Lady.

So who was this Dolly Madison?

Dolly's upbringing in a strict Quaker household was very sheltered. She was the second born of the six children of John Payne who left home early in life to manage a plantation in North

Carolina given to him by his father. Dolly frequently recalled her childhood home. The great black marble mantelpiece supported by white figures. Her mother Mary Coles, daughter of William Coles from Enniscorthy in County Wexford, Ireland was once wooed by Thomas Jefferson himself.

Dolly Payne as she was known then was born on May 20, 1768. She lived a simple country lifestyle until she was twelve. Reading, writing and arithmetic was considered sufficient for her as it was the fashion to ridicule learned women of that time.

Her father became so obsessively scrupulous about the morality of slavery he sold his plantation, freed all his slaves and moved to Philadelphia with the family in 1786 when Dolly was only eighteen. He moved into business with the cash he received from the sale of his plantation but the revolutionary money depreciated in value leaving him poor. Depression set in and he never left the house again. Dolly in the meantime grew more beautiful, with a fair complexion, black hair and blue eyes. Her vivacious personality was her crowning glory.

Her father in his final months of life asked her to marry John Todd. Being the obedient daughter Dolly complied with his request leaving him a very happy father for the remainder of his illness. The marriage was only three years old when John Todd died. Soon after his death Dolly met Madison.

However although news spread quickly of the courtship between herself and Madison, Dolly hesitated about marriage. Martha Washington, Lucy's aunt from her marriage to Washington's nephew enquired about the courtship and expressed happiness and support for the event. "Be proud," she said, "he will make a husband all the better for those seventeen years."
Perhaps her delay in making her decision was the sacrifice that came with it. Dolly knew she risked being disowned by the "Society of Friends" for marrying outside the Quaker family; a fate already suffered by Lucy her sister, even though she had married into the great George Washington's family. But Dolly remembering that her Papa had been disowned for becoming bankrupt thus hastening his demise felt no particular ties to such an unfeeling Society. She eventually made up her mind and the marriage was on. It took place on a beautiful day in September 1794. Now Dolly had become part of the Madison story as the most colourful First Lady ever to enter the White House but that was for later.

Meanwhile she was faced with her biggest trial of all – meeting Madison's family. The visit was put off for a while waiting for drier roads. The account of his homecoming goes something like this. At last the carriage crossed the Susquehanna River on the ferry and was soon pounding south. Madison pointed out some old familiar landmarks to his new bride. Then there at the top of a long slow hill stood a brick house. Cries of welcome greeted them. Their long time bachelor was bringing home his bride. His parents, brothers and sisters saw that he had chosen well. Dolly was pretty and openhearted. The word that came closest was innocence.
And so life began for Dolly in the heady company of Washington, Jefferson, Madison and Munroe who had come to live near the Madison's. Jefferson was only thirty miles down the road and was a frequent visitor to the house of the gentle Quaker girl.

The first sad engagement was to attend the funeral of the great George Washington himself. Soon after Madison became Secretary of State. The new life suited Dolly and she thrived on it. She was humble, sincere and popular and a great support for Madison. Washington DC was at that time a wilderness. There were few houses and the roads were regularly impassable by mud but this did not prevent nightly entertainment lasting from 7 p.m. to 10 p.m. in the great houses around.

Closest of all to her was her four year old son John Payne Todd, good looking, clever yet destined to almost break her heart. But for now that was sometime in the future. I have no record of what sort of life John Payne Junior led. Was he spoiled? Or was he just ignored and isolated in Dolly's new circle of friends? Who knows? To lose Dolly's attention, when his mother was all he had just then could have long term consequences psychologically for him in the future.

Meanwhile "Jemmy" Madison as he was known to intimates, lost himself in their 560 acre farm Montpelier growing tobacco. Dolly loved the life too and became engrossed in her flower garden. Social life was stimulating, centred as it was around the mansions of the planters.

5Guests numbering twenty or thirty were often entertained, winding up after some sumptuous meals with a Ball. Strangely Dolly never learned to dance but caught the mood of the revelry just by watching. Those parties were interspersed with wolf, hare and fox hunting and in the summer outdoor barbeques. Of course there were also the carriage trips to Monticello visiting Jefferson, where profound discussions on the state of the nation were the norm. Dolly sat with Jefferson's daughter almost her own age and joined in. They were very close and often just strolled around the house chatting. Montpelier was a welcome respite from politics and like Adams before him, Madison relaxed at every available moment to him on his farm, building stables and meadow dams, sowing apple trees and vegetables instead of tobacco. When politics called he and Jefferson faced the long horseback ride to Philadelphia together. Today the same trip would have been covered by helicopter surrounded by heavy security and planned over state of the art mobile phones. Does it not make you shake your head and sigh for what used to be?

Because of Jefferson's widowhood Madison found himself drawn more and more into Jefferson's social life. Dolly was indispensable to Jefferson for shopping and acting as hostess at his parties. Madison also was a great asset at these soirees with his anecdotes. Sometimes Dolly invited political opponents to dinner and succeeded in providing the benevolent atmosphere to heal political wounds. She was like a buffer State between great powers.

The approaches of Jefferson and Dolly Madison to these banquets were worlds apart.

Dolly dressed glamorously in formal gowns the colours of the rainbow. Jefferson true to form irritated the sartorially sensitive by receiving the guests in blue coat, thick grey coloured waistcoat, green velveteen breeches with pearl buttons, yarn stockings and slippers down at the heel.

The food was laid out in covered dishes by numerous servants while the guest's eyes covered the area from the roast to Dolly, whose beauty and vivacity were always stunning. Meanwhile Dolly laughed heartily at Jemmy's jokes even though she had heard them before such was the quality of his storytelling. Dolly was as extrovert and trusting as Madison was measured and cautious.

Another social event was a day at the races which occurred every year. It was so popular it closed Congress for the three days it lasted. There were booths and tables on which the spectator loved to stand. The crowd were a motley collection of humanity mainly made up of different classes and colours. Some sat on coaches. Others sat on horseback. The rest were made up of bohemians, the most elegant people who were served by numerous attendants and servants. Vast sums of money were bet and lost.

Dolly, as we have seen, could not participate in the dancing but she did learn to dip snuff and play cards. The men favoured Brag and the ladies a game of Loo.

Yet another social occasion arrived every St. Patrick's day when the city was over run by the "Sons of Hibernia" with shamrocks stuck in their hats. Many of Madison's guests loved his party piece in which he very often identified the name of the wine and the year of vintage by taste for every bottle in his wine cellar. That could be a bit of an exaggeration but given the social world of the planters in Madison's time I am pretty certain it happened.

Madison's philosophy on life in those late 18th century days have been saved for posterity over the years. Perhaps he entertained his guests with these thoughts during social evenings at Montpelier so here are a few chestnuts from his reservoir.

On Peace:
"A universal and perpetual peace it is feared is in the catalogue of events which will never exist but in the imagination of visionaries and philosophers or in the breasts of benevolent enthusiasts." – (National Gazette Feb 2, 1782)
On Religion:
"Where there are such a variety of sects there cannot be a majority of any one sect to oppress and persecute the rest. The United States abounds in such a variety of sects that it is a strong security against religious persecution." - Virginia Convention June 12, 1788)
On Tyranny:
"The concentration of all powers, legislative executive and judicial in the same hands whether of one, a few, or many, and whether hereditary self-appointed or elective may justly be pronounced the very definition of tyranny." – (Virginia Convention June 14, 1788).
On Temperance:
"The task of abolishing altogether the use of intoxicating and even exhilarating drinks is an arduous one ...... It is remarkable that in countries where the grape supplies the common beverage habits of intoxication are rare; and in some places almost without example."– (Letter to Thomas Hertell, December 20, 1819)
On War:
His words on war and the fragility of peace have a sobering message for leaders today, "War contains so much folly as well as wickedness that much is to be hoped for the progress of reason; and if anything is to be hoped everything ought to be tried."

Winston Churchill said something similar though not in the avalanche of words Madison used. He said "Jaw, Jaw is better than War, War."

Madison's inauguration at the 1808 election was something his friends and supporters were looking forward to and they were not disappointed. Boisterous crowds arrived to enjoy the salute of cannons and troops in dress uniforms. Thousands of his supporters swarmed all over Pennsylvania Avenue. Madison's coach and four was pulled up Capitol Hill by four burly grey horses. Nobody stood on ceremony pushing and jostling for the best seats.

Jefferson smugly detached himself observing the scene wryly "I am much happier at this moment than my friend," he grinned. His friend the unfortunate Madison bowing constantly from the waist to well-wishers soon developed a severe pain in his weak back. Then came the inevitable Grand Ball, a precedent set by Washington, which was so crowded dancers were almost crushed in the melee. Dolly was her usual dazzling self. Fainting guests left them no option but to break the window panes to allow in the sweet nectar of precious fresh air their lungs were gasping for.

President Madison just looked in Dolly's direction and smiled "How stands the glass." But the chaos went unnoticed by the revellers eating and drinking as if there were no tomorrow. Jefferson left early leaving behind an envious President. "I would much rather be in bed," Madison sighed. Today such a scene would never be tolerated. Security would see to that.

Earlier Madison's address held no surprises in his inauguration speech.
1. To cherish peace.
2. To maintain neutrality.
3. To prefer discussions to arms.
4. To hold the Union of the States
5. Finally to support the Constitution.
Mixed in were many other aspirations; to promote agriculture, commerce, science and education. Finally, a last complimentary word of tribute to Jefferson.

Next day it was time for Dolly Madison to step on stage for her part in the Madison story as the First Lady of the White House.

She lost no time refurbishing the Presidential home being allowed $26,000 for the work including a piano costing $2,150. Her word was law in the decorations. The President's Palace was taking shape and was soon to be called "The White House". On May 31, three months after Madison's inauguration, Dolly wasted no time in holding her first Wednesday evening "Levee". The couple were described by a British guest as "In striking contrast to each other, Mrs. Madison was plump, tall and affable. Madison was small, thin, pale and rather sour of countenance but talks a lot without any stiffness." The Levee was to be a regular event in the social calendar of the White House.
But Madison's political life, like a long free-flowing river, was becoming turbulent and very like an approaching waterfall ahead. A war with Britain loomed. This possibility coincided with his election for a second term in the Presidency. Madison was nailing his colours to the mast saying "The time might come when war would be preferable to the evils of forbearance." Jefferson's policy of peace was to be jettisoned. America's safety in the international world of warring giants was paramount.

U.S. British relations had been deteriorating for some time because of Britain's policy of intercepting American ships on the high seas, the cargo plundered and the ships sometimes ordered into British ports and the U.S. crew press-ganged.

Ironically Madison's declaration of war was made on June 18, 1812; two days after the British had revoked its restrictions on American shipping on June 16. But the declaration was not rescinded.
Coincidentally the Presidential campaign of 1812 was also taking place at this time. War was the main issue of his campaign and he again defended it as being "Just and necessary." He was duly re-elected President beating Governor Clinton of New York by 128 electoral votes to 89. Is it any wonder they called it "Madison's War"?

During the war one anecdote comes to mind about it. The Battle of Fort Henry inspired a budding poet Francis Scott Key to pen a few lines about it. The name of the poem was The Star-Spangled Banner, now the title of America's National Anthem nearly two hundred years later.

The War

Another spectacular story emerged from the war regarding the invasion of Washington by the British. It was a humiliation that has passed into American history as an embarrassment of incompetence by the top U.S. Generals which eventually pushed the President into the front line himself while Dolly was left behind to save the Cabinet files and treasures from the White House before she fled to avoid capture.

It was truly a remarkable threat to the Presidency never before experienced since Washington's time in power. James Madison and his wife Dolly met up again at an inn called "Wiley's Tavern". Madison returned with the army to Washington having spent almost four days in the saddle.

He found the White House, the capital, and all the public buildings a blackened ruin. Admiral Cochrane it seems was following a system of war laid down by the British Navy "Burn their houses, plunder their property, block up their harbours and destroy their shipping in a few places and before you have time to proceed to the rest you will be stopped by entreaties for peace."

But the Americans were not that easily conquered and the war was finally brought to a close by the Treaty of Ghent.

Meanwhile the White House needed serious repairs so after the war Madison went to live in the house of Colonel John Taylor called "The Octagon House" for the next twelve months. His Presidency continued from there until March 4, 1817 when James Munroe took over as the 5th President. These final years were very productive ones for the economy. Madison improved the infrastructure with new roads and canals and tariffs to encourage new industries that helped to increase revenue into the exchequer. The outcome of the war and the Louisiana Purchase waiting to be ratified by his successor were other reasons which helped to promote a "feel good" factor and his popularity ratings soared just before his 2nd Presidential term came to an end.

Madison retired to his family estate Montpelier with his wife Dolly on March 4, 1817. He was sixty-six years old and she was forty-nine years of age.

As Montpelier was to be Madison's base for the rest of his life perhaps you may like to know what the mansion was like in 1817. It had been built on a slope of land surrounded by the Blue Ridge Mountains and nestled on the hilltop as it had done when Madison first brought Dolly his new bride to meet his family there.
A telescope was often used to view the carriages of visitors as they wound their way up the long twisting road from the valley below. Visitors were only allowed in to view the house and meet Madison from 2 p.m. each day. They were always made welcome by the servants.

The running of the house was always managed superbly by its reigning matriarch Dolly Madison. The gardens were immaculately laid out over the years. Weeping willows concealed the outbuildings and a vegetable garden was laid out some distance from the house. It contained fruits of all kinds growing in abundance and figs, flowers and rare plants grew in profusion everywhere.

Inside the house you could never feel alone with the eyes of great men looking down on you from their places in the hall. There were portraits of Napoleon, a favourite slave, Madison,

Dolly and Jefferson his old friend to mention but a few.

Madison always dined at a small table placed near the dining room to allow conversation with guests dining inside. Next door was the "Clock room" called after an English clock that regulated the household for years. It was quite a spacious house for along the walls were an amazing number of fifty statues or busts of great men including Washington and a framed copy of the Declaration of Independence. A carved oaken staircase led upstairs to a library crammed with rare books brought from Paris by Jefferson. Some of them overflowed untidily onto chairs and tables around the room.

Looking out the windows ninety miles distant was a panoramic view of the rolling Blue Ridge Mountains. It was the ideal location for Madison to return to for peace and tranquillity from his demanding political life. Homecoming to Montpelier from Washington was for both of them like a return to the Garden of Eden. They attended dinners and Balls in their honour for a full month after Munroe's inauguration travelling down the Potomac River by the most recent invention – The Steamboat. During the voyage he joked with everybody like a schoolboy on vacation rejoicing in his new found freedom from the cares of public life. Having less salary now, they budgeted for the simple life dispensing with the French cook. Both of them were very happy and still Jefferson lived quite near. Yes, they had lost little and gained much.

But life in retirement presented Jemmy Madison with financial difficulties. Rich in land and slaves but not in money, his $25,000 per year could not cope with the river flow of guests and relatives walking, riding and napping in the house. The guests fended for themselves most days yet their stay was expensive for they had to be fed and their horses must get their hay and oats. Reducing his slaves was the solution to his money problems especially since Madison considered slavery a dreadful evil.

Ironically freeing their own, well-fed and educated slaves would only worsen their conditions. He often argued about it with friends late into the night to the barking of lone foxes and the howling of prowling wolves outside. Madison's first Christmas at Montpelier after the Presidency was typically Virginian with holly, running cedar and eggnog. Christmas trees were not used. Singing broke out now and then when someone played the guitar or a black musician played the fiddle. The mind of Madison found plenty of scope for reminiscence. Many memories haunted him.

The tragedy of the Indians or Native Americans preoccupied him as much as the slaves. They were never very far from his thoughts. He often talked about them in his retirement. He sometimes recalled his speech made as President back in 1812 when he addressed the Indian or Native American question.

His Speech
"My regards for all my red children has made me desirous that the bloody tomahawk should be buried between The Osages, The Cherokee and The Choctaws. I wish also that the hands of the Shawnee and the Osage should be joined in my presence as a pledge to cherish and observe the peace made at St. Louis.

I have further advice for my red children. You see how the country of the eighteen fires (eighteen States) is filled with people. They increase like the corn they put in the ground. They all have good houses to shelter them from all weather, good clothes suitable to all seasons, and as for food of all sorts you see they have enough and to spare. No man, woman or child of the eighteen fires ever perished of hunger. Compare all this with the condition of the red people. They are scattered here and there in handfuls. Their lodges are cold, leaky and smoky.

Why this mighty difference. The reason my red children is plain. The white people breed cattle and sheep. They plough the earth and make it give them everything they want. They spin and weave. Their heads and their hands make all the elements and productions of nature useful to them. Above all the people of the eighteen fires live in constant peace and friendship. It is in your power to be like them. You will be well-fed, well-clothed, dwell in good houses and enjoy the happiness for which you like them were created."

Five years later Red Jacket of the Seneca tribe bitterly rejected Madison's well-meaning blue-print for a new Indian culture. His reply was recorded in Gloria Jahoda's wonderful book Trail of Tears as follows:

"I am about to leave you and when I am gone and my warning shall no longer be heard or regarded the craft and avarice of the white man will prevail. Many winters have I breasted the storm but I am an aged tree and can stand no longer. My leaves are all fallen and my branches are withered and I am shaken by every breeze. Soon my aged trunk will be prostrated and the foot of the exultant foe of the Indian may be placed upon it with safety; for I have none who will be able to avenge such an injury. Think not I mourn for myself. I go to join the spirits of my father where age cannot come but my heart fails when I think of my people who are soon to be scattered and forgotten."

In 1832 this was a sad commentary on the plight of the old Indian nation.

But profound as these heart-rending words may sound for the sadness and tragedy of a dying nation, Madison was trying to come to terms with his own disaster, the family black sheep John Payne Todd Madison, son from Dolly's first marriage.

Madison's maverick stepson, now a man, had become a loose canon in the family circle. He was getting into debt and turned to Dolly for help. He lived away from home which brought them heartbreak. He also pursued a young lady who did not return his affections. Dolly wrote in desperation "Your papa thinks as I do that it would be best for your reputation and happiness as well as ours that you should have the appearance of consulting your parents on subjects of deep account to you and that you should find it so on returning to Philadelphia."

But now a second problem troubled Madison. His loyal friend Jefferson's health was deteriorating. This coupled with a harvest that failed and the nomadic Payne in trouble again was almost too much for the gentle Madison. This time Payne had to be helped with a $500 debt which Madison kept from Dolly. Here was this most distinguished man of letters, honoured and feted by the nation, having the same family heartache as the common man and helpless to solve them.

Time was fading for Jefferson fast and yet again Payne was in trouble. He had been arrested for a gambling debt of $200 and sent to prison.

Torn between love for Dolly and letting Payne rot in jail, Madison whose own fortune was declining fast just scraped the money together and paid the creditors. Payne was released from the debtors' prison and returned home. The sands of time were fast running out for Madison. His own life was showing signs of ebbing away and one day he took to his bed covered with blankets. "Was it the chill of April," Dolly wondered, "or the cold of death." Madison revised his will which was quite modest by the standards of rich planters around him.

His was really the political shame of an under-valued public service which should have been priced in millions. Unfortunately Payne was a spendthrift who could squander any inheritance quite easily. Madison decided to leave him tangible objects such as a case of rare medallions struck by Napoleon and an ivory headed walking stick. To Dolly he left his lands and slaves and other properties subject to special bequests.

He sold three farms to pay off debts. He also sold sixteen able-bodied slaves with their consent for $6,000. His other slaves he ordered to be kept and freed on his death.

Meanwhile, John Payne Madison was on a perpetual spending spree bringing his friend's home to Montpelier to wine and dine as he felt like it.

But one day the end came for Madison like an angel tip-toeing across the lawn in the morning dew. At 6 a.m. on June 28, 1836 Madison was sitting up in bed. Outside birds were singing in the tree tops and the window was open. As he raised the food to his mouth he paused. "What is the matter Uncle James," Nelly his niece enquired. "Nothing my dear but a change of mind," he murmured. Madison smiled and his head dropped. He passed away gently like a candle in a mild breeze.

Dolly lived for another fourteen years. Shortly after Madison passed away she was lucky to survive a fire that broke out in Montpelier. She had to be rescued by one of her servants who carried her down the stairs. However, despite the danger Dolly refused to escape until she had rescued Madison's precious personal papers which would have been a tragic loss for future historians.

She was eventually placed in a corner of the garden until the fire was extinguished. During her 81st year when approached by a niece on some trivial problem she advised, "My dear do not trouble about it, there is nothing in this world worth really caring for. Yes," she repeated, "believe me I who have lived so long repeat to you there is nothing in this world here below worth caring for."

Soon after, Dolly's health deteriorated and she lapsed into a coma from which she surfaced now and then to smile lovingly and embrace the family surrounding her.

But slowly she slipped into a sleep of final peace. It was July 12, 1849. She was eighty- one years and two months old. Another part of the Madison story was gone. Dolly was buried beside the monument erected to her illustrious husband James Madison in the cemetery at Montpelier.

Sadly, her only son the black sheep of the family died of typhoid fever two years later. I somehow cannot help feeling a sense of pity for the young lad. Once Dolly spoiled her son, the apple of her eye then unwittingly abandoned him in the glamour of her new love affair and the excitement of the Presidency with Madison and his exclusive circle. Could he have been saved by counselling? Who knows what secret hurt lay buried deep inside him. Then again, perhaps he had inherited Dolly's outlook on life that she had expounded to her young niece earlier "Nothing in this life is worth caring about, nothing at all."

But let us finish on the main player in the whole story of the 4th Presidency "Jemmy" Madison who was the last surviving member of the Founding Fathers of the United Sates of America. Was the great little Madison "The Father of the Constitution", truly the most under-estimated political scientist ever produced by America. Really it is very hard not to come to that conclusion.

A publication called The National Intelligence in its obituary wrote the last words for us on Madison with its own sad farewell. "The last great light of the Revolution has at last sunk below the horizon."

5th President   James Monroe

"Old Man America"
Born 1758
Died 1831
73 Years of age
2 Terms
1817 – 1825
Age 59

Party: Democratic Republican
Profession: Soldier, Lawyer and writer
County: Virginia
Ancestry: Scottish
Estate: None
Hobbies: Unknown

Physical Description: Height 6 foot; rugged physique; blue-gray eyes, well-shaped nose, broad forehead; stooped shoulders, slight limp, freckled face.

Extracts from his inaugural address Tuesday March 4, 1817
"I should be destitute of feeling if I was not deeply affected by the strong proof which my fellow citizens have given me of their confidence in calling me to the high office whose functions I am about to assume…… Never did a Government commence under auspices so favourable nor ever was success so complete. If we look to the history of other nations ancient or modern we find no example of a growth so rapid, so gigantic of a people so prosperous and happy."

JAMES MONROE

As the last of the Founding Fathers James Madison passed into history most people would have been entitled to ask, where do we go from here? Nevertheless James Monroe, the last of the Virginian dynasty who took over the mantle of Madison was voted into power by an astonishing voting count which was an all-time record. His popularity even before he started his Presidency was firmly established.

Monroe was a man of sound judgement and of the highest integrity and was affectionately nick named "Old Man America".

His land-slide victory decimated the Federalist Party yet not long before that he had been a loyal member of that very same Party before joining the newly formed Democratic -Republican Party which now practically ruled unopposed.

All his predecessors had been wealthy men of the colonial aristocratic class. Monroe was the first of the working class stock.

James Monroe was tall by the standards of the time – five foot eleven inches – but with a slight limp. His exceptionally broad shoulders were disfigured by a slight sag where the right one had been ripped open by a musket ball when fighting as a Lieutenant in Washington's army. The battle was one of many he had fought in White Plains, Yonkers; Brandywine, Germantown and Trenton to mention but a few. Monroe had curly neatly cropped hair on a large head and a highly freckled nose.

They say he endured years of pain from his battle wounds but turned this into an asset by developing a passive tolerant nature in his attitude to life.
He met his wife Elizabeth Kortright, a Dutch immigrant from Amsterdam when he was a Congressman in New York. They married in the spring of 1786 and had three children, two daughters and a son who died in infancy.

In fact his marriage inspired him to settle for a more secure lifestyle by retiring from politics early to open a law practice. However he missed the challenge of politics and eventually returned to it. What a giant could have been lost to the American people! Monroe in fact had a rural background. His father Spencer Monroe was a carpenter and his mother's name was Elizabeth Jones Monroe. He grew up on a small farm his parents owned at the edge of a forest in rural Westmoreland County. They reared him on their modest income in a simple lifestyle something for which he was always proud.

James helped on the farm when he was six and at thirteen his parents managed to send him to a private school run by Parson Archibald Campbell. One of his classmates there and later to become a lifelong friend was Chief Justice Marshall. At sixteen despite the expense he moved to that famous academy for scholars at that time "William and Mary". He joined the army when he was eighteen in the Virginia Militia and it was said of him he spent the rest of his life "changing little chances to big deeds."

Monroe often talked about his schooldays hearing the town crier shouting out the current news of the Battle of Lexington and also remembered his father joining a group of protesters on a walk to Leedstown, a tobacco port on the Rappahannock River objecting to The Stamp Act. "No taxation without Representation" was their catch-cry. Sadly his father to whom he was much attached died when he was only seventeen years of age.

He was a bit of a rebel at eighteen and went out of his way with fellow students to taunt the British Governor by marching and drilling openly on the Palace Green in front of the Governor's house in a protest against the British troops at Williamsburg. The turbulent nature of the times was contagious to a young lad of eighteen so it was not too much of a surprise to see him leaving school to join the Virginia Militia. He seemed to have a flare for army life for he moved swiftly up the ranks from enlister to Lieutenant Colonel. His combat record was outstanding. Command of the regiment passed to him at the Battle of Trenton when his Captain was wounded. Later during the same battle Monroe himself was seriously wounded by a shot that grazed his chest and ripped open his shoulder. He was Aide-de-Camp to Major General Lord Stirling and later fought alongside Washington at Valley Forge.

His next change of lifestyle was a move to the law office where he studied law under Jefferson. A seat in the Virginia Legislature was next and then a place on the Continental Congress. Meanwhile he continued to enjoy the friendship of both Madison and Jefferson. He was certainly moving in the right circles.

His political career now took on an upward spiral as Governor for Virginia. He spent four years in that job where he became interested in expansion westward. His talents by this time had come to the attention of those in power. His friend Madison recognized them by sending him as United States Envoy or Minister to London, Paris and Madrid. He was later asked to accept the dual role as Secretary of State and Minister of War in Madison's Cabinet. But his luck deserted him. Despite his recognition by Madison, his Paris trip was wrecked by controversy and failure. Sent to act as a re assuring influence to the French who thought America was over-indulging the British it seems his placation attempts went too far and he offended major politicians back home including the great George Washington himself. He was politely reprimanded and recalled, something he was bitter about for a long time into the future.

But his fortunes improved dramatically soon afterwards when he returned in triumph to Paris given the responsibility of negotiating the most lucrative and important real estate deal in history. You will remember that famous land deal I told you about under my previous notes on Jefferson – The Louisiana Purchase. It was the gift of Napoleon's sale to America of one million square miles of lush virgin land, rivers, forests, mountains and prairies for the amazing sum of $15 million dollars.

Then at this point, history took a new change of direction. It was a strange act of fate which led to Florida being finally given to America by the Spaniards, an event which increased the boundaries of the Louisiana Purchase still further right out to the Pacific Ocean.

It came about as a result of a clash between the Seminole Indians in Florida and U.S. troops led by General Andrew Jackson who was sent out to drive the Indians back into Florida. Jackson overstepped his brief and swept into Florida capturing two towns Pensacola and Saint Marks taking two Britons prisoner one of whom was seventy years of age. Their names Ambrister and Arbuthnot. One was eventually shot by firing squad; the other was hanged from the topsail yardarm of a sailing vessel. Needless to say all hell broke loose back in England and it took all the diplomatic skills of John Quincy Adams to mollify the British.

Tough negotiations then followed with the Spanish. They were finally convinced they were incapable of policing Florida. It was agreed to have a $5 million debt to American citizens written off and the deal was completed. A vast country of 59,268 square miles changed hands for something like 17 cents an acre.

The Louisiana Purchase and the Purchase of Florida effectively doubled the size of the United States and heralded the vast covered wagon exodus or migration westward with terrible consequences for the Native American people, the Indians were uprooted in thousands and driven out of their homelands to distant reservations. It was something akin to moving the people of Berlin to the Steppes of Russia. But that migration westwards was to come later under the 7th President General "Old Hickory Jackson".

These times were indeed controversial political times in America.

When Monroe finally returned from his second trip to Paris, time was running out on Madison's Presidency. Monroe found himself cast as the hot favourite to succeed him. His forty years in public life serving in the army, his service as a Diplomat, and skilled politician made him the ideal candidate for the 5th Presidency.

And so it came to pass. On March 4, 1817 two old school mates met once again when Chief Justice John Marshall swore Monroe into office as the 5th President of the United States of America.

The newly inaugurated President Monroe then travelled by sailing sloop and stagecoach when he took on a tour of New England. A strange and unusual story can be told here of his meeting on his travels with the President of Dartmouth College. It transpired the President's wife had been a nurse at the Battle of Trenton who treated him for his war wounds. He recalled "five months of fighting and five months of dying" with her. Then he wept openly and kissed Mrs Mary Wheelock spontaneously and thanked her for saving his life.

His first task as President was to set about strengthening the army and Navy to maintain America's neutrality with dignity in the wars of other powers. He swore to be a peace keeping servant and vowed to make his presidency a memorable one as "The era of good feeling."

However Monroe's life was not going to be easy for besides the Indian problem, the slave situation was a gathering storm of discontent he inherited from Madison's Presidency. Dissatisfaction with slavery was spreading nationwide and Monroe wrote prophetically to Jefferson. "I have never known a question so menacing to the tranquillity and even the continuance of our Union as the present one. All other subjects have given way to it." He was also deeply disturbed by the deteriorating plight of the Indian or Native American for the expansion westward was bringing with it increasing wars and conflict. More than many other Presidents his understanding of their situation was so profound he tried desperately to resolve the problem by the creation of Indian Reserves on which the Native American could live in his own environment and culture protecting and preserving its civilization for years to come. That indeed was a visionary attempt he made to set up a nation with its own language, traditions, folklore, music, dances and morality developed over hundreds of years. Yes, time has proved Monroe to be a man light years ahead of his time.

What a pity he could not have succeeded in spreading his concept geographically and politically as the ideal alternative to a Civil War.

However despite those war drums sounding in the distance the "era of good feeling" continued right through his first term and on into a second term with another resounding landslide Presidential victory.

A deep original thinker, Monroe's second term was famous for the publication of his Monroe Doctrine.

Helped by his Secretary of State, John Quincy Adams and other Cabinet personnel Monroe had spent months writing what he believed was not just a list of laws but a set of philosophies that would help America progress onward into the future free from outside invasion or interference.

The motivation behind Monroe's plan can be traced to the Russians who claimed all the lands along the Pacific Ocean from The Bering Strait to 51 degrees north latitude. Cheekily it included a large chunk of Oregon. But Russia was stopped in its tracks by a blunt "hands off" warning from Quincy Adams, Monroe's Secretary of State. In Quincy's warning was a similar caution to any European power thinking of laying claim to any part of the United States. The principal of a unified independent political and geographic entity was now firmly established and was reinforced by the Monroe Doctrine. No more was heard from the Tsar. The Monroe Doctrine thus became the basic tenet of U.S. foreign policy. But let us explain further what the Monroe Doctrine was all about. I will attempt a short summary: as The Doctrine spelled it out. America is no longer open to Colonization.
We never have and never will take part in European wars or interfere in European affairs.
Any attempt by European Powers to extend their political systems to America is an unfriendly act.
Any attempt to oppress or control the free states of America would be considered an unfriendly act.
To maintain friendly relations and recognize de facto European Governments.
Any attempt to extend the European political system in this hemisphere will endanger our peace.
New States are to be left to themselves by us the U.S.

Monroe went on as follows, "Fundamentally regardless of the great Atlantic Ocean standing between us, the colony-grabbing lust of Europe imperilled America." This was never more so than with the old colonial States now independent in Latin America. Pan American survival demanded their protection from Colonizers.

When he wrote this document, Monroe was very much aware of the changing scene in the Latin American States in South America. The desire of these Spanish Americans to be free was leading to independent movements or uprisings in Chile, Mexico, Buenos Aires (or Argentina), Peru and Venezuela. Now Latin America would come under the protective umbrella of the United States.

Of course anger and rejection was inevitable from certain European powers especially the Colonizers there. France described the Monroe Doctrine as "Monroe's madness" and called for it to be resisted. Vienna condemned it bitterly. The Germans described it as "That American Pretence and an empty threat", yet they never risked violating American territory afterwards. Without the Monroe Doctrine would we have today a German-Brazil on the map? After all the Germans later built an Empire based on its colonies. Who knows?

Kennedy, centuries later was faced with a breach of the Monroe Doctrine by Cuba in the Cuban Missile Crisis. In 1960, the New York Times quoted the Doctrine in its headlines about a diplomatic row with Russia. The Monroe Doctrine was later adopted by Nixon as the basis for foreign policy decisions.

The irony in all this is almost amusing. While Monroe was aware that "such a threat," as he put it "would have to be backed up by bared swords, loaded muskets and fighting ships," he well knew the deplorable inadequacy of America's war machine to fight the might of Europe and the funds to build one just were not there. To quote Monroe again "Every dollar looks as big as the moon and is not much easier to lay your hands on." The only ships they had were busy patrolling against the slave traders from Africa to the Caribbean. The Latin American countries were worse off. In the light of all this did Monroe know he was dicing with a brave but outrageous gamble? It certainly seems like it today.

The day for reading The Monroe Doctrine to Congress was December 2, 1823. Being a man of immense popularity many Congressmen gathered round to share small talk and warm hearted greetings with him. He really was popular or as he said himself – "He had fewer enemies than dollars."

He also sheepishly displayed his new suit for the occasion which he claimed he had been bullied into buying by his daughter Lizzie. Most of the house had only a fair idea of what his special message would be about in a general way for there were many momentous problems simmering away in this young and developing continent. Projects like building public roads, river ports, canals, welcoming new States, expanding new territories, the problems of public mail and new lands for homesteading and not forgetting the thorny problems of unpaid war veterans. Most contentious of all setting up Indian Treaties and settlements. And of course setting up Non-Slave or Free States above the 36 degrees; 30 minutes north latitude.

Unfortunately his talents as a public speaker were not as brilliant as James Madison's, in fact they were quite ordinary, and having a sore throat that morning did not help. He therefore assigned the task of reading the script of this momentous manuscript into the record by an ordinary clerk of the House as is normal procedure when the President is unable to fulfil this duty.

But that was Monroe. Totally without fuss, pomp or pretentions. The most striking thing about Monroe seems to have been his unbelievable popularity as a nice guy. His plain humble uncomplicated attitude to his role as President and his access to his Congressmen colleagues completely defused any conflict. He was so well liked one young Congressman rashly voiced the opinion, not particularly liked by the President but accepted for its well meant intentions that voting against Mr. Monroe was like voting against God. J. Clyman the Congressman said, "It is possible but not politically feasible."

Monroe dressed spoke and lived the part of a humble man. He was known to be as accessible as the fresh air. Yet he did not deliberately court popularity for he often took on even his own powerful supporters by fighting quite successfully to stamp out the slave trade from which they earned their living. The Monroe magic in administration never ceased to amaze everybody.

In fact his White House fireplace was known to be surrounded by many comfortable chairs on which any visitor could come and sit and as Monroe put it "Spit out, whatever they had to say." He always requested but never ordered that public money should be carefully supervised. He usually got his way in this.

During his retirement Monroe, despite his forty-eight years of politics and public service always looked on the Monroe Document as his greatest accomplishment and hoped it would be a working tool for the future. And so it has proved to be.
Speaking of retirement Monroe was sixty-seven years of age when he passed the Presidency on to John Quincy Adams, the son of the 2nd President and the most brilliant Secretary of State in the history of the United States.
Monroe retired to Oak Hill in Loudoun County, Virginia and like three of the five Presidents to

date he was submerged in debt at the time. "Ash Lawn", his estate was considered to be on a par with Jefferson's Monticello, Madison's Montpelier and Washington's Mount Vernon. Sadly unlike Jefferson he had to sell Ash Lawn to discharge his debts. Although he received $30,000 overdue expenses from his time on diplomatic duties he never recovered from the financial burden of Public Office. I am afraid there was no benevolent sponsor waiting in the wings to rescue him from selling his mansion as happened to Jefferson.

Yet despite his financial predicament his personal philosophy never changed in retirement. Humility and "ordinariness" was second nature to him. He returned to Virginia and took up the most modest of jobs – Justice of the Peace, and loved it. When his wife died and despite his ageing years he moved to New York to work with his married daughter and her husband running a small home store in their district.

Here I have to pause to give Monroe's decision closer scrutiny. Is it not hard to believe that no one in his shop among his customers even guessed at the fame and fortunes of their simple shopkeeper? Nobody knew about the wonderful estate he once owned and lived in. It is hard to believe the humility of this man who lived unsung and unknown among ordinary people when he had once shared the glamour, the pomp, and the high society of Paris on diplomatic duties, signing a treaty that doubled the size of America. Here wrapping up vegetables or groceries for a housewife were the hands of a President who wrote The Monroe Doctrine which was to outlaw many more foreign Presidents for two hundred years. A document that made history.

Here was a man whose horse was shot from under him as he fought alongside the illustrious George Washington and whose dropping shoulder was actually shot away at the Battle of Trenton. Yet he was happy to spend any sunny morning exchanging local gossip with homely New Yorkers. Fact can indeed be stranger than fiction.

Retirement did not affect the lifestyle of his wife Elizabeth either. She had seldom appeared in Washington society as First Lady and in fact she secluded herself in the White House most of the time because of her reserved personality and her ill health. She was the total opposite to her predecessor in the White House Dolly Madison but she was always considered gracious, charming and quite regal looking.

Elizabeth Monroe was not only beautiful she had all the sophistication of any Paris beauty where she had been known as "La Belle Americaine". One reason Monroe fell into debt could have been his wife's tendency to live in style, buying her dresses from Paris at $1,500 each (Today's money $35,000). Naturally this caused envy in other women. Sometimes they blamed her beauty on her use of cosmetics which at that time was considered "wicked" on a par with Dolly's past time of taking snuff. Like her husband she was indifferent to criticism especially the row about her daughter Maria's wedding in the White House. The usual family upheaval occurred when she confined the guest list to one family only. Even the Diplomatic Corp got involved but Elizabeth Monroe was not for turning. I do not know if she was as popular as the President but it certainly did not bother her.

Returning to James Monroe's retirement in New York it was not generally known by the neighbours there that he was a great friend of President Quincy Adams.

In fact President Quincy Adams still acted as advisor from time to time.

But history still has one more surprise in store for us, an unbelievable coincidence. Monroe died aged seventy-three on July 4, 1831. He had joined an illustrious trio of Presidents who passed away on Independence Day. And he was the third of the first five Presidents to do so. The other two were Adams and Jefferson.

James Monroe was buried at Marble Cemetery, New York City, NY that July in 1831 but twenty-seven years later his body was exhumed and interred in Richmond, Virginia in 1858. Yes, "Old man America" had returned home where he was finally buried among his own people.

6th President   John Quincy Adams

"Old Man Eloquent"
Born 1767
Died 1848
81 Years of age
1 Term
1825 – 1829
Age 58

Party: Democratic Republican
Profession: Lawyer
County: Massachusetts
Ancestry: English
Estate: $60,000
Hobbies: Swimming

Physical Description: Height 5 foot 7 inches; bald, pot-bellied, round faced with a halo of white hair and side burns.

Extracts from his inaugural address Washington DC, Friday March 4, 1825

"I appear my fellow citizens in your presence and in that of heaven to bind myself by the solemnities of religious obligation to the faithful performance of the duties allotted to me in the station to which I have been called.

I am deeply conscious of the prospect that I shall stand more and oftener in need of your pure indulgence, intentions upright and pure of heart, devoted to the welfare of our country."

JOHN QUINCY ADAMS

As James Monroe sold up house and moved to New York the spotlight focuses on his successor John Quincy Adams.

What can you say about a President who started his public career as a fourteen year old interpreter and secretary to Francis Dana, a U.S. Envoy to Russia in 1781. This teenage French linguist after two years in St Petersburg then returned to his studies in The Hague. One cannot start any younger than that.

The road to greatness stretched before him right up to the Presidency itself. Strangely enough the final prize eluded him for another forty-four years for he didn't become President until he was fifty-eight years of age in 1825.

Quincy was born in Braintree, now renamed Quincy on January 11, 1767 to very illustrious parents; John Adams, the 2nd President of the United States and successor to George Washington and Abigail Smith Adams the most formidable First Lady ever to grace the White House.
His wasn't a normal childhood however for his boyhood years were not spent in the woods and meadows around Braintree or fishing the rivers and streams with other lads his own age in America of that time. Being the son of a Diplomat he found himself sharing the company of other Diplomats from ten years of age until he was eighteen, during his father's stay in Paris.

It must have been a lonely world for a young boy of his tender years as he studied under private tutors while he attended school in France and the Netherlands, a long way from America; he couldn't help but become an expert French speaker, almost a second tongue to him. But at what a cost were these missing years of his young life. Perhaps his three young sons could give us the answer – but let us not fast forward our story too far at present.

Quincy followed his father John Adams to Great Britain to where his father had been appointed by President George Washington as Minister. He then returned to America entering Harvard College for two years and duly graduated. He opened a law practice in 1791 but abandoned law for a career in public life for which he was so obviously well groomed. Incidentally, while in Paris he had enjoyed the personal tuition of his father John Adams and Thomas Jefferson himself.

When war broke out between France and Great Britain, Washington preferred to take no sides and chose neutrality instead. Quincy anonymously defended Washington's stand in a letter to the press under the pen name "Publicola". Washington got to know who "Publicola" was and appointed the brilliant young lawyer as Ambassador to the Netherlands. Knowing the intricacies of European affairs so intimately and having studied international law plus his fluency in French the Dutch job was tailor-made for him.

It was now for a fleeting moment in time that politics took a back seat to romance when he met and married his wife Louisa Catherine Johnson, the daughter of the U.S. Consul in London. They subsequently had three sons Charles, Thomas and George Washington Adams and one daughter Louise Catherine Adams who died aged one year old.

Notwithstanding his successful career and his world travels between European capitals; London, the Netherlands and St Petersburg in Russia, his mother Abigail Smith Adams included him constantly in her thoughts and her letters. His exalted political company and sophisticated lifestyle didn't spare him a literary tongue lashing for his neglect in writing home to Braintree and the Adams family. But that was Abigail.

Quincy Adams was a mature young man of thirty when his father was elected second President after George Washington. Quincy had impressed Washington enough for him to describe Quincy as the most able of all his Diplomatic Corps.

The failure of his father to secure a second term as President prompted Quincy to return to Boston to resume his law practice. However politics was still his first love and it wasn't long before he was called upon by James Madison to go to Russia as U.S. Representative. Here he made great friends with the Russian leader Tsar Alexander I.

These were exciting times to be in Russia and Quincy witnessed first-hand the triumphant advance of Napoleon's armies and his retreat from Moscow. In a letter home Quincy wrote to his mother "The two Russian Generals who have conquered Napoleon and all his Marshals are General Famine and General Frost." But it is difficult to paint a picture of the time without Quincy Adams appearing everywhere in the landscape. He was again recruited as U.S. Representative this time to negotiate the Treaty of Ghent in Belgium to bring the war between America and Great Britain to an end.

We next find him in Britain for a two year spell as a Diplomatic Representative. His next journey was a trip back to America to become Secretary of State in Madison's Cabinet.

Once again Quincy Adams was in the thick of controversy when he was involved in the addition of Florida to the "Louisiana Purchase".

Finally, the famous Monroe Doctrine was launched and Quincy's fingerprints were all over it. They say it was the second Declaration of Independence; this time against all would-be Colonizers with ambitions to colonize States in North and South America.
At long last Quincy's Presidential ship came sailing home on March 4, 1825. But true to form he was once again the centre of controversy. The Presidential election had to be settled by a vote in Congress which resulted in Quincy being elected. Unfortunately the cry "corrupt bargain" was coined and haunted him throughout his Presidency. Some say it contributed to his defeat by "Old Hickory" Andrew Jackson in the election of 1828. The "corrupt bargain" was the suspicion that he had made a deal with Henry Clay of Kentucky. In return for Clay's support he made Clay Secretary of State. Well that is the background to their "corrupt bargain" accusation.

Let us leave the infighting of politics to the historians and move on with our story about the President Quincy Adams.

Politics can be a cruel and indifferent task master and this is the fundamental lesson of public life which came as a surprise to a winner like Quincy Adams. Past glories are a very fragile base to depend on. So despite his brilliance in his past jobs he soon discovered the role of President was a one-off.

It was a frustrating and disappointing experience for Adams. Confronted by hostility from day one from Jackson's supporters inside Congress still bitter from the "corrupt bargain" debacle they suffered in the election of 1824, they forced Quincy to fight a constant rearguard action to assert his authority.

The contrast between his personality and that of Andrew Jackson didn't help. Compared to Jackson the extrovert bemedalled General; Adams seemed reserved, cold, pompous and aloof. Another handicap was the image of the Adams family. They were cautious, practical, meticulous, intellectual and academic. The General was a reckless, flamboyant, colourful soldier-politician. In these circumstances the stiff and formal Quincy found it almost impossible to make friends, which in the Presidency was a major drawback.

Adams was undoubtedly a man far ahead of his time and recommended Government money to be used to fund improvements to the infrastructure such as canals, roads, schools, universities, harbours and the sciences. For such a visionary, Congress almost broke his heart. When he introduced tariffs to protect industry he was savagely and unfairly criticised as a friend of the wealthy. The election of 1828 was a bitter one and ended with the triumph of his political tormentor Andrew Jackson.

It had been the dirtiest election ever. During the hustings both Adams and Jackson were described as "The one who could write and the one who could fight".

However in 1825, at fifty-eight Quincy Adams was at the start of his Presidency. He was small five foot seven inches, pot-bellied, round faced and bald except for a crown of white hair and sideburns. His eyes where permanently red and watery which today we would attribute to conjunctivitis, yet he never wore glasses. If we add to all this a chronic cough, rheumatism and lumbago Quincy was reduced to a very mundane and ordinary individual indeed. However he had one major asset, energy in abundance which belied his age. So healthy was he some days he was seen skinny dipping in the Potomac River, swimming against the tide, for ninety minutes. A half mile daily swim was nothing to him between Daniel Greenleaf's upper and lower wharves in a time of sixteen minutes at sixty-five years of age. That was some achievement. It was a daily target most men in retirement without the cares of public life would gladly steer clear of.

To write about his life in a short anecdotal way, now that I have tried it is impossible. How can you cover fifty years of political greatness alongside the leading figures of history on both sides of the Atlantic closely enmeshed in all the historical events around him even as a spectator to Napoleon's assault on Moscow. It seems easier to look at his career in two distinct halves before and after the Presidency.

He has been described in many colourful terms by his contemporaries. Ralph Waldo Emerson called him "A bruiser who loved a good fight" – someone who loved sulphuric acids in his tea. Southerners denounced him as "The mad man from Massachusetts". Yankees loved him. To them he was "Old man eloquent, the conscience of New England". His son Charles called his stern "poker face" an iron mask and never was sure what his father's true feelings were. His wife only discovered his passion for the theatre after twenty-five years of marriage. Theirs was a strange relationship. Although historians paint her as a frail wilting violet, Quincy thought otherwise. Here is a story to intrigue you.

Louisa Adams was stationed in St. Petersburg while Quincy was called to Ghent to settle the Peace Treaty to end the war of 1812. When he had finished his work he ordered Louisa to sell everything and meet him in Paris. It was the middle of winter and trouble still raged on the roads between Russia and France. Regardless of this she set off by carriage from St. Petersburg. Her only company was her eight year old son and three servants. Her journey was filled with danger, intrigue and tales of murder on the very road she travelled. She refused to stop and overcame snowdrifts, her servants leaving her and fearing to sleep lest she be murdered in her bed. She was even surrounded by crowds loyal to Napoleon and the cry went up "Kill them they are Russians." She showed them her American passport and said "Vive Napoleon" and was let go. She finally arrived to greet her husband at Hotel Du Nord in Paris. The journey had taken her forty days and she arrived in Paris at the height of the French revolution. So much for historians!

Quincy recounted many of these things in his diaries which ran to twelve thick volumes and like his father and mother painted a lucrative picture for historians when he wrote about the times he lived through.

However there were contradictions in Quincy's makeup between the nit-picking, meticulous, prim and proper, stiff-backed New Englander and the ramshackle lovable, untidy but kindly old man of his later years. You can take your pick. His remark to his older son was "There is much in the life of every individual which for his own comfort and that of others should be forgotten." And so he drew a veil of secrecy and caution over his private affairs.

Those people even in his family who probed the reason for his return to politics after the Presidency got very few answers. His wife was incensed. His son Charles nagged him.
His wife Louise dreaded the thought of her home becoming once again the focus of intrigue. She threatened to refuse to go with him to Washington but after a threat by Quincy to sell both his houses in Washington she relented.

His family however should have known better. Their opposition challenged this stubborn "fighting bruiser" streak in him that Waldo Emerson had described so eloquently. And that was that.
His wife in a resigned analysis of the situation concluded that the life of a country gentleman pruning his roses and writing his memoirs and that of his father's would have been his death knell. His insatiable passion for politics could not be blown out like a flickering candle. And so on November 1, 1830 one year after he left the Presidency Adams returned to Congress with a landslide victory. He also returned on a revenge mission because both he and his father were given only one term each which left him a very bitter man.

So much so, like his father, he had not wanted to see "old Hickory" Andrew Jackson sworn in as the 7th President. "Why did defeat for a second term only fall to the Adams family," he asked. He blamed the power of the slavery lobby on their defeats. Quincy Adams criticism went like this. Was it a coincidence that the Virginian President before him had hundreds of slaves in their estate and therefore could be trusted? Yes, maybe he was a paranoid cantankerous old man but historians are coming around to Quincy Adams view today. The 3/5ths rule for counting slaves in the vote helped slave owners determine the State electoral votes in each State. The Adams family because of their lack of slaves were handicapped by this Constitutional rule. The political power of statistics.

But could his rejection after one term be the result of his style of Presidency which some Republicans considered a flagrant violation of their faith. Quincy always claimed that his program of Government was "For the improvement in the conditions of those over whom it is established."

So what were his sins? He constructed a National system of roads and canals, created a National University and a Naval Academy, encouraged exploration westwards, put in place a universal standard for weights and measures, introduced a patent law to encourage inventors and finally built astronomical observatories and all at Federal expense. Not bad at all. But his enemies claimed all these measures with Federal funds were limited by the Constitution. Adams disagreed and so was accused of "Treachery of the most sacred trust." Worse than that, the tax he introduced to protect trade was like a red rag to a bull. Were these the straws that finally "broke the camel's back" and lost him re-election for a second term?

Yes, perhaps his was a cruel political demise but should Quincy Adams have seen it coming? Here was a man who had been a brilliant linguist, an intellectual giant, a world famous negotiator who was so skilled he solved the problems of at least three major international crises. Yet he failed to monitor his own political downfall waiting in the wings. Why?

First of all he didn't enjoy mixing with a crowd. Charles his son said, "I never saw a family which had so little of the associating disposition." But perhaps his greatest mistake was to fall out with his Party machine. As one supporter put it "Mr Adams during his Administration failed to cherish, strengthen or recognise the Party to which he owed his election. Nor with the great power he possessed did he make one single influential friend."

I'm afraid there may be many explanations but, to this day as a politician you offend the Party machine at your peril. Yet somehow the sheer resilience of this man Quincy Adams is astonishing. His story should end here with his defeat and disillusionment but Quincy had other plans.

A new career lay ahead of him for seventeen years into the future. In this role Quincy Adams proved to the world what a unique man he really was.

But something else prompted his return besides a mission of revenge, as some commentators would have us believe.
First, the awful tragedy of his eldest son's suicide and most important of all, a marriage that was not as compatible as the one between his father and his mother.

His wife's diary seems to reflect a marriage failure. The ghost of Mary Fraser, a woman he was discouraged by his mother from marrying, hung heavily all over her diary. To this was added her inferiority complex within the illustrious Adams household. Her fainting fits and morbid moods some said were attention seeking ploys to get affection from a cold indifferent family. Quincy's preoccupation with his own agenda in Congress drove her away from him leaving both of them living in unhappy isolation.

Well that is what her diaries seem to imply. Quincy Adams himself seemed to have no idea how to handle this unhappy woman who just couldn't measure up to the standards of her mother-in-law the formidable Abigail Smith Adams. Louisa's single life was easy-going and family orientated where Quincy had been reared with long parental absences and the pursuit of excellence, hard graft and intellectual studies.

So immediately we had a style and philosophy of child rearing which was a threat to the marriage if left unhealed. Apparently it was left unhealed but the Adams formula for success was far from perfect. All Quincy's sons it seemed were social failures. Charles died a wastrel and a drunk. Thomas deserted his own family regularly and also drank too much bringing disgrace on the Adams family, a problem not unlike the problem of the Madison family.

It seemed the family name was more important than happiness to John Quincy Adams. He was a compulsive controller and demanded standards of his sons which were incompatible with their natural abilities. Despite his attentions not one of his three sons responded with success.   The tragic story of George was one of "might-have-been".   If only Quincy had encouraged him to follow his true vocation, reading drama and poetry at Harvard.   He went into the law business given to him by his father but after some years he went broke and had a nervous breakdown.   The shadow of his father was George's hardest task master.   Quincy's only solution was self discipline, a gift George did not have.   He jumped or fell off a luxury steamboat on his way home from his travels and was drowned somewhere off Long Island.

Quincy's wife Louise blamed him for the tragedy because of the impossible dream he had nurtured for his boys and of his blindness to George's real needs.   It is a story that is commonplace today.   Ambitious parents seem to have a built-in blindness that only their own insatiable egos can inflict.

Last but not least some say his return to Congress was based on money or to be more specific debt.   Although he died in 1848 a very rich man leaving an estate in the region of a quarter of a million dollars – $2 million in today's money – one year after he re-entered Congress in 1831, Adam's financial affairs were in chaos.   He dreaded becoming another broke President.   All of his predecessors with the exception of George Washington had suffered a similar fate - the curse of the White House.

I am afraid the people who managed his money did him no favours for he owed $40,000 when he went back to politics.   But it was not the money he earned there which beckoned him back. It had to be the cut and thrust of debate that would release the demons of worry and tragedy that smouldered inside him.

And so Adams entered a new and exciting era in the growth of America.   He became a folk hero for the anti-slavery campaign which was gathering momentum.   So much so he received a dozen assassination threats per month with letters from far flung places promising "To cut your throat from ear to ear" or "To cut your damned guts out in the dark" or others more restrained but just as dangerous "To put you away."

One Georgian who threatened to shoot him accused him of wanting to disgrace the country by putting into Congress "A big black thick-lipped, crack-heeled, woolly headed, skunk smelling damned Negro."   Yes the pot of rebellion and future Civil War was bubbling nicely on the back-burner.   The duelling grounds were also in great demand for those lost for words.   This was really a Southern trait that was a common pastime even among great men of those times. James Hamilton had fourteen duels on his record resulting in having a perfect score of no deaths but fourteen wounded.   The pulling of one's nose accompanied by a slap in the face was the invitation to war.   Refusal brought social ignomiuy.   Unfortunately for Hamilton his fiftheenth duel was his last.   So much for statistics!

Another story worth telling of Adams's life after the Presidency concerns thirty-nine Negroes who seized a slave ship off Cuba.   Adams defended them in court.   The Judge ordered them to be taken back to Africa.   The case went to the Supreme Court and despite Adams legal rustiness he had them freed.   His role as protagonist and tormentor of the vicious pro-slavery lobby was a constant source of irritation to them.

Finally a momentous piece of unfinished business came along, the ceding of Texas as a new State out of the province of Mexico.   As President in 1825 Adams had tried to buy out the Mexicans but to no avail.   He opposed the annexing of Texas fearing it would spawn as many as five slave-holding States.   In Adams day Texas was a land of freedom untainted by slavery. He was pleased when Mexico banned slavery but slave power was rampant and vested interests were pressing hard for the introduction of slavery to the province.

The area of Mexico included present day Texas, New Mexico, Colorado, Utah, Nevada and Arizona. The problem was that although the land was underdeveloped, Mexico was too poor to develop it and decided to encourage immigrants in from the U.S. by selling the land dirt-cheap at ten cents an acre. Naturally this attracted an avalanche of buyers for elsewhere land was going at $1.25 an acre.

Then alarm set in and migration was stopped by a law that was too weak and inoperable. Next followed a Texas revolt which became a war of independence resulting in 188 martyrs murdered at the Alamo giving rise after that to the catch cry "Remember the Alamo". The new Texas that emerged turned to the United States for recognition as a new State. Adams was not in favour of the rebels because he suspected Jackson's hand was all over the rebellion supported by slave masters. The evidence came from a Quaker Benjamin Lundy who had detailed evidence of the plot, he claimed. Then came the tragic war against Mexico which Senator Robert Kennedy in 1960 described as "A war of U.S. aggression and utterly disgraceful."

Despite Adam's battle, annexation of Texas eventually took place. Slave power had won. But Quincy Adam's part in the story can never be underestimated for its morality and courage.

It must be remembered that through all of his battles in Congress and his travels to meetings covering long distances, Quincy Adams used the very basic transport of the day - stagecoaches, steamboats and trains. Quincy Adams even then was an old, old man by 19th century standards.

He arrived home one day on holidays from Congress after spending most of the year in Washington and had decided to continue his long distance swims. His old haunt on the Rappahannock River had been taken over by a younger generation so he tried elsewhere upstream. He could see the past fading fast behind him and the sands of time quickly running out.

One day while visiting his son in Boston he collapsed from a cerebral haemorrhage and was in a coma for days. He decided to write his last Will and Testament soon after, leaving most of his estate to his wife, his last surviving son Charles and his granddaughter. It was written in painstaking detail proving he was still full of vigour. That was in November 1847. But in February 1848 he was off to Congress again travelling by train and steamers to Washington.

He entered the House to a standing ovation. The treaty with Mexico was being signed, taking from her one million square miles and one third of her territory. Then he collapsed in the Chamber and was removed to the Speaker's Room. His whispered words were barely audible, "This is the end of earth but I am composed," he said. He slipped into a coma and was unable to recognise his wife Louise when she arrived. Two days later the old man died at 7.20 p.m. on the evening of February 23, 1848. He was eighty-one years old.

Here was a venerable old man whose eyes had witnessed the war of Napoleon, the French Revolution, the glamour of the Diplomatic Banquets and the hurly burly of pre-Civil War politics in Congress. A man with a lot of historic memories to leave behind. Now gone forever.

Quincy Adams was buried with all the expected pomp and circumstance for a great man. The air of a national pageant prevailed. The marching military funeral bands, long lines of mourners, politicians in their hundreds including his old political foes all paid their genuine respects calling him "A sage, a patriarch and a great man" in their graveside eulogies. Alas the cantankerous old man never heard the glowing tributes that made him a hero at long, long last.

He was buried in his hometown Quincy but passions he aroused by his fearless anti-slavery fight would only smoulder for another thirteen years.

One day some future generation would fan these smouldering embers into life sending many young men to their graves in pursuit of a cause that was always Quincy Adam's dearest dream – a Slave Free America.

7th President   Andrew Jackson

"Old Hickory"
Born 1767
Died 1845
78 Years of age
2 Terms
1829 – 1837
Age 62

Party: Democratic Republican
Profession: Soldier
County: Tennessee
Ancestry: Scottish-Irish
Estate: Value unknown, Land Poor
Hobbies: Riding

Physical Description: Height 6 foot 1 inch; weight 140 lbs; bushy iron-gray hair, brushed high above forehead; clear, dark blue eyes; prominent eyebrows, carrying a sabre scar on forehead.

Extracts from his inaugural address Washington DC, Wednesday March 4, 1829
"With veneration to the lights that flow from the mind that founded and the mind that reformed our system. The same diffidence induces me to hope for instruction and aid from the co-ordinate branches of the Government and for the indulgence and support of my fellow citizens generally.

It will be my sincere and constant desire to observe towards the Indian tribes within our limits a just and liberal policy and to give them that human and considerate attention to their rights and their wants which is consistent with the habits of our Government and the feelings of our people."

ANDREW JACKSON

The only problem you will have with Andrew "Old Hickory" Jackson when you read about him is whether to like him or hate him. But rest assured you will not be alone in that dilemma. The fact that he became President at all is a mystery for his path to the White House was nothing like those of his predecessors. Most of those Presidents came from privileged positions, with educational grooming and impeccable backgrounds. They say Jackson had an aristocratic family but his rise to power was rough, tough and uncompromising.

He made no bargains with anyone, not even his own Presidents, and all his life he was a virtual prisoner of his own volatile personality. Some said he was an angry young man who grew up to be an angry old man. Yet his blunt impetuosity was coloured by the frontiersman's honesty. Washington had it in abundance but in Washington's case it was dressed and presented with dignity.

Jackson was a bully who liked to get his own way. Heaven help those who confronted him as some duellists found out to their cost. If you got in his way you could wind up dead. When told he was going for President some people just stared incredulously. "Jackson? Andy Jackson?" they scoffed. They even denied they knew him with any intimacy. "My husband might drink a glass of whiskey with him but would never bring him into the house, he was such a rake. Well if Andy Jackson can be President anyone can!"

Jackson was straight and tall, six foot one with reddish hair that fell over his forehead like the mane of a lion just hiding a sabre scar inflicted on him by a British soldier when he was in his teens. He had deep set blue eyes that could blaze in a temper. A sort of fury that could frighten or paralyze the victim of his wrath. His temper tantrums could be so controlled it looked separate from the man and to some observers a well rehearsed fake. But it worked for him.

He was a multiplicity of contradictions. In fact one historian described him as impetuous, cautious, ruthless yet compassionate, full of towering ambition, fierce loyalties and stern self discipline. A great General ignorant in the art of war. A great writer who could not spell. A law defying, law abiding citizen. An atrocious saint. It was not till he married Rachael that he learned the art of self-control from her.

Andrew Jackson was born of Scottish-Irish parents in a log cabin on March 15, 1767. His father was a linen weaver before emigrating from Carrickfergus in Northern Ireland to a farm in the backwoods settlement of Waxhaw on the borders between North and South Carolina. His mother was Elizabeth Hutchinson also from Northern Ireland. They had three children; Hugh who died at eighteen, Robert who died three months later at fifteen and Andrew who was born just after his father died. Jackson's mother now a widow moved into the home of a relative nearby named James Crawford, with whom Andrew spent his boyhood years. He soon gained the reputation of having a fiery temper and willing to fight all comers.

He attended the local frontier school and at thirteen became a dispatch rider for the South Carolina Militia. His brother Hugh was killed when the British raided his hometown Waxhaw. Both Andrew and Robert were roughly treated in the same raid. Soldiers broke up the house and furniture and when Andrew was ordered to clean the boots of an officer he refused. The officer in anger at such insolence from a fourteen year old lashed out with his sabre and Andrew ducked taking the blows on his forehead and arm, leaving him with scars he carried for the rest of his life.

Robert and Andrew were taken prisoner and transferred to South Carolina. Their mother heard of their plight and travelled forty miles to rescue them. Meanwhile Robert had contracted smallpox. This wonderful woman placed Robert on a horse and rode another one herself. Andrew who was also incubating smallpox walked behind barefoot, the full forty miles back home, drenched by a sudden storm.

Robert soon died and Andrew took three months to recover. Soon his mother set off again, this time to nurse some American prisoners at Charleston, 160 miles away. While doing so she contracted cholera or "ships sickness" as it was known and died leaving Andrew an orphan at fourteen years of age. Just why would a mother take such risks in army camps a long way from home, especially camps full of infectious diseases? I have just no answer. They posted her few belongings back home to him. At that critical moment who could have guessed this young fourteen year old firebrand would become President of the Untied States, forty-eight years later. However being alone, he now had to earn his living and soon got a job as a saddle maker. His luck changed and he inherited $300 from his grandfather but this was soon spent on high life in Charleston, one of the biggest cities in the South at that time.

But Andrew's youth was not all doom and gloom. On the contrary, Andrew Jackson was about to make a name for himself as a wild fun loving "devil-may-care hell-raiser" in gambling, drinking, cockfighting and losing money at the races. I guess we have here the answer to his mother's travel bug. She saw enough of Andrew Jackson's emerging personality to see he was completely self sufficient – even at fourteen years of age.

But the resilience that was to serve him so well on the battlefield soon surfaced, and many were surprised when this wild fun loving youth changed his lifestyle completely and decided to study the law. At twenty years old he was admitted to practice and after a further period of six months was examined by two prominent Judges who authorized him to practice as an attorney at the County courts. Soon he was on his travels again this time with a lawyer friend John McNairy whose connections helped Jackson to become a Judge. As solicitor General Jackson made a name for himself prosecuting debtors. He not only built up a law practice but also speculated in land deals.

Our fourteen year old orphan boy had truly come a long way on his own self-sufficiency and ambition. A remarkable journey so far.

But the most eventful time of his life was about to happen. Something, that years into his future would cost a man his life in a duel. Andrew fell in love.

The girl in question was the daughter of his landlady. At that time she was separated from her husband and her name was Rachel Donelson Robards. Believing Rachel had obtained a divorce and was free of any impediments they got married in 1791. Both were twenty-four years of age. But trouble lay ahead when they discovered no divorce had gone through and they had to re-marry in a second ceremony. Later this led to clouds of doubt, rumours and malicious gossip which turned into a scandal. The stress on Rachel was unbelievable. But life went on and although they had no children of their own they adopted four nephews and a little Indian boy whose parents had been killed in one of Andrew Jackson's campaign wars. But all that came later. It was five years before Andrew Jackson entered politics as a delegate for Tennessee at the State Constitutional Convention and the same year he entered the House of Representatives.

He was not long about voicing controversial opinions there when he criticized Washington himself for being too lenient with the Indians or Native Americans after the revolution. He next became a Senator to complete a meritorious triple – Congressman, Senator and Judge.

For such an active, almost reckless man it surprises you to read about him retiring at thirty-seven for eight years from 1802 to 1810. These were happy years for him and Rachel which he spent improving his plantation The Hermitage and breeding racehorses. The Hermitage, his plantation mansion was really a two storey three bedroom house built in the middle of rolling hills outside the Tennessee capital of Nashville and on the Cumberland River. Andrew Jackson was also reported to own other property outside Nashville.

During his retirement the number of his slaves increased from twenty to one hundred. It was at this time he was given the title of Major General of the Tennessee Militia. It was the start of his illustrious military career which was so full of victories and triumphs that it formed the basis of his reputation on which he depended in his bid for the White House.

Here it might be no harm to paint a portrait of army life in Jackson's time in the 1820s.

A soldier once he joined the army was placed in a regiment which was his for life. Since there was no contact outside his company he had to make his enemies and friends within it. His friends in the Cavalry were the men he rode with and the friends he made in the infantry came from his squad. He could not survive unless he was good with his fists. If tough he could find himself promoted to a non-commissioned officer. Unfortunately soldiers were constantly at the mercy of the Officer class. The Court Martial was the punishment reserved for major indiscipline and usually it ended up as a trial by the Officer himself supported by his army friends.

Punishment could mean marching double time around the parade ground. Robbery or desertion called for something more severe like branding a man with a hot iron. You could be the victim of more sadistic punishment like being suspended by thumbs, wrists or arms for a full day. If you were unlucky, a spell in the Guard house with no windows and plunged in darkness all day long was your sentence.

As we can see a significant gulf existed between the ordinary soldier and his Officer. The caste system was built into everything and fraternization between the two was taboo. This isolated the Officer and even his dating opportunities among the girls were confined to his trips home on leave.

The competition in the upper ranks for promotion was even sharper. Jealousies, intrigue and "pulling strings" for promotion was rampant. Important connections were highly desirable but heroic feats on the battlefront helped enormously. Success in handling the Indians was another credit for promotion purposes.

An anecdote worth telling describes life in Jackson's army. It concerns a man called George Cook. Cook was so unusual he got himself promoted from Lieutenant to Brigadier General not for the orthodox career of an Officer but for his original tactics, his thought, and the innovation he put into his job. George could pack a mule, mend a saddle, throw a lariat or eat in the field with his fellow soldiers. He created the war of speedy pursuit in small numbers using men well trained for the task. He even employed Apache scouts to track Apaches. His small mobile units were very similar to modern commando warfare. In fact these units proved so successful they earned him many honours and promotions. Andrew Jackson's first promotion to Brigadier General may have been based on privilege but whether true or not he certainly proved himself in the field later and feared nobody not even his boss the President.

Let us look at Jackson's career. They say about the Irish that all their wars were merry and all their songs were sad. Jackson's swashbuckling style had a touch of both. To the Indians the sadness and to Jackson the glory.

The story of Florida is fascinating. Aaron Burr a leading politician on a visit to Jackson's house The Hermitage discussed his broad plan to expel the Spaniard from Florida suggesting the Secretary of War; Henry Dearborn was in agreement and would provide U.S. soldiers to complete the job. Hate of the Spaniards went back to the post-revolution years when Spain had pinched western trade from the United States by closing off New Orleans to American shipping. Jefferson's deal to purchase Louisiana from France had solved the problem but resentment still ran deep.

Jackson had already threatened to take New Orleans by force before that Louisiana deal. However Spain still had control of the waterways from the Gulf of Mexico into the southwest. For the United States this situation created a vulnerable point in its defence against any power that tried to make war on her. It was actually an open door into America. Another problem was the very lax control by the Spanish against raids by the Seminole Indians. The Seminoles freedom to operate across the border from Florida became a deep source of concern to the U.S.

Jackson ever the conspiring politician saw the situation as a heaven sent opportunity to enhance his political reputation with the help of a military campaign. Funds were agreed with Aaron Burr for the expedition. But rumours came to Jackson's ears that Burr was not in it for America but a slice of Florida over which he would preside. Andrew Jackson did not mind breaking laws to further his country's interest but "Would have no truck with traitors" as he put it. Rumours led to accusations and accusations led to a trial at which Burr was acquitted. The whole case was a thorn in Jackson's side for years into the future. The Government's soft peddling over Spain rankled with Jackson's impulsive personality. Cleaning up the problem became his obsession.

One day orders came through from Washington to defeat the Seminole Indians who were causing havoc in South Georgia and to use any means necessary. Jackson needed no further encouragement now he had the green light to lay the ghost within him at last. Unfortunately Jackson overstepped his authority by invading Florida and executing two British subjects Arbuthnot and Ambrister. One was hung from the yardarm of a sailing vessel and the other was shot by firing squad. The executions almost caused a war with Britain that was only averted by the diplomatic skills of Quincy Adams, the Secretary of State.
"Old Hickory" was fast building a reputation on the battlefield which would steer him all the way to the White House.

But Jackson, the Indian fighter was still in business. One of his most notorious perhaps shameful victories came against The Creek Indians. That battle took place on the bend of the Tallapoosa River called Horseshoe Bend. After allowing the Creek women and children cross to safety Jackson eliminated the fighting Indians by a pincer movement behind them, and then proceeded to a massacre that all but wiped out The Creek nation. What happened afterwards is best forgotten by history. It was shameful because Jackson received many plaudits from Washington for having ended the Indian problem in the southeast once and for all. But the treaty that followed in which Jackson was allowed a "first and final say" all but robbed The Creek Indians of twenty-three million acres of their land now ceded to the United States.

Jackson told The Creeks that the U.S. was entitled to every acre they owned but he would take only half. All previous solemn promises were broken. They pleaded for easier terms for their defeat but Jackson's contempt for them would not allow for mercy. They then offered Jackson three square miles himself as a gift which he accepted with the approval of The White Father in Washington. The President James Madison approved of it but Congress did not. Now Jackson was beyond shame. He did not know how much land he was taking.

Records show it was about twenty-two million acres. What a devastating humiliation for the Creeks! Initially there was a doubt about its ratification by Congress but after his victory in New Orleans any opposition just melted away and it was ratified on February 16, 1815. It was known as "The Article of Agreement and Capitalization". But do not be too unhappy for the Creek Indians because there is a happy ending to this terrible tale. In her book Trail of Tears Gloria Jahoda rejoiced in the news that once more the Creeks are dancing in the pinewoods. "They sing the old songs and attend classes in the language spoken by their ancestors." The year is now 2009, a year when the surviving fragments of their civilization are coming together again nearly two centuries after the Battle of Horseshoe Bend.

The victory or tragedy of Horseshoe Bend won Jackson promotion to Major General in the regular U.S. army. Once again he was ordered to New Orleans to ward off an imminent British attack. Jackson attacked New Orleans immediately finding the city practically defenceless. Jackson then declared Marshal Law for which action he was later reprimanded and fined only to have the fine cancelled. He dug in with a motley collection of 5,000 multiethnic troops consisting of Creoles, Frenchmen, pirates and a "sharp" shooting Tennessee and Kentucky Militia. The British forces numbered 8,700 most of whom were veterans of European warfare under their Commander–in–Chief General Sir Edward Pakenham himself a veteran of the Napoleonic wars. There were 2,000 British casualties to 71 American casualties of whom only thirteen were killed. As far as the powers in Washington were concerned Jackson could walk on water.

But Jackson was soon to find out that political battles were far dirtier than military ones and did not carry the same code of honour.

The 1824 election for the Presidency found Jackson in the field as a Democrat opposing the Secretary of State, John Quincy Adams. It was a battle only settled by Congress and sank to abysmal depths of defamities and lies by both sides.

One of the unfortunate victims was Jackson's wife Rachel, who came under fire from an attack on her character in which the old wounds were reopened about her double marriage fiasco because of a divorce mix up. It was one of the most irresponsible vicious and ruthless Presidential elections ever. One story underlines the level of gutter politics that was practiced judging by an extract from the public prints. Reading from one of the cuttings, Jackson's guard disintegrated in a totally uncharacteristic way. He broke down in tears. Rachel had just entered the room and asked what the matter was. Jackson pointed to the article and said, "Myself I can defend. You I can defend but now they have assaulted the memory of my mother." They had written "General Jackson's mother was a common prostitute brought to this country by British soldiers. She afterwards married a mulatto man with whom she had seven children of which number Jackson was one." A cruel and heartless lie given the way his mother had rescued her two sons from prison in their teens, rode forty miles through pouring rain back home, and sadly died nursing wounded American soldiers later. The story was a disgrace and unforgivable when told in pursuit of the highest office in the land – The Presidency.

As mentioned earlier the election was finally settled by Congress and Quincy Adams won the day becoming America's 6th President. The mental wounds inflicted on both Quincy and Jackson haunted the lives of both of them for years.

This brings the story of General "Old Hickory" Jackson to the pinnacle of the mountain he was climbing all his life ever since he was an orphan of fourteen. After losing his foothold near the summit in 1824 he finally scaled the peak and planted his flag on the holy ground of the Presidency itself in 1828. But Rachael was soon to discover she, along with her husband and his staff were not welcome in Washington. The snooty Washington residents known as "The Cave Dwellers" made sure life was difficult for these outsiders into their precious city.

But Jackson's joy in becoming President was extinguished by the death of Rachel his wife on December 22, three days before Christmas. Jackson always claimed she died of a broken heart.

Rachael Jackson abhorred these "Cave dwellers". But during her time it must be said the quality of the Congressman had little to recommend them. Being from the frontier their education and behaviour were rough and ready. Robert J. Hubbard, a New York Congressman told his wife in 1817, "They sit through debates with their hats on and only remove them to address the speaker." This behaviour caused the people of Washington to demand certain rules of good manners. They kept themselves aloof and apart from these immigrants into Washington's social life. Unfortunately Presidents' wives fell into the same category to be shunned.

Rachel Jackson, wife of President Jackson resigned herself to Washington life saying "I would rather be a doorkeeper in the house of my Lord than live in that Palace in Washington." Maybe it was her earthiness that rankled with the snooty "Cave dwellers" for she was of frontier stock, had leathery skin and preferred to ride on a horse instead of in a carriage. Rachel did not bother with cosmetics and her only social pursuit was sitting at home with her husband Andrew Jackson smoking a pipe. As one person observed she was fat, forty and did not fit in.

Just like his father John Adams, Quincy, the outgoing President did not take part in the inauguration ceremonies for Jackson who took the oath on the East Portico of the White House on Wednesday March 4, 1829. The oath was administered by Chief Justice John Marshall and the ceremony ended with the firing of cannons.

In a theatrical stage–managed scene Andrew Jackson made his regal journey down Pennsylvania Avenue on a white horse surrounded by veterans of the revolution. It was a warm spring day and out of respect for Jackson's wife who had died two months earlier no celebrations had been planned. But an evening reception was held in the White House and a crowd of twenty thousand people got in jamming the corridors, ruining the rugs, furniture and glasswork causing damage amounting to thousands of dollars.

Jackson the man of the people, the first commoner outside the aristocratic circle of his predecessors had arrived. Many of the gatecrashers were seeking jobs and favours from their hero. After his inauguration speech in which he pledged to pay off the national debt, a promise he later kept, the crowd became unruly and Jackson had to flee to the safety of the nearby Gatsby's Hotel. A supply of beer had to be placed on the White House lawn to lure the crowd outside. Some people sneered "The reign of King Mob is triumphant." Others said, "It is a proud day for the people. General Jackson is one of our own."

If anyone thought Andrew Jackson was going to change now that he was President they were going to be disappointed.

All his life, unorthodoxy and Andrew Jackson were comfortable bedfellows, and true to form he proved this when he set up his first Cabinet. It was called the "Kitchen Cabinet" because its personnel consisted of people he could trust or had known all his life. There were men from all walks of life not necessarily politicians. Tennesseans from his own county, newspapermen; the editors of The Patriot and The Washington Globe and of course Van Buren, his protégé for the next Presidency and personal friend. It was an informal "Think Tank" of various shades of opinion. But the system seemed to work for Andrew Jackson.

Jackson liked to believe he represented the people against aristocracy and privilege and no group was entitled to special political or economic advantage. "Jacksonian Democracy" was on the launching pad. In this it was the Democratic Party that attracted a broader base of votes from mechanics, labourers, farmers, intellectuals, businessmen and professionals. All these groups looked to Jackson for leadership and protection against the privileged advantages of the few. An honest referee so to speak. The Jacksonian age was a new dynamic in society which fostered new awareness of fair play for prisoner's rights, insane asylums, women's rights, public education and care of the poor. "A romantic age of hope and promise" as quoted in Robert V. Remini's book Andrew Jackson.
But there was a downside too. A dark sad, illogical, selfish almost cruel story that unfolded from the depths of Old Hickory's military past. During it, Andrew Jackson was known by many nick names. "Old Hickory", "Sharp Knife". The Choctaws called him "The devil". From his experience down all the years fighting, hounding and hunting the Native American he became a man obsessed by one unrelenting ambition, the destruction of the Indian nation. It was a dream he put into law during his Presidency. The law was called The Indian Removal Act.

In it any Indian who remained on his ancestral lands east of Mississippi would be considered a criminal. America's frontiers would always be just that - frontiers, while the Indian confronted, embarrassed, and annoyed the settlers. To this end fifty tribes of all cultures were uprooted lock, stock and barrel rounded up and placed in stockades until a sufficient number was ready for the great trek westwards. These were herded to the far reaches of America, west of the Mississippi.

It was a journey to unknown alien lands, hundreds of miles away from their "grassroots". Hundreds died on the long journey West suffering from disease and starvation. On their arrival at their destination they were planted on lands that for them were a total disaster. This exodus was known as "The trail of Tears". This banishment to distant lands was an official Government decision under the policy of "Manifest Destiny" and "The Louisiana Purchase" carried out by Andrew Jackson. I think I have already explained "The Doctrine of Manifest Destiny". It was an excuse for America to march into the West in thousands. It implied that America had a God given right or destiny to conquer the West.

Strangely for such a rollicking, party-going, death-defying extrovert Jackson's Presidency was a quiet and sober affair and his entertaining was on a very modest scale. Food and drink were left on side tables for receptions that usually started at 11 p.m. He met his guests shaking hands with the man and bowing to the ladies. Jackson himself ate little and liked to show off the grounds and gardens to his visitors.

He worked hard at the Presidency sometimes burning the midnight oil on his duties. Later his war wounds and weak lungs and old age left him bedridden and taking most of his meals in bed.

But even in his Presidency Andrew Jackson led a charmed life and was the subject of an unsuccessful assassination attempt by a mentally deranged house painter named Richard Lawrence. On January 30, 1835 Lawrence fired two pistol shots at Jackson from a range of six feet but misfired.

Lawrence was then tried and sentenced to jail and a mental hospital for life. As I have already mentioned he was luckier than Thomas Hickey who was hung on the scaffold before twenty thousand people for an attempt on the life of George Washington.

It seems Andrew Jackson had such a disdain for his own safety the Gods seemed to have smiled on him all his life. He is reputed to have survived brawls and duels numbering up to one hundred. One man died at his hands in a duel which he fought defending the integrity of his wife Rachel. Charles Dickinson reputed to be one of the best pistol shots in the United States confronted him twenty-four feet apart. At the signal Dickinson fired first, breaking some of Jackson's ribs. Jackson never flinched, fired back, and Dickinson fell dead.

As his frail and ailing bones were paying the price of his past wild life the pace of living became much more genteel for Jackson as his Presidency came to a close. In the evenings he liked to sit in the large parlour of the White House smoking his reed pipe while nearby the ladies of the White House would pass the time sewing. Children played in another corner.

His style in the Presidency was based on the formula of aggressiveness, patience, attention to detail, threat of force when his patience ran out and compromise. This approach earned him resounding victories world wide in State affairs.

Jackson nominated Van Buren, for his loyalty and service, as the next President and so it came to pass.

As we said at the start of this piece he was a man who generated intense and contradictory emotions and the only problem you will have with Jackson is whether to like him or hate him. But no one can deny the impact he made on the history of the Presidency.

His final address to the nation expressed his personal philosophy – "But you must remember my fellow citizens that eternal vigilance by the people is the price of liberty and you must pay the price if you must secure the blessings."

He also referred to "The priceless value of the Union." "My own race is nearly run. I thank God that my life has been spent on a land of liberty and that he has given me a heart to love my country with the affection of a son. I bid you a last and affectionate farewell."

The Whig press was not so charitable. One quote goes "Happily it is the last humbug which the mischievous popularity of this illiterate violent vain and iron-willed soldier can impose upon a confiding and credulous people." Most Americans disagreed with these words for twenty thousand people turned up for the inauguration of his protégé the new President Martin Van Buren. But as Senator Benton wrote afterwards "There was no room for mistake as to whom this mute and impressive homage was rendered. For once the rising was eclipsed by the setting sun."

After the inauguration ceremonies for the 8th President was over Jackson started for home and retirement in The Hermitage. The journey took three weeks. Today he would have been home in one hour. Cheering crowds met him wherever he stopped. It filled him with a grateful emotion. He was now seventy and a very infirm old man, constantly in pain. He arrived home with only $90 in his pocket. His plantation had been mismanaged by his son in his absence and he was lied to as to the extent of his solvency. Does this story sound familiar my dear reader?

In his retirement he was constantly under pressure from his son's debts despite setting him up in business for a new start "hoping he had profited by his mistake". He had not. Jackson suffered acutely from head pains and he could not even lie down in bed. Visiting Rachel's grave was one of his few comforts. Hearing Texas had been finally accepted as a State in the Union, Jackson smiled – "All is safe at last," he murmured. Job seekers continued to pester him despite his illness. He could not sleep and drugs were useless against his pain. He was now seventy-eight. There were tears from his family as he lay dying but ever the old warrior; he lifted his head off the pillow to remonstrate with them. "Oh do not cry, be good children and we will all meet in heaven," he whispered.

Just before 6 p.m. on the evening of June 8, 1845 Andrew Jackson closed his eyes and was gone forever at the age of seventy-eight.

Andrew Jackson was buried beside Rachel on the lawn in front of his house The Hermitage in the tomb "Old Hickory" Jackson had himself prepared for the occasion a long, long time ago.

8th President   Martin Van Buren

"Little Magician"
Born 1782
Died 1862
80 Years of age

1 Term
1837 – 1841
Age 55

Party: Democratic Republican
Profession: Lawyer
County: New York
Ancestry: Dutch
Estate: Value unknown
Hobbies: Riding

Physical Description: Height; 5 foot 6 inches; erect, slender; red and graying hair, bald spot, deep wrinkles, sporting sideburns and wore high fashioned clothes

Extracts from his inaugural address on Monday March 4, 1837

"I am approaching then, in the presence of my assembled countrymen, to make the solemn promise that yet remains and to pledge myself that I will faithfully execute the office I am about to fill. I bring with me a settled purpose to maintain the institutions of my country which I trust will atone for the errors I commit..................I must go into the Presidential chair the inflexible and uncompromising opponent of every attempt on the part of Congress to abolish slavery in the District of Colombia against the wishes of the slaveholding States and also with a determination equally decided to resist the slightest interference with it in States where it exists."

MARTIN VAN BUREN

You have just read about Andrew Jackson, the colourful 7th President. As they say in show business, after a great act – How do you follow that?

Insignificant as he seems nowadays Martin Van Buren, 8th President of the United States was far from insignificant. In fact he was one of the leading founders of the modern Democratic Party.

Van Buren was yet another of the early Presidents who was both liked and disliked intensely. Charming, genial and wise was one description. "A man of ability, courage, honesty and strict personal integrity," said Thurlow Weed, the Whig and yet one of Martin's bitterest political enemies.

But for all the praise there were as many opinions which were not complimentary. Many disliked and distrusted him considering his talent to be mediocre and his career conspicuous by the political trickery he indulged in whilst chasing the spoils of office. An unprincipled manipulator, a magician and a Talleyrand. Harsh words indeed from his critics but in a way they gave him no credit for real achievements. Few Americans recall his name yet American politics is understood today by many to be 9/10ths composed of cant, force, corruption and sham and for this revelation Van Buren can take credit. Yet taking credit for cynicism like this is questionable.

Perhaps he was too dull and lifeless a subject for historians to tackle simply because he was never debunked yet never exalted. As President he behaved with nobility but failed to live down his record and methods in getting there.

But what were these methods; after all he was a Democrat to his fingertips. Martin Van Buren was never a gambler at the races or at cards. Elections were the only flutter he ever had but these gambles were riskless because of his sleight of hand in ensuring their outcome. And herein lies the reason for his unpopularity. The power to ensure victories in elections was due to Van Buren's own creation – the first Party political machine ever invented. It was called The Albany Regency.

The revised Constitution at the time placed a great deal of patronage in the hands of The Bucktails. These were followers of Van Buren who were so named because of the Bucktails they wore in their hats when they attended political meetings. Martin developed great skills in manipulation and controlling caucus meetings where Party policy was decided. The Albany Regency spread out to touch all corners of political life in New York at that time. Of course being chief of the Regency he had power to appoint people into plum political positions. He was the Godfather or spin doctor who it is said won the election for his predecessor "Old Hickory" Jackson. The members of The Regency were bursting at the seams with the very best political talent which Van Buren is said to have exploited to the full.

To crown it all Van Buren learned early the advantages of a compliant press and managed to gain ownership of The Albany Argus, a newspaper that kept him in the forefront of public popularity. He now had the support of an obedient press. You could say he was a man light years ahead of his time.

But Van Buren's early poverty gave him a heartfelt sympathy for the suffering masses. He was responsible for getting rid of debtors' prisons and often defended the vulnerable common folk against bankers and "Robber Barons". Sadly the good he did perished with his bones because of his lifelong reputation of acting only out of political expediency.

But let us go back to where the story of the Van Burens really started back in the early 1600s when his Dutch ancestors came to America as settlers in the New World. The place they chose to live was a little village on the outskirts of New York called Kinderhook. It was here Martin was born on December 5, 1782. Two sisters preceded him, Derike and Jannetje, two brothers Lawrence and Abraham were born later. His father had married Maria Van Alen who took three more children into the marriage from her previous marriage before she was widowed. It was certainly a very crowded household to live in.

Food was prepared in a small cookhouse beside the main house. They owned six slaves, two of whom helped in the kitchen. Funds were scarce although Martin's father owned a small farm and a modest tavern in which Martin helped out. The customers were laced with well-known politicians, a factor which attracted him into politics as he listened constantly to gossip and stories on current affairs while he worked. Martin's father also subsidized the household budget with part-time work as the town clerk.

It seems his father was an easy going man and much loved by the family. But Martin's mother was the driving force behind the family and she had other ambitions for them. A revealing insight into her thoughts can be seen in her quote "A petty farmer's income and a declining tavern have no future and little to recommend them."

Martin was a handsome child delicate in appearance with reddish brown hair worn long, as was the custom at that time. He had light blue deep set eyes, a merry disposition and was quite popular with his friends.

His school was a run down one room wooden cabin. He always regretted not having had "A good systematic education," as he put it, "to sustain me in my conflicts with able and better educated men." But there was no lack of effort on his part in pursuit of his goals from the limited opportunities open to him. Soon he was working in the law office of a leading lawyer Francis Sylvester helping in Sylvester's store as well as clerking and sweeping floors. In return for his services Martin was tutored in the law profession, showing flare and talent for his calling at a very early stage.

One anecdote worth telling comes from early historians and relates to Martin in court during a minor trial. Apparently the Judge turned suddenly to Martin asking him to sum up. Being small he was placed on a bench and told by the Judge "There matt beat your master." I do not know how the story ends but it proves he had come to the notice of his legal peers.

He eventually moved to New York in 1803 at twenty-one years of age and was admitted to the State Bar as an Attorney. He had to practice for a further four years to qualify for work in the Supreme Court. Martin then returned home to Kinderhook and went into law practice with his half-brother James Van Alen.

But not even Martin Van Buren could escape the arrows of cupid and romance caught up with him in the person of Hannah Hoes, a distant cousin. Martin was thirty-two and Hannah was twenty-four when they married in Catskill, twelve miles outside Kinderhook to avoid the expenses of a village wedding. In those days the whole village would have expected to be invited. The happy couple then moved to Hudson, a new city with easy access to the countryside and of course the promise of a lucrative mercantile market from the blossoming trade on the banks of the Hudson River. The city of Hudson flourished and so did Van Buren's new business.

Soon they had four children all boys Abraham, John, Martin and Smith. The law practice boomed but like John Adams the second President, when he was in practice extensive travelling was an integral part of the job. He too was becoming a legal nomad moving from one court to another.

Van Buren was a methodical rather than a brilliant lawyer. He compensated for this by a comprehensive study of the law. Added to this he had a charming personality, a ready wit and an analytical mind. By this time he was bald, rotund and sported sideburns and high fashion clothes and worked constantly on the art of compromise. The grooming of the devious manipulator, a form of self defence – being all things to all men was now complete. There was nothing vicious or harmful about Martin, just a man with an exaggerated caution against mistakes. From his law training he developed into a clinical organizer and an astute strategist in everything he did.

But there were low points in Van Buren's life too. His wife Hannah had a difficult childbirth on their fifth child and doctors suspected she had tuberculosis. The prognosis was not promising. Life was black for him just then having a new child and a sick wife to contend with. Of his other children Abraham was easy to handle, quiet and reserved like his mother. John however was a handful. He was his father's favourite, precocious and full of laughter and mischief.

But life even for the famous and successful is not insulated from personal grief. Van Buren was no exception and his life fell apart two years later when Hannah lost her battle with tuberculosis and passed away on February 5, 1819. Seventeen further years would pass before Van Buren achieved his ultimate goal - The Presidency.

When he was nominated he was immediately the subject of vicious attacks on his character, his appearance, his political style, his alleged lack of scruples and even his parentage. For the first time the word "magician" was used. Some implied it meant the less complementary - intrigue. But one of his colleagues defended him as follows – "If a quick penetrating mind and a cool judgement, quiet and practical wisdom and honourable success be indices of a magician then the name has been properly bestowed."

The election was a close run affair despite being to his enemies a subject of scorn and hate. Comments in the taverns were much courser than the one his supporters liked "The red fox of Kinderhook." However he won through by 170 votes to become the 8th President of the United States, an outcome fully endorsed by the outgoing President "Old Hickory Jackson". Later celebrations were low key for the economy was showing signs of trouble. But let us leave that for later.

A description of his inauguration ceremony is worth hearing and the significance of his inauguration speech will strike you as almost being out of touch with the storm clouds on the horizon for America in the years to come.

March 4, 1837 was a beautiful day. Van Buren spent the night in the White House with "Old Hickory". The coachmen and footmen and the team of matched grey horses were ready. The city was thronged and excited for the spectacle ahead. Delegations of Cherokee and Potawatomi chiefs were there complete with native costumes, feathers, beads and paint. The carriage moved forward preceded by a detachment of mounted Dragoons clip clopping down a crowded Pennsylvania Avenue to the Capitol. Both men were bareheaded. Jackson with his shock of grey hair; Van Buren balding and a half head shorter. The tall Jackson could be seen mounting the steps but Van Buren was lost from view. They took their place in the front row of the Chamber followed by the Cabinet, the Supreme Court, the Army and Navy Officers and the Diplomatic Corps in their colourful uniforms of gold lace. Twenty thousand people heard Van Buren's distinct voice make his inauguration speech. He would "Respond to the new dynamics of a changing society," he said in his half hour speech.

And despite the years that lay ahead to Lincoln and the Civil War, Martin Van Buren seemed to reflect the blindness of a nation to future events, so much feared by Quincy Adams. He said, "I am an inflexible and uncompromising opponent of every attempt on the part of Congress to abolish slavery in the district of Colombia against the wishes of the slave-owning States and also with a determination equally decided to resist the slighter interference with it in the States where it exists. If Congress should pass such a Bill I will veto it on grounds that they were political and sectional rather than Constitutional." He condemned abolitionists but did not name them. The oath was administered and after some sharp short orders from the Captain of the Dragoons, the carriage transporting Van Buren wheeled and turned south towards the White House through the crowded streets full of well-wishers. As usual the reception festivities were filled to capacity, and yes I am afraid the lifestyle of Martin Van Buren had now changed forever – if only he knew it.

The major cause of his discomfort was probably known to him beforehand. He had taken over the reins of State at the worst possible moment of time. Depression was one of his legacies inherited from his predecessor President Jackson. New York banks in 1837 began refusing to convert paper money into gold and silver and panic set in. However the banks refused to co-operate with Van Buren and he was forced to appeal to Congress to deal with the crisis. But he had no friends there either. Congress simply refused to help and it seemed all his political expertise which led him to the White House had deserted him.

In desperation Van Buren ordered expenditure cuts of 20% and cancelled projects like canals and roads that could have improved the employment situation. Even Van Buren's sons were suffering. They had agreed to deal with the correspondence that came into the White House but they never anticipated the volume that flooded in. Documents had to be copied by hand in their hundreds in those days and Martin and Abraham complained bitterly about their new workload.

Meanwhile unemployment hit the cities and villages and a depression loomed. Life was not quite the same on the bridge of State as it had been on the decks below. This was a fact of life that stripped the gilt and glamour from Martin Van Buren's new found crown. Yes, reality can be a hard taskmaster.

There is an old saying "Those whom the Gods wish to destroy they first make mad." Martin Van Buren was no exception. When you hear what happens next you may well scratch your head with incredulity and say, "What in heavens name was he thinking about?" In the middle of what can only be described as a national emergency Martin decided to redecorate the White House. In ordinary times this would have gone unnoticed but doing it just then was a monumental public relations blunder for a man so calculating and astute. Where were the crafty political advisors he mixed with in the old days of The Albany Regency?

Now armies of paper hangers, painters, interior decorators and upholsterers were seen swarming all over the White House. His formal levies continued to bring entertainment unabated. Guards were posted to prevent gatecrashers until the inevitable happened. The public press moved in to give him a torrid time for his thoughtlessness and insensitivity at a time when the country was in such difficulties.

He seemed to have withdrawn into a world of unreality, totally disconnected with events outside the White House. Now he was derided by the nick name Martin Van Ruin. But things got worse. The pro-Southern policies foisted on him by his sponsor Andrew Jackson were bearing bitter fruits. Sadly he was finally deserted by his shallow pre-Presidency friends in his darkest hour.

But Martin Van Buren must have used up all his luck on the way to the White House for from now on fate would not be very kind to him.

The Depression of 1837 was not the only problem Martin Van Buren had inherited from Jackson. He also took on board an Indian chief called Osceola and a frightening Indian or Native American disaster, the relocation of thousands of Indian families east of the Mississippi. Osceola led the Seminole Indians who refused to emigrate westwards. The tribe was often described insultingly as a band of fugitive slaves.

Besides the removal policy he also had to contend with a corrupt Indian affairs Commissioner called Carey Harris who speculated in Indian lands. Disgracefully the removal of all Native Americans east of the Mississippi was not based on sentiments or humanity. Van Buren sacked Harris and installed a new Indian agent Thomas H. Crawford and a career soldier named General Scott, old "Fuss and Feathers" himself.

In the meantime Osceola became an embarrassment winning battle after battle, fighting a more sophisticated war combining his knowledge of the land with Guerrilla tactics against old fashioned European military techniques. He became a symbol of liberty, bravery and ability which drew the admiration of the very officers he fought against year after year.

Meanwhile the removal westward of so many Native Americans was an unpleasant task that had to be carried out but with understanding and efficiency.

Scott was an arch-disciplinarian and his task was horrendous. His duty was to move over 150,000 people away from their homes and native environment. They were rounded up and placed in stockades until sufficient clothing, wagons and supplies were available. Scott's soldiers unfortunately were undesirables, the dregs of society who carried out unspeakable atrocities on defenceless Indian farmers. Hundreds of Indians died on the journey and when they finally arrived at their destination they were met with a wilderness, no tools, no forage and nothing to erect shelters before they could prepare the virgin forest for a crop. In fairness to Van Buren he was really carrying out a policy that went back to Jefferson's Administration and over the Presidential lifetimes of four Presidents.

And so we return to Osceola, our rebel Indian chief. One day he was captured after his flag of truce had been violated.
He died in prison in 1838. The whole story of his capture was exploited by the Whig press and Van Buren was presented as a heartless cynic bringing dishonour on a nation. The cost of the removal was a colossal $50 million which in the heart of a Depression was a major talking point. Nothing was going right for "the magician". To be fair to him the people who criticised him for the removal as being a "heartless policy", were the very ones who voted for it in Congress some time before.

Martin Van Buren's final few days is taken from John Niven's wonderful book The Romantic Age of American Politics. His final years in office are best left to the political scientist who can make a more enlightened contribution about them than your writer.

Retirement day was fast approaching when Van Buren dropped a hint to a friend that he expected to be in New York on March 23. The news somehow found its way into the public domain. Surprise, surprise.

One admirer of Van Buren's carefully orchestrated farewell said "He played the last scene, always a very difficult one, with the greatest skill; he has been at fault in nothing."

When he landed on the New Jersey side of the Hudson River, a biting nor'easter blew in a heavy storm and a torrent of rain. "This should put a damper on any demonstrations," he thought. To his astonishment even with the rain pelting down, vast crowds turned out to greet him. A ride in a closed carriage was suggested by the rain-sodden reception committee. However Van Buren was having none of this while his fellow citizens were wet to the skin.

Bareheaded he waved to the crowd while escorted by mounted militia in full regalia flanked by hundreds of firemen. The carriage was hemmed in by the crowds as the horses jogged through the teeming slums of New York into the Bowery to Tammany Hall a five storey building beside City Hall. Short speeches were made here before making for Butler's House in Green Street. It was evening time when he sat down to a late dinner.
After dinner he attended the Bowery Theatre where he was cheered and clapped from the pit to the gallery. All this euphoria for a "lame duck President" two years after a Depression. Extraordinary!

The next five weeks were hectic for him, attending operas, plays and the theatres of New York including visits to furniture shops, china and glassware specialists and of course visiting old political friends.

On his return he travelled by boat up the Hudson River standing on deck in the rain taking it all in. The villages and towns, the factories and the farmlands along both banks of the river sailed past. A large crowd of Kinderhook residents waited to greet him at the pier. A very respectable procession of four carriages, buggies and wagons followed the farm folk some on foot and some on horseback. The Kinderhook bells were pealing from three churches.

At Stranahan's hotel in the glare of torch lights Van Buren responded in a brief speech to the welcome he had received. Then he settled down to life in his newly decorated mansion bought a year earlier and filled with expensive French wallpaper, Brussels carpets and a library full of his favourite political books, novels, poetry and histories. In the entrance hall he hung a portrait of Andrew Jackson and in the dining room one of Jefferson himself.

Van Buren had purchased the house for his retirement in Kinderhook because he had never had a permanent home during his career, though he owned a few farmhouses in the vicinity. He added 150 acres to the 50 acres that went with it. That summer was the happiest of Martin Van Buren's life. There was John's marriage to look forward to and lots of social activity among family and friends. There were picnics and fishing expeditions to the small lakes on his estate. There was music, singing and laughter, fine wines and sweet liquers at dinners he held. The only cloud on his horizon was John's financial debts incurred by luckless or injudicious speculation. Yet another President's son with no flair for business.

Bizarre though it seems the son's of the Presidents, only seemed to bring heartache to the retired President. I refer here to Quincy's three sons, Madison's stepson, Old Hickory's son and now Van Buren's. But let's not spoil the party.

Now Van Buren would find things different. No more the worries of carrying out the social functions of the White House dinners without a hostess. His first year in the White House had not been a happy one without his wife. His unhappiness was not missed by one young lady who observed – "He goes out little and then seems to take little pleasure in society. His only distraction was a quiet drink of madeira or sherry with his son's Abraham and Martin in a private drawing room."

One ray of sunshine was the marriage of his son Abraham to Angelica Singleton, the younger daughter of a rich South Carolina planter related to many of the leading families of the day like the Cabells, the Prestons, and the Stevensons. Martin Van Buren had come a long way from his humble roots to be accepted by such exalted stock. We wonder what his mother would have made of it all. Angelica was a ray of sunshine in the White House and her impact as substitute First Lady was immediately noticed by the way House parties livened up. A fact that was not surprising being a distant relative of Dolly Madison.

Angelica got rave reviews for her New Year's Eve reception of 1839 from The Boston Post. "A lady of rare accomplishments, perfectly easy and graceful in her manners, vivacious in her conversation......." A little bit overboard I thought, almost bordering on the threshold of canonization. I guess life in the Van Buren household was not as dull as some historians had painted it after all.

Rumour has it that Van Buren retired a very rich man with a fortune of $200,000 in the bank from investments in real estate, his earnings as a lawyer, plus the income of $10,000 per year from his newspaper The Albany Argus while he owned it.

In 1858 his health began to fail and three accidents, one off his horse, and another which inflicted a broken arm, did not help. He just laughed them off. "Does not this speak well of my skull," he joked. But gout and heavy colds sapped his vitality. Bouts of influenza were long lasting leaving him weak. He had never been sick in his life and found it hard to come to terms with his illness.

In 1861 Civil War raged and Van Buren gave Lincoln all his support for the maintenance of the Union. Old and frail as he was Van Buren called for "The democracy of the Empire State to support the Federal Government" in an impassioned plea to save "The Union".

Had his sentiments come many years too late one wonders when we read again his inauguration speech on slavery which he embraced passionately apparently oblivious of the tragic consequences of such views twenty years later? Sadly his bouts of illness increased in frequency and intensity.

But when midnight came on the night of July 24, 1862 the waiting was over for his three middle-aged sons pacing restlessly around the house. The 8th President of the United States suffering acutely from asthma passed away two hours later at 2 a.m. that morning.

He was laid in a rosewood casket and carried downstairs. Five days later on July 29, 1862 eighty-one carriages trailed the hearse into town. The shops were closed in Kinderhook and over the pulpit in the church hung the American flag. The choir sang "God our help in ages past" and the local firemen carried the coffin to the nearby cemetery. Despite the pageantry it was really the funeral of an eighty year old man forgotten by everybody for over a decade. Forgotten for ten years. Yes, a tragedy for a man who had held a breathtaking spread of influential political positions both national and international. In his time he had been President, Vice President, Secretary of State, Senator, Ambassador to England, Governor of New York, Grand Sachem of Tammany Hall, Boss of the infamous Albany Regency and finally enemy and advisor to fifteen Presidents from John Adams to Abraham Lincoln.

Since Martin Van Buren died just after the Civil War started perhaps we should leave the last words to the illustrious Abraham Lincoln, the 16th President.

"Grief of his patriotic friends," wrote Lincoln, "will measurably be assuaged by the consciousness that while suffering with disease and seeing his end approaching, his prayers were for the restoration of the authority of the Government of which he had been head, and for peace and goodwill among his fellow citizens."

"The little magician" would have appreciated that tribute since he himself had always offered due respect for the departed – with one eye on the next election. But once again the Presidency would cause controversy, for Van Buren's successor was destined to spend only one month as President in the White House. Read on.

9th President   William H Harrison

"Old Tip"
Born 1773
Died 1841
68 Years of age
1 Term
1841(1 month)
Age 68

Party: Whigs
Profession: Soldier
County: Ohio
Ancestry: English
Estate: In Debt
Hobbies: Hunting

Physical Description: Height; 5 foot 8 inches; long, thin face, irregular features.

Extracts from his inaugural address Washington DC March 4, 1841

"Far different is the power of our sovereignty. It can interfere with no one's faith, prescribe forms of worship for no one's observance, inflict no punishment but after well ascertained guilt the result of investigations under rules prescribed by the Constitution itself...... You will bear with you to your homes the remembrance of the pledge this day given to discharge all the high duties of my exalted station according to the best of my ability and I shall enter upon their performance with entire confidence in the support of a just and generous people."

WILLIAM H. HARRISON

The scene now moves from the village of Kinderhook to the hustle and bustle of a new Presidency.

In early January 1841, the city of Washington was gradually filling up with expectant office seekers. William Henry Harrison, the 9th President of the United States and grandfather to the 23rd President, Benjamin Harrison in 1889 arrived in town by train on February 9, 1841 and took up residence in the nearby Gadsby's Hotel. The slushy streets, oyster houses and hotels were jammed with visitors some to witness the inauguration but many were looking for any crumb of patronage they could get. Such were the times they lived in.

Harrison at sixty-eight looked tired and harassed by these opportunists. He called on Van Buren, the outgoing President for a quiet chat and Van Buren, being the generous person he was, courteously met him with the full Cabinet. He entertained Harrison to dinner and offered to vacate the White House earlier than February 20, to give Harrison a little peace and quiet.

Harrison afterwards amazed Washington by going out shopping for his own groceries on foot. These were the times when there was still a gap in the railway line connecting Washington and New York. In the opinion of his friends, Harrison was considerate, genial and over generous.

Previous Presidents from Washington to Van Buren lived on the crest of a glorious wave of U.S. history. They lived and endured, fought and survived the most challenging battles in America's march into the future.

Some lived for years after their time on the pinnacle of political power. All of them shared most of their lives with the greats.

Alas, for William Henry Harrison the Gods of fate had other plans. To the grief and disbelief of millions the 9th President was destined never to know or experience more than one month in the White House.

Yes, William Harrison's stay in the White House was cut tragically short, having had no more than a month in office, which did not leave his daughter-in-law Jane much time to establish her skills as First Lady. Anne his wife had been looking forward to Harrison's retirement so when he became the next President she was appalled at the prospect of uprooting her family life to live in the White House. How times have changed. She preferred to await milder weather to travel to the White House. Unfortunately he died before she got there. So it was William's daughter-in-law Jane who was remembered as First Lady in the White House.

Some people say he invited disaster by a foolhardy approach to his inauguration. Perhaps he was already incubating pneumonia but standing for thirteen hours without a hat or overcoat despite the bitter cold and stormy weather on that Thursday March 4, 1841 was asking for trouble for a man of sixty-eight years. He picked up a severe chill that deteriorated into pneumonia which ended the shortest Presidency of all forty-four.

Perhaps being a fighting General on the frontiers of the American West for almost fifty years lulled him into thinking he was indestructible, who knows!

I am afraid Harrison was not a very impressive holder of the office although that assessment may be unfair to a man who spent such a short spell in the White House. It is said Harrison was the first in a long line of Presidents from Ohio whose weakness in the job was only exceeded by their ambition to capture it.

It seems a bit cruel to dwell on the failures he suffered before the Presidency but I must be true to the storyline. One of them was his job as diplomatic representative to Columbia, a perk of patronage he received from President John Quincy Adams who is quoted as saying "Harrison's thirst for lucrative office is absolutely rabid."

Not for the first time in his career was he utterly unperturbed about his route to success. He was found to be totally unsuited for the job and had to be hastily withdrawn by President Andrew Jackson. It is said being withdrawn saved him from expulsion from Columbia after he fell foul of Simon Boliver, the Columbian President.
But let us get back to his early days. Like many other Presidents it seems destiny was his best friend for he actually set out in life as a medical student in the University of Pennsylvania in Philadelphia.

Harrison had a uniquely privileged family tree for besides his future grandson becoming the 23rd President, his father Benjamin was one of the signatories of the Declaration of Independence. He was born and reared on his father's plantation Berkley in Virginia and enjoyed the usual lifestyle of the planter class by studying under private tutors and going on to the prestigious college called Hampden-Sydney for three years. As mentioned he studied to be a doctor to fulfil his father's wishes but when his father died he switched to a military career instead.

It seems Harrison's planter pedigree gave him access to influential friends to whom he did not hesitate to turn for help in his career at every opportunity.
His first job in the army came about with the influence of a friend of the family Senator Richard Henry Lee of Virginia resulting in Harrison receiving an ensign's commission in the First U.S. Infantry.

However, he did have military talent as a soldier which the army was quick to recognise when he was promoted to Lieutant and Aide-de-Camp to the notorious General "Mad" Anthony Wayne. He moved on to the Northwest Territory where he made quite a name for himself. His achievements on the battlefield here was later to serve him well in his quest for the White House. He helped to defeat a contingent of Native Americans in the Battle of Fallen Timbers near Toledo as it is known today. Harrison was cited for bravery in the battle and promoted to Captain. Later he was appointed Commander of Fort Worth in Ohio.

His army life was suspended temporarily around this time to add another perk to his career by marrying Miss Ann Symmes, the daughter of a Judge John Cloves Symmes, who by coincidence happened to be a wealthy land speculator. You can see by now that Harrison always moved in the right circles. The marriage produced ten children one of whom became the father of Benjamin Harrison, the 23rd President.

Harrison then ended the first phase of his army career in 1798. Conveniently once again political influence helped him land the plum job as Secretary of the Northwest Territory. The friend in question was Robert Goodloe Harper, a Congressman from South Carolina.

Here we must give credit to Harrison because he was eminently suited for the job after his army career fighting the Indians in Ohio. Lady luck had smiled on Harrison for this was a tremendous opportunity for him to develop his career and he soon became immersed in the day to day records dealing with land transactions which he presented to Congress periodically. Soon he became one of the most powerful figures in the westward expansion of the United States. By treaty and military conquest, millions of acres of land were transferred from the Native Americans to the settlers who came West seeking a new life. Politically the job rewarded him by increasing his popularity and his share of votes from the frontier voters who were grateful to him for pushing through legislation legalizing land deals. Soon he was also rewarded with the Governship of a new block of States to be called The Indiana Territory embracing five present States- Indiana, Illinois, Wisconsin, and parts of Michigan and Minnesota.

Harrison was well known to Jefferson who authorized him to make treaties and to acquire the lands of the Native Americans. Jefferson further instructed him to promote friendly relations with them. However this dual role was a poison chalice and proved an impossible mission. It was bound to end in not only failure but bloodshed.

Trouble came to a head when the famous Shawnee Chief Tecumseh and his brother Tenskwatawa known as "The Prophet" rebelled against the slow painful and inevitable erosion of their sacred lands into the greedy hands of the settlers while the whole process was legalised and encouraged by Washington. The two brothers established a village near the confluence of Tippecanoe Creek and the Wabush River. Harrison received instructions to break up the settlement, so at the head of 1,000 men he marched to a spot outside the village and requested a parley. History tells us the 1,000 soldiers were taken by surprise in a night attack.

History also tells us that Harrison retaliated viciously by sacking the entire village. The whole tribe was decimated and everything was burned to the ground. Harrison's casualties were 180 men killed or injured.

It was not a very glorious victory but Harrison became famous for it as the victor of "The Battle of Tippecanoe".
Perhaps the so called battle should in all decency be airbrushed from the history books today.

A sad anecdote to this battle happened later. Harrison once again through the patronage of Henry Clay, a Congressman from Kentucky received a new commission into the army in 1812. In a famous battle fought on the Thames River in Canada, his old foe, the distinguished Indian warrior Tecumseh was sadly killed.

Two years later Harrison again resigned his commission, left the army for the last time and returned to civilian life at his home in North Bend a town founded by his father in law. Here he lived in the lavish style of a Virginian planter. He kept servants and indulged himself in expensive and foolish hospitality which he could ill afford. But perhaps here we should pause awhile with our story. Before continuing with Harrison's career I feel we must ask these questions; what happened to the Red Indians or Native Americans during Harrison's jurisdiction over the Indiana Territory? What was life like on these Western frontiers? How did the settlers arrive in Indian Country? What were the stories connected with the families who went West?

The America of Harrison's times as Secretary of the Northwest Territory must now be described to give the reader a clearer wider picture of life in Harrison's Presidency as the Louisiana Purchase kicked in and changed the face of America forever.
The answer to these questions should enlighten us and help us understand the problems

confronting twenty-four Presidents over a period of 125 years since the Revolution of 1776. The anecdotes are many. The hopes, the heartache, the dreams, the victories and failures played out over billions of square miles from the East Coast to the Pacific were legendary. The job of each President going back to George Washington was to build a country and create the laws to satisfy the moving masses westward while also finding a just solution that would appease the millions of Indians or Native Americans fighting to hold on to their disappearing culture built over hundreds of years. I am afraid it was an impossible mission. There was just no compromise between the two. Tragically every President had to live with that depressing reality.

Expansion westward moved relentlessly from the East during these Presidencies. A constant stream of humanity came from as far away as Ireland, England, Poland, Germany and Eastern Europe. This immigrant wave was created by the expectations of a new life, a new climate and a new dream they could never fulfil at home in their native lands.

These were a people who had run away from famine in Ireland or the hardships of the Industrial Revolution back in England. What had they got to lose after surviving the hazards of sea, travel on rough and ready sailing ships never built for passengers?

So here they were in America, the land of sunshine and plenty. Disillusionment awaited many but hope sprang eternal in the hearts of others as they moved on.
A comedy song of the times went something like this, "Come along, come along do not be alarmed, Uncle Sam is rich enough to give us all a farm."

Among the half million immigrants were the Irish with their own tragic story to tell. Back home in Ireland, the potatoe crop upon which they depended just to exist was hit by potatoe blight for two years in a row. By eating less they could just about have enough potatoes to sow for next year's crop. Those were the lucky ones. Elsewhere whole families were found dead in their cabins. Soup kitchens were set up by the landlords for a modest price consisting of a stirabout made of meal, water and rice. When they could not pay their rent "wreckers" arrived to pull the roof off their cabin and tear the walls apart with crowbars. One farmer's experience tells his own story. A Michael Kelly faced with a future of uncertainty and desolation went to the landlord's agent and had his families passage paid to America in the most atrocious conditions as steerage passengers. But anything was better than what they were leaving behind. His story was the tale of thousands. They walked fifty miles to the ships waiting in Wexford, a port in southern Ireland.

Every passenger was to receive a daily supply of fresh water, biscuits and flour or oatmeal or potatoes which they cooked themselves. The ship "The Dunbrody" had a crew of twelve; the Captain, first and second mate, a carpenter, a sailmaker, a cook and six seamen. Discipline as you could expect was rough. The rules were tough. No knives, no smoking, no washing clothes on Sunday. Living quarters were below deck, two metres by two metres for a group of four to six people.

Old men, grannies and children were cluttered together for the five week trip. Many were sick before they even got on board. They could cook their food on the deck but heaven help them if fire broke out. When the seas were rough the hatches were locked down with only two lanterns for light below deck where up to 170 passengers were accommodated. Sea sickness added to their misery. On a fine day they were allowed on deck for twenty minutes for fresh air if only to get away from the awful stench below deck. Unbelievably sometimes someone played a fiddle and others tried to dance to the music but that was seldom. Men, women and children died around them and their bodies were thrown to the fishes wrapped in rough sacking. The sailors seldom did the cleaning leaving that to the passengers themselves by giving them buckets and mops to do the job.

A thirty-eight day crossing was considered fast, yet their ships arrival in New York did not end their troubles. The American's sometimes delayed their landing as a precaution against fever raging on board. Passengers too sick to disembark actually died in the harbour, a terrible price to pay for dashed hopes just as they had found their cherished dream. But our friend Michael Kelly now had to search for lodgings in this new world for his wife and family. He found work but not for longer than a few weeks. Others found work in the coal mines of Pittsburgh. Eventually Michael got a proper job on the railroad. Many others headed for the gold mines of California. The women found jobs as servants and waitresses.

Many more found themselves in Pennsylvania. Many were treated so badly they formed themselves into secret societies called "The Molly Maguires" who dealt out rough justice in defence of their members. It was an unbelievably appalling journey. Many had left behind friends and families they would never see again. But for those who succeeded in their American dream, the hardship in achieving it was well worth suffering for.

This flood of settlers was justified by John L. Sullivan, a leading editor and a well-known advocate of the Young America Movement. He wrote of "The fulfilment of our Manifest Destiny to overspread the Continent allotted by providence for the free development of our yearly multiplying millions."

And so the Doctrine of Manifest Destiny was born and was embraced by expansionists to justify their trek westwards. To these fanatical expansionists "God was on their side and the side of the restless millions marching to a new life beyond the Mississippi".

But there was another side to their story – the pledge of the Indians whose confiscated lands they would occupy. Confronting them throughout their journey West were heartbroken, desperate and angry Indian tribes or Native Americans who saw their homes, their lands, their culture and their very livelihood heading for extinction. They had little option but to fight.

Among the settlers or pioneers, as they were known were prospectors looking for pay dirt. Railways began to crisscross the Continent. Land was cheap. Cultures were crushed and new States were carved out of virgin country. By 1900 forty-five States were created leaving only three – Arizona, Mexico and Oklahoma as territories. A great colonial empire was growing with the help of international money. New cities and Paris fashions blossomed. The land of cowboys and quick fortunes had arrived.

In the mid 1800s the West had only reached the borders of Missouri. Beyond lay billions of acres of rolling prairies, parched deserts, rugged majestic mountains and fast flowing rivers. Rich soil and rainfall were in abundance from the Plains to the foothills of the Rockies on the other side of which lay the temperate and fertile lands along the Pacific coastline.

These rugged determined travellers had to contend with a climate they had never experienced before. Hot winds burned the prairie grasses in the summer. Blizzards and hailstones froze them in the winter. Wild life roamed freely – antelopes, wolves, coyotes, prairie dogs and jack rabbits. The buffalo grazed in enormous herds. Fifteen million, it is estimated, wandered the wide expanses of rich grasslands between Mexico and Canada every year.

Expansionism was in its heyday and Indian tribes had been forced further and further West to accommodate the settlers in their journey to a new life in the West. Most of these intruders had little cash but they did have an insatiable appetite for the romantic adventure of it all. Whole families, grandparents, parents and children travelled in groups. Some walked, others rode horses. The majority rode in groups of covered wagons called wagon trains numbering twenty or thirty, for safety reasons.

The settlers knew no boundaries. They even crossed the Appellation Mountains on the trails blazed by the trappers and frontiersmen who went before them. Some followed in the footsteps of Daniel Boone until they reached the tributaries of the Mississippi where they built rafts and flatboats to continue their lemming like journey towards the Pacific.

Here is another graphic story to describe the times and the emigrants who came ashore into Harrison's America as told by Terry Coleman in his book Passage to America.

In 1849 The Illustrated London News in its Christmas edition wrote about the New World where the sons of Britain had founded a new empire. An empire twenty, thirty or fifty times as extensive and as rich as Britain which was enticing to its bosom the best British blood, the young, the hardy and the persevering young men of England. Sir Frances Drake had said in 1847 "The heavens of America appear infinitely higher, the sky bluer, the clouds whiter, the air fresher, the cold is intense , the moon looks larger, the stars are brighter, the thunder is louder, the wind is stronger, the mountains higher, the rivers larger, the forests bigger." Yes and many hundreds of other such pen pictures were written which any would-be emigrant down on his luck just could not resist. So they gambled on the unknown and set out on a horrendous journey totally unprepared for what lay ahead with only hope to spur them on.
They found the American ships were best. Better built, better commanded, and punctual in their sailing times. Those leaving from Liverpool were crowded with people and cargo such as iron, coal, salt and manufactured goods. Soon the cargo was dropped. People paid better. Vessels with three masts square rigged. The clippers shipped water and were wet. Built for speed they suffered badly from the gales of the Atlantic. "The Washington" carried one thousand passengers and there were smaller ships too but in those there was no guarantee you had a Captain or a crew who were humane or competent. In some the Captain could be a tyrant. Usually the American ships could be trusted as being far superior to the others.

But the crew of some smaller lines could be brutal to their passengers. Many beatings were witnessed; some were kicked without provocation or soaked in water from a fire hose. One agent acting for the Black Star Line complained they had the very worst of sailors. "We get a class of men who go more to pilfer from the passengers than for the purpose of going to sea. One passenger, a twenty-one year old Irishman was hit by a second mate with steel knuckles and received a blow to the head from a weapon known as a "crown cracker". He was nearly knocked overboard. Nobody could look at the officers without getting knocked down. The forecastles held the riff raff, convicts and foreigners."

The passenger's welfare was left mostly to the tender mercies of the mates. Inside one week conditions bring a change to the passengers. Huddled together without light, without air, wallowing in filth, and sick in body and spirit were men, women and children alike. The food was half cooked through lack of stoves. The beds were filthy and the room between them was miniscule. Drunkenness was never discouraged because the Captain sold the stuff. Water was at the very minimum. The passengers were usually ignorant of their rights and powerless to assert them. They were also friendless and penniless. Their only aim was to complete the journey alive. Some smoked tealeaves, others were unshaven and dishevelled.

All were nothing less than prisoners in their overcrowded floating jail until their journey ended. The poor ones depended on begging from the better off to eat over the five long weeks sailing. One brave passenger on one of these ships managed to see the Captain after running the gauntlet of blows from the second mate. He read his letter of complaint and was promptly accused by the Captain of being a trouble maker and a pirate. He was put in chains for the rest of the voyage. Dysentery was often rampant and the bodies of those who died were put in a course sacking and thrown overboard without a service. On arrival, racketeers robbed them of their luggage and this included the customs officers and the police ashore. They could also be ripped off at selected boarding houses sometimes with violence. Boarding house owners paid a fee to be sent such unsuspecting passengers. Sometimes they were sold forged canal tickets into the interior but were thrown off these canal boats after half their journey. Often whole boatloads were sold by the Captain at a profit to the racketeers. Finally, the unfortunate immigrant at the end of his journey would run the gauntlet of bag snatchers who thrived on separating immigrants from their luggage on the New York pier.

After all this the immigrant had to face the dangerous journey into the unknown on the trail westward in covered wagons. Life on these wagon trails was rough, tough and dangerous. On the trail westward the immigrants faced the hazards of winter and summer. Hot, dusty days over prairies, deserts and towering mountains, trying to beat the winter before settling in Sacramento Valley. The trip could take six months crossing half a Continent. Trains replaced wagon trains in later years and the traffic was two dimensional – the hardy and the hopeful going out, passing the weary and defeated coming back.

The notorious cities we know about from the film industry were beginning to make a name for themselves. Deadwood, Nevada, Colorado and Tombstone to mention but a few. Great cattle ranches thrived on the vast grasslands. Branding, roundups and roping skills, became part of a new folklore and the cattle meat fed hungry millions after the Civil War. The cattle drive of animals in their thousands was soon replaced by the shipments of cattle by train across America. At the risk of robbing millions of their cowboy heroes, booming cow towns never produced more than five shootouts per year. Doc Holliday and Bat Masterson killed nobody and Sheriffs like Wild Bill Hickok and Wyatt Earp repaired the sidewalks more often than they would use their guns.

But one thing is for sure. The pedestrian pace of the old planter society was gone forever. In 1865 over 250,000 Indians or Native Americans lived in the West. The Cherokee, the Hopi, Zuni, Navajo, Apache, Chinook and Shasta tribes were then native to the region. Most of the powerful tribes ceded their lands to the United States and settled on Reservations.

Contagious diseases carried by prospectors in the California Gold Rush decimated many. Soon fewer than twenty thousand Indians lived in all of California. Two thirds of the Indians in the West lived on the Great Plains such as The Sioux, Blackfoot, Cheyenne, Crow, Arapaho, Pawnee, Kiowa, Apache and Comanche. They lived a nomadic life style hunting the buffalo and excelled in horsemanship even greater than the U.S. Cavalry.

Though tribes numbered thousands they preferred to live in bands of three hundred or so. They used the Buffalo for food, shelter, clothing, shoes, and even fuel. Some tribes developed a warrior class. Other tribes were run by gender. The men hunted, traded and planted. The women reared the children and indulged in creative artistic work. They also worked in camp, grew vegetables and prepared buffalo meat and hides as well as farming roots and berries. Men were renowned for their hunting skills, women for their skills with quill and paint. The location in which they lived was known by the Government as Indian country.

The hunger for more land grew ever more intense. By the mid 19th century boundaries were set for each tribe within which they would live, hunt and practice their culture. A place to be born in and a place to die in.

But this arrangement led to problems. First to be effected was the hunt for buffalo and soon the Indians were refusing to stay within "their boundaries". White settlers then moved into these Indian lands given to the Indians for "as long as waters ran and grass shall grow". Gold miners also trespassed. Soon wars and battles flared between the Indian and the Federal Government against whom the Indians were no match.

Some confrontations were horrendous like The Chivington Massacre by a Colorado militia led by Colonel John Chivington who attacked a camp of Indian men, women and children on the morning of November 29, 1864 killing 700 of the unfortunate people. The Government openly condemned "this gross and wonton outrage" and the Sandcreek Indians had to move elsewhere to a new Reservation. The great Sioux nation was next to go on the warpath when it was decided to build The Bozeman trail connecting several mining towns right through the heart of the Sioux hunting grounds.

The angry Sioux lured a column of eighty-two soldiers led by Captain William J. Fetterman into the wilderness, ambushed them and wiped them out. Control and punishment was the only solutions put forward. Approximately 54,000 were to be moved from the Northern Plains to beyond the Blackhills and 86,000 Indians on the South Plains were moved to Oklahoma. But that solution only created other problems. Once again gold prospectors encroached on their lands in the Black Hills Gold Rush. The miners were confronted by three great Sioux chiefs "Rain-in-the-Face"; "Crazy horse" and the famous medicine man "Sitting Bull". On the morning of June 25, 1876; 265 men led by the now famous Colonel George Custer were killed under a hot midday sun on the banks of the Little Bighorn River in Montana. It was called Custer's last stand by blazing newspaper headlines and dire revenge was threatened.

Within a month the Sioux were defeated bringing to an end the major Indian warfare in the West but not before the final tragedy took place at an army camp at Wounded Knee in South Dakota. The firing of an accidental shot that killed a soldier resulted in the massacre of two hundred men, women and children in the snow from the muzzles of the army's newest deadly weapon – the machine gun. Towards the end of the century came the "re-education" of the Indian granting them new farms out of tribal Reservations "Provided they lived apart from the tribe and adopted the habits of a civilized life". This was the Dawes Act of 1887, in which forty-seven million acres of land were redistributed. The other ninety million acres left from the Reservations was the most fertile land, but it was sold to white settlers. The elimination and almost extinction of the buffalo completed the death throes of the Native American and finally eliminated the old Indian nation as historians know it.

By way of anecdote and to conclude this piece of background to the America of the 19th century in the Presidency of William H. Harrison, it is impossible to write about the Red Indians or Native Americans of 19th century America without mentioning one name that stands head and shoulders above any other warrior that graced the battlefields of U.S. history "Geronimo".

In his book The Geronimo Campaign Odie B. Faulk writes generously about Geronimo. "He came to symbolize the brave fight of a brave people for independence and ownership of their homeland," writes Faulk.
Maurice Saltzman, a native of Arizona and a lawyer wrote in 1909, the year Geronimo died, "few men deserved as much of a powerful Government's attention." The war to finally subdue

Geronimo, known as "the Napoleon of the Indian race", cost over one million dollars, a substantial amount in the 1800s yet he left the Generals Crook, Miles, Gatewood, Lawton, Chaffe, Willcox and Bourke, the best Indian fighters of the era, filled with admiration for this proud fighter of a lost cause.

General Crook is on record as saying "I venture to prophesy that as time passes and all the available material collected and properly compiled.... When we shall be able to look back upon this Indian war Chief with a historical perspective, we will decide that he was one of the greatest Americans that ever lived."

"Geronimo has fulfilled the prophecy with the passing of time. Novels, movies and television portray him frequently in a sympathetic light," writes Odie B. Faulk. During World War II, paratroopers of the U.S. army used the cry "Geronimo" when they jumped from their planes into battle thus enhancing his reputation. While the Generals I mentioned previously have long since faded into history nobody has forgotten the name "Geronimo".

"His dignity and heroism in the face of overwhelming losses," Odie B. Faulk continues "brought him to the forefront of his own people and enabled him to survive as a great American."

The task of achieving the final defeat of the Red Indian race reached back one hundred years since the beginning of the 18th century and beyond. The final outcome was inevitable. The time span outlived the lives of at least twenty-four Presidents.
The folklore of this great Red Indian nation was finally exploited on the stages of America and Europe, in the "Buffalo Bill Cody Wild West show" in which "Sitting Bull" himself performed. A sad, sad epitaph to the broken dreams of a beautiful nation.

To conclude this piece on the Native American, the Pioneers, and Manifest Destiny, before returning to William Harrison, the 9th President let us hear a poem by Archibald MacLeish. He lamented bitterly the growth of America from a revolutionary to an international power and expressed his sadness in the following lines.

Freedom that was a thing to use
They have made a thing to save
And staked it in and fenced it round
Like a dead man's grave.

You Thomas Jefferson
You could not lie still
You could not bear the weight of stone
On your green hill.

You could not hold your angry tongue
If you could see how bold
The old stale bitter world plays new
And the new world old.

Now let us return to William Harrison.

You may remember we left William Henry Harrison, the retired General and a 9th President living the lifestyle of a rich planter and unfortunately getting deeper and deeper in debt.
I am afraid Harrison's farm to which he had retired was not doing too well. He made several

unsuccessful attempts to enter politics again. Pulling strings as usual he canvassed the new President James Munroe to appoint him Secretary of War but to no avail.

His career just stumbled and stuttered along. In 1819 he entered the Senate but failed to hold his seat in 1821 and 1822. He also failed to get into the House of Representatives. His undistinguished political career rose to a peak when he was appointed Diplomat to Columbia but we read earlier how that post ended for him.

Help was again at hand, however in 1836 when his old political friends felt his illustrious career might just about make him a suitable Presidential candidate against Van Buren. He failed, but his sizeable popular vote made him an ideal candidate for the next election in 1840.

For this election the Whigs dressed him up in fancy slogans and a false identity for the benefit of the poor farmers and frontier settlers who knew him from the days when he was secretary of the Northwest Territories with the power to settle land disputes. The ageing hero of Tippecanoe was wheeled out as a log cabin dweller and a drinker of hard cider. These were blatant lies. Poor Van Buren was characterised as a "Well to do" President lounging on silken cushions drinking imported wines – a despicable falsehood.

Despite this, the 1840 campaign for the Presidency is known for being the first of the modern elections. Two well-organized Parties, speeches, demonstrations, and fierce media participation mobilized the votes. Amazingly 80% of the voters went to the ballots and the hustings were exciting. When a politician came to town his supporters would parade down the main street, pitch a huge tent and a barker invited the curious spectators inside. Itinerant revival preachers roused the crowd, for the clergy were reputed to be the experts in public relations.

These methods were afterwards adopted by travelling circuses. Inside the tent the crowd were entertained to colourful speeches and loud music. Neither candidate made public speeches or attended rallies. In fact it was another fifty-six years before William Jennings Bryan in 1896 canvassed and campaigned publicly and solo. The next was Theodore Roosevelt in 1904. Of course there was the inevitable symbol of the log cabin and the barrel of cider by the Whigs. Since Harrison was obviously of aristocratic stock I doubt if people were fooled by the image makers. Even so a Baltimore newspaper got in on the act.

They wrote "Give him a barrel of hard cider and settle a pension of $2,000 a year on him and he will sit the remainder of his days in his log cabin." They say the 1840 election was also one of the most corrupt elections ever with rampant vote-buying in operation everywhere.

As I said at the start of this piece – all his life, destiny smiled on Harrison. Against all the odds he somehow won the 1840 Presidential election by a landslide to become America's 9th President. But alas he made one fatal mistake.

The new President like the flamboyant General that he once was rode to the Capitol on a white horse hatless and coatless in the bitter cold. Standing for one hour and forty-five minutes he addressed the crowd with the longest inaugural speech on record – 85,781 words.

In it he deplored office seekers and their lust for power. Perhaps he said this with tongue-in-cheek. Yet he did firmly nail his colours to the mast when he spoke out vigorously against the anti-slavery lobby. He called it an intrusion into State affairs.
After his inauguration he led a parade of his supporters back to the White House and later

attended three inaugural Balls in his honour. One was in a converted theatre called The New Washington Assembly Rooms and another in Carusi's Saloon attended by one thousand people at $10 per head.

But here I must pause a while to tell you a strange anecdote worth recording about Harrison. It is from a prophetic speech he made on January 26, 1841. He said "Gentlemen and fellow citizens, perhaps this may be the last time I may have the pleasure of speaking to you on earth or seeing you. I will bid you farewell, if forever, fare thee well."

This was two months before he became President.

In the month before his inauguration Harrison had formed an impressive Cabinet led by Secretary of State Daniel Webster. He also arranged for a special sitting of Congress to tackle the economy.

John Tyler his running mate was installed as Vice President. Like Washington before him Harrison's First Lady did not arrive for the Presidential ceremonies. She still had not arrived when on Sunday morning April 4, 1841 Harrison's severe chill deteriorated into pleurisy fever or pneumonia. Despite the best medical attention, including blistering and bleeding which they say did more harm than good, Harrison passed away and shocked the nation.

He had spent exactly one month to the day (March 4 to April 4) in office as President of the United States.

William Henry Harrison was the first President to lie in State in the White House. Later his remains were brought for burial in what is now called the William Henry Harrison Memorial State Park in North Bend, Ohio.

10th President   John Tyler

"Accidental President"
Born 1790
Died 1862
72 Years of age
1 Term
1841 – 1845
Age 51

Party: Whig
Profession: Lawyer
County: Virginia
Hobbies: Hunting, Fishing, Fox hunting
Estate: $142,000
Ancestry: English

Physical description; Height – well over 6 foot tall; thin; light brown hair; blue eyes; light complexion; high-bridged nose.

There was no inauguration

JOHN TYLER

The scene now changes to John Tyler's Presidency. His predecessor William H. Harrison was a man with all the right connections. To put it bluntly poor John Tyler had none.

There was no inaugural address by Tyler because the Presidency automatically passed to him when William H. Harrison died in office.

And so we come to our 10th President of the United States, the first President to step into a dead man's shoes, John Tyler.

Just after Harrison's election Tyler had returned to his hometown of Williamsburg, Virginia not expecting to be needed for duty for a while. When Harrison died suddenly fate took a hand in Tyler's Destiny on April 4, 1841 and catapulted an unsuspecting man into the lifestyle he could never even have contemplated or planned two days earlier.

But here he was, packing his bags making urgent preparations to return to Washington to take up his place in history.

Not even the greats of U.S. history such as Hamilton, Clay, Webster or Franklin had reached the very pinnacle of politics - the Presidency of the United States of America.

Such were his thoughts we presume as he set out on horseback to ride the 230 miles from Williamsburg to Washington in twenty-four hours a great tribute to his physical well-being at fifty-two years of age.

But the spoils of destiny were not wholeheartedly handed over to him because it seems the Constitution of the United States was vague on the procedure. Perhaps he should have declared himself acting President and called for new elections. But who could blame Tyler for reaching out to snatch the ultimate political prize so tantalisingly dangled before him. It was an opportunity for greatness that might never come to him again.

And so Tyler ignored the first option of a new election and decided to have himself sworn in as the 10th President of the United States. This action was bitterly denounced at the time but it was an action which was to set a precedent for all future Presidents to this day. One modern beneficiary was President Lyndon Johnston after the assassination of President John F Kennedy.

John Tyler is also famous for another historical event in his Presidency - the annexation of Texas but that is a story for later. So who was John Tyler? What was he like? How did he come to be Vice President? What was his background?

John Tyler whose family settled in America in1650 was the sixth of eight children born on his father's plantation at Greenway in Charles City County on the James River in Virginia on March 29, 1790. Like all planters sons he was given a quality education.

His first school was a small private one who's Principal was a great advocate of flogging to aid education. Tyler later remarked "It was a wonder he did not whip all the sense out of scholars. But the pupils had the last laugh when they finally rebelled and set about the unfortunate Principal and thrust him up like a turkey on Thanksgiving Day. This seemed to solve the problem and no more whippings were administered after that."

He was later sent to the crème de la crème of private schools in Virginia the College of "William and Mary", the alma mater of many Presidents.

Tyler turned out to be a very talented student and eventually graduated at seventeen years of age before entering law practice with his father and his cousin Chancellor Samuel Tyler.

His father was made Governor of Virginia when Tyler was only nineteen but at twenty-one, Tyler was helped into politics by another successful politician Edmund Randolph. This first political post was in the Virginia General Assembly.

While there he became a great admirer and supporter of Andrew Jackson which proved a great help to his career.

Later showing that stubborn streak lurking deep inside him he followed his own path where he believed himself to be right. Tyler fell out with Jackson over the removal of State funds from The Bank of America. Later he left the Jackson camp calling it "A rule by mob." It was this type of steel and commitment which would help him to survive four years in the Presidency under enormous pressures. Of course by that time Tyler was financially independent earning from his law practice the colossal sum of $2,000 per year.

After his row with Jackson, Tyler joined the Whig Party and the bad feeling between them was reflected in his decision to run on an anti-Jackson ticket as Vice President in 1836. He was also a great believer in States rights. It was hoped this fact might attract the Southern vote away from New Yorker, Martin Van Buren. The Whigs lost the 1836 election yet Tyler emerged from it with his reputation untarnished. Since both Harrison and Tyler's fathers were once Virginia Governors, and since the Whigs once again needed a Southerner to balance their ticket, Tyler was the obvious but cynical choice for the Vice Presidential ticket. It seems when selecting a Vice President the possibility of him becoming a future President never crossed their minds. Such was the insignificance of the role of Vice President, as Adams Vice President to Washington, complained about with disdain.

But Tyler was a strong-minded, almost difficult character with opinions very much his own. He bowed to no man on this. He disagreed with the Democrats on Constitutional issues and with the Whigs on financial matters. This left Tyler riding two horses when he agreed to be a Vice Presidential candidate in 1840, but the prize of getting revenge on Van Buren for his 1836 defeat was sufficient for Tyler. Political problems could be solved later. Harrison duly won the 1840 election with Tyler as Vice President.

Tyler was known and respected as a very kind person, a laid-back individual who forgave his enemies easily. He could be very warm in private and very cautious and aloof in public. He had to have that special gift of being able to ride the storms of life, for how else could he have survived the turmoil of his Presidency that hounded him for four long years. His secret was in his personality for he was without a trace of malice or bitterness in his make-up. Tyler stood well over six foot tall, with blue eyes, silky brown hair, a lofty brow and a firm set mouth. A rather uncharitable description of his nose says it was prominent enough to land him the role in any film as Cyrano De Bergerac.

Charles Dickens wrote on a visit to America "Tyler looked somewhat worn and anxious, and well he might be, being at war with everybody but the expression on his face was mild and pleasant. I thought that his whole carriage and demeanour became his station singularly well." However what Charles Dickens failed to add was how happily married Tyler was. He had married into a very wealthy family when he became the husband of Letitia Christian, the daughter of a planter and then moved into his new plantation house which they named Sherwood Forest. They were both roughly the same age at twenty-three when they married on March 29, 1813 at New Kent County. They had eight children Mary, Robert, John, Letitia, Elizabeth, Alice, Anne and Tazewell. All except Lettia, his daughter, died young. Letitia lived to a ripe old age for those days of eighty-six years.

Harrison's successor brought a large family with him when he succeeded William Harrison. It seems the two never agreed on anything in the politics of that time. Letitia, his wife had suffered a stroke so her daughter-in-law Priscilla, a top actress took over as hostess. She was so carried away by her new role she wrote to her sister, "I look at myself like a little old woman and exclaim can this be I?"

However, a French Minister was not so impressed remarking pompously, "How can a woman pass from an actress to what serves as a Republican throne." A little too dismissive of Priscilla I think, for she had already established herself with honour on all the stages of the East Coast of America, one of the leading actresses of her time.
The marriage ended in 1842, two years into his Presidency when Letitia his wife died from the stroke she had had three years earlier.

Tyler mourned his wife sincerely but he seemed determined to remarry and two years later he married Julia Gardiner, the twenty-four year old daughter of a U.S. Senator on June 26, 1844 in New York. He was fifty-four. They had seven children David, John, Julia, Lachlan, Lyon, Robert and Pearl. Tyler was the first President to be married in office while living in the White House and his family increased to fifteen children. One anecdote is told of how lucky the couple were ever to get married for they escaped death by inches four months before the wedding in February 1844, while on board a naval ship, "The Princeton", for a demonstration of a huge gun capable of firing a ball 225 lbs in weight. Something went wrong that day and the gun exploded with tragic consequences to those standing nearby. One of these was the Secretary of State. Another two killed was the Commodore and a State Senator. Luckily Tyler was downstairs below deck with his future wife to be Julia Gardiner and both were unhurt.

Another story about Tyler which completes the picture of the man was his love of horses. So much so he actually had two horses imported from England and named them Romulus and Pantalon. In fact on his estate at Sherwood Forest he is reputed to have buried his favourite horse "The General" over which he nailed a plaque with the following inscription: "Here lies the body of my good horse "The General". For twenty years he bore me around the circuit of my practice and in all that time he never made a blunder. Would that his master could say the same."

John Tyler had a great love of life and was a great socialiser. He was an accomplished violinist and enjoyed many hobbies including hunting, fishing, and, fox hunting. Julia Gardiner also enjoyed her role as First Lady for like Priscilla she too was known to have been a famous belle before her White House days. In the White House her entertainment is said to have been very similar to the court of Louis Philippe of France. She was also renowned for her dancing of the Polka.

To round off the family contribution to the White House life Robert, Tyler's son presented the Tylers with a grand-daughter, the first grandchild born in the White House. If there were problems in Tyler's Presidency it certainly seems he and his family didn't take them very seriously. Returning to Charles Dickens, the problems of the Presidency to which he alluded, were not of Tyler's making entirely. There were two problems which were inherited from his predecessors. The problems out West, and the National Bank.

However beneath the surface was his most serious problem which caused him trouble throughout his Presidency - the acceptance of John Tyler the man by his peers. Unfortunately respect from the people surrounding him was never given. You may now ask why the President of the United States should be in such a situation, after all, the Presidency was the most powerful job in the country completely distinct from the office holder.

His situation can now be blamed on the shadowy figures on the periphery of the Presidency who to their utter amazement and anger found that the puppet they thought they had groomed during Jackson's Presidency never saw himself as a puppet. Now you just have to ask yourself how could they have totally underestimated Tyler? Surely this was the man who in all his political life was never in any mans pocket so to speak – not even the formidable and imposing personality of Old Hickory Jackson. They were soon to have a rude awakening and it came at the first Cabinet meeting. It was the most devastating "put down" in American history. Tyler sat silently at the Cabinet table as the Cabinet entered the room and sat around him.

Some of them made very eloquent speeches laying down conditions and expectations they intended as to how the Government was to be run. He of course would be allowed one vote – his own. So far so good. Then came the bombshell they never expected. Tyler listened respectfully then rose slowly to his feet and looked around him. Taking a deep breath he proceeded to burst their bubble of carefully manipulated dreams leaving those dreams broken into irreparable smithereens around them. The Cabinet was dumbstruck. He spoke quietly but firmly, as had always been his style, with the following words. "Gentlemen, I am proud to have in my Cabinet such able Statesmen as you have proved yourselves to be. I shall be pleased to avail myself of your counsel and advice but I can never consent to being dictated to as to what I shall be held responsible for in my own Administration. I hope I shall have your hearty co-operation in carrying out its measures. So long as you see fit to do this I shall be glad to have you with me. I will be equally glad to receive your resignation."

The scene was now set for a very rocky Presidency indeed. His enemies both inside and outside the Cabinet had discovered too late and to their horror that this man John Tyler could not be held on a short leash by his old political backers. The slogan "Tippecanoe and Tyler too" didn't help since by implication it tied him in with Harrison's policies.

Naturally his views were different but these couldn't be expressed by Tyler because of his fear of the press who by now was giving him some stick. Being the youngest man to sit as President up to then, aged fifty-one also left him vulnerable by the presence of the seniors around him.

But by now Tyler had made up his mind. He would not be intimidated by anyone. He declared "The barking of the newspapers and the brawling of demagogues can never drive me from my course." And so the battle was on.

As I have said earlier Tyler was a politician of some experience yet he never got close to the people. His strength lay in the power of his oratory with which he had swayed the voters in his political campaigns. Unfortunately a gap existed between himself and the populist view. He was a rather aloof politician of the old patrician school and he was also handicapped by the reckless manner in which he dispensed political patronage to nine members of his family with jobs in his Administration.

But were these really political mistakes or acts of arrogance towards his opponents? Who knows? Perhaps it was the maverick confrontational streak in his makeup just simmering below the surface that made him a loner all his life. In fact it constantly afflicted his Presidency when a more conciliatory approach might have reaped richer rewards and made more friends for him.

Yes it was a sad, sad Presidency both for Tyler and the United States. His detractors never really forgave the manner of his inauguration. They constantly wrote to him with derogatory titles like "Vice President acting President" or "Ex Vice President Tyler" in their letters to the White House. Eventually he left them unopened. Some even referred to him as "His Accidency". Shamefully he was then abandoned by advisors and friends. Now Tyler was ruling in a Party riddled with hostility towards him. He even suffered the ridicule of some fellow politicians calling him "A President without a Party".

Through it all the patriotic fervour of the earlier Presidencies shone through accusingly. Those were patriots who also had passionately held opinions but cast them aside for the greater good of their newly born America. I'm afraid real patriotism in Tyler's America was painfully missing. Political games were more important than the dignity of the office. Relationships deteriorated and Tyler resorted to the veto. The Whigs Bank Bill was the first casualty of his many vetoes. The Bill was designed to resurrect the Bank of the United States but Tyler's veto resulted in the resignation of his whole Cabinet with the exception of Daniel Webster who was engaged in sensitive negotiations with Great Britain. The Globe surprised everyone by coming out in support of Tyler writing as follows; "The veto punishes the most atrocious fraud ever attempted on a nation." Amazingly even his own Party the Whigs called for his resignation but Tyler retaliated defiantly with the words "My back is to the wall but I will beat back my assailants."
Over the full four years of his Presidency Tyler seemed to be fighting an unending battle for survival. Foolishly or maybe recklessly he committed the cardinal sin of any politician by taking on the press. He issued orders to the Postmaster General not to appoint as postmasters certain editors of newspapers he didn't trust.

Indifferent to the outrage he caused he added a further two vetoes to his record against another Bank Bill and a Tariff Bill.

Tyler by now was not leading the country facing forward but walking backwards into the future keeping his enemies at bay behind him as they snapped and snarled around his ankles like a group of baying hounds.

Eventually the ultimate in condemnation happened when a move was made to impeach him. It is not necessary for me to explain the politics behind Tyler's many vetoes, but his opponents were sufficiently enraged with frustration to label them "A misuse of veto power". Like a roman gladiator Tyler waded into his attackers with gusto defying his tormentors with a taunting challenge – "Impeach me. Any lesser charge would have no Constitutional standing." Tyler had called their bluff.
Then the inevitable happened. The impeachment resolution was introduced by John Minor Botts, a Representative from Virginia on January10, 1843. Tyler was charged with corruption, misconduct in office, high crimes and misdemeanours. The nine charges were rejected and the resolution was defeated by 83 Ayes to 127 Nays.

It is significant to note here that even this impeachment resolution referred to Tyler as

"JohnTyler Vice President acting as President". That was three years into his Presidency. The old wound inflicted by Tyler in assuming the Presidency seemed to be a sin that was unforgivable.

My description of Tyler as a man blessed with that special gift of being easily able to ride the storms of life is now vindicated. And so he went on to complete the most inexplicable Presidency of his time.

But Tyler had one more unfulfilled ambition to achieve, The Annexation of Texas. He persisted in his mission because he feared European nations might gain control of Texas, abolish slavery and set up a buffer State of their own between the United States and Mexico. He succeeded in his ambition by the payment of a Texas debt of up to $10 million in exchange for the millions of acres to be annexed. Just in time the Bill was signed into law on the last day of his Presidency.

Yet even this triumph was tainted with forebodings and dire warnings. The New York Tribune wrote that the annexation was a ready made war situation with Mexico. War with Mexico did eventually take place and the millions of extra acres gained were paid for in lives and bloodshed. I am afraid such an outcome must be left to the historians.

Writing about the political infighting that went on during Tyler's Presidency it would be easy to form the opinion of an Administration totally out of control. A system in chaos. An insurrection going on daily in the Cabinet and in committee rooms of Congress. You may say "What Government could run a country successfully in the midst of this ongoing political disarray?"

Well the answer to this question can neatly be summarized in the words of Tyler's Secretary of State Daniel Webster. He said "I admire his caution with money. In all things respecting the expenditure of public moneys he was remarkably cautious, exact and particular. He left a very sound economy behind him." Remarkable words since Harrison had called a special meeting just before he died to "tackle the economy". It seems Tyler had done a very efficient job on the economy for him and faithfully carried out Harrison's wishes. Most of all he did it entirely on his own.

A very revealing anecdote can be told here about Tyler's tongue-in-cheek sense of humour. True to his sunny personality far from being desolated with bitterness and engulfed in despair, he stood head and shoulders above it all. "He found it so easy to forgive all his enemies" is the character reference I wrote about him earlier. How accurate were those words!

As his term came to an end he threw a huge Ball at the White House to mark the occasion of his retirement. It was his bonfire of triumphal survival.

As to be expected, human nature being what it is, the East Room was crammed with people. Perhaps they were not even supporters but hangers-on and office seekers who never missed an opportunity to flaunt themselves at times like this.

Nothing was lost on Tyler. He was jubilant and light-hearted and his one-liner just about sums up the tenor of the man. "They cannot say I am a President without a Party now," he laughed.

As the new election approached he still had his supporters who urged him to run again. He allowed his name to go forward but James K. Polk was the Party's selection and Tyler withdrew his name.

In retirement he still wrote regularly to the press. Civil War was approaching and Tyler was in the thick of its debate.

He was even elected to the Confederate Congress but before he could participate he was confronted by one enemy he couldn't handle - death, the Grim Reaper himself. He died of a stroke on January 13, 1862 aged seventy-two, one year into the Civil War.

By now I am sure you have deduced Tyler was truly a colourful and controversial figure. Whatever you may think of him he straddled the Presidency with dignity and courage and in the face of overwhelming opposition from jealous enemies and political manipulators he still managed to complete the course with honour.

I can not let this piece end just there for later events were to prove what pygmies even great men can be.

When John Tyler died on the January 13, 1862 at Richmond V.A, the new Government comprised of many great men under John Knox Polk, saw fit to ignore his death. No announcement or proclamation and no official notice of his death were taken. Extraordinary!

Lest one takes the view that this was an unfortunate oversight by the powers that be at the time, the following story taunts him in his grave one hundred and fifty years later. It wasn't until another fifty years had passed since his death in 1862 that a monument was finally unveiled to this once embattled and persecuted President.

The unveiling of the monument took place in 1915 at Hollywood Cemetery Richmond, Virginia. Sadly only five Congressmen and five Senators had the guts to attend the ceremony. If the roles were reversed Tyler I'm certain would have defied Convention and forgiven the black sheep in his grave. His personality would have called for nothing less.
I just wonder today what another illustrious Virginian George Washington would have made of it all. The words "rage and disgust" would not be far from his lips, I'm quite certain of that.

11th President   James Knox Polk

"Napoleon of the Stump"
Born 1795
Died 1849
54 Years of age
1 Term
1845 – 1849
Age 50

Party: Democrats
Profession: Lawyer
County: Tennessee
Estate: $100,000 - $150,000
Ancestry: Scotch- Irish
Hobbies: None

Physical Description: Height 5 foot 8 inches; nearly white hair, worn long; sharp gray eyes; high forehead, thin, angular brow.

Extracts from his inaugural address Washington DC, Tuesday March 4, 1845

"I am deeply impressed with gratitude for the confidence reposed in me. Honoured with this distinguished consideration at an earlier period of life than any of my predecessors. I can not disguise the diffidence with which I am about to enter on the discharge of my official duties. Our people increasing to many millions have filled the eastern valley of the Mississippi, adventurously ascended the Mississouri to its headsprings and are already engaged in establishing the blessing of self Government in valleys of which the rivers flow to the Pacific. To us belongs the duty of protecting them adequately wherever they may be upon our soil."

JOHN KNOX POLK

Our next story introduces us to the 11th President of the United States, "The Napoleon of the stump" as he was called. It was a title he earned for his eloquence and oratory in Congress and in the hustings. Sadly, although popular early in his Presidency, he ended up like Tyler the previous President, unwanted by the people.

As a child James Knox Polk was the apple of his father's eye. He was a fiery little lad and like any normal boy was never afraid to have a fist fight, despite the fact that his frailty made this a rather one sided and precarious pastime. However young James excelled in other areas one of which was his insatiable passion for reading the comprehensive library of books kept by his father Samuel Polk.

Pastor McNeill was the first to notice the extraordinary potential of young James which at that time looked like staying dormant for want of money to educate him properly. As a poor farmer his father could not afford such a luxury. But somehow Mrs. Polk held firm to her one ambition of seeing her son James looking down from the height of the pulpit and preaching just like Pastor McNeill.

Despite his mother's plans for young Polk junior, her husband Samuel had other ideas. He knew the hazards of frontier life and so being a practical man spent many hours with James teaching him how to handle guns. He considered such skills as important as schooling or even riding a horse. James Knox Polk was a very good pupil and became quite proficient with the gun for a little boy. His mother was not too impressed.

Here we can tell you a story of how useful such a skill could be in an emergency.

His father one day decided to move on to a different territory, hoping to make a better life on richer land further West as was the custom of the people at that time in America. He duly joined a wagon train heading West ready to confront the hazards that awaited them through wild and dangerous country.

Sitting alone in his wagon one day James noticed a movement in a bush some way off which aroused his suspicions. It was an Indian complete with war paint preparing to attack.

Taking his rifle James aged eleven, took aim and fired. Whether by fluke or skill the young Indian dropped in his tracks, shot between the eyes with deadly accuracy.

James became an instant hero to his father and the rest of the families in the wagon train.

But the incident did have a sequel later. On reaching their destination his father invested his life's savings of $1,700 buying 200 acres of land after checking out the nature of the country - the soil, the rainfall, the roads, the markets and the availability of local labour. None other than the great Andrew Jackson was the Judge signing the papers.

News of the shooting had reached Jackson's ears and to James's embarrassment Jackson made a big fuss of the young hero. Playfully he challenged young James to a shooting match and again whether by fluke or skill the boy beat the man. Andrew Jackson took his defeat with great humility and perhaps with tongue in cheek promised him a place on his army staff later. He also gave him a present of a gun which the little lad cherished for the rest of his life.

Anyway Samuel's business thrived and he became a very rich man from land speculation which later helped him to put James through college. But at twenty James was still a farm labourer helping on his father's farm and frustration with his life was eating away at him. Around this time an incident happened which changed the direction of the life of James Knox Polk.

An agent from Washington arrived in town, rather dishevelled after a confrontation with local farmers. His mission was to announce the creation of a new road through their county. To say he was having trouble getting his message over would be an understatement. It was a very relieved man who was told about the persuasive skills of one James Polk. The agent came knocking on his door and together they went out to confront a very angry crowd of townspeople in the local town hall. Rough weather beaten cowhands, farmers and the townsfolk confronted them. The mood of the meeting started ugly but after some words of sheer oratory young James Polk won the day. Nerves were calmed down and the situation was defused. Skilful arguments and debate by James managed to solve the problem by peaceful democratic means.

The agent brought word back to Washington and almost by accident James had entered the world of politics and the start of a journey all the way to the White House.

To fill in some further details of Polk let us say he was yet another of the early Presidents born in a log cabin. His family dated back to the late 17th century in Mecklenburg County near Pineville on the frontier of North Carolina.
James was the oldest child of ten children born to Samuel and Jane Knox Polk, herself a descendant of John Knox, the founder of the Presbyterian Church of Scotland.
James was born on November 2, 1795 and I am afraid had a very lonely isolated childhood of poor health. He carried a frail body as a daily handicap which left him with few childhood pals.

Yet his physical weakness was his greatest strength for it bred in him a fierce determination to compensate in another way - the development of his mind and wits. All the time he was constantly assailed by pain and cramps in his stomach.

Then came a horrifying experience he had to endure. His father, ever his loyal supporter, took him at seventeen to Kentucky where a famous frontier surgeon had his practice - Dr. Ephraim McDowell. Here he was diagnosed as having gallstones which had to be removed. Anaesthetics were unheard of and the only path to oblivion lay in the contents of a bottle. Not an ether bottle but one filled with Brandy. So strapped to a bed and held down by a heartbroken father surgery was accomplished. The operation proved to be a success and James enjoyed much improved health from that day on.

Now that his father was wealthy, James's education began at eighteen. The years spent improving his mind with facts and information from his father's library paid off. He was a brilliant pupil. Starting at a school near his home he mastered many subjects in a very short time including English, Greek and Latin. His next school was the University of North Carolina.

At that crucial point in his career Andrew Jackson who had become a lifelong friend stepped in to help him. James was entitled to a scholarship but was confronted by reams of red tape. Jackson cut through this red tape for him and he succeeded in getting bed and board plus law lessons. This was a miraculous bonus for one so poor. He was a very committed student and worked part-time to buy the textbooks he needed. And so began a brand new lifestyle for him in the University of North Carolina.

James had an unorthodox beginning in his first few days at university when he was challenged to a duel by a fellow student which reluctantly he had to accept. Thanks to the tutelage of his father in swordsmanship he was far too good for his challenger and managed to disarm him. From that day on the two became great pals, a friendship which continued for the rest of their university days.

James Knox Polk graduated in 1818 with a first class honours degree in mathematics and the classics which was a tremendous achievement. It meant he had reached this standard of qualification only five years after commencing any sort of studies. Now at twenty-three, with the backing of Jefferson and Andrew Jackson, James Polk was elected to Nashville and the Tennessee General Assembly.

As a further bonus, in less than a year James had his own law practice in Columbia, Tennessee.

Let's take time out now for something a lot more serious – the love life of James Knox Polk. It may not be well known but our hero was quite a ladies man. This had not gone unnoticed by some people. At twenty-seven he was quite handsome and much in demand by the fair sex in his spare time from politics.

He had one particular girl in mind for marriage but nevertheless he was a little perturbed at his own reputation as a ladies man. Taking up his courage he approached his old friend Andrew Jackson.

"How do I further my political career," he asked the old warrior.
With a twinkle in his eye Andrew Jackson didn't beat about the bush with a glib answer. "Just stop the philandering," he said bluntly. "You must settle down as a sober married man."

"Which lady shall I choose," said James. Looking him straight in the eye "Old Hickory" barked out his advice.

"Choose the one who will never give you trouble. Her wealth, family, education and health are all superior to yours. You know her well."

"You mean Sarah Childress?" James was amazed by now at the subtle insight Jackson seemed to have into his affairs.

Perhaps this was not so surprising for anyone to guess, since James was by now wearing his heart on his sleeve for all to see.

"I shall go at once and ask her to marry me."

According to Thomas Fleming when he wrote his piece in that marvellous book To the Best of My Ability, meeting Sarah Childress his lifelong partner in both marriage and politics was the defining moment of his life.

This tall, dark and highly intelligent woman was so influential to his later life she deserves a spotlight of her own just like Abigail Adams or Dolly Madison. However, she had something these two illustrious First Ladies did not have – an almost insatiable passion for politics and the sheer love of all that politics was about. She not only stood beside him throughout his debates, the intrigues, and the cut and thrust of political life, but learned the craft well enough to become an astute advisor to him even as President.

Yet this role paled into insignificance later to the one dictated by her heart. Knowing her husband's frail and vulnerable health she kept a caring eye on him. She was the unchallenged sentinel watching over his ever-increasing workload. When it came to his health she always had the last word.

Just as you would expect Sarah took a keen interest in the White House when Polk was President having it renovated and decorated to standards "befitting the house of the President".

In fact she soon became famous and admired for the glittering house parties and receptions she hosted.

One famous story is told of the first gaslights that were installed in the White house. Being a woman of independent opinions she refused point blank to allow workers to convert the chandeliers in the Blue Room to gas. However her first gaslight reception duly took place and it was a glittering affair. But that very night the burners went out at 9 pm. It seems no-one had asked the gas company to remain on duty in their plant. Later Sarah was well and truly vindicated as she stood under her chandeliers in the Blue Room fully illuminated by her beloved candlelight. That night Sarah measured up to some of her illustrious predecessors such as Dolly Madison and Abigail Adams. She was the belle of the ball so to speak. Her candlelight had saved the party.

Certainly Sarah Childress Polk deserves a mention all of her own in the James Knox Polk story.

She was quite a formidable figure. Unlike Polk, money was no object in her educational development. Because of this she was quite self-sufficient and totally unfazed despite Polk's seniority by eight years on her wedding day, New Years day 1824. He was twenty-nine and she was twenty-one.

Growing up in pampered surroundings, her parents being prosperous planters and tavern keepers, she had her own private tutor and then along with her sister rode the full two hundred miles to enrol at the best school in the South, "Salem Female Academy" in North Carolina. But sadly her stay was cut short by her father's death and she returned home. Incidentally, although she was a warm home loving person life in the kitchen would never be her strong point. She was much more at home in the cut and thrust of politics from alongside her husband.

James's fragile health may have been responsible for this choice because her constant concern was always in evidence especially in their letters. Around that time the problems of Manifest Destiny placed unseen difficulties into the job of the Presidency. How to distribute and govern the new lands and most important of all what role slavery would have on them. It was not the best environment for the wife of the President to live in because of the demands on her husband.

She had a fierce loyalty towards James and defended him vigorously against any criticism. Even Martin Van Buren's son was banished from her guest list for crossing her. She also could not help "showboating" for she often insisted on meeting guests seated on a large armchair placed on a slightly raised platform with three feathers in her hair. Despite her eccentricity, Sarah made a lasting impression on some of the greats of politics who valued her opinions and judgements as much as her husbands. She was also a breath of fresh air because of her youthful exuberance.

Despite Sarah's popularity with many there were others who found her personality a little too extrovert. George Dallas, Vice President-elect thought "She dressed rather too showy for my taste." Because it seems she committed the cardinal sin for a woman in those days of forcefully expressing her opinions she obviously made the men around her feel more than a little uncomfortable. "She wears the pants at home," they sneered but dare not tell her to her face. I wonder why. Sarah was a bit puritanical in her religious beliefs and even on their victory trip after his inauguration she cancelled the playing of music on board the boat on which they were travelling because it was Sunday.

The most complimentary praise we can give to Sarah Knox Polk is to compare her with Abigail Adams, that dynamic First Lady of John Adams the 2nd President. Sarah was described by the national publication called Peterson's Magazine in a poem which ended with these words, "You are modest yet are all a Queen should be."

Sarah survived James Polk by forty-two years after the Presidency. Although her name was linked to bachelor James Buchanan she never married again. When the Civil War came along she sold her estate and slaves (her people) as she called them for $30,000 and her house "Polk Place" was visited by both sides in the battle. She died in August 1891 with her mind undimmed to the end.

Leaving that wonderfully colourful First Lady Sarah Childress Polk for now let's return to her husband James Polk, the 11th President.

How did he become a Jacksonite?

His father Samuel was a great admirer of Jefferson and a follower of Jackson so it was bound to happen that Polk would model himself on both men.

While riding on the judicial circuit with Felix Grundy his tutor, James became very aware of the effect the Depression was having in the agricultural regions of the West. Being the son of a farmer, the drop in cotton prices and the power of the banks made him a severe critic of paper credit which he distrusted intensely after that.

Being a Jackson man to his fingertips he became a passionate supporter of Jackson's policies and politics. While it did not cost him his political career, his loyalty to Jackson lost him many friends who misread loyalty for servility.

One of Polk's major assets in his political life was the eloquence of his oratory which brought him the nickname "Napoleon of the Stump" and also because of his smaller than average size. At this time around 1825, politics was splitting into two camps. One side representing the farmers, labourers and debtors. The other side represented big business, merchants, speculators and wealthy planters. James Polk supported and championed the former class inspired by the people he met in his travels around the courts of the land. He was perhaps the socialist of the day, a champion of free public education, hard money, gold and silver. As we can see he was a staunch supporter of the Andrew Jackson school of politics.
However the admiration was mutual as can be seen from the following quote from old Hickory himself to Congressman John Bell on October 22, 1844.

"You say sir that James K. Polk is a slender reed and so he is. Buffeted by the fierce winds of his enemies he bends, but his spine is strong and supple and does not break; partisan gales tear at him and the foreign foes of his country would break him, if they could, but his great roots are planted deep in the fertile soil of Union and Democracy. He points to the stars and this slender reed will lead our people to new glory. This sir is James Knox Polk."

Polk had his own stubborn views. He opposed vigorously the use of Federal funds to build the infrastructure of roads, bridges and canals. He was a typical farmer's son with his roots in the soil and so opposed all the pressure groups that he felt sought unfair advantages for commercial and financial gains.

It should come as no surprise then to find he was a great supporter of the policies of Andrew Jackson and was involved in all Jackson's political battles. He condemned the banks as tools of vested financial interests as I have already pointed out.

The Jacksonians by now were called Democrats and voted Polk leader of the House. It is not hard to understand why Polk was called some nasty names such as a "servile tool of Jackson". His enemies even accused him of being "a cancer on the body politic". When Jackson retired from politics by coincidence or design Polk himself resigned from Congress to seek the Governorship of Tennessee. Then again perhaps it was political guile to choose this ideal platform from which to run for the Presidency. It proved he was now a national figure to be reckoned with.

So when Martin Van Buren failed to win a two thirds majority Polk was substituted as a dark horse for the Presidency. The compromise worked for James Polk and he was duly nominated to run for the Presidential election of 1844. In those days America's problems were much less dangerous than today. Western expansion was very much the topic of the day as was the annexation of Texas and the acquisition of Oregon from Great Britain northwards to the 54/40 parallel. His slogan for the Presidential campaign was "54-40 or Fight".

As described in previous notes on John Tyler 10th President, the Doctrine of Manifest Destiny was on everyone's lips as a moral claim of the American people to expand westward. They were saying it was a God given right to satisfy the land needs of an expanding population. This seemed to capture the mood of the people and Polk or "Young Hickory" as they were now calling him duly won the election of 1844 by a whisker to become the 11th President of the United States. It is said, Polk during his Presidency, secured so much territorial growth he is now considered one of the most important of American Presidents. However all that comes later. Meanwhile let us listen to his inauguration speech.

Polk's inauguration speech was electrifying. During this speech Polk set out his stall welcoming Texas as a State as soon as conditions permitted it. He set out his claim to a fair share of Oregon territory and hinted about help and protection for the thousands of Americans moving West to California. In a reference to the Monroe Doctrine he belligerently made it clear that the United States reserved the right to discourage any aggressive steps by any country who threatened the internal security of the United States from North America, South America or from any other part of the world.

"Such interference will be regarded as an unfriendly act," he bellowed. He prefaced these words with one significant sentence. "Let me make my meaning plain." James Knox Polk meant business and Europe better sit up and take notice. He was not going to be a President to trifle with. Yes, he was certainly in fighting mood. Maybe he was feeling tetchy for earlier he had differed sharply with one of America's best known Generals in the previous forty years. General Winfield Scott. Scott, always a flamboyant colourful extrovert character succeeded in turning what Knox Polk intended to be a modest ceremony into a military tattoo.

General Scott turned up in a dazzling gold trimmed uniform accompanied by a battalion of cavalry which converted the march up Pennsylvania Avenue into a military affair. Knox Polk was dancing mad and rounded on the unfortunate General not too concerned about who was listening with the following words "General, you have interfered with policy making. I particularly wanted no martial display as a gesture to Mexico. Hereafter, please be good enough to follow instructions." Harsh words indeed. But the General had had his day in the sun and I doubt if it bothered him too much. What is more the band continued to play jaunty airs for the entertainment of the VIPs sitting around.

Such displays of bad temper did not go unnoticed. It was the kind of public dressing down that hurt and could be regarded as petulant. His popularity ratings were already on the way down and that kind of truculence made co-operation with him more and more difficult. But that was Polk the man. Straight, blunt and single-minded. A man determined to put his stamp on the highest office in the land. He pressed on with his ambitions which he succeeded in achieving but at a terrible price to his personal health.

So what were these personal ambitions? We can list them as follows.

1. To pass a tariff acceptable to both North and South.
    2. To reconstruct the country's financial system
    3. To settle the dispute with Great Britain on the Oregon Boundary
    4. To acquire California.
    5. To annex Texas.

The problem of Texas was to prove the greatest obstacle to overcome and unfortunately he would have to tackle it without the help of his good friend "Old Hickory Jackson" who had died in the Spring of 1845 just as Polk started out on his Presidential journey.

Yet achieving all the forgoing triumphs now poses the puzzling question. Why was he consigned to relative obscurity by historians in the annals of the Presidencies?

The war with Mexico may enlighten us on this. Polk was not a pupil of "Old Hickory" without acquiring some of the old General's cunning and duplicity. An anecdote confirming this might be worth telling. Polk's reason for going to war with Mexico was to expand U.S. territory by acquiring both California and New Mexico. He did not even divulge his intentions to his Secretary of State James Buchanan. Polk wished to promote the idea that America went to war to secure peace with the olive branch and sword. This was not true. Being an expansionist, Polk had his own agenda. Duplicity. I do not know how authentic the following story is but I will tell it to you as far as I understand it.

The route for the railroad to California to avoid the Rockies and Sierras was through New Mexico. The main target was California. First of all it seems a military expedition was launched twelve months before the war. I understand a Colonel named Stephen Kearny went with five companies of Dragoons to the Rockies. Apparently Kearny was told to prove that cavalry units could operate effectively at great distances from their base.

As soon as the war on Mexico was declared Kearny was ordered to take infantry and cavalry units along the Santa Fe Trail occupy New Mexico and make the 1,000 miles leap over the deserts to California. The story continues. Kearny began to march over the unmapped desert towards California with 200 Dragoons on September 25, 1845 with Kit Carson as guide and with the help of the U.S. Navy.

However he was met in California by a Mexican attack which killed eighteen Americans and wounded fourteen others. The whole war was delayed by this attack and as a result lasted much longer than expected because the patriotism of the Mexicans had been badly underestimated. The outcome was as follows; while Kearny and Zachary Taylor were brandishing swords Polk and his Cabinet were waving olive branches. The war was eventually concluded for $18 million, the price for which the U.S. acquired New Mexico and California. It was an exercise in duplicity that lost Polk many, many friends. Yet today perhaps the combination of military and diplomatic tactics would be quite acceptable, who knows.

One casualty of the war was Texas which became a slave State. Polk was unperturbed by this as he always considered slavery a necessary evil.

A little story of Texas might be appropriate here. It concerns one of its greatest citizens Samuel Houston after whom the city of Houston has been named. The story of Samuel Houston is fascinating. Sam Houston was a native Virginian and a heaven sent leader of the army in Texas after the siege of the Alamo and the slaughter of 350 prisoners at Goliad.
At fifteen years of age Sam ran away from home and lived for three years with the Cherokee Indians. He then returned home and became a member of Congress. He returned to his old tribe the Cherokees and became a fully fledged Indian warrior with the Cherokee name "the Raven". In the hostilities in Texas perhaps because of his Cherokee training he emerged as Commander-in-Chief during its war of Independence. After the war Texas was declared a Republic and Samuel Houston was elected its first President.

Meanwhile Polk's unwavering dedication to his goals helped him accomplish his amazing legislative targets set out by him very early in his Presidency. He was not unlike Woodrow Wilson during the First World War who also sacrificed his health in pursuit of political goals.
Yes, the work Polk demanded from his frail body was downright foolhardy. Like many other Presidents the demands of the office began to extract the inevitable price from a constitution that was not built for such ravages. His health went downhill.
You may remember me telling you earlier that Sarah Childress Polk lived for the full term of the Presidency. But now she shared his life with a growing sense of despair for the health of her husband. Throughout these four years Polk's health grew steadily worse brought on by the demands the President placed upon himself. His bowel and stomach ailments became more frequent. What'smore, his unpopularity in the job did not help. Even on holidays nobody showed any interest in meeting him.

Whig newspapers lampooned him with the name "Jim Thumb" a midget in the circus of Barnum and Bailey, and not one in the Democratic Party defended him against the sneer. Isolated in the White House he had to negotiate everything without the help of influential Congressmen. The price of being a strong President made a cruel and unfair demand on his ageing bones. Polk wrote on March 3, 1848 in his diary "This day closes my third year in the Presidential office. They have been years of incessant labour and anxiety. Should any President feel like this?"
The day of retirement was fast approaching and Polk had no intention of running for office again. Compounding his sense of defeat and disillusionment was the election of his arch enemy Zachary Taylor who took office in March 1849. Strangely enough although his roots in Presbyterianism went back to his childhood he became a Methodist just after retiring.

Despite all his years of dedication and commitment under extraordinary pressure due to the frailty of his health it is sad to record one final anecdote about him. James Knox Polk sensitive to the reception his unpopularity would receive from the people was forced to take a circuitous route home from Washington after his Presidency ended to avoid troublemakers. It was an exit sadly reminiscent of John Adams, the 2nd President. How futile and bitter must have been his thoughts on that long, lonely horse drawn journey from Washington knowing he had won the greatest political prize in history only to lose the thing that mattered most to him – the love of the common people. What a price to pay for the pursuit of excellence. The end came three months later. One day while tidying up the shelves of his library Polk felt unwell. Even such a mild exercise brought on an intestinal attack.

One wonders what damage was done to his intestines during that barbaric operation without anaesthetics at seventeen years of age. Officially he died of diarrhoea.

On June 15, 1849 three months after his Presidency ended, the 11th President of the United States passed away aged fifty-three. They buried him in the garden of his Nashville home "Polk Place". One word only describes his end. Heartbreaking. However forty years later in 1893 the remains of both James Knox Polk and his beautiful wife Sarah were re-interred in the grounds of the Tennessee State Capitol in Nashville. Later Woodrow Wilson remembered Polk's life with the following words, "Though in no sense a man of brilliant parts, he may be said to have been a thoroughly representative man of his class, a sturdy upright straight forward Party man."

Perhaps the illustrious Woodrow Wilson was right. The feeling I have for the man is one of compassion for yet another President abandoned in office by his people.

12th President   Zachary Taylor

"Old Rough and Ready"
Born 1784
Died 1850
66 Years of age
1 Term (1 year)
1849 - 1850
Age 65

Party: Whigs
Profession: Soldier
County: Louisiana
Ancestry: English
Estate: $142,000
Hobbies: Riding

Physical Description: Height, 5 foot 8 inches, weight, 170 lbs; black hair; grey eyes, squint; ruddy complexion; short legs in proportion to body.

Extracts from his inaugural address on Monday March 5, 1849

"..... Chosen by the body of the people under the assurance that my Administration would be devoted to the welfare of the whole country and not to the support of any particular section or merely local interest. In conclusion, I congratulate you my fellow citizens upon the high state of prosperity to which the goodness of Divine Providence has conducted our common country. Let us invoke a continuance of the same protecting care which has led us from small beginnings "to the eminence we this day occupy."

ZACHARY TAYLOR

The successor to James Knox Polk was Zachary Taylor, his arch enemy. He was the fourth General to become President of the United States.

Taylor was no politician and had no experience whatsoever in the cut and thrust of politics. The discussion that will preoccupy us therefore concerns Zachary Taylor, the soldier, who had straddled the battlefields of history across America in pursuit of military goals all his life.

So let us look closely at Zachary Taylor, a legend to his Generals who is reputed never to have lost a battle.

His main claim to fame was his success in the Mexican War. His greatest victory took place on February 23, 1847 at Buena Vista when he defeated an army of 20,000 with his own contingent of 4,700 men. His relations with his Commander-in-Chief and President James Knox Polk deteriorated rapidly after that battle for reasons I will explain later.

It was at this time, when he was at the peak of his military success, that he was approached by the Whigs to run for the Presidency based on his army career record. Taylor refused, choosing loyalty to his army as the reason.

Meanwhile Taylor continued to fight and win battles against the Seminole and Black Hawk Indians in which he earned his nick name "Old Rough and Ready". He was a real soldier's man and was often seen side by side with them wading in mud surrounded by soldiers – mostly privates.

His philosophy "Do whatever needs to be done." As a soldier he was courageous in battle and inspiring to those around him. He never shirked danger and was constantly found where the fighting was at its fiercest. This fearlessness was carried into his job in the Presidency.

Like all great characters he had a mind of his own and didn't suffer fools gladly. Another reason for his nick name of "Old Rough and Ready" – a description used affectionately by his colleagues was his utter contempt for pomp and ceremony.

In appearance Zachary was really a small muscular man with a craggy weather-beaten face. The nature of the man was blunt and unorthodox, sometimes wearing an overcoat or straw hat on the battlefield. You might even say he was eccentric and noted for his tobacco chewing habit. He had a particular concern for his troops and of course for his old War Horse "Whitey". So attached was he to "Whitey", the horse was given pride of place grazing on the White House lawns during his Presidency.

Zachary Taylor had a unique aristocratic pedigree. His ancestors can be traced back to 1640 when they came to Virginia to live. His father, Richard, served as an officer in Washington's army in the revolution of 1776. Zachary was the third of nine children. When the war was over Richard Taylor received a war bonus of about 6,000 acres of land from the State of Kentucky. The family moved when Zachary was born on a plantation on the muddy fork of Beargrass Creek near the present city of Louisville. Being of such aristocratic stock, the family became quite influential in Kentucky and Richard, his father, was nominated as a delegate to the Territorial Constitutional Convention. He also served in the State Legislature. George Washington himself appointed him as collector of customs for the port of Louisville.

Strangely Zachary did not go the usual educational route of the planter's son. He had no formal education and only enjoyed the services of a private tutor for a short period. Most of the time his only education was in helping his father run his tobacco plantation – yet he never took up farming.

Zachary's talent for army life soon emerged when he joined the Kentucky militia in response to a call to arms by Jefferson during the crisis created by Aaron Burr, a prominent politician of the day. Burr had created a private army to seize land further West. Taylor's unit was eventually disbanded. But he had tasted army life when his second cousin, a certain James Madison, later 4th President of the United States, appointed him lieutenant in the 7th Infantry. Taylor jumped at the job. It was to be the start of a wonderful colourful career, spanning forty years which ended in the White House undefeated.

Zachary, as we can see, came from a very auspicious upper-crust, the ruling "aristocracy" so to speak. These frequently intermarried, usually integrating one power base with another; one wealthy dynasty with another. Zachary Taylor was no exception and true to form married the daughter of a Maryland planter, Margaret Mackall Smith. Zachary and Margaret had six children, five daughters and a son. However, there was a lot of sadness attached to the children. Octavia died aged four, Margaret died aged one, three lived to a good age; Mary (85), Richard (53) and Anne (65).

His second eldest daughter almost broke his heart. Sarah Knox Taylor fell in love with an army officer, a man who was to play a major role in Zachary Taylor's life. He was a young officer called Jefferson Davis. When news of their intended wedding came to Zachary's notice, he was not too pleased. He bellowed "I'll be damned if another daughter of mine will marry into the army." His eldest daughter was already married to an army surgeon. Sarah defied her father, eloped with Davis and married on June 17, 1835.

Shortly after, Davis resigned his Commission having been first appointed to Taylor's staff in 1832 three years earlier. But tragedy struck the marriage. On September 15, 1835 after three months of marriage, Sarah died. Jefferson Davis was reconciled with the General soon afterwards and returned to the army where he fought alongside his father-in-law at Bueno Vista.

But the story of Jefferson Davis does not end there. Although having strong pro-slavery views and committed to the spread of slavery westward with the new territories, he still supported Zachary in his Presidential campaign and won sizeable support for the General in the South.

He did make one mistake. He was foolish enough to dabble in the Secession Movement and Zachary was infuriated. He was so incensed he promised to personally hang Davis if he threatened the Union. Who knows how serious this threat was, but addressing all secessionists, he promised them he would personally lead an army against any person who endangered his beloved Union.

Davis however was also a man of very stubborn views and over ten years later he became President of the Confederate States of America, a rebel organisation set up in opposition to Congress and the Union. By then, Zachary Taylor was ten years in his grave.

But all that was years into the future. Let's return to Zachary Taylor for now.

It took Taylor forty years to become a General. His progress up the ladder was slow and his commands were mostly minor ones on the frontier. He did cross swords, so to speak, at the head of fifty men against 400 Indians, lead by Shawnee Chief, the famous Tecumseh himself. It was yet another battle he won and the widespread acclaim he received resulted in him being promoted to Major. Here perhaps we could digress a little to capture that other world out there that Zachary would leave behind as he stepped into the White House.

While awaiting his inauguration, Zachary Taylor walked the streets of Washington just thinking of all that used to be as he went shopping or just looked around. What a complete change it was going to be. Not like his old life living in the saddle all day long and at home with his old army friends in the familiar surroundings he had come to know so well on the barrack's square. Now it was all to change forever he thought, as he prepared for life as a politician.
He knew so intimately the life he was leaving behind him, observing the Indians who were constantly hunting and struggling to keep around them a fast fading culture threatened on all sides by those setting up their homesteads on a fast disappearing landscape. He would miss the job of keeping the peace and sometimes waging war against his will to control events in their lives. Many he knew as friends right to that day.

The social revolution would still go on when he was sitting at the Cabinet table or speaking in Congress. He knew he would always remember the characters he left out there on the prairie and would never forget them. Yes, life would still go on for the cowboy as he rode behind his herd on the trail northwards on the cow route to Kansas, known as the Chisholm Trail, named after John Chisholm, a New Mexican cowboy. The cattlemen today would still be in charge of one solid mass of cattle as far as the eye could see. The numbers of herds on the trail were many and it was a miracle how the cowhands kept them apart.
A steaming world of dust and insects mixed with the sound of bawling cattle, the cry of calves and the hooting of the riders each with their own peculiar catch cries that imitated the howls of the wolves that kept them company at night. But there were other dangers such as the Indians of Oklahoma – the Land of the Red Man. The Indians were a bitter people against the tide of determined white adventurers invading their space. Thinking of them made Zachary sad and even more determined to do something for them from his exalted position here in Washington.

The Indians introduced their own tax of ten cents a head for permission to cross the plains, their plains. When this tax was rejected by the cowboys there was trouble. The Indians rode bareback with bows and arrows among the long horns cutting out and confiscating bunches of them. Cowboys were ordered "Go ahead – shoot to kill" by their bosses but there were so few cowboys and so many Indians. That's when Zachary Taylor was called in. But fights were commonplace on the Chisholm Trail. It didn't take much to spark off a gun fight between different outfits, whose main aim in life was to get their cattle to the end of the Trail at North Cottonwood and Abilene.

At Abilene, buyers and shippers took the cattle, paid the cowhands and released or retained them on the payroll. June 1871, Wild Bill Hickok was Marshal of Abilene. Historians have built some folklore around him, most of it fictional, mixed with a few true facts. A marksman, a rough and tumble fighter yes, but somewhere along the line the fiction writers had their day. There are some who said he was a cold-blooded killer. Selfish, silent and deadly was one C.V. of him.

Buffalo Bill was another butcher according to the pen of Thomas Ripley in his book They Died With Their Boots On. According to Ripley "Cody was a yellow coward who never killed an Indian in his life." This was also the view of many old hands on the cattle trail. But Hickok however, was "A paid gun hand surrounded by the worst set of men who ever lived" and all in the pay of Abilene's Founding Fathers. Politics in Washington would be just as ruthless but at least democratic. Out there was the world of the so-called Wild West, one hundred years after Washington's Revolution in 1776. It was well-known to all the U.S. Presidents spanning many Presidencies.

Zachary Taylor continued to build a reputation at that time during his wide experience in Wisconsin, Louisiana and Minnesota. Another promotion came along, this time to Colonel. He saw further conflict with the Indians in the Black Hawk War. It was during his battles in Florida that he earned the nickname "Old Rough and Ready". In the Mexican War he was promoted to the rank of Major General. Polk and Taylor were still good friends until now. But Taylor ever his own man agreed over-generous terms with the Mexicans promising not to pursue the retreating soldiers for eight weeks.

All hell broke loose in Washington. As an act of revenge most of his command was transferred to General Winfield Scot, Taylor's superior. But again Taylor confounded his critics by winning the Battle of Buena Vista. This victory pushed him not only to the upper ranks of military men but brought him to the notice of the Whig politicians. His initial reaction to them was to refuse to be a Presidential candidate but he did reluctantly relent saying "I will not say I would not serve if the good people were imprudent enough to elect me." Zachary Taylor was now learning to speak like a politician.

Before now Taylor had never even voted in an election. He put this down to the fact that being a career soldier; he had never stayed long enough in any one place to qualify. He did, however, have his own political opinions. Most people expected these to be pro-slavery being a slave-holder himself. The Civil War camps were just starting to take root but Taylor duly disappointed them all; in fact he outraged them by turning out to be a committed nationalist. Once again political manipulators had got it wrong.

Taylor was an immensely rich man. For fourteen years he had travelled from post to post in his army career, but eventually he settled his family on a 2,000 acre plantation with eighty slaves at Cypress Grove near Baton Rouge.

Peggy Taylor, his wife was known to have prayed for his defeat in the Presidency, hoping to stay permanently at home in Louisiana. But Peggy Taylor had no say in subsequent events. Jefferson Davis joined his campaign and was instrumental in winning a lot of Southern support for him. Davis had returned to the army and fought under Taylor's command but he had now found his way into politics.

There is an interesting story told about Taylor's nomination as Presidential candidate by the Whig Party. News of Zachary Taylor's nomination for the Presidency never arrived due to the postal system. The nominating letter had no stamp, a common fault which was punished by either the non-delivery of the letter or a claim for non-postage paid by the receiver. Taylor was receiving so much unstamped mail from admirers he told the local post office not to deliver them to him. The crucial letter sat for six weeks in Baton Rouge post office before being discovered and acknowledged by the General.

Zachary Taylor's wife Peggy looked on in despair. She was sidelined by forces beyond her control. She was adamant her husband should not enter the Presidential race. She hated Washington and as his wife instinctively knew that the job would be too much for him at his age. What's more she disapproved of the pomp and nonsense of the White House circle, and when told the inner circle in Washington would disapprove of her pipe smoking she was unapologetic ..... "I don't care what they think about that. I disapprove of them for lots of reasons….." Talk of her lack of sophistication persisted long after her death in 1852. The real fact was she so abhorred tobacco she never even allowed anyone to smoke in her presence.

When Taylor eventually won the election, he had to make the journey from Baltimore to Washington alone. Peggy, because she dreaded the fanfare and ceremonies, would take no part in them. He went by carriage, river boat, train and sleigh on a journey that took three weeks. All this was a new experience for Zachary, a man who also disliked such a fuss. How he hated the well-wishers with bonfires, the blisters from hand-shakers and the indigestion from banquets. Fireworks and booming canons greeted him on his arrival at Washington station. So irritated was he by the lack of respect and recognition he had received during his war days, he refused to meet Polk. The Cabinet was ordered by Polk, the President, not to meet him and the impasse was only resolved by the diplomacy of Taylor's son-in-law, Jefferson Davis.

However the army were there to give comfort to their old friend "Rough and Ready". He was escorted to the Capitol building by a dozen units that had fought alongside him. Bands serenaded him at street corners – a group of Chippewa's, a tribe defeated by Taylor, gave a victory dance in his honour which lasted for hours.

But absent from everything were two wives, Peggy Taylor and the wife of Taylor's Vice President, Abigail Fillmore who was ill. Zachary Taylor insisted on taking the oath of office with his hand on Washington's bible, such was his admiration for Washington. Zachary took the oath of office on the East Portico of the Capitol on Monday March 5, 1849. The Presidential carriage moved from Willard's Hotel to the Capitol watched by 30,000 people who came to witness the inauguration. After the parade everyone adjourned to the White House for a reception. There were three different inaugural Balls which Zachary Taylor attended. Millard Fillmore was selected as Vice President, little knowing he himself would assume the office of the Presidency sixteen months later.

Among the crowd of well-wishers were the usual office seekers and under pressure from advisors Zachery mistakenly adopted "The Spoils System" by awarding Party loyalists with posts in his Administration. Much of his time later was spent trying to mollify unsuccessful Whig Party applicants.

Taylor's main concern during his sixteen months in office was the question of slavery in the new States of California and New Mexico. Both of them wanted to enter the Union as Free States. Taylor's solution was simplicity itself. If California wanted Statehood it should get it. If they wanted a slave-free State they the people were entitled to choose this path not Congress. Compromises were unnecessary. The anti-slavery lobby were delighted with this ruling. The Southern slave trade lobby "The Diehards" as they were known, rebelled and for the first time talk of secession was in the air. Taylor confronted them with the threat that he would personally lead an army against any State that carried out this threat to the Union.
He made many enemies by his stand on California and New Mexico and was constantly and unfairly criticised and harassed by bitter vocal Southern inspired factions in favour of slavery. Life on the battlefield was a lot more honest and uncomplicated. At least there, his enemies wore uniforms that distinguished friend from foe.

Zachary Taylor was not easily intimidated. In those times, security was unbelievably casual and Taylor during his Presidency was often seen strolling by himself on the streets of Washington. If only Peggy could do the same but unfortunately she resented Washington too much. As far as she was concerned Washington was taking her Zachary away from her.

Another little anecdote is about Peggy's revulsion and total rejection of life in the White House which was always directed by the First Lady. Margaret Mackhall Smith Taylor, known to us as "Peggy", was a loyal wife all her life. Frontier and army life didn't come easy to her.

She had enjoyed a New York finishing school before forsaking the fashionable sophisticated city life for the harsh realities of army life. She also bore him six children. But political life in the White House was something she did not want. After years on the road fighting wars beside her husband with all its dangers and drawbacks, now was the time to relax into a mellow old age. She was appalled at the prospect of the humbug of Washington society. Now she opted for a background role only, in her rooms upstairs in the White House. Betty Taylor Bliss, her daughter, newly married at twenty-two, took over the hostess role with ease.

But for Zachary Taylor, life was now different. He, metaphorically speaking, rolled up his sleeves and took on the politician's role head-on. It was said of him at the time "General Taylor never surrenders and his first surrender will only be to death itself." Zachary Taylor inspired firmness in the cause of freedom. He was the first U.S. President elected on his military reputation. Later Eisenhower was another. He was not a political animal and so any errors he made in office were down to inexperience.

Time would have taught him the complicated art of politics had he lived. He was wise, temperate, sincere and honest and a great Union supporter out of love for it. He would surely have died for it if asked. Simple in habits, blunt in manners and with a body language that impressed everyone who met him. He was as fearless in Administration as he was on the battlefield.

His very unworldly view of the political horizon, perhaps because he was no Statesman, helped him to see the future more incisively and with a clearer vision than some of his world renowned political colleagues. He was never credited with this by some condescending "experts" around him.

Although a slave-holder himself, he worried for its future and felt it should have its limits. He could be described as an honest patriot trying to be right. Unlike Knox, he was a natural friend of the common man. Had he lived, there is no knowing how he might have changed American history. His was a practical approach to the storms gathering on the issue of slavery. Such a key to the future was lost with this warrior's death.

Zachary Taylor bore the responsibilities of office bravely for a man more suited to the world of a soldier than that of a Statesman. Eventually such a lifestyle took its toll on a man too old for the change from one career to another at sixty-four years of age.

He first fell ill in September 1849 during a visit to Pennsylvania. But his passing was not a gradual process. Standing beneath the hot sun listening to patriotic speeches celebrating Independence Day 1849, he fell ill. That night he had an attack of cholera morbus or acute indigestion. He hung on to life for another five days. Some people blamed the long afternoon sitting in scorching sunshine while Independence Day was celebrated around him. Some even thought his over-indulgence of many helpings of cherries and milk brought on cholera. However, with no detailed scientific evidence to prove the cause of his sickness, posterity can only speculate today.

As the end drew near, during the next five days, the worry of office aggravated the President's condition. It turned to fever. It is unbelievable that on his death bed his tormentors threatened him with censure if he didn't support the slave interests he had opposed. But Taylor was too much of an old pro on the battlefield to allow himself to be intimidated like that, not even on his death bed.

Next afternoon he was shown to be dangerously ill and both Houses adjourned waiting for the worst. Taylor died that evening, July 9, 1850 - aged 65, with the last words – "I have endeavoured to do my duty." Even his enemies were moved by the stubborn bravery of an old man who refused to be bullied on his death bed by the Southern slave trade.

The pall bearers Clay, Cass, Webster and Benton followed him slowly down Pennsylvania Avenue, reminding many of the military fame associated with this illustrious General. Coloured plumes of white, red, blue and green waved in the breeze. The various uniforms representing the different military companies filed by with reversed arms to the brass band music of the funeral dirge.

Chief mourner among the officers was his old friend and colleague General Winfield Scott "Old Fuss and Feathers". Duncan's light artillery, who is claimed to have fired the first and the last shot of the Mexican War, was there. Behind the hearse or funeral car was Zachary's war horse "Old Whitey" richly adorned but with the saddle empty and stirrups reversed, never to be filled again, prancing along behind.

This scene was repeated all across America in the chief cities of the Union. One wonders if Zachary Taylor's daughter Sarah had not met Jefferson Davis all those years ago, would Zachary have happily retired a famous General? Without Jefferson Davis to encourage him, would he have opted for the Presidency against Peggy's wishes? Peggy declined Millard Fillmore's offer to postpone his entry into the White House as President. Her mind this time was made up. She had no wish to remain in a house with her husband's memories all around her. She moved out on July 13, the day of Zachary Taylor's funeral without attending the funeral ceremonies.

Zachary's remains were taken by train from Washington to Cincinnati and from there by steamboat to Ohio, then on to Louisville, Kentucky. He was buried in the family grave alongside his parents, brothers and sisters on the grounds of his home "Springfield" in Louisville. He could not now veto the 1850 Compromise or personally bring an army to stop the invasion of Texas as he had vowed to do. History would surely have re-written itself had he lived.

A final bizarre twist in the storyline is about a post-mortem that took place in 1991, one hundred and fifty years after Zachary Taylor's death. The question of his death by poisoning was, up to 1991, a vague suspicion. But the post mortem produced no evidence of such a conspiracy theory which had always considered Zachary Taylor's sudden death at that precise moment in American history a little too fortuitous to say the least for the pro-slavery forces in 1851. But the slavery issue would not go away. Webster in a foreboding speech to the Senate said "There are many other evils in the world besides slavery and the worst of them is war."

But time moves on as the new President takes up office. That was the Presidency Millard Fillmore was now about to inherit as the 13th President since Washington.

13th President   Millard Fillmore

"His Accidency"
Born 1800
Died 1874
74 Years of age
1 Term
1850 – 1853
Age 50

Party: Whig
Profession: Lawyer
County: New York
Ancestry: English
Estate: Value unknown.
Hobbies: Hunting, fishing swimming.

Physical Description: Height, 5 foot 9 inches; finely proportioned body; thin, greyish hair; blue eyes; light complexion; smooth forehead; well-developed chest.

No inaugural address:
Fillmore assumed the Presidency on the death of Zachary Taylor in office.

MILLARD FILLMORE

Zachary Taylor's short career in the Presidency of one year and twenty-seven days left Millard Fillmore the Vice President in command of the ship of State in the White House at a time of mounting controversy on the slavery issue. Peggy, Zachary's beloved wife, was so upset with Zachary's new found friends and his alien lifestyle as a politician in his final days, she could not wait to shake the dust of the White House from her shoes and walk away. So badly did she want to leave she didn't even wait to say goodbye to her beloved Zachary in his coffin.

For forty years she had endured the lifestyle of a soldier's wife with all its discomforts and drawbacks bore him six children and shared a companionship together with people she loved and respected. The fundamental core of her life was happiness. For his sake, she turned her back on her military friends, male and female. Blunt, honest, God-fearing people, a world away from the political humbug of Washington. Now protocol had no more hold on her and she left quickly.

Millard Fillmore, her husband's successor, had a completely different career path to Zachary. It was a world Fillmore was quite at home in. Yet his offer to delay his entry into the White House was genuine and quite typical of the man, which we will appreciate later.

But now let us discuss Millard Fillmore.

In 1798 Nathaniel Fillmore, father of the 13th President, settled in the township of Milton, Onondaga County with his family at twenty-seven years of age. Milton was a virtual wilderness then, in which they lived in a log cabin, 16 feet long and 14 feet wide. Behind the cabin a line of maple, pine and cedar trees grew. His nearest neighbour lived four miles away.

Millard later recalled how cut off from civilization they were during his childhood. He was truly the first of the hardy pioneers who started the nation.
Millard was born on January 7, 1800 and he wrote of that day as follows: "I cannot learn that event was marked by any striking signs in the heavens above or the earth beneath calculated to alarm the superstitious fears of the scattered inhabitants of that howling wilderness."

It is not generally known that the late Princess Diana Spencer, who married Prince Charles, heir to the throne of England, was related to President Fillmore through Fillmore's grandmother Ellen Wood. Lady Diana was a direct descendant.

Later, his father lost the land through a defective title but Millard saw no catastrophe in that because of the remoteness, coldness and roughness of the region. Incidentally, so remote was his home, his father had to walk seven miles in snow, two feet deep in the dead of night through the woods, with the wolves howling in the dark around him while he searched for a doctor the night Fillmore was born.

The region did have its advantages for Millard however. He lived for hunting and of course fishing and swimming in the local lake. Because of all this hardship, it is easy to understand why Fillmore's education was almost non-existent. His first school was an old deserted log house with only a few benches. And his lessons were based on reading and writing. School was only open for three months in the winter. He could not go in the summer because he could not be spared from his work on his father's farm. His main education until he was fifteen was clearing the undergrowth, hoeing, chopping wood, ploughing, mowing, reaping and logging. He was apprenticed to a trade, cloth-dressing, until he was twenty.

The family grew bigger and funds grew scarcer but Millard was happy enough. He spent every leisure moment reading and studying and his thirst for knowledge became insatiable for he read by firelight well into the night. The most important happening in his life was meeting his future wife, Abigail Power. Starting to study law under Judge Walter Wood was the second most important event in his life. Abigail was a teacher in the local school in Kelloggsville. She had a quick mind and intellect and Millard was a sitting duck as a student two years younger to fall for his teacher. She also helped to tutor him in all his weaker subjects.

Millard was 5 foot, 10 inches tall, had a rugged physique as would be expected of someone who spent so much time in frontier life. He was erect and had the frame and complexion of a woodsman. His blue sparkling eyes and thick blond hair gave him a handsome appearance.

Judge Wood owned most of the village of Aurora. He was very wealthy from his various business interests in the area having farms and tenants spread over a large part of the county. It was Fillmore's father who approached Judge Wood to teach his son the fundamentals of law in between his work as a clothier's apprentice, and so it was almost by accident that he found himself following his new career. In fact when Millard was told about his good fortune he broke down in tears. Balancing this emotion was a feeling of disappointment to know that reading the laws of England was compulsory for his studies. His initial reaction was to consider the whole thing a waste of time. But Judge Wood had every confidence in Millard; so much so, he managed to persuade him to drop his trade in cloth-dressing to concentrate on law full-time. Eventually he parted with Judge Wood and headed for the uncertain playing fields of New York.

Meanwhile Millard's father bought a seventy acre farm, one mile south of the village of Aurora. The area consisted of a small sawmill, a schoolhouse, a Baptist church, a tannery, a blacksmith shop, a general store and a tavern owned by Millard's uncle Calvin Fillmore. There were also a few houses scattered around.

One year later Millard arrived back from New York in the Autumn of 1821 and took a job teaching in the local school at Aurora for the winter. He combined this with part-time work on the lawsuits before Justices of the Peace. But once again his itch for travelling got the upper hand and Millard was off to greener pastures, this time to Buffalo. He awoke each morning early enough to study law before breakfast after which he headed for work in school teaching.

To widen his studies in law, he tried his hand as a law clerk for which he received no payment. His sacrifices paid off and he graduated. Returning to Aurora he opened up a law practice on Big Tree Road.

Millard was not the only one making sacrifices at that time for in far off Moravia a certain girl was one hundred and fifty miles away. Carrying on a love affair by post is a frustrating, painful way to share a romantic relationship but to Abigail Power's credit she endured it bravely.

The day arrived for their painful separation to come to an end when Millard set off by stagecoach which left Aurora Tuesdays, Thursdays and Saturdays for distant Moravia. He could not afford this journey before this. There in the house of her brother, Cyrus Power, they married on February 5, 1826. There were twenty guests at the wedding party. Some of these guests didn't quite approve of Millard who they thought was below the family in social standing, Abigail being the sister of a Judge. Imagine snobbery in the wilderness. How peculiar can the human race be? However, Abigail's sister approved of Millard enough to tell Abigail "Give my love to my new brother."

The happy couple went on to have two children, called Mary Abigail and Millard Powers Fillmore. Young Millard was born on April 25, 1826 two years later and Mary was born six years after that on March 27, 1832. Sadly, the little girl only lived until she was twenty-two years old for she died on July 26, 1854. Sadly short lifetimes seem to have been the curse of many young people in the America of those days.

The love of Millard and Abigail for each other was reflected in different ways. Observers couldn't help notice the attentiveness he showed to her, treating her with the gentle courtesy bestowed upon a guest. He would kneel before her adjusting her overshoes before she entered their carriage. An old friend remembers the smile of welcome she reserved specially for Millard but more significant was Abigail's letters, which revealed a heart-warming affection. Here is an extract from one of them;

January 12, 1834, 11 p.m.   I am now alone having put our little son to bed. Though I regret the loss of your society more than I can express, I am far happier having you at a distance with the assurance that you love me.

Their house in Aurora was known to locals as "the honeymoon cottage". It was restored in 1930 by Margaret Evans, wife of Irving Price, the Fisher-Price toys' tycoon, after he found it empty and deteriorating badly. It seems there may have been a church wedding held nearby for there is a plaque in St. Matthew's Church stating that the couple were married there.

After they settled down to married life, Abigail managed to get a job teaching in East Aurora which helped to supplement their income while Millard attended to his law practice.

As time went by, they became a much respected family in the community. Fillmore earned the admiration of everyone with his temperate habits and professional ethics. He also dressed the part of a well-educated pillar of the community. His thoughtful speech and good looks completed the picture of a well-groomed candidate for the political stage.

He soon came to the notice of some Anti-Masonic politicians headed by newspaper publisher, Thurlow Weed. They put Millard up for a seat in the New York State Legislature and he was elected at the first attempt. Thurlow Weed became his mentor and again put him forward for the House of Representatives and Fillmore once again won the seat, this time as a Congressman. Now a Whig (his Anti-Masonic Party had just merged with the Whigs), he found himself supporting the Whig Party in their compromise over slavery.

The big names of American politics were now part of the political stage on which Millard's life was moving. People like Jackson, Van Buren, Clinton, Quincy Adams, to name but a few. Yet there was always a reluctance on Millard's part to push for the major prize of President. His laid back personality just wouldn't allow Millard to claim the job he was perfectly groomed for. However the Gods had their own plans as we are about to find out.

Millard Fillmore came a step closer to the highest seat in the land when he was nominated as Vice President to Zachary Taylor who eventually won the election leaving Fillmore himself in the centre of the 1848 Presidential inauguration ceremonies.

When news reached his hometown of Buffalo about his election as Vice-Present, there was a great sense of pride and excitement everywhere. One neighbour told him with elation "Your friends here all felt they were almost Vice Presidents themselves." She was so carried away by the news she even proposed setting his house and barn on fire to make a bonfire suitable to the occasion. Mere tar barrels were too small she reasoned. Zachary Taylor was impressed by Fillmore and said so. "Your nomination will prove a tower of strength in all the Northern States." Notice how the United States of the 1850s was already polarizing into two factions, North and South, even in the vocabulary of Presidents.

Preparations for Zachary Taylor's election campaign got under way. A "Rough and Ready" club was formed at the Eagle Tavern in Buffalo's main street. They were also formed in other areas – New York, Harrisburg, Pennsylvania, Louisiana and Mississippi, to name but a few. Southern Whigs wrote to reassure Fillmore that the charges of abolitionist made against him had no foundation in their eyes. They talked of an abolitionist as if it was a dirty word. Even the great Henry Clay admired him as being "full of zeal and indefatigability".

A Whig through and through was the verdict. Undoubtedly a safe pair of hands, they concluded. All the newspapers wrote of him as the most calm, rational and safe candidate there could be to partner Zachary Taylor. In fact they went so far as to say he was known in Maryland as the abolitionists' most obnoxious opponent. I have found no record of Fillmore disputing this claim. They even named Fillmore as the greatest influence in the North to secure Taylor's Presidency. It is easy to see how the Presidency in the 1848 election was under a deep and penetrating expectancy for a lead on the slavery issue.

As we now know, victory went to Zachary Taylor. Fillmore wrote an almost prophetic letter to Zachary Taylor congratulating him on having made no pledges to his followers. He wrote "It is true that pledges form the footsteps by which mere partisans and faithless demagogues ascend to the highest political elevations but when the object of their ambition is attained, they find themselves so trammelled with the voluntary obligations which they have incurred in reaching it that they are no longer free to act for themselves or their country".
Did Fillmore suspect the kind of pressures out there waiting to bully Zachary Taylor to implement the Spoils System? Were these the same type of political parasites that lurked around the Presidency of John Tyler until he stamped his authority on his Cabinet? Were the same manipulators standing in the wings of Zachary Taylor's Presidency?

Unfortunately, they succeeded. Was this because of Zachary's political inexperience? Who knows? Sadly, Fillmore's Vice-Presidency was the main casualty as we shall learn later.

Millard Fillmore duly took the oath of office of the Vice President. The day was cold and snowflakes were falling. He missed Abigail who couldn't be there to share his triumph because of ill health. She didn't miss much. The usual obnoxious people were present deriding Zachary for his English pronunciation. To this snooty element he was still "Old Rough and Ready". Then how could he be anything else? Fillmore was acutely aware of these whispers designed to hurt and humiliate a great General.

He just marvelled at the dignity of Zachary Taylor through all the ceremonies. Millard could not help a flashback to his own early childhood on the frontier wilderness. The poverty and hardship his own family had to endure in those days struck him forcibly as they descended the stairs together and walked into the banquet to receive the congratulations of the guests – Senators, Congressmen, Governors and foreign Diplomats. Where were the pygmies now who taunted their President out of ear-shot? Millard couldn't help a wry smile at the thought.

And so Millard's Vice Presidency began. Strangely it was a carbon copy of the Vice Presidency of John Adams who, despite eight years in the job, always considered it so immersed in powerlessness and futility that boredom was an ever-present companion. Just like John Adams, Fillmore also found himself by-passed by his old mentor, Thurlow Weed who enjoyed the luxury of a direct line to the President in distributing political perks to his cronies. "My advice is neither sought nor given," Millard complained.

A light-hearted anecdote on his other frustration can be told here. It concerns the use of snuff in the Senate. By tradition, the snuff boxes provided for Senators were sited around the Chamber and filled by pages. (Incidentally the use of snuff in the Senate was accepted right up to 1976). In the 1850s one was placed just behind the Vice-President's dais. The rush for the snuff caused both noise and congestion.

Anyway it became so irritating, Fillmore complained about it to Isaac Basset, a page. "Take this snuff box away from here. I can't understand what is going on in the Chamber because of the interruptions and conversations of Senators who come here for snuff." I think the box was moved elsewhere after that. Also in the Senate Chamber at that time in 1849, some Senators were seen to enter the Senate with tobacco juice running down their chins. To cater for these Senators, spittoons were supplied and set up in strategic areas. Charles Dickens, during his visit to Washington, described the city as the headquarters of tobacco tinctured saliva.

There was, however, one exciting event which brightened up the Vice Presidency of Millard Fillmore, the Californian Gold Rush, which began in January 1848.

Get rich quick gold miners descended on California in thousands. They were nicknamed "The Forty-niners". These "Forty-niners" undertook some amazing journeys right across the Wild West of America from Europe and other distant places to try their luck at gold prospecting. Clipper ships were their main mode of travel and upwards of 700 clippers made the journey in one year. They carried people from not only Europe but as far away as Australia, South America, China and the Eastern seaboard of the United States. They faced colossal hardships on sea and land, sometimes braving the notorious sea route through the stormy oceans off Cape Horn. These hardy people could be as much as six months travelling West before reaching California.

Not all of them were successful. However, the early arrivals were lucky and enjoyed easy pickings but as the supply of gold dried up, mining companies took over with superior equipment. Soon the immigrants numbered at least 80,000 causing a breakdown in law and order. Eventually the chaotic situation led to Zachary Taylor changing the status of California from a territory into a State.

But destiny was now about to take a hand in Millard Fillmore's life that would change it forever. Suddenly Zachary Taylor's health went into decline and the whole ship of State was floundering in confusion.

Without warning he died. Now poor Millard was unbelievably the next President of the United States. It is a strange, strange story. Things were quite normal on the morning of July 4, 1850 when Zachary Taylor set out for the usual celebrations marking Independence Day. It seems during an afternoon of soaring temperatures he asked for a bowl of cherries and a pitcher of milk and he demolished the lot. The very lax sanitary conditions at that time have been blamed for the illness that struck him down with an attack of severe stomach cramps. That evening he was diagnosed as having a form of cholera which was not an unusual illness for those times. There was no panic. Five days later Zachary Taylor was dead.

There have been many suspicions and fears built on a conspiracy theory that Zachary Taylor,

12th President of the United States, was murdered by poisoning. These rumours persisted for one hundred and forty-one years until his body was exhumed in 1991. The post mortem proved fruitless however and the myth is still nothing more than an ancient rumour. And so the highest prize in the land went to Millard Fillmore - almost unwanted. It was said he was an accidental President and nothing more than a dark horse running mate of Zachary Taylor but by nature, Millard was a modest, unassuming man. He has been described as a man with little pretentions to the crown and was permanently surprised at where he found himself near the ultimate seat of power, one he never expected and never strived for.

Millard was also a loyal supporter of the Constitution. His philosophy was summed up in his inauguration speech for Vice President in which he promised that "The Constitution would be his guide and all its provisions would be equally binding." Neither of the following two Presidents, Pierce or Buchanan would be so loyal to the Constitution.

Fillmore's intention was to move into the White House straight away from Willard's Hotel where he was staying temporarily.

But on the day of Zachary Taylor's funeral, Fillmore's family had not arrived and he stayed instead in a villa in Georgetown, two and a half miles from the White House to where he commuted daily between the Villa and the White House. His day started at 6 a.m. in the White House and ended at 6.15 p.m. for his return to Georgetown in the evening by carriage.

One last word on poor Peggy Taylor, widow of the President. Peggy never did want her husband to go for the Presidency and had not spared Zachary her opinions on the subject. She had travelled the length and breadth of the land without complaint having no permanent home until just before he was elected President. Life seemed to have moved into the last tranquil journey towards Zachary's retirement. Together they purchased a large 2,000 acre estate at Baton Rouge and employed eighty slaves on the staff.
The last thing she wanted was a new career for her sixty-five year old husband, the champion of so many battles, and the victor of so many glorious conflicts.

But to her horror he accepted the challenge placed before him by politically astute handlers. Against those she had no hope. And now all she had left was the ashes of her broken dreams.

Peggy turned her face towards her beloved Baton Rouge. She couldn't face the funeral pomp and ceremony for a dead king, her king.

Leaving the funeral scene behind her she walked away from Washington forever.
Yet Millard Fillmore's transition from Vice President to President was a lot smoother than that of the 10th President, John Tyler. You may recall the precedent of the handover of power to the Vice President had been firmly set by Tyler after the death of Harrison in office in 1841. This time there was neither political begrudgery nor administrative jealousies like the unrest that soured Tyler's time in office. Thanks to Tyler, Fillmore would have a smooth transition to the Presidency.

Just one observation at this point in our story of the Presidents. What an amazing set of events effected the Presidency of the United States at that point in history! Two Presidents had died suddenly in nine years between 1841 and 1850 leaving the new Presidents to rule America while around them fear of Civil War was an everyday nightmare.

Poor Fillmore had every reason to be over-awed by his new situation. Surrounding him now were some of the greats of American politics in those turbulent times. Men like Henry Clay, Stephen A. Douglas, Jefferson Davis, John Calhoun and Daniel Webster to name but a few. Fillmore also realized he did not have the authenticity of an elected President.

Still Fillmore plunged on courageously into the cauldron of political debate going on about slavery. The gathering storm he saw just over the horizon was like an approaching cyclone. The unpredictable winds and surging tidal waves of opinion were already crashing on the lawns of the White House. Opposing camps had been established and the antagonists were growing in their midst. The challenge to his strength as a President was formidable.

The word abolitionist was on everyone's lips. Like a restless flock of geese settling down in the marshlands of Washington after a long journey, nobody was satisfied with their roosting place. Finding some certainty was the search that troubled abolitionists and anti-abolitionists alike. It would take time for this flock to rise and fall, squawk and gaggle, hover and circle, till they finally settled down on their own chosen greenery, separated by no definable line. Nobody was sheltering from the coming storm - eleven years away.

Judging by Zachary's pronouncements during his Presidency, he was going to be a real stumbling block to pro-slavery forces who must have been relieved at his parting and glad to be dealing with a more flexible Millard Fillmore as President. Yet despite Millard's easier personality, tensions still continued within the Cabinet. How fortunate Millard Fillmore was to be such a laid back personality. Not only had he to contend with his new role as President but, because of a simmering animosity within his Cabinet on issues that carried over from his Vice Presidency, he was forced to accept the resignation of the entire Cabinet. I say forced, because he did make a request for a stay of one month on their decision. They gave him one week. The same fate decimated Tyler's Presidency nine years before in 1841. Where were the George Washington's the country cried out for in those days?
I'm sure Millard must have smiled wryly at these gestures which were an insult to their dead President; especially when he remembered the advice of his old tutor, Judge Woods. "Tread lightly on the ashes of the dead." It seems his Cabinet had never heard of the saying or if they did, they only wore hob-nailed boots.

The question of Mexico was an ongoing saga like Vietnam, Korea and the Iraq war today. Even the decision of going to war was the subject of much criticism and debate. The saying that history repeats itself is not far from the truth, is it? The whole question of whether new States like Texas or California should be let into the Union, slave-free, was at the centre of hotly held opinions which threatened to boil over into Civil War.

Fillmore tried successfully to keep the lid on the boiling pot with "The Compromise" of 1850 and managed to build an uneasy peace that lasted another eleven years. In the meantime, the Industrial Revolution came to America as in Great Britain and turned society upside down. The North became more industrialized and its new power helped to defeat the South when Civil War did break out. But that tragic event would not happen for some time into the future.

Millard Fillmore's main source of trouble was The Compromise of 1850, the problems of which had been debated by some of the most powerful people in Congress for five months before he became President. It was a complex piece of legislation which aimed at defusing the mounting hostility between North and South on the slavery issued. But being a compromise, it was sure to satisfy nobody – coupled with it came the fugitive law as a sop to Southern slave-holders, making it easier for them to round up escaped slaves.

The Compromise was duly passed allowing California to enter the Union slave-free. It would not therefore split into two States - one allowing slavery, the other half banning it. Trouble piled up for him because in the middle of it all, Texas threatened to invade New Mexico and take land they claimed was rightly theirs. To discourage this invasion, Fillmore despatched 750 Federal troops to New Mexico. He then made a speech threatening to call in the militia and the U.S. navy to help keep the peace, if necessary. Yes, he had passed his first test. This was certainly not the style of the inept, indecisive President history painted him.

In fact it totally disproves the charge of Horace Greeley that "Fillmore lacks pluck. He means well but he is timid, irresolute, uncertain and loves to lean." Fillmore it seems has been hard done by in this type of criticism which in retrospect seems totally untrue and unfair today.

As well as The Compromise of 1850, the Fugitive Slave Law was ended, a major headache for Fillmore when he took up office on July 10, 1850.

This was a law that struck fear into the hearts of escaped slaves. Hundreds of them escaped northwards even before its enactment on September 18, 1850. Before this, every Negro was presumed a free man until proved a slave. The new law now made them the subject of persecution by slave-catchers trying to re-capture them. Thousands had fled to Canada. They achieved this by what was known as the Underground Railroad. To this day, Ontario has a small black community, the descendants of those who fled there in the 1850s. Mobs defended some prisoners in mass rallies. Some jails were openly attacked and the Negro prisoners set free. The President appealed for moderation but to no avail.

Fillmore's handling of the crisis established him as a strong President in contradiction to the usual criticism of a weak individual by some writers. He worked for compromise in all the contentious areas and acted honestly for the preservation of the Union. He abhorred slavery and the threat of war and felt the view of those down South should be understood better by the North.

The word compromise is a constant mantra we hear connected with Millard's Presidency. Passions ebbed and flowed not only within his Cabinet but out there beyond the walls of the White House where the issues on slavery were not being resolved by rational debate. Around that time the classic bestseller Uncle Tom's Cabin by Harriet Beecher Stowe was published stirring up the issues on slavery making Millard Fillmore's task even more difficult. Some people have claimed that the Civil War of 1861 was not about slavery yet the thirty years debate that tore the country apart in the years leading up to the Civil War was about nothing else.

Yes they were challenging times indeed for any American leader, yet the Presidency did have its compensations.

In the 1850s, Washington was a straggling, untidy shambles of a town and had no pavements whatsoever. Shops and private houses intermingled in an untidy crush of buildings. Yet, strangely enough the facade of the White House was just as you see it today. Elsewhere there were great empty spaces covered liberally with swamps, creeks, Cyprus trees and marshland.

While the location and environment was not very glamorous outside the White House, inside it the new residents strived to make the lifestyle of the President as comfortable and up to date as modern ideas would allow.

The first liability Fillmore tried to eliminate was the total absence of books in the White House when he arrived. It seems all his predecessors owned their own collections and made sure to take them with them when leaving. To rectify this ridiculous state of affairs, Millard Fillmore, with the help of Abigail, made a claim for $2,000 to the Senate for the purchase of books. The first three were a Webster's dictionary, a Bible and an Atlas. Soon the list grew to 270 books and 258 periodicals covering history, science, literature, art and the classics. The White House Library never had it so good.

Of course, the modernization of the White House by Fillmore didn't end there. There are many stories, some of which have become White House folklore embellished as they are by the passage of time. The tale of the first White House bath tub is one of the most notorious, even hilarious. There are even some cruel critics who say the creation of a bathroom in the Presidential mansion was among Millard's most noteworthy achievements. One writer wrote an essay in the New York Evening Mail on December 28, 1917 to celebrate the 75th anniversary of the bath tubs first arrival. It was really meant as a light-hearted piece of journalism written for laughs during the First World War to help lift the gloom of those depressing years. Unfortunately to the surprise of the journalist, it was taken seriously. As he put it later, it was comparable to the myth of George Washington and the cutting down of the cherry tree. Nobody really knows if Fillmore was responsible for the bath tub story but with the help of biographers and historians alike the myth now enjoys a reality it doesn't deserve.

A true anecdote worth telling is about the social life in Fillmore's White House. It seems Millard was fond of entertainment. Morning receptions saw the Marine Corps' Band sitting at the foot of the great stairway playing waltzes, dances and polkas together with operatic and classical pieces for the pleasure of the residents. They listened to songs such as "The Star-Spangled Banner" and "Auld Lang Syne" among many others. Hundreds of dignitaries attended New Year's Eve parties there including well known names like Henry Clay and General Winfield Scott, "Old fuss and feathers" himself. Celebrities from right across the social and political spectrum were commonplace. Distinguished visitors such as the writer William Makepeace Thackeray were invited to the White House. International stars of the stage at that time like Jenny Lind, the Swedish nightingale on tour in America played "Gigs in the White House".

Abigail, whose health prevented active participation at times, attended many receptions. Because of the wide range of celebrities, both national and international, attracted into the White House, the Fillmore's it is said, using modern parlance, were "The coolest first family" to occupy the White House in the 19th Century.

Another feature of Fillmore's Presidency was the rate of growth of the United States. At that time many States were expanding rapidly westward. In the previous fifty years the number of these States had doubled and the population explosion quadrupled. This new land of opportunity now extended from the Atlantic to the Pacific.

A sign of the times was the demise of some spurious age old traditions. For instance two of the oldest traditions of the Navy were abolished. The distribution of a rum ration to the crew – one tot per sailor – was discontinued. The other tradition to thankfully go was that of flogging. The abolition of this barbarous practice was criticised by the old "die hard" brigade who feared a disciplinary backlash as a result. Of course the backlash never happened.

Finally another milestone was when Commodore Perry set sail under Fillmore's orders in November 1852 to open up trade with Japan whose ports had been closed to foreign trade for two hundred years. The trip was successful and trade with Japan was opened up again.

After nine months in office, Fillmore decided to take a break and accepted an invitation to tour over the railway line just completed between New York City and Dunkirk. "Prosperity came with peace" was to be his message to the people as he travelled.

Crowd reaction for the President was quite an experience that took him by surprise. Wherever he stopped, large crowds met them. A banquet was held at Brainard's Hotel where he met the people. Security guards were non-existent as they sat in easy chairs on the train with a pleasant view of the passing countryside. On arrival at Dunkirk, they were welcomed by gunfire whistles, bands and an oxen roast in that small town of 800 people on the shores of Lake Erie. They later continued by steamboat to Buffalo whose people threw flowers into the Presidential carriage as it passed. A local newspaper commented "Never since the tour of Monroe in 1817 has a President been received throughout the county with such hospitable warmth, such universal cordiality and heartiness."

Once again, security was amazingly absent. "People thronged around his car with dirty faces and shook hands freely with him" was the report. At Rochester, church bells pealed and bands played. "The sun was shining," wrote one reporter. "Man and nature and art seemed to rejoice as if a jubilee were come." The response of the people on the trip refutes the contention that Fillmore was unknown and disliked.

Millard Fillmore's time in office, despite his political difficulties, had many enjoyable social events. One such banquet attended by 3,000 guests had on the menu turkeys, tongues, pigeons, ducks, geese, pigs, peaches, oranges, grapes, pears, apples, ice cream and bread. Such extravagant wining and dining was like a feast before a famine. It more than made up for the difficulties and pains of a country moving headlong towards Civil War in the not too distant future.

The death knell of the Whig Party tolled on the slavery issue after the 1852 election bringing to power Franklin Pierce as the 14th President of the United States. In four years it had been replaced by the new Republican Party led by Seward and Weed.

In March 1853 Pierce took over the Presidency and what a tragic year it proved to be for Millard Fillmore. Not because he lost the Presidency but because he lost something infinitely more precious and close to his heart. Abigail died. In the cold and penetrating winds of Pierce's inauguration ceremony, Abigail caught a chill and died. One month later, Millard returned home without the Presidency but worst of all without his best pal Abigail. Except for a half-hearted final try for the Presidency in 1856 won by James Buchanan, Fillmore settled down to retirement in Buffalo. He did take to the stage temporarily during Lincoln's reign, trying desperately for conciliation between the warring Parties, even opposing some of Lincoln's measures. After the Civil War he supported Andrew Jackson and took an interest in the University of Buffalo which made him its first Chancellor.

When pressed to push for the Presidency once again in 1860 as the only one with a chance to defeat Lincoln, he refused. "I have no desire under any circumstance ever to be President again. I feel I should have something to lose and nothing to gain."

Tragedy is as much a part of life as banquets. No man, no matter how famous escapes it. For Millard Fillmore it was the sudden death of his daughter Abby, aged twenty-two, at her grandparents' home in East Aurora which twisted the knife of sorrow in his heart. You will be familiar with Abby when I tell you she often acted as hostess in the White House in the absence of her mother through illness. The awful part of our story was that Millard never knew she had died until it was all over. That was the way news travelled or sometimes didn't travel in those days. Then, without warning cholera struck the family. Cholera was a dreadful disease to bring you down in those days, for medical science had no known cure to give hope to the victim. Not only had the powerful figure of Zachary Taylor succumbed to this monster, but Millard's brother, Charles fell victim to it on the very day Abby was buried. He was thirty-six. Twelve months after that triple tragedy and having no further Presidential responsibilities to bother him Millard decided to fulfil a long held ambition of his to travel abroad. So on April 24, 1855 he set off for Europe.

His passport papers read briefly "Millard Fillmore, ex-President of the United States, pass freely without molestation." Unfortunately nobody had told Mother Nature about this protocol and fierce storms were waiting for him in the shipping lanes between America and Europe. Three lifeboats were destroyed on his ship and the wheel house was damaged, injuring several sailors. Icebergs were another hazard that terrorized the passengers on a crossing that was commonplace for some seasoned old "sea salts" aboard.

Millard made no pretentions to bravery. At the height of the storm he just prayed. "If I ever reach Buffalo, I'll remain there." England couldn't appear quickly enough for him.

But England did eventually materialize from the darkness and stepping on shore, Millard headed straight for London with his entourage.

On June 12, 1855 six weeks after setting out from America, Millard was being introduced to Queen Victoria who was so impressed with his appearance she remarked "He is the most handsome man I ever met." But then again much had been written already about how handsome Millard was. One writer, having seen every President from Washington to Grant, praises his "massive figure, taller than average with fair complexion and Grecian mouth and the bearing of a Statesman." His presence at any function even after the Presidency was attended by vast crowds eager to see and hear him. There have been romantic stories attached to Fillmore too.

In 1967, one hundred years later, papers were uncovered showing correspondence with three different women, Rhonda Fuller, Dorothea Dix and Anna Ella Carroll, among others. Dorothea Dix was really a passionate crusader for the institutionalised insane and travelled over 10,000 miles seeking improvements in their conditions in State institutions. She was in constant touch with Fillmore on these issues and has been credited with founding and enlarging thirty-two mental hospitals in fifteen States as well as in Canada, Great Britain, Turkey and Russia. She was always considered a good friend of the family. Of the other two, I doubt if they stood a chance of winning his affections for his love affair with his beloved Abigail was far too intimate and permanent a memory for him in 1855.

While passing through England, Millard Fillmore was offered an Honorary Degree by Oxford University. When he saw the citation was in Latin, he declined saying "I had not the advantage of a classical education and no man should in my judgement accept a degree he cannot read."

He was very honest in his humility when writing to a biographer. "I have frankly stated the facts of my early history and as no man is responsible for the circumstances of his birth, they furnish nothing of which I should be ashamed or proud and therefore while they require no apology, they can justify no boasting."

Incidentally, later you will hear about a similar tour made by another ex-President, General Ullyses Grant, thirty years later, but let's continue with this one.

On June 14, 1855 the second day of his tour, he attended a concert featuring the music of all the great masters including Mozart, Mendelssohn, Verdi and Rossini, to mention but a few.

Dinner followed, attended by future President, James Buchanan and past President, Martin Van Buren. For one fancy dress function, Millard was given a cocked hat, sword, knee breeches, silk stockings, and silver-buckled shoes to wear. Looking in the mirror, he remarked to two friends, "Well, gentlemen, I never expected to come to this." His other places to visit were Windsor Castle, Westminster Abbey, the Bank of England, and a dockland tour of wine cellars although he didn't drink. His tour also included places as far apart as the Isle of Wight, Wales, Scotland and Ireland.

One glamorous event was a night at the opera in special boxes filled with distinguished guests and of course the Royal family. Finally a visit to the House of Parliament was essential. After London, Fillmore went on to visit Brussels, Cologne, Switzerland, Prague, Vienna, Berlin and Paris. His four week visit to Rome concluded with a visit to Pope Pius IX. He arrived back in New York on June 29, 1856 to a tumultuous welcome which took him completely by surprise. He had been away for twelve months.

Millard Fillmore was truly a popular President with his colleagues and charmed those who met him socially. He was an attractive man of distinguished appearance and has been described as gentle and affable. Horace Greeley sneered at him as weak and timid but as President Truman said about the pressures of the Presidency, "If you can't stand the heat get out of the kitchen." I doubt if Mr. Greeley ever stood in a kitchen like Fillmore's. Yes talk is cheap and criticism is easy for the one sitting on the fence.

But even more uncomplimentary is the opinion recorded by some "Americans" who look on his memory as a bit of a joke. They have now set up a Millard Fillmore Society that meets annually on his birthday to celebrate his invisibility. They say he takes his place among the unique group of Presidents such as William Harrison, Zachary Taylor, Franklin Pierce and James Buchanan, whose ineptness in the pre-Civil War Presidencies has now been derided by history. Unlike some of them, Millard was indeed truly working class. You can't help having sympathy for Millard Fillmore for he truly was one of the few American Presidents born in a log cabin.

Worse than that, his father even lost title to his humble cabin and was forced to return to his land as a tenant to which Fillmore returned also to work, helping out the family. His really was a humble beginning. Millard spent his latter days just strolling around his beloved Buffalo meeting his fellow citizens daily as an equal among friends. His end came as a sad surprise to all of them.

One Tuesday morning on February 13, 1874 he was shaving when his left hand fell powerless by his side. The stroke soon spread to his face on the left hand side. Breathing and swallowing became difficult. A second stroke inevitably followed. On March 8, 1874 just over three weeks since his first stroke, he had a second one. After declining rapidly he passed away at 11 p.m. on the night of March 18, 1874, aged seventy-four.

His obituaries in the local papers were full of praise for his priceless common sense.

One newspaper in Buffalo wrote a beautiful piece full of simplicity and sincerity. "His death creates a void that will not easily be filled. His stately form and fine presence will be missed by our citizens in their daily walks about the city."

There were many such tributes. The Richmond Dispatch referred to him as "a public man of the very best type… He leaves behind alas too few of his style of man."

A Buffalo newspaper posed the question "Could it be that living near to him we failed to adequately appreciate his greatness?" One went as far as to say "Had Fillmore been President in 1860-61, there would have been no Civil War."

At the funeral parlour in his hometown, a reporter described Millard "Lying as if in a profound slumber." His body was taken to St. Paul's Episcopal Cathedral where it lay in State. Three U.S. Senators were sent to attend the funeral which was accompanied by the army, court officials and other civic dignitaries on that cold windy March day in 1874.

Schools and stores were closed, and the streets were draped in black. The sorrow was heartfelt and universal. He was interred in the family plot in Forest Lawn Cemetery in Buffalo where his grave is now surrounded by a black iron picket fence.

The respect and dignity with which he was treated in death by the people and the newspapers defies the logic of those who try to tell us he was "infinitely forgettable".

He left office having left a surplus in the financial affairs of the nation for every year of his Presidency. His retirement after the Presidency lasted twenty-one years. A long time to be admired and loved. Most of all he died as he had lived, an honourable and decent human being. History will not forgive those pygmies who dare to deride him for they could only be people who never really knew Millard Fillmore.

But lets move on now to the 14th President Franklin Pierce.

14th President   Franklin Pierce

"Handsome Frank"
Born 1804
Died 1869
65 years of age
1 Term
1853 – 1857
Age 49

Party: Democrats
Profession: Lawyer
County: New Hampshire
Ancestry: English
Estate: $70,000
Hobbies: Unknown

Physical description: Height, 5 foot 10 inches, erect bearing; penetrating dark grey eyes, light complexion; smooth forehead; well-developed chest.

Extract from his inaugural address on Friday March 4, 1853

"Let it be impressed upon all hearts that, beautiful as our fabric is, no earthly power or wisdom could ever reunite its broken fragments. Standing as I do almost within view of the green slopes of Monticello, and as it were, within reach of the touch of
Washington, with all the cherished memories of the past gathering around me like so
many eloquent voices of extortion from heaven I can express no better hope for my
Country than that the kind providence which smiled upon our fathers may enable their children to preserve the blessing they have inherited."

FRANKLIN PIERCE

Away in the distant future now, the storm clouds of the coming Civil War were gathering, but the thunder of that catastrophe that lay ahead was neither heard nor noticed. Secessionists were hard at work trying to sunder the Union from its roots in the Constitution. While all this was taking place Congress stood idly by apparently powerless to act.

And so entered Franklin Pierce into the 14th Presidency on March 4, 1853.
Millard Fillmore's America was now beginning to polarise into two camps, those who supported slavery and the abolitionists who opposed it. Later, Lincoln the 16th President, was confronted with the prospect of two Americas. Those who supported the secessionists and had already formed a new Constitution and elected their own President. These came mainly from the Southern States.

The block of States that remained were loyal to the Union and were prepared to fight for their beliefs. Perhaps I do the secessionists an injustice for they too were prepared to fight for their beliefs.

Looking at the world through the eyes of the Presidents in the 1850s the landscape ahead was very bleak indeed.

The reason I start this little piece on Franklin Pierce drawing attention to America in the 1850s is to point out the strength of opinion that was gathering momentum pushing people, whole families, sometimes whole counties into two opposing sets of people, holding points of view that burnt like a forest fire within them, but it was a time for caution, a time for prudence. Yes it was a time for sensitive diplomacy so"Tread carefully" should have been the watchword in towns, taverns, villages and cities throughout the length and breadth of America. Unbelievably those at the top of politics failed this test of prudence. For the last two Presidencies before Lincoln, the people somehow contrived to place in charge of the nation two individuals, Pierce and Buchanan, with distinctly Southern or pro-slavery points of view. If this statement upsets the purists perhaps I've got it wrong, but these two Presidents can only be remembered with despair for the opportunity they lost between them over eight years to defuse and solve a political problem that was drawing America over the precipice into Civil War.

This article is about Franklin Pierce, the 14th President who by some fluke of the ballot box got himself elected as President despite not even being considered as a candidate for the Democrats in 1852.

Normally the voting in any election would not rate a mention as a significant feature
of the Presidency, but surely in this of all elections, it is right to highlight the fragility of the voting structure at the very pinnacle of American politics in such a seriously volatile situation around the America of the 1850s. Why, given the times that were in it, was it so easy to pick a low key dark horse when common sense cried out for a political heavyweight? This is a question that I am sure the historians and political analysts have debated since the 1850s – over one hundred and fifty years ago – without getting a satisfactory answer.

Later I will discuss in greater detail the dramatic ballot to select Pierce as the Democratic candidate for the Presidency in 1852.

Franklin went on to win the election. Who was Franklin Pierce you may well ask? Well he was a very affable personality and a great orator. He was the type of man who could be described as the politician's politician. A man with a strong magnetic chemistry in his make up, a good bar room companion with a definite desire to please. He was five foot ten inches tall, usually impeccably dressed with strong features; penetrating dark – grey eyes, an erect frame and a definite crowd pleaser with Washington society.

Franklin had all the right connections too, so let's return to his roots. He was born on November 23, 1804 at Hillsboro of pioneer stock. His ancestors arrived in Charlestown, Massachusetts in 1630, the year the Puritans set sail for America from England.

He was the sixth of eight children in the second marriage of his father General Benjamin Pierce. His mothers name was Anne Kendrick Pierce. Barbara Bush wife of the 41st President is said to be related to him.

Franklin's father, a soldier in Washington's army in the American Revolution had the greatest influence on him. His father had also been Governor of New Hampshire, a farmer and a tavern owner. Franklin's father actually sent him to Bowdoin College because he disagreed with the political philosophy at Dartmouth, a college his older brother had attended.

General Pierce it seems left nothing to chance in the education of Franklin who settled in well and soon made a wide circle of friends at Bowdoin including his future life long friend the novelist Nathaniel Hawthorne. Franklin duly graduated from college to choose law as a career in the practice of Levi Woodberry of New Hampshire. He also attended law school under Judge Edmund Parker and proved to have a definite aptitude for the subject. It was around this time in 1827 that his father was elected Governor of New Hampshire.

You can see why it was a natural event for Franklin to be attracted into politics. He duly made his first steps in that profession when he was elected to the Hillsboro County Convention as moderator where he served for six years. His father was a Jeffersonian Democrat and naturally Franklin followed in his fathers footsteps as a Democrat. It was then only a small step to move from the New Hampshire Legislature to the Congress of the United States, which he did when he was twenty-nine in 1833.

To read the foregoing I am sure you the reader shake your head in bewilderment after all it is almost a standard formula for many of the early Presidents to follow. School, college, law school and politics. None chose economics or history or even literature as a profession for graduation but now at twenty-nine here was Franklin Pierce with an impeccable pedigree for politics and an attractive personality that endeared him to Washington society. The only jewel missing for his crowning glory was an army career, a gap he was to compensate for in his adventures into the Mexican War.

The army career of Franklin Pierce was typical of the Spoils System that polluted American politics in those days. Yes, even the President was expected to participate in it. Pierce was no exception. It was always understood that progress in the army very much depended on one's family connections and background. With a father who was an ex-General, a wife with an aristocratic background and the personal friendship of ex President Polk himself, rapid promotion was a foregone conclusion. Apparently during the Mexican War his horse managed to fall on him and this accident coupled with various illnesses precluded him from further active service.

His rapid promotion therefore is not too surprising and his army career can be pieced together as follows: Enlisted as a Private in early January 1847, became Colonel on February 16, 1847, promoted to Brigadier General two weeks later on March 3, 1847 and almost three weeks later he resigned from the army on March 20, 1848. Duration of army career: fifteen months from Private to Brigadier General. What an insult to the serving soldier. And so it seems America lost one of the greats of military history when Pierce thought his talents too precious to be the preserve of the army. The stripes and the pips were really meant for his political career planned with precision for him by his father.

Those sponsoring him seemed to have no shame for the contempt they showed towards the real serving soldiers who in 1861 would die for their principals and their country. But that was politics in the 1860s. With the grand design for his career now formally in place the missing piece of the jigsaw was marriage. Pierce would not have found it hard to land an eligible mate given his obviously colourful personality, education and good looks. He could choose a wife from the crème de la crème of Washington society. He duly did and was married on November 10, 1834, aged thirty.

Of course the girl in question had the required pedigree being the daughter of Jesse Appleton, the late President of Bowdoin College, his old Alma Mater. Here I have to write a more sympathetic view of Pierce and give him credit for sincerity in his choice of soul mate. His new wife's name was Jane Means Appleton who was also his lifelong childhood sweetheart. They settled down to married life in Washington DC. Five months later they moved into their new home given to them by his proud father. The marriage was twelve months old when Franklin had to return to Washington leaving behind Jane his wife who was suffering from health problems which forced her to remain at home. But tragedy stalked his marriage from the start. On February 2, 1836 his first child a son Franklin was born but the joyful celebrations were short lived for Franklin junior died three days later on February 5, 1836.
Their second child Frank Robert Pierce was not born for another three and a half years on August 27, 1839. This little fellow was only four years old when on November 14, 1843 he passed away leaving both of them broken-hearted. Just who would want to live in America in those times carrying a little white coffin to the grave yard. The scene was repeated by thousands of Dads and Mams all over the country and the heart aches were unbearable to witness.

One persistent thread that runs ruthlessly through the lives of the early Presidents is the awful mortality rate of their young. The sweet nectar of success drained away quickly when Robert died and fate prevented them from ever having children or grandchildren again.

On January 6, 1853 tragedy struck a third time to Franklin and Jane when their last remaining little boy Bennie aged eleven, was killed just two months before Franklin was elevated to the Presidency. This was the last of their children who died before reaching his teens leaving them with no children after nineteen years of marriage.

Benny's tragedy happened in a freak train accident caused by the derailment of their carriage. Both parents escaped but little Benny was crushed before their eyes, a scene that had a lifelong effect on both of them. It leaves the writer choking back tears at the picture. So distraught was Jane even God was blamed for manipulating events to deprive her of her loving son Benny to leave Franklin free to concentrate on becoming President without distractions. But what man or woman can survive such memories. As you can gather she was inconsolable and after that, harboured a bitter resentment against Washington in general and politics in particular.

So much so she refused to attend his inauguration on March 4, 1853. However her anti-social behaviour towards Washington and politics had been known for some time by those around her. Nine years previously in 1842 the pressure she exerted on Franklin was so intense he was forced to resign from his Senate seat in deference to her wishes for him to get out of politics.

He returned home to New Hampshire in 1842 and resumed his law practice there for the next ten years. Although absent from Washington Franklin still took an active interest in politics. His support of the 1850 Compromise gained him many friends in the South who were quite useful to him later in his bid for the Presidency.

However Franklin was really a very generous human being whose eyes were not always reoccupied by the pinnacles of power. A nice little story is told of his sympathy for a sickly girl whose ill health deprived her of a proper education.

Franklin took her into his care and looked after her welfare. His kindness and support reaped rich dividends for he was instrumental in creating a wonderful human being named Mary Baker Eddy. She later was the founder of a new branch of Christianity called Christian Science. What a wonderful outcome to an unselfish act of love and comfort by Franklin Pierce.

All this took place in the life of a man who was suffering from a terrible affliction himself, the disease of alcoholism. High living seems to have given him a liking for alcohol bordering on addiction. Sharing a home with anybody suffering from this terrible sickness can be very difficult. Sadly his wife Jane was suffering from her own kind of melancholy, and she just could not cope with or understand the disease of her husband. It is easy to appreciate why Franklin's life on the Presidential scene was truly amazing despite his personal and marriage problems.

Franklin had a rough and tumble career in politics and never seemed to have the same charm offensive for politicians, as he reserved for the social butterflies of Washington society. Unfortunately, the positions he took on many issues reassured and alerted the people who selected him for the Presidency. Sadly he held the type of views that pleased them. Choosing him therefore was no accident.

However his politics drew him into the pro-slavery camp. In Congress he actually voted against the Bill recommending an end to slavery. The Bill was defeated. He also held an anti-West bias and showed it by voting against the National Roads Bill and after that a Rivers and Harbours Bill. His pro-slavery views were known to many and his closest friend was Jefferson Davis who was later to be voted President of the new Confederate Parliament and who was also known for his radical pro-slavery views. To even recommend Pierce for the Presidency was disastrous in a world crying out for a steady hand on the bridge of State. So how was he elected?

Franklin was no wilting violet for like Van Buren he was a great believer in a well oiled, well run political machine. He liked to think of the Party, like an army which couldn't operate effectively without a tight chain of command. But the slavery debate was now so polarised and passionate it was already ripping the Democrats into factions. The main problem was bringing together all those opposing factions under one roof so to speak. When nominations for the next Presidency were sought Franklin was not even considered for the job. We will discuss later how he was elected. At this point since the question of slavery is the main theme running through this piece it might be helpful to discuss the whole history of slavery and plantations. What sort of inhuman system was it that drove a million men to fight for four years in one of the bloodiest wars in American history leaving half a million casualties behind on the battlefields of America, and where were the leaders who could have cooled the passions and lead the nation away from those battlefields in the years leading up to the Civil War?

Let's go back to the beginning and investigate the fabric of slavery in America during the Presidencies of Pierce and his successor Buchanan. Let's have a look at its history as far as it makes sense to you and me. When Africans were first brought to Virginia in 1619 their status was confusing. Some were looked on as slaves for life. Others were treated as indentured servants. Many bought their freedom from their masters and some even became planters themselves. Access to black slaves from Africa was a mere trickle because most of them were sold in Barbados where slave traders received a better price for them.

One important factor can be noted here. What made their lives more bearable was the way they integrated as families into plantation life with their own language that blended English with their African tongues. Here another clash of cultures emerges.

Native born blacks treated black slaves with disdain. Despite this the black slave was a more rounded character who embraced Christianity and expressed it with vibrant African feelings especially through their music. It is easy to understand rebellious clashes between these two groups of blacks though they were very rare. However the fear of uprisings was constantly there on plantations and tough defensive measures were always in place to discourage them. Now comes the sinister side of the system. Built into it was the understanding that not only were slaves to be slaves for life but so were their children after them.

As the plantations expanded and plantation owners became wealthier, the demand for slaves increased. But in 1808, thanks to a man in far off England called Wilberforce, a law was passed banning the importation of slaves which caused a severe restriction in the number of slaves available to the planter. To compensate for this, slaves were encouraged to increase their offspring. Since these offspring would also be slaves for life, the system had truly become corrupt and evil. Fear however stalked the plantations. Fear of uprisings and conflicts among the slaves. Because the master had access to the power brokers, laws were passed to facilitate life on the plantation that was illogical, illegal and downright immoral. For instance a master who killed a slave was excused on the grounds that no rational person would deliberately destroy his own estate. The master's "estate" in this case was the slave who was just as much his property as his house or his carriage.

While a good relationship was usually enjoyed between the master and his slave families, a lot of the master's trouble emanated from his overseers or plantation managers.

Overseers were usually the younger sons of other planters working for experience of plantation management. They also came from the ranks of middleclass farmers.

There was a great mobility in this class of labour and many had no interest whatsoever in the plantations welfare or that of the slave.

Now let's look at some statistics: -

A survey was carried out at that time as follows. To be called a planter required the ownership of twenty slaves. In 1860 there were more than 46,000 plantations registered. Of these, 8,000 plantations had fifty slaves. There were 2,000 plantations with 100 slaves, 11 plantations had 500 slaves and 1 plantation actually was registered with 1,000 slaves. The planter was looked up to as a leader of society not unlike the status enjoyed by the British Aristocracy back in England. Only 4% of adult white males owned all the slaves in the South mostly producing cotton, tobacco, hemp, sugar and rice. Out of a white population of eight million people 400,000 were small farmers who had ambitions themselves to become planters in time. They aspired to the planter's privileges of easy access to education, the arts, music and integration into politics. So they were sympathetic to all the planters' decisions and would never challenge any injustice they saw. But discipline based on fear was ruthless.

One of the most heartbreaking methods of discipline against the slave who got into serious trouble was to send him away forever to other plantations hundreds of miles away never to be seen again by his family. Just think of it. A sister, a brother, a son or daughter, was gone forever. Surely an act of pure evil. The fabric of society was complex and free blacks and black slaves were about equal in number. The difference was that the free blacks were the skilled artisans like cobbler's, carpenters and blacksmiths. The vast numbers of small farmers were known as Yeomen Farmers and were also known as poor whites or "White Trash".

The Yeoman Farmer moved constantly seeking better land and marketing outlets and passionately opposed the setting free of slaves. "If they were free they would think themselves as good as us" was their "mantra". This underbelly of a privileged society for the rich was corrupted with greed, fear and self-preservation among this underclass. Most important of all they posed no threat to the planters who they were glad to support for selfish reasons.

Ironically some of the free blacks who had been slaves became prominent in the "Underground Railroad" famous for spiriting away runaway slaves to North America and Canada to help them escape the fugitive laws. These fugitive laws were legislation created to help agents to recapture slaves and return them to their masters. Slaves were truly chattels. Remarkably, even Indians or Native Americans came to own slaves and later fought against the North on the side of the Confederate army. Well that is my amateur attempt to describe roughly the kind of complicated society that bubbled away down South in 1860, seemingly oblivious to the injustices they lived with daily and the plight of their fellow men.

Now we can return to the Presidency of Franklin Pierce. To another world which was oblivious to the South's festering wounds crying out for attention as America moved almost helplessly towards Civil War. But history will always have a wealth of retrospective wisdom built into it. A deep seated wisdom that is seldom revealed until it is too late for corrective action. The exception of course was Churchill and Roosevelt in recognising the evil of Nazism in a sleeping world but that's a story for later.

Now we come to that crucial ballot in 1852 at the Democratic Party Convention. Given this background dear reader I am sure you will scratch your head amazed at the vulgar horse-trading for votes at the Democratic Convention to select their candidate for the Presidential election of 1852. Cheap and undignified might be a better description for it. Hot debates and frantic canvassing went on for days in an effort to find a united front for the Presidential election. Only at the 35th ballot was Franklin Pierce's name introduced for nomination. On the 48th ballot his total votes were still only 55. We don't know what undercurrent or hard nosed bargaining took place but there was a sudden overwhelming change of voting pattern which nominated Pierce as the Democratic candidate for the Presidency by the extraordinary majority of 283 votes from 289 votes cast. The dark horse Franklin Pierce had won and the die was cast for another slumbering Presidency.

How did it happen? It seems Pierce being a Northerner with pro-slavery views and acceptable to the South would now be presented by his influential friends as the ideal candidate for the times that were in it. A pledge to end all further debate on the slavery issue was the icing on the democratic cake that would stitch everything up.

Sadly the struggle to find a compromise candidate mainly to suit the needs of the Democratic Party, but not the need for a strong experienced visionary as required by the people, leaves us with a sense of grave misgivings for the future and no one seemed to be worried. There was now only one hurdle to be negotiated and that was the Presidential Election itself.

Support for "The 1850 Compromise" a law I will explain later was as important for the Whigs as it was for Pierce's Democrats so there was no clash on this issue between Pierce and his opponent General Winfred Scott. The dramatic collapse of the Whig Party which later became absorbed into the new Republican Party headed by Lincoln gave Pierce an easy passage to the White House giving him victory by 254 votes to 42.

The one sinister outcome of the election was the way everyone had sidestepped the question of slavery, despite the fact that it should have been the main problem to be tackled and one that just wouldn't go away. The easy passage Pierce enjoyed leaves many question marks about the ballot for Pierce hadn't even been considered as a dark horse before the election. Up to then he was merely an insignificant player hovering on the edge of the hustings. Now he was the willing tool of the pro-slavery camp as President.

While it took tallymen by surprise the shock result simply bowled his wife Jane over. She fainted. But who could blame her. She had prayed to her old friend God hoping he had forgotten the criticism she had heaped upon him earlier on the death of Benny. Unfortunately God hadn't forgotten her harsh words and once again put her to the test by ignoring her pleas to stop Franklin getting the Presidency. Franklin won through, Jane lost once again, and her relationship with God deteriorated another notch. The rest is history.

Inauguration day arrived on Friday March 4, 1853 when Pierce took the oath of office on the East Portico of the White House. A cold biting northeast wind was blowing when Chief Justice Taney swore him in as the 14th President of the United States. Pierce made a 3,319 word speech without notes. Early on the crowd numbered about 80,000 but the cold weather and the falling snow reduced the audience to 15,000 before he finished. The loss of Benny had a devastating effect on Pierce though he did not show it. Apparently the young lad had been looking forward to inauguration day and his father's speech. The ache in his father's heart can only be guessed at as he stepped up to the podium in the falling snow.

Franklin couldn't help referring to his dead son. Perhaps as a father he had promised Benny on the other side of eternity that he would give him a mention. Any father would. It was misunderstood by cynics who accused Franklin, not to his face, of seeking sympathy. I am sure the President had more respect for his dead son's wishes than the mercurial loyalty of the hangers on. Jane wasn't too impressed by the critics either and she dismissed them with indifference preferring to choose her own lifestyle and social circle from that day on.

After his inauguration speech the grandstand erected for the occasion at a cost of $322, including the cost of paying sixteen extra policemen, was taken down. Because the inaugural Ball, originally meant to take place at Jackson Hall was cancelled, a reception was held in the White House instead. It was a very low-key affair since Franklin was still in mourning for his little son Benny. Jane didn't attend the reception or the inauguration. She was still angry with everyone. Yes, it was a very low-key day indeed.

The first decision of his Presidency was to retain the same Cabinet for four years. His Vice President created history when by a special act of Congress he was allowed to take the oath of office in far off Havana in Cuba. William Rufus Devane King died out there six weeks later on April 18, 1853. He never carried out any of the functions of his office and therefore never presided over the Senate. I suppose you could call him the Vice President that never was.

The New York Times described this period of American history with a very cynical quote "We have fallen on great times for little Men." It was a very inept style of Presidency Franklin Pierce practiced. He continued his policy of limited Government with a definite bias bordering on the deferential towards the powerful Southern wing of the Democrats. It was said he piloted the ship of State right onto the rocks of secession.

We have mentioned this earlier, that this was the time of "Manifest Destiny". Expansionism consumed everyone as they used "Manifest Destiny" to justify adding millions of acres to the frontiers of America. "Manifest Destiny" was the "Mantra" used to claim that God supported America's right to expand westward regardless of the Indians in their path and Pierce fully subscribed to this mantra.

His three targets were the acquisition of Alaska, Cuba and Hawaii, and the building of the Transcontinental Railway which required land held by Mexico. Pierce failed to acquire Cuba, Hawaii or Alaska, and by refusing land grants to settlers and aid to the westward railway line before he left office he managed to alienate the Western Democrats into the new Republican Party.

However the biggest blunder of his career was still to come when he made a speech in his retirement viciously denigrating Abraham Lincoln. At the end of his term of office Pierce became the only President elected to office who was not re-nominated. Except for the twelve months he spent travelling around Europe in 1857 - 1858 to Portugal, Spain, France, Switzerland, Italy, Austria, Germany, Belgium and England the rest of his retirement he spent sniping at Abraham Lincoln.

In one reckless speech he accused Lincoln of attempting "To butcher the white race to inflict freedom on the Negroes who were incapable of benefiting from it."
He lost all his friends after that. All that is except two people, his lifelong friend the writer Nathaniel Hawthorne and his ever faithful wife Jane. When she died of tuberculosis on December 2, 1863 he had but one friend left, Nathaniel Hawthorne.

But on May 19, 1864 Hawthorne died too. Franklin now had no friends, no wife and no children for the remaining lonely six months of his life.

Death came mercifully to him at his home in Concord on October 8, 1869 of complications from chronic stomach problems and dropsy. Perhaps today it might have been diagnosed as cancer. No one will ever know.

But at least the remaining unhappy years of his life were thankfully over. At last he could be reunited with his five best friends, Nathaniel Hawthorne, his own long suffering loyal and loving wife Jane, and of course his three children, Franklin, Robert, and his tragic little son Benny. Franklin Pierce was buried in the old North Cemetery, Concord, New Hampshire in October 1869.

15th President   James Buchanan

"Sage of Wheatland"
Born 1791
Died 1868
77 Years of age
1 Term
1857 – 1861
Age 66

Party: Democrat
Profession: Lawyer
County: Pennsylvania
Ancestry: Scotch-Irish
Estate: Value unknown
Hobbies: Not known

Physical Description: Height, 6 foot; imperfect vision; light complexion; protruding chin; short neck; muscular appearance.

Extract from his inaugural address Wednesday March 4, 1857:
"What a happy conception, then was it for Congress to apply this simple rule – that the will of the majority shall govern to the settlement of the question of domestic slavery to exclude it therefore, but to leave the people thereof perfectly free to form and regulate their domestic institutions in their own way subject only to the Constitution of the United States."

JAMES BUCHANAN

The successor to Franklin Pierce, James Buchanan was born at Stony Batter, Franklin County, Pennsylvania on April 23, 1791. Franklin County is on the borders of Maryland and lies in a picturesque rural countryside covered generously with valleys, mountain springs and a fertile farming soil. The area boasts an immense mountain range running from north Georgia and Alabama to north-eastern New York. Buchanan's birth place was in a house situated in a gorge of these mountains over which towered the hills which surrounded it protectively. Being one of eleven children was no handicap to James whatsoever. Writing about the surrounding areas is like a stanza from a beautiful poem which describes meandering streams and an ancient cabin in the midst of true American grandeur and cries out to be treated with eloquence.

It is impossible once again to separate the hardship from the beauty, the poverty and self-denial from the richness of nature, in the life of another early U.S. President.

Buchanan's father was an Irish immigrant from Donegal, another rugged beauty spot on the west coast of Ireland, who came to live here as early as 1783. He was poor when he came to start a new life in a new land but his commitment to hard work was part of his character. He felled the trees that made a clearing for his log cabin and with his young wife brought into the world a little boy who was to grow up to become 15th President of the United States.
It would be a romantic beautiful beginning for any fairy story but those primeval forests, mountain streams and loving tough God-fearing parents really did produce a little boy, then the youth and later the man who would one day hold sway over the Senators of the United States in ruling this new and far flung Continent.

Buchanan had one advantage however that was to prove the jewel in his crown; a father with an excellent English education and the intellect to appreciate such an advantage.
His mother was familiar with the leading poets and writers like Pope, Cowper and Milton among others. Her Irish background gave her a fervent religious outlook to mould the character of young James. She was certainly a major influence on his life.

When James was eight the family moved to Mercersburg three miles away and it was here he took his first lessons in English, Latin, and Greek and soon displayed a remarkable mind. At fourteen he entered Dickinson College at Carlisle, Cumberland County and rapidly rose to the top of the class in his studies.

Acquiring knowledge came easy to the lad. Daily, he learned the art of fact-finding and memory which would serve him so well in later years. He was a natural boy in his private life and was often in trouble for his practical jokes.

His well-balanced personality projected a kind and even tempered disposition which made him very popular with his school mates and he eventually graduated with honours in 1809 at eighteen years of age.

James was quite tall, slim and handsome and like many frontier boys learned to use his rifle skilfully. So skilfully he demanded pin point accuracy of himself even when shooting squirrels. Life in the rough and ready world of the wilderness built up his stamina and health, a fact he would come to appreciate when long arduous hours in politics demanded great staying power of him later. James Buchanan also had an eye defect which caused him to close one eye to read and being short-sighted didn't help either. He has been described as a sound, honest, generous and uncomplicated individual.

His next step into the future was on the road to a law degree which he duly acquired on November 17 1812, three years after leaving college. He was now twenty-one years old. The competition was tough in the State of Pennsylvania where the legal profession had its own vast fund of leading lawyers famous throughout the land.

It seemed Buchanan's life to this point was a long succession of personal triumphs. But poverty was always a close and depressing companion for him, so his exertions in the job were always tinged with that extra urgency to succeed if only for the rewards involved especially for his family.

But still his star continued to rise. At twenty-six he defended a Judge, unassisted by Senior Counsel, and won. At thirty-one he eventually reached the pinnacle of the legal profession. He was now the crème de la crème of the lawyers with a wealthy far flung legal practice to prove it.

Pressure was now on him to take up politics full time. At the age of forty he retired from the legal work and only came out of retirement once to defend an aged widow being ejected from her home. He won the case against all the odds and then refused any payment for his services. To those who knew him that was not surprising, for Buchanan was always a very kind and generous person. But let's turn the spotlight on his early years.

Up to this time his career had been a very constructive and successful one but into every man's life a little rain must fall and Buchanan was no exception, for a very bizarre incident happened to him in 1819 when he was only twenty-eight years of age. At this point he was quite wealthy and trustworthy, and a "pillar of society" when he met his first and last love Ann Coleman. Despite his fame, her father, a very wealthy iron mill owner suspected James Buchanan of being a "Gold Digger" or fortune hunter. Nevertheless Buchanan and Anne Coleman fell deeply in love and were engaged to be married.
A strange quarrel broke out between them and like many lovers quarrels it was based on a misunderstanding. For some reason Anne was consumed with jealousy they say and she broke off the engagement. That was in early December 1819. The tragic end to this story is that they never resolved their differences. Sometime near the end of that December 1819 Anne took an overdose of drugs and died.

The episode affected James Buchanan for the rest of his life for he never got married though he was always a very eligible bachelor. There was a mystery about the whole affair which has never been satisfactorily explained. The two tragedies were heartbreaking, the breaking off of the engagement and her suicide. Underlying everything was her insane jealousy and her father's objection to her relationship with James.

Perhaps there was another woman involved, who knows? Whatever the reasons could have been, they pushed her over the edge and to any caring human being nothing in this life could ever merit such a horrible ending. As Dolly Madison wife of the 4th President used to say "Nothing in this life is worth worrying about."

Anyway let's move on. Having painted a portrait of James Buchanan from his birthplace through his boyhood years and on into his legal career it would seem his story should end right here at the age of forty-two but there is more to come, much more. His challenge for the White House in 1857, twenty-five years later is worth waiting for. It is said that when he finally turned the key of the White House door to start his Presidency he was easily the most accomplished politician around. Not only because of his legal career but because of the wide experience he had acquired in public life up to that time.

Buchanan's political life so far reads as follows: - Besides being an ex-member of the Pennsylvania State Legislature for many years he had spent five terms as Congressman before he was thirty years of age.

He had been Minister to Russia in the Andrew Jackson Administration for eleven years. He had also been a U.S. Senator from 1834 – 1845. President Polk recognised his talents making him Secretary of State which was a plum job that enhanced his future Presidential prospects. Now a Democrat, he was just beaten by President Pierce on the 49th ballot for the Democratic Nomination in 1852. Because of his impressive showing in 1852 he was promoted by Pierce as Minister to the Court of St. James in London and that completed a wonderful international portfolio for his 1856 Presidential Election campaign.

I have tried to be as accurate as possible about all the foregoing but the object of the exercise is not to claim political super stardom for Buchanan but to lead my reader to the question that comes easily to the lips of a critic of his Presidency as follows.

Why, given all this background, did Buchanan fail in the Presidency? Why did he fail to read the signs of history, not written in the stars, but in the political cauldron around him?

In view of all I have written what quality was missing in the last two Presidencies before Lincoln to avert the terrible Civil War of 1861? What questions can we ask Buchanan? Why did he not use his vast legal and political expertise to head off the catastrophe? Could it possibly be he had not got the stomach for the job? Perhaps we can get the answer to our dilemma before I finish this piece on Buchanan. I'll have to leave it to you the reader to study the evidence and make your own mind up.

Meanwhile, his inauguration was taking place on Wednesday, March 4, 1857 so let's go there.

The usual festive crowds turned up with large unusual floats. Models of battleships and "The Goddess of Liberty" were among many such inventions on display. Regardless of hype or haggling on political issues the people of the mid 19th century just loved their elections every four years to crown a new Commander-in-Chief. Issues faded into obscurity as they gathered from all over the country to celebrate the occasion. It was one great big party. A Razzamatazz that just could not be missed by anyone. Visitors from hundreds of miles away usually made the journey for this one big day in Washington. Those who organised the event were never lacking in their imagination on how to present it.

In Buchanan's case a special building to hold six thousand people at a cost of $15,000 was erected on Judiciary Square for the inaugural Ball. In Madison's day they danced in the White House, broke the windows in the crush, and ended up drinking on the lawns.

Now for Buchanan's inauguration Two halls were needed to run the show - one for supper, the other for dancing. The dimension of one may seem irrelevant but 235 feet long and 75 feet wide is quite an area for dancing. Its ceiling was covered in gold stars and its walls were painted red white and blue.

The P.R.O. was quite accomplished and engaged a forty piece orchestra. It may be worth mentioning the quantity of food and drink consumed at this lavish event - 40 gallons of oysters, 60 saddles of mutton, 4 saddles of venison, 125 tongues, 75 hams, 500 quarts of chicken salad, 500 quarts of jelly, 1200 quarts of ice-cream and a cake four feet high. The cost of the wine alone was over $3,000.

It looks like some very rich supporters paid for it all.

There is no record of any special admission card to get into the banquet. I'm sure there was but, if previous inauguration feasts are anything to go by I'm sure there was no shortage of gatecrashers.

Before we place the crown on Buchanan's head let us pause for a moment to ponder on his career to date. When we do it is easy to see how fortune had constantly smiled upon him. The fates were always with him. Each new achievement was a logical progression upwards but little did he know now that the Gods of fate were no longer smiling on him. Perhaps they were bored. The rising graph of his achievements since he first set out as a fourteen year old boy going to college in 1805 was about to come to an end. Yes the Gods had chosen an ignominious end for the 15th President James Buchanan.

But what went so badly wrong that he left office the subject of derision and contempt? So flawed were his final years in politics even the great Lincoln, his successor, blamed him for the chaotic, vacillating, rudderless ship of State he had inherited from Buchanan.

It is one thing to be a brilliant academic and lawyer and even an able Minister to Russia and England but it requires a special talent of courage foresight and vision to be President. Unfortunately when the time came for James Buchanan to ascend to the final pinnacle of power he found he was for the first time short of the qualifications he needed most for the ultimate job in the land, leadership.

Leadership I hear you gasp? Yes Leadership and there was nothing he could do about it. Because leadership is a truly instinctive talent or gift bestowed only on the very few. James Buchanan sadly was not one of these.

And yet are we being fair to the 15th President when we say this? Perhaps it was only the quality of leadership that was at fault.

Maybe he was just unlucky to be President in an era that called for different talents. In any other age with his vast intellectual and political background he would have had a glorious opportunity to develop America westward alongside the covered wagons of the pioneers. In 1861 America was in a state of turbulence sitting as it was on the edge of the Industrial Revolution. It had a developing infrastructure of rivers, railways and canals with commerce ready to launch the country into the explosion of an economic boom.

Would a different leader have had the vision to foresee the future like this and so harness all the powers of State, manpower, and machines to reach out to that vision? Yes maybe a different leader just might.

Perhaps a Washington, a Jefferson or even a Franklin D. Roosevelt could have defused the ticking time bomb of pro and anti-slavery camps and diverted peoples energies into a more peaceful and productive dream that all of the above named once cherished.

That type of President, history and America needed just at that time simply wasn't there. Yes perhaps we were expecting too much of Buchanan, Pierce, Fillmore, Polk and Harrison at what was truly a crossroads in American history. Perhaps the expectations were just too much for all of them.

Here let's pause for a moment and ponder what Buchanan had inherited in the Presidency. It might be helpful to realize the festering passion about slavery and abolition and all the attendant fears that played havoc with the hearts and minds of ordinary people in Buchanan's day. Passions which were just simmering beneath the surface of society in 1856 had been gathering momentum for the previous thirty years all through other Presidencies.

Evidence of this was recorded in a publication in the 1830s called Niles Weekly Register which described the mob riots that flared up from time to time. One such report referred to an attack which took place on the printing office of the local press in Cincinnati in 1836. The owner was Achilles Pugh who had openly supported the abolition. Niles Weekly Register wrote as follows "The machinery was broken up and flung into the streets." The mob accused the owner of being in the pay of autocrats in Europe.

The other owners were warned "If any of you are foreigners you are advised to be silent on the question of slavery." Later the mob assembled on the corner of Main and Seventh where Pugh's press was located. They broke into the shop then headed for his home. Finding nothing there they paid a visit to the other owners' homes. They then returned to Pugh's press took out the machinery and threw it into the river. The second phase of the mob rule got ugly. They picked on Negroes rather than abolitionists huddled together in a seedy part of the city. Here the mob was repulsed by gunfire but they attacked again and demolished the houses. Only the intervention of the Mayor prevented serious bloodshed and the Negroes returned again to their homes but not before the mob attacked six or seven Negroes, broke up their furniture and smashed all their windows. That was America thirty years before Buchanan.

Another incident much more serious happened in September 1841 in Cincinnati. It started with a row between a few white and black boys. A battle followed in which four white boys received serious knife wounds. The white community was enraged and a riot began which lasted from Friday evening until Monday morning when Cincinnati was at the mercy of the mob numbering anything between 200 and 1,400 people in which dozens were killed on both sides.

Yet another disturbance is written about this time it happened in New York. In 1834 there had been trouble brewing about abolitionism as abolition mobs roamed the streets of New York. The blacks armed themselves and waited for the night assaults. As news spread about the stock of ammunition guns and other hardware held by the blacks questions were asked as to how they got them. Mobs assembled in the street and marched on the Negro quarter at Broadway and Sixth Street. A canon was fired followed by the guns of both sides.

The whites began to dominate the riot and the blacks fled to the hills outside New York. Rigid enforcement of the Black Laws of 1807 was called for "To protect the people from this evil development of modern abolitionism." More stringent measures were introduced. The anti-abolitionists formed themselves into a society and declared war against "Abolitionist white men who, disregarding the misery of the whites make a parade of their kindly feelings towards the blacks." It seems the riots were organised by respectable middleclass citizens who wished to preserve the status quo rather than change it.

Buchanan himself acknowledged that this undercurrent of agitation had been going on for some time. He said "It can not be denied that for five and twenty years the agitation in the North against slavery has been incessant."

In 1835 pictorial handbills and inflammatory appeals were circulated extensively throughout the South of a character to excite the passion of the slaves and in the language of General Jackson "To stimulate them to insurrection."

Last but not least is the story of John Brown whose name has long since entered into Civil War folklore and Buchanan himself believe it or not played a major part in the fate of John Brown who became renowned in song and story.

It was Sunday October 16, 1859 when a tall gaunt man fifty-nine years old entered Harpers Ferry with what looked like a small army. There were five blacks and thirteen whites.

The man was John Brown. This was the same man who twenty years earlier had stood up in a church in Ohio and said, "Here before God and in the presence of these witnesses I consecrate my life to the destruction of slavery." Perhaps the congregation thought he was a nut case at the time.

The little army that arrived in Harpers Ferry had 200 rifles, 200 pistols and 1,000 pikes in a wagon they pulled behind them. They then seized an armoury belonging to the Government. The arsenal building which they ransacked was to be a base for fleeing blacks and a centre for launching an insurrection throughout the South against slavery. But they were only amateurs and the first person they killed – I don't know if it happened by accident, was a black man who had already been given his freedom. Things deteriorated and the town's people armed themselves and surrounded the building.

That morning ninety marines arrived under Robert E. Lee called in by Buchanan. Later Lee would become a General in the Confederate army. The rebels held out for two days but were eventually killed or captured. Two of Brown's sons were among the dead. Brown was slashed with a sword. His anti-slavery anger had been festering for some time until he decided himself to do something about it. Seeing a white man beat a slave boy with a shovel made up Brown's mind.

Before this Brown and his sons had killed five pro-slavery supporters in retaliation for the deaths of five anti-slavery protestors.

His bleeding from the sword wound left him too weak to stand. So he had to lie on the floor of the courthouse to receive his sentence of death after being found guilty. However his weak condition and sentence for murder and treason didn't stop him making a very moving speech after the trial. 1,500 troops guarded him at the scene of the hanging. The note he handed to his guards before he died was uncannily prophetic for the times that were to come. "I, John Brown, am now quite certain that the crimes of this guilty land will never be purged away but with blood."

To his wife he had said, "I have been whipped but I'm sure I can recover all the lost capital occasioned by that disaster by only hanging a few moments by the neck. I feel quite determined to make the utmost possible out of a defeat."

His plea for slaves and his dignity at his trial impressed many in the North and some say swayed the uncommitted to join the ranks of the abolitionists who regarded him as a martyr to their cause. Some even say Brown's raid on Harpers Ferry was the start of the Civil War.

The people in the South thought the opposite they were outraged by John Brown's raid on Harpers Ferry. Somebody actually wrote a song about him the chorus going something like this – "John Brown's body lies a-mouldering in the grave (repeated three times) and his soul goes marching on. Glory, Glory Hallelujah and his soul goes marching on."

John Brown was hanged on December 2, 1859. To the North he became an abolitionist martyr, but to the South a warning of the chaos to come if the blacks were not kept under control. Hanging him was the worst thing Buchanan could have done and was another of his political insensitivities in such very dangerous times.

Horace Greeley described Brown's act as the work of a madman but went on to praise the grandeur and nobility of Brown and his men.

The Southern whites were beside themselves with anger at the millions of Yankees who seemed to approve of a murderer who tried to set the slaves free. A Baltimore Newspaper bellowed loudly "Could the South afford any longer to live under a Government, the majority of whose subjects or citizens regard John Brown as a martyr and a Christian hero." "The Harpers Ferry invasion has advanced the cause of disunion more than any other event since the formation of the Government" cried the rival Richmond Newspaper. Basically the outcry was really about the constitutional rights of the South to have slaves and not about the unfortunate John Brown. But the lid could not be kept on a boiling pot for very much longer.

Historians have called attention to the sharp increase in disorder and riots in the Jacksonian period. Some assumed it happened even in the mid 1820s with the advent of Andrew Jackson's "rise of the common man".

Travellers to the United States filled their notes with clippings from newspapers about knifings, shootings, riots and internal wars and suggested that America was not a land of friendly neighbours for its citizens who were habitually lynched, editors beaten up, convents burned, and Negroes tortured. Even the Montreal Herald drew attention to "The strife's and hatreds which exist in that miscalled land of Liberty."

Later Lincoln was to say in a speech at Illinois – "In this land so lately famed for law and order, violence and disorder has become the everyday news of the times." "Mobs," said Lincoln in another speech, "have pervaded the country from New England to Louisiana alike, they spring up among the pleasure hunting masters of Southern slaves and the order loving citizens of the land of steady habits."

Many blamed the phenomenon of rioting on strong drink, poor upbringing, foreigners, Catholics, gamblers, or even the bankers, but strangely enough it has been recorded that most men blamed it on organized anti-abolitionist mobs. The abolitionist was commonly thought to be "Directly responsible for provoking slave insurrection, race riots, anti-abolitionist mobs, and the tension that lead to attacks on Mormons, Catholics, prostitutes, gamblers and other outcasts." The divisions now were open chasms of hate in the brickwork of a once happy society.

Not withstanding all the foregoing events well documented and well-known by the leading Statesmen in Congress, Buchanan entered into the Presidency with a strange contradiction in his behaviour. He promised in his inauguration speech to serve as a peacemaker yet he then set about creating a Cabinet of mostly Southerners which made it extremely difficult to have an impartial policy in handling the volatile times that lay ahead.

He seemed to set his face against any compromise in his views turning a deaf ear to radical opinions in the North. The very people he ignored would eventually end up voting for Lincoln in the 1860 Presidential Election. In a Cabinet of seven, four were Southerners and of the remaining three, one was a "Dough Face" that is a nickname for a white with Southern views.

It was Buchanan's pro-slavery behaviour that spoke even more eloquently than his choice of Cabinet. His action to endorse a Kansas Constitution written by pro-slavery settlers, in itself, gave encouragement to Southerners to expect special support for their cause. More and more he painted himself into a corner as the controversy between North and South spun out of control around him. Even his pronouncements were full of contradictions. On one hand he denied the legality of secession yet did nothing to force Federal troops of which he was the Commander-in-Chief to stop the secession.

Despite all this James Buchanan had a deep sympathy for the plight of the slaves and showed his feelings openly by persistently purchasing slaves in Washington only to set them free in his home State of Pennsylvania proving he was a very generous man at heart.

Another wonderful anecdote is told about James Buchanan to support this picture of a genuinely decent human being concerns his niece Harriet Lane. It seems when Harriet was only a little girl of nine her mother died. Her mother was Buchanan's sister Jane. To make matters worse the little girl's dad died two years later. Despite the fact that Buchanan was and would remain a bachelor for the rest of his life he took on the tricky task of rearing the young girl to womanhood. The little orphan grew into a very attractive young lady and graced the White House as hostess during Buchanan's Presidency. This human story reflects great credit on James Buchanan and just has to be acknowledged.

In defence of Buchanan perhaps he was really a casualty of history and history's wilful neglect over many Presidencies going back to the 1830s. These pathetic Presidencies were responsible for the time bomb left ticking on the back burner which eventually exploded in the face of Abraham Lincoln with disastrous consequences.

Buchanan spent the final months of his Administration trying to mollify and appease the Southern States despite their direct challenge to the fundamental authority of the Union. They proceeded to occupy Federal Posts, Arsenals, and Navy yards and even to confiscate U.S. property within the seceded States. But Buchanan was frozen into a state of thrombosed inactivity. His appeasement like Chamberlains before the Second World War only fed the ambitions and arrogance of the rebels.

On December 20, 1860, three months before Lincoln took over, the reins of State, a Convention held by the secessionists in South Carolina voted to leave the Union. But it was worse than that. Not only were they leaving the Union but they were setting up a whole new nation which would have left the old Union sundered into two halves.

These people were serious about their alienation to the Union and proved how deep their bitterness was when they then proposed a new Constitution and a new President. One by one each State dropped out. South Carolina in December, another five in January; Mississippi, Florida, Alabama, Georgia and Louisiana. Inaction and compromise was Buchanan's only weapon against this combined institutional rejection of the old Union set up by the Founding Fathers in the early days of America.

Since these States also took half his standing army with them it left Buchanan with serious difficulties of warfare should he decide to take the secessionists on? Well they were Buchanan's reasons for his inactivity. The situation was not unlike global warming in 2009 watching icebergs in the North Pole break up in large chunks to go crashing into the Arctic

Ocean.

The new Constitution of the Confederate States was duly adopted on March 11, 1861 a week into Lincoln's Presidency.

Just a small historical note about these early days of Lincoln's Presidency. On March 20, 1861 Charles Francis Adams, grandson of the second President John Adams and son of the 5th President Quincy Adams was appointed Ambassador to Great Britain, a position previously held by his illustrious predecessors. Perhaps in the middle of this terrible crisis looming in the country it was a significant reminder to many that this great family of yesterday were still standing in the wings and still working for the same Union. What, I wonder, were their thoughts at that time? Bewilderment perhaps or even despair.

As Buchanan's days in office went slipping away, appeasement seemed to be his only way to buy time and peace for his Administration. But one must ask the question. Could any self respecting nation be expected to stand idly by and watch the geographical, political, administrative and financial parts of its own structure as a nation built on the blood of brave and glorious patriots in its past history literally tear itself in two for one prize and one prize only – legalized slavery? That was the country Lincoln inherited in 1861.

In the final futile gesture of his Presidency Buchanan turned to Congress as a last resort for solutions to his problems.

He addressed the Senate and the House of Representatives warning them of the dangers that threatened the Union. "The tranquillity of the country was urgent to protect it from the perils that lay ahead." He described it as a calamity recognized by every intelligent citizen. It infected everyone throughout the length and breath of the land. Alarm had reduced imports dramatically as if in time of war. Money flow was affected and trade was paralyzed. Manufacturing had stopped. The stock market had dropped and unemployment was biting hard as a result. As the prospect of a bloodless settlement started to fade public distress became more aggravated. The fear of Civil War is more destructive than the most formidable foreign war.

Buchanan appealed to Congress as the only one with the power to declare war or remove grievances leading to war. Delay would be disastrous but it was now already too late. The die had been cast and the storm clouds of Civil War were already rumbling overhead.

By now James Buchanan was tired and totally disillusioned with the Presidency. In a letter to Mrs Knox Polk, the wife of the former President he wrote: - "I am now in my sixty-ninth year and am heartily tired of my position as President. I shall leave it in the beginning of March 1861 with much greater satisfaction then when entering on the duties of office."

He had not changed his mind on Lincoln's inauguration day. As they shared a carriage that took them from Willard's Hotel to the Capitol he turned to Lincoln and said:-

"If you are as happy my dear sir on entering this house as I am leaving it and returning home to Wheatland you are the happiest man in the country." The flames of rebellion had already been lit. James Buchanan disappeared into history after that but supported Lincoln throughout the Civil War from the house he called Wheatland where he lived right through a Civil War he couldn't prevent.

It started on April 12, 1861 one month after Buchanan left office and lasted for four years until April 9, 1865. Lincoln, his successor, was assassinated five days after the war ended on Good Friday April 14, 1865. Buchanan continued to live at Wheatland for another three years after the Civil War ended in 1865. He died at home in Wheatland of pneumonia and heart failure on June 1, 1868 aged seventy-seven years and was buried at Woodward Hill Cemetery, Lancaster, PA.

16th President   Abraham Lincoln

"Great Emancipator"
Born 1809
Died 1865
56 Years of age
2 Terms
1861 – 1864/ 1865 (1 month)
Age 52

Party: Republican
Profession: Lawyer
County: Illinois
Ancestry: English
Estate: $110,974
Hobbies: Town ball, walking, wrestling
Physical Description: Height, 6 foot 4 inches (tallest President); weight, 180 lbs; beard; black hair; grey eyes

Extract from his inaugural Address, Monday March 4, 1861

"It is seventy-two years since the first inauguration of a President under our national Constitution. During that period fifteen different and greatly distinguished citizens have in succession administered the executive branch of the Government. They have conducted it through many perils and generally with great success. Yet with all this scope of precedent I now enter upon the same task for the brief constitutional term of four years under great and peculiar difficulty. A disruption of the Federal Union, heretofore, only menaced, is now formidably attempted. I hold that in contemplation of universal law and of the Constitution of the Union of these States is perpetual".

ABRAHAM LINCOLN

Of all the Presidents of the United States, Abraham Lincoln's life must be the most written about story in American History. That is why this little piece will not go down in history as a world shattering detailed comprehensive original literary masterpiece. How can it be? One can only attempt to wade through the stories about him to solve the puzzle of the man in pictures that give an accurate image of someone so famous. His place in politics is synonymous with the heartbreaking human tragedy that exploded across the American Continent in 1861. So let's proceed to find out just who this Abraham Lincoln really was. How did he come to be leader of so many famous Generals at a turning point in U.S. history?

The Lincoln story starts in 1806 when his father Thomas Lincoln met and married a neighbourhood girl called Nancy Hanks. The traditional Kentucky wedding feast was laid out consisting of bear meat, venison, wild turkey and maple sugar lumps. Of course the wedding included the customary race for the whisky barrel. It was a day of painful contrast compared with life before and after the wedding. The Lincolns lived a nomadic lifestyle of ever changing scenery as they moved from place to place, living frugally off the land. To say the Lincolns were poor is an understatement but Tom, his father, had a sense of humour and a love for a good story that sustained him in the rough, tough life of the wilderness. Nancy, deeply religious and serious, was an obedient wife who worked hard setting up new homes in place after place as they moved around the country. She also became mother to three children while struggling to cope with a life imposed on her by her husband's restlessness. Tom Lincoln worked as a hired hand and carpenter on nearby farms. He eventually bought a place of his own for $200, but the three hundred acres he bought demanded many sacrifices and backbreaking toil in an environment where one storm could wash a month's work away. Abraham Lincoln grew up in this uncompromising lifestyle of his father and he was never impressed by farm life in Kentucky after that.

When he was seven, Abraham went to school at Knob Creek, a building with no windows and one door, where he learned reading, writing and some spellings. In December 1816 the family moved across the river to farm a richer land in Indiana. It was a landscape of virgin forests and having prepared the site, his father returned up-river to collect Nancy and the three children, Abraham, Sarah and Tom. There they stayed for fourteen years until Abraham was twenty-one. Homespun clothing and bare feet in the summer was the norm. Only the better off had household luxuries such as pots, pans and cutlery.

That winter was Nancy's last. She contracted milk sickness for which there was no cure. With no doctors within reach she died in great pain and Abraham helped his father make her coffin. Together they buried her in a plot not far from their back door. Undeterred by this tragedy, Tom set off for town twelve months later and found himself a new wife. Abraham's stepmother was Sara Bush Johnston, a widow with three children of her own. Sarah transformed their cabin into a more civilized way of life. She greatly influenced Abraham who never forgot her kindness, love and attention during those years. He called her "My Angel Mother". It was a fragile, frightening environment where a horse's kick or an attack by a wild animal was commonplace and fatal. Attacks by bears and wolves often destroyed the livestock. The only consolation for them in their sufferings was the words of a passing preacher but these visits were few and far between.

Education was the hard toil of the frontiersman and in his youth, Abraham held no other ambitions than to survive a hostile country. But there was a silver lining for Abraham – his love of reading. The bible was his chief source of contact with other civilizations in ancient times.

Still, life went on for Abraham grubbing, hoeing and making fences. He also picked fodder for the animals and while resting during ploughing, practiced reading. But Abraham Lincoln never had the appetite to follow in his father's footsteps. In the nearby town of Troy business bustled. Steamboats took on supplies, boatmen gambled in nearly every tavern and the excitement gave Abraham the idea for making his own boat. When it was built he used it as a sideline, ferrying passengers to nearby steamers. This was so different from the lifestyle of his unfortunate father. Abraham drifted into store jobs, enjoying the stories of people who passed through, travellers, missionaries, traders and politicians heading for St. Louis. So when he was asked to take a trip down river to New Orleans he jumped at the chance.

Then came catastrophe. The first finger of fate plucking from him a terrible price. His sister, Sarah died aged twenty-one. She had been a kind of mother and constant companion to him, sharing in all his plans and dreams. Now she was no more. He sank into a deep depression at the terrible loss and pain his grief inflicted on him.

Abraham was, at nineteen, a tall gangling youth. He had dark eyes and black wavy hair and hard work had developed his physique and stamina. He swam well, and wrestled with and out ran his friends. Sometimes a man needs psychological defences against the disappointments of life and Abraham's shield was that of a built in comic. His story-telling, mimicry and conversation entertained neighbours and friends alike. Imitating the mannerisms of preachers and politicians gave fun to many in a town where boredom was never very far away. Today he might have been a top TV comic for he had practiced the art since he was fifteen. But Abraham was actually learning the skills of the orator that were to surface in years to come with remarkable results on the political stages of the future. Abraham often suffered from mood swings that transported him to highs and lows between grief and happiness.

But far away hills were still beckoning to Thomas, his father and the family were soon on the move again, this time to Illinois. More trees had to be felled to tear out a new settlement. But nothing had changed. The milk sickness they were running away from was there to meet them in Illinois. Then came a change of direction when Abraham was offered a deal ferrying a cargo to and from New Orleans. His parents being settled and Abraham being of age, he decided to leave home. He now compared himself to a piece of floating driftwood ready for anything just to escape his father's way of life. Friendless and penniless he was glad to be on his own at twenty-two years of age.

It was a strange feature of life in those days that wherever there were settlers a whole new breed of trader was spawned. Speculators, promoters, traders, all with fertile ideas for making fortunes. Warehouses and factories, banks and wharves blossomed. Out on the sun-baked prairies an occasional roving Indian band rode by. New Salem, where Abraham settled, was no exception. New houses were built and attracted blacksmiths, wagon-makers, doctors, hat-makers and other trades. Hogs, sheep and cattle clogged the roads of Salem. Whiskey flowed freely to drown sorrows, and while wrestling, cock-fighting and debating societies spread rapidly, temperance clubs just didn't stand a chance.

When he was twenty-two, Lincoln arrived in New Salem in late July 1831. He got work piloting a raft down river and walking back. He bought a general store in partnership with a man called William F. Berry but his partner was the firm's best customer, helping himself freely to the whiskey they sold. They went broke leaving Lincoln embroiled in debt. But New Salem was folding up anyway. Settlers were no longer coming and Lincoln's first and last business venture ended in Court writs.

Lincoln's honesty in the town made him popular and his ability to read gave him an added advantage. His opportunities for work had broadened with his literary skills, his use of the axe, and as the pilot of a flatboat. He became postmaster at the post office and also mixed the job with that of postman, delivering letters to distant farms. At this time he was expanding his education reading deeply in trigonometry, geometry and surveying and he was frequently able to settle boundary disputes and mark roads. In his easy frontier fashion, he signed notes, bonds and mortgage agreements on trust. This was dangerous for he was liable for them on default. The inevitable default happened and almost destroyed him leaving him facing enormous debts which were only cleared in 1848, sixteen years later. His relaxed approach to business as in life floored him. Despite this setback he was drawn imperceptibly into politics.

His gift of mimicry, his easy manner with words, his popularity, and last but not least, his undoubted honesty, were his tools for the future. Lincoln ran for the State Legislature on a platform of improved transportation, banks, schools and the needs of the community. In short, he was selling his dream in politics based on his tough upbringing in an honest presentation of Lincoln "the man to be trusted". He talked to local farmers, pitched horseshoes and mixed socially with everybody. Sadly his only reward was this caustic quote. "He looks just like another layabout with a big mouth and nothing to do."

Needless to say, Lincoln failed in his first bid for Congress but he was learning. Who could ever see him becoming President of the United States at that stage! All the illustrious Presidents before him like the Adams family, Jefferson, Madison, Pierce and Buchanan were academics from the greatest Universities of America. Lincoln was a floating, uneducated, uncertain drifter, a rail-splitter, whiskey salesman, frontiersman, a store man, a farmhand and even a penniless boatman.

But gradually Lincoln began to hone the skills of a national politician by dint of hard work and attention to detail. It was a personal approach based exclusively on his own honesty, accessibility to his neighbours and his ability to communicate widely. He was eventually elected to Congress but not until 1847. At last he had mastered the art of campaigning.
Worth mentioning is Lincoln's first outing to Vandalia, the State Capital, on an Education Convention. For him it really was an education. The population there had almost doubled and the social life was buzzing. Frequent Balls took place. Lawyers, lobbyists and office seekers crowded the inns and taverns in abundance. Disorder, rioting and drunkenness were rarely penalized. A jail was erected with the luxury of iron bars and a place for debtors was set up. Also provided were fireplaces for the jailers.

Lincoln didn't take part in the high life but was an interested spectator and was completely taken aback by the drunken revelry he saw around him that left him sad and perplexed. It was a far cry in time and distance from his home in Indiana where Thomas Lincoln, his hard-working father, was living. However his road took another direction in 1836 when he decided to become a lawyer. It was to him the missing link in his equipment for life as a politician. Work on the ground with the farmers proved how easily their ignorance of the law became their downfall.

An attorney's life would also copper-fasten his status within the community. But his approach to graduating was unorthodox to say the least. He bought all the books that contained legal knowledge and read them thoroughly. Books such as Blackstone's Commentaries, Chitbyes Pleadings, Greenleaf's Evidence and Story's Equity were ones he recalled in later years. Practice in the courts was to do the rest. He passed his first examination in September 1836 before the Supreme Court and the final one in March 1837. He then set off for Springfield, the town where he was highly regarded in politics and opened up a practice with a John T.

Stewart.

The final product for a career in politics was now ready for the fray. Abraham Lincoln was really a man's man, preferring masculine company and pastimes such as swapping stories, drinking, horseplay and practical jokes. Bachelorhood to him was a skill to be cherished to protect him from the wiles of women. But one story proves how vulnerable he was. He was absolutely useless against one Mary Owen, a pretty young visitor from Kentucky. Unfortunately there was a slight hitch in the matchmaking by Mary Owen's sister. Having set up a marriage to the pretty girl Lincoln remembered years previously, her sister returned from Kentucky with a totally different version.

This Mary Owen was now plump, weather-beaten and missing some of her front teeth. Being away from town a lot, he conducted the romance by letter. Now alarm bells were ringing and he defended his bachelorhood with gloomy morose pen pictures of himself to Mary Owen. He tried to convince her of the risk she took if she married him. He even wrote to her with a horror story of the depressing lifestyle of Springfield. Not a nice place to live in at all. Mary hung on for a while but eventually his tactics seemed to work and Mary Owen duly returned to Kentucky and out of Lincoln's life forever. He often joked later about his narrow escape.

Although Springfield was now the new Capital, it was still surrounded by raw wilderness with the prairies on one side and the forests on the other. A population of 1,500 lived in small cabins and hogs, cows, chickens, and other farmyard animals wandered freely in the muddy streets. It had four taverns, six churches, eighteen Ministers, and eleven lawyers. But frontier life was polished a little for the inhabitants by lessons in Spanish and Latin. They were an unsophisticated people but happy, and life unfolded gently around them. Meanwhile A. Lincoln, as he was known, was now thriving in the rough and tumble of State politics.

One of the colourful events that livened up Springfield was "The young men's Whig Convention". Wagons and horses headed for Springfield from everywhere in the county. The inevitable parade behind the band gave the war veterans of 1812 a chance to preen themselves in public. Barbeques, speeches, and of course endless drinking, made it a meeting to remember. Churches and courthouses attracted the soap box orators who may not have persuaded many, but they certainly entertained their listeners. Verbal wars ended in fist fights and minor riots. Lincoln was in his element and the social life of Springfield bubbled and blossomed in this rip-roaring joyful turbulent America of the 1830s. But now lightning was to strike A. Lincoln a second time. The Gods of fate he had thwarted in 1836 were unforgiving and not to be trifled with a second time.

Enter Mary Todd of Lexington, Kentucky, the daughter of a well to-do family. The year - 1839. Mary lived in a lively house on a hilltop where aspiring lawyers and politicians came to picnic and debate. Molly, as her friends knew her, was well-educated, recited poetry and danced and talked with ease. She did have her "moments" when she threw feminine temper tantrums, behaviour that was accepted as the norm in those days.

One day Lincoln accepted an invitation to the house on the hill by his law partner, John Stewart, who happened to be a cousin of Mary. Lincoln was thirty and considered "a mighty rough man". Mary was twenty-one and her chatter dazzled and bewitched Lincoln who was secretly considered "a gawky bumpkin" by Mary's well-to-do relatives. Cupid struck and Lincoln was hooked. He had fallen in love. She had always wanted "a man of the mind with bright prospects". She needed no wealth, just warmth and affection, loyalty and sensitivity and Lincoln had all those assets in abundance. She satisfied a need in him that neither bachelorhood nor politics would ever achieve.

Yet some relatives cruelly made it obvious how much they frowned upon the engagement. Self-doubt became a burden he couldn't handle. He sank into depression and eventually released Mary from their engagement. "If what I feel were equally distributed by the whole human family, they would not have one cheerful face on earth," he wrote to his partner Stewart. It can safely be assumed he was on the verge of a nervous breakdown. Let's now fast forward a couple of years. The coming of the railroad linking Springfield and Jacksonville was a momentous time in the life of Abraham Lincoln. As fate would have it, he met Mary Todd again at the celebrations and our story is complete. On November 4, 1842 three years after they first met, our romantic couple were married. Writing to a friend a few days later, he wrote "Nothing new here except my marrying which to me is a matter of profound wonder."

They settled down in a rented two-storey wooden structure far below the standard expected for their daughter by Mary's family. But life for Abraham Lincoln had changed forever. Funds were meagre from Lincoln's law fees and four children soon followed with Lincoln still paying off his New Salem creditors. Although a staunch Whig and a solid citizen, Lincoln refused to go to church. Another thing he couldn't change was their money situation which was still precarious. However, his problems eased dramatically when eventually he was elected to Congress.

In October 1847 he left for Washington with the boys intending to stay with Mary's family in their mansion at Lexington. It was his first experience of slavery at work. There was a tension in the air because of the lawlessness and pilfering in the district and because of the trial of some slaves for attempting to poison their master. It was a tension that was heightened by advertisements in the local press for the capture of runaway slaves. Lincoln heard Henry Clay describing slavery as an irremedial wrong to its unfortunate victims.

After Washington, Lincoln was glad to return home to Springfield. Glad to discard all the veneer of Washington life, sometimes to Mary's annoyance. Worn out carpet slippers, a blue cloak ten years old and worst of all for Mary's peace of mind, reading the newspaper lying on the ground in front of the fire. His manners to her genteel senses left a lot to be desired. But that was Lincoln at home. They both spoiled the children, blind to all their faults and conscious of the child mortality rate of the time, worried abnormally about their well-being. Lincoln also had nightmares about "the fate of his little rascals". Mary's temper was volatile and her explosions cost them many a servant, a fault she always regretted. His absences didn't help her feeling of isolation, especially during thunderstorms, for Lincoln often sought refuge in the banter and conversation of the local grocery store.

But it seems all their concern for the children only attracted the hand of fate. Eddie died aged four on February 1, 1850 after a brief illness lasting two months.
Strangely for a man of Lincoln's compassion, he seldom wrote to his own family although he helped them out with small sums of money. He never went back home because, as he put it, "The ghost of a painful past would be too much to bear." He answered no letters and his words explaining this has a hollow ring. "It appeared to me, I could write nothing which would do any good......" When pressed to visit his dying father, he declined, blaming his absence on Mary's ill-health. He then wrote "If we could meet now it is doubtful whether it would be more painful than pleasant. Let Thomas call on the maker and if it be his lot to go, go now. He will join many loved ones gone before."
Five days later Thomas died; an old man, perhaps even a rejected old man. Around this time, Lincoln's thoughts were becoming preoccupied with slavery "That inescapable malignancy imbedded in the Republic," he concluded. But his absences in Washington had undermined his law practice and he pulled back from politics for a while. Yet slavery again persisted in his

thoughts when he pronounced the eulogy over the grave of Henry Clay at Clay's funeral. In it Lincoln made some veiled references to abolitionists. Clay himself had been aware of "The fire bell in the night that warned of the threat to the Republic".

But in the tug of war between his law business and politics, the winner was always going to be politics, especially as the danger to the Union surfaced. Slowly his opinions were being formed and solidified by events around him such as the refusal to allow Cassius Clay, the Kentucky abolitionist, use the State House for a talk. It seemed sinister forces were gathering to frustrate freely-held opinions. The book Abraham Lincoln and the Union by Oscar and Lilian Hamlin, gives an intimate view of Washington in 1847, roughly like this:

Lincoln's arrival as a freshman Congressman in Washington in December 1847 is worth noting. The Capital at that time was really a rambling chaotic village. Garbage littered the streets and hogs, cows and other animals roamed freely in the alleyways. Well-built houses and others in disrepair stood side by side. Coaches avoided Pennsylvania Avenue to avoid the bone shaking bumps over its uneven cobblestones. Disturbingly, gangs of slaves in chains attracted little attention. The shops were filled to capacity with farm produce from the fields outside Washington, yet Baltimore was the main shopping centre for the higher class goods over two hours coach ride away. Unbelievably street lights were only lit when Congress was sitting. The security force depended on fifteen policemen to keep order during daytime but they all went home at night leaving the city without one policeman for night duty. There were thirty-seven churches covering the needs of eight denominations and the men far outnumbered the women because Congressmen left their wives at home maybe hundreds of miles away.

Dinner was at five each evening, but the British Ambassador dined at six, when his richly dressed liveried servants arrived with dinner laid out on huge silver platters. Sometimes Buchanan entertained lavishly and Dolly Madison was one of the most famous names on his dinner list of up to 1,500 guests. On the steps of the White House, the Marine Band played for the entertainment of passers by daily. It was all truly a culture shock for the man from Springfield, one Abraham Lincoln.

But events were moving rapidly. The vast spaces out West won by the Generals left the burning question uppermost in everyone's thoughts – should the new areas be slave free? Party unity was shaky on the issue.

Even now Lincoln took no clear stand on slavery to the point where back home he was being charged with disloyalty and duplicity. The name "spotty Lincoln" was heard everywhere. It hurt Lincoln so much he was thinking of getting out of politics. Even the Congressman's lifestyle wasn't to his liking. Mary left Washington and took the two lads to stay with her family in Lexington. Lincoln missed her. He worried about her health and the children's. Mary wrote back to reassure him giving him details of family life back home. He longed for reunion with her so much he again considered quitting politics. But the slavery issue would not go away. Quotes from John C. Calhoun didn't help his peace of mind. "The superior white race required the enslavement of the Negro lest the section become the abode of disorder, anarchy, poverty, misery and wretchedness." It seemed the Negro was to be blamed for everything.

Disillusioned with Washington, Lincoln looked for a Judgeship but failed. It seemed the blood, sweat and tears he had put into having President Zachary Taylor elected had come to nothing. He returned home in disgust and wrote to Taylor but got no reply. In September 1849 he finally returned to the law circuit. Although it had never been lucrative for him, the stress of family life and the uncertainty of Lincoln's future was getting to Mary. Her temper wasn't getting any better.

Servants left after being on the receiving end of a tongue lashing and Lincoln had to pay extra to hold on to some of them. Her depression often forced Lincoln to seek solace in the house of a friend. He even brought his breakfast to the office. Friends, even his most intimate ones, avoided the house leaving him heading for the grocery store to engage in his favourite pastime of banter, story-telling and conversation. She had become quite neurotic even with tradesmen whose goods she returned frequently. As I said earlier catastrophe struck the household in February 1850 when their son Eddie died after a short illness. But Lincoln still refused to go to church.

Lincoln's father was nearing death too but still Lincoln refused to visit his folk back home. Because of Mary's illness he was anchored to his own life but anyway he was doubtful of the good a visit to his father would do. "Besides," he wrote, "his father would meet many loved ones gone before." And so, his father died and was buried, ignored by Lincoln. Perhaps because he was a great believer in the law of inevitability "You cannot shun a danger that was appointed, nor incur one that is not," he wrote. This might have been directed at his departed father but perhaps it was a prophetic finger of fate pointing towards history to come.

But the question of the Union always intruded on his personal decision to return to his career in law. Strangely his living quarters or neighbourhood of South Illinois was quite complacent on the slavery issue. The storm across the nation was raging and still Lincoln remained neutral. He was still preoccupied by the mundane issues of his law circuit; divorce, the sale of unlicensed liquor, addressing juries and dealing with correspondence.
But his ideas were forming gradually. His thoughts recorded privately reflected this. He wrote, "Bondage was not a matter of colour, of intellectual superiority or of interest, otherwise men with lighter skins could enslave those darker than themselves; the more intelligent could enslave the less, any person could seize any other." Invitations to speak at rallies grew. The campaign was growing. North versus South was dividing the nation. Lincoln continued to antagonize many with his speeches, especially when he declared that "If runaway slaves crossed his path, he hoped they could run faster than he."

The State Fair in Springfield on October 3, 1854 opened as usual. Farmers exhibited, cattle dealers were many and out to make a fast buck. Women sold jellies and jams but the real business exciting attention was the speeches by politicians. Lincoln spoke for three hours in the rain. Douglas took two hours to answer. Twelve days later Lincoln made the same speech but it was greatly improved by the emerging conviction in his ideas. Even Jefferson and the Founding Fathers were quoted as being "Against the monstrous injustice of slavery." Another quote of Lincoln argued that "Man's freedom was conditioned on denying himself the forbidden fruit – of despotism." The fire was now alight in Lincoln's belly and it was only a matter of time before he returned to politics.
The first real spark of trouble came when violence erupted in Kansas. Pro-slavery Missourians poured in. Terror spread and the rival camps armed themselves. Gunfire in the distance disturbed a worried Lincoln. Worse than that, pro-slavery legislators enacted pro-slavery legislation. The poison was spreading and the patient was dying fast. The inability of the great men of past history to wield a restraining influence on inflamed passions was the next casualty of the terrible dilemma. The peaceful extinction of slavery was becoming a lost cause. Gradual emancipation was out of the question. Was the fourth of July to become nothing more than a fireworks day with no substance any more. Lincoln now feared the one basic question must be "Could the nation remain half-slave and half-free? May God in his mercy superintend the solution."

Lincoln was now coming to national prominence addressing crowds of 10,000 and 20,000. At some State fairs, crowds queued over a mile to hear his speeches. They somehow knew the hand of history was upon them. Lincoln was now called the high priest of abolitionism. Yet he continued his law practice which was now becoming prosperous.

Meanwhile the economy was expanding. The Michigan canal linked up the Great Lakes with the Mississippi in 1848. Eleven railroad lines reached Chicago whose population quadrupled from 1,900 to 112,000 between 1850 and 1860. Most significant, immigrants replaced Southerners in Illinois and the political balance swung in favour of the abolitionists. Illinois was making headlines for the rest of the country. The New York Times praised Illinois as the most interesting political battleground in the country.
Now Lincoln's time had come and he was nominated for the Presidency under the banner of the new Republican Party for the election of 1860.

Meanwhile Lincoln was being referred to in Columbia, a Southern plantation town as the Black Republican. It didn't bother Lincoln but it bothered Mary. He was attacked in the South as vulgar, illiterate and unqualified. Scaremongering grew to fever pitch in warnings of "Robberies, rape and murders of the poorer whites by emancipated blacks, disfiguring this smiling face of a happy Southern land." But Lincoln was convinced common sense would prevail. To relieve the tension of our narrative, perhaps you would like to hear a little anecdote many times told about an eleven year old girl asking Lincoln to grow a beard because "Ladies liked a beard and would tease their husbands to vote for you." Lincoln wrote back and chided her saying "Such a thing as a beard now would be thought of as a silly affectation." Despite these protests, he allowed a beard to grow. You can decide yourself whether the story is true or false.

But let's move to the Convention of 1860. It was held in the Wigwam. Here Lincoln was nominated by a crowd of about 20,000 to rapturous applause. His speech was cautious as he chose to mend fences by adopting a reasonable approach on the slavery issue. Fiery tub thumping oratory was put on the back burner for now. His autobiography was due to be published by two newspapers The Chicago Tribune and the New York Tribune which later sold over one million copies. His whole platform was a subdued low-key affair stripped of all past glories in office. He now chose to reach out to the people as a working class candidate who had risen to his present job out of genuine poverty. He was an ordinary citizen you could trust.

His nomination had seemed incredible to many at the time. Here was the little-known Abraham Lincoln standing before them in place of the talented, distinguished, experienced and towering figure of William H. Seward, former Governor of New York, twice a Senator and the national leader of the Republican Party. The choice of those mid 19th century politicians defies analysis yet who would choose otherwise today.
The rise of the dark horse has always been a bizarre inevitability of many a Presidency since Washington. It still remains inexplicable. How to hold the Union together was now Lincoln's task. I won't dwell on the hustings for the battle lines had long since been drawn up. As the history books record, Lincoln was duly crowned United States 16th President, beating Breckenridge by 173 votes to 73. Lincoln had already set his stall out in a speech he made in 1858. Today we call it "The House Divided Speech". "A House divided against itself cannot stand. I believe this Government cannot endure permanently half-slave and half-free. I do not expect the Union to be dissolved. I do not expect the House to fall. But I do expect it will cease to be divided. It will become all one thing or all the other."

In another speech in his campaign which opened in Chicago, he recalled the Declaration of Independence upon which the nation was founded. He lashed out at those seeking to place one man superior to another on the basis of colour or race. "Let us discard all these things and unite as one people throughout the land until we shall once more stand up declaring that all men are created equal." Whether it was before 10,000 people in the blazing sun at Ottawa or 15,000 people standing in drizzling rain at Freeport or in the small towns where 6,000 people often turned out to hear him, the message was the same. The Union stood supreme and was made sacrosanct by the Declaration of Independence.

Distance was no problem; Ohio, Indiana, Kansas, Iowa, Wisconsin and New York City, all heard the brilliance of a marvellous orator. He travelled thousands of miles without helicopters or jet planes.

As Lincoln walked through the doors of the White House in March 1961 the hand of history on his shoulder, Mary at last was about to re-discover the old grandeur to which she had been born. She didn't waste much time admiring her surroundings in the White House and soon took over the job of redecorating it out of the $20,000 budget she was allowed. Not only did she use State money but even spent her own on elegant gowns, clothes and gloves and by Christmas the White House was sparkling. Sadly Mary, ever the complicated enigma in his life, didn't get happier. She missed old friends and only relaxed in the company of her black seamstress, named Elizabeth Keckley, confiding in her completely.

Unfortunately, she over-ran the $20,000 budget by $6,700 and Lincoln was furious "For spending such money on this damned house, when soldiers can have no blankets." Yet despite Mary's difficulties they never fell out. The children, Willie and Tad, didn't help. Not used to such opulence they ran free and wild inside the mansion to the irritation of Mary. To add to the confusion, their pets grew almost out of control.

It was not unlike the White House under Theodore Roosevelt one hundred years later. Just like "Teddy" Lincoln's children were also thoroughly spoiled by their indulgent parents in many ways.

Later Lincoln took them to visit the troops along the Potomac River and often took part in their games. Willie loved poetry but Tad was like his mother – sensitive and hyperactive. He also had a speech impediment.

Back to the business of the White House. Lincoln after four months was still playing it cool and cautious. But he was sticking to his principles of no slavery.

The inevitable happened in January 1961 when the Deep South seceded. "Guaranteed slavery in perpetuity" was their bottom line. At that time Lincoln was only President-elect and could do nothing about it while Buchanan was in office. But he was determined not to allow the destruction of the Union. Already assassination plots were surfacing before he reached Washington for his inauguration. Mary reacted hysterically when hearing of the plots. There were even rumours of an invasion of Washington to prevent Lincoln's inauguration. Three hundred threatening letters against him had been received by Vice President Hannibal Hamlin but Lincoln pressed on regardless and made his first speech as President. Once again he reaffirmed that "The Union of these States is perpetual." Anyway, the pro-slavery seceders were in the minority. To accept their interpretation of the problem would lead to anarchy. He pleaded for calm. To quote a part of his speech "We are not enemies but friends and mystic chords of memory are stretching from every battlefield and patriot grave, to every living heart and hearthstone all over this broad land."

At the start of his Presidency, Lincoln did an unusual thing which would challenge the patriotism of his former opponents who considered themselves superior to this "backwoods President". He took them into his Cabinet; Free Soilers, Whigs, Democrats and Republicans, representing every section but the Deep South who had seceded. Some were Conservative and some Radical. Lincoln was indifferent to their arrogant attitude towards him and used them for their specialized talents now working for himself and the Union. Despite the inaugural speech of Lincoln's which took place on Monday March 4, 1861, thirty-nine days later all his pleas for caution and cool heads was blown sky high like confetti in the wind.

The fuse to the powder keg between North and South was ignited with an attack on a little barracks on Charleston Harbour called Fort Sumter at 4.30 a.m. on Friday April 12, 1861.

The historic shot came from a white-haired elderly Secessionist fanatic named Edmund Ruffin who was determined to fire that first "shot of honour" as he called it. The shell embedded itself in the wall of the Fort just above the head of the second in command Colonel Doubleday. The only casualty was a Confederate soldier whose gun barrel blew up in his hands because its owner Daniel Howe did not swab the cannon down. When Anderson, the Fort Commander realized defeat was inevitable he abandoned the Fort taking with him the torn and tattered flag that flew above Charleston Harbour.

The supply ship "Star of the West" returned home without landing supplies. The notorious Edmund Ruffin is credited with being the first to enter the Fort after its surrender though perhaps the narrative writer got carried away by the excitement and added a little padding to that story. Most important however was Lincoln's reaction to the situation for after hearing the Fort had suffered six hundred direct hits he realized the Confederates meant business. The Civil War had started. A last postscript on Edmund Ruffin. An agronomist by profession he specialized in agriculture after the war and died on June 17, 1865 aged seventy-one.

The Confederate General in charge of the attack was Jefferson Davis who had fought alongside his father-in-law, Zachary Taylor in the Mexican war. Zachary you may recall later became the 12th President of the United States. After a thirty-four hour siege the Commander of Fort Sumter, Major Anderson, was forced to surrender. As Commander-in-Chief now of the whole U.S. army, Lincoln had no intention of sitting wringing his hands in the White House like Buchanan the previous President had done. This he concluded was an open act of warfare against the Union itself.

Army Commanders were immediately given their orders. 3,000 miles of coastline and two hundred ports were to be blockaded. An additional 43,000 troops were recruited on a three year contract to supplement the 75,000 already called up – just like Washington's War the army was understaffed, underfunded, inexperienced and badly managed. It was a slow torturous affair. Even the Cabinet had its flaws for being of opposite factions they were jealous of each other. The Navy however, stayed loyal. England true to form was stirring it up, siding with the rebels, refusing to recognize it as an internal insurrection. Lincoln gave them a hands-off diplomatic broadside on the quiet. Everything was happening now in a sensational way around Abraham Lincoln.

Meanwhile, unbelievably, the news of Lincoln's declaration was greeted with great excitement in Britain which was described in a newspaper report as follows – "A storm of enthusiasm was heard everywhere even in the Music Halls to welcome the announcement that Lincoln had declared war on the Confederate forces rebelling against the Union. Here shouts arose, hats and handkerchiefs were waved. Women sprung to their feet to give more energetic utterances to their joy. Three cheers were called for again and again for Mr. Lincoln. Such scenes were never before seen in a British Music Hall." The media in Britain just went mad. To add to the confusion, help from volunteers far outstripped the uniforms available. The prospect of a short war also attracted glory hunters.

The question of allegiances surfaced and even Robert E. Lee was faced with a decision he didn't relish – loyalty to the South or loyalty to the Union. This wasn't surprising for great men of all ages and professions were forced into two gigantic camps on both sides of the political divide. There was no in-between. To Lincoln's disappointment Lee chose loyalty to the Confederacy. Experienced Commanders joined the Confederacy but Northern West Pointers like U.S. Grant, William T. Sherman and the popular Winfield Scott joined the Union forces. At seventy-five years of age "Old Fuss and Feathers" was still among the first to enlist.

There were many buffoons and charlatans among the volunteers to the army who, unlike the Navy, needed no special skills to join up. Every State demanded its share of titles, commissions and political capital and these patronage demands would exact serious penalties on the troops. Amazingly, nobody seemed to be taking the war too seriously thinking it would be short, quick and a bit of fun. Were they in for a rude awakening!

Was it all a bit of fun? Let's look at the lifestyle of both armies and see what lay in store for the Civil War soldier for the next four years. The wages of these young conscripts and volunteers were $12 for a Confederate Private and $13 for a Union Private per month; First Lieutenant $53 plus $36 subsistence per month. First Lieutenant's wages in the Union forces was roughly the same $90 per month. Sergeant Major's wages for both armies was $21 per month.

At first enlisting in the army was a light-hearted affair. Three months training, the election of their own officers, a rudimentary medical test, a speech by a local politician, then into the railway cars or a march down the road carrying flags they promised never to dip in shame, leaving weeping relatives behind. Using their slang they were "Off to see the elephant" i.e. seeing some major event "like Barnum's Circus and side shows". Early in the war those under eighteen and over thirty-five were allowed to return home after only three months service.

They were mostly housed in tents, before barracks were built, similar to the Plain's Indian's tepee. A stove stood in the centre of an 18ft diameter space, housing about twenty men and their equipment. Lower grade officers shared a tent, a fold-up desk and a chair. Confederates rarely used tents but slept in the open under a tree or near a fire. Reveille started the day with drums or bugles. Fifteen minutes was allowed for dressing, washing and roll call. Mounted men first dealt with their horses, while foot soldiers had breakfast. Infirmary call allowed the sick to report to the surgeon's tent. Fatigue call meant cleaning, chopping wood or other such chores. "Roast Beef" was the call to dinner after brigade drill. A final roll call at 5.45 p.m. and a dress parade finished the day. At 8.30 p.m. the bugler sounded "Attention". Assembly followed then "Tattoo" finished the day with a last roll call and a return to their quarters. "Taps" was sounded and all lights were extinguished.

The routine only changed on Sundays when knapsack drill meant minute inspection for particles of dirt. Also included in these inspections were quarters, grounds, kitchens and hospitals. Spare time was spent writing letters or singing songs, playing cards or sight-seeing locally. Some units actually published their own newspaper. Finally theatrical companies catered for stage entertainment.

Discipline was firmly applied by the men with gold rank insignias, giving orders such as when to get up, what to eat or where to sleep. It was something for which the raw recruits were completely unprepared. All misdemeanours came under Articles of War. Most offences were drunkenness, insubordination, theft, leaving a post without authority, and absence from camp without a pass.

Court Martials distributed punishment such as dirty jobs like emptying latrines or burying dead horses to mention just a few. Officers could find themselves demoted. Flogging was banned in 1861. An execution for murder, rape, mutiny or treason was carried out by a firing squad of a dozen men; the victim sitting on his own coffin after a short prayer ritual.

Front-line duty sees men getting increasingly nervous as they approach the smoke covered front; hearing the crackle of small arms, the booming of cannon; seeing the pile of severed arms and legs outside field hospitals and hearing from inside the cries of the wounded as the army marches past. Not a very comfortable experience. Veterans became unusually quiet, and novice rookies made jokes loudly. Many just prayed and hoped.

The time has come and mounted officers try to calm nerves with shouts of "close up". Drums beat a steady pace. Bands sit behind the lines playing patriotic tunes. Confederate bands at Gettysburg played polkas. Some try to drop out into ditches or bushes only to be prodded out with the sword by "File closers". Such deserters usually return to ranks to serve well for the rest of the war.

The noise of battle leaves men deafened for hours after by the explosions of artillery and the rattle of rifle muskets. Heavy sulphur smells pollute the air. Black powder clings with bitterness to the lips and the musket barrel becomes too hot to touch. No matter where the soldier looks he sees smoke fire and mutilated bodies. Strangely as battle commences they have control of their lives for the first time and their nerves calm down dramatically. Some actually enjoyed it for the buzz it gave them. Sometimes men fighting for hours, keel over fast asleep before they hit the ground. "Survivors guilt" affects many, throwing them into severe depression afterwards.

Those who are wounded are eventually taken to prison camp hospitals for operations without anaesthetics. If they become prisoners for too long they are always in danger from sanitation diseases such as cholera and dysentery which took the lives of more than 40,000 prisoners during the Civil War.

Medical services were carried out by a surgeon and assistant surgeon who would walk behind the regiment picking up the wounded. They usually selected a suitable hospital building out of the line of fire, e.g. a farmhouse which was then marked with a yellow flag, 6 foot by 4 foot with a green H marked clearly in the centre. The job of the surgeon was to control the bleeding wounds with ligatures. 94% of all wounds were bullet wounds of which 70% were fatal. Chest wounds were three times the number of abdominal wounds.
The wounded were then brought to the field hospital down a lane of buntings, usually yellow. Bullet forceps were used to remove balls imbedded in wounds. Shattered bones and bullet wounds called for amputation. Chloroform was used extensively when they had it. Unsanitary conditions caused many infections. A rubber ground cloth was thrown over a table. The instruments were washed in a pan of bloody water and sponged off with a dirty sponge. The reasons for so many amputations were the soft nosed bullets being used. By 1862, one million farm workers joined the Union army to be replaced on the farms by women. "Change the tactics or lose," said Lincoln.

About 97% of those who contracted pyemia – pus in the blood – died in the hospital. The lucky ones were taken out by specially designed railcars acting as an ambulance for full recovery elsewhere. When recovered they could be returned to the battlefield for further action.

A gruesome sentimental song was popular with the troops and went something like this –
Into the ward of the clean whitewashed
Where the dead slept and the dying lay
Wounded by bayonets, sabres and balls
Somebody's darling was borne one day.

The Navy had a job to do too. The Confederates planted torpedoes in rivers and harbours which were dismantled by chains dragged along by rafts pulled behind monitor ships. Other methods of warfare were the ram or long pole at the end of which an explosive device was detonated at close quarters sometimes electrically. The naval war was usually confined to a restricted area like harbours or rivers. Ships were never successful in attacking forts.

Yes, life in the Civil War, like any other war, was no picnic and certainly not the "bit of fun" the recruits were naive enough to expect on joining. The scene of the first battle seems to reflect the light hearted mood of the people who had never known war since 1812 and before that since 1776. This first military conflict was called the Battle of Bull Run which happened thirty-five miles southwest of Washington and believe it or not attracted hundreds of sightseers – reporters and picnickers all gathered together for a family day out to witness the battle between 35,000 Union soldiers and 22,000 Confederates wearing multi-coloured uniforms.

It was here at Henry Hill, Stonewall Jackson got his nickname. Confederate re-enforcements then caused confusion and even the spectators got caught up in the melee and had to make good a hasty retreat. Things got more serious after that and battles with casualties numbering thousands took place. 24,000 at Sharpsburg near Maryland and 16,000 at Fredericksburg were the norm all across the land for over four years. However, the optimists were still thinking of a war that would be short and sweet like a donkey's gallop. The years that followed painted a sorry contradiction of their expectations. Survivors of battles often struggled back to Washington without knapsacks, cross belts or even uniforms wrapped only in blankets. It became a familiar sight everywhere. Self-doubt affected Lincoln who had hoped for a quick victory to restore constitutional Government and mend bridges. An armistice would be a defeat. There was no other route but Scott's anaconda policy "Surround the South and squeeze it to death."

Yet in the midst of Lincoln's worries and doubts God was listening after all for the most illustrious group of soldiers ever to fight for America emerged to fight for Lincoln. It was called "The Fighting 69". This 69th Infantry Regiment was a military unit originally from New York City. Its nickname The Fighting Irish was coined by Robert E. Lee himself and for good reason. Since 1861 it has fought in four wars; The Civil War of 1861, The First World War 1914-18, The Second World War 1939 – 45, and the Iraqi War of 2008. The army crest consists of two wolfhounds and a red shamrock. During Lincoln's war its regimental colours were green with the golden harp of Ireland.

It was founded in 1851 when its first soldiers "The Young Irelanders" failed in their rebellion against the British in Ireland causing them to emigrate to America where they founded the 69th Infantry in New York. Its leaders were General Michael Doheny, Colonel Thomas Francis Meagher and General "wild Bill" Donovan. There was another illustrious figure called Father Duffy, the fighting chaplain. In France in the Battle of Meuse – Argonne in 1914, he was offered some grenades to protect himself which he refused and continued to give the last rites to the wounded. Father Duffy is memorialized today in a statue at the north end of Times Square. Some people still call it Duffy Square.

In the Civil War a Confederate officer noted that "The 69th held their ground" like a rock in a whirlpool and they fought like heroes!! Confederate General Hill was heard to complain during a battle "There are those damned green flags again!!" The fighting 69th were known to be brave to the point of being suicidal. So brave, 4,000 died in the Civil War.

I don't know how authentic this is but at Gettysburg, a Father Corby was seen giving them mass and absolution before the battle. He gave a promise "To refuse a Christian burial to the soldier who turns his back upon the foe."

A statue of Father Corby was erected later in Gettysburg. At one point only the Irish stood between the Confederates and defeat at Gettysburg. They stepped into the field and with banners flying came within yards of the Confederate line. Even their opponents were heard to praise the Fighting 69th. Lt. Colonel Bland of the 7th South Carolinas said "Is that not a magnificent sight" after watching the 69th charge. It has been described as one of the greatest fighting units in American history.

The Irish played a major part in the Union Army for over 170,000 Irish and Irish Americans joined up. Irish priests and nuns served as chaplains and nurses in the field. It's hard to believe that during one of their battles, a Confederate General was heard to say "Why, we forgot they were fighting us and cheer after cheer went up along our lines." In another battle one man was heard to say "What a pity, here comes Meagher's fellows."
Following Gettysburg the Fighting 69th disbanded in June 1864. However many new volunteers joined its ranks and were present at the surrender of General Lee at Appomattox. Out of more than 2,000 regiments in the Union Army only six regiments had more casualties than the Fighting 69th which finally marched in glory in the Civil War victory parade in Washington DC.

Let's bring the story of the Fighting 69th up to date. Their final appearance on the streets of America came when they were specially appointed on September 11, 2001 to active duty once again. They served to protect U.S. nuclear power plants, airports, bridges, tunnels and trains throughout New York as part of Operation Noble Eagle after the attack of 9/11.

So let's hear two final citations of honour to them from two of America's greatest citizens General Douglas MacArthur and President John F. Kennedy. General Douglas MacArthur, gave the following address to members and veterans of the 69th at The Waldorf-Astoria Hotel in New York City via short-wave radio from Manila, The Philippines, on January 24, 1940:
"No greater fighting regiment has ever existed than the One Hundred and Sixty-fifth Infantry of the Rainbow Division, formed from the old Sixty-ninth Regiment of New York. I cannot tell you how real and how sincere a pleasure I feel tonight in once more addressing the members of that famous unit. You need no eulogy from me or from any other man. You have written your own history and written it in red on your enemies' breast, but when I think of your patience under adversity, your courage under fire, and your modesty in victory, I am filled with an emotion of admiration I cannot express. You have carved your own statue upon the hearts of your people; you have built your own monument in the memory of your compatriots."

John Fitzgerald Kennedy in his address to the Irish Parliament on June 28, 1963 expressed America's praise and admiration for the Fighting 69th:
"The 13th day of December, 1862, will be a day long remembered in American history. At Fredericksburg, Virginia, thousands of men fought and died on one of the bloodiest battlefields of the American Civil War. One of the most brilliant stories that day was written by a band of 1,200 men who went into battle wearing a green sprig in their hats. They bore a proud heritage and a special courage, given to those who had long fought for the cause of freedom. I am referring, of course, to the Irish Brigade. General Robert E. Lee, the great military leader of the Southern Confederate Forces, said of this group of men after the battle, "The gallant stand which this bold brigade made on the heights of Fredericksburg is well know. Never were men so brave. They ennobled their race by their splendid gallantry on that desperate occasion. Their brilliant though hopeless assaults on our lines excited the hearty applause of our officers and soldiers."
In view of all the foregoing, I guess history has long since shown that Lincoln had no need to fear the future.

But the Gods would not relent and tragedy struck not just Lincoln's army but his beloved sons

Tad and Willie who came down with fever. Willie died on February 20, 1862 leaving Lincoln devastated with grief. Mary, who couldn't attend the funeral, had a nervous breakdown. Mary gave away all Willie's toys and turned to religion and séances for consolation.

The hour was a dark one indeed and even Lincoln's resistance to a higher power relented. He began to communicate with Mary's God more intimately. Mary meanwhile tackled her own grief by visiting hospitals to comfort wounded soldiers, thus sharing in their suffering.

But meanwhile fraud, corruption and mismanagement riddled the army with a different kind of disease – incompetence. Lincoln moved to stamp it out – "This army has got to fight," he said. "The champagne and oysters on the Potomac must be stopped." He ordered the army to march on Richmond. McClellan, a politically ambitious General had other ideas. He procrastinated.

Getting together the right blend of Generals to do the job was one of Lincoln's main headaches as the fortunes of war vacillated. Frustration forced him to command the Commanders but McClellan demanded 100,000 more men and again procrastinated. McClellan was withdrawn from the fray temporarily but after another defeat was reinstated.

Lincoln questioned God's purpose. "God cannot be for and against the same thing at the same time," he thought. But if God willed this contest it would only end when God wanted it to end. Yes, even God was causing confusion.

McClellan's commitment was to a compromise settlement in which both sides, North and South, would go back to the status quo. But to Lincoln this would leave the nation half-slave and half-free. Lincoln had thought profoundly as a politician on this dilemma for the past few years. He had had plenty of time to come to terms with it. He had long since found the answer by a long complicated process the General had never tried. Lincoln's mind was made up. The ultimate emancipation of the slave without endangering the Union was the only route he concluded. Some of Lincoln's decisions were criticised as those of a man born of white trash and educated in a slave State. Waste and corruption in the army continued to flourish. Lincoln sacked General John Charles Fremont, a one time friend. The fact that blacks were employed as labourers but not as soldiers didn't help.

A compensated emancipation plan went before Congress. The New York Tribune hailed the measure as "The day star of a new dawn". Congress approved it and speed was demanded in legislation. But Lincoln refused to be hassled into mistakes. "I can only go as fast as I can see how I go," he said.

In July 1864 Lincoln's ideas were clarified even further – "Human bondage," he said, "was incompatible with the Union. A gradual compensated emancipation was the only long term route." He was becoming cynical now, saying "I distrust the wisdom if not the sincerity of friends who would hold my hand while my enemies stab me. These professed friends have paralysed me more in this struggle than any other one thing. But whatever else they did slaveholders would not part with their human property," he concluded.

Poor Lincoln then came under fire from some of his own supporters who accused him of deference to rebel slavery. Not even Nixon or George Bush has been confronted with such a nationwide conflict of opinion. It was like riding an unbroken runaway racehorse with the rider trying desperately to protect it from its own self destruction.

Patience and moderation continued to be the mantra Lincoln preached. "The Union could not be saved without destroying slavery." There was no in-between. He was also worried about the increasing riots against Negroes in the North.

Lincoln addressed Negro leaders in the White House. Surprisingly he said "The blacks in America would never be truly free in a white man's country." A puzzling admission from a

President fighting as Commander-in-Chief to achieve such freedom. Lincoln was still riding that runaway racehorse. Once again he was criticized for his blunt honesty when Frederick Douglas accused him of inconsistencies, contempt for Negroes and canting hypocrisy. But Lincoln's words were words of sympathy not contempt.

Other more practical post war problems surfaced. What would happen to the slaves when they were free? How would they be fed? What would happen to the South deprived of its labourers? Lincoln's critics continued to confront him for change to which he replied – "I am a slow walker but I never walk back."

He continued to jail anyone who helped the rebellion and more than 13,000 of them filled Northern prisons. His Generals still manipulated to prevent victory and bring about a compromise and thus save slavery but to no avail. This negotiated peace was attacked by Lincoln. "Must I shoot a simple minded soldier boy who deserts, while I must not touch a hair of a wily agitator who induces him to desert?" Despite the riots, violence, slaughter, burning and looting against the Emancipation Proclamation it was pushed through Congress on to the Statute Books.

The Ratification dates for the Proclamation were as follows:

1865 - Illinois Feb1, Rhode Island Feb 2, Michigan Feb 3, Maryland Feb 3, New York Feb 3, Pennsylvania Feb 3, West Virginia Feb 3, Missouri Feb 6, Maine Feb 7, Kansas Feb 7, Massachusetts Feb 7, Virginia Feb 9, Ohio Feb 10, Indiana Feb 13, Nevada Feb 16, Louisiana Feb 17, Minnesota Feb 23, Wisconsin Feb 24, Vermont Mar 8, Tennessee Apr 7, Arkansas Apr 14, Connecticut May 4, New Hampshire Jul 1, Sth Carolina Nov 13, Alabama Dec 2, Nth Carolina Dec 4, Georgia Dec 6, Oregon Dec 8, California Dec 19, Florida Dec 28.

1866 - Iowa Jan 15, New Jersey Jan 23,

1870 - Texas Feb 18,

1901 - Delaware Feb 12

1976 - Kentucky Mar 18

1995 – Mississippi Mar 16** Mississippi ratified the amendment in 1995.

Meanwhile the dead mounted in the war. To Lincoln "God had not yet reached His ultimate purpose in these terrible times. Waiting for God's journey to finish was in the future." He was encouraged by such thoughts as "When we give freedom to the slave, we assure freedom to the free." The word God came easily to him now.

On November 19, 1863 Lincoln went to Gettysburg where only four months previously 170,000 Americans had been locked in battle which ended only after 51,000 had fallen as casualties. He intended to make a short sincere explanation to the relatives and dignitaries present as to why their loved ones had fallen. Through his steel rimmed spectacles he read a speech that has gone down in the history of the American people as one of the most movingly eloquent speeches ever written, "The Gettysburg Speech".

Starting with these words "Four score and seven years ago (1776) our fathers brought forth on this Continent a new nation. We are met on a great battlefield – of a war testing whether any nation so conceived and so dedicated can long endure." He finished with the words "That we have highly resolved that these dead shall not have died in vain – that this nation under God shall have a new birth of freedom. That Government of the people, by the people, for the people shall not perish from the earth."

Lincoln continued to live an open life despite the traumatic nature of events he lived through. To confront threats and outspoken passions released in a cauldron of hate, confusion, despair and tumult from friends and enemies alike must have been frightening. To walk oblivious of the dangers he was surrounded by was the very essence, the very heart of a very brave man. Yet Lincoln was not oblivious to the storm clouds that daily hung over every waking moment of every new day.

The list of would-be assassins could come from any part of the society he lived in. Republicans, Democrats, Copperheads abolitionists, office seekers gathered like a rabble babbling about the pain of their failure. Failure to change the course of history their way. Hostility even spewed from a Democratic newspaper preaching in hand-wringing pros against Lincoln's re-election with words that encouraged sedition. "If elected to misgovern for the next four years some bold hand would pierce his heart with dagger point for the public good." An open invitation to kill him after the next election!

Lincoln nevertheless was re-elected at fifty-six years of age. Mary knew he was broken-hearted and exhausted. His dry humour ever present came to his rescue when on incubating smallpox; he laughed "Where are the office seekers now I have something to give to everyone." But when asked to take a holiday he replied "The welfare of the country would always pursue me."

Inauguration day approached and Lincoln admitted to what others could clearly see. He was unwell. "My feet and hands are always cold. I suppose I should be in bed." Because of the persistent rumours of assassination, his safety was taken more seriously now, so extra guards were posted on him. It was no surprise therefore that the first Cabinet meeting of his second term was held in his bedroom. He was propped up on pillows.

One story refers to a premonition he had four years previously in 1860 waiting for the first election results. Lying full length before a mirror he perceived the illusion of two faces, one pale and haggard. When he stood up his reflection was normal only to return to the double image when lying down. Mary ever the clairvoyant had become upset saying the images told he would survive his first Presidency but not the second and she became very upset. They could also have indicated seriously high blood pressure from stress.

Another theory asks another question. Could these symptoms really denote a low blood count in Lincoln? Who knows? The war continued outside. General Grant fought with tenacity and to a complaint about Grant's drinking problem, Lincoln replied, "If I but knew the brand I would send every other Commander a barrel of the same whisky. The war is eating my life out. I have a strong impression that I shall not live to see the end." Another dark prophesy. But 540,000 had been killed as Lincoln watched the wounded coming into town while on his way to a Soldiers Home to visit his troops. But good news did filter through now and then.

Trains proved a major asset in getting troops moved in large numbers to distant battle zones. About 24,964 men operated 419 locomotives and 6,330 cars over 2,105 miles of track. A further 137,418 bridges were built and 641 miles of track was laid.

Yet despite the casualties that sometimes saw 40,000 or 50,000 killed or wounded in one battle, amazing stories emerged. Like the magnanimity of General Grant when he ordered 25,000 rations to be distributed to General Lee's hungry troops proving how a soldier's kinship is boundless towards his fighting opponent in a different uniform. Then again they were all fellow Americans who deep down in their secret thoughts must have questioned the cost of it all.

They may even have questioned by now, in the midst of the carnage why they were fighting fellow Americans. Their thoughts more profound now as they matured in battle. Time left them searching for real answers as each day came and went.

The cost of it all was mind boggling. So far 360,000 Union Troops and 260,000 Confederates were dead. Amazingly, visitors still invaded the White House to question, debate and hear Lincoln's replies in yarns and stories. One lasting impression was his solemnity through it all. People even thronged the corridors. He disliked reviewing Court Martials for cowardice. "Leg cases" he called them, having great sympathy for the young boys who ran away under fire.

Lincoln's sympathy for the young soldiers was not unusual for in a Civil War you were not fighting a foreign foe but your own countryman. Here are a few anecdotes that tell their own stories to embellish what I say.

The following anecdotes are taken from The American Civil War Source Book by Philip Katcher.

Returning from the front a soldier was asked where he was going. He replied that his father lived four miles down the road and he was going home to speak to his brother who had returned from the Southern Army on sick leave and he intended to take him prisoner.

Another similar story was somewhat different. Passing some newly taken prisoners a soldier heard a shout "Tom, what are you doing in such bad company?" However Tom's reaction was to mix with the POW's, shake one of them by the hand and engage in a little banter before walking on to fight his own battle in the Civil War.

Sympathy was another emotion shown from one soldier to another. In a barn just after "The Battle of Slaughter Mountain" two badly wounded soldiers lay, one in blue, the other in grey. "Johnny where are you shot?" said one. "Lost my leg," was the reply. "Ah, you're in a divil of a fix for dancing, I've only lost my arm." "I'm sorry for you Yankee," the soldiers in blue said. "You'll never be able to hug your sweetheart again. Why are you fighting us anyway?" "For the old flag," was the reply. "Well take your darned old flag and go home with it, we don't want it."

A bizarre picture is written about a Ball attended by well-dressed neighbours celebrating in the middle of the battle going on around them. Two twelve inch shells fell in the front yard. The dance stopped for five minutes only.

One heart-breaking picture comes through a story about a brave little girl who defied the Confederate soldiers facing her by waving the Union flag taunting the soldiers with "Traitors, Traitors, Traitors. Take the flag off me." Fearing a serious reaction from his troops the Commander saluted the flag and the men cheered. The young girl broke down and cried "Oh I wish I had a rebel flag. I'd wave that too." Perhaps in this little cameo we are experiencing the heartache and pain of a nation torn apart who didn't really want to fight.

Still Lincoln defied the odds of assassination despite the threats. He daily took his ride in an open topped carriage with Mary. It was not hard to plot his whereabouts for often he turned up at a Soldiers Home to meet the wounded. Evening receptions still took place. Hundreds of people turned up. When not socializing he was working. He was an easy touch for clemency whenever possible. John Murphy, a seventeen year old son of a father killed in the war, was due to be shot but on the appeal of his mother, Lincoln cancelled the order. A great cross-section of promoters, inventors and storekeepers trooped before him daily, the line of such visitors was never ending. He even debated the Indian question. "I'll deal with that after the war," he said.

But other more serious work went on. A pardon was negotiated for all Confederate Troops provided they took an Oath of Allegiance to the Union. The 13th Amendment to the Constitution was also drawn up to ensure no future Government could reverse the Emancipation Proclamation. It was passed by three votes on January 31, 1865.

The possible aftermath of the Civil War haunted Lincoln. When he looked out across the Potomac he mused "If the people over the river had behaved themselves I could not have done what I have done." The impact of the war didn't escape anybody countrywide there was a national debt of destroyed bodies and broken families. "The heavens are hung in black," he observed. "Husbands, sons, fathers, brothers dead and for what? Was the punishment inflicted hurting the complacent, the self-sufficient and all who had forgotten God in their presumptuous sins?" There's that word God again. Somehow, he seemed to blame an ungrateful nation for turning its back on an angry deity.

Lincoln gently chastised America for its treatment of a God he believed in but seldom prayed to when he wrote as follows: We have been the recipients of the choicest bounties of heaven. We have been preserved these many years in peace and prosperity. We have grown in numbers, wealth and power as no other nation has ever grown. But we have forgotten God. We have forgotten the gracious Hand which preserved us in peace, and multiplied and enriched and strengthened us; and we have vainly imagined, in the deceitfulness of our hearts, that all these blessings were produced by some superior wisdom and virtue of our own. Intoxicated with unbroken success, we have become too self-sufficient to feel the necessity of redeeming and preserving grace, too proud to pray to the God that made us.

Perhaps a speech that needs repeating daily today in a pagan world that just won't listen anymore.

Four years is a long time to be fighting against your own countrymen but the end of the war arrived to leave us with stories which are heartbreaking. The Confederate army fell apart at the end. There were no retribution or mass hangings. Southern leaders like Robert E. Lee just packed up and went back home. But the ordinary Confederate soldier had to walk home as best he could with no money and little food. One Lieutenant didn't get home until late 1865. "The morning after I arrived home," he said, "I put on some of my father's old clothes armed myself with a corn knife and waged war on the standing corn as if I had only been away a day or two."

Some arrived home to find their small things like pens and pocket knives were impossible to replace. Many civilians shut their doors on the Confederate soldier when he came to beg for food for the journey home. Large plantation owners ended up in menial jobs, cleaning streets or working for the U.S. army. Some like the James brothers of Hollywood fame became desperados and gun fighters out West. Some went to Brazil, others went to Mexico. The Union soldiers were much better off getting a gratuity of $250 each. Officers received more. Many lost their gratuities gambling or were robbed by thieves.
I feel I must find space here for the son of the forty years undefeated General and 12th President Zachary Taylor. His name is Richard Taylor. You may remember the warning Zachary gave to Jefferson Davis his son-in-law against any threat to the Union. In fact the 12th President threatened to shoot Davis and lead an army in support of the Union.
Zachary's son Richard graduated from Yale University in 1845 after which he served his father as military secretary. He later became a Louisiana planter and State Senator.
His first role in the Civil War was as Colonel of the Louisiana Infantry. Although he never reached the military greatness of his father amazingly he chose to fight on the Confederate side in the Civil War. This, knowing the life of Zachary Taylor his father, was an extraordinary decision reflecting the deep divisions of heart and mind in even the most illustrious family fighting in the Civil War. After the war Richard canvassed for leniency for the south and especially for his brother-in-law Jefferson Davis. Richard Taylor died in New York in 1879 aged fifty-three.

The Union soldiers came home victorious and idolized by an appreciative population. Support groups sprung up to help the needy with museums, reading rooms, social centres and libraries with a ready exchange facility for war relics. However, for many the war was far too painful and most of them preferred to just forget it. Many just escaped into depression and drink in some far distant hut in the wilderness. Today these symptoms are treated by modern medicine as post traumatic stress disorder (PTSD). Old Soldiers' Homes were a great help to both sides as were the pensions payable for their lost limbs and eyes. Yes, war can never be the answer to an unresolved political problem. Broken minds and broken hearts will always serve to remind us of the sheer futility of war when the last gun has been silenced.

The fact that hostilities took over half a million lives – the lives of many young, exuberant, happy, innocent, fun-loving young lads on both sides, with their whole future ahead of them, was a sacrilege. The whole ghastly mistake was finally put to rest when on December 18, 1965 the 13th Amendment to the Constitution was ratified setting every slave in the United States, North and South free forever. Would that Congress had been allowed to resolve the problem four years earlier before the first gun shot was fired at Fort Sumter on April 12, 1861?

But war or no war politics still went on. While the gunfire of the Civil War was still crackling inauguration day came in March 1865 for Lincoln's second term. In his speech, Lincoln's words revealed his heartbreak at the horror of the battlefields. "A terrible price to pay for the sin of slavery," he said. "Let us strive on to finish the work we are in, to bind up the nation's wounds, to care for him who shall have borne the battle and for his widow and his orphans to do all which may achieve and cherish a just and lasting peace among ourselves and with all nations."
One month later disaster struck. The final curtain in the life of Abraham Lincoln, 16th President of the United States came down on Good Friday evening April 14, 1865.
John Wilkes Booth, an actor, decided to play God. He was never a soldier in the cause of the South but a man filled with some kind of insane hatred by taking on the role of Lincoln's executioner.

The description of the assassination made horrific reading. Under the headline of "Assassination of President Lincoln" the following is an extract of the printed newspaper report.

At 1.30 this morning Mr. Stanton (Secretary for War) reported as follows: 'This evening at 9.30 President Lincoln while sitting in a private box at Fords Theatre, with Mrs. Lincoln, Mrs. Harris and Major Rathbone, was shot by an assassin who suddenly entered the box and approached behind the President. The assassin then leaped upon the stage, brandishing a large knife and escaped in the rear of the theatre. A pistol ball entered the back of the President's head penetrating nearly through. The wound is mortal. The President has been insensible ever since the infliction of the wound and is now dying.
Wilkes rode off victoriously into the night hoping to be hailed as a hero should he reach Confederate lines safely. Wilkes wasn't to know his trigger finger was to do the South more harm than good.

He had planned the assassination for months openly and flamboyantly inviting detection. He had originally planned to kidnap Lincoln and take him to Richmond but when Richmond fell he changed his plan to murder. He had Grant Johnston and Seward lined up also but his fellow conspirators were too useless to carry out even a smash and grab raid at a corner news-stand.

Stephen B. Oats gave a dramatic account of Lincoln's assassination in his book With Malice Toward None, a book of historic significance. I give here an abbreviated version of that terrible night. Mary Todd Lincoln and Julia Grant just did not get on. Mary insulted Julia in front of officers in one of her tantrums. It was impossible therefore, for General Grant to accept the invitation to them to go to the theatre. So, who to invite? The Stantons too were unable to go. Lincoln told Mary at lunch he had half a mind not to go. But Mary insisted since it had been in the newspapers they had to go. They finally found a handsome young couple, Major Henry R. Rathbone and Clara Harris his fiancée, the daughter of a Senator in New York.

Lncoln spent the afternoon labouring over pardons and reprieves and other mundane jobs, for the usual stream of visitors. Around five in the afternoon, the Lincolns rode out of the White House gates into a bitter cold windy night. They sat close together and Lincoln was in good form. "You seem so gay, so cheerful," said Mary. "And well I might be. I consider this day the war has come to a close. We must both be more cheerful in the future. Between the war and our darling Willie, we have been very miserable."

On the way Lincoln met the wife of the manager of Groters Theatre which was showing a new play called "Aladdin". Hess, the manager, had invited Lincoln but Lincoln would not change his plans. He wanted something that would make him laugh.
In the carriage Mary and Abraham Lincoln talked about the future. What they would do after his second term. Travel to Europe with their sons. Visit Jerusalem, he had always wanted to see it. Then out West to California where the soldiers discharged from the army would find jobs in the silver mines. After that, return to his law practice to make enough to provide for them. Back to the quiet of the office and the Supreme Court; to the circuit; to discussion with old friends around hotel fireplaces. Mary was doubtful if she would go to the theatre. She had had a headache. However, she went and here they were in the carriage to the theatre. Anyway, what rest would he have back in the White House from the visitors? Crook offered to go as an extra guard when Lincoln had refused to call it off. Premonition was thick in the air "No," said Lincoln, "You have had a long hard day." He had then said goodbye to Crook on the White House steps.

Street corner lamp lights glimmered in the swirling mist. They were late and the play had started without them. The theatre was packed tonight. On entering the theatre the orchestra spotted him and struck up "Hail to the Chief". Lincoln sat in a rocking chair provided for the occasion in his box which was left unlocked behind him. The guard slipped away for a while. Some say to get himself a drink. The Lincolns let themselves relax into the play and Mary laughed a lot. Lincoln felt a chill at one point and stood up to put on his overcoat against a slight breeze. Mary nestled into him. "What would Miss Harris think of my hanging onto you so?" she whispered. "She won't think anything about it," he replied. The scene was now set for the real life tragedy that was to come. Behind Lincoln the figure of a man stepped into the box and aimed a derringer at the back of Lincoln's head not six inches away.

The gunshot in the State box was heard and interrupted the dialogue. Lincoln's arm jerked up convulsively. The man stood in a smoky cloud behind them. Lincoln slumped forward. Mary screamed in terror. The killer now had a dagger, a wild looking man in black felt hat and high boots with spurs. He yelled and slashed Rathbone's arm to the bone. He jumped for the stage, a short distance down, but caught his spur in a regimental flag and crashed on to the stage, breaking his left shin bone.

The audience recognised the actor, John Wilkes Booth and thought it was part of the play. They heard his cry "The South shall be free" or something like that. As Rathbone dragged himself out the back door of the box he shouted after Booth "Stop that man, won't somebody stop that man." Miss Harris cried "The President is shot." Screams and panic came from the crowd as they shoved and jostled in the aisles heading for the exit. "Keep your places," a voice cried in vain.

A young army doctor fought his way into Lincoln's box. His name was Charles A. Leale. Mary was there weeping hysterically. Leale lay Lincoln on the floor and attended to him. The bullet had struck just below Lincoln's left ear, passed through his brain and lodged behind his right eye. Another doctor arrived and helped with artificial respiration. Leale massaged Lincoln's left breast. Finally Leale gave him mouth to mouth resuscitation. At last Lincoln was breathing faintly on his own and his heart began to flutter into an irregular beat. Leale shook his head and whispered "It is impossible. His wound is mortal." They carried him out into the mist and across the road to William Petersen's Boarding House opposite and laid him diagonally on a four poster bed. Mary ran to his side, dropped on her knees and begged him to speak to her. Robert, her son, came and comforted her. Other assassination attempts were tried elsewhere and Stanton placed the country under Martial Law and called for the police and Andrew Johnson, the Vice President, now the new President. Mary was recalling Lincoln's dream of mournful voices and a corpse in the White House .....

She remembered Abraham's dream now. It was April 1865 and he fell asleep while working late. He recounted his dream to Mary. A weird dream he also told to his friend and bodyguard, Ward Hill Lamon. In his dream he was walking around the White House and somewhere he heard the sound of people crying. He wandered down the stairs. All the rooms were lit but empty. The weeping was coming from the East Room, usually used for funerals. There was a corpse there on top of a platform, surrounded by guards and mourners. Lincoln asked who had died "The President" was the reply. "He was killed by an assassin." "My God," Mary sobbed, "that was prophetic."

At last when Mary left the room at 7.22 a.m. Lincoln was accepted to be dead. The Pastor said some prayers and Stanton said tersely "He now belongs to the ages." The nation mourned. Those who had castigated him as a dictator, a baboon, stupid, incompetent, now were unified together in a terrible grief. The Chief was dead.

His bitter words about his own patriotism had now come true. "I'd rather be assassinated than lose one star from the flag."

Meanwhile, one of Booth's accomplices, Lewis Payne, forced his way into Seward's room at his home where he was convalescing from a carriage accident. Payne slashed him with a knife but failed to kill him. The plan for Johnson and Grant also failed. Payne and his four accomplices were later imprisoned. Booth was shot dead two weeks later in a barn some miles away by a Sergeant Boston Corbett.

Naturally there were many other different accounts of that terrible assassination night and of course much speculation on Booth's background in the newspapers. Some reported Booth as saying he had links with the underground Confederacy. They also claimed he was familiar with Fords Theatre since he used it to collect his mail there. The moment of assassination was to take place at a highlight in the play "Our American Cousin" when there was loud noisy laughter, thus drowning out the fatal pistol shot.

They speculated further as follows. "Booth being familiar with the stage hands was also able to lure them away with a bottle of whisky left for them at a local saloon." After the assassination things began to go wrong for Booth. He got entangled in a curtain as he jumped from the box to the stage and broke his ankle. A speedy getaway was essential and Booth limped to a pre-arranged destination to meet up with another of his gang, a man called Herold. They rode to the house of a Doctor Samuel Mudd, who treated Booth's ankle.

As I later point out in my piece on Andrew Johnson, Lincoln's successor, there were eight people brought before the courts. The fate of all nine was as follows: - Booth shot dead in a barn; Herold, Atzerdot, Payne, Mrs. Mary Surratt, Arnold, O'Laughlin, Spangler and Mudd were charged with complicity in the assassination. Payne, Atzerdot, Mrs. Surratt and Herold were hanged. The rest got lesser sentences.

The Secretary of War, Stanton, enters the picture and becomes the subject of much criticism by the historians for his handling of events from now on. It is easy to criticize in hindsight a Party who was cruelly deprived of their leader at the moment of his triumph. In the passions that were released who could blame Stanton for wanting revenge on those who not only challenged the Constitution laid down by the Founding Fathers; Washington, Adams, Jefferson and Madison, but formed their own Government and placed an army in the field which resulted in carnage and the loss of half a million lives. They sullied the very name of America by shooting dead the very man who spared the lives of their defeated army. This was unforgivable.

Stanton was convinced Lincoln's assassination was a plot hatched by the rebel Confederate Government itself but unfortunately after his investigations he was never able to prove it. He was certain it only came about as a result of the dying Confederate war effort. Stanton spared nobody and stirred up much anti South feeling. The chances of voices being heard to promote a peaceful outcome to this terrible deed as Lincoln himself would have wished were not going to happen. As we said earlier, Booth never truly understood how much damage his bullet would do to reconciliation in the South for years to come. Meanwhile Stanton took charge of Lincoln's funeral procession.

For six days Lincoln's body lay in State in the East Room of the White House. All of this I will describe in more detail under the Presidency of Andrew Johnson, Lincoln's successor. On the seventh day, Lincoln's coffin was placed aboard a train which would travel all over the country going by circuitous route to Springfield, Illinois, Baltimore, Philadelphia, New York, Albany, Buffalo, Cleveland, Columbus, Indianapolis and Chicago. It also took in many minor stops on the way.

Lincoln's remains went on display in New York, Chicago and many other cities in its travels. Millions of Americans paid their respects as his body lay in an open casket. Many others watched in tears by the side of railway tracks as his coffin passed by. The funeral procession lasted for two weeks. Shock and indignation showed in the faces of men and women everywhere across the North. They knew they had passed through four years of hell. Their President being struck down at the very moment of victory, left them with an anger that blacked out Lincoln's vision for reconciliation after the war.

It surfaced in a frightening way that Abraham Lincoln would never have tolerated.
Mobs gathered outside the homes of anyone who failed to drape their houses in black. One newspaper editor who publicly abused Lincoln in print was killed.
Even ex-President Fillmore didn't escape their attention. He explained to the mob that he had not heard the news of Lincoln's death because he was so pre-occupied with nursing his sick wife. They accepted his explanation and withdrew. Such were the passions that were aroused by their President's assassination.

To conclude the story of Lincoln's burial, the funeral cortege finally made its way back to Lincoln's home town of Springfield where he was buried in a hillside crypt on May 4, 1865 in Oak Ridge Cemetery, one month after his inauguration for a second term as President of the United State.

But even now we have a bizarre twist to our story of Abraham Lincoln. Shortly after his burial, his crypt was invaded by kidnappers or body snatchers who almost succeeded in removing the remains of Lincoln, which they intended to ransom for money. They were disturbed and chased away. But now, Lincoln's body, lying in a burial chamber, became a potential target for future kidnappers or body snatchers and the authorities became paranoid with fear that the ultimate sacrilege would be accomplished. It was eventually re-interred fourteen times before it was finally laid to rest at a palatial resting place, worthy of the great man, at Oak Ridge Cemetery, Springfield, his first and now his last resting place.

Life went on for America after Lincoln's weary bones were finally laid to rest. The tragic Civil War officially ended at Appomattox on April 9, 1865. Reconstruction got underway with the new President, Andrew Johnson.

But should we not spare a last thought for someone else? Someone, who was closer to Lincoln than any of his political friends. Someone who lived through the crazy heartbreaking turmoil of not just the past four years but the highs and lows, the joys and the sorrows of family life with Abraham Lincoln.

In the avalanche of words written and spoken about her husband, the fate of his wonderful loyal, heartbroken wife, Mary Todd, has been ignored even dismissed. She wasn't the architect of U.S. history. Her name was irrelevant to the tapestry of events that exploded around her. Yet, she lived every painful moment which hurt her deeper than it hurt any of the famous Generals who fought for Lincoln. She also fought for Lincoln but unheard of and unseen.

So when that fatal shot rang out in Fords Theatre, who asked her what were her thoughts? When she returned to an empty White House again, who asked her how she felt? When she stayed at home during his funeral which because of her grief she couldn't face, did any one dry her tears and comfort her? No one seems to have recorded these awful moments in her devastation.

Yet the years that followed told their own story. Like any widow, she feared for her future. Like any widow she worried about her financial security now that her breadwinner was only a memory in a photograph and in the images she cherished in her heart.

People who would have shown no disrespect for her while her husband was around took from her past a hurtful rumour about a girl called Anne Rutledge. She was a girl who died years before Lincoln met Mary Todd. Lincoln it seems had never extinguished the flame of love he held for Anne Rutledge. Lincoln's law partner, William Herndon, Mary's cousin claimed to have a deeper more intimate knowledge of this than Mary, Lincoln's wife of twenty-three years. How the hell could he know? What a treacherous bastard he was to bring it up now. Mary's instinct was to escape from it all. One day with Tad, her youngest son, the one needing special attention all his years, she sailed away to Europe where she stayed for over a year. A very heart-searching, lonely twelve months it must have been for her.

Meanwhile, Congress was divided on the question of her pension and how much she was due. They dutifully settled on $3,000 per year for the wife of a martyr. Mary finally returned to America only to suffer the greatest cut of all six years later. Tad died, aged eighteen, on July 15, 1871. Mary had always been erratic, unpredictable and a manic depressive. Now her world disintegrated so dangerously, Robert her son, a Harvard Law School student, decided to commit her to a mental institution for her own good. The home had no bars but Bellevue had no cure either for a woman already caged in her own prison with the ghosts of three dead children and a husband shot before her eyes.

She fought for and achieved her release but lived on, a broken woman. As broken as any of the soldiers who had survived the horrors of the battlefield. She lived on for another seventeen years until she mercifully died on July 16, 1882 at Springfield, Illinois, aged 63 years and 215 days.

Lincoln's legacy to future generations is significant. Without his victory, the United States as we know it today might not exist. The Republic endured and slavery was ended forever. But at what a cost! Well, that cost is the subject of the story we read about under Lincoln's successor, Andrew Johnson, the 17th President of the United States – coming next.

Yes, this has been an astonishing story, laced with anecdotes about a man who achieved everything he set his heart on. But it is more than that. It is also the story of a tragedy. The tragedy of the Lincoln family – all six of them; Abraham, Mary, Robert, Edward, William and Tad. It is also about the tragedy of a country torn apart with wounds that took another one hundred and fifty years to heal, if at all.

What a pity nobody understood the warning in the words of another colossus of the American Political Dynasty, 3rd President of the United States, sixty years previously, Thomas Jefferson, when he wrote on the injustice of slavery.

"I tremble for my country, when I reflect that God is just and

that his justice cannot sleep forever".

17th President   Andrew Johnson

"Tennessee Tailor"
Born 1808
Died 1875
67 Years of age
1 Term
1865 – 1869
Age 56

Party: Democrat
Profession: Tailor
County: North Carolina, Raleigh
Ancestry: English
Estate: $50000
Hobbies: Unknown

Physical description: Height 5 foot 10 inches; stocky; brown hair worn long; high forehead

Extract from inaugural address:
None. Johnson was not elected due to the assassination of Abraham Lincoln.

ANDREW JOHNSON

Normally up to now I have begun the story of each President at his childhood but the assassination of Lincoln was such an abomination in American history I think we should continue the story of Lincoln as it affected his successor Andrew Johnson on Good Friday April 14, 1865 the day of the assassination.

Very early on Easter Saturday morning April 15, 1865 a loud banging on the door woke Andrew Johnson from his sleep. It was the morning after Lincoln's death.

The stories of plots and counter plots were numerous and implicated Johnson as well as the conspirators. But all those stories surfaced after the assassination of John F. Kennedy and could not be substantiated. The knocking became louder. Much more urgent. "Is that you Farwell?" he called out, recognizing the voice of former Governor Leonard J. Farwell of Wisconsin. "Yes let me in," was the reply. Farwell had just come from Fords Theatre. Soon guards arrived to protect Johnson as Seward was already seriously injured and no one knew how wide the assassination plot really was. Johnson sent Farwell to Fords Theatre ahead of him for more news while he dressed himself. Although offered the army for protection Johnson declined the bodyguards and with Farwell and O'Beirne set out at a run to see the stricken President.

He found Lincoln breathing heavily lying diagonally on a bed that was too small for him. Doctors and Cabinet Ministers came and went. Mrs. Lincoln was next door devastated by grief. Charles Sumner was holding Lincoln's head. Johnson did not stay long but returned to his own hotel room and paced up and down threatening dire consequences on the perpetrators. "They shall suffer for this," he said repeatedly.

But Lincoln died at 7.22 a.m. on the morning of the 15th and Johnson arranged for his own immediate inauguration at his hotel which happened at about 11.00 a.m. Johnson made a short dignified address and it was all over. He was now 17th President of the United States.
He went at noon to his first Cabinet meeting and asked Lincoln's men to continue in their posts. That is one version of events. Now for another version. You can take your pick. Senator Stewart of Nevada a man of profound prejudice always accused Johnson of being "The most untruthful, treacherous and cruel person who had ever held a place of power in the United States." This was Stewart's version of what happened on Saturday April 15, 1865. "Myself, Senator Ford and the Chief Justice were the first persons to bring Johnson the news of the assassination."

Johnson at the time was half dressed, dirty and shabby with matted hair as though from the mud in the gutter, trying apparently to overcome a hangover according to Stewart's story the Chief Justice gave Johnson the bad news. They went off to inform Secretary of War Stanton and when they returned Johnson was asleep again. They then dressed him, took him to the White House where they sent for a doctor, a tailor, and a barber. They then bathed him and dressed him in new clothes. Johnson they said "Didn't properly recover until that afternoon."

All of this horrific account has long since been proved wrong by the Chief Justice's papers, and various newspapers who confirmed there was no sign of drunkenness at Johnson's first Cabinet meeting. This was recorded in several places. It is also a well known fact that not only was Johnson not in the White House that day; he didn't enter it for three weeks.

It is well to record these accounts to highlight the distrust with which Andrew Johnson was held by his enemies of which he had many when entering the White House.

Secretary of State for War Stanton was left a free hand to pursue the perpetrators and organise the funeral arrangements. As we shall discover later the wisdom of giving Stanton such a role is questionable. Stanton was disliked and considered devious and imperious but nevertheless was trusted by Johnson to carry out his task. Besides Johnson was anxious to cause no waves and was content to keep Lincoln's men around him.

To be courteous to Mrs. Lincoln Johnson didn't enter the White House for three weeks. His patience and diplomacy were widely appreciated. Anyway he was too busy for the first few weeks attending to the new Cabinet and helping Stanton with the funeral arrangements. The casket was placed in the East Room on a catafalque 15 feet high and the room was decorated in black crepe by expert flower arrangements. On the day of the funeral the family were seated in a semicircle at the foot of the catafalque surrounded by Congressmen. Governors, military officers and other dignitaries. The funeral was as described by me in my piece on Lincoln.

Not surprisingly suspicions were rampant about those thought to have been implicated in the assassination, one of these being Jefferson Davis himself. A reward for the arrest of Davis was set at $100,000. One million dollars in today's money.

However this was really a gesture to satisfy popular demand. Davies was captured and jailed awaiting trial. There were other people apprehended too. All were sent for trial. Their names are now lost in the passing of time since that Good Friday, 1865.

People like David Herold, George Atzerdot, Lewis Paine, Mrs Mary Surratt, Samuel Arnold, Michael O'Laughlin, Edward Spangler and Dr Samuel Mudd. They all were brought before a military commission in a trial that lasted six weeks. Herold, Atzerdot, Paine and Mrs. Surratt received death sentences and the others got lesser punishment.

Just a small postscript to all this. Andrew Johnson later complained he did not want Mrs. Surratt executed but had been "hoodwinked" (that's his word) by his Secretary of State for War Stanton. The hanging of Mrs. Surratt to this day is considered to have been a gross miscarriage of justice.

However it seems the jury recommended mercy due to her sex and age. Johnson claimed he was never told of this. But the Judge advocate Joseph Holt said "Johnson read it in my presence and he said 'she kept the nest that hatched the egg'." Captain Christian Rath the hangman did not expect to have to hang the unfortunate woman and left her rope until last. He only made a five turn knot instead of the regulation seven turn knot but found it did its job satisfactorily. Mrs. Surratt's last words on the scaffold were "Please don't let me fall." At the end she was wearing a black dress and black veil.

All the death sentences were eventually carried out by hanging despite the vain protests by Mrs. Surratt's heartbroken daughter on behalf of her mother. Davis although not considered to be a conspirator received three years jail at Fort Monroe.

The high point of Johnson's first few months in the Presidency was the victory parade celebrating the end of the Civil War. That took place on May 22, 1865. The viewing platform was set up near the White House on which sat the President, members of the Cabinet and a list of Generals. It was a beautiful sunny day during which each army corps saluted the

President with lowered swords and dipped flags. To celebrate the wars final conclusion the last Confederate troops in Texas surrendered symbolically to the President.

The war was now truly over. Sadly missing from it all was the Commander-in-Chief himself Abraham Lincoln. Johnson received a glowing press approval especially by refusing the gift of a carriage from some New York merchants as "an unseemly act if accepted by him".

So far the new President had survived his baptism of fire by filling the shoes of an immortal with dignity and honour. Unfortunately time was to be a hard task master on Andrew Johnson as we shall see later.

Before getting carried away with the aftermath of the Civil War what about Andrew Johnson and his life story to date.

Andrew Johnson was unique in the Presidency for he was the only President ever to be impeached. He never attended school and was one of the few Presidents whose log cabin credentials could not be disputed so poor were his beginnings. He also enters the record books as the ex-President who returned again six years after his retirement to become a Senator. Another I can recall also returned also returned to Politics after retirement. He was the sixth President Quincy Adams. So ahead of us we have quite a formidable character to love, hate, pity and wonder about.

Andrew Johnson was born on the frontier in Raleigh, North Carolina on December 29, 1808 into a poverty that was unrelenting during his childhood and youth.

Raleigh was just a small town containing a courthouse, two hotels, a few stores and a small expensive school which most of the town's youngsters couldn't afford to attend. His first disaster was the death of his father Jacob when he was only three leaving his mother Mary McDonough Johnson penniless with two young lads to rear. The locals called her "Polly Weaver", I don't know why.
Polly was illiterate and showed no inclination to having the two boys educated. They remained uneducated for the rest of their childhood. Polly married again and this time to another poor uneducated white so nothing changed for the family.

Andrew's first job was as an apprentice in a tailor's shop where he was indentured to a James J. Selby. It was only through a visit to his workplace, by a Dr. William Hill that Andrew first heard of the classics which Dr. Hill read aloud to him.

He learned to read and became interested in following a career outside tailoring. He gathered periodicals and memorized them until one day he found himself sacked for a prank that misfired. After that he left home and made for South Carolina but with a trade as a journeyman tailor.

He returned home to Raleigh again to confront some family trouble but soon was on the move again to avoid arrest for disserting his tailoring apprenticeship.

So setting out again Andrew took with him his mother and stepfather and another apprentice aboard a cart pulled by a blind donkey. They eventually found themselves in Greenville where they settled down to a new life. But cupid had other ideas and was waiting to strike in the guise of a beautiful girl called Eliza McCardle. After a short courtship our romantic couple got married on May 17, 1827 aged nineteen. Andrew and Eliza moved into a house on Main

Street, Greenville and when the local tailor moved elsewhere Andrew used the front room of his own house as a tailor shop. The building still stands today in the year 2009 with a sign over the door that reads "A. Johnson Tailor". A new arrival Martha completed the happy family.

But Andrew was made of stern stuff and soon he prospered enough in his tailor shop to invest in some property including a Smiths shop, two houses and a farm where his mother went to live in the comfort she had never before experienced. Soon Andrew Johnson's Tailor Shop became the focal point for political debates by any of the locals that cared to drop in.

It was only natural for him to become a member of a debating society to which "he walked four miles" each way to participate. Soon his oratorical skills become obvious as was his talent for making friends.

There was nothing particularly special about Andrew Johnson. His appearance was not handsome; dark eyes, black hair, swarthy complexion and a broad face. However he did take life seriously and so was not blessed with a sense of humour. He was stubborn and unshakeable in what he believed in and perhaps because of his working roots identified easily with the ordinary man in the street including the small farmer. He had an instinctive suspicion, almost dislike for people of wealth and privilege.

At twenty, Andrew became an avid Jacksonian Democrat and soon won the local elections for Alderman in Greenville. His lack of education wasn't even noticed. Around this time he had further additions to the family - Charles in 1830, Mary in 1832 and Robert in 1834. He was now a very busy man with his tailor shop, his family and his politics. Andrew's talents were recognised when he was elected Mayor of Greenville and soon he became at twenty-six years of age a member of the State Legislature in Tennessee. Looking back down the hill he had ascended Andrew Johnson could congratulate himself on a life of no mean achievements since his humble beginnings in Raleigh, North Carolina.

Andrew Johnson soon learned from the local Greenville people their brand of resilience and independence. They were a tough class of mountaineers who moulded young Andrew's personality for further battles. Slavery was only next door in the region but so far Andrew was uncommitted.

However he didn't go unnoticed in the State Legislature as a speaker and a dresser and very soon he was a really polished performer.

He now had a national reputation and his potential was sky high. The ambitious Johnson changed Parties and became a Democrat in 1840 and one year later he was elected to the Tennessee Senate. The year was 1841.

For some strange reason Johnson was so impressed by this promotion he remarked, "I have reached the summit of my ambition." It was an opinion he still held right to the end of his Presidency. So perhaps we have a reason for his come back into politics as a Senator six years after he retired as President. Maybe election to the Tennessee Senate really was the zenith of his ambitions.

His final step up the ladder in politics was to Congressman in 1843 a position he held for ten years. But his journey was still in an ever-rising spiral and soon he was elected in 1853 as Governor of Tennessee. A little anecdote or two here must be told of Andrew Johnson and the sort of person he was. The retiring Governor of Tennessee kindly called to deliver him by carriage to the inauguration ceremony. Andrew politely declined the offer preferring as he put it "To walk with the people."

It must have been good political electioneering for he was re-elected Governor of Tennessee two years later in 1855. As Governor he was now in an ideal position to use his power to help those who like himself had failed to receive a decent education. He asked for a tax on all the property of the State for a common schools fund. A reluctant legislature agreed to the measure, and direct taxation for education became a new feature of life in Tennessee from that time on.

Johnson introduced many other radical ideas as Governor which were light years ahead of his time. Certain educational standards were set for teachers not unlike those of Bill Clinton late in the 20th century. Prejudices against women teachers were overcome and teaching jobs were opened up to women on the same pay as men. Another wonderful innovation was the introduction of State Libraries. Ever the friend of the farmers he introduced the first Agriculture Fair to be held in Tennessee to promote their produce and still he was looked down upon as a crude, low-class upstart by so called Southern Aristocrats. In such a crude and unsophisticated environment, where child mortality and hygiene caused the death of thousands, snobbery existed like a comic opera.

An amazing story of Johnson during his campaign for a second term as Governor of Tennessee reflects the man's almost insolent courage towards his enemies.

His life had been threatened by someone unknown so just before a meeting he was about to address he laid a pistol on the table before him for all to see. Telling his audience there was a would-be assassin among them he then proceeded with his speech as follows:
"If any man has come here tonight for the purpose indicated I do not say let him speak but let him shoot." The challenge was never taken up.

Well that is the personal story of Johnson and how he came to scale the dizzy heights of politics from very humble roots so poor that it seems to the writer he achieved the impossible.

What should be remembered is this. Andrew Johnson was a Southerner, and a slave-holder who because of his roots had a built-in certainty of the superiority of the white race. Sadly another form of snobbery.

So how did he come to be selected as Vice President when Lincoln won the 1864 Presidential Election? It seems there was a split in the Democratic Party ranks on the slavery issue. Johnson emerged by opposing the secessionists and declaring for the Union. His small group was known as the "War Democrats". This was an amazing and very courageous stand to take for his own Tennessee had joined the ranks of secessionists and the times were dangerous, full of hatred bitterness and violence. To his Tennessee people he was considered a traitor but when the Nashville Mayor refused to swear allegiance to the Union Johnson, as Governor replaced him with a Unionist. For his loyalty to the Union Johnson was nominated as Lincoln's running mate and in November 1864 he was elected Vice President to Abraham Lincoln.

However Johnson's commitment was to the Union and to the Constitution and only later to Emancipation. Johnson's very complicated reasoning would lead him into very troubled waters later.

He was now replacing Hannibal Hamlin who was Vice President to Lincoln in Lincoln's first term of office. But far from being a moment of triumph to be inaugurated Vice President to Abraham Lincoln, the whole show turned out to be a monumental disaster for Andrew Johnson. Why you may ask? Well it was because Johnson turned up for the big Ceremony drunk.

Events took place as follows: - Johnson left Tennessee for Washington quite ill and made a few speeches on the way while his family stayed behind in Tennessee. The night before the big day he shared a few glasses of whiskey with a friend.

Inauguration day was raining and dark and Johnson rose, not too well, from his activities the night before. Not feeling well he asked for a glass of whiskey and drank it neat. He then had another drink and on his way to the ceremony ran back for a third. Being already sick with Typhoid trouble didn't help. An array of foreign dignitaries in full court costume plus military and Navy officers in full uniform were there. Lincoln serious and austere sat in the front row to complete an intimidating picture for the unfortunate man.

At noon he entered the Chamber arm in arm with his predecessor ex-Vice President Hamlin. He was now drunk and proceeded to remind the top brass by name how indebted they were for their privileges to the people who elected them. He almost flaunted his grass roots belligerently to all and sundry. It was a virtuoso performance of petrifying embarrassment for all present.

The reaction of the press next day said it all. The New York World writing about Johnson's performance said "In comparison even Caligula's horse was respectable." "Democrat Senators were seen to chuckle" wrote the Richmond Sentinel. Later even though he retired into seclusion with his typhoid fever it was widely rumoured he was still on a binge. Certain Judges were forgiving however.

Benjamin Truman who knew him well said "I shared a table with him at Nashville and I never knew him to take wine or liquor at any meal I had with him. Some days he would consume two or four glasses of whiskey but on others no liquor at all." Yet the Assistant Secretary for War said "I saw him imbibe heavily throughout his Governorship of Tennessee but never saw him drunk." His sons did suffer from alcoholism but unlike a true alcoholic Andrew could take it or leave it. Some days later Lincoln spoke very protectively of Johnson. "I have known Andy Johnson for many years. He made a bad step the other day but you need not be scared Andy ain't no drunkard."

One note of criticism was heard from Zachariah Chandler "I was never so mortified in my life."

Frederick Douglass had a disturbing personal experience to tell after being introduced by Lincoln to Johnson during the inauguration ceremony.

The body language of Johnson troubled Douglass. He wrote "I concluded right there and then that the Tennessean was no friend of the black race." A very disturbing observation by a complete stranger.

Stage 1   The Presidency of Johnson

The story of Johnson's Presidency was played out on two geographical stages. One stage covered the vast landscape of post-Civil War America in the South in the middle of the true reality of life for people in a conquered war ravaged land. All around him were the free blacks and slaves now with new hope, new ambitions and new horizons ahead and most of all new mountains to climb to reach their stars.

In the other half of this picture the planters were trying to piece together the broken remnants of their once thriving exciting society full of laughter, riches and comfort and the security of a promising future. Now it was all gone swept away in four years of hardship and death. Swept away by Generals marching back and forth across their cotton fields leaving thousands of soldiers lying dying on the black earth bleeding in defeat or glory.

Stage 2

The second geographical stage was one on which "actors" posed in the spotlight of power strutting their stuff, posturing and pontificating in the victorious North in the hallowed halls of Washington. Johnson saw the South as a problem to be solved. A country to be rebuilt. A people to be rehabilitated. A place waiting for the miraculous touch of a visionary to blow the smoking embers of its dreams into life again.

All that was needed were the right methods, the right people, the right laws and the right expertise to rebuild the fabric of a new society. After that everyone would live happily ever after. Unfortunately Johnson was not the visionary they cried out for in their need.

Because their true leader was now lying sleeping in a peaceful spot in Springfield and as Stanton said "belonged to the ages" people on both stages North and South would reap no reward for victory but share together the bitter fruits of failure in the years ahead.

The Southerners now lived in the desolation of their beautiful lifestyle which was now only a memory. Let's walk again among the ruins of a conquered continent where once a beautiful land blossomed and flourished. You would find it a painful experience had you known it before the war. The best way modern readers can understand it better is to see the newsreels and films of Germany and Europe at the end of the Second World War in 1945.

To understand Johnson's dilemma let's look at the carnage he faced in his mandate to solve the problem of the mind shattering human tragedy spread before him. It was a journey that ended for him not in triumph but in the failure of his Presidency which ended in his impeachment four years later.

The scene was approaching anarchy. No previous President had been faced with the problem of reuniting, rebuilding and binding up the wounds of the victims as Lincoln had put it.

The landscape was covered in the ruins of broken homes that stretched as far as the eye could see. Plantations were wrecked. Major cities like Atlanta and Richmond were now only fire blackened spectres of war. Factories destroyed, railroads torn up and uprooted families wandering the country confused and homeless.

Alas, where were flag waving abolitionists or the defiant rebels of Fort Sumter now? Was there nothing left but the drums? Sadly drums will only make a lot of noise, they don't rebuild cities. Wisdom only comes when the noise abates leaving nothing but a helpless silence. That has always been the language and sheer futility of war when the last gunshot has sounded.

Two thirds of the Southern Railways were destroyed. One method was by heating the rails and twisting them around nearby trees. Over one hundred and forty miles of Memphis Railroads were the victims of this treatment. The Savannah and Charleston lines had no trains for five years after the war. South Carolina railroads were destroyed to the tune of $1.5 million. Billions in today's currency.

Old country mansions were burned or stripped of their furnishing. Even stately oak trees didn't escape the vandalism when they were cut down by soldiers for firewood. Plundered belongings turned up in Northern pawnshops. Stolen plates, pictures and books, clothes and even pianos were found later in the homes of officers and chaplains.

Northern papers pleaded for the return of such property. The price of peace was expensive too. Confederate currency became worthless and Confederate bonds were repudiated as the price of re-entering the Union. These bonds could be a major part of a life's savings to the owner. One hundred million insurance investments evaporated. Families unlucky enough not to be present when the army marched into their property found themselves confiscated of their lands for abandonment.

The Southerners greatest loss was his property in Negroes amounting to between one and four billion dollars in money value. Only those Southerners who could prove that he had never helped the Confederates could file a claim for war damages. Out of $60 million in claims only $4.5million was allowed.

Agents were appointed to tour the South during the war to take possession of all abandoned property especially cotton. Much of this was resold by Federal Agents. Dishonesty by these Federal Agents beggared belief.

It was described as the most stupendous swindle ever perpetrated and totally disgraced the Government in Washington. Secretary Hugh McCullough was forced to say "I am sure I sent some honest Agents South but it sometimes seemed very doubtful if any of them remained honest for long." Although they were allowed 50% commission even that amount didn't satisfy their greed for profits. Out of $20 million seized and sold only $8 million found its way into the United States Treasury. When no cotton was found livestock was taken instead as Confederate property. The biggest cotton thieves were Simeon Draper, Agent for the Gulf States with headquarters in New York and William P. Millen, Agent for the Interior with offices in Cincinnati. Draper, bankrupt starting the job was a millionaire in a few years. Even Government officials got rich beyond their wildest dreams but few were punished. The North also gained at least $68 million from cotton tax from the surrendered Confederacy. It was excused as a financial punishment for causing the war.

All this happened from the day the Union soldiers got a foothold in the South. Agents ran amok and collected taxes ruthlessly by seizing properties for which they paid ridiculous amounts and reselling them for huge profits which they embezzled. One estate worth $15,000 was claimed for $3,000. Another worth $24,000 was bought for $8,000. A whole town was sold for $10,608 but the sale was later disallowed.

Even pensions for past wars were confiscated and that included the widows of the Revolutionary soldiers of 1776. The right to practice in Federal Courts was nullified by a law of Congress in January 1865.
We praised the Union soldiers for being magnanimous in victory but the behaviour of the ruling class after the war reduced a dignified victory to the depths of shame. Their dead President would never have tolerated it.

Over a quarter of a million young men out of a white population of five million never returned from the battlefields. Many of the top Confederate soldiers were arrested or fled abroad to escape arrest. Jefferson Davis became a "hot potato" and was finally jailed for three years in Fort Monroe. A brother of Joseph Holt, the Judge Advocate General wrote in April, 1865 "Our fields everywhere went untilled. Splintered chimneys and charred ruins all over the land marked the spot where happy homes, the seats of refinement and elegance once stood, their former inhabitants wandering in poverty and exile. Old aged Widows and helpless orphans beggared and hopeless are everywhere." One editor wrote "Those who strew flowers over the graves of departed heroes will feel that the quiet dreamers in the dust are far happier then those who will walk the rugged paths of a distracted world."

In George C. Rable's book But There was no Peace there were many opinions quoted which went to the core of the problems facing the North. One quotation said "The Confederacy never really surrendered beyond the laying down of arms. Your idea of governing the conquered States by the force of the bayonet may serve for a time but it fills the future with blood." Again he quotes the moderate Ethelbert Barksdale "An army of one hundred thousand men could not maintain the Reconstruction Government in the South. The North would not support such a large military establishment and would abandon Southern Republicans to their fate."

That was another observation which had the ring of truth about it and future events proved it right. During Reconstruction political economic and social turmoil produced disorders. Frustration and anger was rampant among old Confederates. Race riots in Memphis and New Orleans was a symptom of this anger during the Reconstruction period. "The foreigners must be driven from our soil" was the mood of many. White Southerners launched taxpayer's protests and joined white line organizations.

George C. Rable goes on "The failure of the Republican Party to remake the South was evident but at least it was tried." Now there was a unity in the South that didn't exist before the Civil War. The war against the Yankee continued long after they had abandoned Reconstruction. As George C. Rable again said "They embraced a new culture in which they developed an intellectual and moral defence of slavery. The nationalism that was shattered at Appomattox was reborn in the soil of defeat and bitter disillusionment."

This was the broken spirit and desolation of despair that was deep in the heartbeat of a defeated people whose conquerors demanded a terrible price for their past failures and injustices. As Paul Hamilton Hayne wrote "Southerners will hate Northerners forever" and went on "Why in the mysterious providence of God we were allowed to be conquered by them? It was the puzzle of puzzles."

One old aristocrat made a new living raising flowers and selling them. Others had their splendid mansions burnt down and their plantation divided among the Negroes while the owners became wanderers upon the face of the earth glad to earn a dollar to keep them from starving.

Finding out what was happening in the South meant a slow long distance carriage drive from the North.

A short visit South by General Grant saw him reporting back "A very fine feeling is manifesting itself towards the North" and he recommended the South should be entrusted with its own Government as soon as possible. Congress was unimpressed. Instead the army was sent in with a Major General head over each State. But even here law and order broke down because Negro soldiers became openly hostile to the inhabitants and were known to freely insult the whites. They were nothing more than uninformed thugs. Because of this General Grant ordered all black troops to be withdrawn and they were all gone before December 1866.

The South was now descending into chaos. Corruption was fuelled by lack of capital for investment. Money, material, and labour to replace the slaves, now free, were desperately needed. In five years the wealth of the country had been cut in half. Slaves would not work for their former masters and took to the roads. The labour market was non existent. Planters knew fear too. They feared their lands would be taken from them by force.

But eventually agreements were reached on an annual contract for employment but these contracts usually favoured the employer. Share cropping was another system tried by the employers in which the labourer worked for a share of the crop. But this meant sharing losses as well as profits and debts multiplied for the croppers.

After the visit of General Grant another tour of the South was undertaken by Chief Justice Chase in the summer of 1865 to see conditions for himself.

Chief Justice Chase reported the same picture I have painted. Ex-slaves who refused to work for their old masters were seen strolling in the streets living in squalor. The local gentry showered the Judge with lavish hospitality and bouquets of flowers. Black delegations urged him to get them a voice in Government and he promised them equal rights at the ballot box.

General Lee, the Southern General made a study of the Negro. He wrote very sympathetically "The Negro is like a helpless child easily amused by little things such as brass finger rings, earrings, gaudy handkerchiefs, tobacco and whiskey. The Negro is an amiable and social race, a spendthrift and gullible. He is easily influenced by peddlers and storekeepers. Nothing gave him greater pleasure as a mark of freedom than to carry a pistol and be followed by a dog he could call his own, an indulgence he couldn't enjoy in slavery. Owning deadly weapons and the use of whisky increased his lawlessness. To leave his slave cabin and wander was another mark of freedom he quickly embraced!"
As can be seen education was not the Negro's strongpoint but this was ignored by the radicals in their Reconstruction plans. Very cleverly and cynically they praised the Negro to capture his sympathy because it worked well at the ballot box.

The power of the ballot box gave the Negro an undreamt of feeling of control he never had before. One commentator wrote "It was a wonder that his very head did not burst with its amazing grandeur and every rink of wool turn to a golden diadem."

Mockingly the white man now began to wish he were a Negro. Here is a typical bit of doggerel written at that time.
"Oh, if I were a nigger I'd do just as I please
And when I took a pinch of snuff all Yankeedom would sneeze.
Then Congress too would worship me and bow down at my feet
And swear that since the world began there was nothing half as sweet."

But Negro enthusiasm for a new life was exploited gradually by vested interests.

The pendulum swung violently back when the contempt of the whites for the uneducated Negro came to the surface. One comment goes as follows, "Allowing them to vote now would be little short of madness...." The good-natured doggerel above was getting nasty. An Augusta editor when writing about the Negro being able to govern himself finished with these words "Good God the thought is horrible."

Now the Negro's fate was about to take a frightening turn for the worst when the South descended into anarchy. As feared, unreconstructed white Southerners began to deal with the blacks in their own way. Unprotected by an inadequate number of soldiers and with little heart in Washington to become seriously involved in protecting them, the blacks and the slaves were left to the tender mercies of former Confederate veterans thirsting for revenge. The slaves and blacks were now being blamed for the war. That last sentence is the only conclusion one can come to.

How the North could so insensitively abandon them to their fate is beyond comprehension. It was a licence for murder and mayhem. At a moment when Southern leaders were weak and expected punishment, a golden opportunity was lost by the North for a lasting permanent solution to the problem.

Instead blacks were shot down in broad daylight, lynched, burned slowly over open fires because they had fought against them for a Government that now abandoned them.

This for them was the second Civil War, the one which overthrew Reconstruction. One of the survivors an Albion Tourgee said, "There were enough killed like this to cover a battlefield, woken from their sleep at midnight at public assembly, on the river bank, in the woods, shot, stabbed, hanged, drowned, tortured and mutilated beyond recognition. The wounded numbered more than those that covered the slopes of Gettysburg."

City blacks suffered most and were segregated from the white society legally and illegally; some establishments, like hotels and restaurants began to favour only whites. The Civil Rights Acts were not rigorously enforced by the Republicans leaving sinister black segregation to creep in

Even the schools became segregated. Blacks and whites were now living in separate worlds. Private violence and attacks on blacks happened on a massive scale. Thousands were murdered without trace. Few tormentors were brought to justice. The military rule that was introduced to protect the blacks and former slaves was useless. The soldiers brought in made little progress. Voting in the South by the blacks was crushed by the violence and intimidation of white supremacists. Corruption by bribery for lucrative contracts became rampant. The final evil was the immergence of the Ku Klux Klan. In short Reconstruction was abandoned. The slave society had now been replaced by a radically divided society based on white supremacy. One evil had been replaced by another.

Before leaving the problems of Reconstruction for the last time let's reflect on some aspects of slavery that are not generally known.

The free Negro was an anomaly bitterly resented by the whites. He was feared in the towns as a competitor by white tradesmen. Slave owners thought they were a bad influence on their slaves corrupting them by selling them liquor. According to the slave owners, the free blacks were thieves and receivers of stolen property and set a bad example. Later the legal position of free Negroes deteriorated as his evidence in court was now invalid and he was subject to curfew laws.

 Yet many of the blacks remained unmolested after the emancipation of the slave perhaps because a considerable portion of them were skilled workers such as blacksmiths, shoemakers and barbers.

However they were later drawn from these trades by the whites after the Civil War. I'm afraid the lot of the Negroes didn't improve after the war. It was even seen to be illegal to teach free Negroes to read or write. In fact he was constantly in danger of being kidnapped and sold. This contradictory standing among the population got more complicated. Bizarrely he was at the same time allowed to own slaves, accumulate money as a businessman or even become a planter.

Some modern scholars claim vigorously that the old view of the plantation slave was degrading and only a partial truth. They say the letters and diaries of planters and plantation records often discredit the stereotypes of the typical Southern slave as being a lazy unreliable individual, which was not true. Many records tell of slaves so intelligent that their masters consulted them as advisors on plantation policy.

There were even slaves who were competent overseers, or slaves who had a passionate attachment to the plantation, and a pride in the crops. One well-known planter wrote in his papers for example of a remarkable Negro slave of his. "Andrew is such an intelligent man – and one of principal – it is a pleasure to see his work." Numerous plantations had slave merchants and carpenters who were even hired out in the cities. Although this caused such a reaction from worried white tradesmen they canvassed the Legislature complaining of the competition. One remarkable slave called Horace was such a brilliant bridge builder throughout the black belt that his master applied to have him emancipated. He was successful in 1845 – 1846 and Horace went to work for him as an Artisan.

But, and here is the awful truth, according to John H. Moore, "With the coming of freedom these top Negroes lost their unusual opportunity to rise above the ranks of manual labour in the old Southwest." Yes, I shake my head as I quote another of his recorded comments. "From 1863 onwards all positions of authority were reserved only for whites."
The blacks remained abandoned for the next one hundred and fifty years until the birth of the black activists in 1955. Desegregation was established by Judge Earl Warren in the 1957 case Board of Education of Topeka V Brown. Tactics of obstruction and intimidation were resurrected from the past but to no avail. It was another General, President Eisenhower, who took on the South by sending in troops to Arkansas to assert the Courts ruling.

I can now write of the Negro's final journey to respectability. The African – American, as he is called now, voted for one of their own to become President of the United States in 2008. But that will be a story for later in this book when we hear the story of Barack Obama, the 44th President.

As we can see Congress and the Supreme Court finally took a hand in 1957 to ensure a national policy of racial justice. It had been a long, long journey since Lincoln but that journey can best be seen through the eyes of later Presidents.

Now let us return to the politicians in the North and the stage on which they were living, far from the awful reality of life in the post-Civil War South. Life in Washington DC was the world Andrew Johnson lived in.

Let's look at some events that preoccupied President Andrew Johnson in Washington during the Civil War aftermath. William H. Seward the Secretary of State badly wounded by Lincoln's assassination gang bought Alaska from the Russians for $7,200,000.

It was ridiculed at the time as "Seward's Folly" but history has since more than vindicated him. The oil reserves now lying there has proved a lucrative payback for his investment.
Another international story shortly afterwards concerns a raid into Canada by of all things a group of Irish revolutionaries based in the United States known as "The Fenians".

In June 1866, 1,500 of them crossed over the border into Canada only to be defeated by an alert Canadian military. They returned to New York where they were arrested by the authorities but were soon released and the adventure was never repeated. As you can see much can happen in the life of a President. Research into the reason for the raid so far has produced nothing.

Meanwhile the social tragedy of the blacks in the South continued as if the North was another country and the successor to Lincoln, Andrew Johnson, seemed to have lost the Civil War. Down South they were not to know their new President was himself engaged in a different sort of war with his own political foes at Congress. In this battle, while the blacks of the South desperately needed his help, he was disagreeing with everything brought before him for debate.

Johnson's behaviour in office has been explained by numerous historians in various ways. He came from Southern roots and has been accused of being a white supremacist and a saboteur of the Government Reconstruction programme. Harsh words you may say but could there be another view of his perceived obstructionism.

Remember Johnson came to Washington as an outcast himself from his beloved Tennessee because of his rejection of Tennessee secessionists. So how could a man so loyal to the Union be accused of setting out to destroy the very platform on which the South was to be finally slave-free, the platform of Reconstruction?
One finds it hard to understand therefore why he opposed Congress for four years. During all my research into Johnson's political infighting I have never found one explanation from him justifying his opposition to and obstruction of the Reconstruction Acts. Some simple words of explanation as to why he decided everyone in Congress was wrong in their ideas for Reconstruction. Yes, why was he so convinced in his opinions that he bitterly attacked Congress right up to his very last speech as President?

Perhaps someone else has explained this somewhere so I am open to advice.

Anyway life still went on for Johnson. In fact at that time a century old problem was cleared up by agreement with the Sioux Chief Red Cloud. The agreement was known as the Treaty of Fort Laramie.

The Sioux nation in return agreed to end their raids and war parties for total control of their Dakota homelands which included their sacred black hills in perpetuity. The raids stopped but the promises were never honoured. I am afraid that is history we can never rewrite now.

But Andrew Johnson's behaviour in office still puzzled and angered everyone. Was he aware of the new evil of white supremacy that was fermenting in the South? Being at the heart of power perhaps he saw the complete lack of commitment to the South all around him.

Was he disillusioned by this hypocrisy he saw in operation in the hearts and minds of so called friends of Lincoln. Perhaps being of Southern roots he understood the South better than most of those in Congress. Without explanations in a clear cut statement from him the vacuum has left only suspicions as to his motives. But his character was never criticised for lack of patriotism. The incident of the gun proves he was a man without fear in that little hall somewhere while he was on the hustings.

So do we blame him unfairly? Were his vetoes alarm signals warning of the potential downfall into corruption that eventually overtook the South? Judging by the final outcome of the North's Reconstruction programme his accusers have not exactly covered themselves in glory. Yet it is easy to understand his attitude towards the conquered South.

General Grant himself displayed the same honourable magnanimity to his defeated opponent General Robert E. Lee when he supplied special rations to Lee's defeated soldiers, allowed them to keep their horses, and never even suggested a war crimes tribunal. The whole post-war thrust by Grant's victorious army was one of reconciliation. Everyone went home to pick up the threads of their old life peacefully. Was Johnson's approach to reconciliation any different? Would Lincoln's approach have been any different?

So let's dig a little deeper. Let's look at events as they unfolded for Andrew Johnson from day one of his Presidency. What Presidential problems did he face in the following four years?

His day began in the customary way for a President in 1865. A continuous river of visitors trooped into the White House daily. Southerners seeking pardons, politicians manoeuvring for patronage. Deserters looking for leniency and well-wishers seeking his handshake, and this continued day and night until his advisors grew restless ad worried about his health.

To tackle the job Johnson found himself in a very vulnerable position. He couldn't rely on popularity like Lincoln enjoyed, nor could he depend on the public respect as an elected President to sell his own policies. He was very much on his own doing a solo run.
But few Presidents had his wealth of experience. Unfortunately he only had a vague idea what Lincoln's intentions were for after the war. Yet he knew he differed from Lincoln on the slave issue. Lincoln preferred protection and civil rights for the blacks. Johnson preferred entrusting them to the tender mercies of their former masters by resurrecting the old political structure without delay.

He was now about to embark on four unbelievable years trying to realize the unknown dreams of Lincoln now lying in his grave in Springfield, Illinois. The fundamentals of these dreams and the seeds from which a new America would emerge were to be known as the Reconstruction.

So now we have Andrew Johnson a man from the poverty stricken roots of an uneducated childhood about to grapple with the greatest challenge in American history for any President.

Fighting with guns and bullets and swords was easy in comparison. This time America was fighting not for glory but the hearts and minds of millions.
The task he faced was almost insurmountable. And why? Because forgiveness and reconciliation are two ingredients in the makeup of mankind that have never been mastered. At first Johnson made loud "fire and brimstone" noises against the Confederate leaders "sword rattling" for their personal punishment.

It was an unfortunate misjudgement to think that the wounds of the Civil War would heal so quickly. There were too many bitter memories to be overcome. Perhaps it was Presidential inexperience that brought him failure; after all he had only been in office for six weeks.

Johnson's actions so far pleased the radical Republicans. Words he used like "Treason must be made infamous" and "Traitors must be impoverished" were music in the ears of the Republican militants. However his desire for speedy change based on Lincoln's policy of conciliation saw Johnson promoting measures that were far too lenient and impulsive for the Republican Party at that particular time. Yet Congress found itself unable to oppose his policy.

Why, because Congress simply was not there.

Yes, unbelievably it had been adjourned from April until December 1865, a gap of nine months which Johnson took full advantage of.

Nine months holidays while the South was bleeding in a post-Civil War shockwave leaves the writer dumfounded.

Matters came to a head when on May 29, 1865 while an adjourned Congress was empty; Johnson issued a general amnesty to all participants in the Civil War.

This is my abbreviated version of the amnesty passed on May 29, 1865 which reads as follows; "I hereby grant all persons who have directly or indirectly participated in the existing rebellion, amnesty and pardon with restoration of all rights of property upon the condition that every such person shall take the following oath 'I do hereby solemnly swear in the presence of almighty God I will faithfully support and protect the Constitution of the United States and the Union of States'."

By the time Congress reconvened in December 1865 all the Southern States with the exception of Texas had established new Reconstruction Governments under Johnson's programme. But far from appreciating Johnson's leniency none of the Southern States introduced a vote for blacks at the ballot box. But worse than that, they introduced new State laws known as "Black Codes" which were designed to tie blacks even tighter as unpaid labourers to the slave owner just as before the war. Nothing was to change.
The Chicago Tribune reacted with anger and warned the State of Mississippi with the following words: -
"The white men of the Mississippi is being told that the North will convert the State of Mississippi into a frog pond before they will allow any such laws to disgrace one foot of soil in which the bones of our soldiers sleep and over which the flag of freedom waves." In short the codes were pro white and under them no law could force a jury to believe Negro testimony. However common sense prevailed and these obnoxious Black Codes were never enforced and were finally taken off the statute books by the radicals.

But the day of reckoning came when Congress reconvened in December 1865. The suppressed anger of the radicals exploded into a vicious back lash against the President and a four year battle of minds began. On one side was Johnson defending the rights of the Presidency under the Constitution. On the other side was Congress claiming the right to make all laws relating to Reconstruction.

The Congressional Election of 1866 saw the Radicals increased in number and everything went sour for Johnson from that moment on. The Radicals scrapped his Reconstruction programme and introduced their own more punitive measures. Military Governments replaced Johnson's Reconstruction Administrations. The South they maintained could not be trusted with their own Government.

Things got worse for Andrew Johnson but this time it was a family problem. He had brought his son Robert to Washington to act as his private secretary. Unfortunately poor Robert was an alcoholic and had a breakdown. He returned to drinking heavily and brought disgrace on himself and the family.

It was a sad time for Andrew Johnson. Not only had his son inflicted pain on him by his lack of loyalty and appreciation for his father's kindness but the Confederate friends to whom Johnson had been so trusting and generous let him down badly. To complete his cup of woes Johnson's own brother William shot himself dead in a hunting accident.

Still Johnson's war went on. There were two camps now in Congress bitterly opposed to each other. All matters relating to Reconstruction was now handed over to a "Committee of Fifteen on Reconstruction".

This left Johnson completely isolated in the White House. However Johnson was always a dour antagonist going back to his days in Tennessee when he opposed the Southern establishment regardless of the consequences. He fought on. This time he fought with a veto. He used it against every Bill on the Reconstruction Acts they put before him.

Isn't it strange how one man can influence the destiny of a Nation? Only a few succeeded in doing so; Washington, Jefferson, and Lincoln and in later years Roosevelt and Kennedy. To include Johnson in such exalted company seems bizarre when historians have hinted darkly Johnson was responsible for the South remaining white mans country for the next one hundred and fifty years.

But it is hard to agree completely with this judgement when we read about the corruption, the swindles, the dishonesty and the violence that politicians in the North either could not or would not control.

Could it be that the South was betrayed by get rich quick opportunists in the North and the South and more interested in graft than the political purity of a George Washington or an Abraham Lincoln?

Surely it wasn't the sins of one man that brought down Reconstruction but the folly and greed of many.

Unfortunately Johnson's personality in the job cannot be left out of the chemistry either, for he even fell out with General Grant so bitterly he refused to share the carriage with Grant on Grant's inauguration day.

Sadly I feel his personality was to play a major part in his Presidency from now on. His vetoes were causing grave disruption to the running of Congress and everyone's patience was running out fast. It was becoming almost impossible to operate normally as long as Johnson was President using his veto to strangle the very life out of the Government. Civil War was being enacted all over again this time on Capitol Hill.

Stanton, the Secretary of War was sacked to be replaced at first by General Ulysses Grant and then by Brevet Major General Lorenzo Thomas.

The Radicals finally lost their patience and to end this political stalemate they finally moved to snatch back the Presidency from Johnson by voting for impeachment.

Impeachment proceedings were instituted against Johnson by the House of Representative on February 24, 1868 with the following resolution "That Andrew Johnson be impeached of high crimes and misdemeanours." The charges were usurpation of the law, corrupt use of the veto power interference at elections and misdemeanours. Bringing Congress into disrepute and failing to implement the Reconstruction Acts. The trial opened in a blaze of publicity. Tickets to the trial were in hot demand especially for gallery seats which were sold by scalpers or black marketeers for enormous sums of money.

One sin that was not up for trial however was Johnson's unrepentant conviction that the white race was superior to the black. This was his one dangerous flaw which would not allow him to compromise leading him to alienate even the moderates in Congress. The view he took was that no constitutional changes could take place as long as the Southern states were without representation. But let's return to the impeachment of Andrew Johnson. The scene was set for a wonderful stage show and the public were not going to be denied.

It was a great event in Washington circles and the real test was whether the charges amounted to violations of the Constitution. But it is worth mentioning that if Johnson had lost, his successor would have been a man called Ben Wade, President Pro tempore of the Senate, a very unpopular figure who was not a very attractive alternative for Republicans. In fact they feared and reviled Wade. The trial began on March 12, 1868. Final arguments took fourteen days from April 22 to May 6, 1868.

Johnson's lawyer, William Groesbeck made a colourful address in Johnson's defence. He said, "Johnson's view of Reconstruction was as follows. He was eager for pacification. He thought the war had ended. The drums were all silent. The Arsenals shut. The roar of the cannon had died away. The army had disbanded. Not a single enemy confronted us in the field. He was too eager, too forgiving, too kind. The hand of Reconciliation was stretched out to him and he took it. Is kindness a crime? Kindness is the high statesmanship of heaven itself."
But still the managers of the impeachment were optimistic. Wade and prosperity are sure to come with the apple blossom was the catch-cry.

Like any good story there is a kick in the tail. Rumour has it that Johnson made a private deal with some Senators promising them he would not continue interfering in The Reconstruction Acts. This is not borne out by the result for after all if he made a deal it would not have ended with a cliff hanger.

But now one name was to surface from the trial that took everyone by surprise. He has since been glorified in a book entitled Profiles in Courage for which John F. Kennedy received the Pulitzer Prize.

I've no intention of reproducing the article in full. Suffice it to say the story is a fascinating one. The man in question was a very big player in the Andrew Johnson saga. Going back in time, let's stand beside this man Senator Ross and listen to him speaking his mind after the impeachment resolution was passed.

Senator Ross was honest but not very prudent. Turning to a fellow Senator Sprague of Rhode Island he remarked casually, "Well Sprague, the thing is here; as far as I am concerned, though a Republican and opposed to Johnson and his policy, he shall have as fair a trial as any accused man ever had on this earth."

Senator Ross was a marked man after that, for from that day until just before the trial began, his life was a nightmare. The Radicals were furious at the possibility that Senator Ross would sabotage the vote because they were hell bent on the destruction of Andrew Johnson. Now Ross might rob them of their prize. Only 36 votes were necessary to achieve their goal of a 2/3rd majority but only 35 votes could be guaranteed. Senator Ross might vote Yes but what if he might vote No?

For weeks they spied on him, bullied him, bribed him, threatened him, watched him, hunted him, and all that time he remained neutral refusing to commit himself one way or the other.

The Philadelphia press reported an avalanche of telegrams demanding he join the "Yes" vote camp. Still Senator Ross said nothing.   A bribe of $20,000 was offered to his brother. "There's a barrel money," they said. "How much does the damn scoundrel want?"

Of course Senator Ross knew that voting NO would mean political suicide for him.   But still he said nothing. They even tried to get a Bill passed to introduce six new States whose voting power was bound to destroy Johnson. Luckily for the President this was not an option for them and their move was overruled.

The tension was electric as the speeches rang out one after the other when the debate moved around the Chamber. Passions flared from a meandering village stream to a raging river in flood, and only ended when the inevitable vote was called for.   As expected the 35 votes for conviction lifted the hopes of the Radicals. One more vote was needed for that magical 2/3rds majority.

But that crucial vote now rested with Senator Ross from Kansas. Not a single person in the room knew what way he was going to vote. Was it to be "Wade and the apple blossom" or Ross and disaster for the Radicals?

As a hush descended on the House time stood still. All their hate, loathing, bitterness and fears rested on this one unfortunate man whose whole future was hanging by a thread. Not a foot shuffled. Not a garment rustled. The Senators leaned forward to catch the voice of the Chief Justice.

"Mr. Ross, how say you?" The reply came in a whisper. "Not guilty." Shouts from the far side of the Chamber cried out for clarity. "Is the respondent Andrew Johnson guilty or not guilty of misdemeanour?" repeated the Chief Justice.

The answer this time was loud and clear.   "Not guilty," said Senator Ross with steely conviction.

Senator Ross by a remarkable quirk in the voting procedure was the last vote to come in. His answer blew the Impeachment charge right out of the water. Believe it or not Johnson himself was not even in the Chamber to hear the verdict.
But there was a terrible price to pay by Senator Ross for his bravery. When he returned home to Kansas he was subjected to appalling abuse. Called a traitor by his neighbours in the street. Ostracized and shunned like a leper. He was eventually forced to leave Kansas in poverty, driven out of politics permanently, and forced to settle into a new life in Mexico.

The worth of the man was recognised years later by his new found friends in Mexico who appointed him Territorial Governor there.   However Senator Ross' vote of conscience was not forgotten by one of his illustrious colleagues in the Senate, who admitted remorsefully years later "Great injustice has been done to a Statesman of spotless character." The remorseful colleague was none other than the famous James G. Blaine.

So how do we as jury judge Andrew Johnson, one hundred and forty years later? The question we are now left with is this. Did Johnson deliberately sabotage the Reconstruction Acts? His sins according to the critics were many. They say he destroyed the opportunity to remove the stain of three centuries of slavery and create the national unity for the post-war years based on justice, human rights and racial adjustment. His actions encouraged Southerners to believe white supremacy could be preserved. It was an incitement to darker forces in the South to fight for white supremacy. Well I have presented all the facts North and South as best I could. The result of the acquittal was said to have set back progress for the Negro in the South for the next one hundred and forty years. Worse than that Reconstruction was eventually overthrown!

But U.S. Presidents have always been special and Johnson was no exception. Undaunted by events he went on to finish out his Presidency to his retirement. Yet retirement was the last thing he was thinking of. As if to underline his amazing resilience and to prove conclusively his undiminished popularity in his native Tennessee, the 17th President Andrew Johnson was elected again to the Senate on March 4, 1875 six years after he left the Presidency.

Yes, despite his so called sins he was still embraced by his own people. I'm sure they were glad they did for after only five months as a Senator he died on July 31, 1875. Like the rest of us he had lost his final battle in this world.

The epitaph on his tombstone in a peaceful Greenville graveyard is brief unambiguous and simple. It reads "His faith in the people never wavered".

As we leave Andrew Johnson to rest in peace in a Greenville graveyard, the General who won the Civil War Ulysses Grant was now in power as America's 18th President of the United States. Please read on.

18th President   Ulysses S Grant

"Hero of Appomattox"
Born 1822
Died 1885
63 Years of age
2 Terms
1869 – 1877
Age 47

Party: Republican
Profession: Soldier
County: Ohio
Ancestry: English/Scottish
Estate: Nil (Manuscript of book "Let us have Peace" - income: $500,000)
Hobbies: Sleighing, skating, swimming and riding.

Physical Description: Height, 5 foot 8 inches; beard; square straight brows; large head; heavy nostrils, firm-set mouth.

Extract from his inaugural address Thursday March 4, 1869.
"The responsibilities of the position I feel, but accept them without fear. I shall on all subjects have a policy to recommend but none to enforce against the will of the people. The proper treatment of the original occupants of this land, the Indians, is one deserving of careful study. I will favour any course towards them which tends to their civilization and ultimate citizenship."

ULYSSES S. GRANT

After the colourful turbulence of the Presidency of Andrew Johnson, the future now looked to be in the steady rock like hands of a successful General but nothing could be further from the truth.

The life of General Ulysses Grant constantly surprises you. It may not be well known that the man who led Lincoln's army to victory in Americas Civil War was not even in the army when Lincoln called for troops on April 15, 1861. He was working as a shoe salesman for his father's leather store on Main Street, Galena when hostilities broke out. Irony is a strange bedfellow of history.

It was now fifteen years since the Mexico war from which Ulysses had returned home a hero. He had retired from the army and took the job offered by his father as a shoe salesman in a joint business venture. But one chilly Tuesday morning in April 1861 he sat in on a citizen meeting in Galena, Illinois which was discussing the amazing events at Fort Sumter which had sparked the Civil War. Speakers varied in their opinions. Nothing was a foregone conclusion. The crowd in the hall was split between those who only wanted peace and those who were determined to march under the flag in protest. Compromise was out of the question was the conclusion of one famous speaker John A. Rawlins, a lawyer. Walking home from the meeting Ulysses Grant told his brother Orville "I think I ought to go into service." "You should you should," said his brother, "I'll mind the store."
Within months the middle-aged Grant was a Brigadier. Four years later he was a four-star General.

Grandma Simpson was responsible for his name. Grandpa Grant suggested Hiram so he was christened Hiram Ulysses first child to Jesse and Hannah Grant. Time found him being called by his second name Ulysses by popular usage. The lads he played with had great fun calling him "useless" to tease him but that's the world of children for Ulysses was anything but useless.

His father Jesse was a bit of an extrovert but a likeable one. Without education but with no lack of ambition or opinions Jesse was an avid reader of everything he could lay his hands on. Modest factory owner converting raw hides into leather he also dabbled at writing and amateur poetry that everyone knew would never find their way into the classics. Ever the colourful character Jesse almost courted unpopularity with his controversial views on local politics.

Hannah on the other hand was devout, modest and a completely balancing contrast to Jesse with her quiet disciplined philosophy on life. Like all frontier mothers she was hardworking and home loving. Home life for Grant was simple and clean; bare walls, tiny windows, rough and ready furniture and a living space that was very basic. The cooking was done on an open fireplace. Outside cobblestone streets were easily flooded in stormy weather and the background scenery was picturesque with rivers flowing through nearby mountain passes.

The Ohio River moved slowly past them going West to join up further with the Mississippi known to neighbours as "The highway to the new West" beyond. Settlements along the banks were amply served by the steamboats and barges that passed by. The town Ulysses was reared in was called Point Pleasant where Ulysses' grandfather was known locally by his fame as Captain Noah in Washington's revolutionary army. Sadly Noah was unable to keep his large family together when his wife died and suffered the awful loss of his children scattered among relations and neighbours from that day on.

Jesse, Ulysses' colourful father ended up with the Brown family whose eldest son was the tragic John Brown of song and story who became an inspiration in the Civil War when he was martyred on the gallows for his beliefs. It was in that family Jesse learned his trade as a tanner. More important, because of his life with the Brown family Jesse became a vigorous critic of racial discrimination and preached that Gospel to anyone who cared to listen to him.

Ulysses moved East with his dad to Georgetown when he was two years old to be close to a forest that would help in his father's business as a tanner. The trade was very important for the making of saddles boots, harnesses, stirrups and other leather items which were so essential to life in the West at that time.

Ulysses disliked his father's business and his father's talkative personality and grew up more like his mother, quiet and reserved. Anyway soaking, washing, rinsing and curing bloody hides was just not for him.

However he loved horses from an early age and his mother once boasted to a neighbour who found Ulysses swinging from the tail of his horse...... "Horses seem to understand our Ulysses." He watered them at noon and night and although having to stand on boxes to achieve the task, he regularly harnessed them at the age of seven. By the time he was ten he was a free lance teamster and earned a great reputation locally as a horse tamer.

Into his teens Ulysses was much in demand for long distance hauling of freight and passengers through the wild frontier countryside. This helped him get to know the large towns and cities where he sometimes stayed such as Cincinnati, Louisville and Toledo picking up freight or new passengers on the return journey. "He will take good care of himself" was his father's reassurance to worried passengers who were unsure about trusting themselves to this undersized delicate looking youth with the handsome sensitive features. They were in marked contrast to his self-confident air that said "I am at home with these horses". His brown hair and steady grey blue eyes eased any remaining doubts.

Ulysses grew up with the usual advantages of rural life, swimming, and fishing in the summer, skating and sleighing in the winter. Being the driver of the sleigh for local boys helped bridge the silence his reticence and shyness created. He would never join in the shooting of animals on a hunt being very upset that "The animals were mostly wounded and left to crawl away and starve," he said. Foul and game were off his menu completely after that.

School lasted only three months in those far off days and only then at a "subscription school" provided by the parents. Teachers were usually paid in beef, flour, port or corn. Reading and arithmetic were his strong points and he was lucky to be so gentle and well-behaved because it saved him from the beech rod which was used freely by the teacher. Ulysses was mainly a "thinker" rather than a frustrated shouter when in difficulties. When he was fourteen his father sent him to prep school while he stayed with his relatives who gave him free board and lodgings.

In prep school he learned to enjoy a new activity to him the debating society. Well that was the boyhood life of Ulysses Grant which went a long way to moulding the man he was later to become quite shrewd, thoughtful, gentle and a great horseman.

His father was a great influence on Ulysses as a young lad. Although their contrasting personalities often clashed they never seriously fell out. In fact it was on his father's advice he applied for West Point. Entrants at that time used West Point for later careers, like teaching and engineering, so resigning after graduation day was a good option.

His father got him nominated to West Point by a Congressman but Ulysses was not too happy about all this. He had no intention of staying there but because his father had other ideas he relented.

Ulysses duly got in to West Point and began the almost cruel demanding West Point training that could nearly break a man. The brainwashing or hazing consisted of a barrage of orders, questions, reprimands and almost insults from what were known as "Upperclassmen", his seniors. Mentally and spiritually Ulysses was really unsuitable for the job. His laid back frontier background was too casual and he rated 150th out of 223 when he graduated. His drill, tactics, military discipline and French studies were dismal but he excelled at Mathematics and naturally was sensational at riding school.

But now fate was to take a hand inflicting its first major surprise on him which left his whole world turned upside down. Fred Dent Junior who roomed with him at West Point invited him home. Significantly for our West Point soldier Fred had three sisters but only one mattered to Ulysses, Julia Dent.

Young Ulysses had a doll like look although he was now a young soldier five feet six inches high. Julia was attractive but with a slight squint. An expert horsewoman they had something special in common. Grant called it in later years "Love at first sight."

At this point in time I'm afraid Ulysses' love affair with the army could not match his love affair with Julia. The army just had to go. Now Cupid had other surprises waiting for him for in May 1844 he became engaged to Julia. They had to wait four years to marry because of Ulysses' army commitments. It seems that love affair with the army had never really ended.

The first conflict of his adult life struck Ulysses like a thunderbolt. Julia's father Colonel Dent rejected him and his father Jesse. Unsurprisingly this didn't bother Jesse. The row was a political one. Dent was a slaveholder and Jesse was an abolitionist. It was "only a skirmish" in army parlance and a truce eventually solved it. Meanwhile another war in Mexico had to be fought and Ulysses was posted there against his will because he felt the war was immoral. Nevertheless, in battle he impressed another officer later to become a Confederate General who said "You could not keep Grant out of a battle. He was in the thick of every fight: one particular feature of his courage was his coolness under fire and acted as though he was in a hailstorm not a hail of bullets."

Ulysses learned many skills in the Mexican War which helped him in the Civil War. Practical ideas like feeding and clothing an army, and living off the country to save supplies. Zachary Taylor he noticed was always unhurried under fire and always applied common sense when interpreting army regulations. Yes, he always learned lessons from many of the great Generals around.

He wrote to Julia "I'm deeply moved by Mexico she has so many poor and starving subjects. The rich keep down the poor with a hardness of heart that is incredible. Walk through the streets of Mexico for one day and you will see hundreds of beggars but you never see them ask any of their own people. It is always of the Americans they expect to receive."

With the war over Ulysses returned home to Julia and married. It had been four years of lonely separation. They had "a small old fashioned wedding" according to Julia's sister. Despite the truce Jesse and Hannah gave their blessing but would not attend the wedding. Yet when Ulysses brought Julia home his parents were bowled over by her and insisted she could stay with them whenever Ulysses was away on duty. Their first born was named Fred after the brother who had introduced them to each other. Another baby and a distant posting to the Pacific arrived. The posting was a terrible shock.

For the modern soldier it was like being posted to South East Asia today for the journey was unbelievable by modern standards. A trip by ship to Panama then overland to another port then by ship up the West coast of America in the middle of a tropical summer and after that a journey by dugout canoe and mule back. On the way his party of soldiers were struck with cholera and Grant had to arrange hospitalization for them. Army wives praised him profusely saying "He was like a ministering angel to us all." Devastatingly nearly a hundred soldiers died in the outbreak. Another lesson learned. Disease was a greater danger than battlefield hazards. A day in San Francisco followed observing the Gold Rush excitement of that town.

They ended up in a real Wild West Fort complete with stockade. Their job now was to entertain and re-equip the surveying parties crossing the Rockies to map the new country beyond. Now he had to cope with another problem. Without his wife Ulysses was lost despite the magnificent splendour all around him. Fishing on the lakes and riding alone was no substitute for a new young wife back home. Julia's letters were seldom and he scolded her gently for this. Loneliness created a dangerous habit for Ulysses when whiskey became his substitute for Julia and his resistance against it deteriorated. He gave it up at first but gradually his resolution to resist it disintegrated. Sadly whiskey as a cure for loneliness was no help. In fact it was disastrous.

His drinking came to the notice of his superior officers after he was promoted to Captain and he was transferred to San Francisco. Being a man of the highest principal he had no option but to resign.

We have no records to show if he was requested to do so. Jealous rivals in the Civil War later tried to exploit this story. Funny enough it never seemed to bother Ulysses. All that mattered to him at that time was the elation of going home to Julia. It was good to be a family man again.

Around that time The Fugitive Slave Law, which allowed Sheriffs from the South to invade Northern States in pursuit of escaped fugitive slaves, was whipping up angry opposition to slavery more then any stories about distant plantations. Jesse his father, now a wealthy man was disappointed in his failed soldier son yet he didn't need much persuasion to help out Ulysses whose funds were now low and work was scarce without a skill or a trade. Despite Jesse's help a row between father and son blew up and Ulysses moved out into his wife's farm, a holding of sixty acres given to her as a wedding present by her father. Ulysses rolled up his sleeves and built a house on it for his family.

It was a picturesque setting with rivers streams oaks and elms under a blue sunlit sky. Slave plantations were all around him but he never lost his concern for racial justice. He once wrote home from Oregon, "It is really my opinion that the whole Indian race would be harmless if not put upon by whites." He even protested in San Francisco about the slavery conditions of the imported Chinese labourers – for Ulysses Grant soldiered with his heart as well as his head.

Yet somehow in the midst of a slavery environment he managed to keep himself free of major conflict among his family on the subject.

Anyway, he was too busy cutting firewood for a living chopping, sawing, loading and hauling it to St. Louis for sale.

One ex-colleague who met him on the road and was now a Brigadier General shouted out "Why Grant what in blazes are you doing here?" to which Grant answered drying "Well General I'm hauling wood." Incidentally Jesse his father had written to Jefferson Davis asking about Ulysses' relationship with the army and was told the way was still clear for his son to return to the army. Despite all his critics army life was still open to him.

Nellie Grant was born on of all dates July 4, 1855 and she was to become famous for her White House wedding. However that would be years into the future.

Meanwhile the new house was now ready for the "raising" – today we call it a "housewarming". He named the house "Hard Scrabble" as a tribute to his own hard work in building it. He was very proud of this four roomed log structure which has a story all of its own. He soon became well known in the district for his help as a mediator in family problems sometimes giving his own cash to subsidize with practical help, the advice he gave counselling them. Later Grant was known to reminisce nostalgically after two terms in the White House with the words "Those were happy years."

Economic Depression hit business in 1857 and Grant was forced to sell "Hard Scrabble" to go to St. Louis. He rented out "White Haven" from his father-in-law Colonel Dent who had left his plantation and had moved to St. Louis.

Again he failed as a business man when he tried his hand as a real estate broker and a landlord's agent – in short a rent collector. He also tried his hand as a county engineer for which he was qualified by his West Point training. Because of his father in laws connection with slaveholding he lost his job. Yes his luck was really down at rock bottom. His friends, all Southerners, often angered him when they talked glibly about secession. He promptly set free the one slave he had although he could have sold him for over $1,000 which he needed badly. "Hard Scrabble" then exploded in his face when the cheque he was to receive for it bounced. It tied the whole sale up for years into the future. Life wasn't getting any easier for U. S. Grant. With the funds so low he again had to return to his old pal his father Jesse Grant who gave him the job of salesman in his Grant Brothers store.

Well that's the story so far. As you can see, after all its surprises, it finally arrives back on the streets of Galena where we left Ulysses Grant saying goodbye to Orville before riding off to rejoin the army.

Now during the 1860s the conflicting opinions that were debated everywhere were not unusual. Many talked in a state of confusion on the reason for the war. Some said it was a war to protect the Union. It was even said it was about tariffs. But Ulysses knew deep down with a gut instinct that it was about destroying slavery to save the Union. Both could never again live side by side. Grant's mind constantly wrestled with this horrific Civil War puzzle. Most people in the North Grant felt were against slavery but were only noisy not numerous. They certainly were not thinking of war to get rid of it. But slaveholders were different. They had to expand to survive and their nuclear weapon was to secede. It was rule or ruin for them. Although in a minority they could manipulate the wheels of power by their control of the ruling Parties, the Whigs and the Democrats. To them the ownership of slaves was something that conferred nobility on them, like some sort of divine right. The last few paragraphs were really the thoughts of Grant himself on the whole Civil War question. The Unionists were against secession but the slave owners were for slavery.

When Grant in his later travels around the world discussed this problem with Bismarck in Germany he had to explain to Bismarck what it was all about. "It was," he said "Not only to save the Union but to destroy slavery." Grant wrote to his father "There are two parties to this traitors and patriots."
People like Jefferson Davis did not help when he boasted "One Southerner was equal to five Yankees."

But Ulysses was like others in grave error when he said the war would be short. He soon learned his mistake because militarily all the cards were stacked against the North. The South could not be outflanked because it was one geographic whole that must be invaded. The North also suffered from a lack of military might at the top – under qualified Generals.

But Grant came under political fire early in the war when the press in the North criticized him for the shocking casualty lists. He was a logical scapegoat for cowards who had scattered to the rear. His drunkenness was one of the untrue allegations against him by The New York Times who were complaining about the "8,000 dead at Shiloh." The Boston Traveller complained of a "Universal dislike for him as a leader of men." The New York World described him as "an imbecile."

The problem was largely Grant's naive public relations skills. General Sherman was a great friend of Grant throughout the war who Grant noticed very seldom defended himself against press criticism. From that time on only once was he heard to say to a press man "Your paper is very unjust to me but time will make it all right." Lincoln rejected criticism of Grant saying "I can't spare this man he fights." But unbelievably Grant received help from an unusual quarter – the slaves themselves.

As Grant said "They follow in the wake of the army. I use them as teamsters, hospital attendants, company cooks and so forth thus saving soldiers to carry the muskets." They cheerfully helped as guides to the army in any unknown county. Every path, hill and hollow was mapped by them. Other Generals were not so far seeing and even allowed civilians into their camps to "retrieve their property". Official records show over 185,000 slaves joined the Union ranks. As the army advanced the freed slaves did not know how to handle their new found freedom. In modern parlance Grant was really tackling the problem of refugees.

The man he placed in charge of this was a John Eaton, a Divinity School student who met Grant in private at his headquarters. Grant was actually tackling a problem head on in the battlefield that would eventually wreck the South, the tragic failure to integrate the slave into society. The very future of the Negro in the Southern States depended on his rehabilitation. They were gathered into camps by Eaton on Grant's instructions. Army rations and clothes were requisitioned and he met with Grant daily to help these wandering men women and children. The whole thing was to be paid for by selling cotton. Fortunately Eton was a brilliant organiser. Slaves were even helped to read and write. Disgracefully these teachers and helpers were later ostracized from Southern post-war society for helping Grant. They were contemptuously called "carpet baggers". What a deplorable unfair world it can be!

But that was post-war Confederate territory after the movement for Reconstruction had been overthrown by white vested interests that was to flourish for the next one hundred and thirty years. Grant's foresight and political genius on the battlefield was never fully appreciated. Who could believe such profound ideas could produce only bitter fruits. This world of hate that strangled hope was the South's everlasting shame.
Another more pleasant anecdote is recorded about Grant just before the Battle of

Chattanooga. As he rode with his bugler past a Unionist camp the order "Turn out the guard was given." "Never mind the guard," said Grant and rode on and the men went back to their tents. But within earshot just across the creek the man on Confederate guard duty heard the order and repeated it to his men "Turn out the guard for the Commanding Officer General Grant." The battle-worn rebel soldiers front-faced and gave the salute which Grant returned. The bizarre relationship between the two sets of solider rebels and Unionists can be seen in this one little war story. Grant was still their Commanding Officer was the message from the rebels to the world.

Grant was eventually given the highest award that could have been bestowed by Lincoln. He was made a First Lieutenant General with permanent rank since George Washington and Commanding Officer of all the armies of the United States.

Lincoln told him "All I want is someone to take on the responsibility and act and call upon me for all the assistance he needs; I pledge you that I shall use all the power of Government in giving such assistance." The date was March 9, 1864.

The war was to continue for another twelve months but statistically Grant's prospects of a victory were now overwhelming. The Union with a population of 22 ½ million people had the added advantage of superior war production behind it.
The Confederacy had a population of 5 ½ million but its 3 ½ million slaves could not be armed. Unfortunately its industries and raw material were pitifully small. To crown all this the Union could call on twice the cash required to pay for the war. The North could with its superior naval power blockade vital ports dependant on the import of war materials. The South's survival for so long was really a tribute to the courage of its fighting soldiers.

Despite these disadvantages the South had a monopoly of the officer class from its many plantations. Its top General Robert E. Lee has been recognized by historians as the best in both armies.

After four years of bloody carnage 650,000 men were killed, 150,000 more than the total American casualties in the Second World War, the final surrender was signed at Appomattox Court House by General Robert E. Lee. Grant was magnanimous in victory allowing Lee's army to keep their horses. He also gave them an allowance of rations to take them home. Finally, no war crimes court ever resulted. It was a time for healing and reconciliation. The date was April 9, 1865 twelve months to the day Lincoln had made Grant Commander-in-Chief of all U.S. forces.

Within four years General Ulysses Grant was to become President of the United States. His pedigree, fame and illustrious army career behind him made him a natural candidate for the job. Yet he wasn't the first choice of the Republican Party. Despite this those who voted against him respected him. As a victorious General in the Civil War he had earned himself the reputation of a no-nonsense administrator. In army life he had been single minded and ruthless in selecting his officers and ensuring they carried out his orders. The ideal strong man for the turbulent times of post-Civil War America or so it seemed. He was expected to run his office with the same unswerving precision of a masterful General leading a well-disciplined army.

Well they were the expectations on which Grant was elected by a sweeping majority of 73% to 27% or 214 votes to 80. To his manager's despair he achieved his victory despite taking no part in his election choosing to return to his hometown Galena to await the result.

Grant's inauguration on Thursday March 4, 1869 on the East Portico of the Capitol was the most impressive ever seen up to then. A parade of eight full divisions of troops took part in the march past. Once again an outgoing President Andrew Johnson refused to attend the celebrations for his successor but was seen leaving the city that very day. The usual Ball was held in the new Treasury Building at which the expected vast crowds of supporters and well-wishers attended.

In his victorious inauguration speech Grant said "The office has come to me unsought, I commence its duties untruamatised." But perhaps the highest office in the country came to him a little too easily, for he was soon to discover that the world of the military gentleman in which he had lived for so long was a very unsound training for life in the alien world of politics populated by high rollers and unscrupulous ruthless opportunists.

Time would prove it was no place for an honest broker like Ulysses S. Grant.
Not long into his first term Grant found himself compromised by the Spoils system which had tainted and weakened many Presidencies before his. He also had to surround himself with "machine politicians".
Had the challenges he faced been military ones his skills in that field would have been unopposable. But financial economic and diplomatic problems called for different expertise for which he was totally unprepared. The verdict of history, though today a little more sympathetic, seems to say he was a great General but a useless President.

So why this verdict especially since he was re-elected for a second term with an even larger majority.

His main critics were the reformers in his Cabinet who were deeply disappointed with his "hands off" attitude on public issues. This approach left his Party drifting and even breaking up. Worse than that, the ex-Confederates in the Southern States just refused to co-operate with him. His Cabinet became frozen and divided urging neutrality against the South's growing racism and anti black bigotry. Worse than that, his Cabinet even apposed action to restrain the violence against the blacks.

One would have expected the General in him to step in and bark out orders. His detractors' major criticism centred on the fact that Ulysses had not the same genius as a politician that he had as a General. Expectations in Ulysses Grant, now dashed, encouraged an intolerance for his smallest errors.

Inevitably people began to desert him. Opinions had changed now and old latent racial prejudices surfaced. They didn't take kindly to Grant's determination to enforce Civil Rights laws. Ulysses came more to depend on ambitious professional politicians to help him govern. Unfortunately an economic slump which lasted for the whole of his Presidency didn't help. Profiteers had already hijacked the high ground of commerce and political life in pursuit of small fortunes. Scams like "The Gould and Fisk Gold" scandal left a bad odour around the President although he had never been involved in that scam. Speculators got their fingers burned. It was raw ruthless capitalism in all its sordid selfishness. The old pride and honour of Washington's America was fading fast. Depression and hardship for many was the price they paid.

Scandals continued to rock the White House even in upper circles. Bribery for contracts was rampant but the one which hurt Grant the most was the so called "whiskey ring". New taxes had been imposed on whiskey to pay for the Civil War. Inspectors were bribed who were involved in certifying whiskey output. The figures were juggled to give the whiskey barons enormous profits and Grant was an unfortunate victim of this corruption among his friends.

Yet not withstanding his uninspiring first term Grant was re-elected, as I said earlier to a second term this time by an even bigger majority of 286 to 66.

Far from being surprised Grant expresses a feeling of vindication by his victory against those who had criticized his first four years.

In his inaugural address he complained of being criticized with such malignancy for his first term. Grant was glad to castigate his critics by telling them during his speech "I have been the subject of abuse and slander scarcely ever equalled in political history which today I feel I can afford to disregard in view of your verdict which I can accept as my vindication."

For Grant's second inauguration on Tuesday March 4, 1873 the parade was a great disappointment because of blizzards that hit the city. During the ceremony several West Point cadets collapsed with the cold. The now famous Ball was held in Judiciary Square in a temporary building so cold the guests danced in their overcoats. Even the musical instruments were affected by the freezing cold. But the 1872 election saw a changing America. The first black Presidential candidate was nominated by the Equal Rights Party at the Democratic Convention, that year a Roman Catholic was nominated for the first time but he received only 300,000 votes from twenty-three States. A further sign of the times saw the first woman Presidential candidate.

Unbelievably the political Civil War in Washington still continued around Grant in his second term. The same war he had already won on the battlefields of America he was losing to the politicians in Washington. Now he found that the slave, the abolitionist and the plantation owners were no longer an issue. A new world was been rebuilt in the South by the white supremacists and radicalists which was to last for another one hundred and fifty years and Grant was unable to turn the tide of history without his soldiers.

By the end of his Presidency all the glories of his military victories were now just drums and bugles sounding the last post. Sadly the Presidency had been confiscated from him by corrupt politicians, swindlers and the old Confederate establishment that half a million brave soldiers had fought to replace and failed.

So called experts have blamed Grant for this disaster as loudly as they trumpeted his military triumphs but the changing times and the greed of vested interests were the real culprits.

As his second Presidential term came to an end the whole fabric of the South was being challenged by business interests in the North who complained selfishly about a perceived threat to commercial stability by conditions in the South. "Leaders of property and intelligence" as they were called would not accept racial equality. For their own ignoble reasons "Leniency towards the South" became their war cries. Today we would call it "The appeasement of the speculators".

There was a saying abroad "Where economic interests jibed men of business were men of peace." Railroad interests, cotton interests and investment interests were pushing for disengagement with the whole problem of the South choosing to leave it on the terms laid down by white racists for future generations to sort out.

Crafty supporters of the next President Rutherford B. Hayes exploited the new mood in the country and an abandonment policy was in the air. But that is a story for another day when we read about the life of Grant's successor in later pages.

But let's change the mood a little and write about lighter events. We can't leave Grant's Presidency without mentioning what life was like in the White House during his stay there. It was his first permanent home for thirty years. This is not unusual for an ex-General. You may remember a predecessor of his in the Presidency Zachary Taylor had the same experience. He too had not enjoyed such grandeur so different from the rough and ready life he knew as a soldier. Sadly for Zachary he did not live long enough into his Presidency to enjoy such grandeur.

Grant's son Fred was now a West Point Cadet and his other son nicknamed "Buck" was a freshman at Harvard. His other two children were Nellie aged fourteen and young Jesse. Grandpa Dent the ex-planter now a widower settled into the White House as part of the family. Getting on in years now he never let go of his opinions of the new rights given to blacks. Yet Grant's father Jesse was an easy match for him being an avowed abolitionist since his early days. Many were the verbal jousts between the two grandfathers. Today it would have been ideal material for a TV show. Some things in the White House took Grant by surprise. He walked out of his room one morning and was a little irritated to find sentries posted along the corridor of the White House. He confronted one sentry about this and was told "Sir it is a precaution taken since the war." Grant had them removed. He wanted to be a civilian leader. They were indeed amazing times. Despite the assassination of Lincoln Grant sometimes went window shopping in Washington without a bodyguard. He often sauntered outside the White House with or without Julia and became quite familiar as a cigar smoker around the place. He also preferred to go personally to his Senator or Minister to discuss problems with him rather than calling that person into his office. He preferred the hands on approach, a habit he acquired from his military days.

Grant's day started early. He rose at seven read the papers, and waited for Julia who usually wasn't down yet. The announcement of "breakfast being served" saw him heading for the dining room. Another cigar after breakfast, a short stroll and then back to his office to deal with Presidential business and the visitors. His secretaries were former soldiers who had kept their rank since the war years with him. His contact with civilians had always been limited but outside the White House a new lifestyle had changed society since the Civil War. A new millionaire class full of ostentation and the flaunting of wealth which the new business boom rebuilding the country had spawned. It was a new vulgarity Ulysses barely tolerated. The new social circle that had infiltrated the White House was completely alien to an ex-army man like Grant.

But let's move on a little further. Nellie now a teenager was making a name for herself as the leader of a young social set. Press criticism of her boisterous behaviour caused her to be shipped out to Europe by Grant with the Secretary of the Navy and his wife. We don't know how Nellie felt about this but one thing was for sure Nellie's vivacious personality wouldn't be suppressed. Her illustrious name still shone like a jewel on her travels.

It did not prevent her having a wonderful time and she did the usual round of parties at Queen Victoria's court. Her journey to England however was to prove not only exciting but romantically fruitful. The truth is her fame was no defence against cupid. The boy was a passenger she met on the ship and she returned to America got engaged and eventually married Charles Frederick Sartoris in a famous White House wedding. Someone had a little peep behind the scenes that day and saw her father the rough and tough old war horse

General Grant sitting in Nellie's room sobbing softly for his "lost daughter".

A final word on the White House children concerns nine year old Jesse. He liked to play with the neighbourhood lads in the White House grounds in good weather and in the basement during bad weather.

The story of the gold watch is now well-known from consistent telling. It seems his grandfather Jesse had promised him a gold watch to encourage young Jesse's concentration on his studies. But somewhere along the way the gold watch remained nothing more than a promise to the lad's obvious disappointment. Ulysses was annoyed enough to intend asking his father about the watch but decided against it. Instead he bought a gold watch for Jesse and kept it a secret hinting he would give it to Jesse at Christmas. But one night Grant's self-discipline, usually a rod of steel, gave way and he produced the watch at dinner. "But you said it was for Christmas," said Jesse with delight. "You didn't want to wait for Christmas did you?" retorted Ulysses with a grin. "Neither did I."

We can't leave the White House and the Grant family without mentioning the First Lady Julia Dent Grant who became a very popular White House hostess. In fact the dinner parties thrown by Julia Dent were legendary and were reputed to have run to twenty-nine courses. They would indeed have impressed the Queen of First Ladies the great Dolly Madison herself.

Yet Julia is also renowned for the political clout she wielded. Proof of this was the appointment of the most talented Secretary of State ever to grace the U.S. Cabinet, Hamilton Fisher, at the suggestion of Julia. She was also ahead of her time as a great supporter of women's rights. There are many other family stories concerning Grant's term in the White House which are not recorded here. Eventually Grant's days in the White House came to an end and perhaps his story should finish right here. But just like George Washington his retirement is for me a fitting end to a wonderful life story and if you will bear with me I think it merits another small chapter to complete the picture.

As Grant left the Presidency the deal to abandon the Southern blacks was sealed by the incoming Democrats led by Rutherford B. Hayes. Ulysses Grant now free of the whole distasteful baggage decided to tackle his one remaining ambition – a world tour.

Let's continue the Grant story at Philadelphia as he set out on his epic journey abroad. He sailed away on the warship "Indiana" on May 17, 1877. Only two other members of his family were on board, Julia his wife his youngest son Jesse, and the brilliant journalist and writer John Russell Young who was to write a column in the home papers describing the great adventure. As Grant's touring party moved from country to country John Russell Young became famous for his column which was one day to become a brilliant travel book. I rely on his book Around the World with General Grant for my contribution to the final chapter of my Ulysses Grant story.

It was originally intended to be a six month visit to Europe but because of Russell Young's column which reflected how popular Grant was in Europe the journey was extended another two years. Grant went everywhere in style having at his disposal the best and biggest war ships available. He was feted everywhere he went as the guardian of American liberty which was a great boost to moral back home.

His travels were not unlike the diary of another illustrious player in American politics, Abigail Adams, wife of the second President of the United States.

The best way I can approach this job is to stop wherever I can in the houses and festivals of people and places that stand out for me personally. My stop off place may not be to everyone's taste but once written about I can do no more than leave the judgement of my selections to you the reader.

Grant was seen off by thousands of well-wishers in Philadelphia, supporters who had long since forgotten his failures as a politician being happy instead to cheer on their hero of the Civil War General Ulysses Grant. It took ten days to cross the Atlantic in a Navy warship a significant improvement of four weeks on the sailing time of Jefferson and Adams years before.

Because of fog they had to lay low for eight hours just outside Queenstown now Cobh, Co. Cork. They had temporarily landed in Ireland on May 27, 1877 but after the brief welcoming ceremonies were over they pushed on with their trip promising to return again later which they did. Waiting for him were crowds of well wishers as he landed in Liverpool and again when he spoke in Manchester. Queen Victoria lost no time inviting him to Windsor Castle but made the unfortunate error of seating young Jesse with the servants. Realizing the mistake of protocol Jesse was then placed with the adults. After that Julia was glad to leave the Windsor Castle circle far behind her when they left.

Ulysses quickly realized he would need to take great care in his eating habits as he was lavished with banquets and invitations to banquets wherever he went and he had yet to travel north to the midlands. The speeches all had the one theme a welcome to a victorious General who had always been magnanimous to the vanquished. General Grant acknowledge the praise telling his listeners he represented the thousands of British subjects now in America and he was merely a humble representation of their offspring.

Ulysses then paid a visit to Tyneside, Newcastle to see the opening of the Tyne Swing Bridge. The band of the Northumberland Volunteer Artiliary played from a boat which left the new quay to the cheers of thousands. Although the weather was cold the river banks were crowded with no fewer than 150,000 people who had left their work and their homes to join in the great occasion. The General stood in the bow of the boat while all around him the shipping was bedecked with buntings and flags of welcome for the General. The noise was deafening as guns, mortars and even fog horns were added to the din. Again in his speech Grant connected the cheering crowds with their grandchildren in far off America. Newcastle itself assumed a holiday atmosphere. Walls, cabs, windows and balconies held a cheering crowd of 80,000 people to hear the speeches. Ulysses Grant was overwhelmed by the turn out.

His entry into London was like a triumphal procession. The arrival of a tanner's son from a two roomed cottage was like the parade of a mythical king.

One reporter got carried away a little when he wrote "That he should rise to the exalted position of President from such humble beginnings" went right to the heart of the heaving masses.

Yet another party was arranged for the Grants in London where they were entertained by the Lord Mayor in his country house in which they had stayed overnight. The Prince of Wales took him to the races to watch the Oaks, an English horseracing classic. Another highlight was meeting The Duke of Wellington who was actually the son of the famous Iron Duke; naming the dignitaries Ulysses met were too numerous to be interesting. Suffice it to say he met MP's, Lords, Marquises and many representatives of the nobility and British society including the Primer Minister of the time Mr. Gladstone. His stay in England was finally crowned by receiving the honour of freedom of the City of London.

At this stage I would like to introduce a book Transatlantic Crossing by Walter Allen in which the London of Grant's visit was vividly described from which I now quote: "Every type of cockney shuffled along its dark dingy looking streets. The hackney coachman and cabman with their own peculiar language and a hundred other characters straight from Dickens. What a contrast to Paris and the elegant flower covered restaurants. There the tables are set in elegant galleries among the trees of a garden. There, waiters spring from table to table as noiselessly as shadows. But London dining rooms are where you can swill porter and devour roast beef." Walter Allen then took us to the top of St. Paul's. Here is how he describes the scene. "I went to the top of St. Paul's. Standing on a mountain top I have enjoyed unbroken forests right to the horizon. But looking down from St. Paul's you see the tiled roofs and steeples half hid in smoke and fog and a filthy river covered with boats. There is an incessant din and the smell of coal smoke that pollutes the air. The smoke you see streaming in the wind from 10,000 chimney pots obscure the landscape like a veil. Church spires disappear into a far off horizon. It was an indistinct but limitless panorama. Here I thought I had under my eye the greatest collection of pimps prostitutes and bullies. Was there ever such a cursed hole and overhead covered with cobwebs and smoke dust half dropping from their staff the flags that were borne at Nelson's funeral."
Yes a very ugly melodramatic picture indeed but maybe Walter Allen was just a little too hard on the London of the 19th Century. Who knows?

Now let's return again to Ulysses Grant and the people he met in a society that was worlds apart from the London of Walter Allen. I am afraid the unfortunate General had to endure dozens of long winded boring speeches as he moved from banquet to banquet on a treadmill of functions specially laid out for him in his honour.

As you can see the sheer adulation and respect offered to Grant was truly amazing coming from so many of the so called exalted people. It seemed a long, long way back to Jesse and Hannah Grant's humble home life in their cottage beside the Ohio River.

Of still greater contrast in his mind in the midst of all this splendour were the visions he had of the battlefields of America, the heart-breaking carnage around him, the shouts and screams of dying soldiers and the sounds of battles he had witnessed. Nothing in the glitzy Palaces of Europe could ever fade these pictures from his memory and he knew it.

His visit to Southampton to meet his sister was much more low key and informal away from the fuss and celebrations of the cheering mob. This was the highlight of his whole exotic journey. How he enjoyed the long pleasant drives in the horse-drawn carriage he shared with her to the many quaint picturesque hamlets and towns along the coastline.

But his world tour was attracting more and more interest because of the newspaper reports of John Russell Young to the people back home. Never before had they read of such pomp and pageantry among the Kings, Emperors and Viceroys who feted Ulysses in Europe. There were pen pictures of truly touching scenes about little girls in an Indian school learning and singing the Civil War song called "John Brown's body". So successful and happy was the tour, the six months planned for it was extended to two years to include every continent except Australia.

But let's not get too far ahead. Right now the Grant party was still in England and preparing to move on to Europe. On July 5, 1877 they finally headed for the Continent and Paris where there were many adoring fans waiting to greet them.

Paris was a culture shock that Grant was not expecting. What a contrast from England. He left London with his wife and son and journalist John Russell Young on a special train put on for them from Charing Cross. On landing at Boulogne, after a short rest, the party moved on towards Paris settling in at the Hotel Bristol in heavy rain. Because of political undercurrents Grant's visit to Paris was very uncomfortable for him. The last thing he wanted was politics on this a holiday visit. However Victor Hugo did not help when he accused the ex-President of supporting the Prussians in the France-Prussia war when he was President. This was untrue and embarrassing but that's politics. Grant kept a low profile after that just window shopping and lazing alone on the Champs Elysees watching the world go by. Mostly he dined with the American colony there. He continued his Paris sightseeing around the usual tourist highlights such as the Louvre, Notre Dame Cathedral and the gardens of the Palais Royal no doubt with Julia and Jesse by his side.

At that time, the American colony in Paris numbering 3,000 was one of the most influential collection of Americans gathered together in one city. Sometimes this floating colony could rise to 10,000 depending on the tourist season. At that time in the late 19th century Paris was becoming a focal point for the world American traveller so it is easy to understand the concentration of fashionable coffee houses, newsagents and bazaars catering for this particular trade.

So numerous were they Grant found it hard to resist the patriotic fervour of so many wanting to entertain him.

One intriguing feature of his visit was that everywhere he went there were businessmen ready to greet him hoping to gain a foothold through Grant in the rapidly expanding trade between the U.S and the Continent. It seemed to him he had not left the "Spoils system" behind him in America after all. Even King Leopold of Belgium notoriously known as "The Butcher of the Congo" politely described by Grant as "A man of more than ordinary gifts", canvassed him for a shipping line he was promoting from Antwerp to America.

After Paris, Grant followed the usual tourist route from the Cathedral of Cologne down the Rhine and on to Frankfurt where he was again entertained to dinner by the American community. Once again he was inundated by sightseers determined to see him in the flesh. How different his travel plans would have been today. Then it was on to Switzerland, where in Geneva he laid the cornerstone of the American Episcopalian Church of George Washington's faith which is still there today one hundred and thirty years later. The stamina of Grant was truly remarkable for he also found his way to Edinburgh where, to the General's surprise, the Scots claimed him as one of their own.

Back in Paris again it was soon time for him to head for the Mediterranean so at 5 p.m. on December 13, 1877 he boarded a new man-of-war the "Vandalia" a gift from President Rutherford B. Hayes, and pulling up anchor the ship set sail for Italy, Egypt and the Holy Land.

They cast anchor in Naples where Ulysses and Julia went on a tour of the city. It was a week before Christmas 1877. They stood on the balcony of a summer Palace specially opened for them and gazed out on the splendour of the Bay of Naples with Vesuvius beyond in a shimmering blue sea. Vesuvius was dormant refusing to crackle fireworks, not even for a Yankee General. They were disappointed with Naples which they found picturesque but a dirty city at that time. A carriage drive up Vesuvius was the highlight of the day. To modern readers most of this journey with an ex-President on board would have been taken by helicopter and army jeep today. The weary horse-drawn carriage drive was no match for this for it left the passengers cold and hungry and the horse exhausted.

They were glad to return to the comfort of the Vandalia with all its lights ablaze in the harbour.

One of the most memorable experiences laid on for him, by special permission for visiting dignitaries, was a private dig in one of Pompeii's buried houses. Although only a couple of vases and a loaf of bread wrapped in cloth were unearthed while they were there the find was such a treasure any of our present day Archaeologists would have paid a fortune to acquire it.

Now let's look at what life was like on board a man-of-war. Grant as an army man was fascinated with the way it operated. Routine was a way of life for the sailor and everything happened to the beat of a drum. The watches, the calls, the drill, the discipline, the ceremony, the sense of command and obedience. It was all so new to Grant despite his own experience of army life back home. Life on board was like being a cog in a wheel. You rise to the beat of a drum. The drum even calls you to dinner. Everything is strict and precise. Young sailors here live for years away from home in a space no bigger than a New York drawing room. They listen constantly for the drum tap that may call them at midnight to fight a storm or tackle an enemy at day break. "How weary it all must become after six months," mused Grant.

Yet moral never dropped among the good companions on the "Vandalia".

Everyday at noon Grant comes on deck. At 6 p.m. he has dinner. Then it is a cigar and a conversation. He is permanently in a state of good humour and speaks well of both enemies and friends. Magnanimity describes his Philosophy. Cadet days and old friends, Sherman and Lincoln inspire great animation in him.

But life aboard the Man-of-war was not always "perfume and roses". Nights could be cold. Rain bubbled in pools on the deck. When the wind blew the old ship trembled and high in the dripping rigging a Jack Tar would peer into the night. Now and then a call answered from the bridge.

On the quarterdeck the grey head of the quartermaster stared grave faced into the swirling rain. They feel safe when he is on deck. In the comfort of the ward room some of the officers are writing home, others try to read. All outside is blackness lit periodically by a flash of lighting on the horizon towards Sicily. The good ship strains and twists on course for Alexandria where they anchor before moving on to Cairo, The Nile and the Holy Land on Christmas morning 1877.

Christmas morning was spent on board the Vandalia. In the early hours he was greeted with a fifteen gun salute. At half past five in the evening a sumptuous festive dinner was laid on in the wardroom followed by the inevitable cigar to end the evening. New Years Eve was celebrated on board the Vandalia as she was speeding down the Mediterranean and finished with the singing of "Auld Lang Syne". That night Ulysses and Julia had their first pangs of homesickness.

As you will appreciate it is impossible to condense 438 pages of John Russell Young's fascinating book into one chapter at the end of Grant's life story. Russell Young recounted in minute detail all the events of Grant's world tour. I have only sketched out selected stories, as I said I would earlier, to give a bird's-eye view of his progress around the globe.

And so we move on towards the Holy Land. Even in the remotest Arab villages Grant was amazed to be greeted with a banner on which were scrawled the message "Welcome General Grant". Torches blazed rockets and fireworks exploded as they approached the gates of the Missionary College of the United Presbyterian church where they stayed.

The party duly arrived in Calvary where a dome had been built over the place of the Crucifixion. You must remember Grant's visit was a long time ago and naturally everything has changed since 1877, one hundred and thirty years ago. At that time Calvary was within the old town walls and stood sixty feet above the lower streets of the city. Grant was surprised to find that despite the reverence for the place this did not deter the everyday commercial activity that went on there. Beggars crying out for alms; workmen building, merchants selling, camels, asses and other beasts of burden adding to the confusion. Finally a large barracks was now sited where Pilate's Palace once stood. The Grant party entered the enclosure where the whipping, scourging and crowning with thorns took place almost two thousand years previously. It was from here Jesus was released to the mob for Crucifixion. The hill to the summit of Calvary was even for a fit man like Grant, without the burden of the cross, a climb that knocked the breath out of him.

A visit to Bethlehem and Nazareth completed his tour of the Holy Land. The party then returned to "The Vandalia" to prepare for the next stage of the tour to Italy and Rome. It was now March 1878.

Arriving in Italy, Ulysses was only now getting used to the dignitaries, the pomp and the well-meaning welcomes and banquets which were now unavoidable. All ideas of a private pilgrimage to these foreign lands in secret and unnoticed had long since been abandoned by the party. On April 15, 1878 all the Ambassadors and Ministers attended a State dinner given by King Humbert to welcome the ex-President of the United States.

Holland, Germany and Scandinavia were Grant's next ports of call. He was finding it difficult to resist many invitations from leading Americans in Europe. Because Prussia had figured so much in the news in the recent twenty years Grant took a great interest in Berlin where Bismarck was in his ascendancy and the Brandenburg gate was already erected. The Chariot of Victory sat on the top of it ever since being returned to Germany after the Battle of Waterloo in 1815. It seems strange today to be discussing such "current events" in Grant's time. The truth is Napoleon's defeat at Waterloo was only sixty-three years previous to Grant. To understand the time factor better today just as the end of the Second World War in 1945 is still only sixty-two years of age for us today.

His trip to Russia could not neglect a visit to the wonderful Winter Palace of St. Petersburg. Nothing in his beloved America could prepare him for the Hermitage Housing as it still does today one hundred and thirty years later, the astonishing treasures, paintings, jewels and precious stones in one dazzling room after another. A marvellous tribute to the genius of the most famous Russian of all - Peter the Great. Napoleons defeat on the outskirts of Moscow in 1812 was still the topic of conversation even as it faded into history. The final revolution and the annihilation of the Russian Royal family was still to come in 1917 nearly forty years later although Grant was not to know this. Talking about their native Moscow they said "Though Moscow now be great it never can be as it was before it was burnt." They were talking about 1812. Little did they know Hitler's siege of Moscow in 1942 was still to come. The Kremlin so impressed Grant he agreed it was the one lasting impression left on any traveller there. That was in 1878.

But here we must call a halt to Grant's tour in this article for there are too many other lands he travelled to for me to do it any justice here. I will leave that to the pen of the illustrious writer

John Russell Young. The missing countries will be India, Spain, Portugal, Ireland, Singapore, Burma and China to mention just a few. So let's just finish with his visit to Japan.

Japan although not rich displayed very little poverty among the ordinary people. He remarked to his party on the wealth of minerals and its abundance of fish that swam in its many fine harbours. The country had indeed a very promising future he concluded. How lucky he was to be seeing Japan in all its beauty in 1877 and not in the terrible aftermath of the war between their nations in the Second World War. Or, seeing the terrible abomination that history had hidden from them in the devastation of Hiroshima and Nagasaki just over sixty years later. How hard he would have fought to change that history. It was good he was not to know.

The time was fast approaching when sadly he must bid farewell to this lovely people and head for California and home. Soon the last line that held them at anchorage was thrown off and surrounded by a convoy of Japanese man-of-wars, Grant's huge ship moved out to sea. Seamen ran up the riggings to man the yards. The guns rolled in salute and were echoed by others all across the bay. Finally the guns of the awesome Monongahela thundered goodbye. Cheers rang out from nearby ships and Grant's Steamer "City of Tokio" answered with a shrill salute on her steam whistle. Then they breasted the incoming waves, pointed their stern towards California and headed for home.

They arrived in San Francisco on September 20, 1879, two and half years after leaving Philadelphia. After receiving a grand banquet of welcome General Grant's party moved eastwards through the Midwest for another three months prior to stopping at Philadelphia before 350,000 people cheering him home. One commentator compared it significantly to a Presidential campaign. However that was one road Grant knew he would never travel again. He finally landed in his hometown of Galena, Illinois in the Spring of 1880. The nomination for the next Presidency went to a dark horse named James A. Garfield. Sadly Garfield was destined to be assassinated on September 19, 1881 a year and a half into the future. That was to be another traumatic experience for America and a story we will be unfolding for you later.

America was now a far different country to the one he had left behind in May 1877 over three years previously. The Civil War wounds were healing but only very slowly, and Ulysses Grant despite his free spending world tour was not a wealthy man.

What money he managed to hold on to was swindled from him by Ferdinand Ward, a partner who proved to be a crook. Yet again this great man of astute judgement and decisive brilliance in war was conned by someone he completely misjudged and trusted in civilian life. Once again the flaw in his armoury let him down just as it did in his Presidency when he was the victim of the very shady people who managed to gain his confidence. It seems his trust was too easily given and too easily betrayed.

But the story of Ulysses Grant, victorious General, hero of the Civil War, twice President of America just could not end with a whimper.

Mark Twain, that great American writer managed to persuade Ulysses to put his thoughts on paper. For two years he laboured in long hand pages that are now locked away in the Library of Congress – which produced what is recognised by the literary world as a masterpiece of writing. The title Let Us Have Peace was to ensure a pension fund for his family and he succeeded beyond his wildest dreams. His book is now a Civil War jewel and earned him half a million dollars in royalties. It was completed during his last two years struggling with the diabolical pain of cancer.

During the writing of the book he knew he was in a battle with time. As the remaining months, then weeks, then days faded away for him his last hours drew vast crowds outside his home in Galena. They had gathered in respectful silence as news of his illness leaked out.

It was a spontaneous outpouring of love for a great warrior. Work on his memoirs continued and was only completed two days before he died. As the illness progressed his voice began to fail him and he spoke to his family in notes only.

It is a sad commentary on Ulysses Grant that he had smoked twenty cigars daily during his lifetime. It is easy today to link his throat cancer to this habit. They say his smoking habit dated back to the Battle of Donelson in 1862 when he was reported in the newspapers to have smoked light cigars during the battle. The publicity of the battle resulted in Grant receiving boxes of choice cigars which were numbered in thousands. "I gave hundreds away," said Grant but the ones he kept must have inflicted the fatal craving for the killer weed.

Shortly before his death Ulysses called his son to his beside and handed him a note being unable to speak. It was a last request which sadly could not be granted by the authorities at West Point. He wished to be buried there but he also wanted his faithful Julia to be buried alongside him. However West Point could not allow this so he was buried instead on Saturday August 8, 1885 in Riverside Park, New York City sixteen days after he died on July 23, 1885. Perhaps West Point may someday grant him his wish. Both of them Ulysses and Julia now lie at rest beneath a memorial overlooking the Hudson River. Engraved in stone over the entrance are the immortal words "Let us have peace".

19th President   Rutherford Birchard Hayes

"Rutherford the Rover"
Born 1822
Died 1893
70 Years of age.
1 Term
1877 – 1881
Age: 55

Party: Republican
Profession: Lawyer
County: Ohio
Ancestry: Scotch
Value of Estate: Unknown.
Hobbies: Reading, Croquet, Shooting, Driving, Hunting, Fishing and skating.

Physical Description: Height 5 foot 8 ½ inches, Weight 170 lbs, Brown hair, sandy red beard, deeply set blue eyes, large head, high forehead, straight nose, circling brows, mild but very audible voice.

Significant Extract from his Inauguration Speech on Monday March 4, 1877
"......With respect to the two distinct races whose peculiar relations to each other have brought upon us the deplorable complications and perplexities which exist in those states, it must be a Government which guards the interest of both races carefully and equally......"

RUTHERFORD B. HAYES

As Grant sailed away into the sunset on his world tour he left behind him a country in a state of confusion and conflict as it faced into the problem of healing the wounds of the Civil War economically; socially, racially and legally.

The Native American or Indian problem had been tackled with some success with the Dawes Act designed to improve the lot of the 260,000 Indians living on Reservations. But the Negro problem went a lot deeper. It was still festering thirteen years later in 1899 when Frederick Douglass an ex-slave and outspoken champion of the Negro, asked this question of future generations.
"Can American liberty and American civilization, American law and American Christianity be made to include and protect alike and forever all American
citizens in the rights which have been guaranteed to them by the organic and fundamental laws of the land?"

But in 1877 Rutherford B. Hayes was only beginning the journey that Douglass had already travelled. Before him was the formidable task of reconciling so many opposing factions in a Southern society blown apart from its very roots. Of course there was also a slave problem being solved in Europe in the 1870s but for France, Holland, Portugal and Spain, theirs was a mere trickle compared to the numbers that had to be accommodated in America. Furthermore, the flood of immigrants from Europe was daily being integrated into American society until there was a general outcry to stop the movement altogether.
Since most of the Civil War had been fought on Southern soil the entire area was impoverished and devastated. Yet the North's economic activity had expanded, increasing its pre-war economic superiority over the South. When he looked into this cauldron of change, Rutherford B. Hayes was faced with a Southern part of the nation unable to pay a living wage out of the depleted resources left available to them and a Northern State thriving commercially.

Sadly very few of the architects of the Reconstruction understood the situation down South and were of little help to him. Rumblings of war on the other side of the Atlantic and the scramble for Africa by greedy nations left America isolated in her troubles. No help was coming from that quarter either. Over there they had their own kind of Reconstruction problems based on political greed.

The establishment of white rule was now seen as the only road to stable Government in the South. Northern public opinion was coming around to the acceptance of the Negro as "a second-class citizen". And nobody was protecting his "second class rights" despite the pious platitudes of a succession of weak Presidents between 1877 and 1901.

So the scene has now been set for the Presidency of Rutherford B. Hayes, 19th President in line since Washington.

They say he vacillated between devotion to the Constitution and democracy on the one hand and pacification of the country coupled with concern for the fortunes of his beloved Republican Party on the other.

One thing is for sure he was the principal Presidential architect of white supremacy in the South according to some historians. Perhaps this will come as a relief to the supporters of poor old Andrew Johnson, the 17th President who attracted all the blame for white supremacy by his veto policy in the Presidency.

Rutherford's problems seemed to be insurmountable but the one fear uppermost in his mind; the one that haunted him almost on a daily basis was how to prevent a second Civil War.

The seeds of his ambivalence and his easy accommodation to vested interests have been noted by some commentators in his inauguration speech. An extract reads "The moral and material prosperity of the Southern States can be most effectually advanced by a hearty and generous recognition of the rights of all, by all, - a recognition without reserve or reservation."

But the country in the South was like a tinderbox and on the very day of Hayes' inauguration speech, the town of Hamburg, South Carolina, was the subject of bloody rioting. Another race riot occurred on September 15, 1877, six months into Rutherford B. Hayes Presidency. Bloodshed was being defended by the rioters as the only means by which the whites could redress the perceived wrongs inflicted on the whites by a Negro majority.

Grant's Attorney General Taft wrote in September to Hayes claiming – "It is a fixed and desperate purpose of the Democratic Party in the South that the Negro shall not vote and murder is a common means of intimidation to prevent them."

Hayes wrote in his diary "Bloodshed and Civil War must be averted if possible." Another entry underlines his misgivings. "The coloured man's fate will be worse than when he was in slavery." Words that were not far from the prophetic. Another entry in Rutherford's diary articulated these worries further. "I would require absolute justice and fair play for the Negro but I am convinced that this could be got best and almost surely by trusting the honourable and influential Southern whites." It is hard to explain how naïve these words sound today one hundred and thirty years later.

The troops were withdrawn on April 10, 1877 from South Carolina and in his diary, Rutherford B. Hayes writes "I can hope for peace and what is equally important, security and property for coloured people." At the end of his entry, he writes, "Time will tell." But this gamble with the future was fiercely criticised in the Washington Evening Star by two of the most dedicated abolitionists, William Lloyd Garrison and Wendell Philips.

However, before we read their comments, perhaps we should understand the make-up of Rutherford B. Hayes and how he arrived in the ultimate office of State in those notorious times. Here I would like to acknowledge the source of my observations on President Hayes from the book The Presidency of Rutherford B. Hayes by Kenneth E. Davison.

Strangely it is only in recent years that historians have decided to re-appraise the Presidency of Rutherford B. Hayes. Up to recently any claim to fame has been sabotaged by the sleazy events surrounding his election to the Presidency, details of which we will discuss later. Despite these criticisms, our modern historians place him as high as third in their rankings behind Lincoln and F.D. Roosevelt, among Republican Presidents.

Before he entered the White House, Rutherford had lived a regal lifestyle in his mansion called "Spiegel Grove" back in Ohio where high imposing gates opened on to a long winding driveway leading to an estate of remarkable beauty in a country setting of large oak trees, unusual shrubs and beautiful well-kept flower gardens. Although Hayes entertained all the great men of his time; writers, politicians, soldiers and Statesmen there in this stately Victorian mansion, he seems to have been neglected, even ignored, by the scholars of politics whose time was been spent among the exciting economic giants of the later 19th Century. His was an almost forgotten era of the past, or so it seems.

Rutherford B. Hayes was born in Delaware, Ohio, on October 4, 1822, the first born child of Rutherford and Sophia Birchard Hayes who came to Ohio five years previously from Vermont. But Rutherford was never to know his father who died of fever just before he was born. Rutherford's mother survived and her brother, Sardis – later to become a rich merchant – became guardian uncle and father to him. Sardis played a central role in Rutherford's life, providing him with funds for his education and legal career.

The house belonged to Sardis who generously left it to Rutherford when he died in 1859. Rutherford was thirty-seven then. His mother, a strict Presbyterian, brought him up in her hard-working religious church-going lifestyle. She too was a major influence on him.

As a boy, Rutherford went to school in Delaware, then on to Norwalk Seminary School, Ohio. He then moved to a Methodist school, finally finishing college at Isaac Webb's private school in Connecticut. He opted for Kenyon College instead of Yale at his mother's request and graduated on August 3, 1842 when he was just twenty. Like Lincoln he went on to the read the famous Blackstone's Commentaries until he ended his studies in Dane Law School of Harvard University. He completed his studies at Harvard in February 1845 at the age of twenty-three.

Like some of his illustrious predecessors in the Presidency, Rutherford B. Hayes was born with a silver spoon in his mouth so to speak for he enjoyed a very privileged upbringing indeed. Later he associated with intellectuals and being an avid reader, built a significant library at his home. He was humble enough to regard himself not as a scholar, but a man with scholarly tastes. He constantly encouraged his four sons in their careers with a fatherly eye on their welfare. Rutherford moved in exalted circles, sharing the friendship of other great academics like Quincy Adams, 6th President of the United States and Daniel Webster. Rutherford Hayes was not unlike William Jefferson in his thirst for knowledge, delving deeply into French literature, politics and even the theatre. To crown all this, he set up a very successful and lucrative law practice just after being admitted to the Bar in 1845.

But setting up business was not as easy as academic life and proved a very frustrating time for him. He didn't enjoy the experience until he moved on to Cincinnati four years later. Here he set up a partnership with a local Whig leader, Ralph P. Buckland, who was to actively promote Rutherford's later political career.

When he was twenty-five, Rutherford began a love affair with Lucy Webb, his childhood sweetheart, later to become his wife. They married after five years courtship in 1852.

But Rutherford's plans for an army life in the Mexican war was discouraged by his doctors so he joined the Sons of Temperance and moved in local circles of Whig society supporting passionately the "Zachary Taylor for President" platform.

A trip with his uncle on horseback around Texas gave him a deep sympathy for Southerners for the first time. He attempted to set up another law practice in Cincinnati and only established himself after two years. Success he found didn't come easy outside academia in the hurly burly of commercial life. His breakthrough came in the case of Nancy Farrer, a woman accused of four murders by poisoning. Rutherford said "It will give me a better opportunity to exert and exhibit whatever pith there is in me than any case I ever appeared in."

But the Gods would not smile on Rutherford just yet. Nancy Farrer was found guilty and sentenced to hang. Still, Rutherford couldn't accept defeat and asked for a new trial. The

Supreme Court granted him one in which he based his case on her insanity.

His moving speech, here abbreviated, went something like this: "The calamity of insanity is one that may touch very nearly the happiness of the best of our citizens …….. We must all wish to see rules as would satisfy an intelligent man if instead of this friendless girl his own sister or his own daughter were on trial."

He spoke with first-hand experience having seen mental illness already in one of his own family. His sister Fanny, was the victim of a post-natal childbirth depression.

Anyway, Rutherford was successful and Nancy Farrer was sent to an asylum. But Nancy, a resourceful character, escaped from the asylum after making significant recovery and was never seen or heard of again. Rutherford's career took off after he won two further murder trials.

Rutherford's very short army career dated from the beginning of the Civil War when he joined Lincoln's army as a volunteer officer in the Ohio Infantry. It was not a very illustrious or glamorous place based as it was in the mountains of West Virginia.

Still it was different. A little more hectic than usual for up to now everything about Rutherford's lifestyle was quiet, reserved and low-key. Amazingly, he reached the rank of Brevet Major when his army career ended. He was a popular officer and enjoyed the experience so much he considered the time in the army of the Union as the best years of his life. His career, he said wryly "Was a very humble one and a place utterly unknown to history." However, his army friends would say "Colonel Hayes was known to have led numerous charges against enemy lines and had several horses shot from under him. In fact he could be intense and ferocious in battle." He carried the scars of three bullet wounds in his right knee, left arm and forehead which pained him constantly throughout his life, especially in damp weather. Mrs. Hayes was much admired by his fellow soldiers for her work among the wounded.

It was an ideal credit to add to his political career CV as politicians seldom got far without an army career in those days. Almost reluctantly, Rutherford found himself nominated to Congress by friends while still in the army. He was duly elected and he didn't even canvass for his election. He rarely took part in Washington's social life but he did achieve great work for soldier's bounties and pensions and earned himself the title "the Soldiers' friend".

But it was in the cultural world of Washington that Rutherford B. Hayes earned his greatest distinction. I suggest we pause here to ponder the world of post-Civil War, America and the turmoil of the South, the political conflicts, the treachery of white racists, the wheeling and dealing of business opportunists and the final history making abandonment of the Negro for the next one hundred and fifty years.

As we consider those years that lay ahead for Rutherford, isn't it fascinating to observe the early years in his political career in Washington and marvel at the sheer tranquillity of these times in the North and the almost innocent pursuits with which he was now preoccupied.

Before diving into the world of Rutherford's Presidency, let us look at his pre-Presidency achievements. It was a pleasant life among the faculty members in Washington University, gentlemen and scholars, doing work far removed from Lincoln's nightmare. They covered many fields; the arts, paintings, the library and the botanical gardens among a cultural circle. Through his contribution, two new wings were added to the library. The Smithsonian Institute's collection of books and documents were transferred to it. He was also involved in the purchase of works of art for the Government. Rutherford just wasn't a verbal politician debating the great issues of the day in Congress. He hated that scene and called it "That noisy exhibition." Why he ever entered politics amazes me though he was almost born to be a back-bencher, a perennial hum-drum insignificant Congressman for he thrived in that role.

So how did he become President in the most aggressive debates in American history? The mind boggles. To quote Rutherford himself, he said "Washington parties were all a bore generally...... Being errand boy to one hundred and fifty thousand people tires me so by night I am ready for bed instead of soirees." He took no part in the bitter speeches that was the red meat of congressional life mostly about "The Plan for Reconstruction" in 1867.

But one day Rutherford B. Hayes set out on a momentous journey during the mid-winter recess of 1866. He was then forty-four years old and in the company of several other Congressmen and their wives he toured the Deep South, New Orleans, Lynchburg, Know Deville, Chattanooga, Nashville and Memphis. It was both a social and political trip to inspect conditions in the South and to meet Southern leaders in their own home towns so to speak. On this trip Rutherford came of age as a politician and sowed the seeds of future success for his Presidential tour of the South ten years later in 1877. But on this trip with the Congressmen and their wives to a war-torn South, Rutherford was still the reluctant Congressman with little ambition for the profession. It was really only two years since the Civil War ended.

We quote him once again when he confided to his uncle "I have no ambition for a congressional reputation or influence – not a particle. I would like to be out of it creditably."
It is unbelievable that it was again some friends who suggested his name for the Governorship of Ohio. He thought about the idea and only looked on it as an escape route from Congress. He said "If this nomination is pretty likely it would get me out of this scrape and after that I am out of political life decently." So Rutherford Hayes capitulated to the urgings of his friends and at the Republican State Convention in Ohio, he was nominated for Governorship on the first ballot. Once again he was reluctant to run against "other more deserving Republicans" but was persuaded to go for it "To leave Washington worries behind me for good," as he said. It was July 1867. Needless to say he was duly elected.

Yet Rutherford enjoyed being Governor......"It strikes me at a guess as the pleasantest office I have ever had. Not too much work, plenty of time to read, good society, etc..." He was re-elected two years later.

But it is time to move on to the Presidency. Just how did Rutherford Hayes move from reluctant Congressman, twice successful Governor of Ohio, to the gates of the White House? It was certainly some achievement for a reluctant suitor.

Here we might ask the question "What talents did the Republican Party see in Rutherford B. Hayes when Hayes himself seemed hell bent on getting out of politics altogether. He spent the three years after his Governorship improving his Spiegel Grove estate, founding the Birchard Public Library in Freemont and attending his properties in Ohio, Minnesota and elsewhere. Once more I quote from Hayes "I shall make a few talks. I wish to drift out of the political currents and shall do as little in a public way as I possibly can." One again, yielding to Party pressure, he accepted the nomination for a 3rd term as Governor of Ohio. It seems comical today but during the hustings the Catholics became embroiled in an accusation of being part of a conspiracy to destroy the public schools system and take over America for the Pope.

Despite the side show, Hayes was duly elected Governor of Ohio for a third time.

Events were now unfolding rapidly and pushed Rutherford into the centre of America's political stage. The public resentment against the corruption of Grant's Administration left the Republicans looking for a safe pair of hands. Rutherford's army career and his three successful terms as Governor of Ohio and most of all his new availability out of retirement pointed to him as the obvious Republican Presidential candidate. But Rutherford's diary was speaking of his unease with the prospect of running for President. He wrote "This would make my life a disturbed and troubled one for six or eight months until November next year." Lucy agreed with Rutherford's views and sympathised with him. Winning the nomination as Governor of Ohio meant two possible outcomes. Losing it he would win his cherished dream of retirement and obscurity. Winning would give him the Presidency should he wish to run for it.

A few days later the Governorship of Ohio was his. By the end of the month he was on the stump speaking to large crowds and getting growing mentions as a Presidential possible. As usual Rutherford was leaving canvassing to his managers, choosing to play a low profile at home in Spiegel Grove.

By March 1876, 750 delegates to the Ohio State Convention unanimously endorsed Rutherford Hayes for President. Rutherford's worst nightmare had arrived. But votes meant nothing to Rutherford it seems. Again he was yearning nostalgically for the quiet life. "In politics I am growing indifferent. I would like it if I could now return to my planting and books at home" he wrote in his diary. It was as if he was now a prisoner of the Party. How far America had come from the white hot enthusiasm and commitment of the Founding Fathers Washington, Adams, Jefferson, Madison and company a century ago.

The day of the Republican Convention is worth talking about. These were exciting and colourful times indeed. Thousands of supporters for all candidates came to town. People milled about the streets and traffic was gridlocked. Bands played, crowds surged, and orators blared through loud-speakers. Cheers and fireworks fed the euphoria. The din and the noise left the speakers inaudible and the managers moved among the delegates quietly garnering votes. The famous Blaine fell ill with sunstroke and lay sick for days. Everybody now held their breath praying for his life.

"Create no enemies" was the fundamental strategy of Hayes' supporters. Professionally working on his low profile approach, they were glad to be looked on as second choice candidate. They made sure they were on good speaking terms with everyone, but hidden from the future lay indescribable heartbreak. Samuel J. Tilden, a bachelor and multi-millionaire, was to be the Democrat's candidate. The stage was now set for the most extraordinary Presidential election in American history. The heartbreak was still to come.

When the votes were counted on the evening of November 7, 1876 Tilden appeared to be victorious by 250,000 votes. But next morning Hayes' supporters claimed victory in the Southern States of Florida, Louisiana and South Carolina where they controlled the electoral machinery. If the electoral votes of these three States could be certified for Hayes, he would just barely win the election 185-184.

Here the George W. Bush story pales into insignificance. In order to solve the problem, an Electoral Commission was set up to adjudicate consisting of five Supreme Court Judges, five Senators and five U.S. Representatives. Seven were Republicans and seven were Democrats and Justice David Davis was accepted as being neutral. But before the Commission even started its considerations there were complications – Davis became a Senator. Unfortunately, the Judge who replaced him was a Republican, leaving the format unbalanced with eight Republicans and seven Democrats. It awarded all the disputed electoral votes to Hayes, giving him victory by one vote. How did this happen? Well, it seems the House controlled by the Democrats accepted this verdict due to a suspected deal between Hayes' supporters and the Democrats to withdraw the troops in the South if Rutherford became President. This effectively ended Reconstruction officially, for Hayes immediately withdrew troops in the South not long into his Presidency. A cloud hangs over "the deal", and later over Rutherford's Presidential decision to this day.

About dawn on Friday March 2, 1877 Hayes was awakened and told that the joint session of Congress had finally declared him President-elect. Two thousand people met his train in Washington to welcome him despite a devastating rainstorm. He was escorted to General Sherman's home by carriage to await inauguration day. Being Sunday, he had to take the oath of office in private in the Red Room of the White House. He repeated it publicly before 30,000 spectators on the Monday. The memorable line "He serves his Party best who serves his country best" was coined by Hayes and so ended the Grant Presidency. A new era had begun in America.

The usual lavish White House lunches followed and the evening's torchlight procession came later but there was no White House Ball. It seems a spirit of contrition hung over the whole proceedings for although Hayes and Tilden were both honourable men whose credentials could not be disputed, political morality was in the dock.
Both men were not winners but losers. Hayes' reputation was tainted thereafter and poor Tilden withdrew from public life completely seeking consolation as a recluse among his books. His morbid obsession with his perceived failure never left him. He went into physical decline and died of a broken heart it is thought ten years later in 1886.

The troops of South Carolina – 34 officers and 316 enlisted men, were withdrawn on April 10, 1888 a month into Rutherford's Presidency. On April 20, 22 officers and 271 listed men were withdrawn from New Orleans. Hayes wrote in his diary on April 22, 1888 "Since the troops have been ordered away, I can hope for peace, security and prosperity for the coloured people." Actually the movement of the troops was really only a symbolic act of returning them to barracks and not transporting them out of the county altogether.

But the Washington Evening Star next day, April 23, had no illusions. William Lloyd Garrison and Wendell Phillips, two committed abolitionists, and Senator Blaine, who had since recovered from his illness and one of Hayes' Presidential opponents, declared openly that Rutherford had betrayed the trust to which the Republicans were pledged. Senator Wade of Ohio, one of the radical Republicans we spoke about during Johnson's trial, said that this failure to protect Negroes after they had been emancipated was a crime as infamous as enslavement itself. Without the votes of the people he had betrayed, he would never have had the power to do this injustice. That was the unvarnished truth as far as Wade was concerned. Yes, it was a worrying start to Rutherford's Presidency. To be fair to Rutherford Hayes in what seemed like appeasement to abolitionists, his bringing the army back to barracks were genuine gestures of goodwill. Unfortunately it was a ham-fisted approach that caused the problem. Rutherford was still on trial.

The Democrats in Congress now voted as a bloc and opposed any changes that threatened the supremacy of the South. This became known as the "Solid South" a vote that remained a phenomenon in American politics right up to the 1950s.

But let's leave the politics to Rutherford for the present and look inside the White House, to life with the Hayes' family in 1877.

One thing can be relied upon. Rutherford Hayes enjoyed a very happy marriage regardless of the path on which destiny had taken him. He always referred to his marriage to Lucy Ware Webb as "the most interesting fact in my entire life." They had eight children, seven boys and a girl. Four boys and the girl, Fanny lived their normal life span but like many couples in those days, they too lost children, three boys during their infancy. Later Lucy acted as Rutherford's confidential secretary during the Presidency. Birchard Hayes Junior practiced law and Rudd attended college.

Rutherford at fifty-four was at his prime for the inauguration, five foot eight inches with broad shoulders and a powerful build, with a high forehead, blue eyes and a full sandy beard. His fair hair turned silver white during his retirement. His lifestyle didn't help a tendency he had to put on weight – 12 lbs during the Presidency. He needed spectacles but never wore them causing him to suffer from sore eyes occasionally. Yet he did have an exercise routine, long walks and a brisk rub down before sleeping. One army pal remarked "Hayes was always young to me." A fellow Judge described Rutherford as having "A fine sunny countenance."

He dressed simply except for public occasions when he wore a silk hat, frock coat, lien shirt and black shoes. Yet, like Jefferson, in private he could be careless and comfortable in old worn jackets. Not unlike Millard Fillmore, the President was quiet in mannerism, calm, agreeable and mild. He made friends readily and avoided confrontation. Yes, Rutherford seemed to have a serious liking for the quiet life. He had a remarkable memory for names and one of his favourite greetings was "Well, what do you know." One of his more unusual habits even during his Presidency was to buy an ordinary day coach railway ticket and to travel incognito talking casually with everyday passengers. But somehow, despite his private popularity, Rutherford seemed to rub the journalists the wrong way so to speak, drawing unfair criticism on himself and thus creating a harsh public perception of him in the press. That was a great shame for Rutherford was really a very nice guy.

Perhaps his unpopularity was really because of the Presidential election debacle. Perhaps it was down to currency disturbances or economic panic in 1873 and the necessary essential reforms he pushed through which actually helped his Party through the 1880 elections. Who knows?
Pastimes were varied for him; social visits to old friends, musicals, sport, travel, genealogy and of course books. The White House seemed to be always crowded, for his son Rudd who often remembered the many times he had no bed to sleep in making do with the billiard table, a couch or a reception room, because Rutherford had requisitioned Rudd's bed for a visitor. In spite of this, Rudd had many happy memories of White House life.

Hunting was another of Rutherford's hobbies being a great shot with a rifle. Even skating, fishing and swimming was on his entertainment agenda. However, he definitely had a special love affair with travel, making many extended trips into the South or to the central plains and rejoiced in his first trip as a President to the West coast. Today, air travel would have bowled him over. Visitors to the White House would never have found him in. In those days the only means of spanning two destinations was a slow tedious journey by railroad or stagecoach over a couple of hundred miles. Trips to New York, Boston and Philadelphia just to visit county fairs and army reunions where he met old friends were no problem to him. Lucy often accused him teasingly of being scenery mad. The Chicago Tribune called him "Rutherford the Rover". I think when we read all the foregoing; you the reader will be in no doubt that the Civil War South did not rob him of much sleep while in office. He reserved life for living and enjoyed it to the full.

But then again Rutherford had the money to indulge his passions for he was a very wealthy man through his uncle Sardis, from his own investments and from his law practice income. He entertained on a grand scale far beyond a President's salary. One month of his expenses alone cost $6,000. He earned $20,000 during his four years as President but managed to hold on to a mere $1,000 when his term came to an end. Despite their lavish lifestyle, Lucy, because of her passion for the Temperance Movement, was never known to serve alcohol at their receptions. She was affectionately referred to as "Lemonade Lucy".

It is said Rutherford dealt generously with begging letters, clearing the debt of strangers and friends alike.

He turned to his wife's faith, Methodism, and was seen to regularly attend Sunday Service with her at the modest Foundry Methodist Church in Washington. It is said they started their day with prayers and ended it singing hymns. Lucy's happiest memory was their honeymoon trip up the St. Lawrence River to Quebec and Montreal, returning via Vermont, New York City and Philadelphia. She enjoyed most of those early years free from public office when they could go to concerts, lectures and numerous church activities alone. For her it was marriage bliss back in her Cincinnati days. Then came Fanny's death which inflicted on them a painful heart-wrenching sadness. Somehow they got over it.

Civil War years came, bringing further personal tragedy for the family with the death of another infant Joseph Thomas Hayes in 1863. Lucy was particularly interested in prison reform and hospitals for the mentally ill. Visitors to the White House were quickly put at ease for she possessed a vibrant personality complementing her husband's more sombre mood. Not unlike the relationship of Jimmy and Dolly Madison, Lucy enjoyed people and was a big help to Rutherford as someone who had long experience of coping with many important people during her husband's public life, both as Governor and President. She also loved to fish and ride horseback. She was blessed with a lovely singing voice and was often called upon to make her contribution to the evening's entertainment.

Family life in the White House for the Hayes family had to include pets. They were many and varied. Scott went everywhere with his goat and two dogs. Lucy kept a mockingbird and Siamese cat which was a great White House favourite. Rutherford himself owned two black horses brought from Ohio. The Hayes family were renowned for keeping a good table and were reputed to serve 2,000 meals per month to house guests, the President's family and domestic servants. Some public receptions had over 1,000 people wining and dining in the White House. One of its distinguished guests was Thomas A. Edison on a visit to Washington to demonstrate to the Academy of Sciences his new phonograph invention. Now let's talk about his children.

Rutherford had to ride thirty-eight miles to get home in time for Fanny's birth when he lived in Cincinnati. Fanny was only nine when Rutherford became President and being the only girl, she was greatly pampered by her father and the rest of the family. She nevertheless grew up a lovely young lady.

Scott was the youngest to survive infancy. He was almost 180 lbs on his fiftheenth birthday and loved riding his pony. He went to private school before going to Cornell University and later became a businessman in railroad equipment but dying prematurely aged fifty-seven.

One harrowing experience probably led to his death. He was caught in a storm at sea while on an extensive business trip to South America. To make matters worse, the ship before it sank released a collection of wild animals being transported on the trip. Tigers, Boa constrictors and other wild animals worsened the chaos and hampered the rescue operations. The passengers lost everything before they were set down finally in Peru. Scott never really recovered from this shock.

Birchard Junior married at thirty-three and specialized in taxation and real estate law. He also graduated from Harvard Law School. He was a shy type of lad and was very conservative. Webb was the favourite son and liked to visit his father while he was soldiering in the Union Army. He became his father's private secretary and also supervisor of the Spiegel family estate.

Rutherford Platt Hayes was like his father; witty, good company and loved social life especially in the White House. He became a banker and trustee of the Birchard Library and sponsored travelling libraries. He later dabbled in real estate in North Carolina. His tastes in books reflected those of his father and he also graduated from Cornell. Unfortunately, he didn't enjoy good health and even went to New Mexico to improve it. He ended up living in Florida in 1920.

There was much to be admired about the Hayes family which, because of its wealth, education, magnificent family mansion and lifestyle, could be judged to be one of America's aristocracy of the 1820s.

Perhaps we can finish this section with a nostalgic look at the President. It is not generally known that Rutherford Hayes, despite his solemn exterior, was really a romantic at heart. Why? Because on December 30, 1852, on his silver wedding anniversary, with the help of his friend Reverend Lorenzo McCabe of Wesleyan University who had first officiated at his wedding to Lucy in 1832, Rutherford re-enacted and re-affirmed his marriage vows in an intimate wedding ceremony in the White House. In his diary, Rutherford has entered this comment about his marriage "These ties, these affections – nothing in life to equal them."

But what was life like outside the White House walls? Despite Rutherford's optimism, injustice and cruelty was rampant in the South. The landowners, planters and the old master class didn't come up to expected standards of justice and morality towards their black employees. Their labour once free had now to be paid for. It was paid for but grudgingly. The Negroes were the dupes and victims of cunning and fraud signing contracts they couldn't read or understand. Goods were doubled in price to them and landowners were in league to prevent the Negro owning land.

No provision was made for education and teachers were prohibited from teaching even their own children privately. The jury box was closed against them and the murder of a black man by a white man incurred no penalty. A midnight raid on the defenceless black man was commonplace and was encouraged by whites. The chain gangs reappeared, spurred on by the use of the whip once again. The Negro now despaired of any change for the better and his only prospect of change was to flee the South.

But Douglass, the most vociferous voice they had, urged them to stay and trust President Hayes to deal with their problems. But if the same President had already withdrawn their only protection by taking away the army, how could they have faith in the law. Hopeless, penniless and in rags, these poor Negroes were crowding the wharves of St. Louis to get aboard steamers on the Mississippi that promised them an escape to a world of freedom. But even there they weren't wanted and were encouraged to go even further north to Canada or even to Liberia.

The word "migrant" became a label as despised as the word "abolitionist" was years before. They found work in coal mines, railroads and as domestic servants. A few Negroes were warmly welcomed by the Indians and in 1880 they built homes, schoolhouses, churches and farms in Indian Territory. But soon the Indians became alarmed at the numbers entering their territory so plans were set in place to push the migrants elsewhere in the United States.

The social upheaval and the terror released by the new laws and new freedoms were almost uncontrollable. Time and history can only be the judge of how much or how little Rutherford Hayes achieved or could achieve with this political Pandora's Box that had been opened before him. Was Rutherford the reluctant President as helpless as the Negro he had abandoned down South?

The suggestion by General Grant to impose tough military measures and wide army control had by now been consigned to the dustbin of history. Besides Grant had now moved on.

The common view of the unfortunate Southern Negro was one of "A lazy, improvident, childlike, irresponsible, chicken-stealing, crap-shooting criminal." A tragic misconception. Mark Twain underlined the Negroes insignificance in Southern society by this conversation in Huckleberry Finn between Huck and his Aunt Sally after a steamboat blew out a cylinder.
"Good Gracious! Anybody hurt?
    "No'm. Killed a nigger"
    "Well, it's lucky because sometimes people do get hurt"

Perhaps, history has been unkind to Rutherford Hayes. Perhaps he has not been credited with many political achievements during his term of office while he struggled daily with the tide of history surging outside the gates of the White House.

He was well aware of the exodus northwards of the Negro. In his diary he wrote "Let the emigrants be scattered throughout the North and West; let them be encouraged to get homes and settled employment." While he did nothing to encourage the emigrants, he vigorously opposed moves that would weaken existing laws. He even vetoed an attempt by the Democrats to withdraw protection by the army in their job of keeping peace at the polls. He pointed out the dangers of depriving citizens, regardless of colour, from the right to vote peacefully. He vetoed eight Bills and won his fight. Because of his stand, he helped pacify the country but most important of all he eliminated the fear of a new Civil War. But in pursuit of this pacification, he did abandon the poor blacks to the tender mercies of the Southern whites. Perhaps he found himself helpless to do otherwise in the mess that was the post Civil War South. In short, he left the South to decide for years to come the status of the Negro in American society.

But let's listen to a more mundane story of Rutherford. Apparently he took a vigorous interest in the building of the Washington Monument which had stalled due to a design dispute among rival engineers. It was thought the foundations would not support the project. Some called it "A tall and awkward smoke stack". Others wanted it torn down and replaced by an arch or museum. Under Rutherford's persistence, all opposition to the monument evaporated and the present 550 feet high obelisk was finally erected. Beneath its cornerstone lies a half dollar piece marked R.B.H. on one side and 1880 on the other. Incidentally, Rutherford is also acclaimed for his work in reforming the Civil Service, a pledge he had made on taking up office.

The Spoils System was his main target. His aim was to stamp out the Party hack placed by patronage in key positions. Dishonesty and inefficiency was rampant everywhere in the Civil Service. As a result, the notorious Senator Conkling was a fierce critic of Hayes and was surrounded by henchmen who attempted to sabotage Rutherford's efforts to reform the system. Top officials were replaced in the Customs House and a majority of Senators supported Rutherford's decision to replace these officials. In his diary Rutherford wrote "I have had great success because my sole right to make appointments has been tacitly conceded." The patronage lobby had been finally defeated and appointments to jobs, strictly on merit was introduced for the first time and considerable graft and corruption was ended.

Amazingly, one of those sacked was Chester Alan Arthur, later to become the 21st President of the United States. Rutherford finally tackled the Indian problem head on. One of the problems he had to confront was the closing of the Western frontier against America's expansion westward. Because of this unabated flood of immigrants, the Indians could no longer move further West from his old Reservation. He now lived in the path of the white covered wagon going westward. The Indians thus became compressed into an ever diminishing area of freedom and quite naturally became alarmed and felt menaced watching his hunting grounds getting smaller and his lands and buffalo also diminishing. The Indian's pride and fear made him despair for his culture and his future. Even the politicians in Washington became alarmed.

So enter Rutherford B. Hayes into the problem. He saw that with the building of the Pacific railways, the consequent disappearance of the buffalo, the wild horses, and the other wild game, the whole way of life of the Indian – his precious hunting was threatened. Rutherford set about teaching the Indian modern agriculture, herding and freight hauling. An Indian police force emerged along with the tribal ownership of land. The ending of the Indian wars meant the time for healing the wounds inflicted on the Indian had come at last:-

(i)   He introduced a programme of education for Indian boys.
(ii)   He introduced land allotments for a set period
(iii)   He gave compensation for Indian lands, and
(iv)   He created Indian citizenship.

Two failures can be placed on his record, the Southern black and his own Presidential election. Nowadays we must include some other successes.
(v)   The solution of the Chinese immigration problem
(vi)   The rebuilding of the South's infrastructure
(vii)   The reform of the Civil Service
(viii) Last but not least the Indian question which had neglected for two hundred years.

All this was achieved against a backdrop of his Party's minority position in Congress. I think we'll rest our case for Rutherford Birchard Hayes' Presidency right there.

While he did not accept blame for the previous two hundred years, he did concede having enough responsibility now to help in the treatment of the Indian. This left him with the duty of redressing the wrongs he saw. Congress appropriated $165,000 as a compensation fund. The old philosophy towards the Indian as an "alien" was now passing. Hayes, to his eternal credit, fostered and implemented a whole range of measures in a new national policy which unfortunately was not fully implemented after he left office. At least Reservations now had a police force manned by Indians.

Rutherford's entry in his own personal diary underlines his commitment to urgent, generous action for the rehabilitation of the Indian people. He called it "an Indian policy for justice and fidelity to engagements and to placing the Indian on the footing of citizens." It seems to me for this achievement alone, Rutherford B. Hayes' courageous Indian policy gives him a rightful claim to fame and congratulations. To balance the criticism he received for his handling of the post-Reconstruction problems, it must be recorded that his Presidency took place at a time of rapid political and economic change. It straddled America's industrial revolution with a society divided by class, cultural and multi-national movements. It was a much more complex society than one any previous President had to contend with.

It should come as no surprise that Rutherford was not nominated for a second term because of the unpopular decisions he made during his Presidency. But true to form, he certainly lost no sleep about it. I guess Rutherford B. Hayes always had a colourful life so the opinions of critics had no impact on him. He simply went out and made things happen. Reading about his life in retirement will convince you of this.

At the end of his Presidency Rutherford B. Hayes sat back and watched with pleasure the festivities surrounding the inauguration of the 20th President of the United States of America James Garfield. Now he could afford to be serene and contented. Four years earlier he had taken up the reins of a divided, confused and unhappy country riven by strife and hardship. Today he was handing over a country united, harmonious and prosperous. Well that was Rutherford's claim. Next day in the company of their children and friends the Hayes family boarded the Potomac express and headed home for Ohio and Spiegel Grove. However, the story of Rutherford does not end there.

Life will always hold unexpected surprises in any age and in any walk of life. For Rutherford there was to be no exception. As they neared Baltimore, they had a head-on collision with another train. Many carriages were wrecked and Rutherford, the retiring President, found himself with sleeves rolled up tending the injured. One engineer died and the other was badly injured but survived. He received from Rutherford a few months later a beautiful watch on a gold chain engraved with the inscription "A token of gratitude of your timely reaction which saved the lives of many". Rutherford had not had such a narrow brush with death in the whole four years of his Presidency despite the dangerous times he lived in.

Rutherford's summary of his four years in the Presidency was expressed in a letter he wrote to Guy Bryan, an old school friend on January 1, 1881. "Nobody ever leaves the Presidency with less regret, less disappointment, fewer heart burnings or more general content with the result of his term of office than I do." He went on "We have on the whole enjoyed our four years in the White House. I am soon to become a private citizen, to have the right to manage my own affairs without intrusion." At fifty-eight and with an estate large enough to leave him independent from money troubles, he was glad to be home in his beautiful wooded estate in Fremont. Now that he was retired he had time on his hands to improve and enhance Spiegel Grove given to him by his uncle Sardis, surrounded by deep primeval woods teeming with wild life. American trees particularly the oak grew wildly there with hickory pines and elms. Willow trees were added later as were tulip trees from Montpelier, the home of James Madison the 4th President.

The house was constantly being added to over the next twenty-five years until it became a large rambling three storey mansion. He built a new kitchen, woodhouse and a privy to the rear of the structure, added on a front porch and installed a library. Like Washington, Rutherford practically doubled the size of his house in retirement and supervised the re-decoration of the whole mansion. One of Fremont's first telephones was later installed in it. He then set about extending the lawns to encourage more sunlight into the surrounding areas and finally his beloved avenue to the house was planted with a long line of hemlock, spruces and pines, installed to welcome the many visitors to his humble abode. Even today in 2009 I understand Spiegel Grove fascinates and enthrals the visitor.

It seems a contradiction but as he grew older Rutherford became a dedicated opponent of privilege. Immersed as he was in the trappings of upper class living, it can be noted that his income from his law career and his investments were hard-earned but well spent. Exploitation by any group was always severely criticised by him.

To this end he became a great supporter of education in the South and became the first President to promote a Negro Education Fund set up by John F. Slater, a Connecticut manufacturer. This fund for scholarships produced many distinguished people in later years. He became a member of the Board of Trustees in many colleges and universities and often was called on to speak at their functions. The National Prisons Association was another project close to his heart while he also kept a watchful eye on political tampering with court cases. But his deepest affection was always reserved for comrades in his old army regiment and he never missed a meeting of theirs.

Rutherford had endured many losses among these friends as they passed on. But the greatest loss of all was that of his beloved Lucy on June 25, 1889 after forty years of marriage. Somehow he never really recovered from that tragedy. But the end came for Rutherford himself almost four years later while standing at a railway station on January 10, 1893. After a trek through deep snow in zero temperatures he was struck by severe chest pains. He sensed the end was near so he was determined to board the train for the journey home with his son Webb.

"I would rather die at Spiegel Grove," he murmured "than to live anywhere else." He got his wish for at 11 p.m. on the night of January 17, 1893 one week later, Rutherford Hayes passed away aged 70 years and 5 months. Three days later on the morning of Friday January 20, 1893 Rutherford was buried. It was a bright clear morning after a night of sub-zero temperatures and the webs of frost on the veranda of Spiegel Grove caught the morning sunlight. Yes, Spiegel Grove was at her most beautiful when Rutherford B. Hayes, 19th President of the United States was laid to rest in Oakwood Cemetery beside his beloved Lucy, gratefully together once again.

20th President   James Abram Garfield

"Martyr President"
Born 1831
Died 1881
50 Years of age
1 Term (88Days)
Age 50

Party: Republican
Profession: Lawyer
County: Ohio
Ancestry: English
Estate: Value Unknown
Hobbies: Billiards, Hunting, Swimming, Reading and Chess.

Physical description: 6 foot, light brown greying hair receding hairline. Blue eyes, large head, high forehead, strong frame, broad shoulders left handed.

Significant extract from Garfield's Inaugural address on Friday March 4, 1881:
"We stand today upon an eminence which overlooks a hundred years of national life – a century crowded with perils but crowned with the triumph of liberty and law. Before continuing the onward march let us pause on this height for a moment to strengthen our faith and renew our hope by a glance on the pathway, along which our people have travelled ….. The Civil Service can never be placed on a satisfactory basis until it is regulated by law."

JAMES ABRAM GARFIELD

Eighty-eight days gives very little room for embellishment in the life of James Abram Garfield. Yes that was the duration of his Presidency until it was brought to an appalling end at the hands of an assassin. The name of the assassin was Julius Guiteau, a man who will dominate this story of the 20th President of the United States. I am afraid there is only one happy note in the story. The death of Garfield ensured the passing of the Pendleton Act which put an end once and for all to the "Spoils System" in American politics. This was a method by which Party activists were rewarded with jobs in the Administration regardless of their suitability for the job.

But let's start at the beginning of this tragic story by tracing the life of James Garfield and his seventeen years as Congressman before being elevated to the Presidency on March 4, 1881.

Post-Civil War political corruption hardly touched Garfield. So it defies logic that a disgruntled reject for a job under the Spoils System should end the life and career of a potentially great man. Demands for the elimination of the Spoils System throughout America grew to boiling point as a result of the assassination.

Garfield, yet another President from Ohio was the son of Abram Garfield and Eliza Ballou Garfield, both New Englanders who had settled in Northern Ohio years previously. His father also named Abram was a farmer and part-time canal construction worker who died when James was an infant of two years old. He left a widow and four children to face life working a small farm on the frontier. Ahead was a very precarious future for the Garfields. Needless to say young James born on November 19, 1831 had a rough and poverty stricken childhood and was the last of the Presidential line who was reared in a log cabin. He worked as a farm labourer and part-time on a canal boat when he was sixteen years of age.
Learning to read was a big thing in those days. Garfield managed to achieve this for the sole purpose of going to sea but somehow he never got further than the canal boat on which he worked.

His mother, faced with the problem of educating James sent him to Geauga Academy in Chester, Ohio. "No greener boy ever set out to school," he observed in later years. At eighteen he had a religious transformation being baptised into a congregation called "The Disciples of Christ". Two years later he moved to the Western Reserve Eclectic Institute, later called Hiram College under the auspices of the Disciples of Christ. He taught here for a while and also combined this job with work as a lay preacher, a highly unusual role for a young man. This helped him to become quite a polished public speaker.

It was not until 1854 when he was twenty-three years old that James Garfield had enough money saved to enrol at Williams College in Massachusetts. Two years later when he was twenty-five he graduated with honours and returned to his old college (Hiram) to teach ancient languages and literature for by now he was a brilliant linguist.

But another role was to impose itself on the unsuspecting James Garfield. He fell in love with Lucretia Rudolph, a childhood friend and fellow student at Geauga Academy. He married Lucretia on November 11, 1858 when he was twenty-seven years old. She was a farmer's daughter aged twenty-six.

But Garfield's marriage for whatever reason was not exactly a success early on for a serious doubt had crept in. He had vacillated for years before making up his mind to marry Lucretia who he nicknamed "Crete". His doubts infiltrated into the relationship for years but it eventually blossomed into a happy marriage.

His seven children, five sons and two daughters were Harry, James, Irvin, Abram, Edward, Elizabeth and Mary. Elizabeth and Edward died when they were two. James, Rudolph Garfield later served as Secretary of the Interior in President Theodore Roosevelt's Administration and Harry Augustus Garfield became President of Williams College. However let's concentrate on the main player President Garfield.

Early in his life Garfield's mother married again but this was a disaster for Garfield as he grew to intensely dislike his stepfather. Like many frontier men his hobbies were open air ones like fishing and hunting. He also liked reading, chess and billiards. Garfield was a tall well-built handsome man. In later years he grew a full growth of beard and developed into a skilled speaker and a fashionable dresser. Like Rutherford Hayes Garfield had no ambitions to become a politician. This is not surprising for he had a cynical distrust of politics. He wrote "I am exceedingly disgusted with the wire pulling of politicians and their total disregard for the truth in all their operations." Later he had some scathing opinions of Abraham Lincoln describing him as "A second rate Illinois Lawyer."
Nevertheless, he joined Lincoln's army in the Civil War and rose to the rank of Major General in a distinguished army career but more of that later.

Meanwhile James Garfield, while cultivating political friends also concentrated on a new career. He went to work part-time in the Cleveland law office of Albert G. Riddle and went on to graduate in law in 1861 when he was twenty-nine years of age. A truly remarkable achievement. Two years before his marriage Garfield's contempt for politicians had abated enough for him to enter politics for the first time supporting Senator John C. Fremont of California for President.
He was only three years in politics when he ran for the Ohio State Senate as a Republican. This was no surprise for by now James had honed his skills as a debater and a polished orator which he had developed while acting as college preacher. He won by a significant margin and went on to make friends with all the prominent Party leaders of the day. Looking back at this point to his very poor childhood we can see James Garfield was a man of single-minded dedication and ambition coupled with a liberal capacity for hard work and a brilliant grasp of languages.

When the Civil War broke out in 1861 Lincoln used Garfield's oratorical skills to recruit troops for the Union army. He was then appointed Lieutenant Colonel and was later promoted to Commanding Colonel of his regiment. He saw active service in Kentucky and won a further promotion to Brigadier General of Volunteers. It seems James Garfield's star was an ever ascending one. He ended his army career as Major General in 1863, when he was elected to the House of Representative. Here he proved himself capable enough to be re-elected eight years in succession.

When the war ended Garfield sided with the radical Republicans who favoured a hard-line policy in the South. This left him totally opposed to President Andrew Johnson's moderate policy towards the defeated South. He also became an enthusiastic supporter of Negro voting rights.

Garfield was now swimming in the upper layer of Republican politics and was becoming a force to be reckoned with. The year was 1876 and he was now Republican leader in the House. A further indicator of Garfield's status in the Republican Party was his appointment to the special commission set up to decide the election of Rutherford B. Hayes to the Presidency, the story of which we have already discussed when writing about Rutherford B. Hayes in the previous chapter of this book.

But Garfield was a complex individual. He was thought to be part reformer and part Spoils man, part moralist and part corruptionist. Some people described him as a powerful politician financially burdened with five children which tempted him to yield to those willing to buy his influence. One questionable payment was a dividend from the Crédit Mobilier of about $300 which he claimed was a loan. There was also a $5,000 fee paid to him from DeGolyer McClelland Company, a firm which had received a contract for paving Washington's streets.

The fact that he was a member of the House Committee on appropriation left questions of undue influence. Garfield was not exactly the friend of trade unions for he opposed an eight hour day for Federal workers and didn't hesitate to call for strikes to be halted by Federal troops. In fact he constantly opposed the trade union movement. He was also in favour of the impeachment of Andrew Johnson. Yet despite his radical opinions Garfield was always constantly assailed by self-doubt just like John Adams the 2nd President of the United States.

Another story expresses the belief that Garfield when separated from his job as preacher in civil life was an easy prey to temptation when in the army. Here he played cards, drank and was reputed to have had an affair with a young widow. However none of these human flaws seems to have mattered too much to those who wanted him to be President.

It was also well known that James Abram Garfield was no shrinking violet. Two incidents were to prove his fearlessness when confronted with hostile heckles or agitated crowds.
The first challenge came during one of his controversial speeches in support of the abolition of slavery. He came under fire from a barrage of eggs thrown by an angry opponent of his views. Garfield interrupted his speech to confront his antagonist with the words "I have just come from fighting brave rebels at Chickamauga; I shall not flinch before cowardly rebels." The opposition melted away as he continued his speech.

Another more serious situation happened on April 15, 1865 outside the Customs House in New York City where an angry crowd of 50,000 people had gathered to mourn the death of Lincoln and at one stage threatened to take the law into their own hands. To underline how dangerous tempers were, two unfortunate men who voiced their disapproval of Lincoln were set upon. One was killed and the other seriously injured. A breakaway section of the crowd numbering 1,000 headed for The New York World crying "Vengeance, Vengeance."

Garfield who was just a visitor to New York as a member of Congress raised his arms high and in a loud voice addressed the mob. His theme was Abraham Lincoln.

"Fellow citizens," he shouted, "clouds and darkness are round about him. His pavilion is dark waters and thick clouds of the skies. Justice and judgement are the establishment of his throne. Mercy and truth shall go before his face. Fellow citizens, God reigns and the Government of Washington still lives." The crowd stopped in their tracks greatly touched and moved by his stirring words. The threatened riots just faded away.

The most important day of the hustings is the Party Convention. The Republican Convention attracted the usual gathering of exited delegates to the Exposition hall in Chicago on June 2, 1880.

The breakdown of the Republican Party delegates was important as future events will prove.

There were two factions - the Stalwarts, the followers of General Grant and the Half-Breeds who supported Senator Blaine and were known as "the Plumed Knights". There was no political difference between the two factions. They differed only in the way the Spoils of patronage was decided for Federal jobs in the Administration later.

The day started badly for James Garfield. He didn't get a single vote on the first ballot. But still the voting continued. He didn't receive one vote from the 14th to the 18th ballot either. Further ballots were more generous to him and it was not until the 36th ballot when Blaine's supporters switched to Garfield that victory was his. Yes, it took thirty-six ballots to select him as the Republican candidate for the Presidency. Ironically Garfield's delegation had come not to support the Stalwarts or the Half-Breeds but the Secretary to the Treasury, John Sherman.

As Sherman said later "The only shade that rests on my feelings about Garfield is that he went to the Convention by my selection and comes away with the honour I sought."

Garfield as you have seen was a very powerful orator and it was his speech to the packed Convention hall that brought about his victory.

Here is a small extract in which he compared the emotions of the delegates to a storm at sea.... "This assemblage seemed to me a human ocean in tempest. I have seen the sea lashed into fury and tossed into spray and its grandeur moves the soul of the dullest man, but I remember that it is not the billows but the calm level of the sea from which all heights and depths are measured. When the storm is passed and the hour of calm settles on the ocean. When the sunlight bathes its peaceful surface then the astronomer and surveyor take the level from which they measure all terrestrial heights and depths."
I'm not too sure if the flamboyant and flowery phrases used in 1880 would grab the attention of modern politicians one hundred years later. But that's just your writer having a little fun with language.

Nevertheless the feeling in the hall was like a tidal wave. Surely here was the man to bring peace and success to the Party.

Yes, James Garfield was an accomplished performer who actually campaigned for the German American vote by giving speeches in German. A delegation of five hundred people paid him a visit during the hustings and he was delighted to address them in their own language. He was also a Latin and French scholar.

Garfield went on to be elected President by 214 electoral votes to 155 for Winfield Scott Hancock. Chester Alan Arthur was nominated for Vice President, a selection which had significant implications in the historical events that followed. Arthur's selection as Vice President was also the subject of controversy but more of that story later.

Inauguration day in America is always an exercise in nostalgia for those lucky enough to be able to attend the ceremony, simply meeting with old friends and swapping nostalgic stories of past Presidential inaugurations. The marching bands, the fireworks, the razzamatazz, the sense of history unfolding around them was like a patchwork tapestry to be remembered in later years in stories told to their grandchildren.

It was Friday March 4, 1881 when James Abram Garfield was sworn in as President by Chief Justice Morrison Remick Waite.

The weather was depressing to say the least. Strong winds blew a heavy snowfall into the faces of the crowds sitting there frozen to the bone watching the parade. The numbers were estimated at about 20,000 people. The usual fireworks display entertained the people that night and the inaugural ball was held that year in the Hall of the Smithsonian Institution. A new fangled gadget called an electric lamp fascinated everyone as it hung over the main entrance. On the stage was an orchestra in which a huge collection of the finest musicians played. It was the German Orchestra of Philadelphia.

Also on stage was the United States Marine band, $5 was the entrance fee and for an extra dollar they were served supper consisting of pickled oyster chicken, salad, roast turkey, roast ham and beef, ice cream, cakes, jellies, bread and butter, tea, coffee, lemonade and French fruits. Cakes and biscuits sold in tens of thousands. It must have been the best fed audience ever to sit at a concert. Incidentally, Garfield's mother was there, the first mother of a President to attend an inauguration. In fact she was the first person he greeted shortly after the inauguration ceremonies finished.

Garfield's mother could not climb the stairs of the White House so Garfield just carried her in his arms up the stairs and down again. This sort of old world simplicity seems to have been lost in today's sophisticated world of politics and pretence. The lack of an elevator didn't go unnoticed by Garfield who wondered out loud why the White House didn't have one.

When armed guards were suggested to him as extra security Garfield refused point blank "Assassinations can no more be guarded against than death by lightening and it is best not to worry about either," he said.

The problem of patronage overhung the new Garfield Presidency from the outset. Some say he had mistakenly reintroduced this old tradition which had already been dropped as an option for a job. Thousands lined the corridors of the White House to the President's room. The crush became a worry and he was blamed for encouraging the practice that saw long lines of office seekers stretching right out into Pennsylvania Avenue.

And so the scene is set for the next stage of our story about James Garfield, 20th President of the United States. Into the picture now comes Charles Guiteau. He stayed at Mary Lockwood's Boarding house but considered it so beneath him he had his mail posted to "Riggs Boarding House", a more upmarket establishment to suit his agenda.

As we said at the outset Garfield spent only about eighty-eight days in the Presidency, but from the beginning, the two factions into that which the Party had split the Stalwarts and the Half-Breeds, were to give Garfield trouble. The question of patronage was the problem and Roscoe Conkling, leader of the Stalwarts in Congress became his chief antagonist.

Being a powerful figure in New York Conkling lost no time in trying to block Garfield's own appointments from the ranks of the Half-Breeds. But one lesson Conkling never learned was written in a wise old saying – "You can't fight City Hall." Conkling's attempts at frustrating the will of the Presidency failed and soon after he resigned from the Senate and left politics a broken and bitter man.

Before Conkling's resignation however Senator Dawes tried to heal the breach between Conkling and Garfield but throwing up his hands in defeat he was heard to say "For a great man, our President has some of the weakest and Conkling some of the ugliest streaks I have ever seen. The one wants to be watched like a child, the other like an assassin." The consequences of Conkling's demise, was only understood on the morning of July 2, 1881, three months into his Garfield's Presidency.

The awful tragedy waiting to engulf everyone is almost upon us. The story of Garfield's Presidency now takes on tragic undertones. It is nearly three months into his Presidency and the place is the Baltimore and Potomac railway station. Garfield is about to board the train for the Jersey shore. The date is June 18, 1881. Somewhere on the platform a shadowy figure stalks the President. Charles J. Guiteau had come to assassinate him. But Guiteau cancelled his plans for that afternoon. When asked at his trial why he did so Guiteau replied "When I saw the First Lady she looked so thin as she clung tenderly to the President's arm that I did not have the heart to fire on him."

But Guiteau's compassion lasted only two weeks. At this point I would like to acknowledge the help I got from a fascinating book on the subject called The Murder of James A. Garfield written by James C. Clark. The scene was very similar to June 18, 1881 as James Garfield stood on the platform of Baltimore and Potomac railway station on July 2, 1881. Garfield had always despised the station describing it as "A nuisance that ought long since to have been abated."

July 2, 1881, Garfield was to board a special carriage added for the convenience of the VIP's in his Cabinet. But today Garfield had more than VIP company. He was being stalked by a killer, a bitter revenge seeking gunman there to balance the books of justice for a perceived wrong he suffered – rejection of a job application. There were so many other injustices out there far crueller, far more personal and injurious suffered by millions in America at that time. Ones that might justify someone to take the law into their own hands and dispense justice to their tormentor without Judge or Jury. But the sheer insignificance of the complaint here leaves the reader of the event with a frozen uncomprehending look of disbelief when he reads it. A man's life for a lost job!

What complications in the warped logic of any human mind could justify the act of murder for such a triviality?

The man Charles Jules Guiteau was the premeditating killer that morning of July 2, 1881. Garfield died a few weeks short of his 50th birthday on September 19, 1881, two months and seventeen days after the assassin's bullet ripped into him.

But let's look at events on the fateful morning of July 2. At 8.30 Guiteau entered the station and the ladies waiting room. He eventually handed two packages and an envelope to a nearby newspaper seller.

Garfield duly arrived ten minutes early checking the time he had to spare with the policeman on duty, Patrick Kearney, standing nearby. In retrospect an unbelievable act of reckless indifference to his own safety bordering on madness. As Garfield passed through the ladies waiting room on his way to his carriage a shot was heard. The bullet passed through a glazier's tool box on the back of its owner Kristoph Plockschis, a fifty-one year old Prussian who ran away panic stricken.

But Guiteau was not leaving matters there. Stepping closer, he took aim ruthlessly and fired again.
The second bullet was the fatal one for it plunged into the side of Garfield, four inches from his spine. The station janitor rushed up to where Garfield had fallen and the ladies waiting room

attendant Sarah White placed a pillow under Garfield's head and attended to him until Garfield's son Harry arrived soon after.

As Guiteau rushed from the scene saying he had a letter for General Sherman his passage was blocked by the astute policeman Kearney. "Look here," he told Guiteau, "you are coming from the scene where there is firing and I will stop you until I see what the result will be." Twenty officers from the nearby police station soon arrived when told by a small boy of the events. Bizarrely some people thought the shooting was the result of a lovers quarrel.

But Guiteau was quite blatant in his act for he fired in front of the assistant train master Joseph K Sharp, so closely the smoke from the gun went into Sharp's eyes. All through the confusion the medic a Dr. Smith Townsend was able to hold a conversation with the stricken Garfield on the ground to ascertain the seriousness of his injury. It all seemed almost too casual.

Dr. William Tindall was told by messengers that Vice President Arthur had been shot. Confusion reigned supreme.

Tindall arrived and a further conversation took place with Garfield complaining about a tingling sensation in his feet.

Lincoln's son, Secretary of War Robert Todd Lincoln sent his carriage for Dr. D. W. Bliss, the city's leading doctor who was found walking in Pennsylvania Avenue. One hundred and twenty years later it is hard not to curse the lack of a mobile phone, computer technology and a fast helicopter to the nearest state of the art hospital with a wide collection of senior surgeons on stand by. But then again that back up was useless in saving the life of President John F. Kennedy years later. In Garfield's case perhaps his lesser injury might have saved him.
The whole scene was unreal. Another doctor sent for refused to come thinking it was a prank. Now surrounded by twenty doctors, the traumatic scene got to Garfield's son Jim who began to cry while his brother Harry comforted him. Back at the White House extra guards were placed at the gates which were now closed. Panic had set in.

Meanwhile Garfield was losing his patience with the handling of his situation and repeatedly asked to be taken back to the White House.

He decided to tell his wife by telegraph of his position not wanting her to learn the news second hand from reporters. "Tell her I am seriously hurt but I don't know how seriously," he told his Aide Almon Rockwell. "Tell her I hope she will come soon. I send my love." Doesn't it seem farcical that a dying President surrounded by dozens of Aides should have to dictate a personal telegram home to his wife? Just who was in charge?

Eventually eight men carried the prostate figure of Garfield through the station to the waiting ambulance which drove not to a top of the range hospital as we would expect today but direct to the White House itself. The ambulance could drive only slowly for the comfort of its patient over the uneven streets of Washington. Inside the ambulance was Navy surgeon, General Dr. Philip S. Wales. At the White House they carried him on a mattress up to his bedroom and on the way there came one of those simple gesture that make one marvel at the sheer beauty of human nature. Passing Mrs. Blaine, his housekeeper, who was standing in the hall, he put a hand to his mouth and blew her a kiss, then pulled her close and kissed her.

At that moment in time who could say the shot was to be fatal. But the truth seems to be that Garfield was surrounded by people who didn't seem to have a clue what to do with him or know how seriously he was hurt. It was now at least two hours since the shooting and he still was not in hospital.

Garfield was given morphine injections. The Washington Post had already reported his death. In the meantime Guiteau was taken to the police station by two policemen. Unbelievably he still had his pistol. They had forgotten to take it off him.

Guiteau described the scene of the assassination to the guards. Almost child like he said "I show you." By this time angry crowds had gathered outside, so to prevent a lynching the military were posted inside and outside the jail. His photograph was taken by a photographer but Guiteau had the audacity to look for a royalty payment of $25 for it. In the streets outside the jail people were filling up Washington in preparation for the Independence Day celebrations at the weekend.

Some of the letters received were quite bizarre. One enclosed a collection of bed bugs to be placed in Guiteau's bed. Another offered to be the executioner should Garfield be condemned to die. A more positive one was a suggestion to get a New York surgeon in immediately since New York surgeons were the best.

By now Garfield was vomiting continuously throughout the afternoon. Only now did they decide to take his grey suit off.

Garfield asked Mrs. Blaine when she entered the bedroom – "Why did he wish to shoot me?"
At 6.45 a.m. next morning Arthur, the Vice President asked to be kept informed if Garfield's condition deteriorated. At 7.00 a.m. they thought he would die within the hour. At 9.00 a.m. he seemed to be getting better. Opinions changed by the hour. Garfield was in a good mood telling his son Jim "The upper storey is not hurt only the hall."

Leading surgeons arrived from New York and Philadelphia. The most constructive thing they seemed to achieve was to insert a finger into the wound only to offer conflicting advice. Too many doctors were in attendance stated The Boston Medical and Surgical Journal later.

Another complication was the war going on at that time between traditional medicine and homeopathic medicine when qualified doctors were deliberately denied access to hospitals. The Homeopathic doctors were described by the qualified doctors as "gauchos". However the gauchos did attract support from the public and some real doctors risked expulsion for consulting with them.
The problem was that Garfield championed the cause of Homeopathy as did his wife. To make matters worse Garfield's personal physician arrived expecting to take charge of the situation. After a near fight between the doctors in a room next door to Garfield his personal physician stormed out never to return again.

The bulletins from the hospital were deliberately falsified to prevent Garfield being upset by news he read. Doing their duty to the President personally and to the public in general was not easy. All this despite the fact that his weight had dropped by over 80 lbs.

The search for the missing bullet preoccupied everyone but to what purpose they didn't know. Bullets had been known to remain inside a shot victim before now and they lived.

One week later the problem was one of keeping Garfield cool in soaring temperatures. A large box of ice was placed in his room. It didn't work and was removed. Air conditioning in those days was still a long way off. Strangely enough almost up to the end Garfield's doctors were convinced he would live. Mrs Blaine even wrote on July 8, "No danger now, no anxiety about paralysis or bullet in the liver and every prospect for a speedy recovery in all parts." Three days late on July 11, Hamilton and his surgeons said "Ultimate recovery is beyond all reasonable doubt." Five days later more progress was reported. In mid July Garfield ordered his own breakfast of steak, eggs and milk with a liberal sprinkling of holy water supplied by the devout White House cook. The Navy were now preparing a Steamer - "The Tallapoosa" to act as a floating hospital for Garfield. Meanwhile he was still in a jovial and polite mood and still in the White House.

Even a barber was called to cut his hair but this was cancelled by Dr. Bliss. In mid August he commented on the fact that it was now six weeks since the shooting "Here I am six weeks today," he said.

When told that "Sitting Bull" was starving himself to protest at his imprisonment Garfield replied "Oh no, send him my oatmeal." Oatmeal was not exactly Garfield's favourite food. He was often fortified by glasses of rum with an egg. A cow had been parked on the White House lawn to ensure fresh milk daily.

But back to Guiteau. When he discovered his papers had not been published he made his own statement. "I had none but the best feelings for the President. I had no malice and no murderous intent. I acted solely for the good of the American people. Not a soul in the universe knew of my purpose to remove the President." Next day he wrote again.
 "The idea that I am a disappointed office seeker and that I shot the President from malice is too preposterous for a moment's consideration. My motive was purely patriotic." He confirmed also that it was Patrick Kearney who had arrested him and not six others who claimed the honour.

He gave special instructions for the publication of his life story in New York and Boston. The books title was to be The life and theology of Charles Guiteau. He had upped the royalties expected from 10% to 20% because of the extraordinary circumstances in which it was written. Guiteau inhabited a world of make believe.

Sadly he was baited by many letters with words and sentiments that were cruel and false, hoping for a personal reply. Words like "All Boston sympathises with you." "You ought to be President." Given a man of such a frail and vulnerable mentality, it was like poking a stick through the bars of a cage into the face of a wounded animal.

By this time infection had set into Garfield's wound and there was now no hope for him. He was suffering from blood poisoning. Yet Mrs. Garfield continued to comfort him with conversation about renovating the White House or their Ohio farm and still they hoped. On August 1, his daughter wrote "Papa doing gloriously, improving all the time but they don't allow him to talk much now. He sleeps regularly and wakes only when his pulse or temperature is taken." On August 1, he signed an Extradition Treaty to return a forger to Canada...... Garfield was bored. But Congress was not in session so lack of duties for him didn't matter. One blessing was a more united Party outside.

But the public were beginning to fear the worst. The Medical Record declared bluntly that the chances of his recovery were very grim indeed. Mrs. Garfield herself was expressing misgivings about the President's treatment. The infection spread to his face until it swelled so much his eye closed. He was now being fed rectally.

But Dr. Bliss when asked by reporters "How is the President today," replied, "He is doing nicely."

Garfield was demanding to go to Menton. To go down the river on the Tallapoosa but his wish was not granted. Pus and mucus threatened to drown him. Multiple abscesses were everywhere.

The bulletins still misled the reporters. When Garfield enquired about the news outside he was told there was no news. "Affairs in the country are dull right now," he was told. He was too sick to bother asking again.

Now sanitary conditions in Washington were atrocious at that time of the year. Raw sewage was now passing into the Potomac because of the summer rain. The increased odours from the river flats were repulsive. It drifted into the White House on the prevailing wind. Elberon, his home town was the only option now. Garfield wanted no more delay and Bliss relented, setting plans in motion for Garfield's removal from the White House.

The railway line to his cottage was extended practically right to its front door. Three hundred workers completed the job in three hours. Slowly they picked up the mattress and carried him from the White House as he waved to White House staff.
His train was converted to a four carriage train. Seats had been removed in Garfield's carriage to accommodate a bed. Ice was placed inside to make it cooler. The train moved at 60mph to Garfield's delight. He arrived at 1.00 p.m. at Elberon station. It was now five hours since they first woke him that morning. Garfield was tired. It was now 94 degrees. Settling into the cottage he smiled "It is nice to get where I can look at the sea," he said choosing where his bed should be.

Unbelievably the staff was cut to five and Mrs. Garfield supervised the kitchen. But now sleep was the problem for everyone as they worked in shifts.
Garfield had developed pneumonia. Nevertheless, the Cabinet arrived to report on the country to give Garfield a feeling of being involved. They didn't stay long.

But a strange incident occurred back home in Guiteau's Washington jail. A guard called Mason shot at Guiteau missing his head by inches. William Mason who took the shot claimed "He was tired of guarding a dog such as Guiteau." He was instantly court marshalled and sentenced to eight years in prison. Protests were made to have him pardoned.

Meanwhile Dr. Bliss was once again issuing encouraging bulletins for Garfield who was now sitting at the window for thirty minutes a day – "This is delightful," he murmured, "it is such a change."

But he was not fooled either. When Dr. Bliss returned from holiday on September 18, Garfield told him "Your anxious watching will soon be over." To Rockwell he put the question "Do you think my name will have a place in human history?" "Don't talk like that," said Rockwell to which Garfield after a short silence replied "No my work is done." Deep down he had the feeling it was the end. On the morning of September 19, the end was approaching. Hamilton was sent for. That night at 10.00 p.m. Garfield put his hand on his heart and complained of pain..... Mrs. Garfield came into the room "Is there no hope," she asked. Dr. Bliss was a worried man and admitted to the reality of the situation. His reply was graphically blunt.

"Madame, he is dying". At 10.30 p.m. on September 19, Garfield was breathing heavily.

Shortly after this Garfield's breathing stopped. "It's over," said Dr. Bliss. Garfield was just a few weeks short of his 50th birthday.

As befitting such a great man he had fought a great fight but sadly he lost it. Molly wrote "Dear little mama bore up with heroic courage and bravery until the very last. She was completely broken hearted for about an hour, then she went to papa's room to watch with him."

Mrs. Garfield had been asleep when the messenger arrived with the news.

The first thing she did was read her bible, then dressed and went downstairs. Her granddaughter Ellen turned to her and said "Are you prepared for bad news!" "No" was the reply. Ellen insisted "Grandma his spirit has passed away last night." "Oh no, it cannot be," Mrs Garfield sobbed. "It must not be. I cannot have it so. My James, my James's dead. I cannot believe you; let me see the dispatch." And she read it for herself watched by Ellen.

Eighteen hours later the autopsy discovered the bullet had fractured the 11th rib but missed the spinal chord completely and lodged below the pancreas. The doctors denied evidence of pneumonia or blood poisoning leaving Bliss and Boynton disgusted with the whole proceedings. Questions were raised and there were plenty of medical opinions in conflict with one another. Criticism of Garfield's treatment rumbled on for a number of years afterwards. Mrs. Garfield never commented on her husband's medical care again. Bizarrely the calendar on Garfield's desk in the White House has never been reset since the day of his assassination July 2, 1883. However fact is stranger than fiction. Garfield's death didn't end the family link with the Presidency. On November 16, 1961 eighty years later his great grandson Newell Garfield married Mary Jane Harrison Walker, granddaughter of Benjamin Harrison, the 23rd President of the United States back in 1889.

But the Presidential office must continue in perpetuity. Next day at 2.15 a.m. on the morning of the September 21, 1881 the serving Vice President Chester Alan Arthur was duly sworn into office as the 22nd President of the United States at his New York townhouse 123 Lexington Avenue by New York Supreme Court Justice, John R. Brady. The ceremony was repeated in Alan Arthur's office two days later on Thursday 22, December before Chief Justice Morrison Remick Waite in the company of ex-Presidents Hayes and Grant.

Now it was the turn of Charles Julius Guiteau to become the central character in the story of this terrible tragedy.

On October 14, 1881 he was brought before Judge Walter S. Cox to answer the charge of murder.
(1)   He had an unusual defence. First of all he blamed God for his act leaving him without free will to do otherwise.
(2)   He blamed the doctors for malpractice.
(3)   He claimed since Garfield was moved out of the jurisdiction of the court by moving him to Elberon and since he died in New Jersey, he was beyond the jurisdiction of the court. It seems everything was God's fault and God's responsibility. He had every confidence in God's power to set him free.

However Guiteau who had a formidable battery of top lawyers ranged against him was defended only by his brother-in-law who had no experience of criminal cases having defended only two in his three years of practice.

He proceeded to drop defences two and three - Garfield being moved from the jurisdiction of the court and the malpractice of the doctors. Insanity was the only defence left to him. His lawyer George Scoville, his brother-in-law claimed "If he is not insane and cannot be clearly made to appear so he ought to be hung." Guiteau confusingly said "I do not pretend to say that I am insane but on the 2nd of July I was insane. That's the issue. Can you go from being insane to being sane in three months?"

One wonders if the quality of Guiteau's defence team was so poor, why a Senior Counsel was not provided to him. Perhaps this was done but I'm afraid your writer found no evidence of this.

The prosecution just called him a cool, calculating blackguard.

Guiteau's defence was weakened by his plea of insanity. Why? Because insanity was hard to prove in 1880. Garfield himself had put his contempt for this defence on record about a year previously saying "All that a man needs to do would be to tear his hair and rave a little – and then kill a man." Temporary insanity defences were considered a dodge used only by the wealthy and well-connected. A precedent for temporary insanity as a defence was upheld in the case of Congressman Daniel E. Sickles in 1859, who had killed a man for having relations with his wife. He was acquitted some say because of his wealth.
The trial of Charles Julius Guiteau opened on November 14, 1881. It was the biggest event in Washington since the impeachment of Andrew Johnson. They even reconstructed the courtroom to accommodate the journalists and guests who would attend.

Most of them were very famous people from all walks of life leaving standing room only for the public. Picnic baskets were brought by some who lunched in the courtroom. Guiteau just sat reading the New York Herald or the Washington Post. He had an amazing capacity for detachment from the real world. First of all he wished to make a statement but was refused. He then handed a copy to the press in which he again blamed God for his firing the shot.

Both he and his brother-in-law tried to have the trial stopped because George Scoville realized he was not competent enough to conduct the case. Guiteau, in consternation, asked to have his co-counsel Robinson also dismissed. Impatiently the Judge ordered the trial to start. Guiteau even wrote to Chester Arthur the President for help. Arthur never replied.

The jury taken from a panel of 131 had already made up their minds. "Nothing but the rope," said one. "He ought to be hanged," said another. And still another "No amount of torture is good enough." "The pleas of insanity are all bosh," said a fourth….. and this was before the trial began. How times have changed.

Guiteau again objected to Robinson his assisting counsel because he wanted to defend himself. At this, the exasperated Judge threatened to remove him from court and proceed without him.

"I wouldn't trust my case to the best lawyer in the world," he retorted to the Judge. But he became contrite and promised not to interrupt again.

But this didn't last long. Soon he even abused his brother-in-law and had to be restrained by guards shouting at them "Mind your own business…." It was both a tragedy and a pantomime with a man's life at stake.

Later, further drama added to the excitement when a gunman on horseback tried to shoot Guiteau but failed. The would-be assassin was called a hero by the Washington Post after he was chased on horseback down the street and arrested. It turned out to be a drunk.

It seems for the purpose of Guiteau's defence Scoville attempted to downgrade Guiteau's ability in everything - religion, politics, earning a living, but it was useless as long as Guiteau's pride got in the way causing him to jump up and down with a denial. He just could not separate the defence by his lawyer from himself as a man. In fact at one stage he shouted "I protest solemnly against your trying to make out that I am a fool." Again he blamed God for the murder.

Guiteau took the stand on October 28 and testified for a week. Confrontation with the Judge, the prosecution, and even the press continued. When he didn't like the type of questioning he heard he called it mean and sickly, then simply sat down and read a newspaper.

Later on Guiteau was allowed to read lengthy portions of his book The Truth. The press accused Guiteau's behaviour as being "filled with insufferable egotism, arrogance and insolence". It transpired that while he was seeking work, four Presidents had been contacted by Guiteau – Arthur, Harris, Grant and Garfield.

One of the medical experts called Spitzka was adamant that Guiteau was insane. "His brain is not diseased but imperfect," he said. Even here Guiteau interrupted claiming he was a good Christian and not afraid to hang. Unfortunately Spitzka fell foul of the prosecution by refusing to answer a question on God, claiming it to be an impertinent question in a country that guarantees civil liberty.

Then the case took a bizarre turn when Scoville's wife intervened and asked to question the witness. The Judge allowed her pass the question to Scoville but Scoville ignored her and didn't ask it.

Time and again Guiteau attacked and insulted his brother-in-law whose patience by now must have been at breaking point. "Get off my case you consummate ass," Guiteau had raved not once but many times.

The case was dragging on towards Christmas. When the court adjourned for the holiday Guiteau wished everyone a Happy Christmas. If this was all an act then the world had seen the greatest artist that ever walked the boards. Guiteau's behaviour was beyond belief. It was unreal.

After Christmas Guiteau was moved to the dock for prisoners from the bench reserved for counsel. But the interruptions went on.

The New Year came and went and Guiteau again addressed the court telling them what a happy New Year he had with visitors that included the "high toned, middle toned and low toned people." "That takes in the whole crowd," he said. "Public opinion doesn't want me to hang."

Again he asked for money and complained that some cheques he had received were duds. A sick joke by those who thought it was funny.

The address to the jury began on January 12, and took two weeks. Guiteau finished his own address sitting down saying "I am not afraid of anyone shooting me. This shooting business is declining. I certainly was a lunatic on July 2, when I fired on the President and the American people generally think I was..... I would not do it again for a million dollars. When the President was shot his Cabinet telegraphed to foreign nations that it was the act of a madman and it will be far better in every way that it be officially decided that it was the act of a madman!!"

The jury deliberated for less than one hour. On return the foreman a John Hamlin replied to Judge Cox "Guilty as indicted". Each juror said the same. I now pose the following question. How many guilty people were in the court room that day? Surely the deliberations of the jury called for more than one hour for the prisoner – even for the death of a President.

Guiteau rose in a rage shouting "My blood will be upon the heads of that Jury don't you forget it. That is my answer. God will avenge this outrage." Then the audience seemed to cheer in sympathy for as he left the courtroom the gallery applauded. The last theatrical outburst came from Guiteau, "The court in banc will reverse this business." Scoville asked for a retrial on the grounds of further evidence about Guiteau's insanity.

Judge Cox rejected the appeal. Before passing sentence Guiteau was asked if he had anything to say. Again he said the shooting was God's act. "Kill me tomorrow if you want. I am God's man and I have been from the start. I care not what men shall do with me."
Donning the frightening black cap Judge Cox made his final deliberations. The execution was set for June 30, 1882, two days short of a year since the assassination.

When the Judge intoned.... "And may the lord have mercy on your soul," Guiteau shouted back, "and may God have mercy on your soul."

I find the behaviour of Guiteau a sad and sorrowful one for everyone. So many people suffered. Despite the leading part he played throughout his trial no one seems to have uncovered the real thoughts of the man. Was he angry? Maybe afraid, even hopeful or sorry? Who did he think of in his lonely moments or had he any. Was his mind the mess he portrayed at his trial? In this day and age would he have responded to intense counselling.....Sadly I'm afraid we will never know.

Scoville's patience finally broke and he withdrew from the case on April 24, 1882. The Supreme Court of the District of Columbia refused to order a new trial and a final appeal to the United States Supreme Court was rejected on June 19, 1882.

Yet somehow Guiteau never really believed he would be hanged. Not a patriot assassin.

He wrote again to Chester Arthur finishing with "I made you and saved the American people a lot of trouble." Meanwhile the White House received a visit from George Beard, a leading New York neurologist to ask for a pardon for Guiteau. It lasted twenty minutes. His appeal was sent to Arthur's Attorney General but it was also rejected.

A final plea came from Mrs. Scoville direct to Mrs. Garfield herself. They refused to see her and little Molly was furious and unrepentant towards Guiteau.... She said, "A year ago today papa had returned to Washington from Elberon and was getting ready to go to Williams College, and but for that villain he would have gone." Still they fought on for Guiteau's life. Over one hundred and sixty physicians wrote to Arthur but he rejected their call for clemency. Inevitably Guiteau was to have the last performance. On June 30, he ate a large breakfast and ordered his lunch prompt for 11 o'clock. He planned to pray on the scaffold, to read a poem he wrote and then drop the paper as a signal for the trapdoor to eternity to open. At

10.00 a.m. he had a bath, still under the eyes of the guards. He asked for writing paper and began writing his prayer. He had his boots blackened and ate lunch. The death warrant was read to him and his arms tied behind his back. Then a bizarre moment of black comedy. He tripped on the first step and turning round said to the chaplain Hicks "I've stubbed my toe on the gallows."

On the gallows he read from the bible, then he read his prayer composed earlier which ended with the words "Farewell ye men of earth."

He finished reciting his poem on the line "Glory Halleluiah I am with the lord."

He then sobbed and stopped for the benediction. His final words were "Glory, Ready, Go." He dropped the piece of paper and the trap door opened as he had arranged. It was all over. He was either a very brave man or he was utterly mad. Charles Julius Guiteau had achieved the first successful act of his life. His last moments on the stage of life were pure theatre and the choreography was all his very own.

His body hung for thirty minutes before it was taken away to the prison chapel and the required autopsy. But even in his going there was consternation and disagreement. The three doctors who carried out the autopsy just couldn't agree on the report.

The final sequel to the whole sorry tale relates to the many bills left behind. The medical bill paid for by the Government was settled for $6,500 and not the $25,000 that Dr. Bliss had claimed. Two other doctors each received $5,000 and two more received $4,000 each. The only woman on the case received $3,000, not the $10,000 she claimed. Ralph Jennings settled for $939 of the $6,154 he claimed for his air conditioning invention and so it went on.

The ice, the curtains, the carpets and even Garfield's embalming bill was cut from $500 to $75. Yes it all descended from the banal to a pathetic farce.

But our story of Garfield remains incomplete if we don't know anything about the main player in his life Charles Julius Guiteau. I'll end here with a quick painful pen picture of the man which will challenge you to ask the two questions never really resolved at his trial.

Was he mad when he assassinated Garfield? And most crucial of all was he mad when he was executed?

The childhood of Charles Julius Guiteau was a turbulent one. He was born on September 8, 1841 in Freeport, Illinois. His father was a Circuit Court clerk and a cashier at the second National Bank. His mother never recovered her health following the birth of Charles. After bearing two further children she died young at the age of thirty-five. Charles was seven at the time – a very impressionable age to lose a mother. He grew up a very lonely and hypersensitive little boy.

Unfortunately his father was cold and aloof and couldn't handle Guiteau's upbringing which was accomplished by punishment and indifference. His father even beat him for his inability to pronounce words.

Then life promised better things when his father remarried. Charles was eleven years old but he could attract no love. His new mother also was cold towards him. Even his older brother couldn't relate to him, nobody wanted him so it was left to his older sister Frances to rear him.

He worked hard for his father but when Frances his sister left home he followed her to Chicago.

He returned to his father's house for a while but grew restless and moved back to Chicago to live with Frances again. He started studying at Bells College but failed his exams. Just then he had a stroke of good fortune when his grandfather left him $1000 in his will. At last he was free of his father. He then failed the entrance exam to Michigan University and became a very lonely and frustrated human being. Feeling desperate he joined a religious cult called the Oneida Community run by a very peculiar man called John Noyes who preached about the second coming of Jesus having already taken place. The community took Guiteau's money into their funds. But here Charles Guiteau began to display eccentric behaviour. When he fell out with a room mate he drew a chalk line on the floor and ordered his room mate to stay on his side. This was another episode which reflected the schizophrenic thoughts in Guiteau's mind. Just then another resident of the house picked up a piece of paper Guiteau had thrown away. On it Guiteau had written "Chas J. Guiteau of England, Premier of the British Lion will lecture this evening at 7 o'clock."

At this stage it seems Guiteau was in urgent need of psychiatric treatment. Later his father wrote in despair "My son is a fit subject for a lunatic asylum." Finally the Community could take no more of Guiteau's strange behaviour and wrote a long letter to his father finishing with the words "We consider there is much evidence of an unsound and insane mind..... We are unwilling to take responsibility for him...." They returned $900 in bonds to Guiteau in three instalments non-negotiable to prevent him selling them. They then dismissed him from the Community.

Charles Guiteau now with nowhere to go headed for New York and soon his $900 was gone. He spent the next few years travelling between his father's home and his sister's house seeking odd jobs and blaming everyone else for his failures.

He went on to marry Anne Bunn, a YMCA librarian in 1867 when he was twenty-six. She thought he was an attorney who didn't drink, smoke or gamble but to her cost found she had married an erratic unstable man who abused her and used her to borrow money. He forced her to sleep in a closet when she clashed with him. He hit her, pulled her hair and kicked her. "You are in subjection to me," he shouted. "I am your master." She claimed he tried to kill her. He contracted syphilis from sleeping with prostitutes in his teens and told no one to avoid the disgrace it would bring on him. Always in pursuit of money he created his own lecture tour with speeches designed to shock and stimulate his audiences. Subjects such as "Is there a Hell", "Paul the apostle", "Martin Luther", "The origin of evil", "Christ's second coming". Throughout his travels he was only one step ahead of the police for refusing to pay his bills and most of his lectures lasted no more than ten minutes. His wife Anne finally could take no more and divorced him in 1874.

When Guiteau was thirty-one in 1872 he hit upon another scheme for making money, political patronage. He tried his hand at the Spoils System by supporting Horace Greeley for President in the hope that Greely would appoint him as Minister for Chile. Outrageous arrogance you might say but it has to be remembered Guiteau was a Walter Mitty character who believed in the illusions he lived with daily.

Greely lost and Guiteau disappeared from politics until eight years later. In 1880 he surfaced again haunting the headquarters of the Republican Party in New York.

All those who remembered him were left with the impression of a man who was not quite right. They humoured him gently but he mistook their politeness for respect.

At this point I must point out again the fatal part Garfield played in his own demise. He mistakenly revived an old tradition of people's right to meet the President. It had been abandoned because of the shear crush of people who came to see the President, mostly job seekers. Now Garfield himself was faced with thousands of office seekers who queued right down Pennsylvania Avenue to see him. John Hay said "The noise they made was like the sound of beasts at feeding time." Garfield suffered so much he began to lose sleep. He called them "A Spartan band of disciplined office seekers."

Into this picture again came Charles Julius Guiteau hell bent on his perceived right to a job.

He did the usual rounds to the State department and the White House on a regular weekly basis. He built his expectations up to such a crescendo of make-believe the blunt refusal when it came, exploded like a time bomb inside him. It was one rejection too many for a lifetime of failure.

In the place of his ambitions there now was a cold seething anger at the establishment, his father, stepmother, the Oneida Community, his divorced wife, his pathetic broken childhood and now Garfield himself who was to pay the price of this final insult. Perhaps these were not the thoughts of Charles Guiteau. Perhaps we will never really know his true thoughts one hundred and fifty years later. Then again who will ever know the mind of a madman. Well that is the pathetic picture of Garfield's assassin, the schizophrenic Walter Mitty who stalked Garfield not once but twice on the Baltimore and Potomac railway station. This man with the twisted mind badly in need of psychiatric help who had actually held a dress rehearsal of the murder he committed.

Sadly Garfield's death on September 19 left him maligned as a shady politician yet deified now as a martyr. I guess it isn't right to sit in judgement on a man whose future in the Presidency will never be known. So may he rest in peace.

I have no doubt he was brilliant enough to have risen to the very pinnacle of achievement, dignity and honour just like all his predecessors right back to George Washington. There is one thing of which I am certain however; Garfield would never be impressed by opinions about him today if you listen to one of his quotations about himself. "I do not care what others say or think about me but there is one opinion which I very much value and that is the opinion of James A. Garfield. Others I need think about. I can get away from them but I have to be with him all the time. He is with me when I rise and when I lie down, when I eat and talk, when I go out and come in. It makes a great difference whether he thinks well of me or not."

And so just like Kennedy, Lincoln and McKinley we can only speculate on how history was changed by Garfield's assassination. Yes we can speculate about history but we will never have the power to rewrite it.

James Garfield had three funerals. One at Elberon NJ, another at Washington DC where his body rested in State for three days and the final one was at Cleveland, Ohio where he now lies at peace in Lake View Cemetery.

21st President   Chester Alan Arthur

"His Accidency"
Born 1829
Died 1896
67 Years of age
1 Term
1881 – 1885
Age 52

Party: Republican
Profession: Lawyer
County: New York
Ancestry: Scotch- Irish
Estate: Unknown
Hobbies: Fishing

Physical Description: 6 foot 2 inches, full side whiskers and moustache, handsome and well proportioned.

There was no inaugural address for Chester Arthur as he was the Country's next in line for the Presidency after the assassination of Garfield. The Constitution did not require another election.

CHESTER ALAN ARTHUR

Around midnight on September 19, 1881 Chester Arthur heard a knock on the door of his New York townhouse. He answered it and was told Garfield had died. "I hope...... Oh my God I hope it is a mistake," he said.

Moments later he read a telegram from Attorney General MacVeigh. ".....it becomes our lawful duty to inform you of the death of President Garfield and to advise you to take the oath of office as President of the United States without delay. If it concurs with your judgement we will be very glad if you will come here on the earliest train tomorrow." Five Cabinet members had signed the telegram.

At 2.15 a.m. a New York Supreme Court Justice John R. Brady administered the oath to Chester Arthur. Early the next morning trains arrived in Elberon bringing Cabinet members from Washington and Chester Arthur from New York.

Two days later the oath was repeated on Thursday September 22, in the Vice President's room at the Capitol before Chief Justice Morrison Remick Waite in the presence of ex-Presidents Hayes and Grant.

So began the Presidency of Chester Alan Arthur, 21st President of the United States of America. Because of the circumstances surrounding his elevation to Commander-in-Chief, the news of Garfield's death nearly two and a half months after the fatal bullet struck him down came as a bolt from the blue. To Chester Alan Arthur mentally he had not prepared himself for the possibility he would be the next President of this vast Continent.

It is easy to understand Arthur's incredibility at the position he found himself in. Shock was a better description than surprise. Before this he was Vice President to a man of vigorous health with a secure life expectancy, certainly long enough for a Presidential term. Suddenly Arthur had been catapulted into the glaring spotlight of the most powerful job in politics. It was a transition of unbearable proportions for him. His vision for the future had been a comfortable four years on the fringes of a job for which he had no ambitions. Now that vision was no more. From now on he was the President. Life would never again be the same for poor Chester Alan Arthur.

"Chet Arthur in the White House". That was the newspaper headlines that bamboozled the readers on that September morning in 1881, almost in disbelief.

Chet Arthur, the Conkling lieutenant and the dismissed "Collector of Customs" was now in the highest seat of power in the land. The man, who had opposed the President to his face calling him "A man of broken promises". The man referred to as a "Pot House" politician during the campaign for Garfield's Presidency and who had not even been defended by the papers, so little esteem did they have for him. The main question was would he be Conkling's puppet? More importantly how could a machine politician end up in the White House?

No man was to regret the turn of events more than Morton Levi, a committed Stalwart who at Conkling's instigation failed to accept the Vice Presidency immediately when it was offered to him by Garfield. It was Levi's hesitancy in saying yes to the offer while he conferred with Conkling which doomed him as being too timed. Arthur was canvassed instead and he had no such hesitancy. Morton Levi did however get his chance again and was made Vice President under Benjamin Harrison but that was as far as he would ever go in American politics again.

But the situation Arthur found himself in was not unique to the Presidency in those days. The reason can be explained like this. The Vice Presidency was looked on as a minor job for someone who would not be considered leadership material.

In Arthur's case as a "Stalwart" he was just a sop to Blaine's "Half-Breeds" who had backed Garfield for the Presidency. It is easy to see why "Accidental Presidents" could easily come to power if for some reason the Presidency came to an abrupt end before its term was over. What better examples have we from the past than the Presidencies of John Taylor, Millard Fillmore and John Tyler.

But unlike them Arthur managed to steer clear of conflict and his is actually remembered as a tranquil Presidency. However it took at least another five more Presidencies before the powers in U.S. politics began to seriously address the credentials of a running mate for the highest office in the land.

But perhaps we can understand the political climate in Washington a little better in 1881 by looking at "Chet" Arthur's grass roots.

Chet's father was an Irish born Baptist Minister and school teacher. His mother's name was Malvina Stone Arthur. Arthur's family was not unlike that of Lincoln's in their nomadic lifestyle travelling around the towns of Vermont and Northern New York when Arthur was ten years old. He attended school at Union Village now called Greenwich and reports describe him as a genial but fairly average student. Incidentally, they say one reason for his father's nomadic existence in which he preached in eleven parishes was the outspoken views he expressed on controversial topics of the day from the pulpit. They didn't always endear him to the parishioners a situation he had to extricate himself from many times by moving on quickly. Chester could perhaps have changed his faith to Episcopalian as a result.

Arthur graduated from Union College when he was nineteen and began studying for a law degree while teaching in a local school. His first promotion in the educational field was as Principal of an Academy near Albany, New York. A year later he moved to New York City to work in the law office of Erastus D. Culver, a friend of his father. In 1854 Arthur, now twenty-five, passed his Bar exam and received his license to practice law. One outstanding achievement was his famous victory in court which guaranteed the rights of blacks to ride any street car in New York City. The year was 1855. In 1856 he opened his own law firm.

Arthur by this time was a very imposing handsome figure of a man. He was tall with black eyes, brown hair, ruddy cheeks, mutton chop sideburns and a high forehand. A bit of a dandy who liked to dress in the latest fashions and being articulate, well informed and amusing was welcome in any social gathering. Three years after he opened his new law firm Arthur married the daughter of a naval officer in 1859 when he was thirty years of age. Her name was Ellen Lewis Herndon. Soon there were three extra people to cloth, feed and care for. Two sons he named Chester Alan Arthur and William Lewis Arthur and a daughter named after her mother Ellen. Sadly William died aged almost three the curse of infant mortality in those times. Arthur's first excursion into politics was with the Whig Party at the Convention called to protest against the Kansas-Nebraska Act which was aimed at allowing new slaveholding States to emerge.

After angry heated debates at the Whig Convention the ground work was laid for the formation of the Republican Party.

The new Republican Party was firmly opposed to the expansion of slavery so from then on

Arthur became a committed Republican and joined the Republican Party. He even went on to campaign for Abraham Lincoln in 1860.

Maybe it was luck or maybe it was Arthur's talent for being in the right place at the right time. Anyway he chose to support Edwin D. Morgan for Governor of New York. Having backed a winner once again Arthur enjoyed the fruits of his labours by being appointed by Morgan as engineer in Chief of Morgan's Military staff even if it was only an honorary position. Well, once again fortune seemed to favour Chet Arthur because Lincoln placed Morgan in command of the New York Volunteers in his Union Army. Arthur was then asked by Morgan to be Inspector General and later Quartermaster General of this New York Militia. Arthur supervised the equipping of nearly a quarter of a million volunteers up to 1863 when he resigned refusing to work under the new Democratic Governor proving Chet had a bit of an independent streak. He found his way home to resume private life in his law practice in New York City.

You will have guessed by now that "Chet" Arthur was well and truly entrenched in the New York Republican political scene and it is no surprise that he soon came to the notice of one Senator Roscoe Conkling. Mr. Conkling at this time was at the height of his powers dispensing political favours and patronage to all who contributed their services to his political machine. Those loyal workers who organised votes for his chosen candidate were of course rewarded by Conkling. It was like a State within a State. The outcome of Arthur's success in the machine when it supported General Ulysses Grant for President was to be appointed Collector of Customs for the port of New York.

So Chet Arthur almost without even trying had landed the plum political patronage available at that time. Being the boss of the New York Customs House meant he was now the undisputed political leader of New York City. Two thirds of all U.S. customs receipts passed through the port giving Arthur an income from fees and perks amounting to what the President himself was earning $50,000 per year. He had more than 1,000 employees under him all of whom owed their jobs to the Conkling machine which made Arthur a very powerful figure indeed. Whatsmore he was grossly overstaffed with people who were seldom seen at the Customs House.

Yes, Chet Arthur had come a long way from the humble beginning he had as a clergyman's son.

Soon he was being connected to the corruption around him. The reason he was suspected of such a connection was his apparent oblivion to the shakedown kickbacks and bribes that went with the job. His greatest asset was his knowledge of everyone's secrets. It has been recorded that in 1881 he confessed as follows "If I get going about the secrets of the campaign there is no saying what I might say to make trouble." But for his own good reasons he had his personal papers of events burned. His philosophy was "the world is the world" and like others around him he took everything as he found them warts and all.

But the movement to end political patronage was gathering momentum and Arthur was to be the main victim of the purge of President Rutherford B. Hayes, Garfield's predecessor against the "Spoils System".

In his campaign to clean up the System, Rutherford removed Arthur on the grounds of corruption. Rutherford had no qualms about calling it as he saw it. Well that was the background to Arthur as he entered the Presidency. The reformer Edward L. Godkin had something to say about the situation when he described Arthur's past associations as "A mess of filth". He also considered Arthur's Presidency, with Conkling the power behind the throne, as a recipe for disaster. Another of Godkin's observations was made about Arthur's Vice Presidency saying "There is no place in which Arthur's powers of mischief will be so small as in the Vice Presidency. After all," he suggested "the prospect of a healthy James Garfield, two years Arthur's junior dying in office was plainly "too unlikely a contingency to contemplate"." So much for clairvoyance.

However the script for this political melodrama was about to get interesting as the new President Chet Arthur decided to shock the complacent people around him with a few surprises they had never anticipated. Arthur was not the first President whose behaviour in the Presidency would not conform to the image they had projected outside the Presidency. From some inner depth of "Chet" Arthur's restless soul stirred a mischievous spirit born in the Presidencies of the distant past which somehow directs the occupant of the White House to live up to the demands of that august role when he enters that cathedral of power. The President just can't help trying to live up to the expectancy millions of Americans place on him. Today is always part of a glorious yesterday.

The first thing Arthur did was to sign the Pendleton Act of 1883 which put a bomb under the Spoils System forever by handing over the Civil Service appointments system to competitive examinations. Surprise, surprise Chet Arthur was determined to be in nobody's pocket.

Needless to say all hell broke loose, and the chief mourner in this weeping and knashing of teeth was poor Roscoe Conkling. To say he felt betrayed would be the understatement of the century. Rubbing salt in the wounds of the now disillusioned Conkling Arthur, then gave jobs in his Administration to "Half-Breeds". This was too much for Conkling and he resigned his seat in the Senate in protest. Sadly for Conkling he never returned to politics. Like a Captain on a ship that was in danger of sinking Chet Arthur decided to jettison all useless baggage.
Yes, Arthur was now a much different person in power. His first decision was to detach himself from Conkling who had ambitions to be made Secretary of State and he never forgave Arthur when this did not happen. Arthur still chose his own Stalwart apprentices but they were of a much higher calibre. Before the Presidency Arthur's personal life received a devastating blow. His wife Ellen died on January 12, 1880 from pneumonia. Arthur was only Vice President at the time but fifteen months later on March 4, 1881 he achieved the unbelievable to become the 21st President. Sadly Ellen would never enjoy the experience of being his First Lady. The duties of First Lady of the White House were undertaken by Arthur's sister Mary Arthur McElroy.

One thing Chet Arthur had never deprived himself of was the exciting pleasures of high society. This didn't change now that he was President. He continued to pursue his favourite hobbies of hunting and fishing and was always at home in the bohemian social life of Washington in the 1880s.

According to White House historian William Seale "Arthur certainly had taste." According to some reports he was appalled at the condition of the White House he had inherited after he had made a tour of the building.

What he saw prompted him to say "I won't live in a house like this" and true to his word he moved elsewhere for the next three months while it was being renovated.
He then supervised daily that historic building's redecoration programme. A year later he introduced Louis Comfort Tiffany to take charge of the work. Tiffany was at that time the country's most fashionable designer. He was the one responsible for a stained glass screen

for the hallway. Even the White House furnishings were patrician. The reformers outside were enthusiastic about Arthur's changes inside the White House even if they found it hard to live with his tainted past outside it.

It was a cruel act of fate that Ellen, known as "Nell", would never get to share the White House social life with him, but there were already rumours anyway that the marriage was about to be terminated just before she died.

She came from Virginian stock and always considered herself a Southerner. Most of her family took up arms against the Union and this prompted Arthur to refer to her as "My little rebel wife". This Civil War ghost between them and Arthur's love of the good life "Feasting into the night with his cronies" as she put it, caused a constant tension between them. "I feel abandoned" was her complaint. Well despite Nell's discontent, their legal separation never came about because of her unexpected death. At that time momentous events were also taking place all around him in New York. Edison's electric light invention was soon lighting up the city with incandescent signs – neon lights. Steel ships were the new invention for the Navy to replace the old wooden ones now no longer being built.

It was almost a national day of celebration when President Arthur and the future President then Governor of New York, Grover Cleveland opened up the new Brooklyn Bridge in 1883 after fourteen years spent in its construction.

Finally, the introduction of Time zones was implemented on railway lines right across America by U.S. and Canadian Railroads to standardize clocks from the Atlantic to the Pacific.

Yes, America was certainly changing rapidly as it approached the 20th century. But it must be understood how much the wheel of fortune still favoured Chet Arthur, as his ship of State sailed merrily on a sea of calm. Not even the tiniest political squabble threatened his idyllic voyage into the future. He sailed on autopilot right throughout his term of office. But why would he make changes - "If it's not broken why mend it" was his philosophy. Amazingly Chet Arthur basked serenely in a sunny voyage and lived his whole Presidency without any major criticism.

Perhaps the country was yearning for this period of calm; a stepping back from the turbulence of the times just gone, that cataclysmic clash of ideologies between two halves of a warring population. Arthur managed to run a neutral Presidency long enough to allow all the protagonists time to review their situations. The three year vacation of Arthur's Presidency from the passions of Civil War politics was just what the country needed. Chet was never encumbered by a political crusade like Washington or Lincoln. As a Republican he had supported the Party line on Reconstruction. Now as a President he was glad to cooperate with the final dismantling of this failed enterprise. To him politics was a profession not a theology worth dying for. So Chet Arthur's style was ideal for the times that were in it whether you agree with it or not.

As America moved into an exciting future Chet Arthur, never one to blush unseen, was busy making his own waves. For the first time in American history Chet was the President who left the comfort of the White House to visit the Native Americans or Indians in their own hometown, their Reservation in Wyoming. As usual Chet Arthur was there not on business but pleasure. The tribe he was visiting was the Shoshonis who had for eighty years been a close ally of the U.S. Government. True to his bohemian personality he was on a fishing holiday for trout and salmon. The location was Yellowstone National Park. A dozen friends, a seventy-five man cavalry escort and seventeen pack animals made up the party. Next morning on August 7, 1883 he reviewed a welcoming procession and was treated to a spectacular display of Indian fighting skills in a mock battle between Indians and Cavalry men.

He finally paid a visit to Chief Washakie in his Lodge. Chet received a gift of two pinto ponies for his daughter Nell. His gift to the Chief turned out to be an army scout. Previous grand battles between Shoshonis warriors and the U.S. army were forgotten. The President emerged from the Lodge describing Chief Washakie as amazing.

His journey to Yellowstone Park was very successful for his hosts made sure Chet went home with three antelopes, a bear, a treasure trove of small game, and all the trout he could carry.

There wouldn't be another hunting trip by a President until Theodore Roosevelt paid a visit to a Comanche Reservation, under the rule of its leader Chief Quanah Parker, twenty years later.

But with history and America moving quickly out of the past into a promising future, whatever became of the giants of yesterday Blaine and Conkling, now that the Stalwarts and the Half-Breeds were heading for extinction as a result of the Pendleton Acts.

The brilliant Blaine leader of the Half-Breeds was still a Senator. He got his final chance of glory in the Presidential contest of 1884 but was defeated by the Democratic New York Governor Grover Cleveland. After that election he returned to the Senate. Like the glowing embers of a once blazing bonfire the "Plumed Knight" spent his remaining years achieving the only ambition left to him, the completion of twenty years in Congress. It was one he passed with gentle dignity.

Whatever happened to Boss Conkling? Well, for the seven remaining years left to him, Conkling could be found nightly in Stokes Café in New York surrounded by a group of old buddies sharing old stories of triumphs and failures in his brilliant career, now sadly ended. It was for him a nostalgic period of soul searching. Conkling did indeed have the ability to take him to the White House itself but unfortunately his personal charm never transferred itself into his politics.

After Garfield died Conkling was asked if he intended to continue his fight with the Presidency. His reply was profound. Looking into distance space he thought for a while and murmured.

"How can I speak into a grave? How can I battle with a shroud? Silence is a duty and a doom."

But what was Conkling's weakness which deprived him of the ultimate prize?

It is said that nothing is more dangerous in politics than the quick hurtful retort. Conkling used words as a prize fighter used fists and made himself many enemies in the process. Too many. Sadly, almost inevitably Conkling died like a prize fighter battling the unconquerable still convinced of his superiority to the opposing forces that confronted him. This time it was Mother Nature.

The great blizzard of 1888 buried New York in an avalanche of snow. Transport came to a halt and few people ventured out. But true to his character Conkling was the exception. He trekked the two miles from the City Hall to Madison Square through the storm for two to three hours. Heartbreakingly, he paid the ultimate penalty. He was found lying in the snow and died of his foolhardiness later. For his friends sitting around the table in Stokes Café life would never be the same again. The end of a glorious era just died with a gentle whimper.

But I wouldn't be wasting too much time feeling sorry for Conkling. He knew that the world of politics can be a very cruel one. And now to President Arthur. What a strange verdict of history it would be to paint Chet Arthur as a "cad" or "a good time Charlie" with no particular talent for the role of President of the United States. That verdict would do the man a grave disservice. He was a skilled debater, charismatic and highly educated. A brilliant lawyer, with common sense and a comprehensive knowledge of Constitutional law. Throughout his term of office he had to work with a Congress evenly divided between Democrats and Republicans. Regardless of what his reputation had been prior to his Presidency he was courageous and honest in his decisions as President. So honest was his approach in eliminating political patronage he lost many supporters who would otherwise have supported him for a second term. His political independence had a price for which he paid later.

If you are searching for words to describe Chet Arthur's Presidency I am sure you will conclude like me that while it was rather undistinguished it was truly practical. It brought in moderate reforms, a modernization of the Navy, and an expansion of America's world trade. In short he re-established the assertiveness of the Presidency to heal the wounds that had been inflicted on it by Reconstruction. If you pause to think of it he must have done something right for they erected a bronze statue to him in New York City's Madison Square Park in 1899.

Nevertheless, although near the end of his Presidency when he was suffering from Brights disease, an incurable kidney complaint, Chet Arthur still hoped to be nominated for a second term as President. Despite his illness Arthur continued to live the life of a bon vivant. His office hours were limited to six per day from 10 a.m. to 4 p.m. He loved good food and held his liquor well. He also loved the reputation of being the last man to go to bed regardless of the event being celebrated. He was a true loner always preferring to keep his lifestyle and his sorrows private. Nobody knew the pain of his grief on losing his wife Ellen or even that he had Brights disease.

Despite all this he still looked for a Senatorship after he lost the nomination as Presidential Candidate in 1884 to Blaine. This request was refused and in retrospect Brights disease which took his life two years later in 1886, would not have allowed him to finish the job. Knowing Arthur's light-hearted approach to life the loss of these two top jobs would soon have faded into the background without bitterness.

Chester Alan Arthur faded into obscurity in retirement unlike many of his predecessors. His major contribution to the Presidency was his steady hand on the tiller of State bringing peace and common sense to the world of post-Civil War America. Like all U.S. Presidents, time allows historians the luxury of second thoughts about them. They now have granted him a more exalted place in history through the wisdom of hindsight and sober reflection.

Yes time is a great healer. Chet Arthur died on November 18, 1886 in his beloved New York aged sixty-seven. He was laid to rest in Rural Cemetery Albany, New York alongside his beloved Nell. I am quite certain in death there was a beautiful reconciliation between them.

22nd President & 24th President Grover Cleveland

"Veto President"
Born 1837
Died 1900
55 Years, 351 days
2 terms
1885 – 1889: 1st term
Age 48
1893 – 1897: 2nd term
Age 56

Party: Democrat
Profession: Lawyer
County: New York
Ancestry: English/Irish
Estate: $250,000
Hobbies: Fishing.

Physical Description: 5 foot 11inches, weight 260 lbs, corpulent, greying hair, going bald, heavy drooping moustache, short neck.

Significant Extract from his Inaugural Address:
"The people demand reform in the Administration of the Government and the application of business principles in public affairs. As a means to this end, Civil Service reforms should be in good faith enforced. Our citizens have the right to protection from the incompetency of public employees who hold their places solely as the reward of partisan service."

GROVER CLEVELAND 1ST TERM

As Chester Alan Arthur's term came to an end his good natured Presidency was about to be replaced by a man with some very strong opinions and unlike Arthur he never hesitated to express them. That man was Grover Cleveland.

His mission in life seems to have been to prevent dishonest things from happening almost to the point of obsession. Despite this rather confrontational style, the people seem to have appreciated his blunt honest approach enough to give him two terms as President.

Thomas Bailey, the historian, defends the negative style of Cleveland on the grounds that the positive approach did not necessarily guarantee effective leadership. William Lichtenberg concluded that Cleveland's leadership was largely negative but went on to say – "Even that was something of a virtue when too many politicians were saying "yes" to the wrong things." Cleveland may not have been brilliant but he will be remembered for his courage, toughness and sense of duty. A very formidable character indeed.

Grover Cleveland had the brawn to go with his fiery personality weighing in at 260 lbs – 30 lbs short of twenty stone. He had a bull neck, thick swarthy body and fists like shovels. He would not have been out of place in the old prize ring.

Stephen Grover Cleveland was forty-eight when he arrived in the White House as the 22nd President of the United States.

He was born in 1837 at Caldwell, New Jersey, the fifth child of Richard Falley Cleveland, a Presbyterian Minister and Ann Neal Cleveland. He was four years old when the family moved to Fayetteville, near Syracuse, New York, where his father worked as a Presbyterian Minister. Young Grover went to school locally before moving on to a nearby college in Clinton. When Grover was thirteen his father died which threatened his chance of further education.

However, Grover was resourceful and earned money by teaching at a State institution for the blind, work that also contributed towards the household bills. Two years later at eighteen years of age, Grover went to Cleveland, Ohio, to seek work but he got no further than Buffalo, New York. His uncle, a well-known cattle breeder there employed him to write up the herd books of his company for $10 a month. Luck was with him because friends of his uncle gave him work in their law offices and encouraged him to study law. This paid off for in 1859 at twenty-two years of age, he was licensed to practice.

Now a young lawyer, Grover Cleveland became an active politician in the Democratic Party. At thirty-three he became Sheriff of Erie County and was soon showing that independent streak so characteristic of him. His uncle was the best known figure in the Buffalo Republican Party since former President Millard Fillmore. Despite his family's Republican background Grover, true to his maverick tendencies, joined the Democrats.
In later years he explained his decision by claiming that the Democratic Party in 1856 represented solid conservative thought. Anyway he was not too impressed by John Charles Fremont describing him as too flamboyant and theatrical. Nevertheless, during his two year term of office 1870 – 1872 as Sheriff of Erie County, Grover succeeded in stamping out routine graft and earned the name of being incorruptible. His political principles were now well and truly established for the future.

Around that time there was a tragedy in the family when two of his brothers were victims of a fire at sea on board the "SS Missouri", bound for Havana, Cuba from New York City in 1792. Over eighty lives were lost in the shipwreck. His two brothers' names were Richard Cecil Cleveland aged thirty-seven and Lewis Frederick Cleveland aged thirty-one.

But life had to move on for Grover. To say he was committed to reform is an understatement. It was an obsession. He carried his mission to ruthless lengths for he was reputed to have personally acted as executioner at the gallows for one criminal. On September 6, 1872 he supervised the hanging of Patrick Morrissey, convicted of stabbing his own mother. The Buffalo Express reported next day that the Sheriff, Grover Cleveland, stood at the gallows with his right hand on the rod attached to the trapdoor and at fourteen minutes past twelve Mr. Emerick gave the signal. Six months later, on March 14, 1873 Cleveland took charge of the hanging of a gambler convicted of shooting a man dead during a card game. The condemned man's name was Jack Gaffney. Grover's reason for doing such a distasteful job was to show others he would never shirk from any task a deputy was asked to do.

Service in the Civil War was always considered an asset to any aspiring politician in those times. Most Presidents at that time had military credentials whether earned or not. However, this was one of Grover Cleveland's liabilities for because of family commitments – looking after his widowed mother and his two sisters – Grover chose to sit out the war. He was able to do so by hiring a substitute to serve in his place for $150, an advantage that was allowed by the Conscription Act of 1863. Incidentally, two of his brothers served in the conflict. The man who took his place was a Polish immigrant who actually survived the war. An attempt by the Republicans to exploit this in the Presidential campaign was stillborn for their own man; James G. Blaine had also hired a substitute.

During the war in fact, Grover became Assistant District Attorney for Erie County, New York in 1863 and although a successful attorney he was generally recognized for his hard work rather than brilliance. He did however attract attention as a crusader against crime and corruption. Grover was soon recognized enough to be made Mayor of Buffalo in 1882 and his next election was as Governor of New York. This was three years before he became President and even then he was opposing legislative wastefulness in the improper use of public funds.

His favourite saying was "Public Office is a Public Trust". As Governor of Buffalo, Cleveland had plenty of ammunition for his crusade when he was confronted by a shady circle of corrupt politicians from both Parties unlucky enough to have to face him in full flow. In one single year he saved the Buffalo taxpayer $200,000 which was quite a bit of money in those days. This money was to be earmarked for street cleaning contracts which those dishonest aldermen thought they had cornered for their own personal profit.

His trusty veto was used fearlessly and the Bills were withdrawn. He became known after that as the veto Mayor of Buffalo. As you can see he must have made quite a few enemies so his chances of further political progress was not very promising.

But fortune does have a habit of favouring the brave and lady luck seemed to approve of him. A rift occurred between two candidates wanting the Democratic nomination for Governor of New York. The powers that be looked around for a new name to reconcile the quarrelling Parties and Cleveland was nominated. He went on to defeat the Republican candidate nominated by President Chester Arthur.

Imperceptibly, despite his full frontal approach to any political chicanery, Grover Cleveland marched on. It is a bit of an uncanny coincidence that a person like Grover Cleveland should find himself at the pinnacle of political power in New York, a position from which the President himself had been dismissed for corruption. The Spoils System was still fighting in hand to hand combat with the reformers and it is no coincidence either that Grover Cleveland took them all on. He gave out the jobs on merit only and not based on Party favouritism. His answer to those foolish enough to question him was invariably met with a stock answer of his "I don't know that I understand you."

Yes, he wielded the veto axe with a flourish in New York just as he had done in Buffalo. His most notorious veto was used in 1883 against the Five Cent Fare Bill which would have lowered transit fares in New York. He claimed he couldn't pass it because it was in violation of the Transit Companies Charter. He was heard to say after the vote "I shall be the most unpopular man in the State of New York." He later fearlessly opposed Tammany Hall, the Democratic political machine in New York, when he vetoed its Bill revising the City Charter. Yes, famous names were totally irrelevant to Grover Cleveland. In 1884 the Presidential hustings arrived and the Democrats had to decide between two candidates for nomination. James G. Blaine, the brilliant but controversial leader of the Half-Breeds in Congress was the Republican choice. It wasn't a good one because Blaine was remembered for corruptly accepting bribes from railroad companies in the past. A group called "The Mugwumps" or "Big Chiefs" asked voters to vote for any honest candidate put forward by the Democrats.

Lady luck was again smiling on Grover Cleveland for with his background of public honesty he could not be ignored by the Democrats. He was duly nominated at the National Convention in July 1884.

The campaign was a vicious personal one. Grover was accused of fathering an illegitimate child and he openly admitted it to be true which defused any debate on the matter. Perhaps it was honesty or it could have been an astute political brain at work, who knows. Blaine's supporters were reduced to a childish chant –

> Ma Ma, where's my Pa
> Gone to the White House, ha ha ha.

Later Cleveland's supporters got their chance of their own retaliation when he won the Presidency. Their chant was –

Hurray for Maria
> Hurray for the kid
> We voted for Grover
And we're damn glad we did.

Cleveland does not come out of the story of his illegitimate child too well. The light- hearted banter at the polls does not disguise his cold-hearted response to the child and its mother. It seems the unmarried mother's name was Maria Halpin. Far from caring for her and the little boy he had her committed to an insane asylum and the child was housed in an orphanage at $5 per week. On her discharge from the asylum she tried to claim her child but Cleveland for whatever reason had him adopted by a "leading family" in Buffalo. Maria Halpin had the last laugh, however, for she had the little boy named Oscar Folsom after Cleveland's father-in-law, Oscar Folsom. Perhaps we are reflecting the socially bereft culture that existed in 1880 America. Such behaviour would have dire consequences for a President today and just would not be tolerated. But let's continue with Grover's election campaign.

Not only was Blaine attacked for his questionable railroad connections but Grover's campaign was given a real shot in the arm by one of Blaine's men, the Reverend Samuel D. Burchard.

The Reverend it seems got carried away by his enthusiasm and called the Democrats the Party of Rum, Romanism and Rebellion.

It all happened like this. In an address of welcome at an old Fifth Avenue Hotel in New York City, the night had been set aside for a banquet given by a group of businessmen James Blaine was addressing. Sleuths heard the speech and reported back to Cleveland. By the evening, the city was flooded with sensational circulars intended to arouse the ire of Catholic voters and they succeeded. The Southern Irish Americans were not very pleased with the outburst and considered it an insulting reference to them. It lost Blaine the critical Irish American vote in New York and some say 50,000 votes swung the election Cleveland's way, helping him to win the Presidency by 219 electoral votes to 182. The year was 1885. He was the first Democratic President since Andrew Johnson in 1865.

Incidentally, the whole style of Grover's Presidency was dictated by his lack of trust in those around him and an analytical caution in studying every problem for himself. This ultra cautious approach was also a nightmare for the press. After twenty-five years of Republican control, political correspondents were despatched to Albany to keep a watching brief on Cleveland's progress as President-elect for they visualized trouble from day one from the South. But Cleveland was not a news hound's idea of the open book. Playing communication games, absorbing much and giving little, he was a newsman's nightmare. However, Cleveland revealed later in private letters how unhappy he was with the job. "I am sick at heart and perplexed in the brain," he wrote. He never lost the suspicion that everyone who approached him had a sinister purpose. However, whenever he was out with friends just duck shooting, he relaxed and was a congenial companion.

The thought of assassination was never far from his thoughts and his inauguration day is worth a story to prove this. Heading for Washington in secret for his inauguration was a further proof of the isolation with which he surrounded himself. Leaving on March 1, for his inauguration on March 4, chased by frustrated reporters, he chose to travel by sleigh to Kenwood railway station, south of Albany, and arrived in secrecy in Washington. It was his first visit to the city and he was never seen walking on its pavements in all of his first term in office. Harrison, who succeeded Cleveland, found a double shift of Secret Service men on guard night and day when he arrived. Security had become a fixation with the unfortunate Cleveland.

Grover was duly inaugurated holding his mother's bible in his hand on Wednesday March 4, 1885 on the East Portico of the White House in a ceremony administered by Chief Justice Morrison Remick Waite. The new President reviewed the usual parade from the platform set up on the White House lawn.

But life was not going to be simple for Grover's celebrating supporters; for once again Grover's controversial demons were let loose when he formed his Cabinet. Grover's new Cabinet contained many "time bombs" that nobody was prepared for. Yes, to everyone's consternation he installed Thomas F. Bayard, an advocate of lower tariffs on imported goods. Once again the power of big business manifested itself when he appointed William C. Whitney, a financier as Secretary of the Navy. He then proceeded to incur the wrath of the Northerners in the Party when he brought Lucius Q.C. Lamar of Mississippi and Augustus H. Garland of Arkansas into the Cabinet. He made Lamar Secretary of the Interior and Garland Attorney General. The pain of the Northerners didn't seem to bother him even though both Lamar and Garland had seen service as Confederates in the Civil War. Grover continued to flirt with controversy regardless of what enemies he made.

But let's not get ahead of ourselves.

It was not only life in the controversial world of politics that fascinated Grover. Early in June the following year 1886, Grover married his sweetheart Frances Folsom, the daughter of a former law partner. He was the first President to be married in the White House. Later the couple were to have five children; three daughters and two sons. Ruth died at thirteen years of age, Esther lived to eighty-seven, Marion died aged eighty-two and Richard died at seventy-seven. Finally Frances Grover, his wife, died in old age.

Despite all his troubles Grover Cleveland had one compensation in Frances, his very gracious wife who became so popular she was even compared to the great Dolly Madison. They came in thousands to get a glimpse of her at White House receptions. So much so Grover sought to divert attention from her by setting up a private residence outside the White House. "I shall buy or rent a house near here, where I can be away from this cursed constant grind," he said. "Red Top" was the name of the new house built with a panoramic view of the Potomac River and they lived there most of the time. When Frances was leaving the White House after Grover's defeat she gave orders to the Staffers to take good care of the furnishings as she expected to be back in four years. She was right. They returned again in 1893 for another four years.

The circumstances surrounding the relationship were unusual. His father-in-law, Oscar Folsom, died when Frances was only eleven years old and Grover took over the care of Folsom's family immediately. Nine years later when Frances was twenty-one, Grover proposed to her by letter. He was forty-eight years old. She was more than happy to accept. That was in August 1885 just after he was inaugurated 22nd President of the United States and in June the following year 1886, they were wed in the White House. But Grover Cleveland didn't waste Presidential time on their wedding day for there was work to be done. Believe it or not, Grover continued to work his full Presidential hours and didn't shut up shop until 7.00 p.m. on the evening of his wedding ceremony. Mind you, he was romantic enough to take the rest of the evening off to devote to his new wife. You can't get any more eccentric than that – can you?

Yes, life went on for Grover Cleveland and marriage did nothing to mellow his approach to politics. Because of his dislike for paternalism in any shape or form, it was not long before he was again in trouble with the people. He was not impressed by "Lobbies" to aid citizens in distress and so vetoed the 1887 Texas Seed Bill to give relief to farmers suffering losses from severe drought conditions they had recently survived.

It is hard to look back now and not describe Grover as being controversial in a "You be damnedness" way. This was what he was admired for. But if he was to drive the country onwards away from Civil War politics, he only did what he had to do. It was now full speed ahead implementing the Pendleton Act of 1883, designed to kill the corrupt "Spoils System".

Grover continued to keep a watchful eye on the purse strings which lead him to veto more than two hundred Bills on Pensions. Even disabled veterans of the Union Army were blocked to stop pensions being given to people regardless of the cause of their disability. The veteran's organisation "the Grand Army of the Republic" was incensed by Grover's actions and never missed the chance to remind him that he had never served himself. The money to placate the farmers would have been a mere $10,000 but Cleveland declared indifferently "I find no warrant for such an appropriation in the Constitution." His theory was that "Federal aid weakens the sturdiness of our national character". "While the people should support the Government, the Government should not support the people" was another quote of his. Yet here is a fascinating theory about that. Herbert Hoover, America's 31st President used the same "mantra" word for word in 1930. Perhaps he was using Grover Cleveland's script from 1885, forty-five years earlier.

Unfortunately, Cleveland's two terms straddled a period of widespread serious strife in the Trade Union movement. One of these was the General Strike of 1886 which was fought for an eight hour day. There were two violent episodes fuelled by these strikes. One was the Haymarket Riot in Chicago and the other was the violent Pullman Strike of 1894 sparked off by the proposal for a 30% reduction in wages. This took place during Cleveland's second term. He had to call in the army to break up this strike to avert a nationwide boycott of trains carrying Pullman cars. Using the excuse that the strike interfered with the delivery of mail Cleveland trumpeted. "If it takes the entire army and Navy to deliver a postcard in Chicago that card will be delivered."

Around this time a new world was emerging in America which previous Presidents never had to contend with in the past. Grover found himself in an environment of escalating economic problems triggered off by opposing commercial forces. The demands of labour for a share in the rising prosperity of the new America were loud and articulate. It is easy to see how a tough President like Grover Cleveland was like a crag of rock jutting out of a turbulent river as the rapids crashed wildly around it.

The story of Cleveland's two Presidential terms seems to have been taken up by his political conflicts and vetoes. He was the first President who used his veto far more vigorously than all his predecessors. All of their vetoes amounted to 205. Cleveland rejected 414 Bills in his first term of office alone and 584 in total. Most of these were Pension Bills for Civil War veterans inspired by some Congressmen to reward cronies. It was a mild form of corruption but nevertheless Cleveland insisted on reading each Bill thoroughly before rejecting those he thought had no merit.

As the new America arrived like a squalling baby from its mother's womb, old wounds still needed attention. The famous Dawes Act came before him and was passed. This was a Bill designed to favour the Native American Indian by settling land on him. But somehow it failed in its purpose because it failed to ward off dishonest white speculators who took advantage of the illiterate Native American leaving him even poorer than before.

This was not Cleveland's fault but it reflects the lower standards of American society that Cleveland was consistently confronting. Just like the question of lower tariffs which was another hot potato he tried to tackle. To cure a treasury surplus he went all out for lower tariffs but eventually this spilled over into the next Presidential election and his lower tariff policy lost the election for him.

The row on tariffs continued for the next four years right into his second attempt at winning the Presidency which he won by 277 electoral votes to 145. His words on leaving office after his first term was remembered by a White House butler. Cleveland had told him "We'll be back." But that's a story I have already told you about earlier.

Normally we end here closing our Presidential story with his eventual death and subsequent burial. But Grover was not ready for his own demise just yet for he returns again as America's 24th President in 1885. Meanwhile we continue the story of the Presidents as we welcome on stage our 23rd President Benjamin Harrison, so just read on.

23rd President   Benjamin Harrison

"The Centennial President"
Born 1833
Died 1901
68 Years of age
1889 - 1893
1 term
Age 56

Party: Republican
Profession: Lawyer
County: Indiana
Ancestry: English
Value of Estate: $375,000
Hobbies: Hunting and Billiards

Physical Description: 5 foot 6 inches, blond, greying hair, full beard, small bright blue eyes, short neck, short legs.

Significant Extract from his Inaugural Address:
"I will not attempt to note the marvellous and in great part happy contrasts between
our country as it steps over the threshold into its second century of organized
existence under the Constitution and that weak but wisely ordered young nation
that looked undauntedly down the first century when all its years stretched out
before it."

BENJAMIN HARRISON

Benjamin Harrison was the last of the Civil War Generals to become President of the United States after Grant, Hayes and Garfield. In fact the 23rd President was a veteran of the Civil War when he was in his thirties.

Harrison had fought alongside Sherman in the Battle of Atlanta and was still bitter about the Civil War rebels and called the Democrats "the Party of the Leprosy of Secession". These were the times when Presidents could walk window shopping in Washington as Grant had done despite the tragic assassinations of Lincoln and Garfield.

The background Harrison possessed was a classic pedigree for any Presidency, just as the 19th century was drawing to a close. To add an extra layer of quality to his C.V. his grandfather, the 9th President was the signer of the Declaration of Independence – "Old Tippecanoe".

Harrison was born in his grandfather's mansion in North Bend in southwest Ohio in 1833 and grew up on his father's farm only a few miles away. His mother Elizabeth Irwin Harrison married John Scott Harrison, another who had a political background; John having served two terms in Congress. Both Benjamin and his older brother went to Farmers College near Cincinnati. Benjamin had the talent for a university education and was sent by his father to Miami University in Oxford, Ohio from where he graduated in 1852 at nineteen years of age. He married a college friend, Caroline Lavinia Scott and the marriage produced a son, Russell and a daughter, Mary for the happy couple.

Grover Cleveland and Benjamin Harrison met twice for the Presidency. Harrison won the first battle in 1885 and Cleveland made a comeback four years later in 1892 to win the second one. Both elections were fought against the background of the necessity for higher or lower tariffs as a cure for the economic instability of the time. But more of that later.

Harrison had other interests to pursue when he defended Indian homesteaders against aggressive railroad interests. Like most Republicans who had fought in the Civil War, Harrison favoured black rights. He backed the young Henry Cabot Lodge in his bid to enforce civil rights in the South but a Southern filibuster killed the Bill in Congress.

One of Harrison's first acts as President was to release millions of acres, once Indian land, in Oklahoma to thousands of new Americans from as far away as England, Wales, Greece, Poland, Italy and Russia. One hundred and sixty acres each was given away free for a minor financial registration requirement. So many came for this free land, that on February 10, 1890 a second parcel of Indian land had to be released to them by President Harrison. It is also hard to believe that this was only a little over one hundred years ago. It is also hard to understand Harrison's feelings as he gave away Indian land for practically nothing to non-American immigrants.

The day of celebration opened when a gunshot rang out signalling the opening of the Indian Territory to white settlement. At the sound of the gun 50,000 people are reputed to have set off on a journey westward to claim a share in the two million acres of land, later to be called Oklahoma. The ones who tried to beat the gun were staking illegal claims and were known as "Sooners". Six months later on November 2, 1889 two more States joined the Union - North Dakota and South Dakota. These were the first of six new States to join the Union under Benjamin Harrison's rule.

The flood of immigrants from Europe and the east coast was unstoppable and although the Indian was protected by the Dawes Act, they were the biggest losers because nobody seemed to care what the Indian wanted.

Still writing about the Indians, another incident concerning them took place when Harrison was President. They call it today "The Battle of Wounded Knee" which took place in 1890.

The Battle of Wounded Knee was a painful story of misunderstanding, accident and sheer murder that does no credit to the army. It seems after Sitting Bull was killed at Standing Rock, the last of the Indian Chiefs Big Foot, led a group of 100 men and 230 women and children across the frozen badlands. At the time, he was haemorrhaging blood from pneumonia. The 17th U.S. Cavalry came across them and took them prisoner. A young foolish brave "Black Coyote" objected to his gun being taken from him and in the struggle it went off killing the officer. All hell broke loose and about 300 of the 350 Indians, men women and children were killed. The newspapers praised the soldiers for their bravery and twenty of them received the Medal of Honour. Just what bravery was necessary, I don't know! Once more they had been "heroes in deeds of daring" wrote the Chicago Tribune. It is still known erroneously today as "The Battle of Wounded Knee".

Incidentally, the Indian did not become officially an American citizen until an Act of Congress bestowed it upon them in 1924.

There is a strange footnote to this story for in 1973 descendants of the Sioux of Wounded Knee protested at the loss of their lands by corruption in the Bureau of Indian Affairs. Up to 1973 dozens of murders had already taken place of FBI men and Indians. In this ongoing ancient dispute the fight by the American Indian Movement continued and a report was set out in a book called The Spirit of Crazy Horse which was then suppressed for six years.

But let's not get too far ahead of ourselves and return to the young Benjamin Harrison as he started up in business. Because of his deeply held religious convictions, the young Harrison considered becoming a Presbyterian Minister but like some other Presidents before him he renounced this role for a career in law. This was a good choice for Benjamin who was admitted to the Ohio Bar in 1854. He was then only twenty-one years old. He opened a law office in Indianapolis which wasn't too much of a surprise for Harrison's grandfather served there as the first Governor of Indian Territory, where he had also fought in the Battle of Tippecanoe.

Harrison consolidated his roots in Indiana by forming a partnership with William Wallace, whose father just happened to be the ex-Governor of Indiana and whose brother, Lew Wallace, was the writer of Ben Hur the film epic. The business prospered because Benjamin specialized in Indiana laws. Later he joined the Republican Party and very soon after that he was appointed Assistant City Attorney. He may not have become the finished article just yet but Benjamin Harrison's pedigree was slowly shaping up to be Presidential material.

Politics was in his blood now and he became immersed in the campaign to elect John Charles Fremont, the very theatrical Senator from California. The following year in 1857 when Harrison was still only twenty-four, he was elected City Attorney of Indianapolis. The graphs of his political and law careers rose in parallel and both seemed to have peaked in 1860 when he campaigned for Abraham Lincoln. Then came the Civil War.

He didn't enter the Civil War straight away but did so one year after it started. In 1862 he was commissioned as Colonel into the 70th Indiana Volunteer Infantry which he commanded.

Despite the time lapse of one year, the true patriotism of Harrison burned bright as he showed in his promise on July 9, 1862 "To raise a regiment, drill it and move to the front with a knapsack on my back and a musket in my hand." Harrison's thoughts on the battlefront in the Civil War reflect the thinking of many brave men in that terrible war. He wrote home to his wife on August 21, 1862 - "We are proud of Indiana and hope we make Indiana proud of us. I hope you all remember us at home and that many prayers go up to God daily for my Regiment and for me. Ask Him for me in prayer my dear wife." Harrison's letter home captured the spirit of the battlefield – the monotonous marching soldiers, the pungent smell of sulphur and the steady pom pom pom of the drummer boys. Still the memories of home were never very far away.

Here are some of the nostalgic homesick words he wrote on Christmas Eve 1862.... "And this is Christmas Eve and the dear little ones are about this time nestling their little heads upon the pillow filled with high expectations of what Santa Clause will bring them and Papa is not there. How sad and trying it is for me to be away at such a time as this. And yet I cannot allow my complaining spirit to possess me. There are tens of thousands of fathers separated like me from the dear ones at home battling with us for the preservation of our noble Government......."

Caroline Harrison, wife of Benjamin Harrison was not a very strong woman and later died of tuberculosis just at the end of Benjamin's first term. She is remembered for her decorations on the White House China collection.
Benjamin Harrison's "Bloody Shirt" speech in response to the taunts of the Democratic Party for waving it captures the passion and reverence he felt about the Civil War soldiers. He said "For I accept the banner of the bloody shirt. I am willing to take as our ensign the tattered worn out old grey shirt worn by some gallant hero stained with his blood as he gave his life for his country. We will bury the bloody shirt in the grave with the honoured corpse who wore it and not before........."

Harrison found it hard to forgive the failures of Reconstruction. Finally, on the Civil War and its aftermath, Harrison the speechmaker supreme had this to say in 1885 twenty-four years later. "If any prophet had arisen during the war and had predicted such a condition of things as we now see, he would have been stoned to death without the camp. No soldier would have credited a prophesy, which involved the placing of the rebel who was confronting him in battle, over the Pensions Office."

Harrison went on to distinguish himself with honour in the army, especially in the bloody Atlanta campaign under the command of General Sherman. He returned home to go into another battle on the political front against the Pro-Southern Democrats. Today we would call that a sabbatical from the army. He then returned to the army just as the war was coming to an end in 1864 and finally retired from the army with the rank of Brigadier General.

He returned once again to a blossoming law career in which he became famous for two well known court cases in one of which he was the defending Assistant U.S. Attorney. By now he was thirty-one years of age, with the proud distinction of a brilliant education, a famous law career and a successful army life plus the advantage of his family background. He was surely an ideal candidate for the Presidency.

It was inevitable that Harrison would find his way back to politics after his army career but it wasn't until 1881 at forty-eight years of age, that he became a Senator. In the Senate he fought on the side of Native Americans and Homesteaders against the might of the railroads. He also took a keen interest in Civil War veterans. His first appearance opposite the cream of U.S. politicians was when he met the great James G. Blaine, a heavyweight he was glad to campaign for in the Presidential Election of 1884 won by Grover Cleveland.

Benjamin Harrison had indeed arrived and what is more he had another nugget to add to those Presidential qualifications of his – he was born in Ohio! Yes, here was a descendant of a past President, with the support of Civil War veterans, a voting block from both Ohio and Indiana where he lived, was blessed with a brilliant legal mind and enjoyed superior political contacts in Washington, yet it took eight ballots to finally nominate him for President in 1888. Harrison's acceptance speech on July 4, 1888 was the usual masterpiece of simple eloquence recalling the beacons lit on the hills of history now known to all Americans. "The Republican Party has walked in the light of the Declaration of Independence. It has lifted the shaft of patriotism upon the foundations laid on Bunker Hill. It has made the more perfect Union secure by making all men free. Washington and Lincoln, Yorktown and Appomattox, the Declaration of Independence and the Proclamation of Emancipation are naturally and worthily associated in our thoughts today..... As soon as may be possible I shall by letter communicate to your chairman a more formal acceptance of the nomination."

Benjamin's life, despite his comfortable background was not without its tragedy. His wife Elizabeth suffered from all the horrors of tuberculosis while they lived in the White House, but that's a story for later.

Harrison although rising to great eminence in the legal world did not always own the trappings of success. In his early days work was very scarce when he wrote to his young wife of twelve months in September 1854. "You do not know how disheartened I feel sometimes at the prospect of sitting in my office for long months without getting anything to do. I would almost be willing to work for nothing just for the sake of being busy. Write often and let us know how you and the babe get along." Yes, that's how honest Harrison was. He told it as he saw it, without excuses.

It seems he was forever offending the family, for early in his political career he had abandoned the beliefs of the old world as enunciated by his father and grandfather by joining the Republican Party. He claimed to "Prefer the young Republican cult" of anti-slavery and temperance strain. Needless to say this shocked the family, especially when he spoke out against the "Slave Oligarchy and Slave Aristocracy". He wrote with great affection of Lincoln "The Rail-splitter Flatboat man and country lawyer born in a log cabin and reared among the unlettered...... so sure was he of his high purpose that he moved forward calmly to his appointed work not with show and brag, neither with shrinking." What a lovely tribute to a hero!

Well, that is the well signposted path that Benjamin Harrison had travelled up to the Presidential election of 1888. So far he had done everything right. His was a blue-print for the White House that defied opposition. In racing parlance, he had an impeccable pedigree, all he had to prove now was – could he win the race?

But what was Benjamin Harrison the man really like? Surely this was important to the voting public. Well, unfortunately he had a major personality defect for a politician – he could never make an outward show of his feelings – what he said he meant, and what he meant he said. Looking back today he seems to have been very badly misunderstood by many. For example,

Theodore Roosevelt who was a Republican was not too impressed by Benjamin Harrison and didn't pull any punches in this description of him. "He is a cold-blooded, narrow-minded, prejudiced, obstinate, timid, old psalm-singing Indianapolis Politician." Not very complimentary you will agree. Harrison also had another image problem to overcome for he was short, stocky, bearded and had cold humourless eyes. His aristocratic polish somehow added to the perception of a haughty aloof disposition. So here was a man blessed with all the political assets, but the subject of ridicule for all the wrong reasons.

Maybe Harrison was a product of his times when it was wrong to dance and even wrong to spend Sunday on anything but religious duties. Life was really a very serious business to him. Even four years in the army didn't change him. He was straight-laced, formal and reserved. Yet he could not resort to pretence to mask his formality but make no mistake he was a splendid type of American citizen. A friend tried to change him one day. General John C. New was sending him on his way at a railway station "Now Ben," he said, "I know you will capture them with your speech but for God's sake be a human being down there. Mix around a little with the boys after the meeting." Harrison met him on his return. "John, I tried it and failed," he said, "I'll never try it again, I must be myself." I think that story just about sums up Harrison the man.

However Harrison did have his sense of humour. Halford, his secretary and close friend, came back from London wearing English plaid clothes. At that time, Harrison was promoting trade protection for American made goods. "Halford," chuckled Harrison, "you can wear those clothes down here but if I wear them in Chicago at the Convention they'll beat me on the first ballot."
Perhaps what Harrison needed was a modern spin doctor, for even his pastimes of cigar smoking, billiards and duck shooting came under fire from a critical press who wrote "They were the hobbies of the 'well to do of the times." Actually his polish and sophistication were really part of his family upbringing. It didn't help when he went on a racoon shoot and ended up shooting a pig to the media's delight.

This idea of a spin doctor is not as far-fetched as it may seem. Far from being a new art form of today's media, back in 1888 it was very much alive and kicking as you will gather from the following piece of information.

In those days it was Matthew Stanley Quay who was looked to as the master strategist. A great reader of the classics, he still managed in the rarefied atmosphere of his reading room to plan the slaughter of his political enemies. He was known to hold a "Sunday morning school" made up of politicians and legislators from different sections of the State gathered for the purpose of discussing impending measures. Quay was asked to manage Harrison's first campaign and he agreed but with the stipulation that Harrison was to make no speeches. But, Harrison's speeches were so good Quay telegrammed him on the stump "Keep at it you're making votes." So what's new you may ask. History just doesn't change it only repeats itself.

As we saw under Grover Cleveland's first term as President, he had introduced lower tariffs to curtail the rising power of the railroads. Tariffs were still the political "hot potato" for debate in 1888. Nevertheless, it was Harrison who beat Cleveland by 233 electoral votes to 168. Yet Harrison was still a minority President, polling 100,000 votes less than his opponent, the sitting President Grover Cleveland who was destined to return to power again four years later in 1892.

Despite his success, Harrison was still being criticized on personal grounds. In political circles he was described as a human iceberg. Even his hand-shake was ridiculed as being "like a wilted petunia". Visitors were said to be fixed with a cold steely stare but those on the receiving end of this unfriendly treatment had the last say. When one visitor was told Harrison could not be seen he scoffed "My God has he got as small as that."

Some say this "personality iceberg" people met was the result of Harrison's legal training. An anecdote to prove what a cool customer he was is told as follows:-

In the final nail-biting hours of the voting for the Presidency early returns were not too encouraging. Harrison looked at the unsmiling faces around him and tried to lighten them up. "Cheer up everybody," he said. "This is no life and death affair. I am very happy here in Indianapolis and will continue to be if I'm not elected. Home is a pretty good place." He then went to bed. Next morning when asked by a friend why he had retired so early, Harrison reasoned it this way. "Well I knew that my staying up would not change the result if I were defeated, while if elected I had a hard day ahead of me. So I thought a night's rest was best in any event." It seems Harrison was elected President while he was fast asleep in bed and the celebrations put on hold. Can you believe it?

It is not until the second Monday of January following the election, that the President and the Vice President are formally elected by the Presidential electors of all the States gathered for the purpose. Harrison once again proved what a cool customer he could be. Some say it was his legalistic way of doing things that gave others the impression of a detached coldness in his approach. Harrison proved this by not accepting the assumption of being the President until after the formality of events on the second Monday in January. He took nothing for granted, not even the official poll result.

Now let's talk about Harrison's inauguration. Once again it is always a pleasure describing all the festivities of a Presidential inauguration with special thanks to that fantastic publication Presidential Fact Book written by Joseph Nathan Kane. Despite the pouring rain, Harrison rode in an open-topped carriage to attend his inauguration on March 4, 1889. Because of the inclement weather, the post parade fireworks had to be abandoned. It always amazes me when I read about the thousands of people who always turn up for this exciting event from all over the country. Twelve thousand people turned up for this one to be entertained by an orchestra of one hundred. Describing the food available will always be of interest to many. The hot food included bouillon in cups, steamed oysters, oysters A La Poulette, chicken croquets, sweetbread pate, Philadelphian style. The cold food included assorted rolls, sandwiches, lobster, salad and cold tongue en Bellevue. I'm not forgetting of course the usual breast of quail, assorted ice creams and fancy cakes, fruits and coffees. A one hour fireworks display to end the evening was held on the lawn of the White House but as I said earlier this had to be abandoned because of the bad weather.

Perhaps in the midst of so much celebration it seems churlish to mention Grover Cleveland who attended it. One cannot help but feel sorry for the man who was tasting his first defeat in public life. Observers noted just how little he tried to cover up his feeling of disappointment. But at least he turned up despite his downfall – something some other defeated Presidents had failed to do.

Harrison's inauguration speech reflected the deeply held convictions he had and the battles he had fought in Congress. He promised to enforce the Civil Service Law against the Spoils men, pledged social justice for all men, a free ballot for Negroes, and pensions for veterans. He was a great supporter of the Munroe Doctrine to protect the national honour of Americans everywhere, vowing non-interference in the affairs of foreign Governments and the arbitration of quarrels as a move towards world peace.

This speech was no coincidence for at a meeting he attended in Paris on July 4, 1899 he repeated his conviction that America had no commission to police the world. What a different way of thinking to 2006. However, Harrison was true to the promises of his inauguration speech and there were many war widows, veterans and their families throughout the length and breath of America who were deeply grateful for the doubled allowances he granted in the Dependent Pensions Act in 1890, two years into his Presidency. Even those disabled, not from the war, were looked after. Grants and allowances of various amounts went to their children, dependent parents, widows and veterans. It was a wonderfully generous gesture amounting to over $50 million extra added to the $81 million already being spent on them.

To consolidate his very caring Presidency, the Sherman Antitrust Act was passed by him to deal with the injustices perpetrated against the people by the power of large business corporations which were already getting out of hand. This was a powerful instrument in the hands of the 26th President Theodore Roosevelt. I wonder did Roosevelt appreciate Benjamin Harrison's wonderful gift to him.

The forming of the President's Cabinet can have a significant impact on his term of office ahead. In Harrison's case his selections were very controversial just like Grover Cleveland before him. First of all, he gave Party managers no say whatsoever. Age and experience is what he went for. Two became future Presidents, Theodore Roosevelt and Howard Taft. It also included the brilliant James G. Blaine. One disappointed candidate for Cabinet was spin doctor, Matt Quay whom he rejected. Quay later proved a spiteful adversary in blocking Harrison's attempt at re-nomination four years later. Party leaders looking for rewards were also to be a constant source of irritation. After his election victory, Harrison was heard giving praise to providence but the shady disgruntled Quay had his own ideas. "Providence hadn't a damn thing to do with it," he growled. "Harrison will never know how close a number of men were compelled to approach the penitentiary to make him President." To this day nobody seems to have challenged such an inflammatory statement.

A few entertaining anecdotes of life in Harrison's Presidency may intrigue the reader. It is a strange quirk of history that the flags which today hang in the schoolrooms of America are there because of a speech made by Harrison at the centennial anniversary of Washington's inauguration on April 30, 1889. The effect was nationwide. He is now called "The Centennial President". The celebrations for the centenary were held in New York City and colourful pageantry, parades and public speeches were a feature of them. Harrison landed in the city, just as Washington had done, from a barge rowed to shore at the same landing place. He stood where Washington had stood when Washington was inaugurated. He attended services at St. Paul's Chapel using Washington's pew and was able to address a big audience at the Metropolitan Opera House. It was here he made his "Flag" speech as follows – "But may I not ask you to carry these banners that now hang on the walls into the homes, into the public schools of your city and into all your great institutions where children are gathered and to drape them there that the eyes of the young and the old may look upon the flag as one of the familiar adornments of every American home."

Another anecdote concerns Halford, his secretary, who recounts an incident that reflected family life in the White House under Harrison. He said "In the afternoons when we would need the President's signature or have some information for him, we would often find him seated at the window of his sitting room reading. Opposite him would be Mrs. Harrison, engaged in decorating china. Often he would be reading aloud to her while she kept on with her painting." Yes, the White House did not change the family life of their Indiana home. Caroline his wife was a very sick woman at the time with tuberculosis. Sadly she never saw his term out, for two weeks before his Presidency ended she died. But he hurt his children later by marrying his first cousin, the niece of his wife. Her name was Mary Lord Dimmick, a widow who actually lived with the family and helped nurse his sick wife during her illness. His children objected to the relationship, for Mary was twenty-five years his junior. Just as Roosevelt had said, he could be very obstinate but eventually the couple went on to have a happy marriage.

Incidentally Harrison and his new wife were married at St. Thomas's Protestant Episcopal Church in New York City and later had a child named Elizabeth, born on February 21, 1897. This caused another rumpus in the family for Elizabeth was actually younger than four of Harrison's grandchildren and her father, now the ex-President, was sixty-three years old. I don't know if he ever made peace with his family for he was a strange enigma of a man, a rich public brilliance yet a wilting violet in private. I will try to explain that observation like this. A friend of his once said "He can make a speech to ten thousand people and everyone of them will go away his friend but let him meet the same ten thousand people in private and everyone will go away his enemy." Yes, his discomfort with people always puzzled his friends. Some said "He had a fine sense of humour but he kept it a carefully guarded secret."

One of the foremost commentators in the 1890s, Chauncey M. Depew in his book My memories of eighty Years claimed that in his opinion "Harrison was the profoundest lawyer ever at the head of any Government. He is considered among America's ablest Presidents. Harrison had an extreme distaste for what is called 'playing to the galleries'." "Wholesale indictments of his character were therefore unfair," wrote Henry L. Stoddard, the seasoned political journalist in his book As I Knew Them "Pretence," Stoddard said, "was something Harrison really detested." That secretary of Harrison we spoke about earlier, gives this pen picture of the man – "I think I have him sized up, when I see him in the morning and he greets me 'Halford, how are you today'?" I sit by his desk for a pleasant talk about matters. When he greets me with, "Good morning Mr. Halford", I bolt for the door and wait until after lunch for a talk." Harrison was a past master at the art of speech making, for he always seemed to have something worthwhile to say and knew how to say it.

Here is another example "A community where law is the rule of conduct and where courts not mobs execute its penalties is the only attractive field for business investments and honest labour." That particular speech reflected deeply his concern about the state of social unrest caused by working conditions and the workplace anger which festered at that time between the forces of labour and big business.

But you cannot please everyone all the time. Despite his very "hands on" approach in looking after the needs of the army veterans and workers rights in the Sherman Acts, he signed into law the McKinley Tariffs Act which was a highly controversial measure to protect trade. Tariff reformers never forgave him for that.

By the end of his Presidency, Harrison's enemies within the Party tried to block him from being re-nominated.

The violent Homestead Strike in which the company guards shot into picket line killing several workers added to Harrison's already full plate of woes.

But these were the times when the sleeping giants of American commerce were now immerging to the fear and disillusionment of many especially the poor. In the centenary celebrations of April 30, 1889 which went on for three days, the sermon of Henry Codman Potter, the Episcopalian Bishop of New York gave a grim warning to the representatives of big business in church that day.

The editor of The New York Times gave a wonderful pen picture of the body language of Harrison and the discomfort of big business people sitting beside him in the front row. The Bishop's sermon was a classic of its kind. Up to that point Harrison's eyes were wandering around the church but during the homily his eyes became riveted squarely on the Bishop for the rest of the sermon.

It is worth recording this historic sermon here as follows: "The growth of wealth, the prevalence of luxury, the massing of large material forces, which by their very existence are a standing menace to the freedom and integrity of the individual, the infinite swagger of our American speech and manners, mistaking bigness for greatness and sadly confounding gain and Godliness...... all this is a contrast to the austere simplicity, the unpurchaseable integrity of the first days and first men of our Republic."

It was a sermon that could strike a chord in any century and deserves to be honoured up there beside any of Harrison's classic speeches.

In forty years time that speech by Henry Codman Potter, the Episcopalian Bishop of New York which signalled the flaws and arrogance of the new ruling class proved disastrously right. In societies depths Codman Potter could see the seeds of its own destruction – The Wall Street Crash of 1933. Worst of all no one was listening.

The legal mind of Harrison however was keenly aware of this decay in American society and here is his verdict on big business of the late 19th Century.

If our corporations would more scrupulously observe their legal limitations and duties they would have less cause to complain of the lawful limitations of their rights or of violent interference with their operation. The society of the unemployed now holding its frequent and threatening parades in the streets of foreign cities should not be allowed to acquire an American domicile.

The later influences that were to engulf McKinley were already beginning to assert themselves with Benjamin Harrison.

One famous commentator made this amazing observation about the Presidency. It is the fascinating insight of J.L. Stoddard the most experienced political journalist of those times. "A gun is held at the head of every President metaphorically speaking from the moment he is elected. Every corporate or banking interest in New York City and Chicago, every railway system manoeuvre for the influence of 'a friend in court'," Stoddard said. "The first target was usually the Treasury Department. A close second came the State Department but the White House itself was always the main one. If the President is proving difficult he will find certain changes taking place in his power base. No threats are made, no open opposition is shown but suddenly the President finds the wheels are not turning. Any President who fights these pressure groups has a rough ride."

Harrison fought this invisible pressure group in a legalistic way or by ignoring anything that didn't come before him. Roosevelt, the next President after McKinley met the problem head on. His abrasive "up and at em" style brought him victory at the polls in 1904. Harrison's legalistic approach resulted in his defeat in 1892 brought about by elements within his own Party who resented his resistance to the big business bullies. Cleveland was considered a much safer pair of hands, an advantage which was to see him returned for a second term.

But no man confronted by the heartbreak of a terminally ill wife could have any desire for conflict. In fact Harrison was looking forward to going home to his beloved Indianapolis and to share the remaining hours that were ticking away for his beloved wife Caroline. A wish that time and God could never give him. As we said earlier Caroline died two weeks before the end of his Presidency.

After his defeat for the 24th Presidency Harrison returned to Indianapolis and resumed his law practice as an international lawyer.

When his Presidency ended and Caroline's final peace took place, the sun came out again for Benjamin Harrison. His retirement was quite a lucrative one, for in January 1898 he accepted Venezuela's request to act as Chief Counsel in the country's boundary dispute with British Guiana. A retainer of $20,000 was stipulated and a total fee of $100,000 was agreed. Incidentally his speech of summation for Venezuela was so impressive Counsel for the British resigned itself to its inevitable defeat as a result. His well-earned fee would be in the region of at least one million dollars in today's money. A stark contrast indeed to his early days starting out on his legal career with a wife of only twelve months and nothing to do but look out his office window and fret all day.

He also spent his retirement writing two books entitled This Country of Ours and Views of an Ex-President. He died of pneumonia on March 13, 1901 aged sixty-eight at his home in Indianapolis in the arms of his second wife, Mary. She was the niece of his first wife who married him despite the opposition of his family in 1896, three years after he retired. Right to the end Benjamin was unpredictable for a daughter was born to the couple on February 21, 1897. Benjamin was sixty-two years and 225 days at the time. This daughter Elizabeth died in 1955 in New York. Mary survived Benjamin by forty-six years and died aged eighty-nine in 1948.

Benjamin was buried in Crown Hill Cemetery, Indianapolis alongside his first wife, Mrs. Caroline Harrison. President McKinley headed the nation's mourners and Hoosier poet, James Whitcomb Riley, delivered the Eulogy.

22nd President & 24th President Grover Cleveland

"Veto President"
Born 1837
Died 1900
Age 63
2 terms
1885 – 1889: 1st term
Age 48
1893 – 1897: 2nd term
Age 56

Party: Democrat
Profession: Lawyer
County: New York
Ancestry: English/Irish
Estate: $250,000
Hobbies: Fishing.

Physical Description: 5 foot 11 inches, weight 260 lbs., corpulent, greying hair, going bald, heavy drooping moustache, short neck.

GROVER CLEVELAND 2ND TERM

The pinnacle of success in American politics is the ultimate crown of the Presidency. To achieve this award for a second time after four years out of office is something that is unique. It has never been won in this way by any President before or since. Twenty Presidents later it has still never been done and the statistics of modern politics in the 21st Century tell me it will never happen that way again.

But ask yourself this question. What makes a man subject himself to such a life of rigorous scrutiny for a second time, especially during the turbulence and drastic changes in society of the final years of the 19th Century? My only answer can be an unquenchable ambition and burning patriotism which hadn't been exhausted in his first term of office.

We must also remind ourselves of his last words to a butler when leaving office in 1889 – "We'll be back." You may also recall at this stage a very disappointed ex-President at Benjamin Harrison's inauguration party. He was very much a man with unfinished business on his mind.

Since then, Harrison had left office to retirement and the writing of his political memoirs Views Of An Ex-President and later to enjoy family life with his newborn child in 1897 at sixty-three years of age. But Grover Cleveland ploughed on, for he had no intention of changing his lifestyle. He was still the proverbial confrontational watchdog against all comers. His good ship Cleveland sailed on full tilt into the oncoming Depression of 1893 just as he took office.

The variety of problems he now took on was an indication of the changing role of the Presidency. One international event that came to his office to be solved was the annexation of Hawaii by a group of planters with the support of U.S. marines. Cleveland stepped into the controversy without hesitation to restore the Queen of Hawaii, Liliuokalani, to her throne.

It was an astute move that achieved peaceful reconciliation. Cleveland was very much aware of what a crucial position these islands held for the Asian markets. Trading ships of many nations stopped there. It was known as the crossroads of the Pacific. Cleveland's action came only two weeks before the end of his first term and soon after Hawaii declared itself a Republic. Sixty years later in 1959, she became the 50th State of America. We will cover the story of these Pacific islands under a later President.

Cleveland's second term was to prove a very rough ride indeed for him. Trouble lay ahead in the form of a financial crisis and Depression caused by the over-expansion of the railroad industry. Businesses failed and unemployment soared bringing poverty and suffering to many. This lead to a wealthy man called Jacob Coxey proposing a Public
Works programme to solve the crisis. He even marched with five hundred unemployed men on Washington to canvas Cleveland to support his plan but nothing came of it. In fact, poor Jacob Coxey was arrested for his trouble and charged with trespassing on the White House lawn.

The whole area of railroads in Cleveland's second term as President is worth explaining. They criss-crossed America and unfortunately were allowed to expand in a laissez faire atmosphere of non-Government intervention. The owners grew richer and developed vast financial empires on their investments while unfortunately greed and corruption engulfed them. Their freight rates became grossly excessive which penalized unfairly the farmers who used the railroads to get their goods to market.

But it wasn't only the railway companies who exploited their monopoly. William Jennings Bryan who was always worth listening to declared in 1896 "The East with its moneybags is the enemy of the country."

In this, the late 19th century, 3/5ths of the seventy-six million people living in America were scattered and isolated in towns, villages and farms with only dirt roads separating them and slow covered wagons the only lifeline between them. Into this scene came the railroads taking hogs and grain to the cities and returning with goods from the factories. Wherever they passed the village became a town or the town became a city. But the monopoly of the railways just bred arrogance. Grover Cleveland and his successors were now sitting on a simmering backlash against the naked power of these tycoons which manifested itself in the Chicago riots.

Grover was also coping with unrestricted immigration. New York of the 1890s had as many Irish as Dublin, as many Germans as Hamburg and half as many Italians as Naples. Fifteen million had arrived in the previous fifty years and twelve million were still to come in the following twenty years. The trouble was he also inherited the slums of Europe which came with them into New York and other cities. Sweatshops mushroomed where young girls worked for a few cents an hour. Sweatshops spawned by the corruption of an unscrupulous new America. Meanwhile, far away on the Plains of America an Indian nation was in its death throes. This will be the last we will write about this tragedy, so perhaps we should pay them the honour of remembering them for the last time.

Despite Cleveland's best efforts the Indian nation was in despair. Red Cloud, a Sioux Chief declared "They made us many promises more than I can remember but they never kept one: they promised to take our land and they took it." Chief Joseph said "You might as well expect the rivers to run backwards as that any man who was born a free man should be contented when penned up and denied liberty to go where he pleases."
Chief Gall went to Washington with twenty-one other chiefs in 1889 to discuss the division of their great Sioux Reservation into small farms for the Sioux families and white settlers. Chief Gull made this comment – "I went to your great city and saw many people. Some had fine clothes and diamonds; others were barefoot and ragged. No money to get something to eat. They are beggars and need your help more than the Indian does. I gave them the money you gave me. All people are alike among the Indians. We feed our poor."

Before we move on to the new vibrant emerging economic colossus that was America at the end of the 19th century, let us spare a last thought for the Indian as he disappeared into the pages of history in the Presidencies of Harrison, Cleveland and McKinley.

While Cleveland was busy in his fight against all the vested interests of big business that confronted him, he had to endure the loss of many political friendships. He knew he was confronting the same culture of ruthless arrogance that had sabotaged the efforts of Congress to reach a fair and honourable settlement with the Indian nation. The forces he now fought against were too powerful for his political friends who had no stomach for the fight and just faded away. It seemed the Indian nation was nothing more than the folklore of the Old West they had left behind.

But that they can never be. They were real people in 1889 when Grover Cleveland first took office. Both Cleveland and Harrison met the Chiefs and introduced them to the delights of American hospitality. They were promised 160 acres of their own tribal land, two cows, a yoke of oxen, seed for five acres and schooling for their children. They would become what the

Dawes Act envisaged, good Christian American citizens. Twelve million acres was to be given to them and the remaining nine million acres were to be sold at fifty cents an acre to white settlers. They were shown the delights of the National Zoo and even introduced to the new American discovery – the cigarette. This they enjoyed sitting around the hotel lobbies smoking from fancy cigarette holders.

Harrison on February 10, 1890 signed away the surplus land as North and South Dakota. Needless to say it was a disaster for the Sioux who knew little of farming. By the winter of 1890 – 1891 they had no food. The Shoshone Chief, Washakie expressed the disgust of the other nomadic Indians, who had given up their old hunting lifestyle to be farmers specialising in three words "God damn potatoes".

But the end was never nearer for the Sioux nation. Unrest was reported and Sitting Bull was blamed. His arrest was ordered and carried out by Indian police on December 15, 1890. It happened on the watch of Grover Cleveland who was still grappling in the White House with the forces of big business.

The Indian police came to Sitting Bull's cabin under the command of Lieutenant Bull Head and his aide Shave Head, followed by Sergeant Red Tomahawk. Sitting Bull's people were furious and "Catch the Bear" shot Bull Head in the side. Bull Head falling to the ground managed to shoot Sitting Bull in the chest, something General Custer and his men failed to do. Sergeant Tomahawk shot him in the back, and then murdered his seventeen year old son. Now there were four policemen and eight Sioux warriors lying dead on the ground. Sitting Bull's head was smashed in and he was scalped by the Indian police. Crazy Horse, one of the heroes of Little Big Horn was bayoneted by his guard. Another Indian, Chief Gall, who we read about earlier survived a bayonet thrust but died mysteriously later of "an overdose" of medicine.

The famous Geronimo, the last Apache Chief, survived until his old age. Subduing the Apaches took another twenty-five years until the Presidency of Woodrow Wilson in 1915. Geronimo eventually took to the hills but his followers gradually dwindled to 24 out of an original 6,000. He was pursued by 5,000 soldiers and even the Mexican Army to no avail. The Great Geronimo was finally persuaded to surrender on September 3, 1886 with the promise of a return to Arizona. But Arizona would not have him and he ended up in Fort Sill where he became a Sunday school teacher. He had one last day of glory in Teddy Roosevelt inauguration parade. Technically he was still a prisoner in Fort Sill where he died in 1909. The Indian wars ended with ignominy as we have described at the Battle of Wounded Knee in 1890. The heartbreaking story of the Indian comes to an end right here. And so we return to the second Presidential term of Grover Cleveland and the America of the 1890s with all its rampant capitalism, factory sweatshops, labour unrest, strikes, riots, private armies and greed.

Looking at this pen picture of Grover Cleveland's America just before the turn of the new century makes very depressing viewing. So powerful were the industrial tycoons they even hired private armies who fought pitched battles outside mines and factories against scabs and trade unionists drawn from the ranks of exploited immigrants. These were battles so violent; thousands of lives were lost during the fighting.

Knowing all this, it is easy to understand the confrontational style of Cleveland as a crusading President in a corrupt and gilded society spawned in the conditions that prevailed at that time. It is even easier to forgive Cleveland his numerous vetoes.

Unfortunately for Cleveland his abrasive "take no prisoners" style of rule lost him many political friends. Slowly they dropped away almost imperceptibly. Whether Grover realised this is not clear but the White House had become a very lonely place for him, as he watched his dwindling circle of political friends. This should never have happened for his own Democratic Party was in full control of the Executive Legislative and Judicial branches of the Government for the first time in fifty years. His personal habit of complaining of "The burden of office" didn't help. He moaned "I look upon the four years next to come as a self-inflicted penance for the good of my country. I see no pleasure in it." Looking at the Democratic Houses of Congress, Benjamin Harrison commented wryly "Perhaps he'll be able to break that team of wild horses to harness." Another commentator replied "He couldn't. They made ribbons of the harness and kicked the buggy into splinters." Poor Cleveland now without sympathy had finally isolated himself from his friends in Congress. But the fierce independence of the man was reflected in an amazing way, in an unbelievable event in his life when he went missing from Congress without an explanation to anyone. He was on "The Oneida", the yacht of a friend, which was anchored in the Hudson River. It wasn't until twelve months later that he revealed his secret operation for cancer in the roof of his mouth carried out on board that boat. He arrived back in Congress with an artificial jaw made of vulcanized rubber.

Only when he had sufficiently recovered did he address Congress. No one even guessed at the personal suffering he had undergone from July 1 to August 17 – in secret. It was a wonderful act of bravery from a man who found it so easy to complain publicly about the discomfort of his job yet suffered his own personal disaster in silence. It seems he shared this frightening experience with only his closest friends. Knowing his caution with the press perhaps it reflects even more tellingly his total lack of trust in journalists.

Another example of Cleveland's maverick tendency to go it alone without consultation can be seen in his decision to send in Federal troops from Fort Sheridan to Chicago on July 4, 1894 to break up a strike at the Pullman Car Company. Sadly his pursuit of the powerbrokers only seemed to alienate him from Congress as vote after vote went against him. Congress even went on holidays at Christmas in defiance of his plea to stay on and support him. As President he could never manage to dominate and never learned to persuade.

Yes, I'm afraid Grover was not a happy man in his second term. They were years of unending heartbreak and humiliation. But still he continued the unequal fight between himself and his Party leaders looking forward to the day when his Party's rival would succeed him. By now the Democratic Party had deserted him completely.

It is significant to read his quote on leaving the White House in 1897 ... "I am tired of abuse. I am going to know now how it feels to be really a sovereign for that is what every American citizen is."

I can't help being aware of how often the President has been abandoned or attacked to the borderline of impeachment. Perhaps Presidential scholars can explain this phenomenon. Deep down inside me one question troubles me sometimes. Is the Presidency too powerful for one man?

One Senator was worried about it.

This one lesson Grover Cleveland never learned was highlighted by Senator James A. Reed of Missouri, when he said "The most dangerous trend today is the custom of omnipotence about the Chief Executive whatever his Party."

Another quote from another distinguished commentator is very interesting. He said "The President should not be the Tsar of his Party but the product of his Party placed in the White

House to carry out what Congress, representing the people directs. Any President who runs counter to the wishes of his Party is doomed to disappointment and is fortunate to escape disgrace." That was the observation of none other than the great James Blaine. He was talking about Andrew Johnson in his book Twenty Years Of Congress. So the lessons of history were there for all to see if only Grover Cleveland had bothered to learn from them. Sadly, he didn't!

By now Cleveland's time in office was running out and his love affair with the Democratic Party was over. The Party nominated Nebraska Congressman and journalist, William Jennings Bryan for President, but despite the brilliance of Jennings Bryan he failed at the ballot box. Cleveland stepped back from the election and Ohio Congressman, the Republican William McKinley, easily won the prize by 271 electoral votes to 149 for William Jennings Bryan.

Grover Cleveland retired to a new house he had bought in Princeton, New Jersey on an estate he called "Westland" and found time to become a member of the Anti-Imperialist League. However, when talk of a third term was in the air, Cleveland showed no interest and devoted his time to his book Presidential Problems a defence of his two Presidential terms.

Just some final words to bring the fascinating story of Grover Cleveland to a conclusion -

Grover spent some time as Trustee of Princeton University where he shared a deep and lasting friendship with the great Woodrow Wilson, who was Princeton's President at the time.

While on the subject of Wilson, let us note something he said about Cleveland's Presidencies. His verdict was summed up in the following words. "Having observed the Presidencies of Johnston, Grant, Hayes, Garfield and Arthur, I felt there was no hope for the office." Later he changed his mind and said "Having lived through Grover Cleveland's two terms, Cleveland was the only President between 1865 and 1898 who played a leading and decisive part in the quiet drama of our national life." Some praise indeed.

Grover Cleveland lived for about twelve years after he finally retired from office. On June 24, 1908 he passed away aged seventy years, after an illness lasting three months. He died at his home in Princeton and was buried in Princeton Cemetery.

His last words were "I have tried so hard to do right." I guess that just about sums up the controversial life of an honest, brave and courageous 22nd and 24th President of the United States.

25th President   William McKinley

"Napoleon of Protection"
Born 1843
Died 1901
58 Years of age
1st Term
1897 – 1901
Age 54
2nd Term
1901: March – September
Age 58

Party: Republican
Profession: Lawyer
County: Ohio
Ancestry: Scotch-Irish
Value of Estate: $215,000
Hobbies: Riding

Physical Description: 5 foot 7inches, high forehead, receding hair line, prominent chin, broad forehead.

Significant Extract from his Inauguration Speech:
"Most of our financial laws are the outgrowth of experience and trial and should not be amended without investigation and demonstration of the wisdom of the proposed changes."

WILLIAM McKINLEY

William McKinley was the third of four Presidents to be assassinated, the others being Lincoln, Garfield and Kennedy. All of them were murdered by someone whose insignificance was only matched by the enormity of their crime. In fact, they were political nobodies whose names were almost unpronounceable and easily forgotten. No link could be made to any political or social grouping. They belonged to no association big enough to set in place such an awesome act. So, how could one individual be so angry, so bitter, so disenfranchised or so badly treated by society to be driven to such an act of finality regardless of the consequences to himself?

I'm afraid these are questions that have never been fully explained. Perhaps the seeds were sown by the condition of society at the time. Perhaps by the stark contrast between rich and poor. Or the arrogance and indifference of the power brokers who flaunted their wealth and privilege so ostentatiously they unsettled a happy contented people. Were these power brokers a nation within a nation who lived by a different Constitution and a different code of ethics than the ones our Founding Fathers handed down to us in a golden bygone age? Perhaps the story of McKinley may give us the answers.

Morton Keller in his essay on William McKinley in that brilliant book To the Best of My Ability about the U.S. Presidents posed a possible solution for us. He wrote "Political enemies accused McKinley of passivity and lack of purpose – of being a puppet of Ohio businessman, Marcus A. Hanna". Hanna was the spin doctor or King-maker of the late 19th century who is reputed to have made or broken politicians by his political insight and manipulations. John Hay, Lincoln's Private Secretary made this observation of Hanna "There are those who think Mark Hanna will ruin William McKinley."
McKinley was a typical product of those fertile turbulent years in the 1890s. He was described by his colleagues as a Christian gentleman. He dressed formally and had a friendly sunny disposition.

Like most of the Presidents in the 1890s he had a Civil War army record and was promoted at the age of twenty-two to Brevet Major, on the army staff of ex-President Rutherford B. Hayes. This of course was one of the assets necessary for the Presidency, a distinguished army career. He was also born and bred in Ohio – another political plus.

Looking back now, the America of the history books in the reign of Rutherford Hayes, Grover Cleveland and William McKinley must have seemed a million years away from the society of the planters, the age of Jefferson and the world of George Washington. The intellectuals like Adams and Madison and the casual laid back lifestyle of small town America was truly a golden age full of nostalgia. The speed and greed of the new society that now straddled the 19th and 20th century changed everything forever. It can best be described as the dramatically changing face of the New America. Expanding businesses, railroads that reached from the Atlantic to the Pacific, and most of all the industrial revolutions; massive wealth, the new inventions like telephones and skyscrapers, the moving masses westward and sadly the exploitation of the new poor. Life was all about the hopes and ambitions of millions searching for their own particular dream. At the head of it all was William McKinley as he led America into the turbulence of a new age at the start of the 20th century.

Way out West, the population on the plains tripled between 1870 and 1900. Compared to the luxury lifestyles of the tycoons and industrial barons in the East, life on the Plains to the West was harsh and friendless. Wood was scarce for building houses and farmers had to make do with prairie sods as building blocks. Cloth hung over the windows which very seldom had glass. Outside the weather was harsh and unfriendly. Summer temperatures reached 110 degrees for weeks on end.

In winter, savage storms swept the open plains with perpetual winds that howled across wide open prairies as far as the eye could see. Fearsome rain came down in a deluge and grasshoppers blocked out the sun, eating everything in sight.

With the coming of technology, huge farms financed by outside capital hired armies of workers, brought in machinery and planted the soil on a colossal scale. But drought between 1885 and 1900 destroyed everything. Discontent grew as the farming boom collapsed. Further droughts followed and thousands of farmers were wiped out. The farmers grew restless and angry especially as railroad rates spiraled. There was now, as one commentator remarked "A sullen rebellion against God and the Government." The Government of course was headed by William McKinley. As the Indians were driven westward into smaller and smaller Reservations, land West of the Mississippi and on to the Pacific became the bread basket of the nation and exports of surpluses boomed. Yes the West became a powerful influence in the making of America in 1900s.

This was indeed the golden age of plenty which McKinley inherited. It was also the age of the elevator, the typewriter, linoleum and the first penny farthing bicycle. America now had a manufacturing output that exceeded that of Great Britain, France and Germany combined. The one flaw in all of this was the reluctance of the U.S. Government to rein back the run-away horse, by leaving the necessary regulation of industry to another day. In this climate railroads boomed from 35,000 miles after the Civil War to 254,000 in 1916 -fifty years later. Up to now America had lived in isolation from world affairs. Soon it was to emerge as one of the foremost powers of world politics.

Although extremely popular, McKinley was a weak President in comparison to Governor Cleveland. He refused to declare war on Spain to liberate Cuba, but when the war was inevitable he did nothing to prevent it.

At home his farmers and labourers were being victimized by big business men with their fast growing economic muscle. But let's start at the beginning. William McKinley was the seventh of nine children born in a town called Niles on January 29, 1843 to William and Nancy Allison McKinley who were of Scottish-Irish descent. Both his grandfathers fought in Washington's Revolution between 1775 and 1783 after which his paternal grandfather opened a pig iron foundry in Niles, Ohio. When William was nine he moved with his mother to a place called Poland, Ohio. His father stayed for a few years to manage the foundry where William went to his first school, a private one in Poland. He studied there for eight years. "A quiet and unassuming lad with a gift for public speaking" is how he was described by his mother who, being his constant companion became a great influence in his life demanding high moral standards of him. Her basic belief was that wealth was a reward for virtue, and poverty was a punishment for sloth. Nancy had high expectations for young William hoping he would one day become a Methodist Minister, an ambition I'm afraid she was destined never to achieve.

The Civil War broke out in 1861 when young William was only eighteen, but his age didn't deter him from enlisting in the 23rd Ohio Volunteer Infantry.

While in the army his path crossed with the illustrious Major Rutherford B. Hayes, the future President of the United Stated. His regiment was then sent to Western Virginia to fight a cluster of small Confederate units, and it was here he met with Rutherford B. Hayes again when Hayes promoted him to Commissary Sergeant for his bravery under fire. But McKinley's talents as a soldier were once again being talked about when he drove a mule train loaded with meat and coffee through enemy fire direct to the front line troops. Hayes was so impressed with McKinley he immediately promoted him to second Lieutenant and installed him as an Aide on his own staff. In 1865 after the war McKinley left the army with the rank of Major, a title he was proud to hold into civilian life.

Back in Ohio, William entered the law office of County Judge Charles E. Glidden of Youngstown. The following year he attended law school in Albany, New York and within another year he was admitted into law practice in Canton, Ohio. Despite his average success as a lawyer he soon became prominent in civic affairs in Canton.

McKinley was quite a popular personality and soon came to the notice of another Canton citizen, the daughter of a wealthy business man. Her name was Ida Saxton and very soon wedding bells were ringing for both of them. They had two daughters but one died when she was only five months old, the effect of which brought a mental breakdown to poor Ida. But the family tragedy was not to end there, for their second daughter also died. This tiny tot died of typhoid fever, a set back from which Mrs. McKinley never recovered, leaving her susceptible to bouts of mental depression and epileptic seizures for the rest of her life.

But despite the sadness in his life McKinley pressed on and soon became prosecuting Attorney for Stark County. By now he had also joined the Republican Party. His parallel career with the life of Rutherford Hayes continued and in the year of Hayes's election to President, McKinley became a Congressman. By now McKinley had become a very formidable public speaker.
Unlike the Democrats, the Republicans were great supporters of high tariffs, the theory being such tariffs protected U.S. business from foreign competition by increasing the cost of imported goods. But the other side of the same coin meant that the poor agricultural community in the West had to pay dearer for badly needed clothes and other foreign necessities. They also paid more for their farm goods which was passed on to the cost of food in higher prices. In short they were importing inflation. McKinley believed in the laissez-faire approach which promoted the minimum of Government intervention in business. Later his "McKinley Tariffs Act" imposed the highest ever known taxes on imported goods which was like using petrol instead of water to douse the embers of a Forest fire. Yet economic history has a way of fooling even the experts because America's foreign policy of expansion overseas in later years required caution in the market place especially in the use of tariffs.

Now a new phenomenon was born which was to haunt politics for years to come – the political sponsor or spin doctor. We are quite used to it in our politics today but the idea of subsidizing top politicians in the hope of hijacking their very own President and thus become the power behind the throne, was a new one in those days. In fact it was a well known fact that an industrialist named Marcus Alonzo Hanna helped to have McKinley elected to the Governorship of Ohio in 1891 and 1893, a very prestigious prize indeed.

He also threw his weight behind McKinley's bid for the Presidential nomination in 1889, but when Benjamin Harrison's victory looked assured they both gave their support to Harrison instead.

History speaks a lot about this man Mark Hanna, as the shadowy figure and President-maker hovering around William McKinley, but let's get it clear who this man really was.

First of all he was a long time friend of the President before McKinley came to the White House. He wanted no Cabinet portfolio and never hid the fact he was first and foremost a businessman. He sought no office or title, just to be a plain citizen and friend of the President. This was Hanna's intention, and to Hanna there was no ambiguity. But McKinley was worried. He was long enough in politics to know there could be no overlord and only one President in the White House.

"It would never do Mark. You know everybody would be running to you before or after seeing me," McKinley told him. "You owe it to me to come to Washington with a title to office or not at all." The solution was to persuade John Sherman to resign as Senator for the job of Secretary of State, thus allowing Hanna to take Sherman's title as Senator. Hanna would then be in Washington in his own right and not as Presidential spokesman, a role McKinley was anxious to distance both of them from. So McKinley was seen to have nobody else controlling him. Only once was Hanna disappointed with McKinley's reading of the situation when McKinley would not recommend Hanna for the Vice Presidency, but here-in lies a fascinating story.

There had been an amazing reluctance by the eligible candidates to become Vice President. Even Teddy Roosevelt tried to dodge the nomination. He eventually agreed and thus became the 26th President of the United States after McKinley's assassination. It is now mind-boggling to realize what all the reluctant suitors for the Vice Presidency never seemed to contemplate. History could well be different today and Hanna could well have been the 26th President and not Teddy Roosevelt, had McKinley nominated Hanna as the Vice President.

Another major problem surfaced when McKinley became responsible for a friend's debts of $130,000 relating to bank notes McKinley had endorsed. McKinley's political career was gravely in doubt but once again Hanna and his rich friends came to his rescue. Meanwhile, McKinley was busy making over 370 speeches throughout America and was becoming the leading Republican candidate for the next Presidential election. Again Hanna came to his aid by leaving his business to canvass for him. The Eastern industrialists they say were not too happy with McKinley's selection as candidate for the Republicans because McKinley was really unknown to them. Furthermore they were now getting used to controlling the candidates of either Party. Then William Jennings Bryan emerged from the Democrats to oppose McKinley, giving fiery passionate speeches against the wealth and political privilege enjoyed by big business in its dealings with the Government.

Big industrial barons were frightened by Bryan's speeches which caused $3.5 million; some say $16 million to be suddenly injected into the Republican Party funds. Pamphlets, posters and speechmakers were found in abundance throughout the country. Bryan's politics was labeled "A social rebellion of fanatics" hell-bent on destroying the Government. Even factory managers joined the slanderers with unfounded accusations and scare tactics that warned of Depression and job losses to follow the victory of William Jennings Bryan. The outcome was a win for McKinley by 271 electoral votes to 176. Not since Munroe's Presidency was there such an air of good feeling. Conducting his electioneering from his own home was a masterstroke. His "front porch" politics, receiving over 100,000 visitors to his front garden, had paid off. They say this 1896 election was the first modern Presidential election in America.

On the train from Canton to Washington for the inauguration Mrs. McKinley, William's mother, had some simple homespun advice to give to her son in the midst of all this praise. Asked by some reporters what she prayed for, her answer was simple. "I pray to God to keep my boy humble."

So who was this man chosen to be part of American royalty in the history books of the future?

McKinley was unique in his memory for names and faces. When George B. Cortelyn, his close confidant was asked for McKinley's major strength, he unhesitatingly used one word "Courage". He was known to resist pressure from Cabinet on committees in situations the public never even heard about although he was no intellectual giant. Perhaps he was the prototype of Tom Reed's idea of a President, "A man representing the average of Party opinion." "The average man was always a safer selection," Reid said. McKinley had no soaring ambitions and his meekness was often mistaken for weakness. But when principles were at stake he could be as tough as steel. During his fourteen years in Congress he was someone who preferred to please rather than displease, to help rather than hinder, to smile rather than frown. But when it came to persuasive debate he had no equal in presenting statistics in an interesting way.

His inauguration was celebrated on Thursday March 4, 1897 on the East Portico of the White House. The oath was administered by Chief Justice Melville Weston Fuller on a mild day that promised an early spring and followed by the usual razzamatazz of pure spectacle in the military march past.

Ida Sexton, McKinley's invalid wife, because of the state of her health was now entering on a harsh demanding role as First Lady, which would one day end in a personal nightmare. But that story is for later.

At the inauguration ceremony Ida was elegantly dressed in stylish royal blue velvet, sealskin cape, and black bonnet edged in white. Her face in contrast was a pallid white and her unsteady steps revealed the fact that here was a very sick woman indeed.

Later at the ball she was resplendent in a silver and blue dress, diamonds, a lace face fan and a cape richly trimmed in white fox fur. A quick turn around the dance floor on the arm of the President, then into the supper and out of sight for the rest of the celebrations. Mrs. Garrett Hobart, wife of the Vice President substituted for the First Lady.

At formal receptions later Mrs. Hobart met the guests instead of Ida who always sat quietly in a blue chair while her husband eased the visitors wide of her, gently and diplomatically.

Lest she catch cold Ida always travelled in a closed carriage and lived with closed windows in stuffy rooms. But despite Mrs. McKinley's ill health, life was quite pleasant in the White House.

The McKinley's loved to surround themselves with flowers as well as children and spent some time in the conservatories at the side of the White House. Among the vines and tropical foliage, orange trees and even pineapples there were also the rare orchids introduced by Mrs. Garfield. The gardeners were always encouraged to fresh efforts and inventions and of course there were also the various receptions to cater for. The Diplomatic Corp, the Cabinet, the Supreme Court and the army and Navy receptions were the main ones. It was a hard job keeping the guest list down to 9,000 at a time and there were always howls of protest from those left out. Explanations were useless. Gatecrashers were monitored by "spotters" since the President flatly refused the use of admission cards. Bringing along relatives and friends also complicated the job of the "spotters" and caused some confusion.

Unfortunately the size of the guest list sometimes forced the banquet to be held in the main corridor which was subject to a gale whenever the front door was opened.
Yet some people who attended these receptions were not too impressed. Some top people were not too complimentary describing the Washington dinners as horrible. One such guest,

John D. Long groaned "Language cannot express the reluctance with which I stretch myself out on the altar of these sacrifices; the same food, the same dishes, the same waiters, the same courses, the same long hours, the same men and women, exactly the same conversation; the same everything!" But the Washington season was definitely enjoyed to the full by the First Lady, Ida McKinley, despite her frail health.

One significant record to note was the tendency in those times for a candidate from Ohio to be elected President. Six of the seven Republican Presidents elected between 1876 and 1920 were from Ohio. Perhaps this was because it had a population that blended the cultures of the East/South and Mid-West, having a rich mixture of agriculture, mining, manufacturing and retail businesses. To become Governor of Ohio was a great political plus and McKinley was lucky enough to be made Governor of Ohio twice. Another significant factor in his election to the Presidency was his easygoing, friendly personality and his moral code of honour based on his Methodist faith and a certain public sympathy for his unfortunate epileptic wife. People accepted him as a "Christian Gentleman". There were two theories about McKinley. Some saw him as a passive puppet of businessman Marcus A. Hanna. Others thought his mild passivity was a mask for political cunning. Both observations were hard to prove.

Life as President was without incident for the next two years, until McKinley found himself in the middle of an international crisis which some people say changed the course of American history forever. Cuban revolutionaries had brought it about in their struggle of many years fighting. At first McKinley resisted getting involved in Cuban independence, saying "I have been through one war, I have seen bodies pile up and I do not want to see another." McKinley did however send one battleship "The Maine" to evacuate American citizens but it was thought to have been blown up in Havana Harbour.
The outcry that followed through the newspaper headlines, especially in New York, forced McKinley's hand to avenge the deaths of 260 sailors. It is worth recording here that in 1976 a scientific investigation came to the conclusion that it was not the Spanish who were responsible for the sinking of the Maine, but spontaneous combustion in a coal bunker aboard the Maine. However, McKinley was stampeded into declaring war on the Spanish on April 25, 1898 and so ended American indifference. Always the religious moralist McKinley justified the war as "A righteous crusade."

Yet with one eye on his new American empire, he proclaimed "We are conducting a war and until it's conclusion we must keep all we get. When the war is over we must keep what we want." Trade he knew would follow the flag, consequently at the outbreak of the war with Spain; Commodore George Dewey sailed into Manila Bay, sunk the only ten ships available to Spain's Pacific fleet and captured the Philippines.

Incidentally, the future President of the U.S. Theodore Roosevelt was at that time Secretary of the Navy. More of that later.

McKinley then dispatched 11,000 troops and on August 13, they captured Manila. To be fair to McKinley, he had now inherited the brand new political philosophy in that time of acquiring empire colonies and expanding westward in the 1900s. The pressure for further markets had now become serious. In 1870 exports had amounted to $393 million. Now in 1900 it had reached $1400 million. There was a worldwide hunger even by the European powers to acquire new colonies and so there was a worldwide hunt for new territories.

The change in political thought did not bypass McKinley and he too could not resist the call for westward expansion into the Pacific Ocean to capture the markets of South Africa and Asia that were needed to fuel America's growing productivity. Now I must rely on the historians. According to them the Spanish-American War was deeply significant to McKinley because America emerged from it with her first colonies. Spain not only gave independence to Cuba but also ceded Puerto Rico and the Pacific Island of Guam to the U.S. and handed over Manila to complete the package. Bizarre as it may sound; of the 5,000 casualties in the war 4,600 were caused by yellow fever and typhoid. Finally McKinley had no alternative but to annex the Philippines.

The war with the Philippines ended with the Diplomats meeting in Paris to discuss a peace treaty. This resulted in America taking on a new role in world politics. On December 10, 1898 the Treaty of Paris was signed and not only did it declare America the victor but in the negotiations, America acquired the Philippine Islands of the South Pacific which it was claimed Spain could not afford to administer themselves. Spain passed them to American control for the payment to Spain of twenty million dollars. America was now an imperial power with its own colonies spread far into the Pacific Ocean. But McKinley had also inherited trouble in the rebellious Filipinos and a three year guerilla war followed costing 4,300 American lives and 57,000 Filipino lives at a financial cost of $175 million. An outrageously expensive price to pay for bigger markets.

Sadly, as in all such wars, the consequences were just as happened in Vietnam fifty years later. The people became the enemy, when whole villages were burned and its inhabitants killed in the guerilla warfare that followed the occupation by the Americans. Samoa was next and resulted in Pago Pago becoming an excellent naval base for America. Hawaii too was annexed but Grover Cleveland, the successor to McKinley, blocked it as being dishonourable. Well, I am no historian so if you disagree with all the foregoing perhaps you should take it up with the academics. Nevertheless I hope you have tasted the impact of war on the White House in 1900 despite McKinley's abhorrence of war.

But let us pause for a while and hear the inner thoughts of McKinley when he openly confessed afterwards his reasons for keeping the Philippines.

Charles S. Olcott in his Life of McKinley recalls this scene with a committee of Methodist Ministers who had called to pay their respects. As they were leaving the White House McKinley said, "Hold a minute longer I would like to say a word about the Filipinos." He continued as follows – "When I realized the Filipinos had dropped into our laps I confess I did not know what to do with them. I sought counsel from all sides, Democrats as well as Republicans, but got little help." He then made an amazing confession. "I dropped to my knees and prayed so worried was I." He remained untouched by divine inspiration for here is how he came to his decision to hold the islands. "In summary, they fall into four main categories - (1) To give them back to Spain would be cowardly and dishonourable. (2) Turning them over to France or Germany would be discreditable as they were our commercial rivals. (3) They could not be left to themselves as they would be subject to anarchy and misrule even worse than under Spanish rule. (4) I was left now with only one alternative – to take them over, educate, civilize and Christianize them." A bit like Iraq today, 2006, would you say? Does history ever change?

But let's return to Paris and the Peace Treaty. On the Saturday night, before the signing of the Treaty, fighting broke out between American troops and Filipino insurgents demanding immediate independence, this time from America. It was a unique historical event in McKinley's Presidency for the guerrilla war that followed was the first conflict with a colony but this time America was the occupying Empire. I wonder what Washington felt?

However, as McKinley promised, and to America's credit, he introduced sweeping infrastructural changes throughout the Philippines. He reformed the Judiciary, built schools, roads and bridges, re-constructed the tax system and instituted widespread vaccination programmes. Yet it was not until 1946 that the Philippines finally gained their independence – a good forty-six years later.

Incidentally, the Spanish-American war, which lead to America's new Empire status reflected quite badly on McKinley's troops. While it proved America could not be trifled with as a world power, the war exposed the soft underbelly of a run-down U.S. army which was grossly under-prepared for the fighting. Its behaviour was characterized by clumsy bungling inefficiency. Food and clothing, medical care and sanitation were so inadequate; for every soldier who died in battle ten died in hospital of disease. The word Empire also did not sit easily on the conscience of a nation who in 1776 had fought as a colony against the British Empire.

One final word on this episode in McKinley's Presidency. The war changed the American Presidency forever. The once modest clerical staff in the White House mushroomed from six to eighty people and overnight it became the new White House press corps we know today, because the President was now leader not only of America but of a new Empire. His economic policy of isolationism and protectionism was now no more. The U.S. was now part of the global markets of world trade and expressionism was the name of the game. The two words "global markets" are now in everyday use today – 2009.

The road to his second term in the White House was now that much easier. A weaker Williams Jennings Bryan, more Hanna money and his own pleasant personality gave McKinley victory by 292 electoral votes to 155. "Prosperity and Empire" was the new mantra and flush with victory, McKinley made preparations for a triumphant tour of the West in September 1901.

William McKinley was now on a roll. As head of an imperial power for the first time and being on the doorstep of China, America was now also an Asian power.

By way of postscript, the Philippine Islands proved invaluable in the Second World War as America's front line of defence against the Japanese.

However, to be fair to McKinley, he resisted much well-meaning pressure to annex the whole archipelago, an idea vigorously presented by both Parties, Republicans and Democrats in Congress.

Spurious reasons were put forward, one by the churches who were madly enthusiastic about converting these "heathens" in the Pacific – even against their will.

Another excuse for the takeover was to protect the Filipinos from the mis-rule of the Spanish. But the expansion of world trade was the real catalyst. Introducing history into our Presidential story is fraught with the danger of getting it all wrong as an amateur historian. However, this time it was worth the risk to try to explain the sort of complicated world of international politics and business surrounding McKinley. Unfortunately, this was the sort of world which would one day turn vicious and violent, releasing sinister forces into his path in the year 1901.

But before we deal with these coming tragic events, let us take a look at the America I'm talking about in the early years of the new century – a world McKinley tried so hard to understand.

The change McKinley had to contend with was exponential. Historic events were exciting everyone, only this time they were not political events. Henry Ford created his first four horsepower car. Two bicycle mechanics, Wilbur and Orville Wright, were on the brink of conquering air flight with their new invention.

Mass production which was aimed at producing vast quantities of goods at rock bottom prices was the new innovation in the workplace. Assembly lines manned by thousands of workers under one roof was never heard of before. Mass production of automobiles came on stream in the early years of the new century with the founding of the new Ford Motor Company. Ford even raced his own cars, setting a land speed record of ninety miles per hour. The small unit profit and large sales triggered a financial bonanza of multimillion dollars for Ford.

It was called "The progressive era" but factory conditions spawned hardship, boredom and danger. Yes, times were changing rapidly during the Presidency of McKinley. It was a time of great ideas fermented in the fields of law, economics, sociology, psychology and science. "Pragmatism" was the new buzz word. Man was master of his own destiny, so outdated practices were challenged where they stood in the way of "progress". Factory legislation was introduced to protect the workers from overwork or unhealthy work practices and places. A whole new way of life was emerging in which the greed of the few was on a constant collision course with the rights of the many. Yes, they were indeed exciting times which were developed still further under later Presidents. To many historians, this became known as "The Gilded Age".

But the darker forces of fate were creeping up on William McKinley in a way he never expected in the midst of such prosperity and plenty.

It was while he was visiting a Pan American Exposition in Buffalo that time stood still for the American people, when he was gunned down by an assassin's bullet. He was the third U.S President to suffer such a tragedy at that time. Lincoln and Garfield were the other two. Kennedy came later.

The name of the assassin was Leon Czolgosz, a twenty-eight year old unemployed anarchist. McKinley was talking to the mill workers at the fair when the assassin struck. One bullet grazed his ribs but a second bullet fired from point blank range entered his stomach, and later killed him. Czolgosz was almost murdered by the crowd but he was saved by McKinley's cry of "Don't let them hurt him." McKinley was operated on in a Buffalo Hospital but gangrene set in and eight days later he was dead. Theodore Roosevelt the Vice President was then sworn in on September 14, 1901. Yes, the corrupt society of the Gilded Age had extracted a terrible price for its indifference to the disintegrating standards of fair play and decency once common in America's illustrious past.

Let us pause events here and look back on American history that led up to this terrible crime. The Doctrine of "Manifest Destiny" which had been used in other circumstances to justify America's march into the West over the villages tribes and homesteads of its true owners, the Native American Indian, was now being used to continue this march westwards beyond the shorelines of America. The march westward no longer stopped at the Pacific but continued onwards to colonize the Midway Islands and beyond until it consumed fifty Island outposts in the prairie-like seas of the Philippines.

It was hard to believe in the euphoria of these wonderful times that McKinley's life was now in danger. The sickly taste of power and prosperity had dulled the conscience of a nation into thinking that it was in charge of its own destiny.

But in the undergrowth of this business jungle, evil forces were at work which leads us to a man called Leon F. Czolgosz, the "ASSASSIN".

He enters the picture now on August 31, 1901 when he booked into J. Nowak's saloon hotel on the east side of Buffalo. He posed as a tourist attending the Pan American Exposition, a glamorous highly political event, which was to be America's shop window to the world. He gave his name as Joe Doe which the hotel clerk didn't need to guess was a lie. But Czolgosz had reasons for his duplicity; for he was an anarchist whose sole philosophy was the annihilation of any ruler, any Government head, any capitalist magnate, or even any church Bishop. No person was safe. To-day Czolgosz's target was no less a person than William McKinley, the U.S. President himself. In Czolgosz's opinion it was to be nothing more than a noble act.

Like Lincoln before him, McKinley dismissed security or the threat of assassination as impossible to guard against, despite the fact that fears for his life had become more acute, given recent events. There was a worrying undercurrent of unrest and anger around since the naval victories over the Spanish. But the major fear centered round the Anarchist Movement which had been growing rapidly since 1875. Already it had turned from theory to violence and so far two Monarchs had been murdered. The Anarchists saw themselves as champions of the poor against the arrogance of the swaggering rich.

So now take your place with us at the Exposition as the Assassination time draws near.
The bells and whistles that greeted McKinley's train as the Presidential Special entered Buffalo, rose to a crescendo. His train stopped at the Exchange Street depot to take on the U.S. Ambassador to Argentina. At the Terrace Station, an artillery Captain touched off a twenty-one gun salute. But bedlam was awaiting the train when it was struck as if by a hurricane. Splinters of glass flew everywhere, confusion reigned. Someone raised a glass to Mrs. McKinley's lips to steady her nerves in the hope of avoiding a serious seizure brought on by the sheer shock of the moment.

The train restarted and moved towards the Exposition grounds. The cry of "Anarchist, Anarchist" was in the air. But it seems the explosion had been caused by accident, because the twenty-one gun salute went off too close to the train.

The train duly stopped at the Exposition Station where a column of mounted plumed Guardsmen greeted the dignitaries. The area was full of alert detectives as McKinley stepped off the train to the adoring cheers of thousands. He looked every inch the President. Mrs. McKinley waved a wheelchair away saying "Thank you Mr. Buchanan, I'll walk." Somebody draped her shoulders with a light wrap. Before him McKinley saw the 389 foot electric tower of the Exposition dominating the skyline. "The grounds are beautiful," he said. "I'll see the buildings tomorrow."

Leon Czolgosz rose early next morning, bought a cigar in a local shop and walked to the Pan American grounds. Police were non-existent there. People flowed through the gates at about five hundred per minute and stewards were getting anxious. One committee man declared the situation as deplorable. Three further committee members jumped into the crowd and tried to get some sort of order.

Just then the President arrived. Marines and National Guardsmen in a riot of colourful uniforms, red, blue and gold, their rifles glinting, marched into view to the rhythm of the martial music of a number of army bands.

313

In courtly splendour the Diplomatic Corps dressed in frock coats joined the Duke of Arcos and his richly dressed entourage on the Stand. Liveried footmen were everywhere. The Mexican Ambassador, with his entourage, filled the ranks of gold braided splendour. The Columbian Envoy was there, as was the Turkish Minister, complete with red fez. The Orientals stole the show dressed as they were in blue, grey and yellow silken robes.

But in the midst of the celebration and excitement, one man was moving stealthily through the crowd towards the Grandstand where the President would deliver his speech. Finding a spot to carry out his evil intent was difficult for Leon F. Czolgosz.

The twenty-one gun salute boomed and was followed by the bobbing red plumes of the mounted military in shining metal helmets that reflected the morning sunlight. It was 9.30 a.m. The crowd surged forward as McKinley, arms protectively around his wife, was led through a cordon of gold braided officers to the Stand.

Czolgosz was jostled by the crowd but pushed relentlessly forward gun in his pocket and his hand holding it at the ready. His quarry was taking some papers from his pocket ….. The crowd pressed forward as the President spoke ….. Czolgosz would have to wait his chance until later …. The President finished with "Our earnest prayer is that God will graciously vouchsafe prosperity, happiness and peace to all our neighbours and like blessings to all the people and powers of the earth."
The crowd began to break up as McKinley moved to his carriage his arm around Mrs. McKinley. Czolgosz moved forward too late ….. Yet others were greeted by the President. From inside his carriage, McKinley stretched out his hand to greet one who shouted "I'm Hawaiian Joe, this is my son." Another man held up a small boy for the President's attention. The security was ridiculous. McKinley, good natured smilingly shook all hands. An old woman pushed forward but was turned away by Secret Service men. Their task was impossible as the Presidential cavalcade moved along at a snail's pace. Popcorn boys, souvenir sellers, all joined in the greetings. One man pushed forward shouting "Howdy Chief." McKinley just laughed at the buffoonery. Riding in his carriage behind a battalion of horsemen, McKinley left the stadium.

He then moved to the "Hall of State Hotel" where an orchestra played "Hail to the Chief" and he was entertained at a festive function. The waiter was to be Harry Winter who served him at the 1896 Republican Convention. This is significant because ever after Harry remembers a strange sense of unease in the body language of the President, like some vague apprehension.

Everywhere McKinley went at the Exposition, he was met with pomp and pageantry, gunfire salutes, marching soldiers and cheering crowds. His day moved swiftly from one function to another. Each attraction was preceded by the precision marching of brilliantly uniformed soldiers in complicated marching routines and the almost ever present military bands. There must have been 115,000 people to see him. They really glorified their President.

The night ended with an incandescent display of crimson spray as a myriad of fountains reflected the hidden lights in their depths. Searchlights beamed as the music rose to a crescendo with the final bars of the National Anthem "The Star Spangled Banner". The night reached its climax with a breath-taking fireworks display.

Next day was set out for a visit to Niagara Falls and the Presidential Special train was waiting to take him there. The usual surging horses and crowds were waiting to greet him.

McKinley's next stop was to the Temple of Music which glittered and gleamed in the afternoon sun. Strangely in contrast to the usual lax nature of security, soldiers and mounted police were very much in evidence at the entrance. He was surrounded by Secret Service men and his own four bodyguards who hovered nearby. In the area between the stage and the Temple's grand entrance even more guards and police were posted. At least eighty guards would scrutinize the visitors as they lined up from the entrance to the reception area. Everything was water-tight, or so they thought.

The one missing ingredient in the whole scene was a handkerchief. The number one rule for meeting the President was to approach him with clearly seen hands but because of the heat and the use of handkerchiefs to mop one's brow or dry one's hands, the rule was waived. Even the President was carrying three extra handkerchiefs that morning. Thousands of others used them to wave in welcome.

Czolgosz stood in line ignoring small talk from the man next to him, a James Parker. The killer was too preoccupied with the impending doom of two people, himself and the President. No one paid him any particular attention. Suddenly there were shouts from across the esplanade – The Chief had arrived. Cheers and fluttering handkerchiefs greeted him. Raising his silk topper, he saluted the crowds in return for their welcome. He was glad to step inside away from the heat outside. Although it was morning, it was already 82 degrees. "It's much cooler in here," McKinley remarked. An organist played Bach's Sonata in F. "Let them come," said the President to his Aides.

The great heavy doors of the Temple swung back and the crowd filed in hot, dusty and excited. McKinley's technique, learned from President Hayes, was to shake hands with his right hand and move his well-wisher courteously on with the other. The variety was amazing; Doctors, housewives, youngsters. Cortelyou, one of his Aides, was fidgety. He moved to an exhibition committee member and said "End the reception in five minutes. There are too many people outside. The President couldn't cope," he said. Word went out "Speed up the line." The guards were ordered into action to close the doors. Parker, the black beside Czolgosz was sweating profusely and became agitated. "If you can't go faster at least let me by," he admonished.

But Czolgosz was already moving urgently forward in the queue. "Get in line," a guard said to him. Casually Czolgosz slipped his handkerchief around his right hand. Soldiers and guards flanked him so close he could almost touch them. Ahead was the President smiling and unsuspecting. There was no retreat now. Only a few people were left. A John D. Wells checked the time on his open-faced silver watch. The dull shuffle of shoes on the pine floor was drowned by the organ music. Everywhere the babble of voices mixed with laughter filled the air.

The President paid particular attention to the children yet isn't it astounding that every move was watched with intensity by McKinley's Secret Service men. A suspicious looking Italian was roughly checked then passed "OK" for greeting the President. Wells noted it was 4.07 p.m. A youngish man with tousled blond hair and a bandaged hand moved as if to take the President's hand. His left hand joined his right as if extending both to the President for his handshake. Time froze for Wells as the young man withdrew his right hand like the flash of a poised rattlesnake. Two shots in quick succession rang out in two split seconds. A mushroom of smoke rose from the handkerchief in the hands of the assassin. The President rose on his toes, clutching his chest and pitched forward. A flaming handkerchief was floating to the floor. Czolgosz was poised ready for a third shot, ruthlessly determined to finish the job. But an alert Private O'Brien dived in when all around him had frozen into a trance of disbelief. With

Detective Geary to help they brought Czolgosz to the ground – too late. The black spectator Parker swung a great fist to the assassin's temple before he hit the ground. Geary caught the President as he staggered back with the force of the second bullet. "Al, get his gun" a Secret Service man yelled to his colleague. They walked the President the few feet to a chair "Cortelyou, Cortelyou," he gasped at his Aide.

"Be careful about my wife," the President instructed him. "Do not tell her." He slipped his fingers inside his shirt and withdrew them covered in blood which was now oozing from his chest. His head dropped to his chest. Energy was draining away. "This wound it pains greatly," he complained. His great head fell back. He was unconscious. Before this he had saved Czolgosz life for the moment, murmuring to his bodyguard "Go easy on him boys." The revolver number 463344 was placed in a box tagged and sealed. Meanwhile Czolgosz was dragged to a room at the side of the stage dumped on a table and searched. He had little of consequence on him. Outside the manager, Frederick Cummins told the crowd the President had been shot and all their tickets would be refunded. No one claimed.

The audience streamed silently towards the exits from all the shows. They didn't disperse but took vantage points on top of fountains and trees. All around were cries of "Kill the assassin....." "Hang him....." "Kill the bastard....." A band of Indians with head feathers and war paint rode to the closed Temple doors crying "Big White Feather has been killed." The mob grew ugly and beat upon the Temple doors. A hastily formed line of Marines beat back the rushing mob. An ambulance was allowed through to collect McKinley. They lifted him tenderly onto a stretcher. A quivering pain-racked McKinley was picked up by twenty men and carried outside before a dumbstruck crowd. It was now exactly 4.14 p.m. The ambulance headed towards the Exposition Hospital at the Elmwood Avenue gate. At the Buffalo Inquirer the presses were held over for "An Extra".

Back at the Temple the mob now stirred to a frenzy banged on its doors in a muffled thunder. The doors held and survived the angry fists. Those guarding the assassin blanched with fear knowing a lynching was the only thing the mob wanted. Those surrounding the Temple were ordered to load rifles by Captain Leonard. The mobs were now shouting "Don't let him get away...." "Get the rope....." "Kill the son of a bitch...." "Burn him......" Their anger was incandescent. It was a terrifying spectacle as these baleful shouts came from the throats of a hundred thousand people gathered outside the Temple.

Inside, vague plans were suggested to get the assassin to Police Headquarters. A carriage was seen out front but the coachman, when contacted, refused point blank to risk it "I can't get through that mob," he protested. Finally, he agreed and galloped his team towards the west entrance. The mob turned in his direction only to be confronted by police, soldiers and marines. "Don't let that carriage get away," the mob shouted. At a signal, the marines stood with fixed bayonets. The guards hurled Czolgosz into the wagon like a piece of baggage. The thwarted crowd cried with such anguish it was a sound never to be forgotten by those who heard it.

Time after time the carriage tottered by the weight of the mob against it as it moved forward. They tugged at its fenders and even the horses' reins. It swayed as if pounded by a raging surf but the Irish coachman was equal to anything. He wielded his whip so savagely the crowd fell back. The crush of humanity was now so dense it seemed an impossible task to break through. The crack of the whip and the crash of flashing hooves rent the air. Soon the carriage reached the entrance and rolled down an incline into the narrow streets outside. With six powerful horses they gathered speed and began to out distance the remnants of the mob, except for some persistent cyclists who followed shouting curses at the assassin inside.

What finally saved the carriage was the astuteness of a guard who opened The Lincoln Gates and let them through, then closed them in front of the chasing mob. At Police Headquarters the assassin was dragged out and frog-marched up stairs to the second floor. But word had got around and people poured out of buildings heading towards the Police Headquarters. The small grey Spanish Renaissance type hospital received McKinley after an unhampered run helped by spectators shouting "Keep Back" – "Make Way."

Inside the ambulance, McKinley probing his wound said to his guard "Doesn't that feel like a bullet." The man felt along the breast bone, locating an oblong object inside. "Yes it does Mr. President." "Well, we have got one of them," McKinley whispered. It was eighteen minutes since the shooting when the President was carried into the building. They whipped him into the operating theatre and retired to the outside hallways to wait. But the main surgeon, Dr. Park was doing another operation at Niagara Falls. A special train was arranged to get him back to the President. The use of a Presidential helicopter would have changed history alas, it had not been invented yet.

Dr. Herman Mynter was the first to examine McKinley's wound. One bullet had glanced off the skin. The second bullet had entered his stomach. This was the wound that might prove fatal, Mynter thought. Surgery was imperative.

"Be careful about the doctors," said McKinley, aware of Garfield's neglect. "I'll leave all that to you," he told Cortelyou. But doctors were everywhere. It was not a question of quantity but quality that was the problem. The trusted help was at hand when Dr. Matthew D. Mann arrived. He was a world renowned gynecologist, trained in the U.S. and Europe. However, he had limited experience in upper abdominal surgery. But speed was essential. When told of the decision to operate, the President said, "I am in your hands."

But later Dr. Park said "I do not recall anyone in the room who wore a cap or gauze." The light was bad and the sunlight they were depending on was waning. The operation began at 5.20 p.m. in the evening. The surgeon dug deep to locate the bullet but the electric light was a disaster, so search for the bullet was abandoned. Outside the crowds were held under control 150 feet from the hospital. Dr. Park duly arrived. Dr. Mann was growing petulant with the strain. Dr. Park offered his services. "Hello, do you want me to get my hand in?" "No," was Mann's curt reply, "it's practically finished."

Mann was short of instruments which Park fetched from his office, sterilized them and handed them to Mann. Mynter advised drainage. Park advised flushing the cavity with a saline solution. The tetchy Mann refused both sets of advice and closed the wound without drainage. The hospital was clearly inadequate for the task. Electric fans were installed at "Milburn house", where McKinley wanted to be taken. Dr. Mann jealous of his role didn't help.

All the doctors involved were sworn to silence to avoid the misunderstandings of Garfield's case. Dr. Park was asked to take charge but felt it would be unfair to Dr. Mann who had done the operation. Dr. Mann was left in charge, with the assistance of Dr. Mynter and Dr. Wasdin. At this point I am sure you the reader will begin to grow angry at the bungling surgeons.

The plight of Mrs. McKinley was sad and serious. How was she to be told and when? It was decided to stall the news. The house was cordoned off and the telephone was disconnected. The crowds must be kept away and clubs were used to keep unruly ones behind the ropes. But seeing it was getting dark at 6.30 p.m. that fatal evening, she blurted out "I wonder why he doesn't come!"

"I have bad news for you Mrs. McKinley," a doctor told her reluctantly. He could delay no more. "What is it," she asked. "Is anything wrong? Has he been hurt?" "Yes, he has been hurt," replied the unfortunate doctor. "He has been shot." "I must go to him," she whispered. "No," was the reply. "He is coming here and his life depends on you to help us." The expected collapse of Mrs. McKinley never took place to the relief of everyone.

When the President's wounds had been bandaged, Mrs. McKinley entered the room. She dabbed her eyes and exchanged intimate whispers with her husband.

The final piece of the drama concerns the assassin. Back at Police Headquarters, he gazed out the window at the crowds outside. In the city, in downtown Buffalo, crowds were again gathering to discuss the assassin's fate. Even prominent citizens were there. Ringleaders emerged but with the help of the 6th and 74th National Guard and police from outside precincts, and the Trojan work of Captain "Big Mike" Regan, calm was restored. "Go home," they were ordered. Back at the Police Headquarters Czolgosz confessed that he alone carried out the deed. "Anarchy," he had concluded "was the only saviour of the working people."

He had decided to come to Buffalo eight days previously. He made enquiries at his hotel how he could meet the President and had only decided on his evil deed a few days ago. He would have shot a third time if he had not been struck to the ground. Throughout the interview, Czolgosz showed neither remorse nor emotion. "Did you intend to shoot the President?" District Attorney Penney asked "Yes" was the reply. "What was your motive?" "I am an anarchist, a disciple of Emma Goldman. Her words set me on fire."

Back at Czolgosz's home, the family was aghast. "I can't think it of Leon," his elderly father kept muttering. "He had not been home for months." His stepmother thought differently .... "I always thought Leon was crazy. Not like an ordinary boy. He was timid, a regular coward." Even friends and neighbours were astonished at Leon's murderous act. They recalled Leon as a boy who would catch flies then release them. "How could such a man kill anyone?"

The most wanted woman now was Emma Goldman. A police net was stretched from coast to coast to find her.

It was six o'clock on Friday evening when they admitted that hope had been abandoned for McKinley and the telegraph instruments in the press tents clicked out the message that the President was dying.

In the late afternoon, the President surfaced from his coma. "It is useless gentlemen," he told the doctors. "I think we ought to have prayers." As the twilight deepened McKinley asked for his wife Ida. She leaned over the bed holding his hands, kissing his lips. In the background, a group of his family and friends stood whispering. McKinley said in a faint voice "Good bye – good bye all. It is God's way. His will not ours be done." He put his arm around Ida and smiled at her. He began to say in a feeble voice the words of his favourite hymn "Nearer my God to thee – nearer to thee." These were the last words she heard him say. His arm still drooped around her as he smiled at the face hovering over him. Mrs. McKinley was led away. For two more hours his heart faltered. One last laboured gasp and it was over. Dr. Rixey said "The President is dead."

It was 2.15 a.m. on September 14, 1901. One must be concerned that there was more than one assassin in that hospital in September 1901.

The funeral ceremonies of William McKinley, 25th President of the United States of America, took place on September 15, 1901 in three different locations – Buffalo, Washington and Canton. The hearse drew up to Milburn house, surrounded by an armed escort of soldiers and sailors. The new President, Theodore Roosevelt arrived and went direct to the oblong drawing room where the massive mahogany coffin lay in State, the lower half covered in masses of flowers and roses. The upper half was open. McKinley's remains bore the signs of suffering on his face, his left hand lying across his breast.

The First Presbyterian Church Quartet sang softly "Lead kindly light" one of McKinley's favourite hymns. The twenty-five minute prayer service finished with another of McKinley's favourite hymns "Nearer my God to Thee". As the coffin was carried outside to the waiting hearse, the 65th band just across the avenue took up the theme "Nearer my God to Thee".

Overnight the city had filled up with people in their thousands who lined Delaware Avenue almost ten deep. A few drops of rain fell. Strangely, the black buntings had become enmeshed in the City Hall clock stopping the hands at 2.15, a bizarre coincidence. McKinley had died at 2.15 the day before. There were now at least 150,000 behind the rope barriers. Sobs and in some places curses rose quietly from the assembled mourners; curses that quietly rained down on the head of the absent assassin, Leon Czolgosz.
Mourners filed past the coffin lying inside the City Hall well into the sunset. The First Lady had consented to her husband's body remaining at City Hall as a mark of respect to the public. The coffin was surrounded by four almost statue-like figures, rifles at attention. The funeral train headed for Washington at 8.30 a.m. the following morning. Darkness fell as the cortege neared Washington. Beside the track Negroes had lit a line of fires and their silhouettes stood out against the burning brush.

All night long in Washington, the casket lay in the East Room of the White House guarded by a continually changing succession of marines, soldiers and sailors until dawn filtered through the windows.

Rain cascaded down next morning, drenching the crowds lining Pennsylvania Avenue, under dripping umbrellas. Streamers on the buildings, sodden from the rain just added to the gloom of the occasion. Down the avenue, cavalry men with sabers upraised were followed by artillery men astride their mounts, ahead of the horse-drawn guns. Plumes, bayonets and sabers glistening in the rain moved at a respectful pace. All the dignitaries of high office, including the previous President Grover Cleveland were there.

Despite the respectful discipline of the crowd before this, when the Cathedral doors were opened to allow the crowd in, control slipped for an instant and many were trampled underfoot, arms were broken and women fainted in the crush. It was hard to believe that thirty-six years previously another murdered President had passed through here – Abraham Lincoln. The train route planned for McKinley was not to be so morbidly prolonged on its way to Canton as was Lincolns. The train passed through York, Harrisburg, Philadelphia and New York City. Those lining the route could still be numbered in their thousands. In the twilight they flanked the tracks to see the illuminated casket go by.

On Wednesday September 18, just before noon, the funeral train arrived at Canton Station where the same crowd who had cheered his departure only a short time ago, waited in grief and disbelief. Once again McKinley lay in State for the thousands who lined up for a last goodbye to their martyred President. Then the casket was closed for the last time and taken to the McKinley residence. There it lay at his home until the final rites were carried out in the

Methodist Church the next afternoon.

Remarkably and to her enduring credit, Mrs. McKinley had kept her gentle dignity throughout her terrible ordeal. The funeral had been impressive as had Mrs. McKinley, America's First Lady, who only at the last minute was persuaded by relatives and Dr. Rixey not to endure the final moments when William her husband was laid finally to rest. She made her final farewells before his casket was carried outside to the hearse, leaving her to her personal grief and private memories as she walked inside and closed the door.

At 3.30 p.m. that afternoon, the casket was received into the gigantic vault in the family plot situated on the crest of a knoll overlooking the City of Canton. That day was declared a day of national mourning throughout the land.

To underline his importance in the new international world, he had graced with such dignity, demonstrations of sorrow also took place in Berlin, St. Petersburg, London, Bombay and Constantinople. Even the guns of distant Gibraltar boomed out a last farewell.

Now to the final scene of this harrowing story of William McKinley. The trial of his murderer Czolgosz was organized by the prosecution before McKinley died and there was some debate that the assassin would get only ten years if the President survived.

These conjectures were now irrelevant. Czolgosz had been moved secretly to the Erie County Penitentiary on Trenton Avenue, a mile west of the city. He had been moved casually by two appointed officers, Chief Bull and Chief Cusack who would take him on their own to the Penitentiary. He was warned by Cusack that he would not hesitate to use the gun in his pocket if Czolgosz tried to escape.

They walked out of the building that had been besieged by thousands only some days before, as three casual pedestrians. No handcuffs were used. Inside the waiting carriage Cusack again warned his prisoner "You move and I'll kill you. You understand?" There was no reply. The horses moved off without undue haste and so not attracting attention. Sheriff Caldwell booked the prisoner into his care and he would remain under his care until his indictment.

The Grand Jury interviewed the witnesses and none were held for more than ten minutes. Twenty were heard inside two hours. Of course, there were many more from the ranks of those on duty at the Temple of Music.

Judge Emery was now waiting in the County Courtroom. The clerk called the roll of twenty-one Jurors. "Have you any report to make?" asked the Judge. Theodore Krehbiel, the foreman, answered "Yes your honour we have a partial report." It was on a typewritten document which he handed to the Judge. The Judge dismissed the Jury after glancing at the document. Murder in the first degree was to be the charge.

To maintain the security of the prisoner he was transferred from the City Hall through a tunnel under Delaware Avenue, 9 feet high and 6 feet wide, called the "Tunnel of Sobs", built in 1878, twenty-three years earlier at the jail's construction. He was also guarded in the passage by a squad of policemen. A barricade of police covered the door of the courtroom to prevent intruders from entering. The prisoner looking disheveled and the worse for wear, in clothes not his own, stood before the bench. He was compulsorily assigned two counsels, Lorin L. Lewis and Robert C. Titus. He showed no interest and seemed to be indifferent to life or death. Perhaps he was right. It seemed hopeless, even the counsel provided had not been a trial lawyer for years. They were also elderly. To make matters worse for Czolgosz they both were repulsed by the assignment given to them.

After much wrangling and the prisoner's total silence, a plea of guilty was the outcome. But the Buffalo press had already headlined the speculation "Czolgosz Sane Beyond Doubt". That was to be the one avenue of escape the press made sure in their estimation could not be used by the assassin.

A Dr. Carlos F. MacDonald was called. He was Professor of Mental Diseases and Medical Jurisprudence in the University and Bellevue Medical College. He was recognized as being at the head of his profession – a leading alienist in the United States.

Czolgosz's counsel, Robert C. Titus, was not much help with the statement "We are not calling adverse witnesses."

At the trial the two counsels again bleated about their distaste for a job imposed on them "by law".

MacDonald declared as a veteran observer of murder trials he had never witnessed such an anomalous defense. Practically no defense had been made on the prisoner's behalf. Dr. Allan McLane Hamilton in his autobiography Recollections of an Alienist denounced the trial out of hand, saying "I really do not think in all my experience that I have ever seen such a travesty of justice." He went on to say with scorn "The two superannuated, self-satisfied ex Judges assigned for the defense apologized freely and humbly for their appearance on behalf of this wretched man....." But a witness, Louis L. Babcock described the writer as "A disappointed job seeker."

The death sentence was duly pronounced. Czolgosz woke on the morning of October 29, 1901 when two priests, Father Hickey and Father Fudzinski, entered his cell. He refused to ask forgiveness. A few hours before the execution his brother, Waldeck, came to visit him.

"Tell us Leon who got you into this scrape?" he asked.

"No one," came the reply. Czolgosz began pacing the cell.

"Do you want to see the priest again?" asked Waldeck.

"No," his brother snarled. "No damn them. "I don't want them praying over me when I am dead. I don't want any of their damned religion."

Czolgosz listened as the warden read the death warrant. His request to see his brother Waldeck again was refused.

He told Superintendent Collins "I want to make a statement with a lot of people around." Collins shook his head. "Well then I won't talk at all." Perhaps he was going to make a political speech. Perhaps he was again going to implicate Red Emma Goldman. But we will never know now.

He was half-led, half carried to the electric chair which was sitting on a rubber platform. As the straps and electrodes were fitted, he cried out. "I am not sorry. I did this for the working people. My only regret is that I haven't been able to see my father." Some accounts say he went to his death foaming at the mouth, screaming curses. In view of his constant calm silence throughout the trial it seems a third version is more accurate. He went to his death with outward composure as 1,700 volts of electricity burned the life from him. He was buried in the prison cemetery and as provided by the law of the State, a carboy of sulfuric acid was dropped into his casket ensuring his remains would disintegrate in twelve hours.

As we come to the end of this sordid chapter in McKinley's life, it hurts even more to think of a conversation he had some time earlier.

When talking to Henry L. Stoddard, a leading journalist of the day, McKinley had expressed a vote of confidence and pleasure in greeting people who lined up to greet him in White House receptions. "Everyone in that line has a smile and a cheery word," he said. "They bring no problems with them only goodwill. I feel better after that contact. It is the visitor to the Cabinet room pressing some policy or seeking some office that tires ..... I have to meet all that force not once or twice each day but all day without interruption."

Yet, the disturbing fact was that McKinley met his death, not in his Cabinet room but at the hands of an assassin in such a casual lineup.

Perhaps the last piece of this sorry jigsaw is Emma Goldman. She was released from jail minus one of her teeth, fifteen days after Czolgosz was executed. She was let go without being charged with anything. Rumour has it she was offered $20,000 for her story by the great newspaper baron Randolph Hearst. It seems Hearst felt he himself was suspected of inciting the assassin and his offer of an interview to Emma was an attempt to exonerate himself of the charge. Emma's reply was dismissive. She claimed "The people are asleep. They forge their own chains to do the bidding of their masters to crucify their Christ."

Her view was the Czolgosz had acted unselfishly and idealistically. It seems both Emma and the assassin were unrepentant. Emma taunted the public "Is it possible that in the entire United States only the President passed away on this day? Surely many others have died at the same time, perhaps in poverty and destitution, leaving helpless dependents behind ..... But why had the assassin chosen the President rather than some more direct representative of the system of economic depression and misery," she asked. "Was it because he saw in McKinley the willing tool of Wall Street in the new American imperialism that flowered under his Administration? He sent troops to strike regions. He typified a hostile and reactionary attitude to labour ..... All those circumstances must have exerted a decisive influence upon an impressionable Leon."

But by these very words she repeated once again the role she had played in similar speeches just before the assassination, which roused a young man's naive passion to murder. By her own words now she was truly guilty of incitement.

Emma was ostracized even by her own Anarchist Movement who felt the assassination had done them irreparable damage. Even her father suffered. His furniture business went downhill and he was excommunicated from his Synagogue.

Let's finish with a final postscript on Emma Goldman. Emma Goldman nicknamed "Red Emma" was hated by most Americans. She arrived in New York when she was sixteen after fleeing from anti-Semitic Czarist Russia in 1885 and was an unbending anarchist. She spoke all over America in favour of free love and birth control, homosexual rights and anything she felt made victims of the underdog in society. Women's rights were high on her agenda though she scoffed at the suffragettes.

Anything that shocked the establishment she did with venom; from praising murdering anarchists to smoking twenty cigarettes a day in public. "Red Emma" was a misnomer for she was opposed to socialism and capitalism at the same time. She finally destroyed herself by praising McKinley's killer as "A man with the beautiful soul of a child." She fled to England after the murder and was never allowed to return to America again.

Strangely the two shots that killed McKinley on that fateful day - September 6, 1901 had its repercussions in the actions of his successor, Theodore Roosevelt, the new 26th President of the United States.

How he reacted will be the next story in our book "The Forty Four Presidents".

26th President   Theodore Roosevelt

"Teddy"
Born 1858
Died 1919
60 Years of age
2 Terms
1901 – 1905
1905 - 1909
7 Years, 171 Days

Party: Republican
Profession: Rancher, writer, public official
County: Illinois
Ancestry: Dutch
Value of Estate: $811,000
Hobbies: Boxing

Physical Description: 5 foot 7 inches tall, pince-nez eyeglass with thick lenses, prominent teeth, bushy eyebrows, drooping moustache, high voice.

Significant Extract from his Inaugural Address (2nd Term) March 4, 1905
No inauguration for his 1st term due to the death of his predecessor in office
"My fellow citizens, no people on earth have more cause to be thankful than us and this is said reverently … .Much has been given to us and much will rightfully be expected from us … .Justice and generosity in a nation and as an individual counts most when shown not by the weak but by the strong."

THEODORE ROOSEVELT

The 24th and 25th Presidencies had almost been hijacked by "Vested Interests" whose only motivation was naked greed. Now America badly needed a fearless no nonsense President to take them on. Welcome aboard Theodore Roosevelt. We find him being sworn into office on September 13, 1901 as the 26th President of the United States.

On September 13, 1901 the tragedy of William McKinley was coming to a close as he lay dying from the gunshot wounds inflicted by his assassin. At six o'clock on that Friday evening preparations were already underway for the swearing in of his successor, Theodore Roosevelt, as the 26th President of the United States. The new technology was busy clicking in the press tents encamped on the lawn outside the house where McKinley lay.

Once again, America had at the very pinnacle of power, a man who had been dumped into the office of Vice President on the presumption he would fade into oblivion on the political stage at the end of the 25th President's expected four year reign.

Now the wild extravagant multi-talented personality, called Theodore Roosevelt, had arrived on the scene very much alive after his political burial.

Theodore was a descendant of Claes Martenszen Van Rosenvelt who had migrated to New Amsterdam (now New York City) from Zeeland, Holland in 1649. Theodore Senior his father, a New York businessman married Martha Bulloch, a Southern belle, from a prominent Georgia family. Like all Civil Wars, the American one split not only the whole country but whole families within that country and the Roosevelt's did not escape the curse. Both of Mrs. Roosevelt's brothers fought for the Confederacy. Theodore's father opted not to fight for reasons we will outline later.

"The Roosevelt family fortune, derived from trade and banking, rested squarely on the twin pillars of law and property and rejoiced in heaven's approval" wrote David Burton about Teddy Roosevelt. Born into the wealthy family in New York City in 1858 Theodore emerged as the leader of reform Republicans in the New York State Assembly in the early 1880s when he was only twenty-three years old.

Theodore, or "Teddie" as he was known in his childhood, was born on October 27, 1858 the second child of four children at 28 East 20th Street, New York City. It was in this house all his formative years were spent as a young lad shaping his future personality. Although he never rose to academic heights in his private education, he did show particular talents for acquiring knowledge. This could have been his brilliance at speed reading which helped him cover a wide area of knowledge at enormous speed. One subject he excelled in was natural history. He travelled widely as a boy of fourteen when he paid a visit with his family to Europe and Egypt in 1872. He went on to Harvard University when he was eighteen, graduating through hard work rather than brilliance. Perhaps this was because he also gave a lot of his time to Harvard's club activities in athletics, horse riding, camping and hunting trips, burning up his bursting energies with a gusto and a sheer joy of life he found it impossible to suppress.

Incidentally there is an interesting story attached to the Roosevelt homes in New York. The family homes were at 26 and 28 East 20th Street which were originally bought as wedding presents for both Robert and Theodore. Theodore moved into No. 28 with his bride in 1854 where they lived until 1872. From there they moved to No. 6 West 57th Street. A commercial firm demolished number 28 for an office block. Some rich benefactors rebuilt a museum and memorial to Theodore on the site in 1919 and it is now called The Theodore Roosevelt Rotunda as a declared New York landmark.

Yes, Theodore Roosevelt, New York's human rocket, was ready for take off. But before take off, just after his graduation he married Alice Hathaway Lee, with whom he had fallen in love while at Harvard. They returned together to live in New York but I'll be telling you more of this story later. At this point in time Theodore's life had not yet found a political direction so he found himself dabbling in several careers. At first he attended law classes at Columbia University but he didn't enjoy them at all.

Around this time the dormant writer in him was now awakening and he produced his first book called The Naval War of 1812 which he had researched back in his Harvard days. It was eventually published in 1882. He broke into politics the year before in 1881, when he was elected to the State Assembly in Albany, New York as a Republican. But perhaps we should be a little more respectful about Theodore's writing career because his writing achievements were truly remarkable for a man whose later job was leader of this vast country on the political stage for over seven years.

It is hard to believe that no critic of literature of his time measured up to Theodore Roosevelt. His opinions on literature were very much respected. He read an amazing quantity of books, plays, magazines, sermons, adventure stories, children's books by poets, historians, philosophers and even romance writers and his reviews were widely accepted by the whole writing fraternity.

It is easy to look at Theodore's life and wonder what to leave out, for every anecdote competes with another for inclusion. In the midst of all the stories his writing talent can easily be overlooked. His output was truly prolific for he had no less than thirty published volumes to his credit. It was an art he learned by sheer hard work and practice. His writing had a compelling accuracy that grabbed the reader's immediate attention. His raw material came from many sources – his youth, his politics and his travels. But his real life experiences themselves, were a wonderful background that any aspiring writer would be more than grateful for.

The "list" of his books included – The Naval War of 1812, Essays on Practical Politics, The Winning of the West in four volumes, The Rough Riders and finally for now Fear God and Take Your Own Part among many others. Yet for some strange reason he chose politics as a career when a life as a naturalist or as a writer would have been so much more suitable to his academic qualifications and aristocratic family tree.

But what sort of a character was Theodore Roosevelt? We could start with another quote from David Burton, who said "Two ideas drove the life of Theodore Roosevelt – rugged individualism and the welfare of mankind." Roosevelt was such a colourful dynamic character, he has been described in many different ways; a fervent nationalist, a consummate moralist, and a Nobel Prize Winner in 1906 for his services to peace. It seems he was the first in everything; the first to ride in an automobile, the first to be a passenger in an airplane, the first to dive in a submarine.

Oliver Wendell Holmes Jr. described Theodore in 1921 as follows: "Roosevelt was very likeable, a big figure, a rather ordinary intellect, with extraordinary gifts, a shrewd and I think a pretty unscrupulous politician. He played all his cards if not more." His intense nationalism often escaped his lips in speeches he made. One of Roosevelt's most popular ones was made on Appomattox Day in response to one made by William Jennings Bryan, denouncing American Imperialism. It was a long and intense speech which I won't cover in full, but here is one extract. "It is a base untruth to say happy is the nation that has no history. Thrice happy is the nation that has a glorious history. Far better it is to dare mighty things to win glorious triumphs even though chequered by failure."

Teddy Roosevelt has often been compared to Andrew Jackson, whose skills in self-projection and self-dramatization were also legendary. It was the coming of the popular press that played the biggest part in building his image. His teeth, his eye-glasses, his tremendous vitality, his sponsorship of the rigorous lifestyle and of course his gift for the telling phrase "Speak softly and carry a big stick" was one of them.

The press of course loved him for he was the ideal foil for leading cartoonists and political commentators of that time and Theodore soon learned to manipulate his relationship with them in a way that made him years ahead of his time.

In a strange way, Teddy Roosevelt's flamboyant personality and undoubted expertise in using the press for the good of his own politics only made trouble for his successors, William H. Taft and Woodrow Wilson.

It seems the expectations he raised could only be achieved by a similar media personality as himself. There has even been criticism of Woodrow Wilson's failure to sell the League of Nations idea to the Senate because of his inability to mobilize the press in its support just as Theodore Roosevelt would have done. I'm afraid there are some skills that are not always passed on by "old masters".

To round off the piece on the press and Theodore Roosevelt, here is a wonderful tribute in his favour, by one of the most experienced political correspondents ever doing the rounds among the greats of American politics in the years straddling the 19th and 20th century – Henry L. Stoddard. He said, and I quote –

"Of all the men in public life I have known and met during nearly half a century of active newspaper work I can recall none more ready to listen to the views of others, more willing when convinced to put aside his own ideas, more ready to accept group judgment in preference to his own than Theodore Roosevelt. Once you had his confidence, you had an open Sesame to his mind. Roosevelt lived in today and tomorrow."

Stoddard goes on – "His yesterdays served only the purpose of building up his tomorrows."

Roosevelt's legendary energy, vitality and knowledge of many subjects were amazing but his fundamental asset was his loyalty to friendships. The greatest hurt he could suffer was to discover a friend had let him down. Yet he carried no revenge in his heart. He loved an honest confrontational debate on a problem but always made sure he walked away from the exchange of views with the friendship still intact. "We'll talk of something else" he would say. If you wanted to offend him all you had to do was agree with him because he was the President. Opinions were sacrosanct to him so long as his opponent didn't capitulate too easily.

It seemed the whole world knew Teddy Roosevelt. No one anywhere from Greenland to India knew him as anybody else but "Teddy" Roosevelt. Through him they also knew America and the American people. His mission to get a square deal for the average man at home was widely understood abroad and greatly appreciated. Amazingly, his circle of friends wasn't confined to politics but spread like a ripple in a pool in ever wider circles to embrace people from all classes. Bucky O'Neil of the Rough Riders – Roosevelt's outfit in the Spanish War, Viscount Grey of Fallodon, and Joe Murray, a district leader who gave him his start in politics. Men in the ordinary walks of life revered him. Even the famous John L. Sullivan, the prize fighter, was a personal friend.

Theodore also had a very special relationship with the church. He once said "It is a historical fact that a community becomes of less worth if the church ceases to be a force in it and until I can believe that the people of our country are better off without churches, I shall try to uphold them in a practical manner."

So convinced was he in the dominant part the church played in the fabric of a nation he became fascinated with the work of missionaries. In the course of his trips abroad hunting in Africa, he never missed an opportunity to visit a nearby mission station and discuss their work with the missionaries themselves. He himself could recite at will long passages of scripture and he often quoted from the Bible text in his speeches just like Lincoln did.

Corinne Roosevelt, his sister, recalls an address given at a function she attended in Japan. "One of the great Statesmen present said something that will always remain in my memory," she said. "To him Theodore seemed to interpret the true meaning of the Japanese Shinto religion." The word Shinto means "The Way". "Theodore Roosevelt," said the Japanese Statesman "was the way to be followed not only by the American people but by the nations of the world ....." Some praise indeed. It would be absurd to imply he was looked on as a deity by the Japanese but the sentiments expressed captured the reverence with which he was treated by people thousands of miles away.

But we are not writing about a deity. It is impossible for a man of such swashbuckling fearlessness and energy as Theodore Roosevelt to live a life in the hurly burly of American politics and be right all the time and nobody was more ready to acknowledge his own mistakes quicker than Theodore. Perhaps his indiscreet speeches for a more militant America, is not easy to excuse in a man so steeped in pure Christianity. As we said above, we are not writing about a deity. Roosevelt was a man with all the passions and fallibility of a human being.

Before we condemn him as a warmonger, we must remember he has already been judged by his peers as a peacemaker and rewarded for this with the Nobel Peace Prize for bringing about a peace treaty between Russia and Japan. That award was not the judgement of angels but the verdict of his fellow human beings throughout the world. Roosevelt's response to the accusation of being a "war bully" was as follows: "I would never advocate war unless it was the only alternative to dishonour."

Individualist Theodore may have been "blazing his own trail" but no one ever imitated a father-like Theodore did. All through his life he measured himself against his illustrious dad, sometimes saying "I tried faithfully to do what father would have done." When seated together on the favourite family sofa, the one most privileged was the one who sat in "the cubby hole": That was the place between his father and the arm of the sofa. Another delightful family scene happened on Christmas mornings when they opened their Christmas stockings in the presence of a smiling father. It was one of his sister's fondest memories. Believe it or not this delightful scene was enacted by the family for a further thirty years.

Strangely enough, although reared in the city, Theodore's love of nature dates from his time in New York City. His early travels abroad to Egypt with the family gave him a first-hand experience of nature and he returned home from that holiday to New York City with his bags packed with stuffed specimens he had collected. That seemed to whet his appetite for, on entering college he decided to be a naturalist. At that time anyway, Theodore had no particular interest in politics. That was to come later when he joined the Republican Party.

It was in 1881 at the age of twenty-three that Theodore ran for the New York Legislature for the first time and won a seat. He was also successful the following two years. It wasn't a simple job for a rookie politician because New York politics was in the hands of saloon owners, dodgy lawyers and gang leaders. Certainly not a place for a family man. But this was a challenge. The young Theodore just couldn't resist a challenge. He was now confronting the Spoils men in their own backyard.

A revealing insight into how they thought can be seen in the words of one leader. "I am in politics working for my own pocket all the time, same as you," he boasted unashamedly. The arrival of someone, whose life was ruled, not by the cynicism of the day but by the Ten Commandments laid down by Moses, was really disconcerting for them. It must have been a tough one for the hard-boiled professionals to cope with. This young upstart who demanded so much integrity and truly believed that rank and privilege had its obligations, not to the ruling class but to the humble and less well off in society. This was unheard of in a New York that made a mockery of American Institutions and freely defiled those noble principles every day.

The story of the Supreme Court Judge he confronted when still a raw rookie in politics became a part of New York folklore. It seems Theodore received into his possession a written letter by a corrupt Judge written to the railroad bosses saying "I am willing to go to the verge of discretion to serve your vast interests." Theodore pressed for the Judge's impeachment in the Legislature. It came as a bit of a culture shock to a politician as naïve as Theodore to discover that businessmen and lawyers and others of high standing, he himself knew socially were not on his side and even resented his actions.

Here you may wish to read again my opening paragraph. The unholy alliance of the corrupt and the powerful were his everyday target from that day forward. Given the society that existed in New York at that time, it is not surprising that the Judge escaped impeachment but Theodore was the real beneficiary. To the downtrodden, a redeeming star had appeared on the horizon. The case of Judge Westbrook, the corrupt Judge in question, showed Theodore just what a hell-hole he had entered.

Later, cases such as the case of cigar making in a tenement house convinced him even further that the courts had no respect for the needs of ordinary people. In fact, the courts only tended to extend their misery.

The press was ecstatic with Theodore and the editorials reflected their excitement daily. Cartoons appeared in which he was presented shearing the claws of the Tammany Tiger – and he was only twenty-four years old. He went all out to prove that politics and honesty were not unnatural bed-fellows. He called to honest men to join him in his crusade "Every man who wishes well to his country is honour bound to take an active part in political life" were his words. "The real service is rendered, not by the critic who stands aloof from the contest but by the man who enters into it and bears his part as a man should undeterred by the blood and sweat." As he grew more experienced, he lived by the principle of compromise, realizing that a man must sacrifice something of his own opinion to his associates if he hopes to see his desires take a practical shape.

Theodore Roosevelt's next major role was his appointment by President Harrison to the Civil Service Commission where he served six years. He was now just past thirty years of age. Soon he became its leader and now he had all the raw material he needed to fuel his campaign of cleaning up politics. The Spoils System, first tackled as long ago as four Presidential terms, was still unwilling to die a normal death. The doctrine "To the victor belong the Spoils" had now been rampant for sixty years. Replacement of those favoured by jobs under the previous Party in power resulted in a permanent turnover of staff into and out of Government. Nobody was permanent regardless of how qualified or competent they were.

Of course the opposition was soon challenging him and clashes occurred on an ongoing basis. Those at the top of the pyramid of privilege were his first targets and despite the wiles of war they used against him, Theodore marched on regardless. One young widow was sacked from her $800 per year job at the request of an influential Senator, leaving her penniless. The Bureau Chief, a humane man, stalled on the dismissal but was threatened by the Senator with dismissal if he refused to sack the woman. She was sacked, but Theodore intervened as he did in many such cases with his applied Christianity. Democracy, as it existed up to then had been replaced by the autocracy of the privileged.

Roosevelt's cure of applied idealism, gradually infiltrated into the actions of those in charge. The trickle became a flood until his philosophy was accepted as a permanent cure for the malaise. He was now much in demand as a fearless reformer. The Mayor of New York City gratefully called on him to help clean up the city. To do this he was made President of the Police Commission. What a job he was faced with for even the police were corrupt. Graft in appointments and promotions for which large sums of money changed hands was quite commonplace.   There were 12,000 saloons which defied the Sunday closing laws with impunity. It was a very similar situation to Prohibition days thirty years later. The Municipal Council was made and unmade by saloon keepers. These saloon bosses also controlled the police who in their turn had the fruit vendors, prostitution dens and gambling casinos at their mercy. Reform the police and you reformed the city, but the question was - how? Others had tried and failed but the underworld now had Theodore Roosevelt to contend with. His base in Mulberry Street was to become feared and famous.

First came the Sunday laws. They were on the statute books and that was good enough for Theodore. The saloons to him desecrated the Sabbath and encouraged crime and misery. In Theodore's eyes, it was an affront to the Lord's Day.

One of his now favourite sayings was coined in a speech he made to a Chicago audience on April 2, 1903 "Speak softly and carry a big stick; you will go far." Yet Theodore was full of strange contradictions in Christian terms. Although he was a caring human being, the giving of undeserved pity was totally alien to him. Such a person he said did not make a good citizen. He looked on such weakness as attention seeking. It seemed to him "When the cause was just – let battle begin". A little like the Crusaders of the Middle Ages – the ends justified the means be they peaceful means or war. "Preachers who preached peace at any price were destroyers not builders". "Righteousness was everything". "He that hath no sword, let him sell his garments and buy one" was another quotation he used from St. Luke to justify his militancy in pursuit of justice. To all this we can add his belief that America must be prepared for war by building up the Navy for he likened pacifists to the Pharisees.

But this apparent lack of compassion and an undercurrent of aggression in his make-up seems to question the authenticity of his Christianity. It seemed so divorced from the Christian message of peace he preached, it is hard not to level criticism at our Theodore.
To sum up the life of this extraordinary man, I will let the words of his hardy backwoodsman friend, Bill Sewall, who was his companion so often in the solitudes of nature, do it for me. "I think he read the Bible a great deal. I never saw him in formal prayer but, as a prayer is the desire of the heart, I think he prayed without ceasing, for the desire of his heart was always to do right."

But let's get back to Theodore's crusade. The cries of pain that went up in his crusade against corruption were music to Theodore's ears. "You have wrecked the Republican Party." "You will never be heard from again." But Theodore carried on ploughing into the turbulence of a raging river of criticism. His reform of the police by a system of recognition and rewards raised it to levels of excellence that took everyone by surprise. Roosevelt's greatest personal reward came from the improved conditions in the tenements. His actions fed back into other areas too. There were less people injured in drunken brawls. Police courts and pawn shops had fewer customers. The city of blackmail, bribery and perverted justice was no more. One of his sayings sums up his whole approach to reform "Play the fair game."

Roosevelt did not apply the brakes with anyone when speaking out against injustice. He never even placed Party above principle. Wherever he found dishonesty, he would straddle his horse called "righteousness" and with his war cry of "the square deal" rode into battle armed with his big stick. His main targets were men of power and influence who stepped out of line in pursuit of a bigger bank balance.

It has been said that these were America's most exciting times. Roosevelt's major confrontations with the frightening powers of big business and large Corporations were front page news almost daily.

In retrospect, the forces he confronted were formidable but the reason for his success, like Lincoln, was the weight of justice behind him and the instinctive confidence of the voters supporting him. The contribution he made to the good name of America cannot be measured because the corruption of unscrupulous people at the top in all walks of life in the USA had become worldwide common knowledge. He not only saved a runaway ship heading for the rocks but managed to take control of the bridge and sail it into peaceful waters.

The arrogance of the times can be summed up in a remark made by the richest man of his time, Mr. Vanderbilt. President of one of America's largest railroads – "The public be damned." One great cartel, the United States Steel Corporation, was capitalized at $1,100,000,000, a position repeated many times over by other combinations of companies. This power base helped them to evade the law in certain situations.

Once again the press was part of the Teddy Roosevelt story when they complained vociferously against social injustice. Yet he didn't mince his words against those pressmen he felt were exploiting the stories of scandalous conditions in business and politics for the good of their editors. He called them "muckrakers". However, by stirring up public opinion in genuine cases, they helped Theodore to tackle these social problems.

Two pieces of legislation came about as a result. One was the Meat Inspection Act. The second was The Pure Food and Drug Act 1906. Politics was in the forefront of debates just as it is today to ensure that privileged interests did not interfere with the popular will of the people. Yes, indeed there was plenty of meat for a reforming politician like Theodore Roosevelt to get his teeth into for these were times of radical change in an emerging industrial giant that was America in the early 1900s.

But life went on for Theodore Roosevelt, the family man.

February 14, 1884 was a Valentine's Day Theodore would remember for two terrible reasons. It was the day a double disaster tore his heart apart. His mother, Martha Bulloch Roosevelt, died at his home in New York City of typhoid fever and providence chose that day also to take his wife, Alice from him at the early age of twenty-two years, 192 days. She died in childbirth; giving life to a little girl he called Alice.

It was arranged that Alice be taken care of by Theodore's older sister and Theodore then lost himself in another venture. Going West for a while, he bought himself a Ranch which he named Elkhorn on the Little Missouri River in Dakota Territory and here he lived the hard rough life of a cowboy. From here he travelled back and forth to the East Coast writing of his experiences in his book Hunting Trips of a Ranchman.

Theodore's restless spirit could not be suppressed for long and after his marriage in London to his second wife; he returned to his new home, he had built on Sagamore Hill in Oyster Bay, Long Island.

I'm sure you would like to hear about Sagamore Hill, the mansion he bought in August 1886 just after he married for a second time. Built in a rural area, there were forty-two different varieties of birds counted there. It formed the basis of his home life just as Monticello did for Jefferson and Mount Vernon did for Washington. It had a beautiful panoramic view built as it was on top of a hill, with a clear view of greenland and woodland, Long Island sound and the distant Connecticut shore. It was the ideal getaway for a born naturalist like Theodore furnished with his trophies of hunting – stuffed animals, wild animal pelts and many weapons and souvenirs including numerous photographs of his worldwide hunting scenes. His library covered a wide range of his interests on poetry, literature, philosophy, history and many other subjects.

Also displayed were mementos of his children, especially his fighting boys in the services. One son, Quentin, never returned home for he was killed in an air battle over German lines. This tragedy hit him very hard, but he proudly and publicly expressed his satisfaction that Quentin had died on active duty, fighting for the America he loved.

Before leaving the subject of Theodore's second marriage – a fascinating story is told of the circumstances surrounding this marriage to his second wife, Edith Carow. It seems they grew up as close neighbours on East 20th Street in New York City and even formed a romantic relationship before they drifted apart when Theodore moved to Harvard. There he met Alice, his first wife. When Alice died, Edith Carow and Theodore became acquainted once again. Soon the embers of the old love affair were re-ignited and they were married in London in 1886.

Incidentally, when Alice, his daughter of the first marriage, was discovered by the media to be a smoker and fond of a gamble, Theodore just shrugged and told the newsmen "I can do one of two things – I can be President of the United States or I can control Alice – I cannot do both." His second marriage produced five children, Theodore Junior, Kermit, Ethel, Archibald and Quentin.

This seems to have been a time he drifted from politics and back to writing when he produced two of his best books Essays on Practical Politics and The Winning of the West in four volumes, published in 1899. Theodore's grief for his first wife never really subsided for he never mentioned her name again not even in his autobiography. But I must add a few words about her here.

Theodore Roosevelt's sister Corinne was a friend of Edith Carow Roosevelt before Edith married her brother Theodore. They lived on the same street in the Union Square neighbourhood of New York. Edith reared five children for Theodore but always claimed he was the sixth. She was responsible for the role the family house on Long Island played, as an extension of the Governor's mansion where foreign dignitaries and politicians were part of its constant flow of visitors. Despite the Roosevelt riches, Edith was constantly aware of the cost involved and often opposed Theodore's ambitions for high office because of this. Yet she never seemed to be able to control her unruly children sliding down the banisters of the White House or confronting their guests with a collection of family pets. Once, Kermit produced his kangaroo rat from his pocket to send him hopping down the breakfast table in front of a famous journalist. Edith was a natural part of the team without whom Theodore could never have flourished.

But the lure of politics was in his blood and soon Theodore found himself back in the fray. This time, on the Presidential campaign in support of Benjamin Harrison in 1888. Harrison won and because of Theodore's condemnation of the patronage system he very soon found himself appointed by Harrison as a trouble shooter against patronage in the role of U.S. Civil Service Commissioner.

Despite opposing him for the Presidency, Theodore was next called on by President Cleveland to head the New York police force as Police Commissioner. We have already discussed these jobs and the impact Theodore brought to them. Theodore was now recognized countrywide as one of the foremost reformers around. Once again he was stirred by a book. It was called How the Other Half Lives by Jacob Riis with harrowing stories of poverty in America.
Suddenly a new window of opportunity was beckoning the ambitious Roosevelt. With the election of another President after Cleveland – William McKinley from Ohio – Theodore pushed hard for the job of Assistant Secretary to the Navy. McKinley reluctantly agreed to give him the job and Theodore immediately set about building the Navy in anticipation of a war between America and Spain.

We have discussed the war in detail under the notes on William McKinley, so there is no need to go into the events here.

As war fever rose the one infected by this disease most was Theodore Roosevelt himself. He resigned from his Navy post and raised volunteers among his cowboy and socialite pals. Cutting through the red tape "The Rough Riders" Roosevelt's own fighting unit was born and launched with Theodore leading the invasion on transports to Cuba.
The humanitarian reasons against intervention in Cuba were moving. The spectacle of utter ruin to a landscape so beautiful and fertile would not be too readily forgiven by the people of America. But debates based on sentimentality were a poor substitute for the wealth that had been invested in Cuba. Some say $30 million to $50 million had been invested up to that time in plantations, railroads, mining and other business enterprises. By 1894 this had risen to $96 million the year before the insurrection broke out. It is easy to understand therefore that the colossal power of the vested interests lobby in America would pull no punches in achieving intervention.

Well, that is some of the background to the story of Cuba in the life of President McKinley and President Roosevelt.

But, what about Theodore's Rough Riders? Where does Theodore Roosevelt fit into a picture that just could not take place today? Just read on.

The Rough Riders

Young Arthur, Theodore's son, remembers his father lying on the lawn at Oyster Bay taking rifle practice at a life sized target pinned to a tree. The children watched with fascination, some even stopped to look over his shoulder along the rifle to the target. When brother Edward cheered out loud at a particularly good shot, Theodore rebuked him gently. Shh! "Bunnies mustn't talk. I must practice if I am to kill enough Spaniards to win the war."

Theodore's enthusiasm for the war was so urgent he had sacrificed his job as Assistant Secretary of the Navy to form the Rough Riders. Yet it is a strange quirk of family history that Theodore's forebears had avoided service in the Civil War and the war of 1812. Theodore was not too happy with his father's decision to buy his way out of the Civil War under the Conscription Act of 1863. He paid a young German immigrant $1,000, quite a large sum at the time to replace him. The immigrant, Abraham Graf, also received his weekly wage of $38 for the privilege. He was later captured by the Confederates but died of fever and scurvy in a Union Hospital in 1865 just as the war was finishing.

Theodore's father never met and never knew the fate of poor Abraham Graf. Strangely, Theodore's mother, Mittie, was a Confederate at heart and insisted that Theodore's father must not take up arms against the family. Roosevelt Senior acceded to her request. Perhaps this little story reflects an underlying hunger in Theodore to make amends for this perceived dishonour in the family. Who knows!

Theodore actually allowed this enthusiasm to overflow into downright disrespect for the officers in the regular army outside his Rough Riders outfit. He said in his book Rough Riders that the majority of these officers were not improving, some were even going backwards. This prejudice of his towards the professional soldiers became outright insubordination on his part. The recklessness of his own unit had a brief and bloody history. Seventeen Rough Riders fell in the battle of Las Guasimas. Burying the dead inspired this comment from Theodore. "Here together in the common grave lie Indian and cowboy, miner, packer and college athlete. The man of unknown ancestry from the lonely western plains and the man who carried on his watch the crest of the 'Stuyvesant and the Fisher'." "The common grave," he said, "was a metaphor for all that is best in America." Incidentally eighty-nine of the one thousand casualties in the conflict were Rough Riders. Could such a high casualty rate be attributed to bravery or could it be down to the reckless foolhardiness of their leader, Theodore Roosevelt – I guess we'll never know!

The war was a short one with Spain, but the one in the Philippines (discussed under our notes on McKinley) dragged on for another three years. The biggest winner was Theodore himself, who added even further to his growing reputation as the hero of the press room. They coined the name "Teddy" as an affectionate reference to someone they now considered "an old buddy". Strangely, Theodore didn't like it.

But now another man enters the life of Theodore Roosevelt and without knowing it he was instrumental in "Teddy" becoming the 26th President of the United States. His name was Senator Thomas C. Platt.

Platt didn't like Theodore's reforming zeal but he swallowed his pride to invite Theodore to accept the nomination to run for Governor of New York. It was going to be a hard contest but Theodore with his war record to back him won by a small majority. The deal was that in office, Theodore would consult Platt on difficult issues. Anybody who knows our Theodore at this point in the story could have told Platt that this was a non-runner. Theodore immediately set about pushing for a tax on public service businesses. His independent assertiveness rubbed a lot of people the wrong way. At that time, Theodore's book The Rough Riders came on the market and became a big hit. But Platt was having his own private nightmares about Theodore so he conceived a devious plot to bury Theodore in the political wilderness of the Vice Presidency. From there nobody could return.

Theodore accepted the nomination as McKinley's running mate and after the election became Vice President to William McKinley.

But here we re-introduce an old friend of ours. You may remember reading about him under the McKinley notes. A great friend of McKinley, a successful business man and reputed to pull all the strings in the background of the McKinley camp.

Yes his name was none other than Mark Hanna. The personality of Theodore however, disconcerted Hanna, for Teddy's career to date had been all action and achievement. New York State Legislator, a Western rancher, a City Police Commissioner, Assistant Secretary of the Navy and a one term Governor of New York State. Yet despite all these achievements, Theodore's unpredictability did nothing to comfort Hanna. It eventually proved a doomed relationship for Theodore and Hanna were completely incompatible.

When placed in the Vice Presidency by the orchestration of Senator Platt, Hanna was heard to say "Don't you realize there is now only one heartbeat between that damn cowboy and the White House!"

The tragic events that removed McKinley from this life vindicated all Mark Hanna's fears. "That damn cowboy" was now the 26th President of the United States.

On the morning that McKinley passed away at 2.15 a.m. Saturday September 14, 1901, the Vice President Theodore Roosevelt was high in the Adirondacks and he could not be reached until late on Friday September 13 with news of McKinley's relapse. He had to ride all night by horse-drawn wagon to catch a special train, waiting to take him to Buffalo.

But while he was travelling, McKinley passed away. Next day on Saturday September 14, 1901 Theodore Roosevelt was sworn into office at the residence of Ansley Wilcox at Buffalo N.Y. and the oath was administered by Judge John R. Hazel of the United States District Court.

Theodore's reaction when he was finally given his lifelong ambition of President was written in a letter to his friend Senator Henry Cabot Lodge. "It is a dreadful thing to come into the Presidency this way; but it would be a far worse thing to be morbid about it. Here is the task and I have got to do it to the best of my ability and that is all there is about it."

Theodore had indeed the determination, ambition and experience having served under three weak Presidents, who were really captives of their Congress and prisoners of conventional outmoded ideas. The bullets that killed McKinley also killed the dinosaur of conservatism, opening the way for a new style of Presidency under Theodore Roosevelt.

Roosevelt, unlike his predecessors, had the will to control any environment that crossed his path. He met his adversary in a one to one combat without pity, just as he had tackled in private his own grief at the death of his mother and his first wife in childbirth.

He had one failure ticked against his record however, when he was confronted by a young bear cub on a bear hunting trip in Mississippi; he just hadn't the heart to shoot it. The story reached the ears of Clifford Berryman who promptly drew a cartoon of the incident for the Washington Post. A Brooklyn Toy Store Manager, Morris Michtom, placed a copy of the cartoon next to a stuffed baby bear. Morris called it Teddy's Bear.

However later events proved a new star had been born. The Teddy Bear became a major market leader for years to come.

But let's get on with the Roosevelt story.

Up to that time, Theodore was the youngest President at forty-two to live in the White House. He liked to skinny dip in the Potomac but expected his Cabinet to share his hobby with him. As I pointed out earlier, Roosevelt was loyal to his friends regardless of where they came from. One old friend, a cowhand from his ranch in Detroit came to the White House and was refused admission. Theodore's advice was typical of the man. "The next time they don't let you in Sylvane, you just shoot through the windows."

Incidentally, his father's personality played a big part in Theodore's life. A lovely little story is told here to underline that relationship and is told by his sister, Corinne Roosevelt about Theodore's first night in the White House as President. Sitting around the table for dinner were his two sisters and their husbands. Theodore spoke feelingly of his father "Do you realize that this is our father's birthday, September 23. I have realized it as I have signed papers all day long and I feel that it is a good omen that I begin my duties in this house on this day. I feel as if my father's hand were on my shoulder, as if there were a special blessing over the life I am to lead here."

There were some strange parallels in the lives of both men. His father taught Sunday school, so did Theodore. Social reform was the driving force of his father, as it was with Theodore. His father's life was one of rectitude and honour and this was the model followed by the new President.

The White House was now Theodore's new home so he set about renovating it into a mansion of aristocratic class and smartness, something that had been missing for generations. Soon, Theodore and his family were to become a national institution.

The sounds of children's laughter were now a ripple of joy not experienced by the staff for years. Games were played and being Roosevelt's children, the rough and tumble was loud and boisterous – cowboy shoot-outs could be seen on the staircase, in the bedrooms or behind the furniture and even in the President's study. True to form Theodore did not need too much encouragement to join in. Celebrities were an ever-present feature in the social life of the Roosevelt's. Because of Theodore's comprehensive interest in the arts, literature, sport and politics and of course those friends from his cowboy days and hunting trips; the variety of personalities that passed through the front door of the White House was breathtaking. Poets, writers, financiers and stars of show business rubbed shoulders with his pals from the Rough Riders as well as one or two prize fighters and church Bishops.

His expeditions to Rock Creek Park never diminished and continued to challenge the fittest among his friends and Diplomats in walking, climbing, running and swimming under the harshest of trials! Throughout the treks he could be heard in his high pitched voice debating and discussing events of today and yesterday.

Life in the White House was so colourful during Theodore's seven year stay, a day without something exciting happening was worth a cartoon in the press. Such a cartoon did appear in the daily press. In it the head of the family leaves down his newspaper to get on with his breakfast. "The paper must be dull today," said his wife. "It is, not a thing doing in the White House." It was as if every day White House observers expected some new activity of their live-wire President to hit the headlines.

Of course, his choice of Cabinet had to be an unorthodox one. Over his two terms he put together an informal group of people whose main quality for membership was the trust and friendship he enjoyed from them. It was known as the Tennis Cabinet and included Leonard Wood, a Major General; James A. Garfield, son of the murdered ex-President; Gifford Pinchot, Chief of the Forestry Service and two Ambassadors, one of whom was a French historian. Although he promised to continue McKinley's programme, change was soon to overtake that promise.   He discovered he was courting a serious row with Southern politicians by entertaining the black educator Booker T. Washington to dinner at the White House. Such was the uproar that erupted he never repeated the invitation.

Theodore seldom made mistakes a second time. In his lighter moments he often accounted for his astute politics to his association in his early days, as he put it, with liquor sellers, a butcher, a pawn broker, twenty low Irishmen and even the Democrats he met in the New York State Assembly. He also included as his educators, such down to earth personalities as his Rough Riders, cowboys and felons alike.

Harold Evans records in his fascinating book The American Century the level of wealth around just as Theodore Roosevelt came to power. Some of the statistics Harold Evans produced paints an astonishing picture of the kind of America Theodore now had to grapple with as the Chief Executive. Up to 1901, he shot from the hip fearlessly at a level just below the top layer of politics. Now that he had been handed the ultimate power, how would he handle it?

He was now aware that the gilded society had spawned four thousand millionaires by 1901. Half of America's wealth was in the hands of only 1% of the population. The money barons shamefully shunned the past and its idealists. Fifth Avenue displayed ostentatiously its vulgar riches in the form of mansions, one more ridiculous than the other. Imitation French chateaux were everywhere built by the glue kings, the copper kings, the railroad kings and were a source of awe to the rubbernecking tourists that came to see them.

Their prices in today's money would be astronomical. One at 52nd Street and Fifth Avenue has been valued at forty-one million dollars in today's money. The inner French carved woodwork had been torn from their moorings in a real French chateau and transported to America regardless of the expense. It was now part of the new American architecture. By World War I in 1914, Vanderbilt houses throughout the country were valued at 513 million dollars for seventeen of them. There were three on Fifth Avenue alone. Reading about this extravaganza in opulence would be depressing if I were to continue. In sixteen years time (1930) the whole edifice would crumble and fall with a crash not of bricks and mortar but of the cash tills of the greedy and selfish. But that's a story for another President, Herbert Hoover to deal with.

John Pierpont Morgan, Rockefeller and Andrew Carnegie were three of the top barons of finance, sometimes called the "Robber Barons". "U.S. Steel", maker of everything from machine tools to battleships was America's first billion dollar corporation. Buying up the smaller companies to form these Corporations was called "Morganisation". The price of course was very much in favour of the purchasing monopoly owned by the robber barons. But the paper money generated had the seeds of that great future stock market collapse built into it as early as the year 1904 but no one suspected it.

The biggest mistake these finance barons made, was to flaunt their wealth and power outrageously as they cornered the market of anything you can name – glass, rubber, whiskey, flour, sugar, meat and on down to the humble coffin. Most sinister of all, they had power over labour and its conditions, its pay and its locations. Morgan's arrogant boast was not gratitude but a contemptuous "I owe the public nothing." This contempt for the people was like a red rag to a bull and very dangerous when that snorting bull was Roosevelt.

He took action five months later when he instructed his Attorney General to prosecute Morgan under the Trust Act. I won't dwell on the details. Morgan attempted to fix a deal with Roosevelt but was told "We don't want to fix it. We want to stop it." The Detroit Free Press claimed that "Wall Street is paralyzed at the thought that a President would sink so low as to enforce the law."

The Sherman Anti-Trust Law of 1890, from the Presidency of Benjamin Harrison, that some people thought was dead, was now about to be tested. The law had some frightening teeth. Theodore won and more anti-trust cases followed, more than from Harrison, Cleveland and McKinley combined. Later, when Roosevelt had left the White House, Morgan petulantly remarked "I hope the first lion he meets does his duty." I presume the lion in question was not on Morgan's payroll for Theodore survived for many years afterwards. Yet this triumph of Theodore did not end there. He was up to his armpits in direct confrontation in his efforts to solve labour disputes. He even invited Labour and Capital to the White House where he acted as mediator to solve the coal strike of 1902 that was turning to violence.

A pen picture here of J.P. Morgan is not triumphal but a sad one. He was pompous, imperious and moody as power became boring. Yet he was a lonely man ever since his first wife died of tuberculosis, a woman he married knowing she was dying. His second marriage was loveless. He was a snob, an anti-Semite and loved yachts, elegant women and paintings, in that order. He avoided service in the Civil War yet sold defective rifles to the Union army. One feels deep down that his wealth and power as life went on must have seemed a great big useless delusion to him. He died in 1913, aged seventy-six.

Theodore's major claim to fame has been his role as "Trust Buster" for he seemed to spend his entire Presidency in showdowns with vested interests. One of his most controversial battles was with the meat packing business. He himself had objected during the American-Spanish War to the putrid beef sold to the army. Now incensed by a bland report about the business by the Department of Agriculture, he appointed his own Commission headed by two men he trusted, a commissioner of labour and a socially conscious lawyer.

He was also inspired by a book called The Jungle by the famous Upton Sinclair on the vile conditions that prevailed in Chicago meatpacking houses. Better packing and dating was the outcome for all meat packed in these big warehouses. Naturally the beef lords objected since their markets served all of Europe. They fought back but Theodore released part of the sickening second report by his own people. Fears for their reputation in Europe pushed the meat cartels into a compromise. This art of compromise was always one of Roosevelt's trump cards in getting progress. He was always happy to accept half a loaf to get half his way.

By tackling the privilege system at its roots in the Civil Service, Roosevelt succeeded in attracting a much more impressive individual to the Civil Service and so aiding his reform campaign enormously.

One of Roosevelt's quotes sums up neatly his unchanging attitude towards dishonesty and corruption in the corridors of power. He said "There is a widespread conviction in the minds of the American people that the great Corporations known as Trusts are in certain of their features and tendencies hurtful to the general welfare .... Corporations engaged in interstate commerce should be regulated if they are found to exercise a license working to the public injury."

Roosevelt had every reason to be worried about these monsters at the end of the 19th century for statistics showed that 185 of them together had a total capitalization of three billion dollars. The speed of their growth in the previous three years had been frightening.

But Roosevelt's fight with the major Corporations was not confined to Trust busting. His welfare campaign in defense of the weaker section of society found a voice in new legislation. He introduced laws to protect the lives and health of miners, streetcar conductors, motormen and factory employees. Also enacted was a Women's Compensation Act, a compensation law for Government employees and a law to investigate children and women's labour. Another law came on stream to regulate hours for railroad employees. Now it was truly a war between his Administration and big business and it must have been successful for vast sums of money was set aside by these Corporations to prevent his re-election as President in 1904. They failed. Roosevelt's observation later was "The hearts and minds of the people had spoken in favour of him."

Yet despite his all out war on corruption in business, in which he even threatened to nationalize the mines to force a settlement in a trade dispute, he was often accused of inconsistencies by using troops to break up legitimate strikes and by entering private agreements with U.S. Steel. In fact, near the end of his Presidency, he began to run out of steam and according to some progressives became less dedicated to reform as time went by. Perhaps this was not so surprising given the vast spread of his areas of interests, such as his natural resources programme, foreign policy, the Panama Canal, his role as Trust Buster, his African hunting trips, his work as a writer, and his role as mediator between Russia and Japan for which he was awarded the Pulitzer Peace Prize.

Strangely enough, although he was known as the Trust Buster, Theodore initiated no more than forty-four suits while in office. His successor, Howard Taft, initiated ninety suits and Woodrow Wilson eighty suits under the Sherman Anti-Trust Act of 1890. Statistics tell one story but right or wrong, they could never match the passion of Theodore in pursuit of justice. Anyway, your writer has not run out of steam for Theodore Roosevelt's story still has a lot of mileage left in it, so let's move on.

While Theodore was still in the White House, John Morley, an astute British observer, wrote "Do you know the two most wonderful things I have seen in your country – Niagara Falls and the President of the United States. Both great wonders of nature, creative in harness and rampant in flood."

But despite these glowing tributes by foreigners to Theodore, it is the simple human stories that paint the most intimate pictures of the man.

Here are some moving little anecdotes about Roosevelt's tour out West. One concerned a little prairie town in Kansas, where two children without seats stood near his pew in church. Theodore invited them into his pew and together they sang the hymns from the one hymn book. Another one happened on the Dakota prairie. As his train slowed on passing a little brown schoolhouse, he noticed the teacher and children waiting to get a glimpse of him. Throwing his lunch napkin on the table, he hurried to the train platform and waved to them. "Those children wanted to see the President of the United States and I could not disappoint them. They may never have another chance. What a deep impression these things make when we are young." Another story can be told about the time he was shaking hands with a group of children that swarmed around him. He noticed a lonely little girl on the fringe of the crowd, shabbily dressed, and a look of hopelessness on her face, being so far away from him. He promptly jumped down from his car and pushed his way to the little girl whose face lit up with joy when he grabbed her hand and shook it vigorously.

Despite Theodore's friendly disposition, he could be a real stickler for morality in public life and refused point blank to entertain Maxim Gorky to the White House because Maxim was travelling with a woman not his legal wife. The Russian Grand Duke who led a notoriously scandalous life was also treated with the same disdain. When he came to visit the White House the President made sure Mrs. Roosevelt was not around and she never met him.

Strangely, despite his high profile career and public popularity, in 1904 Roosevelt was not to be an automatic choice for a second term. Unbelievably that political pygmy, the wily businessman, Mark Hanna, who bank rolled McKinley's rise to power was being suggested for the Republican nomination. However, this bizarre possibility never arose for Mark Hanna died shortly before the Convention and Theodore was nominated with a comfortable vote for a second campaign. Alton B. Parker was his Democratic opponent and Roosevelt was re-elected President by 336 electoral votes to 140.

Theodore in one of his Presidential campaign speeches was introduced to an audience as the poor man's friend. Before he even began his address he was quick to gently correct the compere. "Let me announce," he said, "that I am the poor man's friend if the poor man is straight. I am the rich man's friend if the rich man is straight. If a man is crooked I am against him, rich or poor."

Theodore's inauguration for a second term took place on Saturday March 4, 1905 on the East Portico of the White House. As usual the Chief Justice administered the oath; this time it was Justice Melville Weston Fuller. The parade lived up to its glorious expectations, lasting for three hours between 3 p.m. and 6 p.m. in the afternoon. 200,000 people attended, more than the crowd capacity of a modern sports stadium. Despite that windy day on March 4, 1905 Theodore gave his inaugural address bareheaded, the first to do so of the twenty-six Presidents to date.

Theodore's second Administration opened up as his first one had ended, with an undiminishing energy and zeal for domestic reform.

In 1905, the year his new term began, a maximum rate was introduced in the railroad freight industry, thanks to Theodore's efforts to curb and cap over-the-top freight rates that were crippling business, especially for the farmers using the railways to transport their goods.

Ever the pragmatist, Theodore preferred action to words. The Panama Canal was one of those challenges to his restless spirit. Since he wanted results and not debates, he threw himself into the project and let Congress catch up with him. The Canal was to be Roosevelt's most historical achievement. J.L. Stoddard, our old friend from the press, had this to say "In view of his passionate interest in the canal it is strange he has not been honoured with a plaque or monument to identify him with this achievement." Stoddard felt that the structure was so important a tower of light should be seen on each side of the isthmus from both the Atlantic and the Pacific. Such was Roosevelt's input into the canal, according to Stoddard the beams from them would be a constant reminder to voyagers of the man who made the canal possible.

Theodore was constantly aware of America's right to security on the shores of both Oceans. In one speech he said "We should have it clearly understood by our own people especially, but also by other people that the Pacific is as much our home waters as the Atlantic."

Another project of Roosevelt's was one of the most dynamic and successful programmes ever launched in America. In fact it is still one of the many that future generations of Americans are deeply grateful for. This was his programme of radical reform in the running of National Parks and Forests from the Atlantic to the Pacific Oceans. He succeeded in introducing schemes for irrigation, reclamation and preservation which were never heard of before this. The Inland Waterways Commission was established to promote the area of water power development, the connection between the rivers, soil and forests and their place in the environmental landscape. His biggest contribution in this area however, was the transfer of 125 million acres of public land into forest reserves thus doubling the number of National Parks. Also, something that would appeal to the lifestyle of the ordinary citizen was the creation of fifty-one wildlife refuges over fourteen States. Modern environmentalists would have loved him for it.

Sometimes, Theodore could be so passionate about his particular project he was prepared to bend the rules a little in his favour. Not dishonestly but perhaps deviously. The intention he had to send American battleships around the world as a public relations exercise was thwarted by lack of funds in the Treasury. However, Theodore was not to be frustrated by the Senate Finance Committee. His side of the story goes like this "Loeb and I got to work on the job of digging up funds out of unexpended balances in different departments. We finally found enough money to take the fleet around South America to Japan and China, possibly a little further. It would then be half way round the world. I made up my mind to send the ships that far and then later Aldrich (Secretary of the Committee) took responsibility for leaving them there at anchor or appropriate the funds to bring them back." Aldrich would have no option: he would have to bring them home by way of the Atlantic which was exactly what Theodore wanted. Aldrich and his Committee of Senators surrendered handsomely and the fleet sailed around the world to be greeted everywhere in a friendly spirit. Yes, Teddy duly got his way.

Referring to this voyage around the world, Roosevelt said "The show of force had its intended effect. It was the most important service that I rendered to peace." Critics disagreed. They said "The Japanese welcomed the fleet into Tokyo Bay. Had they been bellicose they could have blown it out of the water or at least interpreted Roosevelt's gesture as a provocative act." In either event it would have been Roosevelt and not others who had endangered the peace.

Incidentally, Roosevelt's "Great White Fleet" of warships that set out on their 46,000 mile journey in December 1907 consisted of sixteen battleships.

But a world famous event far more important than Theodore's adventures with the American Navy took place twelve months earlier on the West Coast of the Pacific.
In April 1906, America suffered a devastating earthquake in San Francisco which razed two-thirds of the city to the ground, killing many and leaving half a million people homeless. There were 28,000 buildings destroyed, the rebuilding of which created millions of jobs but unbelievably the building codes to protect future generations from a repeat of this tragedy were

torn up in the rebuilding and ignored. Today the city is built on the San Andreas Fault, the tectonic plates of which are still building up stresses that will one day tear themselves apart.

There is almost an accepted certainty that this will happen before the year 2030. In October 1989, a minor quake 7.1 on the Richter scale lasting ten seconds, destroyed hundreds of buildings and the underground water system. Only the help of local citizens pulling fire hoses six blocks saved the day – and that was for a ten second shock. The Bay Bridge and the Golden Gate Bridge have been reinforced since but they say an earthquake of 8 on the Richter scale could topple both of them. Back in 1906, 6,000 troops were brought in to blow up houses to make fire-breaks against a fire raging at 2,000 degrees Fahrenheit. Looters were ordered to be shot on sight which resulted in the tragic death of many. The fire-break didn't work and water had to be pumped miles from the Ocean to the fire. The battle was finally won but not before 498 people died. Today seven million people now live in the danger zone.

Hurricanes and volcanoes can be predicted but earthquakes can not. The web of crisscrossing faults threatens the superstructures of thousands of buildings at present and the cost of such devastation could be astronomical. One worry prevails however. Complacency and denial of a potential future disaster can be a more lethal fault than anything the Andreas Fault can bring. Will future tourists arrive there some day to view the ruins like another Pompeii or Atlantis, and will they when they come, shake their heads and ponder at the awful folly of mankind? Let's hope my speculation will never come to pass.

Now let's return to a lighter and much happier subject.
It is not very well known that the whole Roosevelt family had a remarkable history. Edward J. Renehan Jr. in his book called The Lion's Pride gives a very accurate insight into the Roosevelt family, some of it heartrending stuff.

Kermit grew up a carbon copy of his father. The similarities were remarkable. He loved hunting, exploration, history and languages such as Greek, Romany and Sanskrit. He even wrote just like his father and travelled far into foreign places. He was destined to be a great pal of his father all down the years. Sadly he drank too much. Theodore always had grave misgivings about Kermit. Disturbingly, he had brilliance balanced by weakness peculiar to most alcoholics.

The truth is, drink to the Roosevelt's was a curse that followed the family everywhere. Strangely, Winston Churchill became Kermit's close friend and generously gave him a commission in the British Army. Unfortunately, due to a medical condition Kermit was invalided out of the British Army in 1941. He returned to the war in the American Army thanks to the influence of F.D.R. Tragically, he finally ended his quest for fulfillment with a service .45 revolver.

Archie at forty-eight still suffered from his war wounds of 1918 but again with the influence of FDR was commissioned as Lieutenant Colonel and posted to New Guinea. He was such a success as a soldier, the Australians named one area of a battle after him in his honour. They called it "Roosevelt Ridge".

Colonel Theodore Jr. was promoted Brigadier General in 1942. Theodore's grandson Quentin was awarded the Silver Star and the Croix de Guerre. Ted, as he was known, went on to play a major role on D Day, June 6, 1941. The boat carrying Ted was first to touch down on the sand and he not only led his men up the beach under fire to establish them inland, but went back to re-direct different waves of troops onto the beach. For this he was given the

Congressional Medal of Honor. When asked for his opinion on the greatest act of bravery he saw in forty years service, General Bradley unhesitatingly chose Ted Roosevelt's actions on Utah Beach that June day in 1941.

Theodore Junior was the most decorated soldier to serve in World War II. At the age of fifty he had been complaining of heart trouble while still keeping his problem from the doctor. He dropped dead after a rigorous day on the front lines. "The Lion is dead" Quentin wrote to his mother. He was buried in the military cemetery at Saint Laurent sur Mer near Normandy on Bastille Day. It was also the 26th Anniversary of Quentin's father who was killed over Germany in 1918. An army band played "The Son of God Goes Forth to War". General Bradley and General Patton were pallbearers and two buglers played taps. After the war, Kermit's son Kim, was a leading figure in the C.I.A. masterminding the fall of Mossadegh and the return of the Shah to Iran. Later, Archie had a successful career in Wall Street.

Alice, the eldest of the generation known as "Auntie Sister" remained controversial and unpredictable to the end. I'm sure you will remember Theodore's words to the press I wrote about earlier "I can do the President's job or control Alice. I can't do both." She was the wild, independent, irreverent daughter of Theodore's first wife Alice, who died in childbirth. Well, Alice survived to the ripe old age of ninety-six and when she died in 1981, she was still practicing yoga.

Yes, truly a royal family of the American ruling class. An aristocracy the Americans can always be truly proud of.
But retirement was looming down the road now for Theodore Roosevelt and he was anxious to select a successor as soon as possible. It was January 1908 when William Loeb paid him a visit after breakfast one morning. He wanted to discuss the National Convention with Theodore. Loeb was worried about the right kind Presidential candidate to surface, one who could be selected with the full backing of the White House since Theodore had already made it clear he would not be entering the race. Loeb feared a deadlocked Convention which would force Theodore out of his intended retirement back into the fray. Theodore was adamant Elihu Root was the man for the job but Root while flattered at the suggestion felt he would not be electable.

Thoughts then moved to William Howard Taft as the next best. True to form Roosevelt said "Right we've all talked about a candidate long enough, its time for a decision." "Put yourself in Loeb's hands," Roosevelt told Taft. "I'll let it be known I'm backing you. I'll lighten Loeb's load so that you two can work together." The decision had now moved from a vague "favourably disposed" opinion towards Taft's candidacy to a public backing of Taft for the Presidency. It was a relief to get that out of the way for Teddy was anxious to get back into private life again, a feeling that was also shared by his whole family.

At last, Theodore would be free to indulge in his second dearest passion – his ambition to be a writer. His life's colourful story line was to be his raw material and the instrument for this communication would be a magazine called Outlook. Of course his planned African journey on safari would be the cream on his literary Christmas cake. But any man who hopes to hear God laugh will surely hear Him if such a man indulges in making long term plans. For Theodore Roosevelt, the outcome was no different.

But let us return to events in 1908. Theodore did not want to experience that lessening of commitment to his Presidency as the time for change approached and the ambitious ones scanned the horizon for a possible successor or a loosening of his hand on the tiller. With his successor in place, a smooth run up to the Convention was essential to Theodore's ambition to achieve a smooth handover of power and policies to the friends he left behind.

But George Cortelyou, Secretary of the Treasury, had his misgivings about how Roosevelt would handle his own role when the time to vacate the Presidency arrived. He said to Roosevelt "Next March 4, you will ride up Capitol Hill with all the power of office: a moment later you will ride down that same hill stripped of power – with your temperament it is going to be especially hard."

But Theodore had the answer to that one. "I am not going in for politics. I've made up my mind to go for the things I like and have neglected. I've had my day and I know it."

But it was not going to be an easy ride up that hill and down again. The name William Howard Taft would see to that. Protests against Taft's nomination flowed into the White House by letter and in person by jealous rivals of Taft. Roosevelt was puzzled how little they understood Taft. "I've had to explain him to nearly all of our fellows," he said. "There's more red blood in Taft's little finger ….. than any of them."

But Theodore won the day and Taft was duly nominated. He resigned as Minister of War, thanked Roosevelt profusely and later even sat with him in his retreat at Oyster Bay to put the finishing touches to his acceptance speech. No man was happier than Roosevelt. After the sunshine of Oyster Bay they did not talk again until they met at the White House, five months later. But the gap between them gradually widened until Taft's election as President proved that the Roosevelt era was well and truly over.

Taft's acceptance speech had said it all, as follows – "Mr. Roosevelt led the way to practical reform. The chief functions of my Administration shall be to complete and perfect the machinery by which the President's policies may be maintained." It was a seamless transition of power. The speech could have been written by Roosevelt himself. But the rift between the two camps widened into a gulf and later to complete Roosevelt's humiliation, all his measures were thrust aside until it became plain to Theodore he was now only a lame duck President. Now only his title of President remained.

Two or three days before he left office, Roosevelt ordered a very important visitor to the White House, Henry L. Stoddard. "Sit down," said Theodore, "we'll hold up the procession for a while." He was referring to the line of well-wishers who had come to bid him farewell and waited outside. "I suppose I could have had another term," he mused, "to break the solid South vote would end it forever. Thousands of Southerners who wanted to vote Republican could do so without fearing safety to their local conditions." Roosevelt went on "They told me I could cause such a break. I do not know that I could but I felt that I would like to try. It was the one real temptation to run again. But I don't want four more years here. I have been a crusader here. I had to challenge and destroy certain influences or we would soon have had an intolerable condition imperiling everything. I believe I have raised the standards. The conscience of business had to be aroused. The authority of the Government asserted. We have had four years of uprooting. The country has had enough of it and of me. The ground is cleared for construction work. The man who clears is never the man to do the rebuilding. I am going off to Africa for a real fine time. I will be footloose and fancy-free in Sagamore in a year; I'll be the happiest man you ever saw."

Writing about the Presidency to a friend after seven years in office, Roosevelt revealed his private thoughts about what he felt the President's role should be. He wrote "I think it should be a very powerful office and the President should be a very strong man who uses without hesitation every power that the position yields ….. But he should be sharply watched by the people and held to strict accountability by them." However, it seemed to work differently in practice for Theodore who used what he called the President's "Bully pulpit" to "Hold everyone else accountable such as powerful Corporations, noisy Trade Unions and irritating foreign Governments he didn't approve of."

Before Roosevelt, the Presidency had been occupied as a sedate dwelling for low key chief executives but Theodore changed all that. At the time of McKinley's death, Theodore had good intentions to continue McKinley's policies but as soon as he felt the reins of power between his fingers, he took a much more forceful approach, especially to those Corporations, hostile and indifferent to public accountability.

The story of Theodore Roosevelt should finish here with the end of his reign as 26th President of the United States. But fate had organized that Theodore would not disappear into retirement entirely just sitting on his lawn looking out to sea over Long Island Sound for the rest of his days. Theodore had other ideas.

In 1909, the year he closed the door of the White House behind him for the last time, Theodore set off for Africa on that hunting safari trip he had promised himself. The hunting trophies he gathered provided a unique collection of animals for the Smithsonian Institution.

Another memorable trophy he gained from the trip was his firsthand account of it, which he published on his return. The book was called African Game Trails. Before returning home, Theodore managed to fit in a triumphal tour of European cities, reviewing armies and giving lectures at many universities. But you could not keep Theodore out of the news for long.

His return from Africa was a remarkable event. Some commentators said "an Emperor of old could not have got such a regal reception." Cheers were deafening as his ship entered New York Harbour. A quick hello by a reception committee, then a colourful parade up Broadway. But not a word about politics would Roosevelt utter.

But alas those inner demons thirsting for adventure and new challenges could not be quenched for long. Four years later he didn't even wait for Christmas when he headed for the jungles of Brazil in December 1913. At that time the Brazilian jungle was a place full of savage wild animals, reptiles, poisonous snakes, insects and worst of all swamp fever which was to eventually kill him at the early age of sixty. The trip was a disaster for him. Why he took on this dangerous and demanding challenge at fifty-five years of age is impossible to explain. It would be considered an act of lunacy by any normal human being. At that point in time he could have enjoyed a life of adulation and easy living on the laurels he had more than earned up to then.

But then again Theodore was a lot larger than life as lived by the average man. Only one year previously a demented fanatic John Schrank shot him at point-blank range in an assassination attempt. Luckily for Theodore the bullet was deflected by a manuscript and a spectacle case before imbedding itself in his chest. Surgeons marvelled at his amazing physical condition saying it was superb pectoral muscles in his chest that saved him. He insisted on continuing the speech he was giving despite his blood-stained shirt, growling "I will deliver this speech or die, one or the other. Friends, I shall ask you to be very quiet and please excuse me from making a very long speech. I'll do the best I can but you see there is a bullet in my body, but its nothing. I'm not hurt badly." Amazingly, the rest of his speech lasted fifty minutes before he was taken to hospital for the surgeons to work on. Schrank was committed to the Northern State Hospital for the Insane where he lived as a patient until he died on September 15, 1943, thirty-one years later.

I'm afraid I have digressed a little from the second adventure of Theodore's into the jungles of Brazil, one year after the assassination attempt. Why did he go we were asking earlier? Well, Theodore as usual had the best answer to that question. "I had to go. It was one of my last chances to be a boy," he said. I guess it was the heady adrenaline of danger that drove him on while hunting on safari.

This seems like padding but Theodore often shot charging lions, buffaloes and elephants at a time when accuracy and coolness only stood between him and certain death or a severe mauling. He certainly was no shrinking violet, for he was reputed to have killed eight elephants, six buffaloes, thirteen rhinoceroses and nine lions under very dangerous conditions. True to his reckless character he loved it when the odds were stacked against him. Poling through the rapids on the River of Doubt in Brazil, now called Roosevelt River, surrounded by hidden dangers from head hunters on the banks and jaguars and serpents in the undergrowth, were commonplace hazards he and his hunting party had to confront. My words do no justice to the very real dangers he experienced outside the pages of his book Through the Brazilian Wilderness which once again was a bestseller.

Again he returned home with hundreds of specimens for the American Museum of Natural History. But Theodore had paid a terrible price for this adventure, for he contracted swamp fever and never seemed to recover from it. Some say it led to his premature death.

So, how do we sum up the life of Theodore Roosevelt, 26th President of the United States? There were those who accused him of being a warmonger because of his permanent warning to America not to be caught napping. Yet that seems to have been the very fate of America in World War II, when she suffered a surprise attack on Pearl Harbour or even the tragedy in the heart of New York in September 2001 (9/11). Was fate returning to remind us of his warning and vindicate Theodore's call for vigilance at the start of the last century?

Despite all the foregoing achievements Theodore's greatest pride was his contribution to the welfare of the American people. His reign can be summed up in his speech in Syracuse, New York, on September 7, 1903. "We must treat each man on his worth and merits as a man. We must see that each is given a square deal because he is entitled to no more and should receive no less."

Sadly, those super charged batteries of bubbling joyful life were gradually losing their energy. The wheels of his life were turning ever more slowly. He lost his hearing in one ear and was complaining of being old. He was hospitalized in 1918 and the undiminishing pain of bereavement still hurt a broken heart for his lost son, Quentin. Nevertheless, he remained active right to the end. Theodore Roosevelt finally passed peacefully away in his sleep the night he died of inflammatory rheumatism at his Oyster Bay home on January 6, 1919, three months after his 60th birthday. He was laid to rest in Young's Memorial Cemetery, Oyster Bay, N.Y. His last words were "Please put out the light."

27th President   William Howard Taft

Born 1857
Died 1930
73 Years of age
1 Term
1909 – 1913
Age 52

Party: Republican
Profession: Lawyer
County: Ohio
Ancestry: British
Estate: $475,000
Hobbies: Golf; Basketball; Skating & Theatre

Physical Description: 6 Foot, Huge frame, weight 300 – 322 lbs, deep set eyes; ruddy complexion; turned up moustache

Significant extracts from Inaugural address, March 4, 1909
"I should be untrue to myself to my promises and to the declarations of the Party platform upon which I was elected to office if I did not make the maintenance and enforcement of those reforms a most important feature of my Administration … The suppression of lawlessness and abuses of power of the great combinations of Capital……."

WILLIAM HOWARD TAFT

If you care to ask any sailor who has sailed the mighty Atlantic Ocean or crossed the vast open spaces of the Pacific I am sure he will tell you many a yarn of turbulent storms and tempests that lifted his ships high on the waves of uncertainty, as they crashed around him, onto the foaming decks in a cascade of frightening grandeur.

But one thing is for certain. He will also marvel and even wax lyrical about the peaceful windless calm that always followed when the storm was over.

Well those are the images that strike me whenever I think of the tempestuous personality that was Theodore Roosevelt followed by the calm calculating legal intellectual called William Howard Taft.

They say he was a placid man in restless times. So laid back, so relaxed he could easily fall asleep, and often did, in the most unlikely places. In concert halls, at church or attending dinners even among his fellow politicians. He found it hard to get used to being addressed as Mr. President. "When I hear someone say Mr. President I look around expecting to see Mr. Roosevelt," he chuckled.

The fiery leader of the House, Joe Cannon accused him of political clumsiness. Cannon said, "Taft was so conciliatory he would have had Protestants in the College of Cardinal had he been Pope."

History has long since proved that Taft was no politician and was far more comfortable among the Judges and Barristers of the Supreme Court. In fact he dreaded the political limelight. Some commentators say he accepted the nomination for President only because he could not resist the juggernaut that was Theodore Roosevelt. Others say he took up golf as an escape from Roosevelt's attentions saying "The beauty of the sport lies in the fact that you cannot permit yourself to think of anything else."

A worried Roosevelt was not too happy however. He criticized Taft for procrastinating about starting his campaign for the Presidency.

But let us start the Taft story back in the mid 19th century when he first saw the light of this world.

He was born on September 15, 1857 in Cincinnati, Ohio to Alphonso and Louisa Maria Torrey Taft who were themselves descendants of an old New England family of British origin. The flare for law which William enjoyed was not surprising for his father a native of Vermont, was the son of a Judge and practiced law himself. His mother was his father's second wife. William Howard Taft was the seventh child of ten children, five of whom were born into the second marriage. His father eventually became a Judge in Ohio. Ulysses Grant was impressed enough to make Howard Taft's father Attorney General and later Secretary of War and Minister to both Austria and Russia.

William Taft was known to be even-tempered and intelligent. In 1874 at seventeen years of age he entered Yale University. When he graduated four years later in 1878 he came second in his class. His next step on the road to being a leading lawyer was the Cincinnati Law School and finally his law graduation in 1880 by passing the Bar examinations the same year. You can easily see that Taft's whole career path and talent was to be a lawyer in a family of

Judges. Politics at that stage in his career was not even considered. Law was his first and last love.

Going down the career route of his illustrious family the following appointments took no effort on his part. Assistant Prosecutor Hamilton County and Assistant County Solicitor all at twenty-eight years of age. But his career took a background seat at this stage when he met and married twenty-five year old Helen Herron, who he called Nellie, on June 19, 1886. She just happened to be the daughter of a well-known Cincinnati lawyer who was a law partner of President Rutherford B. Hayes, 25th President. Their three children were named Helen, Charles and Robert. The marriage lasted over forty-three years and Helen was reputed to have played a major role in his career at every stage. Besides her connections were impeccable.

Again I must point out Taft's total love affair was with the law. He once said "I love Judges and I love courts. They are my ideals that typify on earth what we shall meet hereafter in heaven under a just God!"

His next stop on the legal ladder he was climbing was to serve as a Judge in 1887 in an unfinished term in the Ohio Supreme Court. The following year he served a full term. Now only twenty-nine he had acquired highly placed connections in the legal profession. Thanks to his father's influence, Benjamin Harrison, the President appointed him Solicitor General of the United States. Taft modestly attributed his achievements to his well-placed connections and his good standing with the Republican Party which he had now joined. He claimed "Like any well-trained Ohio man I had my plate the right side up when offices were falling." Yet despite this humility on his part it was his undoubted brilliance that really attracted such recognition by the legal world of his time.

It seems Taff was quite successful in the job of Solicitor General winning eighteen out of twenty cases. But his thirst for the real bread and butter of the law saw him once again return as a Circuit Court Judge which he loved enough to continue on the bench for another eight years. While it was a happy time for him, his injunctions against trade unions and labour leaders earned him a very poor reputation as an enemy of the worker. Pleasing the courts and the people simultaneously is never easy. But it was as head of a Peace Commission in the Philippines that he acquired his first political experience. There he came into conflict with the military Governor General Arthur MacArthur whose cruel handling of the native Filipinos was not to Taft's liking. McArthur was replaced and Taft became Civil Governor General of the Islands. He then threw himself into reorganizing a very shoddy political system and succeeded in improving central and local structures in the Judicial, educational, tax and Civil Service areas. He even bought four hundred thousand acres of land from the Roman Catholic Church which he redistributed among the Filipinos. Incidentally when the job in the Philippines was first offered to Taft his wife Helen is reputed to have advised Howard to take it. To quote Helen "It is an invitation from the big world outside America." I half suspect, knowing Helen, she had other long term ambitions for him not unconnected with the White House. Future events will explain those words as the story of Howard Taft unfolds later.

Despite his success Taft continued to dislike politics preferring instead to be a Justice of the Supreme Court of the United States. As I have already pointed out his wife Helen had other ambitions for him – to become President of the United States. She had always wanted her husband to be President ever since her visit to the White House when she was a young girl as a guest of Rutherford B. Hayes. While still in the Philippines, Taft was actually offered a place in the Supreme Court but he declined it. This must have been a very traumatic decision to have to make but Taft felt his work in the Philippines remained "unfinished business".

Helen Herron, Taft Williams's wife really enjoyed her four years in the Philippines. Half her biography book was written about the Philippines but she had to go to Europe to rest from nervous exhaustion despite the luxury of life there. Helen controlled the domestic budget and so when Taft was recalled to Washington she worried at how he was going to pay the bills in Washington on a Cabinet salary as Secretary of War. The diffidence with which she was treated within the Philippines was absent in Washington. But it was all worth the sacrifices for she had one ambition only – to see her husband become President. Helen who loved travelling found her sacrifice paying off because during Taft's Presidency she journeyed around the world more than once. Yet somehow she never used her office to support reform movements. Perhaps she couldn't spare the time.

Later, in 1903, Taft returned to Washington as Roosevelt's Secretary of war. Yes he was indeed a very talented man very much in demand. The story of William Howard Taft from that point on is inextricably linked with Theodore Roosevelt who considered Taft "One of the country's most valuable assets." Taft himself remarked "The President seems really to take much comfort that I am in his Cabinet." As for Roosevelt he felt free to leave Taft "sitting on the lid" as he put it while he was away from Washington. Taft continued to be groomed by Roosevelt when he was made Roosevelt's personal Ambassador. He was often sent on diplomatic missions by Roosevelt. Taft was also very much involved in the peace negotiations between Japan and Russia which earned Roosevelt the Nobel Peace Prize.

Both men seemed to be in complete harmony as the new Presidential elections approached. Taft considered his job in the Presidency would be to consolidate Theodore's reforms. But one day Roosevelt was asked what he thought of Taft. Out came his answer outrageously blunt and undiplomatic. It was typical. Roosevelt told fearlessly exactly as he saw it. There wasn't a vindictive bone in Roosevelt's body but sadly his comment was misunderstood by Taft's family as contempt. Here is what he said. "Taft was an excellent man under me but he has not the slightest idea of what is necessary if this country is to make social and industrial progress." Roosevelt being Roosevelt just did not realize how deeply wounding that remark about Taft was to prove especially to Taft's family. How hurtful we shall see later.

Now at this stage of the story I must ask you to cast your mind back or better still return to our notes on Roosevelt. In the final chapters of his story we pointed out the way William Howard Taft had been selected for the Presidency polls against the better judgement of others. The undercurrents surrounding Roosevelt's sponsorship of Taft were not easily disguised so Taft's relatives were suspicious of Roosevelt's plans for the Presidency. Another incident increased their suspicion further. Taft's brother's decided to raid New York politically and take as many delegates as possible from Governor Hughes. They succeeded in persuading ten Senators to change sides. Roosevelt was angry. It just was not done to go into the home State of your rivals. "You will need Hughes," he cautioned Taft. This wise advice was again suspected by Taft's family to be a weakening of support by Roosevelt. Yes, political intrigue can indeed be fascinating.

As we said earlier, Helen Taft was very much a central figure in the Howard Taft story and her opinion on any decision concerning his career was always taken on board by the Taft family. Now her fingerprints were everywhere in the conflict between the two camps.

Her consuming ambition never wavered and was fully focused on him being the next President. A story that underlines this was when Taft was again offered a place on the Supreme Court in 1906. When asked if his father would accept the offer one of his son's replied, "Nope." "Ma wants him to wait and be President."

An unrecorded interview between Theodore Roosevelt and Taft's wife Helen resulted in Theodore not appointing Taft to the Supreme Court. It seems she had managed to persuade Theodore that her husband was White House material. Theodore wrote to Taft saying "After a half hours talk with your dear wife I have decided against appointing you to the Supreme Court." Yes Helen was a very formidable force indeed in the Howard Taft life story.

But the time for fulfilment of Helen's secret dreams was fast approaching. Convention day was here at last and the excitement of the occasion was captured in a book written by Joseph Bucklin Bishop called Presidential Nominations. In his book Bishop gives a very vivid picture of events as they unfolded in Taft's office on the afternoon of the Convention. Bishop had been invited there by Taft and sat with Taft's daughter and his younger son Charlie plus half a dozen personal friends. Helen sat at Taft's desk clearly agitated. The duration of the cheers for Roosevelt lasted forty-nine seconds which she had timed, it disturbed her painfully.

A bulletin arrived from the Convention hall. "Mrs. Taft's face went deathly white," wrote Bishop, as with a visible effect she read from a bulletin. "A large portrait of Roosevelt has been displayed on the platform and the Conference hall has exploded." It was bad news for Helen. Silence struck the room. An awestruck silence. The gloom deepened even further when another bulletin was read describing the march around the hall by Roosevelt supporters carrying a large American flag with Roosevelt's portrait on it. Helen's spirits rose on hearing the twenty-five votes had been given to Taft from Massachusetts. But when news of Taft's nomination finally came through Helen's face was the personification of pure happiness. I write all the foregoing to explain the anti-Roosevelt bias in Taft's camp, despite knowing that Theodore Roosevelt had no intention of going forward for a third term in the Presidency. It may also in some way, explain the drift away from Roosevelt soon after. Yet isn't it puzzling that despite all Roosevelt's goodwill towards him one "throw-away" opinion of Roosevelt's implying Taft would have no idea how to make social and industrial progress could cause so much damage.

As Taft's Presidency began, an ongoing resentment fuelled suspicion. Somehow all was not quite right between the two camps. But the drift that later developed into an open split in the Republican Party and would later hand the next Presidency to Woodrow Wilson the Democrat was now obvious. Amazingly nobody seemed to realize the danger to Party unity of having two camps inside one Party warring with each other.

But let's continue.

Taft hurried outside to meet Roosevelt to pour out his heartfelt appreciation for all his help. He repeated his thanks to Roosevelt next day at the White House when tendering his resignation as Secretary of War. Roosevelt and Taft talked of old times and new ones. The mood was euphoric. Taft duly left for Hot Springs, Virginia to prepare his acceptance speech in Cincinnati on July 29, 1908. But on July19, ten days before his speech, Taft stopped off at Oyster Bay to get Roosevelt's opinion on his final draft and to make the amendments as suggested by the President. That was the last Taft would see of Roosevelt for five months.

Perhaps that was because Taft now had someone else to answer to. Those people who still didn't approve of his friendship with Roosevelt. His round trip to Oyster Bay had not gone down too well with the family. They resented the impression he gave of being in Roosevelt's pocket. Poor Taft, he couldn't understand this criticism which took him completely by surprise. Eventually "blood proved thicker than water", to coin a phrase and Taft reluctantly distanced himself from Theodore. The abrupt separation of the two old friends was manipulated into a boycott of everything and everybody connected with his old boss. The new direction of the Administration was complete. Surprisingly nothing changed. Taft's acceptance speech was still Roosevelt's. That was significant when he said "The chief functions of my Administration shall be to complete and perfect the machinery by which the President's policies may be maintained."

The hustings for the election of the 27th President of the United States was soon underway. But Taft's lack of enthusiasm for politics or the Presidency lay just beneath the surface and was to be reflected in his almost indifference to the campaign work necessary to be elected. He left the enthusiasm and the speeches to the people in his camp and his mood was one of indifference. His heart was no longer in the job. The worrying development to all this resulted in a serious split in the Republican Party into two camps, one pro Theodore Roosevelt and the other pro Taft. The pre-election silent boycott by "Taft's people" of the Theodore Roosevelt regime was now irreparable. The two words "Taft's people" says it all. The sad exit of a once great President like Theodore Roosevelt makes you ask, who would be a politician? Underlying it all was the feeling that the Presidency had been hijacked from poor William Howard Taft.

The 1908 election held no surprises and William Howard Taft was duly declared victorious over his Democratic opponent William Jennings Bryan by 321 electoral votes to 162. The bizarre reality of the election was Howard Taft's indifference to the Presidency. He simply never shared the anti-Roosevelt's sentiment of his own family.
One real surprise, in view of the anti-Roosevelt camp in the new Administration was that all the major Cabinet Ministers held onto their posts carried over from the old regime. (Secretary of State, Roger Bacon), (War, Luke Wright), (Attorney General, Charles Bonaparte), (Postmaster General, George von Lengerke), (Navy, Truman Hardy), (Interior, James Garfield), (Agriculture, James Wilson), (Commerce, Oscar Straus), all were Roosevelt's men.

Before Taft took over, Roosevelt talked confidently about how he saw his new protégé performing for the next few years. "He knows what has to be done and will know how to build on the foundations that have been laid," Theodore said enthusiastically. "He has a legal mind. He can round out and shape up the policies of the last four years better than if I were to remain here. He has a big majority in Congress to back him and the country is with him."

But Theodore was whistling in the dark. Future events would not unfold exactly as he had forecast. Here I would like to remind everyone of the old saying "When man makes plans God just laughs". Well God was now laughing uproariously.

The day of Howard Taft's inauguration Thursday March 4, 1909 dawned a very stormy one. Gale force winds, rain, snow and sleet halted railroads and broke down telephones and telegraphs along the Atlantic seaboard. Most Presidents made their speeches on the steps of the Capitol but this part of the choreography of the inauguration ceremonies had to be abandoned by Taft. Republicans overflowed into the half-empty Democratic side of the Senate Chamber where Taft's inauguration speech was to be made. The oath was administered by Chief Justice Melville Weston Fuller.

The pivotal figures were Roosevelt and Taft. They wished well of each other but the feelings of the old friendship were gone and they knew it. There were whispers of trouble ahead but right now they were only whispers. Theodore said years later "Taft and I knew the true situation and its cause." The new President viewed the parade from the White House reviewing stand. Unfortunately the weather was so atrocious all incoming trains to Washington were cancelled. It seems there was never at any stage a personal split between Roosevelt and Taft. This can be seen by Roosevelt's later remark "Taft and I knew the true situation and the cause." I'm afraid only the historians can explain and elaborate on this little nugget.

Taft waved his silk hat in time with the rhythm of the song "In the good old summer time". But Theodore was not waiting around and was seen sitting in the train battling its way against the storm back to Oyster Bay having heard all the speeches since early morning especially the inauguration speech which he was hearing for the first time. The speech pleased Theodore.

Tariff revisions. The saving and restoration of our forests and waterways. Relief for railroads. They were all there. But the beginning was also the end and the hopes aroused by Taft's speech wilted like a full blown rose in an autumn wind. Now it was obvious to both of them that the autumn winds of the Roosevelt era had also begun to blow. The men chosen to be "A most important feature of my Administration" to quote Taft Joe Cannon and Senator Aldrich, were two of Roosevelt's most vociferous opponents. Once again the press got it right in a cartoon entitled "Carrying out Roosevelt's policies" showing "My Policies" being carried out on a stretcher from the White House by dutiful stretcher bearers.

One significant feature of Joe Cannon's appointment as Speaker was the power it gave him to allow a Congressman to speak on the floor of the House. Those unfortunate enough to be "tainted with Teddyism" as Cannon termed it, under existing rules, unless you had Cannon's favour you might as well have been in Timbuctoo on Safari with Teddy as on the floor of the House.

Except for Wilson in Agriculture not one of Roosevelt's Cabinet was returned. Their time had not even lasted beyond the first Cabinet meeting. A similar fate awaited the Cabinet of the illustrious Franklin D. Roosevelt later in 1945, so newly appointed Presidents are no respector of tall reputations.

Unfortunately Taft left it to the goodwill of both Cannon and Aldrich to change the rules. So the battle for rights began. The insurgents inside the House gained a partial victory which gave every member the right to recognition. But the protestors soon found that Taft was firmly ensconced in the camp they had been attacking. Taft had not only surrendered to Cannon and Aldrich but in fact had walked away completely from the field of conflict. The pessimism of the Progressives increased, realizing now they were floating free severed at the umbilical chord from the White House. Theodore Roosevelt's name was unmentionable and his policies quietly jettisoned by the new man in power. The insurgents were now not against Cannonism in the House but against the new Administration itself.

But let us take a lighter look at William Howard Taft, 27th President of the United States. In the latter part of these political skirmishes Helen became a very dominant personality in the story. What of Taft himself? What do we know of this husband and wife team that once we thought resembled that of John and Abigail Adams, our 2nd President and his wife.

Taft was a huge man of great bulk whose breadth of belt was always linked to a sunny disposition. Reserved and private he weighed in at an extravagant 330 lbs - nearly 24 stone, but because of his disillusionment with the job of President he sought escape from his misery in binge eating. As his troubles grew so did his frame. Food became his only solace and he regularly cheated on his dietician – his wife Helen – by sneaking out of the White House on secret missions that resulted in lavish banquets. His weight shot up to 355 lbs, a full 25 lbs increase over the last two years in the White House. His excuse for spending so much time on the golf course was that he was exercising to lose weight. The charitable commentators were those who claimed his girth was a political asset on which there was neither an ounce nor a gram of deceit.

Poor Taft was always the butt of gentle humour but never seemed to mind the fun poked at him especially about his size. One such anecdote gives a light finish to this piece on William Howard Taft. While Governor of the Philippines, Taft had gone on a trip around the colony finishing with a mild boast of having "Travelled twenty-five miles on horseback – stood trip well" he wrote home. To which Secretary of War, Elihu Root replied, "How is the horse?"

On the other hand, the laid back William Taft was very much in need of the prodding his ambitious wife Helen gave him. As the daughter of a U.S. Attorney she was intelligent, tough and the ideal type of woman to manage Taft. In fact she dominated him and he loved it. White House historian William Seale said "She was quick witted and energetic. But she also dispensed with the charm when she wanted her way." Sadly she paid for the intensity in her personality, for in May 1909 she had a stroke from which she was recovering all through his Presidency. However this did not prevent her "sitting as a Pope and directing me as of yore" Taft was glad to observe. Before this Helen Herron Taft was a suffragette and was always greatly interested in the world at large. She boasted not in a pompous way, that she had the satisfaction of knowing almost as much as her husband about the politics and intricacies of any situation. Maybe this was because she went everywhere with him to political and official conferences.
But now a tragedy took place in the Presidency of Howard Taft that would burn itself into his memory for years to come. The sinking of the Titanic.
Helen was particularly moved by this heartrending tragedy that happened in the Presidency of her husband which was in all the newspapers and on everyone's lips worldwide in 1912.

The story of the Titanic really began on May 31, 1911 when the White Star liner was named and launched with pomp ceremony and fireworks before a glittering collection of the rich, the famous and the powerful of that time. Its owner J. Pierpont Morgan was one of America's most illustrious bankers who had travelled from America to Belfast to be at the launch. All the dignitaries viewed the launching from three stands designed and built for the occasion.

Special trains were laid on and the banks of the Lagan River were lined with people, almost 100,000 to see the spectacle.

The Titanic stood at Slipway number three which was specially prepared with tons of soap, grease and train oil an inch thick. At 12.14 on the morning of May 31, 1911 a rocket was fired when the props, made of huge wooden supports, were knocked away and the Titanic stood motionless like a majestic cathedral of windows and smoke stacks. "There she goes" came the roar from a hundred thousand throats as she began to move slowly into Belfast Harbour. She did not set out on her maiden voyage for another twelve months. Sadly it was to be a voyage from which she would never return. On Wednesday April 10, 1912 the world's greatest liner The Titanic set sail from Southampton bringing emigrants to Taft's America to start a new life there. It was a maiden voyage that was to end in the greatest maritime disaster ever known. Four days into the Atlantic on Sunday April 14, 1912 the sound of the celebrations drowned out a strange sound. It was an imperceptible jolt which was hardly noticed by the passengers. While the laughter, music and card playing continued the crew noticed a shadowy shape ahead. "Icebergs," they shouted but it was too late. One mountainous "growler" as the sailors called these icebergs, struck just below the waterline. With a sound of rending metal, the bottom plating of the doomed ship was ripped away from stem to stern.

Chief Officer Wild on finding that the Titanic had no hope promptly took out a gun and shot himself. A cry went up "Women and children to the boats." Children clung to their fathers. Women held onto by their husbands. The Captain and his crew helped by male passengers started the job of separating the families for the boats and those for eternity.

Two hundred miles away The Carpathia picked up the S.O.S. sent by Jack Philips, Titanic's radio officers and immediately turned around and headed for the disaster area at full steam.

Meanwhile what was happening on board the Titanic?

Although this magnificent maritime masterpiece was the talk of the world nobody knew it was equipped with only half the lifeboats required for a time like this. The crew spent the next two hours banging on cabin doors. Rescue ships were non-existent with the exception of The Californian which although visible in the distance failed to respond to the S.O.S. calls. The reason for this was because the Titanic was at the height of its own celebration party with fireworks, rockets and music and certainly didn't look like a ship in dire peril. Everything started slowly as the lower class passengers wound their way up stairs to the lifeboat stations. One passenger was told to wait by a lifeboat and it was only when she was looking back from inside the lifeboat did she realise the Titanic was going to sink. Another passenger Mrs. Isidor Straus chose to stay with her husband. "I won't go without you," she told her husband and she didn't. Millionaire Benjamin Guggenheim gave his lifebelt away and dressed up for the occasion to go down in style. The orchestra could be heard playing in the distance "Nearer my God to Thee" then the bow of the Titanic rose skywards and there was silence.
There were sixty-five to seventy in each boat and it was heartbreaking not to have room for those drowning in the water around them. But there was a wonderful outcome for one lucky mother whose husband had absconded with her two children. The father placed them in a lifeboat and sent regards to their mother back in France and then waited for his date with destiny. The children were united with their absent mother in France sometime later. What a homecoming reunion that must have been for all concerned.

On board the Titanic some disobeyed the rule of the sea - "Women and children first" and were promptly shot. This floating city, lights ablaze was poised listing downwards in the last throes of its short life. The lifeboats struggled to get away from that awful plunge to avoid being sucked into the cold depths of the North Atlantic with her. She spent three hours in her final death throes. Amazingly the band played on heroically selecting well-known dance band tunes, mingled with hymns like "Nearer my God to Thee" until that final moment I have already described.

Some people counted sixteen lifeboats and two rafts filled with women and children in a calm freezing sea. The wireless operator, Jack Philips was brave to the point of madness as he sat before his Morse code instrument ignoring orders from his Captain to save himself, the only link between this terrible tragedy and the civilized world beyond it. A real life hero when compared to the First Officer Wild who had chosen the easy way out through the muzzle of a revolver. Meanwhile, The Carpathia was steaming valiantly south, threading her way through icebergs some fifty feet high, others one hundred and fifty feet high.

They found lifeboats waiting for them over a radius of four miles. Strangely when asked by Mr. Ismay at the enquiry how many lifeboats should The Titanic have had, the Captain of The Carpathia said "Enough to be required." He had fourteen lifeboats aboard The Carpathia, a liner of only fourteen thousand tonnes. Larger liners of forty-five thousand tonnes like The Titanic were supposed to be unsinkable. Thus the lack of lifeboats.

The Chief Officer of the Titanic, Captain Edward J. Smith floundered in the sea. His final act was to lift a baby from the water and hand it up to a lifeboat before slipping beneath the waves forever.

Army officer Colonel Gracie hit the water at 2.22 a.m. He knew he would be sucked down as the great ship plunged. Here is his story. "I was propelled by some great force through the water," he told a reporter. "I thought of those others at home as if my spirit might go to them and say goodbye forever. I came to the surface. Dying men and women were all round me crying. I found a raft, climbed aboard and began helping others to climb on but it became too full. The crew had to refuse any more from climbing on board. The piteous cries of those around us rang in my ears. I will remember them to my dying day."

The News of the World for Sunday April 21, 1912 had many harrowing tales to report. Here are some further true stories it printed; "The radio operator Phillips vacated his post at last and managed to climb aboard a raft only to be found later frozen to death. The key to the crows nest was not handed over due to a change in staff. Unbelievably the view from the crow's nest would have prevented the collision. The only dangerous moment for Boat 13 was when it hovered ten feet above the water half full of women while orders of "Level", "Aft Stern" came from the seamen lowering the boat. It plunged downwards with a crash under Boat 14 which was being lowered. "Hold Boat 14" was the cry. One passenger touched the bottom of Boat 14 as it swung above his head. They were mostly cooks in white coats who manned Boat 13. A stoker was elected Captain of Boat 13 and all agreed to obey his orders."

There have been many stories, even books and films written about the survivors of the Titanic disaster. One particular story has been revealed to us after ninety-six years. In The Irish Mail dated April 10, 2009 the spotlight fell not for the first time on a senior surviving officer Charles Lightoller, the 2nd officer of the Titanic. He was still aboard the Titanic when it went into its final death throes as it stood perpendicular like a mini skyscraper or a giant Christmas tree. One passenger aboard the lifeboat managed to produce a pencil sketch of its last moments before it plunged into the black depths below.

Later he gave his sketch to Lightoller appearing before the Senate Committee Enquiry in America. Charles Lightoller was closely questioned. Where were you when the Titanic sunk? Lightoller's answer "In the officer's quarters." "Were all the lifeboats gone at the time?" "All but one," was his reply. "What was the last order you received?" "Put the women and children in the lifeboat and lower away." "What did you do?" was the next question. "I obeyed my orders," said Charles Lightoller. "Why was so many crew saved?" "They climbed aboard lifeboats from the sea after the Titanic sunk" was the reply.

But the life of Charles Lightoller was a charmed life as I can now reveal. It seems Lightoller was the hero who organized the drowning passengers into a lifeboat after he surfaced and escaped the terrible suction in the sea around the sunken ship. There were thirty survivors. But the best was still to come. Charles Lightoller went on to become the Commander of a torpedo boat in the First World War. In 1918 he attacked a Japanese U boat by ramming it with the stern of his vessel "HMS Garry". His ship was so badly damaged he had to return to base one hundred and sixty miles away sailing in reverse. In the Second World War an S.O.S. from the first Battle of Dunkirk saw him sailing to France aboard his own yacht built to hold twenty-one passengers. Lightoller crammed it to the gunnels with 139 soldiers and got back from France safely. One of the soldiers wrote him a letter of thanks after the war. He was awarded the Distinguished Service Cross not once but twice for his exploits. Charles Lightoller died in 1953, not at sea I understand, but in his own bed.

But let's return to the Titanic again.

There was no moon in a starry sky. Out there in the blackness the lights of the Titanic blazed from every porthole. The ominous tilt of that leviathan robbed her of her beauty as she plunged into the cold depths below. The time of the final death throes of this modern mercantile masterpiece was 2.22 a.m. Fortuitously, because the radio operator of the Carpathia, Harold Cotton did not go to bed early, he was awake and fully alert for the S.O.S. of The Titanic. Because of this many more lives were probably saved.

Having satisfied himself that his job was done the Captain of the Carpathia headed for home.

With the arrival of the Carpathia in New York there were pathetic scenes. Forty thousand anxious people waited on the Wharf. So devastated and traumatized were some survivors as they were brought ashore they could not recognize their own friends or relatives waiting for them. The news travelled around two Continents and the sympathy the survivors received was never before experienced in maritime history. Notable people at different levels in society were moved to sorrow at this catastrophe. The King and Queen of the United Kingdom, the German Emperor and the people of Southampton, where most of the crew were born and reared, were plunged into despair and mourning. Later over ten thousand people attended the memorial service held in St. Paul's Cathedral. Nearly all the Embassies in London were there including the Lord Mayor of London who immediately opened a Distress Fund for the relief of the widows and orphans left behind.

For the record out of the 2,224 passengers and crew that set out from Southampton on Wednesday April 10, 1912 only 711 arrived in New York five days later on April 15, 1912. This left 1,513 souls that perished on that terrible night of the April 14, 1912.

In September 1985 the Titanic was found with the aid of modern technology and many personal effects were brought to the surface. However the families of those lying in the deep have already expressed a wish to leave the watery tomb undisturbed.

The conclusion of the terrible saga of the Titanic disaster ended in a U.S. Enquiry presumably ordered by President Taft. The U.S. enquiry under Senator William Alden Smith called eighty-two witnesses of which fifty-three were British. The Enquiry began in the Waldorf Hotel in New York. More witnesses were examined in New York than its sister Enquiry in the UK. The U.S. report was also more comprehensive than its British counterpart.

Some of the crew enjoyed their stay in New York with their limited hotel expenses and witness fees. They were shown the sights of New York, attended church services and even made visits to the Imperial Theatre. While the witnesses enjoyed their days at the enquiry, the reports final conclusion was devastating. Its findings were as follows.

The Captain of the California was severely censured for failing to come to the rescue. The Enquiry directed that every Liner should have search lights and enough lifeboats for all. It insisted on a revision of the entire rules of the sea. Captain Smith it concluded was overconfident and careless. He shouldn't have left the ship so soon. The crew were undisciplined and untrained. The officers and crew did not know each other. The surviving officers should not have left the Titanic so soon. The passengers knew neither officers nor crew, a grave fault according to the Senators. I guess we should leave the Titanic right there and get back to our narrative on President Taft.

The Titanic will now always be associated with Taft's Presidency. I felt I should tell the story of the Titanic in detail to do justice to the events and just the way they happened on Taft's watch.

At this point let us return to the White House and the Presidency of William Howard Taft. There was a deep and heartfelt sense of shock and disbelief in Washington when news came through of the sinking. Measures were taken not only to offer sincere condolences to the families of the 1,513 victims but to contribute to the relief fund set up by the Lord Mayor of London. The consequences seeped into The White House and did not escape the notice of Helen Taft, The First Lady. After all, the catastrophe was front page news in New York especially when The Carpathia arrived with survivors.

Despite her stroke, Helen led a fundraising drive to erect a suitable memorial for the victims.

But life went on in the White House and once again Helen was involved in organizing a social event on June 11, 1912 for 5,000 guests. The occasion was their wedding anniversary.

However it had been a rough time for President Taft during his Presidency as Helen had become partly paralysed and unable to speak because of her stroke.

She was also too proud to let the public in on her predicament and to avoid the limelight of the White House she returned for awhile to their summer house in Beverly, Mass. But Taft found it hard to conceal his political problems from her. Writing to his old friend Roosevelt he confessed that "My duties are heavier to bear because of Mrs. Taft's condition." But there is a happy ending to the story for Helen went on to survive her husband by thirteen years.

Let us finish with a nice little postscript on Helen's tendency to be involved and interested in other areas besides politics. She acquired the last eight Japanese Cherry trees available to her and planted them on the banks of the Potomac River in West Potomac Park. The Japanese on hearing the story promptly collected three thousand more Cherry trees and posted them as a gift to her from Tokyo City. Viscountess Chinda, the wife of the Japanese Ambassador helped her to have them planted along the Riverside Drive in East and West Potomac Parks.

Not to be outdone in the public relations field, William Taft was the first President to pitch a ball to open the baseball season on April 14, 1910 between Washington Senators and the Philadelphia Athletes. Incidentally for the baseball fans The Senators won the game 3-0 before a crowd of 1,226.

Meanwhile the battle in Congress continued. One commentator made the following despairing observation of events as they unfolded. "There were two fundamental reasons why Taft did not get on well in the Presidency (1) His nomination was not that of the Party, but was the selection of his predecessor. (2) His boredom with the job - The problem was he liked the title but not the work of the Presidency. All his life he had been appointed to positions mostly legal ones but not elected to any. His election to President had been as standard bearer of his old boss Roosevelt."

His second reason was the fatal one for it led to drift, drift, drift. The change from decision to indecision undermined his Administration. Furthermore suggestions were not welcome in the White House. In fact Taft did not even try to be a success. He smiled his way out of every situation. They said the only thing to improve at the White House was Taft's golf handicap though he was not too good at golf either.

The one amazing thing about William Howard Taft was his three times refusal of the Supreme Court job where he really wanted to be. The words of the President was always important but Taft was not good at them. He always seemed to be giving little thought to grave public questions of which he was the chief trustee to millions of people.

When asked by a reporter what was to be the outcome of the labour situation given the grave economic times that worried everyone in America in 1910, the reality of rampant unemployment and deep Depression left him completely unfazed. Instead of a well-informed, well researched answer to the newshound asking the question the best President Taft could say on the subject was "God Knows."

Taft did wade into the economic mailstorm in Congress but soon he was waist high in deeper waters that he couldn't handle.

Our old friend that illustrious press man J. L. Stoddard's verdict was damning. "Washington is a place of keen, cold judgement and it quickly came to the conclusion that Taft was a mistake in the White House." He continued. "It was as sure in this verdict as it was later, that Chief Justice of the United States was the job better suited to his abilities and inclinations." Soon the country came to the same conclusion. The 1912 election saw his vote plummet from the largest electoral and popular vote of any President to a pitiful minority vote behind Wilson and Theodore Roosevelt. His main blunders were largely down to inexperience and his inept use of words. It is a strange irony that the man who needed to be an expert in the use of words as Chief Justice could have such a political flaw in the use of words. It was enough to lose him the Presidency because of this weakness. Yet Taft's Presidency was not a complete failure for he did chalk up some notable achievements in office.

To his credit was the introduction of the eight hour day for Government contract workers, the establishment of the postal savings account and the introduction of parcel post. He also carried out rigorous prosecutions of illegal combinations when preventing Government lands from falling into the hands of private speculators. He also had twice the number of lawsuits initiated as Roosevelt under the Sherman Anti-Trust Acts. He was responsible for many other significant improvements but received no credit for them because of his failure to sell himself as a politician. History may yet recognize his genius as an administrator something I am sure the people of the Philippines can verify.

And so the story of William Howard Taft, 27th President of the United States draws to a conclusion. In America in 1910 some people had become worried with the direction of the Republican Party and were lining up with protests for the return of Theodore Roosevelt from retirement. Theodore read their letters and listened to their complaints but did nothing. What's more, these complaints were not confined to the rank and file. Elihu Root made the deepest impact. He had declared bluntly that the Administration had broken down and expected to see Congress go heavily Democratic. "The Party needs you" was the message to Roosevelt but he was unmoved, in fact the very idea that he should replace the President at the next election appalled him. He had retired and that was that. But history was not going to accept his decision. Action was needed to stop the drift of the Republican Party onto the rocks and Roosevelt was finally persuaded to enter the next election against his will, a decision he regretted later. Yes Roosevelt should have stayed with his original decision which had reluctantly changed against his better judgement.

So one day Roosevelt announced "My hat is in the ring." The rumours had been there for some time. Many asserting it. Many deploring it. To those who knew him Roosevelt's heart was not in it. He did not want the nomination. He had been bullied by events. Bullied by the bizarre twists of history. Going forward had been put to him by some, as his duty to the Republican Party. Yet others fiercely attacked him. Roosevelt could not understand this change in his popularity. And so he formed another Party to lead those who believed in him. He called this new Party - The Progressive Party. The Party was also launched to express the need for all candidates to be nominated by the people and not by the shadowy figures in the background of the White House. It was a sad outcome for a Republican Party that had almost torn itself into oblivion. The forecast split resulted in a three Party Presidential election in 1912 which resulted as follows Woodrow Wilson - Democratic Party - 435 votes; Theodore Roosevelt - Progressive Party - 88; Howard Taft - Republican Party – 2 votes.

What a terrible price to pay for turning your back on a brilliant President like Theodore Roosevelt and all he had to offer America and the Republican Party.

Taft duly returned to his first love by going back to Yale where he began teaching Constitutional Law until June 30, 1921, nine years later. That was the magic date the Republican Warren Hardy, now the 29th U.S. President named him as the Chief Justice of the Supreme Court to fulfil Taft's only remaining lifelong dream. He had finally arrived where he truly belonged. He resigned later after nine years service as Chief Justice on February 3, 1930. A few weeks after that he died from heart disease aged seventy-two. He was buried in Arlington National Cemetery in North Eastern Virginia. The first President to be buried there. His wife Helen was buried alongside him thirteen years later on May 22, 1942 aged eighty-eight.

28th President   Woodrow Wilson

"Professor"
Born 1856
Died 1924
68 Years of age
1913- 1921
2 Terms – 8 years
Age 57

Party: Democrat
Profession: Teacher & Lawyer
County: New Jersey
Ancestry: Scotch/Irish
Estate: $600000
Hobbies: Riding, Golf & Swimming

Physical Description: Height 5 foot 11inches, weight 170lbs, eye glasses, clean cut, ascetic face.

Significant extract from his Inauguration speech on Tuesday March 4, 1913:
"Men's hearts wait upon us: Men's hopes call upon us to say what we will do …… God helping me I will not fail them if they will but counsel and sustain me."

WOODROW WILSON

In comparison to Roosevelt and Taft, Woodrow Wilson the 28th President was like an insoluble crossword puzzle.

The general opinion on Woodrow Wilson comes through consistently. No matter who you listen to very few people really knew him. His landslide victory for the Presidency seems to contradict this statement, after all his approval rating came from the votes of six million people. There have been many contrasting opinions but the diversity in these leaves the listener scratching their heads in bewilderment.

Some called him "A cold intellectual" others said "An inspiring stimulating companion." "The most curt opinionated man of all I know" and yet another "A man of superb ability and the most workmanlike man I was ever associated with." Some similar opinions came from his closest companions in Princeton University who thought they knew him intimately. Finally to complete the selection how about the following quote "A many-sided man, so many sides that there is room for a variety of honest opinions." He simply mystified some with his speedy, pitiless, inexplicable changes of personality from friendly to cold and dismissive.

You were either for Woodrow Wilson or against him. One element of his style was a tendency not to listen for he treated everyone with an air of condescension. Strangely enough this was something he readily admitted to. When one of his supporters in his first year of office tried to improve the communication zone between himself and Party leaders his conclusions were almost mind boggling arrogance. "Utterly futile," he pronounced decisively. "A waste of time. I would never get anywhere if I should do that. Every fellow has his own views; I would be swamped!" But when pressed to try out the suggestion designed to improve relationships he persisted "Futile I tell you, futile." This final answer encapsulates Woodrow Wilson to perfection. "I can make better headway by giving consideration to my own ideas, whipping them into shape, testing them out in my own way and insuring their adoption by their own fairness and merit. I waste no time while I am engaged in such work."

Another view of Wilson's personality came from Stockton Axson in his book Brother Woodrow.

According to Axson, Wilson's personality invited trouble for he followed his own path in quiet silence.

If this did not suit the press so be it but he really did have a naturally warm heart. The consternation his personality generated never gave him a moments thought. He went about each task in a simple unassuming manner. Some say the opposition to his League of Nations was really a dislike for his personality.

So let's try to capture this mercurial make-up of the 28th President of the United States of America. In other words what made him tick?

First of all let's look at his CV in some detail. Thomas Woodrow Wilson was born the third child of a Presbyterian Minister on December 28, 1856 in Staunton, Virginia but grew up in Georgia, South Carolina.

His father was a Confederate sympathizer so Woodrow grew up a staunch Southerner throughout his life. As a boy he struggled with a learning disability but he did have a flare for writing and speaking well. He went to a small Presbyterian school known as Davis College before moving on to the College of New Jersey now called Princeton University, from where he graduated in 1879 at the age of twenty-three. Woodrow always envied his father's glorious gift of public speaking in church and of course he was impressed by the overwhelming ego that went with it. His father was a hard taskmaster and demanded a standard of perfection that Woodrow knew he could never achieve. However this did not deter him from acquiring the skills of oratory from his father and all the tricks of presentation that went with it.

So life seemed to be set for Woodrow's career in the church following in his father's footsteps but Woodrow had other ideas because from a very early age he wanted to be a politician. One of his early heroes was not a footballer, boxer or a baseball star but the British Prime Minister, William Gladstone.

With this political idea in mind Woodrow studied and graduated in law from the University of Virginia but he soon discovered law was not for him. It bored him. He only practiced for one year in Atlanta, Georgia and soon abandoned law altogether to enter John Hopkins University. Here he studied political science. It seems he had a talent for this subject for he graduated with a PHD in 1886.

He was now thirty and despite his earlier ambitions he had not yet set up a career path in politics for he found himself in a new role as teacher at Wesleyan University, Connecticut before returning to his old Alma Mater, Princeton in 1902. For a man who had an obsession since childhood to be a politician he was certainly leaving it late.

His interest in the academic world however didn't wain until he was fifty-four years old when the Democratic Party nominated him as a candidate for Governor of New Jersey. It was 1910. He resigned his secure job in Princeton and immediately took the plunge into politics for the first time.
He duly won the election for Governor and took on the job like an old hand. He was a reformist Governor taking on and breaking the power of established Party bosses while introducing new laws to regulate elections and business activities.

Yes, Woodrow Wilson had arrived where he truly belonged.

Around that time Woodrow wrote one of his many books. It was entitled Congressional Government based on his Thesis for his PHD degree written five years earlier in 1885 and became a bestseller. It was a classic in political analysis and was followed by further books.

Although he had entered politics pretty late in life his whole academic background made him ideal material for the top jobs in politics. Soon he came to the attention of the Democratic Party bosses who saw him as a possible Presidential candidate. Unbelievably his political career was still only three years old.

The turning point for Woodrow Wilson was the turbulent state of the opposition. The Republican Party was tearing itself apart in a faction fight between the President's men and Theodore Roosevelt's Progressives. But Woodrow was having his problems too and only tough talking by his Democratic Party managers knocked sense into his opponents within his own Party. Woodrow Wilson went on to win the Presidency by the colossal majority of 435 to 96.

The inauguration took place on a cold Tuesday March 4, 1913 as usual on the East Portico of the Capitol and the oath was administered by Chief Justice Edward Douglass White.

At this point just a short anecdote to lighten up our story of Woodrow Wilson. The usual razzamatazz of the inauguration ceremony has been an ongoing feature of these notes. The sheer joy of the occasion, the banquet, the crowds, the fireworks and the excitement of the day was something to be shared by everyone.

Yes, people came hundreds of miles to take part and turn it into a glorious day of celebration.

But back in 1912 there was a rule that the new President elect has no authority over any of the White House possessions or means of transportation until he had actually been inaugurated President. Up to 12 o'clock that day all the automobiles of the White House belonged to the outgoing President Taft. So Wilson therefore had no way of getting his family there. How they managed was up to them.

One relative of Wilson's rode to the White House on a street car. A cousin, Mrs. Florence Hoyt had a companion whose leg had been amputated, so Mrs. Hoyt had to find another way of getting her to the White House. She found a rickety old one horse wagon with an old Negro chestnut seller in charge and she hired him. To improve their comfort he spread some gunny sacks on the floor of the wagon and set off for the White House.

Now the two ladies intended to alight two blocks from the White House but the driver, caught up in the novelty of it all, went right through the gates which were unguarded and drove all the way up the drive to the White House front door.

Before reading about Woodrow's new job in the White House perhaps we should slow up a little and backtrack to his marriage day to Ellen Louise Axson aged twenty-five of Savannah in 1885. They met in April 1883 at the Georgia home of his cousin and became engaged five months later. Ellen was quiet and domesticated preferring work in the garden to socializing. She was later to be responsible for the White House rose garden.

Ellen before this was inundated with Woodrow's love letters; the greatest in history said a historian. But on coming into money she left for New York to study art. He had gone to Baltimore to study political science. While Ellen went to a modest school in New York, Woodrow went on to graduate from Princeton University. He showed jealousy in his letters using the excuse about her staying out at night as being dangerous. She eventually admitted her feelings to him as follows "I was indeed meant for you – that I may do you good and not evil all the days of my life." In June 1885 Ellen accepted Woodrow's calculations that two could live as cheaply as one and a half. What a romantic couple I hear you say. But they duly got married and brought Ellen's brother and sister to live with them because she had been caring for them since her mother died. Life went on and Ellen continued to paint and sell her work to help the finances. Sadly Ellen died on August 6, 1914 of Bright's disease. The marriage had lasted twenty-nine years. As you can see by that time World War I had just started when Ellen died.

Woodrow was to marry again during World War I. His second wife's name was Edith Bolling Galt who was to nurse Woodrow through many bouts of illness. Despite the abuse of critics she all but took over the Presidency when nursing Woodrow after a heart attack. This arrangement was very unpopular and earned the derisive description of "The Petticoat Government" and also caused an outcry. Because of her role Edith was known to many as "The Gatekeeper Extraordinary". Amazingly two full length biographies were written about her. I still feel however his first wife Ellen always played a more human part in his life, and his marriage to Ellen was the real love story. Their only children were the three by Ellen –

Margaret, Jesse and Eleanor. Edith went on to live a long life and died aged eighty-nine in 1961.

Woodrow Wilson didn't waste much time acting on his belief in strong Government and began to push through a major domestic programme. Lower tariffs had been resisted for years but Woodrow Wilson lowered them for the first time in forty years inside weeks of taking up office. The Clayton Anti-Trust Act which strengthened earlier laws to curb the power of large Corporations was another Act to have the dust brushed off it and implemented immediately. Various groups expressed immediate support for his reforms.

Shortly after he became President, Wilson found himself paying the price of fame at the top of America's political tree. This was no Princeton University for now his problems were worldwide. Coincidentally he now began to suffer from various maladies, indigestion and blinding headaches probably caused by stress. Meanwhile he filled his Cabinet with Southerners and reformed the banking system to help him monitor the nation's money supply and balance fluctuations. They were indeed the years of wonderful accomplishments that deserved a generous applause.

Here may I make a mischievous remark? Isn't it amazing that this professor of politics included so many Southerners in his Cabinet. If the Confederates had won the Civil War surely we would be writing about two America's today with two Parliaments, two Constitutions and two Presidents. History can be a bizarre bedfellow indeed.

But his controversial installation of Southern Democrats into his Administration brought him trouble. Born and raised in the South, Wilson turned out to be a white supremacist although not a militant one. After a sitting watching D. W. Griffiths "The Birth of a Nation" which extolled the virtues of the Ku Klux Clan his quote was revealing about the way he saw that illegal gang of thugs. He described the film as "History written with lightening." Woodrow set out on a path of anti-imperialism and promised that the United States would never again seek one additional foot of territory by conquest. Yet he still became as historian Walter LaFeber put it "The greatest military interventionist in U.S. history."

Soon events in far off Europe were heading for trouble and the shifting sands of power there were about to engulf the whole world. Yes, fate was about to take a hand in Woodrow's life from 2,000 miles away and after only two years of his Presidency had elapsed.

The trouble was to escalate into World War I. As everyone probably knows it was all triggered off by the assassination of Archduke Frances Ferdinand, heir to the throne of Austria and Hungary. It developed into a global conflict involving twenty-eight nations including the UK, France, Russia and Italy on one side and Germany, Austria-Hungary, Turkey and Bulgaria on the other.

America was affected by the strict supervision of the sea lanes to prevent goods getting to Germany. British sea Captains set up blockades controlling the trade routes of America and even confiscated the goods of American exporters. Germany retaliated by sinking British ships through the use of hunting submarine packs she let loose in the sea lanes of the Atlantic. The most tragic consequence of this was the sinking of the Lusitania with the loss of 1,198 lives, 128 of which were Americans. Yet rumour has it that the Lusitania was carrying ammunitions as well as passengers.

But life still went on in America. In November 1916 Wilson had an election to fight to be re-elected President for a second time. His opponent was ex-Supreme Court Judge Charles Evans Hughes, who had left the regality of the bench to indulge in the rough and tumble of politics. The new updated media methods were coming on stream such as billboards, magazine ads, and newsreels. However Wilson didn't campaign himself but his backers made sure the country were voting for the man "who kept them out of the war" so far.

Wilson was returned to power by a narrow majority of 277 to 254. One worrying possibility arose for Wilson in the run up to the election. There is always a gap in time between Election Day in November to inauguration day on March 4. Had he lost the Presidency to Hughes he would have had to resign immediately to avoid a power vacuum between November 1916 and March 1917 at a very sensitive time in world affairs. The victory however plunged Wilson into a much more critical situation.

He was re-elected on March 4, 1917 but on April 6, 1917 "the man who had kept America out of war" changed his mind and declared war on Germany. That's politics.

The sinking of the Lusitania changed everything and has been a much debated tragedy for the past ninety years. So what really happened on that fateful Saturday May 1, 1915? The Captain of the U boat was fifty-nine year old Walter Schweiger. One of the Lusitania famous passengers was a member of one of America's richest families Alfred Vanderbilt reputedly worth over $100 million; some say one billion dollars in today's money. The Lusitania was about ninety miles from the Irish coastline when at 2 o'clock in the afternoon, the U boat struck. Nobody took any notice and continued eating their lunch unperturbed. A second torpedo followed it up and the double explosion that followed could have been the secret armaments going off on board.

The biggest shock was how quickly it sank, almost eighteen minutes at the most. For such a powerful ship this should not have happened. By the time rescue boats arrived from Cork on the South coast of Ireland it was all over. There were 769 survivors out of a total passenger list of 1959. Unbelievably for such a cowardly act against a civilian ship, the Commander of the U boat Schweiger and his crew were greeted like heroes on their return to Germany and were even given medals for their handiwork. Schweiger went back to sea and met his death when his submarine hit a mine. Poor Captain Turner died a broken man condemned for not going down with his ship the Lusitania.

But an amazing revelation has come to light in 1973. It was revealed by investigating journalist Colin Simpson, that nearly the whole cargo was contraband left out of the ships manifest which was falsely written up.

Simpson actually dived to the wreck in 1980 and brought up some of the explosives which were part of 10 ½ tons aboard including 4,927 boxes of cartridges from Remington Arms Company. Also aboard according to Simpson were 1,250 cases of shrapnel and 1,000 rounds of bullets. Evidence of all this was confirmed by the submarine log entry "An unusual heavy detonation follows with a very strong explosion cloud." Nevertheless the Germans had the sole right to search the ship so if they intended to sink the Lusitania they were duty bound to evacuate those on board first. After the sinking it did not make it easy for Wilson to stay out of the war as was the wish of the country. But circumstances were slowly forcing him down that path.

Woodrow Wilson would find himself a little later on a battleship headed for Europe sitting in the sailors mess for a sing-along and shaking hands with 800 sailors. Yet he still harboured doubts about rescuing Europe from her self-inflicted wounds. "People will reluctantly endure their tyrants for years but they will tear their deliverers to pieces if a millennium for peace is not created immediately," said Wilson. "Post-war, these ancient wrongs are expected to be remedied in a day or a wave of the hand." That was a deep and profound view of history by Wilson that can be applied in any age or any conflict even in the Iraq of 2006 – ninety years later.

Yet Wilson could not stay aloof from this threat to American shipping and managed for a while to persuade the Germans to moderate their submarine warfare but when the Germans resumed hostilities Wilson took it as a declaration of war. He had no alternative but to enter the war on April 6, 1917.

In his address to Congress on April 6, asking for this declaration of war Woodrow Wilson fell back on the Lincoln format of appealing to the emotions and gut feelings of the American people. He said "We shall fight for the things we always carried nearest our hearts – for democracy, for the right of those who submit to authority to have a voice in their own Governments, for the rights and liberties of small nations, for a universal dominion of right by such a concert of free people as shall bring peace and safety to all nations and make the world itself at last free – the world must be made safe for democracy." Three million men were then conscripted many of whom went straight into battle in France during the summer of 1917. But the war for them only lasted until October 1918.

The new German Chancellor Prince Maximilian accepted Wilson's Fourteen Point Plan as a way to surrender without admitting defeat. An armistice was signed on November 11, 1918 by discontented Allied forces who would have preferred total victory.

Out of it all came Woodrow Wilson's ideas for a league of nations that was to play such a tragic part in his life as we shall see later.

Let's pause here a while and look at history as it unfolded around Woodrow Wilson for the First World War did play a significant part in his life story.

War hysteria triggered violence countrywide although the war itself never touched American soil. German-Americans were attacked in the street. Dissenters and those who voiced opposition to the war were also victims of abuse. Imprisonment was not spared on dissenters for breaking the newly passed laws of sedition.

Declaring war is easier than fighting one. First of all speed was essential. Two million troops had to be shipped to Europe immediately. The Allies were going broke which had encouraged Germany to fight on and risk American intervention. The American casualties for the whole war were only 5,000 as against four million Russians, French and Britons. Yet America paid a severe financial price. Thirty-three thousand million dollars were pumped into the war effort 2/3rds of which were new Government war bonds. There was increased taxation 4/5ths of which came from large Corporations. But every cloud has a silver lining and there were many winners. Wages rose on the farms and in the factories and a redistribution of wealth took place thanks to the war, something they couldn't do in peace.

The impact of war on America was dramatic. In order to run the war the money needed was raised by Liberty Loan bonds. Sedition laws brought about a curtailment of civil liberties which resulted in the imprisonment of the socialist leader and war critic Eugene V. Debs. Times indeed had changed significantly not only for the President but also for the man in the street.

Incidentally after the war Wilson refused point blank to reprieve Debs who had received a sentence of ten years for sedition (i.e. speaking out against the war). He served about four years.

He had to wait until the term of another President Gamaliel Harding to be released in 1922 approximately. More on Debs in my piece on Gamaliel Harding. Debs was lucky and eventually died of natural causes in 1926. While public opinion thought Debs hard done-by; other people were forced to kiss the flag, were tarred and feathered or even killed for antiwar activity.

When the war ended Woodrow Wilson undertook a European tour of the major capitals. It was supposed to be a triumphal tour but it also included six months of tough negotiation for a peace agreement that finally led to the Treaty of Versailles which would impoverish Germany leaving the Allies to reap the bitter whirlwind of Hitler's rise to power.

The Allies won the war but lost the peace. Although the war was declared "A war to end all wars" Wilson was forced to accept measures like the confiscation of German colonies and punitive war damage.

To all this failure, Wilson's Fourteen Point Plan and his vision for a league of nations was thrown out by Congress. No one was prepared to get involved again in other people's wars. Well that was what Congress thought at the time. It was left to another generation to come up with an organization to police the earth – The United Nations.

Woodrow Wilson had become well-known in Europe by now. President Georges Clemenceau remarked with disdain "He thinks he is another Jesus Christ come upon the earth to reform men." It seems that the personality of Woodrow was still operating against him.

Wilson eventually returned to the cut and thrust of Congressional politics away from the world stage. By now he was behaving like a lighthouse, blinking reassurance to ships at sea – and like a lighthouse he was isolated completely from the people on the shore.

This was borne out by J. L. Stoddard, the experienced political editor on a chance meeting he had with Franklin K. Lane, Secretary of the Interior. Franklin was deeply engrossed with a speech he was reading given by Wilson. "Great stuff, great stuff, I like to have him talk that way." "Did you know that he was going to say it," asked Stoddard. "Not a word of it," Franklin replied, "I haven't seen the President for a month and don't know when I shall."

This admission of ignorance to what was going on by one of Wilson's own Cabinet Ministers may leave you the reader perplexed. How could the cream of the country's top politicians be happy to play the role of mere puppets to "Wilson the Puppet Master"? More sinister was the fact that it was becoming an accepted rule of thumb for speeches made by the Cabinet to be seen only after the event. Any views the Cabinet might have offered beforehand were never encouraged. Worse than that never even sought by Wilson.

For a man who was so academically brilliant with a PHD in political science, Government by typewriter could never have come from any of his text books.

The cut and thrust of honest open debate among ones political friends and foes is absolutely essential for rounded opinions especially ruling a country the size of a Continent with all its diverse cultures and problems. The isolated world of the cloister is an ideal setting for mediation among abbots and monks but the post-World War White House was anything but a cloister.

So why had it come to this? Did nobody challenge Wilson? If not, why not? My only answer can be fear. When reminded of his curtness or rudeness Wilson seemed surprised.

This fault of his grew worse as he tasted the heady nectar of power. Sometimes he even asked for views to be given in writing. "In that way," he said "I can consider them dispassionately." A short written reply was their prize two weeks later. Of course the inevitable happened, Wilson became a recluse in the White House.

Yet not only was his Cabinet isolated from him, his Ambassador in London was also feeling the cold winds of indifference in 1914.

Here is a little anecdote I discovered in Trinity College, Dublin when going through the papers of Woodrow Wilson (page 410 Volume 29) in a letter from the American Ambassador in London, Walter Hines Page. It was a bitter letter of complaint about the cost of living in London as an Ambassador and was dated April 7, 1914. In fact it was almost the identical problem John Adams the second President had to deal with when he was in London in 1776. The fragility of the funds available in comparison to those of other countries was still the problem. While Page and Adams were willing to live modestly and that illustrious lady Abigail Adams was quite expert in making ends meet – the sheer expense of ambassadorial entertainment put a terrible stain on the Governments entertainment allowance.

While other countries enjoyed vast amounts of expenses, somehow the Treasury in distant America were very reluctant to match them. Page wrote ..... "I have many times considered taking a small house in some respectable cheaper part of town and living on say $25,000 per year, but no Ambassador does it, here or in any other European Capital.... The Government and the Court entertain me. I must entertain them. The other Ambassadors entertain me; I must entertain them. This purely official entertainment requires a large house. Then the King must be entertained I fear once a year. This is an enormous expense. These things must be done or the U.S. must drop out of the ambassadorial class. As it is, I lose a great deal because our Government has no house."

"The Japs for instance and the Spaniards play the game by the accepted rules. Of course the French, the Russians, the Germans and the Austrians play it even better. The greatest country of all has the meanest method of all...." he finished "..... this increase of office rental has brought the subject up sooner than I should have mentioned it..... Most heartily yours, Walter H. Page."

Here let me remind you of another milestone that happened in the reign of Woodrow Wilson that almost went unnoticed – "Prohibition". Although this caused a major countrywide upheaval that later haunted the Presidencies of Harding, Coolidge, Hoover and Franklin D Roosevelt it is not generally known that it started on Woodrow Wilson's watch, when the 18th Amendment to the Constitution was signed on December 18, 1917. The amendment title reads "The Prohibition of the Manufacture, Sale or Transportation of Intoxication Liquor". It was ratified after much debate by thirty-six States on January 29, 1919 and came into effect one year later on January 16, 1920.

Despite the fact it took three years to be finally put into law it is amazing that nobody in America had the vision to forecast the terrible unbelievable social disturbance it would cause and the gangsterism it would ferment over its fourteen years on the Statute books until it was finally repealed on December 5, 1933 by Franklin D. Roosevelt. At the time Wilson signed the 18th Amendment, it crept onto the statute books stealthily like the mild symptoms of a terminal disease.

Talking of disease reminds me of Wilson's health in 1919, two years into his second term as President. Woodrow was never a very robust man but he was now about to launch himself into a frenzy of political pressure that was to become a self-inflicted journey of pain and self-delusion. From now on he was to be driven by two all consuming obsessions in his life that would lead to his self-destruction.

His Fourteen Point Plan for Europe and his vision for a League of Nations. Throughout this journey he did everything medical science cried out for him not to do.

The story of Woodrow Wilson in Paris must now be told, so let's walk around with Wilson in his hectic life in Paris struggling to make sense of the peace negotiations.

The citizens were glad to welcome the peace negotiations, for only a year before they were in a panic fearing the German army marching into their city. A million people were running away from them certain nothing would hold back the enemy. But the arrival of the Americans changed everything, not only for the men that contributed to the war effort but for the volume of ammunitions the Americans produced without which the Allies would have been defeated.

While at dinner one night word of the murder of the entire Romanov family in Russia reached Wilson's table making him abandon his meal saying "A great menace to the world has taken place." He didn't elaborate but hurried away abruptly as was his style. But the peace agreement was the only thing that mattered now. Wilson's Fourteen Point Plan was received with great joy and excitement by the war weary soldiers and civilians on both sides of the trenches. Wilson became a veritable deity and he was greeted everywhere as a hero.

Making Woodrow a war hero for his Fourteen Point Plan is understandable coming from broken soldiers who had fought in despair in the trenches for the previous four years. At last they had a champion of hope now.

Wilson was very much aware of the terrible stories and tragedies coming out of the war zone. The statistics appalled him. Half a million men had marched into war in 1914. By 1918 250,000 had perished. Ten thousand human beings stepped off the war ships in Gallipoli. By the time the gunfire stopped they were all dead.

The awful mess created by the Generals of both sides was ridiculed in songs and stories from the trenches. None more so than the song "The Band Played Waltzing Matilda".

Here is a short extract you will remember which I produce with grateful thanks to the author.
Then in nineteen fifteen my country said Son
It's time to stop rambling cause there's work to be done
So they gave me a tin hat and they gave me a gun
And they sent me away to the war
And the band played Waltzing Matilda
As we sailed away from the quay
And amidst all the tears and the shouts and the cheers
We sailed off to Gallipoli

How well I remember that terrible day
How the blood stained the sand and the water
And how in that hell that they called Suvla Bay
We were butchered like lambs at the slaughter
Johnny Turk he was ready, he primed himself well
He chased us with bullets, he rained us with shells
And in five minutes flat he'd blown us all to hell
Nearly blew us right back to Australia
But the band played Waltzing Matilda
As we stopped to bury our slain
We buried ours and the Turks buried theirs
Then we started all over again

And for ten weary weeks I kept myself alive
But around me the corpses piled higher
Then a big Turkish shell knocked me arse over tit
And when I woke up in my hospital bed
And saw what it had done, I wished I was dead
Never knew there were worse things than dying
For no more I'll go waltzing Matilda
All around the green bush far and near
For to hump tent and pegs, a man needs two legs
No more waltzing Matilda for me

So they collected the cripples, the wounded, the maimed
And they shipped us back home to Australia
The armless, the legless, the blind, the insane
Those proud wounded heroes of Suvla
And as our ship pulled into Circular Quay
I looked at the place where my legs used to be
And I thank Christ there was nobody waiting for me
To grieve and to mourn and to pity
And the band played Waltzing Matilda
As they carried us down the gangway
But nobody cheered, they just stood and stared
Then turned all their faces away

But Wilson knew he could not remedy the situation overnight. To complicate matters trouble was brewing for him in the shape of the French President Clemenceau who accused him of being pro German because Wilson didn't want a harsh Peace Treaty. Walking in the streets at 4 a.m. one morning, three people received a rough draft of the new Peace Treaty. They were convinced it spelled doom. The three people were General Smuts of South Africa, John Maynard Keynes the world famous economist and Wilson's successor Herbert Hoover. The press of the world attacked Wilson because he had allowed Lloyd George and Clemenceau to water down his proposals.

Now it pleased neither pro nor anti-treaty politicians. Hoover was filled with admiration and sympathy for Wilson who was in a constant fight with the forces of hate and all because Wilson had not failed but half succeeded. Even the Nazi's after World War II complained the harsh conditions of the Treaty had pushed them into war. It seems Wilson should never have listened to Lloyd George or Clemenceau.

The strain was colossal for now Woodrow a professor of political science, had to rewrite the Treaty. He even typed his own statements squatting on the floor to cut up maps of Europe and worked eighteen hours per day non stop.

In doing this he had to cope with the enmity of Clemenceau who used his own French press to vilify Wilson for Clemenceau apparently ruled France by fear.

Now the pressure of it all got to Woodrow. On April 3, 1918 Wilson collapsed with a temperature of 103. Though he was exhausted he persevered in his determination to save his plan. He finally consoled himself by saying "It's the best that can be gathered out of a dirty past." But the deepest cut of all was inflicted by his own countrymen. When he set out for the talks in Paris in December 1918 he left behind him two enemies who would plot and succeed in bringing his every effort and every exhausting heartbreaking minute struggling with ambitious European politicians, to nothing. Some commentators claimed that the two men waiting for him on his return to sabotage whatever he brought back to Congress were Henry Cabot Lodge and Theodore Roosevelt.

It was suggested that the reason for their sabotage was their fear that Wilson would bring back for the Democrats an international diplomatic triumph on top of victory in the war. Somehow I find it hard to agree with that theory for it runs counter to all the noble aspirations of Theodore Roosevelt and his life story we have just read. Now the final chapter in Wilson's life was about to be written with his tour out West to appeal directly to the American people nationwide. But by then Wilson had defied his doctor's for far too long as we shall see shortly.

Strangely Wilson's austere personality changed on his tour West. Thirty correspondents went with him including all the top newspaper journalists of the time. David Lawrence of the Evening Post destined to become the most noted of Washington Correspondents. Jack Neville of Randolph Hearst's International News Service and James Haggerty of the New York Times whose son was to become the best press secretary of them all and Hugh Baillie of the United Press who recalled Wilson's sessions in the press car surrounded by loud talkative reporters.

He answered them without hesitating, without prevarication. He would reach over and tap you on the knee and say… now look here and confront his opponent nose to nose …. Perhaps the change of personality was due to the package he was selling on this crusade or perhaps it was something to do with his illness. That is until one reporter William C. Bullitt quoted Secretary of State Lansing's criticism that some provisions in Wilson's Peace Treaty would not be accepted and that his mission was "useless". All Wilson's old suspicions returned and once more he retreated behind his shell of reserve.

But there were few reserves left in Woodrow's exhausted body. Something serious was wrong with him and he returned home. The 8,000 mile journey West would have felled a younger man. His train immediately returned to Washington stopping only to change engines. The cover up for his illness began; over work, nervous exhaustion, etc. The truth was he was heading for a massive stroke.

His solitary role was his physical downfall but nobody dared have the courage to tell him he was defying nature.

Wilson's truly amazing work schedule in the twelve months from December 1918 to October 1919 is listed hereunder: -

December 4 1918 – Sailed for Europe
January 18 1919 – Addressed Peace Conference
February 1919 – Returned to America
March 1919 – Returned to Europe
June1919 – Signed Peace Treaty
July 8 1919 – Returned to United States
September 26 1919 – Collapsed with paralytic stroke
October 2 1919 –Second massive stroke and paralysis in his arms and legs
October 4 1919 – Complete physical breakdown

This represents eight sea trips of over 15,000 miles in total, enduring all its storm-tossed conditions both ways aggravated by six months intense in-fighting negotiating a mentally demanding formula for peace. Back home a further unrelenting pursuit of his favourite project the Fourteen Point Plan followed by a physically and emotionally charged 8,000 mile speaking tour by train across America.

At this stage you may want to know more about this Fourteen Point Plan. It reads roughly as follows:-

(1)   Open treaties through International Diplomacy.
(2)   Freedom of the seas.
(3)   Free International Trade.
(4)   Reduction of armaments.
(5)   Adjustment of Colonial claims.
(6)   Evacuation of Russian territory.
(7)   Evacuation of Belgium.
(8)   Return of Alsace-Lorraine to France.
(9)   Italian frontiers readjusted.
(10)   Autonomy for Austria and Hungary.
(11)   Evacuation of Romania, Serbia Montenegro (Security of the Balkans).
(12)   Self-Determination for Turkey.
(13)   Independence for Poland.
(14)   Formation of a General Association of Nations.

Despite his unstinting and passionate pursuit of his goals his efforts were destined to be fruitless. Devastatingly fruitless. The League of Nations concept was rejected by Congress now dominated by the Republicans. But even in the face of this defeat Woodrow Wilson refused to water down his Fourteen Point Plan.

As we said he was a man on a mission, so almost rebelliously he launched a countrywide tour to mobilize public opinion for his League of Nations plan. But sadly he had pushed himself beyond the limit. While still on tour he awoke one morning after a highly excited speech in Colorado.

He was experiencing frightening facial twitches and acute nausea. His doctors ordered him back to Washington without delay but the damage done was now irreparable and he suffered a massive stroke that paralysed his left side and confined him to bed for six weeks with orders to be seen by no one except his wife and his physician.

At this point we must ask ourselves this question. Was Wilson's medical collapse inevitable? After his six months travelling between America and Europe and the stress of the peace negotiations in Paris, the major stroke he suffered came as no surprise to those who knew him. But going out West to fight for his Fourteen Point Plan was for Wilson an act of medical lunacy.   It was not generally known that he had already been diagnosed with a cerebrovascular disease as far back as 1896. Nevertheless he still undertook a journey out west of 8,000 miles between September 3, 1919 and September 25, 1919 over a period of twenty-two days.

Previous strokes had lost him the dexterity of his right hand. These were followed by a series of small strokes and a serious condition in his left eye in 1906. Dr. Cary T. Grayson who examined Wilson just after the election of 1912 expressed his doubts that Woodrow would see out his first term alive. Dr. Grayson's Programme of diet, exercise and rest was blown out of the water with the arrival of World War I. Woodrow now had uncontrollable hypertension (blood pressure to you and me).

Even in Paris he suffered a small stroke during the Peace Conference in April 1919 and another one in July 1919. All these strokes plus his major one in October 1919 medical experts said left him totally unfit to comprehend political realities. A totally fit Wilson could have easily sold his Fourteen Point Plan to his Party. The strange irony was that his successor Warren Harding, although a handsome figure of healthy manhood sitting beside Wilson on inauguration day, was an "intellectual bankrupt" compared to the sick and ailing ex-President. Yet the sickly frail Wilson was the one who outlived the healthy Harding.

But here let us pause a while to study an amazing constitutional conflict Wilson's sickness caused in the Cabinet.

There was no public row about the problem his final stroke caused the Cabinet but the tension was there. Wilson's unavailability left no one in charge for eight dangerous weeks. A similar situation had happened before when Garfield lay dying between July and September 1881 after the assassination attempt on him. Today at the start of the 20th Century, Lansing the Secretary of State did take action by calling together the Heads of Departments to discuss the situation.

To his surprise he received a rocket from Wilson in a note dated February 7, 1920. Here is a small extract from the note to Lansing; -

"Is it true, as I have been told that during my illness you have frequently called the Heads of the Executive Departments of the Government into Conference? If it is I feel it is my duty to call your attention to considerations which I do not care to dwell upon until I learn from you yourself that this is a fact. Under our Constitutional law and practice as developed hitherto no one but the President has the right to summon the Heads of the Executive Departments into conference and no one but the President and the Congress has the right to ask their view or the views of any one of them on any public question."

Harsh words indeed! Was it because Lansing had offended Wilson by his criticism of the Peace Treaty to reporters out West? Of course Washington was full of rumours of Lansing's dilemma. Had there been no Vice President as happened under Roosevelt and Coolidge, what a temptation there would have been for Secretary of State Lansing to declare himself President fuelled by an unscrupulous ambition.

If the doctors could not pronounce the President fit for office Lansing could have become President in a virtual coup. Of course this did not happen despite the fact that Wilson was incapacitated physically. If Wilson, his wife and his physician did not run the country then no one was in charge. It was a bedside Government.

Evidence of this is revealed by Secretary of the Treasury, Franklin Houston in his book Eight Years with Wilson's Cabinet. Here is a rough extract from it – "One Sunday in January 1920 a telephone message came from Mrs. Wilson to Houston asking him to the White House at 4.30 that afternoon. She said "You are wondering now why I sent for you. I did not ask you to come merely to drink tea. The President asked me to tell you he is anxious for you to accept the Secretaryship of the Treasury and who you think should succeed you as Secretary of Agriculture......" That was just a peep at Wilson's Presidency during those eighteen precarious weeks when his health was at rock bottom. Enquiries even as to how badly the President really was became a very delicate operation. But who had the right to know? The law could not cater for the situation. Later Houston declared "It is clear some machinery should be set up to deal with such a situation in future."

Wilson's outburst certainly proves the difficulty of tinkering with solutions not written into the Constitution. As one commentator put it had Wilson's Vice President Thomas Riley Marshall decided to tackle the situation head on he would probably have had to take the White House by storm.

However Woodrow did win honourable recognition outside America. The Nobel Committee thought enough of his mission in pursuit of the League of Nations and his work in Paris as Peace Negotiator, to award him the Nobel Prize for peace in December1920. What a glorious prize you may think. But at what a terrible price. I am sure your thoughts are now returning to Woodrow Wilson the almost manic recluse in the White House we spoke of earlier.

He constantly claimed he had no time for discussions. He got angry when people tried to change his mind losing many old friendships as a result. One description of him was uncomfortably true..... "Such a man, too fond to rule alone, Bear, like the Turk, no brother near his throne." Friends drifted away like falling leaves at the end of a fading autumn day. Sadly these separations from the branches of his friendship were his choice alone. His interpretation of such an outcome was now part of his personality. Friendships meant service to him not by him. To quote Henry L. Stoddard once again "Friendships were bridges to be burned as he himself moved on a solitary traveller."

One of Wilson's supporters made the following comment when asked to explain this lonely President "Public office was to his mind most emphatically a trust..... He had the stern sense of duty that would lead him to send his best friend to the scaffold though it would break his heart to do it."

But what of Wilson the private man. "How did he tick?" Well it seems he was great company, genial and witty. He could tell a story magnificently and had a highly developed sense of humour according to one source. A lively companion by all accounts.... Some wag shouted from the crowd during his stumping days "Woody." That pleased him. It was the Woodrow Wilson he really was, a friend of the guy in the street. But sadly he just could not sell the package he really was inside. Unfortunately he would always be the schoolmaster aloof and detached from his pupils. His dress alone gave him away. Pale face, hair groomed perfectly, slender figure, frock coat, dark grey well-pressed trousers and even wore a top hat and white gloves at the Paris summit.

The war seemed to be his crowning glory. It was an opportunity to stand with the greats like Washington, Jefferson and Lincoln in the noble hall of history.

But Woodrow Wilson was different. For even on the foreign stage he sat alone, worked alone and made his decisions alone. The result of his solo run was that America left him acting alone and didn't join the League of Nations. Historians can now use that well tried cliché "If only". If only he was accompanied to Paris with the top political representatives of America with full power to negotiate. After the Lusitania his proclamation "Too proud to fight" was another diplomatic disaster he would not have fallen into if only he had listened to his advisors. He didn't even listen to Franklin Roosevelt. It was a "Do as you please" message to the Germans, "Holding Germany to strict accountability" were other words he used that would not stop a single submarine in its tracks. Alas if only he listened. His words only encouraged defiance. Although truly a patriot who loved his country he just loved his own opinions more. The value of other opinions equally patriotic he dismissed with contempt.

Woodrow paid a terrible price for this arrogance however when he returned home to face the might of Congress. For once he had to listen. To listen to reality. To watch Congress smash his dreams into smithereens. Then to almost kill himself in pursuit of these broken dreams that could never mature into reality. It would have been easier to walk on water as he had tried to do – alone.

Somebody summed up the man that was Wilson just after his inauguration for his first term – "He will make a fine President so long as he is right, but God help the United States should Wilson be wrong."

Some quotes reveal Wilson's total disregard for genuine friendship. Like the politician trying to be of help to him on board the SS George Washington going to Paris for the Peace Conference. His cruel words "Never offer the President advice; never plead a cause with him. He is interested only in what you know, not in what you think. He will listen to your information but not to your opinion."

But a further gesture of defiance to the elements of fate was his liking for the number thirteen. He spoke in the White House frequently of the thirteen letters in his name. The thirteen States that were in the original Union. He thought why not arrive in Brest on December 13, so gave orders for the ship "The George Washington" to be slowed down to meet his wishes.

But fate is a hard taskmaster and nothing will ever alter its wishes. Not even Woodrow Wilson. Now shattered and struggling with his life on a thread running the White House with the aid of his wife and his physician the final blow to his ego was still to come if only he knew it. He was certain all lesser candidates at the Democratic Convention in 1920 would be put aside for the world leader Woodrow Wilson. Alas, although he waited expectantly for the call to come hour by hour, day by day, that call never came. It took some time for the news to sink in. The awful realisation that the crown he had worn with such a single-minded distinction had quietly passed to another in far off San Francisco, was gut wrenching.

The date was June 28, 1920 one year exactly since he signed the Versailles Treaty. Sadly Woodrow Wilson had now passed into history.

Woodrow Wilson opened up his inner thoughts to very few. Yet in a family conversation on the rear Portico of the White House, Woodrow expressed some unusual views of the Presidency that were worth recording. He didn't agree that the office of President was so powerful that it would be dangerous for any man to be handed the job for more than eight years. To explain this it is easier to quote Woodrow word for word for to paraphrase his conversation would risk taking it out of context:

"I insist that the Office in and of itself is not the most powerful of Offices," said Woodrow. "It is nothing like so powerful as the Premiership of England for the simple reason that the Prime Minister of England can, at any time dissolve the Parliament and appeal directly back to the British people. Thus he has a hold on Parliament utterly unlike and superior to the hold the President has in Congress." Profound thoughts indeed from a Professor of politics. A fascinating book by Gene Smith called When the Cheering Stopped pulls back further the curtain of secrecy behind which Woodrow lived and allows us to peep behind it to share Woodrow's early days in the White House. Sitting in his favourite chair these memories were among his sweetest dreams.

These were the only dreams that mattered now as his thoughts returned again to those happy times when "Nellie" his First Lady was shaping the White House for family living. She filled it with furniture from the Princeton he loved. The rough and tumble of play with his little daughters Nellie and Margaret. Undignified it may have looked but he enjoyed the chase around the table after the squealing girls; Nellie, the First Lady tolerated it for a while then chastised him loudly "Woodrow what is the matter with you", Jessie his sensible one only watched. She was the one classified alongside her mother as one of the "proper members" of the family as opposed to himself and Nellie Junior. He and Nellie junior were the vulgar section of the family circle.

He liked to ride in the afternoon in one of the White House Pierce-Arrows. This was a big open car with a right-hand drive complete with the Presidential seal on the door. Nellie saw things that shocked her on the journey. She was a product of village life and the crowded big city bustle of Washington's back streets was a revelation to her. She fearlessly walked through the slums and loved to talk to Negro servants. After one such trip she urged her husband to clean up the slums which he dutifully did. She wouldn't spend more than $1,000 on her clothes which was regarded by friends as eccentric. But even for an ex-professors wife this was a colossal sum. She spent no more than $50 per week during her Princeton days. She was a tiny gentle woman who spoke in a soft Southern accent and was blessed with long golden hair.

He remembered how she loved to potter around the White House lawns planting boxwood, rose trees and tall cypresses. She even clipped the hedges but she worried constantly over Woodrow's health which was never very robust.

Sadly Mrs. Wilson's own health deteriorated and the daughters rallied around her. In August 1914 she was dying and Woodrow often sat by her bed writing about the situation in Europe. He made sure she didn't know about the war. She was glad to hear his "Slum Dwellers Bill" had been passed by Congress for she knew she was dying of Bright's disease. On August 6, 1914 just as the first German soldiers went into battle against the Belgians, she took her doctors hand drew him towards her and said "Please take good care of Woodrow doctor."

They were the last words of her life. It was twilight and she died that evening. Woodrow had known her when they were both children and said "I have loved her since she was in her cradle." The funeral was a simple one at Myrtle Hill Cemetery. School girls all in white lined the route. Woodrow had wanted it quiet but almost the entire population of his wife's hometown was there. He stood with the girls beside a large oak tree. A breeze moved the flowers by the grave as workmen began to shovel clay on to the casket below while Woodrow, his head bare stood there quietly weeping. Ellen was gone. Gone forever.

Not having many male friends Woodrow had become very emotionally attached to Ellen but seven months later he met Edith Bolling Galt, widow of a Washington Jeweller who completely bowled him over.

In a whirlwind romance that caught Edith so completely by surprise when he proposed to her she gasped "Oh you can't love me for you don't really know me." But this response did not deter Woodrow and on December 18, 1915 one week before Christmas, Woodrow and Edith were married in Washington. His whole life had changed in sixteen months since Ellen's death on August 6, 1914. Edith didn't have the intellectual background of Woodrow's first wife Ellen but she proved a very loyal companion after he had a stroke in 1919 and even assumed a lot of decision making responsibility for him during his illness, the background to which I have already told you about.

But every painting deserves a splash of colour to balance the dark and gloomy brushstrokes. Yes, it is always fair to show a man's personality from both sides. Sometimes the mask he wears can be a defensive shield against the world. Woodrow Wilson was no different. Far from being the aloof Head of Princeton College, he was called Tommy by his devoted classmates even after he was elected President of Princeton. He sometimes blamed his father's nomadic job in the church ministry for not having time to form boyhood ties of affection with other boys for he was always pulling up stakes and moving on. The closing of the door of any friendship always caused him so much pain he couldn't go back. Sadly the friendship always ended for life.

Perhaps the Scots were like the Indians – they do not forget easily. Somehow despite the pain of parting he could not be reconciled although without anger or remorse. They say this vulnerability went back to an experience he had with a Princeton Colleague John Grier Hibben, his sole best friend at Princeton which damaged his trust in friendships forever. When discussing his suggestion for changes within the college his friend opposed him. His dependence on this friend was irretrievably shattered. The row left him shocked. His friend was hurt deeply too by the crisis of friendship but Wilson never again gave that friendship to any other man. That friend John Hibben tried desperately afterwards to mend fences but all to no avail. Their friendship and Woodrow's future trust in friendships was finished for life.

Yet it wasn't the bitterness of lost friendships that preoccupied Woodrow's final days as he sat in his favourite chair on S. Street lost in thought. His dreams were about his childhood. He was only three years old when the family moved South to Augusta. Woodrow played the violin and had a good singing voice. When he got married he continued the family prayer group and musical sessions singing together. The behaviour of Union soldiers under Sherman polarized his family into outright support for the Confederation.

Perhaps here is the reason why he became a White Supremacist and his family Confederate sympathisers. The Yankee soldiers' behaviour under Sherman really hurt the heart of a little boy for the rest of his life.

Sitting in his chair he thought of his childhood days full of the normal boyhood games and pastimes enjoyed by the town lads. Games he had often shared with them. There were no professional coaches as we know them today. They learned swimming, horse riding, shooting and fishing by just doing it. Boxing with gloves was the favourite. They enjoyed baseball clubs among their pals and these bore bizarre and glorious names dreamt up by the lads themselves. Of course like all boys they managed to swing from the branches of trees and walk backyard fences with varying degrees of daring and skills especially after the travelling circus had left town.

The boys enjoyed being involved with the circus carrying pails of water for the animals. Games of Indian fights or hide and seek among the cotton bales in the local warehouse were commonplace. Bows and arrows, kites and marbles got their undivided attention. Yes, they were no different than the boys of their time the world over. Southern boys fought at the drop of a hat and found it hard to take part in team play. But modern boys can lose out on what these lads enjoyed – the sheer invention and imagination that went into their individualism. This kind of unmolded singularity of thought and action helped to turn Woodrow into an individualist in everything he tackled later in life.

Another man recalled more of those memories Woodrow dreamt about in that favourite chair back home in S. Street. Writing about Wilson's childhood Mr William Bayard Hale says "Woodrow was a real boy while he was a boy." Tom Wilson, as Hale recalled him, found his fun in all the sports and games just mentioned above. His baseball club was called "Lightfoot". He rode horseback and when on the streetcars loved to work the brakes. He played "Indians" with his tomboy cousin Jessie Bones. "They would stain their faces," Hale said, "with pokeberry juice, carry bows and arrows and perform the "Leather-stocking tales" they read about in the book of that name. In fact Woodrow had a traumatic experience when playing with Jesse a game called "squirrel in the tree top". Jesse tumbled to the ground "shot" by Tom's arrow. He carried her home in terror crying "I am a murderer". It wasn't an accident I killed her." Fortunately she recovered inside a few minutes and all was well."

Woodrow's health even in his Princeton days was never very robust and sometimes his vitality ran so low he had to take to his bed. It was a stomach bug which had to be treated by almost pre-historic remedies. Antibiotics would have done the job nicely today. Perhaps these early badly treated ailments accounted for Woodrow's frail health in later years. Who knows?

As he grew older in his retirement Woodrow was subject to mood swings. He had always been highly strung and intense so his nervous disposition was not unusual for a man as sick as he was. Yet he had his moments of childlike affection that radiated with kindness. These happy moments were a pleasure to all who met him. He always sat at the library of his house on S. Street Washington and always in the same chair by the same nook near the fireplace. It was a varnished armchair upholstered in brown leather from where he beamed at everyone in placid acceptance of life. The sunshine was still there after all the hard battles. The core of his life was definitely Mrs. Woodrow Wilson. In a strange way, for someone so stern, Woodrow needed love, close personal love, daily love. Mrs. Edith Wilson knew just how he ticked so what he would have done without her in these declining years God only knows!

In a strange way Woodrow Wilson was a bigger man in defeat than he ever was as President. He lived to see two Presidents follow him into that August office uncomplaining and philosophical about the fate of his League of Nations. He consoled himself as follows. "It is all right.....It might not have worked just yet. We are still in darkness but I'm sure it is a darkness that eventually lightens. I realize now I am an empty tenement, a tool that has served its purpose in God's hands. I was stricken because it was his way of doing things. It was his will to set me aside. He knows what is best. I am content with the record as it stands."

Woodrow Wilson died aged sixty-eight years in Washington DC on February 3, 1924. He died in the house to which he had retired on S. Street after his years in the White House and where he had lived quietly taking no further part in public affairs. He is now buried and at peace in the National Cathedral in Washington D.C.

The verdict of the historians has been that Woodrow Wilson was a prophet of peace who wasn't listened to. In fact they concluded that the modern United Nations is really the fulfilment of Woodrow Wilson's broken dreams for a League of Nations. Some have even claimed that only Franklin D. Roosevelt emulated him such was his importance in the U.S. Presidential and world history.

And so dear reader, we can't always walk in the company of giants so bear with me as we move on to our next President, the much maligned Warren Gamaliel Harding our 29th President.

29th President   Warren Gamaliel Harding

Born: 1865
Died: 1923
58 Years of age
Term 2 Years
1921 – 1923
Age 56

Party: Republican
Profession: Publisher
County: Ohio
Ancestry: English, Scottish & Irish
Estate: $487,000
Hobbies: Golf

Physical Description: 6 foot tall, high forehead, greying hair and bushy eyebrows.

Significant extract from Inauguration speech March 4, 1921
"We are ready to associate ourselves with the nations of the world great and small. Our eyes never will be blind to a developing menace, our ears never deaf to the call of civilization."

WARREN GAMALIEL HARDING

Warren Harding's Presidency is remembered for the corruption associated with it. To me the writer, having travelled along the long unpredictable road through the lives of twenty-eight other Presidents so far this seems to be a very harsh and unfair reflection on a man who was morally and basically decent. Why he should have to shoulder the blame for the deeds of others less patriotic than himself needs some explanation by the historians.

Having studied Harding the man it is not surprising that this unpretentious, easygoing, trusting individual was an easy prey for the unscrupulous "friends" with whom he surrounded himself.

A little more cunning, a little extra sharpness might have alerted him to the sharks swimming around his pleasant swimming pool. But I am afraid hindsight is a luxury nobody enjoys and when it does arrive it is nothing more that a vision that comes to taunt you.

So perhaps we should discover in Warren Harding's journey from boyhood to the White House the explanation for this judgement posterity has come to. It all started for Warren when he was born, the first child of Dr. George and Phoebe Dickerson Harding on the family farm near Corsica, Ohio in 1865. When he was a boy of seven, the family moved a short distance to nearby Caledonia where he first went to school.

He played in the village band some of whom remembered him as a jolly sunny little chap full of fun who made friends easily. His future personality was already beginning to take shape.

He then went to Ohio Central College where he spent his spare time working on the family farm and in the local sawmills to subsidise his college expenses.

The most significant event in Warren's life was the family move to Marion, Ohio in 1882. Here he studied law, sold insurance and had a job as teacher in the local school. But these were jobs in which he had no particular interest. Lady luck smiled on him however when he discovered the newspaper business with his first job on the college rag. It proved to be a love affair for life. His next job was working part-time for The Caledonia Argus. Later he moved to a job as a printer, pressman and reporter at the Marion Democratic Mirror.

By sheer chance he had found the type of work he was to cherish for the rest of his life in the exciting world of the news hound. But Warren had his own political views which didn't always agree with that of The Democratic Mirror, so he formed a partnership with a friend and together they bought a minor four page newspaper called The Marion Star. Lady luck again smiled on Warren Harding when The Star prospered and developed. The town of Marion and The Star Newspaper grew in parallel.

Harding's next step up the ladder was to buy out his partner. Finally his greatest stroke of luck was his marriage to a wealthy widow Mrs. Flossie Kling-DeWolfe. After that not only did his modest Marion Star flourish and grow into a very influential newspaper, his bank balance also grew to astronomical proportions. So much so, his estate after he died was estimated at about $487,000. Not bad for a once lowly news reporter.

Harding's good looks and male testosterone attracted the women of small town Marion like bees to a honey pot. But one woman had decided Harding was hers even if Warren didn't know it. Her name was Florence Kling-DeWolfe. Unfortunately although he gave a qualified love to "Flossie" as he called her, it was never a wholehearted relationship. But there were problems waiting for him down the line. Amos her father rejected him point blank as a suitor for his daughter. To Amos, this newspaper upstart with empty pockets and reputed to have Negro blood in his veins was an appalling prospect to have in the family.

But Flossie was having none of it. A row followed and Amos forbade his wife and sons from having anything to do with Flossie, and for seven years he would not even recognise her when they met on the street. It would be another fifteen years before reconciliation took place. On July 8, 1891 Flossie and Warren married in the front hall of the house they bought at 380 Mount Vernon Avenue and Flossie's mother helped her buy some furniture for it unknown to Amos.

Incidentally, this very house on Mount Vernon Avenue has since been lovingly restored to what it was when Warren Harding and Flossie Kling first entered it to hold their wedding ceremony. Almost $75,000 was spent on the restoration by the Ohio historical society in 1964. Since Harding's death it has become a kind of museum, housing the usual bric-a-brac given to a President while in office. Vases, glass bowls, goblets, stone ashtrays, inkwells, canes and trinkets in gold and silver. Even the Duchess's Ostrich plumes that embellished her hats sat there beside his evening slippers. The restoration of the house was so accurate and sympathetic to Harding's domestic lifestyle should Harding return to it today he would find it exactly as he had last left it. The brown Victorian wallpaper, his rocking chair, his tobacco jar including his enamel coffee pot. They are all there now in their old familiar places.

It was at this moment in time just after he married Flossie Kling that the life of Warren Harding was to change dramatically for he was a prime candidate now for the wide exclusive social and business circles open to him.

To this end he joined those special influential clubs and fraternal orders called "The Masons" and "The Elks". He became a director of the Marion County Board, the Telephone Company, the Marion Lumber Company and because of these respected positions in Marion's commercial life he was made Trustee of the Baptist Church. Here you may have noticed two very important things about Warren Harding's life. He had no ambitions to acquire an academic qualification and his interest in politics is hardly noticed. To predict that he would ever be President of the United States would surely at that point in time, be greeted with a few good old belly laughs, and I am sure Warren himself might very easily have joined in the merriment.

But Warren had developed a number of other assets not found on the University campus or in the law courts of the United States. His new exclusive connections made him the hub from which the social life of Marion society radiated. More importantly the wheelers and dealers of Marion politics now began to take notice.

Yes he was now the centre of an impressive circle of friends, in all walks of life. He joined the Republican Party as part of this circle and built up a very polished style of public speaking in the process. In 1898 and 1900 he found himself elected to the Ohio State Senate. The scene was now set for the most important event in Warren Harding's life - his meeting with Harry M. Daugherty, an influential lawyer and politician in the city. Yes, Warren Harding had now come to the attention of major State politicians drawn by his friendly personality, his public speaking oratory and of course the most important asset of all, his influential Newspaper The Marion Star.

Daugherty proved a very impressive political wheeler-dealer for Harding won election as

Lieutenant Governor of Ohio in 1903. For the first time however, Warren Harding gave evidence he was not too overawed by politics, for after a two year term in 1905 as Lieutenant Governor of Ohio, he retired from politics for five years and returned to his one and only love, the newspaperman's city desk. The fact that he had lost a third term as Governor before he made this decision wasn't the reason for his retirement. He actually missed the buzz of the newsroom.

Warren had now reached the pinnacle of political life and this was proved when William Howard Taft, the sitting President invited Warren to nominate him for a second term as President. This Warren was only too glad to do, so he came out of retirement to campaign vigorously for the President. But as we know poor Taft polled only a handful of votes leaving Woodrow Wilson of the Democrats victorious. Warren Harding gained from this connection, and with Daugherty's help he was elected to the U.S. Senate by a large majority.

Life in the Senate was a great help to Warren's political future for he was well liked there. Because of his conservative approach to politics he offended no one. His humble low profile approach to politics was appreciated even more because he represented the important State of Ohio.

It may sound cynical but the passing of highly protective tariffs and import taxes favoured the rich multinationals so it was no surprise to see the businessman Warren Harding supporting them. In fact he supported any measure he felt was most favourable to big businesses. He continued to vote conservatively when the Versailles Treaty and the League of Nations came before Congress. Warren made sure his uncontroversial but safe "go with the flow" politics invited no flak or disruption to upset his peace of mind.

So, how could someone with so little leadership potential be nominated to represent the Republicans to replace an intellectual giant like Wilson? Most of the credit seems to be due to his political mentor Harry M. Daugherty. Late in 1919 Daugherty set up a well-organized plan called "Harding for President Campaign". True to his laid back personal philosophy of life, Warren accepted the plan and set off into the country making speeches with the slogan "Not nostrums but normalcy". Warren's word "normalcy" coined by himself embraced a return to free enterprise and all that this "non-restraint" implied. Going back to the old America meant a return to isolationism in international politics leaving America free from involvement in the messy troublesome world of European politics.

The Democrats analysed this message of Harding's describing it as "An army of pompous phrases moving over the landscape in search of an idea." Warren didn't get the full support of his Ohio delegation but he wasn't too disappointed. Again we see Warren's lack of total commitment to the Presidency beginning to surface. It was all too much like work for him. Hard work. His lack of enthusiasm didn't help his confidence and at one stage he wanted to pull out of the race altogether. Going back to the Senate seemed to be a much more pleasant proposition.

But two people were looking for results Daugherty and Flossie who both persuaded him to keep going. Unfortunately he kept going and it was a decision he paid dearly for. After all this staggering and stumbling on the hustings Warren finally arrived at the National Convention. The famous phrase "smoked-filled room" was common currency there. It was coined to describe Suite number 404 in the Blackstone Hotel where political deals were supposed to have been made. The outcome in this smoke filled room dominated by Republican Senators was to nominate Warren Harding for President.

An amazing prediction by Harding's controversial manager Harry Micajah Daugherty just has to be mentioned at this point.

Daugherty's prediction went as follows "At the proper time after the Republican National Convention meets some fifteen men, bleary eyed with loss of sleep and perspiring profusely with excessive heat, will sit down in seclusion around a big table. I will be with them and will present the name of Senator Harding to them and before we get through they will put him over."

On Saturday June 12, 1920 Daugherty's prediction came true. Perhaps that prediction was not as uncanny as it seemed. It took ten votes to eventually select him. One quote is almost pathetic when placed alongside the historic magnificence of the title President of the United States of America. It reads "He was nominated to the best of my ability because there was nothing against him and the delegates wanted to go home." Does it not leave you almost despairing that the most exalted position in American politics in November 1920 should be treated so flippantly? The delegates wanted to go home!

So when they say today that Harding was the manipulated choice of a collection of Party leaders on the 13th floor of Chicago's Blackstone Hotel, it is easy to see how easy it was to be right in a political prophecy.

Circumstances around Harding's selection threw up another controversy. This time the focus was on the fate of the Vice Presidency. Hiram Johnson was nominated for the Vice Presidency and had he accepted he would have changed the history of the Presidency itself because the next President would surely have been Hiram Johnson and not Calvin Coolidge. But Johnson refused Harding's personal request to be Vice President and the rejection by Johnson was pretty blunt. "If I cannot be named for President I prefer to stay in the Senate." The tactics of Harding's campaign managers also irritated Johnson. So robust was Johnson in his refusal to go on the ticket, Harding's men feared he would not support Harding at the Nomination Convention. But their fears were unfounded.

Harding stood for no particular issue and was willing to cooperate with whatever the Party wanted. He somehow managed to project the image of being the least concerned person in the race. The other people did the hard work and the worrying. Why do I think we've been here before with Howard Taft? Senator Lenroot was nominated for the Vice Presidency, but now comes an amazing twist to the story. A groundswell of opinion in the hall rooted for the unknown Calvin Coolidge which started with a call from Oregon. They had come to nominate Coolidge for President. Now they at least wanted him as second best. It was an uprising from the floor which couldn't be defeated and Coolidge was duly nominated for the Vice Presidency. Once again we have the Vice Presidency complicating the situation – challenging the Gods of fate to do their worst. And they did.

Destiny had certainly made its presence felt as future events will prove. After the excitement of the Convention it was now down to mundane matters.

One week after the Convention political reporters paid a visit to Harding in his home town Marion. Harding enquired of the reporters what length his acceptance speech should be. He had a large sized page spread out before him. "About half that size," said one of them. Candidates are inclined to say too much in acceptance speeches was the advice. But Harding wasn't too happy with that. "Let them know it all," he retorted. "Let them decide 'Don't let's cheat them'." The speech filled two newspaper pages.

"Don't let's cheat them" became a formula in all his speeches. It spread back to National Headquarters and was turned into a catchphrase and a guide for everyone on his team.

Harding's frank honesty was a particular trait of his. He even worried about his credibility before making a decision. Had he said something different in his campaign speeches? "I don't want to be accused of breaking faith," he told his campaign advisor Will Hays. Later he ordered research into all his speeches before he vetoed one particular Bill in case he should be accused of breaking faith with the voters.

The style of Presidential campaigns was rapidly changing in the 1920s. New media inventions like billboards, newspaper adverts and printed handouts were supplemented by a new fangled gadget called radio which was arriving for the first time on the political stage and was later used with brilliance and sophistication by Franklin D. Roosevelt to remarkable effect.

Harding was the pioneer who first used radio when he broadcast from Washington D.C. to twenty-eight countries. Proving he could have ideas of his own.

He was very cleverly managed by Daugherty his sponsor, and despite the new gadgets decided to conduct his own campaign from home. It was to be a "front porch campaign" from his home in Marion, an approach that had proved successful for previous Presidents Benjamin Harrison in 1888 and William McKinley in 1896.

Harding, the master of confusion in his Presidential speeches, seemed to excel himself. Being of limited Presidential talent was no handicap to him at all in an election where all the cards were stacked in his favour. The League of Nations was already an issue that was hard to sell by the Democrats. Having entered the war was another minus for Fox, his opponent. High inflation, soaring unemployment and a leaderless state of the nation due to Wilson's stroke was a disaster for the Democrats. The result was a victory for Harding by a record-breaking margin of seven million votes.

The day of the inauguration duly arrived. A peep inside the White House just after Harding's victory gives a revealing insight into the personalities involved that the laid back Harding had to contend with. Edith Wilson could not conceal an aloof contempt for the Hardings when they came to tea in the Red Room after the Presidency had gone to Harding. Edith Wilson was a plantation bred Virginian with a soft almost English accent. "The Duchess" as Harding called his wife, had a rasping voice with a nasal twang. It seemed Harding was ill at ease in her company.

Yet Harding was an impressive sight himself in the Red room. Lusty black eyebrows, steel grey hair, massive shoulders and bronzed complexion gave the impression of rude good health. If he was wearing a toga he could easily have filled the role in any production of "Julius Caesar". That remark I'm afraid is not original for back home Harding was known affectionately as "The Roman from Ohio."

Behind him was the determined Duchess holding him on invisible strings. She was five years older than Warren. For the inauguration she had worn a sealskin coat with a vast chinchilla collar. Her thin hair resembled a well groomed wig and her crowning glory was a wide brimmed blue hat complete with spiky feathers like the ones I wrote about earlier. Her face was made up with a heavy layer of paint and one would be forgiven for thinking that her regal look was triumphant when she entered the room. Edith Wilson had a flair for clothes too in fact she looked like the Duchesses' daughter. The frail Wilson took Harding's arm as they stepped outside and angrily displayed a tired, cranky and petulant independence.

Warren Harding had carried every State except those in the Democratic South and eventually won by a landslide 404 electoral votes to 127. It was the largest popular majority in American Presidential history up to that time.
It has always been impossible to explain the thinking behind some victories in the Presidential elections looking back over the years since Washington. Harding's election still puzzles the experts. I suppose people will always look for change but in Harding's case it was surely because he was as different from Wilson, the man in power, as it was possible for a personality to be. Wilson seemed tired, old and frail there in the Red room.

Wilson let go of Harding's arm but had to be guided, almost lifted into the official car waiting for them. Harding's Chesterfield top hat was tilted jauntily as he sat beside Wilson. Four troops of Cavalry set off in front to the orders of the Cavalry Captain, as they rode down the White House drive ahead of the two Presidents. Two more troops trotted beside them on either side of the Presidential car, a fourth troop closing in behind. Five official cars and five secret service cars followed. The Duchess was heard calling out through her window to the reporters. "My boys," she confided to Edith Wilson who showed absolutely no interest sitting in her stole. Wilson stared straight ahead ignoring the applause of the crowd but Harding acknowledged it happily. Harding, uncomfortable beside this cold ravaged figure beside him talked about his dogs. The old President forced to endure this State led ritual of rejection and succession listened politely.

Only one incident marred the day of the outgoing President Wilson – the arrival of Henry Cabot Lodge who had boasted about his part in the downfall of Wilson's League of Nations. "I appreciate your courtesy, good morning sir," said Cabot Lodge. "I have no communication to make," Wilson snapped at him in answer to his greeting. The tone was icy with contempt as was Wilson's last cold stare after him as he left the room. But who could blame Wilson's contempt. Here was the man who had danced on his political grave.

Wilson's relationship with Harding was so much different, after all Harding was a kindly gentleman.

"I would not consider it discourteous of you if you do not appear at the inaugural," Harding said to Wilson kindly.

"I guess I had better not try it, I'm afraid I shall have to beg off," Wilson murmured apologetically. Harding said he understood and was met with a warm smile and an "all the luck in the world" farewell as he left. Woodrow left behind him the assembled Ambassadors in the peacock splendour of their uniforms of blue, red and gold.

Harding was marching forward into history while the old and feeble warrior Wilson stumbled into the wings forever.

It seems grossly unfair to criticize Warren for his weakness as a President since the man himself was honest enough to recognize that fact. His state of mind was reflected in one opinion he expressed to a friend before his election. "The only thing I really worry about is that I might be nominated. That's an awful thing to contemplate." To another he said "I'm not fit for this office and should never have been here." Even his wife Florence expressed grave doubts about Warren's limitations and she being his wife should know.
She said "I can see but one word written over the head of my husband if he is elected and the

word is tragedy." But like all those around Warren she too failed him. After all when Warren Harding tried to withdraw from the nomination why did she and Daugherty persuade him to go forward when all he wanted to do was to return to the Senate? It does seem that their agenda was more ambitious than Warren's.

But life went on for poor Warren Harding and a Cabinet had to be installed. He needn't have worried however; the people who supported him were going to make certain he was cushioned by heavyweights. Nothing was going to be left to chance. We can divide the Cabinet into two layers. The top professionals who had proved themselves outstanding leaders like Charles Hughes, a Justice of the Supreme Court and Presidential Candidate in 1916. Henry Cantwell Wallace an Agricultural expert of impeccable character and future President Herbert Clarke Hoover.

The flaw in the Cabinet which would bring so much pain and recrimination on everyone after Harding's death, were the people brought in to repay political debts such as Albert B. Fall later to serve time in prison for corruption, Edwin Denby another who let him down later. The group of his friends he favoured with jobs of less than Cabinet status were known as the Ohio gang. Included in these was Charles R. Forbes head of the Veterans Bureau who resigned later and fled the country only to be repatriated and sent to prison for defrauding the Government of $500 million. His best friend and political manager now Attorney General, Harry M. Daugherty who disgraced himself and was found to have made a profit by allowing alcohol to be taken out of Government supplies. He got off scot free.

It must be emphasised that despite all the criminals around him no wrongdoing was ever traced to Warren Harding. We will cover these post-Presidential investigations later in the story about Calvin Coolidge the next President.

One thing Warren was always consistent about was his brand of politics, a sort of middle of the road conservatism in which the ship was always sailed to avoid the turbulence and bad weather zones that would endanger an otherwise uneventful voyage. Peace with Germany was sealed by both houses of Congress and the Republic of Colombia was appeased for their loss of Panama in 1903 under Roosevelt with a payment of $25 million.

But in 1923 his ship was about to encounter major storms ahead, storms which were completely unavoidable – the corruption scandals. Before discussing these perhaps we could deviate a little to talk about some other anecdotes in Warren Harding's life and the times he lived in.

One that comes to mind is the case of Eugene V. Debs, the Socialist Party leader imprisoned under the 1917 Espionage Act for speaking his mind when opposing America's decision to enter World War I. Debs' imprisonment while perfectly legal was an acute embarrassment to all shades of political opinion. Wilson vindictively refused to free him as we have pointed out under our notes on the 28th President. Harding provided the more humane solution and released him from prison to everyone's relief. The Act under which he was jailed was very harsh even for a wartime measure for it authorised sentences of up to twenty years in prison for aiding the enemy; obstructing recruitment of a soldier or encouraging disloyalty.

But there was no reason to be concerned for Debs known as convict 9653 in jail. He was almost canonized in prison and was idolized by guards and convicts alike. He told them "There are no bars and no walls for a man who in his heart is free, and there is no freedom for the man who in his own heart is a slave." He returned home when Harding pardoned him and he retired to Terre Haute, Indiana where he died aged seventy in 1926, eight years after the war.

Harding's desire to please was praised for its success in pacifying a crisis-ridden Government and his re-nomination for a second term for the Presidency was not out of the question. Even his successor Calvin Coolidge later maintained most of Harding's policies. It seems a shame today that history has rubbished Harding for although he might not have been an intellectual he must have been doing something right.

The relationship of Harding and his wife Florence Kling-DeWolfe was a strange one. She was the daughter of a very wealthy man by Marion standards and was a divorcee with one young son when she met Warren. There seemed to have been an element of contempt in her for the simplicity of Warren Harding. Her haughty attitude towards him to outsiders seemed to betray a coldness that did not deserve his warm friendly personality. But he understood his woman as she understood him. She had proved her loyalty a long time ago so perhaps any criticism does "Flossy" a disservice for she obviously was the tough practical woman that a "laid-back" Warren Harding needed to spur him on. Who knows?

Here is a small anecdote or pen picture of Flossy Kling to help embellish the story. Florence Kling Harding was really a great extrovert and the oldest woman at sixty-one years of age to become First Lady. Some people said she was better than her husband Warren Harding as a politician. A joke by Warren was revealing when he said that his automobile was the only thing he possessed that "Flossie" did not have a desire to run." Cosmetics played a major part in keeping her looking young and her flamboyant plumed hats and pearl studded satin gowns could have come out of Hollywood. Smoking cigarettes and flying in aeroplanes were other features of a woman glad to be noticed by the crowd. A "devil may care" extrovert lady with a larger than life personality and she knew it.
Needless to say she had the wealth to be reckless with public opinion. It's hard to believe that such a colourful woman was reputed to have kept a little red book of people she intended to get even with when she got the chance – perhaps as First Lady. But Harding was a disappointment to her for his Presidency ended in scandal caused by the crooks in his Cabinet. Someone said "George Washington could not tell a lie but Harding could not tell a liar."

In all the Conventions he attended be they County, State or National he was a very popular figure. The Legislature at Columbia, the Lieutenant Governorship and the Senate in Washington came the same to him. Through them all he never forgot or drifted far from his roots even though he soon outgrew these people as his political career took off. They clung to him even when they had become an embarrassment to him. Still his loyalty never wavered and he could not change his friendships even if he tried.

Unfortunately his trust was not reciprocated with loyalty in return. Through it all he worked with that blood pressure dangerously high, defying his doctors in the process.

But the war was to claim the lives of two President's Woodrow Wilson and Warren Harding. The final ravages of the conflict landed on Harding's desk for solutions. Without the required experience to tackle the situation while battling with severe blood pressure he depended entirely on the experts around him. Yet slowly he got to grips with the problems and despite the critics his two years in office were quite successful given his limitations. Scandals erupted which he tackled fearlessly yet he viewed his greatest triumph to be a reduction of the twelve hour day to an eight hour day in the iron and steel mills for 200,000 men. Poor Harding was an unlucky President, for in his first term of office all hell broke loose in a miners' strike at a mine owned by the Rockefeller family.

This was a particularly vicious strike when the UMW (United Mine Workers of America) were turned away from the striking mine. Rockefeller Junior "Mr. John" as he was known, was running the show while his father was out playing golf. Mr. Rockefeller decided to cut up rough and sent in a private army of three hundred gunmen he had hired for the purpose. These were backed up by eight machine guns and an armoured car nicknamed "The death special". Twelve thousand men, women and children were then evicted with their shabby belongings from their company owned shanties, in a thunderstorm.

Believe it or not Rockefeller's father rewarded him for his toughness by gifting him with 10,000 shares in the company. The State Militia were then ordered in to bring the scabs to the mine where thirty miners were killed. The newspaper
The Cleveland Leader then exulted in the picture of the charred bodies of two dozen women and children with the headline "Rockefeller knows how to win." This story is from that illustrious publication The American Century by Harold Evans. So the event did happen. But later the war news was much worse for Warren Gamaliel Harding.

The first bodies brought home from World War I for burial was a heartbreak to him for he was visibly agitated as he walked the length of the pier along the rows of coffins. Then he brought tears to many eyes by the speech he made. "They have earned everlasting gratitude which is in the supreme solace in dying. There is ringing in my ears like an abomination eternal, an insistent call. It must not be again. God grant that it will not be and let a practical people join in cooperation with God to the end that it shall not be."
Referring to war he reflected "How can humanity justify or God forgive." These were tough times for Harding. "Directing post-war America, bringing it back to normalcy," as Harding put it, "was just as difficult as in war times." The reason for this is easy to understand. The unity of a country at war ceased. Railroads were almost bankrupt and he was left with a surplus of ships destined never to sail the seas again. Now came another headache, millions of men had been demobilized from the forces onto the streets creating industrial and agricultural overcapacity. Through it all the country was staggering but not falling.

Meanwhile Harding's troubles intensified when the Duchess' old kidney complaint flared up so seriously he spent many nights by her bedside. Eventually the Duchess recovered. A touching story about this is the visit of the so called cold aloof Woodrow Wilson accompanied by his wife Edith to see the Duchess. Harding was deeply moved by this sympathy visit by a very sick man. Like Harding, Wilson had not lost the common touch either.

Some time later just before a visit to Canada he was surrounded by reporters doing the usual job of a newsman. Harding's inner thoughts were reflected in this conversation with them and his thoughts were full of nostalgia. He said "It is hard for me to realize I shall never be editor of The Marion Star again. It's the finest job in the world. I envy all you fellows. You have a better job than I have." And he really meant it. They continued on for some time, the hacks and the President, reminiscing and talking shop. The President left two hours later on a trip from which he would never return. Something was hovering over him was the impression he gave as he said goodbye to them.

J. L. Stoddard the world renowned newsman, despite his inside knowledge of events, never suspected Harding was a sick man. But Harding's strength was fading away as was the colour from his face. "I realized," Stoddard said later "that the man needed rest. I also made up my mind that Harding was not happy as President."

Like Taft, the honour and prestige of the job would never compensate for the void in his daily life, that separation from old friends and haunts inflicted on him.

"Although Harding received the biggest electoral majority recorded so far fate was very unkind to him" wrote J. L. Stoddard. "Nothing could replace the memories he carried from his days as editor of The Marion Star. There he was the best known man in town at the club and in the shops where he was known as Warren. His office was the gathering place for his friends and visitors alike. He knew everyone in town by their first name. The sheer joy of small town life was his elixir of happiness."

Harding's heart never really left Marion. He often talked nostalgically about the city. "There never was a day in all the years I ran the newspaper that I didn't get some thrill out of it," he told William Allen White. "Everyday at 3.30 here in the midst of State offices I wondered what kind of layout the boys have got on the front page. How much advertising there is? I would like to walk out in the composing room and look over the forms before they go to the stereotyper. How I would love to go there without the Secret Service, just on my own, stopping to chat with the people along the way." But that was no longer possible for the President.

In the middle of his troubles in the Presidency, an impending railroad strike and a three month old coal strike was not going to keep him away from Marion's Centenary Festival or so he thought. But a week before he went, violence erupted in the coal
strike. At Herrin a strip-mining centre in Bloody Williamson County the "absentee mine owner" decided to up the anti against the strikers by bringing in armed strike-breakers mostly from Chicago's seamier side to run his mine. But he completely underestimated the calibre of the miners he was confronting. The miners retaliated with rifles, dynamite and even a plane dropping bombs on the blacklegs. County sheriffs and deputies wisely lay low. The strike-breakers were forced to take on the enraged miners and when it was all over twenty-one of the strike-breakers had been beaten to death. The miners were not going to be bullied that easily.

Red Agents and Bolshevik saboteurs was the easy answer to the troubles. But that was Daugherty's line. Harding vowed to use the Government "To prevent the Labour Unions of the country from destroying the open shops."

One of the most sweeping injunctions ever drafted by the United States Government was issued. No loitering near any railroad stations, offices, yard, or shop would be tolerated. But Hoover, the next President was angry with Daugherty for violating the basic rights of the shop men. Hoover proved to be right and a General Strike was called by the Unions, but Gompers the Union Leader rejected this choosing instead to move for the impeachment of Daugherty. Once again Daugherty resurrected the spectre of a Red plot. By the end of the year however the strike was over. Significantly the labour movement vowed revenge at the next election.

Despite this carnage at Herrin, Harding nevertheless set out for Marion in his official Presidential car for the festivities of the Centenary festival. He was accompanied by a car load of Secret Service men and a car load of reporters. But there was no need to worry about Harding's safety. The President was stilled revered by everyone. Twenty-five thousand spectators filled the Grandstand at the fairground cheering, whistling and shouting their greetings to the incoming Presidential motorcade. American flags were everywhere. In his speech Harding did not refer to the Herrin massacre and a fireworks display finished off the nights celebrations of the Centenary Festival. Everyone enjoyed themselves.
Yet America was still a rip-roaring turbulent whirlpool of opinions and passions as the ordinary American fought for his right to a decent living in the early 1920s.

Back home in Washington Harding soon realized his temporary escape from the reality of his Presidential responsibilities on his visit to Herrin changed nothing. Fears of a cold winter from lack of coal supplies, and industrial chaos from a railroad shut down, haunted Congress. The country was turning to oil now and although the mines won the wage rises they sought, they could not win regular daily work. The country was slowing down and by the end of the 1920s the number of miners had dropped from 400,000 to 150,000. These were dark portents of times to come, as the signs of downward decline gathered momentum.

The trains still ran without going on strike but trouble brewed beneath the surface which erupted now and then into isolated strikes. At one point 2,500 passengers on twelve continental trains were stranded in the Arizona desert. In the 113 degrees heat babies were born in the aisles and people collapsed. Harding was later applauded in Congress for his condemnation of the lawlessness of both sets of strikers - the miners and the railwaymen. Yes, I'm afraid Warren Harding's Presidency was a very troubled one indeed.

Trouble no one expected back in that smoke filled room on the 13th floor of Chicago's Blackstone Hotel and certainly it was trouble well outside the power of one Harry Micajah Daugherty to fix.

Reading about the characters who flitted into and out of Warren Harding's Presidency is like reading a script from a Hollywood B movie. I have now followed their role as best I could right through to the State Penitentiary. For most of them, no doubt I have missed some names, and many strokes and shady deals, but given the sort of twilight world they moved in the whole truth may never be exposed.
One name that should be added I feel is that of Gaston Bullock Means, a clown prince among con men whose only claim to fame is the book he wrote about Warren Harding entitled The Strange Death of President Harding.

I have already recorded Harding's death from very authentic sources, which leaves me in no doubt about the real tragic end of this gentle President. So who was this man Gaston Bullock Means? Of all the intriguing characters who infiltrated into the White House in the Harding years this man had no equal.

Here is his story. One description of him was this "A wastrel cherub with a round dimpled smile, sharp chin, and beaming eyes that flickered and darted with a kind of madness." He was a swindler, a proud liar, and a cheat who made deceptions a work of art. He blackmailed bootleggers, promoters, erring millionaires, and peddled his so called influence for thousands of dollars before his career came to an end in the State Penitentiary. His book The Strange Death of President Harding was another money making scam.

In this book he tried to persuade the American people that Harding had been murdered by his wife and doctor if you could believe him. He liked to boast that he had been accused of everything from murder down and was convicted of nothing. Gaston was six foot tall and weighed in at 200 lbs. He went to the University of North Carolina but dropped out. However he was known as a hot-shot salesman.

He started in a small way selling Department of Justice reports and papers claiming he could offer protection for a price. He couldn't because he had no power to do so. He had up to now a wide clientele of underworld contacts and spread the word among them that he could fix prosecutions having connections to the Attorney General. He had none. He was able to travel in his own chauffeur driven Cadillac on $7 a day wages. He even had a clash with the young

J. Edger Hoover who ordered him to stay out of his office.

He had in his possession endless supplies of forged documents which he used to con clients from his bootleggers circle into believing he could secure them liquor licenses which he could not do. He made odd amounts of money out of false promises sometimes $50,000 sometimes $11,000 and $13,000 given to him for promises he never delivered on. He couldn't, because it was all a con.

Gaston again surfaced in a dispute with Secretary Melon who had accused him of trying to infiltrate the Treasury Department. Gaston accused Melon of issuing illegal liquor permits after claiming he was Harding's investigating agent. But amazingly Gaston managed to convince an investigating committee of the truth of his accusations. Daugherty, the Attorney General was drawn into the investigation but the wily Attorney General refused to appear before the committee investigating the charges. The charges were eventually dropped.

But lady luck was running out for Gaston. His creditability was beginning to be questioned. His stories demanded more and more verifications but after much stalling he arrived at a Senate committee meeting one day saying his files had been robbed. They went back five years. Word had got around about Gaston's reputation being the swindler of the century. He was put on trial for some misdemeanours and instantly lashed out with accusations against the Administration implicating many. With his easy access to the inner circle of Harding's political machine he could well have been a great embarrassment to a lot of people. But is it not surprising given the type of world inside the White House at that time that a character like Gaston Bullock Means should emerge from it.

However the story of Gaston Bullock Means came to a tragic conclusion when he made the outrageous claim that he had made contact with the kidnappers of the Lindbergh baby which he had not. Again people believed him out of desperation as the story of the baby had been headlined across America coast to coast. His deal was as follows – for the payment of $100,000 and a few thousand dollars expenses he would produce the missing child which he couldn't. The money was paid to Gaston and when he failed to produce the money or the child he went on trial for larceny. He refused to testify for fear of his life and he was duly sentenced to fifteen years in the Leavenworth Penitentiary, Kansas. He died of a heart attack there six years later but the money was never recovered.

Well that's the story of Gaston Bullock Means, one of the many shadow figures visiting the White House under Harding. A Walter Mitty character that would never have appeared in these notes if it wasn't for his book – The Strange Death of President Harding and of course the freedom he had inside Harding's Administration.

But let's move on. Because of the unsavoury characters Harding had surrounded himself with there was an undercurrent of gossip about their activities which suggested Harding had been hijacked by shady politicians so the question remains. How much did Harding really know about what was going on in his Administration? It seems he turned a blind eye to what he did know accepting this kind of petty law-breaking as common enough to be ignored.

"It was the way political business was done," he thought. He was like a man helplessly watching a train crash in slow motion. It is hard to believe he did not know that Harry Daugherty, his best friend, was involved in widespread graft. Early in his Presidency it seems Warren was persuaded to approve the transfer of Western Oil Reserves from the Navy to the Department of the Interior. But Secretary Fall grabbed this opportunity to make a profit and was soon busy leasing out Government oil he didn't own to Harry Sinclair and Edward Doheny, two other rogues.

It became known as "The Teapot Dome Scandal" which only came to light after Harding's death. The fact that the Administration was full of minor officials stuffing their pockets with public funds didn't help. By now the sickly odour of corruption was even beginning to waft around the occupants of the Cabinet room.

One story doing the rounds was that the unfortunate Harding was so worried he was seen on the back lawn of the White House crying. The story may be suspect for the man claiming to have seen this happen was busy in his own field of corruption Charles Forbes, head of the Veterans Bureau. Later a sordid story surfaced around the same Charles Forbes when one of his employees, a lawyer named Charles Cramer shot himself.

The story gets murkier. Cramer it seems left a suicide note for Harding who refused point blank to have anything to do with the note and would not read it. The plot thickens for another death occurred in suspicious circumstances later when Daugherty's lifelong associate Jesse Smith died suddenly. The death however could not be confirmed as suicide or murder. Strangely it was shortly after this that, Fall the Secretary of the Interior, the one leasing out Government oil that he did not own, tendered his resignation. It was a sad, sad situation that an Administration so promising to start with deteriorated into such a shabby disgrace.
The final consequences were dramatic. Daugherty and the Secretary to the Navy resigned. A dozen Administration figures including Fall and Forbes went to jail. But as you could expect in any B movie Harry M. Daugherty, the biggest rogue of all got away scot-free.

Although being eulogized as the greatest commoner since Lincoln, subsequent events after his death destroyed Warren Harding's reputation completely. The Harding scandals up to then were known only to the few but the truth emerged and blew the Administration apart leaving America in a state of shock. Senate investigations lasting some years resulted in prison sentences for many. Charles Forbes received a two year jail sentence for his part in the Veterans Bureau Scandal. Oil deals were the next for investigations into Harding's officials. The most notorious scandal was the Teapot Dome in Wyoming concerning oil reserve lands which were leased to two oil men Harry F. Sinclair and Edward L. Doheny without competitive bids for the rights.

The Secretary of the Interior responsible Albert Fall received a year in jail and a $100,000 fine for having accepted bribes of $400,000 for his services. An even more serious investigation which was started by the Senate in 1924 one year after Harding's death involving the Justice Department was amazingly frustrated by a "fortuitous fire" in a bank that destroyed crucial evidence. Did Harding participate in these frauds or did he know about them? Well because these questions were never answered satisfactorily Harding's reputation was left in smithereens.

As for Harry M. Daugherty, he was cleared of all charges in a criminal trial despite suspicions he had bribed the jury. When confronted by the press on the steps of the court house they were ruthlessly blunt as only newsmen can be. "Harry," they shouted. "Have you been maligned badly or are you the cleverest crook of the lot?" He shrugged and grinned unperturbed. "You can take your choice," he replied.

One final thought for consideration. If Warren Harding's pedigree was so flawed and I don't for one moment believe it was, why did it not come to light after fifteen hours all night debate in that smoke filled room 404 of the Blackstone Hotel before his selection for the Presidency?

Warren Harding's pedigree was cleared that night as articulated by journalist William Allen White – "Because there was nothing against him and the delegates wanted to go home."

I'm more inclined to accept the verdict of Teddy Roosevelt's daughter, the outspoken Alice when she said "Harding was not a bad man he was just a slob."

By the spring of 1923 Harding's health was failing and his intended trip to Canada was only approved by the doctors provided he got some rest. However his Party bosses had other plans for him and used the trip to Canada as the groundwork of the 1924 Presidential campaign. Not even his fears about his health could stop Warren being the willing tool for his Party manipulators so he went on tour.

As usual Warren gave a star performance in his speeches in Canada. At Vancouver in British Columbia on July 26, three days before he died he impressed his listeners as a man of sentiment, patriotism and friendship according to the press. Here is a short extract from that speech – he said "What an abject lesson of peace is shown today by our two great countries to all the world. No grim faced fortifications mark our frontier. No huge battleships patrol our dividing waters. No stealthy spies lurk in our tranquil border hamlets. Only a scrap of paper recording hardly more than a simple understanding safeguards lives and properties on the Great Lakes and only humble mile posts mark the inviolable boundary line for thousands of miles through farm and forest. Our protection is our fraternity."

But that trip was fatal for Harding. As the world knows Warren Harding died in the Palace Hotel, San Francisco on July 29, 1923 in circumstances that were downright careless by those who should have had his interests at heart. Some say his death should never have happened given his medical conditions.

He was agitated and worried about events back home concerning the scandals surrounding his officials. Coupled with his ill health, the stress in his job, the pressures of a coming election and his dangerous but neglected hypertension a coronary was no surprise to those close to him especially his doctors. However his deteriorating health during his travels in Alaska could not cope with the programme set for him by his mentors. It all ended in disaster. That journey to Canada in 1923 with Flossie turned out to be Warren's last one.

So much had happened over the years, the Romanesque physique of Warren was now showing severe signs of the wear and tear of life in the Presidency. The Canadians in their love for this peace President, the first one to visit Canada, were overwhelming in their welcome and unfortunately for Warren his programme had been geared to meet their numerous demands. During reviews and march-pasts in front of 40,000 people at Stanley Park he appeared exhausted. Then a ride in an auto-parade after which another speech to 60,000 people followed. Halfway through it he dropped his manuscripts which Hoover his successor recovered for him.

Then another address to the press club followed after which he sat down in a state of collapse. He complained of violent cramps and indigestion and his programme was suspended for two days. Further speeches had been planned for him in Portland, San Francisco and Los Angeles. But his train was ordered to run straight through to San Francisco. He was now examined and the verdict of the doctors diagnosed a very enlarged heart. So alarmingly large, Doctor Ray Lyman Wilbur the President of the Medical Association was asked to meet him at San Francisco. Dr. Charles Minor Cooper the heart specialist was also waiting for him. The God like figure of old, now a flabby faced aging old man, slack chin, puffy eyes and utterly drained, came forward to meet them.

Harding went to bed later in Room 8064 at the Palace Hotel. The Duchess had her own suite across the corridor. Next day his pulse rate was 120 and his temperature was 102. With the rapid development of bronchial pneumonia likely, the California programme was cancelled.

Early in the evening Colonel Stirling found him propped up in bed. Warren's one regret was not having caught one fish in Alaska. The Duchess came in to read a piece from The Saturday Evening Post written by Samuel Blythe. "A calm view of a calm man". The theme pleased Warren, depicting him holding a steady competent course quietly pursuing his task deaf to the howls of his critics…. "That's good," he told the Duchess, "Go on read some more." After finishing the article she crossed the corridor to her room leaving him resting on some pillows. His nurse shortly afterwards came out of the bathroom with a glass of water for him.

She noticed Warren's face twitch sharply and his mouth drop open. Then his body slumped forward and his head lolled to the right. She screamed for the Duchess who came into the corridor and shouted "Get Doctor Boone." The doctor found the Duchess sitting on the bed sobbing "Warren, Warren, Warren." Harding's body had now been placed lying flat on the bed, his eyes closed, his face relaxed in peaceful repose. The time was 7.32 a.m. The diagnosed cause of death was a cerebral haemorrhage. Other doctors however disagreed. Doctor's Sawyer, Wilbur, Cooper and Boone finally agreed. Death was due to some brain evolvement probably an apoplexy. The Duchess refused to allow an autopsy or death mask to be made. An announcement was made in the hotel "Your President is dead."

Diners stopped eating and left the restaurant. The Duchess rode in the first carriage as "The superb", Warren's Presidential train, now his funeral coach, moved out of San Francisco station to head East across the Continent heading for Washington covered in black and white buntings. At the clanging of the brass engine bell those clustered on the station platform sang Warren's favourite hymn "Lead Kindly Light". The Duchess spent the long journey home grieving the loss of her lifelong companion, the one who was first rejected by her family when her heart knew with a woman's certainty the man with whom she would spend the rest of her life. Today the memories would come flooding back nostalgic but triumphant.

Now for what is only a pale description of Harding's homecoming to Washington as told by Francis Russell in his book President Harding: His Life and Times; a book that can only be described as deeply moving and beautiful. In it Russell captures the sense of loss experienced by ordinary Americans across America. Harding like Lincoln transforms from a badly slandered President to a deity overnight. The lining of the track by Civil War veterans. The millions who watched his funeral train pass by. The tolling of the Liberty bell as his train passed through Desert Mountain and Sage Country, slowed down by the thousands who crowded the rails.

Workers in the field stood bareheaded. Boys just like boys would climbed onto telegraph poles, trees and the roofs of barns and outhouses to watch his train go by. Most amazing were the robed and hooded members of the Ku Klux Klan who held midnight services gripping flaming torches of red fire in the form of a fiery cross. Not until nightfall did the remains of Harding arrive in Washington to be greeted by the new President, Calvin Coolidge and his Cabinet. A band played "Nearer my God to thee" as Harding's body was placed on a bier in the East room where Lincoln had lain in State. At half past one in the morning the Duchess arrived downstairs "To keep Warren company," she said.

With her head close to Harding's she started a gentle conversation with him. "No one can hurt you now Warren," she whispered. When day broke she arrived to take her place in the first limousine which moved ahead of the cortège down Pennsylvania Avenue. The roads around Marion were choked with traffic when the funeral arrived there.

Hundreds of newsmen struggled to write their copy with originality. Warren would have understood their plight. How can one achieve originality? There are limited ways to describe a common grief. The Duchess countermanded the Secret Service. "Keep the parlour open until the last well-wisher has come and gone," she said "even if it takes until daylight." This was her moment. Hers and Warrens.

Finally the marines carried Harding's body into the Crypt reserved for him. Taps were sounded. The Duchess slipped quietly inside to say her last goodbye. The new President waited outside. She reappeared unbowed, her veil thrown back and her proud head held high. No one knows what her parting words to Warren had been. No one ever shall.

The official verdict on Harding's death was a blood clot on the brain. But besides that book I have mentioned by Gaston Means accusing Harding's wife and his doctor of collusion in his death, rumours did actually persist at the time that even Daugherty had a hand in it. Some even thought it was suicide. Perhaps this speculation was the fault of Mrs. Harding who refused to allow an autopsy to be carried out on Harding. "Why did he die?" they asked. I think historian David Jacob got it right when he wrote "Perhaps he died because it was the best thing to do."

The story of Warren Harding is not quite over yet. The Memorial Association in Marion far from being discouraged from building a memorial to Warren Harding, despite the withering winds of disrepute blowing around him, pressed on with determination. Three quarters of a million dollars ($750,000) had been raised and they managed to persuade Vice President Dawes to come from Washington on April 26, to lay the cornerstone. Its size and grandeur was already inviting criticism.

But the climate was not quite right for the politicians. This magnificent marble statue that the Marian Memorial Association erected to him from contributions by his friends remained undedicated for years because they could not find a Republican figure to risk his reputation in carrying out the ceremony. It was left to Herbert Hoover, the Republican and 31st President to come to Marion later in 1931 to do the job.

It seems Hoover had cause to be grateful to Harding for help received earlier. Behind him sitting on the platform totally unperturbed, was one of the men to escape censure after that "fortuitous fire" - Harry M. Daugherty. President Hoover to his everlasting credit didn't mince his words. Let's listen to what Hoover had to say about Warren Harding.

"Here was a man whose soul was seared by a great disillusionment. President Harding had a dim realization that he had been betrayed by a few of the men whom he had trusted, by men he believed were his devoted friends. It was later proved in the courts of the land that these men betrayed not only the friendship and trust of their staunch and loyal friend but that they had betrayed their country. That was the tragedy of the life of Warren Harding."

Could there be a better epilogue written than that for the years of Warren Harding? There is one remaining anecdote that remains to be told. It is an amazing coincidence concerning his death. On November 21, 1924 his wife Florence Kling-DeWolfe died, less than fifteen months after Warren. Both were re-interred on December 27 1924, to a vault in Marion Cemetery, a mausoleum costing $800,000. Both had died within the expected four year lifespan of Harding's Presidency.

Now as Calvin Coolidge stepped into Harding's shoes, preparations were already underway to bring to justice the shady people who disgraced the Harding Presidency. Our next story about the 30th President Calvin Coolidge should finally tie up all the loose ends.

30th President   Calvin Coolidge

"Silent Cal"
Born 1872
Died 1933
61 Years of age
2 Terms - 5½ years.
1923 - 1929
Age 51

Party: Republican
Profession: Lawyer
County: Massachusetts
Ancestry: British
Value of Estate: $500,000
Hobbies: Fishing, Golf, Indian Clubs Trap Shooting, Mechanical Horse.

Physical Description: 5 foot 10 inches tall, large clear forehead, thin nose, tightly set lips

Significant Extract from his 2nd Term Inauguration Speech Wednesday March 4, 1925
"No one can contemplate current conditions without first finding much that is satisfying and still more that is encouraging….. Confidence has returned, business has revived, and we appear to be entering an era of prosperity which is gradually reaching into every part of the nation. Wage earners are in a state of contentment seldom before seen."

CALVIN COOLIDGE

Yet again we are confronted by an old problem; another President has died before he has completed his full term. When Warren Gamaliel Harding died in the Palace Hotel, San Francisco on the night of August 2, 1923 word went out to contact Calvin Coolidge, the Vice President. Coolidge at that particular time was on a visit to his father in Plymouth Notch, a remote family homestead. So remote and so simple it boasted no electricity, no indoor plumbing and no telephone. It took the Calvin entourage two hours to contact him. To make matters worse, the phone they rang belonged to a Mrs. Cilly, whose store was just opposite to where Coolidge was living. Somehow it failed to wake Mrs. Cilly from her slumbers but persistence paid off and soon a party arrived at Calvin's house banging on his door.

"Ok, ok," the Vice President's father shouted impatiently as he arrived to open the door resplendent in a long nightgown wondering what the hell all the commotion was about. When told the news of Warren Harding's death, he shouted upstairs to the new President who duly hurried downstairs to greet his visitors.

First Calvin crossed the road to Mrs. Cilly's store and sent a message of sympathy to Mrs. Harding. He also phoned the Secretary of State who advised him to take the oath of office immediately. Calvin's father, being a Notary Public obliged by swearing him into office. It was a historic scene. A fourteen foot by seven foot room where the visitors stood on a worn Wilton rug; nearby was a wood stove, a rocker and a marble topped table. A kerosene lamp threw out a yellow light leaving flickering shadows on the faded wallpaper as Calvin's father carefully spoke the oath sentence by sentence which Calvin repeated "I Calvin Coolidge," his father read. "I Calvin Coolidge," repeated Calvin till finally, "so help me God." It was over. The rococo clock on the mantelpiece gave the time as 2.47 a.m. The Notary seal was affixed and Calvin Coolidge was now the 30th President of the United States.

After a few hours sleep despite the comings and goings of the press, politicians, some curious neighbours and a bodyguard sent from Boston; Calvin got up, shaved and dressed, got into a waiting automobile and with Grace his wife, set off for Washington. He had only travelled a short distance when he ordered the driver to stop the car outside the local cemetery. There he got out and walked to his mother's grave and stood silently for a while in prayer. "She seemed very near to me that morning," Calvin confessed later. Crowds greeted him at every one of the train's stopping points on the way. He went out on the footboard and returned their waves enthusiastically.

The oath was repeated for official purposes on Tuesday August 21, 1923 in his suite at Willard's Hotel, Washington D.C. that historic building which had seen so many Presidents pass through its doorway. Justice Adolph August Hoehling of the District of Columbia Supreme Court officiated at it. But these were very serious times for the Presidency for the hunt was already on for all those implicated in the gathering storm about corruption and scandal in Harding's Administration.

As the Congressional investigations got underway, Coolidge proceeded to implement a damage limitation policy so skillfully he achieved what was considered his greatest contribution to the Presidency – a new-found respect for the office. In so doing he assured the Republican Party ascendancy would be in power for another eight years and better still his own re-election by a landslide victory in 1924.

The mid 1920s were widely renowned for the sheer exhilaration and prosperity of America during those years and Coolidge was President for most of them. His "laissez-faire" philosophy of economics with little or no Government intervention to the market forces that prevailed was the basis of his approach to the economy. Nothing should get in the way of business was the credo he preached. He was the second President following Theodore Roosevelt, a man who would have had much to say about this dangerous freedom given to big business operators had he been around. But that's a debate for another day.

Coolidge's famous mantra was always "The chief business of America is business." He was no different in his approach to the Presidency than was Warren Harding before him, just happy to float along on the crest of the wave of prosperity bubbling around him. If it didn't need mending, why mend it! Little did anyone know that deep within this philosophy lurked the seeds of long term destruction which we shall read about under Herbert Hoover and Franklin D. Roosevelt.

Calvin Coolidge was comparatively unknown in politics in 1923, so what was his journey like to the pinnacle of the Presidency itself. John Calvin Coolidge, 30th President of the United States, who coincidentally was born on Independence Day July 4, 1872, was the only son of a storekeeper. John Senior his father and his wife Victoria Josephine Moor Coolidge lived in the dwelling at the rear of their general store-cum- post office in Plymouth Notch. Calvin went to school at Plymouth Notch and in Ludlow Vermont. Like President Fillmore before him, his schooling in Plymouth Notch only took place on days the pupils were unavailable for work in the fields. He didn't set the world on fire at school either for his examination successes were average. I suppose like any other boy, there were too many things to enjoy for Calvin to be concerned about that.

Here I must add a little picture of what life as a boy in Plymouth Notch was like. It has been nicely captured in a book by Donald R. McCoy, called The Quiet President. Apparently his boyhood years were very happy ones during which he worked on the family farm. Sugaring off in April, mending fences, spring planting, chopping and piling wood for the winter, plucking fruit and even ploughing at the age of twelve. His only ambition was to be a storekeeper like his father. He didn't become a storekeeper but he acquired three assets of greater merit. Tightness with the dollar; economy with words (a feature of Vermonters) and an interest in politics.

Boyhood activities crowded his life, like fishing, exploring the local woods, playing checkers, singing, husking bees, bobsledding, skating and hay riding. He loved acting in plays and being involved in minstrel shows and, like all little boys of mischief, playing pranks. Despite his interest in games he was really a very shy lad. He certainly was not one for the girls or the kissing games. Some blamed his shyness on his grandmother and her penchant for locking him in a dark attic now and then for punishment.

As a youth he was sent to Ludlow to continue his studies which were mixed with bouts of work in his spare time and he stayed in "room and board" for three dollars a week. Yes, it was a hard lonely life away from home missing all the friends and boyhood life he had left behind. But everything improved dramatically for Calvin when his sister Abbe came to join him in his studies. Abbe was great company for him as they had much in common and shared a beautiful relationship.

Alas, it ended in tragedy. Just as fate denied him later of his own son, Calvin, at the start of his Presidency, it also denied him of his beloved sister Abbe when he most needed her. One day she fell ill and to his horror, inside one week she was dead, leaving him brokenhearted. America was a beautiful place to live in those days but the mortality rate for young people was frightening. He wrote home to his father some time later saying "I find it lonesome here without Abbe. We talked about so many things," he remembered to a friend. "She poked fun at me and laughed a lot. She filled my days full of laughter and how I miss her when I have a problem. God how I miss her now," he finished and quietly sobbed. But life had to move on for Calvin Coolidge.

When he was nineteen in 1891, he enrolled in Amherst College Massachusetts, where his favourite subjects were philosophy and oratory. Despite reading oratory, he never did become a good speaker. However he duly graduated in 1895 and then moved on the Northampton, Massachusetts to study law. He opened his own practice three years later in 1898. Incidentally, Calvin became trustee at Amherst in his later years after the Presidency. In his law practice Calvin mainly specialized in debt collecting for businessmen, estate management and some work for the banks.

Around this time, Calvin suddenly had more on his plate than he bargained for. A certain Miss Grace Anna Goodhue arrived on the scene. In fact she came to live on the same street as Coolidge. Aged twenty-six, she was a Vermont girl, teaching in the Clark Institute for the Deaf in Northampton. She was vivacious, clever and friendly with a warm sociable personality and consequently poor Calvin hadn't a chance. They were duly married and were blessed with two children, two boys, Calvin and John. Those who knew Calvin just shook their heads in disbelief, for Calvin Coolidge and Grace were as diametrically different from each other as chalk and cheese.

The contrast in their personalities stood out like a sore thumb. She was a bubbling extrovert full of life whereas Calving was a taciturn loner. Later she became the first "First Lady" to receive an honorary degree from Boston University. So she had brains to go with her looks. As President he had made it clear to her how much he disapproved of her participation in politics, yet he was happy to reap the benefits of her undoubted charms. Being the quiet introvert, Calvin I am sure must have winced when Grace met the press which she did regularly. Yet he was still proud of her and her stylish fashions not forgetting her rapier wit and was happy to promote her to his advantage. Grace Coolidge survived Calvin by twenty-four years after a marriage that lasted twenty-seven years.

Nobody could even guess at why Grace married Calvin Coolidge, not even her mother. At a reception, another young wife there was heard to remark "I cannot see how that sulky red haired man ever won that pretty charming woman." Perhaps what bonded them was an impish sense of humour they shared. How they met gave her a real belly laugh. She was watering flowers nearby when she looked up to see Calvin with a felt hat planted firmly on his head. He was shaving at the window in his underwear. She laughed so loudly he noticed her, made a date and the rest is history. He was taciturn; in fact he was almost wordless at times. When someone was told "She taught the deaf to speak," they grinned and said, "Why didn't she teach Cal?"

Grace Coolidge was fun-loving and rebellious though she made sure she played everything low-key when Calvin Coolidge was around. Some say in her young days she was the first to arrive at parties and the last to leave. By the way she was also a Boston Red Socks fan. Grace tried anything new like smoking, travelling by airplane and bobbing her hair. She was also heard to complain "Being the wife to a Government worker is a very confining position." She did attend a co-educational university at Vermont to cut out a career of her own. It paid off for Grace acquired a bachelor's degree and then went on to have additional training to help her teach the deaf. Yes Grace was a very independent woman indeed but Calvin let her get on with her life and the teamwork went well.

Anyway Calvin Coolidge had plans for himself so his next step was to enter politics. However, he was torn between his law practice and the Republican Party. Despite his colourless personality he still managed to win elections. He compensated for his lack of charisma by personal contact with his constituents with this simple request at the door "I need your vote, please." In today's "Spin Doctor" world of politics, this approach would seem naive but in the America of the 1920s honesty, sincerity and integrity were the only ingredients that interested the voter. So Calvin developed a laid-back style and became known as "Silent Cal". He went on to become well-liked and respected for the tenacity of his convictions, many of which he carried over into his Presidency.

It was common knowledge that he never sought newspaper notoriety or made speeches full of propaganda about himself. That just was not his style and he even refused to go on campaign tours believing his record should speak for itself. His career over the next eighteen years was developed through his political contacts in some high profile jobs like City Solicitor, Clerk of the Courts, the Massachusetts Legislature, Mayor of Northampton, Senator in the State Legislature and finally as Lieutenant Governor during the war years from 1916 to 1918.

Calvin's solid style was now attracting Party "Bigwigs", so impressed were they by his hard work and loyalty to the Party. He also attracted the attention of wealthy Boston Department store owner, Frank W. Stearns. Stearns decided to sponsor Calvin's political career and supported him for the Governorship of Massachusetts which Calvin won by 20,000 votes.

Yes, Calvin Coolidge had arrived almost without effort. In an unexpected way, the job as Governor was to prove a significant turning point in his life. He was now on the national stage and shortly he was to be thrust into the political spotlight unexpectedly when he became deeply involved in the notorious Boston policemen's strike. This started when the underpaid policemen sought a pay rise. Unfortunately, they formed a police trade union to fight their case and this was the Pandora's box that let loose an avalanche of demons hell bent on trouble. But why not judge for yourself. The inside story is dramatic as seen through the pen of Donald R. McCoy's book The Quiet President.

Needless to say the story of the strike was front page news throughout the country while it was in progress. The main protagonists were Mayor Peters, Curtis the Chief of Police, nineteen Union Leaders, and Calvin Coolidge, all of whom should have been acting together for a speedy outcome but didn't for the following reasons. The nineteen union leaders were the newly formed Police Union who launched the strike. It is a fascinating story that simply must be told so important was it in Calvin Coolidge's political career. To start with, Mayor Peters was anxious to please his political supporters by trying to head off the strike. The fundamental demand was for the right to strike. This was out of the question. The inevitable political play of forming a committee was suggested to study police wages, hours and conditions.

The right of police officers to have an organization was also questioned. Curtis, the police chief turned this down flat. The Mayor then turned to Coolidge to support the plan but Coolidge refused to become involved. Mayor Peters was desperate to avoid the strike and correctly warned the Governor that if the nineteen officers who lead the strike negotiations were suspended a strike would take place. Once again Coolidge took no notice of this warning believing he had no mandate to intervene. The nineteen leaders were duly suspended and alarm bells rang for the besieged City Fathers.

They implored Coolidge to act. Still he refused for a third time. The poker game went on. They suggested the introduction of troops if the strike took place. For the fourth time he refused, passing the buck back to Curtis, the Police Chief, as his responsibility. The vote for strike was 1,134 to 2. Negotiations were now at a standstill. Politics was at the heart of everything with all Parties fearing a political backlash before the next election. Tension was sky high. Although Coolidge was legally correct, his aloofness was considered inexcusable. The press was in full cry and caused mild panic with fear stories of looters running amok and law and order breaking down if the strike took place. War veterans offered to help police the city.

Finally, the police did strike and hoodlums and riots hit the streets. The big three bosses were still transfixed in helpless inactivity. Then the Mayor broke the logjam and called in the State Guard. He asked Coolidge for 3,000 extra troops and these arrived in the city by nightfall with bayonets fixed. The atmosphere was electric. Then the stakes were raised higher. A General Strike was threatened. No one knew what Peters, the Mayor would do under such stress. But the poker game had gone far enough.

Calvin Coolidge stepped in and acted regardless of the possible defeat he would suffer at the polls. As he put it in his autobiography "The authority of the law and the obedience to the police and its Commissioner was paramount." But by now the troops had fired on a disorderly crowd killing two and wounding others. Another riot was dispersed in Scollay Square when cavalry with sabers drawn, charged a mob which resulted in one death. Finally, the might of the troops broke the back of the strike. Civic leaders were gravely worried about the consequences of the riots caused by this new protégé in the Governor's house. They paid a visit to Coolidge to discuss the situation. It was agreed Coolidge should take charge and call out the militia even though it was a little late in the day for this contribution. But the outcome was a "coup d'état" for Coolidge – a giant stroke of luck for which he was reaping the credit. He had enforced law and order and avoided a General Strike.

The papers of course headlined "Coolidge takes command". Bolshevism was blamed. Editorials were jubilant. "The nation has been saved by Coolidge who has saved an American way of life". The cream on the cake was when Samuel Gompers, the Labour leader, asked for the re-instatement of the nineteen leaders and was met with this cold reply that made Coolidge famous. "There is no right to strike against public safety by anybody anywhere anytime." This broadside placed Coolidge in the role of a national hero by the press which assured him of success in any election in future.

It is a strange, strange world where the last to act should be the first in line for credit. Perhaps I haven't read the story right but showing no compassion to the nineteen officer leaders seems a little harsh today, ninety years later. Would he have got away with this ruling in 2009? – I guess I just don't know.

By now Coolidge was on safe ground, for he was applauded by all shades of opinion across the nation and he was even suggested for the Presidency by his supporters at the Republican Convention of 1920. But Coolidge was only the new kid on the block and made no impact, getting only 34 votes. Warren G. Harding was selected instead. But like all interesting stories, Coolidge's life was soon to take a remarkable twist of direction. The hand of fate pushed Coolidge's career that day right to the top of politics and without any effort by Calvin Coolidge. It happened like this:-

Senator Irvine Lenroot was nominated for the Vice Presidency but refused point blank to accept a second best nomination. There was also an upsurge of mild rebellion among the delegates because, as they saw it, Harding was forced upon them by Party leaders. In another part of the hall by an amazing turn of events, the Oregon delegation nominated, in a noisy passionate scene Coolidge for Vice President. At this time he was an unconsidered "non-entity" standing in the shadows. To resounding cheers, Coolidge won easily and was installed as Vice President to Warren Harding.

Here could I refresh your memory with a quote about Theodore Roosevelt when he was made Vice President. "That damn cowboy is now only a heart beat away from becoming the next President." And so it came to pass.

Like previous Presidencies, no one gave the remotest consideration to the fact that this man Coolidge could be the next President. Following the vote, many would have scoffed at the idea; after all they were only playing the game of politics. But dying in office for whatever reason had been up to then a distinct occupational hazard of the Presidency. History was destined to carry this probability out with mysterious accuracy and Coolidge, the unknown in 1920, became the 30th President in 1923.

Lucky for America such an "Accidental" President has never let the country down so far but given the wrong man as number two, the danger of a catastrophe is always there.

Yes, as I have described at the start of the story, Harding died suddenly and Calvin Coolidge was duly sworn in. All that remained now was the installation of the Cabinet. After that, the famous corruption scandals had to be sorted out. When they were over, for the rest of his Presidency, Calvin is reputed to have done nothing but enjoy the view from the bridge of his very own ship of State. The Calvin Coolidge of the police strike debacle, the fearless Governor, was gone forever. He became as invisible as he had been in the Boston police strike before he got tough with the warring Parties.

Walter Lippmann, the world famous columnist, put it better about Calvin Coolidge when he said, and I quote "Nobody has ever worked harder at inactivity with such force of character, with such unremitting attention to detail, with such conscientious devotion to the task."

But here I just have to come to Calvin Coolidge's defence. If we turn the clock back to July 7, 1924 less than one year into his Presidency and a few months after the scandals of Harding's regime had been put to bed Coolidge was hit with the most devastating tragedy of his life. His sixteen year old son, Calvin, died of blood poisoning which he developed from a blister he incurred playing tennis on the White House lawn. Just when Coolidge was about to take up the reins of power, the sky fell in on him. Those reins of power just slipped through his fingers. To use Calvin Coolidge's own words "The power and the glory of the Presidency went with him." That is the hidden story of Calvin Coolidge no one ever understood, the love of a father for a lost son truly pulls at your heartstrings. Another President Teddy Roosevelt, the 26th President suffered the same fate with his first wife Alice.

But life does have its compensations. Here I would like to include a beautiful story about how a little boy reacted to the death of Calvin's sixteen year old son, Calvin. This little known story told by one of his bodyguards, Colonel Starling, paints a touching picture of Coolidge. "I saw a boy early one morning, his face pressed to the fence," said Colonel Starling. "What are you doing up so early," I said to the boy. "I thought that I might see the President," was his reply. "I heard that he gets up early and takes a walk. I wanted to tell him how sorry I am that his little boy died." "Come with me," said the Colonel, "I'll take you to the President." The boy took the bodyguard's hand and walked into the grounds. In a few minutes the boy was standing in front of the President awestruck.

With the help of the Colonel he gave the President his message. Calvin was so struck he found it hard to control his feelings. Words just would not come. Later he said, "Colonel, whenever a boy wants to see me, always bring him in. Never turn one away or make him wait." Coolidge may have had a tight formal personality but there were times he couldn't help wearing his heart on his sleeve. At least in the headlong race of time, a little boy had remembered and shared in Calvin's grief. It was a beautiful memory he always remembered.

Now that he was President, the job of investigating the corruption of the previous Presidency could not be avoided, distasteful though it was. There was no need to rely on rumours any more as the investigation team was soon to discover. First of all, the Director of the Veterans Bureau, Charles R. Forbes, stole €200 million of public funds and then escaped to Europe, or so he thought. He was extradited later and jailed.

The Attorney General, Harry Daugherty sold alcohol out of Government stocks and kept the money. He got off scot-free. The most devastating revelation was known as "The Teapot Dome Scandal". Secretary of the Interior, Albert B. Fall and the Secretary of the Navy, Edwin Denby were deeply implicated. It was revealed that Denby had approved the transfer of Federal oil reserves at Teapot Dome, Wyoming to Interior Secretary Fall, who then passed them on to an oil company, Pan American Petroleum for a sum of $400,000. The news even threatened the nomination of Coolidge for a second term as President in the coming elections of 1924.
In April 1922 Robert La Follette rose in the Senate to demand an investigation into the scandal. The Senate adopted his resolution without one dissenting vote after his public tongue-lashing of the Government. All these events happened under President Harding, one year before he died and before Coolidge became President. Enquiries dragged on for another year.

Poor President Harding was not corrupt but was badly betrayed by those he had around him. Just before Harding died, Coolidge was confronted about the scandal when he was Vice President. Coolidge defended Harding as a decent, honest man and declared there was nothing he himself could have done about the scandal. Calvin continued to stonewall, a skill he had displayed previously as Governor of Massachusetts during the police strike there.

He claimed the whole mess was the responsibility of the Senate. Edward Doheny, the owner of Pan American Petroleum, then became involved and soon the whole story was implicating the Cabinet itself. Coolidge was now up to his neck in "Fire Damage Limitation". Although he was not in charge of the White House, when the fraud was going on, Coolidge had inherited the whole sordid scene. Many names were thrown up by the investigation and the case was the talking point of Washington Society in 1924. There was even talk of it involving the whole top layer of Republican officials in authority.

When accusing the Republican Party of corruption, the newspapers were merciless with this piece of doggerel. –

> "There was a dog named Rover
> and when he died he died all over"

It all eventually subsided with the conviction of most of the guilty Parties. As usual, Calvin once again came through it all with flying colours. Prosecutions and jail sentences brought the whole episode to a conclusion which was to everyone's relief.

Despite the apparent insignificance of Coolidge by political commentators in the roll call of Presidents, he certainly had a very colourful existence right up to the first year of his Presidency. One thing that strikes me so far was his silken skills of sitting out each crisis and surviving with honour. He even managed to escape the nightmare years of the Depression by not seeking re-election in 1928. Did he know what was coming down the line? Who knows? Maybe it was just luck.

But let's get on with the story of Calvin Coolidge. Luck did play an amazing part in his career. He had no obvious ambition to be Vice President and by a turn of fate he became Vice President due to circumstances outside his control; the refusal of the hot favourite Senator Irving Lenroot to accept the nomination. Becoming President came about through another accident of fate by the early demise of the sitting President Harding. Except for the scandals of Warren Harding's Administration, which Coolidge inherited, his Presidency seemed to sail along in a golden age of plenty. However, he did make enemies with the western farmers who certainly got no benefits from the prosperity they saw around them. So what was this golden age like you may well ask.

The America of Coolidge's time was an amazing place in which to live. Coincidentally, the weak and inept stewardship of Harding, and later Hoover was the last thing America needed in a period of exponential social change. Prohibition spawned the gangsters who thrived on the illegal liquor sales. They made extraordinary sums amounting to $2 billion annually. The corruption of the cities resulted in the birth of the Ku Klux Klan, really formed as an expression of rural protest against the city. It was not just anti-black but anti-aliens such as Italians, Russians, Jews and Catholics. Beatings, floggings, burnings and murder were openly condemned and they were at their strongest in Texas, Oklahoma, Oregon and Indiana. The roaring twenties just about described the period.

Liquor became expensive and the middle and upper class not only had a greater access to it with their purchasing power but openly flouted the law in doing so. The rewards of the new industrial revolution went to the professional classes such as managers, executives, engineers, doctors and bankers. Their prosperity eventually outstripped their needs and their disposable income led them into speculation in the stock market. The graph of their avarice rose uncontrolled until it all ended in a resounding crash on Wall Street in 1929. History would repeat itself in 2008.

The skyscraper, built mainly by Indian labour, became a feature of city skylines, caused by the soaring price of land. By 1929, the U.S. had 377 buildings over seventy storeys high. It became the symbol of American mass culture.

In March 1929 one of the most magnificent monuments to the golden age of Coolidge's Presidency was built. It was the Empire State Building. It stands as a truly remarkable reminder of all that was incredible about the roaring twenties. The expertise, the innovations, the technology, the harmony, the skills, the leadership and the dedication of the American worker and management lifted it 118 floors high in unbelievably record time.

If only the expertise, the leadership and the vision of its creators could have been harnessed to save the economy, there certainly would have been no Wall Street crash.

Here is a rough and I hope fairly accurate story of its rise from ground level to the clouds. The last brick laid was the end of plentiful employment and the builders knew it. The workers on it walked away from the project, the cream of the American working class, some of them never to be employed again. What a sinful waste!

Yes, the most fascinating story of the roaring twenties has to be that of the Empire Building built in eighteen months. The race to the top was started by first building down. The steel order was the largest that had ever been placed – enough steel to build a railway line 500 miles long. Rivets had to be pre-designed to a fraction of an inch and the fabrication in the mill had to be flawless. Some beams were 44 ton weight. The complete frame of the Empire State Building required 58,000 tons of steel. Each beam had to be numbered and manoeuvred into its proper place by specially constructed cranes. Trucks could not arrive late or the schedule was wrecked; zoning laws and the time plan were that strict. It was built by the five Starrett brothers who launched the project with not even a shovel of their own because new technology had to be specially designed from the start. It took 3,500 men onsite to complete the job. People stood mesmerised on 34th Street just watching, yet sadly this was the early days of the coming Depression. The tradesmen employed were the very best available and the timetable and the building was completed as planned on time and on budget.

As the building neared the top the rate of work was slowed down. Twenty-two storeys of steel were put in place in twenty-two days. Makeshift elevators had to be installed to get the men to the top. New innovations were introduced bordering on genius. Different rivet gangs were working in different places. It was estimated a man would die for every floor so dangerous was the job – 102 floors in all. That only five died was a triumph for the considerations for safety the Starrett brothers insisted on. The derrick cranes used had to be moved upwards with the building and re-assembled on the new floor. On completion, art deco design of limestone panels and over 6,000 windows had to be set in place. The finish was a work of art 1,040 feet high. The sixteen storey high mast to finish it off was built as a moving raft for dirigibles and so become an airport. It never achieved that. The idea was to throw a line from the dirigible out of the airship on to a gangplank. However, the dirigible became obsolete putting an end to that dream but achieving another record instead that lasted forty years – the world's tallest building.

Al Smith, the New York Governor, lead the crowd of dignitaries to the 86th floor to open it. Among them was "The Engineer" himself, Herbert Hoover. Unfortunately, the building was destined to be idle for years to come. The revenue it earned was a disaster, opening as it did in the depth of the Depression. By November 1931, it was known as the empty State building and teetered on the brink of bankruptcy. Then came a worse disaster, a bomber accidentally crashed into it 950 feet up. The steel frame withstood the greatest impact it could have endured. Soon after, it was to become the most profitable building in the world. Today anyone who comes to visit it never leaves unmoved.

Biggest losers in this success story of the economy were the farmers. The war economy saw demand for farmers' produce soar but post-war this demand dipped alarmingly until in 1929, the farmer's average income was $273 per annum compared to the national average of $681 per annum. It is hard to believe today that in 1929 an employer could use what was called a "yellow dog" injunction to prevent workers joining trade unions. The blacks who came North during the war now found jobs in only the menial service areas, collecting garbage, washing dishes and sweeping floors.

Nevertheless, their wages were still a vast improvement on what they would get down South. But the danger signs in the economy were ominous. The unequal distribution of wealth, the new expectations for more consumer goods, coupled with over-ambitious speculation was a world gone mad. The boom was heading for a crash. To add to our story the new American, now wealthy, was hell-bent on pleasure. New crazes were rampant in the night clubs. New singers, new dances, new music – jazz clubs and the multiplication of speak-easys, entertained in a heady mixture of bootlegging gangsters and music hall stars never known in the social life of the once simple American.

Playwrights like Eugene O'Neill and writers like Ernest Hemingway and F. Scott Fitzgerald, came to prominence as did the war lord, Al Capone, striding the saloons of New York and Chicago like a colossus. The permissive society was thriving, exploited by the moguls of Hollywood. It was a bubbling cauldron of excitement and law-breaking almost impossible to control.

Sport took on a major role in the life of the average American during the twenties. The average guy now that extra leisure time to enjoy himself and the spending power to go with it. As well as taking part, millions of people had new heroes to cheer in their lives. Jack Dempsey, the boxer captivated a huge audience of followers; footballer, Red Grange and Baseball legend Babe Ruth, are household names today, ninety years after their exploits were written into American folklore. Great feats of bravery held people spellbound like the flight of Charles Lindbergh solo across the Atlantic. New inventions like the motorcar and the amazing flight of the aeroplane by the Wright Brothers. Radios and telephones were now commonplace. Sex, itself a taboo subject in the receding Victorian age, began to take centre stage in peoples lives as the old standards of morals started to crumble.

Finally, the voyeurs and commentators on the changing face of America, the literary giants analysed it all, wrote profound books and plays on what they saw and experienced around them. The emptiness and shallow hypocrisy of a society stripped of the supporting structure of the old decencies and goodness was reflected in books like The Great Gatsby and Charlie Chaplain's film Modern Times.

One redeeming consolation was the advent of jazz or blues music from the South to bring a joy and vibrancy to people everywhere, a wonderful gift from the black people to the white man, a gift that has never been fully appreciated.

New Orleans exported up North jazz stars like Charles "Buddy" Bolden, Ferdinand "Jelly Roll" Morton and of course Louis "Satchmo" Armstrong, with his own improvisation that had no name. They were all big hits in Chicago. The western was the new image creator of what the old West was supposed to be like. But even the folk heroes of those films like "Bat Masterson" and "Billy the Kid" were no more than the product of the movie writer's vivid imagination. Still they entertained millions and made money which was the end product. Flash Gordon was the hero of the space age movies.

Yes, the roaring twenties were indeed a glorious period of American history. It was truly an age of "Glad to be Alive" expectancy bubbling with new ideas, new hopes and new dreams. The tragedy was that at the end of the twenties far from capitalizing on America's vast future potential, it all ended in the tears of the thirties under Herbert Hoover and Franklin Delano Roosevelt, the 31st and 32nd Presidents of America.

Most historians have vilified Coolidge, saying his inactivity failed to harness the vitality and promise of those times into a much more productive future. They say the consequence of this inactivity led inevitably to the great Depression of the thirties which followed. But as we shall read about later, historians and commentators in 1980 and 1998 are today re-appraising this conclusion, an exercise not unfamiliar in the judgement of past Presidents by so-called experts. To explain this phenomenon I am always amazed, as I write on America's 30th President so far, how many have been returned to respectability after being rubbished in the Presidency. Hindsight always holds the strange seeds of miraculous conversion in it.

During these turbulent rip-roaring times, the press had grave misgivings by experts about Calvin's personality. Somehow, he just could not help being formal. He faced the press with scarcely a nod of greeting. He looked bored. Frank R. Kent of The Baltimore Sun, who was just beginning to make his reputation, wrote a piece that reflected a picture of unfriendliness. "Mr. Coolidge does not smile. He utters no greeting, does not even nod his head ..... He seems not to be pleased. The reporters are respectfully silent. His voice corresponds with his appearance. Even when his replies are defiant, which is rare, they are flat and meatless."

Yet he often caught the press by surprise when answering questions. If he did not know the answer to a question he admitted it with charm and frankness. Information he knew, he passed on with generosity that seemed out of place given his dour presentation. The press eventually warmed to him and his dry "one-liners" even though they disliked his style. But there was an answer to his aloofness and he revealed this private part of his thinking to the press one day. "Do you know I've never really grown up? When I was
 a little fellow as long ago as I remember I would go into a panic if I heard strange voices in the kitchen. I felt I just couldn't meet the people and be friends with them ..... The hardest thing in the world was to have to go through that kitchen door and give them a greeting. I was almost ten before I realized I couldn't go on that way ..... I'm alright with old friends but every time I meet a stranger I've got to go through that old kitchen door back home and it's not easy."

Talking of one-liners – for someone who had so little to say Calvin Coolidge had a deep reservoir of homespun one-liners. In fact, they were so numerous they appeared in a fascinating book called The Quotable Calvin Coolidge, edited by Peter Hannaford. Here are a few of them.

On Persistence (1929):
Nothing in the world can take the place of persistence. Talent will not – nothing is more common than unsuccessful men with talent. Genius will not – unrewarded genius is almost a proverb – education will not – the world is full of educated derelicts. Persistence and determination alone are omnipotent.

On Duty (1919):
Duty is not collective, it is personal. Let every individual make known his determination to support law and order. That duty is supreme.

On Grace, his wife (1929):
We thought we were made for each other. For almost a quarter of a century she has borne with my infirmities and I have rejoiced in her graces.

On The European Union (1931):
If Continental Europe can work out some plan for economic unity it will be of much profit to the world. (A quote seventy years ahead of his time).

On Presidents (1929):
We draw our Presidents from the people. It is a wholesome thing for them to return to the people. I came from them. I wish to be one of them again.

On Honour:
No man was ever honoured for what he received. Honour has been received for what he gave.

To conclude this piece on one-liners, a well known anecdote is always told about one of Coolidge's favourite chestnuts.

Known for the frugality of the sentences he used in conversations or speeches, one unsuspecting guest at a garden party, held on the lawn of the White House, teased him by telling of a bet she had to get at least three words from the President. His answer came out quick as a flash – "You lose."

Being from such a humble background, he detested snobbery. "I come from Boston," a gushing woman cooed at him ….. "Yes," said Calvin "and you'll never get over it."

Coolidge was renowned for his wit; something that surprised many, coming from a man who was never talkative. They say his wit could be rather mischievous, for he always had the classical comedian's deadpan expression on delivery. Another story was of a lady who complained to him as follows – "Mr. President, I was so anxious to hear your speech at the opening of Congress yesterday that I had to stand for the whole forty-five minutes." Coolidge's reply "So did I."

Once when being interviewed by William Allen White at the White House, White was foolish enough to say he wanted to peek at the man behind the mask. Coolidge paused and replied mischievously "I don't know as I can help you. Maybe there isn't anything there."

But there was a man behind the mask. One who revered his mother, whose picture never left his desk. Inside a locket he carried, nestled a smaller picture of her which he kept in his pocket at all times. He talked often about her, recounting every memory as if she was still alive. "I wish I could really speak to her," he said one night. "I wish that often." He worried about his ageing father, especially when his father's health began to fail. However his father just refused to live in the White House with Calvin, so a direct telephone line had to be connected between the White House and his father's home in Plymouth Notch.

When the final crisis came and his father's life was running out, Calvin travelled by express train and by car home to meet him. Sadly poor Abraham Lincoln could never find the time to visit his father back home. However Calvin was different. On his final journey to see his father who was ill arrangements were made for the train to have the green light all the way home to Plymouth Notch. All roads were cleared for his car but it was all in vain. His father John had passed away before he got there. Later Calvin wrote "When I reached home he was gone. It costs a great deal to be President." The cost Calvin referred to was not money – it could not be measured in cash.

Having only one surviving son, did not deter Calvin from treating him with a strict parental control. Once when John was late for dinner by one minute, he asked for permission to dine without formal clothing. Calvin rose to regal heights, pointing out to poor John rather pompously "You will remember that you are dining at the table of the President of the United States and you will present yourself promptly in proper attire." I doubt if modern day culture would approve of such a stuffy put down. But John seems to have accepted it as normal and survived. As far as his father was concerned, John would be brought up right and would always be made aware of whose son he was.

But Calvin's life was really attached to Grace his wife with a deep personal affection. Perhaps his affection for his own mother reflected this. She was the hub of the wheel around which the spokes of his life circled. She was his strength and his support, but most of all his most treasured possession. It sounds unbelievable, almost too sugary, but Calvin carried this act of possession to the point of jealousy. When she was at home he was there. When she was away, he behaved like a lovesick honeymooner, missing her till she returned. Yet she tolerated this situation allowing her life to be regulated and dominated by a strict schedule of behaviour, set up by the master of the White House. He lived for her letters while she was away. Needless to say they were the first he opened when he was dealing with the U.S. mail. He was even insanely jealous of her bodyguards. His relationship with these unfortunated Secret Agents was never cordial.

But Calvin was never really happy with his Presidential lifestyle. In a letter to his father on New Year's Day 1926 he wrote "I suppose I am the most powerful man in the world but great power does not mean much except great limitations. I cannot have any freedom even to go and come. I am only in the clutch of forces greater than I am."

Eisenhower in a later Presidency complained of the same restrictions which made Presidential life like living in a goldfish bowl. Even his discarded waste paper was rescued from the waste paper basket to be recorded for the benefit of future historians.

To escape this world of constriction Calvin took numerous vacations which caused the uprooting of the entire White House staff to accompany him. His family, the domestic staff, the White House press corps, the Secret Service and a force of over one hundred soldiers and marines. The holiday locations were as far apart as Saranac Lake in New York, South Dakota's Black Hills, Cedar Island in Wisconsin, Virginia and Sapelo Island, Georgia. Later he escaped into fishing as a hobby and acquired more than an average expertise in the sport.
He even took up horse-riding to get away from the boredom of the office. He rode so often he fooled himself into believing he was capable of riding wild horses, something Grace and his bodyguard, Starling, made sure he would never get the opportunity to prove. Unfortunately the modern Presidents like Obama, Bush, Nixon and Johnson (LBJ) were too busy fighting foreign wars to have time for golf, boxing or jungle trips like Roosevelt. Perhaps in more peaceful times, when a wiser mankind has discovered the secret of inner peace or technology has discovered a way to the stars. In the meantime I'm afraid he will continue to be earthbound.

But who could blame Calvin Coolidge if he chose to reign benignly and not make waves. Satisfied with the surging bubble of prosperity everywhere, the people also accepted benignly the America they lived in.

It is not surprising therefore that Coolidge riding on the crest of a wave of popularity was elected President in his own right in 1924 by a wide margin. The slogan "Keep Cool with Coolidge" was popular and effective. His margin was 382 electoral votes to 136 for his opponent, Corporation Lawyer, John W. Davis.

As usual, the inauguration took place on the East Portico of the White House, the oath being administered by ex-President, Chief Justice Howard Taft. The date was March, 4, 1925. The forty-five minute speech by Coolidge was broadcast with the miracle of a new invention – a radio network to about twenty-three million people. Still Calvin Coolidge missed the opportunity to change the headlong gallop of American recklessness. It was still spend, spend, spend as never before. Calvin firmly believed that his job was to improve what was already working. Nothing was to stand in the way of big business. "Laissez-faire" was the order of the day. As he put it "Government price fixing once started has alike no justice and no end. It is Government who must live within its means," he said.

Any suggestion of applying the brakes filled Coolidge with dread lest it harmed a healthy economy. And who today could blame him. In those days there was no Alan Greenspan around – our modern economic guru. There would be no shortcuts to curb the rampant prosperity. Respecting the rights of others was paramount. "Departments will be financed for real necessities and not for over extravagance," he said and went on "Our house will always be found ready for any emergency and equal to the test." Since President Harding had had no time to tackle the post-war chaos now it was Calvin's turn. One hundred million people immersed in a surging tide of wealth with rampant ambitions for increasing this wealth on the world stage just had to be restrained. Coolidge coolly tackled the future with quiet and meticulous intuition not by flamboyant gestures for the benefit of the press. He was always willing to wait for results. But waiting was one luxury Calvin Coolidge could ill afford in 1928. The ship was already heading for the rocks. The steadily rising stock market still met with his approval and he failed to hear the alarm bells that were starting to herald the Crash and Depression of 1929. But the experts around him were no help either.

To understand Coolidge we must look at his personal life nearing the end of his Presidency. Like Teddy Roosevelt's lost son, Calvin's lost son was no less painful. Just like Roosevelt he carried the pain with him every waking moment from the time he got up each morning. The type of life Calvin lived was no help to ease his grieving. There were very little White House banquets. Unlike Teddy Roosevelt there were no foreign hunting trips to distract him from his inner thoughts. Calvin was a man of routine sober habits.

He rose at the same time each morning at 6.30 a.m. and was at work from 8.00 a.m. until 12.30 p.m. mid-day. His next role was that of host to about four hundred well-wishers each morning and how he hated that job. He was then glad to retire for his afternoon nap of two hours. Calvin was a workaholic, so the routine continued later into the evening and even into his weekends and vacations.

In his spare time he wrote his own speeches and still managed a press conference twice weekly. There was one consolation only in life – his good wife Grace. An extremely outgoing person, Grace was the breath of fresh air he needed to stop him taking life too seriously. She had a passionate interest in people which was a great asset to him and she was frequently by his side – the first of the Presidents' wives to take on that role. She was easily the opposite side of the Presidential coin - gay, outgoing and vivacious. Calvin was the preoccupied introvert. Her dress sense was a revelation as was her intellectual ability.

Grace's choice to involve herself in politics was not approved of by Calvin yet he allowed her to take her place beside him. But one day there came a surprising, no, a shock revelation. It was while he was on vacation in the Black Hills during which he was elected to the position of Sioux Chief by Elders of the tribe, that Calvin Coolidge made a world-shattering announcement which caught everyone's attention. "I do not choose to run for President in 1928." Even his wife was flabbergasted. "Isn't that just like the man," she said. "I had no idea." And you can believe her. That was Calvin.

It was an amazing decision for a man to turn his back on the greatest and most powerful job in the world. The announcement was made in a modest Dakota schoolhouse. He had now chosen the fireside to the company of the greatest Statesmen in the world.

As Roosevelt had said you don't live in the White House. You are only "Exhibit A" to the country. As his term came to an end Calvin handed over power to the 31st President Herbert Hoover, another Republican.

Now Calvin wanted a real home so he purchased a twelve room house near Northhampton, Massachusetts in 1930 and moved in there. He then spent his retirement writing his autobiography which was published in magazine installments in 1929 and later it came out in hardback. True to himself he continued to lecture in his weekly articles on the merits of "Laissez-faire" and his philosophy for keeping Government out of business affairs. He became a board member of the New York Life Insurance Company and trustee of his Alma Mater Amherst College.

One of the questions history has left us with is this. Was Coolidge really responsible for the Depression of the thirties or should we really give him credit for the golden era of his Presidency? If he was responsible for the golden years why was he pigeonholed by the experts of later years as a failure and why was he laughed at for his one-liner "The business of America is business." The 30th President received a disgraceful epitaph by his Democratic successors who had their own political elections and agendas to think about. Words like cold, disliked people, worshipped wealth, unconcerned about ordinary people, obsessively materialistic, listless, unimaginative, inactive, crabbed and narrow in outlook, no sense of humour. Descriptions like these do no justice to a decent honest human being. In fact they can only be described as disgraceful.

On reflection one cannot help having sympathy with Calvin Coolidge's economic and political philosophy during his years in the White House. You see, he believed that he represented the will of the people. Events at the time conspired to support him in his view. Who can blame him for thinking that old cliché "If it needs no mending why fix it?" His own victory in 1924 was fully confirmed by the strong support of both Republicans and Democrats happy with the policy of unrestricted free enterprise. The society of the 1920s fully rubber stamped his reluctance to hold back the tidal wave of economic expansion by Government Legislation.

Calvin knew such Legislation would have run counter to the wishes of most Americans. In the circumstances was Calvin more right than wrong. It was not until 1980 that he was rehabilitated as being badly maligned. Ronald Regan went so far as to hang a Coolidge portrait in the Cabinet room. In 1998 the Kennedy Library invited nineteen historians to deliver papers to a Conference entitled "Calvin Coolidge Examining the Evidence". His close ties with the labouring class, and the laws he passed to ease their burden and improve their working conditions, is only now being recognized. Yes Calvin Coolidge may have been slow to act but the good works he left behind were legion.

Just before he left office Calvin justified the boom in a spirit of self-congratulations in his State of the Nation speech of 1928. He concluded: "The Country can regard the present with satisfaction and anticipate the future with optimism."

It was January 5, 1933 and Calvin Coolidge's life was running out now. Whatever vitality he had possessed had been spent on his Presidency. The rest he tried to husband into a lifestyle limited by his failing health. In 1932 he suffered repeated bouts of asthma, indigestion and bronchitis, diseases which were debilitating enough in themselves. Now he complained of a permanent throat infection and breathing difficulties which made life very unpleasant indeed. His experiment with his diet was to no avail. He had one consolation – not to be President given the times that were in it.

He withstood many suggestions to serve on Commissions. "I feel worn out," he complained. That was to be his mantra from then on. Sadly on the morning of January 5, 1933 he arose at his usual time of 7 a.m. After dealing with some correspondence he told his secretary Harry Ross he wanted to go home. He then went to the library and paused to fit a few jigsaw pieces into a picture of George Washington. He next went to the kitchen for a glass of water and then upstairs to his room. There Grace, returning from a shopping trip found him lying on his back in his shirt sleeves. He had died quickly of a coronary thrombosis. He was only sixty years of age.

This leaves me perplexed and I ask myself with all the medical support he had from top doctors why did he have a sudden death? Knowing Calvin as we do maybe he chose it that way. As Grace would say "Isn't that just like the man?"

The funeral services were attended by all the top dignitaries including President Hoover. A smaller party went on to Plymouth Notch for a simple family ceremony over the family plot where he was buried among his own people. Grace, as we said earlier survived him by twenty-four years.

After Calvin's death in 1933 Grace gave interviews and published an article "The Real Calvin Coolidge". She began speaking out on issues, something she wouldn't dare to do as First Lady. She sold their brand new twelve roomed house and furniture, toured Europe, and then went to live with at a friend in Northampton, Mass. She died aged seventy-eight years on July 8, 1959 and was buried alongside her old pal Calvin at Plymouth Notch.

31st President   Herbert Hoover

"The Engineer"
Born 1874
Died 1964
90 Years of age
1 Term
1929 - 1933
Age 55

Party: Republican
Profession: Engineer
County: California
Ancestry: Swiss/German.
Value of Estate: Millions (unknown)
Hobbies: Medicine Ball

Physical Description: 5 foot 11 inches, stocky, square faced, with ruddy complexion.

Significant Extract from his Inauguration Speech on Monday 4, March 1929:
"As our numbers increase and as our life expands with science and invention, we must discover more and more leaders for every walk of life."

HERBERT HOOVER

Herbert Clark Hoover, the 31st President of the United States, came to power four years before he expected to in the year 1929. The sudden shock decision by Calvin Coolidge not to seek a second term saw to that.

But Hoover unlike many previous Presidents whose only careers were in politics, had already lived a very successful life in another role as a world famous engineer. So famous in fact, he was thought to be second in importance only to Thomas Edison himself. Hoover was born in West Branch, Iowa, second son of Jesse Clark Hoover and Hulda Randall Minthorn Hoover on August 10, 1874. Both his parents were Quakers. His father was both a blacksmith and a storekeeper but only lived until Herbert's sixth birthday. That tragedy was repeated two years later when his mother died and he was left an orphan to be reared along with his sister May and his brother Theodore by a close relative.

At ten years of age his uncle took him to live in Newberg, a Quaker settlement in Willamette Valley, Oregon. Here he worked on a farm and attended the local school. He later worked in an office in Salem. You may remember Salem's connection with Abraham Lincoln who worked there too as a store owner and raft pilot. Hoover studied mathematics in the local business school there. Like most jobs it was a chance meeting with an engineer in Salem that set him on the career path of engineer.

Later with the help of a Mathematics Professor Joseph Swain, Hoover gained entrance to Stanford Junior University California. Henry Hoover paid for his studies by typing and operating a laundry agency. The link with typing skills got him a job as secretary to a Geology professor. After four years, in 1895, Hoover graduated by receiving his Bachelors Degree as a Mining Engineer so his spare time jobs had paid off handsomely.

Herbert Clarke Hoover immediately set sail on a mining career a million light years from his later path to the pinnacle of the Presidency of the United States. But that is one of the unknown imponderables of life that always leaves the lady of fate scratching her head bamboozled. But she needn't have worried, for Herbert's mining career was an ever ascending tangent of success. First in San Francisco, then with a London Mining firm "Bewick" working in Western Australia, soon he graduated from technical work to Administration bargaining with the Australian Government. His next move was to China. But like many Presidents before him, somewhere in this busy international world of work he met, wooed and married Lou Henry a young woman he met in his student days.

It was in China he had a very dangerous experience. Chinese nationalists, in what was known as "The Boxer Uprising" launched attacks on foreigners living in Beijing. These foreigners took refuge close to where the Hoovers lived and true to their instincts Hoover and his wife risked their lives to transport food and medical supplies to the wounded. Not long after this incident they returned to England.

It was the year 1900 when Hoover received from his company Bewick one fifth of an interest in it. This gift left Hoover the owner of property in Australia, New Zealand, Egypt, South Africa, Canada and Nevada. In short he was now a very rich man. It can be said with confidence Hoover was now a consulting engineer of international repute. In fourteen years by 1914, Herbert Hoover had reached the very pinnacle of his profession as Consulting Engineer in dozens of Mining firms throughout the World. So accomplished was he in his profession, he decided to write a book on the subject Principles of Mining which later became a standard classic text book on ore extractions.

There are many people reading this whose own lives reached a crossroads and a decision had to be made. Some choose right, others choose disaster. Hoover was one of the latter. Had Herbert Clark Hoover retired at this point in his life he could have done so a very rich powerful and successful man and lived on his wealth and his prestige as a Mining genius for the rest of his life. But lady fate was bamboozled this time. She was worried.

You see, the hunger that makes a man a genius also feeds a man's pride and ambition. Unless he can thwart and defeat the demons of these dangerous troublemakers, he is doomed not to be fulfilled by the tranquillity of commonsense, but tormented by the insatiable hunger for power that leads nowhere. And so the logical progression of the story leads us to Herbert Hoover's new career. "I am interested in some kind of public service" was how Hoover put it to his public spirited wife. It was at this point lady fate somehow conspired to have the American Ambassador invite Herbert Hoover to rescue some Americans now stranded in Europe and return them to their homeland.

This he accomplished. The year was 1914. The genius was still at work however and Herbert Hoover was so successful at this work they decided to challenge him at a higher level to get food, shelter and clothing to thousands of homeless and hungry Europeans. For five years Hoover dropped everything and did the job full time and unpaid. I suppose the title "humanitarian" would now be a well-earned description of the man going back to the days of "The Boxer Uprising" but slowly he was entering into the world of politics almost without noticing it and his C.V. for a major political prize was slowly taking shape.

The world of engineering was now receding rapidly into a fading past and before him was an exciting world with a far different future.

Lady fate shook her head in despair. This new job in Europe was not without danger. As Hoover said himself "I moved constantly in and out behind the trenches on both sides of the conflict." As Chairman of a Commission for relief in France and Belgium Hoover distributed millions of tonnes of food and clothing to refugees and met the top men of the military and Civil Service in England, Germany and France. Hoover's job was that of expert supervisor in a gigantic European task force and once again he was gloriously successful.

Now Hoover found himself sucked into the inner circle in Washington as U.S. Food Administrator at the invitation of Woodrow Wilson. It was now his job to feed the Allied armies in post-war Europe, a job he achieved by organizing the administration of the Grain Corporation, the Food Purchase Boards and the Sugar Equalization Board in the production of Agricultural products.

President Woodrow Wilson then came in with another request. He needed someone to take charge of the economic recovery of post-war Europe after the first World War.
Hoover became a major player in Europe taking charge of shipping, railways, coal mines, ports and canals throughout Europe. When he completed his mission he took over yet another organization for Woodrow Wilson, looking after the children of Central and Eastern Europe. This provided him with the raw material for a marvellous book based on his letters to and from thousands of children, boys and girls throughout Europe called On Growing Up.

But the lethal cocktail of Hoover's ambitions and his future fate were still conspiring against him if only he knew it.

The siren voices of Washington were still luring him ever nearer to Capitol Hill by a call from another President. This time Warren Harding, inviting him to become Secretary of State. Hoover finally resigned from that job to pursue what was now his main ambition to become President of the United States of America. Yes, those deceiving demons inside him were as destructive as ever.

Hoover was now ready to jettison his beloved world of Engineering forever for the dubious delights of politics. Now the time had come for the final push to the summit of Herbert Clark Hoover's final dream President of the United States of America.

As we pointed out at the start of this piece the decision of Calvin Coolidge not to run for another term as President handed Hoover the Presidency four years before his time.

Now there was little opposition to challenge him. His success in Europe gave Hoover's name a very attractive ring to it. At the National Convention held in Kansas City, Missouri in June 1928 he won the Presidential nomination by 837 votes to 74 over Illinois Governor Frank O. Lowden. Senator Charles Curtis of Kansas was recommended for the Vice Presidency.

Hoover duly went on to win the Presidency by a landslide victory of 444 votes to 87 for Tammany Hall candidate and Catholic, Alfred E. Smith. Both of these labels were a handicap for Smith who was also opposed to the newly proposed 18th amendment to the Constitution to bring in Prohibition. The story of Prohibition is mentioned later under Franklin D Roosevelt.

The inauguration of Hoover drew the traditional crowds numbering about 50,000 to the ceremonies on the East Portico of the White House on Monday March 4, 1929 at 1 o'clock in the afternoon. Chief Justice William Howard Taft administered the oath of office. Overhead a dirigible called the "Los Angeles" hovered while four Blimps and thirty aeroplanes flew over the city in the rain. At 8 p.m. the usual fireworks display took place, just before the compulsory by now, inaugural ball in the Washington Auditorium. There was also an Indian orchestra from Tulsa, Oklahoma to entertain them. While I don't know how good the music was and what the name of the orchestra could be I'm sure they covered themselves in glory that night.

Around the time of Hoover's inauguration in March 1929 one of the most magnificent monuments to the golden age of Coolidge's Presidency was finally built - The Empire State Building. It stands as a truly remarkable reminder of all that was incredible about the roaring twenties. A rough and I hope fairly accurate story of its rise from ground level to the clouds has already been described in our piece on Calvin Coolidge. The last brick laid was the end of plentiful employment as the builders knew it. The workers on it walked away from the project, the cream of the American working class, some of them never to be employed again. What a sinful waste!

If only the expertise, the leadership and the vision of its creators could have been harnessed to save the economy, there certainly would have been no Wall Street crash. The building of the Empire State Building was the last good news event Hoover would ever attend. His Presidency was to prove nothing more than a poison chalice for him. Yes, down the road waiting for Hoover was disaster, if only he knew it. The bitter fruits sown in the halcyon days of Calvin Coolidge's unrestrained madness was about to engulf him. For the next four years he was to wrestle with a monster so fierce his illustrious career, his past achievements, and even his personal reputation would be torn from his grasp and trampled in the dust of failure and destruction almost to the brink of disgrace.

As I said earlier, retiring as a world-famous engineer would have been infinitely more just and forgiving than the judgement of politics. But then again there is no substitute for hindsight. Not even the experts of today, almost seventy-five years later, have all the answers to what happened to America in the late twenties. Worst hit were the farmers who, despite Calvin Coolidge's world of plenty, were in desperate straits. In order just to stand still, the farmers were forced to increase productivity every year. Hoover tackled the problem by setting up the Federal Farm Board to make loans to Co-Operatives.

He even suggested large Corporations to buy up farm surpluses in order to hold prices static. Isn't it amazing the way history repeats itself. Thirty years on in the 1960s, Europe created the same programme which resulted in food and butter-mountains and wine lakes. Once again the idea has been discredited by events. It didn't help in 1929 either and with the gathering storm of Depression just over the horizon, the bottom was about to fall out of every market. If luck plays a part in any man's career, the choice of leading his country at that particular time in history was surely to be the greatest mistake Hoover ever made.

The Wall Street crash of 1929 led to the great slump. Today, nearly seventy-five years later, that slump has become a deeply ingrained part of the folklore connected with the roaring twenties and hungry thirties in America. It came at the end of a decade when even President Hoover was claiming in his inauguration speech "We in America today are nearer to the final triumph over poverty than ever before."

So what went wrong? Well, during this golden decade of the twenties, unemployment was low and production profits and wages were experiencing a steady rise year after year after year. Prices remained steady but in fact food prices fell because of a huge surge in agricultural activity. Euphoria reigned. This was going to last forever. The greedy and the ambitious decided they wanted part of the action even if they had to borrow their way into debt for the privilege. The more shares you bought the richer you could become. The start of the crash was simple. Day of sunshine and roses carried the merrymakers along on the crest of a wave without any effort. This was going to last forever. But alas that didn't last forever. One day the train began to lose momentum and the passengers began to jump off.

It all began with an insignificant wave of selling which soon began to gather momentum. The ones who had borrowed to take part in this charade were the first to panic. They sold just to repay their debts. One fed off the other. The further share prices dropped the greater was the urgency to sell. In one month share values on the New York Stock Exchange fell by one third. You can only speculate on how fearful the consequences were after two years of this panic selling. 5/6ths of the value of the average industrial shares had disintegrated by mid 1932.

Businesses began to falter. Consumption dropped as the rise in unemployment led to a drop in demand which triggered a drop in production. In three years, by mid 1932 the fall in trade had dropped to half of what it had been in 1929. Before getting bogged down in the broad brushstrokes of the staggering economy, what was much more important to the man in the street was the question of sheer survival. Families now lived in poverty without eating meat or vegetables for months while unbelievably crops rotted in the fields around because the price of harvesting wasn't worth it. Some opted to stay in bed to keep warm and save on fuel costs. Shoes were patched with rubber and many sold pencils on street corners for a living. Those who fell behind in their mortgages lost their homes and those who became tramps were in danger of arrest for vagrancy. The hobos who met at the side of the railroad tracks were glad to share much needed friendship, food and shelter with each other.

Those unemployed and living at home queued for hours for a welfare relief cheque and some lived on just beans and soup from mobile food kitchens. Not so long ago they were a happy vibrant group of neighbours. This was the depressing picture that today is burned into the memory of millions of Americans looking back on history. Those who suffered through the Depression have long since passed away. I will mention this again further on in these notes, but other countries now suffered greatly when the malaise crossed the Atlantic to Europe. This is not so surprising for at home in America, unemployment had soared from 1½ million to 12 million in three years. Workers were bound to look for another country to escape to. But that is not the real reason the melaise jumped the Atlantic.

The disease was passed on to Europe by the debts the continental countries had incurred on loans made to them by American investors who now demanded repayment. Since trade with America depended on American money, the loss of such investments meant the pool of money financing trade in Europe was drying up. Payments of war reparation debts were unpayable. The scramble for money among competing countries led to a rush on gold. But let's not get carried away with all this doom and gloom. The real question for us is how Herbert Hoover handled the situation he was unlucky enough to inherit back in America. The banks now step on to the world stage.

Hoover blamed the banks for his nightmare. He claimed the free flowing and over-generous credit given to speculators had fuelled the disaster. The game of stocks and shares was a reckless gamble played by fools. The normal purchasing method is in four stages. The application, the allotment, 1st call and 2nd call. The full purchasing price becomes due after the final call. However in the mad frenzy of the bank mania at the height of the boom, this method was abandoned. The wheeler dealers simply took short cuts and used the stocks and shares that were purchased as collateral for further loans despite the fact that only 3% of the purchase price changed hands. This collateral disintegrated into useless paper promises when the market collapsed. Heavy investments abroad said Hoover "was fuelled by this indiscriminate loan policy of the banks." One billion dollars per year was speculated under Coolidge. These investments in Europe bankrolled the purchasing power for buying American goods, thus feeding the boom of both Europe and America. When that money dried up Europe inherited the U.S. Depression.

In the 1920s real wages in America rose by 26%. Payrolls, pensions, rents and profits rose from $74 billion to $89 billion between 1923 –1929. "The weakness of the banking system was the real cause of the Depression," said Hoover. But the number of banks actually increased from 1,345 in 1930 to 2,298 in 1931. It wasn't until 1933 that the hurricane down the road was identified. Suddenly banks in Michigan closed down. This trend escalated into twenty-two States soon after. Nobody learned from what happened in the 1920s and we repeated the nightmare all over again in 2005. Again the banks were the culprits. Hoover unfortunately was right after all.

One particular explanation for the Depression among the many opinions offered was that U.S. factories were producing more goods than the American people could consume. While factory production went up 43%, wages rose only 11%. If the speculator's millions had found their way into increased wages, the increased purchasing power of the consumers would have absorbed the surplus consumer goods. The balance achieved would have avoided the Depression.

Well, as I've said earlier, this was just one of many the opinions offered in hindsight. You can take your pick.

But nobody had foreseen the crash and therefore the speculators remained in full cry, encouraged by the irresponsible lending of the banks. As long as nobody foreclosed on their loans, this get rich quick formula could last forever. But there is no such thing as forever in this world. They were all borrowing, buying and selling on borrowed time. Time eventually did run out for them and only those who could jump off the burning ships quickly enough escaped serious injury. For those not quick enough to jump – "bankruptcy". Although Hoover was vilified for the collapse of the country, he should not be held wholly responsible just because he was skipper of the burning ship as it floundered, for he had only six months of Coolidge's golden era passed on to him. When he began the job, life seemed so promising and secure. His inauguration speech as I have already noted, was full of optimism. The start of his Presidency was full of hope. For instance just after entering the Presidency Hoover took a six weeks tour of Latin America which was steeped in the euphoria of the good times.

Two warships were placed at his disposal for the journey, the "Utah" going out and the "Maryland" coming back. In these early days of his Presidency, he was quite popular and he was received everywhere with great courtesy. A spirit of celebration was everywhere. Sadly this was in stark contrast with his treatment at the end of his four years in the Presidency. In retrospect, the Hoover Administration had one major flaw in its make-up. On forming his Cabinet, Hoover had made the mistake of relying on businessmen and economists to solve his problems when what he needed most of all was an understanding with the politicians with whom he had to work. He just didn't have that gift.

What he didn't realize was that he never had control of the politicians who could choose to ignore him whenever they wished. His promise to take politics out of Government had backfired. The businessmen were not the saviours after all. Soon the "Hoover Bull Market", as it was called was at an end. Between October 24 and October 29, 1929, sales of stocks and shares went through the roof. A total of $16 million changed hands in the panic. The drift in the value of stocks was steadily downwards right up to the summer of 1932.
In fact the total value of stocks on the New York Stock Exchange plummeted from $89 billion to $15 billion. Another reason for the chaos has been blamed on the complete shortage of sole entrepreneurs like Ford. There were it seems, millions of owners holding shares in large Corporations in which 90% of America's wealth was tied up. Unfortunately these shareholders discovered they had no real control because control was vested in the hands of dubious directors. Because of this some of the securities thrown on the market were worthless. Decent honest purchasers were conned into buying rubbish for the benefit of the few. But everyone who participated in the buying and selling frenzy of stocks and shares were subject to the golden rule of "Caveat Emptor", which means Buyer Beware. They purchased not for dividends but for quick profits from the sale of shares at a higher price. The velocity of the selling was as uncomfortable as a herd of runaway buffaloes or the surge of a South Sea Tsunami.

But no man and no U.S. President before 1929 ever had to contend with the greatest economic catastrophe to confront America. There was no one on either side of the Atlantic with the expertise to diagnose the illness and prescribe a cure. Like an aircraft without flying instruments, a compass, or radar; Hoover the pilot, had to fly as they say "by the seat of his pants". Some experts had foreseen the crash – Alexander Dana Noyes of the New York Times, was one prophet who tried to warn the country but he wasn't listened to. Sir George Parish, an English economist was another to ring the warning bells.

Paul M. Warburg of the International Acceptance Bank implored the Federal Reserve Board to introduce a restrictive practice policy and to call a halt to the unrestrained speculation. But none of them had a solution to help the survivors after the crash. From this point in our story, the narrative concerns the victims. Like any crash, the plight of the survivors can be truly horrific. The human consequences were indeed heart-breaking for a humanitarian like Hoover to witness. Personal life savings were wiped out overnight. H.P. purchases had to be returned. Homes were lost. Insurance claims were not honoured. Stores closed with no customers coming in. Vandals broke up vacant buildings. Theatres went dark. Universities closed or staff had severe pay cuts. Soup kitchens opened. Bread lines formed. People slept on park benches, jobless. The combination of hunger, cold and fear was a frightening first-time experience for many. This disease spread to Europe where the same stories were written. This may surprise many people who have only read about the American Depression. The money had truly dried up leaving the rich to suffer the same pain as the poor.

Yet Hoover continued to persevere and recommended tax cuts to increase purchasing power. But taxes had already been cut to the bone and further ones had little effect. All Hoover's measures were proving in vain. His pleas to maintain production and employment on lower wages were ignored. Relief for the unemployed diminished as funds diminished.

Some said that Hoover was oversold as a "master organiser", "the irresistible engineer", "the supreme economist". Hoover was apprehensive of such titles. "I am not a superman." "I hope I can live down my reputation as an Engineer." "If the economy does not perform, I shall be the one to suffer," he prophesized in 1929.

So what were the pen pictures of Herbert Hoover like at that time? I'm afraid the press didn't take to Hoover easily.

You see Herbert Hoover was a practical man who could hire and fire wisely but he had no sense of public relations. "He is not for this hour," said one press man. He knew about working with "things" but didn't understand the power of words. He began to avoid talking about important issues and sometimes refused point blank to discuss them. He wouldn't even help the press by posing for pictures. He was still admired as a world citizen who rescued starving millions in Belgium and Europe but he appalled the press with the bigotry he released across the country in his attack on Alfred E. Smith, his opponent in the Presidential election. Smith was a Catholic by religion. Hoover contemptuously dismissed him referring to his religion with the words "It gives violence to every instinct I possess...." Another appalling observation during those hustings was this – "The Pope would rule America if Smith ever sat in the White House." What had happened to the educated mind of the Engineer? Precision had been replaced by confusion.

Hoover's relationship with the press deteriorated still further because of his belief that the press blamed him for the Wall Street Crash. They thought his measures were inadequate as unemployment, hunger and fear of economic collapse took over the country. The press insisted as he left the White House that if he wasn't the man who caused the crash, he had done nothing to curb it. They then went on to say "He is a stiff-necked upper class President." William Allen White, the famous journalist commented "Hoover's disposition is decidedly low voltage." These opinions were shared by the Staffers in the White House as you will gather from the following notes on Lou, his wife.

When Herbert Hoover was managing the food stocks of Europe after World War I, setting up canteens, a war hospital and Red Cross ambulances, Lou Hoover was in the thick of things. In the U.S. she gave speeches to generate funds for their European work, raising $100,000 in San Francisco alone. Unfortunately, when in the White House she was not too popular with the Staffers because they were told to stay out of sight. Bells were actually rung "to warn the servants" the Hoovers were passing through the servant's private quarters. It was up to the servants to nip into the nearest nook or hiding place. The images of shadowy figures disappearing up the chimneys come to mind. Their verdict was how seldom the Hoovers came in contact with them. Some said the Hoovers disappeared for four years not I presume up the same chimneys. Most of the working servants left the White House never to return. Strangely Richard Nixon had the same rules for Staffers – "Don't speak unless spoken to," he ordered the Staffers.

What Humbug!

Great Presidents like Adams, Jefferson and Madison looking down from the walls of the White House would not have been impressed. The gaiety of Dolly Madison or the informality of Jefferson would have laughed at the pygmies.

Some say Hoover's Presidency was a series of disasters. His public pronouncements were totally devoid of P.R. skills given the serious times that prevailed. "The fundamental business of the country – that is production and distribution is on a sound and prosperous basis." This sort of statement did nothing for the morale of the starving people on the bread queues. His determination to balance the budget made him threaten to veto the payment of the veteran's claim. News of his attitude in Congress leaked out and once again he had made himself another group of bitter enemies.

He didn't seem to know that 94% of Veterans had army and navy records. A veteran's song had this to say "In a cage that is fit for a lion he moves with the soul of a mouse." Campaign buttons in the 1932 Presidential election read "Anybody but Hoover". One joke "going the rounds" in the music halls was as follows – "I think the Depression is ending. Why has Hoover died?" But the hobo groups along the railway tracks around the country multiplied and became known as Hoovervilles. Sacks they carried their belongings in were "Hoover bags". The newspapers they lay on at night became "Hoover blankets". Empty pockets turned inside out were "Hoover flags". If you defended him you were a "Hoovercrat".

The fact that Hoover was as stiff as his well starched collars did not help. Speaking of the poor people who sold apples to survive he said "Many people left their jobs for the more profitable one of selling apples." People who disagreed with him were dolts, wrote Richard Norton Smith. "No one," he told the press "is actually starving." As late as 1932 he vetoed the Garner-Wagner Relief Bill of 2.1 billion dollars for public works as direct aid to individuals.

Yet every city at that time was broke. The fact that Hoover had worked for anything he got was a complete deterrent to him acting magnanimously towards those needing handouts on the suspicion it would turn them into sloths. By 1932 the American people were ready to repay him back in spades at the polls. Herbert Hoover observed ruefully "Democracy is a harsh employer."

Another opinion of Hoover went as follows: He was viewed as a splendid humanitarian abroad but had no talent to cope with the economic crisis at home. Hoover described all the criticism as a smear campaign when writing his memoirs. But unfortunately for Hoover he has left behind events that reflect very badly on his Presidency, such as his showdown with the war veterans. Congress failed to pay a promised bonus to World War I veterans in the dark hours at the start of the Depression. The President's veto was by- passed by Congress allowing the veterans to borrow their 50% bonus due to them. As the crisis worsened the veterans demanded 100%. Hoover, ever the practical thinker, persuaded the Senate to reject this and the veterans drifted into Washington to lobby for the Bill.

Congress refused. But the veterans now calling themselves "The Bonus Expeditionary Force" simply squatted in the shanty village on the flats of the Anacostia River in Washington. These shanty towns were called "Hoovervilles". But Hoover was still refusing to talk to them. The scene was obnoxious and Hoover, to clean up this unsightly mess, offered to pay the taxi fare home for the protesters; 6,000 in total. They were mostly wives and children, certainly not the hoodlums they were labelled. Sadly they were really a desolate army of ragged hungry people. Some slept in Government buildings as a defence against the tropical July nights.

Unbelievably, Hoover employed General MacArthur "to clear up the mess". The eccentric Douglas Mac Arthur resplendent in General's regalia arrived at the head of a force consisting of four troops of cavalry, four of infantry, one machine gun squadron and six tanks. Miraculously, only two of the "Bonus Army" was killed. MacArthur's troops burned down the village of huts, shacks and tents, reminiscent of the Indian atrocities out West in days gone by. Their living quarters were eliminated with the help of troops carrying bayonets and tear gas injuring scores of them including women and children in the process. What were Hoover's comments during his 1932 campaign for re-election? "Thank God we still have a Government that knows how to deal with a mob." That sordid event helped to diminish even more a once respected reputation now tarnished forever. The portrait of the great humanitarian had faded into oblivion.

But let's pause here for a while and recall past events.

When Hoover made his pronouncement at the start of his Presidency that "The country was on a sound and prosperous basis" he seemed to be completely out of touch with the true position of the nation's finances.
There are two questions about announcements like that. If he truly believed how good things were, then subsequent events proved he was disastrously out of touch. To be that much out of touch for a man of such international experience and so intellectually qualified prompts one to shake ones head in disbelief. Could he have really believed his own words? Economic information about the banks, the money markets and the international scene must have been available to him. In short, he was whistling in the dark. Surely he had a shrewd idea of what lay ahead.

To give Hoover some credit, he did respond to the crisis with some innovation by increasing loans through the Federal Reserve Banks and increased Government spending, both of which were designed to encourage economic expansion. The $19 million which were pumped into hospitals, roads, waterways and even military bases were brave new attempts to tackle the problem. Another effort of his was a Bill he pushed through Congress in 1932, "The Reconstruction Finance Corporation Bill" to stimulate business. Here we're talking about a colossal sum of two billion dollars extra for the economy.

Alas, throwing money at the situation was not the answer either. The major criticism aimed at him was that he was too rigid in his handling of the crisis. He was especially opposed to Government "handouts" claiming some vague theoretical excuse based on the need to protect "American Individualism" whatever that was supposed to mean. Those standing in the food queues to soup kitchens would have looked at this verbal rubbish appalled. It would make no sense to a hungry man willing to swallow whatever pride he had left just to receive such a "hand out". What words could describe their tragic situation better than the song "Buddy can you spare a Dime".

Another controversial opinion he expressed came out like this "I don't like the idea of making a citizen too dependent on the Government." Well, it is easy to behave like that when you actually expect, as he did, that the "willo the wisp" of prosperity will just come sauntering around the corner hands in its pocket whistling. But that "willo the wisp" never came.

He was running out of options now. To prove this, he vetoed a Bill to give relief and Federal jobs to millions of people because he feared an unbalanced budget and inflation. There it is, that word "fear" again. Unbelievably, he likened the Depression to some prevailing gloom that hung like a blanket over the country. According to Hoover what the country needed was a good joke, a song, or a happy ending to dispel the sense of despair that prevailed. But unfortunately there was nothing to sing about out there and there were no happy endings on the radar screen just yet.

So Hoover tried another solution. In 1931, he suggested a moratorium on inter- Governmental debts for twelve months and this was ratified by Congress. But because it eased Germany's debt repayments, he was savagely attacked as an agent of Germany drunk with power. His suggestion was even condemned by Hiram Johnson, another Republican Senator, as being dangerous internationalism. They all felt it was the thin end of the wedge which would leave Germany free from paying its outstanding balance. Easing up on Germany was designed to calm the banks there and protect America from the backlash of global fury that could be released over the mess in America. This ease up on Germany's banks came too late however. The forces now released had jumped the channel and was rampant in Britain.

The struggle for ideas raged on in 1931. Contrary to some opinions Hoover was not sitting transfixed, though his cautious approach upset many people especially those who clamoured for a great big splurge of public money. Ogden Mills and Robert Wagner, the New York Senators, lashed out during hearings on unemployment relief in 1932. "I want to break the ice by lending to industry so that somebody will begin to spend money," said Mills. "I'm trying to put men to work and you won't co-operate," he accused Hoover.

But Hoover received support from one significant source Milton Keynes; the world-famous economist wrote "I think the argument for public works is much weaker than for Britain." He favoured changing the rate of interest. Yes, every one had opinions and none of them worked.

Hoover made many more proposals but one thing is for certain, he was not idle. Unpopular maybe but not idle.

Perhaps another of Hoover's problems was his tendency to look outside America for his solutions on the international stage where he made his name. Because he blamed the Depression on the 1914 -1918 war, he looked to Europe for his answers. In his opinion, just as America was having hopes of ending the Depression, his fears about Europe came true. David M. Kennedy's book Freedom from Fear gives a deep insight into Hoover's problems in the Presidency. "A gigantic economic explosion took place over there which shook the world's economic, political and social structures. Europe's unbalanced budgets, war reparation payments, frantic public works programmes to meet unemployment and inflation tore their systems asunder."

That is a rough summary of Hoover's 1914 -1918 theory which you will find in his book The Memoirs of Herbert Hoover. Another book worth reading is The Life of Herbert Hoover by

George Nash.

To be fair to Hoover history has proved him right. The war debts did seriously hobble Germany's economy and the excessive reparation payments have been blamed for drastically weakening the Fatherland, paving the way for Hitler's climb to power. If only they had listened to Woodrow Wilson when he warned of this possibility during the Peace talks in Paris. Hoover went on "The Americans were learning too late the inter-dependence of Nations" which resembled a quote from The Writings of Woodrow Wilson. Somebody phoned Hoover one day suggesting the rescheduling of debts as a solution to his problems, even debts owed by the allies to America. Hoover dismissed the idea as politically impossible. The American people wouldn't stand for it.

"You have no idea what the sentiment of the country at large is on these inter-Governmental debts" were Hoover's words and he went on "America's allies would be very slow to forgive the debts they were owed by Germany" so harnessing extra funds in this way was a non-starter. The argument got bogged down in the suspicion that this talk of reparation payments was nothing more than a ploy to shift the war debt fully on to the Americans and so this debate died in a whimper, according to Hoover's memoirs.

Unknown to the American public, Hoover was constantly being confronted by fear and corporate resistance. One example he gives in his autobiography was the story of the Bankers meeting he called to debate a possible solution to the crisis. He suggested to the Bankers "a $500 million pool to help the weaker institutions." The meeting ran into the early hours of the morning. Hoover wrote "They constantly reverted to a proposal, that the Government do it. I returned to the White House after midnight more depressed than ever before. Some time afterwards they dispensed a paltry $10 million in loans," Hoover continued, "The National Credit Association became ultra-conservative, then fearful and finally died. Its members and the business world threw up their hands and asked for Government action."
It's worth noting that the same experience of Bankers reluctance to lend returned again in 2009 like a dinosaur from the past.

The Hoover memoirs revealed many more initiatives he took. My reason for referring to them here is to sympathise with a President who didn't deserve the reputation of a failure. There were too many forces against him, too many voices without conviction pulling in the opposite direction. I think history will eventually judge Hoover kindly about these times. Now in 2009 the story of the world's present economic turmoil vindicates Hoover's helplessness in 1932 in the face of his own lonely battle against Wall Street. The real enemy today is the same one Hoover confronted all those years ago.

F.D. Roosevelt himself can even be quoted to support this view. When asked he said "The problems of the world were caused as much by those who fear change as those who seek revolution. In Government, in Science, in Industry, in the Arts, inaction and apathy are the most potent foes. And Herbert Hoover's Presidency was a constant struggle against all of them."

You must agree coming from Franklin Delano Roosevelt himself that sounds very like an exoneration of Hoover.

Perhaps at this point we should lighten up a little with some positive pen pictures of the President. Here are a couple of anecdotes about him worth hearing. One is about a meeting he had with Hitler in Berlin before the war. He saw through Hitler for what he was and declined the invitation to meet him. Hoover's vast network of contacts during his humanitarian work in Europe were far flung throughout the Continent. He knew intimately even the remotest troublemaker. So I'm sure he knew of Hitler. But somehow Hitler's Ambassador persuaded Hoover to accept this invitation. During the visit, Hoover mentioned the word "Jew" whether by accident or design. It was like a light applied to a petrol bomb.

Hitler took off on one of his Nuremberg Rally type rants. Hoover to his credit rounded on a shocked Hitler and said "Sit down, that's enough, I'm not interested in your views." What a pity some European Statesmen did not give Hitler the same message as bluntly as Hoover phrased it.

Another little anecdote concerns his marriage proposal to his sweetheart, Lou Henry. Hoover was in Australia when she graduated in Geology. Hoover cabled his congratulations plus a proposal of marriage to her which she was glad to accept by return wire. The following year, they set sail for China together this time as husband and wife. What a nice way to start a new marriage and a new job!

By the way they both learnt Mandarin out there and often used it in the White House to confuse their startled guests. I've already mentioned the Boxer Uprisings which they experienced first hand in China. In fact, Lou worked in a hospital there with a Mauser pistol tucked inside her belt. Incidentally, did you know Hoover was quite a fitness fanatic while in the White House and spent each morning before breakfast tossing a medicine ball around for half an hour? It was an ideal way for keeping him fit. Matches were played all year round regardless of the weather on the south lawn of the White House. Unfortunately it could prove an unlucky day for any visiting journalist, Cabinet Minister, or even Supreme Court Judge, who found themselves instantly drafted into the match to make their contributions. I'd say the return journey home for many of them was a welcome relief. No wonder the fitness fanatic lived to be ninety.

But it was not the handling of the Depression alone which made Americans hate Hoover. I'm afraid his personality was disastrous for a President.

Hoover's pomposity was never far from the surface as reflected in an incident with Franklin D. Roosevelt himself who had come to the White House for a briefing meeting. As Franklin pushed his wheelchair around to exit the meeting, he was stopped in his tracks by Hoover's haughty reproof. "Nobody leaves before the President."

Hoover's one pastime which helped him to escape the nightmare of life in the White House was fishing. He said it was "A discipline in the equality of men for all men are equal before the fish......." I wonder did he realize that all pretensions must also be left behind on the river bank.

Warren Harding's assessment of Hoover was pure newspaperman. "He's the smartest geek I know," said Harding.

But leaving aside Hoover's unfortunate personality, the title of "humanitarian" was so well-earned, it would have been a deplorable injustice for anyone to forget what he did from 1915 to 1923 in Europe. So important was his role helping the Europeans the following note was printed into his passport. "This man is not to be stopped anywhere, under any circumstances." This was the result of his browbeating of all the warring nations not to get in his way in saving Belgium from starvation.

He not only took no pay for his work but gave part of his own fortune towards the expenses and even risked his life against hunting submarines while he criss-crossed the Atlantic on the job. When he delivered food to the Russians, he was attacked by critics for "helping Bolsheviks." His reaction was to bang the table shouting "Twenty million people are starving. Whatever their politics, they shall be fed."

Records show he probably saved more people from a slow appalling death by starvation than anyone else in history. Yes, a man's good deeds should never be allowed to die with him. Hoover like Harding was simply a man completely out of his depth as a politician. What is not generally recognised is the way his engineering background gave him an insatiable appetite for new technology. Here is a surprising list of targets he accomplished. He bullied industry into standardisation of everything from screws to bottle tops. He set safety rules for many diverse services, railroads, automobiles, cement and elevators. He even produced a manual for new homeowners and a voluntary building code. All this from a man who flunked every entrance exam except Maths for Stanford University. As we wrote earlier, he eventually became a mining tycoon and by 1918 was worth nearly $4 million.

One thing that could not be disputed was this. Hoover never shirked hard work. As he said of himself "You can't make a Teddy Roosevelt out of me. My boyhood ambition was to be able to earn my own living without the help of anybody anywhere." I think growing up without a mam and dad to spoil him had something to do with his tough approach to life. This was the spirit which raised him to the exalted position as one of the key Americans in Europe and inspired Franklin Roosevelt to say "He is certainly a wonder and I wish we could make him President." What a pity Hoover ever listened to siren voices like Roosevelt's which invited him to enter into the world of politics; he should never even have contemplated it.

Like Taft whose vocation really was that of a lawyer even after his Presidency, Hoover's world was engineering. Yet in these final words on Herbert Clark Hoover, it must be pointed out that despite the volume of criticism tainting his Presidency, he is still the most honoured President the United States has ever had. Being an academic maybe accounts for most of those honours coming as they did from a wide range of Universities, fifty Honorary Degrees came from American Universities and twenty-five came from foreign Universities. Added to these was the freedom of more than a dozen cities.

The list goes on. Seventy medals and awards, and one hundred more miscellaneous Honours. One doctorate was conferred on him in 1958, twenty-five years after his Presidency. That came from General Mark Wayne Clark, South Carolina State Military College. In all, he received eighty-three Degrees covering the areas he worked in as Engineer, Humanitarian, or Statesman. Three months after this, in April 1958, he received his penultimate Honorary Degree while he was recovering from a gall bladder operation. He certainly must have done something right or maybe the blame for the Depression was not entirely down to him after all.

While writing about honours, his intellectual capacity was phenomenal for he translated a 672 page book written in Latin on mining metallurgy. By way of post-script, you may be interested to know that the Boulder Dam built during his term in office, was renamed the Hoover Dam in 1947. That turned out to be his final honour. Still Hoover carried a deep heartfelt hurt about his political criticism into his grave.

But in the period after the Second World War, the astute President Harry S. Truman, gave him the chance to rehabilitate his reputation by appointing him to his old familiar post-war role – "To feed the hungry of Europe" – which he accomplished again with distinction. Hoover's final words in response to this honour were tinged with defiant bitterness at the memories of his

Presidency – "I've outlived the bastards," he scoffed.

After Hoover's death at the age of ninety, the press came up with four words to fit his epitaph, "courage, integrity and humanitarian service." Few tried to contradict them.

Herbert Clark Hoover ensured that after him nothing would ever be the same again either in the White House or the Oval Office. Some say Hoover was eventually overcome by unseen shifting social winds which, despite his many virtues he was unable to cope with. He was caught between left and right wing ideologies. The press it seems, not only created him but also destroyed him.

Sadly he will be remembered as a man too rigid and too remote from the pain around him and the most damaging claim of all, too stubborn to listen. Strangely, three Presidencies shared the blame for the Depression. It was said Coolidge, Harding and Hoover pandered to the rich. To quote Scott Fitzgerald "The rich were only happy in each others company." The shallow lies that emanated from their Administrations turned sour the relationships of the U.S. citizen with the White House. It was left to one of their own, branded by them as a traitor to their class, to rescue them from the hate and anger directed at them from the ordinary American working class – none other than the handsome squire in the wheelchair, Franklin Delano Roosevelt whose story we shall read about next.

Herbert Clark Hoover died in New York on October 20, 1964 aged ninety years and seventy-one days. He was buried in his native West Branch, Iowa. Finally what about his wife Lou?

Hoover's wife Lou had died on January 7, 1944 twenty years previously. She was buried at Alta Mesa cemetery Palo Alto, California but was re-interred on November 1, 1964 alongside her husband Herbert Hoover at West Branch, Ohio. She was 69 years and 284 days.

32nd President   Franklin D Roosevelt

"FDR"
Born 1882
Died 1945
63 Years of age
3 Terms (12 years 39 days)
1933 –1945
Age 51

Party: Democrat
County: New York
Occupation: Lawyer
Ancestry: Dutch
Estate Value $1,085,500
Hobbes: Sailing, Swimming, Stamp collecting

Physical Description: Height 6 foot 2 inches, weight 188lbs, high forehead, greying hair; occasionally wore eye glasses; wore brace on his legs.

Significant Extract from Inauguration Speech on Monday January 29, 1941
"This great nation will endure as it has endured, will revive and will prosper. So first of all let me assert my firm belief that the only thing we have to fear is fear itself. Nameless unreasoning, unjustified terror which paralyses needed effort to convert retreat into advance."

FRANKLIN D. ROOSEVELT

When Franklin Delano Roosevelt became the 32nd President of the United States on Sunday March 4, 1933 note what Walter Lippmann had written of him earlier as follows: "His mind is not very clear, his purpose is not simple and his methods are not direct.....Mr. Roosevelt does not ring true......He is a pleasant man who without any qualifications for the office would very much like to be President."

How wrong can a man be? I am sure what I write about FDR in facts and anecdotes are already known to thousands of people who have read the life story of Franklin D. Roosevelt by hundreds of authors. But let's join him as he started out on his glorious journey as a very privileged youngster living in New York.

It seems Franklin D. Roosevelt was armed with all the disadvantages of the privileged. Money, education, pedigree, parentage, schools, university, social lifestyle and contacts to go with a beautiful house, well-mannered upbringing, and the right genes.

How could anyone succeed in politics with that background? Where was the hunger, the ruthlessness, the ambition, the dedication and the commitment to come from? After all he was a winner from the start with nothing to aspire to.

Back in the time of Washington, Adams and Jefferson, the winning formula for success was to have a planter's family tree. The top families such as the Birds and the Stevensons strangely enough did not produce a President but they all had one thing in common. They were part of the ruling fabric of an emerging Continent. As America grew the ultimate prize always went to men who gave their lives not only to their plantations but to the dream of a new vibrant free America.

So was this the fulcrum of Roosevelt's success – fighting to achieve that dream of a "vibrant, free America". To save it from disintrigating before his eyes into a thousand pieces. The enemy was not on the battlefields of America dressed in uniforms with silver buttons and golden braid. His enemy was an economy in terminal decline and a dictator in far off Europe whose political philosophy national socialism was diametrically opposite to the freedom and self-expression at the heart of Madison's and Jefferson's U.S. Constitution.

Looking over Roosevelt's life it would be easy to list all his assets and conclude that you knew the formula for greatness. Assets any ordinary man would die for. But the ordinary man knows riches will never guarantee success or happiness. If so the lives of the pop stars, film stars and even royalty would be littered with great men leaving behind them a rich tapestry of great deeds. Alas, they never do. So let us search deeper into the Roosevelt family for they really were the royalty of pre-Depression America. They were not a new family on the block for their roots went back two hundred years since they arrived in America from Holland. The American dream was good to them and they became owners of thousands of acres and a fortune from business that turned them into American aristocracy just like the Founding Fathers of the United States.

The tragic part of Franklin's life believe it or not happened during his childhood. But why should having all the trinkets in the shop be a tragedy. Why should having a wonderful father who took him everywhere and taught him everything such as riding, hunting, swimming, skating, sailing not to mention sleigh riding in the winter be a bad memory.

The answer to this lies in the torment of his polio sickness in adult life. Because sadly these were all the things he would never do again. And so he was confronted by the first cataclysmic challenge to his make up. In view of his pampered childhood how could he cope? How would the boy who had his very own train complete with his very own bedroom on board come to terms with an illness that made no concessions to the rich or the famous? For the first time in life he was on his own as a man.

Can you see the heartbreak and dilemma confronting a man who always had everything he ever wanted? He could not turn to his private tutors or servants like he could in those days when he owned a pony, a horse and his own gun before he was fourteen. And even his usual visit to a President would produce no answer.

However, the moulding of his character produced a good natured, good-tempered, well-balanced individual who despite his quiet disposition could be forceful, a leadership trait that would one day blossom when he needed it most. His explanation for this to his mother Sara when she asked him about this outburst of bossiness was a charming one. "Well," he smiled "if I do not give orders nothing ever happens."

Strangely he had the same obsession with the sea as another President, George Washington, who when admitting his urge to be a sailor was told by an uncle – "That is nothing better than a tinker's apprentice." Roosevelt was also discouraged against his ambition but not as bluntly. He was quietly told his job was to look after the Roosevelt family estates. And so he turned to law.

But at this point perhaps we should back track a little to examine Franklin D. Roosevelt's arrival in this unpredictable world.
He was born on January 30, 1882 in the family home Springwood in Hyde Park about eighty miles from New York.
His father James Roosevelt was a business tycoon who all but owned his own railway. He was fifty-four years of age when Franklin was born. His mother was Sara Delano Roosevelt who was twenty-eight when he was born.

As expected he went to private school at fourteen - Groton, the most exclusive in the United States. Emphasis here was on toughness and good manners. Rising at seven o'clock each morning with a cold shower and finishing at night dressed in their best just to say good night to the principle and his wife. Despite being lectured constantly by the principal Reverend Peabody on their obligation to work for the benefit of the poor through politics and their own privileged positions, very few of the pupils took him seriously. To Roosevelt's credit although he himself had no experience whatsoever of meeting a poor or underprivileged person he did take a keen interest in the idea. His smooth good tempered Roosevelt personality and the Roosevelt politics of the Democrats left him very much an outsider in college and a sitting duck for bullies mostly from the Republican families.

But Franklin proved his resilience as he did on many occasions afterwards and managed to survive Groton unscathed. In 1900 at eighteen years of age his next big date with destiny occurred. He joined Harvard University. It was a momentous time for the family that started with heartbreak for Franklin. His devoted father and constant companion died aged seventy-two. A year later his uncle Teddy Roosevelt, now Vice President to McKinley became President after the assassination of Mr. McKinley by a madman's bullet. Teddy, a Republican from the wilder branch of the Roosevelt family was a larger than life character who crashed his way through life like a runaway bull elephant. But a further twist in the map of Franklin's life was to happen before he graduated from Harvard.

In 1903 he announced to his mother his deep feelings for his cousin Eleanor with whom he had grown up in his childhood. His mother was so horrified she took him away from Harvard for a cruise to the West Indies. Thus began a tug of war between Sara and Eleanor. The difference between Franklin and Eleanor was obvious. She was a knickerbocker Roosevelt from the wild unpredictable side of the family. Her mother died suddenly when she was eight and her father became an alcoholic and was never allowed to see Eleanor again. She never was able to let go of him and is reputed to have held imaginary conversations with him in her lonely moments. She was as serious as Franklin was lighthearted.

It was Eleanor who introduced Franklin for the very first time to the desolation of the New York slums on her visits there doing social work. "My God," he gasped, "I had no idea people lived like this." The message of Dr. Peabody suddenly surfaced from his subconscious and took on a life of its own inside him.

At long last the very, very rich young man had come to meet and know the poor. "Something had to be done for them," he thought and it was up to privileged people like him to do it.

It was a strange life moving from the New York slums to the White House as guest of the President, his Uncle Teddy who was a great fan of Eleanor. As a child Teddy taught her to swim by the unorthodox method of throwing her into a river waiting till she sank and diving in to rescue her. There were never any half measures for Uncle Teddy. It was all or nothing.
Franklin duly graduated in 1903 as a Bachelor of Arts and on St. Patrick's Day March 17, 1905, Eleanor and Franklin Roosevelt married in New York. He was twenty-three and she was still twenty years of age. It was the beginning of a partnership that was to last for over forty years. Incidentally, he was an Episcopalian like George Washington before him. His uncle Teddy, the U.S. President gave Eleanor away and it can be no surprise that the very Reverend Endicott Peabody was invited to officiate at the ceremony. The guest list included the Astors, the Livingstones and the Vanderbilts.

But we can only complete the picture of the happy couple by writing a few words about the most dynamic First Lady of them all. Eleanor Roosevelt.

Eleanor is quoted as saying she meant to break some precedents if her husband became President. Teaching in school at East 65th Street, New York would not change.

Eleanor was the daughter of a very beautiful woman but was cruelly described when she was a child as being unattractive. This did not help her ego or self-esteem. Her stern and detached grandmother only compounded the problem Eleanor had with her confidence. What saved her was going to a boarding school in England. Here she was influenced by a kindly Parisian named Marie Souvestre who made a terrific impact on her especially during their travels together across Europe. She returned home to marry Franklin Delano Roosevelt in 1905. She was a distant cousin of his. As we have told you her uncle was the dynamic Theodore Roosevelt, the 26th President. She was totally underwhelmed by life in the Presidency, six children later, despite the help of a nanny for the children. She took no interest whatsoever in politics and when FDR, as he was known, rang her to say Woodrow Wilson had been nominated for President she couldn't understand his excitement.

During the First World War women ran streetcars, delivered mail and did all the jobs men could do. But scarcity of manpower pushed women into different roles. Eleanor chose to care for sick servicemen. "I loved it," she beamed later; "I ate it up." It was the beginning of a new Eleanor Roosevelt. When she discovered FDR's infidelity the marriage was completely sundered and it never recovered. From that moment on Eleanor grew in confidence and joined various women's movements. By now Roosevelt had Polio. Her ignorance of politics soon evaporated when Franklin's Polio pushed her into making speeches to help him. She learnt public speaking techniques and overcame the fear of crowds. The once shy bride and timid housewife was now a personality in her own right and all the papers loved her. Yet she despised being First Lady. "I never wanted to be a President's wife," she told her friend Lorena Hickok in 1932, "and I don't want it now." But this did not stop her from using the First Ladies influence to further her own goals.

Many biographies have covered these roles so I won't bore you with the details. They mostly concerned the lives of other wives living in America. FDR had no influence over her but their son Franklin considered her part of the "Kitchen Cabinet". Just like Theodore had admitted to the press "I can do the President's job or I can control Alice but I can't do both." FDR used a similar excuse regarding Eleanor when he said "Well that's my wife and I can't be expected to do anything about her." Eleanor went on to become influential enough to be suggested as a possible successor to Franklin D. Roosevelt himself. She was thought by Raymond Clapper, a syndicate journalist to be one of the ten most powerful people in Washington alongside John L. Lewis and General George Marshall. Eleanor had come a long, long way since her unsophisticated, fearful days as a young bride in 1905. Her life and her place alongside the great Franklin D. Roosevelt were breathtakingly successful. She was truly one to the greats among First Ladies.

But let us continue our story of Franklin D. Roosevelt.

The first act of obedience to his father was to begin marriage as a landowning gentleman with a law practice. It was not an easy act for him to play with Uncle Teddy barnstorming through America with bands playing "There is a hot time in the old town tonight" dazzling the people with his "up and at em" personality while fighting his way to the ultimate political crown as President of the United States. For Franklin life as a lawyer was very low-key and mundane in comparison.

Yet fate has a way of changing the course of history by the most insignificant and unexpected events.

The one to launch Franklin Roosevelt on his own rocket ship to the stars was a simple knock on his door. It was a Democratic politician named Ed Perkins who stood there. He had called to invite Franklin to become a Senator. Franklin was tempted but such was his reticence he elected to ask his mother first. Perkins was dumbfounded at the contrast between Franklin and the rumbustious President Teddy. He could not believe his ears. "Do you really want me to go back and tell them what you said to me?" Franklin paused, looked at Perkins and said – "Alright, I will stand." The great Franklin Delano Roosevelt had taken his first step into politics.

Franklin's quite smooth laid-back style did not impress some people in the Democratic Party who thought he was a lightweight and would not last the course.

But Franklin was a hands on politician from the start. He learnt the facts on local farm problems and with his aristocratic personality and respect for the voters he won their hearts and their votes to become a junior Senator.

Fate again took a hand when he became an Aide to Woodrow Wilson on his Presidential campaign. "Backing the right horse", so to speak paid off for he was rewarded for his support when he was appointed by Wilson to become Assistant Secretary of the U.S. Navy. It was

Franklin's first foot on the political ladder. Still comparisons were made with the fiery Teddy and people shook their heads and smiled. Where was the fire? Where was the razzamatazz? Where was the guts, the grandeur and showbiz presentation, the hallmark of the Roosevelt style? Yet he surprised many by the expertise he brought to the job of Assistant Secretary of the U.S. Navy. In fact he ran that job from 1912 – 1920 the most turbulent years in world history straddling as it did the First World War years 1914 – 1918.

Franklin's style was truly remarkable because of his man management skills which saw him become popular with both Admirals and shipyard workers alike. Such was his success on the job that not one strike occurred during all his years in charge between 1912 and 1920.

He was fearless when major decisions were needed. Many times he ignored Congress by "forgetting to inform them" when he needed things done. As a result he built a powerful Navy to help fight the U boats that during World War II caused havoc with the maritime ships supplying Great Britain with essential needs such as food, goods and machinery for the war effort.

Soon American ships became the targets too which eventually sucked the U.S. into the war in 1917. President Wilson is known to have cried because his decision to enter the war condemned many young men to early graves. But America, because of Roosevelt, found herself powerfully prepared by a farsighted fearless Secretary of the Navy. "Where was the guts?" they once asked about a novice politician groomed to be a gentleman. Now they knew. You may now recall what I wrote earlier about fate.

It was an everyday casual accident, a bizarre act of fate while out boating with his children that led to unbelievable future consequences for Franklin D. Roosevelt. He fell into the freezing waters of the Bay of Fundy and was almost frozen when he was taken out of the water shivering and blue. Being fit and energetic he went on to read his mail as usual still in his wet bathing suit. Feeling feverish he found himself unable to stand up. It was flu he thought and went to bed to recover. Next morning he was worse, in fact he was paralyzed from the chest down. A specialist from Boston confirmed the worst. He had Polio. Infantile paralysis as it is known is almost unheard of today thanks to vaccinations in childhood but at that time it was rampant in America and was no respecter of person no matter how rich or famous they were.

Had his Uncle Teddy got the disease it would have made banner headlines but the gentle and sunny insignificant nephew from the other side of the Roosevelt family tree did not rate a mention. He was never going to make it as a politician anyway because he did not kick "asses". He was a "softie" they said. But this Roosevelt was no softie. He could have resigned himself to his illness and accepted defeat. He could afford the life of idleness his riches would give him. But all through those comfortable carefree spoiled and indulgent years of his childhood beneath that smiling sunny disposition, a man of mental steel was developing inside Franklin Delano Roosevelt that was never noticed and never seen before.

Now imperceptibly the steel immerged during Franklin's most searching and painful heartaches that challenged his every waking moments from morning until night time. Nobody knows or can even guess at what conversations his silent private thoughts wrestled with as he daily exercised to improve those wasted muscles he once took for granted. His mother had plans for him out of love and a mother's instinct to protect him from the rough and tumble of life. Another loving more practical woman Eleanor his wife had other plans. She kept him exercising and gradually his muscles recovered. His political career also recovered salvaged by an old friend from his Navy days, a Louis Howe. Eleanor also kept Franklin in the thick of politics against the wishes of his doting mother Sara. He went from finger movements to crawling on all fours.

A climb up the stairs on his hands and knees was a call for a family celebration. That man of steel was now operating at full steam in the eyes of a proud and loving family. The new Franklin Delano Roosevelt emerged from his painful shell and a man of steel was revealed. Who were these people who accused him of being a loser with no guts? Those critics were annihilated. Today they were now no more. As he described it "I have rolled in the gutter with death and won."

But FDR never fully beat Polio. He always needed his crutches and his wheelchair but the rest of his talents were undiminished. The power and confidence of the new Franklin D. Roosevelt amazed everyone. He was not only back in politics but he was now a major player. It seems that God had honed and groomed him for the next great challenge of his life - the great Depression; economic collapse and widespread unemployment in the country. The platform he tackled them from was The Presidency itself. (The Depression has also been covered by me under Herbert Hoover).

Wall Street collapsed and ruin came to thousands on the rollercoaster of stocks and shares. Even the small savers suffered. Panic spread, people were laid off and wages were cut which further worsened trade when purchasing power dropped through the floor. Money in Germany became worthless confetti. Anyone who had a job to lose lost it. Contrary to the common belief that speculation was rampant, there were only 600,000 speculators out of a population of 120 million.

There was however one new class of plunger – women. Yes, women held over a third of U.S. Steel and General Motors, 44% of B & O Railroad stock and over 50% of the Pennsylvania Railroad stock. They were known on Wall Street as the petticoat line. The New York Times called them "The Lady Bulls". They embraced many classes in society - dressmakers, hairdressers, stenographers, clerks, private secretaries, department stores assistants, sales women, milliners and even cooks and housemaids.

There were also many household names among the losers in the colossal gamble. Famous names like J. P. Morgan who lost $20,000 to $60,000. The Rockefeller family lost four fifths of its fortune. Winston Churchill lost between $1,000,000 and $5,000,000. Eddie Cantor the film star lost $2,000,000. Jerome Kern the composer was wiped out. Fanny Brice $500,000; Flo Ziegfeld $2,000,000; Groucho Marx $240,000; Harpo Marx $250,000. Rex Stout lost everything only to bounce back with his new character, detective Nero Wolfe.

Railways were the focal point for vagabonds travelling America looking for work. Poor President Hoover became the most hated man in the U.S. as hundreds of thousands faced the stark reality to work or starve. Millions of bread-liners stood in queues for two slices of bread and a bowl of soup from the Salvation Army. The hit song "Buddy can you spare a dime" just about summed up the mood of the nation. New York was the only State to issue unemployment or "dole money". It also helped to feed and cloth the hopeless and the homeless.

The recently elected Mayor had moved fast and decisively. Yes, his name was Frank D. Roosevelt. Reverend Peabody would have been proud of him. At last he was helping the poor. Hoover's ham-fisted efforts to solve the problem led to shanty towns being broken up and attacked by General McArthur and his army sent in by Hoover himself. War heroes in the towns were among them. This has also been covered by me under the Hoover notes.

The next Presidential election was fast approaching in late November 1932. Roosevelt chose to arrive at the Nomination Convention of the Democratic Party in Chicago, Illinois on June 27, 1932 by airplane. It was a ten passenger Tri-motor plane he had chartered. Yes, he arrived at the Convention hall in some style and was duly nominated for the Presidency on the fourth ballot. The Presidential race itself was a stroll for him after the disastrous Presidency of Herbert Hoover and as we told you earlier he won by 472 votes to 59 for Hoover.

Throughout his Presidential campaign he made sure not to be seen in the wheelchair and always chose to appear standing waving a large hat and carrying the obligatory cigarette in the extra long holder, the fashion of the day, and of course grinning as if he was just out celebrating some glorious moment in his life. It was a carefully projected image to lift the spirits of the voters. Wherever he went he promised his listeners a new deal and even had his own band playing "Happy days are here again".

The day of his inauguration however did not take place until four months later on March 4, 1933 as was the custom. His inauguration speech was one that set the tone for his whole Presidency.

As his voice echoed throughout America, there was a solemn confidence in his voice. It belied the sense of helplessness in every face, in every home, in every State from the East Coast to the Pacific. The words he used that day were delivered in a rich tone of hope and optimism that every American was happy to hear. Maybe things were not so bad after all they thought. But Roosevelt knew different. As they listened they found themselves being introduced to a new kind of language they never heard before.

The New Deal; Social and Economic Reform to assist in the development of an economic order. The old familiar catch cries of slavery, Civil War, revolution, planters, "free blacks" and "civil rights were no more". America had moved on since then but now the enemy was different. This was an unseen foe confronting them. Faceless Corporations. Bank collapses, suspected Bolsheviks, poverty, soup kitchens, bread-lines, welfare payments, and the most lethal of all – greed.

That radio message of Franklin Delano Roosevelt was as inspiring as any of Lincoln's speeches. Strangely enough it was made by a rich man from a rich family who had never known and had still not experienced the pain of hunger or poverty. Nevertheless there was a conviction about the man that reached out to those who stood around radios in the Bronx, in Manhattan, in Texas and even in the small towns of rural America where income had been cut in half. Where the crops they grew, however wholesome, had been ploughed back into the ground so bad were the prices offered for them.

His radio message echoed in the slums of New York where teaming thousands lived out their lives in depressing hopelessness. The task ahead for Roosevelt was a mammoth one for any man. It seemed almost impossible for a man in a wheelchair. But then Franklin Delano Roosevelt was not just any man. In time he was to prove the impossible was always the possible all it needed was faith and fearlessness. These were the sentiments with which he began his inaugural speech.

"The only thing we have to fear is fear itself, unreasoning, unjustified terror."

His voice floated overhead in the smoke filled semi darkness of New York and Chicago saloons packed to the doors for his speech. "Only foolish optimism can deny the dark realities of the moment... values have shrunken to fantastic levels..... Stock Exchanges are frozen in the currents of trade, the withered leaves of individual enterprise lie on every side, farmers find no markets for their produce, the savings of many years in thousands of families are gone.....A host of unemployed face the grim problem of existence." "The blame," he said bluntly "fell upon managers of industry and finance who had so blithely assumed credit for the high prosperity of the decade preceding the crash of 1929. Rulers of the exchange of mankind's goods have failed. Through their stubbornness and their incompetence they have admitted their failure and have abdicated. The Money Changers have fled from their high seats in the temple of our civilization. We may now restore that temple to the ancient truths. The nation asks for action and action now. Our greatest primary risk is to put people to work....... I shall ask the Congress for the remaining instruments to meet the crisis...... ...broad executive power to wage war against the emergency , as great as the power that would be given to me if we were in fact invaded by a foreign foe..."

What Roosevelt did not know was this. It would take the best part of eight years to defeat the monster and it would not happen until America had entered the Second World War in 1942. Only then would American business be finally back on the track to recovery.

But in 1933 the Depression intensified. The banks closed to repulse the hoards of investors looking for their money back. This cut the flow of money further and workers were laid off through lack of cash to pay them. Panic deepened into violence between the workless and the police. Even Roosevelt himself became a victim of an attempted assassination. But the action of a woman bystander thwarted the attempt and the bullet hit and killed the Mayor of Chicago to whom he had been talking. The country hit rock bottom, desolation and helplessness when all the banks closed and the Stock Exchange shut down. It was now that his famous inauguration words were remembered "There is nothing to fear but fear."

There were twelve million people out of work now and unemployment increased by over ten thousand per day. Added to this was the terrible tragedy of 24,000 suicides in one year. In two weeks $30 billion was wiped out of the economy, the equivalent of America's final bill for the First World War. This loss of money reduced investment in Europe to a trickle worsening their economic plight for Europe was not only broke but in debt to the United States. In England meanwhile the run on gold was continuing at £2.5 million (Stg pounds) per day. It was truly a vast global catastrophe not just an American one. Meanwhile the poor in America were very hard hit because no system of welfare benefits were in place until Roosevelt introduced them. This may be hard to believe but people actually starved to death. I am sure there are plenty of other anecdotes on the Depression many people can recall.

The "New Deal" was not so much an economic philosophy as a succession of Government actions to solve problems. If the one attempt failed something new was tried. It was a trial and error approach to relieve suffering and it was all accomplished by a decision making President taking actions and issuing Bills daily that changed the jaded unusable debris of the old American way of life overnight. The banks were opened again – under Government supervision.

FDR's social security programme was severely criticized as dangerous regimentation. One Republican complained that every worker would have to wear metal dog tags bearing his or her social security number. Another dramatic outcome of his measures however resulted in the African-American voters transferring their support to the Democrats. A journalist said to them "My friends go home and turn Lincoln's picture to the wall. That debt has been paid in full."

Roosevelt exploited his own popularity saying, "In 1776 Americans sought freedom from the economic royalists who had created a new despotism. What we seek is to take away their power." The Democrats eventually won by 328 votes to 107 in the House. The next Presidential election was soon here and Roosevelt claimed the victory he won on Wednesday January 20, 1937 on a mandate for extensive expansion. The focus now progressed from recovery to reform.

The New Deal in which Roosevelt kept what worked, and discarded what did not work was profoundly revolutionary and changed America in many ways, with its economy more managed than before. The Capitalist structure however remained in place. Severe measures such as the "soak the rich" tax policy prompted affluent vested interests to look on him as a traitor to his class.

During Roosevelt's first year in office the support he received was down to his fireside chats over the radio brought to the people in their kitchens and dining rooms throughout America. The family atmosphere of the White House never before experienced by those living outside its massive walls up to now was passed on to them by the magic of radio. He encouraged them in his travels, his speeches, and his twice weekly press conferences. The remote became the familiar. Distrust became respect. His wife Eleanor played a significant role and in time became the most influential woman of her time. A tall willowy outgoing woman she had her own staff, held her own press conferences and spoke candidly to her husband about the burning issues of the day.

Her syndicated column helped her promote her main passion which was social services and the rights of women as well as rights for the blacks. She really relished her travels in the country promoting Franklin's New Deal. She ate with the blacks defying local segregation laws and was deeply concerned with the plight of unemployed youth. She even invited spokesmen of different persuasions both black and white to the White House after hours. In short she took the political risks Franklin dared not take. One Maine fisherman described her as follows, "She ain't stuck up, she ain't dressed up, and she ain't afraid to talk." Ever ready with one of her colourful memorable quotes she reminded her hearers "The future belongs to those who believe in the beauty of dreams."

There was only one way left and that was up. And it all could be attributed to Roosevelt's smiling optimism when all seemed lost. Somehow he managed to convince the nation that the factories, the machines, the farmland and the people were still there. All it needed was confidence to put all these factors, these assets and of course the people themselves back to work. Slowly like the trickle of a mountain stream after a drought, confidence returned. The trickle became a gliding stream and the stream to a bubbling babbling turbulent torrent that swept all before it. In the waters of confidence new fresh shoots soon blossomed into a rich foliage of greener pastures from which new businesses grew and the economy became a thriving healthy fast growing full blown success.

He next turned his attention to a malaise that had spread like a cancer throughout American society – Gangsterism. Prohibition had spawned this insatiable parasite that fed on the instability of American society. The underworld was quick to recognize an opportunity to exploit the gap now left in the market for booze. Illegal sales grew from their modest beginnings into a nationwide industry run by sinister gangs of hoodlums. By murder, intimidation, exploitation and graft corruption spread its tentacles right into City Hall itself and a gangster called "Al Capone" came to rule his own kingdom as head of the mob.

His influence was so complete a large picture of him hung in the Mayor's office in Chicago.

There were no Democratic elections to decide an overlord of a territory. This was carried out by machine guns, car bombs and fear. Mr. Capone was finally defeated on an income tax rap and was sentenced to Alcatraz where he died some years later of natural causes. Maybe unnatural causes, for some people claimed he died of a sexual disease.

Roosevelt realized the source of this breakdown in law and order was Prohibition and moved quickly against it. As I have pointed out under Hoover's notes it was taken off the Statute books forever. The days of the speak-easy, flappers, illicit boozing clubs, gangland shootouts, police bribery and fear were well and truly finished.

Money was then redirected to farmers. A new building plan for schools, hospitals, railways, and houses to replace the slums got underway. Three billion dollars was voted by Congress for the task. It seems they could refuse him nothing. Dams and power stations for the new electricity network were built. New trade unions were encouraged to fight for fair wages. The Stock Exchange was brought under control to monitor over speculation by greedy investors and the most powerful weapon of all, a Bill to ensure no bank account was ever at the bank's mercy again. Repayment was to be guaranteed in full. It was a new deal alright. A crazy almost reckless spending spree they said but in the long run the risk paid off. The money circulated. The poor could buy goods and even the newly taxed rich found money coming back to them in extra profits. Everyone was a winner.

It did not stop crazy things happening however. Imagination ran riot to generate money for business. Big race meetings only lasted for half the races through lack of money. Even Madison Square Gardens, the mecca of boxing in America opened their doors to a barter system. Pay by goods instead of cash was the idea and what a collection came into the box office. Chairs, sparkling plugs, overcoats and even coat hangers were exchanged for seats in the auditorium.

But Roosevelt's innovations stood the world on its head changing the face of America more radically in a few months than over the previous one hundred years. But time ticked slowly for Roosevelt and unemployment was still stubborn. Eight million were still out of work. Matters worsened when drought hit the Southern States of Kansas, Nebraska, New Mexico, Colorado, Oklahoma, and Texas in 1932. Great dust storms blew three hundred million tons of topsoil away leaving nothing but sand in which to grow their crops. It was a tall order. An exodus of families and their belongings headed for California. "Refugees from nature" they called them. Not unexpectedly California suffered from over crowding and once again Roosevelt was in the breach to feed the hungry wandering multitudes with his Farm Administration Plan.

In 1936, elections meant Roosevelt had to face the angry rich taxed to the hilt to help the poor. They were scared by his spending spree fearing bankruptcy for America. Naturally he had made dangerous enemies but they were not going to undermine Roosevelt's new found confidence. He was not afraid to thump the table and make noisy speeches when it was needed. He was not intimidated by bullies in the opposition ranks and promised to spend even more money on the poor when re-elected. He was returned by one of the greatest landslides ever in a Presidential election 523 votes to 8.

His inauguration speech went as follows:
"This year marks the one hundred and fiftieth anniversary of the Constitution Convention which made us a nation. At that Convention our forefathers found a way out of the chaos which followed the revolutionary war of 1776; they created a strong Government with powers of united action sufficient then and now to solve problems utterly beyond individual or local

solution.

A century and half ago they established the Federal Government in order to promote the general welfare and secure the blessings of liberty to the American people.

Today we invoke those same powers of Government to achieve the same objectives."

He went on to put in place welfare benefits, old age pensions and unemployment relief throughout the whole of America, an unheard of innovation in the 1930s. He became a hero to the ordinary labouring class if not on a par with a deity then the next best thing – the raw material for canonization.

Another reason for this popularity with the masses was his mastery and exploitation of the radio. He learnt to reach the firesides of the family circle by his bedside manner. Eleanor played her part through her newspaper column in which she took her readers into the White House to look around. Another First Lady in the1960s brought the public into the White House through the medium of television. Jacqueline Kennedy wife of John F. Kennedy was bringing the history of the White House to the outside world.

But the greatest challenge to his ever rising list of achievements was his part in the Second World War. His name is now synonymous with these years of danger and terror in the world yet it happened in the second year of Roosevelt's second term as President. This did not allow much time for him to grace the international stage – two years approximately.
Hitler was the new Demigod of Europe. A dictator in his own country and head of a Party machine - National Socialism that preached a doctrine of hate, iron discipline and racial intolerance so different to the sunny and Christian politics of Roosevelt. One based on hate, the other based on love. I need not suggest to the reader who the terrorist was.

Hitler's lust for power was an evil megalomania that infected the whole German people who disgustingly applauded Hitler by the thousands in his mass rallies and torchlight parades. There was only one use for his massive armies to march across Europe as the conquering Emperor. Only one brave and courageous man in Europe dared to challenge this abuse of the democratic rights of millions – Winston Churchill, Prime Minister of England.

Although Churchill was only a back-bencher at the time Roosevelt kept a close eye on Churchill's speeches forecasting what Hitler's intentions would be. But there was little Roosevelt could do about the situation for he was prevented from direct intervention by The Neutrality Act and the mood of the American public which showed little interest in becoming involved in European affairs again. Roosevelt could only watch in astonishment the wars between Japan and China, Franco's war in Spain and Italy invading Abyssima.

The world it seemed had gone mad. Austria, Czechoslovakia and Poland fell to the Germans and neutrality was becoming more and more difficult to maintain. Churchill went from back-bencher to first Lord of the Admiralty, a job Roosevelt had done in his early years in politics. The two men were drawing ever closer to one another in politics and friendship. Besides like Roosevelt, Churchill also came from an aristocratic family.

Almost spontaneously Roosevelt phoned Churchill to offer support and friendship from two thousand miles away. The most powerful country on the planet was reaching out to a stricken people. It was the beginning of a friendship that would last for years. Around this time Albert Einstein had helped to split the atom and the race was on to produce an atom bomb before the

Germans did. But that would happen later.

Because the times were now at the mercy of international events it is hard to avoid recalling Roosevelt without talking about the war years as part of this story of Presidential anecdotes. All the turmoil in Europe from France to the Steppes of Russia and the leader's involved in these historic events were part of Roosevelt's Presidency.

On this journey Churchill reminded Franklin of his wild unpredictable uncle Teddy who also wore his heart on his sleeve and was fearless and almost reckless in his lifestyle. Just like Teddy, Churchill's roar of defiance to Hitler was very familiar "We shall fight them on the beaches. We shall fight them in the fields. We shall fight them in the streets, we shall never surrender."

Reports from Churchill cascaded onto Roosevelt's desk giving him a first-hand bird's-eye view of the war as it unfolded. It was as if everything was happening down the road from Washington.

Soon the Neutrality Act was becoming redundant and Roosevelt made his own mind up knowing what he knew about the war first hand from Churchill. He sent fifty year old destroyers to Britain and although battered and rusty they could float and they could fight.
But life went on in politics and the democratic wheel must keep turning which meant Roosevelt faced a third Presidential election in November 1940, one year after the war started. A third term in office was unheard of since George Washington set the precedent of two terms only. Incidentally two terms now has become law. But in the 1940s things were too volatile and a leadership change in America was out of the question. There was work to be done. A war to fight. At least that was the thinking of Franklin Delano Roosevelt. He threw his cap in the in the ring for a third term and duly won despite the horror of his own supporters who felt twelve years would be too much for any man's health with such responsibilities. Sadly later events proved them right.

The third Presidential election was unusual. While his Presidential ticket was to keep American boys out of any war, an aspiration Woodrow Wilson had but couldn't keep. Anyway it would have betrayed America to take this stance if war was necessary to protect America's vital interest. It was a phony ticket. Nobody really believed what was in effect only campaign oratory. Experience won over change even by a smaller majority. Roosevelt defeated Dewey and promptly introduced "Land Lease" instead of loans to help other countries pay their war debts. This was really to be "A loan of the garden hose to quench the fire in your neighbour's house" as he put it. Goods were only lent. The measure sailed through Congress.

Because America was not yet at war she could not attack U boats on the high seas. However Roosevelt ordered Admirals to fire on U boats who threatened U.S. ships and lives. It was inevitable U.S. ships would be fired on and soon the U.S. was openly attacking U boats in American patrolled waters. The Neutrality Act was swept away leaving America deep in an undeclared war in the North Atlantic.

Full belligerency on the part of America might never have happened if it was not for Pearl Harbour. That debate still rages but it did catapult an unprepared America into a war they never really wanted. Strangely Pearl Harbour was inevitable. Perhaps not at that geographic location but let us say the authorities knew something was brewing. Exports of gasoline had actually been blocked and Japanese assets in America frozen. Troop movements in the East Indies had alerted the Americans to an imminent attack. Diplomatic efforts were tried to persuade the Japanese to drop its aggressive postures against Indochina but to no avail. Then without declaring war the Japanese made a surprise attack on America's 50th State - Hawaii, destroying the whole of the U.S. fleet anchored in Pearl Harbour on December 7, 1941.

Roosevelt it is understood on hearing the news sat for over fifteen minutes just staring at the wall in his office. The time for debate had ended. Roosevelt reached for his pen. America was at war.

In his book American Journey Alistair Cooke, the illustrious journalist and writer described the scene in Congress when Roosevelt declared war. It went roughly as follows. "News of this atrocity was relayed from Congress by President Roosevelt now getting old and weary. Roosevelt climbed slowly on to the dais with the help of his son James who was dressed in the blue uniform of the marines. He adjusted his eyeglasses, opened his loose leaf notebook and spoke for ten minutes as follows, "I regret to tell you that very many American lives have been lost." He went on "Yesterday, the Japanese Government also launched an attack against Malaysia. Roosevelt was visibly shaken when he tersely added to the list of attacks. Last night the Japanese attacked Wake Island. And this morning the Japanese attacked Midway Island. I ask that Congress declare that since the unprovoked and dastardly attack by Japan on Sunday December 7, 1941, a state of war has existed between the United States and the Japanese Empire." The roll call was then taken. The President had left.

In New York every plane was grounded. In Washington black shades were going up at the White House and the floodlights beamed at the Capitol Dome were turned off.

Like any country at war America changed in a way that took the American's by surprise. At the Lincoln memorial a machine gun was mounted outside the State Department. The guards outside wore tin hats which were hard to get used to. The ordinary citizen was seeing a fixed bayonet for the first time in the hands of passing soldiers. Secret Service men now had to be satisfied about the most innocent gestures of harmless older citizen. Once when sirens blared for a routine fire alarm an Englishman was heard to joke "Sounds just like home." Having the peace and tranquility of two hundred years ended, America awoke as if from a long slumber to the terrible reality of Pearl Harbour in Hawaii one of their very own States now as American as Kentucky, Illinois or California. As American as mama's hot apple pie.

The European and Asiatic conflicts were now merged into one global war. On January 1, 1942 the U.S., Britain, the Soviet Union and China signed a Declaration of the United Nations drawing up the Atlantic Charter in which they pledged themselves not to make peace until the enemy had been defeated.

Roosevelt and Churchill formed not just a partnership between America and Britain to fight the war together but developed a relationship that was to grow and deepen. They held at least a dozen meetings. Roosevelt used to tease Churchill at meetings claiming the American's had thirteen destroyers to Churchill's two. It was the sincere vulnerable friendship not unlike that of two small boys who held nothing in reserve. But Roosevelt's respect for Churchill can be summed up in his affectionate words to Churchill on one occasion "It is fun to be in the same decade as you."

At least there was one gain for America which was an unexpected bonus. Stocking up in arms to supply the other nations at war helped the U.S. economy to finally come out of its Depression. Unemployment disappeared overnight. Even the farmer's were working twenty-four hours per day.

I am sure there are many anecdotes told on Roosevelt's life and work during these war years as the world was set ablaze with marching armies and brave glorious soldiers falling in battles that were orchestrated by world famous Generals in a human tragedy too unbearable to recall. Suffice it to say Roosevelt was part of it all side by side with Churchill and Stalin.

But back home in America, far from the turmoil in Europe, life went on for Roosevelt's family. The children came under the influence of Sara their grandmother who lavished expensive gifts on them to compensate for lives deprived by the war of their mother and father. With the cunning of children they managed to exploit the situation to their own advantage. Perhaps they were rebelling at the chasm that had opened up between themselves and their parents now too busy with their own war duties.

The result was speeding tickets, traffic accidents, divorces and smashed photographer's cameras. The press became too intrusive it seems. Even the Mayor of Paris was a victim of their lack of control which Sara, their grandmother had encouraged by her over-indulgence. One young Roosevelt emptied a bottle of champagne over the Mayor. Eleanor after one counselling session with them sighed with despair "As I spoke I knew I might as well have saved my breath to cool my porridge."

Meanwhile Eleanor, their mother feared nothing from detractors. She wrote a syndicated column for seventy-five newspapers. She worked hard and gained more and more recognition for her work as a humanitarian and a public figure. She even paid a visit to London at the invitation of the Queen, having travelled from America by air and enjoyed two days in Buckingham Palace as a guest of the Queen. As usual she held a press conference at which she said she had come to Britain to see for herself how women could help in the business of war. Later that day she toured the city, the East End, St. Paul's Cathedral, the damaged Guildhall, the areas bombed by Hitler and on to Stepney and White Chapel where she was cheered by enormous crowds. She had of course been accompanied by the King and Queen who finally took her back to the Mansion House where they had tea with the Lord Mayor and Lady Mayoress. She finished her trip next day with a visit to the Washington Club where she was cheered by over one thousand American soldiers, sailors and airmen.

In later years President Truman appointed her to an American delegation to the United Nations where she displayed a toughness that impressed all who met her. The U.N. Declaration of Human Rights is a lasting monument to her. In 1964, Adlai Stevenson paid a great tribute to her memory at the Democratic Convention that year. He said, "She thought of herself as an ugly duckling but she walked in beauty in the ghettos of the world bringing with her the reminder of her beloved St. Francis…. It is in giving that we receive and wherever she walked beauty was forever there."

But here we must return to Franklin Roosevelt himself. As the end of the war drew near another monster was in its early pregnancy. Roosevelt's almost naive attempt to harness Russia into a new world order for peace through the United Nations was failing. Stalin had his own agenda which Churchill seemed to understand deeper than Roosevelt. World domination by Communism was in its embryo stages. Expansionist forces were already on the march. Cries against fascism were being replaced by shouts against "Yankee imperialism." One world conflict, sadly despite all the heartbreak and desolation had been replaced by another. The rapid post-war demobilization of American forces left the free world with no defence against Communist advances in Eastern Europe and the Far East. It took until 1947 for the United

States to realize what was happening and so put into place counter measures to resist Communism. The new conflict had already begun as the old one ended. What we know today as "The Cold War" had started.

The cost to the free world was 273,000 square miles of territory taken over by Russia without firing a shot. The countries affected were Poland, Romania, Bulgaria, Yugoslavia, Hungary, Czechoslovakia and Albania. An iron curtain fell around them and liberal leaders had to flee for their lives from a new world tyranny. That story continued to unfold with the new President Harry S. Truman.

Once again Presidential elections were looming and once again the friends of Franklin D. Roosevelt were really worried. There was no way he would survive a fourth term in office. Even Roosevelt himself wondered about his own health and those moments of dizziness, whiter hair, tiredness and debility. But his doctors checked him over and found nothing wrong. It was a close run and vicious election. Big business had never forgiven him for "The New Deal" and was even prepared to sack any man who wore a "Vote FDR" button. To keep their jobs they were forced to hide the button until outside working hours. But the people could not desert this man who was truly the champion of the worker. Roosevelt won a record fourth term and settled down to prepare the world for peace. Sadly it was a peace he would never see. A peace nobody would see.

Russia continued to carve up Europe totally ignored by Roosevelt. He could not bring himself to oppose a friend who had promised support for America in their war against Japan. Still Russia continued to march victoriously across Europe. It was a new type of war, a war of ideologies. Churchill was petrified with foreboding.

But the realization of what was happening did not help Roosevelt's health. Suddenly he felt exhausted and headed for his favorite spot Warm Springs for a break. A portrait session was set up with his artist Mrs. Shoumatoff. While sitting on his chair posing for the portrait he slumped forward and never recovered consciousness.

It was April 11, 1945. The reaction across America was one of shock, disbelief and grief. On Broadway, theatres and cinemas closed down. Shop windows simply displayed signs "Closed - FDR died". Some even read "Closed death in the family". "Why do you not turn on your radio?" An ice-cream seller was asked. "For what," was the reply, "the news is on everybody's face."

Just for the record here is a postscript on the war which ended on May 7, 1945 almost four months after Franklin D. Roosevelt passed away.

It was only in the past year that Churchill and Roosevelt had struggled with Stalin to determine what the future of Europe should be. Stalin refused to allow free elections in the Soviet sphere and to ensure this he created an "Iron Curtain" from the Baltic to the Atlantic. Refusing to grant a $6 million loan to Russia to help reconstruct its infrastructure didn't help. In fact it left Russia bitter which undermined any cooperation between the two blocs far into the future. Also worrying everybody was the fear of nuclear weapons. So the old world of Franklin Roosevelt, the world map, and world politics were now changed forever. More of those thoughts in our piece on President Truman. But meanwhile let us return to the passing of the greatest politician and President of the 20th Century, Franklin Roosevelt.

There were many quotes to reflect the outpouring of grief in their loss of FDR. Most of them by now are part of folklore. Like the reaction of an American soldier in April 1945. It was short and simple "I felt as if I knew him."

Strangely enough Roosevelt during his final days was struck with a homesick melancholy in 1944. "All that is within me cries out to go back to my home on the Hudson River," he said. Somehow he seemed to sense that time was running out on him. Nevertheless despite his failing health, his sense of duty – getting the job done – never deserted him and as I wrote earlier he allowed his name to be put forward for a fourth term which he won. His nostalgia for the Hudson River just had to be put on hold till the war ended. Losing his mother early in the war in 1941 also left him anxious to leave these terrible responsibilities behind him and rejoin the family life he had so much neglected in the cause of mankind. Sadly he only served three months more in the Presidency when he died.

Conrad Black in his book Franklin Delano Roosevelt: Champion of Freedom gave seven reasons why Roosevelt was the greatest President since Lincoln. I will not list them but they were roughly as follows. First because of his support for England in the war who could not have remained in it had Roosevelt not supported them? He extended U.S. territorial waters by eighteen hundred miles into the Atlantic. Attacked German ships and imposed on Japan an embargo on oil and scrap material.

He led America out of deep isolation in 1937 and created the greatest political tour de force in history by partnership with Churchill. The re-invention of the American State was another victory of his colossal welfare programme during the Depression. It was yet another reason to applaud him. Innovations which were resisted as "not possible" before the Depression became commonplace throughout America. Rural electrification, social security, old age pensions, reform of financial institutions, flood and drought control, farm loans, stabilization of farm production and prices, hydroelectric power and Public Sector Development. If his measures were not wholly successful they were a master class in crisis management. He restored the confidence of Americans in their own country. He used the fear of one enemy (Hitler) to conquer another enemy (Depression). By the introduction of his rearmament programme he helped America back to full employment and saved the capitalistic forces from the disgrace they had brought upon themselves. Even his foresight as pre-war Secretary of the Navy was a tribute to a great thinker. Yes I think you will agree he has more than earned and deserves his illustrious place in American history.

The funeral of FDR was an event to go down in history. Before talking about it let us ponder on how they were perceived as a family. The Roosevelt's came from two distinct lines of the family tree. The Oyster Bay line was the one Teddy belonged to, a "rough and ready, up and at em" branch of the family. The all action "gung ho" type. Franklin came from the more genteel sophisticated Hyde Park group. When asked why there was so much sniping and antagonism between them Sara, the Hyde Park matriarch observed "I can not imagine why unless it is because we are better looking than they are."

Franklin was often referred to as the wizard in the White House. His style of Presidency was described as the West Bronx FDR mystique.

As for "The New Deal", people talked about it not so much as an economic philosophy but as a succession of Government attempts to solve current problems. It was a trial and error approach to ideas just to relieve suffering. It seemed to bypass the guru's of the University intellectuals and couldn't be found in any textbook nevertheless it worked. That 's all that matters.

Eleanor could have been nominated for the Senate but she declined. Writing books, articles, magazine contributions and giving lectures took up all of her time. She always complained she had so many things to do and so little time to do it.

It is now my task to write briefly on the funeral of FDR. For a man, no, a giant, with so many successful achievements to his name wouldn't it be great to finish this piece on a world tour with Roosevelt just like President Grant? Perhaps quoting from his world famous memoirs. Or even to hear his wisdom on the lecture circuits of Universities and world Capitals. To have to write about a last farewell to the American people from the grave is an unbearable anticlimax to a wonderful story. But then again this is God's world not ours.

The funeral of FDR was a fitting tribute to Franklin Delano Roosevelt. Though Roosevelt had died back home in Warm Springs, the machinery of State still had to move quickly for it was important that a new President be installed as soon as possible. A call for the whole Cabinet to be present was sent out and most of them arrived at 7 p.m. on the evening of April 11, 1945. Chief justice Harlan Stone administered the oath to Harry S. Truman, the Vice President who now became the 33rd President of the United States. Eleanor Roosevelt made her last friendly farewell to the White House staff and journalists, then got into her car and drove away into history, no more the First Lady of American politics. Just like "The Duchess" President Harding's widow, she too closed the door to the room where Franklin's body lay and spent five final minutes with him. Perhaps there, she had a few tears to shed, some memories to recall, and the future to contemplate. But this is a secret she is entitled to keep in the privacy of her own heart. General George Marshall made the arrangements for the funeral at the invitation of Eleanor. The Presidential train was modified to permit the flag draped coffin of the President to be seen as the train moved slowly northwards in the long 800 miles journey back to Washington.

The local neighbours crowded the railway station to bid a tearful farewell. It was estimated nearly two million ordinary folk lined the tracks on FDR's final journey home. They waved from hamlets and fields through the day and night as the funeral train moved onwards. Whenever the train stopped to refuel or resupply groups of people gathered to sing those lovely hymns "Abide with me" and "Nearer my God to thee" among others.

They were met at Union Station in Washington by the new Commander-in-Chief, President Truman and his Cabinet on April 14. The streets were lined with crowds as the funeral cortege passed by. Dramatically following his gun carriage was the traditional riderless horse with reverse stirrups, the symbol of the fallen warrior. It was 4 p.m. now. The dignitaries attending the service came from every level of American life. Foreign heads of State from all over the world mingled with Princes and Kings of many Monarchies. Eleanor remained dignified and unemotional throughout the ceremonies. She was amazed as she looked through the window of the funeral train to see the cross section of humanity standing solemnly there - children, fathers, mothers and grandmothers watching as the train passed by on its way to Springwood.

A team of horses pulled the caisson up the hill to Springwood in the final climb of its journey home. An honour guard of scarlet cloaked Cadets from West Point fired three volleys. It was a fine spring day as Franklin was buried near the main house in their own familiar rose garden. The crowd melted away and Eleanor was the last to leave. Seventeen years later she would join Franklin in the same grave.

Four weeks after the funeral the war was over. The end came when General Eisenhower, a future U.S. President, accepted the unconditional surrender of Germany's beaten military forces scattered throughout Europe. The signing took place in the early hours of May 7, 1945 at 2.41 a.m. at the Headquarters of General Eisenhower in Reims, France.

But let us leave the last few words to Franklin Roosevelt's old pal Winston Churchill when he wrote to Eleanor with his condolences on the death of her husband.

"I feel deeply for you all. As for me I have lost a dear and cherished friendship forged in the fires of war."

To write further would be an unnecessary embellishment to an already wonderful story – The story of Franklin Delano Roosevelt, 32nd President of the United States.

33rd President   Harry S. Truman

"Give em hell Harry"
Born 1884
Died 1972
88 Years of Age
2 Terms (7 years 283 days)
1945 – 1953
Age 61

Party: Democrat
County: Missouri
Profession: Farmer and Clerk
Ancestry: English, Scotch, Irish
Estate: Unknown
Hobbies: Poker

Physical Description: Height 5 foot 9 inches, 167lbs weight, receding steel grey hair parted on left, hazel eyes, eye glasses with thick lenses.

Significant extracts from Inaugural speech on Thursday January 2, 1949:
"The supreme need of our time is for men to learn to live together in peace and harmony.... The peoples of the earth face the future with grave uncertainty composed almost equally of great hopes and great fears."

HARRY S. TRUMAN

Near the end of the war in the summer of 1944 far away from the gunfire and explosions of marching armies in Europe life went on as usual in the U.S. Nothing had really changed in the social life of the Americans. The Democratic Party was preparing for the next Presidential election and the choice of the Vice President was uppermost in the minds of the Party bosses. FDR perhaps pre-occupied with the war, was in no hurry to appoint a Vice President. It was a bizarre problem to be wrestling with at that time, after all Franklin was busy directing the war alongside Churchill and Stalin and was a major player on the world stage. Having a Vice President of course was never top of the agenda for a very busy President.

But those that knew FDR were very much aware that Franklin Roosevelt had spent twelve years as President and his enthusiasm for politics was also waning with his health. Roosevelt despite this was adamant he must see out the war in office. If a fourth term was granted to him by the people, those around him felt certain he would not complete his term. Here I might hasten to add since he had been passed by doctors as physically fit nobody suspected or contemplated a problem with his health. But for the first time in a Presidential Election the post of Vice President was of ultimate importance because the job was vacant. Then again this begs the question; how thoroughly had FDR been medically examined?

The name of Harry S. Truman had been proposed to FDR but for his own reasons he was not keen on discussing the Vice Presidency.

It wasn't an important issue for him at that particular time but the appointment needed Roosevelt's approval first.

It took some time before Franklin would agree to this commitment but he eventually agreed on Harry S. Truman as his Vice President. The anxiety to have this matter quickly resolved was vindicated for three months after Roosevelt's election to a fourth term – as described in my piece on the life of Roosevelt – FDR died on April 12, 1945.

Following a man of Roosevelt's stature was going to be a daunting task for any politician and it was an anxious time indeed for the people of America. I wonder what Truman's thoughts were when he first sat at the President's desk that morning; after all, it was an office FDR had occupied for the best part of twelve years.

To understand these thoughts lets walk with Truman on the path he had travelled from his birthplace on a farm in Missouri to that very morning sitting at FDR's desk in the White House.

Harry S. Truman the oldest child of three, born to Martha Ellen Young Truman and John Anderson Truman was born on May 8, 1884 in Lamar, Missouri. The truth is Truman really had no middle name but was given the S. to solve a difference between two family members whose names started with S. This gesture of peace seems to have worked between them.

The family moved to Independence, Missouri when Harry was six and while attending Sunday school he is reputed to have met his future wife aged five at that time. Her name was Elizabeth Virginia "Bess" Wallace.

Harry eventually married her after his demob from the army on June 28, 1919 twenty-nine years later. He was then thirty-five years of age. Harry was eight before he actually started school. He wore thick glasses from that age because of his very poor eyesight which was never a deterrent to him reading or playing music, two of his most consuming passions. It's hard to believe he got up at 5 a.m. to practice the piano and read four or five histories a week, a hobby which helped him to become quite an expert on military battles and the lives of famous leaders.

But despite this potential his families financial situation prevented him going to college and he missed another opportunity for a career in West Point due to his poor eyesight. So he had no option but to start work as a timekeeper for the Santa Fe Railroad at $35 per month. He later went on to work as a mail clerk for the Kansas City Star. The job of bank clerk and bookkeeper followed. But even these careers were cut short when he was called home to help his parents run the large farm they were living on which was owned by his grandmother.

Ever the practical man Harry settled down and worked on the farm for ten years with some success. His first taste of politics came in1914 at thirty years of age when he joined Kansas City 10th Ward Democratic Club. Harry wasn't very good as a business man for the following year 1915 he invested in lead mines in Missouri but lost his money. Two years later in 1917 Harry joined the army just before the U.S. entered World War I and was elected first Lieutenant by the men of Missouri's Second Field Artillery.
While in the army between 1917 and 1919 Truman was promoted from Lieutenant to Major after distinguishing himself with his unit at two battles Saint-Mihiel and Argonne.

I am sorry to have to record another business failure at this point in Harry's career for just after being discharged from the army he opened up a men's clothing store. Business boomed for a while but one year after it opened in 1920 prices fell sharply. He struggled on for two more years but eventually was forced to close down. He could have declared himself a bankrupt but refused to take the easy way out and managed to repay all of his debts.
Once again he turned to politics and entered a four way Democratic primary for an eastern Jackson County judgeship. It was actually a job supervising County roads and buildings and the Ku Klux were backing one of the candidates. Truman was advised to join the Klan but refused on the grounds that it championed white supremacy and discrimination against blacks, Jews and Roman Catholics. His entrance fee was returned. But Truman fought it on his military record and won. In January 1923 at thirty-nine years of age he was sworn into his first public office, nine years after entering politics in 1914. One year later his only daughter Mary Margaret was born who would in time become a writer and a concert hall artist. Harry managed to reverse the financial fortunes of the County by repaying $600,000 of a $1,000,000 debt. He continued to have an interest in the National Guard and in time was promoted to Colonel. True to his insatiable appetite for self-improvement he even enrolled in the Kansas City Law School.

But Harry's amazing chequered working life moved on when the Ku Klux Clan brought about his only election defeat. Being out of work again Harry picked himself up, dusted himself down and for the next couple of years earned his living selling automobile club membership and after a while got another job in the banking business. But let's stop here and look back at Harry Truman's life to date. He was an officer, twice promoted in the American army. Before this he had worked on his grandmother's farm for ten years. He was a timekeeper, a mail clerk, a bank clerk and bookkeeper. He was a failed store owner, and lead mine investor, a Jackson County Judge, a salesman and again a bank clerk. In between he learnt the piano, studied history and went to Law School. Finally he had also got married, had a daughter and enjoyed a happy home life.

One thing is for certain Harry S. Truman just never stood still and always managed to bounce back from adversary. It was now he made a significant decision. At this time in the 1920s the Spoils System was flourishing in Missouri and political machines were quite common, one of which was headed by a man called Mike Prendergast. The reward for work in getting politicians elected was usually a Government perk to the loyal Party member. These were almost unstoppable vote getting machines. Tom Prendergast, Mike's son supported Truman for a job as presiding Judge of the County in charge of roads, buildings and taxes. Truman was elected a County Court Judge and he immediately set out to clear up the graft in building contracts and end the flow of money from taxes going into the pockets of Prendergast's supporters.

He fired disreputable workers and hired new ones out of State bank loans. Mike Prendergast died in the meantime and his two sons took over from him favouring Truman with a second term as County judge. But the Prendergast machine had by now been hijacked by gangsters who were involved in gambling, vice rings, bootlegging, police bribery, and even murder. Meanwhile Truman was totally immersed in his job as County Judge and because of the corruption going on around him was impressing his constituents by his obvious honesty and integrity.

Time was also running out on him and I suppose once again he was wondering where his next job would come from. It was now, that Tom Prendergast his close friend asked him to run for the U.S. Senate and on January 3, 1935 he was elected as junior Senator for Missouri. His career in politics had started at last. And the popularity of Roosevelt's "New Deal" helped him enormously.

But his association with the Prendergast machine had damaged him and he was treated with disdain by those who did not know him. Even Roosevelt was worried that the investigation taking place into the Prendergast machine would implicate Truman. But Truman's passion for history from his young days came to his rescue. The knowledge he had accumulated on history and Government had impressed two of the Senate's most influential men John Garner and Arthur H. Vandenberg. They recommended him to two important committees.

These produced the Truman-Austin Bill that led to the Civil Aeronautics Board. His career was assured when he found himself on many other committees which produced The Transportation Act in 1940.

But as long as the investigations were in progress into the Prendergast machine his career made no progress. There was good news for him when the investigations left him in the clear from the sort of corruption and brutality that was uncovered. But Truman was loyal to Tom Prendergast who was indicted by the hearings. Here is Harry Truman's opinion on the situation. "Tom Prendergast has always been my friend and I don't desert a sinking ship." But he did make two enemies from the affair, the two Missouri Democrats who had brought about Prendergast's downfall. They opposed Harry when he sought a second term as Senator. But all Truman's life experience up to then had toughened him up and he decided to fight back with two months of electioneering travelling the State and making speeches putting his record on the line. He finally won a second term in the Senate. His fellow Senators were so impressed they gave him a standing ovation on his first day back in the Senate.

We now arrive at Roosevelt's relationship with Winston Churchill. As we read under our notes on Roosevelt, the aggression of the German U Boats and the situation in Europe was slowly pushing America into war.

Because of this, preparations were being made in the U.S. for war in 1941 but these war preparations were causing problems in the defence programme. Truman toured the camps and discovered dishonesty and incompetence everywhere. He brought back to the Senate his findings and was made leader of an investigation committee. By discovering fraud and waste on a colossal scale his committee made savings of $15 billion for a $400,000 outlay.

These findings pushed Truman right to the top of the political hierarchy on the National stage and his name was now on everyone's lips for Vice President in the 1944 Presidential election. We have already talked about the selection of Vice President. Roosevelt had already had two Vice Presidents in his time as President, John Nance Garner (1933 – 1941) and Henry Agard Wallace (1941 – 1945).

But now the Party bosses wanted someone appealing to mainstream voters and Truman was the man chosen. And shortly afterwards came the death of FDR on April 12, 1945. One of Truman's disadvantages now was picking up the unfamiliar reins of the Presidency for he had spent only eighty-two days as Vice President. He was sworn into the Presidency on April 12, at 7 o'clock in the evening by Chief Justice Harlan F. Stone and as expected no election was necessary because FDR had died in office. Once again Harry Truman was taking on yet another new job. This time it was something completely different, the 33rd President of the United States.

And so Harry Truman settled into office as a war time President, unfortunately with little or no briefing. Before FDR died Truman had only two short meetings with the President after he returned from the Yalta Conference where matters of world significance had been discussed with the Allies. But the trouble was Roosevelt had not discussed the problems of the war or later plans for peace with Truman.
Actually Truman's first few weeks in office were spent being briefed by Roosevelt's Aides. His first historical meeting had been planned beforehand for San Francisco on April 25, 1945. It was the founding conference of the United Nations one of the unfulfilled dreams of Woodrow Wilson. Later his first announcement to the nation was to proclaim victory in Europe day (VE Day) for May 8, 1945 and it just happened to be his 61st birthday. He had only been roughly twenty-six days in office. So he was certainly learned at breakneck speed.

On July 2, 1945 he sent the United Nations Charter to the Senate for ratification. What a momentous beginning for him in his new job. So far so good.

But now Harry Truman was operating on the world stage and America was holding its breath for their new President. Maybe at this point we should leave the history to one side and lighten up a little as Truman meets the newsmen and Eleanor Roosevelt.

The impact of his first days in the Presidency were summed up in Truman's own words to a group of journalist who paid a visit to him on Capitol Hill. "I feel like the moon, the stars and all the planets had fallen on me," he said. He was now familiar with the most intimate secrets of the Presidency one of which was the super secret of the Atomic Bomb Project just coming to fruition off the drawing board.

His first meeting with Eleanor Roosevelt, who was well-known to most of the top men in Washington was revealing. "Harry, the President is dead," she told him bluntly. "Is their anything I can do," he asked. Eleanor just looked at him shook her head and replied almost sympathetically "Is their anything I can do for you, you are the one in trouble now."

Truman was no shrinking violet in his social life for he often sat at a piano to entertain his listeners. A photograph appears in that marvellous book called To the Best of My Ability edited by Jameson McPherson, with Truman at a piano entertaining U.S. servicemen in February 1945. Lying on top of the piano was that famous actress Lauren Bacall. I don't think we should be too surprised at this for his daughter Margaret made many appearances as a concert singer and a television performer. She also went on to become a best selling novelist of murder mysteries based on Washington life.

The transition from Roosevelt's regime was painful for Harry and his White House staff. One staff member said "It was all so sudden. I had completely forgotten about Mr. Truman. Stunned I realized that I simply couldn't comprehend the Presidency as something separate from Roosevelt. The Presidency, the War, the White House, our lives they were all Roosevelt's."

A journalist said "For a time he walked as completely as did any smaller labourer who had been a Roosevelt man in the long shadow of the Presidency." Roosevelt had become so immersed in the life of the White House many Americans thought he would be there forever. Even the papers prolonged the myth when the Chicago Daily News wrote this on Roosevelt "If he was good enough for my pappy and my grand- pappy he is good enough for me." An amusing anecdote is told of one reaction from a father with a newly born son who said "Maybe he will grow up to be President...." "Why," was the angry answer, "What's the matter with Roosevelt?"

Truman was no fool and he must have been aware of all this. One correspondent confessed "It was difficult to address this man as Mr. President so we skirted around the edges by prefacing our questions with the word 'Sir'." The Secretary of Agriculture, Claude Wickard wrote in his diary "I had resolved that I would be very careful when I addressed the new President to call him Mr. President but much to my surprise and somewhat to my disgust I shook hands with him and said 'Harry we want to help you all we can'."
Even Truman's wife Bess was effected. Bess was always very low-key. Despite being known to the White House as the wife of the Vice President she remained unrecognised. When a short plump grey haired woman entered the White House just before becoming the First Lady the chief usher stopped her to ask "Mam, you are Mrs Truman?" Bess replied "Yes" a little amused at the usher's embarrassment at not knowing her.

Naturally the press were not too pleased. She had not the flamboyant material of an Eleanor Roosevelt to whom they had become accustomed. She had no force they complained – perhaps with a play on words – since she failed to break the champagne bottle – after nine attempts during a christening ceremony on a C54 aircraft. Even when she objected to the condition of the White House rooms she had inherited she was met with a disrespectful "Mrs Roosevelt never complained." This was understandable given Eleanor Roosevelt's reputation in the White House.

But Bess Truman was the diametrical opposite to Eleanor. Harry Truman had only been three months the Vice President and Bess could have no idea when she might become the First Lady. This didn't faze Bess for she cherished her privacy jealously saying "publicity was undignified." On her return from the funeral of FDR she confessed to Frances Perkins "I'm not used to this awful public life." When she was told holding press conferences had been a "speciality" of Eleanor Roosevelt she promptly opted out of the ordeal and never held one in her entire stay in the White House.

One famous anecdote is always remembered. So unused to the limelight was she that when asked to christen two aeroplanes it took her eight attempts to swing the bottle without breaking it. But her embarrassment was short lived for her military aide failed in four attempts. It seems the bottle should have been "scored" beforehand. Harry got a good laugh about that.

Unfortunately Bess moved quickly on to the second plane without success. The bottle burst too soon and showered her with champagne. Husband Harry was no help. When he poked some more fun at her later she said ominously "I wish I could have cracked it on your head." But the three Truman's Margaret, Harry and Bess shared plenty of laughter and were known as the "three musketeers".

Staffers said they were the closest family ever seen in the White House, a praise so unique even Eleanor Roosevelt could not emulate it. Her highest praise came from the President himself "I never make a report or deliver a speech without Bess editing them." What the public loved about her was her determination not to allow the job of First Lady to change her. I think she succeeded with flying colours.

Even on Roosevelt's funeral train to Hyde Park criticism and comparisons could be heard. You would think the world had come to an end. One particular voice could be heard in a stage whisper saying "There is no leadership anymore… The country will go to hell." When Truman was asked later "Did he know you heard him?" "I think yes that is what he had in mind," was Truman's reply with a knowing grin. Nothing phased him.

On his second morning in the White House the respect due to Truman, unconsciously was not there. Without realizing it, when Jesse Jones administrator of the Reconstruction Finance Corporation was told by Truman that a St. Louis man had been appointed by the President as a Federal Loan official, Jones looked concerned and asked "Did the President appoint him before he died or after he died." "No," said Truman, "he made it right now." It was a classic put down from Truman who was proving himself quite a master at thinking on his feet.

The ghost of Tom Prendergast was always present however in those early days of Truman's Presidency because the perception around the White House was that Truman was only a nondescript minion of the Kansas City boss Prendergast. The St. Louis Post Dispatch referred spitefully to Truman as follows "Ambassador in Washington of the defunct principality of Prendergast's." It was an unheard of disrespect to the Presidency. Well it wasn't completely unheard of, for that type of disrespect was heard once before back in 1841 when John Tyler, the tenth President was not recognized as the legitimate heir after William H. Harrison, the ninth President. As you will have read earlier in my notes on Tyler's first Cabinet meeting. Tyler's speech to his Cabinet was also a classical put down establishing the pecking order in the Cabinet room once and for all.

Perhaps Truman's past association had brought this misunderstanding that day down on himself but the implication of having shady friends had no place in the Truman story for he was basically proud of his honesty and independence as the following anecdote will portray. Once he reacted angrily to his treatment by Roosevelt as a person. "I am tired of being pushed around and having the President treat me like the office boy," he told newspapermen. "They better learn downtown right now that no Tom Prendergast or anybody else tells Senator Truman how to vote." This was in response to an approach by the President's men demanding he vote a certain way in the Senate. Truman proved that day he was his own man.

So perhaps it is now not too hard to understand Roosevelt's reluctance to sign up Truman for the Vice Presidency. Perhaps he did not think Truman would measure up to the job. Or perhaps like Truman's blunder when he approved the draft of an article criticising Roosevelt's Administration for inefficiency didn't help matters. The article was headlined "We can lose the war in Washington". It took some months for a reconciliation to take place between them. Being an honest broker can be a painful flaw in politics. But Truman was always Truman telling it exactly as he saw it. However the war did bring them together and Truman went to great pains to avoid interfering with FDR's conduct of the war as had been done to Lincoln during the Civil War.

After becoming President one of Truman's first acts of independence from the influence of Roosevelt was his invitation to Herbert Hoover to come to the White House. "Come on over here. I run the White House now not these old friends of Mr Roosevelt." He also made the historic gesture of reversing one of Roosevelt's decisions. This was after FDR changed the name of the Hoover dam to the "Boulder Dam". Today we follow Truman's wishes by still calling it The Hoover Dam again.

But Harry Truman slowly began to put his stamp on the Presidency. He soon made short work of ridding himself of the Roosevelt Cabinet. Some he fired. Other just left town. One, Attorney General Francis Biddle was given twenty-four hours to get out. Biddle demanded to be told to his face and Truman did just that. Truman's opinion of Roosevelt's Cabinet was breathtaking..... "As I look back on the situation it makes me shudder. I am sure God Almighty had me by the hand. He must have had a personal interest in the welfare of this great Republic of ours." David McCullough, the eminent writer's comment on the Truman takeover was blunt and to the point. "To many it was not just that the greatest of men had fallen, but that the least of men, or at any rate the least likely of men – had assumed his place."

However, the least likely of men was not long in forming his opinions of the FDR Cabinet before scrapping it. Here are a few quotations straight from a Truman broadside with no frills attached on why he dismissed them. "Stettinius, Secretary of State, a fine man, good looking, amiable, co-operative but never an idea new or old; Morgenthau, block head nut I wonder why FDR kept him around. Henry Wallace Secretary of Commerce, he had no reason to love me or be loyal to me. Of course he was not loyal. "Honest" Harold Ickes, who was never for anyone but Harold, would have cut FDR's throat – or mine for his high minded ideas of a headline – and did. Agriculture Wickard a nice man, who never learnt how his department was set up. Then there was Leo Crowley whose sense of honour was minus. Chester Bowles, price control man whose idea of Administration was conversation with crazy columnists."

"There was not a man on the list who would talk frankly at a Cabinet meeting! The honest ones were afraid to and the others wanted to fool me any how." Truman commented later even more bluntly "I don't know how I ever got out of that mud hole. Stettinius was as dumb as they come. Morgenthau didn't know shit from apple butter." On another occasion Truman said to his Aide Clark Clifford..... "Most of the people Roosevelt had close around him were crackpots and lunatic fringe..." "The American people have been through a lot of experiments and they want a rest from experiments." Later Ickes who Truman had reinstated into the Cabinet petulantly offered his resignation over Truman's selection of Edwin Pauley to Under Secretary of the Navy. Truman accepted it and gave Ickes three days to clear his desk.

Harry Truman was certainly proving he was no Prendergast puppet. But out there on Capitol Hill those who really knew Truman were not surprised. Truman later remembered The Ickes incident in a memo he wrote "I had to accept the resignation of Harold Ickes because he wanted me to be a Franklin Roosevelt – and that I could not be....." Wallace the last of the

Roosevelt inner circle survived until September 1946. The clear out was now complete..... I have spent some time on the subject of the Cabinet to show how tough and fearless Truman could be. We are to see more of this style in later events.

There have been other great Presidents in the past and life still moved on after the giant in the White House. In my notes on Theodore Roosevelt I pointed out the same transitionary turmoil in Washington when Taft took over from him. Policies, politics and styles are different in individuals. Perhaps the turmoil is not only expected but almost inevitable. Besides all the infighting Truman had to do in domestic politics on the home front in America, he now had to fill the shoes of FDR on the world stage alongside Churchill and Stalin.

Truman was unimpressed about this for he wrote to his mother in July 1945 as follows: "I am getting ready to go to see Stalin and Churchill and it is a chore." He finally set sail for Potsdam aboard the cruiser Augusta. From July 17 to August 2 he sat in at the Potsdam Conference located in a suburb of Berlin. However his position as a newcomer was not unique for Clement Attlee, Churchill's successor was also there. Despite all Churchill's glory on the battlefields of Europe the people replaced him in the first election after the war. As we have said on other occasions in these notes democracy is no respecter of illustrious reputations.

The programme covered in Potsdam debated a wide variety of problems such as the establishment of the Council of Foreign Ministers, settlement of reparation claims and of course The Nuremburg War Crimes Tribunal. He also managed to persuade Stalin to support America in the war against Japan. While he liked Churchill he described the Russians in his familiar blunt non-diplomatic style "pigheaded people". I call his style "Trumanese".

On August 26, he issued the Potsdam Declaration calling on Japan to surrender and listing the peace terms. Significantly, he was now armed with the information that the first atomic bomb had been detonated at Alamogordo, New Mexico. Everyone now knew the awful reality of such a weapon. All that is except the Japanese it seems.

There was now a terrible choice on the shoulders of the new U.S. President Harry S. Truman. Should he use the bomb and save the lives of half a million U.S. soldiers by shortening the war. Japan's refusal to accept the surrender terms left Truman with the only option left to him – drop the bomb.

Here I must pause while I add some thoughts of my own. I am sure you the reader must have similar questions – Why when Russia, America and the whole world were about to confront Japan in battle was the decision taken by Japan to reject the surrender terms? Whose decision was it – The Emperor or his Generals? This we shall learn later. But at this present moment we must ask ourselves, were they not all aware by now through intelligence what a horrific weapon was awaiting them.

But the die was cast and the bomb was dropped as we know today. The following scenes are taken from three terrifying descriptions of the bomb dropped on Hiroshima. One is taken from Harold Evans book The American Century. The second comes from a Daily Mail report of July 17, 2005 on Stephen Walker's book Countdown to Apocalypse. A third account was in a BBC Documentary of August 7, 2005. As you will appreciate they are a rough extract only of events covering that terrible day over sixty years ago. I tried to be as accurate as I could using my own words but the pictures will still burn themselves into your memory forever. Any sane person, knowing the horror it caused, should never ever threaten to use the bomb again.

But does mankind ever learn from history? In June 2009 this awful scene was being threatened by North Korea on their fellowmen from South Korea. Surely they now have video footage of the terrible carnage they would inflict. Surely they realize that this tragedy must never ever be repeated. The following is a picture of what happens in a nuclear explosion.

It all began from an aeroplane the Enola Gay high up in the heavens over Hiroshima. To those on the ground the aircraft was like a tiny silver drop against a beautiful blue sky. It was too high to be a Japanese plane. Height was safety to those in the Enola Gay. Tokyo time had just gone 8 a.m. and the people had finished breakfast. Inside the plane Paul Tibbets the pilot was getting ready for the terrible event to come. No flak he observed. No guns. Put on goggles. Start the bomb run which will last three minutes. Paul released the bomb and banked for home. He was looking forward to the return journey to base.

A teacher was wiping the desk top. It was 8.15 a.m. August 6, 1945 when the bomb hurtled down at 100 miles per hour, the ear-splitting scream coming from the stabilizing plates attached to its tail.

It took forty-five seconds to blow 60,000 people into eternity. After it exploded in an incandescent flash of vivid greens, reds, blues and golds, a woman was seen holding in her intestines with both hands. Nearby a school girl stood with her right eyeball hanging down her face.

Then the firestorms blew. A man stood naked in its wake his clothes burnt off him. A black tubular shape formed in front of his eyes. They were his lips. Then came the black rain from melting bodies in the ashes of the mushroom cloud overhead. It was sticky and poisonous. To quench their thirst people opened their mouths to drink. They were drinking death, for the rain was contaminated in lethal radioactivity. A girl lost her reason in the fields going from corpse to corpse to embrace them crying.

A man sitting on steps outside a bank left nothing more than his pose scorched into the stone like a photograph. The gamma rays released forces by neutrons that destroyed the very structure of living tissues. The kind of death inflicted made the Civil War in America seem like a Sunday picnic. The shockwave alone smashed through everything in its path 60,000 buildings, buses, hospitals, and 50,000 people. The pressure in its path sucking people's eyes and entrails from their bodies on a tidal wave of horror.

It had been a beautiful cloudless day when a whole city crowded with teeming life and culture disappeared instantly. The real statistics have been amended today over sixty years later. They read as follows: 280,000 civilians; 43,000soldiers and 76,000 buildings were obliterated. By 1950, five years later, radiation deaths connected to the bombing amounted to 200,000 and forty years later people still died from cancer attributed to the radiation released by the bomb. A U.S. Navy officer visiting the city more than one month after the bombing wrote "A smell of death and corruption pervades the city..... There is the absolute essence of death in the sense of finality without hope of resurrection." Only three of fifty-five hospitals could offer care with not more than twenty-eight doctors.

The bomb they called "Little Boy" exploded high above the courtyard of Shima Hospital. The time was 8.15 a.m. on that fatal day August 6, 1945. The crowded streets alive with busy shoppers were changed from everything to nothing as a Japanese historian described it. Over 100,000 people within a kilometre of the hypocentre of the explosion were instantly vaporized in the flash. All that remained of them was a scattering of small black piles of carbonized flesh stuck to the concrete sidewalks. People who moved around the city making plans, buying groceries, meeting friends and looking forward to tomorrow were no more. They simply disappeared in an instant to become silhouettes on the walls that were still standing. Photographs afterwards showed a complete absence of rubble as if a giant typhoon had swept it into the bay to look like a bone picked clean.

Four square miles of the city was incinerated and the homelessness created was a war time tragedy. But the horror didn't end there. People began to suffer from an unknown sickness. Some bled profusely and died horribly. They were untreatable. Having no white blood cells left them no resistance. They were literally rotting. Radiation sickness was the name of this terrible monster they had never heard of. The Mayor of Hiroshima bravely read a statement on the radio urging the citizens not to lose heart.

The morning after the bomb fell search teams went out to collect the bodies for burial before disease could spread. There were thousands. The city hospitals had no medicine, no equipment and no staff. One doctor treated three thousand patients in the nearest village. The corridors were full of the wounded. Outside relatives searched frantically for dead relatives among the ruins.

Three days after the bomb was dropped on Hiroshima, the Emperor still debated with his Generals about a surrender. The deadline given by Truman passed and after a futile desperate plea by him to surrender a second bomb was dropped this time on Nagasaki where 50,000 people were killed.

But still the military men of Japan refused to heed the Doomsday clock as it ticked away that summer 1945. The Japanese system of consensus must be obeyed. Hirohito the Emperor called together his top military men. He was urged by them to reject the ultimatum for surrender. Trusting in Russian influence, they harboured hopes of a compromise. This thinking at that critical moment of history was inviting national suicide.
But it was already too late to save the people of Nagasaki. Survivors were pitch black without faces. Worst of all was the thirst. People begged for water but they found none. Just as in Hiroshima the black rain fell. The survivors opened their mouths to the sky but the black raindrops again killed the living for these precious raindrops too were intensively radioactive.

Any area of exposed skin became burning hot. Temperatures of 4,000 degrees were recorded. Victims turned to carbon or were vaporized. There was nobody left who saw it happen. The shockwave turned windows and walls into shrapnel. A jet black cloud came towards them and blew the victims backwards through the walls. Tens of thousands vanished in a fraction of a second and many were trapped and burned where they lay. There was no morning sunshine. The sun was gone. The city was full of corpses in the dark. Many were lacerated by flying glass and fell in the path of the approaching fireball. People walked everywhere and nowhere. They walked in every direction and no particular direction confused distraught and desolate. What a horrible sin is mans inhumanity to man! The next target was to be selected but to Truman's relief it wasn't necessary. Realization of their predicament caused a rethink in the Emperor's Palace. "The time has come when we must bear the unbearable." It seems he was thinking not of the threatened holocaust but his own honour. Helping him also was the thought that to have the bomb fall on Tokyo was unthinkable. "To bear the unbearable" was the Emperors language for "We Surrender".

The news was handed to Truman who read out the surrender note to the sound of exultant cheers. The war was truly over. Surrender terms were signed on board the SS Missouri on

September 2, 1945 in Tokyo Bay.

Incidentally let's finish this piece on the Atom bomb by adding another anecdote about the terrible story as told by a prison camp survivor. He spoke casually as such people do, when he appeared on the BBC programme "The Antique Road Show" on Sunday 29, March 2009. It seems just a day or two before the bombing by The Enola Gay, a document had been circulated throughout the camp to prison guards in which they were instructed to annihilate every last prisoner by any means necessary, hanging, bayoneting, shooting, or knifing should the camp be on the verge of capture by the enemy. Amazingly this ex prisoner of war never heard any explosions despite his camp being sited half way between Nagasaki and Hiroshima. For him the dropping of the bomb was a miraculous reprieve from the atrocity the camp guards were instructed to carry out. Instead of talking on television sixty-four years later he would only have been another statistic.

Nagasaki and Hiroshima are now new cities. There would never be war for them again, that is their vow. It was not just the bombs that killed them but the proud stubborn and aloof army Commanders who were ready to choose fighting and dying with honour to surrender. Deciding the fate of their own people against an unknown holocaust was a gamble nobody had any right to take.

Back home news of the successful detonation was greeted with cheers. People yelled and stamped. Oppenheimer the scientist in charge clapped his hands in the air in a victory salute. The world had gone mad. The crews that returned after witnessing from the air the most appalling devastation in human history were amazed at the celebrations.
A huge party was arranged including a pie eating contest and jitterbug competition. All to celebrate the explosion of a bomb. If only they knew at that time what a terrible price mankind would pay for it. Little did they know the monster they had loosed upon future generations of every nation? So fearful are we of this monster today a protective space shield against incoming nuclear missiles over America was suggested by future President Ronald Reagan but that's another story for another day

Truman never regretted his decision to drop the bomb so bitter did he feel for the attack of the Japanese on Pearl Harbour and the murder of American prisoners of war in Japanese work camps. His reaction "When you have to deal with a beast you have to treat him like a beast." In 1958 he had still not changed his mind when he wrote to the Hiroshima City Council and said "Given similar circumstances I would order the bomb to be dropped again." It was written in a letter to the Hiroshima City Council which he instructed his secretary to send airmail.

But Truman's Secretary of War was not so sure. He urged international control over nuclear weapons because he was certain "If left unchecked they would destroy mankind." But his recommendations were never accepted. At that time in history nuclear secrets were too valuable to share.

Yet Robert Oppenheimer, the exultant scientist after the bomb went off was overwhelmed with grave doubts. A few months later in October 1945 he resigned from his post as director of the Los Alamos Laboratory. He put up fierce resistance to the development of the far more powerful Hydrogen bomb. His protests ruined him and he died a broken man. Very few of the crew had any regrets about their role. Bob Caron, the tail gunner however after seeing photographs of the burned children was disturbed enough to pose the question "I wonder whether we are getting into Gods territory?" No one is certain of this anymore. Even Einstein, the creator of the bomb had second thoughts about what he had released on humanity. Would the world ever get this evil genie back into the bottle again?

Sadly Einstein had a different vision for nuclear energy. With the never ending demand for energy Einstein looked on splitting the atom as the solution to this worldwide energy problem. For example one brick contained enough energy, if harnessed peacefully, to light up a whole city for one year. But that was to be a vision of Einstein's that has never been realized.

For Harry S. Truman August 6, 1945 ended his time on the world stage as a war President. Now he had a whole new list of problems to deal with on the home front.

Four days after the Japanese surrendered on September 2, 1945 Truman addressed Congress. The date was September 6. The drama for Truman was not yet over. In fact it was only beginning.   He stood up and asked for a permanent Fair Employment Practices Commission to aid blacks, wages, prices, rent control, old age benefits, public housing, a national health programme and a higher minimum wage. Still Harry couldn't please everybody for his critics complained he was going too far too fast. Who would be a President? Yet it wasn't Congress who destroyed his Bill but inflation, for prices had risen 25% by now and basic goods by 35%. Now Truman was in the middle of executive orders, court injunctions, strikes and conflicts with labour unions. He was finding that the job was not only different but a rollercoaster of variety and challenges for which he was never prepared. Yet I have already expressed the opinion that "nothing prepares anyone for the Presidency". See my notes on Buchanan the 15th President.

Looking back it is obvious that he was well advised on military affairs when he transferred control of nuclear energy away from the military to the civilian Atomic Energy Commission and reserved the authority to keep the use of the bomb solely under the control of the President. No person in the United States in 1945 was better placed to make this decision.
Harry Truman made a courageous and historic decision to desegregate the armed forces after Congress had refused to do so. After all it defies logic for special units of one colour to be in operation to fight on the battlefields of the world under one American flag. An American soldier was still a soldier black or white. Most discrimination in the armed forces ended after that, in fact the Bill opened up economic areas for advancement denied to blacks prior to this Bill.

But on the world stage Truman was till his own man and clashed with Stalin over reparations, the Polish border and the fate of Eastern Europe. He tried in a subtle way to inform Stalin of his strength by the ownership of the Atomic bomb.

His subtlety was wasted on Stalin for the Soviet dictator was already working on building his own bomb. The Soviets wanted to rebuild the devastated ruins of Russia with German money and negotiations got bogged down on the question of reparations. Truman fearing America would be saddled with the entire cost of caring for the defeated Germans, settled for compromise and accepted the ruling that each occupation zone would pay its own reparations. This however led to the future division of Germany. Daniel Yergin a historian concluded "Because they could not agree on how to govern Europe Truman and Stalin began to divide it."

Fear of nuclear attack was a new nightmare that worried him. A new space defence shield was to be the latest political idea against such a nuclear attack but that surfaced many years ahead in the Presidency of Ronald Reagan.

Memories of the World war receding into history produced statistics of the global holocaust which were unbelievable. The roll call of the dead and missing goes like this thanks again to

Harold Evans wonderful book entitled The American Century.

Killed or Missing	Country
292,131	America
544,596	British Commonwealth
70,000	British Civilians
14,500,000	Soviet Union
7,700,000	Soviet Civilians
1,506,000	Japan
672,000	Japanese
2,200,000	China
10,000,000	Chinese Civilians
279,820	Italy
93,000	Italian Civilians
210,000	France
173,260	French Civilians
2,850,000	Germany
10,000,000	German Civilians

Approximately fifty million people were killed on all sides. Greed, ambition and the lust for power on one side caused it, and a grim determination for justice on the other finished it. The sheer waste of humankind on the battlefields of the world only leads one into a stupefied silence of non-comprehension. It just does not bare thinking about.

Anyway the end of the war saw the establishment of many war tribunals both in Germany and Japan but the main one concerned the ringleaders of the Nazi movement ultimately responsible for the war in Europe.

Eighteen of these ringleaders were convicted of waging aggressive war and crimes against humanity. Their classic defence was that they were only carrying out their duties in their allegiance to Hitler. They expressed revulsion however when confronted by the evidence of atrocities at Dachau, Buchenwald and the Bergen-Belsen concentration camps. One of the accused actually cried out "May God have mercy on our souls. No power in heaven or on earth will erase this shame from my country, not in generations not in centuries." He was Hans Fritsch the press chief sentenced to nine years hard labour but pardoned after five years in 1950. Most of them were either hanged or imprisoned for life by the eight Judges appointed, two each from America, Britain, France and the Soviet Union. There are many books written on this sordid trial which was just as ugly and disturbing as the war itself and are best read as a separate entity to these notes on the Presidents. The monsters who ran this holocaust against the world got meticulously fair trials. Had Churchill had his way they would all have been shot without a trial.

Those hanged were: Von Ribbentrop – Foreign Minister, Field Marshal Wilhelm Keitel - mass murders in Russia, Hans Frank – Governor of Poland, Julius Streicher – Jew baiter, Ernst Kaltenbrunner – Concentration Camps, Interior Minister Wilhelm Frank, Alfred Rosenberg – Eastern Territories, Arthur Seyss–Inquart former Governor of Holland and Austria, Fritz Sauckel – Director of slave labour, Alfred Jodl- Hitler's military advisor, Martin Bormann in absentia.

Those imprisoned: Hess, Funk, Raeder, Doenitz, Speer, Von Schirach, Von Neurath, Fritzsche and Von Papen.

The hangings were grossly unprofessional, some even died by slow strangulation. Field Marshall Hermann Goering escaped by taking poison two hours before he was due on the scaffold. One charge against the German Command for the death of 4,254 Polish prisoners buried in Katyn forest failed. The Russian prosecutor N.D. Zorya had his own answer to the verdict. He immediately took his own life. Perhaps to avoid Russian justice for his failure on returning home after the Trials. The Nuremburg Trials began in September 1945 and ended with the sentences in October 1946, thirteen months later. Some war stories are still being told of this terrible holocaust in our history. Incidentally seven million people are said to have turned out in New York to welcome home General McArthur after his dismissal by Truman. It was to be his last hurrah.

But Truman had yet another problem on his hands as millions of American servicemen came home to mass demobilization just like after World War I. Inflation, scarcity of meat, labour unrest, and the Korean War were also hammering at the White House front door for attention. Truman was under siege and worst of all Congress was not helping. At a time when anti-inflation measures were needed Congress passed a Bill for tax cuts. On top of it all he was now the world leader in the Cold War fighting foreign tyrannies which were suppressing freedom in the weaker nations. The world was now a far different place and far more dangerous than it had ever been and the existence of the atom bomb and its worldwide threat overshadowed everything.

The Monroe Doctrine was replaced by the Truman Doctrine which led to a new Europe built by American money to contain the expansion of Communism everywhere by aid and arms. The money injected was colossal. Twelve thousand million dollars was the price America was prepared to pay to contain the juggernaut of Russian satellite States across Europe. Fear tainted everything in Europe and back home. McCarthyism and the witch hunt he generated against Communist sympathisers grew to ridiculous proportions bordering on panic. A new phrase was coined and was soon common currency in political debate – The Cold War.

The fundamental reason for the Cold War was a breakdown in trust between Stalin and Roosevelt. Both sides broke war time agreements. Stalin refused to honour pledges of free elections in Eastern Europe. So Truman refused to hand over reparation payments by Germany to help the Soviets rebuild a war devastated USSR. A European recovery plan was drawn up by Truman to rehabilitate a free Europe. It was known as the Marshall Plan. Western Germany was to be rebuilt and integrated into a larger Europe. The conflict with the USSR got worse and lead to Russia closing off Eastern Berlin in a blockade that was to last from June 24, 1948 until May 12, 1949.

At a meeting of the United Nations, Trotsky bellowed "We will slam the door so that all Europe will shake." There was much sabre rattling which Kissinger thought didn't make sense in view of America's superiority in nuclear weapons. Gromyko figured the Americans would never use the bomb again.

The Soviets pressed on with their plans and at 6 a.m. on June 24, 1948 all roads, rail and water traffic were blocked off to West Berlin. Even electricity had been cut to a trickle. Truman's decision to create a separate German State was reaping a bitter whirlwind. Unfortunately the row created what is known today as the "Berlin Airlift". As usual Truman showed no regrets. His words were not exactly taken out of the diplomatic text book when he said "I'm tired of babying the Soviets."

Soon Truman was faced with the consequences of his actions. His job now was to sustain continuity of life and commerce in West Germany. Food supplies had to be maintained and 8,000 tonnes of coal per day had to be flown in. The U.S. Air Force and the RAF with the help of civilian American, English and French pilots flew bigger and bigger aircraft night and day in all weathers from as far away as Montana and eventually achieved the magic figure of 8,000 tonnes of coal per day. Factories were kept open and cooking was still possible for two hours per day.

The Soviets finally called off the blockade on May 12, 1949 eleven months after it started. The world sighed with relief as this game of Russian roulette came to an end.

Truman continued to make waves in world politics. The most controversial agreement of his international career was the establishment of the new State of Israel on May 14, 1948 repercussions of which are still being felt to this day nearly sixty years later. Palestine was partitioned to create two separate States one Arab and one Jewish. This went back to the British Balfour Declaration of 1917 which first promised the Jews support for a national homeland. Now it was here. Modern readers will see on their TV sets daily the trouble it is causing between both Parties. As yet there is still no agreement sixty-one years later in 2009. Perhaps Ernest Bevin if he ever returned to us would wag a finger in our direction today and say "I told you so."

All of the foregoing is a breathtaking view of world events that happened on Truman's watch directly after the end of the war, and the two most influential people in Truman's international success were Dean Acheson and General George C. Marshall.

Perhaps they deserve a mention here to understand their personalities and approach working under Harry S. Truman the 33rd President. Both Marshall and Acheson were not crutches supporting a lame duck President but two people who served him out of genuine loyalty. Marshall in particular had a high sense of duty, a natural authority, steadiness of judgment and was a true decision maker. But it was his reserve, self-sufficiency and impeccability that also made him extremely likeable. He was controlled, spoke low, never misbehaved thus making him a person you would listen to. He was never known to lose his temper and accepted his disappointments with dignity. One of those was being rejected for the command of Overlord in favour of Eisenhower. "I have no feelings," he told Dean Acheson "accept those I reserve for Mrs. Marshall." No one found him pompous or priggish. Truman's daughter Margaret who met Marshall when she was twenty before her father was Vice President wrote "I fell in love instantly with this remarkable man.... He was marvellous at making you forget his importance while simultaneously making you feel that you and what you were saying were important to him." He was good not at creating ideas but choosing between them.

Acheson's friendship with Truman went back many years. He was never a crony. A Connecticut gentleman and son of a Bishop. He could be best described as a Patrician of great intelligence. He had no wealth or any aspirations to it and his education was that classical product of the Eastern establishment Groton, Yale and Harvard Law School. He never sought office but then again he did not suffer fools gladly. He had some eccentric and reactionary views but he served Truman with wisdom, flair and an old world loyalty. Acheson's friendship, Truman was later to appreciate, was in stark contrast to the type of Missouri opportunist politicians who had infiltrated his Administration. Acheson was a distinguished cultural man who gave Truman the reassurance he needed during his leadership.

Strange bedfellows were Acheson and Aneurin Bevan. Acheson seemed to have relished

Bevan's earthly style particularly his sense of humour. On the other hand Marshall found Bevan "a rather course fellow".

But even great men have their critics and Marshall was no exception for the Marshall Plan he produced has its detractors today. Historians were the major critics perhaps because of their clinical isolation from the emotions surrounding historical events. They concluded that the Marshall Plan really made no difference. Recovery they said was really based on restocking and would have happened anyway. But others countered "If it did not start the recovery it certainly underpinned it. You can take your pick."

Roy Jenkins, a British Chancellor of the Exchequer in his book Truman tells a story about Truman the year before his re-election to a second term in 1948. "The year 1947 began for Truman on his Presidential yacht steaming up the Potomac. He arrived back at the White House at 8.45 a.m. on that New Years Eve and telephoned his wife and daughter in Independence. He was a lonely man which was nothing new for Harry Truman."

Why he spent so much time apart from his family even when business didn't demand it was never fully explained. Truman was very much aware of the approaching Presidential Election the following year and as Truman implied in his autobiography was very much aware he was still a caretaker President after Roosevelt. "I always knew" Truman wrote "that from April 1945 to January 1949 what I would really be doing was filling out the fourth term of Roosevelt who was a great President, but I had some ideas of my own and in order to carry them out I had to run for re-election and be re-elected and that is exactly what happened." Sam Rosenman a trusted Truman advisor and expert on Roosevelt said "Truman was committed to the idea that he had become President only because Roosevelt had chosen him and he was obliged to recognize that it was FDR's polices the people had endorsed in 1944.

This is why the election of 1948 was so important to him. Harry S. Truman was determined to be his own man with his own policies during his second term.

However despite his ambitions to have a second term Truman would not be Truman if he did not support and say things that were unpopular regardless of the consequences. His loyalty to Tom Prendergast, his blunt language to Stalin at Potsdam, and even his rows with Roosevelt were all part of his honesty. So he did not help his election chances in 1948 by his pro-Zionist stance on the creation of Israel. Even Aneurin Bevan his most powerful ally and friend in Europe was irritated by this.

Bevin made his feelings known in the House of Commons by sneering from the dispatch box "Regarding the agitation in the United States.... For 100,000 Jews to be put into Palestine I hope it will not be misunderstood in America if I say with the purest of motives that that was because they did not want too many of them in New York."

Bevan had another go nine months later which resulted in Dockers refusing to unload his luggage from the Queen Mary in New York harbour and being booed by the crowd at a baseball game in Yankee stadium. But the issue of the Jews challenged Truman's patience to breaking point. In August 1947 twelve months previously, he remarked to Mrs. Roosevelt "I fear very much that the Jews are like all underdogs. When they get on top they are just as intolerant and cruel as the people were to them when they were underneath. I regret this very much because my sympathy has always been on their side."

A couple of months after this Truman deliberately provoked Senator Pepper of Florida by lying to him with the words "I have personally burnt 35,000 pieces of unread pro-Zionist Mail." In an interview with two Senators visiting him in the White House he said "I am not a New Yorker and all these people are pleading a special interest. I am an American..... The Jews themselves are making it impossible to do anything for them."

Truman was once so upset by the words of one visitor, who mentioned the Palestine question after being warned not to, he became very agitated and abrupt. The man in question was shocked by the reaction he had brought on himself "I suddenly found myself thinking that my dear friend, the President of the United States was at that moment as close to being an anti-Semite as a man could possibly be and I was shocked that some of our Jewish leaders should be responsible for Mr. Truman's attitude."

All that turbulence concerning the Palestine – Jewish question was played out throughout his electioneering. Another problem which he never ducked was what he called the Jim Crow laws which maintained segregation in the South. He also proposed laws to punish those responsible for the hanging of blacks without trials called "Lynching"; laws to protect the voting rights of blacks and a fair employment practices commission to end job discrimination. All these measures that were written into the Democratic Party platform by the Northern Democrats almost brought about a split in the Democratic Party. All of them were "hot potatoes" which he never shirked from tackling head on.

His opponents calling themselves the Dixiecrats broke away to form the Progressive Party. Yes, it was going to be a hard uphill fight but Truman set out on a cross country "U.S. whistle-stop tour" to defend his record during which the catch cry slogan "Give em Hell Harry" was invented.

His opponents concentrated on the view that he was incompetent, unappealing and unelectable. "It was his duty to the Party to withdraw" and these were only his enemies inside the Party. Eisenhower was their choice. Truman was tempted to withdraw but when he recovered and he went into battle it was only Eisenhower's decision to issue a comprehensive refusal to go forward that knocked sense into everyone.

In the other camp was New York Governor Thomas E. Dewey. Occasionally Truman addressed large rallies of about 23,000 but mostly he gave short speeches from the back of his train. The train by the way was quite an invention. It had sixteen coaches. Truman travelled in the rear which had been specially converted into bedrooms bathrooms, kitchen, dining room, and sitting room. The old train dining room was now a suite of offices for his staff. Next came a newsroom and a signal corps car. Then the sleeping and living accommodation for travelling personnel including about sixty journalists and photographers.

Thanks to Roy Jenkins' book Truman we learn his trip took fifteen days covering eighteen States out to San Francisco by Chicago, Iowa and the mountain States, down to Los Angeles through the Sunbelt and back by St. Louis. He worked hard starting at 5.45 a.m. with his last appearance at 8.10 p.m. in the evening. Some days he made sixteen speeches. The climax to his daily routine was to introduce Bess and his daughter Margaret to the crowds surrounding his train. In Southern States it was Miss Margaret. The crowds, though not enthusiastic were curious but friendly. Three million people must have turned out to see him.

Yet there was an air of pessimism in the camp when he retired for the last time with a bath, a sandwich and a glass of milk before going to bed early. The husting went on but one morning the depression was lifted when Dewey finally conceded victory to Truman at 10 a.m. Mrs.

Truman arrived back at the White House tired but happy, then in her own humble way she told the White House assistant usher "It looks like you are going to have to put up with us for another four years." More important for Truman he knew his worries were over. At last was the President in his own right.

If Harry S. Truman had any plans for a third term there was no chance he could achieve such an ambition for the year before on March 26, 1947 the 22nd Amendment to the Constitution was passed. This limited the Presidential term to two four year terms per President.

However on Thursday January 20, 1949 Harry S. Truman took the oath of office to commence his second four year term. The oath was administered by Chief Justice Frederick Moore Vinson on a brilliant clear cloudless day. The weather was sharp and crisp with a temperature of between 30 degrees and 40 degrees. There was a newly constructed Grandstand holding the 44,000 people who came to enjoy the spectacle. The three hour parade seven and a half miles long was witnessed by about a million people in Washington. Thanks to television coverage ten million people nationwide looked in and another 18 million listened to it on radio. Over 700 airplanes and five B36 bombers flew past overhead. The traditional inaugural dinner completed the festivities at which nearly 10,000 guests danced the night away in the National Guard Armoury. The White House being under repair was bypassed in favour of Blair House by the newly installed President Harry S. Truman.

Little did Truman know that two years later on November 1, 1950 at 2.15 p.m. an assassination attempt would be made on his life, a depressing occupational hazard for all the Presidents from now on.

Oscar Collazo and Griselio Torresola, two Puerto Rican Nationalists thought they had an ideal opportunity to storm Truman's substitute head quarters at Blair House when they tried to shoot their way in.

A White House Guard Leslie Coffelt was killed and two others wounded. On July 24, 1952 Collazo was sentenced to die on August 1, but his sentence was commuted to life imprisonment. Torresolo had been killed in the assassination battle.

But Truman's life in the Presidency seemed destined to be fraught with war troubles when America became involved in what is known today as the Korean War. The United Nations sent troops from fifteen nations under the UN flag who were commanded by the brilliant but controversial American General, Douglas MacArthur last heard of in these notes marching gloriously into battle against the squatters of Hooverville in the Hoover Presidency. But little did he know that one day Truman would reluctantly have to end MacArthur's army career. This is how it happened.

Truman's intentions had been to confine the war to South Korea only but MacArthur's troops then moved into North Korea. Things became very tense when the UN were warned off entering China. Perhaps it seemed right to head for China as a General but this was politics at its highest level. MacArthur continued agitating to go on into China and publicly defied Truman in the process. Truman had no option but to dismiss him and replace him with General Matthew Ridgway.

Truman's remarks on the dismissal are almost unprintable he said. "I didn't fire him because he was a dumb son of a bitch, though he was. I fired him because he wouldn't respect the authority of the President." Incidentally Truman could not only sack troublemakers but rehabilitate others. Defying convention once again he appointed Herbert Hoover, the ex-President, to a job in Europe and Hoover repaid this compliment in spades by carrying out his duties just like he did as a young man at the ripe old age of eighty-five.

But elsewhere there was another war brewing. Alongside these historic events Truman had another problem which made him act out of character. He lost his temper. Not with the Koreans, not with the Chinese, not with General MacArthur but with the music critic of the Washington Post who had dared to give Margaret "a lousy review" as Truman put it. Truman went on "He put my baby as low as he could and he made the young accompanist look like a dub."

Truman ranted to all who were willing to listen to him. The First and Second World War, Korea, and maybe even the Civil War paled into insignificance beside this slight to his daughter's professional integrity. "I wrote to him," Truman snarled "and told him what I thought of him." Unfortunately General George Marshall didn't help either when he stoked up the anti by adding his opinion about the unfortunate music critic. "The only thing he didn't criticize was the varnish on the piano," grinned Marshall. Later the embarrassed Margaret managed to calm the whole situation down with a joke that put the row finally to bed.

But lady luck was due to smile on Truman. Before the Presidential election of 1948 the Republicans were so convinced that Dewey would win the Presidency they voted for some very generous changes that seemed to them well worth it to see the back of sixteen years of Democratic rule. Truman was really delighted with the bonanza that fell into his lap. For a start they had doubled his salary to $100,000 and added $50,000 of tax free expenses. Overnight life was a bowl of cherries for him compared to his old income. He could now live more easily than before. However the Korean War was to deplete a major portion of the funds available for his bonanza.

Despite the Chinese problem, McCarthy's antics and MacArthur's insubordination, his days in the second term were quite uneventful. Perhaps his handling of world affairs, swift and decisive, contributed to much of the comfort zone he moved in during his second term. In fact Truman has been highly praised by leading figures of the day for his part on the international stage. For instance the creation of NATO under his leadership would in any other period have merited him a third term and justified his re-election.

Yet his final year and a half of the Presidency was downhill. Despite his wonderful achievements over the first six years of political upheaval his later time in office was full of one petty scandal after another sending his poll ratings down to 23% as a result. He had to sack his Attorney General and appoint a third replacement since he got rid of Roosevelt's Biddle.

The saddest loss was an old friend General George Marshall who withdrew from Defence in 1951. His other best friend Acheson was undermined by McCarthy and so his final months were spent knowing time was running out for him and doing things for the last time. One wonders is this really politics or the curse of most U.S. Presidents? Perhaps eight years in office is too long. But there was one final flash of lightening that lit up his receding days in the White House – the visit of a man he revered as one of the greats of world politics, Winston Churchill. He, in Truman's opinion represented "greatness without Roosevelt's pretensions."

Churchill met Eisenhower with whom he would have to work for some time into the future but met him unobtrusively. Back in Washington, Churchill paid Truman a massive compliment. He confessed his dismay when Roosevelt died but added significantly to Truman "I misjudged you badly. Since that time you, more than any other man, have saved western civilization."

What a compliment!

On January 15, 1952 Harry Truman gave his last farewell broadcast to the nation which was televised for the first time. He then drove to Dean Acheson's house in Georgetown where there was a lunch for the outgoing Cabinet. Truman was in great form. [What a contrast this was to the last days in office of some previous Presidents]. Margaret his daughter described it as "An absolutely wonderful affair full of jokes and laughter and a few tears." It was then time for his journey to Union Station, were five hundred people waved him goodbye on his last trip in the Presidents Pullman car.

There was a short speech from the rear carriage, reminiscent of old times, then a few bars of Auld Lang Syne as it pulled away. Still the crowds were lining the track at various towns including Independence and St. Louis. Typical Truman, saw him having a haircut in one of the stations' barber shops on the way. This picture for me lives on long after the other Truman anecdotes have been forgotten. Maybe because no subsequent President would ever again do so much train travelling. Later describing his feelings on his homecoming he said "Mrs. Truman and I were overcome. It was the pay off for thirty years of hell and hard work." He was sixty-seven. In retirement Harry Truman continued his brisk daily morning walks with reporters, those who could last the pace in tow. He also found time to tour the country in support of nominees to State and Federal offices. The nation's colleges and universities were also the beneficiaries of his visits lecturing on American Government some of which were published in his books Freedom and Equality, Truman speaks and Free World and Free Trade. One of his greatest thrills of course was the opening of the Harry S. Truman Library in Independence to which he dedicated himself in July 1957.

So let's summarize what the Presidency of Harry Truman was all about. I haven't done this for previous Presidents but the broad spectrum of his exploits on the world stage I feel merits a summary. Truman the Statesman grew with the job. His ability to master his brief on all aspects of life in post-war America and Europe was impressive to say the least. Looking back on that period and the problems which confronted him at home and abroad makes one shake one's head in amazement and admiration. Although he had not got the legal and sophisticated background of his predecessors his choice for Presidency was a praiseworthy tribute to the wisdom of the American people. His talents reflected the very character of the people itself based on hard work, honesty and common sense.

Listing the problems he tackled may prove my point.

Demobilization of millions of soldiers around the world and absorbing them back into civic life.
Ending the war with Japan and Korea.
The atomic bomb decision which was a momentous one.
Sorting out the economic chaos of post-war Europe.
A "Fair Deal" programme for America. Nothing rattled him. He met the Russians at Potsdam and realized that the treachery of Stalin would demand caution from the Allies in a new Europe.
Signing the Japanese surrender document on September 2, 1945 aboard the battleship SS Missouri. Japan was occupied soon after.
The Marshall Plan.
Fighting the spread of Communism for which he budgeted $ 400 million in the spring of 1947. It was later raised to $700 million.
His Secretary of State, George Marshall set up the Marshall Plan to handle the economic rehabilitation of post-war Europe which was eventually to cost seventeen billion dollars over

four years.

Another problem to be overcome was the Berlin Blockade which led to the Berlin Air Lift.

NATO was formed to protect the West from Russian aggression under the command of a future American President General Dwight Eisenhower.

He took the atomic bomb out of military hands and placed it under civilian control.

He created the Atomic Energy Commission and reorganized the army under one department called the National Defence.

Unfortunately Truman made many enemies at home when militancy in the Trade Unions pushed him into confrontation with the powerful Unions of the Railroads and the Mining Industry. Despite all these conflicts he was re-elected President for a second term by a vast majority.

The spread of Communism was the dominant fear that preoccupied his second term leading to the obnoxious period of McCarthyism personified by witch hunts against suspects at every level of society most of whom were unfairly vilified. Finally the Korean War arrived in the last year of his Presidency. Cometh the hour cometh the man. We can't leave out an attempted assassination in which one of the assassins was shot dead. His handling of General McArthur was decisive and effective when the Maverick General was recklessly threatening to invade China without the permission of his Commander-in-Chief. Truman fearlessly sacked him. Although McArthur was feted as a hero by seven million people on his arrival home to New York, Truman had proved who was boss and McArthur had had his last hurrah. He finally handed over power to a real hero General Eisenhower as mentioned earlier.

The smooth seamless farewell of his departure from the White House was full of nostalgic warmth and goodwill. He gave a real show business goodbye with lots of love to the Staffers who shed genuine tears for both Bess and himself before that last train journey home.

Despite the glory that went with the title "President of the United States" there wasn't too many Presidents who so happily closed the door of the White House behind them like Harry S. Truman.

As we say goodbye to Truman I am sure he will be remembered also for his "in your face" style in the Presidency. It was much more earthy and honest than previous Presidents yet it didn't lose him any friends in the press corp.

Here are a list of one-liners I can recall to emphasise my point. Some one-liners didn't encourage the recipient to like him. Molotov, the Russian Foreign Minister was no exception. After giving Molotov a broadside for failing to deliver on the promises made at Yalta, Molotov complained "I have never been talked to like that." "Carry out your agreement and you won't get talked to like that," said Truman. No diplomatic language there. On his return home from Potsdam Truman told a visiting British Diplomat "I'm here to make decisions and whether they prove right or wrong I am going to make them."

At Potsdam he was surprised to discover Stalin was only five foot five inches high. Truman a little irreverently referred to him as "A little squirt." We referred to the press earlier so here is a one-liner about them. An article in Newsweek by fifty political journalists predicted a landslide for his opponent Dewey in the Presidential election. It pulled no punches and his Aides tried to protect his feelings by hiding it. They needn't have worried. The effervescent Truman came back with all guns blazing. "I know everyone of those fifty fellows. There isn't one of them who has enough sense to pound sand into a rat hole."

When supporters first coined the catchphrase "Give em hell Harry" he corrected them with this advice "I never give anyone hell I just tell the truth and they think its hell."

He could be very amusing in some situations he didn't take seriously. At a serviceman's club he was asked why he became a politician. He joked "My choice early in life was either to be a piano player in a whorehouse or a politician and to tell the truth there's hardly a difference."

His comments about his beloved wife Bess and his reason for proposing to her was pure Truman. "I only had one sweetheart in my life from the time I was six," he said. "It ended in 1917 when I realized I might not come back from the war and that gave me the courage to propose to her." So started a lifelong partnership that only ended when he died on St. Stephen's day December 26, 1972 after a marriage lasting 53 years, 181 days.

In his early eighties, as might be expected, his powers of mind and body were deteriorating. He lost a lot of weight and began to waste dramatically. His last six years found him confined to the house but he continued to read the newspapers everyday until his life slowly faded. On St. Stephens Day December 26, 1972 he died in the courtyard of his beloved library. His memorial stone lists each office he held proudly from Eastern Judge to President of the United States.

His faithful widow Bess survived him by another ten years dying at the age of 97 years, 247 days on October 18, 1982. She was buried alongside her beloved Harry in Independence, MO.

34th President   Dwight D. Eisenhower

"Ike"
Born 1890
Died 1969
79 Years of age
Term: 8 years
1953 –1961
Age 63

Party: Republican
Profession: Army Officer
County: New York
Ancestry: Swiss, German
Estate: Unknown
Hobbies: Painting, Bridge, Fishing and Golf

Physical Description: Height 5 foot 10 ½ inches, 168lbs, bald with fringe of sandy greying hair, blue eyes, ruddy complexion, engaging smile.

Significant extract from inaugural speech on Monday January 21, 1957:
"We live on a land of plenty but rarely has this earth known such peril as today….No nation however old or great escapes this tempest of change and turmoil. The decisive force is international Communism and the power that it controls."

DWIGHT D. EISENHOWER

The world needs no reminding of what Dwight David Eisenhower was famous for before he became the 34th President of the United States. Their isn't a man or woman alive who does not know he was the Commander-in-Chief of the Allied forces in Europe during and at the end of the Second World War. He is rightly honoured for his part as the top General in charge of the invading forces which landed on the beaches of Normandy in France in a multi-nation expedition called "Overlord" which signalled the beginning of the end for Nazi Germany.

What the world may not know however is how accidentally he became a soldier in the first place. For Eisenhower going to West Point was not a patriotic choice to become a soldier but a chance to get a free college education as a lad. He managed to pass the entrance examination but after injuring his knee playing football he had decided to resign from West Point. Had he done so the world would never have heard of Dwight D. Eisenhower? The hand of fate is never given credit for making history but surely it was fate that selected a loyal and persuasive roommate to be on hand to get him to change his mind. Five years later in 1915 he graduated 61st in a class of 164.

So began an illustrious army career lasting thirty-eight years in which he rose up through the ranks to the highest pinnacle of his profession as a soldier in the United States army.

Just like Woodrow Wilson the Academic and Herbert Hoover the Engineer, Eisenhower also switched to another career very late in life when he too turned to politics and a new life as President of the United States. But let's get the story started right at the beginning.
He was the third son of David and Ida Stover Eisenhower and was born on October 14, 1890 in Dennison, Texas. The following year the family moved to Abilene, Kansas which was to remain the family home for the rest of Ike's life. It was here his six brothers were also born. The house was a small two storey one at 201 South East 4th Street. When they moved in it was no more than a shack; with no running water, no inside toilet and no electricity. His brothers went on to become a banker, a lawyer, a pharmacist, an engineer and a bureaucrat each earning more money than Ike did as a Major in the U.S. army. His father had a very modest job as a $10 a week railroad hand until a relative found him a job as a mechanic at the Belle Springs Creamery.

Ike's father David was a very modest man, unobtrusive and almost anonymous but very well respected in the local community. They were a happy religious close-knit family. The only ambitions Ida and David had were for the future of their seven sons. It was only in his later life that Dwight realized just how poor his parents really were. Their philosophy for the boys was "Opportunity is all about you. Reach out and take it." They also taught the boys a few other rules to live by – honesty, self-reliance, integrity and fear of God. To motivate them they were told "If you stay at home you will always be looked on as a boy."

Prayer was an important part of living in the Eisenhower household and the Bible played a major role in family life for they all took their share of reading it to the others at meal times. Washing the dishes was not the sole preserve of mum for all the lads took their turn at this task. Ike, as he was known in the family, looking back remembers how deeply involved his mother made herself in their lives mending their clothes, making meals, encouraging, sympathising with and complimenting all their efforts. She was the hub around which all the family buzzed. It was also a competitive environment for Ike surrounded as he was and challenged constantly by his six other brothers. They even fought together to measure their toughness as fighters. His father though keeping a low profile played a key role by pushing them to win at everything. The town of Abilene although holding only 4,000 people, was self-sufficient and had all the intimate familiarity and security of a small town. Dwight loved the place and often reminisced nostalgically about it. The standards of decency and integrity he had learnt were mostly down to that small town of Abilene.

Later we will discover the part Abilene played as a major cattle town at the end of the 18th Century. Abilene was the end of the journey for the great cattle drives across the prairies bringing thousands of steers for sale to cattle barons waiting for them in Abilene.

Ike's school was just across the road from his house and one of his favourite subjects would not surprise anyone who knew him in later years; yes, military history.

Eisenhower's ambition at that time was to work, save money and go to the University of Michigan. A College education with the chance to play football and baseball. Now what could be better than that? Then he found himself looking up examinations for the Service Academies and chose the exam for West Point which he duly passed. When the time came for him to take the train out of Abilene, Mum held back the tears and dad kept an iron control of his emotions until the train was out of sight. Ike was now 6 foot tall and 170 lbs of muscle, no fat. Clear blue eyes and brown hair which gave him an attractive athletic look to the girls. He grinned easily and his whole approach to life was practical rather than creative. Just making things happen.

One of the exciting things about West Point he found was its glorification of its traditional past especially its history. Every day he lived with it. Grant's room, Lee's Room, Sherman's, Luster's and Winfield Scoot – they were all revered.
It is not possible to cover all aspects of West Point life in a piece as short as this whose sole object is to reflect the essence of the man. Getting the brushstrokes to the painting right is a journey in pursuit of truth. Pranks were many and varied at West Point and Eisenhower in later life loved to talk about them. However, breaking the rules was always a challenge, a sort of inward rebellion to maintain a semblance of individuality in an environment of discipline and conformity.

Take for instance the rule for not smoking. Because it was forbidden Eisenhower smoked, even against the disapproval of his roommate. Inevitably he was caught and suffered the punishments of walking tours and being confined to his room for hours. Still he smoked. Sometimes he was deliberately untidy in his room or a latecomer to guard mounting. The result was he was 125 out of 164 in discipline. This was almost a badge of honour to Eisenhower because it was another element of fear he had confronted – the fear of lower grades. Breaking regulations was in Eisenhower's eyes part of the training. His outburst against one of his classmates was typical. "Christ, he has always been afraid to break regulations," Eisenhower observed with impatience.

He hit his lowest point when his knee crumpled in a game of football. When a plaster cast was removed he was told he would never play again and he almost resigned from the Academy. Life seemed to have little meaning and his studies suffered. But it was all part of character building for he bounced back to become a cheerleader and coach to the football team. Into this role he poured all his energies and analytical skills all of which became part of the General he was to become. Every adversary was his teacher, every setback a challenge that honed his self-discipline giving him a fierce determination to conquer.

He duly graduated, but adversity struck him again in the shape of Gladys Harding, the daughter of a businessman who owned the local freight firm in town.

The reason I use the word adversity was the trouble she caused him. This time he would not win. Some say it was her wish to be a full-time piano player at home while he was away on duty. Others felt it was her father's opposition to her marrying a soldier boy. She eventually married someone else which ended when her husband died.

Now he was going to concentrate on army life or so he thought, but cupid was again too busy for that and on a Sunday afternoon in October 1915 he met Mamie or Mary Geneva Doud. She was as impressed with Ike as he was with her at the their very first meeting. He called every fifteen minutes on the phone next day. Every date he asked for he was rejected but in the end she cancelled her appointments and went out with him. He proposed on Valentines Day, 1916 and she accepted, a milestone that came only six months after their first date. However, her father would not allow her to marry until she was twenty-one years old in the coming November. But Ike being Ike changed the plans and they married in July 1916. Mamie was quite well off in her home life for she even had her own maid, so getting married to a soldier meant a lot of disadvantages for her but she didn't care. She met Dwight's family after the honeymoon and had fried chicken for breakfast. It was a sad time for Mamie as she had just lost one of her brothers before the wedding.

It had been a turbulent year for Ike in 1918. In October he was promoted to Lieutenant Colonel and on November 18, he was to go to France with his armoured unit. One week before he was to go these orders were cancelled for the armistice had just been signed on the November 11, 1918.

"I suppose we will spend the rest of our lives explaining why we didn't get into the war," Eisenhower complained. Little did he know there was another World War waiting for him to get into but he would have to wait nearly twenty-five years for it? Eisenhower was still depressed about the news in 1918. You can understand his frustration for after all he was a new ambitious young eager soldier trained to fight a war. Now it seemed it was a war that would never happen for him. Worse still he was part of an organization that was shrinking and being dismantled.

Then came a tragedy for Ike and suddenly his army problems didn't matter anymore when his son Icky contracted scarlet fever. After many desolate days worry Icky died. Later he wrote about Icky. "He was the one I have never been able to forget completely." Eisenhower wrote this in his old age. It was a tragedy not unlike that suffered by Calvin Coolidge during his Presidency that even robbed Calvin of his will to continue in the Presidency. Eisenhower sent flowers to Mamie on every birthday of Icky's for the next fifty years and made sure his remains would be buried with them when they died. The pain of those days would live with them throughout their marriage. But fate relented and the Eisenhower's were blessed with a second son called John, three years later on August 3, 1923.

But providence is always standing in the wings to surprise you. Providence for Ike was in the person of a General Fox Connor who befriended him during his crisis when he was at his lowest ebb. He made Ike concentrate on serious military literature which Ike did to the letter. He also gave Eisenhower pep talks on tactics in war. Finally he advised him to get himself assigned to a genius – Colonel George Marshall.

But General Fox Connor was a bit of a genius himself for he forecast to Eisenhower in 1919 that the Second World War would happen twenty years hence and that America would fight it with allies. Its no wonder Eisenhower idolized the man. He described his time with Fox Connor as a sort of post graduate school in military affairs. "In a lifetime of associating with great men Fox Connor is the one figure to whom I owe an incalculable debt," Eisenhower said this with pride when he had just reached the pinnacle of success.

Someone else of historic importance was also impressed by Eisenhower – General MacArthur himself. MacArthur said to Eisenhower "The number of personal requests for your services brought to me by heads of many of the army's principal activities during the past few years furnish convincing proof of the reputation you have established as an outstanding soldier. I can say no more than that. This reputation coincides exactly with my own judgement....." Need we say anything further about Eisenhower's qualities as a soldier? Yet it is amusing to observe at this point that later in an outburst of petulance he arrogantly referred to Ike as the best clerk he ever had. No man ever got too close to MacArthur. Nevertheless Ike looked ruefully at the reality of his army life. No matter how high the praise, promotion only came to those in rotation and according to seniority. At his age he concluded his chances of ever getting a "Star" was remote. But as we told you earlier Ike was a master of adversary. He adopted a change of tactics now. "My only ambition in the army is to make everybody with whom I work regret my going when ordered to other duties." It seems at least he had solved the problem of boredom.

Poor Eisenhower's life seemed to have ground to a halt as he saw it. All he really had to look forward to was retirement and his army memories in his old age. But Eisenhower was worrying unnecessarily for his performances had been noticed by others and he was soon in great demand as follows. He was made Aide to General John Pershing and then Aide to General MacArthur in 1935. After that he became Chief Military Adviser to the Philippine Government and Chief of Staff to General MacArthur. Ike was now moving among the top brass in the army.

An expanding army needed Ike's talents and promoted him to Brigadier General after Pearl Harbour. General George Marshall brought him to Washington in charge of the war plans division. His next promotion was Major General in March 1942, then Lieutenant General in the U.S. army European Theatre of Operations based in London. His next job was head of the Allied forces in North Africa fighting Rommel. He was promoted General in 1942 and the following year 1943 cleared the Germans out of Africa. The invasion of Sicily was next on his CV and finally directing the invasion of Italy.

At this point, when we get our breath back, we can see that the progress and experiences of Dwight Eisenhower had been extraordinary and this for a soldier who didn't think he would ever see war back in 1918 when he seemed to be going nowhere with his spirits at their lowest ebb.

On March 10, 1942 Eisenhower's dad died. Somehow time was so scarce for him he hardly had time to record it in his diary.

On hearing this terrible news Eisenhower wrote "War is not soft. It has no time to indulge even the deepest and most sacred emotions." Many boyhood memories of his father came flooding back. Almost as a gesture of defiance as well as respect for his beloved father he quit the job early at 7.30 p.m. noting "I haven't the heart to go on tonight."

On March 12, two days later as his dad David the ex-mechanic and railway worker was being laid to rest in Abilene, Eisenhower closed his office door just to spend half an hour thinking about his father. He sat there contemplating on his father's ever present honesty, pride and independence and most of all his quiet undemonstrative modest lifestyle. "I am proud he was my father" Eisenhower wrote. Then as if on an after thought he noted "It was always so difficult to let him know the great depth of my affection for him." Strangely that's a dilemma many a busy man has to face when the "main man" passes on and realization reminds him of all the conversations that never can be; now leaving a sort of sad emptiness behind. Time gives no man a second chance.

I have glossed over Eisenhower's battles in North Africa, Sicily and Italy among other places out of which I am sure we could have extracted many interesting stories worth telling. My instincts are to find out all about "Overlord" and how it affected Eisenhower for that was truly the pinnacle of Eisenhower's career.

Before doing that it's worth talking about Eisenhower the soldier and the reasons he was so popular with his troops. In Italy while he was outnumbered eleven divisions to twenty-five for the Germans, and his men were bogged down in rain and mud, and without "landing craft" to attack from the sea; Eisenhower's two army units the fifth and the eighth had reached a stalemate. His new headquarters were just north of Naples.

On a cruise around the Isle of Capri a large villa caught his eye "Whose is that," he enquired. "Yours," he was told. "And that one," he asked of a bigger Villa. "Damn it that's not my Villa and that's not General Spaatz' Villa. None of these will belong to any General as long as I am boss around here. This is supposed to be a rest centre – not a playground for the Brass....." He later wired Spaatz. "This is directly contrary to my policies and must stop at once." While Eisenhower was not thought to be a gifted battlefield Commander by his fellow Generals Bradley, Patton and Montgomery, he had one gift which placed him head and shoulders above all his critics – Leadership. He had it in spades.

It was his understanding of men, which helped hold three million soldiers together fighting on a line from the Baltic to the Alps. He was always aware he was leading the armies of many different nations. One story underlines this. After relieving one of his officers of his command for abusing an ally he said "It is all right to call someone "a son of a bitch" but not a British son of a bitch." Word reached the troops of his stand and they were delighted. Struggling in the mud of Italy it was great for the ordinary soldier to hear of the top brass being put in their place by Eisenhower.

The fact that he also swore like a sergeant, something Washington disapproved of, made him more popular with the men than ever. Visiting them in the front line was not something he did out of the war manual – he genuinely loved it. He listened to the troops complaints first hand and when he could he helped them. He enjoyed escaping from the VIP's. "Chatting with the troops cheered him up" he said and "revitalized him". The whole army was proud of him because of his tact, good sense and modesty. But when his sister-in-law wrote and asked him to order Mamie to San Antonio for the winter. He declined. "I give lots of orders," he told Mamie, "but I would stay trying to give you one." I think that meant he wouldn't dare try to give Mamie an order.

But let's return to "Overlord". A decision had to be made on who the Supreme Commander would be. Eisenhower had been returned to a desk job in Washington and he was already getting restless working alongside Marshall. Surely he was not going to watch another war pass him by from the isolation of an office desk in Washington? There goes that ghost again. The fear of being redundant.

Meanwhile Churchill, Roosevelt and Stalin were in Teheran discussing a second front. Roosevelt was trying to reassure Stalin it would take place in early spring 1944. Because

Roosevelt had not yet selected who was to command Overlord Stalin was sceptical it would ever happen so soon.

But Roosevelt committed himself to making the selection inside three days.

This gave him real problems for he was avoiding the decision which up to now haunted him. His preferred solution of Marshall for Overlord with Eisenhower as his replacement in the War Department was just not ringing true with him, Eisenhower would then become Marshall's boss and worse still Eisenhower would be giving orders to MacArthur, another hot potato for him. He so desperately wanted to reward Marshall for his loyalty and good work. Roosevelt dodged the issue again when he canvassed Marshall for his opinion but Marshall was not going down that road. "I could not be the judge in my own case," he countered astutely.

But finally, Roosevelt almost cruelly made the decision for Marshall when he asked him to write a message to Stalin. "The immediate appointment of General Eisenhower to command Overlord operation has been decided upon." Roosevelt then signed it. Eisenhower was now the Supreme General among many famous Allied ones. The die was cast for Eisenhower, for the future politicians, and for the world.

On December 7, 1943 Roosevelt met Eisenhower in Tunis where the President was staying before returning home. In Eisenhower's chauffeur driven car the President turned casually to Eisenhower and said "Well Ike, you are going to command Overlord."

It was electrifying news for Eisenhower, the very pinnacle of his life's hopes and dreams and it came as a throwaway remark in the back of a limousine. Sometimes great men can be indefinable. Anyway at last there was a real job to be done and he would be in charge of it all. It has since transpired that it was Eisenhower's insistence on teamwork and working together which swung it. The integration of a multi-national force of such gigantic proportions, never assembled before in history, demanded a leader with all the talents of a supreme organizer and Eisenhower was the ideal choice. It was also essential to have a leader popular with the men and Eisenhower's hearty personality with his soldiers, his infectious grin, relaxed manner and super optimism more than compensated for any defects in his professional competence.

He was a true leader of men. Later when superiors or subordinates voiced their opinion of Eisenhower they all had one thing in common. Complete trust. They knew Eisenhower always gave wholehearted concentration and analysis to any decision he made, decisions that sealed the fate of thousands of soldiers and civilians, – before he acted. He never failed this real essence of command. A short visit to Washington was his most important task now. Mamie had shared all his heartaches and triumphs up to now so sharing his joy with her was natural. But Mamie was more concerned about his health, his weight, his voice and most of all the abrupt end to their meeting. It was a reminder to her that he had changed.

This love affair of a waiting soldier's wife was no different for Mamie than thousands of other army marriages. They discussed many family issues even down to the family car. One thing worried her. His smoking. He smoked too much she thought. But she was happy to see him on this flying visit because for that present moment in time he belonged to her.

The problem of the Russians bothered Eisenhower. After the war he wanted the Red army's behaviour monitored and under control in occupied areas. Roosevelt disagreed. It seemed Ike was nearer to Churchill in his reading of the Post-war situation, but then again Roosevelt was a sick man.

But meanwhile Mamie was paying the price of their situation. Overlord completely preoccupied her husband. All she had was their painful separation. She watched him pack for yet another trip abroad and her heart was breaking. "Don't come back again till it's over Ike, I can't stand losing you again." Ike wrote several times after that assuring her he was glad he came home despite the upset it caused them. She understood. He wrote 319 letters to her from his headquarters wherever he was. Then he got on with the war.

Mamie Eisenhower

Mamie's wishes to take a background insignificant seat were not going to work out for her however. Ike being made Supreme Commander of the Allied forces in Europe pushed Mamie Eisenhower his wife, into the public arena giving her front page recognition by the press long before Ike became President of the United States. Her breezy personality was a Godsend to them, making her a very popular subject for interview Stars and Stripes the army newspaper, played up her role with headlines like "Eisenhower's wife finds wait tough".

The juicy bit of romance between Ike and his Irish driver Kay was going the rounds and was ideal copy, guaranteed to increase circulation but wasn't too funny for Mamie. His lady driver being posted overseas with him complicated the script. Speculation was therefore easy given the circumstances but Ike still remained married to Mamie right on into his Presidency and beyond. Mamie's verdict on it all was summed up in just three words which were sufficient – "I know Ike."

At First Lady, Mamie was the ultimate in the job of White House hostess. So conscientious, she met the Association of Women's clubs by travelling to their Convention Centre because she couldn't entertain them in the White House. She soon became known to the press as "a family friendly figure". Yet she could give orders to the Staffers as curt, crisp and precise as any five-star General. Mamie first met Ike when he was a second Lieutenant and was with him right up to his promotion to five-star General and beyond. That journey included the loss of their first baby and constant health problems after that, but they carried these burdens bravely. She had other problems which she wouldn't talk about. On coming out of the Walter Reed hospital after an operation a young reporter asked was it a hysterectomy. The White House press secretary on the instructions of Mamie refused to say. That was the private Mamie Eisenhower. The problem of the old conflict between public and private personage never bothered Mamie. She was private and that was how it was going to be.

Just a short anecdote here about a man who is hardly ever mentioned when war correspondents wrote their memoirs. They are privileged to witness up close the deeds of heroism and bravery of great men, the ordinary soldier in battledress who fought and won the war by their sides. The man I write about however is the immortal Harry Hopkins. A small insignificant man who nevertheless, was indispensable to Franklin D. Roosevelt. Known as FDR's shadow he actually slept on the same floor in the White House as Roosevelt himself and often dined with him.

He supervised "Lend-Lease" sitting in on conferences with all the top Generals and Admirals who knew him well by name as FDR's personal envoy. He also was the personal link between FDR and Churchill. Politically shrewd, he impressed Churchill enough to be called by him "Lord of the Matter." Harry called himself "The catalytic agent between two prima donnas." He took day and night journeys sometimes to Moscow in the belly of army planes uncomfortable and unheated. He flew to Scapa Flow and found his launch floated too short for him to embark in the choppy seas but he still managed to bridge the gap by jumping over open water. His dispatches were flung unceremoniously after him. He was constantly living on borrowed time having cancer plus a wasting nutritional disease.

"His soul," said Churchill "flowed out of a frail and failing body." He himself said "I have taken a leave of absence from death" for surgery had taken half of his stomach away. Some say he lived in the White House because FDR refused to allow him to die. Such was his importance to FDR he was also used as Roosevelt's personal envoy to Stalin. His clout was such it was on his recommendation that Marshall was appointed as overseer of the famous Marshall Plan. That was Harry Hopkins. I mentioned earlier that Eisenhower was going to get on with the war. But that was not as simple as it sounds.

Ike was the Overlord. His job was to organize a vast armada of ships, men, guns, planes, explosives and the backup planning necessary to launch the invasion of Europe. His job was to harmonize the work of the Generals from different nations and the fighting men under their command. He was the one chosen by Roosevelt to take on the might of the Third Reich and defeat it. No wonder his armies were cheered from village to village. The reader will already have seen the documentaries and read the story of the war with amazement.

Here is a rough summary of the start of "Overlord".

The invasion of Europe began at 7.30 a.m. on the morning of June 6, 1944. The allies had learnt lessons from other amphibious landings in Dieppe, North Africa and Sicily. The Third Reich was rapidly losing men so the Germans decided to build fortresses along a two thousand mile long front called "The Atlantic Wall". Rommel, right as usual, feared Allied airpower would cripple them and depended instead on mined stakes to impale landing craft on the beaches. This made Eisenhower's task formidable in trying to put over 10,000 landing crafts (4,300 in the British sector and 6,000 in the American one). Miraculously a total of 132,715 men got ashore in the first seventeen hours.

Equipment landed was 6,000 vehicles, tanks and guns, tonnes of ammunition and food supplies for thousands coming through the three beaches called Omaha, Gold and Utah. Eisenhower gave most of the credit for this to "The ingenious mechanical contrivances built for the job." The troops on Omaha were pinned down for six hours until the destroyers came within 800 yards of the beach, firing five inch shells at strong points.

Meanwhile, the invasion fleet had to be protected against attack at night out at sea. The biggest threat was from the Oyster mines dropped from the air. Destroyers, Minesweepers and many other craft were damaged on June 18. Problems escalated as the weather deteriorated to a force 8 gale in the channel hampering the transport of equipment. Specially built Mulberry harbours to solve the problem were designed. However Eisenhower vetoed attempts to repair other Mulberry Harbours to concentrate on Cherbourg.
As we have said, Ike was the lynchpin holding the far flung forces together. Even the mistakes of four years war were analysed and improved upon unlike his opposite numbers Rommel, Rundstedt and Kluge who were constantly undermined with orders from Berlin. Yes, Ike covered himself in glory from Normandy to Berlin in every theatre of war with men, ammunitions and machines. The allies were in good hands under Ike's expert guidance right to the end of the war.

One thing is for certain Eisenhower was a very special man indeed. The outcome we know ended in victory and the trials of the Nazi war criminals at Nuremberg. I have written in detail under Truman about Nuremberg which can be described as the final act of conquest by the Allies. These trials that made the terrible war experiences they experienced, despite their horror, well worth the lesson that came out of them.

To lighten the storyline perhaps we could tell a few anecdotes here which would bring to life scenes of the war familiar to Eisenhower. A fascinating collection of stories and pictures were printed in the illustrated London News a book edited by John Keegan entitled The World at War 1939 – 1945. Here are some of them:

General Eisenhower reported on August 31; 400,000 German losses in the first eighty-one days of the Allied onslaught across Northern France.

Tough house to house street fighting was described in another report. "The Canadians fought most gallantly against hundreds of fortified posts; German tanks were concealed in basements and there were machinegun nests and snipers in house after house. The enemy was dislodged by massed guns and finally by the bayonet in hand-to-hand fighting against crack German paratroops." This battle was for the important Italian port of Ortona which eventually was won by the allies.

A lighter side of the war was the bet Eisenhower lost to Montgomery. It seems "Monty" promised a group of U.S. Generals he would take a town called Sfax by April 15. Ike bet him a flying fortress complete with crew if he succeeded. Monty beat the deadline by four days arriving in Sfax on April 11. The fortress was duly delivered complete with crew for the duration of the war.

Back home in England at Aldwych tube station people used the Underground to shelter from the bombs that rained down on London during the blitz. Later London built amazing shelters 100 feet underground, air conditioned, lit by "daylight" bulbs equipped with canteens and even play centres for the children. Whole families could be accommodated in private railed off areas containing tiers of bunks. Only the distant rumble of the tube trains disturbed the silence.

Approximately three thousand miles away deep down in the Moscow underground were pictures of men, women and children glad of their Underground giving the same protection. Both pictures told the same stories separated by half the globe. Two different cultures under attack by the same deranged madman. Tragic horror stories were shared by millions. The solution of these problems pressed down everyday on the shoulders of one man General Dwight Eisenhower.

Looking through The World at War there were some heartbreaking images. The ruthless evil thuggery discovered by Eisenhower in concentration camps was highlighted by one picture of a little boy of six shot in cold blood by SS officers. His mum and dad were nowhere to be seen, probably executed by the same thugs minutes before.

The sheer futility of war in all its ugly actions, where there are simply no rules, was a feature of this terrible fight for Europe. Smashed up houses, broken homes, scattered families, murdered prisoners and the bombing of densely populated cities reducing priceless historic buildings to rubble and burnt out shells cries out for some explanation for the madness. There will never be any explanation for the carnage simply because the horrific bombing of cities was perpetrated by both sides. What better proof have we than the devastation of Dresden or the tragedy of Hiroshima. Truly a scab on the face of history for mankind to live with. Grand larceny of Germany's wealth was also practiced widely by the Germans. Here is a story to prove it. Two old women in the village of Merkers told a U.S. military policeman on patrol "Down there in the salt mine is all the gold in Germany."

They were not exaggerating for when the story was followed up by the MPs they discovered countless millions of pounds worth of treasure, at least 100 tonnes of gold bullion, paintings by Van Dyck and Rembrandt and priceless tapestries. One of the Nazi leaders Kesselring hoped to beat General Patton's army to the hoard but failed. Another bizarre discovery was 10,000 church bells stolen from churches, convents and monasteries across Europe to be melted down for armaments.

But perhaps we should end this piece on a happy note – the liberation of Paris. It was an event well worth anyone's wildest dreams to be part of. August 19, 1945 was a beautiful day when French police took over the prefecture. Members of the Resistance called the FF seized the Hotel de Ville. Except for a few snipers the Germans surrendered to France's General Leclerc. General de Gaulle then entered the Capital in triumph, as agreed with Eisenhower, who held back his troops to allow this. Again even the politics was planned in detail by Ike. Before his march down the Champs-Elysées, De Gaulle gave a rousing speech to the cheering crowds standing around. He told them "France will take her place among the great nations which will organise the Peace."

Alan Moorehead of the Daily Express wrote "Machine guns began firing again. Young boys with armbands marked FFI were rushing about with Sten guns." General de Gaulle then requested the Americans to send in divisions in a show of force designed to impress the many armed collaborators still at large.

Finally, headlines from newspapers throughout the war are worth reading for their historical content alone. Here are a few "The United States to allow 'Cash and Carry' arms sales"; "King's visit to the British and French armies in France, a perilous but unspectacular task"; "Minesweepers at War"; "Germany invades Norway and Denmark"; "The end of the phoney war"; "The pitiful trek from the Nazis in Belgium"; "The miracle of deliverance"; "The evacuation of Dunkirk"; "War on the African seaboard"; "Italy's advance into Egypt"; "The first Nazi mass air raids on Britain"; "The greatest double cross in history Hitler invades Russia"; "The retreat from Moscow 1941"; "General Winter cooperates"; "Pearl Harbour, the act of treachery of Japan's death warrant"; "The battle of the Solomon's"; "Heavy U.S. and Japanese sea losses"; "The Russian armies press westwards from North to South"; "The Allied assault on the German stronghold of Montecassino"; "Allied advance in the Pacific smashing Japanese strongholds"; "The first wave of the seaborne assault hits the Normandy beach"; "Pre-invasion bombing, day and night precision"; "The battle of the flying bomb"; "Hitler's latest attack on England"; "Mass extermination of prisoners at Majdanek Camp"; "The race for the Seine, the allies close on the enemy retreat"; "First Allied landings in Southern France"; "Germany menaced from the West Luxemburg France and Belgium liberated"; "The Russian Campaign in the Balkans"; "Russia liberates Northern Finland and Norway"; "The great Soviet drive across Hungary"; "British troops land in Greece"; "Athens liberated"; "The Western front advances all along the Allied lines"; "The winter campaign of the Red Army"; "Warsaw liberates"; "The Crimea Conference which sounded the death knell of Nazism"; "Lest we forget some examples of German sadistic inhumanity"; "President Roosevelt dies, Vice President Truman takes over"; "Mussolini meets his deserts"; "The battle for Berlin"; "Scenes from the dying Reich capital"; "The Liberation of Holland, Denmark and Norway"; "VE day celebrations we have never seen a greater day than the journeys end"; "The last act of surrender ratified in Berlin"; "Civilization lets out the atomic genie"; "The International Trial Nuremberg Judges and Defendants".

Looking back on this world wide tapestry of Eisenhower's war experiences with the greatest Generals of four Continents we must recognize one indisputable fact. Ike was a hero, a very special man indeed, and he was at the heart of it all.

However there would have been no heroes if it hadn't been for Overlord. It was the most brutal, savage and frightening invasion in the history of warfare which led to the destruction of an evil tyranny that had it lived would have enslaved mankind for generations to come.

It was on these beaches of Normandy in the smell of cordite gunpowder and seaweed, wave after wave of brave men jumped into the Ocean in full fighting gear and slogged through a hail of bullets that cut them down ruthlessly. Well over 1,000 men fell killed or wounded while their comrades pushed on to batter the German army into submission. Going forward the thunder and carnage of battle brought them through the meadows to the village of Arromanche and beyond.

In 2009 in that very village sixty-five years later the same soldiers who fought here gathered to pay homage to their fallen comrades. Today, in the peace and tranquillity of a warm summers day it is still the same little French seaside village. The ice cream shops and the usual seaside tourists are back. The old quaint little French houses have been rebuilt. The streets are buzzing with the excitement of this annual Remembrance Day complete with dignitaries, television crews and pipe bands.

Ex soldiers come here now on the 6th of June every year from all over the world at the invitation of the Normandy Veteran's Association. It is a visit steeped in nostalgia for all who come here. The dignitaries are many including Barrack Obama, President of the United States, Gordon Brown, Prime Minister of the UK, President Sarkozy of France and Prince Charles of England. These represent Roosevelt, Churchill, De Gaulle and King George – the leaders in 1944.
Interviews with the veterans, now in their nineties, was a traumatic experience for those watching. Many broke down in tears remembering old pals who fell around them in the water, on the sands and in the fields beyond.
The numbers who come now are dwindling fast. One little French boy captured the history around him when he said "These are the very soldiers I read about in my history book. I can't believe it when I look at their faces now."

Just a short distance up the road at the military cemetery in Colleville-sur-Mer; 9,387 American soldiers are buried in sight of the sand dunes on which they had fought. What a tremendous tribute that is to the Americans, who could so easily have stayed at home in America leaving Europe to fight its own battles. The villagers thanked their visitors warmly for their bravery here sixty-five years ago.

The Mulberry harbour intended as a temporary structure all those years ago is still there. Outside the harbour a minesweeper lies at anchor in the bay. The Réveillez was sounded followed by a trumpeter playing "The Last Post". Finally an unrehearsed moment of sadness when the veterans and the VIPs linked arms and sang with gusto as the pipe bands struck up an emotional rendering of Auld Lang Syne. Deep down nowadays everyone knows such celebrations will never be repeated. Modern nuclear warfare will see to that.

One story however must be told at this point. Eisenhower's overwhelming gratitude for the performance of Franklin D. Roosevelt as Commander-in-Chief. He said "I have often thought how fortunate it was that the two great allies of World War II were led by two men Churchill and Franklin D. Roosevelt who had a quality of leadership that inspired people." Of Roosevelt Ike said "The man exuded an infectious optimism. The thought of defeat apparently never crossed his mind despite the fact we were fighting two great wars simultaneously on opposite sides of the world with Japan and Germany. FDR had the nation almost solidly behind him in his conduct of the war."

The news of FDR's death came as a terrible blow to Eisenhower. It reached him on April 12, 1945 at the end of a horror filled day. That day was the first time he had witnessed the degradation of a German Internment or concentration camp. "I never dreamed that such savagery could really exist in this world" Eisenhower wrote to his wife. He was weary and it was after midnight when he turned in at the house of a Nazi Commandant.

But before continuing perhaps we should discuss what Eisenhower saw for it was happening all across Europe by a new ruthlessness, a new political idea that he never learnt about at West Point – the elimination of a whole nation outside the Geneva Convention. Six million Jews to be exact.

One of the most unforgivable atrocities in the war that brought untold shame on the German nation was its treatment of the Jews, the full impact of which had appalled Eisenhower on the day he was told about Roosevelt's death.

Strangely the whole policy seemed to start simultaneously across Europe on the 14th and 15th of July 1942. Survivors told harrowing stories about their part in it during a BBC documentary on November 4, 2006. The first they knew about it was the banging on doors by armed soldiers and a loudspeaker announcement in the streets outside. "You will be taken from your homes, nothing will happen to you, you will be taken to work in Germany." A gut wrenching fear pervaded each village. Nobody knew what was going to happen to them. They had hardly left their homes when looters were ransacking them and robbing their furniture. This was the "master race" at work.

They were put into cattle trucks on trains by SS guards with dogs. Sanitation was nil in these trucks except for a bucket in the corner. The prisoners had seized to be human beings. In Dresden the flats were cleared of Jews. Neighbours could only watch through their curtains with fear. Those Jews who became inmates of the camps were luckier than those who were driven direct to the Crematorium and burned alive, others were gassed beforehand or died standing up in a crush. A child who did not die by the gas let out a whimper only to be searched out by the guards and shot. The SS were determined to carry out their evil mission with ruthless efficiency. Word got out about the Holocaust and it stunned the international world. A statement was read out to the House of Commons and for fully three minutes, afterwards there was shocked silence.

The scenes in the concentration camps were repeated all across Europe until almost six million Jews were burned and gassed into eternity. Hitler was kept informed constantly by radio of the progress achieved by his jackboot thugs. Later suitcases from every country in Europe were gathered up with the victim's pathetic belongings inside. The first part of Eisenhower's career was drawing to a close but his new life as U.S. President was some way down the road yet.

But let's get on with the story of Eisenhower. On the night of August 12, 1945 Ike was hardly in bed when Patton and Bradley woke him to tell him the news of the President's death. It left him with a sense of enormous personal loss. At that moment he became aware of the President's buoyant personality throughout all his troubles. A great mountain landmark had crumbled and was no more as Eisenhower put it. He went back to bed depressed and sad. Two months later Eisenhower told the House of Representatives "From his strength and indomitable spirit I drew constant support and confidence in the solution of my problems."

There were however those who were jealous of Eisenhower's rise to fame. Many people marvelled at the rise of Eisenhower to prominence during FDR's third term. Some said it defied belief if you didn't know it was true. Late September 1941 he was a Colonel unknown to the country even to his fellow officers. The massive military manoeuvres in Louisiana helped Eisenhower distinguish himself but he was still without combat experience. Yet astonishingly he jumped over 366 senior officers.

By March 1942, six months later he was a Brigadier General. Six months after Pearl Harbour he was in command of the entire European Theatre. I have already covered Eisenhower's movement up the ranks in these notes but he didn't receive the Distinguished Service Medal or the illustrious Oak Leaf Cluster for nothing. Yet again there was a connection made with Roosevelt when FDR handed him a fourth Star placing him on a par with the top ranking British Generals. Despite being unknown and with many officers to choose from Roosevelt chose him to command Overlord. Some say Marshall had been Eisenhower's main sponsor for promotion but Roosevelt approved every one of them.

He was projected by the Presidency as being in close tandem with FDR. Ike was publicly praised by Roosevelt too at the annual dinner of the White House Correspondents Association as follows: "I spent many hours in Casablanca with this young General, a descendent of Kansas pioneers. I know what a fine tough job he has done and how carefully and skilfully he is directing the soldiers under him. I want to say to you tonight and to him that we have every confidence in his leadership."

Well I think we can readily dismiss now the contemptible accusations that Eisenhower rode to the top of his profession on the crest of a wave of patronage and privilege.
This is a preposterous suggestion about a man whose glorious record in each job he was given brought honour and glory to the men he led and the nation he loved. I must also emphasise we are writing about the 34th President of the United States and a man who filled that position too with distinction. Anyway, let's move on for there are many more stories and anecdotes to be told about him.

However before we leave the subject of his army career isn't it obvious to any fair minded person that the yardstick for distinction in the army is tough and uncompromising.

It is based on the safety of thousands of soldiers under his command. Thousands of unnecessary deaths would very quickly consign any Charlton to ignominy and disgrace. This never happened to Ike so he must have done something right.

As we all know the Germans surrendered to Eisenhower unconditionally on May 7, 1945 at his headquarters in Rheims, France.

The cable he received from General Marshall is a true and authentic summary of the honour and regard his fellow Generals had for him and their judgement is based on their professional assessment of him as a soldier. The cable reads as follows:

"You have completed your mission with the greatest victory in the history of warfare. You have commanded with outstanding success the most powerful military force that has ever been assembled. You have met and successfully disposed of every conceivable difficulty. You have been selfless in your actions, always sound and tolerant in your judgements and altogether admirable in the courage and wisdom of your military decisions."

Eisenhower's stay in Germany for another three years from 1945 – 1948 as Chief of Staff of the army was not really a happy one. How could it be as he watched demobilization eat into his illustrious U.S. army which shrunk from eight million men and women to less than one million? At the end of these final days he retired a five-star General.

His fame, his charisma, and his popularity with all classes brought the inevitable invitation from both political Parties to go into politics but instead he chose to accept an offer of the Presidency of Columbia University in New York City which he held from 1948 to 1950.

Around that time the North Atlantic Treaty Organization (NATO) was formed as a fighting unit to withstand Communist aggression which threatened the allies of Europe. Harry Truman turned to the now retired Eisenhower to command it and build it up, yet somehow the plight of the Europeans in their post-war poverty and the Korean War thwarted his efforts in the expansion of NATO. Incidentally another ex President Herbert Hoover was brought back from retirement by Harry Truman to tackle European poverty with great success. But his thoughts were now focussed on exciting events back home in America, the 1952 Presidential Election as the Republican candidate.

The Democrats were also in hot pursuit and Truman in 1951 tried again to secure Eisenhower's approval for his nomination under the Democratic banner. Eisenhower's answer was blunt and to the point "You can't join a Party just to run for office. What reason have you to think I can ever be a Democrat? You know I have been a Republican all my life." The die was cast when Ike gave up his NATO post in the spring of 1952 to win the Republican nomination. Truman was furious when he heard this and wrote to Ike immediately. It was a typical Truman broadside shooting from the hip – verbally of course.
"I am extremely sorry that you have allowed a bunch of screwballs to come between us." One thing you could be sure of. When Truman had something on his mind he certainly didn't mince his words. As we pointed out earlier fate always seemed to smile kindly on Eisenhower. At the Convention in Chicago, Senator Robert Taft of Ohio, an isolationist and severe critic of NATO looked poised to get the Republican nomination having, it seemed, 35 votes out of 70 almost guaranteed to him.

But Eisenhower unexpectantly received the help of an unlikely guardian angel in the person of one Richard Milhous Nixon junior Senator for Chicago. Nixon's reward was a place on the ticket as candidate for Vice President. Incidentally Nixon was destined to be Ike's son-in-law and to be a future President of the United States. Ike's prestige did the rest because his name was now being associated alongside the illustrious soldier Presidents of the past such as Washington, Zachary Taylor, Jackson and Grant.

But I'm afraid Ike was about to have a rude awakening as we are about to find out. This was a different fight in a different world to the military one he had lived in for thirty-eight years. Here the rules were not played like a gentleman pugilist of the Officer class but straight out of the bare-knuckle fighting academy of an old time prize ring.

The opening salvo from Taft, unbelievably a member of his own Party shocked Eisenhower - Ike's personal life was vilified by accusing him of a love affair with his driver, the presumed Jewish blood in his veins and the lowest blow of all - his wife's drinking habits. What a sickening contrast to the honourable job he had had for thirty-eight years now gone forever. Being a war hero throughout the length and breadth of Europe meant nothing now. Absolutely nothing.

He talked to Truman, an old political trooper about this on a social visit….. "If that's all it is Ike then you can just figure you are lucky" was Truman's response. Eisenhower ruefully noted what he had secretly feared – he was not going to like politics. Yet he was determined to take on the fight which surprised no one. He followed up on these thoughts with the following words. "Having put my hand to the plough I intend to see the job through to the end of the furrow."

There were two fears about Taft. One was that if he won the nomination he would lose the election to Truman. Also there was a fear that if he won he would pull the Untied States out of NATO. The moderates were supporting Eisenhower which split the Republicans into two camps.

The decision of Eisenhower to run caused Truman to withdraw from the race and his place on the Democratic ticket in opposition to Eisenhower now fell to Adlai Stevenson of Illinois. Eisenhower's supporters hit on a catchy campaign slogan "I like Ike" which was easy for the electorate to believe in, given Ike's soldierly presentation and his relaxed friendly personality. The outcome was a victory for Ike and the Republicans by 55% to 44% for Stevenson. Well Eisenhower was learning the dirty game of politics fast and the master of this type of politics was his future son-in-law who was in the forefront throughout the campaign, "Tricky Dickey" Richard Milhous Nixon. Stevenson knew he could not beat Ike as he remarked sarcastically later "Who did I think I was running against George Washington?"

Nixon stirred up hysteria about Communism, corruption and Korea. Even Eisenhower's former General in arms Omar Bradley later criticised him for hypocritically attacking policies he himself had helped formulate alongside Roosevelt. He condemned Truman for withdrawing troops from Korea, something he himself had been party to and while he had an input into allowing the Russians beat him to Berlin, on the campaign trail he blamed Truman and Roosevelt on this decision.
But the truth about the new Eisenhower was that he was now in a different ball game – politics- and that was how you won elections. Eisenhower was a fast learner. So he duly won yet another battle though not on the battlefield.

Inauguration day was Tuesday January 20, 1953 and Ike took the oath before Chief Justice Frederick Moore Vinson and created a new precedent by offering up a private prayer, a small extract of which I include here as follows "Almighty God as we stand here at this moment my future associates in the Executive Branch of Government join me in beseeching that thou will make full and complete our dedication to the service of the people in this throng and their fellow citizens everywhere."

The usual parade took two and a half hours to pass by the Presidential Stand. 60,000 people were in the Grandstand having paid $3 to $15 per seat. In the parade there were 22,000 servicemen and women and 5,000 civilians from fifty different State organizations. 350 horses beautifully groomed; three elephants and an Alaskan dog team added to the glamour of the occasion. The music was provided by 350 bands. Stars of radio, stage, screen and television also attended. The night was concluded by two glittering inaugural Balls as is the tradition on this special Presidential occasion, which was attended by 14,000 guests.

Sadly the old free and easy night traditionally spent in the company of the President was now in its final year for on August 6, 1956 the concern of the Establishment for the safety of the President had become uppermost in the priorities of those running the event. The maintenance of law and order and the protection of life and property were passed into legislation on August 6, 1956. This Act was to empower the inaugural committee to make watertight plans for the security of all concerned in the running of this auspicious event for the future.

Eisenhower was not really overawed by the Presidency since he had been involved with the policy makers in politics during most of his years in the army. He once said "This idea that all wisdom is in the President, that's baloney. I don't believe this Government was set up to be operated by anyone acting alone; no one has a monopoly on the truth and on the facts that affect this country."

But Eisenhower was lucky. That sounds like a mantra of your writer since I used it concerning Eisenhower before this in my notes. So why was he lucky this time? Well he stepped into the Presidency at a time of an enormous boom in America. National output had doubled between 1946 and 1956 and would even double again before 1970. A whole new middleclass was enjoying spectacular increases in their spending power. Personal income tripled between 1946 and 1955. Thirteen million homes were built and bought between 1948 and 1958.

Over 83% of homes owned a television set now. Two car families doubled between 1951 and 1958. America was making no less than two thirds of the world's manufactured goods. Male life expectancy rose from age forty-six in 1900 to age sixty-five in 1964. The forty million births that took place between 1950 and 1960 meant that 40% of the population were under twenty by 1964.

In a way, Eisenhower inherited an America very similar to Calvin Coolidge's America which spawned the good times of the 1920s. The only difference was that Coolidge's good times ended in the disaster of the Depression of the 30s.
Some people may think that the move to the Presidency would need a period of acclimatization, a period of learning the ropes so to speak in his new job in politics.
But strangely his predecessor Harry Truman found the transition much more traumatic, for Harry had been pitch forked into a whole new world on the death of Roosevelt. But Eisenhower had lived in that world for years. He was used to Aides at his elbows, advisors behind him, and reporters crowding him in all the public places they chose. Photographers were not new to him and the case of watching his words carefully for fear of being misquoted was part of his life as a top General. The power of decision-making didn't faze him either.

Yet some things were new. For example he hadn't eaten in a restaurant for years. The last time he had enjoyed a private life was back in 1942. Even dressing himself was new to him now for in the army he had a valet to do the basic chores like helping him to put on his underwear, socks, shoes, pants, shirt, jacket and tie. Back then he drove no car, had no worries about parking and had never seen a supermarket. Even money was new to him now.

Eisenhower had kept himself quite fit for he had quit smoking, exercised regularly, played golf and went swimming. At sixty-two he looked tanned and erect with a military bearing that impressed his audience especially among his political colleagues. He looked the part of a leader of men. There was one man who saw things differently however. He was that ever blunt and practical friend of his, ex-President Truman who wryly observed. "He'll sit here and say "do this do that" and nothing will happen. Poor Ike it won't be a bit like the army. He will find it very frustrating."
So was Eisenhower about to realize now that he commanded nothing?

He was only a month in the job when he was asked "How do you like your new job?" Ike's reply "I never said or thought that I would like it. It is not a job that I suppose it is intended one should like."

Eisenhower did have his visions based on his experience of war-torn Europe. One of these was the creation of a United States of Europe. His inaugural speech called for a more closely integrated economic and political system in Europe. But Europe had no money to fulfil his dreams. They even asked the U.S. to increase its nuclear weapons in Europe. But Eisenhower was not having any of this and insisted the Europeans would have to pay their own way on defence.

It is easy to understand today why Eisenhower was not getting involved in war in another country while America was booming. It is easy to understand also why an ex-General who had seen all the bloodshed, chaos and fatalities of war firsthand was not eager to repeat that experience.

His first confrontation with the Chinese Communists came therefore, not with a moving army but with a subtle threat that he would not be constrained in the weapons he used to secure not victory but peace. This story has since been refuted. The Chinese signed an armistice in 1953 and both sides in Korea went back to their pre-war boundaries.

His next war was not an international one. It was a political battle with the notorious Senator Joe McCarthy who had become a bit of a nuisance in chasing headlines searching for Communists on the Government payroll. Eisenhower tried to fight McCarthy by ignoring him because of the clout McCarthy held in the Senate. Given enough rope McCarthy would hang himself was Ike's thinking. But Nixon was urging him to follow his instincts to confront McCarthy. Ike knew he was dangerous because of the support he had from millions of Americans. His methods were evil however, because of the innocent victims he left behind strewn in the wreckage of his paranoia. Again McCarthy attacked, this time against another illustrious name Dr. Ralph Bunche, a Negro American who had won the 1950 Nobel Peace Prize when he was working at the UN. Ike was furious.

On May 9, Eisenhower's friend Harry Bullis warned him that Senator McCarthy had unlimited personal ambitions, unmitigated gall and unbounded selfishness. "In the opinion of many of us who are your loyal friends it is a fallacy to assume that McCarthy will kill himself. It is our belief that McCarthy must be stopped." Ike refused. His outburst said it all "I will not get into a pissing contest with that skunk." The Europeans viewed this situation as abject appeasement. McCarthy even attacked the books of many American authors in overseas libraries. Still Ike held back.

In the meantime Ike was fighting another battle for peace. This time his battle was with those hawks within his Administration who wanted to create funds for war. They called it a level of preparation for a feared attack from Russia. The hawks among American politicians seemed to be living in a self-inflicted funk against what? Eisenhower's reaction is a classic for politicians everywhere to study before declaring war. "The jet plane that roars over your head costs three quarter of a million dollars. That is more money than a man is going to make in his lifetime. What world can afford this sort of thing for long? We are in an armaments race. Where will it lead us? At worst to atomic warfare. At best, to robbing every person and nation on earth of the fruits of their own toil!" He wanted to see the resources of the world used to provide bread, butter, clothes, homes, hospitals and schools; all the good and necessary things for decent living, not more guns. He also felt that America and Russia had built armed forces to fight a battle of Armageddon.

Now that Stalin was dead (he had died on March 5, 1953) there was an opportunity for a fresh start. There is no need to say much more on this subject. Suffice it to say Eisenhower had now moved into the area of arms limitation designed to insure the prohibition of atomic weapons supervised by a practical system of inspection under the United Nations.

Eisenhower now found himself in a battle for peace against the hawks in his Administration. Here is another speech he made to bring sense to the situation. Warmongers should learn it off by heart. "The cost of a modern heavy bomber is this. A modern brick school in more than thirty cities. It is two electric power plants each serving a town of 60,000 people. We pay for a single fighter plane with a half a million bushels of wheat. We pay for a single destroyer with new homes that could have housed more than 8,000 people. This is not a way of life at all in any true sense. Under the cloud of threatening war it is humanity hanging from an iron cross." He finished his speech by promising to devote a substantial percentage of the savings achieved by disarmament to a fund for world aid and reconstruction programmes to assist all peoples to know the blessings of productive freedom. The monuments to this new kind of world would be these: Roads and schools, hospitals and homes, food and health for everyone.

The Embassies of the world were inundated with messages of support. British, continental and American newspapers outdid themselves in praising him. His speech, entitled "The chance for peace" was so effective even the Soviets responded favourable. How much we will see later.

But we have skipped over a process of thinking for Eisenhower in which he wrestled with a war problem he had never experienced before. Stephen E. Ambrose, Eisenhower's eminent biographer describes Eisenhower's dilemma with a profound insight of the problem now facing the world. The problem of a destructive force capable of destroying civilization. How to sell this idea of a nuclear holocaust to the world. The idea that war must never happen again. Some advisors wanted bigger bombs, others wanted no more bombs. How do you convince the world it is racing towards catastrophe? Oppenheimer, creator of the bomb, advocated building no more bombs after Hiroshima so devastated was he by the consequences.

Despite his genuine pangs of conscience, the distinguished Oppenheimer was accused of being a Communist. Disgracefully a three man committee was charged with the task of investigating Oppenheimer as a security risk. Instructions went out to block McCarthy from exploiting the situation he had created.

By now it was revealed that the new atomic bombs were not only more powerful than those dropped on Japan but had more explosive force than all the bombs, shells and bullets exploded in the entire Second World War. The sheer disaster of this new threat to mankind was sitting on Eisenhower's desk. No other President had ever had the remotest similarity to this problem waiting to be solved in the whole history of the United States. The solution was simple. The nuclear problem had to be diverted into peaceful purposes. Nuclear energy could not be used for anything else. The U.S., UK and Russians met. They agreed on an Atomic Energy Agency. Eisenhower went to the United Nations and outlined the plan to divert these terrible powers of nuclear fission to peaceful purposes. When he had finished 3,500 delegates rose to applaud him and even the Russians joined in. But sadly it all failed at the negotiating table. Suspicion and distrust saw to that. The nuclear race restarted to the point where both camps had easily enough weapons to destroy the world one hundred times over. Ike's plan for peace was one of his bitterest defeats. Then again was it his defeat or the defeat of politicians who didn't understand the problem as Eisenhower did. Ike was far too hard on himself. History will prove that.

Fifty years has elapsed now since Eisenhower struggled to convince the world in the 1950s the awful reality and danger to civilization of the nuclear bomb. He failed.

The problem was placed on the back burners and left to the nations of the world to sort out themselves. They failed.

Ten Presidents have passed through the White House in those years. The stockpile of nuclear weapons has risen steadily until in the new century 2010 we have 800 launches and heavy bombers and 700 inter continental submarine launched ballistic missiles submerged under the oceans of the world primed to end civilization as we know it, not in a week or a month but in a nano second. This was Dwight Eisenhower's greatest nightmare.

But news has just come to hand from the White House that history at least is taking action. President Obama and President Dmitry Medvedev of Russia have agreed a nuclear arms reduction treaty to replace the 1991 Strategic Arms Reduction Treaty. The new treaty is to be signed on April 8, 2010 in Prague.

At present the U.S. has 2,000 and Russia has 2,500 deployed strategic nuclear weapons. The agreement calls for 1,500 nuclear weapons for each nation, the reduction to take place over seven years.

A new verification mechanism to monitor the agreement seals the deal. The world is now on the road to a nuclear weapon free world sometime in the future. Mankind will now rest a lot easier and I'm sure will be celebrating joyously somewhere beyond the scars.

But let's return to Ike. While Oppenheimer the creator of the bomb was eventually removed from the Atomic Energy Commission, Eisenhower did his best to keep his other scientists happy and untouched by accusations of Communist leaning. Oppenheimer later was cleared of these charges but was still removed from the A.E.C. McCarthy however wouldn't go away and was now knocking on the door of the White House personnel. The modern Presidency was at stake.

In this the nuclear age no information was free to anyone not even Joe McCarthy. The situation was simply unprecedented. Eisenhower was angry and now took unilateral action by deciding his people would not be subpoenaed. It was the end for McCarthy and his career as Communist hunter and baiter died with a whimper. Executive privilege was born to the Presidency forever. Nobody ever again tried to make an Aunt Sally out of the great and the good in American public life.

But Eisenhower still had one more war to fight. What should he do about Vietnam? Dulles was posturing for a showdown with China but one day Eisenhower called his bluff. "If I am to go to war," he told Dulles "there will be no halfway measures. I will declare a state of war with China and possibly there should be a strike at Russia. Any attacks would have to be against Russia and China." He confronted the joint-Chiefs of Staff with the scenario of a Russian nuclear strike. "I want you to carry this question home with you. Gain such a victory and what do you do with it? There would be a great area from the Elbe to Vladivostok.... torn up destroyed without Government, without its communications, just an area of starvation and disaster."

"I ask you what the civilized world would do about it. I repeat there would be no victory except through our imaginations."

When asked later by reporters what did he think of a preventative war. Ike's reply did not need the wisdom of a biblical prophet to anticipate. It was blunt and to the point "Believe me there is no such thing and frankly I would not even listen to anyone seriously that came in and talked about such a thing." A final anecdote completes the picture.

When Syngman Rhee flew to Washington later to tell Eisenhower that the moment had come to strike hard at the Communists; Eisenhower, with a wealth of war wisdom behind him and a profound knowledge of the terrible weapon available to everyone in the theatre of war, confronted Syngman Rhee like a schoolmaster giving a lecture to a foolish student. "Let me tell you," he said quietly and with deadly earnestness, "If war comes it will be horrible. Atomic war will destroy civilization. War today is unthinkable with the weapons we have at our command. If the Kremlin and Washington ever lock up in a war the results are too horrible to contemplate. I can't even imagine them."

All I can say is that history would have been rewritten if there had been anyone left to rewrite it!! Thank God for an Eisenhower at that particular time in the history of the world.

His contribution to civilization today by resisting the crazy clamour of the circling hawks who bombarded him for nuclear war is still not fully appreciated or understood today sixty years later. History will one day thankfully place him among the great statesmen of the nuclear age.

Eisenhower was eventually vindicated by events. The Chinese didn't intervene in Vietnam. On July 21, 1953 a ceasefire was established and Vietnam was partitioned though it didn't solve the problem long term. The domino theory never came to pass either.
Later Southern Vietnam fell to the Communists. That is a story to be told under a future President. One prediction has been remarkably accurate. Today his proposed United States of Europe, made in his inauguration speech, is in place known as the European Economic Community consisting of over twenty-five nations and still expanding.

But here I feel the time has come to lighten up again and shine the spotlight on another side of Dwight Eisenhower with a few stories from his book At Ease: Stories I Tell my Friends.

The stories in Eisenhower's book are so fascinating it is difficult to know which to leave out. I will recall some of them, in my own words of course, to give you the reader an insight into Eisenhower's personality and the people who shaped it during his boyhood days in Abilene. I do hope the ones I have chosen help to complete the pen picture I am trying to capture through all the sources I have consulted about him.
First of all his memories of his home town Abilene are no different than those we ourselves may recall when walking once again among the same old people and the same old bricks and mortar in our memories. The hometown noises once muffled except for the rumble of a distant train has been replaced by other noises. The family can be scattered like lost pieces of a jigsaw never to be put together in the same way. The horse, the hitching rails and posts, the watering troughs, the livery stables, the towering manure heaps all gone. The functional two storey school building complete with bell in a roof cupola still stands out for him, though in those days the expectancy was to educate for the standard jobs available in a small frontier town at that particular time.

Eisenhower had a terrific respect and love for his father and recounted how at forty years of age his father enrolled in a refrigeration engineers course which he studied by Kerosene lamp to prepare himself for new machines manufacturing ice and ice cream in his job in the local creamery. As Ike remembers, most adults in Abilene were born in the Civil War period and were very much aware of their previous President's lack of professional education. Some Presidents only had one year's formal schooling to their credit, even George Washington himself. So education was no big deal. All that was required for success was good clear handwriting, good spelling and a native intelligence.

As we pointed out before in these notes Ike's mother had a very central role in the life of the family. In Ike's book At Ease he recounted how his mum on the arrival of his grandfather to live with them, seldom had less than eight to cater for at breakfast or dinner. Dad's lunch was delivered by one of the lads in a horse and buggy to the local creamery. They were a prayerful family who although poor themselves, always had an intimate prayer for the unfortunate souls who were cold, sick or hungry in the outside world. He speaks proudly of his mother's role in the home. Her serenity, her open smile, her gentleness and her tolerance are indelibly impressed in his memory. An interesting account is told of life in his mother's time during Stonewall Jackson's campaign down the road in the Shenandoah Valley just ten miles from where she lived in Mount Sidney, Virginia.

As a General looking back to those years he could appreciate the background to her life as a spectator of history in the making. The snorting of the horses, the rattle of the gun carriages and the shouts of passing soldiers outside his mother's home must have been passed on by her among many anecdotes of Stonewall Jackson's battleground before wrecking the Union's strategy for the taking of Richmond. One could almost smell the cordite and hear the sound of musket shots when being told about it. What also came over in this account of his mother's childhood was the sheer tragedy of war which she must have passed on to Ike. Burnt out homes, barns and haystacks, orchards uprooted, wrecked bridges and railways. Yes this valley of small farms saw devastating scenes with fire and sword as bitter as any location in the Deep South.

To Eisenhower it was these scenes she had lived through first hand which gave her a deep hatred of war and a burning instinct for peace. His mother eventually went on to high school and college where she met Eisenhower's dad David. They got married on September 23, 1885 in the campus chapel and the college pastor officiated.

But Ike had another hero to look up to as a boy in the person of a man called Bob Davis, a six foot tall easy going gentleman of fifty who taught him all the tricks of the local poacher.
He caught fish illegally in nets and taught Ike how to use a flat boat with one paddle. How to set and anchor a net with the opening downstream? He was full of questions when teaching Ike. How do you find north in a forest of trees when it's raining? How do you catch a muskrat? How do you catch a mink? The lore he passed on was priceless. Ike even learnt poker from Bob which proved a very lucrative asset for him in later years. So good did he become and so consistent were his winnings he had no option but to retire undefeated out of sympathy to his fellow officers. Their losses worried Ike so much he decided never to play poker with them again.

Finally, Ike gives an amazing insight into the Presidency. The timing of press releases was of critical importance. The exact hour of the release was studied to achieve maximum impact. No point in giving a report or announcing public policy if the public were not listening perhaps because other events were more important to them. There was a total lack of privacy he discovered. Every phone call made or received was monitored from start to finish. Except for personal letters from Mamie, nothing reached him without being read and noted. Even the scraps of paper discarded by him were recovered from the waste paper basket for microfilming and examination for the benefit of future historians, nothing was lost. It was now a career in a goldfish bowl. To have every word you say or write scrutinized by others who are complete strangers he found very disconcerting. It was a constant daily guard on him carried out by friends who only had his best interest at heart.

Sometimes he felt their passion for careful recording and observation went too far. Even a ribbon he wore in error on his uniform at some public international event caused major concern to his "minders" resulting in a series of shocked letters from the Department concerned to those responsible to ensure no repetition of this error would happen again. Ike just shook his head and smiled ruefully. Had he treated his officers so pompously he would never have become the General who won the war?

One final anecdote concerns Ike's relationship and love for his mother. After the war Eisenhower wrote "The sight of my mother was one of the rewards of peace. Of course, she had paid the price of a lifetime of caring and working. As I first knew her she was a tall woman perhaps five foot six inches. She weighed about 135 lbs with blue eyes and brown hair untouched by grey. Now her hair was grey and somehow she was a little smaller. To be sure her life was one of almost ceaseless work." These could well have been the thoughts of any front line soldier after the war. Yes that book At Ease truly was a fascinating glimpse behind the scene in the White House as well as a beautiful American story of a little boy's journey from the frontier town of Abilene to the White House and President of the United States.

However there was one historic conflict in which he did order in the troops, something he refused to do outside America. Circumstances left him no option. As President he became involved when a ruling by Earl Warren decided it was unconstitutional for segregation by race in public schools. The Supreme Court Judge had ruled in the case "Brown V. Board of Education" to bring about social change. The Governor of Arkansas opposed the ruling.

In 1957 it was the first Civil Rights Bill since reconstruction back in post-Civil War days that gave blacks the right to vote. Still the authorities hesitated. Governor Orval Faubus of Arkansas took a defiant stance in opposing the Supreme Court ruling by calling out the State troopers to block integration. Eisenhower was appalled. "There must be respect for the Constitution" he declared "or there will be chaos." He called in the Arkansas National Guard for as he said "It was unthinkable for a State Governor to defy a Federal Court Order!" The State Guard had to obey the President and soon Little Rock Central High School was the centre of history. Had this sort of action happened one hundred years earlier reconstruction might have been more successful, as it turned out it was another soldier General Eisenhower who made post Civil War history in 1957.

But the Eisenhower story has not finished yet so let's continue with his Presidency.

The Republicans true to form once again clamoured for a laissez-faire approach to his domestic programme and reverse the policies of Roosevelt in his New Deal programme. Not only did Ike ignore them he expanded Social Security to include seven million self-employed farmers. His public works programme thrived with the Saint Lawrence Seaway project and the Interstate Highway systems - the largest construction project in history. He also launched a nuclear research programme into the peaceful use of atomic energy. He deliberately avoided getting involved in dangerous international situations and refused point blank to interfere in the Russian invasion of Hungary. Intervention in Vietnam was also urged on him by John Foster Dulles and Richard Nixon but Eisenhower was simply not interested.

But on September 24, 1955 two years before the trouble at Little Rock, President Eisenhower was making a different kind of history. On that day in September he was the first President to suffer a heart attack while in office and strangely enough it happened while he was on vacation at Denver, Colorado. He didn't walk for a month at the Fitzsimons Army Hospital where he was treated. The doctors assured him he would be fit for another term in the Presidency.

During the holiday he talked with his advisors about a second term and he wasn't at all keen on the idea. Retiring was a much more attractive proposition right then. Perhaps it was the holiday he was enjoying which coloured his thinking. The weather and the golf were in tandem to perfection. The fishing was good too and some people commented on how well he looked. Always an early riser he cooked breakfast, bacon and eggs at 5 a.m., for lunch he had hamburger and onions between phone calls to John Foster Dulles.

But his stomach was upset. Later he shot some billiards with George Allen then went to bed at 9.30 p.m. He awoke at 1.30 a.m. with severe chest pains. In the hospital he was put in an oxygen tent and Mamie was given living quarters on the eighth floor. She later took over the job of answering every letter personally. Five years more in his pressure cooker job seemed only a remote possibility. Meanwhile, as he lay in hospital there was a month of political infighting between Dulles and Nixon. The press were aware of this and trumpeted that the Party was determined to keep Nixon out of the race.

I wonder what Ike thought of this for after all his grandson was now part of Nixon's family.
Throughout the turmoil that followed the Little Rock decision, Eisenhower chose not to take sides. The segregationists mistook his silence as a signal that he was on their side. He was widely criticized for creating this ambiguity in the minds of bitter men. Some held the view that a strong moral stance by him supporting the decision of the Court openly would have avoided the flare up across the South as desegregation was implemented.

Judge Warren himself concluded that all the country needed was one word from Eisenhower and the transition would have been easier and smoother. But Ike still insisted it was not the role of the President to comment on Court decisions. Could it have been down to the old ghost of one hundred years ago which the country had never really exorcised between North and South during Reconstruction? Then, who am I to wear the shoes of Dwight Eisenhower from the safety of fifty years later. Let's just say the subject will always provoke enough opinions for a passionate debate.

The appearance of unity in the Party was wafer thin. With Ike in hospital Nixon was in a tough situation. Did he take a background seat and look uncertain and unprepared or did he make his own contribution himself and appear to be ruthlessly seizing power in Ike's absence? Nothing had changed from past history. The Vice Presidential role in situations like this still had not been clarified. McKinley, Lincoln and Garfield all left behind them problems in the transfer of power. Once again a similar dilemma faced the Administration.

But retirement into inactivity was unthinkable for Dwight Eisenhower. Mamie, while hoping for a retired Ike, knew a second term was right for him and accepted that situation with unselfish loyalty.

There was a lot of mileage to go and Ike was very much aware of how vulnerable he was after a heart attack and the increasing importance of the Vice President's role. Nixon was still not the popular choice. Ike would not endorse him but with Nixon's worldly experience Ike had a gut instinct that Nixon was an essential part of the ticket. He finally told his advisors of his decision and the race for the Presidency had started.

He again defeated Stevenson; this time by ten million votes twice the margin of 1952.

Eisenhower set off on his second journey determined to have a balanced budget and he was certain it would be achieved by one essential measure – disarmament.

At this point I ask myself what would I have done? Head for retirement with my pipe and slippers? After all Ike had survived over thirty year's army service – a World War, one Presidential term and two heart attacks. Surely he owed himself retirement. But disarmament was an obsession with him now.

Ike told this to the press and the public on every possible occasion. He never failed to lecture everybody, not only about the sheer futility and horror of nuclear war, which he said was not war in the conventional sense, but of the unbelievable waste of public money in stockpiling weapons no one could use. To this end three of his four budgets were balanced. Because his second inauguration date fell on Sunday 20, January 1957 his swearing in ceremony had to be taken in private.

Next day on Monday 21, January 1957 he had to repeat the oath on the East Portico of the White House administered by Chief Justice Earl Warren. That afternoon the celebrations got underway and entertained 750,000 spectators for three and a half hours. These march-pasts were getting bigger and more spectacular. Marching over a three mile route 17,000 people took part including 17,757 in military service; 52 bands and 10 drum and bugle corps. The finishing float was 408 feet long mounted on 164 wheels. The message it carried was "Liberty and strength through consent of the governed!" The inaugural Balls had also increased in number and were held in four hotels. The Armory, the Mayflower, the Statler, and the Sheraton-Park until the early hours of the morning. Two years later in the fall of 1959 the whole Little Rock saga had stabilized and integration in the 466 schools became the accepted norm. Another problem had been solved.

With only a year and a half to go Eisenhower invited Khrushchev to Washington against the wishes of many especially the press. One suggestion was to fill New York Harbour with red dye so that figuratively the Soviet President would come on a river of blood.

But Ike had other plans. He just wanted Khrushchev to see Americans at home in their own houses enjoying their freedom. Happy people that only needed to keep law and order with no other intimidating rules or regulations to make them. He wanted Khrushchev to see first hand Democracy at work. De Gaulle, Adenauer and MacMillan were worried. Eisenhower decided to visit them to reassure them no private deals would be done. The Germans, the French and the British turned out in the streets in hundreds of thousands to greet him. Ike was really moved. But somehow his plan backfired. Khrushchev was unimpressed by the American way of life. At least Ike had tried.

But historians have since criticized Ike's policy of non-belligerence to maintain peace. Non-belligerence against Korea, Vietnam, Cuba and Hungary seems to have been an indictment rather than a badge of honour. They complained not against what he did but what he failed to do. They even went so far as to say his reputation would have been higher today had he listened to advice. But who cares about reputations and glory in the history books if these same history books did not have photographs of devastated cities and unliveable countries and a list of American families blown into shadows on a wall by nuclear retaliation.

No, I think Eisenhower just about got it right and history will one day prove how right he was in the slow certain passage of time.

503

Stephen E. Ambrose, his biographer says "Eisenhower's decade by any standard was the best of the century" and that distinguished opinion is good enough for me. Certainly Ike's Presidency was no picnic.

One quote, of John F. Kennedy just about sums up Ike's Presidency. In a meeting with Eisenhower after Ike had left office he confessed. "No one knows how tough the job is until he has been in it a few months." Eisenhower replied "Mr. President, if you will forgive me I think I mentioned that to you three months ago." Kennedy's reply "I certainly have learnt a lot since."

But lets not jump too far ahead for the Eisenhower Presidency was now well into its second term. His heart was failing and he was well aware of it. In 1957 on November 25 he suffered another stroke this time sitting at his desk signing papers. Dizziness, disorientation and dysfunction is how it was described later. After calling his secretary Ann C. Whitman he found his explanations only came out as nonsense. Aides helped him to bed. His personal physician and neurological specialists arrived to diagnose his condition. A minor spasm in one of the capillaries to the brain was the verdict. The result according to Ike was a gap between what he wanted to say and what he could say. "This is the end," he thought and brooded morosely.

"Mamie and I are farmers from now on," he said. But later that month he decided to test himself by attending a meeting of NATO in Paris in mid December. Mamie worried. "It's foolhardy," she muttered. These frequent illnesses he endured were persuading him to arrange a smooth takeover should he again become incapacitated. That morbid awareness of his own mortality surfaced again and again. "My place in history," he predicted in his final year in office "will be decided by historians and I don't think I will be around to differ with them."
The last ten weeks of his Administration was spent waiting. He was now a caretaker President. The major decisions were left to the incoming President. Kennedy was a respectful listener when he came to the White House for a briefing on how the office was run. He came alone sitting in the back seat of the limousine – Eisenhower was glad. Coming with a group of advisors would be tantamount to a takeover. A celebration of victory. He needn't have worried. Kennedy was a gentleman. On January 17, 1961 at 8.30 p.m. Eisenhower was to make a farewell address on national radio and TV. His theme was the Cold War. He spoke of war and peace, police States and freedom. The permanent arms industry that had developed worried Ike. Lasting peace was in sight but the best he could say was that war has been avoided. On January 19, Kennedy came again to the White House for a final briefing.

Kennedy was told about the man with the satchel that contained the communication equipment to connect the President with SAC and the missiles forces. He was, according to Ike, an unobtrusive man who would shadow the President for all his days in office. Eisenhower like a small boy could not resist giving Kennedy a demonstration of the services available to him. He picked up the phone and said "Send a chopper", six minutes later one appeared on the lawn outside.

On the morning of Kennedy's inauguration John, Eisenhower's son remembers an eerie atmosphere in the White House. It had snowed heavily the night before and the Staffers had spent the night sleeping in the basement. The servants lined up. Eisenhower and Mamie went down the line saying goodbye to each of them. Tears were shed by many of them. The Kennedys, the Johnsons and a small entourage of Democrats arrived for a cup of coffee. After the ceremonies the Eisenhowers slipped quietly out a side entrance and into history. Eisenhower's thoughts were a revelation "We made a fantastic discovery – we were free."

Ike retired to Gettysburg to farm. Remarkably fit for a man who had suffered a major heart attack and major surgery. His mind was as sharp as ever.

Kennedy's assassination on November 22, 1963 saw Ike at a luncheon at the United Nations. The morbid lesson of man's mortality surrounded him in everyone's faces when they heard the news. Their innermost thoughts of the futility of it all remained an unspoken secret in their hearts.

The following day he went to Washington to pay his respect to Kennedy's widow Jackie and stand in prayer at his casket. The new President Lyndon Johnson asked him for advice which Eisenhower was glad to give by letter "Point out first that you have come to this office unexpectantly and you accept the decision of the Almighty" was some of what he wrote. Ike's closeness to the Almighty was instinctive to him ever since his boyhood days in Abilene.

But on Monday March 24, 1969 Dwight D. Eisenhower suffered a severe set back. His heart was fading. Oxygen was administered by tube up his nose. Billy Graham dropped in and they talked about spiritual matters. Three days later on March 27, the electrocardiogram was reading better. His life was being artificially prolonged, but sleep was not improving him. On March 28, 1969 the family was again gathered around his bed. "Lower the Shades," he barked like giving an order on the parade ground. "Pull me up." A doctor and John obliged, one on each arm. Mamie held his hand. The electrocardiogram was fluttering. Ike looked at his only son John and whispered softly. "I want to go, God take me." Soon his great heart finished its life's work. Ike was no more.

One feature of Dwight Eisenhower's Presidency stood out like a beacon in the full eight years of his term of office. Despite being a war time hero who tasted the glory of leading to victory the greatest army of fighting men, from nearly every nation on earth ever to be launched into battle, he used the memory of this terrible experience to keep America out of war during the whole course of his Presidency. To use his own words "The United States never lost a soldier or a foot of ground in my Administration. We kept the peace." People asked how it happened – quoting the Civil War General Robert E. Lee he always replied, "By God it didn't just happen!"

I won't dwell on the funeral of this great soldier and President, suffice it to say it was a funeral fit for a great man and the leaders of the world were gathered together for it. He passed away on March 28, 1969 and was finally laid to rest in his beloved Abilene in Kansas at the dignified old age of seventy-nine years. His beloved First Lady Mamie Geneva Doud Eisenhower survived him by almost ten years and was laid to rest alongside Ike in Abilene, Kansas. The date of her death was November 1, 1979 at the age of 82 years, 350 days.

The story of Dwight Eisenhower, 34th President of the United States and his loving First Lady Mamie does not quite end there. I have to include the one little person who brought so much joy and yet so much heartbreak to their lives. He was little "Icky" or Dwight Doud Eisenhower who died January 2, 1920 aged two years and three months. He was the tragedy in Ike's life about whom he said, "He was the one I have never been able to forget completely." Ike sent flowers to Mamie for every one of Icky's birthdays all through his life. As promised Icky was reinterred with Ike and Mamie. All three together once more happy in paradise.

35th President   John F. Kennedy

"JFK"
Born 1917
Died 1963
46 Years of age
1 Term
1961 – 1963
2 years, 306 days

Party: Democrat
County: Massachusetts
Profession: Author, Sailor, Politician
Ancestry: Irish
Estate Value: unknown millions
Hobbies: Swimming, Sailing and Touch Football.

Physical Description: Height 6 foot, Weight 170 lbs, dark red hair, handsome appearance.

Significant extracts from inauguration speech on January 20, 1961:
"The world is very different now for man holds in his mortal hands the power to abolish all forms of human poverty. And so my fellow Americans: Ask not what your country can do for you, ask what you can do for your country. My fellow citizens of the world. Ask not what America will do for you, but what together we can do for the freedom of man."

507

JOHN F. KENNEDY

We all know just how world famous President Eisenhower was but it is hard to believe that his successor in office John Fitzgerald Kennedy never met Dwight Eisenhower in the entire eight years that Kennedy was a Senator. I have uncovered some amazing facts in my research on the Presidents but that fact is the most puzzling of them all.

By the way I have already introduced you to JFK, as he became known later, in my final notes on Eisenhower. You may remember the conversation which I have already told you about. Kennedy was truly a raw recruit to such an office being the youngest President ever elected in 1960. He was honest enough to admit to Eisenhower how tough the job was even after only three months doing it.

It must have been a traumatic experience for such a man trying to fill the shoes of not only a great President but a colossus of the world military machine he bestrode. So famous was Eisenhower in Europe he only had to pass through the streets of Paris, London or Berlin later to bring thousands of waving cheering fans out to see him.

Yet Kennedy was the first of a new breed of politician and the most charismatic leader of the Democratic Party for years. A smooth polished educated and sophisticated member of what was to become known as the Kennedy Clan.

Sadly he will be forever remembered for his tragic assassination in Dallas at 12.30 p.m. on November 22, 1963 just over one thousand days after his inauguration on January 19, 1961. But let's start at the beginning.
John Fitzgerald Kennedy was born on May 29, 1917 at his home on Beals street in Brookline, Massachusetts, an attractive suburb of Boston. Kennedy's life story like Washington's is another Presidential anecdote that begins much earlier than his birth. Both of his ancestral families, the Kennedys and the Fitzgeralds, reached back three generations and are an essential part of the story.

The famine in Ireland in 1847 had a traumatic effect on the rural people of Ireland. Potato blight was a disease which destroyed the potato crops in Ireland in 1847. The potato was also Ireland's greatest source of income and its loss decimated the population. As a result of the potato blight there was a major exodus on the "famine ships" from Ireland's West coast carrying hundreds of thousands across the Atlantic to escape the death and desolation caused by this farming disaster. America was their only hope of a future. Certainly this dangerous journey was a much better bet than staying behind riding out the famine in Ireland.

The Kennedys and the Fitzgeralds were part of that history. Unfortunately when the Irish immigrants arrived, although many settled in quickly to life in America many, many of them were confronted by a wall of bigotry and rejection not unlike that experienced by black Americans later.

In almost every Boston newspaper after the Civil War in 1861 the job advertisements had one thing in common. All included the phrase "No Irish need apply". Politics seemed to be the only door open to them to overcome the discrimination against them and their children.

There was a fascinating rivalry between two of these families of Irish extraction. Between 1894 and 1900 Rose Kennedy's father, John Francis Fitzgerald had been elected to Congress for three terms of over three years but Patrick J. Kennedy(Paddy the Cooper), the grandfather of John F. Kennedy, who made his living as a cooper thwarted "Honey Fitz" – as John Francis Fitzgerald was called – from getting a fourth term. But by a strange quirk of fate, the son of Patrick J. Kennedy, young Joseph met, wooed and married Rose Fitzgerald daughter of "Honey Fitz" on October 7, 1914 and that put an end to their political rivalry forever.

It wasn't a wonderful match according to "Honey Fitz". Rose was amused by her father's opposition dismissing it flippantly with the words "I suppose no father thinks any man is good enough for his daughter but my father had extravagant notions of my beauty, grace, wit and charm." Joe Kennedy's father, Patrick J. Kennedy was a graduate of Harvard University, having been conferred there in 1912 before setting off on his main ambition which was to make as much money as quickly as possible. By the time he was twenty-five he had become the youngest Bank President in America and his new target was to become a millionaire before he was thirty-five. Fact is stranger than fiction for by some strange coincidence Patrick Kennedy, the political winner against Honey Fitz who landed in America in 1848 died of cholera on November 22, 1858; Assassination day in 1963.

Joe Kennedy, JFK's father stayed married to Rose Kennedy despite being a serial womanizer. His family grew steadily in number until they had nine children. According to the autobiography of screen star Gloria Swanson written in 1980 he even had a love affair with her. She was known as the goddess of the screen in the late 1920s. But that is as far as I intend to go on the subject of Joe Kennedy. He proved to be a brilliant father to a wonderful American, patriotic, well-educated, cultured family one of whom rose to be President of the United States.

Life is a great leveller. It has a habit of teaching us a short sharp lesson in the realities of living usually at a time when pride and arrogance make us blind to the good people around us. Luckily for Joe he had his short sharp shock when young Jack was hospitalized with scarlet fever. Jack's condition deteriorated to the point where Joe offered the almighty half of his fortune with a cheque made out to the church if only JFK lived. Jack recovered to everyone's relief but I found no record of that cheque ever been made out to the local Bishop. All joking aside I am sure Joe found another way of keeping his promise for from that time onwards he was a changed man and never took his family for granted again. After that the marriage became a closer union of two loving people.

But JFK's father Joe having satisfied his ambitions to become a millionaire was now consumed by another ambition – to launch Joe, his eldest son into politics with his money and wide social contacts anything was possible now.

The second eldest son John was also following the same path as his brother Joe. He followed in his footsteps to London but within a month John's health broke down and he returned back home with hepatitis or jaundice so his mother said. His next step in his education was a place at Princeton University although a chance to join an old friend K. LeMoyne Billings known as "Lem" was his main motivation. Lem in later years was to become a life long friend. John didn't have a very academically brilliant stay in Princeton.

His only claim to fame there was to be a member of "The Muckers Club", a collection of notorious students whose only ambitions were to play practical jokes and pranks on other students and faculty members. His comments on Princeton were vague: "Princeton? I didn't do much at Princeton. No, I didn't read much. It was mostly physical. Then I had jaundice........." This illness was to cost him a year out of college. He finally pulled out and found himself in his father's Alma Mater, Harvard University. His average aptitude and scholastic tests could not have opened the doors to Harvard without the help of his influential father Joe Kennedy. Perhaps it was not JFK's fault for his health was always a constant problem. His brother Bobby poked fun at his elder brother about it.

He said "If a mosquito bit Jack the mosquito would die........." The lack of academic success was tough on Jack as he continued to compare himself with big brother Joe. His only area of favourable comparison was football when he became one of four Kennedy brothers to play for Harvard at football. When John Kenneth Galbraith, the famous Harvard Professor of Economics, recalled the Kennedys he picked out Joe as "every faculties favourite" but JFK was gregarious, irreverent and far from diligent. "One did not cultivate such students," he said.

Perhaps it was the environment of Harvard or its thinkers and brilliant Professors but by his third year Jack began to take his studies seriously though he never did give his professors much credit for that miracle. Anyway he blossomed into a dedicated student and in 1939 won an honours degree in political science. His thesis was later published in book form under the title Why England Slept. Arthur Krock of the New York Times who was a friend of his father later wrote "It was remarkable, not so much for the freshness and precision of the supporting data – (which he had extracted from his father's files) – as for the fine perception of the fundamental problems of a peace loving democracy threatened with dictatorial regimes bent on subversive annexation or war."

His father's speech writer also helped. It thrilled Joe Senior no end for he wrote to Jack "You would be surprised how a book that really makes the grade with high class people stands you in good stead for years to come ....." Yes his father, even in this personal triumph of his son was as usual projecting his thoughts way into the future and painting rainbows.
The book became a national bestseller, helped of course by a doting millionaire father who just happened to buy the first 30,000 or 40,000 copies for storage in their Hyannis Port home in Massachusetts. The timing of its release came with Hitler's onslaught on London. "The Blitz" as it was known left thousand of casualties killed and injured in its wake. Sadly the Allies were later guilty of similar atrocities over German cities, a type of warfare avoided if at all possible today.

In a strange way the end product of his book Why England Slept led to something John F. Kennedy had never planned in Harvard when writing that thesis for his political science degree. He was now standing firmly on the national political stage, and he had only just left college. The year was 1940 and America had not yet entered the war. In the summer of that year Jack headed to California for a holiday.

While there he decided to enrol at Stanford University in the school of Business Administration. However his health once again let him down and after only three months at Stanford he returned home to hospital. By spring of 1941 he was off again, this time to South America and got acquainted while on holiday with the daughters of a well-known Argentinean Diplomat. Jack was young and single so could be excused his playboy lifestyle which was natural for a fellow in his age group. But war in far off Europe was raging with fierce intensity and the war drums were getting louder and beating ominously back home in America. Roosevelt's flirtation with Churchill on the political stage and the reports coming from the battlefields of Europe made it almost inevitable that war would come to America.

Roosevelt's declaration of a national emergency changed everything for the Kennedy family. Joe Junior jointed the Naval Aviation Cadet Programme at Harvard. Some say Jack was rejected for both the army and the Navy because of his weak back but this can't be proved.

Others say he got into the Navy after a programme of back strengthening exercises. Perhaps the real truth lay in his father's ambassadorial influence – his father had just been appointed U.S. Ambassador to Britain by Franklin D. Roosevelt. Whatever the truth is John Fitzgerald Kennedy entered the Navy in the office of Naval Intelligence a plum desk job at the time. But here another twist of fate changes the storyline completely when on December 7, 1941 the Japanese attacked Pearl Harbour. This made Jack totally dissatisfied with his "plum job". He wanted action.

The following conversation recorded in Martin S. Goldman's book John F. Kennedy underlines this. "You know what they tried to do? They tried to ship me to Panama. So then I called the old man and told him what I wanted, that I wanted action. And the next day just like that, the very next day, I had orders sending me off to this PT outfit in the Pacific."

Around the same time his elder brother Joe having gone the orthodox route, graduated from flight training school in Florida and received his naval wings as an ensign in the Naval Reserve. It was one of the most elite groups in the forces and he had achieved it all by his own efforts. His father proudly presented him with the gold wings of a naval aviator.

In the meantime JFK was spending a further stretch in hospital. But the handicap with which John suffered was back trouble, one which could have excused him from the hazards of war. But JFK rejected this option out of hand and vowed it was not going thwart his ambition for action. Perhaps he realized once again that Joe had been top dog so he was determined to compensate for this on dangerous overseas PT boat duty.

So what was a PT like? It was known as a gasoline engine torpedo boat; eighty feet long with a beam of twenty feet eight inches. The thirty-eight tonne boat made of plywood had a draft of five feet and carried a compliment of seventeen men with a speed of 41 knots. It had four 21 inch torpedoes and also carried 3,000 gallons of gasoline which made it a floating time bomb.

JFK's exploits with PT109, the boat he commanded has gone down in naval folklore. On the night of August 1, 1943 - PT109 was rammed by a Japanese destroyer. It cut JFK's boat in half leaving two crewmen dead and others badly injured. The crew swam away from the sinking PT109 and headed for Plain Pudding Island, an Atoll over three miles away. JFK it has been reliably reported towed one of his injured shipmates the full three miles holding the strap of his crewman's lifejacket between his teeth.

How he managed it given the handicap of his weak back was miraculous. It was also a very courageous act and one which saved the crewman's life. It is also good to report that all the crew was eventually rescued. For his heroism John F. Kennedy was presented with the Navy and Marine Corps Medal in 1945 by Captain Frederick Conklin. The citation was signed by Admiral William Frederick Halsey.

Here let us insert a character snapshot of Kennedy given by Richard Reeves in his book John F. Kennedy….. "He was intelligent, detached, curious, candid, not always honest and he was careless and dangerously disorganized. He was also very impatient, addicted to excitement and living his life as if it were a race against time. Someone said he was like a man driving a motorbike at 100 mph – on the edge of a cliff. Yet he was a man of soaring charm who believed that one on one he would always prevail."

Naturally, being the son of Ambassador Joe Kennedy, the story of PT109 found headlines in all the national newspapers and was later exploited for political purposes. Historians have since criticised this exploitation but have admitted nevertheless that it was truly a brave act in the course of duty for his country.

As a postscript, here is a little story about the incident. When asked by a little boy in Ashland, Wisconsin "How did you become a hero?" Kennedy replied "It was involuntary. They sank my boat." Sadly the war was to punch an almost unbridgeable hole in the life of the Kennedy family which can never be divorced from the life of John F. Kennedy?
A devastating tragedy engulfed them. In August 1944, Joe Kennedy Junior was killed on a bombing mission over the Bay of Biscay while delivering explosives to the Continent.

By an amazing coincidence Elliott Roosevelt, son of FDR was in the flight escort and came home safely. Later it seems Joe Kennedy tough, hard, bitter, and unforgiving lashed out to Senator Harry Truman about the death of his favourite son..... "What the hell are you doing campaigning for that crippled son of a bitch that killed my son Joe?" However it must be said President Roosevelt later sent a letter of condolence to Joe Kennedy. But forgiveness didn't come easy to Joe Kennedy for on hearing of the death of FDR he wrote to his daughter "There is no doubt that it is a great thing for the country." But this anti-FDR sentiment touched even John F. Kennedy. When asked how he felt on hearing of FDR's death he replied dryly "I had no traumatic experience."

Still, writing on stories of the war years: In June 1948 when he was a young Congressman John F. Kennedy addressed the Polish-American Citizens clubs in which he criticized FDR for not understanding the Russian mind. Next day he was reported by The Boston Herald as saying "Roosevelt sold Poland to the Reds." This repugnance of Roosevelt by the Kennedy Family was also reflected in a speech this time by the words of Robert Kennedy in a seminar paper he wrote on Yalta. In it he accused FDR of accommodating "The immoral Soviet Union who had a philosophy that spelled death and dishonour to the world."
But this well-known bitter hostility between the Roosevelts and the Kennedys was roundly criticized by one of Kennedy's own Democratic Congressmen after JFK voted in support of the 22nd Amendment to limit the President to two terms in office. The vote was seen as an anti-Roosevelt vote and the irritated Congressman complained "My God can't they let the man rest in peace."

We learned earlier how Joe Kennedy's ambition was to have Joe Junior follow a political career. A strange almost prophetic promise was made by John F. Kennedy as a Senator. He said "Just as I went into politics because Joe died, if anything happens to me tomorrow my brother Bobby would run for my seat in the Senate. And if Bobby died Teddy would take over for him."

We know today how that prophesy nearly came true. First JFK, next Bobby, then Teddy. But it ended when Teddy withdrew from the race for his mother's sake. Three of her four sons had died Joe, John and Bobby. She was not about to sacrifice a fourth one.

But there were other events happening in John F. Kennedy's life far more important than politics. He pursued, wooed, won and married a graduate from the Sorbonne University in Paris, a sophisticated lady of beauty and grace who later was to bring style, class and elegance to the White House social scene. Her name Jacqueline Bouvier. She worked as The Washington Heralds "inquiring Camera girl" for $42.50 per week. Marrying her handsome prince elevated her instantly into the Kennedy millions. With her chic "Jackie look" bouffant hairstyle, pillbox hat, she became a leader of fashion for not only the party-going Boston set but later for the whole of the nations young women.

She was a painter, art collector, and linguist and before she met JFK she also studied at Vassar College and the George Washington University in Washington DC. As First Lady she restored the interior of the White House with furnishings of America's traditional past and was proud to display her finished work in a nationwide televised tour of the White House explaining and discussing the treasures of its rooms. She often went on tour with her husband to Europe and Latin America displaying on her visits her genteel manners and charm and of course her command of foreign languages.

Kennedy was very proud of Jacqueline's talents especially her linguistic skills and her knowledge and familiarity with French culture which so impressed General De Gaulle on Kennedy's visit to Paris with her.

His verdict on that State visit was summed up as follows "I am very proud to have been the man who accompanied Jacqueline Kennedy to Paris." This fascinating lady Jacqueline Bouvier was very much a part of the JFK story. A book was written about this famous love affair by Edward Klein, a New Yorker born in Yonkers who had an illustrious career in American Journalism as Editor in Chief of the New York Times Magazine. His brilliant book called All Too Human won for him the Pulitzer Prize.

His book traces the lives of both Jacqueline and JFK from the time they met until that tragic day in Dallas. Selecting some of the anecdotes in its four hundred pages to paint a quick sympathetic picture is extremely difficult. I trust he will allow me to mention a few of them.

Jackie it seems was the daughter of an alcoholic father and a volatile mother whose personality clashes created a very unhappy atmosphere in the family. There were seven children in the marriage with three different mothers.
Jacqueline described herself in a simple self-portrait as being five foot seven inches in height, having brown hair and square face and eyes too far apart for which to find a suitable pair of specs. Modestly she admitted to "Having a sensational figure but can look slim if I pick the right clothes." At twenty-one she was blossoming into a beautiful woman. Riding her show jumper "Sagebrush" almost recklessly over the stone walls of the country seat of the Auchincloss family where she lived, was one of the most exhilarating pastimes she knew.

She met JFK at a wedding they had both attended and was fully aware of his reputation at that time as a war hero, a playboy and a budding politician. The Kennedy's of Massachusetts were of course a famous family whose father had been a pre-war Ambassador in London. Jackie's circle however, was not that impressed by the Kennedys, describing them as "course loud Irish Micks." Jackie wasn't that interested in meeting this John Kennedy as she already had her own date.

It's not well known that Jackie came from a strange aristocratic background when her father Hughie Auchincloss married ten years previously and brought her to live in Merrywood. Unknown to most Americans in 1950, an aristocratic ruling class had existed in their midst for three hundred years. It was known as the WASP ascendancy and was made up of a few hundred wealthy families whose men moved up the educational ranks from private schools through Groton and on to Yale University.

Their journey usually ended in top jobs in banks and law firms and sometimes in the higher reaches of the CIA. It was their accents that gave them away. Jackie was surrounded by servants and it would be difficult to separate her lifestyle from that of the British upper crust back in old England complete with eccentric relations. Vanderbilt, a prominent member of this top three hundred had his own "summer cottage" worth $365 million in today's money.

It would have been impossible to convince this exclusive circle that this was Washington or Lincoln's America they lived in. They were a race apart. Worst of all the Kennedy wealth was looked down on with contempt because of Joe Kennedy's mafia links building his fortune from bootlegging.

Jackie's stepfather, Hugh Auchincloss was the heir to the Standard Oil fortune – "the old money" as it was known. The staircase of Merrywood swept regally down to the grandfather clock in the hallway where the sounds of the Butler and his wife could be heard preparing the dining room for dinner. This was a familiar scene Jacqueline often experienced. Janet her mother was also familiar on a nightly basis with the black tie society dinners she attended. For her it was one endless round of parties from June to September.

Yet nobody was spared Janet's temper tantrums not even Jacqueline Bouvier. As for Jacqueline herself she was quiet and proved herself capable of discussing the intimate lives of famous European artists with National Gallery director John Walker. The language allowed around the dinner table was in French so it is no wonder Jacqueline grew up an accomplished French speaker. But in the middle of so much wealth and opulence Jackie was almost a Cinderella for her only inheritance from the Auchincloss fortune was $3,000 in 1948. Being only a Bouvier and not an Auchincloss she lived her life as a humble poor relation.
Well that just about paints a simple picture of Jacqueline Bouvier Kennedy and the life she lived growing up in Merrywood before she met John Fitzgerald Kennedy, future President of the United States.

But let's concentrate on Jacqueline the woman. As we know she was born in Long Island in 1929 the daughter of a stockbroker whose marriage broke down. Her mother remarried, this time to Hugh Auchincloss who was far wealthier than her real father. Jacqueline was sent to the most exclusive schools, two years at Vassar, a year at the Sorbonne in Paris and finally to George Washington University. She ended up, despite all this education, working in a job arranged for her by Hugh Auchincloss as an "Inquiring Photographer" for a Washington newspaper. From the beginning of her time as First Lady Jackie was planted deep in the elitist camp.

She soon set out to upgrade the White House with the help of the Commission of Fine Arts and the National Gallery. She was unique for a First Lady as a linguist. She was always very well informed on literature and the Arts yet could hold her own usually alongside the sex symbols of Hollywood. The youth of the country simply adored her and copied her hairstyles, her clothes and her hats. Jackie was very much her own woman and refused to cooperate with the Administration by going on holidays solo. They were luxury packed holidays abroad that brought a rocket of protest from her husband when the bills came in.
At her wedding she refused to meet the Auchincloss side of her family. Perhaps the reason for not playing the dutiful wife was because her husband was busy breaking the marriage rules himself. Her final act of independence was to dominate at Jack's funeral directing everything according to her own wishes. She even wore the same blood-stained dress she wore in Texas on the President's Assassination day.

She almost had a disdain for politics and perhaps this was reflected in her choice of partner for her second marriage, Aristotle Onassis, a Greek shipping magnate. In fact she finally went to live in Greece, a long way from the bright lights of Paris, Boston or Washington. Although she lived her life surrounded by the rich and powerful somehow I feel she was always a very unfulfilled woman. Because of the assassination of her husband the 35th President, she left to history the heartbreaking image of a very tragic woman indeed.

John Fitzgerald Kennedy at 170 lbs was quite slim. As a growing young boy, he had tousled brown hair, protruding ears and flashing white teeth. He was boyish for his thirty-four years.

But John F. Kennedy had a different upbringing. His father Joe had a macho, vulgar, and immoral no-holds barred approach to women. He had no respect for them and unfortunately Jack picked up his bad habits. Jack became disparaging about them and seemed to display an utter contempt for the possibilities of romance for instance. He couldn't identify with the letter that passed between his friend and his fiancé. She had written a love letter, a real tear jerker to him but JFK shocked his friend by saying "It may be romantic to you but its shit to me."

Lucky for Jack he wasn't the apple of his father's eye so the broad spectrum of his father's bad behaviour didn't influence him. That sort of spinoff fell on Joe his elder brother. The one female companion that had any beneficial effect on Jack was that of his sister Kathleen or "Kick" as she was called. She was his best friend and when she died it left a jagged hole in his life, uncannily like what happened to Calvin Coolidge.

He missed Kathleen desperately. To him she was the one female he could entrust with his most secret thoughts. About God, his family, his future. But this was good news. There was still really an innocence and vulnerability about him that no amount of his father's grooming had affected. Basically he was still a nice guy.

However Jacqueline was not a hit when she arrived at Hyannis Port to meet the Kennedys. His sisters poked fun at her and everything about her. They had never seen anything like Jacqueline. This was no surprise after all they came from two different cultures.

It was this differentness that attracted Jack and Jacqueline to each other. It was a foreign chemistry cultivated in her WASP upbringing that set her apart and set Jack on fire.

Jacqueline found it hard to handle the Kennedy family's extrovert approach to everything. Insults flew hard and fast. Always charging around, sometimes interrupting conversations with private jokes, bouncing around with noisy ridicule of many victims. Sports, politics, films, books and many other subjects ebbed and flowed like a turbulent river crossing the rapids. Surviving was the name of the game and it frightened her. She could only describe it as an Irish Picnic.

It was a very spasmodic courtship Jackie remembered "Conducted mainly at long distance with a great cascade of coins in dozens of phone booths." The mobile phone was still a figment of some inventor's imagination in the 1960s.

He proposed by telegram while she was in England photographing the Coronation of Queen Elizabeth II for The Washington Times Herald.

So let's describe their wedding day briefly. A crowd of about three thousand people lined Spring Street when Jackie arrived outside St. Mary's church. She seemed to float down the isle on the arm of Hugh Auchincloss. There were some complaints that it was not the gracious Newport happening that her mother Janet would have preferred. Irish politicians were all over the place in their bright blue suits. Brother Bobby was the best man. Jack was in pain for the forty minute ceremony of the nuptial mass celebrated by Cardinal Cushing a friend of the family. Finally they exchanged the customary kiss and headed for the exit smiling at well-wishers on both sides of the church.

Jackie spotted one well-wisher and her heart jumped. It was her real father from the Bouvier side of the family who stood in the shadows as a spectator. Black Jack Bouvier had tears in his eyes as he watched her go by. He could take no part in the ceremony being unsteady on his feet. Outside Jackie recoiled at the frenzy of the mob but Jack basked in the adulation. Jackie was just terrified: On honeymoon in Mexico as a guest of the President, Jackie wrote a loving and compassionate letter to her father. Black Jack's friend described it as "One of the most touching letters black Jack had ever read. Only a rare and noble spirit could have written it."

The marriage had hardly started and JFK was already bored. As he once told a friend "It's the chase I like – not the kill. Once I get a woman I am not interested in carrying on."

Jacqueline captured JFK's restless boredom in a telling poem. Which reads as follows: -
He would find love
He would never find peace
For he must go seeking
The Golden Fleece.

Three children blessed the marriage John, Caroline and Patrick but tragedy struck Patrick down and he died when he was only two days old on August 9, 1963. His body was re-interred in Arlington National Cemetery close to his father on December 3, 1963. The death of Patrick tore JFK's heart apart for he cried and cried for days afterwards.
Jack's loss of interest continued and he often went missing leaving Jacqueline to her own devices. Unfortunately she began to cultivate extravagant tastes such as expensive clothes and jewellery. Her many shopping trips and cavalier spending habits began to irritate Jack and rows flared up about Jacqueline's shopping list. It began to register with their friends that their marriage was not a happy one. The fact that he continued his extra-marital affairs with other women didn't help. An amazing rumour was going the rounds that Jack's father Joe Kennedy had paid her one million dollars not to walk out on the marriage while Jack was President. I find this hard to believe. Being answerable to her husband for clothes would be eliminated for bills would not be necessary given such financial independence of one million dollars. Besides Jacqueline's independence born and nurtured by her Auchincloss upbringing would never have allowed her to wear such a halter round her neck.

JFK's marriage and his politics were creating a strain on his health. His spine was acting up and his days were full of pain. In fact in 1954 he was using crutches to get around. Malaria and fevers from his war days and the onset of Addison's disease just about filled his cup to overflowing. His natural defences against sickness were just not working.

He was eventually confined to hospital for a serious spine operation a stay which hit a serious crisis. An infection set in and he went into a coma. He was so bad he was given the last rites of the Catholic Church. There was confusion as to whether his crises came from Addison's disease or his spinal surgery. But he came through it all and a silver lining shone through when he was convalescing because during it he wrote a book called Profiles in Courage.

This was a book of essays about Americans who fought for unpopular lost causes and it won for him the Pulitzer Prize in 1957. Again it was a book written by him that enhanced his reputation among an audience who up to now did not know him. They now knew a man who had a deep appreciation of American history.

As we can see John F. Kennedy was beginning to make an impact on the National Stage. In 1957 he became a powerful member of the Senates Foreign Relations Committee. The following year he spent his weekends campaigning for re-election in Massachusetts and was eventually returned with a record majority of 874,000 votes, the biggest ever recorded in a Massachusetts Senatorial contest.

Yes, as you can gather John F. Kennedy was fast consolidating his claims to the Presidency. Now the Presidency was to become Jack Kennedy's major goal. The year was 1956. As soon as he had been re-elected Senator for Massachusetts, JFK began to flex his political muscle for a final push towards the pinnacle of American politics. Yet this ambition was not a foregone certainty for Kennedy and his political machine. There were many obstacles to be overcome. Some thought he was too young. Others felt he was too inexperienced. A third opinion, the most worrying of the lot was his Roman Catholicism. In a country mainly Protestant, this obstacle had never been overcome before.

You may remember some previous opinions expressed by critics about this dilemma in other Presidencies. How could he convince his detractors that being a Catholic did not make him a puppet of the Pope in Rome as many people seemed to fear? He also had to contend with the Democratic Liberals in the Party who favoured Senator Hubert Humphrey of Minnesota or his old sparring partner President Eisenhower and even the formidable Adlai Stevenson. He threw his cap into the ring early in 1960, six months before the National Convention, and won seven primaries the most important of which was West Virginia, a predominantly Protestant State. This eliminated the Roman Catholic obstacle at a stroke.
Lyndon B. Johnson was considered his main opponent but it turned out Johnston was only strong among Southern delegates. Kennedy won the nomination on the first ballot and persuaded Lyndon Johnson to be his running mate. The stage was now set for his clash with Richard Milhous Nixon for the Presidency.

Both of their campaigns spared no expense and no geographical limitations on their travels. Kennedy canvassed in forty-six States and 273 cities and towns throughout America. Nixon matched him by visiting every State in the Union as well as seventeen urban areas. In Houston Kennedy said "I believe in America where the separation of Church and State is absolute..... Where no official neither requests nor accepts instructions on public policy from any ecclesiastical source."

Kennedy's slogan was similar to Roosevelt's New Deal. He called it the "New Frontier". His TV debates are now history but they have prompted much intensive analytical discussions. JFK's four television encounters with Nixon is claimed to have held the key to his final election. This seems to me an outlandish claim for two men who had travelled the length and breadth of America meeting a couple of million Americans on their journeys.

There are those who claim that these TV debates finally launched John Fitzgerald Kennedy as a mature, polished, modern politician well capable of the role of President. Perhaps in modern day parlance Kennedy was well-equipped with his spin doctors image makers, and brilliant scriptwriters far ahead of their time. They said that Nixon had been projected as a badly prepared, swarthy, unshaven candidate at these final TV debates.

Once again I consider this a very unfair excuse for defeat especially from Kennedy's side of the debate. It seems to have been overlooked that Kennedy defeated a Vice President who had been around at the top of politics for many years, eight of which had been spent inside the White House. Besides, Nixon was an accomplished lawyer and a formidable debater.

No, I am afraid the time had really come for this new kid on the block, the charismatic John Fitzgerald Kennedy with an eloquent vision of the future to become 35th President of the United States. His victory I am sure had very little to do with the stubble on Nixon's chin.

Finally one ingredient in his favour was the power of the black vote in the Northern States. His support for the release of civil rights leader Martin Luther King from jail, for taking part in a civil rights demonstration in Georgia fed into his power base. Martin Luther King was released from jail soon after. JFK as we all now know emerged victorious in the Presidential election of 1960 by 303 electoral votes to 219 and his inauguration followed in January 1961. The start of his expected four year journey had arrived.

Inauguration day was truly a miserable one weather-wise on January 20, 1961 as the new President John F. Kennedy was sworn into office by Chief Justice Earl Warren. He was the 35th President since George Washington was first inaugurated back in 1789. Snow had begun falling the previous night covering Washington to a depth of eight inches. It was tossed and blown by sharp blasts of icy cold winds. There were 32,000 people including a number of missiles on gun carriages in the march past. Place of honour was given to a PT boat containing eight surviving members of an eleven man crew which Kennedy had commanded in World War II in the Pacific.

Over four thousand Secret Service agents, policemen and plain clothes men mingled with the crowds protecting both the incoming and outgoing Presidents. Four churches were represented in the person of Cardinal Cushing of Boston, Archbishop Iakovos, Primate of the Greek Orthodox Church of North and South America, Reverend John Barclay of the Central Christian Church and Rabbi Nelson Glueck, President of the Hebrew Union College Cincinnati who sang the "Star Spangled Banner". Robert Frost read one of his poems The Gift Outright. Kennedy was the youngest President yet to be inaugurated at 43 years and 236 days. His inauguration speech quoted earlier made quite an impact on his listeners an extract of which is as follows.... "The world is very different now for man holds in his mortal hands the power to abolish all forms of human poverty. And so my fellow Americans ask not what your country can do for you, ask what you can do for your country. My fellow citizens of the world ask not what America will do for you, but what together we can do for the freedom of man."

The usual inaugural balls entertained the crowd in five different hotels. It was an evening shared by the new money clan of the Kennedys and the old money aristocracy we have come to know as the WASP ascendancy, one group barely tolerant of the other.

And now the one thousand days of John F. Kennedy's reign began and there was a lot of work to be done. As mentioned when writing on Eisenhower, JFK met him for the first time just before inauguration day and acknowledged there was a lot to learn from this old pro. Now his learning curve was about to take off.

On January 17, 1961 Eisenhower left the Presidency with a warning of the growing power of the military industrial complex in America. The message became diluted in the euphoria surrounding the incoming Kennedy clan. The glitz and glamour surrounding the new people in the White House became orchestrated by show business celebrities like Frank Sinatra.

But JFK was groping his way in the job. His most controversial appointment to the post of Attorney General was to be his brother Robert. Congress found it a difficult choice to approve. In his Administration there were one hundred and one from South of the border or just on the Southern border with mostly Republican leanings. Much of his foreign affairs problems he inherited from Eisenhower. Cuba had fallen to Castro after a guerrilla war from the hills.

Castro was a popular victor being seen by the Cubans to have defeated Batista's corrupt regime which was backed by sinister underworld figures and cynical corporate interests. He was the Cuban Robin Hood. However over 100,000 refugees fled from Cuba to America. But Castro was no angel for he had told Richard Nixon "The people of Cuba don't want free elections, they only produce bad Governments. The people of Cuba don't want fair trials. They want them shot as soon as possible." It seemed this justified in Castro's mind the five hundred deaths by firing squad in Cuba. Well that was the impression the revolution left.

Cuba was Kennedy's first political time bomb which would cause him much pain and confusion. Kennedy ignored advice not to take drastic action and allowed the CIA to formulate its own policy towards Castro, the final result was the disastrous adventure called "The Bay of Pigs" invasion named after the beach where an abortive landing of troops took place. Significantly Kennedy's Generals over whom he now was the Commander-in-Chief showed no interest. It was supposed to be a low-key invasion but soon the new Republican magazine got hold of the news. Kennedy suppressed publication and it did not print the story.

Bizarrely now it had reached comical proportions where the only thing that wasn't known to Castro was the exact time and place of the invasion. However Castro, a top General himself during his campaign, had already guessed where the troops would land. He placed 25,000 well-trained soldiers and 200,000 militiamen in strategic positions and the rest is history. Only one certainty came out of this debacle – Kennedy had got off to a very poor start with a bloody nose. In December 1962, he was obliged to pay a ransom of $53 million in food and medical supplies for the release of 1,189 prisoners.

Some time later Kennedy and Eisenhower met on April 22, 1961. The subject for discussion was the failed raid on the Bay of Pigs. It was an informal meeting at which Kennedy ruefully confessed the raid had been a total failure. They continued to stroll around the grounds of Camp David called after Ike's son David, and JFK was only now beginning to realize the complexity of the job. He seemed bewildered.

Eisenhower the General, steeped in military expertise asked Kennedy "Why on earth did you not provide air cover?" Kennedy's reply startled Eisenhower. "We thought that if it was learned that we were really doing this rather than the rebels themselves the Soviets would be very apt to cause trouble in Berlin." Eisenhower thought that was exactly the opposite to what would really happen. "If the Soviets sense weakness that is when they press hardest" were roughly the words he used.

Eisenhower then launched into his own military logic.... "Mr. President, how could you expect the world to believe that we had nothing to do with it? Where did these people get the ships to go from Central America to Cuba? Where did they get the weapons? Where did they get all the communications and all the other things they would need? How could you possibly have kept from the world any knowledge that the United States had been assisting the invasion? I believe there is only one thing to do when you go into this kind of thing. It must be a success."

So it fell to Robert Kennedy the Attorney General to act as fire-fighter in the crucial area of civil rights. But Robert was no intellectual either and held no firm belief worth talking about. But he was a tough cookie and loyal to a fault. Robert did not get on at all well with Herbert Hoover, the head of the FBI. Robert it seems was too unorthodox and disrespectful in his approach to running the Justice Department and that didn't suit the great Mr Hoover. Robert had the backing of the President but Hoover was supported by a vast and far flung empire of FBI men. He was a dictator in his own circle to all intents and purposes.

The dark side of Hoover was the files he kept on the liaison between Jack Kennedy and a Danish beauty called Inga Arvad, which a Hoover's Agent had bugged in 1941, twenty years previously. He had plenty of material to go on in the life of JFK and reaped a delicious harvest for his files. It was now a dossier. This included names like Marilyn Monroe, Jane Mansfield and Judith Exner, the girlfriend of Chicago gangster Sam Giancana. Today it is said Hoover maintained his own power by the collection of such dossiers on prominent politicians.

But the personalities of both Bob Kennedy and Edger Hoover were so similar they were on a collision course from day one.
The young Kennedy was impatient, ambitious and driven by detail. In 1961 he had the same personality as Hoover had in 1924. Both were hard taskmasters. It was no secret Hoover didn't like these precocious newcomers to the White House. Their casual dress and attitude horrified him. Bobby even took his beloved Labrador to work with him. This Labrador sometimes soiled on the carpets. Most irritating of all was Bobby's habit of bypassing Hoover to speak directly with the Agents. No Attorney General had ever tried that before. Finally Hoover's access to the President was now limited with Bobby blocking the way.

To return to civil rights, it was inevitable Hoover would be a problem in this field. For years Hoover had resisted hiring blacks as Agents. The ones who served did so as drivers or office clerks. Hoover was an unpleasant, unrepentant racist and related the rise in racial agitation to Communism. The agitation started in 1955 on a bus in Montgomery, Alabama when a black seamstress now revered by blacks refused to give up her seat to a white and was arrested. Her name was Rosa Parks.

The black church leaders flexed their muscles for a year after the arrest but when a boycott of the buses citywide was implemented the blacks were listened to out of economic necessity. One of these leaders was Martin Luther King. His policy of non-violence was a carbon copy of Gandhi's one in India. King had a PHD in Theology from Boston University. But the mob didn't understand the power of non-violent protest and reacted with violence and brutality which was captured on film for the world to see, and the world wasn't amused at what it saw.

There were many sit-ins in places that practised segregation as the world looked on. Soon Robert Kennedy was forced to intervene. His brother John F. Kennedy made a speech on television saying: "If this country should ever reach the point where any man or group of men with force or threat of force could long defy the commands of our court and our Constitution then no law would stand free from doubt, no Judge would be sure of his writ and no citizen would be safe from his neighbour."

The Kennedy brothers were coming out of these civil rights clashes with added glory. The struggle came to a head with the "Freedom Rule" in the South in 1961 and the Kennedys had to take a stand supporting them. Violence flared and Hoover's Agents did nothing. Kennedy called in the Greyhound bus leaders and let them know where he stood on the issue of integration on the buses. John F. asked for a cooling off period to which James Farmer one of the militant protesters replied "We have been busy cooling off for one hundred years."

Robert finally sent four hundred Federal law officers to Alabama to ensure the safety of the interstate freedom riders. Segregation was finally banned from the interstate buses on November 1, 1961. A century of discrimination was over. Kennedy was only nine months in office.

Later the words used at a meeting with Robert Kennedy by civil rights activists depressed him. One famous playwright Hansberry shocked him by telling him she would like to arm all blacks to shoot white people in the streets. A white backlash in the South would not do the Democratic Party or his brother the President any good.

It all came to a head with a march on Washington on August 28, 1963 to give notice that black Americans would have to be taken seriously. Locked arm in arm were Jewish, protestant and Catholic leaders. Stars of stage and screen also participated. Charlton Heston, Marlon Brando, Harry Belafonte and Sidney Poitier walked with fifteen United States Senators. It was on this march Martin Luther King coined the famous phrase "I have a dream." Kennedy, while later supporting the march was criticized for being too cautious. Still he was always applauded as the civil rights true champion.

But another crisis followed. One of the most dangerous times for the world took place in the fall of 1962 "The Cuban missile crisis". It is well-known to us all today but at that time John F. Kennedy was being challenged to prove his true mettle as a leader and he came through it all with flying colours. Russia was the troublemaker. By sending nuclear missiles to Cuba to be sited there they were looking for trouble. It was a direct challenge to America's pride and Kennedy had no intention of shirking it. The cocky Russian leader Khrushchev was deliberately testing the waters so to speak.
He presumed he was dealing with a weak U.S. Presidency under an inexperienced leader. After the Bay of Pigs fiasco who could blame him for thinking this way. Despite all the sermons of Eisenhower on the horrors of nuclear war, Castro took the criminal gamble. Khrushchev and Castro would have been condemned as war criminals if war had broken out and millions of people annihilated. Having missiles appealed to Castro for he could never defeat America with conventional arms. The audacious decision to place missiles in another country was explained by Khrushchev as follows "We carried weapons there at the request of the Cuban Government. These weapons were to be in the hands of Soviet military men.... Our aim was only to defend Cuba." But coming Congressional elections and the awareness of the press combined to push the crisis to the top of Kennedy's political agenda. This time there would be no mistakes.

In late June 1962 the CIA alerted Kennedy to the fact that something new and different was happening on the island. There were now 5,000 Soviet specialists there. The missiles were being installed fifty miles southwest of Havana. The object was deadly serious. American cities were being targeted with nuclear warheads from Cuba and the only light moment at the emergency meeting of his Generals came when General David M. Sharp remarked "You are in a pretty bad fix Mr. President." To which Kennedy came back with........ "Yes and you are in it with me."

Raining conventional bombs on Cuba thus killing hundreds of thousands was a non-starter. There were too many missiles directed at America and literally eighty million Americans would die instantly. McNamara's suggestion of a naval blockade was adopted. By doing that the U.S. would win the propaganda's battle by proving she was not the aggressor.

It is amazing today to find out just how serious Kennedy took the threat. Bombers loaded with nuclear weapons were put on full alert. Quarantine on all offensive military equipment being shipped to Cuba was introduced. The first armoured division consisting of 15,000 men and four tank battalions was ordered to the East Coast; four tactical squadrons were placed at readiness for strikes against Cuba. A fleet of 180 vessels and 250,000 men were prepared for landings if required. Even Polaris submarines armed with nuclear warheads headed for the Soviet Union. The military men, the Hawks, were calling for a Pearl Harbour type strike.

Kennedy appeared on television at 7 p.m. in late October to explain the situation to America. Any nuclear weapon launched from Cuba against any nation in the Western Hemisphere would be considered an act of aggression by the Soviet Union on the United States. Every American city right up to Seattle was within range of these missiles. Perhaps the fact that the crisis was played out on television before the world and not inside the silence of a Cabinet room helped to focus a lot of minds on the danger confronting everybody. Walter Lippmann, the famous columnist questioned Kennedy's approach of direct confrontation. Others felt it was a gamble by Khrushchev to get rid of the missiles the United States already had in Turkey which were targeted on the Soviet Union. The end product of the standoff was to have the Cuban missiles withdrawn in return for a similar move by the U.S. in Turkey.

Fairness and justice among all parties had been achieved but by some very dangerous sabre rattling. The lessons Eisenhower had preached in the 1950s were proved right in the 1960s.

The thirteen days standoff was a solitary lesson to the fools in the Administration calling for war who luckily were tightly controlled by Kennedy. America had stood eyeball to eyeball with the total annihilation of everybody involved. The respected writer I.F Stone however argued that the risks taken had been disproportionate to the threat posed. He wrote "When a whole people is in a state of mind where it is ready to risk extinction – its own and everybody else's – as a means of having its own way in an international dispute, the readiness for murder has become a way of life and a world menace."

Even JFK learned lessons for he issued a statement later. He said "Above all, when defending our own vital interests, powers must avert those confrontations which bring an adversary to the choice of either a humiliating defeat or a nuclear war." If only all parties from East and West had taken Eisenhower's manual for peace more seriously. At least the military hawks had learned that a nuclear strike would never be the answer to an international problem.

One spinoff for the President was his attitude towards Vietnam. On the day before he died, John F. Kennedy had formed his own opinions on the futility of modern warfare. On November 21, 1963 just before he left for Texas he told his Aide Mike Forester "When you get back after the first of the year I want you to organise an in-depth study of every possible option we have got in Vietnam including how to get out of there. We have to review this whole thing from the bottom to the top." John Fitzgerald Kenned was assassinated the very next day.

Why Kennedy ever consented to a trip to Dallas is hard to understand. Like the PT109 experience perhaps this was just another challenge he had to confront. A dangerous challenge I am afraid to say for this was the stronghold of the John Birchers, the Dixiecrats and the ultra right Republicans whose extremist followers had manhandled Adlai Stevenson and Lyndon Johnson in different incidences in the previous three years.

The Dallas Morning News had an inflammatory advert surrounded by black borders accusing JFK of being a Communist tool. It was signed by Bernard Weissman Chairman of "The American fact finding Committee". This was a fictitious organization front for extreme rightists including Nelson Bunker Hunt, a member of an oil rich Dallas family.

On a personal note the doctors were not too keen on Jackie going to Texas three months after the death of baby Patrick which had such a devastating effect on her. But JFK's ratings were down and Jackie knew she was needed by his side. "We are really heading into Nut country," Jack remarked after reading the Dallas Morning News.

"Last night would have been a hell of a night to assassinate a President," he suggested to Jackie strangely prophetic….. "Jackie," he continued "if someone wanted to shoot me from a window with a rifle nobody can stop it. So why worry about it!" Perhaps this was in response to Jackie's misgivings already expressed to him.

At present, JFK had other worries on his mind. The Party friction in the Democratic Party led by Vice President Lyndon Johnson, Governor John Connally and Senator Ralph Yarborough worried him. They intended to shadow the President everywhere on his visit such is the crazy chemistry of politics.

The banality of Jackie's hope for rain surfaced. It seems she didn't want to ride in an open car for fear of ruining her hairstyle. Another prophetic omen. But the sky cleared and they climbed into the back seat. The bubble top had been removed in the now roasting hot weather to give the people a better view of the famous couple. Connally and his wife Nellie sat in front of the Kennedy's behind the driver Bill Greer.

A car full of Secret Agents followed the President's car. Behind that again was the car holding Vice President Johnson and his wife.
Jack ordered Jacqueline to take off her sun specs…… "If you are riding in a car like this with your glasses on you might as well have stayed at home."

The windows of the buildings on both sides of the road were being watched by the First Lady's Secret Agent Clint Hill. He was nervous. Historian William Manchester was also watching the buildings and he didn't like the feeling he had. Yarborough was enjoying himself however shouting at the crowds exuberantly "Howdy there," he hollered. Despite this show of celebration he too was worried and thinking "It will be good to have the President out of this."

Jackie remembered later the triple underpass tunnel ahead "It should be cool there," she mused. Jack raised a hand to wave at a boy. But then the almost unbelievable happened. Gunshots. They shattered a beautiful day. A 6.5 mm bullet struck JFK at the base of his neck just right of his spine exited his throat and nicked his tie. It didn't kill him. "No, No, No, No, No," Connally cried out "they are going to kill us all."

Jack turned round and looking puzzled slumped forward. The second bullet entered the back of his head sending blood and brains everywhere. "My God, I've got his brains on my hands. What are they doing? My God they have killed Jack. They have killed my husband…….Jack, Jack."

Jacqueline jumped up on to the trunk of the car "looking for a portion of Jack's head" was what she told Manchester the historian.

We all lay down in the car and I kept saying "Jack, Jack, Jack and someone was yelling, he is dead, he is dead." These were her words later to journalist Theodore H. White.

She continued to call out "Jack, Jack can you hear me – I love you" to the fatal remains beside her on her ride in the ambulance to the hospital.

She literally ran along the corridor of the hospital. "I am not going to leave him. I am not going to leave him."

"I want to be in there with him when he dies," she insisted. It was her prerogative and she got it.

The surgeon wanted her out. It was a repulsive sight he was protecting her from…. She objected "It's my husband – his blood, his brains are all over me." She covered his foot protruding from the sheet and reaching under the sheet that was covering him she grasped his hand while two priests gave him the last Sacrament. It is called "Extreme Unction" the last rites of the Catholic Church.

While all this trauma was taking place events elsewhere complicated the story. The three day tour of Texas was now over. The shooting took place as Kennedy's cavalcade neared the Trade Mart where he was to address a lunch for businessmen. One Newsman claimed to have looked up to the top floor of the Book Depository after he heard the shots and saw a rifle being withdrawn from the window. Charles Brehin a thirty-eight year old man was standing fifteen feet away and saw JFK waving to the crowd when he was shot. Kennedy became the fourth President to be assassinated during his Presidency. After the shooting the motorcade broke up as both Kennedy and Governor Connolly were rushed to hospital.

The Texas School Book Depository building was to play a leading role in this terrible tragedy while the whole world sat in the audience. The bullet travelling two thousand feet per second entered Kennedy's neck, exited his throat and entered Connally's back before it struck his wrist. That was the first shot. A second bullet was the fatal one tearing half JFK's head off. The shots had come from the upper floor of the Depository building.

Harvey Oswald, the gunman hid his rifle and once on the street outside headed for his rooming house. There he changed his jacket and put a pistol in his pocket. Once again he walked onto the streets only to be spotted by Patrolman J. D. Tippit who got out of his squad car and moved towards Oswald. Oswald shot him dead then slipped into a nearby cinema. It was there he was arrested. The time was 2 p.m. one and a half hours after the assassination.

Oswald was brought to police headquarters where chaos reigned created by the number of people allowed onto the premises, police officers, FBI Agents, the press and unknown visitors. One of these visitors Jack Ruby stepped out of the shadows and pumped a number of shots into Oswald as he passed down an underground passage in the company of his arresting police officers. Oswald collapsed and died. The three people who took part in this terrible event. J.F. Kennedy the President; his assassin Harvey Oswald and Oswald's executioner Jack Ruby, a nightclub owner were now part of American history. Ruby was taken away for questioning as the horror filled day of infamy Friday November 22, 1963 came to a sorrowful end.

The verdict of the Warren Commission set up to investigate the assassination came up with one judgement only. Lee Harvey Oswald acting alone had killed President Kennedy.

At this point rumours were rampant. The most prominent one being Oswald was a fall guy for the mob who had him killed after the assassination was carried out. But the mob was quite capable of executing Oswald much easier than in front of the world surrounded by armed policemen. That theory didn't hold much credibility.

Some people suggested a second assassin shooting from a grassy knoll overlooking Daley Plaza. By 1993 hundreds of books rolled off the printing press all with their own pet theories. Oswald's body was actually exhumed in 1981 to prove that the Russians had not switched Oswald with an impostor look alike when Oswald was returning from Russia. Even poor Lyndon Johnson was suggested as a conspirator in pursuit of the Presidency. The list got longer. Khrushchev, to avenge his Cuba defeat. Castro, for the Bay of Pigs invasion. The mafia, for Russian Cuban gold or to punish the Kennedy's for investigating Jimmy Hoffa, the Union leader.

However, of the hundreds that were published, two books that took another angle drew together some fascinating facts we will discuss later. The books are by a Matthew Smith entitled JFK say Goodbye to America and The Kennedys.

Meanwhile let's return to the heartbroken widow of the murdered President Jacqueline Bouvier Kennedy.

Back in Washington Jacqueline took charge of the funeral arrangements and she was to stay in charge for the next three days.

It was her idea to incorporate as much of Lincoln's funeral as possible into the funeral of her murdered husband John Fitzgerald Kennedy. With this in mind she organized a working group to go into the Library of Congress that night to research Lincoln's Funeral. The library, being closed, left the researchers no option but to study the details by torchlight.
Her first wish was to drape the White House in black just as it was in Lincoln's time. Everything had to be duplicated from the riderless black horse jogging behind to the catafalque and the platform on which the coffin would be placed in the White House. First to last she decided on everything this historical event should be - the greatest pageant in history.

The family wanted him to be buried in the Kennedy plot in Boston. Jackie would have none of that and dismissed the idea out of hand. Jack belonged to the nation now not to the Kennedy family. Arlington National Cemetery was to be his last resting place. Embellishing his grave would be an eternal flame and she would light the flame herself.

Breaking the news to the children was a problem. To protect them from finding out accidentally Jacqueline and her mother delegated Maud Shaw their nanny to do the job. But Maud was finding it hard to hold her own tears back. When told she was delegated to break Caroline's heart she protested in anguish. But the die was cast. After speaking in riddles about their dad now being an angel in heaven looking after Patrick the subtlety was useless. Caroline buried her head in the pillow of her bed and cried uncontrollably. John's turn would come later.

The question of JFK's assassins troubled Bobby. Was it the mob or was it Castro. Lee Harvey Oswald had Cuban connections? Bobby had also hounded the mob. "How responsible was he for Jack's death?" he thought. But the plot thickens. Back in Dallas news came through that Oswald had been assassinated himself by Jack Ruby, a nightclub owner. Ruby also had connections to the mob.

On the morning of JFK's funeral one hundred million Americans watched on television as the gun carriage carrying JFK's body left the White House and headed up Pennsylvania Avenue towards the Capitol. De Gaulle, Haile Selassie, Prince Philip and many other top dignitaries followed Jackie, JFK's brothers and the entire Cabinet as they walked to the steady rhythm of the slow funeral march.

The U.S., Asia, Europe and Russia watched as Jackie with her two children, one on each hand, face drawn, eyes swollen, mouth set in sorrow, walked her inevitable journey on that long to be remembered afternoon in Boston. The whole world focussed on her. At the graveside "John, John" as he was known bravely gave a soldier's salute. It was an image that has been frozen forever in the memory of millions. To ease the tension in our story let's fast forward it into the future.

Five years after this tragedy that brought her marriage to such a horrendous finality Jacqueline Bouvier Kennedy was married again on October 20, 1968 to Aristotle Socrates Onassis in a Greek Orthodox ceremony in the chapel of the Little Virgin on the island of Skorpios off the Greek coast.

Jacqueline Kennedy only ever gave two interviews after she left the White House neither of which has been published. She died on May 19, 1994 in New York aged 64years and 295 days and was buried alongside John F. Kennedy in Arlington National cemetery VA.

The John Fitzgerald Kennedy story should end there but to do so would leave a lot of loose ends to be tied up. The Warren Commission was to be the instrument to do just that so we will take the story just that little bit further. Of all the books written so far the most lucrative source of revelations has been published in two fascinating books by a Matthew Smith called JFK say Goodbye to America and The Kennedys. In these books a number of facts and theories on the assassination of JFK try to explain the mysteries surrounding it. As promised earlier, here are some of the anecdotes Matthew Smith wrote about.

Jack Ruby

Jack Ruby was questioned by ex-President Ford and Chief Justice Earl Warren at the Commission. As the session neared its end after three hours Ruby suddenly asked "Is there any way you can get me to Washington?" Warren was astonished….. "Gentlemen my life is in danger," Ruby pleaded….. "I may not live to give further testimony. The only thing I want to get out to the public I can't say it here." "If you think that anything I am doing, or anything I am asking you is endangering you in any way shape or form, I want you to feel absolutely free to say that the interview is over," said Warren.

When Ford began to question Ruby on his visits to Cuba in 1959 Warren cut in. Later Ruby's lawyer commented "Warren blocked Ford out of it. That was impressive." Ford's response was a hard stare but that line of questioning was abandoned.

Ruby pleaded "I would like to request that I go to Washington and take all the tests….. It is very important…. My life is in danger…. My whole family is in jeopardy….." Warren just stonewalled. Then Ruby made an astounding assertion. "It is something to do with you……." Plead as he did no promise of a trip to Washington could be given to Ruby who continued to insist that he was a scapegoat…….. But for whom?

We can only speculate on Ruby's mental condition. However he did come out with some outlandish remarks…. "If I am eliminated there won't be any way of knowing….. You won't see me again I tell you that….. A whole new form of Government is going to take over the country and I know I won't live to see you another time."

Matthew Smith's superbly researched books are fascinating. It is amazing the stories he reveals. According to Matthew Smith by implication Ruby had accused people in high places but never gave their names. To a psychiatrist later Ruby claimed that the whole assassination was motivated by "An act of overthrowing the Government." He even claimed that he knew who had President Kennedy killed and that he himself had been framed into killing Oswald.... Later Ruby kept his word. He died.

Smith's books then takes us into other areas as mysterious and disturbing as a John Le Carre thriller. Let me mention further anecdotes from Smith's books, which I'm sure, are authentic.

Dorothy Kilgallen
Dorothy Kilgallen broadcaster and writer managed to get a private interview with Ruby. After it she went home to her friends saying "I am going to break the real story and have the biggest scoop of the century......" She died suddenly. There were two medical reasons why she died. One was, it was a heart attack, the other reason was suicide. A third reason was slightly more vague "Circumstances undetermined." Her friend Mrs. Earl Smith in whom she may have confided also died forty-eight hours later.

Cancer Injections
No one has been accused or implicated as a result of Ruby's interviews with the Warren Commission or the Kilgallen death. We will have to leave the matter rest there to await future historians to debate. Now a further twist in the story occurs. Should our historians include the police? .... Police Officer Tom Tilson claimed that it was the opinion of other Dallas police officers that Ruby had received injections of cancer while he was incarcerated in Dallas. Speculation? Hearsay? Gossip? Who knows? Injected with cancer! Is this medically possible?

Police Officer Tippit
Smith refutes the possibility that Oswald had killed police officer Tippit earlier because there were two different bullet types taken from Tippit but only one was sent to the FBI in Washington and that particular bullet the FBI claimed had not come from Oswald's gun. The plot thickens.

Later it seems four more cartridge cases found at the scene of the Tippit shooting were examined. These too had not come from Oswald's gun. Yes, the mysteries seem to pile up.

J. Edgar Hoover
According to Matthew Smith another confusing story emerges about J. Edger Hoover. He is supposed to have rung Bobby Kennedy, the then Attorney General within two hours of the assassination. In this phone call he named Oswald as the assassin giving a detailed pen picture of Oswald's background "An ex-marine nut who had defected to Russia." Yet Captain Will Fritz of Police Headquarters at that exact time had not even ascertained Oswald's identity or background. The mysteries stack up.

Matthew Smith goes on to compile a list of people who died in suspicious circumstances which feed into the mysterious, the puzzling, the coincidental and the downright bizarre happenings surrounding the assassination of JFK.

Warren Reynolds
A Warren Reynolds saw a man fleeing the Tippit murder scene. "It was not Oswald," he

claimed. Unfortunately this was a claim that proved fatal for him. Darrell Wayne Garner shot Warren Reynolds. Then conveniently a club showgirl called Nancy Jane Mooney turned up to give Garner an alibi and Garner was released without charge. Sometime afterwards, the same Nancy Jane Mooney was picked up for a minor offence and put in a cell. One hour later she was found hanged there.

Matthew Smith's books continued to piece together some unknown facts so let's continue. Garner who shot Reynolds was found dead of an overdose in 1970.

Ruby's girls
Another of Ruby's girls who was planning to write a book about the assassination was murdered in 1964.
Earlene Roberts
Earlene Roberts's, landlady of the boarding house Oswald lived in died dramatically and unexpectedly of a heart attack.

Tom Howard
Tom Howard Ruby's lawyer died of a heart attack.

Bill Chesher
Bill Chesher, a business man who was foolish enough to admit he knew of a link between Oswald and Ruby also died of a heart attack.

Deputy Sheriff Roger Craig
The Deputy Sheriff Roger Craig who was present at the Book Depository fell victim to the knowledge he had, when he said he saw someone running from the building and picked up by a green car. He was fired "for talking to newsmen". Later he was shot at and run off the road. His wife left him and one day he was found dead. His death was declared a suicide.

Gary Underhill
Gary Underhill, a CIA agent who claimed to have the fatal information of inside knowledge connected to the assassination never got a chance to reveal it. He was found with a bullet in his head. The verdict - suicide.

Thomas H. Killam
Thomas H. Killam known as "Hawk" made it known in an idle boast that he knew of a link between Oswald and Ruby. He also told his brother "I am a dead man but I have run as far as I am running." In March 1964 "Hawk" was found dead in an alleyway with his throat cut.

Karyn Kupcinet
Karyn Kupcinet whose father was a TV host, picked up her phone two days before the assassination asked for "long distance", and screamed into the phone at someone that President Kennedy was to be killed. Two days later she was found dead in her apartment. Nobody was charged with her murder.

I guess there are hundreds of stories since then just like these going the rounds all totally unsubstantiated.

They are certainly bizarre stories told fearlessly by Matthew Smith in both of his books The Kennedy's and Say Goodbye to America. However Smith goes on to say that the chief research officer of the Warren Commission, Jacqueline Hess was given the job of investigating this strange multiplicity of mysterious deaths and found, absolutely nothing to connect them to a conspiracy in JFK's death. I don't know if she investigated the list produced by the New Orleans Attorney Jim Garrison who carried out his own investigation into the assassination. Some witnesses who were to appear before him with any sort of connection to Jack Ruby or Oswald died mysteriously. People like Clay Shaw, Dave Ferrie, Dr. Henry Delaune, William Sullivan, Sam Giancana and Johnny Rosilly.

This second list was included by Matthew Smith in his second book The Kennedys in which he made the amazing assertion that the whole Kennedy family was targeted for annihilation to change the course of American history by evil darker forces who have never been found to this day. Perhaps when the full assassination secrets locked up in the Warren Commission Report until 2039 have been released another attempt may be made to finally solve the mystery.

One thing is for certain The Warren Commission's conclusion that Oswald was the sole assassin has not been accepted by many. The words of the Police Chief Jesse Curry in a TV interview did nothing to allay these doubts. When asked "Do you have an eyewitness who saw someone shoot the President?" his reply was blunt and to the point "No sir, we do not."

Somehow I feel future American Presidents will not allow this wonderful story of JFK and the Kennedy family to end like this. For many it is still unfinished business. Fate, destiny, history and time itself may one day find the missing pieces of the jigsaw. Then again perhaps the Warren Commission's report consisting of twenty-six volumes containing ten million words may be the nearest we may ever come to a final conclusion on John Fitzgerald Kennedy's assassination.

Just one final milestone to report on the Kennedy family. On the morning of August 26, 2009 the final curtain came down on the Kennedy dynasty when the last surviving son of Joe Kennedy, Ted Kennedy, died of brain cancer. His sister Eunice Shriver died two weeks earlier. Tributes poured in from all around the world claiming Ted to be the most influential man in American politics. A man loved by millions who will surely stand alongside his illustrious brothers Joe, Bobby and President John Fitzgerald Kennedy when American history is written.

So now let's turn another page of history as we stand beside Lyndon Johnson, the 36th President on Air Force One as it flew home to Washington with the body of John Fitzgerald Kennedy on board.

36th President   Lyndon B. Johnson

"LBJ"
Born 1908
Died 1973
65 Years of age
1 ½ Terms
1963 - 1969
Age 55

Party: Democrat
Profession: Rancher
County: Texas
Ancestry: British.
Value of Estate: Millions (unknown)
Hobbies: Hunting.

Physical Description: Height: 6 foot, 5 inches, 200 lbs weight, eyeglasses occasionally, large ears. Mobile, expressive face.

Significant Extract from his Inauguration Speech on January 20, 1965
"Justice requires us to remember that when any citizen denies his fellow saying 'His colour is not mine' or 'His beliefs are strange and different' in that moment he betrays America, though his forebears created this nation."

LYNDON B. JOHNSON

The world stood still on that awful day in November 1963 as millions watched Jacqueline Bouvier Kennedy carry out her final role as First Lady with dignity and heartache during the funeral of her late husband John Fitzgerald Kennedy, 35th President of the United States. She was indeed a credit to her family and the nation in those last traumatic hours and she went through them with admirable bravery.

I'm afraid we cannot say the same for the dignitaries of Dallas as the remains of President Kennedy was kept waiting at the airport before going home. This delay was to clear some technical difficulties put forward by unknown officials led by a Doctor Earl Rose. Unbelievably, he informed Kennedy's people that the body of JFK could not leave Texas without an autopsy. That was the law of Texas. Luckily, Jackie was shielded by the President's men from the bust-up that followed. Tempers were fraying and matters got worse when Dallas police were called in to re-enforce Doctor Rose's ruling.

"As far as I am concerned it is just another homicide" was the verdict given with abysmal insensitivity to a tragedy all America was mourning. These Texans it seemed had no remorse. Two groups of about forty angry men then confronted each other and things got nasty. Kenneth O'Donnell, one of JFK's oldest friends boiled over. "Get the hell out of the way we're leaving," he yelled. The Secret Service men then brushed the outraged Doctor Rose aside. The police backed off and the cortège raced towards the President's aeroplane "Air Force One" which was waiting on the tarmac of Love airfield, engines turning. They climbed aboard.

Back on the tarmac Dr. Rose stood in consternation. Before we continue perhaps we should get to the bottom of the problems from the point of view of Dr. Rose. The reason for the delay was simple. It seems those at the hospital were anxious not to break the chain of evidence which would be endangered if the body of the President was taken out of Texas without an autopsy. This was to protect the rights of the accused. However, the legal papers were actually signed and handed over as Kennedy's men wheeled the casket across the tarmac. The autopsy was carried out in Washington.

But when the party arrived in Washington an astonishing discovery was made. Someone had tampered with the fatal wound, for it was twice the size it should have been. Worse than that, this extra surgery was inflicted by persons unknown. The new wound would now confuse the evidence as to whether the bullet came from in front or behind. "The one bullet, one assassin theory" it seemed could not now be challenged as a result. Matthew Smith's observations were certainly controversial in his book JFK.

The horror of the whole heartbreaking visit to Texas cries out to be obliterated from everyone's memory. My stunned reaction to the story is to protest that it can't be true. That someone could desecrate the corpse of the President of the United States in such a short space of time, surrounded by surgeons, doctors, police, Secret Service men and family members is frightening. If the deed was done in Texas, then we are clearly dealing with very powerful people who were quite capable of achieving whatever they set out to do. To prove there is an element of truth in the whole story, the House Select Committee on Assassinations in 1978, while investigating many theories, actually acknowledged a botched autopsy but debunked the theories surrounding it.

And so we will continue with the story of LBJ on board "Air Force One" in Dallas before taking off for Washington.

At 2.37 p.m. in the cabin of "Air Force One" with the Kennedy casket in the rear of the plane and the bloodstained widow of the murdered President standing beside him, Lyndon Baines Johnson took JFK's bible in his hand and was sworn in as the 36th President of the United States. Sarah Hughes, a Dallas County Judge officiated, as "Air Force One" headed home.

Lyndon Johnson moved quickly into the vacuum that the death of Kennedy left. He met a stream of world leaders and reassured them that America had no political instability as a result of the assassination. At home on November 27, he addressed Congress with these words. "All I have I would have given gladly not to be standing here today." Then he set about enacting Kennedy's Tax and Civil Rights Bill. As a tribute to their fallen leader he said "Let us here, highly resolve that John Fitzgerald Kennedy did not live or die in vain." Johnson was no Kennedy but what he lacked in charisma he more than made up for by his vast experience. His ego was legendry. When a young marine officer enthusiastically directed him to the right helicopter saying "This one is yours Sir." Johnson drawled, "Son, they are all my helicopters!"

It was LBJ's height and powerful personality that dominated any room he entered, yet strangely his camera technique let him down badly. Hard as he tried he always seemed to come across as a cunning old fox not to be trusted.

I've referred to Johnson's ego being legendry but there was another asset he possessed which was also legendary – his skills and ability to handle Congress which far exceeded those of Kennedy. He could work comfortably with both Southern Conservatives and Liberals. He had an extraordinary command of the legislative process and his control of Senators helped him to become the most influential Senate majority leader in history. He never got bogged down on ideologies and more than proved the worth of his thirty year Congressional life. One of his famous cajoling approaches was to use a quotation from Isaiah "Come now let us reason together saith the Lord." Somehow it always worked.

He made every effort to tone down and manage his rumbustious Texas style which many thought to be brash but others described it as the natural up-front, no nonsense approach of a typical Texas rancher. He nevertheless held a middle of the road course, pruned the budget, trimmed foreign aid and ran the Government with economy, so dear to the hearts of the American people. But he was also loyal to Kennedy's dream of advancement for the blacks and aid to the poor. One of his major pitfalls however, was to allow the question of Vietnam to slide from aid to intervention and disastrously from intervention to war itself. It would later prove to be his own Armageddon.

But let's retrace our steps back in time to when Lyndon Johnson arrived on the scene for the first time as a bouncing baby boy on August 27, 1908 on a farm near Stonewall, Gillespie County, Texas. His grandfather Samuel Ealy Johnson Senior, having been born in Georgia, was taken by his parents to Texas in 1846 to live. When Samuel grew up he became a cattle rancher and then met his wife Eliza Bunton. Their marriage in 1867 produced a son, Samuel Ealy Johnson Junior, who found his way into politics in Texas. While serving in the Texas Legislature, Samuel Junior met and married Rebekah Baines from another ranching family. They had five children, one of whom Lyndon Baines was the eldest.

But luck changed for Lyndon's father Samuel when his cotton crop failed and he was forced to get out of farming. He continued to support the family by selling real estate. But politics was always his first love and Lyndon was the benefactor of his passion. The Johnsons were of pioneering English-Scotch-German bloodlines and had left their three room shack on the Pedernales River in the hill country of Texas to live in a small town, population 333, but described as Johnson City.

Lyndon's mother, the daughter of a ruined attorney, was an elocution teacher in Fredericksburg and a "stringer" for the Austin newspaper. Being close to his father, Lyndon often was seen at ten years of age sitting at his feet in the Texas Legislature. To his everlasting credit, Sam was above bribery, even though he had to subsidize his salary by working on a road gang. Sadly, the town was not so generous and upright and sneered at Sam's downfall in business. To add insult to injury, Lyndon's humiliation was worsened when he was forced to go to school on a donkey.

Lyndon wore his father's mantle in politics and if imitation is the highest form of flattery, Lyndon was only too glad to acknowledge this for both their styles were identical. One of Sam's political assets was to take care of the locals. Nothing was too much for them. He helped get pensions for the elderly veterans or their widows and even travelled the road to Houston if documents needed to be located to back up a claim. He was instrumental in having a $2 million Seed Fund set up to help farmers after one natural catastrophe.

Stell Glidon, a newspaper editor in Johnson City recalled "If there was legislation to be passed it was always to Sam they turned." Sam Ealy Junior had the same physique and an uncanny resemblance to LBJ later. They even walked the same. Sometimes it seemed there was an air of tension between them. "That boy is just not college material," Sam would say cruelly, within earshot of LBJ, in an effort to spur Lyndon's concern for his studies to even a flicker of interest. The problem was Lyndon was just plain lazy. Even when assigned farm chores, gathering eggs, putting logs in the wood box, like Tom Sawyer, he somehow coaxed his pals to do the jobs for him and rewarded them with cookies for their trouble. Despite his later macho image, he never liked killing foxes, squirrels or rabbits. His boyhood adventures were similar to other lads around that time, playing marbles, baseball and swimming in the "Baptism Hole", a favourite swimming spot on the local river.

Johnson's mother, Rebekah, spent her life trying to impress upon Lyndon the need for a good education but it wasn't until 1927 when he was nineteen, that he took any notice. As a teenager, newly graduated from high school, he lived up to a wild reputation by buying a car with five friends and heading for California. There he did odd jobs on the West Coast, packing fruit, washing cars and helping in restaurants. He returned home by hitchhiking and I just don't know what actually happened to the car. But Lyndon has been described as a bit of a troublemaker among the five children defying his father's shouts and his mother's scoldings.

He refused to go to college after graduating, wrecked his father's car and ran away twice. He also fell foul of a girl's jealous boyfriend. Perhaps this is a consolation to many parents who have an over-energetic, difficult independent teenager. Maybe the Presidency could be waiting for him too. Anyway, Lyndon finally started trying for a degree by going to a small teacher training college in 1927 at San Marcos, Southwest Texas. This was a turning point for him for he shone as a temporary teacher and he later taught in a Mexican school in Cotulla. Not only was he liked by the students, he was also educated to the hardcore poverty and prejudices in the United States. The LBJ teenage rollercoaster had finally come to a peaceful landing. Incidentally, for the record, he did receive his degree in history in 1930 at twenty-two years of age.

The next stage in Lyndon Johnson's turbulent development was on November 17, 1934 when he married Claudia Alta "Lady Bird" Taylor, aged twenty-one. Life seemed to be set fair for him, for he had also secured a teaching role at the Sam Houston High School, where his uncle was Chairman of the History Department. The personality and determination he was famous for later was rounded off here for he was remembered by students as a tough fair teacher but very demanding of them. Life was even now pointing in the direction of politics and in his second year as a teacher he accepted a political appointment as private secretary to the wealthy newly elected Congressman, Richard M. Kleberg of Corpus Christi.

Incidentally, his wife, Lady Bird Taylor, the daughter of a prosperous eastern Texas family and a graduate of the University of Texas, was to play a major part in his career. They had two daughters Lynda Bird and Luci Baines Johnson. True to his brash impetuous personality he proposed on their very first date, at breakfast, and very nearly broke the bank with a $2.50 wedding ring. Later Lady Bird was always very loyal to him despite his occasional romantic affairs.

Lady Bird Johnson had something in common with many, many First Ladies before her – she never wanted to be in the White House. She told Abigail McCarthy in confidence "If I had known that this was going to happen to me I would have changed my nose and my nickname." Lady Bird finished High School too young for college so she decided to stay on another year. But when she eventually entered the University of Texas she had an exclusive advantage over other students. Her family were very well off so she could buy her own car. She had an unlimited expense account and a cheque book.

But she was not a spendthrift. Later, long after she became a millionairess, she still shopped for "seconds". For the funeral of John Fitzgerald Kennedy she borrowed her black outfit. Some people had a few rude words for her but Nan Dickerson, the journalist, described her as being rich but very frugal. She was careful about everything she did except her choice of husband. This didn't deter her although LBJ was as brash as she was reserved.

One thing about Lady Bird Johnson her husband never fazed her. When asked did she help campaign for her husband, she retorted "No indeed … I just go along with Mr. George and sit on the platform to show them I don't have a cleft foot." LBJ's stint in the army was the turning point in her life proving to her "she could still do things on her own". The major well-known event in her life concerned a bankrupt radio station in Austin. When it went up for sale in 1942, Lady Bird borrowed $10,000 from the bank and with a little of her own cash bought the ailing station. Her University qualifications in journalism were a big help.

The new business she bought eventually became the Texas Broadcasting Corporation and the revenue it generated soared under the watchful eye of LBJ. After Lyndon's death, she returned to her business life and left the family ranch to the National Park Service. Well as I have told you earlier, Lady Bird's marriage was truly amazing. It took place inside two months of their first date. Unlike other wives her husband recruited her as his aide teaching her the ropes in a "Post Graduate" hands on study of the art as per Lyndon Baines Johnson. Yes she managed to learn politics in detail under LBJ's tuleledge. She had to learn by heart a list of Counties, the principal communities in each and their leaders. She also had to learn to cook, for his political visitors to their apartment were numerous.

Lyndon could be overpowering as we have already discovered so life wasn't a bowl of cherries for poor Lady Bird. He wasn't easy to please and sometimes berated her in front of others even criticizing her clothes and her make up. On one occasion, he insisted she leave the room to change her stockings and all because they had a run in them. Any woman could see his petty rules of behaviour for her were ridiculous, but Lady Bird put up with them, saying "What pleases Lyndon pleases me." He was even course and rude to her in front of reporters. Yet Lady Bird accepted this boorish behaviour saying she chose to serve him placidly.

Surprisingly, she had been nicknamed Lady Bird from birth when she was described by her nurse as "pretty as a Lady Bird" and the name stuck after that. Shana Alexander, the historian, rated Lady Bird one of the foremost First Ladies ever, third behind Eleanor Roosevelt and Abigail Adams. As a successful business woman, she more than earned that title.

Now back to Lyndon Johnson, the aspiring politician. LBJ's drive and forcefulness brought him to the attention of the political machine in Texas and he found himself appointed as Director of the National Youth Administration, a newly established relief organization run by Aubrey Williams, a controversial character like Lyndon himself, who was to become his lifelong friend. At this stage Lyndon Johnson was fast acquiring a network of politically useful friends.

The sudden death of a sitting Congressman sparked off a special election in 1937. Lyndon borrowed widely for his election needs and with a $10,000 debt hanging over him he entered the race fearlessly. He ran as an all out supporter of Franklin Roosevelt and won with a 3,000 vote surplus. Ever the opportunist, he met Roosevelt who was in Texas on a fishing trip and conveniently got himself invited aboard the Presidential train. His meeting with FDR paid off for he was given a job on the Naval Affairs Committee.

LBJ followed the normal success formula for any aspiring, young vigorous ambitious Congressman by getting himself close to the President and on the inside track to most of the House Leaders. But it wasn't contacts alone that fuelled his rise to power. The other essential ingredient he possessed was his ability to work close to his own voters and having that enormous drive of energy he put into everything he did. That carbon copy image of his father Sam Ealy Junior was very much the style of our new Congressman Lyndon Baines Johnson.

His own staff will vouch for this because a twelve to fifteen hour day was nothing to him. His favourite mantra was to "Answer every inward letter within twenty-four hours." He became known as the man who gets things done.

An amusing anecdote is told about him when he was at college. Apparently he boasted perhaps with tongue-in-cheek that he would be President of the United States one day. Nobody took him seriously then, for he was known as "Bullshit Johnson" to his amused fellow students. But at twenty-eight as Head of the National Youth Administration he was a resounding success. He found work for 20,000 as well as school places for others.

His Washington knowledge was put to good use in cutting red tape that was holding up the building of a dam. He then campaigned vigorously for electric power for Texas and when the lights went on in November 1939, people were so impressed they actually called their kids after him. It must have been a nightmare for school teachers later to be confronted by so many Lyndons. In 1948 he beat Dixiecrat Governor Coke Stevenson by 87 votes out of 988,000 and was instantly accused by Coke of vote-rigging. Stevenson took the case all the way to the Supreme Court but the accusation couldn't be proved.

He was known as landslide Johnson after that. In the Senate he used his contacts to acquire a rich broadcasting franchise for Lady Bird his wife. In 1955, the Democrats won the Senate and Lyndon Johnson at forty-six became the Senate's youngest majority leader. Somehow, Lyndon was not as indestructible as he thought for in July of 1955 he went down with a heart attack. Weighing 225 lbs and smoking three packets of cigarettes per day didn't help. Well, LBJ recovered quickly and went on to become the most dynamic Senate leader the Senate had ever seen.

In 1941 LBJ was about to fight another battle, a great deal more dangerous than politics. After Pearl Harbour in December 1941, true to his "John Wayne" personality he was the first Congressman to enlist in the army. He went into the Naval Reserve on a seven month tour of duty as a Lieutenant Commander. He survived not one but two near misses in almost fatal air crashes and received a Silver Star for gallantry from General Douglas MacArthur. Back in Washington once again he found himself tackling the modernizing of Navy procedures. Then came a crisis for LBJ – the death of his beloved President Roosevelt in April 1945. He felt it deeply and personally for as he said to a reporter "Franklin D. Roosevelt has been a second daddy to me."

The larger than life personality of Lyndon Johnson is worth one more mention. One anecdote is told of a challenge he felt was an affront to his masculinity. When teased about Kennedy's womanizing being in the super-stud class, he bellowed "Why I had more women by accident than he ever had on purpose." Another challenge to his "top dog" image was really funny. It concerned his limousine phone which had just been installed; the only Senator to achieve this first was minority leader, Everett Dirksen, his principal Senate rival. Dirksen, however, couldn't resist the temptation to ring Lyndon on his car phone to boast about it. Quick as a flash, LBJ was up to the situation "Can you hang on a second Ev, my other phone is ringing" was his amusing put down. All in good fun.

But that old ego was always vulnerable to being hurt. Like many Presidents before him including the illustrious John Adams, Vice President to Washington, he resented the sheer insignificance of the Vice Presidency. Being Vice President to Kennedy left him in a permanent sulk. He didn't appreciate playing second fiddle to a younger and less accomplished politician like Kennedy. But when he became President he proved himself "top dog" as the second most gifted President, next to Roosevelt, in administering domestic reform.

Lyndon Johnson's personality had an in-built contradiction not unlike a previous occupant of the White House, John Adams, who I have already mentioned in relation to the Vice Presidency in his day. He too suffered from a sense of inadequacy in the Vice Presidency. He too needed the reassurance of a woman, his wife, the brilliant Abigail Adams. Johnson sought the same reassurance but not from his beloved wife "Lady Bird". He compensated for this failing of inadequacy by overeating, overdrinking and over-work.

Ever sensitive to any slight to his political contribution and his ability to "make a deal" he confronted Senator Frank Church of Idaho about a White House proposal which Senator Church had voted against. "I voted against you because I was following the lead of Walter Lippmann" (the famous columnist) Church answered lamely. Johnson's reply was blunt and to the point – "Next time you need a dam go ask Walter Lippmann."

In February of 1964, three months after the assassination of Kennedy, Johnson persuaded Congress to reduce personal income tax by more than $10 billion which launched a major economic boom. Consumer spending increased as a result by an amazing $43 million per year. Despite a fifty-five day filibuster he won the Civil Rights Bill which now outlawed segregation of blacks in public facilities, lessened racial discrimination in employment and protected the voting rights of blacks. But all of these measures were also a tribute to Kennedy who launched them. His theme of loyalty to Kennedy by a programme of continuity was to lay the foundations for his own ambitions to the Presidency in his later Presidential campaign.

It is worth recording LBJ's own pen picture of himself
"I am a free man, an American, a United States Senator
and a Democrat in that order. I am a Liberal, a Conservative,
a Texan, a taxpayer, a rancher, a businessman, a consumer
a parent, a voter and not as young as I used to be or as old

as I expect to be and I am all these things in no fixed order."

To understand more fully Lyndon Johnson's quest for the Presidency on his own merits in 1964, perhaps we should review the election campaign he fought alongside John F. Kennedy in 1960. Up to now you will notice how Vice Presidents who arrived in the Presidency unelected were very much aware of the flow in their credentials and so their own goal was to stamp their own style on the Presidency by winning the next election.

Strangely LBJ was not going to enter the primaries until a group of enthusiasts in the South and West pushed him into the arena. Even then his hopes were to be a second choice candidate if there was to be a deadlock. Like everyone else he had completely underestimated the young John Fitzgerald Kennedy who ran a superb campaign and was elected on the first ballot. He was even more surprised to be offered the Vice Presidential nomination by Kennedy. It was a masterstroke by Kennedy given Johnson's Southern connections. LBJ threw himself into the Presidential fight with gusto and was a trump card to counteract the Protestant suspicion of a Roman Catholic in the White House.

History tells us Kennedy won but it doesn't tell us what Johnson expected in his new low-key job as Vice President. Both men got on very well together and Johnson continued in all his old jobs on the National Security Council, The Equal Employment Opportunity Committee and the Space Council in which he took a great pride, especially when its headquarters moved to Texas. Both Kennedy and Johnson worked closely together and Kennedy made certain Johnson was included in all his major decision-making. In spite of mischievous rumours to the contrary they were a loyal team together.

In fact the Vice President's advice was valued only second to Robert Kennedy's, the Attorney General. The age gap between the young guns surrounding Kennedy caused rumours that Johnson would be dropped from the ticket next time around, but Kennedy was quick to step in and declare publicly that was not his intention. In fact one glowing tribute LBJ paid to JFK was his comment "I believe he is more considerate of me than I would be if the roles were reversed."

Later when he was settling into office after the assassination, he replaced the young bloods with his own men, many of them from Texas, although he retained many of the key Kennedy members for over a year afterwards. His budget cutting found a spinoff in the White House, where he was chided affectionately for his new found passion for turning off unnecessary lights in that august residence.

He next turned his attention to his war on poverty, especially in chronically depressed areas like youth employment, food stamps and unemployment relief systems, aid to schools, libraries, hospitals and nursing homes and achieved spectacular results. He knew the personal lives and interests of every Congressman and had no hesitation in contacting them one on one to win a vote. Here are some case histories to go on.

They say that being lobbied by LBJ was an overwhelming experience. He was known to grab people by both lapels, a habit he learned from his father. Next phase was to lean his giant six foot five inch frame to within inches of his victim's nose and try to persuade him gently. Sometimes he had the poor man by the elbow or the shoulder poking a finger in his chest. Even sitting down he was intimidating, giving the impression he was intent on devouring his subject.

Hubert Humphrey, his Vice President, had another juicy anecdote of Johnson's style.

Humphrey's story goes like this. "He'd come at you like a tidal wave, sweeping all over the place. He went through walls. He'd come through a door and he'd take the whole room over. Just like that. Everything. Releasing his grip, sometimes a kick on the shin followed with the order 'Get going'."

Even Governor Wallace had the wind knocked out of him in a White House meeting, according to Humphrey. In March 1965 Johnson put his great arms around him, gripped him by the knee and spoke to him as one populist to another "Why don't you let the niggers vote?" Wallace mumbled something about the authority of the County Registrars to which Johnson roared "Don't you shit me, George Wallace." Knowing every Congressman was important to LBJ. "He knew where the bodies were buried" was one comment. He found the answer to one key vote on civil rights by appealing to the Congressman's black mistress.

His energy was prestigious even though he slept no more than four or five hours per night. Aides would have to pursue him into the bathroom through the shower and even in the toilet from where a constant torrent of orders came through the door. His staff were the best team in Presidential history. To describe LBJ as a whirlwind may do a grave injustice to the whirlwind. Perhaps a category seven hurricane would be more appropriate.

But then again what else could one expect from a man who claimed proudly that "For thirty-two years Capitol Hill has been my home." I'll finish on a final anecdote about Johnson's persuasive powers. He once called a Congressman at 4.00 a.m. to lobby him on a Bill. "Sorry to be calling you so early in the morning," he began. "Oh that's all right came the sleepy reply, I was just lying here hoping you would call." But time in the Presidency eventually ran out for Johnson when he had to present himself for a second term in 1964.
His nomination was never in doubt although there was a substantial protest vote cast in three States, Wisconsin, Indiana and Maryland; for the Governor of Alabama, George Wallace believed that the Federal Government had no right to intervene in the affairs of individual States, an old political chestnut. Segregation policies were designed to keep blacks and whites apart, he claimed. But from the inception of the Union, this separation of State and Federal powers had always been a bone of contention for maverick politicians as I have alluded to above.

With Hubert Humphrey as his Vice President, Johnson ran as a "Consensus Candidate", one who appeals to a large majority of the population. His opponent in the Republican camp was Barry Goldwater. Johnson's election was almost assured so weak was the opposition. His reading of the situation proved correct. Quoting one of Napoleon's favourite maxims, he said "Never interfere with the enemy when he is in the process of destroying himself." The result was the greatest popular vote margin ever won in modern U.S. history, at that time 61% to Johnson, 39% for Goldwater. The next day the Republican Party were sadly viewing the landscape of their political future which was one of complete disarray.

Inauguration day was Wednesday January 20, 1965. The day was cold with a bright sun overhead as Chief Justice Earl Warren administered the oath of office to Lyndon Baines Johnson, the 36th President of the United States. LBJ's speech took about twenty minutes, spoken in a soft deliberate voice. The sign of the times saw a President standing behind a bullet proof screen for the first time. After the ceremonies, Johnson moved down Pennsylvania Avenue to the White House where he watched, with his guests and family, as the parade march-past took place. Fifty-two bands and fifteen thousand marchers including many colourful floats took part. The inaugural parade took two and a half hours to pass, watched by about a million people who lined the streets for that special occasion, always a spectacle since the days of George Washington.

At about 9.15 p.m. the President and his party left the White House to attend five inaugural balls run at five different hotels - The Mayflower, The Statler-Hilton, The National Guard Armory, The Shoreham and The Sheraton-Park hotels. It cost the modest sum of $25 each for admission so it is easy to see how twenty-eight thousand people were able to participate. Johnson, after a tiring day, returned to the White House at about 12.20 a.m.

And so a new Presidential dawn began. Lyndon Johnson was now setting out on his own voyage of discovery with his own concept of the future which he called "The Great Society" an idea he promoted for the first time in his speech at the University of Michigan on May 22, 1964.

The first Richard Goodwin, an Aide, heard of it was when he was called to the White House where he met Johnson at the swimming pool. Goodwin was an ex-Kennedy Aide and first in his class at Harvard Law School. Johnson outlined for Goodwin his vision of "The Great Society" which he wanted Goodwin to articulate in a statement of National Purpose that would inspire citizens to achieve abundance, justice and liberty for all. It was to satisfy the desire for beauty and the hunger for community which would improve the quality of American civilization.

In pursuit of this noble ideal, Johnson delivered ninety of his one hundred and fifteen legislative recommendations. They were the brainchild of former Kennedy Administration academics and Congressmen. The programme, criticized by his critics later as being wasteful, was said to have squandered a great deal of taxpayer's money. The cost of social welfare payments increased from $67 million to $127 million. Yet it was Vietnam that ran the country into the red, costing approximately $885 million.

So what did Johnson achieve with his $127 million dollars? Medicare and Medicaid that protected the health of the old and the poor. It almost achieved the wipe out of elderly poverty at a stroke; Civil Rights laws that empowered blacks as never before; the appointment of blacks to the Cabinet and the Supreme Court; funds for pre-school and higher education. It improved the lot of underprivileged children; cleaner air and water standards; a hike in the minimum wage for the working poor; cultural enrichment through the National Endowments for the Arts and Humanities; the John Kennedy Centre for the Performing Arts; the Corporation for Public Broadcasting and last but not least significant additions to National Parks and Preserved Lands. The icing on the cake was a nice big tax cut for everyone. The Civil Rights Act 1964 was reinforced by the Voting Rights Act of 1965 which suspended literacy and other voter qualification tests which had served to keep blacks from voting.

Some of the credit must go to the secret task forces he had assembled but the vast majority of this domestic programme can go to none other than Lyndon Baines Johnson himself, one of the truest masters of Congressional politics ever to occupy the White House. If only he had retired right then. Alas, he had still four years of his Presidency to come.

It seems a sad commentary on history that despite all these achievements, Johnson, the most masterful politician ever to grace the chambers of Congress, should receive so little recognition for them. The Vietnam War and its consequences on the streets of America, punctured his credibility until it worsened from a trickle to a haemorrhage of public ridicule. But how did an astute mastermind of the political arena allow this to creep up on him?

At home, Johnson was a master of Congress and domestic affairs. But the seed of his downfall can be traced to his first address to Congress on November 27, 1963 as President of the United States. In it he pledged the following:-

"The nation will keep its commitment from South Vietnam to West Berlin. We will be unceasing in the search for peace; resourceful in our pursuit of areas of agreement, even with those with whom we differ; and generous and loyal to those who join with us in common sense."

De Gaulle rubbed him the wrong way by his veto to keep the U.K. out of the Common Market and the removal from French soil of expensive and elaborate facilities for NATO, putting France effectively outside that organisation. De Gaulle had also been a fierce critic of U.S. policy in South East Asia. The Middle East was now a potential powder keg which was damped down by U.S. – U.S.S.R. diplomacy.

But Lyndon Johnson was not always comfortable with foreign affairs. Listening to military advice he began to commit half a million Americans to service in South East Asia. Fury and distrust exploded across the college campuses of America and the Western world. Unfortunately, like so many Americans of that time, he believed it was weakness that led to war. "I am not going to lose Vietnam," he told the American Ambassador to Saigon just after taking office in 1963. "I am not going to be the President who saw South East Asia go the way China went."

Lyndon Johnson, aware of the problems that Castro had caused Kennedy, moved ever deeper into the morass in his pursuit of containing Communism in the Western Hemisphere. When trouble broke out in Brazil, he immediately sent 20,000 troops to the Dominican Republic. But the cost to Johnson politically was substantial. This astute politician, master of all he surveyed on the home front in Congress, only struggled on the international stage pursuing the traditional Cold War policies he had inherited from Kennedy. He was now under attack from Congress, the media and the universities. His inexperience and weakness in foreign affairs contributed to his future failures on the world stage.

But it was Vietnam that became his obsession and his ultimate downfall. How had it come to this? What madness caused him to hold on to the failed policies of Kennedy and Eisenhower? Was it blind loyalty to these two great Presidents? Johnson listened to the Kennedy men and they were all hawks. Even Eisenhower supported the military action he refused to take when he was President. LBJ rejected again and again suggestions for a "Campaign" against North Vietnam. McNamara and McGeorge Bundy played on his insecurity to get their way. Later Clark Clifford who succeeded McNamara as Defence Secretary suggested that the military tricked Johnson into war on the instalment plan.

Others said Johnson was playing it by ear, unwilling to face either the reality of what he was doing or the inevitable public outcry. He sent 175,000 troops to Vietnam telling America that the South Vietnamese troops would do most of the fighting. The scale of the white hot anger he felt on the situation was reflected in the ferocity he showed to Marine General Victor Krulak, a battle-hardened veteran of World War II, when he briefed Johnson on how hard it was to engage the Viet Cong. Johnson's face flushed with anger and he pounded his desk with his fist and shouted "Kill 'em, Kill 'em, Kill 'em." Vietnam was now President Lyndon Johnson's Alamo.

Perhaps at this stage we can look at the Vietnam War as seen by Christian G. Appy in his colossal work entitled Vietnam. Some of his anecdotes are amazing. It shows us events of that time not well known to some of us.
On August 4, 1964, President Johnson appeared on U.S. television complaining about unprovoked attacks on South Vietnamese villages. Two U.S. destroyers were also attacked in

the Gulf of Tonkin, the "Maddox" and the "Turner Toy". As Johnson put it, "All the necessary measures to repel any armed attack against the forces of the United States have been taken." He appeared before Congress some days later requesting permission to take all necessary measures including the use of armed force against North Vietnam. At that particular time, only 16,000 troops were in Vietnam. It was called "The Gulf of Tonkin Resolution."

Many Congressmen later regretted giving their support to the Resolution. William Fulbright, Chairman of the Senate Foreign Relations Committee, became a lifelong critic of the war after that. It was later discovered the attack on the U.S. destroyers never took place. Unbelievably, it seems the reports on the incident were actually written two months before, based on Johnson's expectation of his future need to escalate the military commitment to Vietnam. The whole crisis it seems was a cynical political exercise kept secret from the American public. The non-attack was confirmed in 1995 by Nguyen Giap, North Vietnam's Defence Minister during the war. Anyway, President Johnson got his troops and his blank cheque for the war and the rest is history.

Over the next three years, Johnson raised the U.S. troop commitment in Vietnam to half a million. Yet he always had his misgivings and expressed alarm to Senator Richard Russell. "It scares the hell out of me," he said. "We're losing more everyday. We're getting in even worse."
Johnson genuinely hated the war which was haemorrhaging money ($5,100 billion) so far from his beloved Great Society dream. He described it as "This bitch of a war." The personal cost hurt most of all when protesters chanted "Hey, hey LBJ, how many kids have you killed today?"

Another amazing fact was revealed by Christian G. Appy. The soldiers, who hardly knew where Vietnam was, had to travel on commercial airlines as individuals. Their fellow passengers were strangers as they travelled half way across the world to fight a war they knew nothing about. It was so far away from their base in America it seems to us today to have been military and political lunacy to fight there. They set out as civilians and arrived as soldiers carrying no guns. Sending troop carriers to the war zone would have highlighted the massive troop movements needed in and out of the war. The use of commercial transport conveniently masked this fact. Later Johnson was to disguise further troop additions of 120,000 soldiers by sending them piecemeal at 10,000 per month.

Yet there was no hiding place for hundreds of U.S. troopships waiting for weeks offshore to unload their supplies. As the war escalated, hundreds of airfields and helicopter landing pads were built. The amount of material sent rose to two million tonnes. But how were the Vietnamese affected by the war. Well, millions of them saw their homes razed or burned to the ground. Thousands were scattered far across the country, thus uprooting and destroying the very fabric of Vietnamese society. Children were evacuated from cities where the war was really fought in the streets of South Vietnam.

In the jungles outside, boys and girls as young as fifteen, filled in bomb craters and cut down trees repairing roads to help volunteers get to the front. It was called the Ho Chi Minh Trail. One such worker said "We were so young we didn't know anything but our patriotism was high. We went to war willingly."

The conventional tactics against the Vietnamese ambushes and tunnels was by bombing. But the bombing of these tunnels were ineffective so deep and complicated were they. One Vietnamese remark dismisses the American tactics with these words "A stork can't shit into a bottle so with our tunnels, we shouldn't be scared of American bombers." The tunnels were an underground maze just wide enough to crawl through. Kerosene lamps were used for meetings underground as there wasn't enough oxygen down there for candles.

U.S. planes bombed churches to the regret of the pilots. Yet one war song went like this "Strike the town and kill the people.
 Drop napalm in the square.
Get out early every Sunday
And catch them at their morning prayers".

Phosphorus rockets were used and they were worse than napalm. Its fires did not go out. Blame for all that happened was falling more and more on the leaders in the war. As the war coarsened, the combatant prisoners were the victims.

One American pilot remembered ….. "First they beat the crap out of you to soften you up. Then you were sat on a little wooden stool for days. The thirst was awful but by feigning sleep a prisoner could sip the water thrown over him. Torture meant 'max-cuffs' with arms pulled up behind your back, your upper arms were handcuffed. A rope was tied to your wrists and pulled upwards causing indescribable pain. It ceased when you supplied the information they were looking for. The failure of surrendering left you feeling far worse than the torture."
The war was indeed a military mistake but once the military got involved they had to win. Another mistake! It was really a civilian misadventure but the Generals were convinced of the correctness of the cause. General Westmoreland at a briefing one night said "We have complete air superiority" which couldn't be debated. The Viet Cong had no aircraft. Westmoreland went on "We can do anything we want anywhere we want. It's up to the enemy how much punishment they are prepared to take."

The veterans he was addressing went back to the White House and told Johnson "We're in a helluva mess over there and we gotta get out." Johnson just blew his top in total denial. But later his opinions changed to the humiliation of the top brass.

He blew his top again – this time with the top brass of the army and Navy he had called in for a report on the war. They made the fatal mistake of smugly recommending even more war with their overwhelming naval and air power forcing the North Vietnamese to sue for peace. You may remember Johnson's technique for pursuing others in debate, smile and compromise. But now he got serious. He said quietly "So you're going to bomb them into the Stone Age." He turned to the Army and Marine Chiefs and said "So you fully support these ideas?" "Yes Sir," they said.

Then all hell broke loose "You goddam fucking assholes, you dumb shit. You're trying to get me to start World War III with your idiotic bullshit. Do you expect me to believe that sort of crap? I've got the weight of the free world on my shoulders and you want me to start World War III." He then blasted them with more obscenities, calling them shit heads and pompous assholes. He really degraded them. When he had calmed down, he turned to them again and asked each in turn – "What would you do if you were President?"

He addressed each General but the answer was the same. "More war". When they finished he shook his fist and shouted. "How can you fucking assholes ignore what China might do … You have just contaminated my office, you filthy shit heads. Get to hell out of here right now." For some days the Generals contemplated resigning en masse but feared they would be accused of treachery in the face of the enemy and did nothing. Perhaps had they known the thoughts of George Reedy, quoted in the book To the Best of My Ability, they might have understood better their ordeal in the office of the President?

George Reedy's views on Johnson are revealing. He said "Lyndon B. Johnson is a master of vulgarity which he uses to intimidate and entertain. His lapses from civilized conduct are deliberate and are usually intended to subordinate someone else to his will."

I wonder if conversations like this have occurred over the Iraq war in 2007. There seems to be an uncanny parallel between Vietnam and Iraq. The U.S. going into war under false pretences, then escalating the war with further troops. Who says history doesn't repeat itself.

But let's return again to President Johnson in the White House of 1969. More than 20,000 Americans had now been killed and 50,000 wounded. More than 900,000 Americans had been drafted. The so-called defeated Viet Cong now attacked thirty-six cities with 84,000 troops. The sobering fact was beginning to dawn on everybody that there was no way to win the war in Vietnam. Even if another million men were sent to the war zone and America also fought a war with China and with nuclear weapons, what purpose would it serve and at what domestic consequences. America would still be occupying Vietnam.

Now Johnson was abandoned by all the wise men, Dean Acheson, McGeorge Bundy, Douglas Dillon and Henry Cabot Lodge, who only five months previously had been telling him to hold fast. His new Defence Secretary, Clark Clifford, had become a dove, pressing for speedy negotiations that began in May 1968 in Paris. On June 8, 1969, 25,000 troops were withdrawn and peace was finally agreed on January 23, 1973, five years after the peace talks began.

Perhaps the flaw in Johnson as a foreign policy leader is summed up best by the President himself when he said jokingly "Foreigners are not like the folks I'm used to." Eric Goldman, the Presidential historian reinforces this point saying Johnson viewed foreign policy as "Something you had like measles and got it over with as quickly as possible."

Coming up to the 1968 Convention observers noted a difference to that of 1965. Vietnam was now centre stage. A note of weariness and anxiety could be detected in the delegates. A war-weary country and growing disorder in the streets were to blame. "The Great Society Budget" had accelerated from $7 billion to $21 billion. Vietnam was draining the country of much needed cash for social services.

In late March 1968 the President's fatigue was obvious. "He was slumped in his chair" wrote Joe Califano "and he looked very tired." "My eyes are hurting," LBJ complained. "They always hurt when I'm very tired." The polls however were optimistic. He called the Defence Secretary, Clark Clifford, in while he was dressing for the speech he was about to make. He handed him a note which he intended to append to his speech later on that evening. Clifford read it slowly. Astonishment registered on his face. The note went as follows: "I have concluded that I should not permit the Presidency to become involved in the partisan divisions that are developing in this political year.... accordingly, I shall not seek and I will not accept the nomination of my Party for another term as your President."

It was as unexpected a bombshell as that delivered by Woodrow Wilson in 1929. Clifford looked up from the note and asked "You've made up your mind." "Yes, totally," was Johnson's reply.
At nine o'clock that evening Johnson told his television audience of his intention to de-escalate the war by a substantial reduction in hostilities. Bombing would be halted over 90% of North

Vietnam. The President was effectively sacrificing his own career to unify the nation. 49,000 telegrams and 30,000 letters poured in, most of them favourable. Even De Gaulle praised his courage. The Washington Post wrote "LBJ has made a personal sacrifice in the name of national unity that entitles him to a very special place in the annals of American history." Johnson's popularity sky-rocketed from a 57% disapproval rating to 57% approval. A few days later Hanoi announced it was ready to open peace talks.

But politics is a very volatile chemistry and events have a habit of pyramiding. Two of these events happened within months of each other. The deaths of Martin Luther King Junior and Bobby Kennedy. It was just 6 o'clock on the evening of April 4, 1968 when Martin Luther King Jr. was gunned down on the balcony of the Lorraine Motel in Memphis, Tennessee. The bullet that cut him down was fired by James Earl Ray, a thirty-nine year old criminal who had escaped from a Missouri prison. King died instantly. Ray wasn't caught until two months later on the other side of the Atlantic. There seems to be a murky background connected with the shooting. King had changed direction to oppose the Vietnam War. This didn't please conservative black leaders and his powerful white supporters. What made his death more mysterious was the prophetic vision he portrayed the day before in a speech he made, as follows:
"Like anybody, I would like to live a long life. Longevity has its place. But I'm not concerned about that now. I just want to do God's will. And he's allowed me to go up
to the mountain and I've looked over and I've seen the Promised Land. I may not get there with you. But I want you to know that we as a people will get to the Promised Land. And I'm happy tonight. I'm not worried about anything. I'm not fearing any man. Mine eyes have seen the glory of the coming of the Lord."

For that speech, I'm indebted to Harold Evans The American Century (pg. 48). As Harold Evans implies "It was eerily clairvoyant." Reading slowly through it again makes you ask the question, did King suspect his life was in danger and his days numbered? Perhaps he even knew who would murder him. But that is just speculation on my part.

But let's move on. The reason Martin Luther King had been in Memphis was to help sanitation workers in their strike for higher wages. LBJ was now galvanized into action. He immediately called black leaders to the White House to calm the situation and made April 7, a national day of mourning. He also ordered an acceleration of the Civil Rights Bills through Congress. But racial rage couldn't be contained and riots broke out in 168 cities all over America. Looting was particularly severe. Smoke from arsonist fires could be seen in Washington through the White House windows.

Stokely Carmichael, the extremist, had threatened to burn down Georgetown, the home of liberal and anti-war pundits where anti-war journalists were known to live. Lyndon Johnson still holding on to his sense of humour grinned "Goddam, I've waited thirty-five years for this day." However, he had no alternative but to call out Federal troops to restore normality in the nation's Capital. But as I've already suggested, political activity has a habit of sparking unpredictable events almost unconnected with each other.

First, the Johnson resignation from the Presidential race, then the assassination of Martin Luther King Jr. and then the most awful twist of fate imaginable, a second politician of the Kennedy family was gunned down. On June 5, 1968 while on the crest of a wave, Bobby Kennedy, having won the California primary, was assassinated by a Jordanian – who resented Bobby's perceived pro-Israeli position. He was assassinated in the kitchen of a Los Angeles Hotel, The Ambassador, by Sirhan Bishara Sirhan. Sirhan was a twenty-four year old immigrant from Jordan.

The heartbreaking reality of this awful act is mind-boggling in its consequences for the country. It changed the whole direction of politics and blew into history forever the dynasty of the Kennedy family as a political force for good in America. Here I must point out that we have already been warned of this plan by Jack Ruby in our piece on Kennedy. Edward Kennedy, the only surviving brother of four, (Joe Jack, Bobby and Edward), cancelled any plans he had to seek the Presidency.

Bobby's potential was just beginning to emerge. His following among the young of all races; the poor blacks and the not so poor, had great promise for the future. His "impossible dream", the campaign slogan he adopted, reflected this hope. It was inspired by a Tennyson epitaph as follows:-

The lights begin to twinkle from the rocks
    The long day wanes: the slow moon climbs
    The deep moans around with many voices
    Come my friends, 'tis not too late to seek a newer world.
Yet another writer, Jack Newfield, a biographer and journalist, captured the national sense of the loss of Bobby when he wrote: - "To this day I keep searching for one more leader who might reconcile and re-unite the injured classes still trapped on separate sides of the tracks that run through the American dream." Perhaps that someone is Barack Obama who became President in 2009.

At that time between April and June 1968 the dreams of both, Bobby Kennedy and Martin Luther King Jr. were snuffed out to be engulfed in the blackness of an unknown tomorrow.

Violence was now rampant in the politics of America and LBJ was worried for a sick society. He established a Commission headed by Milton Eisenhower, brother of Ike. One question he posed for it was, "Are the seeds of violence nurtured through the public airwaves, the screens of neighbourhood theatres, the news media and other forms of communication that reach the family and our young?"

The Democratic Convention arrived and sadly when Johnson asked Louis Harris if he should go, the pollster expressed misgivings that LBJ might be booed there. Not only was LBJ not booed, he wasn't even mentioned from the platform.

Demonstrators rocked the party, the city and the nation despite the presence of 11,900 Chicago police, 15,000 Illinois National Guardsmen in reserve and regular troops equipped with rifles and flame throwers. The anti-war demonstrators and police in riot gear clashed in the streets outside the Convention Hall. The TV news caught the swinging clubs, broken glass, sirens and tear gas for the millions back home. "When to stop the bombing" was the main debate inside the Convention Hall. Johnson was praised for bringing North Vietnam to the peace table. "Stop the War", "Stop the War" was the chant outside while embellishing the chant with their own well-known national anthem "We shall overcome". And they sang it with nostalgic gusto. A Newsweek columnist observed "Had Nixon written the script himself, he could scarcely have improved upon it."

Hubert Humphrey as the world knows now was defeated by Richard Nixon who became the 37th President of the United States. Humphrey told LBJ in a phone call "Well Mr. President it looks like I didn't make it after all. I'm sorry I couldn't do it for you. I just want to thank you for all the help." It was now only a matter of time until Lyndon Baines Johnson left the bridge of the ship of State now to be taken over by a Republican

Just as Eisenhower met Kennedy in the Oval Room prior to Kennedy taking over, it was now time for Johnson to meet Nixon there. Lady Bird entertained Mrs. Nixon and their daughter Tricia, showing them around the living quarters of the White House.

And so one last unusual job was left to be done. On December 13, 1968 Johnson strolled a few feet over the border separating Mexico from Texas to meet up with Mexican President, Gustavo Díaz Ordaz. There under a chilly winter sun on the new Paso del Norte bridge that linked the two countries, the two Presidents set off a minor explosion that caused the Rio Grande to be re-routed under a 1963 agreement of President Kennedy and Adolfo López Mateos. The result was a permanent end to an old contentious boundary dispute. Johnson said proudly "We have shown that borders between nations are not just lines across which men shake their fists in anger. They are also lines across which men may cross hands in common purpose and friendship. And we have done so."
I suppose that little scene of friendship and harmony between two old enemies is the best way of ending these notes on a great but very much under-estimated President. If only Vietnam had never happened what a different story we could have told you. Yes and will we say the same of George W. Bush forty years later?

But once again there was talk of faceless men. Bobby Kennedy had pushed the Government to harass and chase down the Mob, Jimmy Hoffa, head of the Teamsters Union and even Castro himself. In truth Robert Kennedy was in the dark about who had shot his brother Jack. He asked John McCone of the C.I.A. had it been a Russian or a Cuban hit. "They should have killed me whoever 'They' are." It sounded like he blamed his own vendettas against the underworld for Jack's death.

But after many rows with LBJ about the Vietnam War, and nine months after JFK's death, Bobby resigned as Attorney General. He was elected Senator in November 1964 but continued his crusade against the Vietnam War. J. Edger Hoover always an enemy of the Kennedy's, planted suspicions in Johnson's mind that Robert was leaking information to Martin Luther King. Johnson's reaction was supposed to have been these words "I'll destroy you and every one of your dove friends politically in six months."

But harsh words are easily taken out of context in the times that were in it. I merely repeat them to highlight the nature of the bitterness generated about Vietnam. Two days before he was murdered, a Harold Weisberg appeared on TV recalling a conversation with a Kennedy Aide. Weisberg said "I asked a Kennedy Aide why Robert supported the Warren Commission Report on his brother's assassination. The Aide made a significant reply. "It is simple. Bobby wants to live. There are too many guns between him and the White House." Whose guns - we will never know. Incredibly, according to the autopsy report, fourteen shots were fired in that hotel kitchen but Sirhan's gun only fired eight.

The eastern intellectuals didn't understand LBJ. The media despised him and millions of citizens blamed him for Vietnam. On his farewell night, however the four hundred guests made up of Democrats and Republicans cheered him as he entered the room. They showered him with affection and praise. Funny enough, so many parties were arranged for him it defied logic how he had been so unfairly reviled in his latter days as President.
His expenses as an ex-President had been set down in legislation; $375,000 to pay for his adjustment to civilian life reducing after a while to $80,000 per year. His pension of $25,000

per year seems small today. Added to this was a $22,000 per year pension for his time in the House and the Senate. Free Secret Service protection for life and free Medicare seems a little mundane but then again life at the end of any Presidency even a great President will always seem mundane.

LBJ's post-Presidential years on his ranch in Texas named "The LBJ" swung between highs and lows, between euphoria and despair. There was now plenty of time for reflection. Too much time. He came closer to his family after giving most of his time away to others in pursuit of his political visions all his life. He now doted on his grandchildren. He grew more tender towards Lady Bird perhaps, only now seeing her for the first time in the full-time role of a wife, mother and grandmother.

But his family didn't always prevent him from sinking into the "dumps". Like George Washington in retirement he too was taking a deeper interest in his estate and his beloved ranch. He now worried about the weather and his hens' egg production. At one time he appeared in his pyjamas and slippers to bombard his long time foreman with questions. The man, Dale Malechek, joked later "Gee I hope he runs for President again." Lyndon tried other activities too like the University of Texas football games, golf, swimming and writing his memoirs. But LBJ's family medic, Dr. Hurst, had predicted that the next heart attack would be fatal and this proved correct. One day, Lyndon called his switchboard urgently for his Secret Agent, Mike Howard. Two other Agents rushed to the room and found him on his back. He appeared to be dead. They applied mouth to mouth resuscitation. External heart massage didn't help either. LBJ was put on a private plane and flown to Brooke Army Hospital in San Antonio, where Eisenhower had been. It touched down at 4.35 p.m. but he was pronounced dead before his body was removed from the plane.

They brought him back to Austin to lie in State.

It was a cold but sunny day in Washington on January 24, 1973 when Lyndon Baines Johnson's grey metal coffin was carried on a horse-drawn caisson from the White House to the Capitol. Black Jack, the same horse that pulled the gun carriage of John Fitzgerald Kennedy, ten years previously, followed the funeral riderless with black boots in reversed stirrups.

Common folk mixed with heads of State as he lay in State in the Capitol. The same common folk of whom he had been so caring. Dean Rusk's eulogy claimed that "In other times long ago he would have been known as 'Lyndon the Liberator'." Hubert Humphrey remembered him as someone "Who could take a bite out of you bigger than a t-bone steak and the very next day put his arms around you like a long lost brother."

The motorcade then took him back to the banks of the Pedernales where he was buried next to his grandparents and parents in the family plot, to the singing of "The Battle Hymn of the Republic". A ninety-two year old black man was there to pay his respects too. He told Luci later "A tree would have to fall over me to keep me from being here today." "Taps" was blown on a bugle by Master Sergeant Patrick Mastrole of the 3rd Infantry. Lyndon was then laid to rest in a spot of ground near an old oak tree.

What better words can we use to finish the story of Lyndon Baines Johnson than those used by Johnson himself in the famous speech at Michigan Stadium on May 22, 1964 to celebrate the University's 120th Anniversary. It was a happy sunny day when Lyndon opened up his heart and his mind to give us an intimate picture of what this ex-President really felt about mankind. These are the words by which we should always remember him. I quote

"The challenge of the next half century is whether we
have the wisdom to use our wealth to enrich and
elevate our national life and to advance the quality of
our American civilization. Americans had the
opportunity to move not only toward the rich society
and the powerful society, but upwards to the Great
Society.

That great society would be something new in the world.
It would be a plea where every child can find knowledge
to enrich his mind and to enlarge his talents, where leisure
is a welcome chance to build and reflect. Not a feared
cause of boredom and restlessness. A place where the city
of man serves not only the needs of the body and the
demands of commerce but the desire for beauty and the
hunger for community. The Great Society would allow
men and women to renew contact with nature … It would
honour creation for its own sake and for what it adds to the
understanding of the race. In the Great Society people
would be more concerned with the quality of their goals
than the quantity of their goods."

What a lovely vision for the future LBJ articulated. As I said earlier – what a wonderful story we could have told you about Lyndon Baines Johnson if only there had never been a Vietnam.

Yes, LBJ would only have been remembered today for his Great Society, there is nothing surer.

When placed beside LBJ's profound visions for America, talk of his wealth seems to me a vulgar irrelevance. But lest we start to feel sorry for our larger than life Texan on his modest pension after the Presidency, I would urge you not to pity the great LBJ. That would be one emotion he couldn't handle. Suffice it to say, LBJ died a very wealthy man for the following reasons.

During his retirement he didn't neglect his business interests and actually managed to double his wealth with purchases of property in Texas, Alabama, Mexico and the Caribbean. To this can be added his photographic supply company in Austin, as well as his T.V. stations. He donated his ranch to the public as an historical exhibit. Also included were those items such as his birthplace and boyhood home and the log cabin in nearby Johnson City that Sam Ealy, his grandfather, had used as a headquarters for his cattle drivers. Finally, for posterity he left the one room Junction Schoolhouse where he had gone to school at four years of age. I think you will agree Lyndon Baines Johnson not only travelled a long way from his one room junction schoolhouse but was truly blessed with a wonderful and very full life indeed.

A final postscript on his loyal and loving wife. His beloved Lady Bird lived to ninety- four years of age and passed away peacefully on July 12, 2007.

Both LBJ and Lady Bird were buried in the family plot on the LBJ ranch in Johnson City, Texas.

37th President   Richard Milhous Nixon

"Tricky Dicky"
Born 1913
Died 1994
81 years of age
2 Terms
1969 – 1974
5 years 201 days
Life after President – 19 years 256 days

Party: Republican
Profession: Lawyer
County: New York
Ancestry: English, Scotch Irish
Estate: Millions (unknown)
Hobbies: Golf, Piano

Physical Description: Height 5 foot 11 ½ inches, weight 172 lbs, receding hair line, bushy eyebrows, upswept nose jutting jaw

Significant extract from inauguration speech on January 20, 1969:
"The greatest honour history can bestow is the title of peacemaker. This honour now beckons America – the chance to help lead the world at last out of the valley of turmoil and onto that high ground of peace that man has dreamed of since the dawn of civilization."

RICHARD NIXON

A little story at the beginning of this piece on Richard Milhous Nixon 37th President of the United States just about summarises the very nucleus of his character. Nixon claims the whole philosophy of his political life was formed by a football coach he so much admired "Chief Wallace Newman". It seems Nixon was encouraged by his father to play football at Whittier College. Unfortunately not only was Nixon just a little guy, a full 50 lbs lighter then his opponents but he was not very mobile. The result was an enthusiastic father but a very knocked about, roughed up lightweight son.

Nixon far from regretting his treatment on the football field never forgot the lesson of his coach Wallace Newman. I quote Nixon as follows: "He drilled into me a competitive spirit and the determination to come back after you have been knocked down or after you lose."

What better training for the Presidency for a man who had lived around the White House for eight years as Vice President to President Eisenhower, suffered a hairline defeat for the Presidency itself by John F. Kennedy and a wait of seven further years before finally becoming the 37th President in the White House.

His endurance and patience had finally paid off after waiting in the shadows for eighteen years between 1951 and 1969.

So how does the Nixon story begin? Richard Nixon was born of Scots-Irish stock on January 9, 1913. His father a tough disciplinarian bought an $800 shack and being a superb odd job man assembled it into a liveable one storey timber house. Five children were born to Frank and Hannah Nixon, a girl and four sons of whom Richard was the second eldest. The address was Yorba Linda, California just five miles outside Los Angeles. The Nixon's had a twelve acre lemon grove there but were unsuccessful in making it pay its way.

Like many frontier mothers of that time Hannah took a keen interest in young Richard's education and taught him to read before he even went to school at six years of age. She was a member of the Society of Friends, known also as the Quakers, and wanted Richard to become a missionary but the lad's only interest at that time was to become a railroad engineer.

Later he got interested in politics for which he credits his father who was a keen follower of the Republicans. So much so Nixon remembers his father getting very upset with his mother Hannah for having voted for Woodrow Wilson in 1916. Perhaps because Wilson was a Democrat.

But from an early age Richard Nixon was a grafter. When his father got out of farming he moved to Hannah's home town of Whittier, borrowed $5,000 and opened a gas station and a store there. The business thrived and Richard was drafted in, aged nine to buy and bargain for fruit and vegetables in the local market. This job required him to set off at 4 a.m. every morning on his mission. It didn't seem to do him any harm however for in school he still managed to become a champion debater, a classical scholar and a student leader. His nickname at that time was "Gloomy Gus" but don't ask me how he earned it.

The Harvard club of California nominated him as the State's best all-round student and offered him a scholarship. However because the family couldn't afford the room and board he went instead to Whittier College, a Quaker Institution in September 1930 at seventeen years of age where he majored in history.

His political career actually began here by winning the student Presidency on the promise of having the ban lifted on college dances. He then delivered his promise by outflanking the college President and appealing to the trustees. One of the trustees Herman Perry was impressed enough to later nominate him as a Congressman. He eventually graduated and won a scholarship to Duke Law School from where he graduated in law 3rd of a class of twenty-five in 1937. His next step was to find a job which he secured in Whittier. But fate was about to take a hand in the life of our whiz kid lawyer for he was destined to meet his match at the hands of a beautiful red head named Thelma "Pat" Ryan.

He fell in love at first sight with Pat when they both read for an amateur part in a play. He was the up and coming lawyer and she was teaching for the second year in high school. But this was going to be his first difficult brief for "Pat" Ryan was no pushover. She had been brought up in poverty on a small farm by her Irish father and German mother who died when she was a teenager. Being an independent little miss it took Richard Nixon, the so called great debater, a full two years to persuade her to his point of view that he loved her and wanted to marry her. They were both finally married on June 21, 1940 and went on to have two daughters, Patricia born in 1946 and Julie born in1948. Incidentally by an amazing turn of events Julie was later to marry David Eisenhower, the grandson of General and later President Eisenhower. The lowest point in Richard Nixon's childhood was the death of his brother Arthur aged seven followed by the death of his other brother Harold eleven years later aged twenty-four. "From that time on it seemed Richard was trying to be three sons in one," said his mother. Both his brothers died of Tuberculoses for which there was no cure at that time.

Before moving on, perhaps we could pause a little to discuss a certain little lady called Pat Ryan in a little more detail. She later was an essential part of Richard Nixon's life during the most turbulent years of his Presidency and they came through it all with their marriage still flourishing.

The relationship of Pat Nixon to her husband was not as servile as Lady Bird Johnson. Being in the White House for the terms of Truman and Eisenhower were an ideal moulding for her character and an apprenticeship for her as First Lady. She was born on St. Patrick's Day 1912 and was described by her school teacher as having a strong personality behind a quiet exterior. She earned money for her studies by sweeping floors and working as a teller in a bank. So here we see two people, one who became President of the United States, and the other his First Lady for eight years, who got nothing easy in their childhood. Certainly they never knew a millionaires lifestyle at that time.

Then a young lawyer came home to town and tried his luck in the local drama group. So impressed was he with Pat Ryan he proposed on their first meeting. "I thought he was nuts," Pat said later. But the guy wasn't nuts just determined. His persistence paid off two years later when she accepted. The young fellows name was Richard Nixon. Like LBJ, Nixon was financed by his wife's hard earned savings when going into politics. Once again we had a reluctant First Lady who hated politics. When Eisenhower, a future family member insisted on a public confession from her husband on his finances before accepting Nixon as running mate her contempt for politics intensified.

His humiliation disgusted her. After that she extracted a promise from him never to run again. He agreed. But it was a promise he couldn't keep for he broke it four times in 1960, 1962, 1968 and 1972. Pat was glad he did, for she enjoyed immensely their trips abroad to many countries afterwards as wife of the Vice President when Eisenhower insisted she go with him.

For a woman of such a genteel personality she did make one enemy in the White House, H R Haldeman. Pat resented not only his puritanical views on smoking and drinking but most of all his hypocrisy in other things. It's not so surprising for she had heard rumours of his criticism of her, pushing and sniping and urging the President to keep her away from the public and pressurizing him not to take her on trips.

He even put his advice in writing. Yet all the hardboiled reporters loved her and saw no threat in her presence abroad. She loved to write personally to the little people, the hometown girls and boys and even signed her letters rather than use a facsimile. But sadly she had to endure ridicule on leaving the White House. One incident in particular was hurtful when they showered her with confetti chanting "If this were Napalm you would be dead."

Like all First Ladies she unfortunately had to endure the brickbats as well as the bouquets. Pat Ryan Nixon was a credit to the White House and lived to see her husband return to reconciliation with the next Administration who was glad to use his profound political expertise well into the future.

Stephen E. Ambrose, the great historian and biographer wrote this pen picture of Richard Nixon.

"He was heroic, admirable and inspiring, while simultaneously being dishonourable, despicable and a horrible example. It was a role only Richard could have invented or played." Criticism or praise? Well, I suppose, a little of both.
Let's continue the story and see how it unfolds and see if we too, will come to the same conclusion at the end of it.
The Second World War started and America entered the fray after Pearl Harbour on Sunday April 7, 1941. Richard Nixon joined up against the wishes of his Quaker family in August 1942. Lieutenant Nixon was very popular with his crews as he loaded aircraft with weapons and casualties. He became completely immersed in army life when he landed on Green Island to help evacuate the wounded. He even opened a beer and hamburger stand called "Nick's Snack Shack" and just like Eisenhower won a lot of pots playing poker.

One thing is for certain however, he never neglected those love letters to his wife everyday, for after all he was only four years married and was away from home for almost fourteen months. He finished up in the army in 1946 as Lieutenant Commander.

Richard Nixon now thirty-three was like thousands of others at that time, a young man in search of a career when he left the Forces in 1946. Californian Republicans had already made their minds up about his career and persuaded him to be their candidate against the popular Jerry Voorhis for his seat in the U.S. State House of Representatives. It was now that Nixon showed the aggressive attacking technique that was to characterise his future political career for the rest of his life. Despite being "the new kid on the block" he came out with all guns blazing accusing Voorhis of being soft on Communism.

Such a charge was damaging to anyone in politics given that the country was then in the middle of a stalemate between America and Russia which we know today as "The Cold War". Pushing Voorhis onto the back foot or defensive position in their debates won the seat for Nixon by 65,586 votes to 49,999. Nixon was on his way and the gamble he took with his wife's life savings had paid off. I'm sure he repaid the loan but I never did find out. His first post was on the European Recovery Programme better known as the Marshall Plan, called after the great General Marshall who administered it. It helped to rebuild a devastated Europe after

World War II.

But the platform that made Nixon's name was the un-American Activities Committee of which he was a member. He personally pressed for the investigation of Alger Hiss, a high State Department official. The evidence he used was revealed by an ex-Communist who was also a writer and an editor, Whittaker Chambers, who testified before the Committee by claiming to be on the inside track in a Communist cell as a courier transmitting secret information to Soviet Agents.

The unfortunate Hiss was accused of turning classified documents over to Chambers to be sent to the USSR. A microfilm of these documents belonging to the Department of State Navy and War was presented to the Committee. The outcome was the downfall of Hiss and the rise of Nixon by him being re-elected to Congress for a second term.

His next victim was opponent Helen Gahagan Douglas in a contest for the U.S. Senate. Again Nixon used the Communist link to defeat the opposition. Helen Douglas just happened to be the wife of screen star Melvyn Douglas and a lover of a younger Lyndon Johnson. She was also a friend of Eleanor Roosevelt. The Nixon smear was classical for him. "She's pink right down to her underwear," he sneered. He followed this up by issuing a half million handbills on pink paper that tied her to Vito Marcantonio, a New York Communist apologist. Nixon won the battle but had earned the dubious distinction of a spurious nickname from that day on. "Tricky Dickie Nixon".

The year was now 1952. It was only six years since Nixon entered politics. It was a measure of his impact on Republican politics that he was selected by the Party as a running mate for Dwight D. Eisenhower in the 1952 Presidential election. Once again Nixon was embroiled in controversy when it was reported that a fund had been collected to meet his expenses as Senator. The charge was that he was "in the pocket" of favour-seeking millionaires. No evidence could be found to implicate him in wrongdoing yet the advisors to Eisenhower were still anxious to jettison him because of the scandal they feared would affect Eisenhower's chances. However the feared scandal did not materialize. Nixon went on television to defend himself in a speech now known as the "Checkers" speech because he used it to refer sentimentally to his dog called Checkers. Nixon made a comprehensive disclosure of his financial records and it seemed to satisfy Eisenhower. After the speech Nixon was still on the ticket.

Well they say "never drop a winning formula" and Nixon knew he was on to a winning one when once again he released the ghost of Communism from his box of tricks accusing the Democrats of being soft on Communism. Eisenhower won by a landslide. Once again Nixon had moved up a ratchet in his climb to the pinnacle of politics. I must make a comment here on Nixon's formula of Communist scaremongering. Surely Eisenhower did not approve of it in view of the hassle McCarthyism later caused him. Then perhaps knowing Nixon even the advice of Eisenhower would be ignored.

The Vice Presidency always a poison chalice for an energetic ambitious high flyer usually drove the occupant to boredom and despair. For Nixon it was different. He used it to hone his already considerable skills in diplomacy and expertise in foreign affairs. He travelled widely representing Eisenhower abroad.

But Nixon being Nixon seemed to attract conflict and media attention. On May 13, 1958 in Caracas, Venezuela he was lucky to escape with his life. It was supposed to be a goodwill tour to balance the bad press America had been having as a bully, a supporter of dictators and a wealthy exploiter of vested interests. He had an easy ride in Uruguay, Columbia, Argentina, Paraguay, Bolivia and Ecuador. Peru was a foretaste of what was to come however but Venezuela was a disaster. The two cars containing Nixon in one and his wife in the other came under attack. Both cars were ambushed and surrounded by protestors in trucks and cars. It was twelve minutes of hell. A mob rushed Nixon's car armed with iron pipes, clubs and rocks yelling "Muera Nixon." Now the car was being rocked with the intention of capsizing it and setting it on fire. The Secret Service men drew their guns. Nixon afterwards confessed he thought he was going to die. But he feared a shooting would be life-threatening. Keeping his nerve he ordered them not to shoot. As he reflected later the crowd would have gone berserk as soon as a gun went off.

"That would have been the end of us," he said. It eventually sorted itself out and Nixon returned safely to Washington Airport where he was met by President Eisenhower and a crowd of 15,000 well-wishers to welcome him home.

As Vice President his second famous incident happened in of all places Moscow, and the guy in the other corner was none other than an ebullient Nikita Khrushchev who mischievously stirring up trouble with Nixon on the merits and demerits of Communism compared to the Capitalist system of the United States. It is known today as the "Kitchen Debate" and in it, Nixon, if he didn't win on points must have won by a technical knockout. He was more than capable of taking care of himself. It took place in a model U.S. kitchen on display which explains the name "Kitchen Debate", the debate was later sent out on both U.S. and USSR TV programmes.

Before finishing the tour Nixon was given an unprecedented appearance on television to address the Russian people. But for Nixon such incidences were just meat and drink to a by now sophisticated polished professional operator. In modern parlance he had become a serial world traveller and as Jonathan Aitken said in his book Nixon a Life, he was a gifted foreign affairs Statesman.

Here is a story from Aitken's book describing Vice President Nixon's visit to Europe with Robert Ellsworth, a Congressman from Kansas, where they met all the leading figures of European affairs, i.e. Harold MacMillan, Edward Heath, Harold Wilson, Conrad Adenauer, Willie Brandt, Pope Paul VI, Charles de Gaulle and Paul Henri Spaak. "I soon realized," said Ellsworth, "the extraordinary mind at work." To Nixon international politics was the highest stakes game in town. He, as we have already mentioned loved poker. This was real poker. He listened with intensity, analyzed everything especially anecdotes and conversations with top Statesmen. Ellsworth was very impressed and saw Nixon as thinking three moves ahead, even a generation ahead. Nixon returned home to America but was soon on the move again to Asia. Next on his itinerary were Latin America, Africa and the Middle East. But these travels of a global Presidential candidate were treated with criticism and disdain. The New York Times asked petulantly "What is he trying to prove. Is it that the road to the White House leads through all the capitals of the world?"

I think what Nixon was proving to those who had eyes to see was that their Vice President was holding his own on the world's political platforms. Anyway it was an ideal training ground for his role to come in the twilight of his years as a world Statesman after he left office.

But more turbulent trials, tears and heartaches were waiting to enter the life of Richard Nixon before he entered that twilight zone of his career. They are the stories for later. Right now in 1960 Eisenhower was preparing to retire from the White House. Everything seemed perfect for his heir apparent to succeed him and Eisenhower was only too glad to nominate his apprentice of eight years Richard M. Nixon. Who could blame Nixon for thinking it was a foregone conclusion, a "Shoe-in" as they say.

He chose Henry Cabot Lodge of Massachusetts as a running mate. We have already covered this election under the John F. Kennedy story. You may remember those four famous TV debates which are reputed to have given victory to Kennedy. I have already expressed my doubts about this under Kennedy for they both had covered a vast amount of mileage on the road before this on the stump. Kennedy proved to be quite a surprise packet and had the sophisticated Party machinery to match his personality. Victory went to Kennedy by only the very narrow margin of 112,803 votes.

There is no need to discuss the tragic outcome of Kennedy's term in office for we have already been over that ground before in our story of John F. Kennedy. Nixon licked his wounds and returned to California to do battle for the Governorship opposing the sitting Governor Edmund G. "Pat" Brown. But this time the winning formula didn't work. Playing the Communist card against the Democrats had become a jaded exercise and Nixon crashed to defeat. At this point any other politician might have returned to his law practice and called it a day. But that old football coach Wallace Newman could not be ignored after all these years. After the defeat Nixon, picked himself up from the pitch dusted himself down and refused to accept the verdict, in fact he refused point blank to acknowledge Brown's victory.

Even in defeat however Nixon was getting the headlines but for all the wrong reasons. He lost his temper with the reporters by his now famous broadside at them "Just think how much you are going to be missing. You won't have Nixon to kick around anymore because gentleman this is my last press conference...." Yes, they seemed like the words of a broken man....Was Nixon actually quitting?
No, politics was not hearing the last of "Tricky Dickie Nixon". He returned to New York and joined a law firm yet still kept in touch with national Republican leaders.

Meanwhile, Lyndon B. Johnson having taken over the Presidency after the tragic assassination of Kennedy held onto it for another seven years as I have already told you. It was now seven years since Nixon had walked the corridors of power in Washington or fought with Khrushchev in that famous Kitchen debate in Moscow. His wounds had by this time healed and he was now more than ready to return to the fray.

I quoted a pen picture of Nixon earlier by that famous historian Stephen F. Ambrose which was pretty harsh but at this point you can't say Nixon was not a trier.

"Returning to the fray" was easier said than done. His former State California had rejected him in 1962.

In New York he was faced with the powerful Nelson A. Rockefeller another Republican candidate. Nixon did have a great following in Congress however especially from the politicians he had helped in previous campaigns. Now it was payback time. Shrewdly Nixon changed his style choosing a middle of the road course.

The Democrats were divided and in enough trouble for Nixon to be able to play his peace card at home and abroad. It was a different America to the one Nixon knew as Vice President seven years previously. It was 1965, National Guardsmen and even regular army troops armed with automatic pistols and bayonets travelling in armoured personnel carriers were commonplace patrolling burnt out ghettos in some of America's biggest cities where there was chaos on the streets. It was an appalling picture of American life in the mid 1960s. It only took a rumour of somebody beaten up by a white cop and thousands of rioters hit the streets torching and looting their own neighbourhoods.

Over two hundred people were killed in one hundred cities and four thousand more were wounded. In the crazy year of the 1968 election Martin Luther King and Robert Kennedy were assassinated. Robert Kennedy had written a book To Seek a Newer World inspired by an epitaph from Tennyson's "Ulysses" as quoted earlier under Kennedy. "The lights begin to twinkle from the rocks. The long day wanes, the slow moon climbs: The deep moans around with many voices. Come my friend's tis not too late to seek a newer world."

The young crowded around Robert Kennedy at rallies even though they were calling for revolution to change everything.

Robert Kennedy winning every primary could have been a threat to Richard Nixon. He had already crushed Hubert Humphrey. Thousands flocked to meet him in the inner cities and that was only the first eighty-five days of his campaign which he called "The impossible dream." He could well have defeated Nixon in a re-run of the 1960 race for the Presidency. To this day it is one of the great imponderables.

Sordidly, sadly and tragically all that was brought to an end in the kitchen of the Los Angeles Ambassador Hotel by Sirhan Bishara Sirhan a twenty-four year old Jordanian immigrant who was convinced Kennedy was a Zionist sympathiser.

Biographer and reporter Jack Newfield after watching Kennedy's funeral train pass through New Jersey on its way to Arlington cemetery saw tens of thousands of poor blacks on one side of the track waving goodbye and on the other side of the track thousands more poor whites crying unashamedly waving American flags tears running down their faces. Jack Newfield wrote "To this day I keep searching for one more leader who might reconcile and reunite those two injured classes still trapped on separate sides of the railroad tracks that run through the American Dream." I have made an observation when writing under JFK when I suggested one name that may yet end Jack Newfield's search, President Barrack Obama winner of the Presidential election in 2009. Only time will give us the answer.

But beside this cultural revolution of the well-educated young on the campuses of America, the Democratic Party had to live with the monster they had inherited from L.B. Johnson and nurtured into its present awful reality – The Vietnam War.

So Nixon continued to play safe riding on the crest of a wave.

But for once lady luck smiled on Richard Nixon. Mayor Richard Daley's police did Nixon's work for him when the anti-war protesters gathered outside the Conrad Hilton Hotel to march to the Democrats Convention Hall. The police went berserk shouting "Kill, kill, kill" as they lashed out with their batons indiscriminately at passing citizens, even doctors, and nurses who tried to help. A London Times reporter wrote "The kids screamed and were beaten to the ground, rapped in the genitals, cops swinging "Billies"." I saw one girl screaming "Please God, help me, help me." A young man who tried to help got his head bloodied by a flailing club.

The sadistic romp was repeated whether crowds legally assembled or not. They were clubbed and gassed. Scuffles even broke out on the Convention floor with the cops hitting delegates and newsmen including the famous TV presenter of CBS, Dan Rather. Reaping the whirlwind Nixon was swept into the White House. Yes, Richard Milhous Nixon had finally arrived to claim his cherished dream in that house on Capitol Hill as 37th President of the United States.

But what an inheritance it was!

Before we follow Nixon into the lions den which was the White House of 1969, with all its Vietnam War troubles waiting for him, let's follow him up Pennsylvania Avenue for his inauguration on Monday 20, January 1969. He had attended two of these celebrations as Vice President to General Dwight Eisenhower. Now he was the main man after being sworn in by Chief Justice Earl Warren, and spent only seventeen minutes on his inaugural speech before he set out for the drive up Pennsylvania Avenue. He had urged those at home to lower their voices. "We cannot learn from each other until we stop shouting at one another."

But the Nixon we have come to know seemed to be the constant bedfellow of excitement. Never in the history of the Presidency has a President been attacked and abused on his own inauguration day. The route was lined with 38,000 spectators who had paid for the privilege of cheering the President. Unfortunately the party was spoiled by loud mouthed anti-Vietnam protesters lining Pennsylvania Avenue.

Burning American flags and screaming "Four more years of death." They even hurled smoke bombs at the Presidential car. But Nixon did not have the temperament to turn the other cheek. As he passed the worst of the demonstrators he stood up threw open the sun roof and defiantly gave the V sign to cheering spectators. He was still the same fighter that had clawed his way to the Presidency. Back in Georgetown's social society anti-Nixon snobbery had already expressed itself.

The host at one party lashed out at Nixon to her fellow guests "Such a common little man" she sneered, words that were greeted by guffaws of laughter. Yet this "Common little man" went out of his way to treat the vanquished Hubert Humphrey with more kindness and consideration than Nixon himself had received as the beaten Vice President in 1960. Mrs. Muriel Humphrey was treated to her favourite flowers in the bouquet she received and the Air Force jet was placed at Hubert Humphrey's disposal in recognition of his twenty-five years of Public service. The softer side of Nixon always took you by surprise possibly because the numerous nicer gestures he was capable of were not very well-known.

It is hard to believe even today Nixon's amazing political resurrection. Yet, given the state of American society right then, was the eighteen year wait and the final glorious victory really worth it? Only time would tell as we are about to find out

Now that Nixon was in the White House, he was going to have to confront the problems he had used as stepping stones to get himself there. Nevertheless his main challenge had to be Vietnam. This war that was tearing America apart right now had been going on since 1959 when Communist guerrillas supported by the Communist Government of North Vietnam launched a bid to overthrow the Government of South Vietnam.

The war escalated into an all out conflict between North and South Vietnam. As we have described under our story of Lyndon Johnson American involvement worsened from the sending of advisors in 1950 to the dreadful situation in 1968 when 536,000 American troops were fighting there. As usual Nixon kept the nation off balance. In August 1969 he brought home 25,000 troops to be followed by a further 65,000 brought home by December 1969. Yet four months later in April 1970 he authorized the invasion of Cambodia to pursue Vietnamese troops there.

Naturally all hell broke loose for him at home. He then authorized the invasion of Laos and the immediate bombing of Laos, Cambodia and North Vietnam. These bombings went on in tandem with a continuation of troop withdrawals from Vietnam. By the end of 1971 U.S. casualties had dramatically declined from 4,221 in 1970. They were now only 1,380. The South Vietnams casualties however were soaring. The war got worse when in March 1972 North Vietnam launched the massive Thet offensive against the South.

So, far from pulling out of the mess as he had promised, Nixon was now ordering air strikes on North Vietnam railroads and the mining of major ports there. Peace talks were started but collapsed which led to massive bombing sorties over Hanoi and Hai Pong. It was now three years into his Presidency and Nixon was in boxing parlance, staggering against the ropes. Extrication was not as easy from the hot seat of the Oval Office as it seemed from the platforms of election rallies.

But Richard Nixon seemed unperturbed for there was other business to conduct elsewhere. He made headlines when he headed up a goodwill mission to both China and the USSR in which he signed trade agreements with both countries and sold huge quantities of wheat to the Russians to ease their crop failure troubles.

At home Nixon was under fire, this time from the economy itself. Prices were rising, but these combined with high unemployment meant hardship was rampant for many people. The usual basic tool of higher interest rates didn't work so he seemed to be flying by the seat of his pants by introducing wage and price controls and devaluing the dollar. It was 1972 and election time was fast approaching for a second term but just in time three things happened for him.

The international tensions eased and the economy improved. But most significantly of all peace in Vietnam suddenly seemed a possibility. With an unhealed division in the Democratic Party, Richard Nixon romped home for re-election by 47,169,911 popular votes to George S. McGovern's 29,170,383 popular votes. Richard Nixon had been given another four years to solve his problems. At this point let us pause for breath for you will need it to take in what happened next.

Richard Nixon was set fair to becoming the most successful President for some time. With peace almost assured in Vietnam he could have taken his place among the illustrious Presidents of the past. But there is an old saying that goes "Those whom the Gods wish to destroy they first make mad" and Richard Milhous Nixon was no exception. But that is a story for later. First let us pay a visit to his second inauguration on Saturday January 20, 1973.

Nixon, an old hand at inauguration ceremonies by now again spent little time on his speech and just like in 1969, Chief Justice Earl Warren administered the oath.

The theme of the parade was "The spirit of 76". True to form, unlike previous Presidents, Nixon again attracted severe criticism not for the Vietnam War this time, but for the $4 million he spent on this, his second inauguration.

The protestors didn't bother the Nixons too much for Nixon and his wife Pat danced the night away at six different inaugural Balls in the Capital.

Unfortunately for Nixon, tomorrow he would still have to wake up to the unresolved problem of Vietnam. I am sure you are wondering by now how this mess came about? It was a strange dilemma Nixon had inherited from the three previous Presidents Johnson, Kennedy and Eisenhower.

It seems their mindset had all been haunted by the spectre of Europe in 1938. Nobody wanted America "to suffer the same indignity" as Chamberlain whose appeasement of Hitler allowed him to march into Czechoslovakia, Poland, France, Belgium, Holland, Norway and Denmark. All three previous Presidents reasoned that the fall of South Vietnam to the Communists would trigger off a similar domino effect across the Far East with the inevitable fall of Thailand, Burma, Malaysia, Indonesia and even India to the Red menace of Communism.

A monolithic Communist threat was envisaged rolling like a tidal wave rippling across the Pacific menacing New Zealand and Australia with bolshevism. Such a perceived nightmare would have to be halted and fought back in Vietnam. Nobody knows who came up with this domino theory, in fact nobody could even say how much this theory was based on conjecture or maybe plain fear. I leave you to ask today forty years later why the theory never happened. And even more importantly, why the genius who came up with the theory never confessed to it?

In tapes just released in 1997 twenty-five years later, Lyndon Johnson is heard to confess wearily "I don't think its worth fighting for and I don't think we can get out. I don't see that we can ever hope to get out of there once we are committed. It's just the biggest damn mess," LBJ complained. He of course could not express that view in public at the time. Then he went on to admit his worry about Congress "They'd impeach a President, wouldn't they?"

No President wanted to risk the pullout. Nixon had said himself he would rather be a one term President than permit America to become a second rate power. All the previous Presidents felt the same way. They dreaded the idea of so powerful a country as America being humbled by, as Johnson put it, "Barefoot peasants in black pyjamas in a damn little peasant country."

Johnson went on to verbalize his other fears "Of a rash of troublemakers everywhere, petty dictators, subversives and red pawns running wild." Johnson actually told Doris Kearns Goodwin "I can see myself in the middle of a long open space and in the distance I hear the voices of thousands of people running at me shouting Coward! Traitor! Weakling!" The scholar John M. Newman suspected that Kennedy had secret plans to withdraw if he was re-elected. Others thought however that Kennedy's determination to be a winner would have stopped him from withdrawing.

Johnson's anguish was expressed dramatically when he said "I am torn between the woman I really love 'The Great Society' and 'That bitch of a war'." The final blunder was when Congress rubberstamped a blank cheque for an enormous expansion of power to Johnson with the connivance, the encouragement and support of three hawks McNamara, Bundy and Dean Rusk.

Johnson found himself going to war far quicker than he and the public realized. Vietnam has continued to torment the conscience of America to this day attracting a wide spectrum of scholarly journalism in pursuit of explanations.

It makes a layman like me shake my head in amazement. Why, after America did withdraw, did the threatened domino effect never take place? How could so, many experts get it so wrong? Who knows my dear reader the conclusions are over to you?

But let's return to Nixon's Vietnam in his second term. News from the front in Vietnam was not always depressing; Nixon was able to reveal to Congress some startling success in captured weapons and documents. For example, a half ton of documents; 22,892 weapons; 15 million rounds of ammunition; 14 million lbs of rice; 143,000 rockets mortars and rifle rounds; 1,955,552 anti-aircraft rounds; 5,482 mines; 62,022 grenades and 83,000 lbs of explosives and finally 435 vehicles had all been captured from the enemy. Don't those statistics beg the question, who supplied them to the Vietnamese?

Henry Kissinger gives an inside view of Nixon at war with the following account of Nixon's monumental rage when things went wrong. For example when Nixon found out about the signal equipment and the CIA representative that he ordered into Phnom Penh on April 1, and again on April 16, had still not been sent, his temper boiled over on April 23. "He must have called me ten times," said Kissinger, "Three times at a meeting I was having with the Senate Foreign Relations Committee." It seemed when Nixon got agitated like this he just barked out an order and hung up the phone. He wanted the offending official relieved and an aeroplane with the CIA aboard sent to Phnom Penh immediately. Everybody to be given a lie detector test and a General appointed to take charge in Cambodia. But twenty-four hours later all was forgotten. That was Nixon.

He could also be guilty of extraordinary insensitivity when he called the student protestor's bums for blowing up campuses and once again blaming students for their own tragedy after four of them were shot at Kent State University.

His cruel offhand remarks were heard and reported by a journalist. The momentum of student protests increased after that, Washington city was under siege now not about Cambodia but about the shot students. It reached a climax when 75,000 to 100,000 people turned up at the White House and only the sixty buses that surrounded the White House front lawns stood between Nixon and a White House invasion. One thousand lawyers lobbied Washington to end the war. Two thousand people sat down on the roads in the rush hour. The mood was picked up by the press. Bonfires of peace were lit on many college campuses. But when they protested in New York, workers in the World Trade Centre attacked them with clubs and other weapons. Somehow through it all Nixon remained convinced that the American people were on his side. He was proved right for in a gallop pole 50% of people supported the way he was handling the war and only 35% disagreed with his handling of it.

Conservatives were demoralized by a war that had turned into retreat. The Liberals' responsible for the sending of half a million troops to Indochina wrung their hands in anguish and were in total denial contributing absolutely nothing to a solution. As Kissinger put it "There was a headlong retreat from responsibility. The Government had now only two options continue its policies or capitulation."

Capitulation left Nixon one option only. To achieve it with honour at the peace talks. How to do this while respecting the lives of 31,000 brave troops killed in action was the mood which permeated the whole peace summit from day one. They must not be made a mockery of. It didn't help when protestors insisted on reading out lists of the fallen soldiers name by name at their rallies. He was now attacked from all sides.

He got no help from another strange source Senator Edmund Muskie of Maine who complained that Nixon's peace plans were ambiguous. Critics from both Parties wanted the President to call a ceasefire. By December 1970 there were calls in Congress for an immediate withdrawal from Vietnam. Kingman Brewster, President of Yale added his voice to those asking for a withdrawal. Even North Vietnamese Premier Pham Van Dong exploited the debate with an open letter to the American people in support of the rebels. The distinguished Dr. Benjamin Spock added his voice criticizing Nixon as having "Limitations on his personality" preventing him from ending the war.

But Nixon hit back in a speech in San Francisco. He said "I saw demonstrators carrying signs reading 'Lose in Vietnam, bring the boys home'." He went on "One of the strengths of our free society is that any American has a right to reach that conclusion……" "But", he continued "for two hundred years the policy of this nation has been made under our Constitution……" "If a vocal minority however fervent its cause, prevails over reason and the will of the majority, this nation has no future as a free society."

The public reaction to this speech was amazing and Nixon was inundated by thousands of telegrams that piled high on his desk in support of him. After that the protests eased off giving him space to manoeuvre at the peace talks.

All of the foregoing just about paints the picture of Nixon's dilemma going into the peace talks in Paris in 1973.

Somehow, miraculously, progress was made in Paris. Sensing this Nixon ordered a halt to the bombing, mining and artillery fire in North Vietnam. They met again, Kissinger and Tho on January 23, 1973. By evening President Nixon was able to announce on nationwide television that a formal ceasefire had been reached. The Vietnam War was over. It went into effect the following week on January 28, 1973. Richard Milhous Nixon was now riding high on the crest of a wave of glorious popularity. Alas if only we could have ended the Presidency right there and then. Nixon could have walked away from the White House in triumph. But while the grand parade was over for Nixon events developing ahead were like a ticking time bomb. Little did he know he was heading for disaster – The Watergate Scandal!

In January 1973, the twenty-three years of turmoil since 1950 had come to an end. The guns and bullets, bombs and mortars, mines and gunpowder were now silent. Two nations licked their wounds and buried their dead. Sons, fathers, mothers, wives and daughters in the depths of despair. Proof of the futility of it all didn't come home until thirty-three years later, when in the newspapers of November 2006 a food crisis was declared in Northern Korea. "The charitable organization called Caritas allocated $600,000 for hunger relief. The Communist Government still in power has cut food rations from 250 grams to 200 grams per day. This is only one third of the calories needed to survive". It seemed the military holocaust North Vietnam survived was all in vain and Communism was proved a failed entity. Did it take twenty-five years of turmoil for millions to learn the sheer futility of war as a solution to mankind's pride?

Some sources reveal that "Three and a half million elderly people, children and pregnant women are existing on vegetable porridge. The world food programme warns that more than six and a half million people out of a population of twenty-two million are in danger of death by starvation. Nearly half the children will die for mortality rates have now risen from 27% to 48%." So does it really matter who won the war. Was it worth hundreds of thousands of lives to prove that Communism does not work? More significantly still that war itself never works. Although we have today reached the 44th Presidency of the United States our narrative concerns the crumbling dynasty of the 37th President Richard Nixon so let's continue now with the story of the Watergate Affair.

The news of Watergate when it broke was nothing more than an insignificant report tucked away on the inside pages of the morning papers. It hardly attracted any notice and ran something like this. "Five men connected to Nixon's re-election committee were arrested during his campaign. They had broken into the Democratic Party Headquarters in the Watergate apartment complex in Washington DC trying to steal documents and place wiretaps on the telephones there."

The details of the break-in which was later to rock the world bore no resemblance to a James Bond operation. It was 2.30 a.m. on the morning of June 17, 1972 when the five men made history as the most inept gang of burglars on record. They used a "Jemy" on the door latch to one of the stairways in the Watergate building. An alert security guard noticed the damaged door and notified the police who arrived armed to the teeth. They burst in with guns drawn.

Behind a partition a voice cried out in panic "Don't shoot, don't shoot." Then all five walked out from behind the partition with their hands up. They all wore surgical gloves, three were Cubans, one was a Miami businessman, and the fifth was a former CIA security specialist. They had come well prepared with a bag of tools among which were as follows. Two 35mm cameras, forty rolls of unexposed film, three tear gas canisters, a walkie-talkie, and radio, electrical equipment including bugging devices, a wig and $5,300 in brand new notes numbered consecutively in denominations of $100 notes. Next day Nixon is supposed to have dismissed it as some sort of prank, a flippant attitude he was later to regret.

He wasn't to know that this little scene he treated so dismissively had the seeds of destruction in it. Time would be his worst enemy and it was slipping away like sand in an egg timer.

But to broaden the narrative a little let's pause right here before continuing with the story of Watergate. The event we return to happened very early in the Presidency.

Let's look back with nostalgia to that time that delighted America only six months into the Presidency of Richard Nixon. In the midst of all the present controversy and conflict surrounding the Presidency it's nice to remind ourselves of better days that seemed to have taken place a century ago. The most amazing event of any Presidency, going back to George Washington himself – The landing of a man on the moon. That fascinating story was replayed in May 2008 over thirty-eight years later in a TV Programme entitled "In the Shadow of the Moon".

In it we learned of the sheer incredible nature of space travel. In retrospect we can see the astronauts had pushed the very frontiers of science to its outer limits. There were shots of practically every nation on earth just standing awestruck faces turned skywards or watching the action on specially constructed giant screens. All of these astronauts are household names today. We watched fascinated as they played out their terrifying roles while they transferred from their mothership "The Columbia" to the Lunar module which then headed for the moon surface 97,000 miles above the heads of the awe-struck spectators on the ground here on earth.

Before this, all sorts of problems were aired openly. They talked about their feelings as they crossed into the shadow of the moon to be plunged into darkness. They looked out the window at the moon and felt it was a hostile place. They worried that they had to land on the moon with barely enough fuel to get back. The word "Go" was announced and the Lunar module called "The Eagle" headed for the moon.

"The eagle has wings," said Neil Armstrong nonchalantly. "See you later."

We watch transfixed as "The Eagle" headed towards the moon. Then there was an alarm with the computer programme. Radar was the problem, but they just said "We Go." The spot to put down was crucial. A boulder field was interfering. Some rocks were the size of Volkswagens. Sixty seconds was allowed to preserve fuel. Sixty seconds or abort. Armstrong would never do that. The cameras focused in on the surface. The words "The Eagle has landed in tranquillity Base" caused NASA to erupt. "They're on the moon" was written in big lights in baseball parks all over America. They said he was now the loneliest man in the universe but Armstrong said later he had too many people yapping in his ears from Mission Control to be lonely.

Dave Scott an astronaut said "We were experiencing the moon landings of the comic strips of fifty years ago." Now the whole world was watching as Armstrong stepped down the ladder of the Lunar module. We all remember his famous words "Its one small step for man, one giant leap for mankind." "The words were appropriate," said Buzz Aldrin. They got the flag out and planted it into the moon's surface without rehearsal.

Buzz told us "We had to do so many things before we got out of that desolate place." Deep down the crew on board the mothership were worried. "Would there be enough fuel in the retrorockets to get them up and back to their mothership" and the whole world watched in ignorance of their thoughts. Amazingly after Apollo II there would be six more attempts at a moon mission and only one failed. Altogether ten other men walked on the moon. Charles Conrad, Alan L. Bean, Edgar Mitchell, James Irwin, David Scott, Charles Duke, John Young, Eugene Cerman, Jack Schmitt and Alan Shepard. All were Americans.
It was one of NASA's greatest moments when they climbed aboard the moon buggy to ride across the moon surface as if on a picnic.

Charles Duke had a feeling of awe. The black sky made it even more dramatic. "Now we were scientific explorers," he laughed. They collected moon rocks one of which would end up in the Oval Office from now on.
Michael Collins was more worried about getting them off the moon as he was of putting them there. Meanwhile, Nixon in his role of President had to anticipate disaster in the mission and pre-recorded a stark message of condolence for the occasion. Thankfully the world never saw or heard it. The mothership crew waited anxiously. What if the retrorockets didn't work? They watched as the Lunar module rose from the surface of the moon until it docked safely. They got ready to kiss the moon walkers on the forehead then changed their minds. "Oh, what the heck," they said and left it at that.

A strange wisdom came to Edgar Mitchell. Suddenly he realized that the molecules of his body, the universe, the earth and the moon were one. "It was an epiphany," he said.

The realization of his own sheer insignificance in the cosmic whole left him with a sense of great wonder. "Oh my God," he thought. And he actually confessed to a feeling of ecstasy as they came home at 26,000 miles per hour – a bullet travels ten times slower. "The journey home was like being inside a light bulb," said Edger Mitchell.

Suddenly they heard three explosions and the three parachutes billowed open behind them. Their capsule plunged into the Pacific Ocean causing Edgar Mitchell to address the earth. "Nice Ocean you have got here on planet earth." "Nobody messed up," said Buzz Aldrin. Now in future they would have to uphold the image of the men who walked on the moon. Afterwards the crew travelled all over the world to tell their story. Europeans, Asians and Africans agreed "We did it". It was not "You Americans did it" it was a universal "We". A shared joy. A triumph for mankind. The total cost of the adventure was twenty-five billion dollars. Incidentally we can't leave Richard Nixon just yet for he was there waiting on the aircraft carrier to welcome them home before the cameras of the world. Not until Reagan's "Star wars" episode in the late 80s would our love affair with space travel be reignited.

Today George W. Bush has set a date of 2020 for a modern programme of space travel. They're calling it "Lunar Colonization".

Looking back with delight on his journey Gene Cernan said "Science and technology had no answers to how I felt. There I was, there you were. I had no answers. I felt there was too much purpose and logic about everything for it to have happened by accident. There has to be someone bigger than you and bigger than me. I mean this, not in a religious way but in a spiritual way. There has to be a creator of the Universe who stands above the religions that we ourselves create to govern our lives."

Charlie Duke said later at a bible study class he attended "The feeling was hard to describe. My walk on the moon lasted three days but my walk with Jesus lasted the rest of my life." "I had a sense of peace," Mike Collins said "because I have flown to the moon some of our territorial quarrels are so insignificant to me now." Dave Scott said "From out there in Space I was aware of urban pollution. Since that time I have not complained about traffic. Why do people complain about the earth? It's so beautiful." Throughout it all Richard Nixon was in close contact with their mission even talking regularly to the astronauts while they were actually walking on the moon. Yes, Richard Nixon never missed a curtain call. Talking of curtain calls Watergate now takes its place centre stage once again so read on.

Now the scene changes. Len Garment was someone Nixon had added to his circle. He was an old buddy from a New York law firm they had worked for as partners. At ease in the world of art he was also a clarinet player and any contributions of Nixon's to the humanities were down to his influence. He was both a decent man and a true friend of Nixon's. "Special consultant to the President" was his grand title though he had no day to day role.

Garment came to Kissinger one day in his office overlooking the White House lawns. He spoke mysteriously to Kissinger. "What would make the problem of Vietnam seem a mere triviality," he asked Kissinger? Kissinger just stared at him. "From today," Garment continued "Nixon's whole career is at the mercy of his lifelong enemies. Watergate has gone beyond the break-in at the Democratic National Committee Headquarters in the Watergate apartment complex."

The story Garment then told Kissinger was unbelievable. There had been more than one break-in which made matters worse. All had been sanctioned by the White House. A plan was discovered for the kidnap of leaders of potential demonstrators against the Republican National Convention and to fly them to Central America. Prostitutes were to compromise and blackmail delegates to the Democratic National Convention. Garment went on to say "This sordid mess has other dimensions I know nothing about." He suspected the Special Counsellor to the President, Charles W. Colson was the evil genius behind it all.

Also involved were two assistants to the President, H R (Bob) Haldeman and John Ehrlichman. Both had been nicknamed by the press as "The Germans". They significantly were the last link to the President. If they were involved it was almost inconceivable Nixon had not known what was going on. A full admission by all the guilty parties was required.

At this stage, though Garment and Kissinger did not know it, the whole episode was to run to its final disastrous conclusion for all those names I mentioned above. As Garment had forecast enemies of Nixon and the Administration would at some time in the future wallow in a feeding frenzy on the reputations of all Nixon's top men. Even the astute, politically brilliant foreign affairs expert, Kissinger could see the whole panoramic vista spreading before him with a sinking heart. Nixon was doomed. When Kissinger asked Haldeman what Watergate was all about he was given the surprising reply "I wish I knew." The story unfolds further.

On the night of the White House Correspondent's annual dinner Kissinger received an urgent phone call from Nixon. This time Nixon asked a question and he didn't hang up, in fact he seemed to be very upset. "Do you agree that we should draw the wagons around the White House?" he said. Kissinger had not been party to an urgent meeting that day between the leading players in this debacle Nixon, Haldeman Ehrlichman and former Attorney General John Mitchell. Being on the outside of this circle Kissinger couldn't answer Nixon's questions constructively. When Kissinger approached Ehrlichman about Garment's story to him some days, earlier Ehrlichman dismissed it disdainfully.

"Garment is a nuclear over reactor," he said. At this stage it seems everyone was either in total denial or were just frozen into immobility through fear and resignation to their fate. As Kissinger put it "We all shared a sense of impotence." This was simply because they were all in ignorance of the looming scandal down the line. Some observers blamed the acts of illegality on the vicious relationship between the Democrats and the Republicans. A relationship made all the more bitter by the Democrats who had got America into Vietnam and were now perceived to be sabotaging Nixon in his efforts to get America out of there.

Nixon feared that his White House Counsel, John Dean, was about to betray him. He immediately announced an investigation into Watergate with no immunity for White House staff found to be guilty of misdemeanour. This was done to counteract any "sweetheart deals" done with the State Prosecutor by Dean.
Henry Kissinger described the mood in the White House at that time as like the titanic; to quote him, "One part of the ship was flooding but no one else was aware or affected, to be aware of the danger and the band played on."

Nixon wanted to sack Haldeman and Ehrlichman. Kissinger paraphrasing Shakespeare's Lady Macbeth suggested that "Whatever had to be done should be done quickly." Kissinger has since praised Nixon for all he had achieved in the Presidency which seemed to be overlooked at that time. Kissinger spoke emotionally about Nixon "For all his ambiguities he had by conspicuous courage seen our nation through one of its great crisis. He had inspired and run the risks for a sweeping and creative revision of our foreign policy. He had affected a dramatic breakthrough to China. He had begun to construct a more positive relationship with the Soviet Union. He had attempted to free America from its historical oscillation between over extension and isolation. His strange mixture of calculation, deviousness, idealism, tawdriness and courage had evoked a feeling of protectiveness among those closest to him – all of whom he more or less manipulated, setting one against the other."

The above pen picture of Nixon's expertise as a President could only be given by Henry Kissinger and I would do no justice to it not to give it as he wrote it. In that way it doesn't lose in the telling word for word.

Such is the importance of it to the Nixon story. But everything was now crashing around Nixon at what should have been the pinnacle of his career.

The final scenes of the tragedy had now arrived. The tapes. The disclosure that Nixon had been tape recording all his conversations since early 1971 came as a bombshell. No one knew of their existence except Haldeman and Alexander Butterfield. It had been a defensive mechanism to protect Nixon from leaks which were designed to attack his character as the villain of the White House. It was now revealed that LBJ had installed one which could be controlled from his desk in a selective way – Nixon had LBJ's one removed, and then on an afterthought he re-installed it. It was mainly to be used by future researchers. But Nixon's tapes activated by sound alone were outside Nixon's control. An emotional man like Nixon was sitting on a time bomb. Outbursts not expected to be taken literally or even acted upon were there for all to hear. In those passionate moments he was oblivious to the tapes.

"After the tapes become known," said Kissinger, "I understood certain things in retrospect both innocent and contrived. I could see occasions when I was set up to prevent my dissociating myself from some course or to get me on record in supporting some complicated design."
"Like the bombing and mining of North Vietnam, a meeting I was called into only five minutes before it closed," said Kissinger. "Haldeman was against it. I defended the decision insisting it was too late now to change it." Nixon remained silent and signed the order without comment.

Rockefeller felt the tapes were a breach of faith with anybody who entered the Oval Office and thought they should be destroyed eventually. A legal process to claim the tapes started. "From then on," said Kissinger "the Nixon Presidency was irredeemable."

The televised Watergate hearing was like a pebble dropped into a placid pool leaving the ripples spreading in ever widening circles. More and more members of the White House staff were sucked into the scandal. The bombing of Cambodia, Operations in Chile. "The plumbers Unit" came to light which was revealed as a unit created to prevent leaks. This was John Ehrlichman domain. J. Edger Hoover, the Director of the CIA was highlighted by Nixon as a man who would stop at nothing to destroy individuals who had incurred his displeasure. Nixon felt Hoover was quite capable of using his information to blackmail a President. He was determined to get rid of Hoover. Wiretaps came out at the hearing as peculiar to only Nixon's Administration but this was not correct for it was a well-known practice in many European countries such as Britain and France.

Judicial warrants for them were only necessary after 1972. The wiretaps were all part of counterintelligence to prevent leaks by Communist sympathizers.

But when you turn a stone in your backyard there is no knowing what may crawl from under it. Watergate like any tribunal was no exception to this possibility.

What emerges at this point is the siege situation that confronted Nixon in the White House. Darker forces were suspected of exploiting the anti-war Vietnam demonstrators, the leaks, and the countermeasures necessary to fight this enemy from within. The fear that most of his troubles were emanating from ruthless enemies inside the Democratic Party left Nixon no alternative in his own mind but to throw the rulebook out the window.

He was wrong to go down a road that was inevitably going to gamble with disgrace if found out. Inevitably he was found out. We may condemn Nixon but in the circumstances he found himself it is easy to sympathise with his dilemma. The culpability of the Democratic Party in its carelessness with Nixon's profile on the international stage has to be questioned. A little more respect would have been expected of the opposition. The wilful unauthorized disclosure of military and diplomatic secrets in the middle of a war was highly questionable and extremely dangerous for U.S. soldiers in the war.

Fundamentally Nixon's line was "If I was caught in some abuse, I was only protecting myself against my enemies who did worse to me but were never criticized. I told my staff that we should come up with the kind of imaginative dirty tricks that our Democratic opponents used against us and others so effectively in recent campaigns." In his book Abuse of Power the Watergate historian, Stanley J. Kutler published 231 hours of tapes, all of which seemed to be emerging from the depths daily. Ignoring the profanities Nixon was revealed in them as being obsessed with three grievances (a) Getting Ellsberg (b) Getting leakers and (c) Smearing the Democratic establishment for starting Vietnam.

In Nixonese "Getting the God damn leakers, the sons of bitches, the cocksuckers and the rich Jews," he lashed out. "We are up against an enemy, a conspiracy, they are using any means. We are going to use any means. Is that clear?" It was to be political warfare. Some of the conversations bordered on the bizarre. Colson actually suggested they go in and firebomb the place and then go in disguised as firemen.

There seemed to be a complete recklessness in discussions seeing Nixon knew they were being taped. "You talk to Hunt. I want the break-in. Hell, they do that (presumably the Democrats). You're to break into the place, rifle the files and bring them in. Just go in and take it. Go in around eight or nine o'clock." Another conversation with Kissinger went as follows, Kissinger: "Brookings has no right to classified documents." Nixon: "I want it implemented God damn it, get in and get those files. Blow the safe and get it."

Haldeman: "They may very well have cleaned them by now." Kissinger: "I wouldn't be surprised if Brookings has the files." Ehrlichman later quietly discounted Brookings involvement. It was a measure of Nixon's paranoia when he said "We have checked and found 96% of the bureaucracy is against us, they're bastards who are here to screw us." But let's slow the narrative down a bit. It is not your writer's intention of replaying seven years tapes here. I think I have given a fair enough picture of what happened in Watergate. The whole episode was a Kamikaze adventure totally reckless and totally unnecessary. Now the cover up.

In his memoirs in 1978, Haldeman blamed Nixon on the cover up from day one. In fact in his own memoirs Nixon covered up for his actions and continued to cover up for the rest of his life. By his legal sanctions thousands of hours of White House tapes and documents have been denied to future scholars. It was a relentless determination on his part to obstruct justice. To this end he went to enormous extremes to achieve success. Strangely it was not Dean who brought Nixon down, described by Senator Howard Baker as "A sleazy lying little son of a bitch, a stool pigeon trying to save his own skin." Damning though his evidence was, it was the chance exposure of the White House taping system by Alexander Butterfield on Monday July 16, 1973 that torpedoed Nixon.

"Without them the State had only hearsay evidence to go on," as one commentator put it. "Watergate struck at the soul of America." How marvellous it was that in the end the Constitution came to the rescue of the Republic it defines. Rose Mary Woods was the first to hear the final outcome that the gladiators in the political arena had been battling to bring about for a couple of years. Nixon rang her on Tuesday August 6, 1974 and asked her to tell his family he was going to resign that night. Nixon received an almost pleading note from his daughter Julie married to ex-President Eisenhower's son David. "Dear Daddy," she wrote. "I love you, whatever you do I will support you. Please wait a week or even ten days before you make a decision. Go through the fire just a little bit longer. You are strong. I Love You, Julie. Millions support you."

George Bush Senior, Chairman of the Republican National Committee at a meeting that morning said Watergate had to be ended. It was a blunt way of saying to Nixon "quit." Kissinger observed later "It was cruel and it was necessary." When the meeting ended Kissinger went to the Oval Office. He also talked bluntly. He suggested to Nixon he should resign.

Nixon later that afternoon summoned to his office Chief of Staff, Alexander Haig and Press Secretary Ron Ziegler. He greeted them with "Well I screwed up good, real good, didn't I." He then told them he would announce his retirement Thursday night. This was followed by a two hour rant in which he threatened to run it out to a criminal trial and jail. It was vintage Nixon.

"You know Al," he said to Haig pausing for breath "you soldiers have the best way of dealing with situations like this. You just leave a man alone in a room with a loaded pistol."

Now for the final scene of this tragedy. The way these last few hours of Nixon's Presidency came to an end has been denied by Kissinger. It was supposed to be one of a drunken Nixon walking the corridors of the White House making speeches to portraits of former Presidents hanging on the walls. I believe Kissinger when he says this did not happen.

Nixon did call Kissinger to the Lincoln sitting room and his demeanour according to Kissinger was one of personal agony. He was anxious to know how history would judge him. To this Kissinger said reassuringly "It will treat you more kindly than your contempories." He sat in the half light with Kissinger who had never got close enough to be called a friend, just reminiscing. They opened up the brandy. Nixon then guided him to the Lincoln bedroom.

"Every night," he told Kissinger "I kneel here in silent prayer," a Quaker custom of his mother. "Won't you join me, an unorthodox Quaker to an unorthodox Jew?" Kissinger reluctantly obliged. Nixon prayed for help, rest, peace and love. Woodward and Bernstein wrote in their book The Final days – "Nixon then curled on the carpet like a child. Striking his fist on the floor he sobbed 'what have I done? What has happened?'"

However this does not square with Kissinger's account in which he was much more gentle with the memory. His version and I quote was "The President was shattered and deeply distraught but in control of himself." I am more inclined to believe Kissinger, the man who was there himself. Another story implies that Kissinger betrayed Nixon by telling his Aides Lawrence Eagleburger and Brent Scowcroft about Nixon breaking down crying. Later a phone call was supposed to have been made by Nixon to Kissinger pleading with him. "Henry, please don't tell anyone that I cried and that I was not strong." Since no record has been found of this phone call we can only trust Kissinger's version of those final hours of Nixon in the White House.

You may remember I have already discussed how irritated Eisenhower was with the Staffers in the White House who rescued every discarded piece of paper from his wastepaper baskets to be microfilmed for the benefit of historians. It is hard to believe phone calls would not also be recorded. The only conclusion one can come to is the phone calls were just guesswork or just never happened. Kissinger's verdict on Nixon's behaviour seems more plausible to me.

But life goes on. The following night Nixon spoke on TV to one hundred and ten million viewers and on radio to forty million listeners in which he confessed his mistakes but not his guilt.

"I am not a quitter," he said in the broadcast. "I have never been a quitter but as President I must put the interests of America first." It was a dignified and honourable farewell. Next morning to the sound of "Hail the Chief" and with Mrs. Nixon at his side he entered the East room full to capacity with White House staff and his Cabinet. He then made an anguished speech which touched everyone deeply. His final words to them were as follows "Only if you have been in the deepest valley can you ever know how magnificent it is to be on the highest mountain." Then to cheers he stepped out onto the South lawn through the last salute of a guard of honour, climbed into his waiting helicopter, waved goodbye to everyone and was gone forever as President of the United States. He was over Missouri at 12.03 p.m. when Gerald Ford was sworn in as the 38th President of the United States.

The reader may be interested in a last postscript giving the fate of the main players in this political drama.

Spiro Agnew
Nixon's Vice President had already fallen from grace having been sentenced to three years unsupervised probation and $100,000 fine for soliciting bribes for public contracts and evading tax.

John W. Dean
He is suggested to have instigated the break-in to gather information on a suspected call-girl ring servicing Democrats. He served four months after doing a deal with the prosecutor. He changed from Nixon's counsellor to Nixon's Judas.

Bob Haldeman
Chief of Staff spent hours alone with Nixon discussing cover up plans. Few bypassed him. Nixon actually called him his Lord High Executioner.

Haldeman acted as a shield between Nixon and any personal confrontations Nixon hated. His proud boast was as follows: "Every President needs "a son of a bitch" and I am Nixon's. I am his buffer and his bastard." Active in scheming Nixon's cover up, he was also a teetotal family man. He was sentenced to eighteen months.

John Ehrlichman
He was Nixon's domestic advisor. He approved the Ellsberg operation. He was a UCLA graduate and like Haldeman he was a Christian scientist. His acid tongue got him hated by Congress. He advised Dean to dump his evidence in the Potomac. He was sentenced to eighteen months and on his release worked in Mexico and wrote bestselling thrillers.

Chuck Colson
Special Counsel to Nixon spent hours with Nixon devising dirty tricks. A brilliant strategist and an unrepentant Kennedy hater. After his sentence he became a lay teacher. He received seven months for smearing Ellsberg as a treasonous conspirator.

Howard Hunt
(Ex CIA) left evidence of his burglary in a hotel bedroom. He was sentenced to thirty-three months in jail.

James McCord
Another Ex CIA man wrote a confessional letter to Federal District Judge John J. Sirica. He served four months.

John Mitchell
The Attorney General. He lied about directing the secret fund for the re-election of the President and for approving Gordon Liddy's programme of sabotage. He offered to be the fall

guy if the authorities would stop the pursuit of Nixon. He was an enthusiastic supporter of Nixon and enjoyed Nixon's affection. He was sentenced to nineteen months in prison. Later he was freed on bond in return for his co-operation.

Gordon Liddy
He supervised the break-in operations and set out a $million programme for kidnapping demonstrators, drugging them and dumping them in New Mexico. He also hired call-girls to entrap Democrats whose pillow talk would be bugged. He also conducted electronic surveillance of Democratic campaign offices. He was a gun nut. He was sentenced to twenty years but in 1977 this was reappraised by President Carter. Liddy was released in September of that year having served four years.

Incidentally, Sirica the Federal Court Judge had threatened to impose major sentences to pressurise Nixon who expressed his incredibility. "You know when they talk of a thirty-five years sentence here is something to think about. There were no weapons right! There were no injuries right! There was no success! It is just ridiculous."

Rose Mary Woods, Nixon's secretary claimed to have accidentally erased eighteen minutes of tape by touching a wrong button. No charges were made against her.

Later Dean revealed a black list to the Senate hearings on June 25, 1973 which was then held by the Administration. The list ran into hundreds and included prominent names of stage, screen, politics and sport. All were considered enemies of the State. Famous names among them were: - Edward Kennedy, Jane Fonda, Walter Mondale, Gregory Peck, Paul Newman, Steve McQueen, Barbara Streisand, Joe Namath of New York Jets, Bill Cosby, the President of Yale, the Harvard Law School and fifty-seven newspapers and TV people.

A final anecdote gives us an amazing glimpse into the crazy world of the White House in 1973 during Watergate. It involves Nixon's loyal secretary Rose Mary Woods, a woman with a fiery Irish temper.

It seems when Kissinger heard he was to be a subordinate to Colonel Haig, the new Chief of Staff, he decided to resign. Rose Mary Woods was appalled when Kissinger broke the news to her. She lambasted Kissinger reminding him of his humble beginning as an obscure academic and how his rise to White House prominence was due to Nixon's patronage. "Why can't you now return that loyalty," she asked. "The President needs you. For once in your life Henry just behave like a man." The broadside stopped Henry in his tracks. Is it any wonder after such a rollicking that poor Henry never got around to submitting that resignation.

Finally for the record the two reporting partners for the Washington Post who exposed Watergate were Carl Bernstein and Bob Woodward.

But let's not forget there was also a kindly lighter side to Richard Nixon. We can pencil in some revealing personal anecdotes of Nixon in the White House that came out of his TV interviews with David Frost as told in his book I Gave Them a Sword. "Do you have a temper," asked Frost. "Yes I do have a temper," he answered "but I have got weaknesses where personal factors are concerned." His comments about the Kennedy family leave one feeling he was snubbed by them.

"You know," said Nixon "that in eight years after Mrs. Nixon and I had served in Washington for eight years as Vice President – I was Vice President and she was my wife – we were never invited to the White House to a dinner or a lunch.... Rose Mary Woods, my secretary nearly went out of her mind when I put Hubert Humphrey on the list for White House dinners. When I for example invited Jackie Kennedy and her two children to come up for a private dinner without any publicity so that they could see where they had grown up and all the rest. When Mrs. Nixon had Rose Kennedy over." David Frost interrupted and asked if Nixon had felt an outsider in Washington, Nixon just laughed and retreated into his shell.

Could there have been a touch of cynicism in the laugh? Another anecdote Nixon told to David Frost was about the note he sent Edward Kennedy sympathizing with him over the diagnosed cancer of Kennedy's son which required a leg amputation. And that other note to Tom Eagleton's son who was depressed after his dad was driven off the 1972 Democratic Presidential ticket. He was also moved by a note he received from journalist Daniel Schorr during his own illness.

Schorr enclosed a "Get well" greeting from Schorr's young son. Nixon's interview with David Frost is revealing. As if to justify the existence of the softer Nixon he went on "Why do I bring this out? What am I trying to tell you are this whole business of am I paranoid about hating people and trying to do them in? And the answer is at times yes. I get angry at people but in human terms as far as I am concerned I believe that an individual must never let hatred ruin him."

Nixon then continued with another little anecdote about Bob Hope's wife Dolores.... "Bob Hope's wonderful wife once said to me when we first came to California after my resignation. She said 'Remember Dick one person who loves you is worth ten who hate you. There's a love hate complex in all of us'," he went on. "I just hope that when they tot em all up before you go to St. Peters or the other way down that maybe the ledgers are going to come out reasonably well in that respect."

Using Henry Kissinger as an example of the loose use of words he quoted him as saying "I will destroy them." This was Kissinger's reaction to someone who suggested the Cambodia bombing leak had come from the Republicans. "Henry was not a mean man" – recounting Kissinger's escape from the Nazis in 1938 – "But he said I will destroy them. Why do we feel this way – Because the people on the other side were hypocritical."

"And they were not serving the best interests of the country. Paranoia for peace isn't bad."

Speaking of paranoia leads me to Nixon's final verdict on these tormentors. "I brought myself down," he told David Frost in that interview. "I gave them a sword and they stuck it in and they twisted it with relish. And I guess if I had been in their position I'd have done the same thing." Strangely LBJ said the same about Kennedy. Praising Kennedy's kindness he said "If the roles were reversed I would not have done the same for him."

But how did all the drama affect the personal life of this human being called Richard Nixon. The ongoing pressure and stress on a man at the pinnacle of power but living inside a goldfish bowl of public and private scrutiny was deeply intrusive and unbelievable in its intensity. How did he come through it all unhurt? The answer to
that one is easy. He didn't. He collapsed and almost died.

Nixon told David Frost "I was emotionally and mentally fagged out after my resignation." He went on to describe how he felt because others had been sentenced to jail and not him. "No one in the world and no one in our history could know how I felt; no one can know how it feels to resign the Presidency of the United States. Is that punishment enough?" he asked rhetorically. "Oh probably not," he answered himself. "We have to live with not only the past but the future and I don't know what the future brings, but whatever it brings I will still be fighting." The pain and heart searching, not only into his present state of mind, but into a future he seemed to fear, was aglow in his words. He seemed to imply that beside a jail sentence which covered only a section of time, this punishment would last a lifetime.

His illness in hospital he recalled, in which he was treated for clots in his legs to prevent them getting to his lungs. His blood pressure dropped to zero and he collapsed. His doctor said to him afterwards "Dick we nearly lost you last night." It was only then he realized how sick he was. Four pints of blood had entered into his abdominal cavity. It took his medical team three hours to stabilize the situation. The reason for his collapse was caused by an internal haemorrhage.

It looks like his constitution had hit rock bottom after the crisis of his resignation. He remained on the critical list for four days and his stay in hospital ran to three weeks. During his hospital treatment President Ford came to see him. As you would expect excitement was never too far away from Richard Nixon. The glass door to his intensive care ward became locked while President Ford paced up and down outside. The Secret Service man was good with the hacksaw and cut his way through the door to allow both the President and ex-President to renew their friendship.
Nixon's philosophy on life came through in his chat with David Frost as a very practical one. Not for him nightly parties, afternoon bridge parties, drink talk and the aimless existence of the jobless rich.

"Retirement? No thank you. Life must have purpose," he said, "A goal, a battle, a struggle, even if you don't win. Playing a role you don't want to play is when you become depressed and unhappy." So retirement was to be a real punishment. Another battle to win.

Yet for another twenty years Richard Milhous Nixon lived in retirement. During this time he travelled widely and succeeded in redressing the damage to his reputation. He became widely respected as a foreign policy expert. To this end he was often called in by the people in power to discuss with them issues on the Cold War and foreign policy. His expertise on China was of paramount importance to them. He wrote several books on politics including No More Vietnams in 1985, In The Arena in 1990 and Beyond Peace the year he died in 1994.

We started this piece on Richard Milhous Nixon with a pen picture by Stephen E. Ambrose the famous historian. So was Nixon "heroic, admirable and inspiring or was he dishonourable, despicable and a horrible example?" to quote Stephen E. Ambrose. There were too many people who loved and admired Richard Nixon for him to be bad. He could never be a traitor. The only flaw that betrayed him was a persecution complex that robbed him of being a truly great President.

Knowing the true Nixon was not always easy. Henry Kissinger pulls back a small part of the curtain in his book Years of Upheaval to give us a glimpse of the mercurial personality of Richard Nixon. There were he wrote "A number of warring personalities fighting to assert themselves". There was the reflective, philosophical stoical Nixon challenged by the idealistic, thoughtful, generous sometimes petty vindictive or emotional one.

They seemed to be always in an effervescent turbulent uneasy balance. Kissinger wrote again "One could never be certain which Nixon would turn up from meeting to meeting. Nor was it wise to act up on an impulsive instruction without making sure that the reflective Nixon had a crack at it." It was the failure of some White House advisors to understand the complex character that was Richard Nixon that pushed the Watergate Scandal so swiftly forward until it had a momentum of its own.

In a contradictory way his darker side seemed to manifest itself mostly during his calmer moments. Jonathan Aitken's pen picture however was a deeply human one. His Nixon was highly intriguing positive and sympathetic. He said "Richard Nixon both as a man and a Statesman has been excessively maligned for his faults and inadequately recognized for his virtues. His life rolled for eighty years like a long and fascinating river flowing into mysteriously still waters in which there lie hidden depths of sensitivity, intellect, spirituality foresight originality and wisdom."

To quote Aitkens once again he said "Richard Nixon had reached the estuary of old age secure in the knowledge that many of his dreams had come true."

In 1990 the wounds had all but healed. Bridges had once again been rebuilt. He celebrated his golden wedding, published a bestseller, was feted by politicians of all parties when he returned to Congress, and presided over the dedication ceremony of his Presidential Library and birthplace at Yorba, California. The years of political upheaval and turbulence had been calmed by a new found respect and affection from his old colleagues who finally blessed him with a sincere forgiveness.

Richard Milhous Nixon died on April 22, 1994 and was buried alongside his beloved Pat on the grounds of the Richard Nixon Library and birthplace in Yorba Linda, California. His age was 81 years and 104 days. His wife Pat had died nine months earlier on June 22, 1993 aged 81 years and 98 days. They now share a common resting place. Two world travellers together again as they had always been in life.

38th President   Gerald R. Ford

"Jerry"
Born 1913
Died 2006
93 Years of age
1 Term
1974 – 1977
Age 61

Party: Republican
County: Michigan
Profession: Lawyer
Ancestry: English
Estate: Unknown
Hobbies: Golf

Physical Description: Height 6 foot, weight 195lbs, square jaw receding sandy hair; contact lenses: left handed, athletic build.

No inauguration speech (No election)

GERALD R. FORD

Since Gerald Ford was never elected President of the United States no inauguration speech took place. I include hereunder a short extract from his speech celebrating the Bicentenary of Independence Day made at 2 p.m. June 29, 1976 "In preparation of the joyous ringing of the Liberty Bell in Philadelphia let us again proclaim liberty throughout all the land to all the inhabitants thereof… as the bells ring in our third century, as millions of free men and women pray, let every American resolve that this nation under God will meet the future with the same courage and dedication Americans showed the world two centuries ago."

The quiet conservative Gerald Ford started his Presidency with a bombshell because one of his first acts was to issue a full pardon to his predecessor Richard Nixon. It was issued on Ford's own initiative despite the fact that Nixon could have pressed for this himself. Because of the delicate nature of events Nixon could not even issue a pardon for his top Aides. Everyone, he concluded must take their medicine. Giving such pardons would have seemed the ultimate cover up.

Nixon feared such a pardon would cause Ford trouble…. As Nixon said "It had exactly the effect that I expected. It exacerbated the issue. It was embarrassing to Ford. It cost him a great deal….."

But Gerald Ford was his own man. When Nixon called him a few days after the pardon to apologize for all the furore, Gerry Ford gave a fiery reply. "I don't give a damn about the criticism; I did it because it was right." Some rumours went around that Nixon had tried to give the pardon back which Nixon denied. Anyway there was no precedent for doing that.

It was certainly a controversial way to have to start a Presidency. So now let's concentrate on Gerald Ford, 38th President of the United States. Let's get to know him better and as soon as possible.

The story of Gerry Ford must start with his mother Dorothy who was known as Dorothy Gardner in her single days. She was born in 1892 in Harvard, Illinois. She went to High School, Finishing school, and then went on to College. When she was twenty she met a Wool Trader called Leslie Lynch King who lived in Omaha, Nebraska. There was a whirlwind courtship and finally they married on July 14, 1913 out of which was born Gerry Ford. Sadly they were not compatible and he was a violent man who beat her a lot.

They divorced two years later and she returned to live with her parents in their large comfortable house in Grand Rapids. But life didn't stand still for Dorothy. She met, fell in love with, and married Gerald Rudolph Ford, a paint salesman working for the Grand Rapids Wood Finishing Company on February 1, 1916. Gerald Ford soon had a brother Thomas Gardner Ford born July 15, 1918. A further two brothers entered the family Richard Addison Ford on June 3, 1924 and James Francis born August 11, 1927. Gerald was now renamed Gerald Rudolph Ford after his new father.

It may seem unnecessary to dwell on the family of the President but the role of Gerald Ford's new father, I feel, is so important to the story of the 38th President. It could have been so much different had his mother continued to live in an unhappy relationship.

Gerald's new father was the linchpin upon which he grew up and matured. Gerald Ford the lad, grew up with a normal childhood, went to school in Madison Elementary School and discovered his love for softball and football in which he almost made a career in later years. After the end of World War I the family moved to East Grand Rapids to a more prosperous home, the first his parents ever owned. Rosewood Avenue was to be his new address for years to come.

The sales career of his father blossomed and he went into the coal business with his nephew. But as usual it was the mother of the family who gave out the lessons of life and she stands out like a beacon of shining integrity and discipline to Gerald as he grew up. They had many skirmishes yet despite their battles he loved her deeply for she was very much the person in charge of the family. As he described her "The most selfless person I have ever known." But then again she was a great favourite with a wide circle of neighbours and friends whose problems she was always glad to share.

His father preferred a low-key existence in the family which must have been a haven for Gerry Ford given his own early upbringing.

Gerry Ford's grandfather had died young leaving his stepfather to earn a living instead of going on to college. However he never complained. He was a devoted "Freemason" and supporter of the local boy scouts.

But Gerry Ford's stepfather was just as much of a stickler for discipline as Ford's mother Sarah and so drilled into the boys one word – honesty. His parents had three golden rules; tell the truth, work hard, and come to dinner on time, and woe to the one who broke any of those rules The summer holidays they went on consolidates what I said about Gerald Ford's childhood for once again we see the part his stepfather played as a great family man. They loved to go thirty miles to a cabin on the little South Branch of the Pere Marquette River shore where they swam fished and played many outdoor games each summer. While they were not rich in money they were emotionally secure, a blessing for which Gerald Ford gives them grateful praise and credit.
Gerald developed a stutter when he was ten which he eventually grew out of. He seems to think it was caused by a dilemma that troubled him – he was ambidextrous; throwing a football he used his right hand, yet when writing he used his left hand. I suppose it was really the fun other people poked at this strange quirk that caused the trouble. When he was eventually left alone by wise parents who had decided it wasn't important enough to worry about it disappeared over time.

But life didn't always run smoothly for the Ford family. In 1921 his father ran into financial trouble and the mortgage people put them out of their lovely home on Rosewood Avenue. They shrugged off the setback like the well-knit family they were. In their new rented home they all got their jobs to do. Gerald's job was to look after the furnace, clean out the ashes and bank it up with the day's supply of fresh coal. There were other jobs too like cutting the lawn, cleaning out the garage, washing dishes and making beds which were shared by everyone. However they were no angels and Gerald was caught by his stepfather and reprimanded with his other pals for playing poker.

Not many of us know what good points we take from childhood to the world of an adult. Gerald Ford is unusual in being able to pinpoint from where he got his tolerant philosophy. It seems there was much rivalry around and many of his pals and competitors hated each other because of the difference in their talents. "I decided," said Gerald Ford, "hating and disliking people because of their bad qualities was a waste of time. Everyone had more good qualities than bad. From that day on I tried to accentuate the good qualities in them." It was an approach towards others he always sustained throughout his career right up to the Presidency and beyond.

Gerry Ford was encouraged to shape his character in the hard grind on the football pitch and in part-time work outside school hours. His part-time job was to slap hamburgers onto a grill, take in cash and wash dishes in a restaurant opposite his school. But a traumatic experience upset him one day when his real father surfaced again. He introduced himself to Gerald, on a visit to Gerald's part-time job to invite him to dinner.

Leslie King had not changed his ways after his mother's divorce. He had promised to pay maintenance money for Gerald's upbringing but dropped out of the payments leaving them to be paid by Gerald's stepfather. Soon the cheques finally stopped coming in and Dorothy in disgust never bothered to press for them. Now, here he was large as life sitting in front of Gerald who was only fifteen.

"Ask your boss if you can get off," his father said. "I am working," replied Gerald. However his boss agreed and the lad of fifteen was now introduced to King's new wife sitting in a newly purchased Lincoln car. They went to a restaurant, had their meal, chatted about trivialities and then King gave Gerald $25 "To buy something he otherwise might not have been able to buy." Then with a wave King and his wife were gone forever.

Gerald broke down crying that night at the contrast between his stepfather and his well-to-do real father who didn't give a damn about him. One was poor and concerned for him; the other was rich and indifferent. A move of house once again had an impact on Gerry Ford because he needed transport for school. He had to use all his savings earned in his stepfather's new firm doing part-time work just to buy an old car. This was to be his transport back to his old school where he had decided to stay. But a calamity hit hard when it went on fire and he had to borrow his parent's car for the next football match. Unfortunately he crashed this one too while reversing with six of the team in the back and worse than that damaged the spare tyre. His father was furious and made Gerald pay for it out of his own pocket money. One lesson he learned from this - some experiences in life never come cheaply.

But football was a thriving part of his life now and the Detroit Lions offered him $2,800 to play for them. It was big money for someone with modest pocket money who had spent his college years in poverty trying to make up the shortfall in his finances. But pro-football was not for him so he opted for law.

The tiresome problem of money once again challenged Gerald Ford. How was he to pay for his studies? Maybe his school would hire him as a coach he thought but the school budget couldn't afford it. So that wasn't an option.

However his school coach contacted Yale who was looking for a line coach and Ford was soon on his way to New York. The Yale campus was stunning to Gerald Ford. The tall gothic towers, the long sweeping lawns. Everywhere, the atmosphere of scholarships, dignity and tradition bowled him over. He was hired to coach both the football and boxing teams for $2,400 per year. But now there was a snag because this job at Yale was fulltime leaving no room for law studies.

However Gerry was getting good at solving seemingly insurmountable problems. He decided to forsake his studies in law, return home to coach elsewhere, save money and return again. It was gut wrenching. Gerald Ford had still not started the career he hoped for. He even considered a job in Yellow Stone National Park which a roommate told him about.

Eventually Gerald got into the law classes at Yale and although he had a fulltime job at coaching, managed to reach the top 25% in his class among which were top performers like Cyrus Vance and Sargent Shriver. Of course what made his schedule much tighter was the arrival on the scene of Phyllis Brown, a slim gregarious blonde who was a student of Connecticut College for Women in New London. Phyllis decided to leave college to become a model in New York City and her photograph appeared in Cosmopolitan and other fashion magazines. She was quite a lady for she had quite a list of strings to her bow so to speak. She could ski. She loved the theatre and played bridge, tennis and golf.

Gerald Ford just had to learn these pastimes just to keep up with her even if it meant taking lessons. They visited each other's homes and generally life went along on a pink cloud for Gerald, so badly was he smitten with the love bug. But both their careers were going in different directions. Her's was in New York and his was destined for Grand Rapids. They parted leaving Gerald convinced he would never meet the likes of her again. Where have we heard that "old chestnut" before?

Gerald's studies had now reached a crucial point. When he finished at Yale he headed for Michigan for Bar exams which he eventually passed. He then set himself up as a partner to Phil Buchen, a friend of his in a new law firm. Then war took over and just as they got established - Pearl Harbour devastated America on December 7, 1941. It seemed Gerald's life was a never ending conveyor belt of challenges to be tackled and overcome. So Gerald Ford found himself being called up for service in the Philippines.

Pearl Harbour has been mentioned elsewhere in these notes on the Presidents so perhaps this might be an opportunity to give some more detailed information on one of the most significant events to shock America in years, perhaps decades. Its unexpected treachery and viciousness caught not only the people by surprise but the politician's, Diplomats and the armed forces too. Like all historic surprises, Pearl Harbour has had its share of conspiracy theories to excuse the lack of defence measures in place on that fatal Sunday morning. Here is what happened as reported in that illustrious publication (p. 312) The American Century.

It was December 7, 1941 when three hundred and fifty airplanes, dive bombers, fighters and torpedo bombers suddenly appeared out of a blue sky over Pearl Harbour in Hawaii. Mitsuo Fuchida led the first wave and Lieutenant-Commander Shigekazu led the second. At the end of the war Mitsuo became a Christian Evangelist and a great friend of Billy Graham. Shigekazu, leader of the second wave, was killed in action later in 1945. The aircraft carriers "Oklahoma" and "Arizona" had direct hits. The Arizona was hit by a torpedo and was sunk with 1,200 men on board. A memorial was later made of the wreck. Seven battleships were sunk or damaged. Three cruisers and three destroyers were obliterated. A total of 2,335 servicemen and 68 civilians lost their lives in the frenzy. Luckily the Japanese bombers missed out on the power station, fuel depots and repair centres. Three other aircraft carriers escaped the attack because they were out at sea at the time. The verdict of the Japanese Admiral Yamamoto was as follows. "What I have achieved is less than a grand slam." Within a time span of minutes half of the U.S. aircraft were destroyed on the ground. They numbered 188 fighters, bombers and patrol planes. Unbelievably there was no ammunition readily available for American anti-aircraft batteries.

It was a frightening scene for the very waters in the harbour exploded in flames as the leaking oil surfaced from the bulkheads below. One piece of good news was the fate of the "West Virginia" which although receiving a direct hit only suffered 105 deaths out of a crew of 1,541. Five died on the "Tennessee" berthed just behind her. General MacArthur received word of the attack at 2.30 p.m. in the Philippines. Instead of striking at the Japanese 11th Air Fleet instantly on their Formosa Base, McArthur did nothing. At 12.37, ten hours later, the 11th Air

Fleet struck at Mc Arthur's base and destroyed sixteen B17 bombers, fifty-five P40 fighters and thirty other planes. But not only MacArthur made blunders. Admiral Kimmel had only 190 of the 780 anti-aircraft guns on his warships manned that morning. Worst mistake of all was the complete inactivity of Kimmel's thirty-six patrol planes and the radar at his disposal was turned off and only used a few hours per day. Here we see an amazing similarity to other war situations going back to Madison's time. Good times seemed to breed a lazy complacency in the armed forces. You may remember our praise for Franklin D. Roosevelt for his foresight in building up the Navy when he was Secretary just before World War II. An alertness for which he was highly praised later.

This time the humiliation of the U.S. military was caused not so much by the surprise of the attack as the sheer arrogance of the American's assumption that such a major attack could not be carried out by what they called "A short bandy-legged race too near sighted to bomb anything with accuracy."

Only reluctantly has the raid been recognized today as a highly dedicated, efficient, daring and formidable accomplishment by a courageous group of men. The final depressing revelation came out later with the news of a last diplomatic ultimatum from the Japanese. The warning arrived at 7.30 a.m., the day before the attack on December 7. Forewarned is forearmed but still the top brass slumbered and many blundered.

The outcome, as we know today, resulted in America being pitch-forked into a World War role they never really wanted. But perhaps Pearl Harbour was a blessing in disguise, for the evil of Nazism could never have been defeated without the Americans.

But let's return to our piece on Gerald Ford and where he fits into the Pearl Harbour story.

As America entered the war Gerald Ford answered the call and early in 1942 he entered the Navy as an ensign. He ended up as a physical training instructor in North Carolina. But this did not suit Gerald who wanted to be part of the action and after canvassing many people he was given a post on the USS Monterey a light aircraft carrier. His next ship was the aircraft carrier Enterprise. Just then an assistant navigator was transferred out and Gerry Ford once again asked for a change for more action. They gave him the job in spades. In his book A time to Heal Gerald Ford gives the reader quite an exciting inside picture of life on the frontline fighting in the Navy. He was kept busy supporting the landing of troops in places with unpronounceable names like Kwajalein and Eniwetok and the Island of Truk. Later in the battle of the Philippine sea he supervised planes taking off to hit targets on Taiwan and returning at dusk. Sometimes he was surrounded by the deafening noise of the gunners fighting off Japanese fighters and dive bombers.

"The heart-stopping shock of near misses by Japanese torpedoes was something you got used to" he wrote, and as if that was not enough he then had to cope with typhoons, and teeming rain mixed with hundred knot winds and the unbelievable sight of three destroyers rolling over and capsizing with a terrible loss of life. Finally the almost fatal roll which threw him across the deck almost shooting him overboard. Who would be a sailor on a wartime aircraft carrier especially in the middle of a Typhoon?

Isn't is amazing how events that cross our paths affect the way we think way into the future. The war years for Gerald Ford made him change his mind about America's role in world affairs. It made him realize how important it was to have well-equipped, well-trained forces ready to go to war instantly wherever America needed them. As I've just pointed out above that was also the thinking of Franklin Delano Roosevelt. Money, muscle and manpower must always be available to help the nations of Western Europe. That's the way he began to think.

Soon Gerald Ford was in Civvy Street again and it wasn't long before he was beginning to get under his mother's feet back home. His brothers were married and raising children, a fact his mother was not too slow to remind him about.

"You're thirty-four years old, when are you going to settle down?" she asked in her own inquisitively teasing way. But lady luck and cupid were not idle and Gerald was already in their sights though he wasn't aware of it.

At a function he attended one night he happened to say casually "Who's around that a bachelor my age can date? You have any ideas?" Peg the host in the house came up with a name "How about Betty Warren, you know she's getting a divorce? Well why don't you call her?" Peg was one of Betty's best friends. "I'll get a phone and see if I can convince her anyway to have a drink," said Gerald.

This was one lady who was going to liven up Gerald Ford's future if only he knew it. It was going to take more fancy footwork than he ever taught to his local college boxing team. Betty was a fashion coordinator for a large department store and she had better things to do with her time than sit drinking with a footballer she never met. Well they were not her words just a perceived sidestep and body swerve that Gerald found it hard to cope with. "Besides," she reminded him "I shouldn't date until my divorce decree comes through. As a lawyer you should understand that." But Gerald was not that easily put off, and after a little persistence on his part she gave up and agreed to "just an hour or so."

Yet even then nothing was too serious for our bachelor of thirty-four. He had no idea something big was happening to him. She was preoccupied with her job and he was absorbed by his work and his new found interest in the Republican Party so at first it was a platonic friendship.
His first major confrontation was with Congressman Bartel Barney Jonkman, a determined isolationist who was considered unbeatable. His scope for dishing out political favours otherwise known as patronage kept local constituents constantly in debt to him. "He can't be defeated, he's too strong. Leave him be" Ford was advised. Meanwhile Gerald's romance continued to blossom just playing bridge and attending dinners and dances together. A two week vacation away from each other gave out signals of something deeper taking place in their lives. They were missing each other. Yes, they were falling in love... He finally proposed in February 1942 sitting on a couch in her apartment. She accepted. Both had reached a certain maturity from their past love affairs and both knew what they wanted from life.

Besides his plans for marriage, Gerald Ford was about to set out on his first journey into politics. It was to be his first adventure into the rough and tumble of Party politics for the Republican Congressional Nomination. Before we get immersed in the complicated world of politics let's discuss the role Betty Ford played in the Presidency as First Lady. To do this I know we are fast forwarding the story to accommodate this pen picture of Betty Ford, his future wife.

The style of First Ladies was changing with the times and Betty Ford was no exception. Betty spoke candidly about subjects that were once taboo particularly women's issues. She also testified before Congressional Committees on mental health. Like many other President's wives the First Lady's life revolved around the family while politics took the President away on political work, speeches, meetings, Cabinet discussions, and press conferences.

When Barbara Bush was First Lady she had plenty of stories to tell about her visits to the local hospital surgery. Betty Ford ruefully told the same stories. Yes, the First Ladies were not much different from millions of working wives throughout the country. Betty Ford was unique in her openness with reporters about the children, her health and her political opinions. She soon developed the reputation of honesty and frankness. "I took a valium a day," she confessed shocking her hearers. This wearing of her heart on her sleeve made her extra popular with the people. Unfortunately Betty was hit by alcohol dependence but to her lasting credit she confessed it publicly and not only rose above it, but set up The Betty Ford Foundation to rehabilitate alcoholics striving to recover from this terrible disease.

Now let's return to our main story - Gerald Ford getting elected to Congress.

His opponent he discovered was none other than the formidable Barney Jonkman, I told you about earlier. Gerry Ford was never one for half measures. Once he had decided to enter the race he wasted no time about getting to know his constituents. A reporter from the Grand Rapids Express Jerald F. Terhorst takes up the story in his book Gerald Ford. Terhorst had a lifelong friendship with the 38th President of the United States after their first meeting.

His phone rang one morning on his desk at the Grand Rapids Press. Gerry Ford was going into battle with Bartel J. Jonkman the established Republican Congressman in the September 14, primary election. Going into battle meant setting off to seven farms in the district to meet the farmers and discuss their problems. Terhorst thought Ford was mad. The morning was bucketing rain, the weather conditions were atrocious but the new young lawyer had his own ideas and he arrived on time rearing to go. The total votes involved were about seventeen. Gerald's conversations with them were sincere and to the point "I'm sure you've got problems Washington doesn't know about," ventured Ford. "Now if I were your Congressman – instead of Mr. Jonkman what would you like me to be doing for you?" The farmer, used to hard bargaining in the marketplace weighed a man up by his honesty.
They made that eye to eye contact that searches a man's face for deceit or arrogance. With Gerry Ford they found none so they proceeded to pour out their complaints and fears about rising food costs, clothing, schools, tax and so on. Ford made notes after listening attentively. His style impressed the hard-boiled reporter from the Grand Rapids Press... Then a final "Remember the name is Ford if I get to Congress I'll remember what you told me..." A simple start but full of promise, integrity, honesty and hard work. That was going to be the Gerry Ford of the future. The newswires picked up the story of this new guy Ford and his methods of campaigning – close personal contact with his people in the barns and in the fields of Grand Rapids. One person who was impressed by this, though Ford did not know it then, was one freshman Congressman Richard Nixon.

Getting the votes out was not easy at the start of a new summer season. With the glorious weather the fish were biting on the numerous small lakes that dotted the region and fat perch were waiting to be landed on the piers of Lake Michigan. Summer cottages were being reopened. Spraying time in the orchards of the countryside, that spread for miles, was here again. The 1943 Spring Tulip Festival was over and the focus of the housewives was more preoccupied with their children home for holidays than two warring Republican candidates for Congress. Besides everyone was more interested in the possibility of a Presidential candidate in the person of their own distinguished Senator Arthur H. Vandenberg.

At that time, Truman touring the nation was shocking local Calvinists and Baptists with the use of the word "Damndest". But for Gerry Ford his first days in politics were every bit as important to him, a young son of Grand Rapids, as were the rantings of Truman. Michigan to him was the heartbeat of the Republican Party since it first was launched in 1854, seven years before the Civil War. After the return of its Unionist soldiers the Republican Party thrived in Michigan for the next one hundred years.

Only during the Depression years did they change their allegiance to the Democrats in 1932 to back Roosevelt's crusade for a better America. Gerry Ford discussed his ambitions and his stepfather, with whom he always discussed his ideas, gave him a little advice "If you want to work in politics around Grand Rapids you had better start by seeing McKay."

Frank D. McKay was a political giant around Michigan at that time. He drove a fancy car but was seldom seen in public. He was a dynamic earthy politician whose tough words made good use of the expletives he loved to use. Having no formal education was no handicap to his political or business life and it didn't prevent him from becoming a millionaire many times over. When he spoke things happened anywhere in the State.

He was a real estate operator, a banker, an insurance broker, bondsman, and main agent for Government contracts in the State. He practically owned everything in Michigan between the 1920s and 1950s. Even the handsome building where his political office was located in later years was renamed McKay Towers. He is reported to have left $10 million when he died. He kindly granted Gerry Ford three minutes of his precious time when Gerry came to offer his services in support of Wilkie's Presidential fight for the White House against Roosevelt. At the end of the interview McKay dismissed Ford and instantly forgot him.

After that Gerry Ford decided a good local man with grass roots support could beat a wheeler dealer like McKay. But those who tried to buck McKay were inviting trouble. To break McKay had been the ambition of a local dentist for years. He formed an organization called the "Home Front" with people who owed McKay nothing. His name was VerMeulen. Together Ford and VerMeulen decided McKay's hold on the Republican Party was not good for it. The war interrupted the "Home Front" work for a time but after the war the McKay organization was losing its power due to the scandals of bribery, corruption and payoffs being connected to the McKay people. The final clout of a newly formed Independent Veterans Organization, consisting of the "Home Front" and the young veterans of World War II helped to defeat the selfish unpatriotic McKay people. Since Jonkman was a lieutenant of McKay the writing was on the wall for him too.

This is where our story of Jonkman ends as Gerry Ford now leader of the Home Front was asked to stand against Jonkman. The war, the times, and the political scene, had now changed America. This was the time for Grand Rapids to move on into a more accountable era. A more visible era. Ford's accessibility and the fact that he didn't speak down to the people from some kind of ivory tower did the rest. On September 14, 1948 the votes of Ottawa and Kent Counties gave their answer to the redundant old world of Jonkman and McKay.

Gerry Ford won the election by 23,632 votes to 14,341 against all the odds. One month later Betty was to acclaim her husband who was also destined to be the first Republican newcomer in the 81st Congress. But there was a price to pay for his victory. During the primaries he had promised in an unguarded moment, to work on someone's dairy farm for two weeks if he won, so for the next two weeks he could be found every morning between 4.30 a.m. and 9.30 a.m. doing all the work of a farmhand - milking, cleaning up and generally making himself useful and perhaps even more important consolidating his votes for the next election.

A pen picture of Gerry Ford as Presidential material was give by his friend from the press Jerald Terhorst. He wrote "Endowed by nature with great physical grace, a pleasant face, a sound mind, the alchemy of genes and environment gave him also a strong will, faith in himself and his fellow man, a gentle disposition and just a dash of vanity."

One boyhood pal Ford remembers was Byrd Gareth, the son of a chauffeur whose family was the only black family on the block. "I think I was the first coloured person Gerry Ford was ever exposed to," said Gareth. "I used to go up that short sidewalk and go in the side door and me and Gerry would sit in the kitchen and his mother would give us cookies, molasses and milk. On school days I would come to the Ford house and whistle for Gerry. Then we would stroll the mile to South High school." On winter days they went ice skating at Madison Park, play "crack the whip", "pom-pom", "pullaway" and "ice tag" with the local boys and girls.

Now a retired auto worker Gareth remembers Gerry Ford as "A rich boy but a regular guy"....... "We played games to win. I was pretty fast and he was kind of clumsy. But with that blond hair the girls were always shooting at him. It didn't seem to buzz him though. He was kind of shy." Later they drifted apart when Gareth dropped out of school.

In a peculiar way it was the Dutch immigrants who had the greatest impact on Gerry's life for they consisted of 30 % of the Grand Rapids population. It was their puritanical approach and sermons from the pulpit that touched the lives of everyone. People were almost bullied into believing they were not of this world. Dutch Colonist's browbeat the people into accepting that the Sabbath was so sacrosanct, drinking, card playing, work, social dancing and even the movies were sinful and to be frowned upon. The Protestants and Polish Catholics were not impressed but this Dutch influence did have a restraining effect on the community. Most of this washed over the Ford family, however it did make him uneasy that such a group of well meaning individuals can succeed in bullying a whole community by their fanaticism.

It certainly didn't stop Gerry from one ambition. To be a famous baseball player was his ambition although football was the game he played best. The Depression years had hit Grand Rapids just as hard as any other district and the Ford Paint company was reduced to part-time work. Gerry was obliged to earn his reduced pocket money by helping out in the factory. With funds so scarce it was a great tribute to Gerry's determination to finish his education by graduating from Yale as a lawyer.

But let's move away from Gerry's early life and join him in his new job in Washington as Congressman for Grand Rapids. Somebody once said to his wife Betty "You won't ever have to worry about other women because Gerry is married to his work. Once while sitting in the car of his good friend Jack Stiles, Gerry asked Stiles what he thought of his marrying Betty. "Well," said Stiles, "she's a wonderful gal. I've known her since she was a teenager but I don't know if she can put up with your damn political ambitions." Later when the same question came from Betty, Stiles said "Well, if you can accept the idea that politics will come first and your marriage second, if you can live with that then I think you will have a good marriage. You will make a good team in Washington."

Gerald Ford's first day in Congress was a little unorthodox. A suspicious policeman blocked his path thinking he had come from an all night party. I suppose dressed as he was in baggy overalls who could blame the policeman for thinking the worst. The trouble was he was accompanied by another suspicious looking individual dressed in overalls. "It's all right officer," said his short stocky friend. Nodding towards Gerald he said "He's the new Congressman from Grand Rapids and I am his assistant."

Ford and his assistant John P. Milanowski, a former Marine Captain from Grand Rapids and a speech instructor before the war put their shoulders to the wheel clearing out their office and setting it up for the new term. Gerry not being too good at making speeches, was hoping to get plenty of help in this field from his friend John P. Milanowski. It was a time when Republicans had lost a number of seats and were in a minority in the House.

Ford took his place in the back row on the Republican side and was overawed just watching household names at work before him on the floor of the House, names he had only read about in the newspapers. Next door was John F. Kennedy, a young bachelor Democrat from Massachusetts. Upstairs another rising star was housed. A second termer who was already impressing Republican elders. His name was Richard Milhous Nixon. House members regularly dropped by to talk to the novice from Grand Rapids. They were exciting times. Nixon and Ford hit it off immediately and Ford was highly impressed by Nixon's political skills. But the ultimate ambition for Ford was not the Presidency but to be the Speaker of the House. The buzz word was to get aboard one of the important House Committees as a platform towards promotion and recognition. Who knows the ultimate Speakers job was always down the line waiting for some lucky Congressman.

Already Ford was shaping his career as an internationalist. We have already pointed out earlier his views on America's necessity for a strong defence budget and a powerful military establishment. He was also an avid supporter of the Marshall Plan for Europe. Before long he became known as a junior expert on military spending. He was now emerging as a specialist in that budgetary field particularly with the advent of the Korean War.

It was a long gradual learning curve for the member from Grand Rapids and under the influence of Milanowski Ford developed an amazing system of contacts between his office and his constituents. The district's regular announcements on births, weddings, deaths, school news, business and civic awards were followed up by letters of congratulations or condolences over his personal signature. He even found time to pen personal notes at the bottom of their letters which were always remembered by them at election time. This intensive concentration on a network of communications between him and the world back home in Grand Rapids ensured he would be returned to Congress twelve years in a row, a remarkable achievement.

It was truly his political umbilical chord back home. Ford's family life was not without its casualties however. The happy news was about the three boys born in 1950, 1952 and 1956 and his little girl Susan in 1957. The darker side of the coin was troubling him for Betty despite her loyal support and her outspoken campaign for the handicapped was forced to admit her secret struggle with alcohol and pain killers.

But the cure she achieved from her illness by perseverance, sacrifice and of course skilled medical care had a wonderful spin off for future generations. "The Betty Ford Clinic", for sufferers of this disease was launched by her - an organization that flourishes to this day 2009.

Gerry Ford opted to spend his time on the floor of the House since his personal machine set up to cater for his constituents was running smoothly. It was here he got to know Richard Nixon and always made sure to be present when Nixon rose to speak. Gerry even got close enough to invite Nixon home to his parent's house for dinner. Nixon slept in Ford's mothers four poster bed and ever after she liked to boast proudly that the President of the United States had slept there.

Another pointer in his career was the phone call he received from President Johnson inviting him on to the Warren Commission to investigate the assassination of John F. Kennedy. It was sure proof he had been noticed by those in high places even among the Democrats. Naturally Ford was honoured to serve on it. The work of the Warren Commission was to prove very interesting. Lee Harvey Oswald's wife, his mother and dozens of other witnesses were interviewed including Jack Ruby, the man who assassinated Lee Harvey Oswald. Ford and the Commission met Ruby in a Dallas jail and Ford found Ruby was unreliable and unstable and rambled a lot in his interview.

Next stop was the Texas School Book Depository Building from where Oswald was supposed to have fired on Kennedy. They reconstructed the scene looking through a similar rifle with telescopic sights down on to passing cars below. It was the summer of 1964 when the final report came out which discounted rumours implicating the CIA and FBI in the crime. The Soviets and Cubans were the next suspects to be considered without any connection being established.

All the facts seemed to point to Oswald killing Kennedy and Officer Tippit. The charge of a whitewash to cover up Government complicity surfaced after the Warren Report was published and ever since it has been the subject of much ridicule and criticism which has lasted up to the present day. But the main job in Congress that the ambitious Ford had his eye on was getting closer - Speaker of the House. Meanwhile "Minority Leader" was offered to him and he grabbed it with both hands.

Nixon's rise to the Presidency came to fruition in 1968 and he promptly made Agnew his Vice President. Soon Ford noticed a sinister trend had crept into personal relationships inside the Republican Party. An "us" and "them" attitude began to emerge and heaven help those who disagreed with the "us" element. Those who voiced disagreement with the "inner circle" were disciplined. State dinners and Sunday Prayer breakfasts were suddenly "no go" areas for the unfortunate victim. This "bully boy" approach was clearly noticeable in Nixon's new Administration.

That was Gerry Ford's opinion of the Party in 1969 and 1970. It was his first criticism of his beloved Republican Party to which he had devoted so much of his lifelong loyalty. It was a shock to discover things were not quite right. Ford himself would not tolerate vindictiveness towards his colleagues and this was well known to Aides, who as a result never asked him to discipline Republican "enemies" in the Congress. They usually drifted away to ask others to do their dirty work. Ford's opinions on this behaviour were dismissed by Aides as hopelessly naïve. Despite Ford's conflicts with Nixon's Aides it didn't prevent Nixon from inviting him to San Clemente, Nixon's home for dinner before returning to Washington. Nixon was at his most relaxed there.

Other guests at San Clemente were Bob Hope and his wife Dolores, Henry Kissinger and Arnold Palmer who was playing in a golf tournament in Los Angeles. Shortly after that came the Watergate break-in. Gerry Ford found himself outside the magic inner circle that I have just written about. He could only pose questions. He asked a retired colleague of his, Jack Marsh about one of the Aides mentioned in the break-in debacle. "Do you think anybody in the White House was involved in this because McCord was one of the Aides arrested?" "I don't know who is involved," was Jack's reply "but I do know McCord. He is a former employee of the CIA and he works for Mitchell now. I think there would have to be some involvement there."

Ford's reply reflected his worry. "You know Jack, I don't give a damn who is involved or how high it goes, Nixon ought to get to the bottom of this and get rid of anybody who is involved in it."

It was an unbelievable conversation to have for someone as close to Nixon as Gerry Ford. Not knowing the inside track had left him totally disconnected with the events that followed. Almost angry Ford confronted Mitchell and asked him the blunt question "Have you or anyone else in the White House anything to do with the break-in at Watergate." Mitchell looked Ford straight in the eye and said "Absolutely not."

The story of Gerry Ford at this stage becomes a re-run of the Nixon story. It is amazing that someone as close to the top as Ford and, was close enough to be later named Vice President, was left outside the golden circle by Nixon leaving him almost in a political vacuum. Ford and others left out were known in Nixon speak as "Don't have to knows." So let's follow our story about Ford as the Watergate scandal unfolds.

Ford was invited to China with his wife and members of his staff in June 1972 by the Chinese Government. He remembers his mother teasing him on the sandy beach of Lake Michigan when he was a boy. "If you dig any deeper," she laughed "you will wind up in China." He had made many journeys overseas but this one capped the lot.
The change in China since World War II was remarkable. No flies, no litter, no dogs. Clean cities, hard-working, friendly, well-fed and well-clothed people were everywhere. Ford's party sat in the great Banquet room in the Great Hall of the People as a guest of Chou En-lai, eating Peking duck and later talked until 3 a.m. in the morning. Chou En-lai knew the pollution problems of New Orleans, the dates of the forthcoming Democratic and Republican Conventions and was even familiar with one of Nixon's speeches in Kansas the year before. International politics at that level was truly an eye-opener to Gerry Ford.

Back home again Nixon was voted in for a second time with a staggering majority. But Ford was not too happy with Nixon's response to his election when he demanded the resignation of all non-career employees in the Executive Branch. Ford said, "Nixon's whole life had been spent struggling for power and now that he had that power he was veering off on a tangent." I don't know what Ford means but they were the views of a worried man on Nixon his boss. Now at this point in time the chances of Ford ever being Speaker of the House seemed to be drifting away, so thoughts of retirement were now uppermost in his mind. One more year, then retirement to business or his law practice to spend more time with his family was his plans. He reckoned he would be sixty-three by then, young enough to start again somewhere. Winding down was a happy thought which he was coming to like.

But meanwhile the Watergate boil was festering and getting worse. Rumours of White House officials scrambling to save their own skins were rampant. The resignations of Haldeman and Ehrlichman were announced. That Dean was sacked didn't trouble Ford for he never liked him. All around him heads were falling and new names were promoted – Kissinger and Haig. Still Gerry Ford knew nothing and supported Nixon as an innocent victim of events.

The Wall Street press got the news of Spiro Agnew, the Vice President before Gerry Ford did. Rumours of his involvement in bribes were everywhere. Ford was approached by Republicans to contact the Democrats to arrange Agnew's impeachment. It was a move to help Agnew avoid criminal proceedings against him,

A meeting was arranged with the House Judiciary Committee and Ford having introduced Agnew to them finished with these words, "You have agreed to meet Vice President Agnew and now I am going to let him carry the ball."

The next stage in the drama was a call from Nixon to meet him in his office. Ford heard for the first time the charges against Agnew. In the Chamber there was consternation at the announcement of Agnew's resignation.

Later, while at home having dinner a phone call from Mel Laird called him from the table with a proposition that hit him like a sledgehammer. Would he consider the possibility of becoming Vice President? The suggestion was obviously coming from Nixon.

Everything seemed to come as a surprise to Gerry Ford. First Watergate, then the scandal, and then the resignation of top officials. Following on from that was the tragedy of Spiro Agnew and now out of the blue, an offer of the Vice Presidency.

Ford began to realize there were many great men in American history who were leaders of the nation and tore themselves apart in their ambitions for the major prize and they never achieved it. Here was he, Gerry Ford watching history re-arrange itself before his very eyes and fate carrying him along towards the Presidency itself without any input on his part to bring this about. It was uncanny. Yes, time was about to lead him to America's greatest political prize and the only thing that would bring it about was an accident of circumstances not of his making. The Gods of fate have a mysterious way of achieving their ambitions.

Nixon finally got around to asking Ford to be Vice President. He listed a wide variety of jobs the Vice President would be required to do - foreign affairs, attending Cabinet meetings and attending political functions to name but a few. It was all choreographed by Nixon right down to the photo calls. Even Betty was not to be told until the right time. Nixon's time. Ford went along with it, side by side with Nixon. Agnew later rang Ford to congratulate him.

Because Watergate was now getting to a dangerous stage for Nixon and because he was being nominated for Vice President under the 25th Amendment, Ford found himself before the Senate Rules Committee and the House Judiciary Committee inside two weeks.

There was severe tension now inside Nixon's Administration. Ford was about to be given a grilling so he made sure to do his homework to prepare himself for this possibility. He even pored over his own financial records for the previous twenty-five years as well as his personal income tax returns. Three hundred and fifty Special Agents from thirty-three field offices interviewed over a thousand witnesses in the production of a 1,700 page report. Even an old football incident was investigated to see if Ford played dirty. The intensity of selecting a Vice President amazed him knowing they might be interviewing or investigating a future President, even Ford's political philosophy was probed.

This seems to underline how serious people were taking Ford's new Vice Presidency. I am sure this is a bizarre experience for you the reader. After looking at Nixon's Presidency through Nixon's eyes, we are now as it were a spectator standing on the sidelines at the edge of Nixon's circle, observing the political death throes of a President. Ford must have felt like an uncrowned King-in-waiting watching the final battle of a dying monarch struggling to hold onto a kingdom slowly slipping from his grasp and there standing in the wings was his appointed heir to the throne, Gerry Ford.

It must have been hard for Gerry Ford not to feel part of the cast waiting for the final curtain to fall. It must also have been heartbreaking to watch this tragedy no matter how great the jewels he could win.

But there was still a long way to go in this drama. When writing on Nixon earlier we immersed ourselves in the personal agony of a President. Now the time has come to look into the heart of his successor as the story unfolded around him.

Nixon's apparent remark which he later denied, upset Ford "Can you see Gerry Ford sitting in this chair," he had said to Rockefeller on a visit by Rockefeller to the White House. It was hurtfully loose and unnecessary and cruelly leaked to Newsweek Magazine. "The press are always exaggerating," Nixon snarled. But surely he knew the remarks were on tapes. "Don't pay any attention to it," he concluded. In public Ford was supporting Nixon's innocence in the Watergate affair but events developing around him were throwing up time bombs everywhere.

Nixon wrote to him "Its tough going now, but history I am sure will record you as one of the most capable, courageous and honourable Vice Presidents we have ever had." But Ford was in a no-win situation. Ford said "I couldn't abandon Nixon because that would make it appear that I was trying to position myself to become President, nor could I get too close to him because if I did, I risked being sucked into the whirlpool myself. It was a day to day balancing act."
Gerry Ford based his position on four observations which he maintained to the end (1) Nixon was innocent of any impeachable offence (2) His tactics were wrong (3) The House Judiciary Committee was trying to do a good job (4) The constant leaks to the press by a few irresponsible members were reprehensible. Nixon's deterioration mentally and physically was becoming obvious and what's more he complained bitterly about how he was being mistreated by Congress and the press. His resolve to fight was weakening.

Tip O'Neill thought Nixon's position was precarious and said so to Ford on a golf outing they attended together. Opinions like these made Ford uncomfortable. At this time Ford remembered a story he had been told by a reporter from the Chicago Daily News about some villagers in Civil War Greece in 1948. One villager emigrating next day asked the weary villagers what he would send back to them from America – Money? Food? Clothes? The answer he received was not too surprising. "You should send us a ton of tranquillity." Yes tranquillity in America right then in 1973 was in very short supply.

Nixon one day faced the inevitable and resigned rather than be impeached, a situation we have already covered under Nixon.

Now Gerald Ford was left with the whole Nixon Presidency in his lap, warts and all. Press conferences were a repetitious mantra on Nixon and his future. Some wanted all Nixon's staff ejected overboard instantly, regardless of their honesty or competence. The transition team report says "It was vital Ford put his people in the top jobs as soon as possible". One unfeeling cynic irritated Ford. "You pipe the old guy over the side," he sneered. "Whether he was a good skipper, or a son of a bitch that doesn't matter. I didn't think a Stalin-like purge was the way to go about it so I made the decision to proceed gradually" wrote Ford later and with understanding.

Despite the resolution of numerous minor irritants like handling the press, the staff problems and the work of Congress, Ford knew there was one major obstacle to a trouble-free term in the White House for himself – The Pardon.

It invaded every thought and every conversation he had with his personal and legal advisors. "How do you pardon a man who has not been indicted or sentenced?" said Ford. Listening to lawyer's endless analysis on questions and arguments about the Nixon tapes would only preoccupy his entire Presidency for the rest of his term.

Suppose he waited until after the Nixon trial "In this situation I am the final authority. There have been no charges made. There has been no action by the courts. There has been no action by any Jury." These were Ford's thoughts as he set them out in his biography A Time to Heal. Some thought Ford would wait and if Nixon was convicted, Ford would act just minutes before Nixon went to jail and grant him a pardon. Kissinger however came up with the most impressive argument for a pardon "The spectacle of a former President on trial would damage our country internationally."

Hartmann, an advisor, pointed out some consequences to this decision "All hell will break loose. You will have to expect a lot of flak for there will be strong editorial condemnation for sure. The White House Press Corps will go up the wall." "I know," said Ford "but the press is going to react that way whenever I announce the decision so it might as well be now."

"Your popularity polls will suffer," came a last warning. "I am aware of that," said Ford, feeling a rising steel and a new clarity of thought deep inside him. "Damn it, I don't need the polls to tell me where I am right or wrong."

His mind was made up. That night at dinner he told Betty of his decision. She gave him her full support... With typical woman's logic and those finer feelings not dictated by legal complications she said "Richard and Pat have suffered enough." Her sympathies were all with Nixon's family.

His legal advisors finally found out that the precedent for "a pardon" before an indictment had been raised at the Constitutional Convention and it was decided then to give to the President the power of the pardon prior to indictment. This was at the beginning of the Republic. In fact as recently as 1927 the Supreme Court declared that the granting of the pardon represented "The determination of the ultimate authority that the public welfare will be better served by inflicting less than what the judgment fixed." Ford's gut instincts were now justified.

In his book A Time to Heal Gerry Ford goes on to describe Tip O'Neill's reaction was to be expected "Jesus, don't you think it's kind of early!" However, when Ford told him he had a country to run and couldn't have this affair dragging on. Tips reply was "Ok Mr. President." One dissenting voice troubled him. It was accompanied by a resignation letter which stated the reasons for his resignation. It was based on the fact that Vietnam draft dodger's, conscientious objectors and the subordinates in the White House, who had not been given the privilege of a pardon, made it impossible to support the President's decision.

It was from his friend of twenty-five years and close associate, his own Press Secretary Jerry Terhorst.

They parted friends and the friendship remained in place years later. Now the TV cameramen and sound technicians had arrived and set up their equipment for the 11 o'clock news. The red light just below the camera flashed on...

"Ladies and Gentlemen I have come to a decision which I felt I should tell you and all of my fellow American citizens as soon as I was certain in my own mind and my own conscience that it is the right thing to do...." Thus began a speech that was to leave America gasping.

The outcry was instantaneous. The bitterness of Nixon's sworn enemies who felt they had got Nixon at last was mind blowing. They wanted a body! Blood, broken bones, anything to give them their symbolic victory at least. A victory they felt they had been cheated of.

Forgiveness was non-existent. It was the one discovery Gerry Ford was most hurt about. The focus on the man and not the nation saddened Ford. The hostility he encountered was something he had not been prepared for even with twenty-five years of Congressional experience behind him.

But Gerald Ford had a lot of pardoning to do. There were Vietnam evaders and deserters to be returned to society. The Presidential Clemency Board came on stream to review these. There were thousands involved. Political privilege was to be eliminated from promotions or appointments in the Civil Service. I smile, for political privilege had already been tackled by other Presidencies going back one hundred years. Bugs were banned and Income Tax returns would be the private right of the individual not the State. A new code of Ethics was drafted for White House staff. The Middle East question, even in those times thirty years ago, was the major problem for all the main powers including Russia.

Donald Rumsfeld, later sacked under George W. Bush, was invited on to the White House staff, but he only came with some reluctance as Chief-of-Staff in the White House.

Ford tells a story in his book A Time to Heal to highlight how isolated he felt from the true opinions of those around him. The story was about Lincoln riding out from the White House to watch a final attack on Washington by the Confederates. "Get down you damn fool" came an order barked out by one of the Union Officers. Lincoln later wrote to thank him for his diligence. His name was future Supreme Court Justice, Oliver Wendell Holmes.

Mind you only a President's wife is likely to call him a fool and get away with it. Yes what Ford was missing was straight talk. Just to be needled now and again, if only to be taken off his pedestal that the nature of the office created for him.

One exception was Pulitzer Prize winner David Kennerly. He always told it up-front exactly as it was and Ford speaks of him with great affection.

Coming back from a speech he had made he began to tell the story of asking Nixon to ring him back on the other phone. The subject was Nixon's offer of the Vice Presidency to him by Nixon. From the back of Air Force One a voice boomed. "After the twelfth time we have heard that story we wish the President hadn't called you back."

He invited opinions from some Aides about a speech he made. Their contributions were a little cautious, but Kennerly true to form gave his unsolicited view. "Too damn long and dull." I suppose had Kennerly lived in the time of Henry VIII in England he could have ended up in the Tower of London shackled in the dungeons underneath it.

One of the blackest moments in Ford's life was not a political one. He was in the middle of a draft on one of his speeches when the phone rang. It was the surgeon confirming the lump removed from Betty's breast was malignant. She had decided to go ahead with the full mastectomy to make sure she was clear just in case the cancer had spread. Ford left his desk and made for the small bathroom next door to gather his emotions together. Hartmann, his Aide noticed Ford's face on his return to his desk. He understood instantly. "Go ahead and cry. Do cry," he urged. Ford immediately unleashed a flood of tears which was a great psychological release for his tortured soul. Sometimes it's easier to be human and let go, than to go on being the President.

David Kennerly's name crops up again in Fords book A Time to Heal.

Betty and Gerry Ford had lost two dogs which gave David Kennerly and Gerry Ford's daughter Susan an idea for Betty's homecoming from hospital. The seller of a new puppy however was a bit conscientious and insisted on knowing that the home his pup would go to would be a good one for the dog.

David shadow-boxed around the issue. "The couple are friendly. They are middle aged and they live in a White House with a big yard and a fence around it. It's a lovely place." "Do they own or rent?" was the next question. "I guess you might call it public housing" was Kennerly's ingenious reply.

Next question. "The dog is healthy. She's going to eat a lot. Does your friend have a steady job?" Well the outcome of the story was the seller of the dog was finally told who it was for.

David and Susan brought it to the Oval office and let it loose running and yelping around the office "Whose dog is that," Ford asked. "It's yours. His name is Liberty."
It turned out to be a great pick-me-up present for Betty and Gerald Ford.

Life went on for Gerry Ford in the White House. It was a difficult time those final couple of years to the next election. While we understand his reasons now for issuing a pardon to Nixon, somehow, although his intentions of ending the Watergate bitterness was well-meant, the electorate seemed to look on it as making Ford complicit in the scandal.

Yet Gerry Ford must have been the only President who really enjoyed the job in total contrast to others who had gone before him. "A splendid misery," said Jefferson. "The loneliest place in the world," said Taft. "A prison," said Harding. Yet Ford actually woke up each day looking forward to the job. The domestic staff had been instructed by the Nixon people never to respond to the First Lady or the President when they were greeted by them. Betty soon put an end to that nonsense and from then on the family atmosphere the Fords wanted settled on the White House and everyone was happy.

If Gerry Ford thought that by issuing a pardon to Nixon Watergate would go away overnight, I am afraid he was a little over optimistic. Past covert actions were resurrected by a blunder Ford made in relation to the CIA when it came to light that the CIA had been involved in plots to assassinate foreign leaders. It seems there had been eight separate attempts to kill Fidel Castro. Ford found himself pushed into defending the CIA in an exercise of damage limitation. When George Bush, a later U.S. President was made the new Director of the CIA, an executive order had to be issued outlawing assassinations as an instrument of foreign policy.

Yes the skeletons in Nixon's cupboard were many and now springing to life with embarrassing regularity.

Unfortunately for Ford he had come to the Presidency with his own record of having opposed virtually every "Great Society" measure to come before him in Lyndon Johnson's Presidency. In a little more than one year in Congress he vetoed thirty-nine separate Bills mainly because he supported "maximum freedom for private enterprise". This legacy and the scandal of Watergate gave the Democrats an added determination to win the Presidency. For them the next Presidential election was a prize well worth fighting for in 1976.

Now rumours were shocking everyone with the news that a literally unknown peanut farmer and Governor of Georgia had become the front runner for the Democrats. His name James Earl ("Jimmy") Carter. He won the Democratic nomination easily with a refreshingly candid and honest approach to the Presidential race. Victory for him in November seemed assured when he began the campaign with a thirty-three point lead over Ford. Another depressing statistic was the fact that Ford's Presidency was the first to have to admit defeat in the nation's longest and most humiliating war – the end of Vietnam.

Ford still found it difficult to take Carter seriously. Carter had no experience in Congress and the Democrats had been out of office since 1964, twelve years previously. To rest their hopes on such an outsider with nothing more than a winning smile was not much of an opposition for Ford. But arrogance in politics can be the most dangerous disease one can have and I'm afraid Gerald Ford paid the price for it. He dismissed this little peanut farmer from Georgia as insignificant. Nobody in Washington had even heard of him.

Unfortunately that was also the thinking of Ford's election team and what a stupid mistake it proved to be. The audacity of Jimmy Carter seeking success based on his own insignificance was certainly working for him. So was the Republican Party suffering from a touch of contempt? And had Ford's own complacency blinded him to the reality of a new kid on the block politically speaking. Then an unexpected event happened leaving Gerry Ford dumfounded. One morning he woke up to a brand new threat. This time it was a challenger from inside his own Party, Ronald Reagan.

It seems Ford received a phone call from Ronald Reagan which went something like this. "Hello Mr. President. I am going to make an announcement and I want to tell you about it ahead of time. I am going to run for President. I trust we can have a good contest and I hope that it won't be divisive."

Ford was taken aback and told Reagan "I am sorry you are getting into this." Ford felt he had done a good job and feared the contest would be divisive thus lessening his chances in the real contest against Carter. Inside Ford was disgusted.

"I don't think it will harm the Party," said Reagan...... "Well I think it will," was Ford's opinion and the call ended abruptly. Now the unfortunate President had two opponents Jimmy Carter and his own Party's Ronald Reagan.

Reagan pulled no punches and went on to take on Ford all over America. The two gladiators from the one Party ran neck and neck for much of the time. Very much like Obama and Hillary Clinton did in 2009.

Another piece of bad news came from John Connally, the passenger in Kennedy's car who came to dinner in the White House with his wife Nellie. It was a remark that brought Ford down to earth with a bump. "Jimmy, you are not going to win Texas," he said bluntly. "The Reagan forces are too popular there." But elsewhere they were also growing formidable. Alabama, Georgia, and Indiana succumbed to Reagan. Sadly Carters not being able to beat back a challenge inside his own Party was not good news for any sitting President. The fact that he had done a great job of reconciliation inside the Party and had turned things around since Nixon didn't matter. What he was now fighting for was the same thing Richard Nixon fought for and failed. Survival.

"You blew it" came one insult from a disappointed bystander on a train station platform. "We blew it in the right direction young man," Ford answered angrily "and those of you who don't agree – if you would go out and look for a job you would get one." The crowd applauded loudly.

But Reagan was still ahead by 528 to 479. The primaries were going down to the wire and Ford was going to have to fight delegate after delegate. Not a very nice prospect for the President of the United States.

But at this stage in the narrative let's lighten things up a little by talking about the joy and the history of the Bicentennial celebrations in America in 1976.

In the middle of the election fever the Bicentennial celebrations were a very welcome distraction. Ford remembered nostalgically many 4th of July celebrations gone by when he was a lad. His brothers and himself would save up their nickels and dimes to buy fireworks to be subsidized later by their stepfather who supplied the extra dollars needed. The flag on the front porch, the ice cream, the parades, the brass bands, the patriotic speeches, picnics, and football games. Finally at night the Roman candles to light up the sky in a riot of blues, reds and golden yellows.

They were three very tired little boys who finally collapsed into bed that night after a super day of celebrations. Never in his wildest dreams as a child could Ford see himself as President of the United States ushering in this momentous year. Jack Marsh had reminded him that one hundred years ago General Grant had not treated the Centennial year with much reverence. Marsh wanted Ford to make a speech much more in keeping with the occasion than General Grant. Over five days, Ford spoke at many functions and paid a visit to the Space Museum and the National archives where the Declaration of Independence, The Constitution and the Bill of Rights were on public display. He finished up on New York Harbour to watch the tall ships from thirty nations pass by in the majestic splendour of billowing white sails. A Cameo straight out of the history pages of one hundred years ago.

Prayers in Synagogues and churches, the traditional ringing of the Liberty Bell, dancing in the streets and a jazz marathon in New Orleans were only some of the events spontaneously celebrated across the land in what everyone agreed was a wonderful historic occasion.

At the end of July 1976 Ford had another event to celebrate. His victory over Ronald Reagan. But that was the last glorious victory Gerry Ford would enjoy as President of the United States. Jimmy Carter the insignificant unknown was nominated by the Democrats as its candidate for the 1976 Presidential Election. He duly went on to defeat Gerald Ford for the Presidency in November 1976.

Reagan's decision to challenge an incumbent President did have a detrimental effect on Gerry Ford's chances but that is all over now. Jimmy Carter had stepped into history as the 39th President of the United States.

Yet the final curtain had not come down yet. Gerald Ford had one more phone call to make. It wasn't going to be easy but for the past four years Gerry Ford had been doing things and saying things that were not easy. With the graciousness he had never lost throughout his Presidency he rang Jimmy Carter to congratulate him on a victory well won. They were both exhausted so the phone call was brief.

Stepping out into the briefing room to face the reporters it was Betty Ford who had the last word. Taking the telegram from her husband's hand she volunteered to read it to the waiting press.

It read as follows. "Dear Jimmy, it is apparent now that you have won our long and intense struggle for the Presidency. I congratulate you on your victory. As one who has been honoured to serve the people of this great land both in Congress and as President I believe that we must now put the division of the campaign behind us and unite the country once again in the common pursuit of peace and prosperity. I want to assure you that you will have my complete and wholehearted support as you take the Oath of office this January 1st. I also pledge to you, that I and all members of my Administration will do all that we can to ensure that you begin your term as smoothly and as effectively as possible. May God bless you and your family as you undertake your new responsibilities."

Returning to the Oval office Gerald Ford was glad to leave it to his son Jack to capture the way he felt himself. Jack said "When you come so close it's really hard to lose. But at the same time if you can't lose as graciously as you had planned to win, then you shouldn't have been in the thing in the first place."

He was a true chip off the old block and Gerald Ford could not have put it better himself.

Ford spent the last night in the White House with the Rockefeller family for guests. Leaving your old home of four years can be heart-wrenching. This scene has never been captured better than Gerald Ford. "After a farewell breakfast with senior staff members I returned upstairs and waited for Betty to leave." Ford wrote in his autobiography.

All the photographs were removed from the walls. All the furniture had been taken away. A last goodbye to the "Staffers" – the White House residence staff. The arrival of the Carters meant it was time for coffee with the Fords in the Blue Room. After coffee it was time to climb aboard the motorcade on which to leave for the Capitol. The weather was windy and cold that morning when Chief Justice Burger met Carter to administer the Oath.

Carter's first words as President said it all. "For myself and for our nation I want to thank my predecessor for all he has done to heal our land."

Gerald Ford gave Carter a smile of appreciation. The moistness he blinked away did not come from the mists on Capitol Hill.

Gerald Ford and Betty walked down the Capitol steps after the inauguration of Jimmy Carter and on to the helicopter taking them to Andrews Air Force base. It was only to be a ten minute flight but Ford asked the pilot to bank around the Capitol Dome just one more time.

At Andrews Air Force base his Cabinet was waiting for him and the band was playing "God save America" then a final wave from the top step of Air Force One. The thirty-three passengers aboard were in festive mood cracking jokes. They were all feeling good about Carter's words to Gerry and the response of the crowds to them. Soon the mood changed and everyone returned to their seats. In their private compartment Gerald and Betty reached out to each other holding hands. The sun was shining brightly and Ford's spirits were high as they flew home.

Except for a small spell as professor of Government at Michigan University and an offer of the Vice Presidency by Ronald Reagan which came to nothing, because the press got to hear about the negotiations, Gerald Ford then retired for good. Nowadays he is happy to devote his spare time between his homes in Rancho Mirage, California and Beaver Creek in Colorado. From time to time he has been seen roller-skating at a Palm Springs public rink to his favourite skating music Me and my shadow.

Yet as he grew older he was glad to withdraw into the background more and more.

Being an ex-football star he was proud of his fitness. Perhaps a footballer's wear and tear lead to problems with his knees which required the replacement of two kneecaps. Right into his eighties he was heard to boast about his daily routine of four laps of the swimming pool; two in the morning and two in the afternoon. For an octogenarian I guess he is allowed such a boast. But father time eventually called him home on Tuesday 26, December 2006. He died at the age of ninety-three, the only unelected President of all forty-four Presidents of the United States.

After twelve years standing on the outside looking in, the Democrats were about to reap the rewards of their political perseverence as peanut farmer Jimmy Carter walked through the doors of the White House to claim the prize. That is where our story of the Presidents takes us next. Before we walk alongside Jimmy Carter in his journey in the White House as the 39th President let's just pause awhile to pay our respects to Gerald Ford thirty-one years later as he lies in State in Washington Cathedral.

George Bush, the 43rd President declared Tuesday January 2, 2007 as a public holiday to honour Gerry Ford on the day he was laid to rest in his hometown of Grand Rapids. Four past Presidents were there with their wives at Washington Cathedral to pay their last respects and say goodbye. George Bush Senior, and George W. Bush the sitting President, ex Presidents Bill Clinton and Jimmy Carter. The eulogies were short, dignified, but full of sincere friendship. There was informality in the air typical of the atmosphere Gerald Ford always projected in or out of office.

Thousands of ordinary people filed into the Rotunda over the two days and a night of the lying in State of Gerald Ford. Afterwards his remains were given a short period in repose outside the Senate Chambers where he had served as Senate President. He also lay in State outside the House Chamber where he had spent twenty-five years as the Congressman for Michigan. The thunder of canon gave notice of his leaving the Capitol, accompanied by a military honour guard carrying his casket ahead of Mrs. Betty Ford who watched with the pallbearers. The Washington Cathedral bell tolled thirty-eight times for the 38th President. The church or cathedral is the size of two football pitches. It has a certain grandeur about it with its soaring towers, 215 stained glass windows and an organ with 10,650 pipes. Former Presidents Reagan and Eisenhower would also be waked in there in the years to come. Crowds jostled outside the Senate Chamber in the historic clock corridor. Ford's Bust from his Vice Presidential days had been removed on the request of the family. Reverend Robert Certain had just come from leading services in California for Gerald Ford. "They are one of the most wonderful families, gentle, kind, thoughtful and self-effacing in many ways," he said. President Bush delayed only momentarily at the casket with head bowed then moved across the street from the White House to Blair House to visit Betty Ford. "Mr. Ford brought calm and leadership in the most divisive time of our national history," Bush reminisced to his listeners.

George Bush Senior likened him to a Norman Rockwell painting. Henry Kissinger spoke about Ford's virtues which reflected small town America. Among the three thousand people who joined family and friends was almost everyone at the centre of power in U.S. politics over the previous thirty years. The President George W. Bush said "His name was synonymous for integrity. It was the reason President Nixon chose him from among his political circle to be Vice President when Spiro Agnew resigned. It was because America needed him and not because he needed the office."

President Bush was fulsome in his appreciation of the job of healing Gerald Ford achieved after the Watergate Scandal. His relationship with the press was honoured too by the presence of Tom Brokaw, the former Anchorman of NBC News on the church podium. As he put it "Gerry Ford brought to the Oval Office no demons, no hidden agenda, no hit list or acts of vengeance." George Bush Senior lifted the spirits of the mourners by telling an old golfing chestnut about Gerry Ford when he revealed how "Gerry knew his golf was improving – he was hitting fewer spectators."

Following the funeral service in Washington Cathedral, the funeral cortège moved back to his home town Grand Rapids, Michigan where he had grown up. A private funeral service took place at Grace Episcopal Church in East Grand Rapids followed by a private burial on the grounds of Michigan's Presidential Museum surrounded by those he loved.

My piece on Gerald Ford has a bizarre ending I'm afraid. At that very moment in time three thousand miles away, Sadam Hussein the Iraq ex-President was hanged. Such are the scripts that only history can write.

39th President   Jimmy Carter

"Jimmy Who"
Born 1924
Died
1 Term – 4 years
1977 -1981
Age 53

Party: Democratic
County: Georgia
Occupation: Peanut farmer
Ancestry: English
Estate: Value: Not known.
Hobbies: Jogging, skiing, swimming, tennis, fishing

Physical Description: 5 foot 9½ inches, 160 lbs. greying, reddish brown hair, blue eyes, prominent teeth, soft voice.

Significant extract from his inauguration speech on Thursday January 20, 1977
"Let us create together a new national spirit of unity and trust. Your strength can compensate for my weakness and your wisdom can help to minimise my mistakes. Let us learn together and work together and pray together, confident that in the end we will triumph together in the right."

JIMMY CARTER

As Gerry Ford faded into history, the spotlight now focused on Jimmy Carter making his inauguration speech at 12.05 p.m. from a platform erected on the East Portico of the Capitol. I suppose we may as well sit in on the ceremony.

Chief Justice Warren Earl Burger administered the traditional oath of office on a clear cold blustery morning. The date was Thursday January 20, 1977 and Jimmy Carter was to be the 39th President since Washington. Believe it or not he was the first President from the Deep South to be elected since Andrew Johnson succeeded the murdered Lincoln one hundred years previously.

Carter's address, in contrast to many inaugural speeches previously inflicted on captive audiences, mercifully lasted no more than seventeen minutes – a bit of a record in itself. Nevertheless, Carter didn't neglect his history referring to Jefferson's own inaugural speech and even quoted the Old Testament Prophet Micah.

He then proceeded to walk hand in hand with his wife Rosalyn, from the Capitol to the White House, dispensing with the bullet proof limousine assigned to him, waving to the cheering spectators all along the route. In fact the whole family took part in the walk.

They all retired to the solar-heated reviewing stand to enjoy the colourful two-hour parade of 30 floats, 50 bands and 400 horses. A visit to seven inaugural balls in his honour that evening was a must for any President and his wife. Those not at the inauguration in person enjoyed the spectacle on radio and television. It is amusing to think that this last final climb to the pinnacle of politics was achieved by someone so unknown in the primaries, people actually asked in amazement "Jimmy Who?"
But in his own book Why not The Best James Earl Carter, Jr. had a very clear vision of who he was. He wrote "I am a Southern and an American. I am a farmer, an engineer, a father and husband; a Christian, a politician and former Governor; a planner, a businessman, a nuclear physicist, a Naval officer, a canoeist and among other things a lover of Bob Dylan's songs and Dylan Thomas's poetry". His vision of what he wanted in the Presidency was summed up by Jimmy Carter himself in a speech he gave to a crowd in Sacramento a year before on May 20, 1976. He said "All I want is the same thing you want: to have a nation with a Government that is as good and honest and decent and competent and compassionate and as filled with love as are the American people."

The difference between visions and reality were obvious. Some said the state of the country's affairs at that time made it difficult to imagine why anyone would want the job. Humorist, Art Buchwald, cracked a joke that summed up the tightrope Carter was about to walk. "I worship the very quicksand he walks on," he quipped. Yes, what Carter had inherited was an awesome economic mess, coupled with a worsening oil crisis that spelt trouble ahead.

But first, let us retrace our footsteps back forty-three years to the birth of James Earl Carter Jr. on October 1, 1924 in Plains, Georgia, a tiny farming community of 686 people. He was the first born of four children to James Earl Carter and his wife Lillian Gordy ('Bessie') Carter. He had two sisters, Gloria and Ruth and a brother, William ("Billy") who was to prove a major embarrassment to him in later years.

His father was a peanut farmer and storekeeper and his mother Bessie, was later to be sent to New Delhi on a diplomatic mission by her son in 1977 shortly after he became President.

Although Jimmy Carter worked in his early days on his father's farm, he was very much influenced by his uncle in the United States Navy, mainly through conversations they shared and postcards his uncle sent from far away places on his travels.

I seem to remember another great American who was in the very same situation and had to be dissuaded from taking up a career at sea because of the Navy stories told to him by an uncle of his. America was the greatest beneficiary of his decision to go into politics instead. The man I refer to was George Washington.

Jimmy Carter took the Navy route to the Presidency, when after one year in the Georgia Institute of Technology he went on to the Naval Academy in Annapolis from where he graduated in 1946, five years later. He was 60th in a class of 820 which was quite an achievement and was assigned to the nuclear submarine "Seawolf". Carter didn't waste time once he graduated. A certain school sweetheart, named Rosalyn Smith also from the Plains became his lifelong partner. She had been with him during his days as a peanut farmer. Now she was about to be a partner in the business of matrimony. Their marriage produced three sons, John William, James Earl III and Donnel Jeffrey Carter and a daughter they called Amy Lynn Ann.

Rosalyn was his sister Ruth's best friend and it was the picture of him in his Navy uniform that attracted her to him. When he came home on leave his sister Ruth set up a meeting with him and Rosalyn. After a picnic, a movie and a kiss in the rumble seat of the car on their way home, the relationship blossomed.

When he arrived home that evening Jimmy Carter announced to everyone that he had found the girl he would marry. True to his prediction, they were married on July 7, 1946. What a strange world it can be. What amazing things can happen to a young bride? Events that would change her life forever lay ahead.

As their own homestead could not be set up straight away because they could only live wherever he was posted, they travelled around the coastline, just following Jimmy's Navy around the country. Rosalyn Carter at eighteen married a local Plains lad thinking she would be a sailor's wife for the rest of her life. The way of life was wonderful for her; taking her to Norfolk, Virginia and then Hawaii and Connecticut. Yet it had its lonely times when he was at sea for weeks or even months at a time. They had three sons and enjoyed a very happy marriage. As she said herself "Jimmy always made me feel he was proud of me. I was more content than I had been for years." But it was all too good to be true when her father-in-law died and she had to return to Plains to look after the President's brother Jimmy who was still going to school. Her husband had to run the family business. But she made new friends, played golf and took dancing lessons and life took a different turn for her. Later her life changed again when Jimmy entered politics, but even more challenging for her, she was learning to make speeches. She went on the road with Jimmy and although she worked hard she wrote when it was all over "It was not a vocation I would want to pursue for life." But the end of the road was worth it, the day she entered the White House. It's amazing to look back and see the transition she made in her life and the new skills she was willing to develop on the way.

Even during the Peace Summit of Camp David, Rosalyn was back home in the White House substituting for the President at pre-arranged events on his schedule. She just helicoptered back to the White House and got on with it. Incidentally, in their private lives they entertained informally and carried their own luggage. Rosalyn has been praised for writing the most human accounts of her time as First Lady, even more telling than her husband, the President. She had certainly come a long way since she set out to be a Naval officer's wife back in Plains in 1946. When living in the North there was one culture shock she managed to survive, watching a white woman doing yard labour or housework. "It wouldn't have happened in the South" she thought. Doesn't that remark take your breath away today in 2009.

To conclude this piece on Rosalyn, biographers have concluded that "By marrying her he could take a little of the Plains with him wherever he went in the outside world."
As he set out on his first career job Jimmy Carter was now about to meet an extraordinary brilliant icy and disciplined man who was to make a lasting impression on him. After a time spent on the submarine Seawolf, he came under the command of this wonderful man, Admiral Hyman Rickover, on a nuclear engineering project.

One story of Carter's time in the Navy was about his refusal to sing or join in General Sherman's battle hymn "Marching through Georgia". Perhaps the song was too painful for a Southerner to sing even today. It seems he received a few good-natured slaps from his fellow cadets for his stubbornness. Nevertheless, Carter enjoyed life in the Navy and was even placed third in the Navy's submarine programme. Because he was assigned to the nuclear submarine Seawolf he volunteered to join a team of Navy personnel to dismantle a Canadian reactor that had gone berserk. Although he was exposed to eighty-nine seconds of radiation by entering the reactor luckily for him he didn't suffer any ill effects afterwards.

Late in 1953 however, Carter was forced by domestic circumstances to resign from his beloved Navy to take over the family peanut business due to the ill health of his father who later died of cancer.

Carter philosophically consoled himself at the time "God did not intend for me to spend my life working on instruments of destruction to kill people."

For the next seven years Jimmy Carter not only saved the business but built it into a successful enterprise, warehousing and shelling peanuts for the farmers of the community.

In 1960 he took his first tentative steps into public life by winning a seat on his local school board. It was a modest start to his political life but even a future President had to start somewhere.

After spending so much time writing about Northern Presidents up to now, it is a strange feeling to find ourselves back once again immersed in Southern politics. One gets the eerie feeling that here time has stood still since the Civil War in 1861. We seem to be walking among the ghosts of a Southern past that never really died even for Jimmy Carter.

But let us look at life with the Carters in the small rural town of Plains and some of the people who shaped the personality of the 39th President of the United States.

Plains, Georgia; Carter's hometown sits in the middle of a vast level countryside of green fields stretching around you as far as the eye can see. These are the cultivated green fields of farmland, the peanut growing Plains of West Central Georgia. It has been described as a shady restful oasis, the streets of which are lined by tall leafy oak trees. To reach it by car leads the motorist through mile after mile of native pine forests.

This was the community that Carter returned to on leaving his beloved Navy; the hometown he found so irresistible. When he arrived home there was just no contest with any other place for his affections. His ambition to be Chief of Naval Operations one day didn't rate a chance when compared to "Those dear folk and gentle people that live and love in my hometown" as the song goes. Yes, they are the words of a famous song sung by Guy Mitchell which captured intimately the sort of emotions generated for him by such a small rural town in the Deep South.

When asked how did he feel about his decision to stay at home? He said "No Regrets, None at all."

Jimmy Carter had a special relationship with his father and had beautiful memories of him. One fundamental he always knew was respect for a man who never had to give a direct order for him to do something. Nothing was up for debate. His father's wishes were always sacrosanct to him.

Jimmy's mother was always a friend of the down-trodden or disadvantaged. She was an avid reader of everything she could get her hands on and Jimmy copied her example to the letter.

When asked about her religion, she revealed a very cut and dried Christianity – "No, I'm not like Jimmy and Ruth. I do a lot of things the ladies of the church think I shouldn't do. I take a drink late in the evenings; I used to do it with my husband before he died and I still do. I'm allergic to tranquilizers; I'm allergic to everything except my little drink of bourbon. But there are just so many things that I do that long-faced, dyed-in-the-wool Christians do not do. Jimmy and Ruth love me and they never try to foist their deep religion on me. Jimmy loves me more than anybody else in the world except his wife. And that's right." "Miz Lillian" as she was known, drew a line between churchgoers and Christians, between religion and Christianity. Referring to her unpopularity with local people for her kindness to the underdog, she concluded "I can go to bed at night and go to sleep thinking I haven't done anybody any wrong. How can people who say they are Christians be so cruel? I think I'm on the right side of God. I think He likes what I do."

Jimmy often spoke nostalgically of his childhood. "It was rather a stern life," he said. "There wasn't much to do in our spare time anyway. We didn't have any movies in Plains. I spent my life out in the woods and in the streams and swamps and fields."

Jimmy's cousin Hugh spoke about the trips they went on to Americus over ten miles away. He said "On Saturdays, we liked to hitchhike to Americus for the movies. We didn't have automobiles and going by bicycle was too long a bike ride."

He painted a beautiful picture of the easygoing lifestyle for the lads in Plains. When timber was cut a pile of sawdust was left behind. "We gathered it up and went to find a creek in which we built a dam. We then stripped off our clothes and swam in the swimming hole. At night we'd get out our cooking gear and cook a meal and spend the night out there under the stars and go back home the next day. Jimmy liked to hunt," Hugh went on, "His Daddy and my Daddy would take us hunting early in the morning and we'd start about sunrise. Jimmy got to be a very good shot and he still likes to hunt." Hugh won a seat in the Georgia Senate the year Jimmy lost his first race for Governor in 1966 and Hugh still held his seat ten years later. When Jimmy made his decision to run for President, he wanted to tell the family first. Let Hugh tell the story to you. "Jimmy came to my house," said Hugh. "He came around and knocked on the back door about two months before he announced for the Presidency. 'Hugh I want to talk to you.' So we went into the Den and he said 'Hugh I've got something to tell you and I want all the family to know it first. I'm going to run for President of the United States'."

"I looked at him in awe," said Hugh. "Jimmy, you mean that? And he said 'Yes I do'." One person in particular so impressed Jimmy Carter, he deserves a more comprehensive pen picture than I have already written, Admiral Hyman Rickover, the Jewish genius who persevered against all opposition to create America's powerful nuclear submarines. Carter came to be one of Rickover's favourites as the one who joined Rickover's team constructing the nuclear submarines Seawolf and Nautilus.

"Rickover demanded of me a standard of performance and a depth of commitment that I had never before realized I could achieve." This was Carter's opinion of Rickover. It also explains the drive and discipline he applied to his politics and he credits this to the man who was once his boss in the Navy. "If I do my best and if I lose, I won't have any regrets. That's what Admiral Rickover and the Navy taught me."

Another lesson the war taught him concerns Truman's decision to drop the atom bombs on Japan. Balancing a choice between two evils, Carter said he too would drop the bombs as the lesser evil. However, I don't think he would have chosen "The Bomb" as the lesser evil had he known the frightening devastation it caused for not only the living generation in Japan but the coming future generations far into the future. To underline my point, not one of the future Presidents of the United States from Truman to George W. Bush would ever dream of dropping the bomb again. That's the verdict of history, sixty years later. Could that be because never again would it be the lesser of two evils?

At this stage, please forgive me for digressing a little. Yet isn't it amazing to read that some of the top American Presidential families didn't always share the same political opinions?

You may remember me telling you about another President, Abraham Lincoln, whose wife never changed her views which were buried deep in her Southern roots, having had relatives who were killed on the Confederate side in the Civil War. When a tombstone separates the memories of Civil War families there can be no compromises.

Here once again, we experience family democracy at work in the lives of the Carters of Georgia.

Jimmy Carter's father unashamedly believed in the separation of blacks and whites. He was a segregationist and made no apologies for that fact. Diametrically opposed to him was his wife Lillian, a nurse. She had some very strong views and in the 1960s she joined the Peace Corps and travelled to India at the age of sixty-eight in support of her humanitarian activities.

It must have been a strange house to live in, almost as if time was frozen in the post-Civil War years. Lillian Carter, Jimmy's mother, openly entertained black neighbours in her parlour for she was a true advocate of racial equality. While these neighbours were enjoying Lillian's hospitality, however, her husband refused to come into the house while they were there. Earl, as he was known, was of English origin and owned a store and four thousand acres near Plains, out of which he derived a good income from two hundred black tenant farmers.

The house they lived in had no running water and no electricity and Jimmy Carter, the future President, worked hard on the farm to bring slop to the hogs. He also cut wood and worked in the fields in summer without shirt or shoes. He had his own pastimes too, for he loved fishing for eel and catfish and when time allowed sold peanuts on the streets of Plains. Jimmy also played with other black kids from the neighbourhood. It does seem the Carters had more in common with their black neighbours than they realized. Not having electricity didn't handicap Jimmy Carter very much for at the age of thirteen he managed to read all of Tolstoy's War and Peace. In later years, that illustrious Senator and Speaker of the House, Tip O'Neill, expressed his amazement about Carter. He said "Jimmy Carter is the smartest public officer I've ever known. The range and extent of his knowledge is astonishing."

Another little story concerns a row he had with the White Citizens Council. In the 1950s Jimmy Carter had made a controversial stand in support of blacks when he became the only man in Plains who refused to join the White Citizens Council, an organisation of influential people set up in support of segregation. They even offered to pay his annual fee of $5. Carter's reply was blunt and to the point. "I'd as soon flush the $5 down the toilet." He did pay a price for his snub to the Council for his businesses were boycotted and the family was kicked out of the local Country Club.

I have a reason for telling the above stories about the Carter family. It is important because being from the South; he was scrutinized very closely on his views during the Presidential campaign.

In 1962, Jimmy Carter stepped into the big league after only two years of public life on the local school board. This time it was the State Senate. But Carter was a man in a hurry, so after only two years in the Senate, he decided to run for Governor of Georgia. Although not successful, he came third in a large field to Lester Maddox, a segregationist restaurant owner. This was no mean achievement for an outsider like Carter. Placed second was a former Governor, Ellis Arnall, who was a defender of those who suffered from racism or poverty.

Nevertheless, Carter was grievously hurt by the defeat and perhaps as a defensive mechanism against the bitterness he felt he became a Born-Again Christian. Ruth, his sister, was the real driving force for this change as he tried to re-think his defeat or failure from a Christian perspective. She herself had found great solace in religion during a personal crisis she had had. During her marriage she seemed outwardly happy and blessed with the good things of life, a modern house, a cabin retreat in the woods, a holiday home in Portugal. But internal peace did not come. With each child, she suffered from severe depression. Her marriage became rocky ..... She turned to religion which pre-occupied her so much she was fired from her job because she spent more time talking about God than about her subject, English ..... Her depression lifted which she attributed to Jesus. She became a faith healer, a preacher, and an orator and for over fifteen years travelled the world on her mission. Yes, Ruth was the main inspiration for Jimmy's religious revival.

But let's hear the story of how his new found faith in God came about. Carter's conflict with his religious feelings manifested itself in dissatisfaction with how he handled success and failure. He said "When I had success, I had no sense of gratification or enjoyment. When I had failure it was a deep personal bitterness and sometimes confusion and despair. There was just something missing in my life – a sense of peace, a sense of higher purpose." He was now giving to God some fresh thinking he never had before.

Ruth sympathised with him, speaking of her own God and the discovery she had made. "My experience," she confessed to Jimmy "was of a God loving and caring. A personal God and a Jesus Christ that I had not known in my life as a Church Minister. He was loving. He was here and now." When Jimmy and Ruth prayed together, the Lord was right there in the car or the room with them. She enjoyed helping people, especially those of troubled minds. If this was possible for Ruth, Jimmy Carter thought, why not for him.

Re-appraising his life, he realized he had gone out to meet thousands in pursuit of politics but he had met only about ten per year over fourteen years for God. The title of one of his sermons in those days he remembers vividly was "If you were arrested for being a Christian, would there be enough evidence to convict you?"

It was a warm afternoon in autumn 1966 when he drove with Ruth into the country some miles outside Plains. They talked about God and the future, especially Jimmy's future. They walked aimlessly through the countryside both sharing the depths of their thoughts. Jimmy's conversion took root that afternoon. The release of God's spirit within their own spirit and the liberation it gave them was the subject of their chat.

God's love displayed through His son, Jesus Christ, by way of the Holy Spirit. He was keenly aware of her inner peace and her sense of the Lord's direction in her life ..... "You've got to accept God's Will no matter what it is. To do whatever He wants," was her advice. The quietness and peace of the woods they walked in touched him ..... They knelt there in the Pine Forest, brother and sister, physically and spiritually and just prayed together, asking for help to conform completely to God's Will ..... From now on he would be completely dependent on the Holy Spirit.

This message re-emerged at a meeting he held during his Presidential campaign. A heckler stood up to embarrass or confuse Carter "Just what is your relationship with Jesus Christ?" he sneered. Carter took his heckler by surprise when he quietly replied "Jesus Christ comes first in my life, even before politics." But Carter was not as committed to his new Christianity as he fondly believed. A few weeks later came the test ..... A phone call came through from the Southern Baptist Convention, asking him to give a week to God on a mission. "Who will pay for it?" he asked. "You will" was the message on the phone..... "No thanks," he told them and hung up ..... Carter recalls that it was next day he changed his mind and said he would do it..... "What do I do?" he asked. It was to be a pioneer mission and he was to give it without strings attached. That is the story behind the famous mission Carter embarked upon after his defeat for the Governorship. Now we know it was a combination of his defeat and a miracle of a resurrected faith in God. The reason I give this story in such detail is to establish once and for all the depth of Carter's sincerity with his discovery of the Holy Spirit on his life ..... With so much bad publicity for his political motives, this is one story that was a true lifelong experience. It was certainly no gimmick.

The following year, Carter was away to his mission once again. This time to Massachusetts, where he worked in a place riddled with poverty in the inner city. He worked alongside a Cuban Minister, Ellery Cruz, who regularly came back to his thoughts when he was Governor. Carter's familiarity with the Spanish language was a great help. Carter often spoke of Cruz "He had a remarkable ability to reach the hearts of people in a very natural and unassuming way. He used to say when asked 'How a man so rugged could be so sensitive? Our Saviour has hands which are very gentle and he cannot do much with a man who is hard'. I thought about this often as Governor of Georgia," said Carter.

During his mission, Rosalyn and Jimmy Carter reckoned they had shaken hands with 300,000 people in six hundred communities on their travels. Of course it was great experience for him in his future political travels on the stump. We are never short of comedians in this world and as usual there were a few lurking in wait for Jimmy and Rosalyn on their travels. "I think Jimmy Carter takes his initials far too seriously," they jibed.

When Jimmy Carter decided to go for the Governorship a second time, he decided to look for the support of the black community. A Cameron Alexander said to him "If you want my people to vote for you, come to church." Not since the times of Tom Watson had a white Georgian politician sought black support. Carter went to church and gave a Baptist sermon. Another great supporter was the Reverend Fred Bennett, who was to work long and hard to secure the black electorate for him. It seemed a shrewd move for the black votes gained far outnumbered the white votes lost.

Fortunately for Carter, his opponent "Cuff Links" Carl Sanders had more concern for his political position in the State than a genuine interest in the plight of the black voter. His affluent lifestyle didn't help since it lost him contact with the blacks. He was always uncomfortable campaigning in black communities. As Governor, he had no empathy with the black community whatsoever.

However, Carter himself did not always please the public either. Once in a shopping arcade, he was hit with a right hook to the jaw by a disgruntled marine who unfortunately had a history of psychiatric problems. Carter went later to the mental hospital his assailant was in to offer him forgiveness. A friend of Carl Sanders, Reg Murphy, thought Carter was self-righteous, ambitious and ruthless. This man Reg Murphy was a dangerous enemy to have, being the editor of The Atlanta Constitution in which he described Carter as a redneck, racist, ignorant bumpkin, whose only talent was growing peanuts.

Carter's chief supporter, the man who flew him around, was with him when he won the Governorship; Carter asked him "What would you like me to do for you as Governor of Georgia?" "Nothing," said David Rabham. "There must be something," insisted Carter ..... "Well," Rabham sighed "In your inaugural address, say something about removing the millstone of racism from around the necks of the Georgia people."

Carter wrote on the edge of a flight map "At the end of a long campaign, I believe, I know our people as well as anyone. Based on the knowledge of Georgians, North and South, rural and urban, Liberal and Conservative, I say to you frankly the time for racial discrimination is over". "How would this be?" said Carter, handing the note to Rabham. "Sign it," said Rabham. Carter not only did that, but included it in his inaugural speech.

On January 12, 1971 on a cold and windy winter's morning, Carter was sworn in as Governor of Georgia. His speech, "The most important of his life" said Carter later, lasted no more than eight minutes. In it Carter made his hearers gasp when he announced "No poor, rural, weak or black person should ever have to bear the additional burden of being deprived of the opportunity of an education, a job or simply justice."

It is worth remembering at this stage of the Carter story, given his religious background; he could never be a racist. In fact, when he became Governor of Georgia, he was quite liberal by Georgia standards. He appointed both blacks and women to many State boards and had a portrait of Martin Luther King Jr., the assassinated civil rights leader, displayed in the State Capitol. The best we can do is to accept that Carter being a Southerner knew intimately what the Southern mind was all about and used his knowledge of it to achieve his own political success down South.

It wasn't long before Jimmy Carter was making some controversial decisions as Governor. He introduced tougher consumer laws, new programmes in healthcare and education and also made improvements in the reform of Georgia prisons. I have already mentioned his more liberal treatment of blacks and women by introducing them into his
Administration. Before writing about Carter's Governorship here is a small story about the Governor's next in command called the Lieutenant Governor, who was none other than the

man he had defeated in the elections, Lennox Maddox, and who was now an elected official.

Jimmy Carter disliked Lester Maddox intensely because Maddox was all Carter despised in Georgia politics. But this was Maddox's day too. As Lieutenant Governor he was a happy man. Now he could continue to lord it over the morals of his fellow Georgians. As Governor he had exercised this privilege as a right. He banned short skirts in the State offices. They laughed at him of course, just as they would when he cycled his bike backwards at public functions. People thought he was insane then but Maddox was candid to the point of simplicity. He blurted out whatever was in his mind, sometimes rude, yet frequently amusing. A funny story is told about one of his ideas which he introduced, as a ritual during his Governorship, like that practiced in Washington, in the days of Abraham Lincoln. Every fortnight he threw open the doors of the Governor's Mansion to all and sundry who wished to shake the hand of the Governor.

A group of escaped prisoners off a road gang used that very day to surrender to him in person. "That was not what I had intended," he told some reporters nearby. One day he received a present of a fruit cake and later told his wife "You know honey, sometimes I guess it's too hard to believe that the niggers love me too." That really was hard to believe for he had already built up a reputation of being a small time George Wallace. Yet he barricaded himself into his office scared stiff when thousands came to Atlanta to attend the funeral of the murdered Martin Luther King. But today was his day. On this, the inauguration day of the Governor, Jimmy Carter, he was a happy man in the knowledge that with all his faults, the Georgians had chosen him as second in command. Yes, today he really felt loved.

But in a strange way, even for politics down South, the religious convert and man of compassion, Jimmy Carter, was not too popular with the blacks after he won the election for Governor. Carter afterwards told friends that he felt bad about his actions during the campaign. He said he prayed for forgiveness for some of the things he felt he had to say and do to get himself elected. He was hard on Maddox and patronized him as a pawn of Atlanta money, portraying himself, Carter, as an intellectual.

Yes, I'm afraid politics can reduce the best of us to mere mortals. He was sparing in his praise of Maddox who was on the same ticket with him. Strangely again for a man of Christian ideals, he claimed to be always an enemy of Maddox. No love lost there – nor forgiveness. He also gave his blessing for private schools designed to avoid the integration of education and was actually photographed visiting one of them. Yes, expediency was the key to his election. He explained it all to friends and to the Lord – "I often had to compromise but I didn't compromise in a back room," he said defensively. The judgement of his black voters was a sad one for Carter. He polled only 5% of their vote. But still he implemented all of his reforms later. It was a complicated world in Southern politics as Carter was beginning to discover.

Jimmy Carter loved being Governor of Georgia. He was certain he knew his people. His grasp of even the tiniest detail impressed those around him. He never floundered at press conferences because his command of any subject was far superior to that of his questioner. He radiated self-confidence. Whenever a crisis broke out, such as a ship crashing into a road bridge or a lethal explosion at a chicken processing plant, he was there "with the people". A reservoir of love and respect grew up between them.

His first big perk was the palatial mansion he now lived in instead of the modest family home back in Plains. Both Jack and Georgia were married while they lived there. Having a relative in the State Mental hospital made it important for him to appoint a Governor's Commission to improve services to the mentally and emotionally handicapped.

Rosalyn his wife missed the old relaxed friendship with her friends and came under strain because of a self-imposed aim for perfection. The ongoing constant official entertaining were also too much for her. She only improved when she dropped her search for perfection. God was a great consolation to her then. Jimmy however led a frantic life in his limousine or airplane that rushed him to scenes of disasters or meetings of sheriffs or health workers. His day started without breakfast at 7.15 a.m. Everything about it was planned to precision. Even his time for reading Time or Newsweek was parcelled out to a half hour each day. Wasting time was a major sin in his pact with God.

The Governorship was the ideal training ground for the Presidency. He met many famous people including the not so famous and unorthodox. Everything was a learning curve with him for the future. Van Cliburn, Paul Simon, The Marshall Tucker Band and some Country and Western singers, Henry Kissinger, Peter Max and Eunice Shriver were all visitors to his mansion. Carter took a keen interest in the church's missionary work and he enjoyed the challenge of improving the quality of life for the people of Georgia. The social programmes he implemented were to him an extension of the Gospels and through it all he had one superb driving force – prayer. Despite all that, Carter allowed nobody too close. Only Rosalyn had that privilege. He was extremely tolerant towards his young staff and rarely abused them for errors, no matter how embarrassing.

A nasty racial problem flared up in Hancock County, southeast of Atlanta. Anti-poverty programmes had been set up and funded by Washington and the Ford Foundation. A network of small businesses was setup employing mainly blacks. A group of white citizens in Sparta felt threatened. The Mayor of Sparta bought ten sub-machine guns for the city's white police officers. McGowan, the black administrator decided to balance the books by buying thirty sub-machine guns. The Sparta police chief, fearing trouble, took a month's leave of absence. Carter was told about all this and realized the potential damage to his "New South" image was dangerously close. He could have used State Troopers but that might have made things worse and thus creating the trouble he wished to avoid. Instead, he dispatched a three man civil disorder unit, with one black Justice Department agent, who was a specialist in the field of civil disturbances. This unit had already defused similar disturbances around the State. The order for guns was cancelled and things returned to normal but only after a tense three weeks of negotiations. And Carter was at the heart of everything. Carter became convinced that with tenacity and skill even the most intransigent situations could be resolved. It was a lesson he would one day take with him to Camp David itself.

Carter was successful in many areas reforming the judicial system. He saw race as the great unhealed scar of American society. He also saw his main role was to improve the lot of African-Americans in the State. At the start of his Governorship there were only three blacks serving on major State boards. When he left there were fifty-three. The number of black employees went up from 4,850 to 6,684. He opened up the State patrols to blacks. When receiving a call from the Country Club to address them he was asked not to bring his black troop patrol. He defied them, brought his black bodyguards and lectured his audience on the evils of racism. He only championed the housing programmes that enjoyed the support of black leaders.

The end of his Governorship was approaching when he was visited by the top men in his Administration in Georgia.

Hamilton Jordan coughed nervously and said "I don't know any other way to say this and its hard to bring myself to say the words, but I guess I will have to say it." He paused, "We think you should run for President." Carter didn't argue with him. Perhaps they were only articulating his own reading of the situation.

His faults and failings were then discussed. He was superb at talking one to one, yet useless to large audiences, especially from prepared text. He also did poorly on television. So Carter agreed he needed help there too. Foreign Affairs were also not his strong point and his comfort with economics would have to be improved. Time was now running out for him they said. The meeting closed at midnight. By Christmas 1972 the plan was in place.

A personal visit from Dean Rusk, then a distinguished Professor at the University of Georgia, copper-fastened the plan.

Support from Washington was now forthcoming. Maybe "Jimmy Who" was not the outsider Gerry Ford had imagined. Maybe Ford was in for a big surprise.

And so to the Carter Presidential Campaign.

From autumn 1976, Carter was running for the Democratic Nomination for the Presidency. He was consumed by it, plotting strategy, making speeches and travelling widely. Carter knew one of his greatest assets was the fact that he was an unknown quantity in Georgia. He was also unknown in a country that had lost faith in Washington politicians. Having a record in Federal office was not in those post-Nixon days a credible asset.

Antagonism towards the Federal Government was deep and strong. Your popularity soon waned when you became a "Washington" politician. So Carter had nothing to explain, nothing to apologize for, and nothing to be blamed for. It was an ideal background for an aspiring President and Carter was not long in realizing this and playing up such strong points to the electorate. Carter went on to construct the image of rigid ethical standards of honesty and integrity. He built this up layer by layer in a brilliant well thought out campaign that caught the Republicans in no man's land. Their complacency was their own downfall.

Averell Harriman described as "The doddering patriarch of the community" by James Wooten in his book Dasher: The Roots and the Rising of Jimmy Carter was told by someone across a dinner table – "Carter seems to be the candidate who might have a chance in the Presidency." He stared incredulously at the one who made this outrageous statement. "Jimmy Carter? Jimmy Carter," he repeated – "How can that be? I don't even know Jimmy Carter and as far as I know none of my friends knows him either." But one day in the future Harriman would not only endorse Jimmy Carter but would call him "One of the great leaders of his generation."

But that ghost in his curriculum vitae had not gone away. There were still some people who only knew him as "Jimmy who". That's why Carter had his work cut out persuading the big guns of the Democratic Party to support him. In Texas he had a bad time, for not one member of the States Democratic establishment was interested. But Carter was willing to accept help from anyone, even George Wallace. Wallace eventually joined the Carter crusade after his defeat by Carter in Florida. Mayor Daly was the final kingmaker. The unknown was "home and dry" in the Democratic race ..... The big one was still to come. Yet the Preliminaries had hardly begun.

Rosalyn Carter gives us an insight into the intense nature of her husband. "His preparation for the job as President started with his search for a comprehensive knowledge of every President since Washington," she said. He even read up on Presidents who ran for office and lost. He studied in-depth the wide range of issues confronting a President and pored over a map of the

United States just to know the exact location of each State of the Union. He realised that knowing the country would not be enough. The country must know him.

Some Democratic leaders were vaguely aware of "New South Governors" but up to 1974 very few voters had even heard of him. Carter's strategists laid out the formula to redress this gap in their knowledge – to run everywhere, go everywhere and meet everybody. Carter's charm and friendly personality would do the rest. To emphasize his independence of Washington they would base his headquarters in Atlanta. He travelled to thirty-two States to help sixty-two candidates and connected with Party leaders in twenty States. He paid for the travel himself and left behind him oceans of goodwill. He certainly learned a lot about the country. Yet he did it on a weekend basis according to Rosalyn. As she said defiantly "Jimmy had a job to do back home as Governor of Georgia."

Fundamentally, what Carter wanted was to be sent to the White House to restore to America its lost soul, its lost moral fabric, its lost trust in the hearts of its people. To give them once again good news stories from Washington. The good news that all their aspirations for an honest, decent, law-abiding leadership led by a decent God fearing man would be rewarded. The man was to be James Earl Carter.

That he succeeded in convincing them is now history. Jimmy Carter won the Presidential Election to be installed as the 39th President of the United States beating Gerald Ford by 297 Electoral votes to 240.

Now he would no longer attend Bible Class to teach eager students as he had done regularly as Governor of Georgia. Those who knew him back home accepted the fact that he would not be giving his usual bible class until after the Presidency. They would also recall with a laugh Carter's boyhood days. Sundays, when a tiny Jimmy Carter of eleven or twelve, collected all his pals who couldn't make it to bible class through lack of transport. Looking into their past perhaps they were one of those laughing little urchins who tumbled out of his mother's old black Plymouth he used to collect them. So big a car, his tiny curly head could barely be seen behind the steering wheel ..... Now he was President of the United States of America. What a tribute to a country like America!

To conclude this section, a lovely story is told in the book The Miracle of Jimmy Carter by Howard Norton and Bob Slosser, two Pulitzer Prize winners. It is about an interview with a journalist in the limousine taking Carter to the airport after making a speech in his Presidential campaign.

The journalist representing The National Courier, a Christian newspaper, posed this question – "I think there are millions of other Christians in the country who would like to know exactly what kind of Christian you are." Carter smiled.

As his motorcade moved through the rush hour traffic, Carter revealed a remarkable insight into his personal philosophy. He spoke of his missionary trip into the North, preaching the Gospels, in which he discovered a sense of complete dependence on the Holy Spirit. Describing his missionary work he said "It wasn't my eloquence that convinced my listeners. I soon realized it wasn't me or my brilliance or my fervour that made a difference. It was something else." Carter continued the story with sincere conviction. "It was the presence of the Holy Spirit. Just when I fumbled or thought I had failed that was the time when people were convinced by the Holy Spirit. I realized it wasn't me." The car journey came to an end at the airport gates. Carter got out and said – "I've got to go … Good luck with the book." It was an amazing new piece of Presidential history.

The journalist had interviewed many Presidents and Presidential candidates going back to Franklin D. Roosevelt over a period of thirty-six years. Never had any of them openly admitted to such a spiritual experience. He had never before heard a candidate or President give so much prominence to the presence of the Holy Spirit in his life.

Well, we have heard about Carter, the family man, the peanut farmer, the sailor, the businessman, the Governor and the Spiritual convert. Now let us talk about Carter, the President.

We have already described inauguration Day, Thursday 20, January 1977. With the festivities over, Jimmy Carter's first day in office was about to start.

One of the peculiarities the White House staff had to come to terms with now in the life of their new President was his unswerving devotion to farmers' hours. Up at 6.00 a.m., leaving his wife behind sleeping he could often be seen walking across the broad hall to the elevator which whisked him downstairs to the basement. From there he would walk quickly outside through the Rose Garden, past the Cabinet room, to the large French door of the Oval room, the seat of power in America.

He ignored the elegance of his surroundings, crowned by the thick blue and white carpet, on which the Presidential Seal was emblazoned and headed for the small alcove used by his secretary and on into a cosy little study which was now the heart-beat of his working day in the Presidency. The Oval room was strictly for visitors, photo calls with foreign dignitaries and politicians. It was also used for lunching with his wife or the Vice President or holding nationally televised speeches. The desk he sat at very seldom was JFK's old model which Carter had retrieved from storage, within a week of his arrival in the White House. His crowded schedule left little time for leisure or time wasting.

Most of his time was spent in the first eight months literally immersed in a ceaseless flow of paperwork churned out by the vast Presidential machine outside the Oval office. To use Carter's own words "Each day was an education."

It was a brand new world far removed from what he had expected and far removed from anything he had experienced up to now. But he enjoyed it. Even Rosalyn said she had never seen him so happy. But time was having its toll. An extra wrinkle, some greyer hair. He was fast approaching the record for the hardest working President in history. His energy and workload did not escape the notice of his staff. In fact, it was remarked that "He worked like a farmer in the final days of the harvest – beginning early and ending late."

One morning after his coffee was poured by a steward in blue blazer with the Presidential Seal on the breast pocket, he answered a knock on the Oval room door with "Come on in." It was a big man who ambled in ..... "You see this," he said to the President. "Yeah, I read it in the car," replied Carter. "Ribicoff and Percy still thinks Lance should resign" was the newspaper headline. "Pour Mr. Lance a cup of coffee too please," Carter said to the steward. Thomas Bertram Lance had worked with him when he was Governor of Georgia. Lance had brought efficiency and honesty with him from Georgia. He was Carter's close personal friend.

They were a strange combination, Carter slightly built, impeccably dressed, well-groomed; Lance a big hulking untidy bear of a man, 250 lbs. at least, a back-slapping gregarious extrovert. Most certainly, not of the Officer class Carter had known in the Navy. But Thomas Bertram Lance was Carter's ringmaster and could not be left out when Carter entered the White House.

Two other of Carter's friends who were invited to join him when in Georgia, were Jody Powell and Hamilton Jordan. They were laid-back unorthodox characters who wore sweatshirts and canvas shoes around the office next to the Governor's in Georgia. Complaints filtered through about their inappropriate dress but they took no heed of it ..... After victory for the Governorship, Carter had asked Powell "You want to try Press Secretary?" "Why the hell not," Powell answered. Political Aides and councillors they became despite their non-conformity. However, the story reveals a tolerance in Carter that didn't change in the Presidency ..... They found out soon enough that Carter's silence meant he was happy with their work, but when they needed to be rollicked Carter could be tough, though not in front of others. The relationship with Carter was like a warm mutual trust.

Lance eventually left Carter that morning, leaving him with just one hour to clear his papers before his next visitor, his security advisor, Zbigniew Brzezinski, an immigrant from Poland. A rival of Kissinger, he was always anxious to distinguish himself from the Kissinger style. Both being foreigners intensified the struggle between them.

Carter himself wanted to shape a different Presidency than his predecessors, so the two had much in common.

But Lance had problems which eventually demanded a Senate investigation. His banking and campaign techniques came under fire yet Carter would not abandon him. However, that's a story for another time.

Meanwhile, as we pointed out earlier, Carter's Administration had inherited a lot of trouble from Ford's Administration, and coming events that were to explode on the world stage in the Far East.

From Ford they had inherited runaway prices, a devalued dollar no longer tied into gold, bankrupt cities and even televisions and motorcars that didn't seem to work. The country's morale was at rock bottom. The good times of the post-war boom after 1945 and the euphoria that had extended into the fifties and sixties would only last until 1973. From that point on it was all downhill. The bottom two thirds of the workforce found their income falling, a problem that continued into the early eighties. It was all made worse by the oil crisis when the Arabs imposed an oil embargo in the Yom Kippur War of October 1973. The unknown sacrilege of petrol queues outside filling stations was now an everyday feature of the American way of life; the country that was once self-sufficient in fuel supplies was now importing 50% of its needs.

Conservation was the buzz word everywhere. Nixon and Ford had already tried price controls, reduced speed limits, slashed air flights and pushed the promotion of solar and nuclear energy but all to no avail. Carter tried to stimulate thrift by announcing the lowering of thermostats in the White House and having televised fireside chats sitting by an open fire in cardigan and sweater. What made it tough for him was a cynical public and selfish vested energy interests in the Senate. Worse was to come, however, for OPEC (the Organisation of Petroleum Exporting Countries) increased its oil prices. Oil that was $1.50 a barrel in 1970 was now in 1977 $32 a barrel. Of course, this sucked billions of dollars out of the western economies eastwards and inflation rose above 10% in 1979. To counteract this, Paul Volcker raised the interest rates to 20%. As Chairman of the Federal Reserve Board he also had a problem with double digit unemployment in many areas. Someone coined an appropriate word for all this misery – Stagflation. (Isn't it unbelievable that as I write this in 2009, 30 years later the price of a barrel of oil is now standing at $100)

Yet ever the optimist, Jimmy Carter announced one day to his wife Rosalyn that he was having his best day as President. No, he had not discovered a nest of oil wells all across America; he had discovered a new friendship and spiritual rapport with a man from Egypt, President Anwar Sadat, the Egyptian President. It was April 4, 1977.

A few months later he also met Prime Minister Menachem Begin of Israel. Six months after that in November 1977, Sadat accepted the Israeli Prime Minister's invitation to address the Knesset while Begin agreed to visit Egypt. Both had risked the wrath of their followers in doing this. Sometime later, Carter followed up with his own invitation to both of them for a meeting at Camp David, a wooded retreat in Maryland called after Eisenhower's son. This was almost a year later. They both arrived with a large supporting cast on September 4, 1978 to begin a learning curve together. Sadat's first move was to produce a document which Begin read in disbelief. "Why don't you sign it," grinned President Carter. "It would save us a lot of time." The joke was enjoyed by everyone. Sadat struggled with the intricacies of democratic discussion. Begin was slow and stubborn but so was Carter as he took them gradually towards an agreement while coping with threats by Sadat to go home. Finally it was agreed. Israel could use the Canal and they would withdraw troops from Sinai. When the Treaty seemed threatened, Carter flew to both countries and got the talks back on track. On March 26, 1979 two years after Carter's first meeting with Sadat, the Treaty ending thirty years of war was signed in a huge tent on the White House lawn. It was a tremendous tribute to the tenacity and talent of the new President, Jimmy Carter.

Carter's next headache on the international stage came when the Shah fled from Iran and the Muslim Cleric, Ayatollah Khomeini landed in Paris heading for home to start the now infamous Khomeini Revolution in Iran which was a nightmare of anarchy, assassination and daily executions. "Foreign Devils" was the wild-eyed chant of millions of Iranians who took to the streets, stirred up by Khomeini's ranting about Americans in Iran. The gates of the American Embassy were stormed by mobs baying for the blood of the Shah and Jimmy Carter. The Shah was in Mexico getting treatment for lymphoma. The mob finally broke through the gates with the Marine Guards under orders not to fire and hostages were taken outside to face the mob and the television cameras. The ordeal intensified for some. A secretary, Elizabeth Montagne, had a gun with one bullet in it put to her heart and the trigger pulled, five times. Mercifully, she survived. The ordeal for others lasted fourteen months.

Now Carter was caught in a dilemma. Use violence to get the hostages freedom and risk their death at the hands of their captors or struggle with diplomacy as Cyrus Vance wanted. Before dawn, it was decided to act "to lance the boil". Colonel Charles 'Chargin Charlie' Beckwith, a veteran of Korea and Vietnam was called in. But Charlie's verdict on the possibility of success was a rasping "Zero, Sir." A dramatic plan was hatched in which a Commando Group was to be sent in and helicopters were to be flown into the Embassy compound to lift the hostages free. All this was to happen at night. "Operation Eagle Claw" began on April 24. But disastrous mishaps happened and the mission was aborted. The hostages were finally released later, just two days before the next Presidential Election which Ronald Reagan won.

The credit for their release goes to Carter who had worked day and night to secure a final deal - the hostages for the return of $12 billion dollars of frozen Iranian Assets. He didn't leave loose ends for Reagan to tie up. Carter stayed with the problem to the end of his Presidency and won the hostages freedom.

But Jimmy Carter was an unlucky President; unlucky with the oil crisis, unlucky with stagflation, unlucky with Iran. Perhaps he was more a moral than a political leader. The Camp David Accord was one of his few success stories. One speechwriter thought that as a house builder to the poor and as a tireless community leader even his critics acknowledged Jimmy Carter was among America's greatest ex-Presidents. His capacity for minute analysis of any problem that confronted him was amazing. He only finished his research when he knew he had the facts. Armed with these he was absolutely focused. But you cannot please everyone, for sometimes this was mistaken for arrogance, even pomposity. But politically this was counter-productive. He admitted "I am pretty rigid. It's been very difficult for me to compromise when I believe in something deeply. I generally prefer to take it to the public to fight it out to the last vote and if I go down, I go down in flames."

When Tip O'Neill gave him a list of Congressmen, he should call during a speech on energy; Carter said "I wouldn't dream of it." The American people would know that he was right. Big Tip confessed "I could have slugged him." It seems, according to Walter Mondale, his Vice President, the worst thing you could say to Carter was that it was "politically the best thing to do".

Routine trading for any other President was for Carter a test of his credibility.

Now just a quick mention of someone we met earlier - Bert Lance. Subjected to "over the top" unfair criticism for his banking practices prior to his appointment, Bert Lance was in trouble. Politically Carter could have saved his career but under Carter's own strict moral code, Bert Lance had to go. Carter's Presidency seemed to be a constant battle between doing what was morally right and being a politician running a country. The two seemed to be incompatible for him. A shrewder politician might have bridged that gap successfully.

Yet, it didn't stop him gaining many successes at home. He banned the dumping of raw sewage into the ocean, created the Department of Energy and Education, deregulated the airlines and trucking, and reformed the Civil Service. Again, with a touch of rectitude, he withdrew the U.S. team from the Olympics in response to the invasion of Afghanistan by the Russians. A moral decision which, in view of the four year preparations required to go to the Olympics, turned out to be a very cruel one for those unfortunate athletes involved. But history makes a fool of everybody. Who could feel then that America would be in the battlefields of Afghanistan thirty years later in 2009? Yes, once again, Carter was unlucky. Had the hostages come home in a blaze of glory before the elections, who knows Ronald Reagan might never have entered Presidential history?

I guess we might blame that on the Ayatollah who some say delayed the hostages' release deliberately, and much too long for Carter to benefit. And yet perhaps, Jimmy Carter would have seen it differently. Perhaps "Just the work of the Holy Spirit". Anyway, he had done enough. It was time to go.

Ronald Reagan became the 40th President of the United States by defeating Jimmy Carter and Walter Mondale overwhelmingly by 51% to 41%.

Before talking about Jimmy Carter, the retired President, perhaps we could tie-up some loose ends.

Billy Carter, Jimmy's brother, was a bit of a loose cannon who lived his own life, exactly as he wanted to. He got into a number of scrapes, one of which was a loan or a gift of $220,000 he received from Libya. Investigations were made into the reason for this $220,000 sum given to Billy but no clear answers ever surfaced. Attorney General Benjamin R. Civiletti was accused of a cover-up but even after a Senate investigation nothing showed up to indict anyone.

Carter did keep America out of foreign wars but many of his promised reforms never took place. Some people say his Presidency was over-cautious but others felt he was thwarted by congressional hostility. Although he was very popular he lacked faith in his own undoubted leadership ability as was proved by the Camp David triumph.

Carter wrote a number of books. Besides the one I have already mentioned Why Not the Best? He also wrote Keeping Faith, Memoirs of a President; The Blood of Abraham; A Nation Come of Age and Talking Peace.

By the way, here are some fascinating insights on Carter told in her book Jimmy Carter by Betty Glad, as follows: "His talents were recognised by many prominent people" she wrote. Theodore Sorenson, a former Kennedy Aide who advised Carter in his 1976 campaign said "He was the smartest man I met in politics since JFK." James Fallows, a former scriptwriter, praised Carter's intellectual skills. "The smartest President this century," he said. "He grasps issues quickly and made me feel confident." Rosalyn Carter was always compared to Eleanor Roosevelt "She gave him advice in private and was Carter's closest confidante." Carter was always devastated by defeat, like his depression just after losing his first Governorship election.

But here are additional opinions to help improve our understanding of Jimmy Carter. He was depressed after failing to receive a Rhodes scholarship in 1940. Even on the tennis court he had to win. He could be a bad loser too. Sometimes his reaction to criticism looked like rage at being questioned. His negative reactions to opposition and criticism suggested a man who could have trouble learning from mistakes. When pressed hard, his eyes and face freeze and sometimes a vein on his forehead or temple visibly throbs as he reaches for defences. The line between fact and wishing was blurred for he had an unconscious tendency to upgrade himself. "I think they feel that I am a good President," he announced – nine months before he was elected President.

Let's summarize what Jimmy Carter was all about. He had his own visions for the nation both at home and abroad but somehow he never translated these dreams into reality. His personal qualities; honesty, integrity, religious conviction and trustworthiness somehow or other remained a private image in the minds of the public. He never translated this into Statesmanship, although all this changed when he left office and devoted his post-Presidential life to trouble-shooting around the world on humanitarian issues.

For example, in 1989 he helped mediate on the Nicaraguan Civil War between the Sandinistas and the Contra rebels. He was on the spot some months later leading an international team of observers, finally declaring Panama Elections a fraud. His next assignment was in North Korea in 1994 on the invitation of President Kim Il-Sung from where he returned with an agreement outlining an end to North Korea's nuclear weapons programme. Unfortunately, this programme came apart in 2009 when North Korea confronted the world with nuclear tests once again. Nevertheless, regardless of geography, Carter impressed negotiators whenever he turned up to sort out the health and human rights problems of the poor among them. So popular has he become for his dedicated humanitarian work they have coined a new nickname for him. No longer is it "Jimmy Who?" Now it is "Jimmy Everywhere Carter".

Well, that completes our portrait of James Earl Carter Junior, 39th President of the United States. Now we move on into show business and the fascinating story of Ronald Reagan.

We normally end our piece on the death and burial of the President. But today June 2009, Jimmy Carter and his First Lady Rosalyn are still thankfully very much with us as we read this. Now it's over to Ronald Reagan.

40th President   Ronald Regan

"Dutch"
Born 1911
Died 2004
93 Years of age
2 Terms
1981 - 1989
8 years
Age 70

Party: Republican
Profession: Actor
County: California
Ancestry: British/Scots/Irish.
Value of Estate: Unknown.
Hobbies: Reading and swimming

Physical Description: 6 foot, 1 inch in height, weight – 185 lbs, brown hair, blue eyes, contact lenses, hearing aids in both ears.

Significant Extract from his Inauguration Speech on Tuesday, January 20, 1981
"All of us need to be reminded that the Federal Government did not create the States; the States created the Federal Government ….. Government can and must provide opportunity not smother it; foster productivity, not stifle it ….. It is my intention to curb the size and influence of the Federal establishment ….."

RONALD REAGAN

The best way we can describe Ronald Wilson Reagan, the 40th President of the United States can be summed up in the words he wrote under his own picture in the High School Year Book. "Life is just one grand sweet song, so start the music." Looking quickly over the landscape I mean to cover to paint a picture of the man; nowhere did I find one note of animosity or rancor in his makeup. He seems to have been true to his instincts from the day he wrote those few words. When that covers a lifetime of eighty-four years, you cannot help shaking your head in admiration at such an achievement.

Ronald Reagan first saw the light of day when at an outrageous weight of 10 lbs he was born in a rented flat over a bank in the tiny town of Tampico, Illinois. He was the younger of two sons born to Nelle and John Reagan, a very ordinary American couple. The date was February 6, 1911. His father Jack Reagan, an Irish Catholic, was a wise-cracking small town shoe salesman whose main ambition was understandably – to own his own shoe store. A great FDR supporter, a vociferous anti-racialist and passionate opponent of religious bigotry. Jack unfortunately had a drink problem. Ronald Reagan's nickname "Dutch" was coined by Jack as a term of endearment when he referred to a pudgy baby Ronald as his fat little "Dutchman". The name "Dutch" somehow or other just stuck to Ronald ever since.

Dutch's mother had a very lively social conscience. Not only was she a deep believer in her religion, the Disciples of Christ, but she practiced faith healing and gave her spare time to visiting mental hospitals and prisons. She also liked to dabble in being an actress. It seems to have been Nelle who introduced Ronald to the stage for she played a big part in his early life, teaching him to read before he was five. This was a great asset to little Ronald for he was then able to immerse himself in the exciting adventure stories he loved to read.

Jack, his father, was a restless personality who was constantly moving on. He changed house ten times before finally settling down in Dixon, Illinois, when Ronald was nine years old. From nine to fifteen Ronald enjoyed a great romance with the open air life around Dixon. He hiked in the hills, loved to watch the teeming bird life in the hedgerows and fields around him, played football at right guard, and became a champion swimmer which got him the job of lifeguard at a place called Lowell Park on the Rock River. Reagan said later, "That job of lifeguard paid for one half of my studies and washing dishes paid for the other half."

So good was Ronald Reagan at his job of lifeguard he built up a remarkable record of saving seventy-seven people from drowning. One such incident was described in Edmund Morris's Book Dutch. It seems Reagan was mentioned on the front page of the Dixon Evening Telegraph under the headline "Pulled from the Jaws of Death" an incident Edmund Morris wrote about.

It happened at closing time in the bathhouse at Lowell Park. Hearing splashing in the river, Dutch returned, dived in and swam about in the pitch black darkness looking for the unfortunate man. Dutch homed in on the sound of the splashing and after a desperate struggle managed to get the man, a James Raider to the bank. Raider was very lucky for he had already gone down once. He responded to artificial respiration and was led outside afterwards. No charges were filed but the danger to Dutch is not understood at the first telling of the story. When one looks at the hazards, Reagan confronted diving off a moving bobbing platform, then finding the drowning man in the pitch black darkness, and then the rescue was a miracle especially since Reagan had to take a detour to ride the currents. Punching him out of his panic he grappled the drowning man into a headlock and towed him upstream and on to the bank.

And to think there were seventy-seven such rescues. What a record to be proud of even if you never became President of the United States.

At seventeen years of age he entered college and had to "wait on tables" to pay his way. However, when he finished at twenty-one in 1932, his grades were only average in economics and sociology. Nevertheless his main talent was blossoming, just getting on with people. In his freshman year the students chose him to speak for them in a strike against academic cutbacks and a ban on dancing, a strike which lead to the resignation of the College President. I seem to remember a very young Woodrow Wilson having a similar experience. Just check it out under Woodrow Wilson.

Reagan won a Scholarship to study at Eureka College, a picturesque 'Disciples of Christ' College near Peoria, Illinois. He loved the place from the very first day with its nine buildings no taller than the elms that surrounded them. Covered with ivy and separated by wide lawns and gravel walks, the blackbirds, the cawing of the rooks and the whiff of cow dung from a local farm completed the picture. It was here Dutch majored in sociology, was President of the student body, a member of the football team and captained the swimming team. After graduating the only job available to him was as local radio sportscaster for station WHO in Des Moines, Iowa.

Even in those days, he was an amazingly uncomplicated man with simple interests. He liked the Olympics, the singer Eddie Cantor, and his next game of football. Yet this laid back element of his personality seemed to attract people to do things for him.
Reagan's first job of sports commentator came about in a way he never tired of telling his listeners.

He turned up for an interview at WHO station in Des Moines and was met at the door by a crusty old individual, a Scot named Peter McArthur, who stood at the door on two sticks crippled with arthritis. After a chat Ronald walked down the hall to be followed by a shout behind him. "Hold up you big bastard." Shuffling after Ronald he asked "How did you get to be a sports announcer if you can't get a job in a radio station," he persisted. "Do you know anything about football?" "I played football for eight years," Reagan replied placidly.

Little did Ronald realize that he was in the middle of an interview? The little old man went on ahead leading him into a little room just off the hall. "Stand in front of that mike," he told Reagan. "When the red light goes on – you are watching a football match – just commentate on it. I'll be in the other room listening." He disappeared next door, the red light went on and Reagan did his piece. Soon the interview and the broadcast were over. The little man re-appeared on his sticks. "Be here Saturday," he said "you're broadcasting on the Iowa-Minnesota game." The interview had been successful after all. Ronald Reagan often smiles when he thinks of it. "I guess radio is the theatre of the mind," he remarked years later. After that Reagan's voice became a household sound, loved and admired by thousands of sports fans.

Now he was a radio announcer as well as an actor. By the way, his first recognition as an actor had come from his school's drama fraternity at Eureka and they were very proud of the nugget of talent they had unearthed.

But meanwhile dark clouds were gathering on the horizon for his parent's marriage was in trouble. By 1929 it began to disintegrate. Perhaps the cracks had already appeared before Jack lost his business, maybe due to drink. Funds were now much lower which put a strain on the marriage. The trouble started when Jack got a job in a firm called the Red Wing Shoe Company for a fairly generous wage of $260 per month. The downside was the amount of time and travel away from home it demanded. Most of his time was spent living in Springfield, where he fell to the temptation of an expensive girlfriend. Meanwhile, Nelle looked after her home on depleted funds working part-time to supplement Jack's occasional cheques from his pay packet. She turned to her religion for consolation and became totally wrapped up in it. The rumours of divorce descended into sad reality and both of them eventually walked away from it all forever.

But in 1937, aged twenty-six Ronald Reagan had decided it was time to move on; to start an acting career in Hollywood. It proved to be a successful gamble that led to a career lasting twenty-five years. It was a traumatic change for him and even a colossal risk for he had already established himself as Sports Director in WHO at $3,900 per year. But radio had been a terrific learning experience for him and when he headed for Hollywood he was already an accomplished and polished performer and had mastered every trick of voice presentation.

On Saturday May 22, 1937 Ronald Reagan set out on his journey West. He was determined to arrive in the fastest time possible and he duly arrived there on the verge of exhaustion. On his first day he drove six hundred and fifty miles to Cheyenne, Wyoming. His second day he drove six hundred miles to Nephi. The third day he finished the final six hundred and sixty miles to the orange groves on the highway of Santa Monica as the sun was setting. Next day he headed for Warner Bros. on the far side of the Los Angeles River. Warner Bros. he found was almost a city in itself. It had its own Police department, Fire Company, power plant, hospital, school, four cinemas, thirty miles of streets and a railroad. It even had a local radio station and two transmitter towers. He had been there twice before but only now was he taking it all in.

Ronald had to work hard separating fact from fiction in Hollywood city. Some streets were tree-lined and their storehouses were filled with amazing gadgets; Tudor thrones, jewels, ingots and dance floors. It was here that the celluloid ribbons would record over the next twenty-five years making Ronald Reagan the Errol Flynn of the B movie. His words not mine. Right now he had nothing to complain about for he had been given a contract at $10,000 per year, more than twice what he was earning as a Sports Director back home. He would eventually appear in fifty-four low-budget movies, the first of which "Love is in the Air" was released in 1937.

The role he played, Andy McLeod, ironically enough was about a news broadcaster. Being a man of conscience, he revealed in his newscast his suspicions of corrupt politicians. Naturally you can't fight City Hall so they say, and Andy McLeod was demoted to minor children's programmes for his honesty. But the crooks were exposed eventually and Andy McLeod emerged the hero. The film got a good reception from the public and Ronald Reagan became famous in a later film for the part he played as Notre Dame Tailback, George Gipp, who on his deathbed says to his coach "Maybe you can ask the boys to go in there and win just one for the Gipper." Reagan has been associated with that little speech for the rest of his life.

Being the good-looking all American guy, Ronald was not short of escorts in Hollywood and among the many "Stars" to walk out with him was Lana Turner. But it was another Hollywood star who eventually captured this eligible bachelor's heart, Jane Wyman. They were married on January 26, 1940 and had two children, Maureen and Michael who was adopted. The war broke out in 1939 but America didn't enter it until after Pearl Harbour in 1941. Reagan, barred from the war because of defective eyesight, was posted to California where he spent the war as 2nd Lieutenant in the Army Reserve making war propaganda and training films.

While Reagan never reached the superstar heights of the Hollywood greats, he was certainly good enough to appear in many movies alongside the likes of Pat O'Brien, Errol Flynn, Olivia de Havilland, Wallace Beery, Lionel Barrymore, Bette Davis, Ann Sheridan, and even the "Dead-End Kids".

"Kings Row" was easily his best and he claims it made him a star after which he received a contract from Warner Brothers of $5,000 per week. However, his three year service in the army which promoted him to the rank of Captain for his background work in training films didn't help. One such film called "This is the Army", the all soldier stage revue by Irving Berlin, meant a temporary return to Civvy Street in Warner Brothers' studio not on film star wages but on $250 per month on the army payroll.

The reason for all this was because the film was to release all its enormous proceeds into the Army Relief fund. From there he went to the Air Force Motion Picture Unit for documentary and training films. The three years in the army meant he was off the commercial screen too long to be able to cash in on his major success in "Kings Row" three years earlier. Roles opposite Eleanor Parker, Patricia Neal, Virginia Mayo and Ginger Rogers followed. That he was amazingly versatile in the acting profession can be seen in the type of films in which he appeared. The Broadway comedy "The Male Animal" and "The Winning Team" opposite Doris Day in the role of an alcoholic baseball player; Grover Cleveland Alexander, and finally opposite the great Barbara Stanwyck in "The Cattle Queen of Montana".

His final career role before entering politics was as host on television's "The General Electric Theatre". But as President of the Screen Actors Guild, Ronald Reagan objected to the attention, much of it unwelcome, given to film stars' private lives. Little did he know he was on a collision course with the Hollywood press? They laid out the rules for him in a scathing rebuke by the Editor of Motion Picture in June 1951, in which he was told in no uncertain terms that as a public figure who received an exotic sum of money, for just that reason he had an obligation to the press for putting him there. It was a lesson he took with him to the heights of politics. Certainly much of his success in politics can be credited to his relationship with the media and his lively friendship with the press.

The trouble in his marriage only became obvious to him around 1948. Perhaps the reason it took him by surprise was his preoccupation with the Screen Actors Guild. In fact one of Jane Wyman's complaints in her divorce papers was the irritation Ronald inflicted on her by his obsession with politics about which he talked at every meal. The divorce she sought ended the marriage in 1948 after eight years together. "You and me Ronnie just ran out of gas," she told him. But this criticism and the break-up of the marriage left him dead inside for years, he confessed later.

His marriage breakdown was shared by all Hollywood. Nobody wanted it to happen. It was a marriage much admired by Hollywood as a symbol of what an American marriage should be, just like that of Mary Pickford and Douglas Fairbanks which also shocked Hollywood when it broke up. When it came, Ronald said "I believe children are better off with their mother. Anyway I'll still have the privilege of seeing them." Those words signaled the end of a beautiful dream. Everyone's beautiful dream.

Ronald Reagan worked hard after that, not only in films but as President of the Actors Guild for which he was elected eight times as President because of his negotiation skills. These were the years when Truman was President of the United States and Reagan, a democratic supporter.

Meanwhile he had a tremendous success in "This is the Army" and "Kings Row" and incredibly became the top box office draw in Hollywood, his rating being nine points above Jimmy Cagney. But at thirty-two, going on thirty-three, he had reached his peak. He was never going to achieve the superstar success enjoyed across America by his ex-wife, Jane Wyman, who would receive an Academy Award for her role in "Johnny Belinda". It was time for Ronald to examine his options.

As S.A.G. President, he worked until three in the morning. The Red scare was rampant and McCarthy's purges with his "Committee on American activities" were homing in on Communists in the film industry and Ronald Reagan took a very strong anti-Communist stand, testifying before the Committee.

But there were other more important things happening to Ronald Reagan which we must talk about. Yes, none other than Nancy Davis, as she was known before she came into his life. Rumours had been going the rounds in 1949 just after his divorce from Jane Wyman that his film career was on the rocks. Around that time he had a serious accident in a charity baseball game which resulted in a badly smashed thigh that left him bedridden for seven weeks. Walking on aluminum crutches meant he wasn't much of a candidate for work. To be brutal, he was unemployable.

Crippled he may have been, but unavailable for female company he was not. Yes, he was still the most eligible man in town. What's more he was still in demand for some screen parts. One in particular was opposite Ginger Rogers in "Storm Warning". There was also a $375,000 deal for five films over five years. With bonuses he could still make $200,000 per year. Yet, he still had a yearning vacuum in his life left by Jane Wyman. Then to use his own words "Along came Nancy Davis and saved my soul." She was the daughter of a conservative neurosurgeon. Nancy was described by an MGM man Sam Marx as being "A tough little broad with a jaw like Mammy Yokum, an ambitious doctor's brat so I decided to keep my distance." According to Marx, she had been hired not for her talent but to repay her father for medical favours. Not a very flattering CV but just a little bit bitchy.

There are several versions of how she got her first date with "Dutch" on November 15, 1949. The one that seems the most authentic was the night they were both guests at a dinner party in her mother's house. Subtlety was never Nancy's forte but when he first rang the doorbell of her apartment that November night leaning heavily on two sticks, the door to a beautiful future beyond their wildest dreams had begun and she knew it.

Actually the date was really a professional meeting with the head of her Union for which she wore an eminently suitable black and white dress. A total contrast to Jane, she had a sense of style, her clothes always expensive, just one step behind the latest fashion. Naturally like most men, Dutch was completely oblivious to the demands of fashion or art and only noticed her widely placed hazel eyes which always mesmerized him. One day that face would decorate his studio in oils.

Years later he waxed poetical about that first meeting. He said "Bells must have rung. It was just that I had buried that part of me where such things happen so deep, I couldn't hear them."

Nancy Davis was no girl. She was at twenty-eight, older looking than Jane Wyman. "Five feet, four inches of pile driver purpose" is how she has been described. On the advice of that old master of the one night stand, Errol Flynn, Dutch continued stepping out with the ladies. Doris Day, Rhonda Fleming and Piper Laurie, to mention just three of sixteen who may have come home to his luxurious apartment high up over the sparkling city of Hollywood. He refers to them all in his old age rather coyly as his "cocker spaniels". They noticed two things about him. One was his verbal avalanches, his unrestrained talkativeness. The second was his political chat and his readers digest brand of jokes. Doris Day complained "It really wasn't conversation; it was rather talking at you. I remember telling him he should be touring the country making speeches."

But Nancy was a born listener. She had had good experience listening to her ex-trooper mother and her egotistical stepfather blessed with a talent for self-satisfaction. In short, she was completely free of the narcissistic tendency to want to be heard herself. She was a complete natural for him. Actually she was just crazy about the man. The answer to her being in his presence was as simple as that and even into the twilight years of his cruel Alzheimer's disease when he had long since forgotten who she was, Nancy still loved him. They were married; I almost forgot to tell you, on March 4, 1952.

Unlike Jayne Wyman, Nancy never complained about Reagan's political life or conversations and demonstrated her all consuming loyalty to him by giving up her own acting career to become one of his toughest and shrewdest supporters. They have two children, Patricia and Ronald.

For eight years from 1954, Ronald Reagan would host the "General Electric Theatre" on Sunday night television. Although he was a card carrying member of the Democratic Party until 1962, Reagan's new job made him the corporate spokesman for the company for which he travelled extensively giving speeches to its employees around the country. Still he considered himself a Liberal Democrat. However, his anger at what he perceived as a live Communist threat to the film industry and his role for eight years representing corporate America pushed him to the right in his politics and in 1962 he joined The Republican Party. That was the real beginning of his political career.

Before we move on to politics in Reagan's life here are some movie stars' opinions some of which I think you may find interesting.

Despite appearing opposite her in films, Patricia Neal is reported to have said "I don't like Ronald Reagan. If he runs for President or Vice-President, I will give up my American citizenship, I really will." When Jack Warner was told Ronald Reagan was running for Governor of California, he replied "No, no, Jimmy Stewart for Governor – Reagan for his best friend." Bette Davis was not impressed by Ronald Reagan's political pedigree; she said "Ronald Reagan gave no hint when we performed together at Warner's. He was a very nice pleasant little guy." John Wayne defended him against President Ford. "They've tried to make him sound like a warmonger on Panama. I've known Ronnie since he was President of the S.A.G. He is no warmonger so I decided not to be quiet about this." Robert Taylor knew him well. "When I first met him he was vitally interested in athletics and in keeping himself in great condition," he said. Finally, we must remember what a different world it was in the Hollywood of the 1970s. Lying in the grass beside Alexis Smith, the director yelled "You both can't be in the prone position at the one time." So Ronald had to play out the love scene propped up on one elbow.

But someone in politics had now noticed him. In October 1964 the Hollywood actor called Ronald Reagan was hired by The National Republican Committee to give a televised speech in support of Barry Goldwater who was being put forward as a Presidential candidate. His theme was "individual freedom" which he delivered in relaxed reasonable language. The speech didn't help Goldwater. In fact, the greatest beneficiary of the speech was one Ronald Reagan. It set him out on a remarkable political odyssey.

It was mainly on the basis of this speech some wealthy friends decided to support him to run for Governor of California. They were proved right in their judgement not only of Reagan's friendly relaxed style but most of all because it was combined with a professional expertise before the cameras, a technique which brought him a landslide victory over Pat Brown, the sitting Governor. He was also in tandem with the feelings and frustrations of the middleclass voters of California who were increasingly disenchanted with the smoothie professional politicians they had experienced up to now. He was also aware of their deep resentment over higher taxes, welfare programmes and bureaucracy.

Ronald Reagan, from somewhere in his past, perhaps as President of the Screen Actors Guild for eight years, or as countrywide speechmaker for the General Electric Theatre, had developed his innate instincts as a politician. He was now the finished product. It had not happened overnight but developed in a long, upward learning curve over the previous sixteen years and Ronald Reagan was an astute learner. More than that, he was now Governor of California.

For the next eight years he was going to add an illustrious chapter to the life of a celebrated movie star in the hurly burly of Californian politics.
One of the many discoveries Reagan added to his repertoire was Kennedy's method of working the crowds. Reagan knew his experience in this area was limited. He learned that touching two hundred people could be done quicker than shaking hands with twenty. Edmund Morris, author of the authentic biography of Ronald Reagan, was his tutor one night in the Fairmount Hotel in San Francisco. Reagan was fascinated enough to question Morris into the small hours of the morning. He became as animated in pursuit of the skill as he would be learning the cameras, the sound or the body language required for a new film script. That was the man called Ronald Reagan. As he wisecracked later "I've never played a Governor before."

The scalp he won when defeating Pat Brown was much more significant than he realized. Brown was a ruthless manipulator of people and power. One of his victims recalled Brown as a man quite adept at savage political in-fighting, capable of dispensing instantly with anyone that he no longer needed. His democratic machine was a well-oiled juggernaut that had steamrollered him to the Governorship twice and was ultra-confident of winning a third term as Governor. The fact that Ronald Reagan was victorious was truly an unbelievable tribute to this new kid on the block, Ronald Wilson Reagan.

In a strange way Reagan's arrival in politics coincided with a change in the population in the 1970s, especially in the Sun Belt region in the South and West. This movement of people to these areas brought with it Conservative supporters of the dominant Republican Party. Most of them were white middleclass and skilled young professionals, drawn by the politics of low taxes and less Government where the market place enjoyed a "laissez-faire" approach embracing the minimum regulations in commercial affairs. People were reacting strongly against Liberals, and their softly softly approach to Communism, and the African American troubles. They cried out for a naked capitalism coupled with all the advantages that a "laissez-faire" economy would bring them.

As I have previously mentioned, Ronald Reagan, whether by design or conviction, carried the flag high for these resurgent Conservatives. As the song says "A spoonful of sugar helps the medicine go down" so his sunny public image and relaxed charm helped to soften the hard thrust of his right-wing ideas.

It wasn't always sunshine and roses in the Governorship, however. Sometimes Reagan was called upon to act a little more seriously than a movie star turned politician. There were some tough decisions to test his steel. Cuts had to be made. The University of California was the first to feel the squeeze when their budget was cut by 15% and this was followed by a one million dollar tax hike for the people of California. The hospitals were cut by 3,700 employees. After an outcry he agreed to cut this to 2,700. Yet he refused point blank to visit those hospitals affected by his cuts and his reputation for niceness suffered permanent damage after that. The most traumatic decision he had to make was his refusal to grant clemency to an Aaron Mitchell, a black who had murdered a police officer. Pat Brown had upheld the conviction just three weeks before Reagan took office. However, Reagan couldn't face Aaron's mother who ran out of the building sobbing "Why, Jesus, why?"

A letter arrived next day to the Governor's house saying "Tough shit for your Hollywood friend." He hoped he'd get an Oscar for his new movie "Capital Punishment" but the last thing seen outside San Quentin prison at dawn was a sign on the gate "Ronald Reagan – no Academy Award for legal murder". It was the first execution in California since 1963. First in the whole country that year in fact! Poor Reagan, although the sentence had been confirmed again and again on appeal, the finality of the execution that night left him with the worst nightmare of his life. "The Sacramento Committee for Life" held a vigil outside his rented house on 45th street with candles and silver bells tinkling.

Nancy was outraged at the effect they were having on young Ron, aged eight. Yes it was the most heartbreaking argument anyone could have made against State executions. There was just no answer to the feeling of helplessness felt by everybody involved. Finally, he was forced to decide on another hot potato just after that – The Therapeutic Abortion Bill. Pregnant women were to be given the right to terminate a pregnancy where there was a danger to their physical or mental health. Others wanted to extend it to include women who had been raped or the subject of incest. The religious consequences were enormous. As decision day drew near, Reagan turned to his Cabinet secretary, Bill Clark, a Roman Catholic. "Bill, I've got to know more, theologically, philosophically, medically." So effective was Bill's comprehensive information Reagan was quoting Saint Thomas Aquinas, the superstar of Christian Theology, before he finally signed the Bill into law. Yet Reagan was left with some very mixed feelings after it was passed. Feelings of frustration and guilt. As he saw it, 82,000 would be aborted that year whereas he had risked his life as a lifeguard to save 77.

Just a happy little note to cheer you up after that. There is a story of a garden party by the swimming pool of his residence, one 4th of July. Nobody noticed a black girl falling into the pool and sinking. The ever alert Reagan peeled of his coat and dived, bringing to the surface another grateful human being to the poolside. She was to improve his record to an amazing seventy-eight rescues from a watery grave. Reagan was heard to remark later "Not one of them returned to thank me."

The primary season was getting started just around that time. It was the worst period of urban rioting America had known. It was 6 p.m. on April 4, 1968 and somebody had just shot Martin Luther King. Reagan reluctantly agreed to allow his name to go forward for the hustings.

Smoke from burning buildings created a fog that almost obscured the Washington Monument as Reagan made his speech to the National Women's Press Club in Washington. He was quickly rushed away from the hall with the words "You'd better get out of here the city's going up." On the way home he could go no further and had to leave his car and walk to his hotel. There is a story that two black youths recognized him in the middle of the sound of distant rioting, broken glass and gunfire. Reagan was lucky however and duly arrived safely back at his hotel. To show how dangerous his walk had been one hundred and twenty nine cities were burning that night as he flew home to California.

Nixon won that election of 1970 and Reagan had learned one more lesson by it "To trust his own instincts from now on." His own feel for what the electorate wanted would be his blueprint for the next Presidential election.

January 3, 1975 was the day Reagan handed over the Governorship of California to Pat Brown's son. He had now relinquished the job of the strongest man in a State more prosperous than some countries. He seemed headed for retirement, after all he had succeeded in everything he tried – President of his high school, lifesaver extraordinaire, college leader, broadcaster, box office movie star, trade union executive, corporate spokesman and Governor with flair and vision. He was now going to develop a new property of about seven hundred acres of leafy valleys high above Santa Barbara. "You feel as if you are in a cloud looking down on the world" was the poetic way he described his new found toy.

It gave him the privacy and loneliness he had craved for now that his public life was "over". But there were trees to fell, ponds to clean up, floors and roofs, walls and furniture to put right if he was to stamp his personality on the place. During his Presidency this magnificent property had long since blossomed into a ranch he could retire to whenever he needed to escape from the cares of office. Because of the special security arrangements that were installed, he could take out his favourite horse and ride unhindered for miles inside its borders with Nancy.

Agents were placed at strategic points within the ranch keeping and eye on the President while communicating by "walkie, talkie" radios. "Rawhide" was his code name to the agents. The President could never drive his own car on the highway but here he was happy to indulge himself free from the claustrophobic security arrangements necessary outside his ranch. That to Ronald Reagan was real freedom.

During his political career, his opinions were not dead in the water and the comments by former Governor Reagan were regularly invited by hundreds of newspapers and radio programmes. There was no way Ronald Reagan would be allowed to disappear into obscurity. Those who pursued him never let up on his chances for success in the Presidential stakes. One day their efforts paid off when he agreed to run in the next election. "I've always been the player on the bench. Its time for me to get into the game," he said.

However, the race for the Presidency is never a foregone conclusion and in 1976 Jimmy Carter, the unknown from Plains, Georgia, beat Gerald Ford in an amazing turn up for the books. You may remember the story I told you of the guy from Georgia they called "Jimmy Who". Yes, Carter certainly took everyone by surprise. It was now 1980 and Ronald Reagan had been out of power since he relinquished the Governorship of California in 1975.

But Ronald Reagan's time had come at last. Now he was the finished product, polished, suave, sincere, relaxed, confident and friendly. He offered the Vice Presidency to Gerald Ford but Ford declined and George Bush Senior accepted it gladly. Reagan beat Jimmy Carter by a landslide of forty-six million votes to thirty-six million for Carter.

The movie star beneath the surface never failed to surface in Ronald Reagan given the slightest opportunity. What better opportunity was there than the inauguration of the President of the United States. Not for him a swearing in ceremony in the shade at the back of the Capitol. For him the only place for it was the front terrace of the famous building where he could feel the golden sun on his face. It was 11.57 a.m. on January 20, 1981 and the weather was on its best behaviour windless, sunny and mild. Reagan didn't spend long on his speech which lasted only twenty minutes. Once again a President was calling for a national renewal. The goodies were laid out in the form of tax reductions and a spending control in Government house-keeping. This meant a cutback on Government staff renewal. The Iranians had timed to perfection the release of the American hostages they held and this news released by Reagan helped to improve the spirit of the celebrations going on around him. After Chief Justice Warren Earl Burger administered the oath, Reagan rode in an open-top car waving to spectators along the route.

Later behind a glass fronted reviewing stand he sat surrounded by his family and guests watching the magnificent parade of 8,000 marchers, 450 equestrian teams, Indians in tribal dress, mountain men in Coonskin hats and twenty-five Alaskan sled dogs. The spectators numbering about 300,000 lined the parade route for miles. Later that evening the President and his wife Nancy, danced the night away at eight inaugural State Balls, watched by millions on television. At eight million dollars it was said at the time to be the most expensive inauguration ceremonies in American history but eight years later President Bush exceeded that amount by over seventeen million dollars. Reagan's first formal duty in office was to pass into law a day of celebration and so January 29, 1981 was declared "A day of thanksgiving to honour our safely returned hostages."

Reagan's eight years on the bridge of the ship of State were not always consistent with his ideological pronouncements. He often strayed from the programme he had set himself to steer a more pragmatic course. He stood for fiscal restraint, tax reductions and limited Government control yet he ran up record budget deficits. Despite being an avowed enemy of the Evil Russian Empire he still managed to moderate the Cold War more than any previous President. Again, despite his famous charming and gregarious personality, he could lapse into a strange remoteness and passivity even with his own family.

He had no intellectual approach to economics and was almost impotent about the details surrounding all his advisors' mathematics. But one thing is for certain; his eye for the broad picture was a special talent in itself which amazed Margaret Thatcher at one of the G8 meetings. He must have been doing something right for he took up the Presidency facing massive stagflation throughout the nation, but at the end of his term America was prosperous and Communism was reeling on the ropes.

His major contribution to all this was not buried in statistics or visionary dreams but in the serenity and pride he managed to impart to the American people. He certainly renewed their faith in the American way of life. Reagan actually left office with an unbelievable popularity rating of 70%. Somebody said about him "When growing up Ronald felt it was his job to make everyone happy." Perhaps that was the secret of his eternal optimism. The speaker of the House, Jim Wright, shrewdly observed him as follows: "I'm appalled by what seems to me a lack of depth, I stand in awe nevertheless of his political skill."

But all this may never have occurred had Reagan not survived an assassination attempt two months after his inauguration at 2.30 p.m. on March 30, 1981. His attacker also wounded Reagan's Press Secretary, James Scott Brady, a Secret Service Agent, Timothy J. McCarthy and a District of Columbia policeman, Thomas K. Delahunty. Reagan was rushed to nearby George Washington University Hospital where he was operated on that afternoon and a bullet removed from his left lung. Bush, his Vice-President, returned immediately from a speaking trip to Texas soon after. All the other wounded recovered. The assailant, John Warnock Hinckley Jr, a twenty-five year old, was overpowered and arrested on the spot. He was charged with attempted assassination and shooting three others. He was duly sent to Butner Federal Prison for psychiatric testing. On June 21, 1983 over one year later Hinckley was found to be insane and therefore not guilty. What a gift that would have been to the assassin of William McKinley who was considered by expert physiatrists to be insane (see my notes on Mckinley). He spent an indefinite period in a hospital for the mentally ill. One of Regan's one-liners was memorable. Just before his operation he turned to the surgical team around him dressed in green aprons and said "Please tell me you're Republicans."

There is an amazing parallel between this scene and the one just eighty years previously involving another shot President. Both Reagan and President McKinley were shot in the chest. Perhaps it was modern surgery that helped to locate and extract the bullet from Reagan's chest to allow him another eight years in the Presidency and beyond. They never found the bullet in McKinley until the autopsy was carried out after he died.

The above condensed account does no justice to the seriousness of the events that took place at the George Washington University Hospital. The reason for the assassination attempt according to Hinckley was to impress a Miss Foster by his hoped for notoriety after the attack outside the Washington Hilton Hotel. The "shoot-out" left the President's Press Secretary shot in the head, his Secret Agent shot in the stomach and Reagan injured. There were six shots in total. One bodyguard grabbed Ronald Reagan and bundled him into an official car, then set off at breakneck speed without a motorcade to the White House.

However, inside the car it was noticed that the President was bleeding from the mouth so the car was re-directed to the George Washington University Hospital. Reagan was in pain from the bullet wound in his left side. Strangely enough no one had yet even suspected he had been shot. It was thought the blood was from an injury sustained bundling him into the car.

Meanwhile in the hospital a phone call came through. The President's motorcade is on the way to your facility. No one knew who was coming. By now the President was fighting for breath in the back of his car for by this time he had lost about quarter of his blood. His blood pressure had now dropped dangerously low. Instead of 110, the reading was only 50-60. Ten minutes after he arrived there had been so much turmoil around the President nobody had checked for a bullet hole.

Outside all was confusion as the media stormed the front door hungry for news. The Secret Service's presence in the operating theatre only heightened the tension which didn't help.

Dr. Joe Giordano took over as head of the trauma team, being vastly experienced in victims of shootings. But the President was bleeding to death unless a solution could be found to stem the flow of blood. He was also on the borders of shock. Needless to say all the top administrators and experts were called to the trauma bay. They cut quickly through the cloth of Reagan's expensive suit.

Meanwhile there was consternation in the White House which had been alerted for a follow-up Soviet Union attack, maybe nuclear. Danny Spriggs, Head of the Secret Agents, was alone with Hinckley and found his personality different from the cold-blooded killers he had been used to. Haig feared over-reaction or miscalculation by the Cabinet.

Nancy rang to check what was happening. "It is not a good idea to come Nancy" she was told. "Are you kidding," she said. It was vintage Nancy. "I'm on my way." After meeting the President she was told about the small chapel in the hospital so she retired there for a while. Meanwhile an examination had discovered a bullet hole in the President's chest. The doctors were very concerned about the condition of a seventy year old man and what his body was enduring. X-rays were called just to locate the site of the bullet but without success.

The greatest piece of luck was the presence on the scene of surgeon Benjamin Aaron, a Senior Consultant who was to be the key man in the operating theatre. He made an incision in Reagan's chest and for three quarters of an hour probed with his fingers covered in blood into the soft tissue of Reagan's lungs. Time was running out. Then he hit upon a master stroke by deciding to follow the track of the bullet into Reagan's lung. The wire he used as a probe struck the bullet at the back of the lung, and then with a forceps he fished out the bullet. The onlookers could barely suppress a shout of elation, but the danger wasn't over yet. The bullet was bent. Could there be fragments in the President's stomach? Another X-ray proved nothing was there. Reagan had now been under the knife for four hours. Nancy was the first to be told all was well.

Just before this, the media had become frustrated and agitated. "Who was in charge of the country?" they shouted. Larry Speakes was getting a torrid time. They suspected him of evasion. Al Haig stepped in to diffuse the situation. The Constitution says when the President is incapacitated the Vice-President takes over. Mr. Bush is still on his way from the West Coast. Then Haig used those fatal words that cost him his job. "As Secretary of State, I am in charge." It was the decision of a General not a politician. But that was only a sideshow.

All the admiration was for the seventy year old President, they were sewing up in the theatre. He had survived an assassin's bullet and after a four hour journey to the very edge of eternity he survived.

He came out of the anesthetic, alone with his nurse, and struggled to speak, then sat up. Gently she held his hand and handed him a notepad. The words he wrote were sad and profound. "Am I alive?" She smiled and said, "Yes, Mr. President, you are going to be all right."

Only Ronald Reagan could be capable of ending his traumatic experience with a joke. Here is a lovely little story from Michael, his son. "Michael", said his father, "if you are going to get shot make sure you don't wear a new suit." "What do you mean Dad?" said Michael. "Well," said his father, "you know son, I had only just bought that suit. It was the first time I wore it." Michael shakes his head and smiles when he tells the story. His father had nearly been killed in that suit and he still managed to joke about it. At least unlike the unfortunate President McKinley, they found the bullet and that is why Reagan survived.

Reagan came through it all still making wisecracks "I'd like to do this scene again – starting at the hotel" was one of them. However, it wasn't over yet. On April 4, Reagan had a relapse in the form of a slight fever and more blood from the lung. Stronger antibiotics were introduced with a wider range of effectiveness over the next week. One week later on April 11, he was walking out of the hospital on Nancy's arm. "Whatever happens now?" he wrote later in the

White House, "I owe my life to God and will try to serve Him everyway I can." And he truly meant it. The support he got in the post was overwhelming. The letters that lifted him most were from old friends calling him by his nick-name "Dutch". Here is one that particularly moved him. "Dear Mr. President 'Dutch' Reagan – I met you in the 20s in Lowell Park III. Do you remember the good times we had in the 20s? You were seventeen years old then and everyone called you "Dutch". Please, please get well soon. We need you to save the country – remember all the lives you saved in Lowell Park."

Ronald Reagan was not too bothered about that old ladies English spelling. What she said was from the heart and that is what really mattered. No press bulletins were issued about Reagan's discomforts. The real news was that the President was alive and working in the White House.

What the public were not told was the change in his body language. His face had collapsed; his eyes were melancholy, his hearing not so good. Chest splints gave him discomfort when he took deep breaths. A respiratory device lay beside his bed. The old immaculate sun-tanned athlete of seventy years was now not quite 100%. The truth was 60% was nearer the mark. Perhaps the shock added a spiritual dimension to Ronald Reagan for he could not come to terms with the narrow escape he had.

He needed somebody spiritual to explain the answers to his searching mind yet he didn't turn to his own rough and ready Baptist Padre. Deaver, an ex-candidate for a seminary life before politics, arranged for a meeting with Cardinal Terence Cooke. The interview and exchange of thoughts seemed to have satisfied Reagan. The outcome was his vow. "I have decided that whatever time I have left is for Him."

Perhaps Reagan's thinking about the evils of Communism intensified after this. He had hated Communism for the previous thirty-five years, basically because to him it was not an accident of history but perniciously ideological. It was a doctrine he said, manipulated by a cynical minority to enslave and terrorize a majority. The confiscation of freedom at the hands of this evil gang at the top of Russian politics was true evil in all its diabolical overtones. "The sure road to peace," Reagan said "was to negotiate from a position of strength" which was to build up his military arsenal.

Critics of the new Reagan accused him of acting as though he was still a cowboy in a B movie. But despite his preoccupation with his health and the Russians he refused to be bullied at home. After promising not to strike, air traffic controllers did just that and Reagan stepped in ruthlessly and sacked twelve thousand of them. Labour leaders were appalled but once again Reagan's gut instinct was right for he was applauded by the public who loved it.

It seems Reagan was a mystery both personally and politically. But how could he be a mystery when he was loved and understood by millions of television viewers. Some say it was because he was an actor. Even Edmund Morris, his personal biographer confessed "Reagan was just incomprehensible." Peggy Noonan, his star speechwriter said, "His life was a paradox all the way down. He was gregarious and liked people but he never allowed them to get close to him. He spoke of God but he did not go to church. He praised family values yet he was divorced, had strange relations with his children, and seldom saw his grandchildren." "He knows so little," Robert McFarland, his security advisor said, "yet he has accomplished so much."

Even two and a half years after Reagan left office Nixon was confessing Reagan was right. Nixon had said the Communist system would not collapse. Reagan said it would and it did.

They said he was the great communicator. Others said he was the great manipulator. His budget director was worried about a two hundred billion dollar deficit, "As far as the eye could see". Yet Reagan seemed to be detached and unaffected by the news. Anthony Lewis a columnist for the New York Times wrote "He was a President with a seven minute attention span." He was even said to dose off at Cabinet meetings. Carter when handing over the Presidency was anxious to list the problems ahead. "Ronald Reagan just listened but made no notes," Carter said. "He refused to be distracted by detail but kept his eyes on the broad picture ahead."

Reagan's acting skills and his rhetoric were the fundamentals of his leadership skills. Some say he learnt his negotiating skills dealing with the movie bosses in Hollywood. He said himself, "Dealing with the toughest movie bosses in Hollywood helped me to prepare for Gorbachev." "After the studios," he said "Gorbachev was a snap." When confronted by the chance of getting most of his demands or nothing he always took a deal. Reagan's triumph with Gorbachev went back to his experience with the Communists he faced in the film industry.

He had to carry a gun then because of threats to his life and quickly learned of the deceit and violence they practiced to further their ideological cause. One anecdote to highlight Reagan's ability to detach himself from the excitement and anger that sometimes surrounded him happened at the Cabinet table. A furious debate erupted about grain exports. The debate escalated as others became involved. Reagan seemed to be sitting outside the "loop" so to speak. He reached out and pulled a jar of jelly beans towards him. "What is wrong with the guy" thought one of the protagonists as he watched Reagan totally focused on his favourite coloured jelly bean oblivious to what went on around him.

A final attempt to describe the man is left to his family. Patti, his most outspoken daughter confronted him angrily and said "We have never exactly been a close family." Reagan pulled out an old photo of them all together smiling and said, "Look we were a happy family." He was truly heartbroken in his failed efforts to be the great communicator inside his own family circle as he was renowned to be outside it. But the fact that he, just like millions of Americans, had family problems made this extraordinary man a much loved ordinary man.

But here are two stories from Kitty Kelly's biography of Nancy Reagan showing Ronald Reagan in a different role.

Reagan was his usual disarmingly honest self who told it as it was with no pretentions. His hosts at Yale, a class of students, were bowled over by Ronald Reagan when he arrived there for a four day lecturing stint. He sat casually on a desk giving a talk on American history and bluntly admitted to having never taught anything before this except perhaps swimming and Sunday school. The Ivy League class gave him a standing ovation and rushed up to surround him and shake him by the hand.

However, his evening turned a little sour when he was called into the room of one particular professor who asked him what drink he would have. "I'll have a Vodka Martini," volunteered Reagan. "Sorry, we make our Martini's with Gin," grinned the professor. "I'm sure that's the way a Martini should be made," smiled Reagan. "But I'm allergic to Gin so I would like vodka please." The professor put up a roadblock. "Sorry Governor but at Yale we drink only gin." But the roadblock was expertly dismantled by Reagan's next reply. "Look I'll make it myself," and he did. Earlier Reagan had learned there was opposition to his presence at Yale and the professor was part of that cabal. I am afraid with Reagan's easygoing style as well as being a polished politician any attempt to humiliate him just hadn't a chance.

Perhaps we can lighten the story of Reagan a bit by taking a look at how he lived when he was at home at Number 1669 San Onofre Drive, Pacific Palisades. You may remember me telling you about the other famous houses built lovingly by earlier Presidents – Washington's Mount Vernon, Jefferson's Monticello, Madison's Montpelier, Hayes' Spiegel Grove and Teddy Roosevelt's Sagamore Hill.

Reagan's residence was just a little different but palatial nevertheless and in keeping not only with a President's lifestyle but the glamorous life of a film star as well. Besides the other trappings of the good life, Reagan's assets included such comforts as a Cadillac, a refrigerator and a ranch stocked with steers. Unlike the cash strapped Jefferson, Reagan was made a present of the house by an employer who filled it full of the most up-to-date General Electric equipment, enough to light up a row of neighbours' houses.

Furnished with a zebra skinned black-slate foyer, sunken living room, shelves full of Boehm birds, a triple car-port and of course the inevitable swimming pool surrounded by a patio engraved with the initials NDR-RR. The house oozed wealth and class. Each glass-fronted room overlooked the pacific. Called by some "The house of the future" it was sure to attract the ire of the jealous, the angry, and the down and outs on the other spectrum of American society.

Why Reagan would choose the trappings of political power given the terrible price those trappings extracted from him, when he could have retired gracefully to his paradise in the sun enjoying the adulation of the film world, is one of those mysteries burned deep in the DNA of human nature and totally inexplicable.
Reagan's two marriages blessed him with four lovely children; however, like many politician's children, they missed that total commitment to them an ordinary father would bring.

Nancy Reagan was no hard-bitten politician. Like any woman in a new home, Nancy set about refurbishing the White House as soon as she arrived in it. Despite the fact that the furnishings were due to be updated, Nancy was helped by some wealthy friends who donated over $1 million towards it. The press didn't reveal this and left Nancy a sitting duck for public criticism. She cried. But soon such a reaction was controlled, and then eliminated altogether as time went by. She changed dramatically into a self-sufficient, confident First Lady.

She changed for Ronald's sake and soon became his protector, adviser and personal secretary who made decisions which placed her between Ronald and his controlling Aides. She always felt Ronald was too soft a touch who hates hurting friends and in this area needed a wife's arm around his shoulders. The President's Aide, David Fischer made his own observations. "It's kinda like that magic that's in everybody's courtship has never left the Reagans. They hug and kiss all the time. They're really in love with each other."

Nancy Davis Reagan was old enough to hear of Mamie Eisenhower's homely image. Press reporters were not so accommodating with Nancy Reagan. While Rosalyn Carter had chaired conferences on mental health, Nancy was determined to push a different public image. One Washington Monthly reporter wrote that Nancy considered it a divine right to make such predecessors as Mamie Eisenhower, Betty Ford and Rosalyn Carter look tacky pushing women's rights. Now caviar and other such delicacies increased exponentially not to mention expensive "four figure", outfits for entertaining at White House parties.

Reporters were not too impressed by the new coteries of Nancy's Hollywood friends. Nancy's announcement that her life had begun when she met her husband and looking after him was her first priority began to sound trite. Critics and feminists dubbed Nancy's loving focus on Ronald during speeches as "The gaze". She was really struggling to please the reporters yet all the political experts agreed later that she had been a major asset in his rise to power.

When she entered the White House she overspent the household budget by $850,000 (the budget was $50,000). You may remember Lincoln hadn't the funds of some of Hollywood's high rollers. Simultaneously cuts in "daycare help", training centers, family planning allowances, and social security benefits unsettled a lot of people who heard of the White House redecoration costs. People were appalled at her timing of $200,000 spent on new White House china the day before cutbacks in the school lunch programmes.

Her first year was not a good one. Now she was being described as the worst of all First Ladies. She was even being referred to as "Queen Nancy". It took a major image refit to heal Nancy's tarnished reputation. She was encouraged to invite community leaders to Washington to discuss the drug problems in April 1985. Nancy's new approach improved her image by twenty points in the ratings. She did not rate highly in her daughter Patti's ratings however; a family rift that triggered off two books. The one from Nancy entitled My Turn. We have already discussed Patti's book earlier. Like all mother and daughter rows this one too ended in fond reconciliation. Her verdict on her role in the White House was as follows "The job of First Lady was one you never get used to."

But before the end of his first term the harsh medicine administered by the Federal Reserve began to work. Personal and individual incomes improved and the stock market had risen dramatically. The cure is now known as Reaganomics which had been ridiculed by many (see later notes).

His success with the economy gave him a landslide victory for a second term as President and all that was left for him was to celebrate his second inauguration.

Ronald Reagan took the oath of office at 11.57 a.m. on January 20, 1985 in the Grand Foyer of the White House. The weather changed all the plans for an outdoor ceremony when arctic winds rocked the city and the temperature dropped to -2o. Yes, Mother Nature was on her most unbelievably ugly behaviour. Even the inaugural parade down Pennsylvania Avenue was cancelled for only the second time since Andrew Jackson's inauguration in 1833. The swearing in ceremony had to be repeated next day because the official inauguration day fell on Sunday. Chief Justice Burger again administered the oath. Reagan's speech was very low-key lasting for only eighteen minutes and in the evening Nancy and Ronald paid a visit to nine inaugural balls held in their honour.

Of all the modern Presidents, Reagan was one of the very few who truly understood the Communist mind. His profound understanding of this can be found in some of his quotations. "Communism is a false religion that seeks to destroy the family, private property and genuine religious faith in order to achieve a kind of earthly paradise." In 1978 he said "Communists are not bound by our morality. They say that any crime including lying is moral if it advances the cause of socialism." Once a person understands this philosophy that black can be white, depending on what advantages the Communist mind can extract from the situation, negotiating with a Communist can be that much easier. Let me point out a story that appeared in a small booklet called Red Star and the See by Douglas Hyde, an ex-Communist. It was all about how China set out to undermine the church from within in order to achieve its downfall in China. In it Hyde described the supreme fear they had of the "Communist expert" who knew how they operated. If such a person was spotted for what he was while sitting at the negotiation table, they asked to have him removed on some pretext. Progress on their terms was always impossible when such a man was at the table.

It was that very factor that helped Reagan "stand out from the crowd" so to speak, no doubt accounting for his brilliant success with Gorbachev to bring about an end to the Cold War. He was that man sitting at the table. Douglas Hyde revealed another insight into the Communist mind when he described the process by which society changed suddenly after the social change brought about by social revolution.

He described society like a bucket of water on a hot stove at that crucial moment it changed to steam. Or that moment it froze and changed from water to ice. It sounds impressive when it is put another way according to the Communist intellectual. The negation of the negation; the interpenetration of opposites and the transformation from quantative to qualative change. Reagan completely understood this way of thinking by the Reds and they knew it. Yet Ronald Reagan has been sneered at with condescension by many even those in his own Republican Party. His own Vice-President Bush, during the primaries in 1980 described his supply side ideas as "voodoo economics". Another of his critics was Congressman John Anderson who joked "Smoke and mirrors are required to make sense of Reagan's policies."

Post-election comments showed no let up from the media "experts". Donovan wrote disparagingly about him being "Nowhere near Presidential", others wrote "A howling idiot, a reactionary kook, a dangerous warmonger." Columnist William Greider joined the bandwagon pronouncing: "My God, they've elected this guy who nine months ago we thought was a hopeless clown. There's something going on here we don't understand." It is amazing, almost criminal, the hysterical contempt some journalists heaped on him "Ronald Reagan is an ignoramus" was the opinion of John Osborne of the New Republic. "A nostalgic figure whose time has passed" Richard Reeves of Esquire wrote in 1979. The Nation was strident and so wrong when it trumpeted "He is the most dangerous person ever to come so close to the Presidency." "A menace to the human race" stormed The Nation on November 1, 1980.

What generally was not known about Reagan was the depth and breadth of his reading material which he looked on as ammunition for his point of view. Among his books were such choices as The World Marxist Review to help him understand as he put it "What the other side is up to." The image Reagan projected of "the laid-back all American dunce" was light years away from his true personality. His selection of authors was really astonishing; Friedrich Hayek and Frederic Bastiat on economic liberty. Whittaker Chambers and Alexander Solzhenitsyn on Communism. His specialty was the American Founding Fathers.

The books in his study were not just for decoration as his biographer Lee Edwards found out when he flicked through most of them. Not only were they all obviously read but significant passages were highlighted and noted in the margins for use later. Memorable quotes were also underlined. He often surprised his Aides by citing the Roman Emperor, Diocletian's policy of wage and price control or by mentioning Islamic historian, Ibn Khaldun's opinions on taxation and Government revenues. But what was more significant than his reading material on Communism was the practical experience he brought with him from his battles with the Communists in his role as President of the Screen Actors Guild. There was one person, a figure of major importance in Congress, who never underestimated him. He said "Reagan is the toughest debater I have ever faced." His name was Robert Kennedy.

Reagan was particularly impressed by Chambers autobiography, reciting from memory passages from Witness which explains why Chambers jeopardized his career and risked his life testifying about his "other life" in the Communist Party. In this publication, Chambers described Communism as "The focus of concentrated evil of our time". Reagan, the Communist "specialist" always had ideas to push and thrust at the Soviet Empire in an effort to rollback its borders to its pre-World War II perimeters.

Distributing literature including getting bibles to the people of those countries trapped behind the iron curtain may at first glance seem eccentric but it can easily be understood when you realize what he was doing – reaching out to the Communist mind beyond the walls of ignorance. A sworn enemy of this evil creed he could be heard muttering with cold fury on a visit to the Berlin Wall…….. "This wall has got to come down." Despite his misgivings about the Communist threat, when others despaired of the future he always had a lighthearted approach to life. Scott Fitzgerald in his book The Great Gatsby, had a quote that could have been about Reagan: "He had an extraordinary gift of hope."
Ronald Reagan's Presidency will always be remembered for two cataclysmic events in world history – the elimination forever of nuclear arms and the disintegration of the Soviet Union. He did so in partnership with an immortal of the Soviet political stage, Mikhail Gorbachev.
Gorbachev was born in 1931 and was too young to participate in World War II. His older brother did so and gave his life in that struggle. His grandfather fell foul of Stalin and spent nine years in prison for his rebellion.

Gorbachev had a normal childhood in Russia, went to school and gained excellent results there before turning his attention to a combine harvester which he drove from fifteen to nineteen years of age. He then went on to Moscow University where he graduated in law. For the next twenty-five years he worked for the Communist Party, rising up the ranks until he reached the very pinnacle of power as Secretary of the Politburo in 1985. When he got there he didn't waste time for soon he was setting about change in Russia so appalled was he by the military cost of the Cold War. He came to the conclusion that the Soviet Union just couldn't afford it.

In the meantime Reagan was relentless in pursuing Soviet totalitarianism wherever it raised its ugly head. But Gorbachev was leading the Soviet Union in an amazing change of direction. Reagan was aware of this and four meetings were arranged for different parts of the globe; Geneva 1985, Reykjavik 1986, Washington 1987 and Moscow 1988. The nucleus of Reagan's star wars idea was originally planted by a visit to the North American Air Defence Command (NORAD) in 1979 when a conversation with the Commander-in-Chief of NORAD shocked him. While American missiles could be sent with pinpoint accuracy, nothing, yes nothing could stop one missile fired from Russia. Commander James Hill said "We can track them but we can't stop them." Reagan left the base convinced there was something flawed about the whole defence policy of the West. Reagan was certain it was immoral to base a nation's security by threatening the complete destruction of another nation's entire civilization. "There had to be another way to defend ourselves" thought Reagan.

He wasn't too far off Eisenhower's way of thinking. As a World War General, Nuclear warfare according to Ike really was an exercise in total futility.

And so on March 23, 1983 he launched a programme to make nuclear weapons obsolete. He called it a vision for the future. Meanwhile he tackled medium range weapons and in 1987 in Washington an agreement was finally reached to reduce the number of medium ranged missiles. In fact, medium ranged weapons were eventually eliminated entirely. Success had almost caught Reagan by surprise. He had been pushing at an open door. His next step was to call for $26 million over five years to launch the programme. Margaret Thatcher said afterwards "Ronald Reagan's decision to go ahead with SDI (Strategic Defense Initiative) was one of the vital factors in ending the Cold War."

Alexander Bessmertnykh, former Foreign Minister of the Soviet Union, agreed with her. Yet although this had been the verdict of many senior figures in the Soviet Administration, at home he was ridiculed. The concept of SDI had been in Reagan's mind since 1967 when he dropped in on the Lawrence Livermore Laboratory in California where he met Edward Teller, the inventor of the hydrogen bomb whose students were experimenting with space-based lasers. It was Teller who told him these lasers would soon be powerful enough to destroy nuclear missiles in space.

Reagan was fascinated with the idea and said "At some point the sword invites the shield." The opposition to his star wars programme said it would take twenty years to develop and the final cost would be astronomical. Top scientists were skeptical. They argued that at least 5% of missiles would get through the laser shield, enough to destroy every city in the United States. Reagan insisted nevertheless that nuclear retaliation was the only other but unacceptable option. He often grew quite worried about the prospect facing mankind, a mood that truly explains his persistence with SDI. Perhaps it explains one of his outbursts which went as follows: "How can we claim to be more civilized today than one hundred years ago if our peacemaking relies on a threat to kill men, women and children in millions without discrimination by either country."
"All we are doing is research but if they really mean it about wanting to eliminate the threat of those weapons, and research can bring us the idea of a weapon that makes these others obsolete then it's good for them and good for us. I wish they would go forward with the same thing themselves because if both of us knew we could stop the others nuclear missiles, we wouldn't have to."

It is inconceivable that Reagan would not have presented all these arguments to Gorbachev and it is no coincidence that Gorbachev set about changing the whole political structure of the Soviet Union at the same time. It only needed the reassurance that Reagan gave him to create a nuclear free society to spur him on. Reagan told advisers "In the past we've dealt with the Soviets on a mirror-image – that will to see they are just like us. And if they see that we're nice, why they'll be nice too – I thought it is now time we talked straight!"

That little speech confirms just how well Reagan understood the Communist mind. Far from being the "popular dunce" he was proving to be better than the Soviets at Russian roulette. Then an amazing change came about in Russia which led to the fall of the Berlin wall. Gorbachev's contribution was comprehensive, ruthless and impressive. All Soviet forces were withdrawn from Afghanistan. Gorbachev's purge continued when Perestroika or restructuring was announced to deal with the flaws in the Russian economy. The next new word the West came to know was "glasnost" which was a new openness in Russian affairs. Criticism was not punishable by death any more. Free elections were next, in which most of the old hardliners were defeated. By the end of 1989 the entire region of Eastern European Communism collapsed.

Because the Russian army could no longer be used to bolster oppressive dictatorial puppet regimes, these dictatorships began to crumble too. The Berlin Wall was next to go. Millions then streamed westwards from East Germany and the Cold War was over forever. The USSR was now election-free which encouraged countries within its boundaries to seek their own freedom. Estonia, Latvia and Moldova were just a few of its component Republics to secede and the old Soviet Union was now formally dissolved. The Communist system was pushed aside by Yeltsin and in December 1991 Gorbachev resigned, not into political oblivion but to a place in Russian history.

It was a triple triumph for both Reagan and Gorbachev, the end of the Cold War, the collapse of Communism and the ultimate ban on nuclear weapons in East and West forever. History has a lot to be grateful for to both of these great leaders. Just before the Soviet Union disintegrated, Gorbachev was at rock bottom in Russia. On a visit to Reagan in retirement in California, he invited Reagan's advice on the situation. Reagan's reply was "stay the course". To his eternal credit, Gorbachev stayed the course and the rest is history.

Meanwhile the space programme was going full blast at the beginning of Reagan's second term of office and money it seemed was totally irrelevant in running it. Carter had budgeted the space shuttle part of it at $5.9 billion to include building three more such spaceships over four years. The frontiers of race and gender were also being extended and in 1983 the first American woman astronaut, Sally Ride, and the first American black astronaut, Guion Bluford, were added to the crew.

After an unbroken run of successes, experimenting with military, industrial and scientific payloads, these flights were now thought of in terms of a commercial platform for making profit out of revenue generating cargo. This would include launching communication satellites into orbit for private industrial projects or ferrying spy satellites into the stratosphere for Washington. It was hoped in the long run that these commercial enterprises would more than pay for the entire space programme. The inevitable outcome was to be the extra pressure on the launching schedule.

Demand for shuttle flights was growing and consequently fifteen flights were scheduled for the launching pads with four shuttles for 1986. It may be wrong to imply that this extra workload was asking for trouble but the first space disaster ever took place on January 28, 1986 at 11.39 a.m. Only seventy-four seconds after the first launch of the year, the Space Shuttle Challenger disintegrated in a ball of fire killing all seven astronauts on board.

History was to be made with Challenger for she was to carry the first private citizens into space – a school teacher from New Hampshire whose name was Christa McAuliffe. A commission was appointed to investigate the disaster to find out the cause and make future launches safer. It was called The Rogers Commission. To be brief, the cold weather on the morning of the launch combined with the failure of the sealant rings on an external fuel tank designed to seal in the booster rocket gases during lift off was blamed for the explosion.

The shuttle programme itself was criticized as being seriously flawed. The engineers had actually pointed out prior to take-off that it should not have been launched when the temperature was below fifty-three degrees Fahrenheit but top administrators in NASA were not told. In fact, some safety procedures were abandoned to meet the hectic shuttle programme. After that, the ambitions of everyone had to be postponed for two years. Reagan ordered the programmne to be switched from commercial projects to military ones. The first shuttlecraft to be launched since the 1986 disaster didn't take place until 1988.

Now let us turn to family matters. Ronald Reagan's daughter, Patti, is very much part of his life story. Patti Davis wrote her life story entitled Family Secrets a very poignant, deeply moving peep behind the spin and razzamatazz surrounding her father, Ronald Reagan. One sentence in her cry to be understood stands out like a beacon the first time I read it…. "I have blamed my father for being there but not really being there and have expected other men to make up for that absence. The truth is it wasn't my father's fault. He did the best he knew how." Later, she wrote about the men in her life... "I'd decided the guy was going to abandon me before he'd even thought of it, so of course he would and then I could blame him and continue my pattern of being a little girl whose father never noticed her."

When one reads these heart-rending thoughts of an adult woman about her relationship with her father, especially a father so famous, so rich, so powerful, so popular as Ronald Reagan, it makes you wonder where it all went wrong. Like any other normal family, all three of them, Ronald, Nancy and Patti searched for answers to Patti's hurt and accusations. The hurt that was a part of their lives wasn't known to the public looking through the celluloid world surrounding the President. It must have been hard to smile at a cocktail party or listen to the cheers in the Convention Hall or maybe read the praises in the press when deep inside there was someone they loved and cherished who told them she didn't belong. Money, riches, fame and glory could never compensate them for the sense of failure they must have felt in the midst of their glorious success.

Patti tried to analyze the problem. In her book, Family Secrets, she blamed her grandfather, Jack and his alcoholic lifestyle. She felt the boyhood experience of coping with such a father left in her own father, Ronald Reagan, a mechanism of blocking out the pain Jack inflicted on him. Unfortunately, this blocking out mechanism was used by Ronald Reagan to escape any other pain inflicted on him by life. It meant the shielding of his true feelings with that film star smile of indifference throughout his life. She suffered as a result, was her verdict. This laid-back style of his has already been articulated by Ronald Reagan in the statement he wrote under his picture in high school, I've already mentioned. "Life is just one grand sweet song so start the music."

But what made his remoteness more unbearable for her were the ugly scenes she endured with her mother that he never knew about. These clashes nearly always ended in tears. Ronald like most fathers left it to mother and daughter to resolve. Whether this was a good idea or not is not for me to pass judgment on. After all, he had some other very important business to attend to as President of the United States. This ongoing unresolved problem in the relationship of Patti and Nancy only got worse as Patti got older. So goes Patti's story as she told it in Family Secrets.

For such a beautiful couple as Nancy and Ronald, so popular with those outside the family circle, it is hard to write about so much pain on the human level inside a family that was the envy of millions. Can there ever be a formula for true lasting happiness in this world you may ask.

But let's look at the lighter side for a change. One funny anecdote in all this comes from Uncle Richard Davis, Nancy's brother.

"It must have been hard growing up with your father," he said to Patti. "One day you'd have to be Mother Theresa just to get his attention." "I don't know if that would have done it," Patti replied, "unless Mother Theresa was a Republican."

Patti finally turned to drugs which resulted in another family confrontation with her father and mother. Shortly after that she moved out for good. No matter how she tried to communicate her unhappiness her father, Ronald Reagan, was too close to Nancy to believe her.

Patti with the wind of freedom now in her hair and the determination to prove she was no longer under her mother's thumb kicked over the traces like a runaway covered wagon in one of his B movies. Patti, going to Europe with a Rock singer appalled Nancy who still played

Sinatra records on a seventy-eight. Patti going to live with him shattered her. Unfortunately, like Ronald, she was totally unaware how life had moved on since their B movie days. This was the age when joints were passed between the kids at rock concerts. Making love at his house didn't cost Patti a thought. Once again there was a Council of War with her parents. Living together outside marriage was incompatible to Ronald and Nancy Reagan with their beliefs in the Bible. It was a sin. But she had turned her back on their culture and once again they were not on speaking terms. A peace council was called between three unhappy people but Nancy walked out. Even in politics Patti chose a separate course and further alienated them by being part of the anti-nuclear movement.

To read of the overwhelming political success of President Ronald Reagan with world famous Statesmen making future history, I feel an awful sadness for a man who could achieve so much in the public eye while he suffered a family life in so much turmoil.

Patti did return to the family for inauguration day and spoke in her book about the White House itself. "It's smaller than I expected," she said. But she also felt a strong sense of reverence for the history of the place. "Everyone seemed to have an urgent task and by walking swiftly, gave an air of urgency to their task" she wrote. "Clearance badges are pinned to everyone, and dark suits and uniforms are evident everywhere." She was fascinated that from the second floor you look down and see the black iron fence surrounding the building with the ever present spectators pressed against it. Patti was an infrequent visitor to the White House after that, only visiting for two christenings, a second inauguration and once more when her father was shot. When she left and said goodbye to him in the Oval office she wouldn't be back there for eight years.

There was one realization that shook Patti when she was flown to Washington by army transport to visit her father in hospital after the assassination attempt. She looked at the family flying with her. "None of us had called each other on hearing the news. None of us had gotten through to my mother nor had she called any of us ..... What kind of family is this, I wondered, even a bullet can't bring us together." Perhaps the answer is in one photograph published in her book of Ronald Reagan and Nancy as he walked away from office on retirement. Under it is her caption "Some people thought it was a sad image but I realized that they don't need anyone else to make their world complete." Yet another sentence from Patti strikes you "Ronald and Nancy Reagan are two halves of a circle: together they are complete and their children float outside."

Patti looked around at her family scattered around the plane and couldn't bear the situation so she changed her seat to sit beside Michael. The thought of what was happening got to her and she began to cry not for her father in hospital but for the sadness of a broken family. Michael slipped his arm around her to comfort her. She never did reveal it until she wrote in her book Family Secrets the real reason for her tears.

In later life Patti became more reconciled with Nancy. Her father, now suffering from Alzheimer's disease, had forgotten her anyway. She became an actress and wrote three novels and a column. It had been a long painful journey. Only God knows why she had to travel that route.

But Nancy had a go at writing a book too. She called it My Turn, so let's hear from her.

There were four children in the marriage – Michael and Maureen, children of his ex-wife, Jane Wyman, and Ron and Patti, born to Nancy and Ronald Reagan. Rearing four children can be a pretty demanding time for any parent, so perhaps we should take that on board when we read about Nancy's relationship with the children.

Nancy always felt things were exaggerated by the ever gluttonous feeding of the media on their ordinary every day difficulties. Perhaps it was part of the territory but knowing that didn't help her live with it. Living away from the White House as two of them did with Jane Wyman, didn't help in bonding them all together. In Ronnie's eyes, they were entitled to their independence and to be left to choose their own path in life. Unfortunately when there was a falling out, like most families have, the press was quick to home in on it making a private row a public one. A trivial tiff became a major crisis. Yes, to use an old cliché, being in the public eye can be like living in a goldfish bowl. Yet when we look at photographs of the family together they come across as a very happy normal American family, no different from millions of other such families throughout America.

Kitty Kelly, in her book Nancy Reagan had many controversial anecdotes on the Reagan Presidency and the people worth a mention in it. I trust she will allow me to use them to paint a picture of the Reagans. Richard Nixon it seems was the first to spot the influence Nancy Reagan had over Ronald Reagan long before Reagan came to power. Here is how Nixon put it to an Aide of his – "Nancy Reagan runs Ronald Reagan. She's a very strong woman and if you make her angry you are never going to pull this guy into the camp. You just can't afford to alienate Nancy. I'm telling you, Nancy Reagan's a bitch, a demanding one and he listens to her…"

However, one personality who had a special relationship with Ronald Reagan and Nancy was another 'show biz' name, famous the world over, Frank Sinatra. Tea and cakes in the afternoon was a regular feature of his visits. However, Sinatra's mob connections had not gone unnoticed by the F.B.I. and a special report was made out with his name on the letter head. It was the job of the security people to screen and investigate all visitors to the White House. The report on Sinatra gave directions that he was debarred from any political position regardless of how insignificant it was. The relationship with the President was to be mainly a social one. However, this didn't prevent Sinatra gate-crashing Reagan's first inaugural celebrations. According to Kitty Kelly, Sinatra was seen barging his way up the steps of the inaugural platform where the Reagan family were seated despite the efforts of the F.B.I. and the Capitol Police to discourage him. No one dared stop him, even without the required admission ticket.

Nevertheless, Nancy still remained the dominant matriarchal power in the Reagan clan. What she said was law. Only one of the Staffers ever had the courage to oppose Nancy, for to do so was to risk being "flash frozen" as they called her icy stare of disapproval. The story goes like this, Bess Truman had died and Jim Rosebush, an Aide, was confronted by Nancy with a "Don't expect me to go to that funeral" warning. But Jim to his credit was not going to be bullied. He told her quietly
"I expect you to go to that funeral because last month you went to Monaco and sat beside Princess Diana at the funeral of Princess Grace …..If you don't go to Mrs. Truman's funeral it looks like all you care about is European royalty and international glitz."

No one had ever disagreed with Nancy before, so it took courage to do this. He got the customary stare but she later agreed to go.

Now let's move on to more interesting anecdotes of Nancy and Gorbachev, the Russian Chief.

Nancy's conversations with Gorbachev, which I recount later, are quite astonishing but even more revealing was how she saw her role beside her husband, the President. She wrote "The Soviet leaders kept dying – Brezhnev, Andropov, Chernenko, until we began to wonder if anyone was going to stay around long enough so we could get something constructive started." It almost paints a picture of her sitting at the table with Gorbachev and Ronnie for business. As she put it "So we could get something constructive started." It was not a political statement. It was how she lived her life alongside her husband until his world had integrated with hers. Raisa, Gorbachev's wife, had become part of the scene in Russia. The relationship between Raisa and Nancy was closely watched for friction and the press was not disappointed. Coming from such different backgrounds, this was inevitable. Nancy wrote – "My first impression of Raisa was that she talked and talked and talked."

Nancy felt she was being lectured on Raisa's favourite topics – Marxism, Leninism and Soviet Art, Raisa's strong points. Nancy didn't like Raisa's body language. If Raisa didn't like her chair she just snapped her fingers and her KGB guard jumped to her attention. Sometimes she repeated the scene shortly afterwards. She seemed to enjoy the power she exercised and this completely threw Nancy. When she returned home to Russia, Raisa made certain to walk one step behind Gorbachev. "That sort of obedience to Russian tradition would not have worked with me," said Nancy.

During dinner one evening, Gorbachev turned to Nancy to admit a certain chemistry between himself and her husband Ronald Reagan. "Yes, I've noticed," Nancy told him. "It's very rare," said Gorbachev. Then an amazing admission "I am familiar with your Constitution but I wish your husband could stay on for another four years." It is easy to see by this conversation why Reagan was so effective in his meetings with Gorbachev. They were almost "buddies". Here is a snippet of one conversation to prove this

Gorbachev: "What is it like to see yourself so young on the screen?"

Reagan: "You've set me up for a great one-liner," said Dutch – like meeting a son you never had."

A fascinating story is told in her book My Turn about preparations for a dinner she was to host for Gorbachev in Russia, with the help of her social secretary, Linda Faulkner. It seems everything had to be brought from Washington; the china, the silverware, table cloths, flowers, even the sugar tongs, salt dishes and ash trays. All the food was prepared by the Embassy Chef in Washington and flown over. The staff was re-trained in the American way of serving food and husbands and wives sat at separate tables. The icing on the cake was the hiring of Dave Brubeck and his jazz quartet who was a great favourite in Russia. Nancy's trip to Russia ended with a memorable visit to The Bolshoi Ballet Theatre which turned out to be a memorable send off. Bridges were re-built between Raisa and Nancy during a final meeting at which sincere invitations were extended by both families to visit each other on a private basis which I don't think ever took place.

Leaving the White House after eight years can be a traumatic experience for any President. This time, to change the format perhaps, we should look at the event for the first time through the eyes of a "First Lady".

As Nancy said "Nothing can prepare you for living in the White House and nothing can prepare you for leaving it." There were many "going away" ceremonies, but one of them impressed her. At the close of the Kennedy Centre Honours Night, Walter Cronkite called the cast back on stage and everyone sang Auld-Lang-Syne to them. When it finished, Ronald was carried away enough to shout "This is better than an Oscar."

Then came the final goodbye – Ronald Reagan's farewell to the nation. Unlike all his previous speeches this one just had to go right. The Oval room was full to capacity. The Media and TV people, writers and celebrities, cables and cameras all added to the occasion. Tension mounted "two minutes to go" was announced. The producer was worried. His concern for this last performance by the President was obvious.

Silence settled on the Oval room feeding the anxiety of all concerned. Another solemn reminder. "One minute Mr. President." Unbelievably the President cracks a joke "Have I time to make a phone call?" A nervous titter. The eyes of the audience were riveted on the hunched up figure of Reagan, head bent down staring into the texture of his big dark desk. Watching anxiously was a frightened Peggy Noonan, his scriptwriter. "What the hell's he doing?" she gasped. But those around couldn't help. Was this to be an embarrassing catastrophe? The countdown continued five, four, three..... The majestic head came up, his big chest inflated, his eyes twinkled a quick wink towards Peggy. Unbelievably he was ready....... "Fellow Americans, this is the thirty-fourth time I'll speak to you from the Oval office." Peggy sank into a grateful exhale of pure relief; her written words were now flowing from Reagan's lips.... "Why in heavens name was I worrying" a relieved Peggy was thinking. To Ronald Reagan it was just another script. Spoken by the consummate professional - President Reagan himself. Another cameo captured on celluloid.

The cameras stopped rolling and the President turned his attention on his audience and grinned widely, back in the real world again.

Only then did his audience realize they had been watching an old pro at work completely at home with the razzamatazz, the lights, the mikes and the supporting cast around him.
It was his final performance.

The last Christmas at the White House had an old fashioned theme. They received a tracing of a John Adams saying, written over the mantelpiece in the State Dining Room "May only good and wise men inhabit this house". Ronald didn't forget to visit the Park Police stables, where the Secret Service learned their trade. They were overjoyed at the stables and agreed they never had such a warm relationship with a President. Nancy had changed a lot of the building on the second and third floor, even going so far as to have thirty-two coats of paint removed from the White House Walls. "I put a lot of myself into that house," she proudly boasted "and I'm leaving a lot of me there."

Saying goodbye to the household staff "The Staffers" was the most difficult task they had to do. Then it was time to meet the Bushes and the Quayles. It was now time to leave for the inauguration. "I hugged the butler" wrote Nancy "and then walked outside". She remembered to ask Sandra Day O'Connor, wife of the Chief Justice, how she was feeling. Sandra Day had had a mastectomy around the time Nancy had hers. The Bushes and the Quayles saw them to the helicopter. Nancy broke away to run to the Chief of the Secret Service, George Opfer, and gave him a big hug. At noon they mounted the steps of AF27000, no longer Air Force One.

The sun almost on cue slid from behind a cloud focusing a spotlight of golden sunshine on Ronald Reagan as would befit any star of a multi million dollar epic. It was just as Hollywood would have written it. He waved goodbye to his audience for the last time as the 40th President of the United States. Then he turned slowly and slipped smoothly inside the door of the plane disappearing forever from his adoring public. As they circled the White House in the helicopter, for one last look from above, Ronald Reagan leaned across and said to Nancy "Look dear, there's our bungalow". If they couldn't stop him wisecracking on the operating table he certainly wasn't going to stop now. They had been eight wonderful frustrating and even frightening years. The crew served cake and champagne and presented Ronald with a picture of the White House. By coincidence this was to be their pilot's last journey on Air Force One.

Back home the first touch of reality that proved their dream was over was when they had to unpack the bags themselves with the help of their son Ron. The Bushes and the Reagans had now two different schedules to meet. Anyway, that is how it always has been in the White House. The President and the Vice President always seem to have their own separate worlds. The only time they really socialized was at State Dinners. That's how it was for the Reagans and Bush Senior as they went their separate ways. One thing was for certain, Nancy would go on being Nancy.

But the story of Reagan's Presidency doesn't quite end there. There is a fascinating, even bizarre twist to the storyline you the reader could never be prepared for. I can truly guarantee that.

Despite their meticulously planned farewell some genius forgot to record the final moments of Dutch's movements after the nerve-racking saga surrounding his epic speech to the country. How could they explain the "cock up" to ex-President Reagan? But they needn't have worried. This was an area that was child's play to any other professional actor. Doing a re-take the next day was the answer, but where would they find an actor? Some other genius came up with the answer. "Would the ex-President be willing to take on that role again for the cameras?" It was a challenge Reagan couldn't resist. Faithful to his art and to his deeper instincts he went through the choreography for the cameras. He can now be seen tapping on an empty desk, walking to the door of the Oval office for "the last time", looking back sentimentally and closing the door behind him as the cameras rolled. It was a performance worthy of an Oscar. Knowing Reagan as we do now I'm sure it all ended with the expected wise-crack to the camera crew brought back on overtime for this last special occasion.

As the world knows, Ronald Reagan contracted the dreaded Alzheimer's disease before he died, a painful period we would rather not dwell on. To see the light burning low and then being extinguished in a brain and a personality as lovable and brilliant as Ronald Reagan is somehow just not right to end a story as illustrious as his. From life-saving lifeguard to radio broadcaster, from movie star to world Statesman, from nearly assassinated President to survivor, was one hell of a journey to make. He couldn't have revealed more of that man he was inside when he confessed his condition to the world: "I now begin the journey that will lead me into the sunset of my life."

Ronald Reagan finally passed away on June 5, 2005 aged ninety-three. His illness was first diagnosed by doctors about October 1994. They told Nancy it was the preliminary stages of degenerative cognitive dementia and for the next ten years his family lived with his increasing incapacity. Some people suspected it was the result of a riding accident in July 1989 which inflicted a massive contusion on his brain. Now he was gone, the world gathered to mourn the loss of a very great man indeed.

"Ronald Reagan belongs to the ages now but we preferred it when he belonged to us," said George W. Bush in his eulogy. The great bells of the National Cathedral in Washington tolled forty times just like churches throughout the country to respect the 40th President of the United States. "Amazing Grace" and "Ave Maria" were sung by Ronan Tynan, an Irish tenor. A twenty-one gun salute took place at noon on military bases throughout the world. At dusk a fifty gun salute also took place at U.S. bases everywhere. Even the Casino lights of Las Vegas dimmed momentarily for three minutes. State offices were shut down in a dozen States. The Stock Exchange and Universities closed for the day while the Alzheimer's Foundation held a candlelit vigil to commemorate its most famous victim. After the funeral, Ronald Reagan's casket was transported through streets lined with Americans paying their last respects as it headed for Andrews Air Force Base to be flown to California for burial.

At the precise time of the burial, in California, thousands of miles away in a little church in Ballyporeen, population three hundred, in South Tipperary, Ireland, all the villagers gathered in prayer to remember an old friend from his historic visit of 1984. They remembered he had come among them to see his ancestral home and graveyard at Templetinney where his ancestors are at rest. The words of James Junkin, thirty-one, who had arrived in Washington from Alabama with his twelve year old son, said it all. "President Reagan connected with the average Americans more than any other President in modern history and he made us proud again. After Vietnam and Watergate along came Ronald Reagan and there was a whole new attitude." Those words from the ordinary people of the Deep South were spoken outside the Cathedral in Washington. While inside four former Presidents, all of Congress, and major figures of the Cold War stood in unity making it a memorial day never to be forgotten by any of them.

It was late evening as the sun went down on Los Angeles. The sunset ceremony Ron always wanted was over and the flag bedecked coffin stood alone outside except for a Marine standing to attention nearby. Nancy leaned over and kissed the coffin, whispering softly "I love you, I love you." Patti, Michael and Ron Jnr. ushered her gently away. "He is home now – he is free," murmured Ron.

The burial service at the Ronald Reagan Presidential Library took place under a cluster of oak trees. A few yards away was a chunk of the Berlin Wall. It was supposed to be a family affair but still seven hundred and twenty old friends attended, including Arnold Schwarzenegger, another ex-film star and present Governor of California and family friend Charlton Heston, who also suffers from Alzheimer's disease. Now united in death, the family held hands together, grief written on all their faces. They had become very close in the past three or four years. Patti was finishing another book on the family A Long Goodbye, a memoir to her father in his declining years. This time, Nancy approved of it. As Nancy says "I think any illness brings a family closer together. It brings things into focus and should reshuffle your priorities."

Patti is still Patti, with opinions of her own. She has just laid into George W. Bush for claiming he talked to God. "It's hard to believe" she wrote in Newsweek "that God would say sure go ahead and invade Iraq. Forget the United Nations". Yes that's Patti.

But today it was all about her father, Ronald Reagan, 40th President of the United States of America, the man who with a lifeguard's sure touch had lifted America over the waves of nuclear and economic peril and breasting the surf of hope, placed her safely once more on the shores of a happier future.

41st President   George Bush Senior

"Have Half"
Born: 1924
One Term
1989 – 1993
4 years.
Age 65

Party: Republican
Profession: Businessman
County: Texas
Ancestry: British
Value of Estate: Unknown (millions).
Hobbies: Tennis, Boating, Fishing, Golf, Horseshoes, Hunting, Jogging and Swimming.

Physical Description: 6 foot, 2 inches high, 195 lbs., brown hair, blue eyes, trim athletic build.

Significant Extract from his Inauguration Speech on Friday January 20, 1989.
"The totalitarian era is passing, its old ideas blown away like leaves from an ancient lifeless tree. A new breeze is blowing and a nation refreshed by freedom stands ready to push on. Great nations of the world are moving toward democracy through the door to freedom."

GEORGE BUSH SENIOR

The changeover of the Presidency took place at 12.03 p.m. on January 20, 1989. The age of the Reagans had passed into history and a new dynasty was about to begin.

It may not be too well-known to you, the reader, but the Bushes are really a very distinguished family, going back to the middle of the 19th century.

George Herbert Walker Bush, the 41st President of the United States, would be too modest to claim such an illustrious background, for he was as unassuming and low-key as his predecessor, Ronald Reagan, was polished, famous and master of the media.

The truth is Bush's family history more than prepared him for the Presidency. Both the Walker and Bush line consisted of old wealthy families who built their wealth in industrial engineering, railroads, financial investments and oil.

The great, great grandfather of George Bush, James Smith Bush went to Yale in the 1850s going on to become an Episcopalian Minister on Staten Island, New York. His son, Samuel Prescott Bush became an engineer. In his biography of George Bush, The Life of a Lone Star Yankee Herbert Parmet recalls how Prescott Bush, George's father down-played his wealth to gain the votes of ordinary voters in his bid for the Senate and duly became the family's first Senator.

However Prescott's claim that his family had not got the money to send him through Law School was a bit of a myth which his friends refuted, being more familiar with Prescott's lifestyle than the voters. Prescott, a six foot four inch giant of a man, dignified and imposing, had a tremendous influence on his family. He was also renowned for his singing, his love of music and his barber shop singing groups.
According to Kevin Phillips in his book American Dynasties in the year 1914, the other side of the family was getting even richer than the Bush's in St. Louis. It was here G.H. Walker and Company was becoming the biggest Investment Company in the Mississippi Valley.

If you wish to pursue the fascinating story of the wealthy Bush-Walker line, I would go no further than American Dynasties. I'm sure you won't be disappointed. Meanwhile I must move on to the real story of George Bush, United States President, for after all a President is really judged on his record in office and not his bloodlines.

The foregoing notes on the Bush-Walkers is an interesting anecdote to highlight the fact that they were every bit as rich and influential in American politics over the years as were the Kennedy Clan.

Meanwhile, I must move on to the real object of my notes, the story of George Bush, 41st President of the United States.

George Bush was born in Milton, Massachusetts on June 12, 1924 and was one of a family of five children; Prescott his older brother, Nancy, Jonathan and William. The family moved from Milton to Greenwich and it was here that George grew up. Talking about his childhood is impossible without including Prescott his older brother. They were inseparable from the day they shared the same bedroom together. Mother, respecting their need for privacy, as she thought, decided to divide the room by a partition but they had other ideas and were glad to see the old room return when she tore down the intruding partition at their request.

George was renowned within the family for his generosity with food, toys and clothes, until he had earned the nickname "Have half". From an early age, however, he was good at sports, yet never lorded it over the rest of the Bush kids.

His first heartbreak was being separated from his older brother Prescott, when school term took Prescott away from him. So miserable was George, his astute and caring father solved the problem by sending George to school one term earlier. He was smaller than his classmates but according to Prescott, his kid brother was never fragile. Anyway, with a big brother to protect him, I am sure that was another plus factor in keeping his schooldays happy.

From day one, according to Prescott, "George was good at sports." He described George as "Coordinated, a good pair of eyes, good hands and natural reactions, and he hit the ball well." We of course can only be talking of the future Yale Baseball Star who could have played in the Major Leagues. "He was a terrible tease," laughed Prescott "and I'd often wanted to pound him."

Although never a teacher's pet, he got on well with them. It seems they liked his outgoing, easygoing personality at Greenwich Country Day School.

Summers were spent at Walker's Point, Kennebunkport, Maine, with the whole family, including the dogs. One local resident said "If Bush was running for sainthood in Kennebunkport there would be no contest." It was here he soaked up all the excitement of the seaside town of one thousand inhabitants, cycling, tennis, picnics, and movies, and of course girls. I guess it was tough for them to return to normality at the summer's end. Yes it was the sort of place that bonded the Bushes into the close knit family unit they are today.
George usually "farmed" the tennis prizes every year but most important of all never lost his temper. No, he never "did a McEnroe". In Kennebunkport, both Prescott and George became a pair of "old salts" as far as sailing was concerned and many an amateur sailor owed their rescue to the seamanship of both of them. Later as Vice President he would return to Kennebunkport and to the frustration and anxiety of his bodyguards would race around almost recklessly in a twenty-eight foot speed boat in the roughest of weather, leaving them behind in their 'pre-historic' craft as they struggled to do their job on security detail.

As usual, Barbara was never very far away just as she was in the days of his childhood, when she played tennis, swam and ran in races with her brood. She was the permanent matriarch in those days, overseeing the family as it grew up and grew older around her. She was always there to impart her wisdom, keeping their feet on the ground as she did with George when he had the temerity to boast about his war medals in her presence. She always liked the fact that George was not in the habit of boasting. It just was not his style. Their grandfather also took Nancy and the other children to New York for films where they all enjoyed movies like "Life with Father", "Louisiana Purchase" and "White Horse Inn" just as millions of other ordinary Americans did in those days. There was nothing exclusive about the Bushes in their upbringing which may come as a surprise to those who like to knock them.

Religion was given a respected place in their family life too. Their dad, Prescott, would read a lesson from the bible every breakfast time and on Sundays they all paid a visit to church. During games there was strictly no gambling as dictated to them by their mother, a dedicated Presbyterian.

One marvellous piece of praise and admiration came from Gelb, a youngster George saved from a bully in their schooldays in Andover. Gelb remembers that incident nostalgically by claiming George was his hero after that. "George Bush has friends like me all over the country. Nothing makes me a more willing loyalist than a guy who sticks up for a little kid and puts a bully down. The reason we stay friends is that he is still George Bush. He knows who he is. Some people forget where they came from."

But life was soon to change dramatically for George Bush and America, for on December 7, 1941, Japan attacked Pearl Harbour without any warning. It made up George's mind to go to war for his country.

Another event was also taking place in George Bush's life of equal importance to him. During a Christmas Dance in 1942 he met someone very special to him. It happened like this. He was circling the dance floor when he grabbed the arm of a friend and asked "Who is that vision in the green dress?" "Want to meet her," came the reply. "That's the general idea," said George. Barbara and George met and danced the night away to Glenn Miller's music until George, who for once was short of skills in a pastime, asked her to sit down and talk. They have been talking ever since.

By the time George was to be shipped overseas, wedding bells were not very far away. George was the youngest Navy pilot in World War II. For the technically minded, he was assigned to the VT-51 bomber squadron on board USS San Jacinto where he piloted a 3-man Grumman TBM Avenger. Life was fairly spectacular for him in combat for on June 19, 1944 he had to ditch the Avenger with four depth charges on board and had just parachuted away when they went off. He had a second near thing on September 2, 1944 when his plane was hit while he was dive-bombing Chichi Jima Island.

But this didn't deter him for he continued the dive, dropped his bombs on a radio tower, and shouted to his crew to bail out. Being last to leave he was lucky to get away for as he jumped his parachute was damaged and he suffered a head wound by striking it off the plane's tail and landed in the ocean. He lay there drifting on his life raft but was saved by the U.S. submarine USS Finback and spent the next month underwater with the sub-mariners while they attacked Japanese ships in the area. For his bravery under fire he was awarded the (DFC) Distinguished Flying Cross. He really was a genuine war hero.

During the war, George had called the plane he flew "Barbara" after his new girlfriend Barbara Pierce, later to become Mrs. Bush. The story goes that they met when he was eighteen and she was a high school girl of sixteen at that Christmas Dance in 1942. One year later they proved they had fallen in love at first sight when in August 1943 they got engaged secretly just before he was dispatched on war duty to the Pacific. When he was twenty on January 6, 1945 they were married in Barbara's hometown of Rye, New York. It didn't stop him from volunteering to join a new torpedo bomber group in the invasion of the home islands but this was aborted by the Japanese surrender.

But let's digress a little by returning again to Barbara, one of the cornerstones of his life. We can start at a no more meaningful moment of their partnership than that of the wedding.

The night before his wedding, his father Prescott gave a nuptial dinner at the Greenwich Field Club, an occasion that proved to be a great relief from the world conflict overseas.

In mid-January 1945 they spent their honeymoon at The Cloisters on Sea Island, Georgia; a popular rendezvous for American newlyweds, with facilities for swimming, tennis, golf and good food. They enjoyed all of the five star treatment.

This should be an ideal spot to talk in detail about Barbara. Barbara Bush was yet another First Lady who had served an eight year apprenticeship as wife of the Vice President George Bush, Senior. Of course, she lived not in the White House but in the Vice President's house. She had no guarantee she would one day be able to cross over to the White House for statistics were all against her. Not since 1830 when Martin Van Buren was top dog in American politics had it occurred. But on January 20, 1989 it happened and Barbara was America's First Lady. As I have already written, her father Marvin Pierce was related several generations back to America's 14th President, Franklin Pierce. Barbara was born on June 8, 1925 in the up market New York suburb of Rye; the daughter of a successful publisher, so she had a fairly comfortable upbringing. Naturally she went to the best schools, one of them the boarding school called Ashley Hall in Charleston. Barbara's heartache in her marriage when she lost one child, Robin, to leukemia changed her life forever.

A sad and heartbreaking account of little Robin's sickness was captured in James Hatfield's book Fortunate son. One morning, three year old Robin woke up lethargic, pale and restless and told her mother she would sit on the grass outside just watching the cars go by on the road beyond the house or maybe stay on in bed. Alas alarm bells rang and the worried Barbara decided it was time to take her little girl to the paediatrician. They both returned to the hospital later that afternoon to hear the results of the blood tests. Dr. Wyvell, a friend of the family met them with tears in her eyes and they feared the worst.

Dr. Wyvell said "I have got some bad news for you, little Robin is suffering from an advanced case of Leukaemia – her white blood cell count is the worst I have ever seen. Robin has not long to live." Then she gave George Bush Senior the best advice anyone could have given but as George Senior later put it regretfully "We didn't take it." Barbara remembers what the doctor said to this day. "Number one - don't tell anyone. Number two - don't treat her. You should take her home, make life as easy as possible for her and in three weeks time she will be gone."

Naturally they told everyone and conferred with the best medical advice they could get when they flew her to New York to see Dr. John Walker, an uncle and a former cancer specialist. Like Dr. Wyvell he also advised them to rest her so as to prolong her life in the hope of medical research solving the problem before she died. A newly developed cancer drug was prescribed. It only partially worked. George Junior was not told of his sister's battle for life so as not to upset him unnecessarily. No more rough play was allowed now since a haemorrhage could be the result of an over-robust joust. Bone Marrow transplants and painful blood transfusions followed and Barbara never left Robin's bedside. George's job in the oil business and his job as father looking after George Junior who was only seven years old and his infant brother Jeb added further pressure. They came together as a family only at weekends when George Senior flew back to the hospital. Finally little Robin died after an unsuccessful operation to stop haemorrhaging. They were both there beside her as Robin finally lost the battle and passed gently away. They donated little Robin's body for medical research.

One final little anecdote to finish this touching story of a family in tears. When George Senior and Barbara drove up to the house George Junior had a bad experience. It still bothers him deeply to this day. "I saw Robin in the back of the car," he remembers, "I thought I saw her but she wasn't there."

Robin had only been given three weeks by Dr. Wyvell but the medicine that prolonged her life another seven months had life-threatening side effects.
Barbara had taken the full burden of living by Robin's bedside and paid a price for it when her

hair went prematurely grey at twenty-eight years of age. Perhaps in private they look back now and wish for Robin's sake they had not fought so hard to save her. Only they can know the answer to that one but they never spoke about it afterwards.

Being a family conscious parent, anything that affected her children was a major consideration for her. I have spoken about Robin but later another child was revealed as dyslexic, an affliction which pushed Barbara into investigating the field of literacy and made it her major plank for her work. She connected society's ills, drug abuse and homelessness, to an inability to read. She also wrote a book about the family dog Fred, the royalties of which she funnelled into her literacy groups. She herself did not avoid her personal worries and one of these was a disease she developed called "Graves Disease" a disorder of the thyroid. Despite her illness she was a tough, no nonsense mother which she needed to be trying to control three red blooded sons with their own independent personalities. One has since become the 43rd President of the United States, so she didn't do too badly, did she?

George seemed to be impressed with his new way of life when he wrote "Married life exceeds all expectations. Barbara is a fine wife." After two years of the war in Europe, George came home and was given the job of training instructor to young pilots.

On the night of August 15, 1945, Barbara and George were enjoying themselves in the Officers Club with other young Navy couples, when word came through that the Japanese had surrendered. A quiet mutual gesture of thanksgiving was called for and George and Barbara slipped away quietly to a nearby church to offer their gratitude to the higher power for His deliverance at last from the horrors of war. They returned unobserved to the party and danced the night away.

Just a little postscript on Barbara. During the war, when George was on service with the Navy, Barbara spent her time in her sophomore year at Smith College. Her friend, Jenny McBride, shared a class with her reading American Economic History. Both were bored but at least Barbara had her wedding to look forward to. Barbara duly dropped out of the class for her wedding but many years later when she was First Lady they met regularly and Barbara had never changed, according to Jenny McBride.

Now it was George's time to go to College and in November 1945 he commenced his studies entering the college to major in Economics. He chose this subject for practical reasons since he had already decided to go into business and it was essential he was familiar with how the American system worked.

Perhaps it was his whiz kid father, Prescott, who inspired him to go in that direction for the country was just ripe for a commercial boom restocking after years of war. One advantage in George's favour was the fact that he was a married man and was not going to be prey to the "distractions" of a campus bachelor. Strangely enough in those immediate post-war years, there were many married scholars tackling their long delayed studies with a new urgency in colleges throughout the country, especially among the war veterans who outnumbered the younger students.

Being married, jobs were more important than the idle happy-go-lucky life of a bachelor student. The scarce housing situation didn't help either, but between them Barbara and George accomplished all they set out to do. Yale for George had all the pressures of fierce competition which raised the standards required to pretty demanding levels so the Phi Beta Kappa he received was no mean achievement in the circumstances. Yet, all his studies did not deter him from success in the sports field. He made the Varsity Baseball Team three seasons running. In fact, his team almost went all the way to become National Champions losing to the University of Southern California in the finals of the National Collegiate Athletic Association. Rumours abound that he even came under the scrutiny of Major League Scouts who came close to making him an offer.

One of Bush's fellow students, later Senator for Rhode Island, John H. Chafee, claimed that the Yale team George played on was no ordinary one. "It was a terrific outfit," he said. To prove this, five of that team went on to play with Major League clubs. Life at Yale saw George Bush working for many charities, especially the United Negro College Fund, an organization he was glad to support when he left Yale.

One comment described him as a "Golden Boy", not in a smarmy way, but mainly because everything he did he did well and furthermore everyone knew him. He even made it to the famous Skull and Bones Club, one feature of which is a clubhouse without windows. Some people described it as similar to the Alcoholics Anonymous Organization where each man reveals something of his inner self to his colleagues. As a result, the members develop into an intimate group or family to one another. The symbol of the club is meant to reflect the fact that everyone dies and life is too limited to neglect using ones talents for the benefit of others. The name of the headquarters is actually called "The Tomb".

In later years, the members are a great support to one another in triumph and failure. One cannot help comparing this club to the Free Masons who are also a secret society that thrives on inner rituals. I cannot help being reminded of the sort of antics my own fun loving grandson gets up to in the secret world only a small boy can inhabit. But life went on, and after leaving college George was looking around for opportunities to cut his teeth in the business world. He was offered a job in Dresser Industries in which his father Prescott was a senior director. It was a job at the very base of the pyramid as a Yale graduate but this didn't bother George Bush. He was excited enough about the prospect of, "cutting it on his own", free of school ties and bloodlines in the East.

Beginning as an ordinary labourer in the brand new petro-chemical industry was to him an ideal opportunity in a world soon to be dependent on oil. Texas he presumed was also destined to be like a new California Gold Rush. This time Black Gold. He headed for Odessa in Texas, taking Barbara and George Walker Bush Junior with him and little did he know he would not be back for twenty years. Incidentally little George Walker Bush was destined to become America's 43rd President in the year 2001.

George's duties were varied and sometimes not very glamorous. As equipment clerk he was called on to clean and paint the machinery which he carried out with all the dedication of a typical military man. The house the Bushes lived in was, as George put it, a typical crude "shot you house" because it resembled a box a shotgun was delivered in. Just bare boards crudely nailed together without insulation. It was partitioned into two sections, on the other side of which lived a family of hookers with quite a noisy boisterous clientele who shared the house's only bathroom. Still a mutually observed social demarcation line was kept and everyone was happy.

Since his total cash assets amounted to no more than $3,000, times were frugal rather than tough for all three of them. However, he does remember being made bartender at the firm's Christmas party and being encouraged to drink an odd one with the customers. Never one for more than a couple of drinks you can understand the unknown territory he allowed himself into that night. He was late home and instead of trimming the Christmas tree, he just fell asleep.

He was delivered to Barbara off the back of a pick-up truck. George is skeptical about the veracity of the story as told by Barbara, but he ruefully admits he still cannot remember the details.

Salesman was to be his next assignment in his new base in California. It's astounding to learn George and Barbara managed to live in twenty-eight houses in seventeen cities before he arrived in the White House. I guess a fellow can't gain experience by sitting at home twirling his thumbs. His stint as salesman covered one thousand miles per week on his rounds. They seemed to like his "nothing is impossible attitude" for he soon found himself promoted. Two and a half years later he took the plunge and went out on his own. He was a little apprehensive about this because his father and his main man, Neil Mallon, had done much for him. Would they think he was ungrateful, even treacherous to them? But he needn't have worried and Neil Mallon, his boss, even showed him how to set up an oil company of his own.

Bush was so glad of this help he named one of his children after him – Neil Mallon Bush. The new firm was called Bush-Overbey Oil Development Co. Inc. Now he had crossed the Rubicon from the security of a senior executive to the lonely road of the entrepreneur. To add to the pressure George now had four children. Perhaps his genes had the businessman's instinct imprinted on them, passed on by his great, great, grandfather, James Smith Bush, who had himself left a secure job as a storekeeper to tackle out the California Gold Rush.

His new base in Midland Texas was full of hungry prospectors from out of State. Most of them were graduates from Yale and Princeton, fresh from University and rearing for fun. They socialized together, increased their families together and talked oil, oil, oil together. They also played the stock market in oil, armed with information about potential finds not yet advertised. Somebody described it as a pretty raw, rough and ready frontier town similar to the old West. As George put it – "We weren't saints but we lived by standards." George and Barbara even began to take a lively interest in the local community for better hospitals, schools, music and such areas that challenged the slumbering political instincts in George. Little did he know he was already starting his political journey. He even took an interest in the Y.M.C.A., the church, the theatre and the prospects of the local children. Baseball of course was a fascinating subject for the kids, especially with George's background, his baseball skills and his anecdotes to entertain them.

The problems of oil speculation in those days were no different from today. Geologically suitable land, royalty rights and finance played a major part in the mix but one of his chief assets was his family connections. His uncle, Herbert Walker, invested half a million dollars in the firm. The two names of Prescott Bush and Herbert Walker rang some very harmonious bells for him. That aristocratic background paid dividends in the oil business for him.

But all this time, George Bush had one ambition, to become a politician, backed by the security of independent means. This he achieved so there was no need to concentrate further on his oil business. He was a millionaire at forty-one years of age.

George Bush entered politics in 1953 being sworn into office by Jack Kennedy. He sought to rein in Senator Joe McCarthy's purge against Communists and became a great buddy of Eisenhower albeit on the golf course, but at least he was moving in the right circles. The final piece of George's political jigsaw fell into place in 1954 when his firm, called Zapata, struck the black gold jackpot finally, giving him the financial security he needed to enter politics.

George Bush found himself sharing life with Dwight D. Eisenhower in 1952 and 1956. Not on the golf course this time but helping Ike in his two Presidential campaigns. Here, you may be interested in a small anecdote about oil and U.S. politics. His father, Prescott Bush, opposed the oil lobby in the Senate when it was pushing for deregulation of their industry. For the first time George came up against the powerbrokers behind the scenes when they threatened to ruin him if he didn't change his father's mind about opposing the Bill for deregulation.

A Sid Richardson reputed to be the richest man in the world called him at two in the morning threatening to destroy his business if his father voted against the Bill. But once again Bush's family contacts moved like a juggernaut to crush the threat to George Bush. The outcome was an apology from Richardson and George heard nothing more from this lobbyist again. There was a happy ending for democracy in all this, for Eisenhower was so irritated by the behaviour of the oil Corporations, he just vetoed the Bill and condemned the lobbyists for low moral standards.

However, it had been an eye-opening experience for George and what politics was all about but it didn't dampen his enthusiasm to persevere in his career as a Texas politician.

Working in Texas, George had to cope with one major prejudice. In the eyes of all Texans, being called a Texan was something that had to be earned and the Yale polish of Bush didn't help. It would have been so much easier for him had he based himself in say Massachusetts a location much more like his own patch. However, the complement to be accepted as a Texan was something he would have to wait for from the natives who lived there all their lives. But he had earned the right to be their politician as a "Mr. Clean". He was not a gregarious man and having been used to having the mantle of approval placed around his neck, now he had to hustle for that mantle. Yes, it would have been so much easier back home or simply becoming a Democrat who were the preferred Party down South ever since Reconstruction one hundred years ago. But George Bush ploughed on making speeches everywhere and the faithful Barbara was never very far away, even while enduring one hundred and fifty renditions of the same speech.

Although George Bush was a millionaire before he was forty-one, when he sold his share in Zapata Offshore for $1.1 million dollars he lost $400,000 on the deal. He could have made that much more had he sold the employees with the firm. But George insisted on a clause that ensured the buyer retained all his staff in Zapata. In fact, as he remarked to Barbara "I could have made seven million dollars if I'd held onto that stock." Getting out of Zapata was a final break with the business world to leave him free of any constraints on his political career connecting him with oil. He could now concentrate fulltime on politics.

In 1966, with the help of Richard Nixon, George's confidence in this move to a new career was fully justified when he was elected to the House of Representatives. He had now entered the major league in American politics for the first time.

George worked with an urgent purpose to establish the Republican Party in a Democratic stronghold. The Party grew larger and richer and his reputation grew. Jugular politics was not Bush's style and there was no rancour or personal criticism of him from friend or foe. Even in business he always maintained when competition becomes cut-throat everyone suffers. What a different world it was for George Bush when compared to Ronald Reagan. Despite all his illustrious connections George Bush found it a hard dour struggle to establish himself Reagan by comparison seemed to float in a glamorous style of living floating on a pink cloud of life surrounded by rich, exciting and famous film stars. Such are the contrasts of lifestyles politics. In politics the climb to the top can sometimes feel downright unfair.

George Bush I'm afraid paid a painful price for the intensity his goals inflicted on him – bleeding ulcers and heartburn. Changing his diet helped but some people were worried that his new lifestyle would even challenge the digestion of a garbage grinder. Well that's what they were saying on his entourage. But now he was coming to the notice of Party leaders who fancied him for a seat in the Senate. However George was still a raw greenhorn in the business and his Yale polish couldn't be ignored. What's more he was still an ex-Easterner. Although he lost his first election against Ralph Yarborough, he still polled 43% which made him the biggest Republican vote-getter in Texan's history.

So what was he doing wrong? Perhaps honesty of expression didn't help him when making speeches but in retrospect he never regretted this tendency. He told it as he saw it.

George Bush could be controversial as he proved when he risked the jeers of angry constituents by making what they considered an outrageous statement. Today, nobody would even question it. He said when talking about LBJ's Housing Act that he didn't see why a black soldier coming home from fighting for America in Vietnam should be barred from owning a decent home. So appalled were his listeners he found himself and his family spitefully expelled from his local Country Club. I seem to recall another President, Jimmy Carter, although a Southerner, getting the same treatment at the hustings down South. Yes, it can be a very painful experience to see things which are a generation behind the current way of thinking.

The Bush household was a very important factor in George's life and Barbara's contribution was paramount to a happy home life for the children. The ghost of Robin was never very far away, especially at night time prayers. Dad George tucked Doro, the youngest up and discussed Robin and both of them would have a little cry. We'll be talking about Barbara later and we will mention Robin and the impact her death from leukemia would have on the family. Meanwhile let's talk about the house. There was always a sense of chaos about the place Marvin recalls. It was the focal point for all the kids in the neighbourhood in which there always seemed to be ten or fifteen people at any one time there.

Both parents seemed to bask in the knowledge that, yes indeed, theirs was a mad house. But nevertheless a house of warmth and love that cascaded over everyone. The worst offence was to ridicule, pick on another or poke fun at them. Jeb published a local neighbourhood newspaper similar to Mrs. Franklin D. Roosevelt who was responsible for her own small effort in a little column she called "My Day" in the 1930s. It was a buzzing, thriving house of activity covering business, politics, charity, church, school and local affairs and Barbara was its manager extraordinaire.

Becoming a Congressman meant a demand on all the family. Everyone down to the dogs had to pull up roots and move to Washington. George's sacrifices were theirs. They left friends, schools, surroundings, pals and daily familiar routines in age groups that were really difficult for young George (19), Jeb (11), Noel (10), Marvin (9) and Doro (6). Barbara found a suitable house by telephone at Hillbrook Lane and as usual her handling of the exodus eastwards was carried out with the expert touch of a professional organizer. New friends, new schools, new tasks and a colder climate were the challenges. But new friends were soon part of the family circle and George Herbert Bush was duly sworn into Congress as part of the forty-seven new freshmen Republicans in January 1967. The resilience of the Bush family was truly amazing.

A new cycle of life had started for the Bush family. George Bush's lighthearted personality was noticed and appreciated by Mrs. Zamaria, who was the manager of his office in Washington.

Although he had only two terms as a Congressman she remembers him well. He was courteous and grateful for work done and was always upbeat. Although, despite his new responsibilities he still managed to return every weekend to his Texas constituents. Once again however, the magic Bush connections were working overtime, landing him the job of a coveted seat on the Ways and Means Committee.

This influential person I refer to was none other than his ever faithful father, Prescott, who made the key phone call. George was the first new Congressman to achieve that honour since 1900. But the phone calls that were more important to him were those from his children and he left orders nothing was to stand in the way of these V.I.P. phone calls no matter where he was. Whenever they were due to go anywhere together, Barbara usually arrived with bags packed, foot tapping and George usually arrived with less than half an hour to flight time and say "Right, let's go." The children thought that that was the reason their Mom's hair turned white so prematurely.

One little anecdote about George's hairline deadlines at airports is told by Marvin. Heading home to Houston for Christmas, George arrived at the airport with three minutes to spare and button-holed a startled baggage attendant. Handing him the car keys George said "I don't know you from Adam, but I trust you. Please do me a favour and park my car for me. I'll take care of everything when I get back after Christmas – I'm George Bush." "Who the heck's that?" the baggage man asked. "I'm the Congressman from Houston," said Bush. Everything worked out perfectly. The attendant was honest and efficient and the car keys were at the reception desk on George's return.

One thing is for certain, his office, no matter where he was, never closed to the children. They were never shut out, no matter how busy he was.

One golden rule of George Bush was never to take part in Washington's social rounds. Home entertainment was the only outings he offered visiting constituents no matter how important they were. And this it is easy to see, given our knowledge of the Bush household, could be a very tricky experience for a visitor. Nothing changed in the family routine. Kids ran everywhere, made noise and didn't have much time for formality. "Perhaps that's why they all still came home when they grew up," George loved to boast.
Bush learned four golden rules of behaviour in Congress from Gerry Ford and the Minority Whip, Mel Laird.

1.   Never get personal.
2.   Do your homework.
3.   Persuade, don't intimidate.
4.   Be considerate of your colleagues above or below your rank.

You may remember my telling you of George Bush on the hustings and how his outspoken opinions on blacks rubbed people the wrong way. As a result he found himself and his family ostracized from his own social club.

He was in trouble again with his constituents and this time it wasn't an opinion he aired but the vote he made in Congress. The subject was the same, the Fair Housing Act, which aimed to stop the prohibition of a sale or renting or financing of a house on the basis of colour, religion, sex or national origin. At the hustings he asked the question "Why should a man be fit to fight for his country and not be entitled to a fair deal on housing."

But this time George had stirred up a real hornet's nest of opinions back home, mostly against himself and against the Act. Hate mail poured into his office but Bush didn't run away. He returned home to face the mob and the rally was a large one. But he didn't flinch – going out to the mike; he confronted them with devastating logic against anyone denying any American the right to live wherever he chose regardless of race or colour. To go against his own conscience in a vote, he said, would not serve his constituents only betray them. Open housing he admonished offered a ray of hope for blacks and Hispanics who were at that moment giving their lives for their country in Vietnam.

He finished with "Somehow it seems fundamental that a man should not have a door slammed in his face because he was a Negro or speaks with a Latin accent."

The speech could easily have been recorded back in 1861 when the Negro question was being hotly debated and people were preparing to go to war for their opinions.

But Bush was not speaking in a time warp. Times had moved on. He ended his speech to a deathly silence. Then, as if a log jam of understanding was crumbling, slowly very slowly there was a sprinkling of applause, that gathered its own momentum until the log jam of opposition collapsed and he was standing on the platform with a turbulent river of applause crashing over it as the audience rose to its feet to cheer the lone man looking down on them from the mike. Jeers had turned to heart-warming cheers and Bush went home in grateful triumph. He had stood alone up there, did it on his own, and triumphed with a deep sense of satisfaction.

Not long after this speech blacks from all over America were converging on Washington to mourn and protest about the death of Martin Luther King Junior.

In front of the Lincoln Memorial they pitched tents in what they called Resurrection City. After the rain that fell it turned to a quagmire. George Bush went to Resurrection City to meet with the black leaders in their poor people's campaign. He got a good press and perhaps that was why no Democrat opposed his re-election to a second term in Congress.

George Bush had a good relationship with LBJ and went to the airport to see him off at the end of LBJ's Presidency. The Presidency was not a happy one in those times of Vietnam and later Nixon, so a friend like Bush coming from the opposite side of the camp was truly welcomed all the more. Bush was the only Republican to see him off and the ex-President shook his hand and said "Thanks for coming." And LBJ really meant it.

Later George and Barbara were invited to LBJ's ranch and were treated to a madcap race around the dirt roads that bordered the Pedarnales River by LBJ. I don't know if Bush threatened LBJ with the same treatment in a speed boat at Kennebunkport, but no one has mentioned it.

Now the time had come even against the advice of his father to leave the Congress and try for the Senate in what he felt was a safer route to the White House. His connections with several States widened his mandate even more. Massachusetts where he was born, Connecticut his home county, Maine his summer resort, Virginia from his army days, and that old rascal Texas he had adopted over twenty years ago. But politics could not be played like a game and Bush lost first time around for the Senate seat.

Bush, now a lame duck Congressman, was saved by Nixon who appointed him Ambassador to the United Nations despite his lack of experience in foreign relations. All those magical connections were still at work for him.

But George's inexperience began to make waves. Adlai Stevenson made an amazing attack on George Bush when Nixon appointed him Ambassador to the United Nations. He said it was an insult that such an inexperienced man should be given such a post. Little did he know that this unknown "small time" selection by Nixon would one day be good enough to be President of the United States. Obviously Nixon could see promising material in George Bush that others hadn't seen.

Maybe Bush's illustrious family contacts had worked the oracle; maybe he had proved his talent in a world where talent was in abundance. I don't know. But in writing these stories and anecdotes going back through forty other presidents, it is amazing how fate seemed to play a major role in the selection of the most unlikely people for high office. Bush was a real winner in everything he touched. Yet he was not pushy. He didn't seem to plot or plan his promotions. I've seen this happen to other Presidents who stood in obscurity unnoticed without fanfare, then as if an unseen deity was re-arranging the chairs in the Cabinet room, the unknown then stepped out of the shadows onto the stage of history; dark horses like Franklin D. Roosevelt, Franklin Pierce, Abraham Lincoln, Howard Taft, Herbert Hoover, Harry Truman, Millard Fillmore, and Jimmy Carter. Smoke-filled rooms in top hotels and compromise candidates come to mind; Vice Presidents chosen as puppets who were never going to be puppets. Yes, the Presidency has its own amazing method of selection outside the power of ordinary men. Most significant of all, the chosen one so far has never failed to be the right one. That to your writer is the magic of the Presidency.
But the dark days of Nixon's Presidency was a serious worry for the Republicans. George Bush had still a little way to go along that road that fate had chosen for him. That torturous road had many pot-holes to be negotiated. The most dangerous and complicated ones were waiting ahead in the dark days of Watergate. The Party and the President are two different entities he said and promptly set about salvaging the good name of the Party itself, despite every effort by those embroiled to save their own skins. He travelled 124,000 miles, gave 118 speeches and 84 conferences around the country to hammer home the message that the time had come for all good Republicans to stand by the Party. He kept the Party flag flying during those darkest of days. Eventually he chose to confront Nixon himself.

The most famous of his decisions was written in a letter to Richard Nixon. "Dear Mr. President, It is my considered judgement that you should now resign. I believe this view is now held by most Republican leaders across the country. This letter is much more difficult because of the gratitude I will always feel towards you ..."

This last sentiment was really heartfelt for Nixon had been responsible for Bush's progress in Government so far. The outcome for Nixon was inevitable and Gerry Ford, his Vice President, eventually took over. Now the hustling for the new Vice President's job was in progress. Ford decided to compile a list of probables which he circulated throughout the country. The votes came in – 255 for Bush, 181 for Rockefeller, the rest were nowhere. But Ford chose Rockefeller as the better known name, most acceptable to the country in a Party shorn of credibility. Bush took yet another defeat in his stride although it looked like his political career had reached a watershed. The only way he could go now was down or so he thought. But those Presidential Gods of fate had still got plenty to say about George Bush. As we are about to find out.

Ford offered him Ambassadorships to London or Paris to compensate for his disappointment. But Bush never did do the obvious and opted for China instead.

By the time he was appointed Mao Tse-tung had already ruthlessly purged China, annihilating millions and the Cultural Revolution had already taken place. He was now involved in diplomacy to stimulate world trade for China.

The star of the show in the diplomatic world, however, was not George Bush but Henry Kissinger, who breezed into China inundated with security guards, was welcomed by beaming Chinese VIPs and whisked off again leaving George standing aimlessly when he was gone. Kissinger really enjoyed the role of Chief Healer Dealer on his world missions and Bush had to admit he was brilliant at his job. He certainly impressed the Chinese.

But George impressed them too, only by a different route.

One story of George Bush is told of his time in China. He had only arrived in Beijing when he made a momentous decision – he would go everywhere by bicycle. So he got rid of his official Chrysler Sedan and chose to ride everywhere on his trusty bicycle. Of course the unfortunate Barbara went with him. But the Chinese loved it and commented with a grin "Busher who rides the bicycle just as Chinese do." Perhaps it was a bigger diplomatic triumph than any of Kissinger's spectaculars.

George Bush's stay in China didn't last long, but he had made a sufficient impression on Mao Tse-tung to be welcomed back any time he came to China. In December 1975 he was heading home to become Head of the C.I.A. He duly passed the screening process and returned to Washington to his old address and his old neighbours and friends. One thing had changed however. For the first time in his life he would not be able to discuss his job with Barbara. Gerry Ford felt the C.I.A. had been undermined by scandal and needed a safe pair of hands and George Bush was that safe pair of hands.

Talking about safe hands, Fitzhugh Green recounts an enjoyable anecdote about Dan Schorr the T.V. news pundit. It seems Schorr's car had slid into a snowdrift during a blizzard. His passenger looked at Schorr wondering what they would do next when a limousine pulled in behind them. "Let's get you out of this" came a voice through the window. It was George Bush, Director of the C.I.A. The car was duly pushed into action again. When his companion exclaimed "Isn't it a wonderful country where the Head of an important agency like the C.I.A. personally rescues you from a pile of snow." Schorr ever the newshound replied irreverently "I guess so but I wonder why the hell he was following us in the first place?"

Bush's stay at the C.I.A. lasted no more than a year when he was replaced by the incoming Democratic President Jimmy Carter in 1977, leaving George jobless for the first time since 1948.

Nothing very exciting happened to him for the next three years. He worked in various jobs, such as the International Bank in Houston and joined the International Bancshares Corporation at Director level, but he was always the politician waiting to return to the fold. I won't clutter up the story of Bush with banalities at this stage but when the 1980 Presidential Election came along he found himself alongside Ronald Reagan as his running mate. As history now records, he was destined to become Vice President for the next eight years. Only once in that time did he come near to promotion and that was the time he sat at Cabinet as a substitute for the almost assassinated President Reagan, still being treated in hospital for his wounds.

Being Vice President did not change him and there were many stories to prove this. Whereas his father Prescott was a little aloof towards the local tradesmen in Kennebunkport, George knew and talked to everyone. One story describes his efforts to get in touch with one of the locals who had lost her husband. Bush despite the high level meeting he was attending persevered and finally got through to her at midnight to offer his condolences.

Walking over a bridge in town he was tooted by a local, given a quick wave by the driver who drove on. He goes to church with the rest of the townspeople whenever he is in Kennebunkport visiting. They don't see him as the Vice President, just George back on a visit to them.

But politics can be so much more critical and much more incisive about its heroes and what is expected of them. Despite George's vast international experience, here are some of the opinions so irrelevant today.

"Wimp, wasp, weenie, insubstantial. Never gets anything done. Been everywhere but left no footprints. Done nothing for eight years; Boring. Doesn't relate to people, especially women. Unelectable".
But George Bush did prove electable, despite his running mate, Dan Quayle. The observation about Quayle was that of a ship which had struck an iceberg. The fear was that the iceberg Quayle would hole the ship below the waterline. Unfortunately, every attack on Quayle also undermined the chances of George Bush. Poor Quayle was treated as a gatecrasher to the Party by the press. His suspected womanizing, his scholastic record, his doubtful Vietnam draft avoidance record, were all exploited for headlines by the press.
During the hustings, George Bush's one gaffe came back to haunt him. His use of that unfortunate punch line "Watch my lips, no new taxes." But that is a story for later.

On November 8, 1988 George Bush was finally declared the winner of the Presidential Election in spite of Dan Quayle's presence on the ticket. He beat Michael Stanley Dukakis by 48,881,278 votes to 41, 805,374 votes.

On January 20, 1989 he was sworn into office on the West Front of the Capitol Building. He dispensed with the morning coat traditionally worn by a new President and wore a blue business suit instead. He took the oath of office from Chief Justice William Hubbs Rehnquist at 12.03 p.m. The mild weather was a pleasant change from the normal cold January day, though the sky was overcast. In his speech, he promised to pursue "A kinder gentler nation", then went to luncheon under a giant painting of George Washington in Statuary Hall, after which Barbara and himself rode up Pennsylvania Avenue together at the head of the inaugural parade. They both stopped the vehicle three times and continued to walk the route waving to the cheering crowds. The cost of the whole show was a record $25 million, for a festival that was the most lavish in the history of inaugurations. The number of inaugural Balls they attended, nine in all, was also a record for the occasion.

While the story of George Bush, the 41st President has now reached its climax and the journey of George Bush ended in the greatest prize American politics can bestow upon a citizen, let's spare a thought and a little time now for the woman who had walked that road with him in trials, troubles, tribulations and triumph, his good wife, Barbara Pierce Bush.

Barbara, the new First Lady, is famous for her forthright opinions on most subjects but only once allowed herself to get involved in matters of public policy. Her opposition to gun control and abortion is now well-known.

Becoming First Lady took her by surprise for although she had had eight years to play understudy to Nancy Reagan, promotion from Vice President to President was statistically against her husband. Not since Martin Van Buren in the 1830s had this occurred.

Speaking of Presidential history, Barbara Bush had her own Presidential pedigree. Her father, Marvin Pierce was related to the 14th President, Franklin Pierce. Her mother, Pauline Robinson Pierce was the daughter of a Supreme Court Justice and Barbara's father became President of the McCall Corporation in New York City, giving to his four children, including Barbara herself, a very privileged lifestyle.

But all this wealth and status could not ensure a trouble-free world for Barbara, for at three years old, their daughter Robin was diagnosed as having leukemia. It was a heartbreaking experience that lived with the Bush family for the rest of their lives. Robin only lived seven more months after receiving the best of medical attention. To Barbara, the family distress this caused was the most difficult time she ever knew. The evidence is still there today. Her beautiful raven black hair turned to a premature white within months of the tragedy.

Men sometimes have a pretty tough approach to personal crises. George Senior carried the after effects of the family tragedy deep in his heart but showed little patience with Barbara's depression. He could have indulged her gently but he knew this was not the way Barbara would respond and come out of it. He chose instead to say "Barbara, just get on with your life." This medicine worked and together they survived their trauma. Young George, aged seven, was of greater help than he knew at the time. She heard him telling a pal "My Mum is so unhappy." This little insight into his heart cheered her up enough to fight back for his sake. He eventually had his old "happy Mum" back again.

"Getting on with her life" as George Senior put it was aptly described by Barbara to an audience at the American University in 1985. She had three more additions after Robin died, two boys and a girl. Barbara told the audience "While George was out having an exciting time; I was sitting at home with these absolutely brilliant children who say one thing a week of interest." Their needs meant more work for her, going to football games, parent conferences, meetings with teachers and the odd trip to the emergency surgery at the local hospital. She described it as "A period of long days and short years of diapers, runny noses and earaches." Yet her neighbours were astounded to see how organized she could be for not only did she mow her own lawn but she found time to mow her neighbour's lawn when they were away on vacation.

Barbara and George Bush were once interviewed together by Reagan's official biographer. George was puzzled about Reagan "One thing kinda bothers me," said George. "The guy never seemed to need anybody" – "Except Nancy" interjected Barbara and continued "They went to Camp David every weekend and she never took the kids with them. We'd go crazy if we found ourselves up there without a whole bunch of the family running around," said Barbara passionately. Later in the conversation, George Bush complained that Reagan never seemed to want them upstairs in the White House. The sense of being isolated or shut out by both Reagan and Nancy during Reagan's Presidency seemed to have hurt them deeply. The happy-go-lucky extrovert nature of the Bush family just didn't gel with the celluloid world of the Reagan's.

I must add to this story a similar complaint from another Vice President Richard Nixon who revealed in his Frost interview how he felt snubbed by the Kennedys when he was Vice President. The 2nd President John Adams suffered from the same isolation.

But the days of diapers were soon over and Barbara Bush at fifty was ready to do something with the rest of her life. Volunteer work grabbed her attention and time for a while. Her dyslexic son made her realize the importance of literacy in a child's life, the lack of which she connected with a child's vulnerability towards drugs, homelessness and crime, so she worked at it. It was not a hobby with her but a fulltime commitment even after she arrived, living near the White House as wife of the Vice President to Reagan. Her charity work had honed her skills for the job of First Lady which she duly became in 1989, at sixty-three she was the oldest First Lady ever but was blessed with enormous energy. She was also complete in her own right.

Other First Ladies started in office learning new skills. Lady Bird Johnson focused on reducing her weight; Rosalyn Carter learned Spanish and Economics, Pat Nixon became a wardrobe fanatic. But Barbara was happy to be just the way she was. Cruel jokes were made about her white hair and being overweight, putting her down with jibes of being George's mother. But nothing fazed her and the public loved her. Of course, comparisons were made with Nancy Reagan. Barbara, never afraid of a joke at her own expense, liked to compare the size of her own thighs to Nancy Reagan's size 4 silhouette. When asked why she fancied a three stranded faux pearl choker, she laughed and told reporters with tongue-in-cheek "It covers some wrinkles." Yes, her irreverence was a real bonus as far as the public and press were concerned.

The AIDS virus and its consequences appalled her and she threw herself into this problem with gusto despite the fact that she herself had been struck down with a thyroid disorder which gave her two red itchy eyes and a frightening weight loss. By being photographed holding a baby with AIDS she helped to reduce the apprehension that AIDS was easily transmitted from human to human.

A lovely story emerges around the family dog which spent most of its time cavorting with famous people or with her grandchildren around the White House, Camp David, the Blue room or Kennebunkport. She wrote a book about it called Millie's book: As Dictated to Barbara Bush. In it she included hundreds of doggie photos. It was not a book meant to have classic pretensions but the proceeds from it earned almost $800,000 in 1991 which went to "The Barbara Bush Foundation Fund for Family Literacy". It was more than any other First Lady had earned while in office.

A slight lapse of style occurred when she departed from her code of silence on political matters by criticizing sarcastically a candidate for Vice President, Geraldine Ferraro. She spent so much time and trouble explaining herself she never allowed this carelessness to creep in again. Of course, she couldn't please everyone for the Feminist Movement wanted her to speak out on various issues. It was precisely because she had outspoken views in private that she was urged to air them. It's a pity her role in the White House prevented her from doing this or we would have had some very interesting debates to discuss here on many controversial subjects, such as gun control and abortion. And why not? A change of style in the Presidency might have been a very healthy development.

Soon the time had come for Barbara Bush to leave the White House in early 1993. Of the other three First Ladies before her, only one, Nancy Reagan, had acquired a college degree. Yet all four of these modern first Ladies, Lady Bird Johnson, Pat Nixon, Rosalyn Carter and Barbara Bush played an essential partnership role with their husbands in the White House. Most of their work was completely undocumented but influential nevertheless.

It was left to the new generation of women to be different. But while this narrative is about George Bush, let's say Barbara Bush, his wife, has filled the post of First Lady with her own distinctive personality. Today in 2005, she still hasn't changed. At present she is in India at eighty-two years of age pursuing another of her all consuming projects so dear to her heart. Her dedication and energy are truly remarkable.

One of the first problems George Bush had to face into as President was the economic consequences of peace. Although the end of the Cold War was set in motion by those two world-famous Statesmen, Reagan and Gorbachev, the final disintegration of Communism took place on George Bush's watch as President of the United States.

It didn't come about in a constructive planned extension of the disarmament talks in Moscow, New York, Reykjavik and Washington. On November 11, 1989 souvenir hunters and those with the pent-up anger of the caged in East Germany celebrated their new found freedom with sledgehammers and chisels. The Berlin Wall, without any prior signal of history about to take place, was suddenly inundated by thousands of busy people. The checkpoints couldn't suppress the flow of 10,000 people who appeared from nowhere.

Just as the Americans of 1776 claimed their freedom from their British oppressors, in 1989 tens of millions claimed their own countries back all across Europe. The Red Army, now impotent by political changes in the corridors of power, just looked on in silence. Poland claimed freedom for Solidarity, Hungary renounced Communism forever. Bulgaria, Czechoslovakia, Romania and the Baltic States followed. The rest of that painfully constructed machine of evil, going back to Lenin and the Bolsheviks in the 20s, just fell apart. It was truly an event of unbelievable historic importance. Millions just cried tears at the first taste of their new found freedom.

But George Bush knew this wasn't the time to gloat. America, the land of the free, was so busy looking over their neighbour's garden wall, shaking her head with contempt; she failed to notice her own shocking failures. Let's look at the picture Harold Evans described in his incomparable book The American Century. He wrote "When the Berlin Wall collapsed; back in America the top 1% of Americans owned more wealth than the lower 90%. Forty million people had no healthcare. The poor were the greatest victims of crime. There were more beggars in the U.S. than in Europe and Japan. Special interests enjoyed enormous favours from those in power." Yes, the speed of reform within the country badly needed a new momentum. Evil had many guises that didn't need guns and bullets to sustain it in the land of the free. "Capitalism had defeated Communism". But as Harold Evans put it – "Could it triumph over its own contradictions?"

George Bush, just like Jimmy Carter some years before, had inherited a looming recession. For years heavy military spending had kept the ship of State afloat, masking a lack of true economic activity in the global economy.

The sudden cutback in defence spending against the surging economic performance in Germany and Japan spelt trouble. The average pay cheque brought home deteriorated from $454 in 1988 when Bush came to power to $440 in 1992. It had people looking to the Democrats for escape from twelve years of Republican Rule. But despite these setbacks the attraction of what Poet Emma Lazarus called "The Golden Door" reflected the limitless possibilities of America.

After the fall of the Berlin Wall, two further events came to fruition in Bush's Presidency, catching him by surprise. One raised his popularity ratings to euphoric heights at 89%. The other sowed the seeds of his own destruction at the polls of the next Presidential election.

Let's deal with the good news first. Trouble in the Persian Gulf had been simmering for some time now and that political maverick of Iraq, Saddam Hussein, was deeply implicated. On August 2, 1990, Saddam played the Emperor straight out of an Arabian Nights fantasy by marching into the Persian Gulf Emirate of Kuwait at the head of his glorious army. World War II may as well have not taken place. No lessons had been learned in the Middle East. The U.S. President, George Bush, had to resort to urgent breakneck diplomacy by phone. Nothing happened; Saddam was implacable and ruthlessly reckless.

But Bush's leadership qualities from his army training his worldwide political experience and his contacts in China, Russia and the United Nations came into play. The stakes were high. Twenty per cent of the world oil supplies were in danger. President Bush called the invasion of Kuwait "A naked act of aggression" and said "This will not stand." The United Nations Security Council responded with a series of resolutions, ending with a threat to use force if necessary. A coalition of troops was built from many nations including Egypt, Saudi Arabia, Syria, the United Arab Emirates, Britain, France, Italy, Spain and Canada. Japan and Germany only made financial contributions. Even the Soviet Union came on board, the first time Cold War enemies were on the same side since World War II. China agreed not to interfere.

"Operation Desert Shield" was launched after the debate to delay the invasion had been defeated. Economic sanctions were just not working. On January 12, 1991, Congress and the Senate agreed on the use of military force and sometimes in the dark night of January 16, 1991, the counter-invasion started. A Massive round the clock bombardment was launched lasting six weeks. Bush's ratings reached the highest point of his whole career just then. "No Fly Zones" north and south were introduced to protect the Kurds and Shiites from Saddam's revenge. But Saddam was still being provocative two years later and Bush had to send in further planes in his final week as President. Today one question remains unanswered. Would history have been different if General Schwarzkopf, the American Commander in Iraq, had been allowed to pursue the Iraqi Army into Baghdad as he wanted to? But his political bosses, refused just like McArthur was refused in North Vietnam in the 1950s.

Well, so much for George Bush's good news. Now for the bad news. Reagan had left him with a $3.2 trillion Federal debt which was increasing annually at $220 billion per year. The recession which accompanied this state of affairs was developing before Saddam took centre stage and it lasted right through George Bush's Presidential campaign for a second term. Bush was in despair. How could America be a leader in world affairs on a foundation of debt which was three times bigger than 1980? Tax increases were becoming increasingly more inevitable although a severe cut in Federal spending was also a solution.

But then came the crisis that proved to be "the straw that broke the camel's back" – "The American Thrift Industry" had been allowed to fall $166 billion in debt because of lax Federal controls during the Reagan years, giving banks a carte blanche to invest depositors' money recklessly in stocks and shares and estate deals. Bush had to bail them out and most of the money to bail them out came from the taxpayer. To remedy the situation Bush had to sign an order, raising taxes. Here you may remember the scene I told you about in 198 when George Bush made that outrageous promise during his Presidential campaign "Read my lips – no new taxes," which he said recklessly.

During the elections of 1992, Big Bill Clinton, his Democratic opponent, was too wily to miss such a golden political opportunity. He reminded Bush of his broken pledge and added a mantra of his own – "It's the economy stupid." George ruefully said later "If I had to do it all over again I wouldn't do it." But taxes had to go up and the damage was done electorally. If only he knew what lay ahead. His economic troubles inherited from Reagan's regime were to deteriorate exponentially leading to a possible global meltdown two Presidencies away in 2009. The golden suntanned years of Reagan it seems were paid for by trillions of debt now coming home to roost. But to be fair we can't blame Reagan alone. The culprits were the same unpatriotic "get rich quick gang of speculation" who almost ruined America in 2009.

Let's finish on two opinions which reveal George Bush as the brilliant politician and George Bush the man.

On January 3, 1993, George paid a visit to Moscow for the signing of the Nuclear Arms Reduction Treaty. Boris Yeltsin, the controversial President of Russia, who had braved the tanks in the streets of Moscow to persuade the Russian army to stand by the Government, now stood not on a tank but on the platform after the signing ceremony. With George Bush by his side, he addressed the world over the mike and on television.

The praise he heaped on the U.S. President standing there beside him was almost embarrassing. He said of George: "His remarkable personal and political qualities and competence have contributed to a successful transition from the Cold War to a new world order."

Some praise indeed for George Bush. Wonderful words but words don't win elections. Sadly for a man of such talent, four years is all he was allowed as leader of the free world.
However, the second opinion coming from Atlanta Mayor, Andrew Young is the George Bush I have come to know in writing this. He said "I've felt if there is one thing you could count on it was George Bush for his decency and fairness." And we can't finish the George Bush story on a happier note than that.

42nd President   William Jefferson Clinton

"Bill"
Born: 1946
Jan 1993 – 2001
2 Terms
Age 55

Party: Democratic
Profession: Law Professor
County: Arkansas
Ancestry: English
Estate: Unknown
Hobbies: Golf, Jogging, Saxophone, Touch Football

Physical Description: 6 foot 2 inches, 230 pounds, sandy greying hair, blue eyes, square jawed.

Significant extracts from his inauguration speech Wednesday 21, January 1993.
"There is nothing wrong with America that can't be cured by what is right with America…. To renew America we must be bold. To renew America we must meet challenges abroad as well as at home. There is no longer division between what is foreign and what is domestic – the world economy, the world environment, the world AIDS crisis, the world arms race – they affect us all."

BILL CLINTON

The stranglehold the Republicans had held on the Presidency for the previous twelve years was at last broken by Bill Clinton the third youngest President ever to be elected since John Fitzgerald Kennedy. In 1996 he went on to be elected to a second term by defeating Republican candidate Robert Dole.

However Clinton had a major job ahead in 1993 with an economy that had been in economic distress for almost the full term of George Bush's Presidency. In fact the major plank of Clinton's election manifesto had hammered home the crisis in economic management by his predecessor George Bush. While this is not to denigrate the record of a President with an admirable record on the world stage, a man who had received the plaudits of world leaders from Mao Tse-tung to Boris Yeltsin, the country's national debt had become an albatross around his neck.

Sadly George Bush paid the price for this with his job. Now it was left to Bill Clinton to rectify the situation. While gloating on election platforms may be good for political posturing, the time had now come for Bill Clinton to convert oratory into action in the school of hard-knocks in the U.S. Congress.

The story of Bill Clinton's life has a very traumatic and tearful beginning. Bill was born during a violent summer storm on August 19, 1946 and was the only child of Virginia Cassidy Blythe and her husband William Jefferson Blythe III, the son of a poor farmer who had died in a car accident three months earlier on May 17, 1946.

Clinton's mother first met his father in the emergency ward of Tri-State hospital in 1943 where she was training as a nurse – anaesthetist. Two months after they met they married. However it seems their love affair was never to blossom for the war intervened and Bill Blythe was called up to fight in Europe.

It is a story that brings a little tear to the eye for a love affair that never really got started. Bill's father spent the war in the invasion of Italy repairing jeeps and tanks with the skills he had. He duly returned to Hope where they lived. After a while both of Bill Clinton's parents headed for Chicago to make a new start.

Life was wonderful as he arranged to get his old job back as a salesman with the Manbee Equipment Company. They bought a little house in Chicago which needed attention before they could move in. Being pregnant Virginia returned to her parent's home in Hope until the house was ready. Soon the day arrived to move in and the furniture was installed. Then tragedy struck, for while driving back home to collect Virginia to start a new life, Bill Blythe's car had a blow out. His car went out of control with a burst tyre and he was thrown clear of the debris but this proved fatal.

The car ended up in a ditch but Bill was thrown into three feet of water and drowned there at the roadside. It was a freak bizarre accident that defied explanation. At twenty-eight years he died by an American roadside when he had survived all off the war in Italy. Dying at the roadside on Highway 60 was a horrendous end that robbed the world of a beautiful love affair with a glorious future. Sadly William Jefferson Blythe would never know that the baby in Virginia's womb was destined to become the 42nd President of the United States. The baby was born three months later on that stormy summer evening of August 14, 1946.

Bill Clinton has always had a special place in his heart for this father he never knew and for all of his life he has tried to fill in the gaps in his knowledge with hearsay and anecdotes, old photos or even scraps of paper he came across.

Some of the information, that has since been unearthed by investigative articles, he could have done without, and were hard to believe. It was the first Bill and his mother knew of his father's life before they married. It seems his father had probably been married three times and had at least two more children. Later Bill met his own half-brother Leon Ritzenthaler and his wife. Leon looked a lot like Bill and they still keep in touch occasionally. A half-sister also surfaced from a marriage that ended in divorce. Her name was Sharon Lee Blythe of Kansas City but so far she has never met with Bill. To his mother's credit although all this news came to light when she was battling with cancer she was still true to the love affair that had ended in tragedy in 1946.

Bill could see she still loved him and she was convinced that he also loved her at the time. That is all we need to know about that part of Bill's life because his mother would always cherish happy memories of William Jefferson Blythe III and that's how it should be.

One anecdote is told of Bill Clinton's father by a man who met him during the war in Italy. He was Umberto Baron of Netcong, New Jersey and he had met Bill Blythe when he was a young boy visiting the army camp in Italy where he loved to go. Bill Blythe used to encourage the little Italian boy telling him how to repair engines. Baron duly came to the United States and started up his own garage business. It wasn't until Memorial Day 1993 when thumbing through The New York Daily News that he realized his pal Bill who had befriended him in those army days in Italy and called him "Little G I Joe" was none other than the father of the President of the United States. Yes there in the corner of one of the pages was his friend of many years ago. "It was like being struck by lightening," he said. It seems Bill Blythe; Clinton's dad was a real sound bloke.

Bill Clinton's mother left him her wedding ring and the inspiration to live life to bring credit to two people, his mother and the father he never knew.

But life for Bill and his mother took different paths in 1946. Bill grew up in his parent's house which is now known as the Clinton birthplace and has now been filled by the townspeople of Hope full of old memorabilia and pictures.

It was heartbreak for her when she had to return to her hospital work as an anaesthetist in New Orleans Charity Hospital. He remained behind under the loving care of his grandparents. On a visit he made to New Orleans, Bill remembers waving goodbye to his mother as she literally knelt by the railway tracks as the train brought him back home and away from her, leaving her crying there on her knees. A very poignant picture full of meaning for both of them.

But Bill Clinton has many other happier memories of New Orleans in later years which he cherishes with fond affection. Memories of meals, music, jazz music and an old friend, Al Hirt, the great trumpeter who gave him a free seat at his Jazz show when no tickets were available for a little boy and his mother. Both of them sat at a table in front of the stage. What a memory for a little boy.

Bill's memories of his grandparents are happy ones. His grandma was a fiery tempered woman who dished it out to her poor husband and Bill's mother.

She seemed to be a frustrated woman tinged with anger. Yet she was always kind to Billy, as Bill was called, making him live by her own golden rules for him, to eat a lot, learn a lot, and stay clean.

His grandfather was Bill's favourite, a man he idolized. He was known as the most generous man in Hope. The local kids remembered him for the 25 cents they received for helping him on his ice delivery round. One lovely anecdote is about one of them who became a Judge later and who told Bill Clinton about it. It seems he asked for five dimes and a nickel to feel he had more money. Unfortunately on his way home he lost one of the dimes and spent hours looking for it. The Judge laughs when he recalls that whenever he passes the spot today he still has a glance at the spot hoping to find the missing dime. And how Bill loved his visit to the Sawmill in which his grandpa was night watchman. He remembers the sandwiches, the sawdust piles and sleeping in the back seat of his grandpa's car. It was in those days he learned the generosity of these two wonderful people towards black people and the kindness his grandpa showed towards them. They hadn't got a racialist bone in their bodies.

But stories can be like pictures of many shades and colours and the story of Bill's mother had all of these.
She came home from New Orleans overjoyed at having her son Bill with her again. It was around that time she met Roger Clinton, a hard-drinking, good-looking, twice divorced hell-raiser from Hot Springs Arkansas. He was generous and kind to her and to little Billy but Billy's grandmother astute and more worldly than his mother was not fooled by Roger. In fact she disliked Roger Clinton intensely. Anyway they got married, his mother and Roger in June 1950. She was twenty-seven years old when they moved into 321 Thirteenth Street.
Roger Clinton did his best to be a good father but although he carried out his role on occasions, his outings with his new son were few and far between. Binge drinking unfortunately came high on his list of priorities. The verbal abuse and violence Bill's mother endured didn't help young Billy's confidence. But one day his father pulled a gun on Bill's mother in a family row and ended up in the local jail. He came out a very contrite man but life went on for Bill Clinton.

Roger bought a farm where the family lived for a while but returned to Hot Springs at 1011 Lark Avenue. It was a huge house and Bill helped maintain the shrubbery and trees surrounding it. The town of Hot Springs attracted some colourful characters at that time such as William Jennings Bryan, Teddy Roosevelt, Herbert Hoover, Franklin and Eleanor Roosevelt, JFK, Lyndon Johnson and Harry Truman. There was also a fair sprinkling of the notorious including outlaw's, mobsters and that famous pool shark Minnesota Fats. Gambling was still illegal and it became a Mecca for the top professionals. But Roger Clinton's alcoholism got worse. One night it started again. The bedroom door was closed. The screaming and abuse frightened little Roger aged four. Bill was now fourteen. The year his father pulled a gun came to mind and Bill grabbed a golf club threw open the door to see his drunken father standing over his mother lying on the ground.

He was beating her. Bill quietly warned him if he didn't stop he would beat the living daylights out of him. His father just fell apart. Again he was taken to jail but there was no more trouble after that. Yet Bill felt sorry for this father who was basically a good guy. Somehow Bill bottled up this anger he felt and tried to understand it in secret. He was living by the family motto "Don't ask, don't tell."

Living with an alcoholic is like living on some wide rolling acres of green countryside full of flowers and bird song. Alongside this picture black clouds of violence and the storm clouds of erratic alcoholism was frightening. Separating the monster from the good man was an ongoing challenge to everyone's patience and tolerance. But Bill tried only to remember the good times. However there came the day when the threats were no danger to the family as Bill got bigger and stronger than his father. Bill's mother could hold out no longer and filed for divorce. Remorse engulfed his father who lost a lot of weight in his desperation to get her back. He was a wreck. He didn't shave for three days. One day he approached Bill and begged for help. He had nothing else to live for.

He cried in the car they shared. Like any alcoholic he promised to reform and hoped he was believed. He had however made the fatal mistake of not admitting to himself he was helpless against drink. The family had a meeting to allow his father back. There were many doubts expressed but Bill's mother opted to take the risk. They remarried and when he became terminally ill they were all glad they had not turned him away forever. I know I have spent a good bit of time on Bill Clinton's boyhood years, as well as his mother and his two fathers and their tragic lives.

I also hope you are not getting too impatient with me at this stage but I honestly feel those years of his life and the people involved in them made a serious contribution to what kind of person the future Bill Clinton was going to be. What saved him from the turmoil of his alcoholic father were three remarkable people, his two grandparents and a unique loyal and loving American mum.

Now let's get on with the rest of his story. The details and the anecdotes I have extracted from several books about him, the major one being My Life, Bill Clinton a wonderful autobiography from which cascade some simple true to life and very moving stories he talks about. Stories I am glad to acknowledge and include in this book of Presidential anecdotes.
One of Bill Clinton's many talents is his love of music and his skill playing the saxophone. The music could be Classical Jazz, Big Band, Rock and Roll, Swing or Gospel. It didn't matter to a guy who had just discovered the key to Santa's treasure trove when he joined a dance band called "The Stardusters". He improved enough to be first chair in the All State Band.

He spent two more years playing in a jazz trio and even played in the Annual Band Variety show. He won medals at several State festivals for solos and ensembles. So whenever you see Bill Clinton on stage with a saxophone in his mouth you can be sure of one thing, he certainly knows what he is doing. He is no amateur in fact I would call him an old pro.

Bill Clinton was a strange mixture of certainty and doubt. This is reflected in an essay he wrote trying to capture the contradictory images of life that troubled and puzzled him. He wrote "I am a living paradox. Deeply religious yet not as convinced of my exact beliefs as I ought to be. Wanting responsibility yet shirking it. Loving the truth but oft times giving away to falsity." It was a brilliant essay which his teacher praised as a beautiful and honest attempt to go way down inside. His pursuit of honesty "getting to know himself" won him a grade of 100. It was the kind of confrontation most of us have attempted from time to time only to stay away from the painful conclusions Bill Clinton had the guts to admit to with the words "I detest selfishness but see it in the mirror everyday."

It is hard to believe today the kind of America Bill Clinton grew up in, yet the events that happened to him were only a few decades before he became President. Martin Luther King Junior's speech on August 28, 1963 when Clinton was only seventeen moved him literally to tears. In those times there was no Civil Rights Bill. No Voting Rights Act. And no Open Housing Law. Schools were still segregated on racial lines and the Poll Tax was manipulated to deny blacks the chance to vote. The word "Nigger" was everywhere, used or abused openly. The final sacrilege of this time in American history was the awful assassination of John Fitzgerald Kennedy in Dallas. So awful, can be summed up in the words of LBJ I have already quoted under my piece on Lyndon Johnson "All that I have I would have given gladly not to be standing here today...." These bitter words when he was just accepting the terrible fruits of this evil act by an unknown gunman. Even the Presidency of the United States didn't compensate him for the loss of a great President and an old friend.

In the summer of 1967 there were one hundred and sixty riots all over America. President Johnson's Commission on civil disorders came to the conclusion that these were the result of police racism and brutality and the absence of economic and educational opportunities for blacks.

The final summing up became famous to millions of Americans "Our nation is moving toward two societies, one black, one white – separate and unequal."

But another event was about to happen in Bill's life in the fall of 1967 when his father's illness degenerated and he was called home from college. Helping his father in these terrible last days created a bond both of them never achieved in earlier days. Roger even worried about the time Bill was losing from College. At one point near the end Bill's mother came into his room, filled up and told him she loved him and then burst into tears. This, after all he had put her through. Funny how his funeral took place in the rain. As Bill put it in his book "Daddy would stare out the window in a storm and say 'Don't bury me in the rain'." "Surely," Bill thought to himself "he deserved better." Funny too how the injustice of the rain never left their thoughts even as the hymns were being sung. Yet as the cortège moved towards the newly cut grave a miracle happened. The rain stopped. All the family could do was rejoice secretly with knowing smiles at each other.

Once again I refer to Bill's autobiography when he wrote "On his last journey to the end that awaits us all, he found a forgiving God. He was not buried in the rain."

The day of the Rhodes scholarship interviews soon arrived. Every year thirty-two American Rhodes scholars are chosen for two years to study at Oxford University. The cost is covered by the Trust established in 1903 by Cecil Rhodes who made a large fortune in the African Diamond mines. It was meant for young men from present and former British colonies who had shown outstanding intellectual, athletic, or leadership qualities. Women were later allowed to compete. I won't go into the complicated details of the selection process but after passing the Arkansas interview Bill moved on to New Orleans for twelve more interviews. Finally he was selected and broke the news to his anxious mother on the phone by asking "How do you think I'd look in English tweeds mammy?" He was so proud and happy for his mother. "For a while," he confessed "the world just stopped."

He set out for Oxford on the SS United States on October 4, 1967. Drinking wasn't a problem aboard ship for Bill had long ago developed an indifference to alcohol. Later in life every one of those scholars that went with him made their mark in some form or another in politics, law and even in the army.

It was to be an amazing two years for Bill Clinton. Strangely enough the man that seems to have impressed him most was Douglas Milling, the head porter at Oxford, a retired Navy man who had his feet planted firmly on the ground. It was from him Bill learned how the college worked, how the professors ticked and the difference between Vietnam and World War II. As Bill wrote in his book "Douglas became a lifelong friend. One day, he returned to Oxford with Hillary and feeling a little self-important having just been made Governor of Arkansas. He was brought down to earth when Douglas greeted him with a robust but good-natured "put down". 'Clinton, I hear you have just been made King of some place with three men and a dog'."

"Douglas was always good for a reality check," said Bill. Years later Bill helped Chelsea unpack her things in the flat directly opposite where he stayed thirty-three years earlier. That was a moment of magic for him. Here is a little piece of useless information about Oxford. Archie, Clinton's "scout" in college jargon, a man who had taken care of visitors and their rooms for fifty years introduced him to Guinness, a beer Clinton developed a distinct liking for. However this didn't stop him soaking up the atmosphere of a University steeped in ancient English tradition. It was good for a visitor coming from 3,000 miles away to study in the same environment as the greats of this ancient Academy.

Names like Shelley C. S. Lewis, Stephen Hawking, Clement Attlee, Harold Wilson, Bob Hawke and film star Michael York comes to mind. Bill Clinton continued to soak up his English experience not only in his course of studies in politics, philosophy and economics but in the very English pastime of Rugby. He also found time to travel up country to Stratford-on-Avon to see a Shakespeare play in the bard's home town. He added a trip to London twice and to Birmingham to play basketball once. As an American he was asked to address some high school students and answer questions on "America after Kennedy". Meanwhile his mother decided to wed a guy named Jeff Dwire, again choosing a colourful character who had been to prison and was divorced.

However Bill liked Jeff and accepted him just as he was by returning home for the wedding. It was 1968 and back in America the draft was uppermost in everyone's mind. Nobody seemed to have any patriotic feeling about fighting in Vietnam just a deep sense of grave misgivings totally different from those soldiers asked to fight in World War II. An excerpt from one letter he received from Vietnam tells the story. "Bill I have already seen many things and been through a lot no man of a right mind would want to see or go through. Over here they play for keeps and it's either win or lose and it's not a pretty sight to see a buddy you live with, and become so close to, have him die beside you, and know it was for a good reason. And you realize how easily it could have been you."

I quote that letter word for word from Bill Clinton's biography not as a lazy substitute for inspiration but to capture that man's heart and emotions describing what a war correspondent could never emulate in a despatch home.

It was the gut feeling of a young man in 1968, far from home in a war he never wanted. Bill Clinton did a lot of reading at Oxford and a lot of thinking. There was so much time to think now. This solitude was something he learned to cherish. Later he was to make it part of his daily life snatching two hours per day just to think and do nothing. It was at Oxford he learned to know himself. It was there he discovered a passion for public service, sympathy for the problems of other people, anger at any measure of violence whatever the cause, and just thinking of his stepfather's violence it resurrected in Bill mysterious demons of self-doubt and impending doom that depressed him. His early days of boyhood had many lovely memories but they were laced with other ghosts he could not quite exorcise from his memory.

Bill was happy with these sessions of loneliness and self-examination. They were good for him. They helped him to find his real self.

A passage from Carl Sandburg's The People consoled him. "Tell him solitude is creative if he is strong and the final decisions are made in silent rooms....." In those hours alone Clinton was doing what Sandburg said was needed to sort out what a good life required.

On April 20, 1968 Bill received his draft papers. They told him he could finish out his Oxford term first. Bill filled in his remaining days in England drinking in the beautiful scenery of the English countryside and paying a visit to the village of Stoke Poges where that famous churchyard is to be found written about by Thomas Gray in his "Elegy written in a country churchyard".

The icing on the cake for Bill was a visit to Paris where he stayed in the Latin Quarter and roamed around the traditional tourist attractions and Paris being Paris there is no need to mention them. Just make a list and take your pick.

But Bills being allowed to return to Oxford for his second year disturbed him enough to cause him deep pangs of conscience.

The decision to go had been taken out of his hands by Colonel Holmes of Army Recruitment. Yet that didn't calm Bill's troubled mind, for in America there were two streams of opposing thoughts on the war. One was to go, out of duty and loyalty to those who went. The other was not to go in rebellion against a corrupt war. Bill didn't rebel but he wasn't going to be there until after his second year at Oxford was completed and he felt pangs of painful guilt about the position in which he found himself. Looking at his position from an outsider's point of view, fulfilling a Rhodes scholarship was an experience he would never again be offered. Fate is a strange conundrum.

What young man could turn that chance down? Bill has been honest enough to say in his autobiography "I am not sure I ever answered the question myself." But in 1970 the war was being wound down and the need for more troops eased off to the point where Bill Clinton's number was never called. I guess fate had had the final say in his future.

Bill's second year at Oxford was uneventful except for one story he tells, about his Ferry Trip to Helsinki while at Oxford. On board, a fight broke out between two men over a girl. When he stepped forward to bring peace a third man blocked his way. "You can't stop the fight," he was told. "If you try they will both turn on you and we will help them." Bill was a big, well-built man well over fifteen stone weight but when he asked why they all would attack him for trying to bring peace to the situation they just grinned and said "We are Finns."

Bill shrugged, walked away and realized he had just learned a lesson about different cultures. But your writer believes Bill Clinton was very lucky not to be thrown overboard. We might never have come to know Bill Clinton 42nd President of the United States. The thought is not beyond the realms of real possibility.

He was not so lucky on another occasion however, when back in America he had a minor car accident and unfortunately had not got his driver's licence with him. The police had no alternative but to lock him in jail for the night. With an "all night" light burning and a stuffed up urinal, his sleep was fitful to say the least on his hard iron cell bed. He was sure glad to be bailed out by his friend Tommy Caplan. It was another lesson on how the other half in this world lives and he made sure never to be without his driving licence again.

Yale was Bills next port of call in his educational odyssey. But for all his experience, and for all his accumulated life skills, combined with his travels and diverse activities around Europe, none of this was of any use to him on one particular day in Law school.

It was the day he first met the lovely but formidable Hillary Rodham, his future lovely partner and wife.

Bill noticed her thick dark blond hair, her eyeglasses and complete absence of make up. Yes not a bad observation for a disinterested bystander. The attraction was obviously a new experience for him. This wasn't just any woman among the many he had met casually over the years. This girl had strength of character and self-confidence that bowled him over. His normal technique of a tap on the shoulder, a friendly smile and a charming opening just wouldn't surface. He was frozen at the point of contact – that tap on the shoulder just never took place.

He was hooked though he didn't recognize the symptoms. Unfortunately she was gone before he had the courage to introduce himself.

His next meeting was in the Law Library when they made eye contact over the distance of the long library. She walked towards him and stopped. "If you are going to keep staring at me and I am going to keep staring back, we ought to at least know each others names."

"Mine Hillary Rodham – What's yours?" She challenged. Bill remembers the words differently from Hillary but I'm prepared to favour Hillary's version.

Then a miraculous thing happened for Bill was gob-smacked into a stunned silence. He exchanged his name with her, and after a few words Bill doesn't recall, she was gone.

They met again when Bill stood in line with her to register for next terms classes. "You have registered already Bill what are you doing here?" said the Registrar. Bill's cover was blown. She knew it and laughed out loud. It was the beginning of a deep and wonderful relationship which grew more and more romantic as the years went by. It was also a political journey together in a world where both of them were getting fed up with the failure of the Democrats to solve the burning issues of the day. Together they resolved to change things. In 2001 Hillary wrote in her book Living History a tribute to her husband Bill which I couldn't improve on and I quote "All I know is that no one understands me better and no one can make me laugh the way Bill does. Even after all these years he is still the most interesting, energizing and fully alive person I have ever met. Bill Clinton and I started a conversation in the spring of 1971 and more than thirty years later we are still talking."

As often happens in love affairs absence makes the heart grow stronger. At the end of the school term Hillary went East. Driving to the airport she drew Bill's attention to a quaint little house off the roadway. That little house will return again in our story later but let's return to Hillary. Back East she had missed Bill and Arkansas, and picking her up at the airport Bill remarked casually "Do you remember that house you liked?"
"Well I bought it so now you better marry me because I can't live in it by myself." Not a very romantic proposal you will agree but it worked. Bill had anticipated her reply and had already bought an old wrought iron bed at a local antique store and some sheets and towels. He turned up the long driveway to the house which was in need of some repairs but having looked it over and made some plans Hillary agreed to say yes.

They were duly married in the living room on October 11, 1975 by the Reverend Vic Nixon – no relation to Richard Nixon of course. It was a simple family wedding attended by a small group of close friends and relatives. For the female readers Hillary wore a lace-and-Muslin Victorian dress she had bought the night before. The reception was attended by a huge gathering of two or three hundred friends in the backyard. Perhaps it was not the razzamatazz style wedding of the Roosevelts, the Astors or the Kennedys but it did have two of the most important ingredients of all, lots of sincerity and buckets of love.

Hillary Rodham Clinton has appeared throughout this piece on her husband William Jefferson Clinton so perhaps she hardly needs a mention here as First Lady. She became First Lady on January 20, 1993 and the first evidence that she was different was the way a popular magazine wrote about the Presidency. The piece was not headlined "A hundred days of the Presidency" but "A hundred days of Hillary". This was the new age of computers, emails, mobile phones and jet planes. Unlike First Ladies of a century ago there seemed to be a closer union between the President and the First Lady especially in the public relationship field.

The remoteness of former First Ladies in the White House from the President himself had completely disappeared as the new century approached. Perhaps it was all down to education for Hillary had not only passed through college but also graduated from Law school. By 1990 women graduates had increased in Medicine (34%), Dentistry (31%), Law (42%) and Theology (25%). They were also prominent in other faculties such as foreign languages, health, the sciences, literature, sociology and the social sciences. Imperceptibly women's names were appearing in positions of power not only in commerce but inside the Cabinet room itself. Sandra Day O'Connor was the first woman in the Supreme Court nominated by the Republican President Ronald Reagan.

Hillary was born on October 26, 1947, in the Chicago suburb of Park Ridge. She is the daughter of a small businessman and fulltime stay at home mother and lived in their comfortable middleclass home all her life. Hillary went on to lecture in Law in Arkansas University. Sadly a Monica Lewinsky took centre stage in their lives which unfortunately was a traumatic period for both Bill and Hillary, something I will be writing about later. Hillary was destined to go on, supported by her husband Bill, to contest the primaries to be the Democratic candidate for the 44th Presidency against Barrack Obama. It was a neck and neck fight all the way and Hillary covered herself in glory even though she just failed. Barrack Obama went on to fight it out with John McCain for the final prize on November 1, 2008 for the 44th Presidency of the United States which he duly won. Incidentally Hillary was appointed in 2009 as Secretary of State by the 44th President Barrack Obama. Bill now comes home to Hillary if she is not already away on business meeting foreign dignitaries like Angela Merkel of Germany or President Sarkozy of France. As Bill admits the roles have now completely reversed. But let's return to the 1980s and the story of Bill and Hillary Clinton I was discussing earlier.

After four years of marriage Hillary became pregnant. The red letter day arrived and Bill turned up with Hillary insisting on being present at the caesarean operation. This was against all the rules of the hospital but being Governor of Arkansas did help. From that day on it became an accepted practice for nail-biting fathers to attend the gruesome event by right. Anyway Chelsea was duly born on February 27, 1980. Bill became the instant doting father, driving everyone nuts taking his bundle on bonding trips around the hospital, showing her off to all and sundry as his special contribution to the human race.

Well that was the general impression Hillary has given in her autobiography. You may have noticed Bill was Governor of Arkansas at the birth of Chelsea but we will come to that later. Bill's entry into politics came about as follows: After several campaigns and midway through his first year teaching at the University of Arkansas in 1974 he put this experience to the test for the first time as a candidate for a seat in the United States House of Representatives. He ran an energetic campaign and gave his main opponent Hammerschmidt the closest fight of his career. Now Bill Clinton was noticed for the first time nationwide so he turned his attention to the post of Attorney General. After another campaign he won the election and entered public office for the first time in January 1977 as Attorney General.

He fought rate increases by public utilities and opposed the construction of a large coal burning power plant and linked in with this was his fight for tougher laws to protect the environment and his voters.

His next opportunity to step up the ladder in politics came when the sitting Governor David Pryor of Arkansas ran for the U.S. Senate in 1978. This created a golden opportunity for Bill to progress higher in the political world and do a job he looked forward to.

Looking around his beloved State Bill realized there was plenty of political improvement needed and he promised to right these neglected areas in his home County. The average wage in Arkansas he noticed was 49th of the 50 States. Schools, highways and job opportunities must be improved and updated. Clinton managed to persuade the electorate to trust him with the job and they gave him an overwhelming vote of confidence. Bill Clinton had truly arrived. As Governor of Arkansas, he was now the youngest Governor in the nation's history.

Tackling the job with all the hunger and inspiration found in the heart of a true reformer, Clinton waded blithely into the quicksand of Arkansas politics. Taxes must be increased to fund his reforms mainly in licensing fees on automobiles and large trucks that inflicted the damage to the highways.

But his political naivety was exposed as the big guns of Arkansas took him on. Big business was not going to take these penalties lying down from this new kid on the block. Compromises were agreed but to the satisfaction of no one. The majority who paid the taxes turned out to be the ordinary car owners.

New legislative initiatives only generated opposition. Putting his environmentalist hat on he next tackled tree felling to protect the environment. This only antagonized the lumberjacks, the largest employers in the State. Physicians opposed his plans for healthcare in poor rural areas and Bankers were penalized for the way they made loans that didn't generate new jobs. It was certainly a steep learning curve our Bill was climbing.

As I wrote earlier he had entered the quicksands of Arkansas politics and in the 1980 elections for Governor, Bill Clinton was about to suffer his first lesson at the hands of disgruntled businessmen. All the vested interests did a classical pincer movement and had the financial clout to confront and beat him giving victory to Frank D. White, a Little Rock businessman turned Republican.

Yes, politics can be cruel or sad, ruthless or caring and sometimes a very humbling experience. Yet it had its compensations. Fisher, the famous cartoonist had a golden opportunity one day making fun of one of Frank White's gaffes. In a speech announcing his trade mission to Taiwan and Japan, White had accidentally told the press he was glad to be going to the Middle East. It was a verbal blunder that just invited trouble. Next day Fisher produced one of the funniest cartoons for years. In it he portrayed White's party stepping off the plane in the middle of the desert.

In the background palm trees, pyramids, robed Arabs and a camel. With a banana in his hand he looks around and says "Splendid. Whistle us up a rickshaw". Frank White then pushed up electricity rates that Clinton had just frozen which didn't help him either. Yet no Governor had ever lost and been re-elected. Promising more of the same in education and jobs, Clinton also promised to listen to the voters in other areas. But it was White who won it for Clinton. When he made the remark "The Blacks would vote for a duck if it was a Democrat." The Church Of God in Christ took exception to this insult by telling its congregation to "Get Old Hog head out of office." Old Hog head duly paid the price for his carelessness and victory went to Bill Clinton. He was Governor for the second time.

This book is about interesting anecdotes, significant quotes and speeches, historic moments, the odd bit of banter and even a little bit of fun in the lives of the Presidents. For this reason I can't leave Clinton's victory there. There was one little speech in his pursuit of the Governorship and one man's name that deserves to be printed again.

In one town Bill Clinton had made a good speech listing all he had done for blacks as Governor. A black lawyer stood up, backed another candidate and ended his speech by calling Clinton a loser. The crowded room was stunned into silence until a small, tough, well-built guy at the back of the room stood up and said something like this "All I know Bill Clinton may be a loser but when he was made Governor, the crap was running open in the streets of my town and my babies was sick because we didn't have no sewer system. When he left office we had a sewer system and my babies wasn't sick anymore. He did that for a lot of us. If we don't stick with folks who stick with us, who will ever respect us again. He may be a loser but if he loses I am going down with him and so should you." This one man's words changed everything that night. So overwhelmed was Bill Clinton with this man John Lee Wilson, Mayor of Haynes, a small town of only one hundred and fifty people, that when he was President, Clinton told the story which was televised nationwide. John Lee Wilson had since died but his widow wrote to say "How proud her John would have been to have the President praise him like that."

So significant was John Lee Wilson's little speech, Bill feels he might never have made it to the Presidency without it. Perhaps that's an exaggeration but what a deeply profound insight it is into the world of American politics. Especially Southern politics.

In all my previous stories about the Presidents there are many I feel who did their best work prior to entering the White House. Bill Clinton was no exception. Just look at the things he achieved for Arkansas in that second term he served as Governor from 1983.

Education was to be his main target for improvement. Bill felt the educational system was not doing justice to the needs of the community. It didn't prepare children for good jobs or encourage the right industries to offer skilled well paid jobs. Hillary was appointed head of a committee to achieve higher standards in the schools. A new curriculum was devised to meet this challenge. New laws were introduced, new taxes were imposed, teachers were paid more money, college scholarships were created mainly favouring where possible the poorer classes. Even teachers didn't escape the demand for higher educational qualifications. There was a bit of anger at first but this time they accepted Bill Clinton's ideas. The drop out statistics swung to the national average from rock bottom averages.

New businesses were developed and new jobs came on stream helped by loans for new firms involved in technology. Taxes were reduced for firms who expanded their business and gave new jobs. Unfortunately these new ideas had to be funded by higher taxes so the changes were not always popular. The big business Combines he had antagonized in his first term used their muscle to block these higher taxes. By now Bill Clinton's power base had expanded to becoming chairman of the National Governors Association. It was time for him to move on. Anyway he had achieved most of what he set out to do in Arkansas. National politics was now to be his new platform on the road to the White House.

In 1988 he was tempted to plunge into a Presidential campaign straight after his Governorship triumphs in Arkansas but Hillary's hand on the tiller restrained him as did Chelsea's tender years, she was only eight – politics would have to wait for the family came first. That is how it has always been with the Clintons. He now had another three years to mature and learn his role for the Presidency and by 1991 he was ready. One aspect of politics fascinates me however. The complications and intricacies of the political infighting and the different shades of Democrats that came and went through the pages of Bill Clinton's autobiography overwhelm me. How anyone can figure out who to vote for is completely beyond me. How do you satisfy the voters? Trying to please five hundred million people is a lot more daunting than trying to please the voters of a small European country.

But playing the hustings in America can best be understood from the simple meetings Clinton had with ordinary folk. A little anecdote may be appropriate at this stage to spotlight his talent for reaching out to people and paints another shade of colouring to the Clinton image. It is an extract from The Natural: The Misunderstood Presidency of Bill Clinton by Joe Klein.

It seems Clinton had just had a rough passage at a meeting of Veteran Trade Union leaders. Stepping down off the rostrum, the first person he met was Joe Klein who just happened to have written a not very complimentary piece about Clinton's inconsistencies in a New York magazine.

William Jefferson Clinton as always the astute aware politician with the human touch couldn't resist little Sophie Klein, Joe's five year daughter. Squatting down he placed one big hand on Sophie's shoulder and said. "I know that your father hasn't been home much these past few months. He has been with me but he talks about you all the time." Joe a typical hard-boiled newsman was impressed by a genuine compassionate gesture on Clinton's part. He could never have been conned by a phoney cynical gesture and accepted the incident for what it was, a spontaneous human meeting with a little girl of five. Like John Lee Wilson we read about earlier who turned a whole gathering of people to his point of view in a speech he never rehearsed that blew apart the oratory of a professional lawyer into smithereens. These seemingly insignificant men and women in remote places expressed ideas in their own simple way that reflected the feelings of their own kind right across America and Bill Clinton never ignored them.

Another story concerns someone he met in the back kitchen of the Sheraton Hotel in New York. As he passed through he was stopped by a waiter Dimitrios Theophanes with a conversation that made Theophanes a friend for life "My nine year old boy can't play in the park across the street or walk down the street to school by himself because it is too dangerous. He is not free. So if I vote for you will you make my boy free?" The waiter's words nearly reduced Clinton to tears. "I told him," said Clinton "that community police officers who knew everybody would walk the blocks and I was committed to funding 100,000 of them." These were the heartbeats that Clinton had a special talent for tuning into. This to him was America, more than all the razzamatazz of a Democratic Convention, and is something the ordinary citizen can never grasp unless he or she can travel with the candidate and hear the common folk tell their stories and express their fears.

Looking at the map one can see the journey would take the candidate over boundaries right across the States from New York on the East Coast to California on the West Coast covering the route taken by the Merryweather and Clark expedition on Jefferson's orders across the heartlands of America.

Bill Clinton undertook that journey in 1988. The thousands of miles he travelled by trains, planes and helicopters leaves me just shaking my head in amazement. Trying to reach and preach to five hundred million people is truly amazing to say the least. Writing about New York alone Bill Clinton gives a bird's-eye view of the territory to be covered. Five very different boroughs; large black and Hispanic populations, and the largest population of Jewish Americans in the country. He met with well-organised Indians, Pakistanis and Albanians and talked to a multiplicity of other ethnic groups. The diversity of each group, including 500,000 from the Dominican Republic, was truly breathtaking. Meeting 950 ethnic leaders for fundraising was another job for the team. This also meant the organization of ethnic groups' right across the country and that included trade unions.

During these briefings came the suggestion to meet "The Irish Issues Forum". Because he had observed firsthand while in Oxford in 1968 the troubles in the North of Ireland, Clinton needed little encouragement to take Northern Ireland politics onboard. He felt confident he could influence the situation in Ireland even if it infuriated the British. President Bill Clinton kept his word and had a real hands-on relationship in the final Irish Peace accord as President. It became one of the greatest passions and success stories of his Presidency.

Bill Clinton's concentration on ethnic groups may not have been entirely an accident. In fact in retrospect it seems to have been a carefully planned design of an astute political strategist. Based on the statistics of 1990, Asian Americans were among the fastest growing minority groups. In America at that time 7.3 million Americans were of Asian or Pacific Island descent and they were growing at seven times the national rate. It was projected that by the year 2050 one in ten Americans would be of Asian Ancestry. Chinese, Filipinos, Japanese, Indian, Vietnamese and Korean would constitute the sic major Asian ethnic classifications, and of 46% of all immigrants into the United States in the 1980s Asian Americans made up an astonishing 64% of any ethnic group. What's more they were all relatively rich and educated so their progress had indeed been remarkable and could not possibly be left out of Clinton's calculations.

However through radio and television shows, the press, and the opinions of the big hitters in the media had to be won over too.

Peter Hamill of The New York Daily News gives a typical helpful quote "I have come to respect Bill Clinton. It's the late rounds and he is still there."

The New York Post surprised Clinton with this one. "It speaks strongly to his strength of character that he has already survived a battering by the press on personal questions unprecedented in the history of American politics. He has continued to campaign with remarkable tenacity.... In our view he has manifested extraordinary grace under pressure......"

Clintons verdict on his campaign "The darker the night, the sweeter the victory." Well perhaps the foregoing can paint an overall picture of the job you take on to become President of the United States. Yes, forty-two Presidents after George Washington life is a little more complicated for the modern Presidential hopeful than it was on the stump in the Wild West frontier days of Jackson or Madison.

If you want to be President today make sure you know exactly what you are letting yourself in for.

But it wasn't all plain sailing and complimentary sound bites by the media. Clinton made the blunder himself of admitting to smoking marijuana in Oxford but not inhaling it. Since he wasn't a smoker he just couldn't inhale. As Clinton said himself I gave the late night TV hosts fodder for years of jokes. In fact he was lucky. Character is the essential ingredient in any President's make up for no President could operate with a flawed pedigree. The lucky break came when Jimmy Carter, whose own reputation was indisputable, supported him for the White House.

The campaign rose to a climax with the usual TV debates of the leading candidates. This one involved President Bush, William Clinton and Ross Perot, an eccentric Texan billionaire.

Bush attacked Clinton's character and his opposition to the Vietnam War and threw in the accusation that "Clinton would use Elvis economics launching America into Heartbreak Hotel." Perot had some great one-liners when told he had no experience running a Government he scoffed "The President has a point I don't have any experience in running up a $4 trillion deficit." But the one-liner that won it for Clinton was "It's the economy stupid." D. day could not be kept away forever and as it moved to within 24 hours of the countdown both Bill and Hillary made one last all-out push in a campaign that crisscrossed the country.
On the way they stopped at Philadelphia, Pennsylvania, Cleveland, Ohio, Detroit, Michigan, St. Louis Missouri, Paducah Kentucky, Fort Worth Texas, Albuquerque and New Mexico. They arrived back at 10 a.m. on the morning of the election staying at the Governor's mansion. At 10.47 p.m. that night Bill Clinton was declared 42nd President of the United States.

There was a flurry of excitement back home and I am not talking about the new Cabinet. Presents were cascading in from all over the world and private belongings had to be gathered up and packed away for the transfer to the White House. Sometimes a shout went up by Chelsea "Wait till you see what has just come in."

A portrait of Bill made from seashells mounted on a red velvet background arrived; among many presents some for the Clinton's very famous black and white cat "Socks". The Bush household you may remember was faced with similar problems re-rooting the family to Washington. Now it was Clinton's turn.

A new school for Chelsea was organized. Hillary resigned from her law firm to concentrate on the office of First Lady. Now it was going to be a radically different social scene for both of them here in Washington.

But inauguration day arrived and Bill Clinton took the oath of office at 11.59 a.m. on the morning of Wednesday January 20, 1993 on the West Front Portico of the Capitol. Chief Justice William Hubbs Rehnquist administered the oath. Clinton's speech which lasted only fourteen minutes included a touching tribute to the outgoing President George W. Bush for his fifty years service to the nation. He went on to say there is nothing wrong with America that cannot be cured by what is right with America. Here is a small extract from his inauguration speech which was being watched by thousands in person before him and millions on television.

"Today we celebrate the mystery of American renewal. This ceremony is held in the depth of winter. But by the words we speak and the faces we show the world we force the spring. A spring reborn in the world's oldest democracy that brings forth the vision and courage to reinvent America. When our founders boldly declared America's independence to the world and our purposes to the Almighty they knew that America to endure would have to change. Each generation of Americans must define what it means to be an American...." Then came

Maya Angelou's poem On The Pulse of Morning.

Lift up your faces, you have a piercing need
For this bright morning dawning for you.
History, despite its wrenching pain,
Cannot be unlived, and if faced
With courage, need not be lived again.
Lift up your eyes upon
The day breaking for you.
Give birth again
To the dream.

Here on the pulse of this new day
You may have the grace to look up and out
And into your sisters eyes, and into
Your brothers face, your country
And say simply
Very simply
With hope
Good morning.

Billy Graham completed the ceremony with a simple brief prayer after which the new and the old President left the stage both of them walking into history. Bill Clinton and George Bush descended the back steps and walked to where Bush's Helicopter Marine I was waiting to take him and Barbara home. For Bill the night was only just beginning. First there was lunch with the Congressional Committee, then the ride up Pennsylvania Avenue to the viewing stand. Hillary and Chelsea joined in the last short walk of a few blocks waving to the crowds that lined the sidewalk. Then it was back to the White House to wash, change and freshen up for the nights exhausting schedule that lay ahead of them. At 7 p.m. they started the marathon festivities together. Bill's brother sang and Bill himself played a saxophone duet Night Train with Clarence Clemons.

Hillary at last got a chance to show off that precious purple gown she had bought for the occasion. Chelsea went to a youth Ball while both the President and the First Lady toured around eleven Balls saying a few words and dancing a few bars of the obligatory dance together before moving on. They finally arrived home at 2 a.m. to the White House.

Congressional leaders held the traditional luncheon to welcome the new President in Statuary Hall and the inaugural parade was one of the longest parades in history. The age old tradition of lavish Balls and banquets were celebrated throughout inaugural week and were attended as far as possible by the new President and his First Lady. The usual open house gala in the White House was attended by thousands. There was one historic moment that almost went unnoticed however when Bill Clinton was given the most amazing tribute at a luncheon arranged by the leaders of Congress just after the inauguration ceremony. He was given the key to the Capitol. The traditional sanctity of the Capitol has always been preserved very jealously by Congress. So special is the preserve of Congress the key is kept only by the architect of the Capitol. Only two duplicates were ever made one was given to Ronald Reagan and the other was now presented to Bill Clinton.

The architect has the special privilege of opening and closing the Capitol doors every day. I have often wondered how he lives with such a restriction on his life or perhaps I am taking his task too literally. But tradition is tradition and it was a gesture of great magnanimity to pass the only remaining replica of this key to the 42nd President of the United States. Speaker of the House Thomas Foley told the President that the key was an open invitation "To come anytime you wish. The key was a symbol of our outstretched hand our pledge of co-operation." Now the President in normal circumstances can only enter the capital by invitation. Clinton saw the humour in the situation for on receiving the key he reminded congressional leaders, given his propensity to lobby the legislature "I may be here all the time," he said with a twinkle in his eye.

The mad rush had begun in moving out the Bushes luggage while the Clintons' luggage moved into the White House. Somehow this must be accomplished between the inaugural ceremony and the end of the inaugural parade. History was now all around Hillary. It was hard to come to terms with the fact that she was now married to the President of the United States. The Staffers or permanent staff carried on the system with the smooth professionalism of people who had seen it all before. Nothing had changed for the permanent engineers, carpenters, plumbers, gardeners, florists, curators, cooks, butlers and housekeepers. The whole show was overseen by the ushers and the administrative staff. This is the unseen but significantly important layer of personnel that keeps the White House ticking over from President to President. People I must talk about later.

Bill's mother had more fun than anyone and made special friends with Barbra Streisand, a friendship that was to continue long after inauguration day. After the final dance Hillary and Bill made their way back to the White House at 2 a.m. in the morning.

As they got out of the elevator on the second floor they realized for the first time it was all true. The White House was indeed their new home. Only one incident caught them by surprise early that morning. After tapping on their bedroom door a man in a tuxedo pushed his way in. Bill shouted "Hey what are you doing here." It seems breakfast for the Bushes started at 5.30 a.m. but on that particular morning that was one tradition that would not be kept. The children, Chelsea and her friend, were entertained that night by the ushers who intrigued them with various games of discovery around the house. One such clue was to find the haunted room which turned out to be the Lincoln bedroom where ghosts have been seen and cold breezes have been known to waft through the room. Living with the Secret Agents appointed to them was also something new they would have to get used to.

Bill's jogging routine gave his Secret Agents some headaches. He had several routes, one of which defied the cold winter winds that came across the Potomac. But his favourite one was out the Southwest gate of the White House to the mall then up to the Lincoln memorial, back down to the Capitol and home. It was all too good to last however for he finally had to accept his security people's concerns and cancel the route.

Bill was particularly affected by the total change in his lifestyle as has all new Presidents. This became clear instantaneously with his opening day in the White House. As he said himself in his autobiography, since he was twenty he had been a free spirit, independent, and with a particular gift for self-sufficiency practiced over the years as a student in college. He had got used to cleaning, cooking and doing all the odd jobs for himself. Even in marriage Hillary and Bill had shared these jobs between them. Driving alone in his car listening to his radio and just thinking could now never be his private domain again; the new system had engulfed him for his own good.

That was the rule and that was how it had to be with troopers following him in traffic in unmarked cars. Funny how the ordinary punter enjoyed these liberties everyday of the week.

It is stories like this that makes one look back to the easygoing uncomplicated lives of Adams, Jefferson or Madison with just a little tinge of jealousy. But Bill Clinton did manage to run alone when out jogging provided it was a predictable secure route surrounded by people even if it was only for a distance of half mile from the White House. But Hillary was determined to stamp her own style on the White House kitchen. She rebuilt it into an intimate family area where Bill, herself and Chelsea could eat together as a family. The upstairs dining room was far too big and formal for the Clintons except when there were visiting guests.

The 42nd President of the United States Bill Clinton was to enter into the quicksand of Irish politics just as sublimely as he had dived into the quicksand of Arkansas politics. In Arkansas he had taken on the big hitters and the vested interests and won. Now he was about to take a journey into the politically turbulent waters of Irish politics no President before him, not even Kennedy had attempted to enter.

First it had to be accepted by everyone on both sides of the political divide in Northern Ireland that no political solution could be made in Northern Ireland without the mutual agreement of both sides. There were some very tough personalities to be coaxed and cajoled into such an agreement. Gerry Adams, Martin McGuiness, Ian Paisley, John Hume, David Trimble to name just a few.

To debate the issues here would take many, many pages and perhaps confuse the reader into boredom. Suffice it to say that Bill Clinton despite his many problems right across the world's international stage with Jordan, Israel, Cuba, Russia, Europe, China, Japan, Bosnia and the Middle East somehow found time for the Irish question and a peace agreement was eventually signed on Good Friday April 10, 1998.

One of the most emotional moments of Bill Clinton's Presidential life was his visit to Ireland in 1997. It was the first ever visit of Hillary and Bill to Northern Ireland.

Bill Clinton became deeply involved in the Irish Peace Accord and so decided to visit Belfast with Hillary. They met and talked to women of the troubles on both sides of the war, women who had already felt the terrible heartbreak of losing their sons, yet trying to heal the wounds by reaching out to each other in a maternal understanding where politics played no part. One person Joyce McCartan, a remarkable woman spoke for many a wife and mother when she said "It takes women to bring men to their senses."

Bill and Hillary went to Derry and tens of thousands of people right across the divide crowded the streets on that cold December day when Bill addressed them. A young naval steward with the Clintons remarked at that Christmas tree lighting ceremony as he looked down on a sea of upturned faces "These people all look the same why have they been killing each other." "We want Bill, we want Bill" they chanted which brought a lump to Hillary's throat with pride for her husband. He spoke of hope and peace and told them his time in Belfast would live in their hearts forever. "It was one of the most remarkable of our lives," he said and Hillary wholeheartedly agreed with him.

Dublin was their next stop and Hillary's verdict just about sums up their visit. "Ireland invigorated and inspired me, and I wish we could bottle up the good feelings and take them back home."

Sadly the extraordinary odyssey of the 42nd Presidency was about to be troubled as dark clouds rolled across the face of their sun casting shadows and thunderstorms of doubt, despair, disbelief, and even disillusionment on their wonderful love affair. Like the vortex of a raging hurricane this one too had a name. The name was Monica Lewinsky.

I have no intention here of entering into the no-man's-land of idle speculation. Perhaps the space I give the story is best filled by the First Lady herself and how she saw it in her autobiography Living History.

On Wednesday morning January 21, Bill woke Hillary and broached the problem of Monica Lewinsky for the first time to her. "There's something in today's papers you should know about," he said nervously. "What are you talking about?" asked Hillary. He explained that besides the affair he was being accused of by Paula Jones, another name had surfaced Monica Lewinsky, a White House intern or trainee. Worse still he had asked Lewinsky to lie about it to Jones' lawyer. Like any good bloodhound with the scent of a kill in its nostrils Ken Starr was interested enough in the incident to request the Attorney General Janet Reno to grant him permission to expand his investigation further in order to pursue possible criminal charges against the President.

Apparently Lewinsky during a meeting Clinton had with her had asked for help in job hunting. "She had misinterpreted my attention" was a mantra from the past he used to defend himself. Well that was roughly what came over in Hillary's book Living History. "I had seen it happen dozens of times before" wrote Hillary. But Bill had always been a very charismatic handsome man so getting women's attention from groupies and adventurous women was not unusual for him.

Bill denied any improper behaviour and told the same story to others. To Hillary it was just another vicious scandal manufactured by political opponents. Yet all the potential fallout both personal and political pre-occupied Hillary leaving her torn apart with worry and inner conflict. "What was to happen in the future?" she asked herself. Gone were the old days of happiness and certainty. Now there was doubt, now there were fears. Impeachment was one of those fears that haunted her and as a lawyer she understood the implications. The ghosts of the Nixons were once again stalking the White House.

Gossip was another enemy she had to contend with. Her imagination ran riot. How could she get up in the morning let alone go out in public? Even if she didn't believe the charges it was devastating just to hear them. The advice of Eleanor Roosevelt that every woman in political life must develop skin as tough as a rhinoceros was easier said than done. It was one long dark night of the soul that left her alone, lonely and defenceless.

Her only consolation was the thought that the enemies of her husband were at work undermining him to regain the political ground they had lost to him at the ballot box.

No, that's not strictly correct. Her friends gave her great consolation too. Their understanding and kind words were far more helpful than they could ever have realized. Tony Blair and his wife Cherie were two people she counted as part of that circle of friends.

But Ken Starr was remorseless and by the end of 1997 he had forced two dozen Agents on the White House staff to testify. Yet the tide of public opinion was turning against Ken Starr. Was his campaign based on conspiracy or coincidence? Newsweek pursued this line. In an article under this title they linked together twenty-three different connections that might be contributors to a witch-hunt; Media executives, Authors, Lawyers and various organizations among others. The media were beginning to get aboard this possibility of a conspiracy against the President. Soon the Paula Jones case collapsed through lack of evidence. Now Ken

Starr's motives were coming under scrutiny. Remorselessly life went on in the Presidency with their trip to Africa. In Ghana over half a million people gathered to hear him speak on March 23, 1998. Bill's charisma in working the crowds was a joy for her to watch. In Rwanda they met with survivors of the genocide that had killed 500,000 to one million people.

The Secret Service had misgivings about this meeting and for security purposes they met at the airport lounge. In Cape Town they met President Nelson Mandela, who pointed out when walking through the prison where he spent years on Robben Island, the powdered rock which he used to teach fellow prisoners to read when their guards weren't looking. Moving on to Senegal and Goree Island, Bill made a speech at "The door of no return" in which he made an apology for America's role in the slave trade. Controversial sentiments but courageously said nevertheless.

Back home they were told he was soon to be on his way to China whose future direction was very important to world trade in a newly modernized Chinese economy. The violation of human rights was a hot potato for the Diplomats on both sides to juggle with. Their meeting in Tiananmen Square could not be avoided but with the memory of tanks confronting rebel students there in 1989 still fresh in their memories it was deeply disturbing and repulsive for them. Hillary's mention of Tibet and the repression of the Tibetans went down like a lead balloon

President Jiang got quite agitated by her pointed questions and launched into a tirade about Chinese history and the Tibetans being freed from religious feudalism. To her credit at least Hillary wasn't afraid to confront him with uncomfortable questions.

Later with Chelsea and Hillary's mother they toured the Forbidden City and the Great Wall of China, finishing with a magnificent dinner in the Great Hall of the People where they were entertained by Chinese and Western music.

They finished their journey in Shanghai, the New York of China, with all its hustle and bustle, ending their visit with a meeting of businessmen in the Shanghai Stock Exchange. And so, from the frenzied heartbeat of Shanghai in China, they made their way back to America. They were relieved somehow and were glad to be back home again.

Hillary Clinton always comes over as a remarkable woman. In the year 2006 she was suggested as a possible candidate for the presidency. Her vast intellectual interests and her wide academic background coupled with her role as First Lady makes her a formidable choice if she did go forward.

Despite her problems in her marriage she launched a millennium showcase in history culture and science. She headed up a series of lectures in the East room for scholars, historians, scientists, and artists in subjects from jazz to genetics, from the Human Genome Project - unlocking the secrets of our genetic make up, to cosmology. She gathered together world famous names like Stephen Hawking, Dr Vinton Cerf and Dr Eric Lander. Even America's poet Laureate was there.

Looking at this wealth of talent of which she felt so proud she made up her mind to face into her future with a renewed hope and a new determination.

But somehow life goes on even when we don't want it to. Hillary's nightmare was to worsen. Monica Lewinsky had negotiated a deal with Ken Starr giving her immunity. Bill had to testify before a Grand Jury and suddenly he knew the game was up. He could no longer deny he had sexual relations with Monica Lewinsky. One morning he woke Hillary and told her the truth. Hillary admitted in her book Living History. "I was dumbfounded, heartbroken and outraged for believing him. Chelsea had to be told." When he realized this his eyes filled with tears. He had lied to her too. Hillary wrote "I remember the times I had sat with women in all parts of Ireland to look for a way to achieve peace and reconciliation." Now she had to do the same herself only this time it was her own life she was talking about. At that time she really didn't know what to do.

But time is a great healer. If this love affair lived out together all over the world was to survive she had to ask herself one question. Did she still love him? The answer came painfully slowly to her over the coming weeks. Yes she still loved him. The gap between them was unbearable. The one she always needed most in a crisis wasn't there. They were living like strangers and even Chelsea was not there. Theologian Paul Tillich was a great help when he wrote "Sin and grace exist through life in constant interplay. Grace strikes us when we are in great pain and restlessness."
"It happens or it does not happen," Tillich the Theologian told her. Hillary had no alternative but to wait. To wait for it to happen. The futility of bitterness was brought home to them on their visit to Northern Ireland after the bombing of Omagh. This final carnage in the midst of reconciliation and forgiveness was truly evil. Yet from their visit they learned lessons for their own lives. Reconciliation was possible from the ashes of bitterness, even bombs couldn't destroy it.

Now Hillary was looking at her marriage in a new light. It had also survived a similar explosion; peace was not too far away for both of them. Yes maybe grace had happened too. Now she saw all the good Bill had achieved and the risks he had taken for good. A new relationship was developing deeper and more profound. Maybe the love affair of Hillary and Bill Clinton may some day go down in history on a parallel with those of Abigail Adams, Dolly Madison, Eleanor Roosevelt or Barbara Bush who knows!

But Impeachment was now a certainty. Ken Starr was about to have his pound of flesh. On January 7, Chief Justice William Rehnquist officially opened the Impeachment trial of William Jefferson Clinton. One week later the House Impeachment managers began their three day presentation of the case. Nobody had articulated the standard for judging. What conduct was impeachable? The media began to put their finger on a cabal of right-wing groups and condemned them for abusive tactics but at least the TV talk shows were more balanced.

Professor Cass Sunstein of the University of Chicago and Susan Bloch of Georgetown released a letter on the unconstitutionality of the Impeachment process. It was signed by four hundred legal scholars. One of the House managers actually questioned the right of the Senate to judge whether Clinton's alleged offences met the constitutional standard of Impeachment. Chuck Ruff a former U.S. attorney argued that the charges were untrue and even if the Senators only thought they were untrue, the offences did not come close to the constitutional standard for Impeachment.

There was also a contradiction in the Perjury charge. The Senate had raised it but Ken Starr had not. When Clinton was accused of obstruction of justice, Cheryl Mills an African-American graduate of Stanford Law School was brilliant. She said "I can't let their comments go unchallenged." Black people all over America knew that the drive to impeach Clinton was being led by right-wing White Southerners who had never lifted a finger for civil rights.

The black voters of the South were now a formidable block of public opinion entering the fray. She also pointed out that the Paula Jones case had been dismissed by a female Judge. Her final statement was deeply impressive saying "Bill Clinton's record on civil rights and women's rights was unimpeachable. I stand here today because President Bill Clinton believed I could stand here for him…" "It would be wrong to convict him on this record," said Dale Bumpers. "We are here today because the President suffered a terrible moral collapse. I am not here to defend him as a friend but to defend the Constitution, the most sacred document to me next to the Holy Bible."

This was the contribution of Dale Bumpers who had just retired from the Senate after twenty-four years and was a careful student of the Constitution. He finished by giving a detailed account of the Constitutional Convention in which Madison was a major architect. He finished with the words "Don't defile the constitution! The American people are calling to you to rise above politics." It was a magnificent speech.

Despite this, the process lasted for another three weeks. Between that and the final impeachment vote Clinton gave the State of the Union Address. Before he addressed the nation he was taken to the speaker's quarters. A delegation of Senators came to take him to the House Chamber. All the traditional procedures were respectfully kept, they shook hands with him and he was announced to the audience as is customary for the State of the Union Address.

Walking down the isle which separated the Democrats and Republicans from each other he shook hands with the Democrats and was surprised to have some Republican hands outstretched to him. On the podium he began with a salute to the new speaker. He had eighteen million new jobs to announce. The lowest unemployment since 1957. Educational reforms, a new pension initiative, more funds for Medicare and finally a promise to reverse the decline in military spending. He specially honoured Hillary for representing America so well on the world stage. Finally he described the times as a new dawn for America.

The waiting was now almost over and the judgment that decided the whole meaning of Clinton's life up to the Presidency and for years to come was now at hand.

On February 12, 1999 the verdict was announced. The impeachment failed, the perjury vote failed, and the obstruction vote failed. The ordeal for Bill Clinton's family and for America was over. Hillary was laughing again and Chelsea was still doing well at University. The bible story of the woman caught in adultery was uppermost in his mind at that time when he recalled the words of Jesus "Hath no man condemned thee." "No man Lord." "Neither do I condemn thee go and sin no more."

Bill Clinton continued in office to the end of eight years in the Presidency. He looks on life now as a transient experience constantly in a state of change.

Today he still remembers the Moon Rock in a glass case in his Oval office. Whenever debates became heated as President he always pointed across the room and said "You see that Rock, its 3 ½ million years old. We are just passing through. Let's calm down and go back to work."

So what will history's verdict be on William Jefferson Clinton 42nd President of the United States? "He was warm, physical, commanding and exuberant" Evan Thomas wrote in his essay in James McPherson's book To the Best of My Ability. Evan Thomas went on; "Clinton was cunning as well as intellectual and a master at manipulating people." To Clinton's credit, looking back on the economic shambles he had inherited, he did extricate America from the mess he took over and can be congratulated on leaving America an undisputed superpower in an era of peace and prosperity. "Perhaps his impeachment was a self-inflicted wound, for as Jonathan Alter of Newsweek observed, "Clinton was really two different people. One was inspirational who could feel a nation's pain. The other one – the one which was responsible for that self-inflicted wound – was a reckless perpetual adolescent."

As you will appreciate many of Bill Clinton's opinions are worth listening to so here are a few of them from his interview with Sir David Frost on his programme "Breakfast with Frost" on Sunday July 18, 2004.

On Arafat: "Arafat thanked me for all my help and told me I was a great man. I replied Chairman I am not a great man. You made me a failure. I meant I couldn't get him to make a conference of peace."

On the wall in Israel: "The evidence in Gaza is that it works to keep civilians alive. So taking the wall down is a pretty hard argument to make to the Israelis."

On Past Presidents: "Theodore Roosevelt complained because he didn't have the Civil War like Lincoln." Frost was puzzled and said "It's difficult to be remembered as a great President if you haven't had a war to cope with." Bill Clinton didn't agree. "In one hundred years from now we may come to value the peacemaker more."

On Africa: He was quite remorseful. "I have spent the last ten years trying to make up to Africa. I should have moved on Rwanda more quickly."

On his Tombstone: "Mr. President what would you put on your tombstone," Frost asked. After a long pause Clinton said "He loved his Family, he loved his country, he left them a world better than he found it."
On the CIA: "It's a different world than during the Cold War. You and I could walk in Warsaw in 1979. We wouldn't last very long in Afghanistan today."

"How many marks would you give yourself out of ten as President?" Frost continued. Clintons reply just about sums up his whole philosophy in politics. "I couldn't answer that, it is better to let history judge me. I have wanted more people to have better stories than when I started and a lot of them did."

I guess you can't get any deeper into the mind and heart of Bill Clinton than that.

In his retirement Bill Clinton suffered a massive coronary. Always a particularly fit guy who took his diet and jogging fairly seriously, this setback came as a bit of a shock to both Hillary and Bill. No, maybe that is a bit of an understatement, Hillary was devastated. His bypass operation left him weak but the worry didn't end there. The following year he had to return to hospital to have six large glasses full of fluid drained from the gap between his ribs and his lungs. Bill was now fifty-nine and Hillary had a career ahead of her that might one day lead to the White House. But Bill was always a tough cookie and he bounced back to take his place beside her. Shrugging his broad shoulders he was heard to say "I am as healthy as a horse now. I have got a couple of big scars on my chest but I have got another twenty or thirty years of life." That love affair was still in evidence when he continued. "She helped me for thirty years and I said 'I will give you the next thirty and then if we are still alive we can argue about the rest'."

So let's finish the Clinton story as Bill Clinton finished his when he said "I grew up with a fascinating mother who adored me. I have learned at the feet of great teachers. I have made a legion of friends and built a loving life with the finest woman I have ever known and have a child who continues to be the light of my life. I think it's a good story and I have had a good time telling it."

As for me your writer I too have had a wonderful time telling the world about a beautiful love story that will only blossom as the years go by. The love affair of Bill and Hillary Clinton.

43rd President   George W. Bush

"Dubya"
Born: 1946
2001 - 2009
2 Terms
Age 55

Party: Republican
Profession: Businessman
County: Texas
Ancestry: English
Estate: Unknown
Hobbies: Baseball

Physical Description: 5foot, 11 inches high, 189 lbs., gray hair, blue eyes, energetic and fit google.

Significant extracts from inauguration speech on January 20, 2001
"Never tiring, never yielding, never finishing, we renew that purpose today, to make our country more just and generous to affirm the dignity of our lives and every life. This work continues. This story goes on and an angel still rides in the whirlwind and directs the storm."

GEORGE W BUSH

By the end of the inauguration ceremony for George Bush the 43rd President, the Staffers of the White House had moved out the personal belongings of Bill Clinton the 42nd President and his First Lady Hillary Clinton. The ritual of completing the transition moved smoothly to a successful conclusion. This needless to say was no surprise, for the people involved had seen it all before with each succeeding tenant of the White House. The younger ones may have wondered about their new President. What was he like? Would he be easy to get along with? What new style would he bring to the Presidency? Some of the older staff already knew him from his boyhood days living there when his dad was both Vice President and President. Now they were welcoming George Bush the man.

But let's go back in time to when the story of George Bush first began in 1946. Who could tell then that the little boy born into the family of George and Barbara Bush would one day succeed his father and follow him into the White House? Only one other man had achieved such an honour and that was back on March 4, 1825 when Quincy Adams became the 6th President of the United States. Quincy's father John Adams had been the second President succeeding George Washington. Yes, George Bush was being compared to some very illustrious predecessors. Bush's family tree also had a touch of the political aristocracy about it for as well as his father the 41st President; his mother had a distant relative Franklin Pierce who was the 14th President in 1853.

His grandfather Prescott Bush was a Wall Street financier who was elected to the Senate from Connecticut in 1952. According to Burke's Peerage there were other talented people in his family tree we could throw into the mix. He was the fourteenth cousin twice removed from the Queen of England. He was a distant relative of Princess Diana and Winston Churchill, while even the illustrious George Washington can be found down the bloodline.

The Bushes were of the American political aristocracy going back to before World War I when New Yorker Samuel Prescott Bush went West to seek his fortune in 1905, eventually rising to be President of the Buckeye Steel Casting Company. He also became an intimate advisor to President Herbert Hoover "The Engineer" just as the terrible Depression broke out in 1930. Samuel had a son Prescott Sheldon Bush who grew up on the vast family estate near Columbus and like many of the wealthy class at that time was packed off to an elite prep school aged thirteen.

Prescott graduated from the exclusive St. George in Newport Rhode Island and became the first of the Bush family to enter Yale University. Academia, Sport and singing were all part of his success story. He was one of those people who was good at everything. Perhaps that is where the genes of George Bush Senior came from. The war broke out as he left Yale and in 1918 he ended up aboard a troop ship heading for Europe. Returning home he married Dorothy Walker whose father George Herbert Walker had founded the private investment firm of Brown Brothers Harriman which became one of Wall Streets largest investment company.

Preston Bush seemed to hit it off well with his potential father-in-law for he became both his golf and businessman partner. This same father-in-law George Walker became President of the U.S. Golf Association and was actually the founder of the Walker Cup competition, one of the most prestigious international events on the golfing calendar today. Dorothy and Prescott eventually married and became parents and grandparents to the two Bush Presidents. It was a fascinating Gatsby type world for both Dorothy and Prescott Bush living as they did in elegant Fifth Avenue mansions owning private railroad cars and turreted summer cottages as exotic as any French castle.

But their lifestyle didn't stop there for they also owned a palatial Long Island estate and to top it off a ten thousand acre South Carolina plantation. Funny enough it was their modest summer retreat on the rocky coastline of Maine Kennebunkport where all the action took place for the family. Their friends could be found on any American aristocratic guest list. Names like the Morgans, the Drescels, the Vanderbilts, the Astors, the Harrimans and the Mellons to mention but a few.

They were never called upon to endure the Depression of the 30s living as they did in a rambling Greenwich Connecticut mansion with a broad veranda, a Porte Cochere and a large household staff. This was considered the norm for the Bushes. Yet Jonathan Bush made his own private observation on all this when he said "We had a cook, a maid and a chauffeur and never thought we were wealthy as other kids we knew had much more!"

Yes, we have come a long way from those unbelievable days of pomp, wealth and prestige enjoyed by the Bush-Walker family circle in the 20s and 30s. It seems light years away from the life of a very ordinary insignificant guy named George W. Bush who stumbled into the Presidency without influence or intelligence just by luck. After all I have just told you I doubt if you really believe that any more. If you still do, well, I just shake my head and smile.

I have written earlier about the WASP families in my notes on Jacqueline Bouvier Kennedy. The Bush-Walker family's social life was no different than most WASP families at that time in the Northeast. George Bush's early childhood memories go back to sailing off the Maine coast and being chauffeured in his great-grandfather's two Rolls Royces. From these early days he was made aware of his Yankee heritage and of the ties that bonded him to another world – an old money world of opulence, privilege, entitlement and influence deep in his north-eastern roots.

George, known later as "Dubya", was only two years old when his father started his career in the petroleum business in Odessa, Texas, a place remotely distant from his lifestyle up to now. Odessa was truly an unforgiving place to live. That part of Texas was vast with a far flung treeless horizon. The only thing to disturb the stillness was the occasional menacing tornado and sandstorm that made everything vanish almost in an instant. A stinging, swirling nightmare of dust blew in when you couldn't see the opposite footpath. These are roughly the words of a Bush friend Earle Craig Junior. Because of this environment families got used to the dust that infiltrated into the houses, offices, schools and hospitals. Even storm windows were installed to keep out the rain and the sand.

Schooldays started by the daily ritual in the mornings of sweeping clean each desktop. Rattlesnakes, scorpions and tarantulas the size of large apples made you wonder how anyone could set up home here. George Junior was also very familiar with the occasional invasion of frogs that he remembered like a biblical plague. The people just made friends with the bouncing bushes of tumbleweed in the streets. Every December they sprayed the clumps with gold and glitter to use as Christmas decorations.

George Senior made one of the very few mistakes in his life in Odessa when he invited a member of the National Association for the Advancement of Coloured People to dinner. The young black civil rights leader knew the district better than the newcomer George Bush Senior and refused the invitation. Later Bush was quietly warned ominously never to try something like that again. It takes one's breath away to realize the depth of the bitterness around at that time. It seemed like the Civil War had only just happened yesterday.

But business then took the family to California. One year later, the family returned to Texas and settled in Midland, a small town about three hundred miles from Fort Worth. The family lived there until 1959 when George was thirteen years old. They were still sadly mourning the loss of George's little sister Robin who had died six years earlier in 1953 of Leukaemia. It was a tragedy that drew George closer to his mother. George, by the way, also had three brothers and another sister to contend with Jeb, Neil, Marvin and Dorothy. I have written earlier about this Bush family tragedy in my piece about George Bush Senior, the 41st President so I won't dwell on it again.

At this point just to lighten things up let's talk about George W. Bush's schooldays.

Many anecdotes reveal the inner irrepressible comedian in George Bush bottled inside of him. Most of the time it struggled to escape even as a young boy. One episode concerned his music teacher who was not amused when she heard George's schoolmates giggling as she wrote on the blackboard. Turning around there was George entertaining the class by drawing a beard and sideburns on his chubby face. Perhaps she should have handled things differently. Then again perhaps on that particular day she had had enough. The outcome was he was marched off to the Principal's office to account for his behaviour in disturbing the class. The Principal Mr. Bizilio's remedy was three swift slaps with a strap on George's rear end. George's swagger and dignity ended with a loud wail. The Principal remembers it like this. "He hollered as if I shot him but he learned his lesson."

However it was only the beginning of George's "on stage" behaviour for the amusement of his admiring pals. I'm afraid Mr. Bizilio was a little over-optimistic, for the mischievous imp buried inside George couldn't be suppressed that easily. As a youth George defied convention and was seen smoking cigars and heard cursing like a Navy deckhand. Always out to shock, he greeted his Sunday school teacher with the greeting "Hiya Little Lady, looking Sexy" which got the desired effect to George's amusement. Barbara couldn't always control him and he spent many an afternoon in his room waiting for dad to come home to deal with some of his over the top behaviour.

Barbara recalls her jousts with George like this "We fight all the time; we're so alike in that way. He does things to needle me." She would only have to scoff sarcastically "Don't be ridiculous" and a new row would erupt gathering steam as it went. It was this constant clash of wills between a steely no-nonsense mother and a super-hyper headstrong son which shaped George's personality. It was I suppose an ongoing battle she had to win, for most times she was the sole disciplinarian in the home when George Senior was away on business. Politics meant his father George Senior couldn't always be at home to play that role.

George had a lively mind and developed the talent for associating faces with names, a trick he learned while working with his father on the stump. It came in useful during George's own political career. He developed another side of this skill by applying nicknames to everyone he met.

As an adult this trait in his personality didn't diminish. The cocky ever-optimistic clown prince of mirth came into his own in Andover. As their self-appointed cheerleader he had only one mission in life there, to lift the spirits of everyone around him. He appeared at football rallies in all sorts of special gear. Once he was seen hamming it up in the gym dressed as one of the Beatles. Sometimes at football matches he gave a running commentary in wisecracks through an outsized megaphone wearing a squashed funky fishing hat.

Ultra conservatives at Andover began to mutter at the way George was defying the sophisticated traditions of Andover. George was becoming embarrassingly good as a cheerleader to such an extent they were going to sack him from Andover. But George had a fan in Dean Benedict who enjoyed George's antics so much his suffering critics had to endure George's unorthodox approach to the job for a little while longer. Maybe it also had something to do with George's Ivy League background – who knows. I think you will agree by the foregoing that our 43rd President was no wilting violet and for most of his life he simply refused to take himself seriously. Furthermore this irrepressible personality didn't change once he became President. I have certainly got one enjoyable story to prove that one.

The story moves on now. In 1959, again for business reasons the Bush family moved to Houston, Texas. It was two years later that in 1961 when George was fifteen years old that he left Houston, Texas for Andover, Massachusetts to attend a boarding school where his father had been a boarder – The Phillips Academy. George seemed to enjoy it here playing a lot of basketball and football. It was here the bug for baseball well and truly bit him. It became his first love which one day would lead him to the ownership of a baseball team but that's a story for later.

In 1964 at eighteen years of age George set off for Yale, although he was still called on to help his dad on his campaign for a Senate seat for Texas. Like his father and grandfather George became a member of the exclusive Skull and Bones society, a club I have covered in previous notes on Bush Senior. At Yale George was only an average student who didn't exactly cover himself with the distinction his father achieved.

It seems he spent most of his time there drinking, watching sport or just chasing girls, not an unnatural tendency for any red-blooded male so young.

Later as President, when being awarded an honorary degree from Yale, dozens of professors boycotted the ceremony while outside protesters booed. But this didn't phase our light-hearted President who we know never took pomp and circumstances very seriously anyway. In his speech he grinned unabashed saying "To those of you who received honours awards and distinctions I say well done. To the C student I say, you too can be President of the United States."

But let's continue his story at Yale. In spite of George's so called erratic study programme and larger than life behaviour he still accomplished his goal by graduating in history. Later he graduated in business studies by being conferred with the MBA in Harvard University in 1975. He was twenty-nine years old then. But this didn't end his almost nomadic family lifestyle for they returned to Midland almost immediately. Now life was to become very turbulent indeed for George. He started work for the first time as a Landsman helping to organise oil drilling ventures which involved gathering together Geologists, property owners, investors and negotiating business deals.

Around this time life became a little more interesting for George W. Bush. Early in 1977 cupid paid him a visit and without warning he fell head over heels in love with a young elementary school teacher who was also a librarian. Within three months of their first date George and Laura Welch became Mr. and Mrs. Bush in November 1977. We will talk about that later.

The marriage inspired George to move into politics as a Republican Congressional candidate in 1978. He lost it even though he had the full support of the oil industry behind him. The loss was hurtful but part of a great learning curve for him. His Democratic opponent criticised him for being out of touch with the needs of Texas voters so George vowed never to be caught out of touch again.

After his defeat George returned to the oil business and opened a number of small firms in exploration as well as campaigning for his father as he fought alongside Reagan for the Presidency. Over the next eight years he worked alongside his father when George Senior was Vice President. In 1981 another event brought him a new source of happiness the birth of his two children; this has another story to it which I will tell you later. The names of his twin daughters are Jenna and Barbara.

Yet somehow his oil ventures never got going and fate found him moving to Washington this time to assist his father in his bid for the Presidency. The year was 1987 and George was now forty-one years old. He had not made a great noise in the business world but then again the great English Prime Minister Winston Churchill was unable to succeed in anything he attempted up to his 50th birthday. One unseen talent he had developed over the years was an amazing understanding of politics which he no doubt must have cultivated over the many years working alongside his father on his campaign trail.

Fate took a hand in his life; for once again he left Washington and returned to Dallas where he bought a small interest in the Texas Rangers Baseball team in 1989. He became a manager and general partner in Texas Rangers and assumed the role of public spokesman for the club which helped to raise his profile in Texas. A new baseball stadium was built and life was at last happy and uncomplicated for George W. Bush. His erratic unplanned lifestyle at last had a purpose.

This did not stop him making the round trip between Dallas and Washington regularly to confer with his father the President. It was now the early 1990s when his father's own political career came to a close with the end of his Presidency. George decided it was now time to take his own political career seriously.

Now a much more mature and experienced politician he aimed his ambitions for the highest political prize available to him at that time, Governor of Texas. It was 1994, sixteen years after his defeat for Congress in 1978 and he was determined not to be mistaken again for an outsider in Texas. He criss-crossed the State and worked hard for the political prize he wanted and eventually triumphed with 53.5% of the vote. He was now against all expectations Governor of Texas. More important still - no longer a political outsider. But far from being a planned family triumph his success caught everyone by surprise. Not for the last time would George W. Bush confound his critics.

His father George Senior actually expressed amazement at his son's success for before George set off on his historic venture for the Governorship even his wife Laura tried to dissuade him from his ambition. "George," she said "it is an ill-advised and ill-fated idea." But once George became Governor of Texas his father was heard to say "The Presidency should now be only a six inch putt" to use golfing terminology.

Amazingly George W. Bush was now no longer a candidate for more business failures in Texas but a live probability for the highest job in the country, President of the United States. Against all the odds an unknown was marching confidently into the unknown.

The year was 1994 and at long last George W. Bush was in control of his own destiny. To do this he had to overcome another obstacle, the limited authority of the Governor's office. By gaining the confidence of some powerful Democrats, especially the Lieutenant Governor and the Speaker of the House, he was ready to bring about the reforms he aimed for by cutting welfare rosters and returning control of the schools to local municipalities.

Yet according to some critics he failed to tackle the environment, children's health and rising poverty. His major goal was to take on board the most influential Democrats in Texas; after all he was still only a Republican sitting in the Governor's mansion. But gradually he gained public support and even went on to serve a second term as Governor of Texas. The death penalty in Texas was his major stumbling block but despite high profile executions on his watch, the public in Texas supported passionately the use of the death penalty.

Karla Faye Tucker was one such high profile victim of this awful procedure and was the first woman to be executed in Texas since the Civil War in 1861. For those anti-hanging people outside America hanging is stomach churning. Strangely Ronald Reagan had suffered the same fate in California when he was also asked to adjudicate on another heartbreaking tragedy, to decide whether a prisoner lives or dies. But let's move on now.

It seems his father the ex-President had been right to judge his chances for the Presidency as only "a six inch putt" for George had now become more and more the focus as a Presidential possibility. How his fortunes had changed in a matter of years. George W. Bush was now describing himself as a compassionate conservative and worked tirelessly in Texas to be re-elected Governor. His strategy irritated the Democrats when he repeatedly appeared to speak in sensitive areas to Hispanics in the Democratic strongholds. He duly won his second term by a majority of 69% of the vote, the first Governor in Texas history to achieve this remarkable distinction and as a Republican too. A Republican in a Democratic stronghold!

Although he was lucky to be head of a prosperous Texas, George Bush's politics were changing rapidly, moving distinctly towards faith-based organizations to do the work generally done by Government. He promoted the idea of freedom for Churches, Synagogues and Mosques to do the work of bringing social services to the people. He claimed his idea was to counter the moral decline that was at the root of society's problems.
It is hard to believe such radical thinking had been buried deep inside a man who seemed to have a futile mission, trying to fill the footsteps of an illustrious father in the oil business. But all that was in the past now as he settled into politics, the real George Bush emerged from that self-imposed shell in which he had buried himself.

Of course George as ever had his critics. As Governor they accused him of exposing the poor of Texas to unnecessary risks by concentrating too much time in pursuit of his long term goal to make sure every child in Texas knew how to read and write. I'd hazard a guess that Barbara his mother was an enthusiastic supporter of this plan. Unfortunately that is the hazard of political choices that most politicians live or die by. But that magical odyssey went on and on. Now George W. Bush was walking on that long straight road to the White House which he had firmly in his sights. How life had changed for him since January 1999.

It seemed such a short time since early January 1999 when he set up the campaign committee for the hustings in August 1999 against the cream of Republican candidates such as Ambassador Alan Keyes, Elizabeth Dole head of the Red Cross, Senator John McCain and former Vice President Dan Quayle. Once again George was underestimated by his opponents when he emerged victorious early in the preliminaries.

By January 2000, exactly one year after he set out on his journey Bush and McCain became the main Republican candidates. Again George had his critics sniping at him from the wings. He was riding on the coat tails of his father they said. Others complained he lacked experience. However George's answer to that accusation was that the economy and the area of Texas had a population bigger than many countries. Furthermore he had run it as Governor for a record two terms.

In June 2000, a year and a half after his campaign began he had attracted $85 million for his campaign so it was now obvious the big guns had jumped aboard. But astute as ever, the following month July 2000, he was making overtures to the NAACP. To you and I that is the National Association for the Advancement of Coloured People. Once again he was reaching out to the disenfranchised minorities especially the blacks. Some people said he had not delivered specific solutions to their problems but whatever the chemistry he used they trusted him. As we know today he picked one of his father's men Dick Cheney to be his Vice President and running mate.

On November 7, 2000 less than two years after he started out on the road to the Presidency he set out his stall for the Presidency itself promising tax cuts, an improved educational programme but most of all he introduced the theme of "morality in Government" which was to appeal to millions across the bible belt of America.

In the Presidential race the polls ran neck and neck and as the results came in Bush had won twenty-nine States, among them traditionally Democratic States such as West Virginia and Tennessee and Southern States Utah, Georgia and Alabama. George was still confounding everybody.

The resurgence of the Republican Party in Texas was a George Bush phenomenon. Texas had always been rock solid Democrat. In east Texas they called them "yellow dog Democrats" meaning they would vote for a yellow dog before they would ever vote for a Republican. This situation had existed for the previous one hundred years from Reconstruction to the 1965 Voting Rights Act. They say that this achievement paved the way to the White House for him. Back at the turn of the century O. Henry, a Texas newspaperman, described the political thinking in Texas at that time as follows "We have only three laws such as against murdering witnesses and being caught stealing horses. The third one is voting for Republicans." And George Bush was responsible for this miracle. The movement to the Republicans came usually from blue collar Democrats and those with strong Evangelican views which George was glad to exploit.

It was indeed a glorious two years for George W. Bush since he first formed the committee to plan his Presidential campaign back in January 1999.

But George's meticulously laid plans could never have anticipated what happened next. Just as it seemed the prize was tantalizingly within his grasp, the two year roller coaster of heady success was about to plough into a brick wall for the counting of votes had run into trouble. I suppose this is a story that has been written a hundred times by other commentators more formidable than your writer. However just for the record here is my reading of the story and of the Court cases that ran for five weeks at the end of the 20th Century.

1. Florida law demanded a recount where the margin between two candidates is no more than half of 1%. After this recount Bush was still ahead by 300 votes. It gets more complicated.
2. The next problem to surface were the votes of the overseas ballot. How many were there and for which Party would they be cast.
3. Meanwhile the Democrats wanted a manual recount because of the inaccuracy of machine tallies.

4. The Republicans opposed this and went to Court to prevent a manual recount because of the danger of human error in the recount.

5. If you are still with me the story continues as follows. The Democrats then went to Court seeking to have all manual recounts included in the final ballot.

6. In the meantime on November 14, 2000 Florida Supreme Court ordered a delay in the certification process until it could hear the case. One week later on November 21, it ruled unanimously in favour of including the manual counts but the result was to be submitted to the Secretary of State before November 26.

7. Bush disagreed with the decision of the Florida Supreme Court and appealed his case to the United States Supreme Court.

8. When the November 26 deadline came about Florida certified its election results and Bush still won this time by 500 votes. Now it was up to the United States Supreme Court to make its ruling on Bush's appeal but it first asked Florida Supreme Court to clarify its ruling.

9. On the same day December 4, a Florida Circuit Court Judge ruled against the Democrats request for additional recounts.

10. Gore immediately appealed the Circuit Court Judges' ruling and brought his request for additional recounts to the Florida Supreme Court.

11. If you think all that is complicated the waters now get muddier for on December 8, Florida Supreme Court ruled that additional counts should be allowed.

Like an old fashioned tennis rally the ball was still in the air and the players were scampering around the Court going all out to win the final rally and smash it over the net for victory. Now Bush went up the line once again to the U.S. Supreme Court which suspended all recounts until after it heard Bush's case which it did on December 11. The next day December 12, the Supreme Court finally ruled that the recounts were unconstitutional on the grounds that the recounts violated the equal protection clause of the United States Constitution because there was no clear standard for how to do manual recounts.

Because of this they ruled not all votes were being treated equally.

This ruling was a huge victory for Bush. The following day December 13, five weeks after the election, Gore had no alternative but to concede the election to Bush. George W. Bush was now the President-elect of the United States which was finally legalized on January 20, 2001 at the inauguration ceremony. What an amazing unbelievable two years it had been for George W. Bush. It had taken several visits to three Courts – the Circuit Court, the Florida Supreme Court and the U.S. Supreme Court to resolve the Presidency.

To say such a situation was unsatisfactory is the understatement of the century. George W. Bush was now moving into the Presidency with a flawed pedigree through no fault of his own. There hadn't been an election like it since 1888 when Grover Cleveland won the popular vote only to lose in the Electoral College. The 1876 election had been decided by an Electoral Commission who gave it to Rutherford Hayes just days before his inauguration. So at 10 p.m. on December 12, 2001 by a Supreme Court ruling of 5 – 4 handed down just two hours before the deadline for State certification, the decision was finally made.

It was a real turn up for the books.

Al Gore, the Vice President had started the race with a considerable advantage, peace abroad and prosperity at home. Unfortunately for him because of his decision to distance himself from Bill Clinton he could not capitalize on Clinton's policy successes. Bush's financial clout was also a telling factor in Gore's defeat. Unfortunately the State that created the problem, Florida, was the one whose Governor was Bush's brother Jeb. Yet isn't it worth thinking about? What if some other State had been the final one involved in a recount? Would there still be the same frantic debate on the outcome? Only time will tell and one day only time will heal.

Many books have been inspired and written on President George W. Bush not all of them complimentary. One such book has been put forward for the prestigious Booker prize Stupid White Men by Michael Moore, author of another anti-Bush publication Fahrenheit 9/11. In the Booker prize favourite Stupid White Men, Bush's campaign team were accused of paying $4 million to Database Technologies to remove suspected felons from the voter rolls. This was ordered by Florida's Secretary of State with the blessing of Governor Jeb Bush. Since felons are not eligible to vote anyway the criticism only becomes relevant when Moore makes the point that 31% of black men in Florida are prohibited from voting because they have a felony on their record.

This rule would keep thousands of blacks out of the polling booths and since blacks mainly vote Democrat, the conclusion Moore came to was that this amounted to thousands less votes for the Democrats. Since Gore had polled 90% of the black vote Moore suggested that 90% of those debarred would have voted Democrat. Then Moore makes a further charge that a false list was used from another State which resulted in 8,000 voters being culled from the voter list. He says that this list contained names of ex felons who had already served their time or who had only been guilty of misdemeanours such as parking fines or littering. He then produced another statistic that takes the gloss off Bush's victory, i.e. 173,000 names were wiped off the register of which 66,000 were black. Moore claimed it was an assault on the voting rights of minorities.

Looking back on my previous forty-two Presidents and the dignity with which they won and held office it leaves me with a profound sense of sadness and unease to have to record the bitterness generated by the election of November 2000. The story of this reaction I now give you.

Inauguration day January 20, 2001 was a cold windy raw day. The protestors ran into thousands still sore about the election result. The footpaths were crowded with people at 4.30 a.m. disgorged from buses specially engaged for various shades of opinion. "The media may project them as low-life criminals, drug addicts, Communists and anarchists" were the thoughts of James Hatfield in his book Fortunate Son. His experience would be vastly different he claimed after watching only mainstream Americans, educated, law abiding and working class people worried about their democracy who were standing around.

The protestors were actually met with cheers by bystanders. The usual questions and answers protest filled the loudspeakers "Did George Bush win the Majority?" "No," the crowd roared as a car passed. A cry went up "It's Bush"; "Boo" came the almost hysterical reaction from a small group of protestors. The overall public reaction can be measured in percentages. Only 25% now believe the TV news, 19% believe newspapers and 12% believe magazines.

Spin doctors were getting a terrible pasting but all the foregoing didn't prevent the $30 million extravaganza of pomp and pageantry with brass bands and marching soldiers down Pennsylvania Avenue from taking place. The eleven inaugural Balls where the President and the First Lady danced the night away were celebrated as joyfully as any of the Balls held in all of the past forty-two inauguration ceremonies going back to Washington himself.

But democracy has a life of its own and is just as unpredictable. Amazingly the protestors of 2001 disappeared from view four years later in 2005 and George W. Bush was re-elected for another term by a landslide. Yes, he was still surprising America. And America was still surprising itself.

But let's talk about George Bush's 1st term. The day after his inauguration was visitor's day at the White House. The first day is always shared with thousands of visitor, who come on a first-come first-served basis. This is a traditional event which throws open the White House doors to the ordinary citizen. It goes back for years through many Presidencies. It was George and Laura's first official outing and it was a great help in returning both of them to everyday reality. The questions were easy to cope with covering the domestic concerns about decorations, colour schemes, intended renovations, and the everyday problems which might confront the First Lady. Laura fielded them with a light-hearted script of her own. George helped her too "It is the peoples house," he told them "and you are very welcome here."

Sunday afternoon was set aside for about 3,000 visitors who passed through the front doors of the White House all day. George was preoccupied also with getting down to work Monday morning and he intended to get started early with some security briefings. Yes he intended to be a very busy man. "The most important thing for this President to do is to focus on trying to get things done, limited things over these next few days." Those were the words of former White House Chief of Staff Leon Panetta.

Life had started for the new President George Bush, 43rd President of the United States.

Just a word of caution. The first days of George W. Bush's extraordinary Presidency were serene and peaceful in comparison with what was to happen later.
With the fire and fury of the Presidential election behind him now George W. Bush set about the tasks he had laid out for himself for his first term as President. He had three main priorities. "Education will be a priority of course," said Bush "swearing in my staff will be a priority, working with people on the Hill from both Parties will be a priority, and as I mentioned during the course of the transition, the first legislation we will be sending up will be an education package."

The Governorship of Texas for George was to prove an ideal learning experience for the Presidency. Part of his plan was the creation of a $5 billion fund to ensure young children learn to read by the third grade. There was even a controversial proposal to give Federal money to low income parents to help those who wished to transfer their children from failing schools to private or parochial schools. "Money needs to follow the child," said Rove.

Another part of his agenda was to introduce a $1.3 trillion tax cut as he had promised in his Presidential campaign much to the concern of White House Chief of Staff Leon Panetta. "You can't slam dunk a tax cut package the size they are talking about," she said on the TV programme "Late Edition".

Sunday was declared a national day of prayer and thanksgiving as the first day of his Presidency began with the prayer service at Washington's national Cathedral. This is a traditional appointment written into every President's schedule.

About 3,000 people attend the religious service.

Also there, were President Bush Senior and Barbara. George Bush and his Cabinet members took their seats in the front row to hear Billy Graham's son Franklin give his sermon. "We have gathered here today with renewed hope for America; I pray that God will place his great hand of protection on each and everyone and especially upon you Mr. President and your family."

"This prayer service demonstrates our recognition and need for help from the Almighty." Frankly Graham went on "We affirm that we are indeed a free and independent people but in a more profound sense, we are a people that are dependent on Almighty God."

The moving hour long service also had Scripture readings by Rabbi Samuel Karff of Beth Israel Synagogue, Houston, Texas and Archbishop Demetrios of the Greek Orthodox Archdiocese of America.

The service concluded with the singing of "America is Beautiful".

Sadly the beauty they sang about only survived about eight months of normality in George Bush's first term in the Presidency. During this time the almost tranquil, everyday events of American life unfolded around him. People loved and laughed, played and got married, went on vacations and celebrated the births of the next generation of Americans.

Suddenly and without warning the bitterness of suppressed anger that had been fermenting for years in the far off lands of the Middle East exploded in a massive fireball over New York when three airliners were flown with devastating consequences into the twin skyscrapers known as the World Trade Centre and the Pentagon.

The date September 11, 2001 will now forever be associated with the 43rd Presidency of George W. Bush. It had the same historic impact as Lincoln's Civil War, the emancipation of the slaves, and the very foundation of the American Republic under the revered George Washington.

Suspects were rounded up and imprisoned in Quantanimo Bay, a centre where suspected terrorists were brought for interrogation. On Monday March 27, 2006 Zacarias Moussaoui confessed at his trial that there was to be a fifth plane which he was to pilot. His accomplice was to have been someone who by now was well-known to the world as Richard Reid the "Shoe Bomber".

You may remember he was taken off a passenger flight and found to be wearing a bomb built into the heel of his shoe which got him the name of the "Shoe Bomber". The flight from Paris to Miami in December 2001, two months after 9/11 was saved when the passengers and crew of the American Airlines jet, tackled and overpowered him just before he ignited the explosion. He was sentenced to life imprisonment and was imprisoned in January 2003.

So Moussaoui was moving in the worst of company. "I had knowledge that the twin towers were to be hit but I didn't have the details," he said at his trial. "I was supposed to pilot a plane that was to hit the White House," he said in answer to a question put to him by the Court attorney. Incidentally, he had already been found guilty and was on trial to determine if he should be executed. He knew all nineteen of the hijackers by face including ringleader Mohammed Atta who was killed in the raid. Strangely Moussaoui had been picked up three weeks before 9/11 but had lied to the FBI in order to ensure the attack went ahead. Even then he was not a qualified pilot, but in the middle of simulator lessons to complete his training for the mission. He denied being a big wheel in Al Qaeda, the terrorist organisation lead by Osama Bin Laden who was emerging as a major enemy of America. Just a pen picture here of Osama Bin Laden may help the reader understand why the attack took place.

It was unbelievable just how bitter and fearless Zacarias Moussaoui was which was reflected in his defiance in the dock. He expressed no regret and no remorse. So unmoved was he on hearing the evidence of some of the victim's relatives at the trial, he lashed out at them saying "I wish you had suffered more." "So would you be happy to see 9/11 again?" Prosecutor Rob Spencer asked. His reply was chilling "Everyday until we get you," the bearded thirty-seven year old Frenchman spat back. He wasn't helping his hard-working defence team. He even spent two hours with the lawyers on both sides arguing whether he was sane or not. He admitted to a dream he had held, in being part of a prisoner exchange for captured troops.

Hearing Lt. Nancy McKeown sobbing just made his day, he declared "I am glad there was pain and I wish there was more pain," he ranted. Defence lawyers tried to promote the idea that he was only seeking martyrdom through execution. The verdict eventually came on May 3, 2006. It was not to be execution and martyrdom as Moussaoui had hoped but solitary confinement for life without any hope of parole. He clapped his hands in derision as he left the Court shouting "America you lost – I won." The panel of nine men and three women failed to reach the unanimity necessary to execute him. It took seven days of deliberations and despite all his boasts three jurors had decided Moussaoui had only limited knowledge of the plot to hijack the four jetliners that caused the atrocity.

The prosecutors asked for the death sentence saying "There is no place on this good earth for him." The verdict was read by U.S. District Judge Leonie Brinkema at the Courthouse in Alexandria, Virginia situated quite near the Pentagon. As she read it out it was heard with a grim stunned silence by a tense packed courtroom where a whole row of seats was taken up with the victims of 9/11. Moussaoui showed no immediate reaction as he sat slouched in his chair utterly refusing to acknowledge the gravity of the moment.

President Bush welcomed the sentencing of Moussaoui saying "Evil has been vanquished. Our cause is right and the outcome is certain. Justice will be served. Evil will not have the final say. The end of this trial represents the end of this case but not an end to the fight against terror. And we can be confident evil will not have the final say. The mercy shown by the Jury," he said "was not extended by Moussaoui to his 3,000 victims."

The act of terrorism that brought down two whole skyscrapers in the centre of New York crushing 3,000 people of many nationalities will go down in infamy in the hearts and minds of the American people.

Unbelievably, Zacarias Moussaoui an educated English Frenchman of Moroccan extraction was the only one charged with the crime of 9/11 that killed 3,000 people of different nations. Details of the casualties were as follows: -

Twin Towers

Perhaps a few facts might help us to have a deeper insight into 9/11.

The Twin Towers were built in 1970
The firms who worked there numbered 430
Visitors to the Twin Towers were 50,000 average a day
2,823 were killed in the tragedy
Underground fires burned a further 69 days
Number of body parts 19,500
Days searching for them 230
Intact bodies found 291
Identified bodies 1,102

Death Certificates without bodies 1,616
Still missing 105
Airplane victims 92

Al-Qaeda

Bin Laden's father Mohammad Awad. Bin Laden's children 52
Fortune left to Bin Laden $300 million
Bin Laden's wives 3
Al-Qaeda founded in 1988
Bin Laden's expulsion from Saudi Arabia 1991
Osama Bin Laden offered refuge in Kabul 1996
Expulsion from Sudan 1996
Nationality of hijackers 15 Saudis from 19 hijackers
Compensation claimed from Bin Laden's family and Saudi Princes
Compensation amount claimed one $trillion

But let's return to the Presidency on September 11, 2001. George Walker Bush had started into his first term as President of the United States. He had settled into the job and was looking forward to a comfortable routine lifestyle to the end of his first four years in office. September 11, 2001 was to be no ordinary day in the Presidency for when he woke up that morning the day was mapped out for him full of ordinary routine events. He was pencilled in for a visit to a school in Florida, mix with the kids, smile and just be the President. But at 9.05 a.m. that morning his whole world was to change forever.

While talking to the children word came through to him that a plane had crashed into the twin towers of the World Trade Centre. A crazy accident he thought as he sipped a cup of coffee. But it was worse than that. Another plane had done the very same thing minutes later so what was happening? This was no accident. His Chief of Staff Andy Card confirmed his worst fears "America is under attack," Card told the President.

The cameras exposed with ruthless indifference the reaction of George Bush's features. His body language said the rest. Shock, disbelief, horror, would best describe his emotions. His affable personality would seem useless in such a crisis. Scowling and frowning might project an image of toughness that the occasion demanded, yet that type of gravity was not normal for George Bush. Today he was being tested with something for which there was no training. This time he was on his own. Would the long turbulent years behind him bear fruit and show the steel in the man?

In far off Lima, Peru, President Alejandro Toledo was sitting down to breakfast with the visiting American Secretary of State, Colin Powell. The main subject was textile quotas which the President was determined to discuss. Suddenly textiles became totally irrelevant when an American Aide rushed into the room carrying in his hand a page torn from a notepad. Two airplanes had crashed into the World Trade Centre. Powell headed for the airport but on the aircraft he found all lines to Washington jammed.

He hated this imposition of inaction but he was helpless. Seven hours of helplessness followed and was more than he could bear for a man who could have been President had his wife not vetoed the idea, threatening to walk out leaving him to the Presidency alone. This vacuum was not his cup of tea. Although he had been an automatic choice for Secretary of State somehow he always seemed to be operating at the edge of the Administration. Now he was heading home he thought "How can I influence the President or will I have to listen to the hardliners surrounding me." Terrorism would be top of the agenda.

Meanwhile back in the White House the First Lady started the day doing the President's job for him by taking the dogs Spot and Barney for a walk. With her walk over she returned to the White House for breakfast with her in-laws George Senior and Barbara Bush.
Laura's diary was full for she was to appear that day before a Senate Committee on the subject of funding for nursery schools. She duly kissed her in-laws goodbye and headed for her official car. September 11, promised to be a beautiful day with warm autumn sunshine lifting her spirits.
Then the day may as well have had cyclonic thunderclouds over head when her Secret Service Agent took her aside and broke the news. "Something terrible is happening in New York," he said. Her husband, 900 miles away in Florida, was getting the same message. Vice President Dick Cheney was rushed to the nuclear bomb-proof bunker in the basement of the White House while flak-jacketed security men ran through the House shouting "Get out! Get out! This is real."

Later Laura sat in Senator Edward Kennedy's office watching the pictures running across the TV screens. "Nothing is ever going to be the same again," she thought. As George Bush watched the same pictures in Florida his face was red with rage "God damn whoever did this, God damn them."
He grabbed his STU-III mobile phone, a black bulbous instrument on which he was sure to have a secure line twenty-four hours a day. First Dick Cheney, then the Head of the CIA spoke to him. Osama Bin Laden was the chief suspect. When Bush hung up he turned to his Aides and said grimly "We're at war. We are going to take care of this boys. That's what we're paid for. When we find out who did this they are not going to like me as President."

This was a significant turn of phrase from George Bush for his sunny nature was his stock in trade. He liked to be liked. One of the few criticisms levelled against him was always the fact he never took things seriously.

Could this frivolous personality stand up to the trouble crashing all round him which he rode like a clipper ship in a storm. He had no military expertise to call upon and there was a wide range of doubters watching for chinks in his armour.

A third passenger jet was reported to have crashed into the Pentagon. Had it been re-routed away from the White House?

"I am going to leave going back to Washington," the President decided. Someone had called the emergency line with a threat "Air force One is next." What made the call authentic was the knowledge the person had to get through to the nerve centre beneath the White House and they also knew the code for Air Force One. These people had done their homework it seems. This time from inside the Presidency. Bush was desperate to know about the safety of the First Lady and instructed his Aides to get her on the phone. "Oh Bushie," she said "how horrible how terrible!" Once again she was his rock when she just said calmly "Don't worry about me or the girls we are safe." For the first time in aviation history all commercial aircraft was grounded to nearby airports. A fourth plane then crashed into the nearby airfield. When the President was airborne Air Force One rose to a different level of 40,000 feet as a precaution. At 11.50 a.m. it touched down at an air force base in Louisiana.

The change in the America George Bush knew before he went visiting in Florida struck him like a tidal wave when he stepped off Air Force One in Louisiana. He was met by a detachment of soldiers in combat gear carrying M-16 rifles. Hummer patrol vehicles with machine guns perched on top were parked guarding the runway.

A decision made at this point by his backup team was a bad one diplomatically and was to prove counter-productive politically later. George wanted to get on with it and return immediately to Washington. But Vice President Dick Cheney had other ideas. He thought, backed up by security advisors that it was dangerous and inadvisable. "I don't care," Bush replied "I don't want some tin-horn terrorist keeping the President out of Washington." He was talked out of it however but his first instincts were right and he should have trusted them. Perhaps it was his phone call home to his father who urged that George protect the office of the President first.

Don't take any chances. And so "Air Force One" suffered the indignity of hopping from airport to airport for the next nine hours attracting increasing media criticism as it went. "Where was the President?" "Why was he hiding?" they trumpeted in their headlines. It wasn't until 7 p.m. that evening that Air Force One came dipping down through the clouds to land at Washington airport where Laura was waiting for him. With eyes wet with tears she embraced him tenderly. At 8.30 p.m. he finally sat in the Oval office to address the nation on TV.

His speech went something like this: "The search is underway for those who were behind this evil act..... We will make no distinction between the terrorists who committed these acts and those who harbour them." He went on "Tonight I ask for your prayers for all those who grieve." George Bush spent some time speaking in anguish about the pain of the children whose sense of safety had been shattered forever and gave a ruthless guarantee of retaliation for this attack on the security of the United States.

His speech finished with: "None of us will ever forget this day, yet we go forward to defend freedom and all that is good and just in the world. Thank you and goodnight and God Bless America." Then hand in hand with Laura they headed for their private quarters. It had been a devastating day for the Bush family and the victims of 9/11. But like a script from that master of suspense Alfred Hitchcock the day did not end there.

"Why not go to the nuclear shelter to sleep Mr. President" was the remark that caused George to flip his lid at about 9 on the Richter scale. The Secret Service man who suggested they sleep in the nuclear bomb-proof basement took a risk above and beyond the call of duty. It was the straw that broke the camels back so to speak. All Bush's frustration burst like a pent-up dam of emotions on the unfortunate man. "Oh, no we're not," he growled "I've had a heck of a day and I am going to sleep in my own bed tonight." Laura fell asleep instantly but a half awake President was suddenly sitting bolt upright when a Secret Agent burst into his bedroom shouting "Mr. President, Mr. President, an unidentified aircraft is heading this way. I think we are under attack." So Bush grabbed his dogs and steered Laura towards the bunker. However it was all just a false alarm and both of them burst out laughing with relief and returned to bed for the final time that night.

The backwash of criticism for his delay in getting home was a little cruel. Laura sensed this injustice and dismissed it with just two words. "Ignore them." She was a tremendous force for keeping things cool. "Don't act rashly," she counselled him "Don't act out of revenge." She was also aware of the plight of American Muslims caught in a maelstrom of retaliation.

Bush took immediate action to deal with that possibility. Laura's instincts had been absolutely true for next day a man was shot dead in Arizona just because he looked Asian.

"Muslims make an incredibly valuable contribution to our country," Bush declared "and they need to be treated with respect." This was vintage Bush for he was reared in a family that believed in rejecting racial bigotry in any situation.

I have deliberately opened with the crisis of September 11, 2001 eight months after George Bush stepped into the White House as its 43rd President because I feel it will be the catalyst around which the 43rd Presidency of the United States will be remembered far into the future. It is almost impossible to separate 9/11 and the war in Iraq, the twin tragedies of modern American history. They were destined to dominate the whole of the George W. Bush Presidency.

So let's move on and watch events unfold around him.

Now that Bush was home in the White House he knew this was different. Not even remotely like anything he had encountered before. Despite all his experience alongside his father out on the campaign trail, and infighting in the politics of Texas this was an international war situation for which he had no previous experience.

The world looking on held its breath and wondered what sort of a President he was going to be as their Commander-in-Chief? How would he handle this new responsibility?

Even his closest companions on the Press Corps who had travelled thousands of miles with him on the Presidential Campaign trail didn't know how he would bear up. Part-scamp, part-adolescent optimist, who seemed at all times more in harmony with the inner child just beneath the surface than the harsh realities of the world at large out there.
In short he loved everyone around him. Frank Bruni of The New York Times remembers the playful clown who found time to forget his august position with practical jokes that invited retaliation in kind such as his habit of placing both hands on the gleaming dome of a bald colleague, looking up to heaven in mock horror and shouting "Heal, Heal." He could be playful, clumsy and irreverent whenever the mood suited him wrote Bruni. Sometimes he even lampooned himself when in mock incredibility he sat behind his desk in the White House and exclaimed "My, Mr. President, you look fabulous today" or "Mr. President that was a magnificent speech."

Yes, how would a President who didn't take himself seriously confront this type of crisis? But one thing is for certain, the people out there calling him a "Bozo" or "a man of straw" had a lot to learn about George Bush. Hadn't he confronted his own personal ghosts of alcoholism alone in the years gone by and won against unbelievable odds not just for one day but everyday he woke in the morning since then? He had indeed been face to face with extinction as a man and as a politician in those days. So when confronted in the Oval office with a question from a reporter about how he felt at that moment he answered with tears in his eyes. It was a display of compassion; his light-hearted personality always masked from the public, and revealed the caring and sensitive person he really was in his most secret thoughts.

Yes George Bush was a strange enigma with a story very similar to another of the Royal family of American politics The Kennedy clan. Here was a man who entered politics and has surprised everyone to become America's 43rd President. His articulate younger brother Jeb was the family favourite to reach the top. Yet it was almost a carbon copy of the Kennedy story when the younger Jack became President after the expected heir to that throne, Joe

Kennedy was killed in the battle of Britain.

Yes who can know what the hands of fate have in store for us? Studying the personality of George W. Bush can be best understood by looking at the formidable task all the sons of George Bush Senior had to contend with. George Senior was a father who excelled at sport, was a top guy in Yale, successful in the oil bushiness, Head of the CIA and President of the United States.

The demands of living up to the standards of such a father must have been colossal for his sons. Jeb was the first to succeed in politics becoming Governor of Florida. George W. always wore his heart on his sleeve among the family. He was very hurt when his two daughters Barbara and Jenna showed no interest in politics, in fact they failed to turn up for one of his speeches. The situation hadn't gone unnoticed by Al Gore who preened himself about how lucky he was to have all his family turning up to support him. It hadn't gone unnoticed by somebody else, the First Lady herself. Laura immediately took action and had some words with the girls who took a closer interest from then on. This story has a happy ending for Jenna came home after one of George's speeches and told him "Dad you were great." Her words had an impact she didn't expect. George just cried.

Another contributor to the man we are trying to understand is none other than John Sargeant, the experienced BBC commentator. On a late, late TV show he gave a surprising answer to his Irish TV host. "George Bush is a guy you would be very happy to have on your side," Sargeant said. For someone with Sargeant's expertise, a man who had straddled four generations of world leaders, and had moved in the most exalted political circles over forty years in Europe and America it had an immediate impact on the listener.

This was a man who met Churchill and DeGaulle, Thatcher and Gorbechev, Anthony Eden and John F. Kennedy himself. Sargeant's opinion revealed a shrewd analysis of Bush when he said "For someone who is the son of an ex-President, a Yale graduate, and a man with such a privileged background he just could not be an ordinary guy "a Mr. Average"."

It was his political brilliance that helped him to project such an image in the circumstances. "Being one of the boys" who loved barbeques, while it may be true, was an astute projection of a public image which was his major triumph and not his liability. Being capable of piloting an F102 Navy Jet and still not appear to be intellectual was something George Bush had worked on. On reflection can anyone honestly believe that a man with Bush's political family background could be so misinformed as to state that World War II started after Pearl Harbour as has been reported? Finally, for Bush to become a fluent Spanish speaker is not bad for a mere American dunce is it?

As we come to know Bush through the eyes and ears of those closest to him we will soon realize the world had no need for misgivings on Bush's personality.

I am writing this after five years of his Presidency and so far the world hasn't exactly imploded.

So let's look at life in the White House as David Frum one of his speechwriters sees it. How America reacted to September 11, 2001 is a story we will have to postpone a little longer if you will bear with me. In his book The Right Man, Frum leads us into a depressing environment of a Presidency which only seemed to attract ridicule. The routine answer everyone used to describe Bush's apparent mediocrity was to call him stupid. But his outspoken opinions had the stamp of honesty about them for he ran as hard against his own Party as he did against the opposition accusing them of balancing the budget on the backs of the poor. Nevertheless the late-night comedians for some strange reason continue to have a field day at George's expense.

Today's bookshelves, so full of anti-Bush hysteria should have dissuaded me from looking for any worth in the man. Perhaps a sheer waste of time. But like Frum I decided to investigate for myself and I am glad I did.

Sometimes Bush exposed his own personal vulnerability his tendency to wildness and sometimes he expressed himself in a way that resembled poetry. "I believe in a God who calls us not to judge our neighbours but to love them. I believe in grace because I have seen it, in peace because I have felt it, in forgiveness because I have needed it." Not exactly the words of a poet Laureate but language that touches a very human chord in the listener.

Here is a fascinating story worth listening to. The conversation of George Bush to become a Born Again Christian was revealed in his own biography A Charge to Keep published in 1999. Nobody who read it could be under any illusions he was a changed man. It was a meeting with Billy Graham the noted Evangelist that changed his whole life. They met when the Evangelist paid a visit to his father when his father was Vice President. "Over the course of that weekend Rev. Graham planted a mustard seed in my soul, a seed that grew over the next year. He led me to the path and I began walking. It was the beginning of a change in my life," said Bush. His wife influenced him to give up the liquor, the substance that threatened to leave him as just one more easily recognizable Texas drunk. This conversion gave him second thoughts about kick-starting a stuttering political career and to start following again in the footsteps of his father and grandfather. The rest is history. But back to Frum and his intriguing peep behind the scenes in the White House as he moved in there.

Walking in the footsteps of David Frum from the day he was invited, against his will, to become George Bush's speechwriter, is an education in itself. Living for a year with any man has to reveal something about him to all but a walking insomniac. But don't take my word for that, listen to Frum.

It was at the Republican Convention that Frum made his first discovery. Bush spoke and the speech was not about denying the prosperity of recent years in a begrudging way. He suggested that the Clinton years of prosperity were all downhill. He put this failure down to a moral failure on the part of the Administration. He summarised his own speech in the following words about Clinton. "Our current President has so much talent, so much charm, such great skill. But in the end to what end. So much promise to no great purpose."

Frum's opinion is the insight no one had captured so far. He called Bush's approach ingenious. But Clinton's Presidency had left Clinton politically crippled, a fate that also befell three other Presidents in the 20th century. Bush's strongest supporters were the people most disgusted by Clinton's behaviour. When asked at exit polls what their most important ingredient should be in their President 80% of them replied "Honesty".

The first information to come to Frum's ears was the rather unfair rumour that the Clintons had loaded hundreds of pieces of White House furniture recklessly onto their removal lorries on the way out. News of it had raised Bush's approval rating to 60%. When discussing the famous desk in the Oval office used by three Presidents Kennedy, Reagan and Clinton, Frum's source implied it was nailed to the floor "that's why its still there." A new style of honesty even a new style of dress came with the new President. Casual and sports clothes were common under

Clinton now it was mainly jackets and ties everyday even at weekends. Laura took no part in politics in contrast to Hillary Clinton who had acted almost as a Vice President.

Now Bush opened every Cabinet meeting with a prayer. When he was in West Virginia he talked about his book A Charge to Keep. Referring to it as "The book I wrote" he corrected himself with a grin "Well, they say I wrote it." Yes the Presidential style had certainly changed. His obsession with telling it as it is often exasperated him. Doing a recording in Washington and saying "Today I am in California" was meant to be broadcast when Bush was in California in two days time…. "But I am not in California…," he protested. Little white lies were not his style not even to suit the tape recorder. Another example was the words "I am happy to be here with you." "What if I am not happy to be here," he said to his scriptwriters!! Why should he pretend was his philosophy.

He wouldn't even take credit for what he did not do. An order was made releasing billions of dollars to pay for the restoration of the Florida Everglades yet he refused to take credit for it. "Today I signed an Everglades agreement with the State of Florida," he said and felt much more comfortable with that speech. Idle self-serving compliments to the audience were not allowed to his speechwriter. Even if he came from the County or had family connections with the town, this was not to be mentioned. Frum was gradually learning the mind of the President and how his President felt. Well that was Frum's job as official speechwriter to the President.

He had to be very true to the personality of George Bush telling it as it was. The pen picture Frum produced was as a result starkly honest and true to life. One quote from a classmate in Andover recalls "He was not a goody two shoes. He partied as much as anybody. I don't ever recall him being depressed." "Everybody knew George and George knew everybody" remembers Clay Johnson, "People just wanted to be around him." This was before George Bush became known. "I was quick with the one-liner," admits George, a skill that earned him the nickname "The Lip". Others say it was because he was never short of an opinion on most subjects. The Dean of Andover had his own opinions of George. One day he asked George where he planned to attend College "Yale," said George optimistically "my fathers Alma Mater." "Well you won't get in there so where else are you thinking of?" the Dean sneered cruelly. George confounded his detractors and entered Yale without help from the family.

You can see why it is not hard to understand how George W. Bush always had a certain disdain for Yale. "I was no fantastic genius at Yale," George admitted modestly "but there was always a challenge to do well there." One significant thing about his stay in Yale was his complete disinterest in the "Vietnam Rebellion" going on there and he never signed the circulars sent out by the protestors. He also had a photographic memory for people and names. Once when asked to name three names from a list of fifty, George named all fifty.

His friend Roland Betts from Yale described George Bush as "Not pretentious, not exploitative, he is just a disarmingly charming person." One political commentator said "He has a great ability to see through guff. Having had the chance to work alongside his father George W. Bush has more political sensitivities, a more political way about him than does the President. He will be much easier to elect when he decides to run for office than his father was!" He called it political instinct.

Frum made this comment about George "Even at Yale despite his mediocre grades George was showing an uncanny flair for getting people to do what he wanted." Mitch Kurz, a friend of his put it like this, "George's leadership was not based on raw brainpower. He had an intangible quality about him that there wasn't a problem that couldn't be solved. One ingredient he had got was an iron self-discipline which was reflected in his scripts as President. Yet sometimes the difficulty of writing for the President had nothing to do with the script." Once after having a joke deleted, Frum challenged Karl Rove about it. "Karl that was funny." "Yes," sighed Rove "but Presidents shouldn't be too funny." Some of the careless throwaway remarks of George Bush to reporters regularly made him the subject of ridicule when printed. But Frum, his scriptwriter just smiles about them and says "That image of George Bush gives no credit to his meticulously well-rehearsed, profoundly thought out political speeches. You may find this hard to believe but he was an absolutely ruthless editor of the words put before him. You will find this fascinating because a President's speeches project the entire importance and impact of the Presidency. This was something George Bush never forgot and never neglected. He hated repetition and redundancy" as Frum put it, "He insisted on strict linear logic.

Disjointed sentences would be corralled with the President's heavy marking pen. Black arrows would explain Education goes here, Tax relief over there, Defence spending here. He liked simple statistics so he added to vague phrases the inevitable questions in black pen 'By how much?', 'From what to what?'"

Finally a little anecdote of a particularly ruthless treatment of a speech meant for a big occasion. The scriptwriters had slaved for hours over the different drafts. There was a $5.6 trillion Federal surplus to be distributed most of which the Democrats had hoped to capture. He walked into the House of Representatives through doors flung open behind him. He kept walking past outstretched hands, past the faces familiar and unfamiliar, up the steps to the gleaming wood of the rostrum. A nod to the
Speaker and Vice President, a quick glance at the teleprompter on both sides of him. As Frum put it "His case was as clear and simple as any of Euclid's propositions. He told his audience: "(1) We have a big surplus (2) We are going to use some of it to increase spending on education and defence (3) We are going to use some more of it to repay debts (4) With the money left over we will cut taxes. Thank you and goodnight"."

Frum went on "If anyone still thinks he is an unfocused, indecisive muddled President after that performance I guess you will never get it right." As John Sargeant has said "He is certainly the guy you would most want to have on your side."

You may remember I promised to return to 9/11 for a final visit and what better place to start than at the national Cathedral where George Bush spoke with dignity and authority. When he finished, the rat-tat-tat of the military drums struck up as a prelude to a military choir bursting into the patriotic music of the "Battle hymn of the Republic". The words:
I have read a fiery Gospel wrote in burnished rows of steel
As ye deal with my contemners so with you my grace shall deal
Let the Hero born of woman; crush the serpent with his heel
Since God is marching on.

With the service over Bush flew to New York City. It was three days after the attack and New York was still in shock. The Brook Brothers' store on Liberty had been quickly converted into a hospital. Bridges and tunnels were closed to all but essential traffic. Photographs of the missing were posted on walls and massive flower bouquets were on the footpaths in front of the Fire Stations.

Bush helicoptered to Wall Street Heliport on the East River then drove to ground zero where a wall of grateful people, rescue workers, police, fire-fighters and Paramedics cheered and waved their flags chanting "USA, USA."

Giuliani, the Mayor of New York pointed out through the window of the limousine in which they were travelling "You see those people cheering you, not one of them voted for you." His point was as clear as day "Right now the whole of America supports you."

Bush got out and toured the ruin in a casual windbreaker. No plan had been set out for him. No microphone, no sound system, no notes. A crowd of workers surrounded him, emotions throbbed everywhere. Bill Beckwith climbed aboard a wrecked fire truck and Bush climbed up beside him. He put an arm on Beckwith to balance himself then left it there. He began to speak "We can't hear you," they shouted. "I can hear you," he yelled back. "The rest of the world hears you and the people who knocked these buildings down will hear all of us soon." The crowd roared. He promised to get the evil killers dead or alive. This was a war, not just a skirmish or a terrorist attack. He finished with "From now on any nation that even harbours or supports terrorism was going to be regarded as a hostile regime." He stepped down to thunderous applause from the workers around.

In General Colin Powell's book My American Journey he defended the decision to end the mission against Saddam Hussein in Desert Storm to save American lives. "There wasn't enough of Iraq's army left to be a regional military threat" he wrote. He was unhappy with charges that the job was left unfinished leading to September11 and excused the decision "not to finish the job" as down to a UN decision.
"Desert Storm" was a UN mission and that mission was accomplished said Powell who then made an astonishing observation when he said "The Arab States had no wish to see Iraq dismembered into separate States of Sunni, Shia and Kurdish political entities." After three years of occupation by Allied troops, a new Constitution, and a new parliament, that is exactly where defeated Iraq, seemed to be heading with a state of Civil War looming on the horizon. Failure was in the air. Furthermore now that Saddam was being demonized by George W. Bush for 9/11 it made the ending of Desert Storm seem even more implausible. But Desert Storm happened under the leadership of his father Bush Senior. Five years later Saddam has been defeated, captured and put on trial for war atrocities. Isn't it amazing the speed at which history evolves?

But let's return to the weeks after 9/11. The White House became an impregnable fortress for a newly declared war President. To the public he could do no wrong. The Taliban in Afghanistan, Al Qaeda and Osama Bin Laden were now arch enemies. Congress gave power to Bush to attack Afghanistan on October 7, 2001. No significant American casualties were expected. Overwhelming U.S. air power brought victory; a new Government in Kabul and a new department of Homeland Security at home in America. That last sentence proves how time can make a fool of any well-meaning political commentator. The UK has now joined America under a new President, Barack Obama, a brand new front in Afghanistan. The year 2009.

Revenge or retaliation has no long term political logic to them and already there are rumblings of doubt about the direction America was going.

Was this new War Administration clamping down too much on basic freedoms to defend America against an unseen enemy? Had the Administration over-estimated their political skills in winning the hearts and minds of the Iraqi people? In Stephen Graubard's book The Presidents, all the foregoing doubts have been raised. Graubard blames the situation on the veterans of the Cold War, the would-be warriors who surrounded Bush. Top people, too vain and inept to recognize their own political frailties and limitations. Anybody familiar with Hitler or Stalin's threats to the world and who had lived through those terrible years only laugh at the suggestion that the Al Qaeda threat had any similarity whatsoever. Most countries in Europe were now beginning to realize that Iraq needed only a police action like that in Northern Ireland especially as the fear of weapons of mass destruction (WMD) was no longer justified "In fact," said Graubard, "they did not exist."

But this is not about the war in Iraq or the people who live there. This story is still about George W. Bush. David Frum living inside the fortress of the White House seemed to understand better than most what was happening there. He said "No matter how many times Bush did the brave thing, his conservative supporters inexplicably continued to expect that next time he would do the weak thing." Some of this mistrust can be blamed on Bush's style of leadership. Frum seemed to think that George Bush allowed far too much latitude to his Cabinet officers which some of them abused to wage internal war on the President's policies.

The New York Times complained that Karl Rove, the President's top political advisor was expanding his White House portfolio inserting himself into foreign policy matters. Colin Powell and Rove were at loggerheads "Why should anyone with a background in domestic politics have an important voice in foreign policy?" Powell in criticism of Rove said. Since the President also came under that heading many wondered why Powell survived. "Bush," Frum went on "was like Babe Ruth who pointed to the stands before he connected for a homerun. He did exactly what he promised." Despite his gaff Powell remained untouched.

Finally this brings us to the core of Bush's philosophy of honesty. In September 2002 he invited three religious leaders to the Oval office a Christian, a Jew and a Muslim. He wanted them to know that the hardest battle still lay ahead.

"You know," he said "I had a drinking problem. Right now I should be in a bar in Texas not the Oval office. There is only one reason that I am in the Oval office and not in a bar. I found faith. I found God; I am here because of the power of prayer."

Frum's opinion on George W. Bush was that while he was not the most obvious man for the job, by some very strange quirk of fate he turned out to be, of all unlikely things, the right man. Leadership, he concluded, was the greatest mystery in politics.

But now perhaps we could lighten the story just a little. Life in the White House was not always dominated by 9/11. Little human things happened which separated the darkness from the light. Here is a story that appeared in The Catholic Digest of March 2006 which to your writer reflects impressively on the humanity of President George W. Bush.

In the middle of a world preoccupied with terrorism, Iraq, Saddam Hussein and Bin Laden a letter dropped on the desk of George Bush in the Oval office. Just a routine epistle among thousands he received. It was from a young girl named Shannon Hickey, her fourth letter in three years. Anyway it seemed to strike a chord with George Bush and with his usual directness and logic which always took his Aides by surprise he ordered a meeting with Shannon from Lancaster, Pennsylvania. The meeting was set for September 16, 2004.

The wheels of the Administration went into action and a voice on the line at her home issued the invitation. What a shock it was for a young fourteen year old girl to get a phone call from the White House to herself personally. The President would be speaking at Valley Forge Convention Centre in King of Prussia, Pennsylvania. Shannon was selected to meet with the President and the First Lady Laura Bush on the tarmac after he stepped off Air Force One at the Willow Grove Naval Air Station, Pennsylvania. It seems Shannon had impressed George Bush with the story of her work in her Outreach Ministry with "Mychals Message" a charitable organization distributing clothing and other help to the poor.

Shannon almost choked with excitement. Her mother just turned pale. Well everything turned out far beyond her wildest dreams.
She duly met the President and the First Lady at the airport. Stepping off Airport one the President kissed her on the cheek and Laura hugged her. Then like a scene from a movie she was whisked by motorcade in the blink of an eye to the Conference Centre. What a thrill it must have been for her mum to watch on television her little girl being so honoured in front of millions. For Shannon just to meet the President was a lifelong ambition fulfilled at last.
But George Bush also made the most of this human story at a time when all around him nothing was going right. Her little gift to him was just right. It was a simple one but George Bush was deeply touched by its beauty – a bottle of holy water. The bottle also contained some ashes from ground zero. "I will truly cherish it," he said and he really meant it. The icing on the cake for Shannon was hearing him call her a "social entrepreneur" who heard a call and acted on it. The President went on to say "I particularly want the young who are here to look at Shannon as an example of what you can do to help America; one heart, one soul, one conscience at a time.

Shannon's summary of that beautiful day in her life said it all. "It was so cool," she murmured. I think you will all agree, those few words just about spoke for everyone.

That little story may sound trite and superficial in a world of hard-bitten politicians, International Dictators, oil rich eastern dynasties, and the intrigues of petro politics but inside the White House there were two human beings whose lives in the Capitol were only an extension of their personal past.
Beautiful things still happened to them. The joy of their families. The friendship of old buddies and the memories George and Laura cherished from their past on the road they had travelled since first they met.

So maybe we should continue on the story of the 43rd Presidency by travelling back in time to the beginning of this extraordinary journey as he set out on it with Laura his wife.

Of all the important decisions he ever made George Bush sums them up like this "The best decision I ever made was asking Laura to marry me. I am not sure the best decision she ever made was saying yes. But I am glad she did...."

Two great friends of theirs had this to say, "George and Laura love each other but just as important they are proud of each other...." Long-time friend Nancy Wiese "It's a pretty overwhelming job but they handle it, they handle it."

I have already described the experience of George and Laura on September 11, 2001 so I won't visit that day again with them. We have seen the world of the 43rd President through the eyes and ears of political commentators. Now let's look at it through the hearts and minds of the President and the First Lady and the words of their close friends.

If I cross the line into stories I have already mentioned I trust you will bear with me. To understand Laura and George you must understand Midland. "All that we are, all the things we believe in come from that one place," George said. His personality comes from Barbara (his mother) they both love to needle and they both love to talk.

You will find when studying George and Laura they appear to be two very different people. She is the serenely calm partner. He is a turbulent ball of energy. She is soft spoken. He is outspoken and to quote George "perhaps obnoxiously so." She is reserved, polite and self-effacing. He is "in your face". Though not unlike President Johnson who leaned into strangers, nose to nose, even hugging and touching them, invading their personal space.

She is a good listener and that had to be a plus with George being the talker he is. In contrast to his predecessor Bill Clinton who had no true relationship with his natural father whereas George was almost handicapped trying to live up to the standards of a talented and successful father, George Senior. Three more quotes help to add a little more to their personal pen pictures. "Without her he would not be where he is" says Paul Burka journalist and friend.

"He is clearly the wild one even today" that quote comes from Karl Rove his advisor. Here is the tongue-in-cheek "one-liner" from George himself. One can almost see the mischievous twinkle in his eye "When I was young and irresponsible, I was young and irresponsible."
His relationship with his mother was an ongoing clash of personalities and his choice of wife reflects that. Laura is the exact opposite of his mother. Warm not stern, shy not assertive, domesticated not political. But nowadays the Presidency cannot be separated from the First Lady. Anyone writing about the top job in the land must be impressed by this modern phenomenon.

The names roll off the tongue naturally like Richard and Patty Nixon, Gerry and Betty Ford, Lyndon and Ladybird Johnson, Ronald and Nancy Reagan, Bill and Hillary Clinton, and George and Laura Bush. Of course it is not a political relationship but a partnership of the heart essential for normality inside the Presidency. With respects to the President and his First Lady I now turn the spotlight on George and Laura Bush as only their autobiography George and Laura can do.
George and Laura Bush's partnership began in Midlands. Laura was working in Austin in Molly Dawson Elementary School as a Librarian. Every Friday afternoon she made the five hour journey back to Midland to spend the weekend with her family.

Nothing unusual about that except in Midland there was a certain cupid at work. In fact there were two of them; Joe and Jan O'Neill. As the O'Neill's remember it. Laura and George were just two of a diminishing circle of single people still unmarried so the O'Neill's decided to do something about it. Jan repeatedly tried to invite them to dinner without success.

Boasting about their friend being a new and promising recruit to politics was useless. Laura was totally disinterested in the subject or even a rising star like George. Besides she had dropped out of the dating scene by choice. Not even George's illustrious family tree impressed her. But neither cupid or the O'Neill's would take no for an answer and one evening in early August 1977 Laura relented and went along to the barbeque the O'Neill's had so cleverly arranged for that evening, meeting the man she had heard so much about.

An old cliché is often used in situations like this "Love at first sight". It sounds ridiculously banal in retrospect but thar description is just about right. George was smitten and why not? Here was a beautiful woman who was different. His observation says it all. "Laura was gorgeous, good humoured, quick to laugh, down to earth and very smart. I recognized those attributes right away in roughly that order." The O'Neill's knew that opposites attract but worried that perhaps this might be different. Too different for them to hit it off together.

George as usual talked and joked the night away but more important Laura listened. Don't take my word for that listen to George W. "When we met I was enthralled. I found her to be a very thoughtful, smart, interested person- one of the great listeners. And since I am one of the big talkers, it was a great fit." His morning three mile run gave the game away. He usually left a party by nine but now he didn't leave until midnight, despite his three mile run due next morning. Laura had her ideas too. "I don't know that it was love at first sight but it was close," she told Jan O'Neill. She admitted that she thought he was really cute and was very funny in an outrageous way. The next stage was biologically inevitable. He started to pursue her, an ancient ritual known instinctively by lovers since time began. However there was a snag. They lived miles apart, he in Midland and she in Austin. She even sat on her mother's bed and discussed George "The thing I like about him is he makes me laugh a lot," she told her mother yet they also knew the distance between their homes was a big negative to further progress in their romance.

He solved that one by driving to meet Laura in Austin to save her the five hour drive. The next stage crept up on them imperceptibly when he blurted out to his gob-smacked parents his fascination for a certain young woman he had met. Jenna Welch, Laura's mother thought things were happening too fast. Would he turn Laura off? But she need not have worried for Laura was more concerned now by something else. How would life be as a politician's wife? Would she cope? George W. promised her she would never have to make a public speech just to reassure her. The wedding day was agreed for November 5, 1977 a bare three months after their first meeting at the barbeque thrown by the O'Neills in early August 1977. That "love at first sight" saying was coming true. The nuptials were unpretentious, just seventy-five guests, no bridesmaids, no groomsmen, no flower girls, no ring bearers, no fuss.

George said "We just wanted to get married and wanted our closest friends and family there to celebrate with us. Each parent was allowed only two guests and of course this caused a minor war among some of the Bush uncles. On Saturday November 5, 1977 George and Laura were married in the Glass Chapel of the First United Methodist church. Instead of a bridal gown Laura decided on a long sleeved street length dress of candlelight beige crepe de chine. She wore a single strand of white pearls and a corsage of white gardenias at her waist. Well that's how it was all described in their book George and Laura. It had certainly been a whirlwind romance very much to be expected of our 43rd President. They now have two grown up daughters aged twenty-eight today and are still together as a family. It seems cupid has done a very professional job indeed.

George and Laura took on the new lifestyle of a Congressman in the world of politics. Incidentally Laura did have another dark secret which she confided to George later yet it didn't even phase him – she was like most Texans at the time a Registered Democrat. Marriage didn't change his schoolboy exuberance however for he thought nothing of demonstrating his ability to wiggle his ears to entertain his friends. Or worse than that to pick on some unsuspecting victim, the more dignified the better and tap him on the far shoulder then disappear into the crowd leaving the unfortunate person looking around and nobody there. A Republican friend Curtis Webster shakes his head at the memory calling it just what you would do as a twelve year old schoolboy.

Sometimes politics was no joke for George, especially when confronted by a real home-bred Texan like Senator Kent Hance who boasted about his local roots, sneering at George Bush as a Yankee in Stetsons and Spurs, the pampered son of a rich and well-connected New England family masquerading as a true son of the Lonestar State.

An Ivy League background stuck in the craw of many hard-bitten locals. But that was the world George and Laura now embraced and eventually conquered between them. The evidence of that became obvious when Kent Hance not only became a great friend of George W. but actually joined the Republican Party to become one of George Bush's most loyal supporters.

The taste of defeat in his first Congressional election came as his first gut-wrenching lesson in humility. He had been rejected by an electorate who had called him an outsider.

The "Non-Texan" jibe was now a reality. It hit him so hard he cried. Seeking some wisdom from Barbara, Laura was told "Don't ever, ever criticize your husband's speeches." Laura followed this advice to the letter but after one not so good showing George insisted she tell him the truth. She did. As they approached the house up the driveway he promptly drove into the wall of their garage. Laura never discarded Barbara's advice again. But George was learning to rethink his arrogant personality after his failure at the polls.

Luckily for him Laura was having a calming effect on him but it took a couple of further years of marriage for her to achieve this. She checked out his way of dressing. Hand-me-down alligator loafers two sizes too big for him was one example of her task. "Why should I change when I am comfortable in them," he said. But she persevered and made some progress. However George was getting quite restless. The oil business had little appeal for him now. Politics was in his blood and he resolved to go back to it. "I am getting back into the game, all it needs is for me to pick the right moment," he said.

Meanwhile a terrible personal heartbreak faced by thousands of other married couples across the nation had hit the Bush household.

Laura painfully recalls the whole episode "When George and I got married we wanted lots of children." For three years they tried for a child without success. Laura blamed herself and her family history since her mother only succeeded in having Laura after many miscarriages. The size of George's family seemed to justify her worst fears. She became so depressed she avoided walking down the baby isle of the local supermarket. "It was too sad," she said. At last the fertility experts told them "It is extremely unlikely you will ever conceive a child." George and Laura were devastated. Adoption was their only hope of children.

They duly made the long drive to an Adoption home in Fort Worth. It was Spring of 1981. They complied with the usual requirements. Letters of recommendation were submitted, financial statements and application forms were filled in and a visit by the local officer to determine the suitability of their home for a small child was arranged. As often happens in the case history of many women in this situation Laura became pregnant.

A phone call was sent to the adoption home. Laura was careful to emphasise their plan for adoption was only put on hold. This to them was a wonderful miracle and they didn't want to tempt fate by a final cancellation. But the miracle became two miracles when on checking the Sonogram they discovered another baby showing itself. George of course dissolved in tears and the usually cool, calm and collected Laura just joined him. The next day she opened the door to the postman. He handed her a bouquet of red roses sent from "The father of twins."

But still she avoided the baby isle at the supermarket. Her twins were due around Christmas and she still had her fingers crossed in case something awful happened. But her fears were not unfounded for after six months she developed severe toxaemia. All three of their lives, mother and two babies hung in the balance. She hung on and cemented another memory for George of a very stubborn woman determined to have the joy of two healthy babies. At 10 a.m. on November 25, 1981 the children arrived by caesarean section. They were both named after their grandmothers Barbara Pierce at five pounds four ounces and Jenna Welch at four pounds twelve ounces. "It was the most thrilling time of my life. It was beautiful, I witnessed it all," said George and once again he broke down and cried.

But now for another story not so pleasant. It happened in a restaurant. At one table was a Wall Street journalist, Washington bureau chief, Al Hunt. Marching towards Hunt's table was a red-faced intoxicated George W. Bush. "You no good son of a bitch," he screamed "I will never fucking forget what you wrote about my father." Hunt's four year old son was frightened…. The diatribe continued for another minute or two then George W. staggered to the door and out into the parking lot outside. This is not just a cheap swipe at George W. Bush. It was the turning point in his life. Word got around and finally back to Laura herself. She was livid. It was yet another public scene that wounded her so deeply she knew her very marriage was threatened. Up to now George only suffered a hangover the next day.

This time it was different. The consequences were much more costly – for both of them. It was in 1985 she gave him her ultimatum. "It's either me or Jim Beam." This has been denied by her friends "Laura would never give a threat like that," they said, "George would not respond to it anyway." But another friend has confirmed the story. It's true Laura did lay it on the line one night. He had gone too far this time.

Others say he listened quietly, stood up walked across the room and poured himself another bourbon defiantly. But the days of defiance had finished forever for both of them. George knew she was a gentle person. Yet she had a strong side that was important to him. The change came imperceptibly. No fan fare, no drama, no public announcement. As Robert McCleskey his lifelong friend put it "You just sort of noticed George wasn't holding a beer anymore. He didn't make a big deal about it never even brought it up." When asked about it George just said he wasn't drinking anymore and changed the subject. There was one vice he did continue to indulge in. It was one Laura enjoyed too – chain smoking and they both never even tried to abandon it.

In April 1987 the whole family became embroiled in George Senior's Presidential campaign and George W. moved the family including his two daughters to a townhouse in Massachusetts Avenue, Washington. Another phase of the George Bush story had arrived shared by Laura his rock in everything he tackled.

In the role of his father's "loyalty enforcer and gate keeper" (Bush's words) one of George's jobs was to vet all journalists who wished to access his father. "Why you?" He would question the unfortunate newsman. "Give me one reason I should let you talk with George Bush." He had no time whatsoever for "that goddamned psycho babble crap" as he called it. Those were the people who delved too deeply into his fathers psyche trying to explain what it was that made him tick. In that job George W. had an easy charm and a total commitment with boundless energy.

He could be a tough disciplinarian too monitoring everyone working on the campaign. He liked to cut "big shots" – people who were too big for their boots down to size. Most of the press found him abrupt, abrasive and presumptuous and heaven help those who didn't do justice to his father's reputation and image. Those observing him in action could have no ambiguity about his forcefulness. He was more than a match for the big guns on Capitol Hill.

Nobody who watched him operate as his father's trouble-shooter in the Presidential race of 1988 could have any doubts they could be looking at another President in action. He was truly the man in charge. When asked about his motivation for his job he simply said "He's been a great dad." A little story here to change the mood. Laura was just getting used to being around the trappings of power and began to look forward to weekend visits to the White House. She tells a peculiar story about sleeping in the Lincoln bedroom. "Everyone who sleeps there says the same thing," she said "You can feel Lincoln's presence in the room."

She also experienced the same worries as Jacqueline Onassis Kennedy, that fear of her children being injested by the Bush clan just as Jacqueline feared about the Kennedy clan. The Bushes had a mutual love and respect for her but she always had a mind of her own. Politics was not in her blood the way it was in her husbands. Strangely enough George showed no interest in influencing his father's decisions in the Presidency and seemed to have no ambitions connected with it. His major interest at that time was the baseball stadium and team he left behind. Actually when encouraged to go for the Governorship of Texas he held out for the job of Commissioner of baseball. It was only when the Commissioner's job didn't materialize that he allowed his name to go forward for the Governorship of Texas. But now let's lighten the story even further for the reader. A much told story is worth retelling as written in the book George and Laura.

The night was in May 1992 and the function was a White House luncheon for Queen Elizabeth II. Barbara, the First Lady, gently warned her majesty that George had been seated as far away as possible and told not to speak. To ask George to comply with such a ridiculous request with his personality was asking the impossible. The Queen asked George about this "Are you the black sheep of the family?" George just grinned and said "Yes your majesty. I suppose that's true." "Well, I suppose all families have one," the Queen smiled.

"Oh does your family have a black sheep?" George cheekily enquired. "And if so who is it?" Queen Elizabeth laughed and turning to the First Lady she shrewdly remarked "I don't know why you think your son is dangerous." Meanwhile Laura was keeping a watchful eye on her husband but she needn't have worried for soon he was seen engaged in an animated conversation with the Queen.

Both of them were laughing merrily without any inhibitions. It seems George "could charm the birds off a bush" no pun intended. But there were two people who gave him orders that George W. couldn't refuse. Their names were Barbara and Jenna his daughters. One evening he decided to cut short his Governorship campaign to do the job other fathers did on a regular basis. They condescended to allow him pick them up after the party they were attending which finished at 11 p.m. Under no circumstances was their famous father to even enter the school. Poor George had to remain outside seated in his car until 11.30 p.m., two and half hours past his own bed time. Then the girls finally came out walked to the car and got in. Adolescent daughters, as any father knows, can be a bit of a mystery sure to test anyone's patience. But it was an exercise in humility the future Governor of Texas just grinned about later and laughed.

However George and Laura's ongoing love affair compensated for everything. Two quotes will confirm this for the reader. One is from George who said "I'll give this my best shot and if people decide, heck if there's someone else they'd rather have as President I know she'll still love me. And that's more important than winning."

Laura's words gives a woman's view of their relationship when she said "What I like best is when my husband says; you look great tonight." Can anyone now deny they're the words of a woman deeply in love?

Sometimes the observation of a friend can be more telling than all the expert's analysis. Here are a few that paint their own picture "My impression is that privately she tells him exactly what she thinks" – Mike Barker West Texas writer and Bush friend.
"She is his safety net for life," – Mark McKinnon Bush advisor. "You see them together and it's like they're reading each other minds," said a family friend. "Laura is quiet but she accomplishes a great deal with that quietness" – Barbara Bush.

Family quotes reflect the togetherness and concern of any other normal family –"I'm concerned about these little girls, I really am" – George on Jenna and Barbara. "If we never saw their pictures in the paper again we'd be a lot happier" – Laura. "In politics you always have an opponent, it shouldn't be your spouse" – Laura.

There are many people who would love to hear what it was like moving into their new house for the first time in the White House. Like any woman setting up house Laura Bush saw everything through a woman's eyes. Cupboards were explored. Curtains were yanked down and walls were repainted. Hidden treasures were discovered in storage such as the desk saved from the British warship HMS Resolute a gift from Queen Victoria to President Rutherford Hayes in 1878.

This was an historic piece of woodwork for apparently Woodrow Wilson had also used it as did Franklin Roosevelt for his broadcast of the famous "fire side chats". John John President Kennedy's little fellow loved to hide beneath it during Cabinet meetings sometimes popping out to laugh at his audience before charging round the room whooping it up. One concession George had to make was to leave behind his six-toed orange and white cat in case he made short work of the precious draperies hanging about the house.

Perhaps for that reason he had the Ulysses Grant furniture moved upstairs to his office. What was hard to get used to were the well-groomed men with earpieces shadowing her everywhere. Luckily for Laura she could shut them out of her consciousness almost completely. The pomp and ceremony of the office disturbed him like the tradition of having "Hail to the Chief" played whenever he entered a room. One little anecdote is well worth retelling of his first week in the White House.

His senior staff were meeting in a room when George peeked in. Chairs crashed back and ten men stood up simultaneously. George motioned them to sit down "Just checking," he said. Two minutes later the old mischievous George Bush surfaced and he returned to peek in again. Once more the chairs crashed back and all ten men were standing to attention expectantly. George just grinned like a schoolboy. "I just wanted to see you do that again," he joked. Irrepressible is one word I can find to describe him. Maybe even clown prince.

One problem did miff George concerning the safety of his daughter Barbara. When on a social night out she gave the security men the slip which caused them to go into emergency mode at 70 mph on a slippery road. They caught up with the offending car carrying the President's daughter. But unluckily for her it was not the President who rang her about it but Laura. She gave Barbara an earful "You put other people's lives in danger when you do something like that. Don't ever do it again." To reflect finally on the Bush family in the White House a little story about Barbara, George's mother, will make you smile and nod your head approvingly.

George rose at 6 a.m. when on a visit to his parents' house at Kennebunkport. He slipped downstairs, grabbed a cup of coffee and flopped down on the sofa opposite his parents committing the cardinal sin of placing his feet on the table in front of him.

"Put your feet down George," barked Barbara imperiously. "For God sake Barbara," his father protested. "He's the President of the United States." "I don't care," replied Barbara with finality "I don't want his feet on my table." George instantly obeyed. It seems fame had not changed the status of the Bush family pecking order and that's exactly as it should be with any healthy family

As Laura remarked to a friend after 9/11 "We're praying more than we ever have but we're not about to buckle under the pressure. George and I have learned one important thing "Whatever happens in life we can handle it"."

Opinions vary on George Bush the President and George Bush the man yet there is one theme that never varies at all. Never underestimate him. Harvard Professor of Human Rights, Michael Ignatieff was quite surprised at the level of anti-Americanism he encountered in Europe. At one of his lectures in Trinity College in Dublin he experienced an unjustified loathing and contempt coming over to him from the audience. His words are amazing when describing Bush. He said "The Irish and the Europeans are making a fatal mistake by underestimating the President. George Bush is a major league politician. He has wiped the floor with everybody in American politics." He described Bush's skill as a kind of political cross-dressing. The President passes himself as a plainspoken man of the people when he really is the scion of one of the biggest East Coast dynasties in the history of American politics. Ignatieff went on to emphasise his dislike of Bush "I don't like him but I am saying Europe underestimates Bush at its peril." Ignatieff was one of the Liberals who supported the war and now he is sorry. This is quite an opinion for a man who as Professor of Human Rights at the Kennedy School of Government, broadcaster, columnist, advisor to the United Nations, author of many books, and a leading international intellectual who wouldn't normally be on the same side as George Bush.

Professor Ignatieff felt "Americans will cut and run late 2005 or early 2006 to shed the problem of Iraq before the Congressional elections in 2006." Only time can judge him on that one and I wouldn't hold my breath waiting for it. I am sure we have covered most of Bush's life in the Presidency to your satisfaction but one remaining puzzle fascinates me.

When confronted by the second victory of George Bush after his electoral roasting four years previously isn't it hard to avoid this question. Who voted for him second time around? Well let's pursue that question in a little more depth. The weight of his victory was almost too much for many. Tom Wolfe American journalist wrote in The Sunday Times November 7, 2004 - "At a dinner party in New York they speak in hushed voices. The hush turns to silence if you volunteer the information "I voted for him" as I did….." Wolfe goes on.

"Those who also voted for him were the Scots-Irish who were not Christian right but just religious. If you are religious you are against gay marriage and abortion," so said James Webb the most decorated Marine to come out of Vietnam with a Silver Star and a Navy Cross. In Webb's book Born Fighting he reckons the Scots-Irish were fighting men from all over the Appalachians and they loved a battle. "My own father was from the Shendendoah Valley in the Blue Ridge Mountains of West Virginia" wrote Tom Wolfe our American journalist "I know the kind of people Webb is talking about." These were the type of country and western people who identified easily with George W. Bush.

Once again the old chestnut of Bush's personality surfaces. Wolfe writes "Despite his wealthy and refined lineage in terms of family and where he went to school Bush still manages to come across to people as one of them. He likes cattle, baseball and stock car racing the most popular sport in the United States. Not that you would know it from reading the New York papers. They don't cover it." In a little place called Bristol, Tennessee a place full of Scots-Irish, it draws 155,000 spectators every year to its baseball arenas 55,000 more than goes to the biggest football game.

"Bush reflects the real America," Wolfe went on. "That's what his critics can't stomach. Bush honestly seems to believe in God; Kerry just said "I am a Roman Catholic so I must believe in God but it was obvious it didn't play a part in his life"." Perhaps the Will-o'-the Wisp answer for his victory may be found in a place called Crittenden as written about by Sarah Baxter a New York journalist. In The Sunday Times November 7, 2004 she wrote "It is a place one mile long and yet spans Middle America. It is a place where people aspire to moral values but don't always live up to them. For them Bush was the all-American family man who overcame his character flaws and drink problems, worked to forge a happy marriage with an admirable "stay at home" wife and brought up two flighty girls who are good at heart."
"In Bush they see, not the warmonger with an East Coast Ivy League pedigree but a man they could sit down and talk to." "Man of the people" may sound a little trite but then how else can you describe that political chemistry he possesses. Democrats didn't bother to try. They just blamed their failure on God, guns and gangs. Yet somehow I feel, despite all the ingredients we have thrown together to explain his victories, perhaps the best explanation lies in one simple answer. This is nothing more mysterious than his hard work and commitment on the stump, something he learned in the aftermath of his first Governorship failure in Texas years ago and a lesson he never forgot. The result was a vote from sixty million people giving him 285 Electoral seats and lifting him to an overwhelming victory. Not bad at all considering how heart-stopping his first election had been. He also won 81% of the Nation's 3,141 Counties second time around.
It is now six years since he became President and people are puzzled where he is leading them. The answer is there for all to see. In George Bush's second inaugural speech his message was crystal clear. His goal for the future was the promotion of liberty and the ending of tyranny across the globe. The speech took seventeen minutes in which he spelt out his intentions. His main theme was Peace and American security by the advance of democracy and freedom.

The speech which went through twenty-two drafts had the word "Freedom" mentioned twenty-seven times and the word "Liberty" fifteen times. It was a truly remarkable speech "For as long as whole regions of the world simmer in resentment and tyranny – prone to ideologies that feed hatred and excuse murder – violence will gather and multiply in destructive power and cross the most defended borders and raise a mortal threat. The survival of liberty in our land increasingly depends on the success of Liberty in other lands. The best hope for peace in our world is the expansion of freedom in all the world." Iran and North Korea were the main targets to which he addressed his intentions to halt the proliferation of weapons of mass destruction. "In the long run there is no justice without freedom and there can be no human rights without human liberty."

Whether the speech was the work of his scriptwriters or the profound thoughts of George Bush himself is for the reader to decide. One thing is for certain, it was the clear blueprint of the direction America intended to take in future under George Bush. From that speech on, there could be no ambiguity of George Bush's intentions for the next four years.

The world has moved on since George Bush's second inauguration speech on the steps of the Capitol. Since then a Civil War rages in Iraq between two sides the Shia and the Sunny tribes. A third faction is the Kurds. Midterm elections have since given power to the Democrats in

Congress and the Senate. The new leader of the House is Nancy Pelosi, a Democrat from California. The fearful reality of the importance of oil now hangs like the sword of Damocles over the West. The world economy depends on it which makes the turmoil in Iraq, Iran and Saudi Arabia all the more frightening. A political meltdown in the region would see the price of oil rocketing maybe to $100 a barrel so the search intensifies for alternative sources of energy with nuclear power taking centre stage once again.

As political turmoil threatens to change the very map of Iraq and perhaps split it into three geographical zones run by the Shiites, the Sunnis and the Kurds. The architect of the whole sorry mess Saddam Hussein was found in a bolt hole by American soldiers in 2003 and handed over to the Iraqi's for trial. He was sentenced to death by hanging and that fatal day arrived on New Year's Eve December 31, 2006.

The world held its breath as the man who had challenged two Presidents of the United States by recklessly leading his country into war in defiance of the United Nations walked to the scaffold.

Here was the man who invaded Kuwait and Iran which led to the deaths of over one million people. This tyrant had a particular perversion of not only killing with impunity but where possible to torture his victims in the most gruesome ways best left out of this narrative. But hate built into Iraqi society over the years must be satiated. The word "avenged" might be more appropriate. At the scaffold a bizarre ghoulish decision was made by the powers in charge of this terrible event.

The hanging scene was to be videoed to the world in a ritual that perpetrated indignity and insult on the condemned man just as grisly as Saddam himself had inflicted on his victims. So unacceptable were the taunts, the public prosecutor was on the point of cancelling the hanging. An investigation is to take place later. Unfortunately the triumph of capturing Saddam by U.S. soldiers was sullied by the scene.

Yet, Saddam Hussein ever the showman, had contributed to the hanging himself when for the sake of the cameras trained on him, and for the sake of his followers, he refused the hood offered to him by his hooded jailors.

George Bush, the President at home in America had gone to bed early in preparation for the State funeral of Gerry Ford the 38th President who had died on December 27, 2006. Bush's statement read after the hanging was as follows "It was the kind of justice Saddam had denied his victims. It marks the end of a difficult year for the Iraqi people and our troops."

At this stage it may appear to the reader that giving Saddam Hussein so much space is irrevelant to the George Bush story. In fact Saddam was the very fulcrum of everything that happened to George Bush's Presidency until this moment in time. For instance the number of American troops who have died in Iraq as of now, December 31, 2006 is 3,000. The cost to date for hunting down Saddam stands at 500 billion dollars. Looking at the cold statistics perhaps we can find some justification for the campaign to see Saddam Hussein's name on a tombstone. The deaths of 600,000 Iraqi's, 180,000 Kurds and 1 million soldiers in Iran are down to Saddam. His wartime use of gas and chemicals breaking every rule of the Geneva Convention is well documented. Worst of all, the cold ruthless terror of his secret police that brought bloodshed and sorrow to every family in the land made his capture by the American troops a triumph for the U.S. Presidency of George Bush and well worth its place in the story of the 43rd Presidency.

But let's reluctantly return to the hanging.

As Saddam Hussein fell through the trap door at 6 a.m. on New Year's Day 2006 at Camp Justice a former military intelligence barracks in Baghdad, the call to prayer was canting out over the rooftops on a cold January morning which required Saddam to wear his overcoat as he fell to his death in an instant. Twenty-five years of tyranny had ended in approximately one second. The Hajj or Muslim feast of Eid-Al-Adha was six hours old.

Most of the world's response was muted except for the celebrations in Baghdad by the families of his victims who danced in the streets in joyful relief at his passing. The UK and others mumbled ambivalently at the use of the gallows instead of a life sentence. But everyone knew that Saddam alive would always pose a threat to stability in the Middle East.

One broken-hearted man Jawad Abdul Aziz, the brave but bitter witness at Saddam's trial was allowed to look into the coffin that held Saddam's corpse. He shed tears of sorrow for his father and three brothers murdered by his oppressor as he spoke to the corpse in the coffin "I told him this is a well-deserved punishment for every tyrant," he said afterwards.

The body of Iraq's tyrant leader was loaded and driven away in a plain wooden box to his burial ground in his village of Awja near Tikriti while the world watches and waits for the backlash.

Here are some extra snippets of news on Saddam Hussein's passing into history. The hunt is now on for 23 billon dollars salted away by Saddam Hussein's family in bank vaults in Japan, Switzerland, Germany and the Far East

Iraqi exiles based in Britain were elated "We have been waiting twenty-five years for this," said Zara Mohammed, a Kurd whose four brothers were killed by Saddam.

Near Detroit, Michigan, the large Iraqi-American community celebrated in the streets outside a Mosque dancing and blowing car horns. "This is the first time I have seen my dad this happy," said his thirteen year old daughter Ali al-Najjar with tears in her eyes. "I have been praying for this all my life."

Residents in Awja, the poor village of his birth however claim Saddam is now a martyr. A former Judge Barzan al-Tikriti and Saddam's stepbrother were to be executed after the four day Hajj. They were eventually executed on Monday January 16, 2007.

Aziz Salih sat in a Kurdish restaurant in North London. She read a text message on her mobile phone "Let us celebrate that Saddam has gone" it read. "It is a triple celebration," said Silah "we saw friends disappear. It was illegal for the Kurds to celebrate or even sing under Saddam. I hated him. Today it feels like I have a fresh life like I am wearing new clothes." His colleague Alan Ali used to live in the Kurdish town of Halabja "My relatives were laughing when they told me he was hanged," said Ali "we are so grateful, I am so happy, this weekend we will celebrate."

Yet what do you say to a broken-hearted girl who is going to miss him. Rana his daughter expressed anger and anguish in her loss and helplessness at what had happened. "I guess I still held hope that by some miracle, by some last minute act of God it would not come to this. I never thought I would never see him again. I used to sit on my prayer mat and pray and plead to God not to deprive me of him. People tell me I should be strong," she said tears brimming in her eyes "but I am human and a woman and not just Saddam Hussein's daughter." All this grief for a man who murdered her husband after Saddam called him back home to Iraq with the promise of safety. Yes, isn't it unbelievable that contemptuous of his daughter's feelings, Saddam murdered her husband thus betraying the daughter who loved such a father so trustingly? But let's move on.

On a happier note, far away on the other side of the world, preparations were being made to honour a world leader of a different age. Gerry Ford 38th President, who had healed America after the Vietnam War and the scandal of Watergate, was now being laid to rest in his own hometown, revered and honoured by his people.

What a stark contrast history was unfolding for us. The great political healer, buried on the other side of the world with dignity, yet 3000 miles away and on the same day a political monster was hung on a gallows at Camp Justice an intelligence centre in Iraq.

You have already read about this event under my notes on Gerry Ford.

The story of George Bush's 43rd Presidency is now coming to a close with the death of Saddam Hussein.

So let's look at the world through the eyes of the 43rd President thousands of miles away in Washington.

He may not stand side by side with the fighting soldiers on the battlefield in Iraq but his role back in America, meeting the caskets carrying dead soldiers back home from the front is the most emotionally draining sorrow that a President must endure.

One such day happened when he was called upon to present a medal to the family of a serviceman who showed amazing bravery in the course of his duties on patrol in Iraq. It was only the second time this top military decoration, the Medal of Honour, has been awarded for action in the Iraq war. Addressing himself to the parents of CPL Dunham George said proudly "He was the guy who signed on for an extra two months in Iraq so he could stay with his squad. He wanted to make sure that everyone made it home alive. CPL Dunham took that promise seriously and would give his own life to make it good." It is easier to understand the President's speech when you know the story of CPL Dunham.

The battlefield report told of how he led his soldiers to the site of an ambush and became engaged in hand to hand combat with an insurgent. In the scuffle a grenade fell to the ground and Dunham covered it with his helmet. The grenade exploded and CPL Dunham died of his injuries a few days after. Mr. Bush looked at the face of Mrs. Dunham, the boy's mother standing beside him and tears of compassion trickled down his cheek. It was a terrible moment for him.

The last time he felt and reacted like that was at "Ground Zero" among the workers and firemen after 9/11. Being President is not always about glory and adulation. Sometimes it really does hurt to be President.
Keeping the storyline personal let's take our place on the Barracks' square listening to the banter or watching the farewells of the ordinary guys heading for the frontline out East.

"If we go again we go again," said specialist Steven Buthram. "We all volunteered for this." The third brigade was leaving Fort Benning for a month of training in California. The soldiers gave farewell hugs to their wives, girlfriends, husbands and boyfriends. Their military family is now their new unit, their new family.

Mrs. Carroll first met her husband when they were teenagers growing up in Akron, Ohio; their three months apart while he was training had been rough. Now they will be separated for a year. He has one consolation "The sooner I leave the sooner I can get back," he said.

The impact of war on a family can be felt in the words of one young woman. "I haven't visited my mom in Connecticut since 2005," said Chandra Waltin. "I don't know when I will see her." Pte Waltin is on her way to Iraq. Her husband has himself just finished his stint there and must now wait at home for her return from duty. His face told its own story.

These are the boys and girls who right now are deciding the destiny and history of the future. Will they quench the smouldering embers of Baghdad or will fate blow these embers into a roaring furnace engulfing the whole of the Middle East. Who knows?

Isn't it strange how history makes a fool of any political commentator? Right now the U.S. soldiers are heading for Afghanistan, the latest theatre of war in pursuit of Al Qaeda

But we can't allow ourselves to get too morbid about the future. Just feel secure in the certainty that the President of the United States is more than capable of solving whatever problems lie ahead.

Meanwhile the final year of the 43rd Presidency was drawing to a close and already the machinery of State was humming away in the Presidential election to install the 44th President. The hustings had been travelling all over the United States to prove to the world of democracy was in full bloom after two hundred years and forty-three Presidencies.

You may remember some pages back, based on past history in previous Presidential Elections, I forecast the possibility of a surprise in America's choice of Commander-in-Chief as 44th President. Well history has not let us down. Now in November 2008, a black American Barack Obama will represent the Democratic Party against the son of an Admiral who was tortured as a prisoner of war in Vietnam where he had been imprisoned for five years. His name is John McCain, a Republican from Arizona.

We will discuss the election and the background of the winner in my next piece on the 44th President.

What a pity the 43rd Presidency got bogged down in a war nobody wanted. Many books have been written about George W. Bush and as can be expected in a democracy not all of them were complimentary. But one thing is certain. George Bush was untouched by scandal and nearly every political commentator will agree he is still a consummate politician.

What legacy he will leave only time will tell.
George W. Bush, the man, you will conclude, was someone the Gods always smiled upon. An easygoing guy with a twinkle in his eye. A qualified Jet pilot of an F102. A graduate, with a BA in history. A fluent Spanish speaker, twice Governor of Texas and one of that rare breed who was given a second term in the Presidency.

One truth can never be contradicted. George W. Bush will not be perturbed in the slightest by anything his critics may say about him. I guarantee not long into his retirement you are bound to find him side by side with his beloved Laura enjoying stock car racing, talking cattle or cheering on to victory or defeat his favourite Texas Rangers baseball team. The icing on the cake will be the weddings of his two lovely daughters Barbara and Jenna in the years ahead.

We now move on to my final President – The 44th since George Washington. I hope you find him just as fascinating as all the previous forty-three. He certainly won't disappoint you.

44th President   Barack Obama

Born: August 1961
1 Term
2009 –
Age 48

Party: Democratic
Profession: Lawyer and Author
County: Illinois
Ancestry: American
Estate: $4 million (from book)
Hobbies: Basketball

Physical Description: Slim, fit, 6 foot 1 inches, black, close cut hair, 170 lbs approximately.

Significant Extract from Inauguration address January 20, 2009:
"On this day we come to proclaim an end to the petty grievances and false promises in recriminations and worn out dogma that for far too long have strangled our politics."

BARACK OBAMA

It was in February 2007, standing outside the old State Capitol building in Springfield, Illinois, that Barack Obama declared his candidacy for President of the United States in the 2008 U.S. Presidential Election. Was the choosing of that historic place called Springfield, Lincoln's hometown, significant and was it specially chosen by Barack Obama.

Symbolism was again his theme, when he linked his campaign to Abraham Lincoln's "House Divided Speech" of 1858. Obama said "That is why in the shadow of the old State Capitol where Lincoln once called on a House divided to stand together where common hopes and common dreams still live. I stand before you today to announce my candidacy for President of the United States of America." I've no doubt that far off history was never too far away from his thoughts in Springfield that day. That should not surprise us; after all he had majored in Political Science and lectured in Constitutional Law at the University of Chicago for a time.

Barack Obama was a totally new face on the political stage in America in 2007 and a big surprise to many today. He had only entered politics four years previously as a candidate for the U.S. Senate and won that seat with a landslide victory becoming only the third African-American to be elected to the Senate since Reconstruction in 1865. There again we come across the jargon of post-Civil War politics. Barack is a fearless critic of the Iraq war which alongside universal health care and energy independence, was to become one of the major planks of his campaign for the Presidency.

Already in July 2008, he had made it clear in one of his election speeches what his Iraq intentions were when he hinted "In eighteen months of assuming office I intend to pull troops out of Iraq and redeploy them in Afghanistan, which now needs more attention." The racial tensions in America between black and white Americans have now come centre stage. Here are some statistics from Annette Witheridge, a New York correspondent, writing in The Irish Mail 17.7.2008.

An amazing 83% of blacks had a favourable opinion of Barack Obama. Only 31% of whites do. Over 60% of blacks claimed race relations were bad. These are very similar to a survey made eight years ago. Nothing has changed. Two thirds of all those polled say they believe America is ready for a black President. Just over one quarter of those whites interviewed said the problems of blacks had been exaggerated. Yet 50% of blacks thought not enough has been done for them.

In his book The Audacity of Hope Barack told it as it was. No embellishments. To him the victims of Hurricane Katrina were the faces of black poverty to be seen in any American inner city neighbourhood. "We didn't have nuthin' before the storm," one black survivor said, 'Now we got less than nuthin'." Only later did President Bush acknowledge the legacy of racial injustice the tragedy had exposed. Two months later Barack was attending the funeral of that brave little woman from the past Rosa Parks. You will remember the lady who defied race laws by refusing to give up her seat on the bus to white supremacists. "Nothing has changed" Barack concluded. However he felt certain that after a strongly debated airing of the grievances of the black community during the election campaign something would change. Barack intended to make that change.

Yet the shrewd and well-informed in political circles seemed to be well aware of this dark horse who arrived out of nowhere for in the first six months Barack's campaign had raised $58 million, exceeding all records for such an opening period in an election. In the first three months of 2008 his campaign brought in another $36.8 million and he told The Washington

Post he would draw more support than Hillary Clinton from Independents. The total funds pledged to him so far, to June 2008, had reached the staggering amount of over $90 million dollars.

But let's back track a little lest the story line gets too far ahead of events.

The Democratic Party was buzzing with excitement for the hustings were in full swing to select their next Presidential candidate. We were watching the weaker candidates drop out of the race one by one until now the field was reduced to two candidates. Not unexpectedly, Hillary Clinton, wife of ex-President Bill Clinton, had come through the pack as the big hitter. True to form the history of the Presidency never lets you down for yet another dark horse, Barack Obama, the Senator from Illinois had surfaced as a major player in the race for the major prize, the biggest in politics. The scene moves on and after a nail-biting scrap across the length and breadth of America, the unbelievable happened. The Queen of Politics, the big hitter Hillary Clinton, was beaten. The page boy had defeated royalty from the dynasty of Congress. The victor was the young, up and coming newcomer, only four years a Senator we told you about earlier, Barack Obama.

I understand the usual consoling hugs and kisses of reconciliation between the disappointed factions has been accomplished without too many tears or heartaches. The Democratic Party is now facing into the battle for the Presidency with Barack Obama the new kid on the block at the helm. Naturally the Democrats were in jubilant mood at their convention as you can see by the following extracts from their speeches.

Convention: Joe Biden
From the platform Joe Biden revealed to the audience of his thoughts on his daily train ride home from Congress as he watched the flickering lights in the homes he passed. He imagined the conversations in those houses. "It now costs 50 – 60 dollars to fill up your car." "How are we going to afford sending our kids to school?" "Women still don't get equal pay for equal work with males." Sky rocketing debts and mounting bills troubled him and Joe said so. Biden's answer to the problems were as follows "Lets make sure for our children there is no chasm too deep, no barrier too great and no ceiling too high to aim for."
Hillary Clinton wanted no more jobs going overseas. She also wanted health care to be written into law. The battle lines were being drawn up as they spoke.

Michelle Obama – "I came here as a wife who loves my husband. I came here as a Mum whose girls are the centre of my world. I feel my Dad looking down on us. He was our hero, who suffered from multiple sclerosis for twenty-five years. His hard work helped me go to college. I was taught that your word was your bond. You treat people with dignity and respect even if you don't know them. Barack introduced me to work he did in neighbourhoods, among ordinary folk. He talked to me about this world as it is and the world as it should be."

Now Bill Clinton had come on board.

Bill Clinton promised in no uncertain terms his intentions to support Barack Obama to be elected. "Hillary has the same commitment – that makes two of us; ... (pause) ... that makes eighteen million of us. The job of the next President is to re-build the American dream. Barack Obama is the man for that job." They were words delivered with a super charged confidence. He continued by referring to the claim that Barack was too young and inexperienced. "I was too young to be Commander-in-Chief Republicans told us. It didn't work in 2002 because I was on the right side of history. It won't work with Barack because he's on the right side of history. Let's not reward the Republicans, for the past eight years," he finished.

The Republican Party chose Senator John McCain from Arizona to go head to head with Barack Obama for the 44th Presidency. And so the battle begins.

Now we have two men ready to make an unbelievable journey across America by rail and air, by road or on the internet, speaking on radio, television or in open air arenas to sometimes thousands of people ………. wherever their road show chose to camp. Long days and sleepless nights lay ahead full of hope and extravagant dreams by both sides. Let's hope their speechmakers can meet their demands for the rewards of their hard work will decide the destiny of America for years into the future. But before setting out on this epic voyage, Barack had one more job to do – select his possible Vice President.

He chose Joe Biden, the senior U.S. Senator from Delaware. Originally from Scranton, Pennsylvania, where he lived for ten years prior to his moving to Delaware. His political pedigree goes back to 1972 when he was first elected to the Senate. He is the current chairman of the Foreign Relations Committee and a bruiser in debate. But Joe Biden's life collapsed around his ears after his first wife and baby girl were killed in a car crash while she was out Christmas shopping on December 18, 1972. For Joe Biden it was the end of everything. He saw no future but to give up politics altogether. He didn't. Joe was a religious Roman Catholic and suffered the ultimate tragedy for him – he lost his faith!
He decided God had no purpose in his life anymore. "I felt God had played a horrible trick on me," he complained. Time went by and eventually his faith returned. But God had his own plans for Joe for he married again. The girl's name is Jill Tracey Jacobs and to complete the miracle Joe now has a lovely little girl named Jill. Incidentally Joe believes in God again.

His recovery from this tragedy is the measure of his quality and mental steel as a man that makes him the perfect material for Vice President.

Senator McCain, the Republican nomination, was almost an automatic choice by his Party. However, the selection of his Vice Presidential Candidate took everyone by surprise when he nominated Sarah Palin, the Governor of Alaska, as his running mate. She turned out to be a forty-four year old ex-beauty queen who brought a new energy to his campaign and was a big attraction to the women voters. She is the youngest ever person to be nominated for the Vice Presidency and is of English/German/Irish extraction. She came to live in Alaska when she was just a baby.

Now let's study the background of both men. McCain's life story is fascinating. He is the grandson of a famous Admiral, "Slew" McCain, who was Chief of the Bureau of Aeronautics in the Second World War in 1942. In 1943 Slew became a Vice Admiral. He had a desk job in Washington for a while but at heart he was really a seaman and a misfit in the office.

Slew returned to his first love when he was posted to the Pacific Theatre of War to command the famous Task Force 38. It was here he earned his Navy Cross for his exploits in battle. Besides fighting he was responsible for a White Paper in co-authorship with Admiral John Thack which recommended air power be used in the support of ground troops which became common practice later. This technique is now in the Navy War Manual.

Slew's son, Jack, John McCain's father, followed him into the Navy. It was at a welcome home party that Slew collapsed and died. He was only sixty-one years of age. Slew was buried in Arlington Cemetery with full military honours. The name McCain is now famous in the Navy and was revered in Mississippi. The McCain Hall was named after him at the University of Mississippi. Jack, his son, was also made a four-star Admiral making the McCains the only American family in history to have a father and son promoted to Admiral.

Because of his father Jack's nomadic trips around the world on fighting ships, John McCain had an odd, unsettled childhood, travelling from place to place with him. Perhaps this may have accounted for his hair-trigger temper from a very early age, a tendency he often talked about. Needless to say John was laid out for a Navy career from an early age, yet he wasn't aware of this life plan designed for him by his parents. His school, Episcopal, was a Confederate establishment that went back to before the Civil War in 1861 and was re-opened again after it. Located across the Potomac river from Washington on a campus spreading into rolling green lawns, it was ideal for his Southern heritage going back to his grandfather in Mississippi. Its code of honour claimed – "I will not lie, I will not cheat, I will not steal, I will report the student who does so." The discipline was almost brutal in its severity but it didn't stop our John McCain from being a ladies man. I suppose, given his good looks, this was to be expected.

He went on to graduate from Flight School, where he had two miraculous escapes in plane crashes. We all know from his war record how traumatic his career in the Navy was with his Prisoner of War background, which is well documented.

It was at the beginning of 1987 that he became a Senator. The Senate has been referred to as the "House of One Hundred Kings" because of the autonomous nature of each Senator's job.

One would never take McCain to be a superstitious character, but according to Paul Alexander, his biographer, John McCain had his own "lucky emblems", like his lucky eagle feather or lucky compass or his lucky ink pen. He wore lucky shoes and never missed a trip to the cinema on the day the polls opened.

In McCain's biography, called Man of the People by Paul Alexander, I found another unusual story from 2004. It seems when asked about a further try for the Presidency, McCain said "I'm sixty-three years old and I will be campaigning for George Bush for a second term for him. As exhilarating as the experience was, the wear and tear and time away from my children, I'm not sure I would ever want to do it again." Added to this, could be his health for he had two melanomas removed, one from his arm and another malignant one from his left temple.

Finally when asked why he wasn't Vice President, his reply was "I asked not to be considered for Vice President. Anyway, the action is in the Senate. That way, I can always speak my mind."

Well, here we are once again with John McCain coming to the winning post for a second time. His political career simply refuses to come to an end without one last fight. But fighting is in his blood as is his mantra of "Honour". According to an article from Time magazine, September 8, by James Curry and Michael Grunwald, McCain was always in conflict with others in pursuit of this ideal of honour. In his young days, the article says, "He was a constant breaker of rules, a brawler and a slob with an oversize chip on his shoulder." Even in the Navy Academy he flaunted authority and accumulated so many demerits, he came only 894th out of a class of 899. Yet, I remember earlier, writing about Eisenhower at West Point. He went out of his way too, to break rules in minor ways to prove his own individuality to himself and the top brass. But McCain had guts and went through hell as a prisoner of war refusing special treatment because his father was an Admiral. Colonel George Day said "He'd been bayoneted and starved and weighed 95 lbs, he just willed himself to live."

He was also the camp troublemaker, cursing at guards despite the constant threat of torture. McCain referred to Vietnam as "An honourable and winnable war botched by spineless politicians." He even believed his father should have resigned to protest Lyndon Johnson's lack of aggression. Another anecdote records a burst of temper brought on by an affront to his honour, when he threatened to beat up an opponent who had phoned his ex-wife in an attempt to look for dirt. Another explosion was against a man who accused him of selling out for special interest contributions. Honour runs very deep with John McCain and goes all the way back to his Episcopal schooldays. He got involved in a campaign against doping in sport because he didn't want American athletes dishonouring their country. His efforts resulted in a dozen athletes being disqualified from the Olympic Games. It is easy to understand that one of his heroes was Teddy Roosevelt. In November 2008, the American people will decide to reject or endorse this obsession with honour.

Cindy Hensley McCain would become First Lady if McCain won. Carol Shepp McCain was his first wife. They married in 1965 and he adopted her two sons. When he was a prisoner of war, Carol was involved in a serious car accident. Later their marriage ended because of John McCain's infidelity. They have been reconciled since and she now carries his "McCain for President" stickers on her car. Cindy met John McCain now her husband at a party in Hawaii and is seventeen years younger. Chairwoman of her family's beer firm, with an overall worth of over $100 million, her chief influence is not with the campaign but with their kids.

The mobile phone never leaves her hand and is her lifeline to the family when she is out on the stump with John McCain. She vows "I want my sons now in Iraq led by a Commander-in-Chief who understands what it means to send young men and women into combat – and more importantly how to bring them home." In a flare up during the campaign, Cindy was quoted as saying "I would suggest that Senator Obama change shoes with me for just one day and see what it means to have a loved one serving in the armed forces and more importantly serving in harms way."

Now for the story of Barack Obama.
Let's start his story off in far away Honolulu, Hawaii, where he was born on August 6, 1961. His father was also Barack Obama of Nyang'oma Kogelo, Siaya District, Kenya, where he grew up herding goats with Barack's grandfather, also a goat-herder. Barack's mother grew up in small town Kansas. Her father nicknamed "Gramps" worked on oil rigs during the Depression in the 30s. Then after Pearl Harbour, he joined the U.S. army and was posted to Europe. While he soldiered in Europe, his wife "Toots" Barack's grandmother worked on a bomber assembly line. We will come to know them as Madelyn and Stanley Dunham later.

Barack's father was a Kenyan of the Luo tribe, born on the shores of Lake Victoria, in a place called Alego, a very poor African village. Barack's grandfather, we discovered, was an elder of the tribe, the medicine man of the village, said to have healing powers. He was a herdsman and the goats he owned were herded also by Barack's father. But herding was not to be his father's destiny, for he won a scholarship to study in Nairobi. Meanwhile as a result of Kenya's newly won independence, Barack Obama senior found his good fortune enhanced when his scholarship was improved and extended to a University place in the United States.

He was to be one of the new graduates of western technology for the future of a modern Africa. When he was twenty-three he arrived at the University of Hawaii as its first African student. Records show that after three years hard dedicated studies he graduated top of his class with an honours degree in Econometrics. Our story now reaches a significant point in Barack Obama's life when Barack's father went to a Russian Language course where he met Barack's mother, a shy awkward American girl, called Ann Dunham. They became attracted, fell in love and married. Their child was Barack Obama. Unfortunately for Ann Dunham, his father's graph of success in his studies continued to rise which saw him gaining a scholarship to pursue his studies further for a PHD at Harvard. However, funds were inadequate to bring his family with him and although still in love, he left them behind, never to return.

We'll return to that story later.

The colour of his skin was a question that was to haunt Barack for years to come. As he grew older he became obsessed with being the son of a mixed marriage. The word for it was miscegenation and it's hard to believe today that it was on the statute books in over half the States in America as a felony in 1960. In many parts of the country his father could have ended up at the end of a rope for the felony of marrying his lovely mother. Yet he had one consolation, when he was told that his great, great grandfather was a decorated Union soldier. Later came an additional bonus to discover his wife Michelle was rumoured to be a second cousin of Jefferson Davis, the notorious son-in-law of Zachary Taylor, the 12th U.S. President and who later became leader of the break away Confederacy. (You can read all about him under my piece on Zachary Taylor.) The Jefferson Davis story was steeped in romance, heartbreak and tragedy.

Looking at the family on his mother's side, "Gramps" or Stanley Dunham, his grandfather, was a God fearing Baptist who worked with his own brother on the oil rigs around Wichita. Gramps had had a wild boyhood and suffered the awful experience of finding his mother's body after her suicide. The suicide was blamed on Gramps' father who had a tendency to philandering. It was said that "Toots" Barack's grandmother was discouraged from marrying the unpredictable Gramps because of his family history. But Toots was not to be dissuaded. They eloped. Pearl Harbour happened at the same time and Gramps was soon off to war to follow Patton across Europe. Barack's mother Ann was born to Gramps and Toots at an army base where Gramps was stationed.

However, Gramps never really saw action in the war for he spent it for some unknown reason in France. As I said earlier, Toots spent the war on a bomber assembly line. After the war, Gramps' restlessness took them from place to place, town to town, before finally they ended up in Seattle, where Toots finished her high school studies. Gramps became a furniture salesman and they bought a house. But that peculiar wanderlust bit him for the last time, when he decided they should go to Honolulu, which was soon to become the 50th State of the Union and where opportunities were to be limitless. As you can see Gramps always wore his heart on his sleeve while his dreams always flew higher than the stars.

Perhaps that was the chemistry that made Toots love him. For Gramps and Toots, it was a perfect match. But they were not ready for Barack's father when Ann brought him home. And certainly not ready for Barack when his mother brought him home. Toots' memory flashed back to another day when Barack's mother was twelve. She remembered the scene with neighbours because Ann had brought a coloured child in to play in the garden. Gramps dealt with the criticism in his own blunt confrontational style.

But everyone they talked to had the same response "White girls just don't play with coloureds in this town." What a wonderful tribute it was to Gramps and Toots, therefore, to embrace Barack Obama twelve years later and make him one of the family. This little story embellishes everything about the Barack Obama story. It also reflected the love and trust his mother had in his grandparents, the two people who would be his anchor for the rest of his life. It also highlights one significant fact of life in Barack's America. It was still tainted by Civil War thinking one hundred and fifty years after the last shot was fired.

The story continues. After his father walked out on his mother, Gramps and Toots welcomed Ann and Barack back to live with them for the next few years. But the turbulence in Barack's life would not leave him alone for when Barack was only four years old, his mother met and married a man from Indonesia, called Lolo Soetoro. Barack remembers he was short, brown, and handsome and his tennis was good. He also had a nice smile and an even temperament. One day, they boarded a Pan Am flight for Djakarta and life lurched into strange and mysterious waters for Barack and his mother in that strange and foreign land.

Lolo and Barack's mother had already had a two year courtship, from Barack's fourth birthday until he was six. They had also met at the University of Hawaii. Gramps was amused about Lolo's name which in Hawaiian meant "crazy". But Lolo was anything but crazy. He was a man of good manners and easy grace who almost looked Samoan. He related well to Barack and spent endless hours wrestling with him and playing chess matches with Gramps. Having proposed to his mother, they decided to live in Djakarta. Arrangements were made to pull up their roots and travel abroad.

Lolo went on ahead while Barack's mother, Ann, arranged passports, visas, plane tickets, hotel reservations and the usual range of anti-sickness shots. It was time for Ann to gather all her things together and head off for a new life in Djakarta. Gramps sat down and went over a map of the Indonesian Island chain that in his day was known as the "Spice Islands". Still with his mischievous sense of humour, his eyes widened and he said in mock awe "Says here, they even got head hunters." Barack's grandmother threw in two boxes of candy for the trip. What lovely, lovely people they were, for I'm sure at that very moment their hearts must have been breaking to lose their little grandson, maybe never to see him again. But that is only your writer speculating.

Gramps and Toots went with them to the airport and soon Barack and his mum were on their way. Their plane touched down in Djakarta and they were cleared through customs. Lolo was there to greet them and the first thing Barack was aware of was the searing heat. It was a different world now from Hawaii; small stores and markets and men pulling carts. On the way they passed "Hanuman" a giant life-sized image of a monkey God which mesmerized little Barack. "A great warrior strong as a hundred men," said Lolo laughing. "When he fights the demons he is never defeated." Yes, for a little boy of six Barack had come to a different world altogether. In the backyard of his new home was a small zoo of chickens, ducks, a cockatoo and two baby crocodiles. They all settled in to life in Djakarta, making another memory for Barack to include in his book Dreams from My Father.

Lolo was a good father whose philosophy of life and its problems always impressed Barack in a down to earth matter of fact sort of way. Barack soon settled in to learn the new language and in six months he managed to become quite fluent in Indonesian.

He got on well with his new friends whose fathers were mostly poor farmers and whose livelihood was dependant on erratic weather pattern. In fact sometimes the rainfall washed away everything they planted, a very precarious existence indeed.

At that time President Sukarno had been ousted from power for corruption in his regime. Meanwhile Lolo worked as a Geologist in the army but his wages were so poor they had to be subsidized by Ann working part-time teaching English to Indonesians working in the American

Embassy.

After awhile Ann became anxious about Lolo, as stories of corruption filtered through to her. Lolo was non-committal to questions she put to him. He just teased her saying "Forget your worries and go shopping. Don't bother about such talk." But she couldn't help worrying knowing Lolo was not corrupt but he was not in charge of the situation. That was the way politics worked in Djakarta.

Frankly, Ann was so worried for Barack; she began to think seriously about the future. The situation haunted her night and day.

Suddenly the answer came to her. Barack's true life really belonged elsewhere – back in Hawaii. Education would always be her obsession for him. So much so she immediately set up a Correspondence course for Barack which saw her come to his room at four o'clock in the morning to teach him. When Barack complained he got a typical Mom's 'no nonsense reply' "It's as tough for me buster as it is for you. If you want to grow into a human being, you're going to need some values. You don't do things just because others do them. You must have values." She preached passionately to him on his father's success and of course his rise from obscurity and hardship in Kenya to Harvard University. She even played for him the speeches of Martin Luther King to inspire him to reach for the sky just as Martin Luther King suggested.

There was always a path that led upwards and onwards in her book. She always used the prominent, successful black man as her inspiration for Barack. She was trying to protect him and he knew that. Her inner conflict was finally resolved one day when she decided to pack up their bags to return to Hawaii. Her programme for Barack was now charted and unchangeable. He must have education. The best education available. He was going home. What a wonderful American Mom was Ann Dunham.

Barack's return to Hawaii from Djakarta was not what he had hoped for. Leaving his mother, and his new sister Maya and Lolo at the gate of the airport was a lonely separation once again which he didn't realize until he was driving home in Gramps new car in Hawaii. When the conversation dried up the silence made him realize that although he had only been back a year ago on holidays, this time it was different. He had grown up, perhaps grown away from them. Now they weren't living in a big rambling house where all his pals loved to come. They had sold it to live in a small rented apartment in a high rise.

Gramps had sold his furniture shop to go into selling Insurance which he wasn't good at. He was still a dreamer. His mood was not as good either – perhaps because Toots now earned more than him. They didn't go to the beach anymore. Maybe they kind of drifted away from him since they sold the old rambling homestead which Barack had loved and settled instead for security in a rented apartment. This was understandable. They were getting old now. Soon it was time for Barack to go to school. As far as his Mom was concerned it was going to be the best school available - Punahou.

Punahou gave everybody a thrill of excitement. Barack was happy to return to studying and better still Gramps and Toots were secretly proud to be stepping up in status. It was Gramps' boss who pulled the strings to have Barack accepted in Punahou. There was nothing sinister in this just a little help to tip the scales in his favour. After several interviews Barack was sent with Gramps on a tour of the school, prior to admission. The place was impressive, with several acres of green fields and trees. The old structures of glass and steel embraced everything. This was a school that lacked nothing and boy was Gramps impressed!

Tennis courts, swimming pools and photography studios really excited Gramps. Pulling Barack to one side he whispered conspiratorially in his ear "Hell, Bar this isn't a school. This is heaven. You might just get me to go back to school with you." The usual school leaflets were handed over for Toots to study in her spare time. A full catalogue projecting Barack's expected targets in the next seven years. It was the core framework that shaped Barack's future. Gramps was having a great time reading the catalogue "Madelyn, get a load of this," he beamed enthusiastically as he unearthed another nugget that rocked him in his slippers. Yet how do you make a little boy happy when his heart is in one place and his Mom is in another, but Gramps was trying hard to bridge the gap that separated Barack from his lovely Mom and his little sister.

Needless to say, Gramps took him to school on his first day. He introduced Barack to a new boy, a Chinese standing nearby. "This is Barry," he said using Barack's nickname from Djakarta. His Granddad made a great hit with Frederick who grinned and said later "Your Granddad's funny." Barack was not of the same opinion. He was just embarrassed. "Yeah, he is," he replied ruefully. The kids were amused by Barack's name and tittered.

Remarks like "Does your father eat people?" or a request by a little girl to touch his hair, left him perplexed about being coloured. It was going to be tough. His fellow pupils came from houses with swimming pools and were together since kindergarten. Nobody played soccer and he couldn't balance on a skateboard. But he soon noticed others had their own kind of handicaps; asthma or being too big or too small. Coretta was glad to see him for now she was not the only black in the class. But even Coretta was vulnerable to child ridicule. Children of ten are not vindictive, I guess they just tell it as it is.

It was coming up to Christmas when Barack heard his real father was coming to stay for the holiday. The news was a shock to Barack but the time passed quickly. Barack's father was invited to speak to Barack's fellow pupils about Kenya and he carried out his assignment so impressively, the lads found a new respect for Barack. Even the teachers glowed with praise for his father's speech. This was not very surprising after all his father was a PHD in econometrics. That was the last Barack ever saw of his father and he still remained an enigma.

Now let's fast forward a few years. It was time for his mother to reveal to Barack the whole uncompleted story of his father. It was like the interval of an epic movie, before Part II. Maya, his sister, was lying down sleeping, when Barack told his mother he intended to write to his father. His mother, suddenly without prompting, told her story. "I hope you don't resent your father," she began. Why would I?" said Barack. The traffic in the street became part of a shared silence for some time.

She then began to trace her story back in time. Barack listened carefully as his mother reminisced nostalgically. She took the blame for the separation and insisted she had divorced him. Gramps and Toots were not too happy with their marriage at the start she told him. However after a time they realized it was best for them. Ann went on to recall his father's good fortune in being offered a place in two Universities.

She had no recriminations on the terrible heartache inflicted on her by his decision. Forgiveness and time is a great healer. Harvard would only pay tuition fees. New York University offered to pay everything including room, board and even a job on campus. "How can I refuse the best education," he said selfishly, then rejected New York University and the family, then headed for Harvard without Barack or his mother.

Barack's mother was still reminiscing and digressed a little. She spoke about their first date. Barack's father was late, so she lay on a bench and somehow managed to doze off asleep. She awoke one hour later with Barack's father standing over her with two friends. "See I told you she would wait for me," he laughed. It was obvious, she was still in love with him and her story was meant to get Barack to see and maybe love his father as she still did.

A few months after Barack's 21st birthday, the phone rang in Barack's flat in New York. It was his aunt Jane ringing from Nairobi – "Barack can you hear me?" she said. "Your father is dead. Killed in a car accident." The line crackled and she was gone.

Now Barack had the unenviable task of ringing his Mom to tell her the man she really loved had died. She sobbed her heart out at the news. (See article Feb 8, 2008 Irish Daily Mail by Barack Obama).

Barack's mother wrote often to him from Indonesia and she was still very aware of how important education was for his future. She wrote "Did you know that in Thomas Jefferson's day and right up through the 1930s anybody who had the price of tuition could go to Harvard? I don't see that we are producing many Thomas Jeffersons today. Instead we are producing Richard Nixons."

It is easy to understand therefore why she was concerned enough about his studies to send him to one of the most exclusive schools in Hawaii. Punahou could be considered on a par with two other similar schools much sought after in England – Harrow or Eton.

His mother returned home to Hawaii but after a while she felt she wanted to return to Djakarta after all that's where her husband was. She left Barack to decide for himself, if he wished to return with her to Djakarta or stay with his grandparents. Barack now settled into school and happy with his grandparents, chose to stay on in Hawaii. That was the most important decision of his life. This time it was Barack who chose education instead of Djakarta. Deep down I'm sure that is what his mom really wanted.

It is easy to see how important these two people Gramps and Toots had become to him. They formed the basis of Barack's stability for they were both very solid and kindly people. After his mother, Ann Dunham, returned to Indonesia Barack settled in to life with both his grandparents and the pals he knew in Punahou School. Incidentally, these grandparents deserve a special mention in the Barack Obama story. His grandmother Madelyn Dunham was a bank vice president in Hawaii. His granddad, Stanley was a salesman known affectionately as "Gramps". His grandmother was referred to as "Toots". Both of them were revered by Barack's friends who found their home an open, welcoming place for any of them to stroll into. Life went on for both Gramps and Toots and they continued to rear Barack for the next ten years. Later his mother died at the age of fifty-three from ovarian cancer in 1985. Barack was thirty-three.

Like any normal boy Barack went to parties when at High School but sometimes he could be found playing checkers with Gramps his Granddad. A very slim athletic lad, Barack loved all kinds of sport including spear fishing in Kailua Bay. He loved surfing and playing basketball. He was quite a skilful mover at basketball too and was good enough to be on the Punahou team that won the State Championship in 1979. However as a sports celebrity, I'm afraid he was only small fry, so to speak, for since his time a famous golfing sensation, Michelle Wie has been a student at Punahou.

Barack's music at that time was Stevie Wonder and Billie Holiday, but later he introduced his pals to George Benson and jazz. One of the highlights of Barack's year right up to the present day has been his visit home each Christmas holiday to his old Punahou friends, his stepsister Maya Soetoro and her husband and of course to that very special lady in his life, his beloved Grandma, Toots, now aged eighty-four.

So let's finish his college years with an extract from an essay he wrote for the Punahou Bulletin in 1999. It just about summarizes his deepest thoughts about Hawaii. He wrote "The opportunity that Hawaii offered – to experience a variety of cultures in a climate of mutual respect – became an integral part of my world view and a basis for the values that I hold most dear."

While Barack was now a mature solid personality it didn't prevent his two grandparents suffering sadness once again when it was time for Barack to leave home for College. I'm sure Barack's Grandma "Toots" Dunham shed a lot of tears when it was time for her fledgling to leave the nest once again and head for Occidental College in Los Angeles, where he studied for two years. He then went on to Columbia University in New York City and finally Harvard Law School in 1988. Soon after he began writing his first book Dreams from My Father, which was published in 1995, he graduated with honours from both Columbia University and Harvard. He graduated from Columbia in 1983 where he majored in Political Science, specializing in International Relations. Barack was now the finished product of his hard work, intellectual abilities and the sacrifices and love of three people Gramps, Toots and his loving Mom. The next phase of his life was about to begin.

Barack always had an inward urge for public service so before entering Harvard he spent three years in Chicago as a community organizer at $12,000 per year.

Barack's religious background has been the subject of debate on many occasions. The charge of being the son of a Black Muslim, because his father was one, is totally untrue. His father just didn't stay around long enough with a son he only knew as a two year old kid for him to have any influence on Barack. In fact, Barack has been so impressed by the power of the Black Church in the community where he worked and the comfort it gave to its members in difficult situations in their lives, he joined the "United Church of Christ". That was in the 1980s, almost thirty years ago.

So the picture changes again as Barack stepped into the cauldron of life in a flat in Chicago far from the cosy nest he had lived in back home with his grandparents. He was about to sample the precarious world of the job seeker in Chicago. That was in 1983, twenty-five years ago. Just after graduating from college Barack found a job for $12,000 yearly with a consulting firm to National Corporations as a research assistant.

Of course, he still felt the need for being among a disorganized black community for he was very much aware that if change was to come, it must happen at the grassroots of these communities. But personal circumstances forced him to join this multinational Corporation, the only black researcher in the company. At least he was now earning money to repay his student loans and put some bread on the table.

His was a strange way of thinking for a highly trained college graduate. He couldn't help this drive within him. It was focused not towards money or a path that led to money, but a political decision based on some vague idea throbbing away deep in his sub-consciousness. As he said himself in Dreams from My Father, "He was like a salmon swimming blindly upstream towards the site of his own conception." Very profound words indeed but what did they mean? He seemed to feel connected to the images and the reality of the black and white footage of films showing protesters of the 50s singing freedom songs.

At the heart of it all for Barack, there was an urgent need for black communities to be developed for their own good. As he said himself – "Communities must be created, fought for and tended like gardens." It wasn't just the house where you had been born but the shared sacrifice that membership of a community meant to the individual. Barack was soon to discover that lofty ideals were not easy to convert into action. It wasn't a very encouraging start for him. While holding down his job he wrote to every black official with a progressive agenda, to every tenant group and to neighbourhood councils without as much as one reply. However, Barack was no quitter.

The people he now worked for were kind and good listeners. So much so, Barack opened up his heart to them. Only Ike the black security guard was honest enough to tell him it wouldn't work. "Why you wanna do something like that?" he said. "Mr. Barack I'm gonna give you some advice. Forget about this organizing business and do something that's gonna make you some money."

But Barack Obama had an idea, no a dream, for his disorganized brethren in the black community. He had made up his mind already. I think he disappointed Ike who thought Barack spoke well. Perhaps he could become a continuity announcer on TV. "All you gonna do is end up as an old man at the end of your days and nothing to show for it." Yes, Ike was worried. Well, Barack was duly promoted but far from being elated, his brief case and dark pinstripe suit left him feeling guilty. Corporate life was a long way from the poor disorganized blacks out there. In his mind, his new corporate image only betrayed them. He resigned.

Then one day, Barack received a letter from a "leading civil rights organisation" in the city. A tall, good looking, black man interviewed him and again the job was in the corporate sector forging links between the Government, big business and the inner city. Again, it was a desk job far from the grassroots he was concerned about.
But Barack was going nowhere. He was now broke, unemployed, eating soup from a can, still searching for that elusive role to put his talents or his dream into effect.

Then he met Marty Kaufman, a white man of medium height, wearing a shabby suit. Marty didn't have a very impressive appearance which didn't inspire Barack with confidence but he did have ideas to share. Marty suspected Barack of being an angry young man and said so. He himself was Jewish and in his late thirties. He was now fifteen years in the business of organizing.

At present he was trying to save manufacturing jobs in Metropolitan Chicago. He needed a black man to work with him. He was concentrating his work around the churches, the only institutional base in town. The Trade Unions were not much use to him. Marty and Barack talked about Chicago a lot and finally Kaufman offered him $10,000 per year plus $2,000 travelling allowance. He would have to take his chances on his salary improving after that.

They next met at the Calumet Community Religious Conference – the CCRC. The excitement and passion of everyone there was tangible, blacks and whites, to celebrate a jobs bank worth half a million dollars that the Illinois Legislature had agreed to fund. The fundamental driving force for Barack was to clear away the media, the politicians and the bureaucrats from problem solving which would leave the ordinary man with a seat at the table and space to find common ground. He took a bus home from the rally wondering if he had at last found the people to share his dream.

But his new boss, Marty Kaufman, was harder to please. After handing in his report, Marty just said "Not bad." A small row developed and Barack left in a bad mood. "Marty was right," he concluded later, "I just had to get closer to the action." Just then an epidemic of teenage shooting caused Barack to call a meeting of senior community elders but his only reward was a verbal roasting at the meeting from the local power brokers. He was just a well-educated, well-meaning greenhorn who wasn't needed. Later they didn't even answer his phone calls. Marty smiled but was sympathetic. He had experienced the same treatment himself. It seems Barack had a lot to learn about the politics of Chicago. Breaking the logjam of administrative resistance was going to be difficult.

But Barack persevered in his quest to pull all the opposing factions together. Now Marty was worried for him. Barack was working too hard and Marty feared a burn out. Barack took no heed. He continued to mix with the blacks, attended their church services, danced at their Christmas parties, counselled their sons and daughters on their studies and even played with their grandchildren as they sat on his knee. Slowly he got to know them and better still they got to know him.

That's where Barack's dream of organization came in. How to harness their modest dreams into reality was his goal for their future.

But now time was running out and Barack's three years were coming to a close as an organizer. He must now return to Harvard for his acceptance papers had already arrived.
As Barack entered Harvard to complete his law studies he thought alot about his role as organizer. Frank, an ageing friend of his granddad and a poet was someone Barack had become attached to. So his counselling was always invaluable. His advice on race to Barack shook him enough to help him come to terms with his dilemma. "Your Grandma Toots understands," he said. "Black people have a reason to hate. That's just how it is," said Frank. "I wish it were otherwise for your sake but its not. So you might as well get used to it."

But Barack didn't have to come to terms with hate. He had none. What he had to solve was a cul de sac full of unanswered questions on race. Questions he couldn't answer honestly to his own satisfaction even as he entered University. Later, in practice, he would come across discrimination cases where he discovered how the principals laid down by patriots two hundred years ago could be used to defend his clients today. These were clients whose stories should never have happened. These law practice cases nourished and sustained his faith and hope for society and the future. Society was healing its own wounds, - maybe too slowly. That song of Martin Luther King had a ring of truth at last. "We shall overcome one day".

But now we come to the best part of the Barack Obama story. Maybe Barack had been taking life too seriously for a young man. Suddenly he began to notice life really did have a blue sky after all.

For the first time in his life the world was full of beautiful music and majestic rainbows he never noticed before. And why did he dispense with the doom and gloom of reality? Why did he walk infatuated for weeks high among the stars? Could it be that Barack had become another casualty of Cupid? Let's investigate.

It all started during his first meeting with Michelle Robinson. Barack Obama's world took on a brand new meaning in June 1988, the month he first met his future wife. David Mendell, the author of Obama from Promise to Power has described Michelle Robinson as a statuesque African-American lawyer. While Barack was instantly sure he loved her, she was far less sure of him as a future husband. He was the dreamer. Michelle was the realist.

It happened while Barack was acting as a part-time summer intern at the law firm of Sidley and Austin. Michelle was already a practicing lawyer and three years younger than Barack. He was still a first year student at Harvard University Law School, because he had lost three years in "Community Organising" straight after college. He arrived at the law firm on a wet drizzly morning in June. She was dressed in a tailored suit and blouse looking lovely, cool and professional. Barack was bowled over. She gave him a tour of the office, then off-loaded him to a partner offering to meet him for lunch later.

Her secretaries had described him to her as cute. She lived in a small bungalow just north of the area where he had worked as an organizer. Her father was a pump operator for the city and her mother was a secretary in a bank. Michelle went to Princeton along with her brother, yet there was a trace of vulnerability about her. She socialized with Barack and tried to fix him up with two friends. She told him that as his supervisor it was inappropriate to go out on a date with him. But Barack wouldn't take that for an answer. He finally wore her down and the match was on. For their first date they chose to picnic, they then returned to Barack's apartment.

On their way home they bought two ice cream cones and were happy to cool down in the afternoon heat. Barack cheekily suggested he meet her family. This pleased her as did his next request which was also granted, so he kissed her, their first kiss, which later he remembered, tasted of chocolate. They happily dated for the rest of the summer. She told him about a school trip to Paris, among other things, she had enjoyed and revealed her love of Stevie Wonder songs. This affair was making fine progress.

The visit to Michelle's home cemented their relationship even further. Frasier, her good-humoured father, was wrapped up in his work and his son's ball games. Her mother Marian was pretty and like most American mothers, she was firmly in control of the family. She was even in control of their schooling, having a real hands-on interest in everything at school. Craig was her "basketball star" brother, tall, friendly and polite. He talked of becoming an investment banker, but his heart was really in basketball to the point of wanting to become a coach one day.

What intrigued Barack was the abundance of uncles, aunts and cousins everywhere. Sometimes the mood changed when they stayed home to listen to her Grandpa's old jazz records well into the night. It was certainly a real family home, maybe because they had endured their own set of past hardships and troubles to bond them together. Race was a subject not far from the surface. The smaller income for blacks in Chicago in the fifties and sixties bothered them as did the violent streets, the under-funded playgrounds and indifferent schools there.

Like most families, the Robinsons quietly lived out their own internal family tragedy which they endured bravely everyday. Dad had been diagnosed with multiple sclerosis. This had lasted for the past twenty-five years and it was steadily deteriorating. Dad Robinson continued with life without self-pity, still smiling and joking through all the personal problems this terrible disease inflicted on him, like getting up an hour earlier to get to work. Now his limp needed the assistance of two canes as time went by, especially as he struggled across the field to watch his son play football or to cross the room to kiss his daughter.

Of course, they were all aware of his struggles and sacrifices but they respected his private wish to live his life with a low profile as if his handicap was not noticed. They respected his pride. As we all know, Barack and Michelle were eventually married. In his wedding speech, Barack grew emotional when he remembered his life with Toots and Gramps. Incidentally Gramps had passed away only a short time before. It was an ideal time for Barack to unburden himself before his guests.

His heartfelt speech brought tears to their eyes when he reminisced about the role Gramps had paid in his life and how he had made a little boy whose real father was not around feel as though he was never alone. I'm sure there are many granddads who can empathise with Barack. Granddads just like Gramps who are wonderful substitute dads in their own way all over America. After Barack and Michelle married, Barack got to know just how stressful life had been for her mother. Every outing had to be planned and the family disguised their feelings daily behind their own secret anguish for their sick Dad

Yet the sheer contentment of the Robinson household shone through everything all the time. The stability of it all was an everyday reminder to Barack of what he missed without a father. To Michelle perhaps Barack represented wide open spaces with his family scattered to the four winds. She had only known this cosy close-knit family unit built by a loyal and loving mother and father. But six months after they met Michelle's Dad died of complications after a kidney operation. As Fraser Robinson's coffin was lowered into the earth in the graveyard, Barack made up his mind – Michelle would be his to care for from now on. He made the same promise to Fraser in his grave that day. Cupid had certainly hit the jackpot.

The impact of Michelle's family caused Barack to re-think many of the statistics connected with American marriages. Her family convinced him of the healthy state of the American family. The decline in marriage rates were down due to later marriages – postponed for educational purposes. Yet divorce rates had declined by 21%. Pre-marital sex was more prominent, yet many men and women chose to live alone. Statistics showed 33% of all children were born out of wedlock and 34% have no biological fathers directing their lives. It's amazing that this trend is more prominent in African-American families where 54% of them live in single parent households.

Because of Barack's experience he realized constantly that many of those single Moms did a terrific if not heroic job of raising their kids alone. Barack Obama says "In light of these facts, policies that strengthen marriage and that discourage unintended births are sensible goals to pursue"; something to remember if Obama ever came to power. Also keep a look out for marriage educational workshops, another of his ideas. The new world argument upsets him. This was a silly theory that erases gender differences and says sex is recreational, marriage is disposable and motherhood is an inconvenience. If so then civilization is resting on shifting sands. It's a philosophy of despair. Well that is how Barack's thinking comes across when you listen. Time will tell.

The modern family life with both parents working was referred to by his work family expert Karen Kornbluh as the juggler family. This is one where the parents struggle to pay the bills, look after their children and struggle to maintain their personal relationships. The comparison with the circus juggler was that both parents were trying to keep all the balls in the air together, the strain of which inflicts tremendous stress on marriages and family life.

I won't bore my readers with marriage anecdotes that are already all too familiar to the average American. I merely mention Barack's views on marriage in America to signal what kind of a country might emerge in Barack Obama's America of the future. But before we get too serious, here is a nice little anecdote to lighten the narrative. Isn't it strange how America's

Presidents seem to have a mysterious love affair with one particular date, Independence Day the 4th of July? John Adams, the 2nd President died on the 4th of July, Thomas Jefferson died the very same day in 1826. Independence Day, July 4, uncannily saw the death of the 5th President, James Munroe, on that very day. The tradition will be maintained with Barack Obama for his first born baby girl, Malia, was born on July 4. Yes, Malia certainly maintained the strange string of mysterious coincidences connected with that significant date in American history. Could it hold good news for the future of Barack Obama? Incidentally your humble author celebrates the same birthday July 4, 1933.

Barack Obama's second book, Audacity of Hope gives us a brilliant insight into the world of a Senator on the campaign trail. So let's take a quick look at how it all works. One of the main complaints of Barack Obama in his campaign to become Senator was the hard work involved. The hours over a period of one and a half years on the campaign trail are awesome. Twelve to sixteen hours hard slog daily with only seven days off in the entire eighteen months, that amounts to almost 8,000 hours. Costed at just $10 per hour he could earn from alternative employment would amount to $80,000 of unpaid work. Michelle reminded him at least three times a week that it just wasn't normal. Fear is the motivating factor according to Barack.

Not only fear of losing but worse than that, fear of humiliation. Barack had such an experience in the year 2000 and the wounds still hurt badly today. The statistics were against him to start with; name recognition 90 – 11 in favour of Bobby Rush his opponent; approval ratings 70 – 8 for Bobby Rush. Everything went wrong that could have gone wrong, including a family tiff with Michelle who as a candidate's wife had to stay close to her husband without the inbuilt fire of a politician's ambition.

So who could blame her flipping her lid? Lobbyists pay the bills on the chance that they may be able to influence some legislation which would make millions for their clients in big business. Money isn't the object for a politician. Most Senators are already rich. But without money, or television ads that soak up money, you are a guaranteed loser. The sheer weight of money involved is unbelievable in big State elections. The most Barack hoped to spend was $200,000 for there were certain interests such as gaming or tobacco interests he had to refuse. Yet one week of television advertising would cost $500,000. The full bill for a primary could be at least five million dollars. After that one needed another ten or fifteen million dollars for a Presidential Election.

Barack's total outlay would come to just $500,000. The only way to get the money you needed was to appeal direct to rich people. This was no fun, just cold calling on the phone and risking being hung up on. The worst opponent to confront was a self-financing rich candidate. I've already covered this ground in my piece on President Bill Clinton. I think Barack has given you a fair insight into the world of politics today should you have any ambitions to dip your toe in the waters. Working to attract the votes of major groups, such as Trade Unions is what demands the leg work and perseverance necessary. I think you will agree that the successful candidate to reach the pinnacle of politics has really earned the right to be there.

Yet Barack, despite the high powered world of politics he moved in daily, was always brought back to reality when he arrived home. Questions like "I don't want to die Daddy" from Sasha. Maybe another like "What happens when you die Daddy?" Barack always struggled with those ones. They always made him glad to have a family to bring him down to earth. Enquiries like "How many stars come out at night, Dad?"; "How do fishes swim?" are questions light years away from the ones during the razzamatazz of an election but they can demand answers. Answers he could never have. Yes, at times like that I guess children are great for teaching a tired politician humility. The sort of lesson you couldn't learn at Harvard. Lessons you could only learn from a little girl as you tucked her up in bed after a hard day's politics.

Could I pause here just a little while to discuss a topic that always fascinated me? In all my words describing the previous forty-three Presidencies nowhere did I get into the Senate or Congress to be able to describe the House as it worked. Barack Obama's book The Audacity of Hope speaks intimately about this gap in my knowledge so here is my effort to capture that picture in words.

The Senator may arrive into the basement of the Capitol by subway train. The elevator takes him to the second floor passing maintenance men and the tour groups on the way. He passes a busy group of reporters permanently found there and enters through some double doors on to the floor of the U.S. Senate.

Barack was not too impressed with its beauty but he finds the Chamber imposing nevertheless. Overhead the ceiling is a creamy white colour with an American eagle etched into it. The busts of the first twenty Vice Presidents can be seen above the visitor's gallery. One hundred mahogany desks rise from the floor of the Senate in four rows shaped like a horse shoe. Some of them date back to 1819 Barack tells us. Unbelievably they are still equipped for 1819 complete with receptacles for inkwells and quills. In any school room desk, the graffiti inside holds poignant memories of those occupants from previous school years. In the U.S. Senate the graffiti is no different. Scratched inside his own desk Barack Obama discovered famous names of the previous occupants, such as Taft, Long, Stenos and Kennedy.

Why graffiti? I don't know. A gesture of intense pride I'd suggest. Flashbacks from the historical past come easily in these surroundings; great names like Hubert Humphrey, Joe McCarthy, LBJ and Daniel Webster's desk from where Webster spoke fiercely against Lincoln's detractors.
And now the clerk starts calling the roll. Work has begun. Later the Speaker can find himself addressing an empty Chamber with just the Presiding Officer and a Senate reporter to keep him company. A blue uniformed page will then silently collect the Speaker's statement for the official record. Nothing stops the action. As one Senator departs, another will take his place, stand at his or her own desk, seek recognition, then deliver their statement. To the newcomer, no one is listening but everything that happens is of vital importance in the ritual of the Senate.

Being sworn in as a member of the Senate for the first time can be a daunting experience for the member concerned. The member's family can be seen looking down from the visitor's gallery. The new member stands by a marble dais, his hands raised to take the oath of office and afterwards he may be invited for a photo call with the Vice President. The day finishes with hundreds of well-wishers shaking hands outside the Library of Congress.

The Rules for Debate are set out well in advance by the majority leader to ensure the smooth running of the House. By the time proceedings start each Senator will have been in consultation with his staff and interest groups and will have determined how he is to position himself on any particular issue. The Senators will have other outside interests to attend to and will not spend too much time on the Senate floor but will return to his office in the building to meet constituents, return phone calls, or maybe move to the Senate Television Studio for a live interview. Perhaps I paint a picture of boring repetition and long rehearsed rituals but it is a system that has evolved over the centuries and has reassuringly stood the test of time. I cannot vouch for the complete accuracy of my summary but if I have captured a rough picture of events inside the Chamber I will be more than happy.

For the completion of the Barack Obama story, I must mention one lady who could become America's First Lady from 2009. I have already written about the other possible First Lady, Cindy Hensley McCain. This time I refer to Michelle Obama, mother of two daughters, Malia aged ten and Sasha aged seven. Besides being a housewife, Michelle worked in public service as Assistant to the Mayor of Chicago. She has two degrees, one from Princeton, from where she graduated with a B.A. in Sociology. Her second degree was from Harvard Law School in 1988. She went on to become Assistant Commissioner of Planning and Development for the City of Chicago. She was also Associate Dean of Student Services at Chicago University where she has been very closely involved since 1996. Nowadays, she is fully occupied in the running of Barack's Presidential Campaign. Her speech at the Democratic Convention, made with sincerity and passion, was very well received by the audience. However, she really is more mother than politician.

Now let us move on to Barack Obama's speech in Berlin of July 24, 2008 with thanks to Irish Independent correspondent, Alan Hall.

John McCain back in May 2008 suggested Barack Obama should go to Europe to sell his foreign policy credentials. As time goes by that challenge may be seen as a mighty blunder. It sounded like a Presidential Election mind game, a throw away remark that nobody would take seriously. But on July 24, 2008 Barack Obama took up that challenge when he appeared on a podium set up at the Golden Statue of Victory in the Tiergarten Park in Berlin. – "This liberal dreamer who wishes away the world problems" – was the way he was described dismissively by his enemies. The Berlin Chief of Police estimated the crowd who flocked to hear him at around 200,000. He received a tumultuous reception from his audience mostly students or young thirty year olds, screaming "Obama today." Dubbed "the black JFK", he stood shoulder to shoulder with the ghost of that immortal who spoke a few hundred yards down the road in 1963 giving that famous speech now called "Ich bin ein Berliner".

Obama strolled confidently along the raised platform to the mike and recalled his own roots in Kenya and those dramatic months of the Berlin airlift in the sixties. He began with the words "I come to Berlin as so many of my countrymen have come before, although tonight I speak to you not as a candidate for President of the United States, but as a proud citizen of the world." He went on to ask Europe to stand by the U.S. in bringing stability not just to Iraq or Iran but to Afghanistan. He spoke out to his listeners by calling on them to reach back to him as Europeans. "America had no better partner than Europe," he said and reminded them of the fall of the Berlin Wall that brought not only hope but danger too. He said "No one nation, no matter how large or powerful, can defeat such challenges alone." He referred to Christians, Muslims and Jews and the walls between them. "We must tear these walls down," he admonished. The audience just loved it. Funny how Ronald Reagan's words come back to us today for he stood on the same spot thirty years previously. Reagan said "these walls must come down", and the walls came down. Today Obama was talking about the walls of ethnic differences, racial differences and religious bigotry.

Barack moved on to London next day.
But alas here I must interrupt the Presidential Story for a political SOS, so major; if it were an earthquake it could only be measured as fourteen on the Richter Scale. I refer to the Banking Crisis in America in September 2008. While everyone was focussed on the White House race to be the 44th President of the United States, a dangerous enemy had emerged form the depths of Wall Street. This was a monster we all thought Franklin D. Roosevelt had destroyed

way back in 1933. This one is frightening. Even more fearful than Al-Qaeda, the Taliban or Osama Bin Laden. It threatens the very fundamentals of the American Financial system, even the world financial system, and the heartbeat of the American way of life. By slow strangulation access to easy credit was beginning to dry up.

Sadly, like 1929, it has been conceived and nurtured by greed and abysmal contempt for history. It would never happen again they said in 1934. But it has returned – resurrected from the past like an extinct dinosaur. They have called Congress to battle stations and world experts have been wheeled in. Finance Analysts are the new super stars of television debates.

It seems the bankers went bonkers! Unfettered by any regulation, laissez-faire America took off, inspired and encouraged by vast pots of gold in the housing market. Loans were issued in abundance and even those banks without supporting assets dished out cash they basically didn't have. It was called Sub-Prime lending. Sub-Prime Lending got so erratic it could be likened to a runaway train that going out of control hit the buffers hard. So hard, in fact confidence flooded out onto the tracks and the runaway financial train could not be restarted. Distrust became immersed in the system like water in a petrol engine. Distrust was a poison that spread throughout the system and the financial machine that operated on confidence literally ceased up. Nobody trusted his fellow banker. Without trust the whole economy throughout the United States was in danger of stagnation. Unlike the 1930s demand and business were there but the money just dried up.

Then President George Bush on the advice of his Treasury Secretary Hank Paulson guaranteed Wall Street a 700 billion dollar fund to get the wheels of the stalled money train moving again. It was logical; perfectly reasonable. But nobody trusted it would work. Partisan politics defeated the Legislation in Congress by 208 votes to 205. Elections only weeks away scared the Congressmen who feared to meet their constituents back home if they voted for the package. A cold fury had been expressed by the ordinary citizen against the folly, stupidity and greed of Wall Street. The ordinary jobs in ordinary firms were threatened and "would get no equivalent hand-outs from Washington" was how the Congressmen saw it. It seems nobody wanted to take the medicine to save the bankers of Wall Street. But when the Bill went to the Senate amendments and sweeteners were added to appease the Senators. The Bill expanded from 3 pages to 352 pages. Partisan politics just could not be allowed to sabotage everything. The Bill was passed by the Senate – so far so good.

The next stage was to send the Bill back to Congress. But trouble was waiting for it there, this time from the Conservatives, known as "The Blue Dogs" who were incensed by the measures added to the Bill to mollify the Republican rebels. Fierce lobbying was needed to close the gap in the vote. The President made another desperate speech to impress upon all sides the urgency of passing the Bill and the economic consequences if it was not passed. Now there were two rebellions taking place at the same time, one in each camp.

In the meantime, Nancy Pelosi, the leader of the House, came to the rostrum and put the case for the 700 billion dollar bail out. Already 750,000 had lost their jobs for the year 2008 (159,000 in September 2008 alone). "They are not the high flyers of Wall Street," she said. "They are ordinary citizens like you and me." Then she turned on the denizens of Wall Street and bluntly warned them. "The Party is over." The Bill was duly passed by 271 Yeas to 263 Nays.

Isn't it a strange quirk of history that President Reagan back in the 1970s helped to destroy Communism the avowed enemy of the Capitalist system and here were the Captains of

Industry, the Bankers, forty years later doing what Communism had failed to do. By sheer reckless greed, they had put a bomb under the vast edifice of the world's financial structure without a shot being fired. Now the scary question is – how do we repair the damage to prevent a meltdown in the world's global markets? Only time will answer that one. Already a world conference of the G7 and a meeting of the most talented economists on the globe have been called to the White House to examine the fall-out which, even as I write this, in October 2008, is swiftly spreading to Asia, Europe and Russia.

Now one week on since that Congressional vote, only some of the banks are actually trading with each other. Confidence is very slow returning, so we are all just holding our breath and hoping. That melt down forecast by the IMF (The International Monetary fund) is still only round the corner. Meanwhile, the Presidential Race goes on. Both candidates have taken on a new importance, for on January 20, 2009 one of them will sit in the Oval office with the nightmare of the world economies on his desk. No President since F.D. Roosevelt has had such a challenge awaiting his four years stewardship.

If only the bankers had heeded the words of the great Adam Smith in his world famous classic on the capitalist system called The Wealth of Nations.

I quote him as follows:-
"The over weening conceit which the greater part of men have of their own ability is an ancient evil. That the chance of gain is naturally overvalued we may learn from the universal success of lotteries."

Another of his quotes on monopolies should have alerted us to trouble ahead:-

"Man made monopolies are a constant threat to prosperity. The high profits they generate are a sign of decay not advancement. Markets exist to serve customers not enrich corporations."

But let's continue with the Presidential hustings so far.

In an earlier chapter we treated the reader to a casual glimpse inside the Senate Chamber for the initiation of a new Senator. As an outsider I found it fascinating to visit that historic debating forum we only read about in the newspapers. You may remember we walked among the seats and inspected the graffiti left there by names from the distant past. We then witnessed the Senate in session, the role of the Speaker and the business of the House in progress. Yes, it was great to view the rituals of politics inside the golden circle.
We are now going to walk inside the golden circle once again at the invitation of television. On January 9, 2010 BBC2 had a programme taking us into the Barack Obama camp on the stump during his Presidential campaign. I hope you enjoy the journey and that you get a real taste of the atmosphere of election fever from the inside.

We open the story with a question put to Barack Obama. "What keeps you awake at night?" "Nothing," was Barack's reply "but the prospect of the problems we have right now."

One surprise to us was how prominent Michelle Obama was in the action, almost as if it was her campaign too. The cameras gave an amazing image of her at work in the frontline talking to supporters.

Later we stood behind the cameras as Barack addressed his troops talking about his life with Michelle living in a small house with two children. Not unlike the struggles of the same young people listening to him who were also trying to make both ends meat while going to college. Iowa was his first victory which saw the whole family walk out on stage to be cheered to the echo by celebrating voters.

Our next scene was to step aboard the plane taking Barack to New Hampshire and right into a press conference he was giving on board. It was marvellous, "in your face" politics as it was happening. Here we saw a President-elect speaking with a quiet self-assured confidence. A man who knew where he was going.

Next scene took us to the apartment on the 10th floor of a high rise building where he had lived life with his grandmother "Toots" and grandfather "Gramps", just as we wrote about in our piece on Barack after he came back from Hawaii.

But politics is a rollercoaster and the cameras didn't spare us the pain on Barack's face and on the faces of his Aides when news came in they had failed to win New Hampshire. We saw his reaction. How he took it warts and all. His fighting words told them they were in it for the long haul. They were not going to have an easy ride.

But what had started in a whisper in Iowa became a victory in Clinton County. Once again the mantra was being chanted outside "Yes we can", "Yes we can." The enthusiasm was re corded instantly and couldn't be phoney. The hustings were getting better for Barack. Everything burst like a kaleidoscope of spontaneous celebration after Ohio and Texas. Now his Aides were heard to say Hillary Clinton is fighting trench warfare now. Unfortunately Pastor Wright entered the fight and was not welcome. He introduced with ferocity the subject of race, something Barack was angry about. He decided to confront the race issue head on. "People may be angry," he told his supporters "but the question is what are we going to do about our anger?"

The cameras next took us inside the colossal Convention Centre crowded with supporters. It was a frightening spectacle. The sheer size of the stadium, the cheering crowd, the noise, the banners, and the razzamatazz left one speechless.

In the middle of all this awesome excitement Barack had to make an articulate major speech. In front of the cameras we saw him rehearse it with his team. The pressure just watching TV was unbearable. This was truly America on the stump in 2008, a wild extraordinary jamboree of sound, noise and music. All captured on celluloid for posterity.

Sarah Palin entered the picture and instantly lowered the tone of the debate by calling Barack a terrorist. Barack refused to be upset even when they called him "Risky". But worse that that was to come. New s from home that his grandma "Toots" had died. Before our eyes Barack made an emotional speech describing how much she meant to him. The faces of the crowd were caught in close-up. Many had tears in their eyes. A chant rose spontaneously rising to a crescendo. "Yes we will." It was tremendous television.

Soon the big day arrived and the long queues of voters were filmed lining up by the thousand around the block to the voting booths.

"This is momentous," one black lady aged sixty-two said into the camera. "Win or lose nothing will ever be the same again. I've been crying since four o'clock this morning." The voting was 207 to 141. The waiting was almost over.

Then came the screams of the voters shouting exultingly. "We have won! Barack Obama is the new President."

When the excitement died down we walked behind the cameras as they followed Barack's manager through the building to Barack's inner sanctum. The manger was crying. Michelle met him inside and embraced him. She wiped a tear from his cheek. "Don't cry, don't cry" we heard her say.

For us TV voyeurs what a wonderful end it was to this stage of the Obama story.

We're not finished yet. The euphoria of the inauguration ceremony is still to come.

The illustrious journalist, Max Hastings, said in his piece in the Irish Mail Oct 25, 2008, the expectations of people in America caused them to gather in crowds of 50,000 and 70,000 just to hear a message of hope from the politicians. Barack Obama has become the deity of hope in this election, to deliver them from evil and maybe lead them to a mythical place of peace and abundance. The name of the paradise is called change.

Max told a security guard he was here from London because those back home were anxious about this new President. He was just as much our President as America's. Not those words but those sentiments. Homes have already been repossessed in Great Britain in a similar recession now hitting America. The health care problem and two foreign wars killing the young of America worries everyone. A Pastor says from the rostrum "Let us not ask whether God is on our side but whether we are on God's side." Will this coloured God we see before us, sleeves rolled up with his dazzling white smile, bursting with energy, oozing with optimism deliver what we in the crowd are waiting for?

"We meet in a moment of great uncertainty for Americans," Obama preached. I've no doubt he has used the same words at many other rallies. That's what scriptwriters do. But his words released emotions of hope in his listeners and persuaded them he understood their dreams and they loved it. That hope has transferred itself into campaign funds of hundreds of millions of dollars which Obama has used to reach out to the remotest unregistered voters in pamphlets, advertisements and Internet propaganda to tell them what he is about.

"Let's leave Iraq, it's now only a Civil War," he told them. "I'm going to slash taxes so you can pay your bills," he promised. A nearby reporter was shocked that neither McCain nor Obama could not alert the American people about how bad things would become and where the money was to come from to pay for tax cuts. Mike Huckabee of Fox TV and runner-up for the Republican nomination denounced Obama as a "Would-be-wealth redistributor". "That's socialism," he screamed from his pulpit on the radio as if socialism was a dirty word. But there are other disasters besides Iraq; Energy, climate change and the economy to name three. Yet there is optimism which says Obama can solve the problems better than McCain and the notorious "hockey mum" Sarah Palin. But there are eccentrics out there too, Larry Fells for instance. Max Hasting tells us about him. He has theories about Kennedy, Martin Luther King and the Twin Towers Tragedy.

"The Twin Towers were destroyed to benefit the Rockefellers. And George W. Bush engineered the Sub-Prime financial melt down. That's the unvarnished truth" he claims. It also seems Obama will be controlled in the White House by sinister forces. Yes the nutters are having a field day. Perhaps they too are entitled to their place in the sun. After all, it helps to stimulate the cauldron of make-believe in the razzamatazz of election fever. In Andrew

Jackson's day in 1825 the clowns and the preachers followed brass bands into town to sell their brand of politics. Elections were always just great fun, full of impossible dreams.

But life is not always serious during elections. One night there was a truce when the candidates Obama and McCain had a night out at the Manhattan Waldorf Astoria Hotel. John McCain poked fun at his own numerous homes. He referred to his new campaign discovery "Joe the plumber" and announced he had, just that morning, sacked his entire team of advisors and handed their jobs over to someone special. The name "Joe the plumber" got a great laugh. Obama would not be upstaged for he followed it up with this nugget of wisdom. "Contrary to the rumours I was not born in a manger. I was actually born on Krypton and sent here - to save the planet earth." That one brought the house down. But next day life went on for both of them.

According to Sarah Baxter Sunday Times Oct 19, 2008, who we have been privileged to quote when writing about George W. Bush, reports that big hitters are already crossing Party lines, not only to support Obama but to offer their services in any new Administration he might form. Names like Bill Clinton, Hillary Clinton, Colin Powell, John Kerry, Larry Summers, and Chuck Hagel to name but a few. However he will have to leave room to reward the loyalty of his own supporters such as his foreign policy expert Susan Rice. Other possibilities are Richard Lugar and General Jim Jones. The voting numbers could stack up giving Obama an overwhelming majority in both the Senate and Congress which would be unprecedented for a Presidential election going way back to 1933.

But right now I'm sorry to have to pass on a sad, sad story, the passing away of Barack's Grandma Toots. "She poured all the love she possessed into me," said Barack Obama of his lovely grandmother "Toots" who had brought him up since he was eleven years old and has been the fulcrum of his life story since babyhood. Now at the very pinnacle of his life, at the very point of time she might have been over the moon with joy for him, seeing her life's work come to fruition she has died. Yes this wonderful keystone of his life story, which so easily could have gone in a different direction, has passed away on the very eve of the Presidential election. I'm sure there is a special seat in Paradise from where she can comfortably, and proudly watch Barack become President of the United States tomorrow November 4, 2008. What a wonderful journey it has been for both of them.

Barack was on the brink of glory now according to the polls but knowing past history he just urged, no pleaded, with his supporters to work on. Complacency would seem to be his only enemy now to snatch the Golden prize from his outstretched hands.

The turn-out for the election was truly astonishing, estimated at 234 million voters. No one expected such a response. At one stage they swamped the voting machines forcing long lines of voters to wind their way slowly into the voting stations for two to three hours.

Some of the TV commentators got carried away. An obscure voice in the background was droning "Judge a man by the content of his character not by the colour of his skin." Another TV commentator pointed out that half a century ago the only measure of a black man was his right to board a bus. Sound bites well-researched and rehearsed for public consumption. But cynicism has no platform for a night like this so full of emotional realization of what was happening all around them. A dazed realization that the history of the coloured American from the Civil War, through the appalling injustices meted out to the Negro after Reconstruction had failed, through the civil rights protests and the death of Martin Luther King, right through the riots of Nixon's and Johnson's America had come to fruition at this present glorious moment.

The journey had now been justified. Their perseverance had its own reward in the singing of the soul music "We Shall Overcome". Everything was no longer a vague hope but an accomplished reality. After 145 years the Civil War was well and truly over.

As City Park, Chicago filled up to its capacity two million faces looked skywards at the giant screens and punched their fists high above their heads in a victory salute. It was 4 a.m. on November 5, 2008 and the electrifying news was there for all to see. Barack Obama was the next President of the United States by 349 Electoral votes to 162. The margin of victory was the green light for a night of incomparable celebration never seen in Chicago "the windy city". They had waited 220 years since April 30, 1789 for this glorious moment.

"Now we have a chance" one onlooker told the cameras. "It should have happened in the sixties. We now have what Martin Luther King wanted. May he rest in peace." The same cameras captured a flash of rare intimacy as it focussed on an unsuspecting Jesse Jackson in tears. Then from far-away Kenya, Barack Obama's paternal grandma Sarah faced the press outside her little country house and broke down in tears, tears of happiness. Kids from the local school were allowed out to run wild with excitement and Kenya's President did the only thing he could do, declare a public holiday. That meant no school for the kids. So they had a double excuse for running wild.

Neil Toibin, an Irish writer was interviewed. Just like another spectator, he also found it difficult to buy a newspaper in Chicago that morning and was convinced they were being bought to mark the date of the occasion. Two days later, they were being sold for $100 a copy. Perhaps in years to come they will probably be historical documents to cherish. Toibin mentioned the impressive organizational brilliance of Barack Obama but anyone familiar with Barack's life story, as told in his book Dreams from My Father will know that for three years after graduating Barack Obama worked as a professional organizer for the coloured people of Chicago. For your writer therefore, this expertise in organizing the masses came as no surprise whatsoever.

The most amazing fact of all I simply must report. I understand that out of two million people gathered in the Mall and beyond on inauguration day not one arrest was needed or made. Human nature never fails to amaze you.

John McCain spoke with dignity in his concession speech. Republican fireworks were left in unopened boxes. "The American people have spoken," he began. "Tonight I have called Barack Obama to congratulate him on being elected the next President of a country we both love. This is an historic election for African-Americans and for the special pride which must be theirs tonight. We have come a long way from the old injustice that once stained our nation's reputation and denied to some the privilege of American citizenship a century ago. Theodore Roosevelt caused outrage by inviting Booker T. Washington, an African-American to dinner." McCain continued "We fought as hard as we could but though we failed the fault is not yours but mine."

Some of his supporters tried to return to the party they had planned but without success, their hearts just were not in it. By midnight the night staff were tidying up. In the foyer of the Frank Lloyd Wright ballroom the stall holders were cutting their losses by reducing the price of their unsold T-shirts to $5. One bitter outburst from a woman just about summed up the mood of desolation in defeat. "I can't believe that I have to call that man my President." She was in tears. But that could also have been the fate of thousands of Democrats celebrating in Chicago. Right now I guess the line between success and failure will always be pain or ecstasy.

To say that Barack Obama's Acceptance Speech was powerful is an understatement. I've read it many times and I just couldn't make up my mind on what to leave out so here is most of – what I've left in.

ACCEPTANCE/VICTORY SPEECH:

It's been a long time coming, but tonight, because of what we did on this date in this election at this defining moment, change has come to America.

And I would not be standing here tonight without the unyielding support of my best friend for the last sixteen years, the rock of our family, the love of my life, the nation's next First Lady Michelle Obama.

And while she's no longer with us, I know my grandmother's watching, along with the family that made me who I am. I miss them tonight. I know that my debt to them is beyond measure. – To my sister Maya, my sister Alma, all my other brothers and sisters, thank you so much for all the support that you've given me. I am grateful to them.

As Lincoln said to a nation far more divided than ours, we are not enemies but friends. Though passion may have strained, it must not break our bonds of affection.

To those – to those who would tear the world down: We will defeat you. To those who seek peace and security: We support you. And to all those who have wondered if America's beacon still burns as bright. Tonight we proved once more that the true strength of our nation comes not from the might of our arms or the scale of our wealth, but from the enduring power of our ideals; democracy, liberty, opportunity and unyielding hope.

Ann Nixon Cooper is 106 years old. She was born just a generation past slavery; a time when there were no cars on the road or planes in the sky; when someone like her couldn't vote for two reasons – because she was a woman and because of the colour of her skin.

And tonight, I think about all that she's seen throughout her century in America – the heartache and the hope; the struggle and the progress; the times we were told that we can't and the people who pressed on with that American creed YES WE CAN.

At a time when women's voices were silenced and their hopes dismissed, she lived to see them stand up and speak out and reach for the ballot. YES WE CAN.

When there was despair in the dust bowl and Depression across the land, she saw a nation conquer fear itself with a New Deal, new jobs, a new sense of common purpose. YES WE CAN.

When the bombs fell on our harbour and tyranny threatened the world, she was there to witness a generation rise to greatness and a democracy was saved. YES WE CAN.

She was there for the buses in Montgomery, the hoses in Birmingham, a bridge in Selma, and a preacher from Atlanta who told a people that "We Shall Overcome". YES WE CAN.

So tonight let us ask ourselves; if our children should live to see the next century; my daughters should be so lucky to live as long as Ann Nixon Cooper, what change will they see? What progress will we have made? This is our chance to answer that call. This is our moment.

And to all those watching tonight from beyond our shores, from Parliaments and Palaces, to those who are huddled around radios in the forgotten corners of the world, our stories are singular, but our destiny is shared, and a new dawn of American leadership is at hand.

Finally, he ended his speech on a human note that connected instantly with everyone in the audience who had children. The soaring poetry of his speech was not needed when he spoke to his two little girls. It gives a beautiful gentle end to the poetry of history we have listened to from the politicians.

"Sasha and Malia I love you both more than you can imagine. And you have earned the puppy that's coming with us to the new White House." Well true to his word he kept that promise on April 14, 2009 when a little puppy FDOTUS, a six month old Portuguese waterdog arrived at the White House to a press conference just for him. In the middle of a recession the reporters had a field day happy to bombard Barack with silly questions not connected to banking. Everyone enjoyed themselves immensely most of all Sasha and Malia. By the way the dog's name is "Bo".

But now back to serious business. The famous Professor Simon Schama reflected with passion on the significance of this historical moment for America.   Schama said, "It was time we lived up to the Declaration of Independence, Jefferson saying all Americans were free and equal and yet he held slaves. It took Lincoln's document of Emancipation (the 14th Amendment), a Civil War and a Civil Rights Movement to wipe out this original sin. Not until now have we finally lived up to that promise. Was there ever a more poisoned chalice to take up the challenge that lies ahead?"

President Bush appeared briefly to greet the news saying "This is a triumph of the American story. Many thought they would never see this day. Barack Obama can count on our complete co-operation in his transition to the White House. Last night Laura and I extended an invitation to Barack Obama and his family to come to the White House and we look forward to meeting them. On January 20, Laura and I will return back to our house in Texas." The co-operation President Bush spoke of was already taking place on Capitol Hill. Already just two days after the election, major moves were happening behind the scenes to install the next Administration.

As the Barack Obama story comes to a climax, the scene now moves to the White House on January 20, 2009, inauguration Day, for the people all over the United States.

There has never been a Coronation quite like that of Barack Obama in the last 220 years of the Presidency.

The crowd on Inauguration day were arriving at 3.30 a.m. on the morning of January 20, 2009. Washington was bathed in moonlight and the weather was bitter cold. They came armed with layers of woollies, hand and foot warmers, folding chairs, rugs, and blankets and most important of all their picnic kits made up of flasks, sandwiches, coffee and soft drinks. They settled down silently under the most convenient big screen they could find for the long wait until 11.30 a.m.

Later Obama awoke in Blair House, the Colonial building opposite the White House, the lodging house of Presidential visitors to the White House. If he pulled back the curtain and looked down he would have seen throngs of walkers making their way down the Mall searching for an vantage point to celebrate the ceremony. Behind him in the house one hundred guests of his shared an experience they would talk about for the rest of their lives. They came from many walks of life, from Kenya, Indonesia, Hawaii and the Plains of Kansas. Poor blacks from the south side of Chicago were also invited reflecting Obama's life from his own past. Working class blacks mingled with family, friends, excited beyond belief. "It's just unbelievable," said one lady. "You have to pinch yourself. It might be hard to go home." What a contrast Obama's visitors made to the slick, sharp suited people surrounding the Republicans. The multiethnic entourage will remember this day for years into the future.

Michelle, the First Lady, besides having ancestors going back to the slavery era also boasts a distinguished soldier from her family who fought in Washington's Army over two hundred years ago.

Barack Obama, after a last farewell chat with George Bush, which delayed the timetable of the inauguration, was eventually whisked away to be driven the short distance to Capitol Hill by a chain of black Cadillacs to a celebrity style adulation from those crowded around the White House gates.

The anger of one spectator with the old regime was buried in a throw away remark he made "Was it a birthday celebration for the rebirth of a nation?" he was asked. He cocked a thumb behind him at the White House "Yeah", he said "but it's also about seeing the back of those cowboys in there."

Cameras set up inside the White House captured the intimacy of the background to inauguration day. Hand in hand, the old brigade were given their place in the sun. The honourable co-stars of past epics marched onto the Presidential stage. Past Presidents, Jimmy and Rosalyn Carter, George and Barbara Bush, Bill and Hillary Clinton and finally George and Laura Bush. Dick Cheney, the sitting Vice President, turned up in a wheel chair, a casualty of an accident back home.

The Lincoln thread embellished every step Obama made on his journey to the Presidency. Both of them Lincoln and Obama were criticised for being too inexperienced for the job. Both of them wrote best sellers but their major strong point was their power with the spoken word. Obama in his farewell to Illinois from the U.S. Senate once again used Lincoln's identical words from the past –

"I ask for your support, your prayers and confidently hope that all will yet be well."

Obama once again dipped into Lincoln's repertoire of eloquence when he said in his acceptance speech –

"As Lincoln said to a nation far more divided than ours, we are not enemies but friends. Though passion may have strained, it must not break our bonds of affection."

Barack Obama even created a theme for his inauguration called "A New Birth of Freedom" taken from Lincoln's Gettysburg Address. Finally, honest Abe's ghost must surely have been standing there beside Barack when he was taking the oath because the bible he used belonged to Lincoln. This was the first time it had been used since March 4, 1865 when Abraham Lincoln last used it. Incidentally, Obama's oath had to be repeated next day. Now Obama was reaching out to unify both Parties in Congress and the Senate and like Lincoln facing into the storm that lay ahead, coping with a political mess of unprecedented proportions never experienced before in the history of the United States.

There are many similarities between the history of both men with which Barack identified throughout his campaign. At the start of this piece, we saw Obama announce his candidacy for President in Springfield, Lincoln's hometown. Quoting from Lincoln's "House Divided" speech was another reminder that Barack was travelling a parallel course to Lincoln, separated by two hundred years of history. Both of them were peacemakers. Lincoln made it plain how he wanted the peace to be used to unify the nation after the Civil War ended in 1865. Alas, anger generated by Lincoln's assassination hijacked the aftermath of the Civil War, leaving the country sundered politically for years to come. Like Lincoln, Obama has also to deal with the heartbreak of war. While Lincoln's war was at home, Obama's war is international in Iraq and Afghanistan, thousands of miles away.

I know there are people who like to read about those insignificant facts we call "trivia" so to satisfy their curiosity here are some strictly forgettable ones.

Presidential Trivia Facts
Six Presidents since the Second World War were left handed.
The U.S. flag has 50 stars for 50 States and 13 stripes for the original Colonies.
Cost of a seat at the ceremony was $8,249.
Books of J.K. Rawlings – he read all seven.
Presidential limousine called The Beast (8 inch armour, tear gas cannon and Kevlar reinforced tyres),
The number of horses in Inauguration Parade – 242.
The number of people in Inauguration Parade – 13,000.
Obama's paternal grandmother gave him gifts of a stool, a fly swat and a warrior's shield from Kenya.
Security officials numbered 25,500 (8,000 police, 7,500 soldiers and 10,000 National Guards).
Soldiers to be withdrawn from Middle East before 2010 are 150,000.
Obama's earnings from his books last year - $4.2 million (€3 million).
Number of people who lined the Mall – 2 million.
Defence Secretary, Robert Gates, designated Obama's successor in case of disaster, had to spend the day in seclusion.
Inaugural lunch included seafood stew, pheasant and duck, with sour cherry chutney and apple cinnamon sponge.
Time to sell out seats on Parade route – 60 seconds.
The number of cigarettes he smokes per day – 3.
The cost of Obama's weekly haircut $21.
The shortest Inauguration speech ever – George Washington in 1793 – 150 words.
The longest Inaugural speech by William Henry Harrison in 1841 lasted one hour 45 minutes.
The number of black shoes, size 11, in Obama's wardrobe – 4 pair
The downbeat news on Inauguration Day – The Dow Jones fell by 288 points.
The number of suits he owns (Schaffner Marx) cost $1,160 each – 6.
No Dad from age of two. His mother and grandparents reared him.
Edition of Spiderman comic in which he appears – 583.
There is one fallacy: Obama is the 43rd President not the 44th. There were forty-three individual Presidents but forty-four Presidencies.
Among the stars from stage, screen and sport, the most illustrious sport's personality of all was there – Muhammad Ali.
It's not well-known but Malia's birthday is Independence Day in America – July 4.
It is a sobering thought in this the third millennium to realize how rapidly the role of the Government of the United States had grown. As late as 1900, the Federal Budget was no more than half a billion dollars. That is less than the budget of New York State in 2000. To put all this into a more telling context it is hard to believe how much the staff of the White House

has risen from six people, four door keepers and two messengers in 1900 to Bill Clinton's reign at the end of the century, the year 2000, when it took 3,000 people to serve the President.

It might be appropriate at this stage to use a little mantra I have used before in these notes.

"Let's lighten the narrative a little".

I'm sure Barack Obama was not short of advisors but the most crucial words of wisdom received by the Obama family were directed at both Malia and Sasha. They came from the best people to give such advice, George Bush's twin daughters, Barbara and Jenna, both twenty-seven years old now. "Fill the house with laughter and go to anything and everything" they wrote in a special letter to both of them. "Just go" were the words. "Four years go by so fast, so absorb it all, just enjoy it. Have fun and enjoy your childhood in what is such a magical place to live and play." They should know for they had played in the White House when their Granda and Grandma lived there. They also played there when their Dad and Mom lived there. The letter went on … "If you ever need a hug go find Ramsey. If you want to talk football, look for Buddy. And if you just need a smile, look for Smiley. Have swimming parties and go play sardines on the White House lawn. We were constantly inspired by the amazing people we met, politicians and great philosophers, such as Vaclav Havel. We dined with royalty, heads of State, authors and activists. We even met the Queen of England."

The twins went as far as to mischievously encourage Malia and Sasha to try sliding down the banisters of the White House. This was not an unusual pastime, for the children of Theodore Roosevelt, the 26th President were so wild and extrovert they gave the "Staffers" a permanent headache by their antics. However, I doubt if the two gentle little Obama girls will ever release a pet rat for their illustrious visitors' entertainment, as did Kermit Roosevelt. I have already mentioned that episode under my piece on Theodore Roosevelt.
More sobering advice was of the grown up variety "Surround yourself with loyal friends and cherish your pets because sometimes you'll need the comfort only animals can provide."

Incidentally there will be a bonus for the President for working from home in the White House he will spend more time with the kids. Besides now he will only have to go upstairs for dinner.

The Bush girls naturally got around to writing about their father. "Dad's public image has been distorted over the years. Our Dad, like yours, is a man of great integrity and love, a man who always put us first" Barbara and Jenna wrote. "We still see him now as we did when we were seven as our loving daddy. He is our father, not the sketch in a paper or part of a skit on T.V. So here is our most important piece of advice – Remember who your Dad really is."

Well how do you follow that!

Somebody said a week is a long time in politics. If so, eight years is a lifetime. Some people forget George W. Bush was popular enough to be voted back to the White House for a second four year term with a landslide vote. Somewhere in that second term things went disastrously wrong. Oil prices went through the roof; Iraq became caught up in a Civil War; the bankers put a bomb under the economy; and a world recession put the clock back to the 1930s. So, is George Bush another Hoover or a President suffering the fate of Hoover? Only the historians can adjudicate on that one maybe fifty years from now.

As for your writer, I prefer to trust the judgement of George Bush's twin daughters. He is still for me a very sound bloke indeed and as some very astute judges have concluded – a consummate politician.

So let's finish this journey we have travelled, through the lives of forty-four Presidents since George Washington was inaugurated on April 30, 1789 right up to the Inauguration of Barack Obama on January 20, 2009, a distance that has straddled four centuries and 220 years.

The time was 11.34 a.m. on January 20, 2009, as Barack Obama arrived at the mike. The crowd around cried, laughed and clapped. Their Messiah had arrived and was acclaimed by millions as "Our Jesus, our Moses." "Obama is the peddler of vile liberal theology" some sneered. Yet all around, soulful Alleluias rose from the throats of the multitude, arms aloft keeping rhythm with their mood – "We heard freedom ring. You heard freedom ring" they sang.

Like all those illustrious Presidents before Obama, I'll leave you with some significant extracts from his Inauguration speech that painted a picture of the present and pointed a finger to the future as he stood triumphantly on the platform set up for him on Pennsylvania Avenue.

Here is his Inauguration speech – My edited version for the record.

My fellow citizens;
I stand here today humbled by the task before us, grateful for the trust you have bestowed, mindful of the sacrifices borne by our ancestors. I thank President Bush for his service to our nation, as well as the generosity and co-operation he has shown throughout this transition.

That we are in the midst of crisis is now well understood. Our nation is at war, against a far-reaching network of violence and hatred. Our economy is badly weakened, a consequence of greed and irresponsibility on the part of some, but also our collective failure to make hard choices and prepare the nation for a new age. Homes have been lost; jobs shed; businesses shuttered. Our health care is too costly; our schools fail too many; and each day brings further evidence that the ways we use energy strengthen our adversaries and threaten our planet.

Forty-four Americans have now taken the Presidential oath. The words have been spoken during rising tides of prosperity and the still waters of peace. Yet, every so often, the oath is taken amidst gathering clouds and raging storms. At these moments, America has carried on not simply because of the skill or vision of those in high office, but because we the People have remained faithful to the ideals of our forebearers, and true to our founding documents.

Today I say to you that the challenges we face are real. They are serious and they are many. They will not be met easily or in a short span of time. But know this, America, they will be met.

On this day, we gather because we have chosen hope over fear, unity of purpose over conflict and discord.

On this day, we come to proclaim an end to the petty grievances and false promises, the recriminations and worn-out dogmas, that for far too long have strangled our politics.

For everywhere we look, there is work to be done. The state of the economy calls for action, bold and swift, and we will act – not only to create new jobs, but to lay a new foundation for growth. We will build the roads and bridges, the electric grids and digital lines that feed our commerce and bind us together. We will restore science to its rightful place, and wield technology's wonders to raise health care's quality and lower its cost. We will harness the sun and the winds and the soil to fuel our cars and run our factories. And we will transform our schools and colleges and universities to meet the demands of a new age. All this we can do. And all this we will do.

To the Muslim world, we seek a new way forward, based on mutual interest and mutual respect. To those leaders around the globe who seek to sow conflict, or blame their society's ills on the West; know that your people will judge you on what you can build, not what you destroy.

Let it be said by our children's children that when we were tested, we refused to let this journey end, that we did not turn back, nor did we falter; and with eyes fixed on the horizon and God's grace upon us, we carried forth that great gift of freedom and delivered it safely to future generations.

It had been a long tiring day for Barack Obama, living up to his obligations as President so it was back to base for a quick shower, a shave and maybe a shampoo in preparation for Part Two of Barack's inaugural day. In front of him there were ten inaugural Balls to be faced. I won't bore you with too much detail but here are the names of a few: the Home States Ball, the Creative Coalition Ball, the Purple Ball. Don't ask me to explain the names for I am sure they have some historic significance. At most of them, well-known celebrities were dancing with the crowd; Mariah Carey, Faith Hill, Demi Moore and Leonardo DiCaprio, among others. I'm sure both Barack and the First Lady, Michelle, were bowled over by one great singer they met. In our earlier narrative they talked about him on their first date together – the famous Stevie Wonder.

Michelle's dancing was like a dream and full of class. While she floated around the floor, Barack just lacked the finesse of the First Lady. However, he more than made up for this with the passion and fire of a demented limbo dancer. Barack's verdict on Michelle's dancing was as follows – "She made all the right moves in high heels going backwards." High praise indeed from the President

The Neighbourhood Dance was run by the locals for the locals and the smallest dance crowd was 3,500. The Home State was a reference to Barack Obama's home in Hawaii. "It represents our roots," said Barack. The Commander-in-Chief's Ball was full of soldiers who received Barack's grateful recognition for the part they were playing for America in the battlefields of Iraq and Afghanistan. "Hit it man," shouted Barack to the D.J. when he took to the floor for the last time. After that it was time to wave goodbye. He had an early rising next morning for his first day in the Presidency.

There is now only one person left in our story of the forty-four Presidents – George W. Bush.

I have already written the inside story of what happens in the White House on any inauguration day, so I won't worry you too much about the farewell protocol for George W. Bush. Cups of coffee will be handed out in abundance. In the past there has been a little friction between the opposing Parties and their wives. Body language can speak a thousand stories. But this year the atmosphere was one of cheerful hellos and tearful goodbyes from the Staffers who are always genuinely sorry to say farewell to old friends as the previous President and his family leaves the White House.

But no matter how watertight and organized the takeover is, embarrassing hitches do take place. You may recall the exit of Ronald Reagan, I told you about earlier. Someone forgot to film Reagan signing the register, closing the door of the White House for the last time and moving to his helicopter. But they were lucky to find a brilliant actor to play the final scene again next day – Ronald Reagan himself.

There were no such hitches when "Dubya", George Bush's nickname, made his final exit. He just kissed Michelle Obama and grinned "Enjoy the apartment. You will have the time of your life, I promise." They were standing in the grounds of the Capitol Building. Later as George Bush boarded the helicopter with Laura, the lip readers took over. "What did they say," a reporter asked a lip reader. He replied for George Bush "Come on I'm frozen." Who could blame George who was standing in subzero temperatures. Another secret was revealed by a lip reader after Bush and Obama embraced briefly, Obama said "You OK" and the reply was startling. "So relieved." It once again was reminiscent of Lincoln's inauguration. I'm thinking of Buchanan's handover to Lincoln, when he told the great man "If you are as happy my dear Sir on entering this house as I am leaving it and returning home to Wheatland, you are the happiest man in the country."

Although the Bushes have been dispatching their belongings to Texas for some days now, the furniture vans were still outside the White House on inauguration day packing away the final pieces before the Obama furniture moved in.

Laura was very pleased with herself. "I'm leaving with a lot of clothes which is great. I'll never have to buy clothes again." I'd say that was said with tongue-in-cheek for given the right occasion, I bet she just won't be able to resist the temptation to buy a new outfit.

It seems money will be no problem for she has just signed up to a megabucks deal for her memoirs.

George, however, has one problem left to him in his retirement; pouring over the catalogues of major furniture firms searching for ideas to furnish his new two million dollar house built on 1,600 acres in Texas.

There are a number of unknown anecdotes to prove the Bushes were a very kind considerate couple. The First Lady, Michelle Obama, was attacked verbally on the campaign trail and Laura Bush defiantly defended her. Laura now has a letter of appreciation from Michelle Obama for Laura's wonderful reaction to that critic. There is a bond of friendship there now.

Now it was time to go and after another round of affectionate hugs, George and Laura boarded the helicopter to take them home. The Marines were lined up the steps of the Capitol Building like a horseshoe. Standing halfway up were four figures, President Barack Obama and his First Lady, Michelle, and Vice President Joe Biden and his wife, Jill. They did not have long to wait before lift off. Then the Bushes' helicopter climbed heavenwards, heading for Texas. At the window George and Laura could be seen waving a nostalgic goodbye to the new President, Barack Obama below while the ex-President now flew homewards into history.

I find it hard now not to have sympathy for this lonely figure of George W. Bush. He has walked from the Presidency with no friends, no credibility and a figure of ridicule for everybody to snipe at. This can only be discarded as the judgement of the ignorant, the gullible and the fools.

Yet how easy it is to become an unpopular and unhappy President and the lessons of history are there to prove it. Just look at this list.

John Adams, the 2nd President, spent his life with enormous success on the International stage, giving meaning to George Washington's dreams only to be rejected for a second term by the people and rejected by his best friend, Jefferson. He left the Presidency by public stagecoach in the middle of the night and drove home to Braintree alone.

John Tyler, the 10th President, left office so unpopular in the Presidency they did not even announce his death in the newspapers until seventeen years later.

James Knox Polk, the 11th President, took a circuitous route home when he left office – to avoid troublemakers.

Franklin Pierce, the 14th President, died without a friend to mourn him – the penalty for his consistent criticism of the great George Washington. His wife and three children had died during his Presidency.

James Buchanan, the 15th President, was a disaster in his ineptitude when dealing with the coming Civil War. Yet he was a brilliant success as a lawyer and Diplomat before his Presidency. Earlier in these notes you will have read his remark to Lincoln on leaving the Presidency. He went home in despair.

Andrew Johnson, the 17th President, successor to Lincoln, fought a running battle with Congress all through his term of office. He gave a blanket amnesty to the defeated Confederate army and was so volatile he even had a quarrel with the victorious General Grant, refusing to share Grant's carriage on the way to Grant's inauguration. Today we realize what a terrible burden he had trying to fill the shoes of a deity like Lincoln.

Warren Harding's 29th Presidency, ended in such ignominy, it was hard to find a Republican politician to dedicate a statue to him fifty years later, because of the criminals who had surrounded him and sabotaged his Presidency. He was much more successful as a newspaper mogul before the Presidency.

Herbert Hoover, the 31st President, was a world famous engineer and humanitarian before he became President. Had he retired then he would have been almost glorified for his work in Europe, helping the starving millions after the First World War. If only he had retired as an engineer he would not have become a President so hated he retired with ignominy. He too, however, was later rehabilitated by Harry Truman.

Lyndon Johnson (LBJ), the 36th President, never quite achieved his dream. Without Vietnam, he might have been famous for his special plan for America, "The Great Society". He left office feeling a failure.

Richard Nixon, the 37th President, needs no introduction as an unpopular and failed President. His C.V. was horrendous. Yet, late in his retirement, he was forgiven and rehabilitated as an advisor to Congress on International Affairs.

I'm sure the foregoing will reassure George Bush in his retirement. As one commentator said when asked "What destroys the reputation of great men?" He replied "EVENTS." Yes, some day we may be glad to look benevolently on George Bush in history, excusing the demise of his Presidency by one word – EVENTS.

But life goes on and the pages of history keep turning.

Barack Obama awoke to his first day in the 44th Presidency. Tradition demanded the President and his family attend the national Washington Cathedral for morning services.

Despite their late night, Barack and Michelle, Malia and Sasha were whisked away in the familiar black Cadillac for prayer in the church only a few miles down the road from the White House.

They arrived home some time later to eat the breakfast served up to them. This was a brand new experience for Michelle who was used to doing this chore herself.

Barack didn't waste time getting down to business and as they say "He hit the ground running."

At 8.35:   He rang the leaders of Israel, Egypt and Palestine to defuse the Middle
 East powder keg.

At 10.45:   He confirmed Executive Orders restricting lobbyists and setting in motion the programme for closing the Quantanimo Bay Prison in Cuba.

At 3.15:   He had a meeting with his economic advisers. He had still to complete his Cabinet.

At 4.15:   His military advisors arrived to brief him on the Wars in Iraq and Afghanistan.

Later he had some more areas to investigate with the specialists for Stem Cell Research, Health care and the Environment.

Yes, the 44th Presidency had well and truly begun.

I'm sure the coming years will be a rich lore of anecdotes to entertain readers of the next edition of the Presidency. Probably entitled The 45 U.S. Presidents.

Well I guess we've reached the end of that wonderful 220 year journey since 1789. They have been fascinating stories that took us into the events of forty-four Presidencies from George Washington to Barack Obama.

I do hope you have enjoyed the journey as much as I have. I feel a sense of sadness at the thought we have no more Presidents to learn about. Saying goodbye to Capitol Hill is like the break-up of an old love affair. Yes, the Presidencies had a special magic of their own.

Meanwhile, we leave Barack, Michelle, Malia and Sasha to share the wonder of the White House for the next four years. It has been a wonderful trip, full of hope, history, celebrations and heartbreaks. A voyage full of surprises, sometimes laughter, sometimes teardrops, yet laced with great deeds by the honourable men and women who made the American dream come true.

Only one problem remains to be finally resolved in the years to come. Reconciliation with the American Indian, crushed and annihilated beneath the wheels of the covered wagons carrying the pioneers westward across America. Gone is a nation of tribes with their own songs, rituals, dreams, legends, warriors and traditions. Tribes we could not live with, side by side, over the past two hundred years: The Apaches, the Osages, The Pawnees, The Mandans, The Blackfeet, The Comanches, The Sioux, The Cheyennes, The Kiowas, The Shoshonis and many, many others.

With reconciliation now accomplished between the white man and the black man, perhaps the time is not too far away when there will be a final reconciliation between the white man and the red man too.

Perhaps it's not beyond the grounds of possibility that visitors to the White House in fifty years time will walk along a line of paintings of the greatest Indian Chiefs in American history hanging from the White House walls. Their selection could be the choice of the Native American community themselves.

Names like:	Geronimo	Chief of the Apaches
	Sitting Bull	Chief of the Sioux
	Washakie	Chief of the Shoshonis
	Joesph	Chief of the Nez Perces
	Dull Knife	Chief of the Cheyenne
	Ouray	Chief of the Southern Ute
	Sky Chief	Chief of the Pawnees
	Plenty-coups	Chief of the Crows
	Quanah Parker	Chief of the Comanches
	Little Mountain	Chief of the Kiowas
	Eagle Ribs	Chief of the Blackfeet
	Wolf Chief	Chief of the Mandans
	Clermont	Chief of the Osages
	Smoke Head	Chief of the Ponces

Our two hundred year journey is over for now. We soar like the eagle searching for a new landing place without the war drums of fighting nations. A land without the dark clouds of financial failure and ruin to threaten us. A land of true and lasting peace to hand on from President to President for the next two hundred years. Yes, this story will go on and on and that angel will continue to ride in the whirlwind protecting us from the storm.

BIBLIOGRAPHY

Kane, Joesph Nathan, <u>Presidential Fact Book</u>. 1998, New York: Random House. 248 p.

Bennett, Lerone, <u>Forced into Glory</u> : Abraham Lincoln's White Dream. 2000, Chicago: Johnson Pub. Co. 652 p.

Divine, Robert Anthony, <u>America, Past and Present</u>. Brief 4th ed. 1998, New York: Longman. xxviii, 622 p.

Handlin, Oscar and Lilian Handlin, <u>Abraham Lincoln and The Union</u>. The Library of American Biography. 1980, Boston: Little, Brown. x, 204 p.

Degler, Carl N., <u>Out of Our Past; The Forces That Shaped Modern America</u>. [1st ed. 1959, New York,: Harper. 484 p.

Adams, Abigail, Mary S. Cranch, and Stewart Mitchell,<u> New Letters of Abigail Adams</u>, 1788-1801. 1947, Boston,: Houghton Mifflin Co. xlii, 281 p.

Sinclair, Andrew, <u>A Concise History of the United States. A Studio book.</u> 1967, New York,: Viking Press. 224 p.

Caroli, Betty Boyd, <u>First Ladies</u>. 1987, New York: Oxford University Press. xxii, 398 p.

McPherson, James M. and David Rubel, "<u>To the Best of My Ability</u>" : The American Presidents. 1st rev. ed. 2001, New York: Dorling Kindersley Pub. 480 p.

Faulk, Odie B., <u>The Geronimo Campaign</u>. 1993, New York: Oxford University Press. ix, 245 p.

Longstreet, Stephen, <u>War Cries on Horseback: The Story of the Indian Wars of the Great Plains.</u> 1970, London, New York,: W. H. Allen. xv, 336 p., 16 plates.

Kohl, Laurence F., <u>The Politics of Individualism : Parties and the American Character in the Jacksonian</u> Era. 1989, New York: Oxford University Press. xii, 266 p.

Bruce, D.K.E., <u>Sixteen American Presidents.</u> [1st ed. 1962, Indianapolis,: Bobbs-Merrill. 336 p.

Morison, Samuel E., <u>The Oxford History of the American People</u>. 1994, New York: Meridian. v.< 2>

Richards, Leonard L., <u>Gentlemen of Property and Standing; Anti-Abolition Mobs in Jacksonian America.</u> A Galaxy book. 1971, London, New York,: Oxford University Press. 196 p.

Craven, Avery, <u>Reconstruction : The Ending of the Civil War</u>. 1969, New York: Holt, Rinehart and Winston. vi, 330 p.

Mahin, Dean B., <u>Olive Branch and Sword : The United States and Mexico, 1845-1848</u>. 1997, Jefferson, NC: McFarland & Co. vi, 233 p.

Gerson, Noel B., <u>The Slender Reed</u>. [1st ed. 1965, Garden City, N.Y.,: Doubleday. 394 p.

Madison, James and Marvin Meyers, <u>The Mind of the Founder : Sources of the Political Thought of James Madison</u>. Rev. ed. 1981, Hanover N.H.: Published for Brandeis University Press by University Press of New England. lvi, 449 p.

Madison, James and Saul K. Padover, <u>The Complete Madison : His Basic Writings.</u> The Library of the Presidents. 1988, Norwalk, Conn.: Easton Press. ix, 361 p.

Adams, A., et al., <u>The Book of Abigail and John : Selected Letters of the Adams Family, 1762-1784</u>. 2002, Boston: Northeastern University Press. xiii, 411 p.

Jahoda, Gloria, <u>The Trail of Tears</u>. 1995, New York
Avenel, N.J.: Wings Books ; distributed by Random House Value Pub. xi, 356 p.

Remini, Robert V., <u>Andrew Jackson</u>. Johns Hopkins Pbks. ed. 1998, Baltimore
London: Johns Hopkins University Press ;
Johns Hopkins Press Ltd.

Merk, Frederick and L.B. Merk, <u>Manifest Destiny and Mission in American History : A Reinterpretation</u>. 1st Harvard University Press paperback ed. 1995, Cambridge, Mass.: Harvard University Press. xviii, 278 p.

Smith, Elbert B., <u>The Presidencies of Zachary Taylor and Millard Fillmore</u>. 1988, Lawrence, Kan. ; London: University Press of Kansas.

Tebbel, John W. and Sarah M. Watts, <u>The Press and the Presidency</u> :From George Washington to Ronald Reagan. 1985, New York: Oxford University Press. viii, 583 p.

Madison, James and Saul K. Padover, <u>The Forging of American Federalism; Selected Writings of James Madison</u>. Harper torchbooks. 1965, New York,: Harper & Row. ix, 361 p.

Ferling, John E., <u>Setting The World Ablaze </u>: Washington, Adams, Jefferson, and the American Revolution. 2000, Oxford ; New York: Oxford University Press. xxiv, 392 p.

Wilson, Charles M. <u>The Monroe doctrine: an American Frame of Mind</u>. 1971: Princeton, London: Auerbach. 155 p.; maps, ports. 22 cm.

May, Ernest R., <u>The Making of the Monroe Doctrine</u>. 1975, Cambridge, MA ; London: Harvard University Press, 1992.

Richards, Leonard L., <u>The Life and Times of Congressman John Quincy Adams.</u> 1986, New York: Oxford University Press.

Adams, John Q. and David G. Allen, <u>Diary of John Quincy Adams.</u> Vol.1, November 1779-March 1786. David Grayson Allen, associate editor ... [et al.]. 1981, Cambridge, Mass. ; London: Belknap Press of Harvard University Press.

Oliver, Andrew, <u>Portraits of John Quincy Adams and his wife</u>. 1970, Cambridge, Mass.: Belknap Press of Harvard University Press. xli, 335 p.

Rodell, Fred, <u>55 Men : The Story of the Constitution </u>: based on the day-by-day notes of James Madison. 1986, Costa Mesa, Ca: Noontide Press. 281 p.

Hagan, William T., <u>American Indians</u>. Revised ed. ed. 1979, Chicago ; London: The University of Chicago Press. xiii,193p.,10p. of plates.

Time-Life Books and Benjamin Capps, <u>The Great Chiefs(The Old West).</u> 1975, New York: Time-Life Books. 240 p.

Ripley, Thomas and J.W. Hardin, They Died with Their Boots On. [on the Life and Death of John Wesley Hardin and Other Texas Desperadoes. With plates, including portraits.]: pp. xx. 285. Doubleday. 8º.

Brogan, Hugh, The Penguin History of the United States of America. 2nd ed. ed. 1999, London: Penguin, 2001. ix, 737 p.

Bassett, Margaret B., Profiles and Portraits of American Presidents. New and updated ed. 1976, New York: McKay. x, 306 p.

Garraty, John A., The American Nation : A History of the United States. 9th ed. ed. 1998, New York ; Harlow: Longman. xx,148p

Brinkley, Douglas, American Heritage History of the United States. 1998, New York, N.Y. ; London: Viking. 628 p.

Hearn, Chester G., The Impeachment of Andrew Johnson. 2000, Jefferson, N.C.: McFarland & Co.

Degler, Carl N., Out of Our Past : The Forces That Shaped Modern America. 3rd ed. ed. 1984, New York ; London: Harper & Row. xxi, 648p.

Coulter, E. Merton, The South During Reconstruction, 1865-1877: pp. xii. 426. Louisiana State University Press: [Baton Rouge;] Littlefield Fund for Southern History of the University of Texas: [Austin. 8º.

Maihafer, Harry J., The General and the Journalists : Ulysses S. Grant, Horace Greeley, and Charles Dana. 1998, Washington, D.C.: Brassey's, 2001. xv, 315 p.

Meyer, Howard N., Grant, Let Us Have Peace. The Story of Ulysses S. Grant. [With illustrations.]. 1966: pp. xi. 244. Collier Books: New York; Collier-Macmillan: London. 8º.

Bruce, D.K.E., [Revolution to Reconstruction.] Sixteen American Presidents. [With illustrations.]. 1963: pp. 336. Weidenfeld & Nicolson: London. 8º.

Taylor, Richard L. and Richard B. Harwell, Destruction and Reconstruction ... Edited by Richard B. Harwell: pp. xxxii. 380. Longmans. 8º.

United States. Constitutional Convention (1787), James Madison, and Jane Butzner, Constitutional Chaff : Rejected Suggestions of the Constitutional Convention of 1787, with Explanatory Argument. 1970, Port Washington, N.Y.: Kennikat Press. 197 p.

Richards, Leonard L. and American Council of Learned Societies., Gentlemen of Property and Standing: 1970, Oxford University Press: New York. P. ix, 196 p.

Hanna, Ronnie, Never Call Retreat : The Life and Times of Ulysses S. Grant, Ulster-American Hero. 1991, Lurgan: Ulster Society (Publications). xi, 150 p.

Niven, John, Martin Van Buren : The Romantic Age of American Politics. 1983, New York: Oxford University Press. xii, 715 p., [16] p. of plates.

Alexander, Holmes M., The American Talleyrand : The Career and Contemporaries of Martin Van Buren, Eighth President. [1st ed. 1935, New York: Harper. 430 p.

Rable, George C., But There Was No Peace : The Role of Violence in the Politics of Reconstruction. 1984, Athens: University of Georgia Press. xiii, 257 p.

Young, John R. and M. Fellman, <u>Around the world with General Grant</u>. 2002, Baltimore: Johns Hopkins University Press. xv, 448 p.

Logan, Rayford W. and Michael R. Winston, <u>The Negro in the United States.</u> An Anvil original, no. 19, 109. 1970, New York,: Van Nostrand Reinhold. 2 v.

Grant, U.S., Philip R. Moran, and United States. President (1869-1877 : Grant), <u>Ulysses S. Grant, 1822-1885</u>; chronology, documents, bibliographical aids. Oceana presidential chronology series, 6. 1968, Dobbs Ferry, N.Y.,: Oceana Publications. 114 p.

Logan, Rayford W., <u>The Betrayal of The Negro: From Rutherford B. Hayes To Woodrow Wilson</u>. 1st Da Capo Press ed. 1997, New York: Da Capo Press. xxiii, 456 p.

Clark, James C., <u>The Murder of James A. Garfield : The President's Last Days and The Trial and Execution of His Assassin</u>. 1993, Jefferson, N.C. ; London: McFarland. 185p.

Allen, Walter E., <u>Transatlantic Crossing: American Visitors to Britain and British Visitors to America in the Nineteenth Century</u>; selected and with an introduction by Walter Allen. 1971: London: Heinemann. 332 p. 24 cm.

Ciancabilla, Giuseppe, <u>Fired by The Ideal : Italian-American Anarchist Responses to Czolgosz's Killing of McKinley</u>. 2002, London: Kate Sharpley Library. 28 p.

Leech, Margaret, <u>In the Days of McKinley.</u> [1st ed. 1959, New York,: Harper. viii, 686 p.

Stoddard, Henry L., <u>As I Knew Them; Presidents and Politics from Grant to Coolidge.</u> 1927, New York, London,: Harper & Brothers. 15 p. l., 571 p.

Blaine, James G., <u>Twenty Years of Congress: From Lincoln to Garfield.</u>

Sievers, Harry J., Benjamin Harrison, and United States. President (1889-1893 : Harrison), <u>Benjamin Harrison, 1833-1901</u>; chronology, documents, bibliographical aids. Oceana presidential chronology series, 9. 1969, Dobbs Ferry, N.Y.,: Oceana Publications. 89 p.

Miller, Richard, <u>American Imperialism in 1898. The Quest for National Fulfillment</u>. Edited by Richard H. Miller. 1970: New York, etc.: John Wiley and Sons. pp. xii, 206. 22 cm. bibl. pp. 191-206.

Willison, George F., <u>Saints and Strangers. The Story of the Mayflower and the Plymouth Colony</u>. [With maps.]. 1966, pp. xi. 306. Heinemann: London. p. 8º.

Renehan, Edward, <u>The Lion's Pride : Theodore Roosevelt and his Family in Peace and War</u>. 1998, New York ; Oxford: Oxford University Press. xii, 289 p.,[16]p. of plates.

Blum, John M., <u>The Progressive Presidents : Roosevelt, Wilson, Roosevelt, Johnson</u>. 1980, New York ; London: Norton. 221p.

Cotton, Edward H., <u>The Ideals of Theodore Roosevelt</u> ... Foreword by Corinne Roosevelt Robinson. [With a portrait.]. 1923: pp. xix. 329. D. Appleton & Co.: New York, London. 8º.

Wright, Esmond, <u>The American Dream : From Reconstruction to Reagan</u>. 1996, Oxford: Blackwell. xix,669p.

Bishop, Joseph B., <u>Presidential Nominations and Elections: A History of American Conventions, National Campaigns, Inaugurations and Campaign Caricature</u>. With numerous illustrations [including portraits]. 1916: pp. x. 237. C. Scribner's Sons: New York. 8º.

Axson, Stockton and Arthur S. Link, <u>Brother Woodrow : A Memoir of Woodrow Wilson : Supplementary Volume to The Papers of Woodrow Wilson</u>. 1993, Princeton ; Chichester: Princeton University Press. xiv,297p.

Hale, W.B., <u>Woodrow Wilson : The Story of His Life</u>, London: Grant Richards.

Oates, Stephen B., <u>With Malice Toward None : The Life of Abraham Lincoln.</u> 1978, London: Allen and Unwin. xvii,492p.,plate.

Graff, Henry F., <u>The Presidents : a Reference History.</u> 2nd ed. ed. 1996, New York ; London: Charles Scribner's Sons. xiii, 811 p.

Houston, David F., <u>Eight Years With Wilson's Cabinet, 1913 to 1920</u> : with a personal estimate of the President. 1926, Garden City, N.Y.: Doubleday, Page & Company. 2 v.

Means, Gaston B. and M.D. Thacker, <u>The Strange Death of President Harding,</u> London: John Hamilton. 294 p.

Britton, Nan, <u>The President's Daughter</u>. 1931, New York: Elizabeth Ann Guild. 399 p.

Thompson, John A., <u>Woodrow Wilson. Profiles in Power</u>. 2002, London ; New York: Longman. xvii, 265 p.

Reeves, Thomas C., <u>John F. Kennedy :The Man, the Politician, the President</u>. Original ed. 1990, Malabar, Fla.: R.E. Krieger. xii, 165 p.

Kaplan, Robert D., <u>Warrior Politics : Why Leadership Demands a Pagan Ethos</u>. 1st ed. 2002, New York: Random House. xvi, 198 p.

McCoy, Donald R., <u>Calvin Coolidge : The Quiet President</u>. 1998, Newtown, Conn.: American Political Biography Press. viii, 472, [8] p. of plates.

Coolidge, Calvin and Peter Hannaford, <u>The Quotable Calvin Coolidge : Sensible Words for a New Century</u>. 2001, Bennington, Vt. ; [Great Britain]: Images from the Past. x, 183 p.

Russell, Francis M.A.H. and Warren G. Harding, [The Shadow of Blooming Grove-Warren G. Harding in His Times.] <u>President Harding:His Life and Times, 1865-1923</u>. 1969: London: Eyre & Spottiswoode. p. xii, 691: plate; port. 25 cm.

Smith, Gene, <u>When The Cheering Stopped : The Last Years of Woodrow Wilson</u>: [S.l.] : Morrow, 1964 (1971).

Kennedy, David M., <u>Freedom from Fear : The American People in Depression and War</u>, 1929-1945. 1999, New York ; Oxford: Oxford University Press. xviii,936p., [32]p. of plates.

Stewart, Michael, <u>Keynes and After</u>. 3rd ed. ed. 1986, Harmondsworth: Penguin. 230p.

Hicks, John D., <u>Republican Ascendancy</u>, 1921-1933. [With plates, including portraits.]. 1963: pp. xii. 317. Harper & Row: New York. 8º.

Butler, W.V., <u>Franklin D. Roosevelt : Nothing to Fear but Fear.</u> 1982, London: Hodder and Stoughton. 128p.

Parkes, H.B., <u>The United States of America. A History</u>. Third edition. 1968: New York: Alfred A. Knopf. pp. xviii, 805, xxiv: plates; maps. 24 cm.

Black, Conrad, <u>Franklin Delano Roosevelt : Champion of Freedom</u>. 2003, London: Weidenfeld & Nicolson. viii, 1280 p.

Evans, Harold, with Gail Buckland, and Kevin Baker, <u>The American Century.</u> 1998, London: Jonathan Cape. xxiii,710p.

Nash, George H., <u>The Life of Herbert Hoover</u>. 1996, New York ; London: Norton. xiii, 656p.

Hoover, Herbert, <u>The memoirs of Herbert Hoover</u>. 1952, London: Hollis and Carter. 3 v.

Leuchtenburg, William E., <u>In the Shadow of FDR : From Harry Truman to George W. Bush.</u> 3rd ed., rev. and newly updated. ed. 2001, Ithaca, N.Y. ; London: Cornell University Press. xii, 413 p.

Truman, Harry S. and Robert H. Ferrell, <u>Off the Record : The Private Papers of Harry S. Truman</u>. edited by Robert H. Ferrell. ed. 1982: Penguin.

Ambrose, Stephen E., <u>Eisenhower : Soldier and President</u>. 2003, London: Pocket. xii, 674 p.

Jenkins, Roy, <u>Truman</u>. 1986, London: Collins. [256]p.

Eisenhower, Dwight D., <u>At Ease: Stories I Tell to Friends</u> [by] Dwight D. Eisenhower. 1968: London, Hale. [13] 400 p. 8 plates, ports. 24 cm.

Larson, Arthur, <u>Eisenhower : The President Nobody Knew</u>. 1969, London: Frewin. 222p.,8plates.

Goldman, Martin S., <u>John F. Kennedy, Portrait of a President</u>. 1995, New York: Facts on File. xiv, 178 p.

Klein, Edward, <u>All Too Human : The Love Story of Jack and Jackie Kennedy.</u> [Updated ed.] ed. 1997, New York ; London: Pocket Books. xi, 403 p., [16] p. of plates.

Unger, Irwin and Debi Unger, <u>LBJ : A Life.</u> 1999, New York ; Chichester: Wiley. v,586p.

Kissinger, Henry, <u>Years of Upheaval</u>. 2000, London: Phoenix. [xviii], 1283 p.

Kissinger, Henry, <u>The White HouseYears</u>. 1979, London: Weidenfeld and Nicolson : Joseph. iii-xxiv,1521p.,[48]p. of plates.

Frost, David A., <u>'I Gave Them a Sword' : Behind the Scenes of the Nixon Interviews</u>. 1978, London: Macmillan. 320p.

Kutler, Stanley I., <u>Abuse of Power : The New Nixon Tapes</u>. 1997, New York ; London: Free Press. xxiii,675p.

Aitken, Jonathan, <u>Nixon : A Life.</u> 1993, London: Weidenfield and Nicolson. xiv,633p.,[16]p. of plates.

Terhorst, Jerald F. and G.R. Ford, <u>Gerald Ford</u>. 1975: London: W. H. Allen. pp. x, 245: plates; ports. 23 cm.

Ford, Gerald R., <u>A Time to Heal : The Autobiography of Gerald R. Ford.</u> 1979, London: W.H. Allen. x,454p.,[16]p. of plates.

Carter, Jimmy, <u>Why Not the Best?</u> 1975, Nashville: Broadman Press. 154 p.

Kennedy, John F., <u>Why England slept. 1962</u>: pp. 192. Sidgwick & Jackson: London. 8⁰.

Smith, Matthew, JFK : <u>Say Goodbye to America : The Sensational and Untold Story Behind the Assassination of John F. Kennedy</u>. 2001, Edinburgh: Mainstream, 2004. 255 p., [16] p. of plates.

Bourne, Peter G., <u>Jimmy Carter : A Comprehensive Biography from Plains to Post-Presidency</u>. 1997, New York: Sribner. 553p., [16]p. of plates.

Wooten, James, Dasher : <u>The Roots and the Rising of Jimmy Carter.</u> 1978, London: Weidenfeld and Nicolson. 377p.

Glad, Betty, Jimmy Carter : <u>In Search of the Great White House</u>. 1980, N Y: Norton.

Norton, Howard and Bob Slosser, <u>The Miracle of Jimmy Carter</u>. 1976, Plainfield, N.J.: Logos International.

Morris, Edmund, <u>Dutch : A Memoir of Ronald Reagan</u>. 2000, London: HarperCollins. xxxii, 874 p.

D'Souza, Dinesh, <u>Ronald Reagan : How an Ordinary Man Became an Extraordinary Leader</u>. 1997, New York ; London: Free Press. x,292p.

Fox, M.V., <u>Mister President : The Story of Ronald Reagan</u>. Rev. ed. ed. 1986, Hillside, N.J. ; Aldershot: Enslow. 160p.

McClelland, Doug, <u>Hollywood on Ronald Reagan : Friends and Enemies Discuss Our President, the Actor</u>. 1983, Winchester, Mass.: Faber. xiii247p.

Reagan, Nancy and William Novak, <u>My Turn : The Memoirs of Nancy Reagan</u>. 1989, London: Weidenfeld and Nicolson. xiv,384p.

Davis, Patti, <u>Family Secrets : An Autobiography</u>. 1992, London: Sidgwick & Jackson. 335,[32]p. of plates.

Phillips, Kevin, <u>American Dynasty</u>. 2004, London: Allen Lane. xii, 397 p.

Clinton, Hillary R., <u>Living history</u>. Updated ed. ed. 2004, London: Headline. xi, 570 p., [32] p. of plates.

Stewart, James B., <u>Blood Sport : The President and His Adversaries</u>. 1996, New York; [Great Britain]: Simon & Schuster. 479 p.

Hatfield, James H., <u>Fortunate Son : George W. Bush and the Making of an American President</u>. 2002, London: Vision. 350p.

Clinton, Bill, <u>My Life. 2005</u>, London: Arrow Books. 1024 p.

Klein, Joe, <u>The Natural : The Misunderstood Presidency of Bill Clinton</u>. 1st ed. ed. 2002, New York: Doubleday.

Hamilton, Nigel, <u>Bill Clinton : Mastering the Presidency</u>. 2008, London: Arrow. xv, 766 p.

Moore, Michael A., <u>The Official Fahrenheit 9/11 Reader</u>. 2004, London: Penguin. xvii, 343 p.

Moore, Michael A., <u>Stupid White Men : And Other Sorry Excuses for the State of the Nation!</u> 2002, London: Penguin. xxii, 281 p.

D'Souza, Dinesh, <u>The End of Racism</u>. 1997, New York ; London: Free. 752p.

Powell, Colin. and Joseph E. Persico, <u>My American Journey.</u> 1995, New York: Random House. x,643p.,[42]p. of plates.

Webb, James H., <u>Born Fighting : How The Scots-Irish Shaped America</u>. 2009, Edinburgh: Mainstream. xix, 362 p.

Bruni, Frank, <u>Ambling into History : The Unlikely Odyssey of G.W. Bush</u>. 2002, New York: HarperCollins World ; London : Hi Marketing. 288 p.

Singer, Peter, <u>The President of Good and Evil : The Ethics of George W. Bush</u>. 2004, New York ; London: Dutton. v, 280 p.

Moore, James and Wayne Slater, <u>Rove Exposed : How Bush's Brain Fooled America.</u> 2006, Hoboken, N.J.: Wiley. ix, 225 p.

Moore, James and Wayne Slater, <u>Bush's Brain : How Karl Rove Made George W. Bush Presidential</u>. 2003, New York ; [Great Britain]: Wiley. xiv, 395 p.

Graubard, Stephen R., <u>The Presidents : The Transformation of the American Presidency from Theodore Roosevelt to George W. Bush</u>. 2006, London: Penguin. xv, 927 p., [8] p. of plates.

Coleman, Terry, <u>Passage to America: A History of Emigrants from Great Britain and Ireland to America in the Mid-Nineteenth Century</u>. 1972: London: Hutchinson and Co. 317 p.: plates; illus., map. 24 cm.

Hyslop, Donald, A. Forsyth, and Sheila Jemima, <u>Titanic Voices : Memories from the Fateful Voyage</u>. 1994, Stroud: Sutton Publishing working with Southampton City Council, 1997. 296p.

Smith, Matthew, <u>The Kennedys : The Conspiracy to Destroy a Dynasty.</u> 2005, Edinburgh: Mainstream. 304 p., [8] p. of plates: ill., ports.

Appy, Christian.G. and C.G.P. Appy, <u>Vietnam : The Definitive Oral History, Told From all Sides</u>. 2006, London: Ebury. xxix, 574 p.

McKitrick, Eric L., <u>Andrew Johnson and Reconstruction</u>. (Fourth impression). ed. 1967, Chicago ; London: [s.n.]. pp. ix. + 534.

United States. Congress. Commission for the Celebration of the 200th Anniversary of the Birth of George, W., <u>The Writings of George Washington.</u> 1970, New York: Greenwood Press. 39 vols.

Obama, Barack, <u>Dreams from My Father : A Story of Race and Inheritance.</u> 2008, Edinburgh: Canongate. xvii, 442 p.

Obama, B., <u>The Audacity of Hope : Thoughts on Reclaiming the American Dream.</u> 2008, Bath: BBC Large Print. 447 p.

Mendell, David, <u>Obama : From Promise to Power</u>. 2007, New York: Amistad/HarperCollinsPublishers. x, 406 p., [16] p. of plates.

Madison, Dolly, <u>Memoirs and Letters of Dolly Madison</u> : <u>Wife of James Madison</u>, <u>President of the United States</u>. 8th ed. 1896, Boston ; New York: Houghton, Mifflin. 210 p.

Fritz, Jean, <u>The Great Little Madison</u>. 1989, New York: Putnam. 159 p.

Trefousse, Hans L., <u>Andrew Johnson : A Biography.</u> 1st ed. ed. 1989, New York: W.W. Norton & Co. Norton. 464p

McCullough, David G., <u>John Adams</u>. 2001, New York ; Toronto: Simon & Schuster. 751 p., [40] p. of plates.

Kaltman, Al, <u>Cigars, Whiskey & Winning : Leadership Lessons from General Ulysses S. Grant</u>. 1998, Paramus, N.J.: Prentice Hall Press ; London : Prentice Hall International. xiii, 322 p.

Franklin, John H., <u>The Emancipation Proclamation</u>. [With plates.]. 1963: pp. x. 181. Edinburgh University Press: Edinburgh. 8º.

Katcher, Philip, <u>The American Civil War source book</u>. 1992, London: Arms and Armour. 318p.

Hess, Stephen, <u>America's Political dynasties.</u> 1997, New Brunswick, N.J. ; London: Transaction Publishers. xi,742p.

Chesnut, Mary Boykin, Comer Vann Woodward, and Elisabeth Muhlenfeld, <u>The Private Mary Chesnut</u> : The Unpublished Civil War Diaries. 1984, New York ; Oxford: Oxford University Press. xxix,292p.

Depew, Chauncey M., <u>My Memories of Eighty Years</u>. 1922, N.Y.: Scribner. 417p.

Kelley, Kitty, <u>Nancy Reagan : The Unauthorized Biography</u>. 1991, London: Bantam. xix,532p.,[32]p. of plates.

Crosbie, Duncan, Brian Lee, and Peter Bull Art Studio., <u>Life on a Famine Ship : A Journal of the Irish Famine, 1845-1850</u>. 1st ed. 2006, Hauppauge, NY: Barron's Educational Series, Inc. 25 p.

Parmet, Herbert S., <u>George Bush : The Life of a Lonestar Yankee</u>. 1997, New York: Scribner.

Cooke, Alistair, <u>Alistair Cooke's American Journey</u> : Life on the Home Front in the Second World War. Large print ed. ed. 2007, Bath: BBC Large Print. xxi, 451 p.

Andersen, Christopher P., <u>George and Laura : Portrait of an American Marriage.</u> 1st ed. 2002, New York: William Morrow. xi, 307 p., [32] p. of plates.

Frum, David, <u>The Right Man : The Surprise Presidency of George W. Bush</u>. 2003, New York: Random House. 303 p.

Frum, David, <u>The Right Man : An Inside Account of the Bush White House</u>. 2005 Random House trade paperback ed. 2005, New York: Random House Trade Paperbacks. 329 p.

Cunliffe, Marcus, <u>American Presidents and the Presidency</u>. 1972, New York: American Heritage Press. 446 p.

Holmes, James, <u>The American Presidents: From Washington to Clinton</u>. 1996, Pinnacle, 378 p.

Adams, Quincy, <u>Extracts From the Diary of John Quincy Adams</u>, 1878, Private Press of F. P. Rice (Worcester), 30 p.

Ida M. Tarbell assisted by J. McCann Davis, <u>The Early Life of Abraham Lincoln</u> , South Brunswick ; New York : Barnes ; London : Yoseloff, 1974. , 240p

Davison Kenneth E., <u>The Presidency of Rutherford B. Hayes</u> , Westport (Conn) : Greenwood P, 1972., xvii, 266p

<u>McCullough, David G.</u>, <u>John Adams</u>, New York ; London : Simon & Schuster, 2001, 751 p

Lewis and Merriweather Reports, Vols 1 – 5, <u>The Lewis Merriweather Expedition</u>: Specially Held at Trinity College, Dublin.

Olcott, Charles S., <u>The Life of William McKinley</u>, Houghton Mifflin Company, Boston, 1916, p. 313

Quackenbush, Robert M.,<u>James Madison and Dolly Madison and their times</u>, Pippin Press (New York), First Edition edition,1992, 36p

Johns, Wesley A., <u>The Man Who Shot McKinley</u>, South Brunswick [N.J.] A. S. Barnes [1970] 293 p.

Blum, John Morton, <u>The Progressive Presidents</u>, 1st Ed., W. W. Norton & Company (1982), 224p

McCoy, Ronald R., <u>The Presidency of Dwight D. Eisenhower</u>, University Press of Kansas; Revised edition (April 1991) 291p

<u>The Jeanie Johnston 1847 – 58: Famine Ship to be reborn</u> (*Helen O'Carroll*)
The Kerry Magazine. Vol: 6 pp:27-29.

Keegan, John, <u>The World at War 1939 – 1945</u>, (The London Illustrated News), Bracken Books, 192p

Newspaper reports of 1912; Authors not named. News of the World, Sunday 21.04.1912, <u>Sinking of Titanic</u>

Microsoft, Encarta Encylopedia

Newspaper Articles by:

Deborah Charles "World News"	Irish Times	Dec 16, 2003
Funeral of Ronald Reagan by Roland Watson, Tim Reid, Ralph Reigel	Irish Independent	June 12, 2004
Article by John Zawadzinski	Catholic Digest	March 2006
Iraq Chaos by Andy Smith	The Independent	Nov 9, 2006
Ghaith Abdul-Ahad	Observer	Dec 31, 2006
Ned Temko & Peter Beaumont	Observer	Dec 31, 2006

Jason Burke	Observer	Dec 31, 2006
Anushka Asthana	Observer	Dec 31, 2006
Larry Margasak	Irish Examiner	Jan 1, 2007
Greenspan Blasts Bush by Graham Peterson	Sunday Times	Sept 16, 2007
Article by Barack Obama	Irish Mail	Feb 8, 2008
Article by Tim Reid & Roger Boyes	Irish Independent	July 25, 2008
Tom Wolfe American Journalist on George Bush	Sunday Times	Oct 19, 2008
Sarah Baxter American Journalist on George Bush	Sunday Times	Oct 19, 2008
Article by Max Hastings	Irish Mail	Oct 25, 2008
Article by Barack Obama	Irish Mail	Oct 25, 2008
Sarah Baxter American Journalist	Sunday Times	Dec 12, 2008
Frank Bruni on George Bush	New York Times	
Bob Woodward on George Bush	Sunday Times	

World Food Report on Starvation in
North Korea

Brochure on Mount Vernon Estate
And Gardens by Mount Vernon Ladies Association

Acceptance and Inaugural speeches of Barack Obama

Programmes and Documentaries:

John Sargeant	The Late, Late Show	
World at War,	BBC	Nov 4, 2006
In the Shadow of the Moon	BBC	May 2008
Capone in 1920s	History Channel	